# EXODUS

**PREACHING THE WORD**
Edited by R. Kent Hughes

*Genesis* | R. Kent Hughes
*Exodus* | Philip Graham Ryken
*Leviticus* | Kenneth A. Mathews
*Numbers* | Iain M. Duguid
*Deuteronomy* | Ajith Fernando
*Joshua* | David Jackman
*Judges and Ruth* | Barry G. Webb
*1 Samuel* | John Woodhouse
*2 Samuel* | John Woodhouse
*Job* | Christopher Ash
*Psalms,* vol. 1 | James Johnston
*Proverbs* | Raymond C. Ortlund Jr.
*Ecclesiastes* | Philip Graham Ryken
*Song of Solomon* | Douglas Sean O'Donnell
*Isaiah* | Raymond C. Ortlund Jr.
*Jeremiah and Lamentations* | Philip Graham Ryken
*Daniel* | Rodney D. Stortz
*Matthew* | Douglas Sean O'Donnell
*Mark* | R. Kent Hughes
*Luke* | R. Kent Hughes
*John* | R. Kent Hughes
*Acts* | R. Kent Hughes
*Romans* | R. Kent Hughes
*1 Corinthians* | Stephen T. Um
*2 Corinthians* | R. Kent Hughes
*Galatians* | Todd Wilson
*Ephesians* | R. Kent Hughes
*Philippians, Colossians, and Philemon* | R. Kent Hughes
*1–2 Thessalonians* | James H. Grant Jr.
*1–2 Timothy and Titus* | R. Kent Hughes and Bryan Chapell
*Hebrews* | R. Kent Hughes
*1–2 Peter and Jude* | David R. Helm
*1–3 John* | David L. Allen
*Revelation* | James M. Hamilton Jr.
*The Sermon on the Mount* | R. Kent Hughes

PRESENTING the WORD

# EXODUS

## Saved for God's Glory

PHILIP GRAHAM RYKEN

R. Kent Hughes
*Series Editor*

WHEATON, ILLINOIS

*Exodus*



Published by Crossway
1300 Crescent Street
Wheaton, Illinois 60187



Cover design: Jon McGrath, Simplicated Studio

Cover image: Adam Greene, illustrator

First printing 2005

Reprinted with new cover 2012

First printing, ESV edition 2015

Printed in the United States of America



All emphases in Scripture quotations have been added by the author.

Hardcover ISBN: 978-1-4335-4872-7
ePub ISBN: 978-1-4335-4875-8
PDF ISBN: 978-1-4335-4873-4
Mobipocket ISBN: 978-1-4335-4874-1

**Library of Congress Cataloging-in-Publication Data**

Ryken, Philip Graham, 1966-
Exodus : saved for God's glory / Philip Graham Ryken; R. Kent Hughes, general editor.
p. cm.—(Preaching the word)
Includes indexes.
ISBN 1-58134-489-9 (hc : alk. paper)
1. Bible. O.T. Exodus—Commentaries. I. Hughes, R. Kent. II. Title. III. Preaching the Word.
BS1245.53.R95 2005
222'.1107—dc22 2005004629

Crossway is a publishing ministry of Good News Publishers.

VP 25 24 23 22 21 20 19 18 17 16
15 14 13 12 11 10 9 8 7 6 5 4 3 2 1

To

James Maxwell Ryken

*who brought joy to his father's heart*
*while this book was being written—*
*the whole first three years of his life*

and to the

Great God of the exodus,

*who alone can rescue us from the Egypt of our sin,*
*redeem us by the blood of the Lamb,*
*and receive us into his everlasting glory*

*I will get glory over Pharaoh*
*and all his host,*
*and the Egyptians shall know*
*that I am the* LORD.

EXODUS 14:4

# Contents

# A Word to Those Who Preach the Word

There are times when I am preaching that I have especially sensed the pleasure of God. I usually become aware of it through the unnatural silence. The ever-present coughing ceases, and the pews stop creaking, bringing an almost physical quiet to the sanctuary—through which my words sail like arrows. I experience a heightened eloquence, so that the cadence and volume of my voice intensify the truth I am preaching.

There is nothing quite like it—the Holy Spirit filling one's sails, the sense of his pleasure, and the awareness that something is happening among one's hearers. This experience is, of course, not unique, for thousands of preachers have similar experiences, even greater ones.

What has happened when this takes place? How do we account for this sense of his smile? The answer for me has come from the ancient rhetorical categories of *logos*, *ethos*, and *pathos*.

The first reason for his smile is the *logos*—in terms of preaching, God's Word. This means that as we stand before God's people to proclaim his Word, we have done our homework. We have exegeted the passage, mined the significance of its words in their context, and applied sound hermeneutical principles in interpreting the text so that we understand what its words meant to its hearers. And it means that we have labored long until we can express in a sentence what the theme of the text is—so that our outline springs from the text. Then our preparation will be such that as we preach, we will not be preaching our own thoughts about God's Word, but God's actual Word, his *logos*. This is fundamental to pleasing him in preaching.

The second element in knowing God's smile in preaching is *ethos*—what you are as a person. There is a danger endemic to preaching, which is having your hands and heart cauterized by holy things. Phillips Brooks illustrated it by the analogy of a train conductor who comes to believe that he has been to the places he announces because of his long and loud heralding of them. And that is why Brooks insisted that preaching must be "the bringing of truth through personality." Though we can never *perfectly* embody the truth we preach, we must be subject to it, long for it, and make it as much a part of our ethos as possible. As the Puritan William Ames said, "Next to the Scriptures, nothing makes a sermon more to pierce, than when it comes out of the inward affection of the heart without any affectation." When a preacher's *ethos* backs up his *logos*, there will be the pleasure of God.

Last, there is *pathos*—personal passion and conviction. David Hume, the

Scottish philosopher and skeptic, was once challenged as he was seen going to hear George Whitefield preach: "I thought you do not believe in the gospel." Hume replied, "I don't, but *he does*." Just so! When a preacher believes what he preaches, there will be passion. And this belief and requisite passion will know the smile of God.

The pleasure of God is a matter of *logos* (the Word), *ethos* (what you are), and *pathos* (your passion). As you *preach the Word* may you experience his smile—the Holy Spirit in your sails!

*R. Kent Hughes*
*Wheaton, Illinois*

# Preface

A book this long at least deserves the mercy of a short preface. The book itself is based on a series of Bible expositions that were preached before, during, and after the sudden illness and death of James Montgomery Boice, my predecessor in the pulpit of Philadelphia's Tenth Presbyterian Church. I praise God for his faithfulness to us as a church during those difficult days, and for all the love and prayers of our session and congregation. Working through Exodus week by week was a triumphant adventure that brought us closer to the God of the exodus and to his Son, Jesus Christ. My prayer for this book is that it will help others make the same spiritual journey. I wish to give special thanks to Jonathan Rockey for the kindness of reviewing and improving this entire manuscript; to Ted Griffin for his painstaking work as editor; to Lydia Brownback, Ted Griffin, and Pat Russell for the difficult labor of preparing the indexes; to the staff at Crossway for bringing the book into print; and to Kent Hughes for the privilege of contributing another volume to his excellent series of commentaries.

# 1

# Into Egypt

## EXODUS 1:1–7

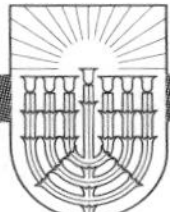

EXODUS IS AN EPIC TALE OF fire, sand, wind, and water. The adventure takes place under the hot desert sun, just beyond the shadow of the Great Pyramids. There are two mighty nations—Israel and Egypt—led by two great men—Moses the liberating hero and Pharaoh the enslaving villain. Almost every scene is a masterpiece: the baby in the basket, the burning bush, the river of blood and the other plagues, the angel of death, the crossing of the Red Sea, the manna in the wilderness, the water from the rock, the thunder and lightning on the mountain, the Ten Commandments, the pillar of cloud by day and the pillar of fire by night, the golden calf, and the glory in the tabernacle.

Once heard, the story is never forgotten. For Jews it is the story that defines their very existence, the rescue that made them God's people. For Christians it is the gospel of the Old Testament, God's first great act of redemption. We return to the exodus again and again, sensing that somehow it holds significance for the entire human race. It is the story that gives every captive the hope of freedom. Thus it was only natural for African-American slaves—many of whom were Christians—to understand their captivity as a bondage in Egypt and to long for the day when they would be "free at last." The exodus shows that there is a God who saves, who delivers his people from bondage.

### Exodus and the Bible

The word *exodus* means "exit" or "departure." It first appears at the beginning of chapter 19: "On the third new moon after the people of Israel had *gone out* of the land of Egypt . . ." (v. 1). When the Hebrew Scriptures were translated into Greek, the verb used for their leaving Egypt was *exodus*. Eventually the word came to be used as a title for the whole book. The exodus, then, is a story of departure, an epic journey from slavery to salvation. As we study this book, the journey out of Egypt becomes part of our own spiritual pilgrimage. So how shall we make the journey? What is the best way to study Exodus?

First of all, our approach must be *Biblical*, which means that we must study the book of Exodus itself. We must study it chapter by chapter and verse by verse, seeking to understand the plain meaning of the text. And we must study the book as a complete literary whole. Some scholars view Exodus as a complicated web of human traditions that must be disentangled to be understood. Others argue that it is really two books in one. Chapters 1–14 contain the original story of Israel's salvation, they say, while the rest of the book consists of material that was added later, somewhat haphazardly.

It is probably true that Exodus was not written at a single sitting. Some parts of the book—especially the stories and songs—may have been passed down by oral tradition. Yet much of the epic seems to have been written by Moses himself. On several different occasions, God told Moses to write down his experiences: "Write this as a memorial in a book" (17:14); "Write these words" (34:27). Moses knew how to write, of course, because he had been trained in Pharaoh's court. So he was able to do as he was told, to write "down all the words of the LORD" (24:4). Some parts of Exodus may have been written down by someone else, especially the parts that describe Moses in the third person. Yet when Jesus quoted from Exodus (e.g., Mark 7:10; 12:26), he attributed what he was quoting directly to Moses, and we should do the same.

The important thing is to receive the book of Exodus as it has been given, which means studying it as one complete story. Like every other book in the Bible, Exodus is the living Word of God. It was breathed out by the Holy Spirit and written down by Moses for our spiritual benefit. What God has given us is not a random collection of documents, but a single book with a unified message.

Taking a Biblical approach also means reading Exodus in the context of the whole Bible, starting with the Pentateuch, "The Five Books of Moses." Exodus often looks back to the promises God made in Genesis. Whereas Genesis tells of the creation of the world, Exodus recounts the creation of a nation. The book also stands in close relation to the books of Leviticus, Numbers, and Deuteronomy. This is how one scholar explains the connection:

> In the Pentateuch, considered as a whole, there are only five major themes: God's promise to the patriarchs; the exodus; God's Self-revelation in covenant and law at Sinai; the wandering in the wilderness; the entrance into Canaan. Three of these five major themes are treated at length in the book of Exodus and, in addition, it looks back to the first theme and on to the last. Moses' vision and call at Mount Sinai are deliberately shown as a fulfilment of God's promise to Israel's forefathers, while the book ends with a promise of God's leading till Canaan is reached. Therefore, while Exodus is only part of a wider and far larger whole, it is a real part and, in a sense, enshrines the heart of the whole pentateuchal revelation.[1]

Beyond the Pentateuch, the book of Exodus has wider connections with the rest of the Old Testament. The exodus was *the* great miracle of the old covenant. Thus many passages in the Psalms and the Prophets look back to it as the paradigm of salvation. The people of Israel always praised God as the One who had brought them out of Egypt. The New Testament writers worshiped the same God, and thus they often used the exodus to explain salvation in Christ. Indeed, a complete understanding of the gospel requires a knowledge of the exodus. As we study the book of Exodus, therefore, we must follow the Reformation principle of allowing Scripture to interpret Scripture. In some ways the whole Bible is an extended interpretation of the exodus. Thus the way to understand Exodus is to study the book itself, in the context of the entire Bible.

## The Exodus in History

Our approach to Exodus must also be *historical*. This book is more than merely a story; it presents itself as history, and thus the only proper way to interpret it is to accept it as a true account of the history of God's people.

Many objections have been raised to the historicity of Exodus. Some of these objections surround the date of the exodus. The Bible says that Solomon began to build the temple in Jerusalem "in the four hundred and eightieth year after the people of Israel came out of the land of Egypt" (1 Kings 6:1). We know that Solomon built the temple in or around 962 BC, which would place the Exodus around 1440 BC. The problem with that date is that it may not fit everything we know about ancient history, either in Egypt or in Israel. Other questions surround the miracles of Exodus. Did the Nile turn into blood? Did the Egyptians lose all their firstborn sons? Still other questions surround the journeys of the Israelites. Did they cross the Red Sea or the Reed Sea? Did they wander around Arabia or travel directly to Canaan?

Adding to the historical difficulties is the fact that Egyptian records make no mention of the exodus. One writer explains that "archaeologists to date have found no direct evidence to corroborate the biblical story. Inscriptions from ancient Egypt contain no mention of Hebrew slaves, of the devastating plagues that the Bible says preceded their release, or of the destruction of Pharaoh's army during the Israelites' miraculous crossing of the Red Sea (or perhaps the Sea of Reeds). No physical trace has been found of the Israelites' forty-year nomadic sojourn in the Sinai wilderness. There is not even any indication, outside of the Bible, that Moses existed."[2] Some scholars doubt whether Israel was ever in Egypt at all. In the words of one professor, "the actual evidence concerning the Exodus resembles the evidence for the unicorn."[3]

Some people don't think it matters very much whether the exodus happened or not. The history of Exodus, they say, is "less important . . . than the quest for the moral and spiritual values that we might extract from this biblical story."[4] This attitude calls to mind a scene from E. L. Doctorow's *City of God* in which two men are discussing the relationship between God and history. "God is ahistorical," one of them argues. He then proceeds to ask, "Do you believe God gave Moses the Decalogue, the Ten Commandments, on Mount Sinai?" After thinking for a moment, his friend replies, "Well it's a great story. I think I'm a judge of stories and that's a great story."[5]

It *is* a great story, one of the greatest ever written. But is it also history? If not—if the exodus never happened—then the book of Exodus has little or no claim on our lives today. If there was no exodus, then there is no reason to believe in a God who has the power to save and no need to obey his commandments. This problem led the Jewish scholar Abraham Joshua Heschel to ask a provocative question: "If Moses . . . failed to find out what the will of God is, who will?" Heschel concluded, "If God had nothing to do with the prophets, then He had nothing to do with mankind."[6]

The truth is that God had everything to do with the prophets, and because he had everything to do with them, he has everything to do with us. One good reason to believe in the prophet Moses is that the book of Exodus fits everything we know about ancient history. Start with the date of the exodus. It is important to realize that the Israelites did not have an absolute calendar in the time of the patriarchs, and that the Bible's method of chronological reckoning sometimes involved some approximation. When the Bible says that Solomon built the temple 480 years after Israel came out of Egypt, it may not be giving us a statistic so much as a symbol. Four hundred and eighty is the product of twelve times forty, and forty is the number the Bible uses to represent a generation (e.g., Judges 5:31; Psalm 95:10). Thus 480 may be a round number used to indicate a dozen generations. However, most generations during the Biblical period were only twenty-five years apart, not forty. If there were twelve generations between Moses and Solomon, that would amount to roughly 300 years rather than 480, yielding a date for the exodus around 1260 BC.

A thirteenth-century exodus would fit the historical situation, including the chronology of the Pharaohs. While the Biblical Pharaoh is not named, it is not hard to guess who he might have been. The harsh Pharaoh who first enslaved the Hebrews may have been Seti I (1303–1290 BC). It was during Seti's reign that the Egyptians began to move their capital downriver to the Nile Delta. This move was significant because it required large building projects—perhaps including the store cities mentioned in Exodus 1:11—in the region where the Israelites are known to have lived (the land of Goshen). Seti was succeeded by Rameses II (1290–1224 BC), who completed the move to the delta, using even more slaves to attempt even more elaborate buildings than his father. It was Rameses who completed the cities of Pithom and Rameses (or Raamses as the ESV has it—presumably the city was named after him).

On the other hand, the arguments for a fifteenth-century exodus are much stronger than is sometimes realized.[7] If the 480 years are taken as chronologically exact, then the exodus occurred in 1445 BC, during the reign of Amenhotep II (1453–1425 BC), with Thutmose III (1483–1450 BC) having ruled as Pharaoh for most of Moses' life. There is substantial evidence that Thutmose, like Seti after him, engaged in major building projects in the Nile Delta. The city of Rameses need not have been named after Rameses II, as some have argued, for the name Rameses was an ancient one. Alternatively, Rameses may have been an anachronism—a name given later to a city built under Thutmose III. But the strongest argument in favor of an early exodus is that the chronological statements in Judges 11:26 (where Jephthah states that it had been 300 years since the conquest of Canaan) and Acts 13:19, 20 (where Paul posits 450 years between the flight from Egypt and the capture of Jerusalem) both support a mid-fifteenth-century exodus.

Like a thirteenth-century date, a fifteenth-century date for the exodus would fit what we know about slavery in Egypt. By the time of Moses there had been Semitic slaves in Egypt for several centuries.[8] The most intriguing reference to them appears in a text called Leiden Papyrus 348, dating from the time of Rameses II, which contains instructions to distribute grain rations "to the 'Apiru who are dragging stones to the great pylon."[9] Obviously, the 'Apiru (*hapiru*) were slaves. Some scholars believe that there may be a connection between the word *'Apiru* and the word *'Ibri* (also mentioned in the famous Tell el-Amarna tablets), from which we derive the word *Hebrews*. At the very least, it is historically certain that people of Semitic origin were enslaved by the Pharaohs during the decades leading up to the exodus.

It is also certain that there were Israelites living in Canaan not long afterward. After a lengthy reign, Rameses II was succeeded by Merneptah (1224–1214 BC). The Stele of Merneptah—a seven-foot, black granite monument celebrating Merneptah's accomplishments—boasts that "Canaan is plundered with every hardship. . . . Israel is laid waste, his seed is not." That is, Merneptah completely destroyed the Israelites.[10] Obviously, Merneptah was exaggerating because the Israelites outlived him by three millennia. What is significant, however, is that there were enough Israelites in Canaan for him to fight against, proving that by then they had made their exodus from Egypt to the Promised Land. To summarize, either a fifteenth- or a thirteenth-century date for the exodus can be reconciled with the archaeological evidence for the conquest of Canaan, although the balance of the evidence supports the former.[11]

Apart from the Bible, we cannot prove the historicity of the exodus; however, we can show that it is historically plausible. Several other archaeological discoveries support specific details from the book of Exodus. A text called "The Admonitions of an Egyptian Sage," also known as the Papyrus Ipuwer, describes a series of disasters that sound very much like the Biblical plagues.[12] Also, a series of Egyptian military outposts has been identified along the coast between Egypt and Canaan. This would explain the logic of 13:17: "When Pharaoh let the people go, God did not lead them by way of the land of the Philistines, although that was near. For God said, 'Lest the people change their minds when they see war and return to Egypt.'" All things considered, whether we adopt an early date or a late date for the exodus itself, the archaeological evidence shows that the book of Exodus fits everything we know about the history of Israel in Egypt.[13]

It is true that there is no extra-Biblical record of the exodus itself, but this is hardly a surprise. The Nile Delta—which is where the Israelites were living at the time—is too wet for many documents to have survived. Furthermore, the Egyptians were a proud people who rarely (if ever) mention their disastrous defeats in their own records, which generally read more like propaganda. We could hardly expect them to set up a monument explaining how they lost a full brigade of their best soldiers in a failed attempt to capture runaway slaves! Indeed, the Bible is unique among ancient documents for providing the most unflattering information about the people who wrote it, a fact that has led Professor Nahum Sarna to conclude that the exodus "cannot possibly be fictional. No nation would be likely to invent for itself, and faithfully transmit century after century and millennium after millennium, an inglorious and inconvenient tradition of this nature."[14] The book of Exodus presents the Israelites as a grumbling, complaining, idol-worshiping people. It does not encourage us to praise the Israelites themselves, but only their God.

## Exodus, God, and Christ

This brings us to a third point: Our interpretation of Exodus must be *theological*. As we study the Biblical history in the book of Exodus, we discover that the real hero of the story is God. God is the one who reveals himself to Moses as the Great I AM. God is the one who hears the cries of his people in bondage and takes pity on their suffering, raising up a deliverer to save them. God is the one who visits the plagues on Egypt, who divides the sea, and who drowns Pharaoh's army. God is the one who provides bread from Heaven and water from the rock. God is the one who gives the law-covenant on the mountain and fills the tabernacle with his glory. From beginning to end Exodus is a God-centered book, a theological history.

To read Exodus, therefore, is to encounter God. The book is about the mercy, justice, holiness, and glory of almighty God, who rules history by his sovereign power and who saves the people of his covenant. When the Biblical writers recall the exodus, they rarely mention Moses at all; instead they speak of the wonders of God. This gives us a hint that the proper way to study Exodus is to pay constant attention to what the book is showing and telling about the character of God. Exodus is an exercise in theology, which is simply the study of God.

If our approach to the exodus is theological, it must also be *Christologi-*

*cal.* In other words, we must understand Exodus in relation to Jesus Christ. The exodus finds its ultimate meaning and final interpretation in the person and work of God the Son. In one way or another, the whole Bible is about Jesus Christ. The theme of the Old Testament is the Savior to come; the theme of the New Testament is the Savior who has come and is coming again. Yet because Exodus is the gospel of the Old Testament, its connection to Christ is especially strong. Jude went so far as to tell his readers that *Jesus* "saved a people out of the land of Egypt" (Jude 5). The Bible also says that after the resurrection, when Jesus talked with his disciples on the road to Emmaus, "beginning with Moses and all the Prophets, he interpreted to them in all the Scriptures the things concerning himself" (Luke 24:27). If Jesus began with Moses, surely he must have said something about the exodus!

In many ways, the exodus set the pattern for the life of Christ. Like Moses, Jesus was born to be a savior and was rescued from his enemies at birth. He also had a sojourn in Egypt, for it is written, "Out of Egypt I called my son" (Hosea 11:1; Matthew 2:15). Like the children of Israel, Jesus passed through the waters of baptism. Also like the Israelites, who wandered in the desert for forty years, Jesus went out into the wilderness for forty days. Upon his return he went up the mountain to give the Law (Matthew 5—7), much as Moses brought the Law down from Mount Sinai.

There are also many ways in which the death of Christ followed the pattern of the exodus. There is a clue about this in Luke's account of the transfiguration. Jesus went up to pray on the mountain, where he appeared to his closest disciples in dazzling majesty: "And behold, two men were talking with him, Moses and Elijah, who appeared in glory and spoke of his departure, which he was about to accomplish at Jerusalem" (Luke 9:30, 31). It is significant that Moses was present because the word Luke uses for Jesus' departure is the Greek word *exodus*. Moses and Elijah were talking with Jesus about *his* exodus. That is to say, they were talking about his crucifixion and resurrection, when he would pass through the deep waters of death to deliver his people from their bondage to sin and take them to the glory-land. This explains why Jesus was crucified at Passover. He was the Passover Lamb (1 Corinthians 5:7) who takes away the sins of the world (John 1:29). Many of the words the Old Testament uses to describe the exodus from Egypt—words like *ransom*, *redemption*, and *deliverance*—are the very words the New Testament uses to describe Christ's work on the cross.

What all these connections with Christ show is that Exodus is not just *a* story of salvation, but *the* story of salvation. Israel's deliverance from Egypt anticipated the salvation accomplished once and for all in Jesus Christ.

The last thing to say about our approach to interpreting Exodus is that it must be *practical*. In order for Israel's journey out of Egypt to become part of our own pilgrimage, we must apply its spiritual lessons to our own daily walk with God. God has given us the book of Exodus, as he has given us every single book in the Bible, for our practical benefit. When the Apostle Paul wanted to exhort the Corinthians to persevere in the faith, he reminded them of the exodus: "For I do not want you to be unaware, brothers, that our fathers were all under the cloud, and all passed through the sea, and all were baptized into Moses in the cloud and in the sea" (1 Corinthians 10:1, 2). Then Paul drew a connection between their salvation and the salvation we have in Jesus Christ: "[They] all ate the same spiritual food, and all drank the same spiritual drink. For they drank from the spiritual Rock that followed them, and the Rock was Christ" (1 Corinthians 10:3, 4). The Apostle went on to explain how, despite the fact that God saved them in the wilderness, the Israelites turned away from God and perished. He concluded by saying, "Now these things happened to them as an example, but they were written down for our instruction, on whom the end of the ages has come" (1 Corinthians 10:11). In other words, Paul was saying that what happened to them was written down *for us*. Exodus is intended for our spiritual benefit.

Since the exodus is a story of deliverance from bondage through the work of a savior, it is the story of the Christian life. Like the Israelites, although we "were once slaves of sin," now we have "been set free from sin" (Romans 6:17, 18). As we trace their spiritual journey, we discover that we need exactly what the Israelites needed. We need a liberator, a God to save us from slavery and destroy our enemies. We need a provider, a God to feed us bread from Heaven and water from the rock. We need a lawgiver, a God to command us how to love and serve him. And we need a friend, a God to stay with us day and night, forever.

## The God of Israel

It is time to start the journey. Since our method is Biblical, that means starting with the Biblical text. In the opening verses of Exodus we are reintroduced to the twelve tribes of Israel: "These are the names of the sons of Israel who came to Egypt with Jacob, each with his household: Reuben, Simeon, Levi, and Judah, Issachar, Zebulun, and Benjamin, Dan and Naphtali, Gad and Asher. All the descendants of Jacob were seventy persons; Joseph was already in Egypt" (1:1–5; cf. Genesis 46:8–27).

The twelve tribes of Israel are listed in a formal way to indicate that this is the preface to some momentous event. From the very beginning it is apparent that these people have a history and a destiny. Exodus begins the way epics typically begin, in the middle of things, with the adventure already underway. In Hebrew the book begins with the word "and," which establishes a connection between the exodus and everything that came before. It is a way of saying that Exodus is a sequel to Genesis, another episode in the continuing adventure of God's people.

Before coming out of Egypt, the sons of Israel had to go there in the first place, and it is worth remembering why they went. How did Israel get into

Egypt? With the mention of Joseph and his brothers, it all comes back to us. Joseph was the first member of the family to enter Egypt. He was the favorite son, the apple of his father's eye, and thus the envy of all his brothers. In a fit of jealous rage they threw him into a pit, sold him into slavery, and took his bloodstained robe back to their father (Genesis 37). Yet in the providence of God, Joseph eventually became the prince of Egypt. When his family later went to Egypt in a time of famine, Joseph was able to give his brothers bread, and the whole family resettled in the Nile Delta. The irony is that eventually the families of the men who sold their brother ended up in slavery themselves, toiling under the hot sun for their Egyptian overlords.

The twelve sons of Israel were never likely to become epic heroes. In fact, the more we know about this family, the more amazed we are that God would have anything to do with them at all. It was not a large family; there were only seventy of them to begin with. They were not very powerful. Joseph had risen to a position of authority, but his office was not hereditary, and the rest of his family were living as strangers in a strange land. They were not especially bright. Certainly they were no more talented than the Egyptians, who built a civilization that could boast some of the world's leading intellects. Nor could this "dirty dozen" claim to be any more righteous than anyone else. Their family history was a sordid tale of treachery, philandering, and violence. Their father Jacob had betrayed his brother Esau by tricking him out of his birthright. Like father, like sons: By getting rid of Joseph, Jacob's boys had tried to deny their father's blessing. The most despicable of all was Judah, who had sex with his daughter-in-law Tamar. The sons of Israel were all sinners—ordinary mortals, as their obituary proves: "Then Joseph died, and all his brothers and all that generation" (1:6).

Joseph and his brothers really had just one thing going for them, and that was their God. What was important about these people was that they were God's people. And what a God they had! Not only was he the God of Jacob, but he was also the God of Abraham and Isaac. He was the God of the everlasting covenant, who turned what they meant for evil—namely, selling their own brother into slavery—into good (Genesis 50:20). He is the same God we will meet throughout the book of Exodus: "The Lord, the Lord, a God merciful and gracious, slow to anger, and abounding in steadfast love and faithfulness, keeping steadfast love for thousands, forgiving iniquity and transgression and sin" (34:6, 7). When this great God is on your side, anything can happen! You can pass through the deep waters unharmed, while a thousand enemies are lost at sea and glory blazes from the mountain.

What made the sons of Israel special, however unpromising they may have seemed, was their relationship to God. They had God on their side, with all his promises. He had given the Israelites the most amazing promises ever. In fact, one of them was already coming true: "Then Joseph died, and all his brothers and all that generation. But the people of Israel were fruitful and increased greatly; they multiplied and grew exceedingly strong, so that the land was filled with them" (1:6, 7). There were only seventy Israelites to start with, but soon the land was filled with them. This was something God had promised when he made his covenant with Abraham: "I will make of you a great nation, and I will bless you" (Genesis 12:2a). "I am God Almighty; walk before me, and be blameless, that I may make my covenant between me and you, and may multiply you greatly" (Genesis 17:1, 2). God gave Abraham two great promises—land and seed. The promise of the seed was fulfilled in the opening verses of Exodus, and all that remained was for God to give Abraham's descendants a land to call their own. Hence his need to get them out of Egypt.

The promise of the seed went back even farther than Abraham, all the way to Adam and Eve, who were commanded, "Be fruitful and multiply and fill the earth" (Genesis 1:28). Now God was keeping his promise to turn one family into a mighty nation. Exodus makes this explicit by describing the Hebrew multitudes with the very words ("fruitful," "multiply," etc.) used in the creation mandate in Genesis (cf. Genesis 1:21, 22; 9:1–7). In his people Israel, God was fulfilling his plan for humanity. As the psalmist later wrote:

> Then Israel came to Egypt;
> Jacob sojourned in the land of Ham.
> And the LORD made his people very fruitful
> and made them stronger than their foes. (Psalm 105:23, 24)

When it comes to the multiplication of the Israelites, some scholars think that the Bible is exaggerating. Niels Peter Lemche claims, "It is generally acknowledged by scholars that the traditions about Israel's sojourn in Egypt and the *exodus* of the Israelites are legendary and epic in nature. The very notion that a single family could in the course of a few centuries develop into a whole people, a nation, consisting of hundreds of thousands of individuals, is so fantastic that it deserves no credence from a *historical* point of view."[15] But this is where theology helps explain history. Historically, hundreds of years had passed since the Israelites had entered Egypt (see 12:40, 41)—enough time for a family to become a nation. But the theological explanation for their remarkable growth is that God was keeping his covenant promises. In the Hebrew original, seven different words are used to describe the population explosion, perhaps demonstrating that the multiplication of the Israelites was the perfection of God's plan.[16] Forever afterward the children of Israel would confess their faith in the power of their promise-keeping God, saying, "A wandering Aramean was my father. And he went down into Egypt and sojourned there, few in number, and there he became a nation, great, mighty, and populous" (Deuteronomy 26:5b).

This brings us to a very practical question: Who is our God? The truth is that we are no better than the sons of Israel. We are envious, ill-tempered people who stubbornly refuse to follow God. We fail to live up to his perfect standard every day. What we need is the God of Exodus. If he is our God, then he has performed for us a miracle of grace, and we can trust him to save us to the very end.

## Saved for God's Glory

We have been saying that the Israelites had only one thing going for them, and that was God himself. What the rest of Exodus shows is that their God had one overriding purpose: namely, to glorify himself. The book of Exodus is so rich that it is hard to reduce it to a single theme or emphasis. Different commentators have made various suggestions about what ties the whole book together, and some have doubted whether there is anything to unify the book at all. However, the theme of Exodus is very simple—so simple it can be expressed in four short words: *saved for God's glory*.

In one sense, of course, God does everything for his glory. In his famous "Dissertation Concerning the End for Which God Created the World," Jonathan Edwards (1703–1758) wrote, "The great end of God's works, which is so variously expressed in Scripture, is indeed but ONE; and this *one* end is most properly and comprehensively called THE GLORY OF GOD."[17] The chief end of God is to glorify himself in all he is and all he does. But this is especially true of the exodus. One of the most glorious things God ever did was to save his people out of Egypt. The exodus was for his glory. As the psalmist wrote, "Our fathers, when they were in Egypt . . . he saved them for his name's sake, that he might make known his mighty power" (Psalm 106:7, 8).

God makes his glorious purpose known throughout the book of Exodus. Whenever Moses told Pharaoh to let God's people go, the reason he gave was so they could glorify God. Pharaoh heard it over and over again: "Let my people go, that they may serve me" (e.g., 9:1). But Pharaoh would not let God's people go. From the human standpoint, this was because his heart was hard. But from the divine perspective, God hardened Pharaoh's heart so that he could glorify himself. Three times God promised to gain glory for himself through Pharaoh: "And the Egyptians shall know that I am the Lord, when I have gotten glory over Pharaoh, his chariots, and his horsemen" (14:18; cf. 9:16; 14:4, 17; Romans 9:17).

God did gain glory for himself—at Pharaoh's expense! And as soon as his people escaped from Pharaoh's clutches, they glorified God. The crossing of the Red Sea was followed immediately by the Song of Moses, in which the people praised God for being "majestic in holiness, awesome in glorious deeds, doing wonders" (15:11). As the Israelites traveled farther into the desert, they saw "the glory of the Lord [appear] in the cloud" (16:10). Finally they arrived at God's holy mountain, where they again witnessed God's glory in thunder and lightning (24:15–17). They also heard it in the words of the covenant, which were given to help them glorify God.

Tragically, while the Israelites were waiting for Moses to come back down the mountain, they started dancing around a golden calf. God was so angry with them that he was ready to destroy them. Why? Because although they were saved for God's glory, they were not giving him the glory. But Moses interceded, asking God to have mercy on them, and he made his appeal on the basis of God's glory (32:11–14). If God destroyed the Israelites, Moses argued, then the Egyptians would not glorify him as the God who saved his people. Afterward Moses went back up the mountain, and there he asked to see the glory of God (33:18–23). And see it he did, glimpsing the back of God's glory. When Moses came back down from the mountain, he himself was glorious, radiating with the brightness of God's glory (34:29–35).

The last chapters of Exodus contain detailed instructions for building the tabernacle. Rather than being irrelevant to the exodus, as some have thought, these chapters explain the whole point of the adventure. We are saved to glorify God, which means worshiping him the way he desires to be worshiped. Concerning the tabernacle, God said, "It shall be sanctified by my glory" (29:43). Thus the climax of the whole book comes at the very end: "Then the cloud covered the tent of meeting, and the glory of the LORD filled the tabernacle. And Moses was not able to enter the tent of meeting because the cloud settled on it, and the glory of the LORD filled the tabernacle" (40:34, 35).

From beginning to end, the exodus was for the glory of God. The whole glorious adventure shows that the God of Israel is the God who saves. Anyone who wants to be saved may call on his name and on the name of his divine Son, the Savior, Jesus Christ. This is what the psalmist did at the end of Psalm 106, the "Exodus Psalm." After recounting the entire epic—explaining how God saved his people out of Egypt in spite of their sin—the psalmist invites us to call on God for our own salvation: "Save us, O LORD our God, and gather us from among the nations" (Psalm 106:47a). We do not deserve to be saved from sin any more than the Israelites deserved to be brought out of Egypt. But God saves us for his glory, so "that we may give thanks to [his] holy name and glory in [his] praise," saying, "Blessed be the LORD, the God of Israel, from everlasting to everlasting!" (Psalm 106:47b, 48a).

# 2

# The New Pharaoh

## EXODUS 1:8–21

NOW THERE AROSE A NEW KING OVER EGYPT, who did not know Joseph" (1:8). With these ominous words, Israel's sojourn among the Egyptians turned from prosperity to persecution. What had once seemed like a promising place to grow into a godly nation became a house of bondage, a wasteland of back-breaking torment.

God had never intended Egypt to become the Promised Land. Joseph had prophesied from his deathbed, "God will visit you and bring you up out of this land to the land that he swore to Abraham, to Isaac, and to Jacob" (Genesis 50:24). Joseph had even made the sons of Israel promise that they would carry his bones back to Canaan. Yet for a time it had been good to live in the land of the Pharaohs. As long as Joseph ruled as the prince of Egypt, the Israelites held a position of privilege. To give but one example, when Joseph went to Canaan to bury his father Jacob, he was accompanied by Pharaoh's highest-ranking officials—"all the servants of Pharaoh, the elders of his household, and all the elders of the land of Egypt" (Genesis 50:7). Obviously Joseph was held in high esteem. Upon his return to Egypt he settled down to a long and happy life in the Nile Delta. And even after Joseph died, the Israelites lived in peace and prosperity. In keeping with God's promise, they "multiplied and grew exceedingly strong, so that the land was filled with them" (1:7).

Then the situation changed. A new dynasty came to power. It was in with the new regime, and out with the old. When it comes to power politics, it's all about who you know. Unfortunately, the new Pharaoh did not know Joseph, and thus he felt no sense of obligation to his descendants. Gradually the Egyptians began to fear the Israelites, and then to hate them, until finally they wanted to subjugate them. This part of Exodus is about Satan's opposition to God's plans and promises for his people. From it we learn how to remain faithful to God, even in times of tribulation.

## The House of Bondage

The new Pharaoh thought he had a problem. "'And he said to his people, 'Behold, the people of Israel are too many and too mighty for us. Come, let us deal shrewdly with them, lest they multiply, and, if war breaks out, they join our enemies and fight against us and escape from the land'" (1:9, 10). Like most dictators, the new Pharaoh was insecure (not to say paranoid). Despite his military superiority, he was worried about getting overthrown. And the more foreigners there were in his country, the more alarmed he became. Soon the immigrant population grew so large that it threatened to destabilize his entire government. Pharaoh worried that the next time he was attacked, the Israelites would join forces with his enemies, outnumber his own army, and bring his dynasty to an end.

Someone has described an excuse as a "thin skin of reason wrapped around a lie," which is exactly the kind of excuse this was. Pharaoh used the threat of warfare as a pretext for persecuting foreigners. Blaming things on ethnic minorities is always convenient because racism is part of our sinful human nature. This is what made it so easy for Hitler to promote anti-Semitism in Nazi Germany. It is why the Afrikaaners were able to use the "black threat" argument to such deadly advantage in South Africa. And it is why each new wave of immigrants—from the Irish to the Indonesians—has faced prejudice upon coming to America.

Playing the race card worked for Pharaoh too. His advisers were only too willing to agree that something had to be done about those Israelites. "Therefore they set taskmasters over them to afflict them with heavy burdens. They built for Pharaoh store cities, Pithom and Raamses" (1:11). It was the ultimate political solution: The new policy simultaneously solved both Egypt's immigrant problem and its labor problem. With their spirits crushed and backs bent with pain, the Israelites would be unable to rebel. As an added benefit, Pharaoh's tyranny would lead to the construction of two great cities. Pithom means "house of Atum," who was one of the Egyptian gods. The city is usually identified with Tell er-Ratabah or Tell el-Maskhutah. An ancient text about it reads: "His Majesty—life, prosperity, health!—has built himself a castle, the name of which is 'Great of Victories.' . . . The sun rises in its horizon, and sets within it."[1] Rameses—which may be the famed city of Tanis, or more likely, Qantir—was the royal residence of the Pharaohs. The sons of Israel built these two great cities with their own bare hands and on their own sturdy backs.

The lust for power is never satisfied, however, and in time the Israelites became more bitterly enslaved. They were treated more and more harshly, until finally "the Egyptians were in dread of the people of Israel. So they ruthlessly made the people of Israel work as slaves and made their lives bitter with hard service, in mortar and brick, and in all kinds of work in the field. In all their work they ruthlessly made them work as slaves" (1:12b–14).

One of the interesting literary features of Exodus is that significant words often come in groups of seven. One example of this occurred back in verse 7, which used seven different words to describe the miraculous multiplication of the Israelites. Another example occurs here in verses 13, 14, which use seven words (some of which are repeated) for Israel's slavery. Umberto Cassuto claims that each word is like another blow from a slave driver's whip. This is brought out in Cassuto's translation: "So the Egyptians made the children of Israel *work* with *rigour* and made their lives bitter with hard *service*, in mortar and brick, and in all kinds of *work* in the field, in addition to all their (other) *work*, wherein they made them *serve* with *rigour*."[2]

With each crack of the whip, Pharaoh was striking another blow against the God of Israel, because ultimately this was a spiritual conflict. Pharaoh was really fighting against God. He resented *God's people*. The Israelites were meant for God's glory. They were supposed to be free to serve him. But by making the Israelites his slaves, Pharaoh tried to prevent them from fulfilling their calling to work and play to the glory of God.

Pharaoh also rejected *God's promises*. God had covenanted to make his people into a great nation. The more numerous they became, the more his promise was fulfilled. If Pharaoh had been God's servant, he would have rejoiced at the birth of each new Hebrew baby. But he did not. Instead the fulfillment of God's promise filled him with fear and loathing.

Pharaoh also resisted *God's plan*, which was to give his people a land to call their own—the homeland he had promised to Abraham, Isaac, and Jacob. It was the same land that Joseph had prophesied for his brothers: "By faith Joseph, at the end of his life, made mention of the exodus of the Israelites and gave directions concerning his bones" (Hebrews 11:22). The land "flowing with milk and honey" was the next phase in God's eternal plan for his people. However, Pharaoh was hostile to that plan from the very beginning. Notice the reason he gives for oppressing the Israelites: "let us deal shrewdly with them, lest they . . . escape from the land" (1:10). With those words, Pharaoh set himself up as the obstacle to the exodus. He was utterly opposed to the one thing God was absolutely determined to do (see 3:8).

In short, Pharaoh is the very picture of man in rebellion against God. He resented God's people, rejected God's promises, and resisted God's plan. Given his proud opposition, it is not surprising that we are never told his name. He is called "the king of Egypt," or simply "Pharaoh." The omission of Pharaoh's name is theologically significant. James Hoffmeier writes: "The absence of the pharaoh's name may ultimately be for theological reasons, because the Bible is not trying to answer the question 'who is the pharaoh of the exodus' to satisfy the curiosity of modern historians; rather, it was seeking to clarify for Israel who was the God of the exodus."[3] The Pharaoh of Egypt was not a private individual; rather, he represented the entire nation of Egypt, including their gods. To be specific, Pharaoh claimed to be the incarnate Son of Re—the sun god—who was the primary deity in the Egyptian pantheon. This means that the struggle between Israel and Egypt was not about politics but about religion.

Pharaoh's strategy for claiming sovereignty over Israel was slavery. In the Egyptian temple of Edfu, there is an inscription from the time of Rameses depicting a god registering slaves for Pharaoh.[4] The picture is a reminder that by enslaving the Israelites, Pharaoh was trying to make a theological point: The Hebrews would not serve their own God—they would work for him. They would not be free to go to the land of God's promise—they would stay right where they were. In effect, Pharaoh was claiming to be the lord of Israel, and by doing so—perhaps without even realizing it—he became the tool of Satan. In his book on spiritual warfare Donald Grey Barnhouse called Egypt "the greatest symbol of Satan's enmity against the children of Israel," and he went on to say: "The devil was in Egypt. The devil was ruling Egypt. Behind Pharaoh there was Satan."[5] The exodus, therefore, was not simply an epic struggle between Moses and Pharaoh, or between Israel and Egypt. Ultimately it was another skirmish in the great, ongoing war between God and Satan.

## Prosperity under Persecution

Satan likes nothing better than to torment God's people, and he used Pharaoh to persecute the Israelites for their faith. It is important to remember how much they suffered, and also how much they learned from their suffering.

There is ample evidence that the Egyptians treated their slaves with barbaric brutality. It was state-sponsored terrorism, for slaves were considered Pharaoh's property. Once they were marked with his royal seal, Pharaoh's slaves were organized into huge work gangs, concentrated in labor camps, and then forced to complete massive building projects—all under the strict control of their masters. Inscriptions in the tomb of Rekhmire at Thebes depict prisoners from Canaan at all stages of brick making: hauling water, pouring clay, cutting bricks, hauling stacks of bricks to a work site, and then laying them with mortar. They are supervised by taskmasters armed with sticks, ready to beat their slaves into submission.[6] Or consider the following ancient text, which describes an Egyptian master traveling down the Nile to inspect his slaves: "Now the scribe lands on the shore. He surveys the harvest. Attendants are behind him with staffs, Nubians with clubs. One says [to him]: 'Give grain.' 'There is none.' He is beaten savagely. He is bound, thrown in the well, submerged head down. His wife is bound in his presence. His children are in fetters."[7]

This is the kind of cruelty the Israelites suffered at the hands of the Egyptians. They were treated "ruthlessly" (1:14), or more literally they were "broken down." The words of the old African-American spiritual "Go Down, Moses" are true:

When Israel was in Egyptland,
Let my people go,
Oppressed so hard they could not stand,
Let my people go.

The oppression of the Israelites raises an important question. It is the question human beings always raise about suffering. Jesus asked it when he was dying on the cross. The question is, "Why, God?" or as Jesus put it, "My God, my God, why have you forsaken me?" (Matthew 27:46). It is suffering that inserts the question marks into the story of our lives.

The first thing to say about Israel's suffering is that the Egyptians were to blame. It is impossible to give an adequate answer to the problem of pain without mentioning the Biblical doctrine of sin. Rather than blaming God for all our troubles, we need to recognize that suffering is the inevitable result of human iniquity. In one way or another, all our trials can be traced back to sin—either our own or the sins of others. In this case, the Israelites were victims of slavery because the Egyptians enslaved them.

This does not mean, however, that their suffering was outside God's control. Could God have prevented his people from ever falling into slavery? Of course he could have, but that was not his plan. It was through God's providence that the Israelites went down to Egypt, and it was by his providence that they became slaves there. Exodus makes this connection by beginning with a quotation from Genesis 46:8 ("These are the names of the sons of Israel"). This is a way of hinting that the God who will get them out of Egypt (in Exodus) is the same God who first led them into Egypt (in Genesis). The psalmist is even more explicit when he says of the Egyptians: "[God] turned their hearts to hate his people, to deal craftily with his servants" (Psalm 105:25).

God had many reasons for allowing his people to suffer hardship. The most obvious was to help them grow: "But the more they were oppressed, the more they multiplied and the more they spread abroad" (1:12). The irony is that this was exactly the opposite of what Pharaoh intended to happen. In verse 10 Pharaoh says *pen-yirbe*, which means "lest they multiply," but in verse 12 God says *ken-yirbe*—"the more they multiplied." The Bible uses this Hebrew pun to show that the joke was on Pharaoh, who had always prided himself on being politically astute. We must "deal shrewdly" with the Israelites, he said to his advisers. What Pharaoh meant by "deal[ing] shrewdly" was politics as usual: pursue military strength, exploit the poor, attack minorities. But the conventional wisdom proved to be folly, because Pharaoh was dealing with the God who says, "I will destroy the wisdom of the wise, and the discernment of the discerning I will thwart" (1 Corinthians 1:19). By keeping the Israelites enslaved, the new Pharaoh actually helped preserve their identity as a close-knit community. Charles Spurgeon comments:

> [I]n all probability, if they had been left to themselves, they would have been melted and absorbed into the Egyptian race, and lost their identity as God's special people. They were content to be in Egypt, and they were quite willing to be Egyptianized. To a large degree, they began to adopt the superstitions, and idolatries, and iniquities of Egypt; and these things clung to them, in after years, to such a terrible extent that we can easily imagine that their heart must have turned aside very much towards the sins of Egypt. Yet, all the while, God was resolved to bring them out of that evil connection. They must be a separated people; they could not be Egyptians, nor yet live permanently like Egyptians, for Jehovah had chosen them for himself, and he meant to make an abiding difference between Israel and Egypt.[8]

Strange to say, one of the ways God preserved this difference was by enslaving his people to Pharaoh. Thus the new Pharaoh was the original rebel without a clue. The more he made God's people suffer, the more God triumphed!

Despite all his clever schemes, Pharaoh ended up being thoroughly outsmarted. By the end of the first chapter of Exodus, we find the Israelites still increasing and becoming more numerous (v. 20). This is exactly what God had promised when he said to Jacob, "Do not be afraid to go down to Egypt, for there I will make you into a great nation" (Genesis 46:3). In future generations God's people would say, "The God of this people Israel chose our fathers and made the people great during their stay in the land of Egypt, and with uplifted arm he led them out of it" (Acts 13:17). And the way God accomplished this saving plan was through suffering. By keeping the Israelites in bondage, Pharaoh actually helped make them into a great nation.

This pattern of growth through suffering has been repeated many times in the history of the church. According to Spurgeon,

> Whenever there has been a great persecution raised against the Christian church, God has overruled it, as he did in the case of Pharaoh's oppression of the Israelites, by making the aggrieved community more largely to increase. The early persecutions in Judea promoted the spread of the gospel; hence, when after the death of Stephen the disciples were all scattered abroad throughout the regions of Judea and Samaria, except the apostles, the result is thus given: "Therefore they that were scattered abroad went everywhere preaching the word." So, too, when Herod stretched forth his hands to vex certain of the church, and killed James, the brother of John, with the sword; what came of it? Why Luke tells us in almost the same words that Moses had used: "The word of God grew and multiplied." Those terrible and bloody persecutions under the Roman Emperor by no means stayed the progress of the gospel; but strangely enough seemed to press forward for the crown of martyrdom. The church probably never increased at a greater ratio than as when her foes were most fierce to assail and most resolute to destroy her. . . . The Reformation . . . never went on so prosperously as when it was most vigorously opposed. You shall find in any indi-

> vidual church that wherever evil men have conspired together, and a storm of opposition has burst forth against the saints, the heart of the Lord has been moved with compassion. . . . Be patient, then, my brethren, amidst the persecutions or trials you may be called upon to bear; and be thankful that they are so often overruled for the growth of the church, the spread of the gospel, and the honor of Christ.[9]

Another reason God allowed his people to suffer was to show them their need of salvation. In a helpful book called *Why Does It Have to Hurt?* professor Dan McCartney notes, "God saw the suffering of his people and then delivered them. But why did he allow the suffering to happen in the first place? Could he not rather have simply prevented it?" McCartney answers by raising another question: "If he had done so, would the Israelites have ever desired to leave Egypt? It was hard enough to get them to leave even when they were suffering."[10] Egypt was the only home they had ever known, and it was not without its luxuries; so it took suffering and bondage to make God's people cry out for their salvation. Once again the joke was on Pharaoh. By enslaving the Israelites, he made them long for the very thing he was trying to prevent: freedom in a new land. Spurgeon writes: "In order to cut loose the bonds that bound them to Egypt, the sharp knife of affliction must be used; and Pharaoh though he knew it not, was God's instrument in weaning them from the Egyptian world, and helping them as his church to take up their separate place in the wilderness, and receive the portion which God had appointed for them."[11]

This teaches us an important lesson about our own spiritual pilgrimage: suffering helps us look for our Savior. If we never have any trouble along the journey, we would never have any reason to long for Heaven. Like the Israelites, we need the house of bondage to help drive us to the Promised Land. McCartney writes, "It is hard enough for us to leave aside the treasures of this evil world even though we suffer in it. How much harder is it for us to desire the new heavens and new earth when our lives here are comfortable?"[12] Our sufferings help us look for our salvation. Or to quote again from Spurgeon, "The whip of persecution is helpful, because it makes us learn that this is the house of bondage, and moves us to long after and seek for the land of liberty—the land of joy."[13]

Once we have been saved, our sufferings also remind us to show gratitude for God's grace. This was another lesson the Israelites could only have learned by languishing in Egypt. After they were released from captivity, they were always to remember that they had been enslaved. For example, when they sat down to share their Passover meal, they ate bitter herbs to remind them of their bitter slavery (12:8). They were to say:

> A wandering Aramean was my father. And he went down into Egypt and sojourned there, few in number, and there he became a nation, great, mighty, and populous. And the Egyptians treated us harshly and humili-

> ated us and laid on us hard labor. Then we cried to the LORD, the God of our fathers, and the LORD heard our voice and saw our affliction, our toil, and our oppression. And the LORD brought us out of Egypt with a mighty hand and an outstretched arm, with great deeds of terror, with signs and wonders. And he brought us into this place and gave us this land, a land flowing with milk and honey . . . you shall rejoice in all the good that the LORD your God has given to you and to your house. (Deuteronomy 26:5–9, 11b)

The exodus was meant to be remembered. We should remember it, too, for we are God's people, and this is part of our history. Praise God for bringing us out of the land of Egypt, out of the house of bondage!

There were many reasons why God allowed his people to be persecuted at the hands of the Egyptians. The point is that God always has a purpose for suffering, and for his people, his purpose is always redemptive. This is the pattern of the cross. It was through his sufferings and death that Jesus accomplished our salvation. It is also the pattern of the Christian life: "Christ also suffered for you, leaving you an example, so that you might follow in his steps" (1 Peter 2:21). We may suffer hatred and persecution; Christians often do. Yet suffering produces spiritual growth: "We rejoice in our sufferings, knowing that suffering produces endurance, and endurance produces character, and character produces hope" (Romans 5:3, 4). It is suffering that makes us long for our salvation and reminds us to rejoice in God's grace.

## Anti-Life, Anti-Christ

Eventually God's people were delivered from the house of bondage, but before things got better, they got worse. Much worse. When Pharaoh realized that captivity was doing nothing to bring the Israelites under control—that in fact their population was growing by leaps and bounds—he devised a new strategy. He turned from slavery to slaughter, thereby usurping God's authority over life and death: "Then the king of Egypt said to the Hebrew midwives, one of whom was named Shiphrah and the other Puah, 'When you serve as midwife to the Hebrew women and see them on the birthstool, if it is a son, you shall kill him, but if it is a daughter, she shall live'" (1:15, 16).

Commentators have raised several questions about these verses. One question concerns the ethnic identity of these midwives. The Bible literally identifies them as "the midwives of the Hebrews," but it does not specify whether or not they were Hebrews themselves. They may have been Egyptians; after all, how could Pharaoh expect Hebrew women to murder their own people? On the other hand, Pharaoh ruled with such an iron fist that it might not even have occurred to him that anyone would dare to disobey. Furthermore, the names Shiphrah and Puah are Hebrew, which makes it likely that these women were indeed Israelites.

Another question concerns the number of midwives. If there were as many

Israelites as the Bible says there were—hundreds of thousands in all—how could two midwives possibly be enough to care for so many pregnancies? The most likely answer is that Shiphrah and Puah were in charge of other midwives. Today we would call them head nurses. Here it helps to know that the Egyptian government, which held tight organizational controls over Egyptian society, employed overseers to superintend nearly every craft or skill—a system not unlike the professional guilds of medieval Europe.[14]

Other scholars wonder why Pharaoh ordered the midwives to kill the boys rather than the girls. If he wanted to stop the Hebrews from having babies, wouldn't it have made more sense to kill the females? But remember that Pharaoh was mainly worried about the Israelites becoming a military threat. The goal of his selective genocide was to prevent his enemies from raising young warriors. So he ordered Shiphrah and Puah to commit infanticide. While the mother was still recovering from her delivery, the midwives were quickly to examine the child, and if it turned out to be a boy, they were to murder him.

When Pharaoh issued this death warrant, he became an enemy of life. He was attempting to countermand the creation mandate, in which God told his people, "Be fruitful and multiply and fill the earth" (Genesis 1:28). Pharaoh also became an antichrist by opposing God's special plan for sending a savior. From the very day that Adam and Eve first sinned, God had always promised to send his people someone to save them from their sins—the offspring of a woman, a son to crush Satan's head (Genesis 3:15). God's people trusted that promise, waiting in hope for the coming of the Christ. Whether he knew it or not, Pharaoh was "the seed of the serpent" that God had promised would strike at the heel of the woman's seed. By trying to prevent the Savior from ever becoming a man, Pharaoh became an antichrist.

Pharaoh's attempt to exterminate the sons of Israel anticipated all the antichrists of history. Wherever there is a reign of terror or a culture of death, Satan is trying to destroy the work of God. The slogans change, but the sin remains the same. Whether it is Adolf Hitler and his "final solution" for eliminating the Jews, or Communist China and its "one family, one child" policy, or the "pro-choice" movement in the West, opposition to life is always hatred of God.

There is also an analogy here to the life of the soul. Pharaoh had two strategies for preventing God's people from growing: slavery and death. These are the same weapons Satan uses when he tries to destroy a human being. First, sin leads to slavery, for as Jesus said, "Everyone who practices sin is a slave to sin" (John 8:34). Then once we are enslaved, sin leads to death: "For the wages of sin is death" (Romans 6:23). What we need is exactly what the Israelites needed: a Savior to deliver us from slavery and to rescue us from death by destroying our enemy. Just as God provided a savior for Israel (Moses), so he has provided a Savior for us (Jesus). Where once there was only bondage and death, now Jesus brings liberty and life. In the words of the Apostle Paul, "I see in my members another law . . . making me captive to the law of sin that dwells in my members. Wretched man that I am! Who will deliver me from this body of death? Thanks be to God through Jesus Christ our Lord!" (Romans 7:23–25a).

### The Pro-life Resistance

It is not easy to stand up to Satan, or even to stand up to one of his lackeys like Pharaoh. This is why Shiphrah and Puah are two of the great women of the Bible. Shiphrah means something like "beautiful one," while Puah means "splendid one." Both of them lived up to their names.

Shiphrah and Puah were splendid and beautiful in many ways. They had a noble calling. As midwives they had dedicated their lives to medical care. The many godly women who throughout history have devoted themselves to medicine are daughters of Shiphrah and Puah. These midwives must have helped many mothers and their babies survive desperate deliveries. No doubt they had also comforted many women upon the death of their newborn children.

The last thing that a woman like Shiphrah or Puah would ever do is take an innocent life. These midwives understood the mind and heart of God. Even though they had not yet received the Ten Commandments, they knew better than to commit murder. Perhaps they were familiar with God's words to Noah:

> Whoever sheds the blood of man,
> by man shall his blood be shed,
> for God made man in his own image. (Genesis 9:6)

In any case, Shiphrah and Puah knew that God is the Lord of life. So they "did not do as the king of Egypt commanded them, but let the male children live" (1:17).

This was an act of civil disobedience. Pharaoh gave the midwives a direct order, and they disobeyed it. But this is what God's people always do when the laws of men contradict the laws of God. Our first allegiance is to God, and as Peter and the other apostles said, "We must obey God rather than men" (Acts 5:29). There are times when Christians not only have the right but also the responsibility to resist. In a way this act of civil disobedience was the start of a revolution, the first beginnings of the slave revolt that ultimately led Israel out of Egypt.

By refusing to follow Pharaoh's orders, Shiphrah and Puah became the first pro-life heroines. The reason these women had the courage to do such a splendid, beautiful thing is that they feared God much more than they feared Pharaoh. Pharaoh was the most powerful man in the world. With a simple wave of his hand, he could have had them executed. Yet Shiphrah and Puah dared to risk their lives because they "feared God" (1:17). They understood that obeying God is always the safest thing. They were acting in accordance with the command of

Christ, who said, "Do not fear those who kill the body but cannot kill the soul" (Matthew 10:28).

Pharaoh, who was not used to having people defy his orders, summoned the midwives so he could accuse them of insubordination. He asked them, "Why have you done this, and let the male children live?" (1:18). What is odd about the wording of Pharaoh's charge is that the midwives had not done anything. Cassuto writes that "in truth they did not do anything, on the contrary they refrained from taking action; but this is the way the wicked despot puts it: he who refused to obey him acts, as it were, against him."[15]

Pharaoh's accusation put Shiphrah and Puah in a precarious position. If they told him the truth, they would undoubtedly be killed. But they also knew that it would not be right to bear false witness. This is the kind of dilemma God's people sometimes face in an evil world, where neither option seems to be free from sin. Notice what these women decided to say: "Because the Hebrew women are not like the Egyptian women, for they are vigorous and give birth before the midwife comes to them" (1:19). The implication was that by the time the midwives arrived, the family had already welcomed the child, and there was no way secretly to put him to death.

A great deal of ink has been spilled over this verse, with many fine commentators taking the midwives to task for telling a lie. Augustine, in his treatise on lying (*De Mendacio*), concluded that the midwives were guilty of deceit. "Gregory also argues that the midwives' lying was reprehensible and diverted their true reward of eternal life into a mere earthly recompense. . . . Calvin argued in his commentary that the lying of the midwives was reprehensible and displeasing to God. Notwithstanding, since no action is free of sin, God rewarded their good works even if mixed with impurity."[16]

A less critical answer is offered by J. B. Lightfoot, the astute nineteenth-century English Bible commentator, who described the words of the Hebrew midwives as "not a lie, but a glorious confession of their faith."[17] Their lie—if it can even be considered a lie—was such a whopper that they can hardly be accused of trying to deceive anyone! Think about it: If what Shiphrah and Puah said was literally true, then why would the Hebrews even need midwives? This is one of the places where understanding the Bible requires a sense of humor. Speaking tongue-in-cheek, the midwives were making sport of Pharaoh by suggesting that the Hebrews were hardier than the Egyptians. What they said was more a joke than a lie. Thus Pharaoh was mocked as well as deceived.

An interesting parallel to the response of the Hebrew midwives comes from the village of Le Chambon, where five thousand French Reformed Protestants rescued some five thousand Jews from the Nazi horrors. It is said that during World War II Le Chambon was the safest place for a Jew in all of Europe. The brave Chambonnais Christians who risked their lives faced many difficult ethical dilemmas. On one occasion the chief of the Vichy police interrogated the ringleader of the resistance, pastor André Trocmé. "Pastor," he said, "we know in detail the suspect activities to which you are devoted. You are hiding in this commune a certain number of Jews, whose names I know. . . . You are therefore going to give me the list of these persons and of their addresses." Trocmé replied that he did not know the names of any of these people. Strictly speaking, this was true, because the Jews had all been given false identity cards. Although this seemed like the only way to save lives, Trocmé and others lamented what seemed to be a loss of their usual candor. On another occasion a Nazi lieutenant demanded to know where the Jewish refugees were hiding. "Jews?" the Chambonnais replied, as if astonished. "What would Jews be doing here? You, there, have you seen any Jews? They say they have crooked noses."[18] To be sure, such a reply required an element of deception, yet it was more like a jest.

But what if Shiphrah and Puah *did* tell a lie? If so, then it might have been better not to say anything at all, for "Lying lips are an abomination to the Lord" (Proverbs 12:22). Yet this lie was told to protect innocent lives from a man who had no right to the truth. They bore false witness, to be sure, but it was hardly against their neighbor! Göran Larsson concludes that "Shiphrah and Puah were lying to Pharaoh in verse 19. But they did so in the service of life and love! In so doing, they saved many human lives, and perhaps they even saved the one destined to become the savior of Israel."[19]

Whatever ethical conclusion we reach about this act of "creative disobedience," what the midwives said satisfied Pharaoh (who seems on this occasion at least to have been a few bricks shy of a pyramid). More importantly, what they did pleased God. In a story one of the best ways to tell whether or not people have done the right thing is to see what happens to them. In this case Shiphrah and Puah received just reward for the obedience of their faith: "So God dealt well with the midwives. And the people multiplied and grew very strong. And because the midwives feared God, he gave them families" (1:20, 21).

By the blessing of God, Pharaoh's attempt to control the population ended up making the Israelites even more numerous! He was outsmarted again, this time by a pair of resourceful women. And God blessed Shiphrah and Puah by giving them families of their own. Whether this was through marriage, childbirth, or adoption, the Bible does not say, but it proves how much better it is to obey God than to fear human beings.

A powerful example of what it means for a Christian to fear God comes from the life of a Dinka tribeswoman from Sudan named Mayen Anyang. This is how she tells her story:

> I was at the market in Abin Dau with my family, including our five children, when the raiders came. We were all taken captive. I was tied by my wrists in a chain to other captives. The journey to the North was very hard. We had to walk for about two solid days. We were given scarcely any food,

> and I and my children were beaten. I have a scar on my wrist from where I was bound. At the end of my journey I was separated from my family and taken to a camp in Shetep. Those who ran the camp put constant pressure on me to convert to Islam. About twice a day they would tell me we should all become Muslim and then it would be possible to live together as brothers, but that if we did not they would kill us all. On several occasions this was accompanied by beatings. I was beaten severely with sticks. The upper bone in my arm now sticks out as a result of this beating. On another occasion, during the night, they came to me again and told me that I must become a Muslim and that they would beat me if I did not. I cannot change my religion. I am a Christian and have committed myself to Christ.[20]

These are the words of a splendid, beautiful woman. They show that fearing God means obeying him even when it means suffering and danger. Mayen's story is a challenge to every Christian who lives in peace and safety. Sooner or later we will be forced to take a stand, to decide whether we fear God or other people. Perhaps it will be at home, where family members are suspicious of our Christianity. Or maybe it will be at work, where we are pressured to lie, cheat, or steal. Then again it might be in our community, where our values contradict the spirit of the age.

When that time comes, what will you say? The splendid, beautiful thing to say is, "I am a Christian and have committed myself to Christ."

# 3

# The Birth of a Savior

## EXODUS 1:22—2:10

DESPERATE TIMES CALL FOR DESPERATE MEASURES. Worried by the rising tide of immigration, Pharaoh tried everything he could think of to stop the Israelites from flooding over Egypt. First he forced God's people to become his slaves, "But the more they were oppressed, the more they multiplied and the more they spread abroad" (1:12). Next he ordered the midwives Shiphrah and Puah to kill every Hebrew boy at birth. But these two splendid women defied Pharaoh, and "the people multiplied and grew very strong" (1:20).

Poor Pharaoh! It seemed that the more he tried to weaken the Israelites, the more powerful they became! Having failed at slavery and infanticide, he finally resorted to genocide: "Then Pharaoh commanded all his people, 'Every son that is born to the Hebrews you shall cast into the Nile, but you shall let every daughter live'" (1:22).

### No Ordinary Child

It was during these desperate times that a young Hebrew couple dared to marry, and when they celebrated the uniting act of their love, they produced a son: "Now a man from the house of Levi went and took as his wife a Levite woman. The woman conceived and bore a son, and when she saw that he was a fine child, she hid him three months" (2:1, 2).

What was a mother to do? Her baby was a fine, healthy boy. Even if she did not realize that she had given birth to a savior or deliverer, there did seem to be something special about him. At least he seemed perfect to her, the most beautiful baby she had ever seen. This made it all the more terrifying that he was born under a death sentence, that at any moment an Egyptian might hear his cries, seize him, and cast him into the great river. For three months the woman lived in constant fear, nestling her baby close to her breast and whispering, "Hush, my child!"

At this point the Bible does not mention the mother's name, no doubt because this story is mainly about her baby. Later we will learn that she was called Jochebed and that she was married to Amram (6:20). But here she is left unnamed, anonymous. She was just an ordinary woman. The only extraordinary thing about her was that she lived by faith. In Hebrews 11—the Faith Hall of Fame—we read that "By faith Moses, when he was born, was hidden for three months by his parents, because they saw that the child was beautiful, and they were not afraid of the king's edict" (Hebrews 11:23). This brave couple feared God more than they feared any man. They were determined to live by faith. But then raising a child is always an act of faith. It is by faith that a husband and wife pray for a child, share sexual relations, and give birth. It is by faith that they train their children and then send them out into the world. Children do not flourish unless they are raised by faith and not by fear.

This particular child was sent out into the world long before his mother was ready. But desperate times call for desperate measures, and "when she could hide him no longer, she took for him a basket made of bulrushes and daubed it with bitumen and pitch. She put the child in it and placed it among the reeds by the river bank" (2:3). For three months the baby had survived, undetected. But the poor woman was at her wit's end, her nerves frayed by the unremitting suspense. The baby was loud, as babies always are, and she feared that the more active he became, the more likely he was to be discovered.

Before she sent her beloved child out to face the crocodiles, the mother did everything she could to protect him. She waterproofed his little boat by covering it with pitch. All the while she must have felt much the way one African mother felt at the loss of a child: "Oh child of my womb and fruit of my desire, it was pleasure to hold the small cheeks in the hands, it was pleasure to feel the tiny clutching of the fingers, it was pleasure to feel the little mouth tugging at the breast. Such is the nature of woman. Such is the lot of women, to carry, to bear, to watch, and to lose."[1]

Then she closed the lid and set him afloat. This was another act of creative disobedience. If Pharaoh had decreed that all the baby boys must be thrown into the river, then into the river he would go! But it still went against every motherly instinct in her body. Jochebed's actions are described so as to emphasize her tenderness. To translate the Hebrew more literally, "she *placed* the child in [the basket] and *placed* it among the reeds" (2:3). When she gently laid her baby down, she was tucking her heart inside the basket. It was the kind of thing a mother could only do by faith, but then she was a woman of faith. Having received her son as a gift from the Lord, she turned him back over to the Lord in faith. Jochebed would hardly have sent her daughter along to watch if she had expected her child to be murdered! If it seemed like she was abandoning him, it was only to God's loving care, as every faithful parent must.

## The Quest for the Historical Moses

Jochebed let her baby go because it was part of God's plan for helping him achieve his destiny. This little child was destined to become Israel's savior. From his birth we learn at least three things about salvation, and the first is that God accomplishes salvation in human history.

Here we need to respond to the objection that Moses (for that was to be the child's name) never existed. Scholars raise this objection in part because he is not mentioned in any of the historical accounts left by the Egyptians. As we have seen, this is not surprising. There are many gaps in the Egyptian records, especially when it comes to their embarrassing defeats. It is also important to remember that the Bible itself provides reliable historical evidence. There are many different types of literature in the Bible: law, poetry, genealogy, gospel, epistle, and so forth. But a great deal of the Biblical material, including the book of Exodus, is presented as history. When it comes to Moses, the Bible carefully records that he was a great-grandson of Levi, who was one of the twelve sons of Jacob and the father of Israel's priests (6:16–20). In time Moses became Israel's deliverer, the great prophet who led his people out of Egypt. These are all historical claims that the Bible presents as matters of fact.

Another objection to the historicity of Moses comes from extra-Biblical literature, where the abandoned child who rises to greatness is a popular motif.[2] The most famous example is the story of Sargon, king of Akkad, who lived centuries before Israel went into Egypt:

> Sargon, the mighty king, king of Agade, am I.
> My mother was a changeling, my father I knew not.
> The brother(s) of my father loved the hills.
> My city is Azuprianu, which is situated on the banks of the Euphrates.
> My changeling mother conceived me, in secret she bore me.
> She set me in a basket of rushes, with bitumen she sealed my lid.
> She cast me into the river which rose not (over) me.[3]

According to the legend, Sargon was later rescued out of the water by a gardener named Akki. The existence of such stories has led some scholars to conclude that "the quest for the historical Moses is a futile exercise. He now belongs only to legend."[4] The great liberator "was a creation of the ancient Hebrews' binding together their own national epic out of the tales of neighbors."[5] He was "merely a character in a grand historical novel, the invention of storytellers."[6]

There are several ways to handle the allegation of literary dependence. One is to point out that "The Legend of Sargon" was actually written after the book of Exodus. Although Sargon himself lived from 2371–2316 BC, the manuscript fragments that contain his birth narrative come from the Neo-Assyrian or Neo-Babylonian period (seventh or sixth century). Perhaps the story originated during the reign of Sargon II (721–705 BC), who cherished the memory of his famous predecessor. But in any case, Sargon's story was not written down until long after the exodus.

It is worth noticing the many differences between the history of Moses and the other ancient stories that contain some of the same motifs. The story of Sargon is the closest parallel, but even here there are significant differences. Sargon was kept in hiding because he was illegitimate, not because his life was endangered. Unlike Sargon, Moses was rescued and raised by real human beings. Besides, his story contains a wealth of specific details about the circumstances surrounding his rescue (who his family members were, how he was discovered, who nursed him, etc.), which are entirely absent from the story of Sargon.

It also helps to know that exposing a child was much more common in ancient times than it is today (especially due to the current prevalence of abortion). James Hoffmeier concludes that "the reason for the multitude of stories from across the Near East and Mediterranean of casting a child into the waters is that it may reflect the ancient practice of committing an unwanted child, or one needing protection, into the hands of providence. A modern parallel would be leaving a baby on the steps of an orphanage or at the door of a church."[7] All in all, it seems unlikely that the Israelites knew the story of Sargon, but it is not impossible that they had heard the tale of some foundling rising to greatness. If so, what happened to Moses would have sounded familiar to them, but this raises no doubts whatsoever about his personal history.

One good reason for believing in the historical Moses is his name, which sounds like the Hebrew verb "to draw out" (*mashah*). Pharaoh's daughter seems to have known some Hebrew, for it was she who "named him Moses, 'Because,' she said, 'I drew him out of the water'" (2:10). Her Hebrew needed a little work, however, because Moses literally means "he who draws out of." Unwittingly, Pharaoh's daughter gave the child a name that hinted at his destiny. Just as Moses himself was drawn out of the water, so he would later draw God's people out of Egypt through the sea. What is interesting historically is that Moses also fits the Egyptian pattern for names in the royal court. The Hebrew name Moses sounds like the Egyptian word *mose*, which is derived from the verb "to bear, to give birth to."[8] The Pharaohs often combined it with the name of a god, as in the name Thutmose (or Thuthmoses, which means "born of the god Thoth"), or the name Rameses ("the sun-god Re has given birth to him"). The name Moses, therefore, has a double etymology that fits the historical context and thus provides further confirmation for the presence of Israel in Egypt.

Some scholars say that it doesn't matter whether or not Moses ever existed; the book of Exodus is still a great story. But it makes more sense to say that if Moses never existed, then the exodus doesn't matter. If the book is nothing more than a historical novel, it might make for interesting reading, but it would not have supernatural power to change anyone's life. *The only God worth knowing is a God who has the power to work in human history to accomplish salvation.*

If God did not raise up a man named Moses to lead Israel out of Egypt, how can we be sure that he has the power to deliver us from our bondage to sin or to raise us up to eternal life? If our problems were literary problems, then a good story would be enough to solve them. But we live in time and space, and the difficulties we face are the difficulties of daily life: loneliness, addiction, conflict, grief. We need a God who can actually do something to help us. We need a God who is at work in our homes and stays with us on the job. If God did not save Moses the way the Bible says he did, it is doubtful whether he can save anyone at all.

## Pharaoh's Final Solution

The mention of the problems we face in daily life brings us to a second lesson: *In salvation God triumphs over evil*. Pharaoh was a wicked man who hated the plans and the promises of God, and because he hated God, he despised God's people. Thus the Israelites lived in dread of this anti-life antichrist, the terrorist who tried to slaughter their offspring.

Pharaoh's attempt to annihilate the Israelites gives us insight into the power of evil, which is never satisfied but always lusts for more. Each time Pharaoh's plans were foiled, he devised a scheme that was even wider in its scope and more deadly in its execution. Plan A was to beat the Israelites into submission with the rod of slavery. Plan B was to have their male offspring killed in secret (possibly Pharaoh thought that Hebrew girls would be assimilated by intermarrying with the Egyptians). Once both of his first two plans failed, Plan C was death by drowning in the Nile. With this final, genocidal solution, Pharaoh's murderous depravity was out in the open. He would not stop until all of Egypt was implicated in his crimes against humanity. This is the way evil spreads, unless it is stopped. What a man at first only dares to do in private, he gradually becomes unashamed to do even in public, with the result that many other people get pulled into the abyss of evil.

This pattern has been repeated many times in the sad history of humanity. In his commentary on the book of Exodus, Göran Larsson draws a comparison between Pharaoh's pogrom and Hitler's Holocaust: "The gradual escalation in Nazi Germany from hate propaganda to trade boycott, the banning of Jews from certain occupations, the steps toward racial segregation, the open violence of *Kristallnacht*, the ghettos, the labor camps, and finally Auschwitz and the so-called final solution, are certainly unique in their ghastly dimensions. However, the basic pattern can be discerned in the tragic drama enacted three thousand years earlier."[9]

The same tragedy is being restaged in the struggle between life and death in our own times. At first the moral outrage of abortion was confined to doctors working in secret. Then it received the sanction of the United States Supreme Court, and death clinics appeared in every city in America. At first euthanasia was only practiced by a health professional stealthily administering a deadly drug. Now the so-called right to die appears on the ballot in state elections, and on at least one occasion a victim has been euthanized on network television. Soon voluntary euthanasia will become involuntary euthanasia, and someone else will determine whether or not our lives are worth living. It is not alarmist to say that unless somehow it is stopped, this culture of death will continue to grow and spread indefinitely, for this is the way of all wickedness.

This is why we need God to be our Savior, for in salvation God delivers us from evil. At the very darkest moment of Israel's captivity—when evil was rampant and the tyrant seemed to triumph—at that very moment God was working in history to save his people. His plan called for a little child to be born in secret and then floated down the river right to Pharaoh's doorstep. In his triumph over evil, God displays his divine sense of humor. Peter Enns comments, "Ironically, this child, once doomed to death by Pharaoh's decree, will become the very instrument of Pharaoh's destruction and the means through which *all* Israel escapes not only Pharaoh's decree, but Egypt itself."[10] Pharaoh was foiled again! Later, when he reflected on God's triumph over Pharaoh's evil, Moses could have quoted his great-granduncle Joseph: "As for you, you meant evil against me, but God meant it for good, to bring it about that many people should be kept alive, as they are today" (Genesis 50:20).

There is a powerful symbol of Pharaoh's failure at Luxor, where an enormous statue of Rameses the Great has fallen down, its face crushed on the ground.[11] Rameses may or may not have been the Pharaoh of the exodus; regardless, his broken statue is a monument to the futility of the pharaohs. Boundless and bare, the lonely sands stretch far away to the empty horizon.

## Salvation Belongs to Our God

The reason Pharaoh was crushed was because God toppled him over. Notwithstanding the fact that this ruler was not mentioned by name, God was at work in every detail surrounding the birth of a savior. Consider the facts: Moses "is spared by being cast onto the very Nile that was to drown him, is treated with maternal kindness by the daughter of the very king who had condemned him and to whose descendants he would become a nemesis, and is assigned as a responsibility with pay to the one woman in all the world who most wanted the best for him, his own mother."[12] Who else but God could accomplish such a great salvation? There are divine fingerprints all over the narrative. Thus the third thing we learn about salvation is that *it is God's work from beginning to end*.

God was at work in the birth of this savior. It was God who formed the child in his mother's womb and safely delivered him into the world. Moses' birth was a reminder of God's creative power. The Bible calls attention to this when it says that his mother "saw that he was a goodly child" (2:2 KJV). This is an echo from the story of creation, when God saw that everything he had made was "very good" (Genesis 1:31). This was no ordinary child indeed (see Acts 7:20; Hebrews 11:23)!

God was at work in the baby's basket. At one moment in history, God's entire plan for triumphing over evil was riding down the Nile River in a little papyrus basket. While it was common for a baby to be put in such a cradle, it was unusual—and not altogether safe—to turn the basket into a boat. His mother made it as safe as she could, of course, but ultimately it was God who protected the precious cargo of redemption. However frightening an experience it was for Moses himself, who was crying when they found him, he was never safer than he was in that basket. God was right there working out his salvation.

The Bible calls attention to God's saving work by calling the basket, literally, an "ark" (*tebha*). The only other place the Bible uses this Hebrew term is in the story of Noah (Genesis 6:14—9:18). This is a hint that God saved Moses in much the same way that he saved Noah. Cassuto writes: "This is certainly not a mere coincidence. By this verbal parallelism Scripture apparently intends to draw attention to the thematic analogy. In both instances one worthy of being saved and destined to bring salvation to others is to be rescued from death by drowning. In the earlier section the salvation of humanity is involved, here it is the salvation of the chosen people."[13] Both Noah and Moses passed through the deadly waters by riding in an ark, the vessel of salvation. They were baptized, as it were, in the same water in which others perished.

God was also at work in the life of Pharaoh's daughter. In the providence of God, she went down to the river at just the right time in just the right place to discover Moses: "Now the daughter of Pharaoh came down to bathe at the river, while her young women walked beside the river. She saw the basket among the reeds and sent her servant woman, and she took it" (2:5). It was a dangerous moment. Despite Jochebed's best intentions, her baby seemed to be in harm's way. After all, the Egyptians had been ordered to drown Hebrew babies, and this woman was the daughter of Pharaoh himself! With mounting suspense we read: "When she opened it, she saw the child, and behold, the baby was crying. She took pity on him and said, 'This is one of the Hebrews' children'" (v. 6). The moment she peeked into the basket, the young woman's curiosity turned into compassion. Either because of the circumstances surrounding the baby's discovery or because he was circumcised, Pharaoh's daughter realized that he was a Hebrew slave. And in direct defiance of her father's orders, she determined to adopt him as her own son.

The pity of this Egyptian woman is a reminder that the exodus was not just for the Jews; ultimately, it was for the salvation of the whole world, including the Egyptians. When the Israelites finally made their exodus from Egypt, a "mixed multitude also went up with them" (12:38). Very likely at least some of those people were Egyptians. This is not surprising, because God had always planned to save people from every tribe, every language, and every nation. The prophet Isaiah later promised that the Lord would "make himself known to the Egyptians" (Isaiah 19:21) and that one day God would say, "Blessed be Egypt my people" (Isaiah 19:25). This promise was fulfilled on the Day of Pentecost, when Egyptians first heard the good news of salvation in Jesus Christ in their own language (Acts 2:10). They have been finding salvation in Christ ever since. Christians everywhere can join their Egyptian brothers and sisters in giving thanks to God for Pharaoh's daughter, a good Gentile who was part of God's saving plan.

God was also at work through Moses' sister, whose name evidently was Miriam (see 15:20). The girl's mother had given her strict instructions not to let her little brother out of her sight, so she "stood at a distance to know what would be done to him" (2:4). It turned out to be an adventure in babysitting, for what happened to her was every babysitter's worst nightmare: the child under her care was kidnapped. But Miriam was a brave, clever girl, and she was determined to save her little brother. There she stood on the riverbank, with her heart in her throat and her breath held tight, waiting to see what the Egyptians would do. When she realized there was not a moment to lose, she ran up and "said to Pharaoh's daughter, 'Shall I go and call you a nurse from the Hebrew women to nurse the child for you?' And Pharaoh's daughter said to her, 'Go'" (vv. 7, 8a). Miriam had someone special in mind, someone she was only too eager to recommend! "So the girl went and called the child's mother" (v. 8b).

God was working through Moses' mother too. (With all these women against him, perhaps Pharaoh should have worried as much about the Hebrew girls as he worried about the Hebrew boys!) "And Pharaoh's daughter said to her, 'Take this child away and nurse him for me, and I will give you your wages'" (v. 9). We can only imagine the joy Jochebed felt as she received her own child back to her bosom. Imagine getting paid to raise your own beloved son, and all at Pharaoh's expense! Jochebed learned that in salvation *God satisfies the deepest longings of the people he plans to save*. Do you believe this? Do you believe that God is doing what is best—not only for his people generally, but for you personally?

God did what was best for Moses as well as for his mother. Miriam made it sound like she was doing Pharaoh's daughter a favor by finding her a wet nurse, but it was really for Moses' benefit. It was all part of God's plan for preparing this child to save his people. His earliest years—the years that shaped his personal identity—were spent with his own family among the people of God. Moses had the opportunity to bond with his mother and to receive basic spiritual instruction from her. She only had two or three years to teach him the most important lessons in life. It hardly seemed like enough time, but no doubt she prayed that when her child became a man, he would love God's people, hear God's voice, and respond to God's call. Her prayers were answered, for Moses never forgot the lessons he learned at his mother's knee. He was living proof of the proverb that says, "Train up a child in the way he should go; even when he is old he will not depart from it" (Proverbs 22:6).

Moses would always be Jochebed's son, but when he was fully weaned, he was adopted into Pharaoh's household. God was working there too: "When the child grew older, she brought him to Pharaoh's daughter, and he became her son" (2:10a). Moses did not grow up as a slave but as a son, safe and secure in Pharaoh's court. There he "was instructed in all the wisdom of the Egyptians" (Acts 7:22). This was the finest training the world then had to offer—a first-class secular education. We know that from the time of Thutmose III (middle of the fifteenth century BC) it was customary for foreign-born princes to be reared and educated in the Egyptian court. The "children of the nursery," they were called; and as a child of the nursery, Moses was trained in linguistics, mathematics, astronomy, architecture, music, medicine, law, and the fine art of diplomacy.[14] In other words, he was being trained for Pharaoh's overthrow right under Pharaoh's nose! With this kind of background, it is no wonder that he came to be "very great in the land of Egypt, in the sight of Pharaoh's servants and in the sight of the people" (11:3). There was a divine purpose in Moses' education, for God was preparing him to lead his people Israel out of Egypt.

"And we know that for those who love God all things work together for good, for those who are called according to his purpose" (Romans 8:28), and the birth of Moses is a perfect example of God working out salvation down to the last detail. More than a thousand years later, when Stephen recounted the story of salvation before the Sanhedrin, he included these details:

> But as the time of the promise drew near, which God had granted to Abraham, the people increased and multiplied in Egypt until there arose over Egypt another king who did not know Joseph. He dealt shrewdly with our race and forced our fathers to expose their infants, so that they would not be kept alive. At this time Moses was born; and he was beautiful in God's sight. And he was brought up for three months in his father's house, and when he was exposed, Pharaoh's daughter adopted him and brought him up as her own son. And Moses was instructed in all the wisdom of the Egyptians, and he was mighty in his words and deeds. (Acts 7:17–22)

None of these things would have happened without God overruling Pharaoh's deadly decree. But these things all happened according to the providence of God in order to accomplish his plan of salvation. God saved the child Moses so that he could save his children the Israelites. From beginning to end, salvation belongs to our God.

## The Birth of the Savior

The story of baby Moses in the basket is a marvelous story of God working in history to triumph over evil, but it is not the whole story. Moses was *a* savior, but he was not *the* Savior. Long after the exodus the Israelites were still waiting for another Savior to be born, a Savior of whom Moses was only the prototype. We sense their longing from the end of Deuteronomy, where we read that "there has not arisen a prophet since in Israel like Moses, whom the LORD knew face to face, none like him for all the signs and the wonders that the LORD sent him to do in the land of Egypt, to Pharaoh and to all his servants and to all his land, and for all the mighty power and all the great deeds of terror that Moses did in the sight of all Israel" (Deuteronomy 34:10–12).

Then a little child was born in Bethlehem, a child "worthy of more glory than Moses" (Hebrews 3:3). He was no ordinary child; he was the Son of God incarnate. This extraordinary baby was born in human history during the days when Caesar Augustus sent out a decree "that all the world should be taxed" (Luke 2:1 KJV). Like Moses, the boy was given a name to match his destiny. They called him Jesus because he would "save his people from their sins" (Matthew 1:21).

Like Moses, this Savior was born under a death sentence. Herod the Great, a tyrant as wicked as any of the pharaohs, was determined to put the newborn king to death. At first he tried to do it secretly, asking the wise men to tell him where Jesus was. When that deadly plan failed, Herod ordered his soldiers openly to slaughter all the baby boys in Bethlehem. But in salvation God triumphs over evil; so, like Moses, Jesus was delivered from death. While the other babies were crushed by the engines of state, the child who was born to save us all escaped to Egypt (Matthew 2:1–19). In all of these events God was working out his plan down to the last detail, for salvation is his work from beginning to end.

The birth of the Savior was only the beginning. Everything else went according to plan too. In time the child was brought out of Egypt and went to the land of Israel (Matthew 2:21; cf. Exodus 4:19). There he "grew and became strong, filled with wisdom. And the favor of God was upon him" (Luke 2:40). He lived a perfect life until finally he died an atoning death. In that death is our salvation, for the cross of Christ is God's ultimate triumph over evil. Do you believe this? The salvation God has accomplished in history becomes our salvation when we receive Jesus by faith. We are called to trust God the way a desperate mother once did when she put her heart in a basket and entrusted it to the God who saves.

# 4

# Moses Takes Matters into His Own Hands

EXODUS 2:11–15

HAVE YOU EVER WANTED TO KILL SOMEBODY? Seriously, have you ever been so angry that the only thing that seemed like it could soothe your roiling hatred was to lay your hands on another human being and take his life? Or have you ever witnessed an act of such brutal injustice that violence seemed like the only answer?

If you have, then perhaps you can understand what led Moses to commit murder. "One day, when Moses had grown up, he went out to his people and looked on their burdens, and he saw an Egyptian beating a Hebrew, one of his people. He looked this way and that, and seeing no one, he struck down the Egyptian and hid him in the sand" (2:11, 12). Moses was so incensed that he took his rage to the *n*th degree, beating the taskmaster to death, spilling his blood upon the sand, and then burying his corpse in a shallow grave.

## In Moses' Defense

Moses was never brought to trial, but if he had been, it might not have been hard to defend him. For starters, what he did was not premeditated; it was merely a crime of passion, if indeed it was a crime at all. Furthermore, from the standpoint of Egyptian law, Moses probably was within his rights. As a prince of Egypt he held the power of the sword, and it is doubtful whether a member of Pharaoh's court would have been condemned simply for killing a slave driver. The Hebrew verdict on Moses would have been even more favorable, for as far as the Israelites were concerned, Moses was a patriot.

Moses also could have been defended on the basis of the ancient legal principle *lex talionis*, or the "law of retaliation." *Lex talionis* is recorded, among other places, in 21:23–25: "But if there is harm, then you shall pay life for life, eye for eye, tooth for tooth, hand for hand, foot for foot, burn for burn, wound for wound, stripe for stripe." In this case it could be argued that the Egyptian got exactly what he deserved. The Hebrew language does not distinguish very precisely between beating and killing; the verb *nakah* refers to both. Thus the word used to describe what the Egyptian did to the Hebrew and what Moses did to the Egyptian are one and the same. This suggests that the slave driver intended to beat his slave to death. If so, it could be argued that Moses did what he had to do to save a life. Perhaps he did not even intend to kill the man. But in any case it was simply a case of retaliation—an eye for an eye and a wound for a wound.

Or consider another possible line of defense. Perhaps what Moses committed was justifiable homicide, a divinely sanctioned act of judgment against God's enemies. Some commentators view it not "as an act of vengeance or rash zeal but as a proleptic execution of divine justice against Egypt."[1] John Calvin, for example, maintained that Moses "was armed by God's command, and, conscious of his legitimate vocation, rightly, and judiciously assumed that character which God had assigned to him."[2] Stephen, the martyr, seemed to hint at this interpretation in his sermon before the Sanhedrin: "When he was forty years old, it came into his heart to visit his brothers, the children of Israel. And seeing one of them being wronged, he defended the oppressed man and avenged him by striking down the Egyptian" (Acts 7:23, 24).

One way or another, an expert legal team could have come up with a winning strategy for Moses' defense. Indeed, many Christian commentators from Tertullian to Aquinas have sought to clear Moses from the charge of murder.[3] But that does not change the fact that what he did was wrong. It was wrong because it was unnecessary. Moses could have protected the slave without resorting to killing the slave driver. It was wrong because it was not Moses' place to do this—it was an abuse of power. He was still a private individual and not an officer of the state administering solemn justice. Rather than appointing himself as judge, jury, and executioner, he should have worked within the system. It was also wrong because it was not God's will. God had not yet called Moses to lead his people out of Egypt. And it was wrong because it was not God's way. God had not commanded Moses to take up arms against the oppressor, as if somehow he could liberate Israel one Egyptian at a time. Later God would smite the Egyptians himself, but that was *his* business, and the time had not yet come.

What Moses did was wrong for many reasons. It was wrong because murder is always wrong, and Moses knew it. This is why he tried to make sure he didn't get caught, looking "this way and that" before committing his crime, and carefully disposing of the evidence afterward. The law that he would later bring down from the mountain was already written on his conscience: "You shall not murder" (20:13).

There are some situations where killing is not murder. One is self-defense against an armed enemy who has the intent to kill. Another is capital punishment, when it is justly administered by the lawful authorities of a sovereign state. Still another example is the killing of military combatants in a just war. *The Westminster Larger Catechism* summarizes by saying that "the sins forbidden in the sixth commandment ('Thou shalt not kill') are, all taking away the life of ourselves, or of others, except in the case of public justice, lawful war, or necessary defense" (A. 136).

The situations where it is permissible to kill are narrowly defined, however, and we are never at liberty to take the law into our own hands. There is a bloody scene in the film version of *The Hiding Place* that illustrates the danger of answering violence with violence. The movie shows how two Dutch Christians—Corrie ten Boom and her sister Betsie—were taken to the Nazi concentration camp at Ravensbrück, where they were imprisoned for harboring Jews in their home. One day as Betsie was savagely attacked by one of the guards for not meeting her work quota, Corrie imagined taking a pickax and hacking the Nazi to death. By this point in the film there is hardly a member of the audience who would not be willing to grab an axe handle and help. But that is not the way God wants his people to combat evil. As Betsie said to her sister, "No hate, Corrie, no hate." Hatred is not the way of the cross; nor is violence the way of Christ, who said, "You have heard that it was said, 'An eye for an eye and a tooth for a tooth.' But I say to you, Do not resist the one who is evil. But if anyone slaps you on the right cheek, turn to him the other also" (Matthew 5:38, 39).

This teaching is hard enough for Christians, who have the example of the willing, suffering, dying Christ to follow. How much harder it must have been for Moses! Anyone who has ever been angry over an injustice can sense how he felt and can sympathize with what he did. Nevertheless, his crime stands as a permanent warning against anger. When Moses allowed his hatred to get the best of him, he was only one short step from grabbing a weapon and bludgeoning a man to death. Murder is simply anger taken to its logical conclusion. Remember the teaching of Jesus: "You have heard that it was said to those of old, 'You shall not murder; and whoever murders will be liable to judgment.' But I say to you that everyone who is angry with his brother will be liable to judgment" (Matthew 5:21, 22a). If we are followers of Christ, then we must live in gentleness and peace. *The Westminster Larger Catechism* puts it well when it forbids "sinful anger, hatred, envy, desire of revenge . . . provoking words, oppression, quarrelling, striking, wounding, and whatsoever else tends to the destruction of the life of any" (A. 136).

## Suffering for Christ

What was so tragic about Moses' impetuous action was that until he took a man's life, he seemed to be on the verge of greatness. His crime was committed "when Moses had grown up" (2:11). The little boy in the basket had become a man. Having been "instructed in all the wisdom of the Egyptians," he was "mighty in his words and deeds" (Acts 7:22). Most important of all, he was not ignorant of his Hebrew heritage. With his intimate knowledge of Egyptian culture and his personal connection with the Hebrews, Moses was poised to lead Israel out of Egypt.

At this time, when he "was forty years old, it came into his heart to visit his brothers, the children of Israel" (Acts 7:23). To understand what God was doing in Moses' heart, it helps to consult Hebrews 11. This is in keeping with our Biblical method, which requires us to interpret Exodus in the context of the rest of Scripture. When we turn to Hebrews, we are surprised to discover this unqualified endorsement: "By faith Moses, when he was grown up, refused to be called the son of Pharaoh's daughter, choosing rather to be mistreated with the people of God than to enjoy the fleeting pleasures of sin. He considered the reproach of Christ greater wealth than the treasures of Egypt, for he was looking to the reward" (Hebrews 11:24–26). Without mentioning any embarrassing details—like the victim buried in the sand, just to name one—the writer to the Hebrews presents Moses as a hero of the faith. For the cause of Christ and in the sure hope of Heaven, he turned his back on sin in order to suffer with God's people.

It is tempting to wonder whether Hebrews has it right. It sounds like a rather romantic view of a man who committed a secret crime and then ran away to hide. But whenever the New Testament offers what at first seems to be an odd interpretation, the thing to do is to go back and study the Old Testament more carefully.

When we look closely at 2:11, we discover several clues that Moses loved God's people. According to standard rabbinic interpretation, the verse shows the prophet's voluntary participation in their sufferings. The most obvious clue is the phrase "his people," which is repeated for emphasis. When Moses visited the labor camps where the Hebrews lived and worked, he felt a sense of solidarity with them. He realized that they were his blood relations, the people of his very own family. The word used to describe his visit is significant: "He went out." This same Hebrew verb (*yatza*) is later used to describe the exodus. There seems to be a connection: before Israel could go out of Egypt, Moses needed to go out of Egypt, emotionally if not yet physically.

Going out to the Hebrews was a life-changing trip, because when Moses left Pharaoh's palace to visit his own people, he took his heart with him. Another indication that he was a Hebrew at heart is that he "looked on their burdens" (2:11). This verb for looking (*yara*) means more than simply "to look or to see." It means "to see with emotion."[4] It is the kind of looking that demands intense personal involvement with what one sees. In a word it requires compassion. Perhaps the best Biblical example comes from the story of Hagar, who, when she feared that her son was about to starve, sobbed, "Let me not look on the death of the child" (Genesis 21:16). When Moses watched the Hebrews, it was more than an eye-opening experience. It was even more than a consciousness-raising experience. It was a heart-transforming experience. When he saw the misery of his own people as they slaved away for Pharaoh, their burdens became the burdens of his very own heart.

What is surprising about Moses' deep sympathy for those who suffered oppression is that he had been raised to show utter contempt for slaves. One of the primary goals of Pharaoh's educational system was to reinforce the pride of those in power. After reviewing the ancient Egyptian curriculum, Göran Larsson notes, "Among these documents one category of educational materials is particularly conspicuous, namely, texts that express a deep contempt of manual labor while stressing the value of study. Studies lead to a life far away from dust, dirt, and toil under harsh taskmasters. These texts emphasize the extremely low status of the working class in ancient Egyptian society."[5] Here is one of the examples Larsson cites to prove his point:

> The maker of pots is smeared with soil, like one whose relations have died. His hands, his feet are full of clay; he is like one who lives in the bog. . . . The carpenter who is in the shipyard carries the timber and stacks it. If he gives today the output of yesterday, woe to his limbs! The shipwright stands behind him to tell him evil things. His outworker who is in the fields, his is the toughest of all the jobs. He spends the day loaded with his tools, tied to his toolbox.[6]

In other texts, slaves are described as the "living dead" or are compared to donkeys. All of their hard labor is contrasted, of course, with the pleasures of the ruling elite, who enjoy a life of ease: "You call for one; a thousand answer you. You stride freely on the road. You will not be like a hired ox. You are in front of others."[7]

This is the historical background for the choice that Moses made "to be mistreated with the people of God [rather] than to enjoy the fleeting pleasures of sin" (Hebrews 11:25). Moses had everything the world had to offer. He had grown up as one of Pharaoh's grandsons, enjoying all the riches of Egypt. One thinks, for example, of the fabulous golden treasures that the English archaeologist Howard Carter found in the tomb of King Tutankhamen. These dazzling artifacts give some idea what Moses left behind the day he left Pharaoh's palace to visit the Hebrews. He had everything to lose and nothing to gain, but the moment he was moved to compassion by the sufferings of God's people, he made his choice. From then on he would be a despised Hebrew rather than a privileged Egyptian. It was a startling reversal. "In most foundling stories the hero is removed from the royal court and raised among the common people, finally returning as a young adult to claim and establish his rightful heritage of wealth and power. In this story, however, Moses did not become the hero, the legitimate agent of God, until he burned all the bridges between himself and the wealth and power of the Egyptian court."[8] He gave up position, pleasure, and prosperity, and by doing so he rejected three of the world's biggest temptations: narcissism, hedonism, and materialism.

Moses still had some lessons to learn, but it was becoming obvious that God had chosen the right man to lead his people—a man, in fact, who was something like Jesus Christ. Remember that our approach to Exodus is Christological. We want to notice the many ways Moses points us to Christ. Hebrews confirms the validity of this approach by stating that Moses suffered "disgrace for the sake of Christ" (Hebrews 11:26 NIV). In Exodus 2 we see Moses identifying himself with God's people in their suffering in order to bring them salvation. Jesus Christ has done the same thing for us, entering into our situation in order to save us. In an earlier passage Hebrews states that God has accomplished our salvation through the sufferings of Christ. Then it goes on to make the remarkable claim that because we are united to Christ in his sufferings, Jesus "is not ashamed to call [us] brothers" (Hebrews 2:11b). We are siblings of the Savior, brothers and sisters of God the Son. Moses condescended to join his brothers the Hebrews, but the supreme condescension is God joining himself to us in Christ, so that we might become members of his own family.

Our approach to Exodus is not only Christological, but it is also practical. So we need to apply the lesson: God calls us to identify with his people, even when it causes us pain and persecution. Some people, if put in Moses' position, would have figured out a way to stay in Pharaoh's court. "With my influence," they would rationalize, "I could do more good for the Hebrews here than I could ever hope to accomplish out in the slave camps." But Moses took a radically God-centered approach to career advancement. As far as he was concerned, there could be no compromise with Pharaoh's evil regime. He was called to forsake sin, with all its pleasures, even if it meant suffering disgrace for Christ.

We, too, are called to suffer for the sake of Christ (Hebrews 11:26). According to Brevard Childs, this "phrase indicates an actual participation by Moses in Christ's shame in the same way as the saints who follow Christ later also share."[9] In other words, as we suffer *for* Christ we are also suffering *with* Christ, enjoying what the Apostle Paul termed "shar[ing] his sufferings" (Philippians 3:10). Such suffering is the inevitable result of being identified with Christ and with his people. Where is our ultimate allegiance? What is our primary identification? If we call ourselves Christians, we must forsake the world to follow Christ, becoming spiritually joined to his people, just as Moses was.

## Not What My Hands Have Done

The more we learn about Moses, the more we realize how tragic his mistake was. For all his admirable qualities—his hatred of injustice, his opposition to slavery, his sympathy with those who suffered, and his deep affection for God's people—with one rash act Moses threw away forty years of spiritual preparation. Although he had a holy zeal to rescue God's people, his zeal was not based on knowledge (cf. Romans 10:2). His failure had nothing to do with his motivation, for his heart was in the right place. Rather, the problem was his method: Moses was trying to save God's people by his own works rather than letting God save them by his grace.

Some commentators have sought to exonerate Moses by comparing Exodus 2:12 with Isaiah 59:16. In Exodus it is when he "[sees] no one" that Moses decides to take matters into his own hands. The obvious implication is that he was checking to make sure no one would stop him. But perhaps what the verse means is that there was no one else to help the Hebrew slave, in which case it was up to Moses to save him. At least that is the way the idea of "seeing no one" is used in the book of Isaiah:

> [The Lord] saw that there was no man,
> and wondered that there was no one to intercede;
> then his own arm brought him salvation,
> and his righteousness upheld him.

Since there was no one to save, the argument goes, it was right for Moses to kill the Egyptian with his own bare hands.

But rather than justifying Moses, this comparison actually serves to condemn him. It is one thing for God to work salvation when he sees that no one else can save, but it is far different for a sinful human being to presume to be the savior. To put it in theological terms, when Moses decided to take matters into his own hands, he was attempting to achieve salvation by works and not by grace. The proof that his way was not the right way was that God sent him into the wilderness for forty years before giving him another chance to deliver Israel. God wanted to make sure that his people would be saved for his glory. When salvation finally came, it would not be through the strength of any man but through the power of God alone.

This principle also holds true for salvation in Jesus Christ. One man who learned this lesson well was the Apostle Paul, who came to abandon any attempt to achieve salvation through his own merits. "If anyone else thinks he has reason for confidence in the flesh," Paul wrote, "I have more: circumcised on the eighth day, of the people of Israel, of the tribe of Benjamin, a Hebrew of Hebrews; as to the law, a Pharisee; as to zeal, a persecutor of the church; as to righteousness under the law, blameless" (Philippians 3:4b–6). Paul listed his religious credentials in order to prove that if anyone could be saved by works, it would be him. But Paul was not saved until he discovered that salvation comes by grace and not by works. As soon as he made that discovery, he took all his religious assets and wrote them off as spiritual liabilities: "But whatever gain I had, I counted as loss for the sake of Christ. Indeed, I count everything as loss because of the surpassing worth of knowing Christ Jesus my Lord. For his sake I have suffered the loss of all things and count them as rubbish, in order that I may gain Christ and be found in him, not having a righteousness of my own that comes from the law, but that which comes through faith in Christ, the righteousness from God that depends on faith" (Philippians 3:7–9).

Moses' spiritual résumé was not quite as spectacular as Paul's (not yet, at any rate), but he could make many of the same claims. "If anyone else thinks he can save himself with his own bare hands," he could have said, "I have more: circumcised on the eighth day, of the people of Israel, of the tribe of Levi, a Hebrew of Hebrews; as for zeal, slaughtering Egyptians." But God showed Moses that it was all rubbish, as anything is that prevents us from receiving the free gift of God's grace. Salvation does not come by works but by faith in Christ alone. We cannot be saved by our ethnic heritage, our family connections, our receiving the sacraments, or anything else that we are or do. This is why it is not enough simply to attach oneself to a church or to work for the cause of justice. Moses had done those things too, yet they did not save him. Nor can they save anyone else.

For salvation to be all of God, it must be all of grace, so that God alone gets all the glory. Horatius Bonar explained this principle in one of his famous hymns:

> Not what my hands have done can save my guilty soul;
> Not what my toiling flesh has borne can make my spirit whole.
> Not what I feel or do can give me peace with God;
> Not all my prayers and sighs and tears can bear my awful load.
>
> Thy work alone, O Christ, can ease this weight of sin;
> Thy blood alone, O Lamb of God, can give me peace within.
> Thy love to me, O God, not mine, O Lord, to thee,
> Can rid me of this dark unrest, and set my spirit free.
>
> Thy grace alone, O God, to me can pardon speak;
> Thy pow'r alone, O Son of God, can this sore bondage break.
> No other work, save thine, no other blood will do;
> No strength, save that which is divine, can bear me safely through.

## The Flight of Moses

Eventually God brought Moses safely through, and all of Israel with him, but not until after the prophet spent forty years in the wilderness. The surest proof that it was wrong for him to kill the Egyptian was his long exile in Midian. This exile began the day after the homicide, when Moses returned, as it were, to the scene of the crime:

> When he [Moses] went out the next day, behold, two Hebrews were struggling together. And he said to the man in the wrong, "Why do you strike your companion?" He answered, "Who made you a prince and a judge over

> us? Do you mean to kill me as you killed the Egyptian?" Then Moses was afraid, and thought, "Surely the thing is known." When Pharaoh heard of it, he sought to kill Moses. But Moses fled from Pharaoh and stayed in the land of Midian. (2:13–15)

This exchange shows why the Israelites were in such desperate need of a savior. Not only did they need to be delivered from Egypt, but they also needed to be delivered from one another. The original Hebrew hints that Moses was surprised to find his brothers fighting ("He looked and behold!"). However, he should not have been surprised that they were quarreling or that they had come to blows. Treat a man with violence long enough and he will become a violent man. After living in a violent culture for so long, the Hebrew community was being torn apart by violence. Their bondage was spiritual as much as it was physical.

The exchange between Moses and the Hebrew slaves also reveals some of the qualities that made Moses such a great liberator. Once again he went out to his people, identifying with them in their suffering. Once again he took the side of the victim, intervening to stop an assault. Once again he sought justice, accusing the man who was in the wrong of instigating the violence. And according to Stephen, Moses was trying to be a reconciler: "And on the following day he appeared to them as they were quarreling and tried to reconcile them, saying, 'Men, you are brothers. Why do you wrong each other?'" (Acts 7:26).

Sadly, and to his dismay, Moses discovered that he was unable to make peace. His crime had been discovered. Perhaps there had been witnesses, or perhaps the man whom Moses rescued had told all his friends. In any case the secret was out, and all the slaves were talking about it: Moses, the prince of Egypt, had committed murder.

Moses faced two problems. One was that his life was in mortal danger. Even if he had the authority to strike the slave driver, it was treason for him to side with the slaves. By joining Israel's civil rights movement, he was cutting off all his ties to the Egyptian aristocracy. When Pharaoh heard what Moses had done, he signed the death warrant that made Moses the most wanted man in Egypt. James Ackerman explains, "In acting to defend the Hebrews, Moses was challenging the basic foundations—social, political, and religious—on which Egyptian society had been established. It should come as no surprise that Pharaoh would seek to crush him."[10]

Becoming a fugitive was bad enough, but Moses faced a second problem that was even worse: the Israelites had rejected his leadership. Rather than showing him respect, they regarded him with utter contempt. Apparently Moses had hoped to start some kind of uprising, but none of the slaves were willing to join the revolt. In his sermon before the Sanhedrin, Stephen commented, "[Moses] supposed that his brothers would understand that God was giving them salvation by his hand, but they did not understand" (Acts 7:25). If this is what Moses thought would happen, he obviously thought wrong, because the slaves treated him with sheer insolence. Stephen tells it like this: "But the man who was wronging his neighbor thrust him aside, saying, 'Who made you a ruler and a judge over us? Do you want to kill me as you killed the Egyptian yesterday?'" (Acts 7:27, 28). As far as the slave was concerned, Moses was meddling and had no right to stick his nose into other people's business. "Who do you think you are?" the man was saying. "Who died and made you the prince of Egypt?"

Good question. Who *had* given Moses authority over Israel? The answer was, no one, at least as far as the Bible indicates. It would be forty more years before God would call Moses from the burning bush. For the time being, Moses was operating as a self-appointed savior, taking it upon himself to lead Israel out of Egypt, and the Israelites wanted no part of it. Although this was the first time they questioned Moses' authority, it was by no means the last. As we shall see, the Israelites often grumbled about their leaders. But on this occasion they were probably right. How could a murderer be a reconciler?

Rather than repeating the Hebrew word for striking, the slave who threatened Moses used the word for killing. In other words, he accused him of murder, plain and simple. Thus Moses could not even settle a simple dispute between two Israelites without being charged with homicide. How, then, could he lead the entire nation out of Egypt? His credibility as a leader was destroyed. By killing the Egyptian, Moses had forfeited the moral authority to deliver God's people.

It would be a long, long time before Moses would regain their respect—almost a lifetime, in fact. His first attempt to rescue the Israelites ended in failure. But God was planning to save his people, and Moses was still part of the plan. Already he was learning that salvation does not come by works. Now he had to go out into the wilderness to learn how to live by faith.

# 5

# Moses in the Wilderness

## EXODUS 2:15–25

MOSES WAS AN OUTLAW, a fugitive from justice. In a sudden rage he had murdered an Egyptian with his own bare hands and buried him in a shallow grave. Not surprisingly, "When Pharaoh heard of it, he sought to kill Moses" (2:15a). Pharaoh did not want Moses dead or alive—he just wanted him dead. And as soon as he heard that he was a wanted man, "Moses fled from Pharaoh and stayed in the land of Midian. And he sat down by a well" (2:15b).

### Moses Learns from His Mistake

The road that led Moses from the palace of the Pharaohs to the wilderness of Midian was paved with good intentions. The Egyptian who was now buried in the sand had tried to beat a Hebrew to death. By coming to the poor slave's defense, Moses had rejected the privileges of Egypt in order to identify himself with the children of Israel. As the Scripture says, "[He chose] rather to be mistreated with the people of God than to enjoy the fleeting pleasures of sin" (Hebrews 11:25). One old commentator eloquently described the choice that Moses made:

> Bred in a palace, he espoused the cause of the people; nursed in the lap of luxury, he embraced adversity; reared in the school of despots, he became the champion of liberty; long associated with oppressors, he took the side of the oppressed; educated as her son, he forfeited the favor of a princess to maintain the rights of the poor; with a crown in prospect, he had the magnanimity to choose a cross; and for the sake of his God and Israel, he abandoned ease, refinement, luxuries, and the highest earthly honors, to be a houseless wanderer.[1]

Yet for all his good intentions, Moses had sinned against God. The only word to describe what he did is murder. It was not Moses' place to kill an Egyptian, even if the man was a slave driver, for God had not yet called him to lead his people out of Egypt. When God did deliver Israel from the house of bondage, he would do it by his own mighty power, so as to keep all the glory to himself. However noble his motives may have been, therefore, when Moses decided to take matters into his own hands, he was outside the will of God. By the time he finished paying for his mistake he would be eighty years old. Yet God still had a plan for Moses, which shows that even failures can be God's followers; even sinners can become his chosen servants.

The thing to do with mistakes is to learn from them. As he fled from Egypt to Midian, the question was whether Moses had learned anything from his futile attempt to save Israel by his own strength. His first test came not long after he arrived in Midian, where he sat down by a well: "Now the priest of Midian had seven daughters, and they came and drew water and filled the troughs to water their father's flock. The shepherds came and drove them away, but Moses stood up and saved them, and watered their flock" (2:16, 17).

Once again Moses was confronted with gross injustice. This time it was not slaves oppressed by their masters, but women abused by men. Apparently there was a long-standing conflict between the daughters of Midian and some local shepherds: "When they came home to their father Reuel, he said, 'How is it that you have come home so soon today?'" (2:18). He was surprised they were back so soon because ordinarily the shepherds gave them trouble. "They said, 'An Egyptian delivered us out of the hand of the shepherds'" (2:19a). No doubt they said, "*the* shepherds" because their father knew exactly who they were. It was a recurring problem. Perhaps these bullies prevented his girls from getting any water at all. More likely, they waited until the women had already filled the troughs, so they did not have to take the trouble to draw water themselves.

Moses may have been a stranger in Midian, but he was not about to let a band of unruly shepherds take advantage of these helpless young women. Courageously he rose to their defense, using the military training he had received in Egypt to save them from their oppressors. Already there are some clues here that Moses had learned from his murderous mistake. He did not kill the shepherds. This time he restrained himself, using only such force as was necessary to drive them off. For the first time in his life, Moses was acting like a deliverer. Furthermore, after he rescued the girls, he came to their aid by watering their flocks. This was to their great astonishment, for in ancient times it was unthinkable for a man to perform such a menial task for a woman. The girls later exclaimed, "[He] even drew water for us and watered the flock" (2:19b). Moses stooped to serve, and by learning to serve he was learning to lead, for all God's leaders are servants.

Service is always one of the first topics covered in God's leadership training course. Anyone who aspires to become a spiritual leader should begin by finding a place of humble service. The perfect example is Jesus Christ, who "came not to be served but to serve, and to give his life as a ransom for many" (Matthew 20:28). Jesus saved us by dying on the cross for our sins. Now the service he rendered on the cross is the pattern for our own servanthood, for Jesus commanded that "the leader" must be "as one who serves" (Luke 22:26).

## Preparation Time

Learning how to control his violent temper and learning how to serve were only the first of many lessons that Moses learned in Midian. God is never in any great hurry to prepare his servants to do his will, especially when he has some great work for them to accomplish. There is no better example of this than the prophet Moses, who spent four decades in the wilderness before beginning his public ministry. The book of Acts explains that forty years passed between Moses' flight to Midian and his encounter with God at the burning bush (Acts 7:29, 30). Forty years! Someone has pointed out that "Moses was 40 years in Egypt learning something; he was 40 years in the desert learning to be nothing; and he was 40 years in the wilderness proving God to be everything."[2] Whenever we are tempted to grow impatient with God's timetable for our lives, we should remember Moses, who spent two years of preparation for every year of ministry.

During the forty long years that Moses spent in Midian, God used three experiences to prepare him for his primary calling, which was to lead God's people out of Egypt. The first was his *living situation*. The precise location of Midian is somewhat uncertain. The Midianites may have lived in Arabia, but more likely they lived on the Sinai Peninsula, near the Gulf of Aqaba. The term does not refer primarily to a place, however, but to a people group—a tribe of desert nomads. Living with the Midianites meant living in the wilderness.

The wilderness is a place for a man to meet his God. Cut off from the rest of civilization and reduced to the daily necessities of food and water, he is forced to throw himself on the mercy of God's providence. It was in the wilderness that Jacob saw a stairway to Heaven (Genesis 28) and Elijah heard the still, small voice (1 Kings 19). The wilderness is where John the Baptist preached repentance (Matthew 3) and where Jesus won his first triumph over the devil (Matthew 4). It was also in the wilderness that Paul searched the Scriptures for the Christ of the Old Testament (Galatians 1:17). But long before that, Moses went into the wilderness to meet the God of Abraham, Isaac, and Jacob.

Moses' wilderness experience was of great practical significance. One of the things he learned was the wilderness itself—its geography and topography. Later, when he led God's people out of Egypt, he knew things like where to find water and how to find his way back to God's holy mountain. But Moses' wilderness experience was of even greater significance spiritually, for before he led Israel out of Egypt, Moses had an exodus of his own. It was in the wilderness that he learned what it was like to be an outcast. The people of God were strangers in Egypt, but Egypt was Moses' home—so much so that the daughters of Reuel immediately identified him as "an Egyptian" (2:19). It was only when he went out to live in the desert that Moses experienced alienation for himself.

At the birth of his first son, he said, "I have been a sojourner in a foreign land" (2:22b). The foreign land Moses seems to have had in mind was not Midian but Egypt, since he was speaking in the past tense. The verse should thus be translated as follows: "A stranger I have been there," with Moses referring back to his upbringing in Pharaoh's palace.[3] It was through his wilderness experience that he learned to identify with God's people in their suffering.

The second life experience God used to prepare Moses for leadership was his *family situation*. Moses was single when he left Egypt, but the priest of Midian did not let him stay that way for long. This was a man with seven daughters, after all, and he was not about to let a man like Moses get away: "He said to his daughters, 'Then where is he? Why have you left the man? Call him, that he may eat bread'" (2:20). What were his daughters thinking, leaving a bachelor alone like that? They were so excited by the gallantry of this strange man from Egypt that they quite forgot their manners, failing even to invite him home for dinner. But in the end Moses enjoyed their hospitality so much that he "was content to dwell with the man, and he gave Moses his daughter Zipporah" (2:21).

Not only did Moses become a husband in Midian, but he also became a father: "She gave birth to a son, and he called his name Gershom, for he said, 'I have been a sojourner in a foreign land'" (2:22). The name Gershom comes from the Hebrew verb *garash*, which means "to drive out or to expel"; thus it may refer to Moses' own experience in being driven out of Egypt. It also sounds like the Hebrew words *ger* and *sham*, a pun that means "an alien there." The Bible does not include these domestic details simply out of biographical interest. Moses' family situation was part of his preparation for ministry. As a husband he learned how to love and serve his wife. As a father he learned how to care for and discipline his children. By settling into the life of the home Moses learned how to be a servant-leader.

It was in the same home that Moses grew in his relationship with God, for when he accepted Zipporah's hand in marriage, he became a member of her clan. The Midianites seem to have worshiped the one true God, the God of their father Abraham. It seems significant that Reuel was a priest and that his name means "friend of God." In all likelihood Moses received spiritual instruction from his father-in-law, so that by the time he saw the burning bush, he had already been reintroduced to the God of Abraham.

Thirdly, Moses learned how to serve God through his *work situation*. Job opportunities are somewhat limited in the wilderness, and since his father-in-law was a shepherd, Moses became a shepherd. We know this because the next chapter begins with him out tending his flock (3:1).

This was hardly the profession Moses would have chosen because he was raised in Egypt, and the Bible says that "every shepherd is an abomination to the Egyptians" (Genesis 46:34b). But the Bible also shows that many great leaders got their start as shepherds. This is because there is a lot to be learned from tending sheep. For starters, sheep are not very bright, which means they need someone to lead them to food and water. They make an easy target for predators, so they need someone to protect them. They are prone to wander, so they need someone to bring them back into the fold. In short, sheep are completely dependent on shepherds for their care, which is why the Bible so often compares God's people to sheep. In the words of the psalmist, "We are his people, and the sheep of his pasture" (Psalm 100:3b). Like so many sheep, we need divine guidance, nourishment, and protection. It was by tending his flock, therefore, that Moses learned how to feed, defend, and rescue the lost sheep of Israel. Since God's people are the sheep of his pasture, there was no better way for Moses to learn how to lead them than by spending forty years as a shepherd. When Asaph later meditated on God's saving work in bringing his people out of Egypt, he said, "You led your people like a flock by the hand of Moses and Aaron" (Psalm 77:20; cf. Psalm 78:52; Isaiah 63:11).

God used the experiences Moses had along his spiritual journey to prepare him in a special way for a special work. By being faithful in small things, he was prepared for something big. It is doubtful whether we will ever lead God's people out of bondage. But even if we are not named Moses, God has a plan for us. The Bible says that "we are his workmanship, created in Christ Jesus for good works, which God prepared beforehand, that we should walk in them" (Ephesians 2:10). When the Scripture says that "we are his workmanship," it means that God is at work in our lives to prepare us for his service.

Not only has he prepared good works for us to do, but God is also preparing *us* to do them, and he does this through the ordinary experiences of daily life. God uses our mistakes, even the kinds of mistakes that send us into the wilderness for decades. As James Boice has written, "God can teach us through the failure of our own plans that He is capable of working for us and in us in spite of us. Only after we fail do we become aware that it is God and not ourselves who is working."[4] God uses our *living situation*. Even when we are living away from home, in a place far away from our ultimate place of service, God is preparing us to do his will. God uses our *family situation*. Those who are married generally learn more spiritual lessons from their spouses than from anyone else. God uses marriage to sanctify husbands and wives. The same is also true of singleness. It is through their singleness that men and women who are unmarried, divorced, or widowed develop intimacy with God and learn to depend on him for every need. God also uses our *work situation*. Becoming a shepherd was not part of the career plan that Moses drew up back when he was the prince of Egypt, but God used the experience to prepare him for his life's work. In order to become the man God intended him to become, it was necessary for Moses to go out into the wilderness and take care of sheep. Even if we are working a job that does not seem to match our gifts or our interests, God will use it for our good and for his glory.

Whatever our present situation, we should try to learn what God is trying to teach us. We may not be doing what we want to be doing. We may not be living where we want to be living—or with whom we want to be living, for that matter. But we should always embrace the attitude of John Wesley (1703–1791), who prayed: "I am no longer my own, but yours. Put me to what you will, rank me with whom you will; put me to doing, put me to suffering; let me be employed for you or laid aside for you, exalted for you or brought low for you; let me be full, let me be empty; let me have all things, let me have nothing; I freely and wholeheartedly yield all things to your pleasure and disposal."[5]

### Meanwhile, Back in Egypt . . .

At the end of Exodus 2 the scene shifts from Midian back to Egypt, where the Hebrews were still in bondage. Forty years of unspeakable suffering are squeezed into the space between verses 22 and 23: "During those many days the king of Egypt died" (v. 23a). As suggested in chapter 1 of this commentary, the king in question was probably Thutmose III, or perhaps Seti I. But whoever the Pharaoh may have been, his death meant that it was now possible for Moses to return to Egypt.

The Israelites needed Moses to come back because they were still enslaved. As much as Moses may have wondered what God was doing in his life during those years, imagine how the rest of God's people felt! Year after year they toiled under the hot desert sun, building monuments to Pharaoh's glory. During their long servitude they must have felt as if they were afflicted by some divine curse, or even abandoned by God altogether. They had nothing—no power, no property, and no prestige. Some people would say, "They didn't have a prayer," but in fact a prayer was the one thing they did have: "The people of Israel groaned because of their slavery and cried out for help. Their cry for rescue from slavery came up to God" (v. 23b). Here the Bible uses three different words to describe the desperate prayers of God's people. Together they express intense grief, bitter distress, and painful agony. Their sufferings were so great that it was all they could do to cry out to God.

Sooner or later every believer ends up in a situation where the only thing to do is to cry out to God. When David was surrounded by enemies, he said, "Give attention to the sound of my cry, my King and my God, for to you do I pray" (Psalm 5:2). Another psalmist wrote:

> Out of the depths I cry to you, O LORD!
>     O Lord, hear my voice!
> Let your ears be attentive
>     to the voice of my pleas for mercy! (Psalm 130:1, 2)

The same prayer was offered in the time of Jeremiah, when God's people were starving in the streets of Jerusalem. The prophet said, "Their heart cried to the Lord" (Lamentations 2:18a). On occasion God's people find themselves in such desperate straits that the only thing they can do is to groan for God's help.

Even a groan can be a prayer, provided it is directed toward God in faith, and not in rebellion. God has promised that even our moaning is articulated at the throne of his grace in the form of a petition: "Likewise the Spirit helps us in our weakness. For we do not know what to pray for as we ought, but the Spirit himself intercedes for us with groanings too deep for words" (Romans 8:26). Even when our needs are too deep or too intense for words, God understands what we are trying to pray. He hears our cries for help and our groans for deliverance, just as he heard them in the days of Moses.

Not only does God hear our prayers, but he also answers them. There must have been times when the children of Israel thought that God was somewhat hard of hearing. For decades—no, *centuries*—they begged God to release them from their captivity. When, if ever, was he going to answer their cry for help? But their cries did not fall on deaf ears. God heard their prayers—he had been hearing them all along. When the time finally came for him to fulfill his perfect plan, he glorified himself in the salvation of his people: "And God heard their groaning, and God remembered his covenant with Abraham, with Isaac, and with Jacob. God saw the people of Israel—and God knew" (2:24, 25).

Here at the close of Exodus 2 Moses steps aside, and God takes center stage. God is ready to deliver his people from their bondage. He is going to act in history for their salvation. To emphasize the power of the living God, the Bible uses four active verbs: God *hears*, *remembers*, *sees*, and *knows*. God is really going to do something! Not only did he have a plan for Moses, even in the wilderness, but his plan for Moses was part of a bigger plan that would result in the salvation of God's people.

When people pray, God responds. First he sees. In the words of one old preacher, "Every blow of the hand that buffets you, every cut of the scourge, every scorching hour under the noon-tide sun, every lonely hour when lovers and friends stand aloof, every step into the valley of the shadow, every moment of sleep beneath the juniper tree, is watched by the eyes that never slumber nor sleep."[6] God not only sees, but he also hears: "The eyes of the LORD are toward the righteous and his ears toward their cry" (Psalm 34:15).

When God sees and hears, he remembers. Thankfully, what he remembers is not his people's sin but the covenant of grace, his unbreakable promise of salvation. The covenant is God's love relationship with his people—his eternal promise that he will be their God and they will be his people. It is the promise God gave to Eve that her offspring would crush the devil and all his evil works (Genesis 3:15). It is the promise God gave to Abraham that all nations would be blessed through him (Genesis 15; 17:1–8). Amazingly, one of the things God promised when he made this covenant is that he would deliver Abraham's descendants from the house of bondage: "Then the LORD said to Abram, 'Know for certain that your offspring will be sojourners in a land that is not theirs and will be servants there, and they will be afflicted for four hundred years. But I will bring judgment on the nation that they serve, and afterward they shall come out with great possessions'" (Genesis 15:13, 14).

Even if his people had forgotten this covenant promise, God still remembered. The story of Moses in Midian shows God's remembrance of his promise to Abraham by drawing a number of connections between the patriarchs and the exodus. There is a direct connection to Abraham because Midian was one of Abraham's sons, by way of his second wife Keturah (Genesis 25:1–4). In other words, the Midianites were Moses' long-lost cousins. There is also a connection with Isaac, whose wife Rebekah was found at the well, watering camels (Genesis 24). The same was true of Jacob, who met Rachel by the well. Like Moses, Jacob was running for his life when he met a young woman, watered her flocks, and was invited to meet her father (Genesis 29). Then there was Joseph, who was first brought to Egypt by a caravan of traders from Midian (Genesis 37:25–36). All of these connections remind us that the God of Abraham, Isaac, and Jacob is also the God of Moses. The God who made his covenant with the patriarchs is the very same God who led his people out of Egypt.

The same God sent Jesus to be our Savior, and he did so because he remembered his covenant. God remembered that he had promised a Redeemer to free us from our slavery to sin, a Son to keep the whole Law for his people, and a Lamb to take the punishment for our sins. From beginning to end, our salvation depends on God remembering his covenant.

If we belong to God by faith in Jesus Christ, then we are part of his eternal covenant. We have a right to every blessing God has promised in Christ, and we are free to claim the benefits of that covenant when we pray, "Dear heavenly Father, remember that your Son and my Savior, Jesus Christ, has kept all the terms of your covenant on my behalf. Remember that he died on the cross for my sins, establishing a new covenant in his blood. Remember that you have promised to give me every blessing of the covenant in Christ—to forgive my sins, to care for my needs, to comfort my sorrows, and at the end of it all, to take me home to glory." We can pray this way because we have God's covenant promise. When God remembers his covenant, he remembers that we are in Christ and that in Christ he has promised to save us to the very end.

Exodus 2 ends by saying that God "knew" the Israelites. He knew all about them. The word suggests intimate, personal acquaintance with all the particulars of their suffering. The God of the covenant, the God who sees, hears, and remembers, is the God who knows our situation in all its desperate need. He is a God who is worth praying to. He already knows all about our situation because he sees everything that happens. He hears all our prayers—even when they are little more than groanings. He remembers that we belong to him by the covenant of grace in Jesus Christ. Then he answers our prayers—not always in the way that we hope or even in the way that we expect, but always in a way that brings him glory.

# 6

# The Burning Bush

## EXODUS 3:1–9

SOMETIMES PEOPLE ARE IN such mortal danger that their only hope is to pray. C. S. Lewis (1898–1963) describes such a time in his novel *That Hideous Strength*. In the story the powers of evil have descended upon England with the intent to destroy creation and reduce man to a machine. Over against the forces of evil stands a small band of virtuous men and women, yet they are powerless to resist the onslaught. Near the end of the novel, one of them says, almost despairingly, "No power that is merely earthly will serve against the Hideous Strength." To which one of his companions replies, "Then let us all to prayers."[1]

It was to prayer that the children of Israel turned when they were slaves in Egypt. For four hundred years they had been under the whip, making Pharaoh's bricks to build Pharaoh's cities. Eventually the situation became so desperate that "the people of Israel groaned because of their slavery and cried out for help. Their cry for rescue from slavery came up to God" (2:23). Their cries did not go unheard. The Scripture says, "When Jacob went into Egypt, and the Egyptians oppressed them, then your fathers cried out to the LORD and the LORD sent Moses and Aaron, who brought your fathers out of Egypt and made them dwell in this place" (1 Samuel 12:8). God cared about the needs of his people, and the time for their deliverance had come. It is this great salvation that will occupy the rest of the book of Exodus. Whereas the first two chapters covered four hundred years of tribulation, the next thirty-eight chapters describe the year of liberation, when Israel came out of Egypt.

### The Fire in the Bush

God's answer to Israel's cry began faraway in the wilderness, where "Moses was keeping the flock of his father-in-law, Jethro, the priest of Midian, and he led his flock to the west side of the wilderness and came to Horeb, the mountain of

God" (3:1). We were introduced to Jethro back in chapter 2, where he was called Reuel. It is possible that the man had two names, which was common in ancient times. It is also possible that Reuel was the name of Jethro's father, which would actually make him Moses' grandfather-in-law (see Numbers 10:29). But perhaps the most likely explanation is that Jethro, which means "his excellency," was a formal title indicating the man's status.[2] In any case, he is called Jethro throughout the rest of Exodus.

Horeb, also known as Sinai, is the mountain where God later gave Moses the Law in the form of the Ten Commandments. Scholars have long debated its precise location. Various locales have been suggested, including not only a number of mountains on the Sinai peninsula, but also several in northwest Arabia (especially Jebel al-Lawz).[3] Since the fourth century, the site most often mentioned is Jebel Musa, which has an exceptional summit—a 7,500-foot peak that rises directly up from the plains near the southern tip of Sinai.[4] To this day, the bedouins who travel in that region call it "Moses' mountain."

The important thing about Horeb is not so much the mountain itself, however, as it is the fact that it became "the mountain of God" (3:1). God was there at that great mountain in all his living, burning presence. "And the angel of the LORD appeared to him in a flame of fire out of the midst of a bush. He looked, and behold, the bush was burning, yet it was not consumed. And Moses said, 'I will turn aside to see this great sight, why the bush is not burned'" (3:2, 3).

The day had probably begun much like any other, with Moses out in the wilderness tending sheep. He was simply minding his own business, but a person never knows when his life might be changed forever by an encounter with the living God. Not a chance encounter, for it was God's providence that led Moses to the far side of the desert. Here it is worth noticing that God did not meet Moses where Moses was but brought Moses to the place where God was. There Moses noticed a burning bush. It may have been a wild acacia, the common thornbush of Sinai, or perhaps a *Rubus sanctus*, a hardy bush that flourishes near Jebel Musa. Whatever kind of bush it was, the amazing thing about it was that it kept burning. During his decades in the wilderness, Moses may have seen a burning bush blazing under the desert sun, but it gradually dawned on him that there was something special about this particular bush. Although it was burning, it was not burnt. It remained on fire without being reduced to smoking embers. It was not even charred; it just kept burning.

By this time Moses' curiosity was piqued, so he went over to investigate. What he discovered was that the bush was not some kind of natural wonder but a supernatural sign. It was a physical miracle that communicated spiritual truth. Even before God *told* Moses who he was, he *showed* him who he was. The burning bush revealed the very being of God. Moses would later say, "For the LORD your God is a consuming fire" (Deuteronomy 4:24). This miraculous sign pointed to God's power by revealing his control over creation. Who else but God has the power to make a bush burn without its being consumed? It also pointed to God's glory by giving a glimpse of the brightness of his splendor. Perhaps it was this experience that later led Moses to ask God to show him all his glory (33:18).

The miraculous sign pointed as well to God's eternity and self-sufficiency. Like the burning bush, God never runs out of fuel. His glory never dims; his beauty never fades. He always keeps burning bright. This is because God does not get his energy from anyone or anything outside himself. He is completely self-existent and self-sufficient in his eternal being. According to Gregory of Nyssa (330–c. 395), what Moses saw in the burning bush was nothing less than "the transcendent essence and cause of the universe, on which everything depends, alone subsists."[5] The burning bush revealed the power and the glory, the eternity and the self-sufficiency of God.

It is not surprising that there was something divine about the bush, for the Bible says that what appeared to Moses was none other than "the angel of the Lord" (3:2). Here is a great mystery. The angel may have been a member of the heavenly host, one of the angelic beings who serve God in glory. But the Hebrew word for "angel" is simply the word "messenger" (*malakh*). Since this angel is identified specifically as "the angel *of the* Lord," there may be more here than meets the eye. Notice the wording of verse 4: "When *the* Lord saw that he turned aside to see, *God* called to him out of the bush." The messenger did not simply see and speak *for* God but *as* God. Here the angel of the Lord is so closely identified with God that the burning bush is generally considered a theophany. In other words, it was a God-appearance, a visible manifestation of the invisible God. For a few brief moments in time and space, the bush was the temple of the living God, the place of his presence on earth. Since the time of the early church, Christians have wondered whether perhaps this was a revelation of God's preincarnate Son, who brings God's saving message to humanity. Whether or not Christ was in the bush, one thing is certain: Moses was in the presence of God.

## Stand Back!

The fact that Moses was in God's presence explains why he had to take off his sandals. He was standing on holy ground:

> When the Lord saw that he turned aside to see, God called to him out of the bush, "Moses, Moses!"
>
> And he said, "Here I am."
>
> Then he said, "Do not come near; take your sandals off your feet, for the place on which you are standing is holy ground." And he said, "I am the God of your father, the God of Abraham, the God of Isaac, and the God of Jacob." And Moses hid his face, for he was afraid to look at God. (3:4–6)

Presumably Moses already knew something about holiness. After all, his father-in-law was a priest, a man set apart for God's holy service. So when God told Moses that he was standing on holy ground, Moses probably had some idea of what God was talking about. On the other hand, this is the first time the Bible uses the word "holy" (*qadosh*) with reference to God. At the burning bush God revealed his holiness in a way it had never been revealed before. Moses was so impressed by this that later, when he wrote his famous victory hymn, he made sure to mention the divine attribute of holiness: "Who is like you, majestic in holiness, awesome in glorious deeds, doing wonders?" (15:11).

*Holiness* means separation. Something holy is set apart. In the case of God, holiness means that he is set apart from everything he has made. Holiness is not simply his righteousness (although that is part of it), but also his otherness. It is the distinction between the Creator and the creature, the infinite distance between God's deity and our humanity. God says, "I am God and not a man, the Holy One in your midst" (Hosea 11:9). His people respond by saying, "There is none holy like the LORD" (1 Samuel 2:2).

In case there was any doubt as to what God meant by talking about holiness, he specifically warned Moses to keep his distance: "Do not come near" (3:5a). God was separating himself from Moses in order to emphasize the gap between the divine and the human. God is transcendent in his holiness, so Moses was not allowed to subject him to close scrutiny. Indeed, if he had taken so much as one more step in God's direction, his very life would have been in danger. Moses needed to stay right where he was. He also needed to take off his sandals, because God was too holy for his shoes. To this day in the Middle East, removing one's sandals is a sign of respect. The proper way for Moses to show his reverence for God's holiness was to take off his sandals.

The Bible does not specifically indicate whether Moses did as he was told, but undoubtedly he stopped in his tracks and whipped off his sandals. Certainly he understood that holy ground is dangerous territory, for the Bible says that "Moses hid his face, for he was afraid to look at God" (3:6b). It's a good thing he did this, because as God would later explain, "You cannot see my face, for man shall not see me and live" (33:20). As much as Moses may have wanted to see God's glory—a theme that will run throughout the book of Exodus—as soon as he realized that he was in the presence of a holy God, he realized that he was an unholy man. The Bible says that God is "of purer eyes than to see evil" (Habakkuk 1:13a). The reverse is also true: God is too pure for our eyes to look upon him.

This is the problem with human beings. We were made to gaze upon the glory of God—like Adam, who walked and talked with God in the garden—but we have fallen into sin. In our unholy condition, it is no longer safe for us to come into the presence of a holy God. But this raises a disturbing question: How will we ever survive a direct encounter with God? The Bible teaches that at the end of history every human being who has ever lived will stand before God's throne for judgment. When that day comes, unless we are holy, we will be destroyed.

Some people deal with this dilemma by exaggerating their own holiness. This is the way most false religions operate. They assume that human beings are basically good, and that if we obey the right rules and observe the right rituals, we will be good enough for God. The trouble is that we are not holy. Certainly we are not holy enough to stand before the Holy One, for the Bible says, "None is righteous, no, not one" (Romans 3:10).

Others try to deal with this problem by minimizing God's holiness, lowering his standards. However, God cannot be any less holy than he is; he would have to un-God himself to do so. Nor should we want God to be unholy. A. W. Tozer, who has written so eloquently on the theme of God's holiness, says, "I tell you this: I want God to be what God is: the impeccably holy, unapproachable Holy Thing, the All-Holy One. I want Him to be and remain *THE HOLY*. I want His heaven to be holy and His throne to be holy. I don't want Him to change or modify His requirements. Even if it shuts me out, I want something holy left in the universe."[6]

The only way for us to come into the presence of a holy God is to become holy ourselves. This is why God sent his Son to be our Savior. He is our holiness (1 Corinthians 1:30). We could never keep God's law, but Jesus kept it for us with perfect holiness. Then he died on the cross to take away all our unholiness. Now when we trust in him, God accepts us as holy in his sight—as holy as Jesus himself: "And you, who once were alienated and hostile in mind, doing evil deeds, he has now reconciled in his body of flesh by his death, in order to present you holy and blameless and above reproach before him" (Colossians 1:21, 22). The grace that God has shown through the cross enables us to approach the Holy One—not as Moses did, hiding his face in fear, but by faith, trusting in the person and work of Jesus Christ.

## Stooping to Save

It is an awesome thing to come into the presence of the living God. When Moses met God in the burning bush, he was not simply gaining new information about God—he was encountering God himself—God in all his greatness. Moses was meeting the glorious God, who blazes with splendor. He was meeting the eternal God, who is sufficient unto himself. He was meeting the holy God, who is perfect in his purity. One would not expect such a great and glorious God to have the slightest interest in mere mortals, especially mortal failures like Moses. Yet the holy God of the burning bush has an unbreakable love for his unholy people, and he revealed himself to Moses in order to maintain his personal, saving relationship with the children of Israel.

We began to see God's concern for his people at the end of chapter 2, where four verbs were used to describe his divine activity. God *heard* the groans of his people; he *remembered* his covenant with Abraham; he *saw* the Israelites in their slavery; and he *knew* about all their needs. These words are repeated in Exodus 3. Obviously God remembered his covenant, because he identified himself as "the God of Abraham, the God of Isaac, and the God of Jacob" (3:6a). Then he went on to say, "I have surely *seen* the affliction of my people who are in Egypt and have *heard* their cry because of their taskmasters. I *know* their sufferings" (3:7). God's relationship with his people is so close, his love for them is so intense, that he specifically identifies the children of Israel as "*my* people." In case there is any doubt as to whether God knows what is happening to them, he repeats himself in verse 9: "And now, behold, the cry of the people of Israel has come to me, and I have also seen the oppression with which the Egyptians oppress them."

When God's people suffer, they sometimes wonder whether God even cares. But the story of Israel in Egypt is a dramatic example of what is always the case: God knows exactly what his people are going through. He is well aware of what is happening to us. He sees our suffering. He also cares about it, which is why he responds to our cries for help. God is full of pity and compassion for the people he loves. What he said to the children of Israel he says to every one of his children: "I am concerned about your suffering."

God's relationship with his people is personal because the true and living God is a personal God who knows his people in a personal way. Notice that when God first called to Moses, he called him by name: "Moses, Moses!" (3:4). Exchanging names is one of the first steps in establishing a relationship, but here there was no need for Moses to tell God who he was. God already knew who Moses was—not to mention where he was and what he was doing. The holy and glorious God has personal and intimate knowledge of each one of his children. When he decides to come and save us, he calls us by name. The prophet Isaiah wrote:

> But now thus says the LORD . . .
> "I have called you by name, you are mine. . . .
> For I am the LORD your God,
> the Holy One of Israel, your Savior." (Isaiah 43:1, 3a)

Every Christian is a Christian by God's calling. Usually God does not meet us at a burning bush or speak to us in an audible voice but uses the preaching of his Word to expose our need of salvation and to compel us—personally and individually—to put our faith in Jesus Christ. Theologians call this "effectual calling," which the *Westminster Shorter Catechism* defines as "the work of God's Spirit, whereby, convincing us of our sin and misery, enlightening our minds in the knowledge of Christ, and renewing our wills, he doth persuade and enable us to embrace Jesus Christ, freely offered to us in the gospel" (A. 31). If you are not yet a Christian, this is what God is calling you to do even now: to receive Jesus Christ. God already knows you, but he wants you to know him, and so he invites you to enter into a personal relationship with him through Jesus Christ.

Long before God entered into a relationship with Moses, he entered into a relationship with the patriarchs. As he said to Moses, "I am the God of your father, the God of Abraham, the God of Isaac, and the God of Jacob" (3:6a). This was God's way of giving Moses his personal history. The God of the burning bush was not some unknown deity; he was the God who always had a personal relationship with his chosen people.

When God identified himself as "the God of your father," he may have been referring to Moses' biological father, Amram. If so, then his point was that he was the same God who rescued Moses from the Nile—the God Moses' parents taught him to serve before he went to Pharaoh's court. Other manuscripts put the word "father" in the plural—"the God of your fathers"—which would refer instead to Abraham, Isaac, and Jacob. It sounds rather impressive to hear God described as "the God of Abraham, the God of Isaac, and the God of Jacob" until one discovers that Abraham, Isaac, and Jacob were deeply flawed individuals. They were liars and tricksters, schemers and dreamers. Nevertheless, by his grace God entered into a personal relationship with them—a relationship of covenant love. God gave them unbreakable promises of eternal blessing. Lest anyone think that it was disreputable for God to associate with such men, the Bible states that "God is not ashamed to be called their God" (Hebrews 11:16a). He is not ashamed because he is the God of covenant love. When people come to him in faith, he is pleased to be known as their God forever.

Incidentally, God still associates with Abraham, Isaac, and Jacob today. Notice the use of the present tense: God does not say, "I *was* the God of Abraham," but "I *am* the God of Abraham." The implication is that on the basis of the eternal covenant, Abraham continues to enjoy a loving relationship with God, even after death. This was the verse Jesus used to prove the resurrection to the Sadducees: "And as for the resurrection of the dead, have you not read what was said to you by God: 'I am the God of Abraham, and the God of Isaac, and the God of Jacob'? He is not God of the dead, but of the living" (Matthew 22:31, 32). To this very day Abraham, Isaac, and Jacob enjoy fellowship with God in Heaven.

God's relationship with his people—the loving covenant he established with Abraham—is a personal relationship. It is also a saving relationship, and this is why God revealed himself to Moses. The God who sees, hears, and knows his people is also the God who saves: "I have come down to deliver them out of the hand of the Egyptians and to bring them up out of that land to a good and broad land" (3:8a). God was reaching down to bring his people up out of Egypt. Here we see that the God who is awesome in glory and fearsome in holiness stoops to save.

There was something God was saving them *from*. He was saving them from their slavery in Egypt, delivering them from the house of bondage. There was also something he was saving them *to*. He was saving them into the Promised Land. His plan was to bring them out of the land of slavery and captivity and into a land gushing with milk and honey. This was the land that God had promised to Abraham—the land of Canaan. He described it as "a good and broad land, a land flowing with milk and honey, to the place of the Canaanites, the Hittites, the Amorites, the Perizzites, the Hivites, and the Jebusites" (3:8b). It was a "good" land. God mentions "milk and honey" because those foods require green pastures and consistent harvests. The land he promised was peaceful, fruitful, and abundant. It was also a "broad" land. The Bible lists the six nations that were already living in the land. These nations had to be driven out, of course, but if the land was big enough for all of them, surely it was roomy enough for the Israelites.

The point is that God not only knew and cared about the plight of his people but was also planning to do something about it. The story of the exodus is the history of how God rescued his people, working out their whole salvation from beginning to end. In this personal saving relationship God brought them out of all their troubles into a good and happy place.

## The God Who Saves

The way God rescued Israel from Egypt is the way God always rescues his people. The exodus is not simply past history but present reality. The God who revealed himself to Moses at the burning bush is the same God we serve today. Whenever and wherever we worship him, we are standing on holy ground, praising the God of Abraham and crying out to him for salvation.

The exodus from Egypt reveals the pattern of salvation in Christ. So whatever God did for Moses has direct relevance for the Christian. John Calvin wrote:

> We again, instead of supposing that the matter has no reference to us, should reflect that the bondage of Israel in Egypt was a type of that spiritual bondage, in the fetters of which we are all bound, until the heavenly avenger delivers us by the power of his own arm, and transports us into his free kingdom. Therefore, as in old times, when he would gather together the scattered Israelites to the worship of his name, he rescued them from the intolerable tyranny of Pharaoh, so all who profess him now are delivered from the fatal tyranny of the devil, of which that of Egypt was only a type.[7]

Israel's bondage is a picture of our slavery to sin. Until we come to God in faith, we are living in the Egypt of our sin, enslaved by its passions and desires. Just as the children of Israel were under Pharaoh's whip, we are under the devil's spell. Therefore, we are in as great a need of salvation as were the children of Israel. If we are to be rescued, God will have to stoop down to save us.

Another word associated with coming down to save is *advent*, and this is exactly what God has done in Jesus Christ. Jesus came down from Heaven to lift us up to glory. It is through Jesus that we enter into a personal saving relationship with God, in which we are saved from the power of sin, the terror of Satan, and the finality of death. We are also saved *to* something: Heaven is our promised land, the place of God's abundant and eternal blessing.

What Moses experienced at the burning bush teaches us about God and the way of his salvation. It is also a great encouragement to prayer. The God who promised to come down and save the Israelites has the power to save us. All we need to do is cry out to him for deliverance. In his sermon on this text, Charles Spurgeon pleaded with his congregation: "Sinner, tell God your misery even now, and he will hear your story. He is willing to listen, even to that sad and wretched tale of yours about your multiplied transgressions, your hardness of heart, your rejections of Christ. Tell him all, for he will hear it. Tell him what it is you want,—what large mercy,—what great forgiveness; just lay your whole case before him. Do not hesitate for a single moment; he will hear it, he will be attentive to the voice of your cry."[8] If we open our hearts to offer such a prayer, the same God who met Moses at the burning bush—the holy God of glory, the God who has entered into a loving, personal relationship with his people through Jesus Christ—will come down and save us.

# 7

# The Great I Am

## EXODUS 3:10–15

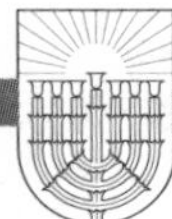

MOSES WAS IN THE WILDERNESS—barefoot at the burning bush—cowering in the presence of a holy God. He had led his flocks to Horeb, the mountain of God. There he saw a strange sight: a bush that kept burning without ever getting scorched. When he went over to look at it, Moses had a close encounter with the glory of the eternal God. He heard the voice of God speaking to him from the bush, explaining that he had seen the misery of his people Israel and had heard their cry to be delivered out of Egypt. The God of the burning bush told Moses that he remembered his covenant with Abraham and that now he was coming down to save his people.

### A Great Commission

At this point the conversation took a surprising turn. God had spoken of his compassion for the sufferings of his beloved people. He had promised to come and rescue them, entering personally into a saving relationship with them. But here was the surprise: God would accomplish his salvation through the person and work of Moses. God said, "Come, I will send *you* to Pharaoh that you may bring my people, the children of Israel, out of Egypt" (3:10). One might have expected God to explain how *he* was going to liberate his people from bondage, but instead he sent Moses to be the liberator.

Here we encounter one of the paradoxes of God's sovereign grace: God uses human beings—sinful human beings—to carry out his saving purpose. Moses had tried to save the Israelites once before, all by himself. The attempt was such a complete disaster that Moses had to leave the country. But God used the events of Moses' life to prepare him for ministry. Now the time of preparation was over, and God was commissioning Moses to lead his people out of slavery. In the end, of course, God was the one who delivered his people. But God raised up his servant Moses to be the human agent of that deliverance.

We have seen before how God can accomplish his saving work through ordinary people. It was Moses' mother who had the faith to put her baby in a basket, Pharaoh's daughter who drew the child out of the river, and Moses' sister who arranged for him to be weaned by his own mother; but it was the hand of God that led Moses to Pharaoh's palace. God rescued Moses—as he would later rescue all his people—through the uncommon faithfulness of common individuals. This is the way God (almost) always operates. His divine sovereignty involves human activity. God does his work through the work of his people, accomplishing his will through the willing obedience of his faithful servants.

The commissioning of the prophet Moses is a reminder that every believer has a job to do. In the previous chapter we saw that whenever God saves someone, he calls that person—personally and individually—to believe in him. Here we discover that God's call to Moses included not only his salvation but also his vocation—the specific task that God called him to accomplish for his glory. The same is true for every Christian. The God who saves is the God who sends. Thus every follower of Christ receives two callings: first to salvation, and then to service. Each of us is called to serve the God of the burning bush. Whether we are preachers or postmen, bridge builders or homemakers, God has work for us to do. The Puritan Cotton Mather (1663–1728) wrote, "Every Christian ordinarily should have a calling. That is to say, there should be some special business . . . wherein a Christian should for the most part spend the most of his time; and this, that so he may glorify God."[1]

Whatever our particular calling happens to be, it is a high calling because it was given to us by the Most High God. God himself has called us to do his work in the world. Therefore, we are to do our work joyfully, cheerfully, and diligently, recognizing that it is God's work we do, and not our own. What the Scripture says about our sanctification applies also to our vocation: "Therefore . . . work out your own salvation with fear and trembling, for it is God who works in you, both to will and to work for his good pleasure" (Philippians 2:12, 13). How remarkable it is that God accomplishes his work through us, using sinners to be his servants!

We find this same paradox at work in our evangelism, for like Moses, we have been given a Great Commission. Jesus said to his disciples, "All authority in heaven and on earth has been given to me" (Matthew 28:18). At this point, the disciples might have expected their Savior to explain how he was going to broadcast salvation around the world. Instead, Jesus commissioned *them* to preach the gospel on his behalf: "Go therefore and make disciples of all nations, baptizing them in the name of the Father and of the Son and of the Holy Spirit, teaching them to observe all that I have commanded you" (Matthew 28:19, 20a). The sovereignty of God's grace does not make our ministry unnecessary—it makes it mandatory! The work of salvation is God's work from beginning to end. Nevertheless, God uses us—as he used Moses—to accomplish his saving purpose.

## Who Am I?

At first Moses seemed ready to accept his great commission, for when God called to him from the burning bush, he said, "Here I am" (3:4b). With these words Moses was not simply letting God know where he was but was placing himself at God's disposal. When he said, "Here I am," what he meant was, "Here I am! At your service!"[2] This is the way young Samuel answered when he was called in the middle of the night: "Here I am!" (1 Samuel 3:4, 6, 8). It is also the way Isaiah answered when God asked who he should send to be his prophet: "Here I am! Send me" (Isaiah 6:8b). With these same words, Moses expressed his readiness to do God's will. Then by taking off his sandals, he let his actions speak as loudly as his words. In ancient times slaves generally went barefoot; so Moses was indicating his willingness to serve. In both word and deed, he adopted the posture of a servant.

But of course this was all before Moses actually knew what God wanted him to do, and as soon as he found out, he started to have his doubts. Apparently Moses was the kind of man who said yes first and asked questions later. He had five questions in all—though by the time the conversation was finished, they were more like objections than questions.

In the first two questions—which will occupy our attention for the rest of this chapter—Moses asked God, "Who am I?" and "Who are you?" These questions come in verse 11 ("Who am I that I should go to Pharaoh and bring the children of Israel out of Egypt?") and verse 13 ("If I come to the people of Israel and say to them, 'The God of your fathers has sent me to you,' and they ask me, 'What is his name?' what shall I say to them?"). They were good questions. Indeed, they are the most fundamental questions a person can ask. Once we know how to answer them—once we know who we are and who God is—we can begin to live for God's glory. John Calvin began his famous *Institutes* by saying, "Nearly all the wisdom we possess, that is to say, true and sound wisdom, consists of two parts: the knowledge of God and of ourselves." Calvin went on to claim, "It is certain that man never achieves a clear knowledge of himself unless he has first looked upon God's face, and then descends from contemplating him to scrutinize himself."[3] This is the kind of knowledge that Moses was seeking: knowledge of himself in the light of the knowledge of God.

First Moses asked for knowledge of himself: "But Moses said to God, 'Who am I that I should go to Pharaoh and bring the children of Israel out of Egypt?'" (3:11). This was not so much an existential question (concerning his identity) as it was a practical question (concerning his ability). Moses knew very well who he was—he just wasn't sure he had what it took to get the job done. The Egyptians were the most powerful people in the world. How could a mere shepherd possibly liberate their entire workforce from slavery? The last time Moses had tried to do something like this, it had taken him forty years to recover! Besides, who among the Israelites would even remember who he was, let alone follow him? And if anyone did remember Moses, what they were most likely to remember was that he was a convicted murderer: "Who am I that I should go to Pharaoh and bring the children of Israel out of Egypt?" (3:11).

Some see this question as a sign of humility. The exodus was a job that only God could do, they say, yet God was asking Moses to do it. Therefore it was appropriate for him to admit that the task was far beyond his abilities, that salvation belonged to God alone. Umberto Cassuto argues, "At this stage, when Moses is confronted with the plan as a whole, and realizes at the outset the terrible difficulties of his commission, his initial response is to voice his sense of humility and to stress his unworthiness relative to the magnitude of the enterprise."[4]

Others detect in Moses not simply a lack of self-confidence but also an element of stubbornness—an unwillingness to trust in God's plan. This was no time for Moses to ask God to review his résumé. He had been given a direct order, and whatever feelings of inadequacy he may have had, whatever reservations about his qualifications, he needed to overcome his reluctance and obey God's call for his life. If it is certain that God is calling us to do something, we must not hesitate. We must do as we are told, trusting God to "equip [us] with everything good that [we] may do his will" (Hebrews 13:21).

## "I Will Be with You"

Whatever we may think of Moses' first question—and he does seem to have asked it more out of fear than from faith—we should admit that we would have asked the same thing. Put yourself in his bare feet for a moment. Would you have wanted to tell Pharaoh to let God's people go? Or to persuade the Israelites that God had called you to lead them to the Promised Land? Moses was a man like us; sometimes he had his doubts.

How encouraging it is, therefore, to see how graciously God answered Moses. God could have tried to prove that Moses was the right man for the job. He could have reminded him of the way he had been trained in Pharaoh's court. He could have pointed to the lessons he had learned as a shepherd out in the wilderness. No one in the whole world was better prepared to lead Israel out of Egypt than Moses, who was Egyptian enough to confront the Egyptians and Hebrew enough to love the Hebrews.

All of that was true, but it was not the answer God gave. If he had shown Moses that he was fully qualified for his calling, that would have led Moses to trust in his gifts rather than in his God. The real question was not who Moses was, but who *God* was, for "He said, 'But I will be with you'" (3:12a). The exodus did not depend on the competence of Moses but on the presence of God.

In his commentary on these verses Peter Enns writes, "Moses' assertion that *he* cannot do this task is correct but entirely beside the point. He is not doing the saving. Moses says, 'I cannot do this.' Yahweh responds, 'You're not, I am.'"[5] Therefore, whatever doubts Moses may have had about his own abilities were totally irrelevant. God had promised to be with him, and "with God all things are possible" (Matthew 19:26).

The call to God's service always comes with the promise of God's presence. There are many examples of this in the Bible. When Joshua inherited the mantle of spiritual leadership, God promised him, "Just as I was with Moses, so I will be with you. I will not leave you or forsake you" (Joshua 1:5). God made the same promise to Gideon, who was too timid to lead the troops into battle. God said, "I will be with you" (Judges 6:16). God also promised to be with Jeremiah, who was only a youngster when he became a prophet: "Do not be afraid . . . for I am with you" (Jeremiah 1:8). But this promise is not just for prophets like Moses and Joshua—it is for all God's people. Just as God was with Moses and the children of Israel, so he is with us, for he has given us the promise of his presence in Jesus Christ, who said, "And behold, I am with you always, to the end of the age" (Matthew 28:20b). In making this promise, God has given himself to us forever and for always. And now that we have the promise of his eternal presence, what more could we need, or even want?

In case Moses had any lingering doubts, however, he was also given a sign: "But I will be with you, and this shall be the sign for you, that I have sent you: when you have brought the people out of Egypt, you shall serve God on this mountain" (3:12b). What is strange about this sign is that it points to the future. In this respect, it is not unlike the sign Isaiah gave when he prophesied the birth of Christ: "Therefore the Lord himself will give you a sign. Behold, the virgin shall conceive and bear a son, and shall call his name Immanuel" (Isaiah 7:14). In the case of Moses, the sign would not be confirmed until he led God's people out of Egypt and brought them back to God's holy mountain. Only then would God's promise be vindicated. So the question is, how did the sign help? If it would not come true until sometime in the future, how could it reassure Moses in the present?

Some scholars have tried to solve this problem by saying that the words "this . . . sign" actually refer to the burning bush. It is true that the bush was a sign. As we have seen, it pointed to eternal truths about God's character. The trouble is that this solution does not work very well grammatically. It is much more natural to take the sign the way the English Standard Version takes it, as referring to Moses' return to the very same mountain. Moses would not see the sign before he undertook his mission but after, because the success of his mission *was* the sign.

What this means is that the sign could only be received by faith. Its validity depended on God's ability to deliver on his promise. If Moses needed to be reassured that he was the right man for the job and that God would be with him, he simply had to take God's word for it, moving forward in faith. That is exactly what Moses did, for the Scripture says, "By faith he left Egypt, not being afraid of the anger of the king, for he endured as seeing him who is invisible" (Hebrews 11:27).

Moses' trust was well placed, for God was way ahead in his planning. Moses was still worried about going back to Egypt; meanwhile, God already had his people rescued from Egypt and back at Mount Sinai, singing his praises! It was God's plan from the very beginning that the exodus would be for his glory. God's plan was not simply to bring his people out of Egypt but to gather them in his presence to serve him with their worship. The central message of the book of Exodus is that we are saved to glorify God.

## Who Are You?

Who is this God we are called to glorify? That was the second question Moses asked. Before agreeing to lead Israel out of Egypt, he first wanted to know who he himself was. Next he wanted to know who *God* was. It was all very well for God to promise to go with him, but who was this God anyway? "Then Moses said to God, 'If I come to the people of Israel and say to them, "The God of your fathers has sent me to you," and they ask me, "What is his name?" what shall I say to them?'" (3:13).

It is easy to criticize Moses for his question. To begin with, he started badly: "If I come to the people. . . ." *If* he goes? What was Moses thinking? He had just received a direct order from the God of the everlasting covenant. Such divine commands are not open to negotiation. There was no *if* about it: Moses was going! He either had to do as he was told or defy God. The reason he gave for asking was equally unworthy. Moses made it sound as if he were asking on behalf of the Israelites, when in fact he was voicing his own doubts. God had given him the promise of his presence—which was all he needed—but Moses was still worried what people would think of him. Notice how self-centered his thinking is: "If *I* come . . . what shall *I* say to them?" Moses was still focusing on his own inadequacy rather than on God's sufficiency. To regain his focus he needed God to say to him, "I AM WHO I AM" (3:14). Then there was the question itself, which was totally unnecessary. Moses already *knew* who God was because God had identified himself as the God of his fathers—Abraham, Isaac, and Jacob (3:6). This whole conversation would have been much shorter if Moses had simply taken God at his word. He still had to learn how much simpler life is for those who simply trust and obey.

Before faulting Moses too much, however, we should put ourselves in his place for a moment. God had made such large promises and placed such heavy demands on him that Moses wanted more information. In particular, he wondered what God's people were going to say when he went back and told them he was going to lead them to the Promised Land. Moses had been raised as an Egyptian, which meant that he had never fully shared in their sufferings. Nor had he been back to Egypt for forty years. Even worse, the last time he was there, the Israelites had rejected his leadership. They were hardly likely to believe Moses when he said he was sent to be their savior. He wasn't even sure himself that he was the right man for the job. So why would anyone else think he could do it? The only thing he could appeal to was God's authority, but how could he persuade people that he had been in the presence of the Lord? He could hardly believe his own eyes and ears, let alone convince anyone else. So he imagined going back to Egypt and saying, "Look, I was out in the desert watching these sheep, you see, and there was this bush, and it kept burning without burning up. Well, anyway, then I heard this voice telling me to lead you out of Egypt."

Moses knew how skeptical people would be, and it was not hard to guess how they would react. They would tell him that he had been seeing things and hearing things out under the hot desert sun. Then what was he going to say—"Well, I guess you just had to be there"? It is easy to see why Moses felt like he needed something more. He wanted the full weight of divine authority behind him. So he asked God to reveal his very name.

It is not certain whether the Israelites already knew God's name or not. It was not uncommon for God to reveal a new name when he accomplished a new salvation or deliverance. However, if the Israelites did not know God's special divine name already, one wonders how much its revelation would have strengthened Moses' credibility. Besides, this is not the first time that God's special name was used in the Bible, or even in this chapter (see 3:2, 4, 7). Therefore, it seems likely that the Hebrews already knew the divine name and that by appearing in the burning bush God was simply reintroducing himself as the God his people had always known.

However, Moses seems not to have known the name of the Lord. By asking God to reveal it, he was seeking to understand God's essence. God's name was more than a name: it represented his entire character and reputation. Thus the answer Moses received was a revelation of God's very being and attributes:

> God said to Moses, "I AM WHO I AM." And he said, "Say this to the people of Israel, 'I AM has sent me to you.'" God also said to Moses, "Say this to the people of Israel, 'The LORD, the God of your fathers, the God of Abraham, the God of Isaac, and the God of Jacob, has sent me to you.' This is my name forever, and thus I am to be remembered throughout all generations." (3:14, 15)

That was God's answer, and Moses probably spent the rest of his life trying to figure out exactly what it meant. Bible scholars have spent the last three thousand years trying to understand it, and they still don't agree, because "I AM WHO I AM" is the kind of statement that raises more questions than it answers.

In fact, Peter Enns thinks that it "can be understood as a near refusal to dignify Moses' question with an answer: 'I AM WHO I AM; they know very well who I am. What a question!'"[6]

One difficulty is determining exactly what the answer is. What *is* God's name? Does it come in verse 14 or verse 15? If it comes in verse 14, then God's name is "I AM WHO I AM" or simply "I AM." But in that case God's name is a verb, which would be highly unusual. It seems more likely that the divine name is given in verse 15, where God identifies himself as "the LORD." "LORD" is the special name for God that occurs more than five thousand times in the Old Testament. One place it occurs is in the Song of Moses, where it shows how Moses himself understood God's answer to his question: "The LORD is his name" (15:3b).

The name "LORD" is sometimes called the *tetragrammaton* because in Hebrew it consists of four letters: YHWH. The Jews considered these letters to be so sacred that later some of them even refused to pronounce the Lord's name, for fear of taking it in vain. Perhaps that is why the proper way to pronounce the divine name has been forgotten (part of the problem too is that the most ancient Hebrew manuscripts do not contain any vowels, only consonants). The King James Version of the Bible sometimes writes it out as "Jehovah," although this is based on a misunderstanding of Hebrew vowels that dates back to the medieval church. The English Standard Version simply prints it as "LORD" in capital and small capital letters. Probably the proper way to say God's special name was something like "Yahweh." But even if its pronunciation is uncertain, God's name itself has never been forgotten. The French Huguenots preserved it in their insignia: a burning bush imprinted with the four Hebrew letters that spell the divine name.

## What's in the Name?

If you want someone to know who you are, the first step is to give him or her your name. The Lord has disclosed his name—*Yahweh*—so that we may know him in a personal way. But what does his name mean? What is it intended to convey?

Exodus 3 is a good place to answer these questions because it is the only place where the Old Testament explains God's name. First, *Yahweh* means that God is mysterious. By giving us his name, God lets us know who he is. But God's name is so hard to comprehend—so inscrutable—that it forces us to admit that there are some things about God that we will never understand. Part of what makes the divine name mysterious is that it is derived from the Hebrew verb "to be" (*hayah*). Although most translations obscure this, the name "LORD" in verse 15 is related to the words "I will be" and "I am." Therefore, God uses variations of his name five times in these verses—once in verse 12 ("I will be with you," or better, "It is I AM who is with you"), three times in verse 14 ("I AM"), and once in verse 15 ("The LORD"). His special name means something like "He who is," or "I am the One who is." But even this is a mystery. The great Dutch theologian Herman Bavinck (1854–1921) wrote, "God *is* that which he *calls* himself, and he *calls* himself that which he *is*."[7] Who is God? God is who he is, and that's all there is to it.

Second, God's name means that he is eternal and unchangeable (or immutable) in his divine being. His name occurs in the present tense of the Hebrew verb "to be." God does not say, "I was who I was" or "I will be who I will be." He says, "I AM WHO I AM." This is because he has no past or future but only an eternal present. God is the One who always is. He is who he is, he has always been who he is, and he always will be who he is. So he could say to Moses that he was the God of the patriarchs—the God of Abraham, Isaac, and Jacob. He could also promise, "This is my name forever, and thus I am to be remembered throughout all generations" (3:15b).

God's name has a third meaning. It means that God is self-existent. The Hebrew verb "to be" is flexible enough to allow the divine name to be translated as "He who causes to be." Everything else owes its life and being to God, but God is independent. He does not owe his being or his attributes to anyone else. He simply exists all by himself. As the Puritan Matthew Henry (1662–1714) observed, "The greatest and best man in the world must say, By the grace of God *I am what I am*; but God says absolutely—and it is more than any creature, man or angel, can say—*I am that I am*."[8] God is who he is in himself. He is not dependent on anyone or anything else because he has his existence from himself.

Another way to say this is that God is self-sufficient. He does not have any unmet needs or unsatisfied desires. He does not need any help. He is not co-dependent. He does not live or move or have his being in anyone except himself. *The Westminster Confession of Faith* says, "God hath all life, glory, goodness, blessedness, in and of himself; and is alone in and unto himself all-sufficient, not standing in need of any creatures which he hath made" (2.2).

As we have seen, this was part of the meaning of the burning bush, which kept burning—all by itself—without ever being extinguished. Like the burning bush, God is perpetually self-existent. Alexander Maclaren wrote:

> The fire that burns and does not burn out, which has no tendency to destruction in its very energy, and is not consumed by its own activity, is surely a symbol of the One Being, whose being derives its law and its source from itself, who only can say—"I am that I am"—the law of his nature, the foundation of his being, the only conditions of his existence being, as it were, enclosed within the limits of his own nature. You and I have to say, "I am that which I have become," or "I am that which I was born," or "I am that which circumstances have made me." He said, "I am that I am." All other creatures are links; this is the staple from which they all hang. All other being is derived, and therefore limited and changeful; this being is un-

> derived, absolute, self-dependent, and therefore unalterable forevermore. Because we live, we die. In living, the process is going on of which death is the end. But God lives forevermore, a flame that does not burn out; therefore his resources are inexhaustible, his power unwearied. He needs no rest for recuperation of wasted energy. His gifts diminish not the store which he has to bestow. He gives and is none the poorer. He works and is never weary. He operates unspent; he loves and he loves forever. And through the ages, the fire burns on, unconsumed and undecayed.[9]

## Jesus Christ, the Great I Am

Knowing the name of the God he met at the burning bush was a great help to Moses. Once he knew God's true identity, he was able to go back to Egypt and say to the Israelites, "I AM has sent me to you." The rest of the exodus is the story of God living up to his name, proving that he is the eternal God of covenant grace.

Knowing God's name is also a great help to us. If God is the Great I Am, who always is who he is, then we serve the same God that Moses served. Whenever we worship, shoes are optional, because we are in the presence of the mysterious, eternal, unchangeable, and self-existent God.

The only difference is that the God of Moses has given us a new name to call him. It is the name—the only name—by which we must be saved: Jesus Christ. On one occasion Jesus was trying to convince some religious leaders that he was the Christ. Finally he said, "Truly, truly, I say to you, before Abraham was, I am" (John 8:58). Jesus was claiming to be the Lord God of Moses, the Great I Am, the eternal and self-existent God incarnate. The religious leaders knew exactly what Jesus was saying, but they did not believe him. In fact, they thought what he said was blasphemy, so they tried to stone him. But what Jesus said is true: He himself is the one "who is and who was and who is to come" (Revelation 1:8).

Do you believe that Jesus Christ is the God of Moses, the Lord of the burning bush? The question is important because its answer is a matter of life and death. Jesus said, "I told you that you would die in your sins, for unless you believe that *I am* he you will die in your sins" (John 8:24). Jesus Christ is the God who saves, and anyone who does not believe in him has no hope of salvation. But Jesus went on to say, "When you have lifted up the Son of Man, then you will know that *I am* he" (John 8:28a). Jesus was speaking about his crucifixion, claiming that his death on the cross for sinners would prove that he is the true God of our salvation. A Christian is someone who believes that Jesus is the Great I Am.

Once we believe in Jesus, we may come to him with our questions, as Moses did. He will not turn us away. But what he wants us to do is to put our faith in him, going where he sends us and trusting in the promise of his everlasting presence.

# 8

# Wonders and Signs

## EXODUS 3:16—4:9

MOSES WAS STILL AT THE BURNING BUSH, but he was starting to lose his inhibitions. In particular he had lost his sense of the awesomeness of God. At first he "hid his face, for he was afraid to look at God" (3:6b). But even if he was afraid to look at God, apparently he was not afraid to talk to him, and even to argue with him.

Exodus 3, 4 recounts a lengthy discussion—not to say a dispute—between God and Moses. Moses was still trying to decide whether he wanted to lead God's people out of Egypt or not, so he asked God five questions. First he wanted to know who he was to undertake such a difficult and dangerous mission: "Who am I that I should go to Pharaoh and bring the children of Israel out of Egypt?" (3:11). God answered by saying that it didn't matter all that much who Moses was, as long as God was with him. Second, Moses asked who God was (3:13). If the success of his mission depended on God rather than on himself, Moses wanted to know what God's name was. God answered by revealing himself as the Great I Am.

Once he had answered those two questions, God proceeded to give detailed information about what he wanted Moses to do. Rarely has a man ever been given such explicit instructions for carrying out God's will. The verses that follow contain a message for the Israelites (3:16, 17), a message for the Egyptians (3:18–22), and three signs for Moses (4:1–9), which—as we shall discover—were given in response to his third question.

### A Message for the Israelites

The first step in God's plan was for Moses to go back to Egypt and speak with the Israelites. God told him exactly what to do and say: "Go and gather the elders of Israel together and say to them, 'The Lord, the God of your fathers, the God of Abraham, of Isaac, and of Jacob, has appeared to me, saying, "I have observed you and what has been done to you in Egypt, and I promise that I will bring you up out of the affliction of Egypt to the land of the Canaanites, the Hittites, the Amorites, the Perizzites, the Hivites, and the Jebusites, a land flowing with milk and honey"'"' (3:16, 17).

If this message sounds familiar, it is because God said all these things to Moses at the beginning of chapter 3. He was simply repeating the promises he had already made. When Moses went back to Egypt, he was supposed to repeat for the elders *exactly* what he had seen and heard. Here is an important principle for the transmission of Biblical prophecy: The men who wrote the Bible spoke from God. They were not writing down their own opinions or making things up as they went along. On the contrary, they wrote and spoke *only* those things that God told them to write and to say. The Bible is not man's word about God, but God's Word to man. The apostle Peter said, "[Know] this first of all, that no prophecy of Scripture comes from someone's own interpretation. For no prophecy was ever produced by the will of man, but men spoke from God as they were carried along by the Holy Spirit" (2 Peter 1:20, 21). This was true in the case of Moses. What he gave the Israelites was not his own personal interpretation of the meaning of the burning bush. The words he repeated, and are recorded for us in the book of Exodus, are the very words of God.

God's message to the Israelites contains many wonderful truths about his attributes and activities. Although we have studied them before, they are well worth repeating. God identified himself as "The LORD" (3:15). This special divine name ("Yahweh") meant that he is the One who is, the eternal and self-existent God. God also identified himself as "the God of your fathers, the God of Abraham, the God of Isaac, and the God of Jacob" (3:15). He was the God of the eternal covenant who established a personal, saving relationship with his people. He knew them by name and had a history of loving and caring for them.

All of that was in the past. In the present, God was at work to save his people. This is why he appeared to Moses at the burning bush, revealing himself as the holy God. When Moses returned to Egypt, he was supposed to tell the Israelites that he had seen a theophany, a visible manifestation of the invisible God. He was also supposed to tell them that God knew and cared about what was happening to them and was ready to do something about it. The Israelites had been enslaved for so long that they feared they were forgotten. But God paid close attention to their suffering. He knew how grievously they had been sinned against, for he said, "I have observed you and what has been done to you in Egypt" (3:16b).

Yahweh was the God of the past who promised salvation to the patriarchs. He was the God of the present who sent Moses to save his people. And he was the God of the future who would bring them into the Promised Land: "I promise that I will bring you up out of the affliction of Egypt to the land of the Canaanites, the Hittites, the Amorites, the Perizzites, the Hivites, and the Jebusites, a land flowing with milk and honey" (3:17). As we have seen, salvation is not only *from* something but also *to* something. When God rescued his people from slavery and captivity, he did not leave them in the wilderness but brought them into the land of milk and honey. After the exit from Egypt, there was the entry into Canaan. The God who spoke to Moses is the God who is active in history—past, present, and future.

We have come to know this same God through Jesus Christ, who is "the same yesterday and today and forever" (Hebrews 13:8). Jesus Christ is the God of the past, who entered human history to save sinners by dying on the cross and rising from the grave in real time and space. Jesus is also the God of the present, who is watching over us and who knows our suffering, including the ways that we are sinned against. The Christ of past and present is also the Christ of the future, who has promised not simply to save us from sin but also to bring us to glory. One day he will return to take us home forever.

## A Message for Pharaoh

When Moses took God's saving message to the Israelites, he was to go first to Israel's elders and gather them in a sacred assembly (3:16). This was partly a matter of convenience. The easiest way to communicate with a large nation is to start with its leaders. It was also a matter of principle. God entrusted the care of his people to a group of men who together exercised spiritual authority over Israel. As we shall discover, even after Moses became their leader, these elders continued to exercise a prominent role in the life of God's people (see 18, 24). In much the same way, the church of Jesus Christ is supposed to be governed by a group of elders who together shepherd God's flock (see Acts 20:17–35; 1 Timothy 3:1–7; 5:17). The Biblical principle of rule by elders (or *presbyters*, to use the New Testament term for it) goes all the way back to the exodus.

There was another reason for Moses to assemble the elders: he needed help to fulfill his calling. God did not intend for Moses to approach Pharaoh alone, but with the support and encouragement of his elders: "And they [the elders] will listen to your voice, and you and the elders of Israel shall go to the king of Egypt" (3:18a). Once Moses had persuaded Israel's spiritual leaders that he had seen the Lord, he would be able to draw courage and receive counsel from them. Then Moses and the elders were to deliver this message to Pharaoh: "The Lord, the God of the Hebrews, has met with us; and now, please let us go a three days' journey into the wilderness, that we may sacrifice to the Lord our God" (3:18b).

What is surprising about this message is that they asked Pharaoh for only three days off. God had already promised to lead his people all the way out of Egypt and into Canaan, but when they first went to Pharaoh they made the exodus sound like a weekend retreat! Not surprisingly, some scholars have objected that God was not completely honest with Pharaoh—indeed, that what he said was a lie. His real intention was to gather his people at Mount Sinai, which was much farther than three days from Egypt.

There are a number of ways to respond to this objection, which must be answered if God's honesty is to be preserved. One is to point out that strictly speaking, the elders did not say anything false. They simply asked to make a three-day journey initially, without saying anything about when they would come back. If what they said was misleading, it was only because Pharaoh had no right to know the truth. Keeping God's people enslaved was an act of aggression, and asking for three days' leave was a *ruse de guerre*—a justifiable stratagem in time of war.

Other possible solutions to the problem of the three-day journey are based on ancient customs. There is evidence that the phrase "three days' journey" was used to refer to any long journey of indefinite duration. It also helps to remember that this was the opening move in a lengthy diplomatic process between Moses and Pharaoh, a process governed by Oriental customs for bartering.[1] It is obvious from their subsequent bargaining that Pharaoh was not deceived and that Moses did not intend to deceive him. Both men were used to this style of discourse, and as they negotiated Israel's withdrawal, they both understood that once the Hebrews departed, they would never return.

These solutions have some merit, but there is another answer that brings out the true spiritual intention of the elders' request. What was more important than the journey's length was its purpose. What the Israelites were requesting was permission to go out and meet their God. In particular, they needed to worship him, to restore their covenant relationship with him by offering sacrifices for their sins. Remember that from the very beginning, the exodus was for the glory of God. Thus the real question was not how long the Israelites would be gone, but whether or not Pharaoh was willing to let them glorify God at all. Ultimately God intended to lead his people out of Egypt altogether; but by beginning with a more modest request, he was able to expose Pharaoh's deep hostility to his glory. Even if it would have been unreasonable to expect the king of Egypt to let his entire labor force leave the country, it was hardly unreasonable to ask for a few days of religious freedom. Yet Pharaoh was unwilling to give God even three days of glory. He wanted to keep all the glory to himself, and he knew that if he granted even this one simple request, it would show that the glory did not really belong to him at all.

This is a choice every human being has to make: Will we live for God's glory or our own? The Israelites had made their choice. Like Moses, the elders had decided to serve the one they called "the Lord *our* God," and when the time came, they would offer him sacrifices of praise (see Exodus 24). Pharaoh had made his choice too. He would not call the Lord his God because he was not willing to give him the glory. Only those who offer everything they are and have to God ever get to know him as the Lord their God.

## God of Wonders

Since he knew how hard Pharaoh's heart was, God knew that the elders' request would be denied. Even if it was only for three days, Pharaoh would refuse to cooperate and let God's people go. God also knew what it would take to bring Israel out of Egypt: "But I know that the king of Egypt will not let you go unless compelled by a mighty hand. So I will stretch out my hand and strike Egypt with all the wonders that I will do in it; after that he will let you go" (3:19, 20). This part of Exodus serves as a "preview of coming attractions," providing an outline for the next eleven chapters. Step by step this is how the Israelites would be saved: "The people will believe, the king will be hardened, the Egyptians will be plagued, the deliverance will occur, and finally the Egyptians will be despoiled!"[2]

This proves that the God who saves is a God who knows the future. This is worth emphasizing because it is becoming increasingly common to hear evangelical Christians say that God does not know the future. Sometimes this idea is referred to as "the openness of God."[3] It means that God is open to the possibilities, that his plans change according to the circumstances. But the God of the Bible, the God who appeared to Moses at the burning bush, is not a God who makes things up as he goes along. On the contrary, he is the God who ordains whatever happens according to the eternal counsel of his perfect will. He is the God who says,

> Remember this and stand firm,
> recall it to mind, you transgressors,
> remember the former things of old;
> for I am God, and there is no other;
> I am God, and there is none like me,
> declaring the end from the beginning
> and from ancient times things not yet done,
> saying, "My counsel shall stand,
> and I will accomplish all my purpose." (Isaiah 46:8–10)

The exodus is a perfect example of God's unique ability not only to know the future, but also to predetermine it. When God sent Moses to Pharaoh, he knew precisely what would happen. Everything would happen according to his plan, as everything always does.

What God would do to conquer Pharaoh's heart also proves his power. For all his stubbornness, the king of Egypt was no match for the God of Moses. The Bible draws attention to this when it speaks of God's "mighty hand" (3:19). Ancient Egyptian texts typically described Pharaoh as "the one who destroys enemies with his arm."[4] But Pharaoh's arm was too weak to wrestle with the arm of God, and God proved his strength by bending Pharaoh's will to his own.

God did this by performing "wonders" (3:20)—extraordinary deeds of supernatural power. The wonders were all the miracles God would perform with his outstretched arm, including the ten plagues he used to afflict the Egyptians. When the psalmist later praised God for the mighty works of his power, he used the same word Moses used to describe the exodus:

> Great are the works of the LORD,
> studied by all who delight in them.
> Full of splendor and majesty is his work,
> and his righteousness endures forever.
> He has caused his wondrous works to be remembered;
> the LORD is gracious and merciful. (Psalm 111:2–4)

Only after God had proved his might by performing all his wonders would Pharaoh let God's people go. Actually he would do more than let them go. The Hebrew phrase suggests an expulsion. Pharaoh would be so eager to get rid of his former slaves that he would practically push them out of Egypt. And when they finally went, the Egyptians would give the Israelites a little spending money for their journey: "And I will give this people favor in the sight of the Egyptians; and when you go, you shall not go empty, but each woman shall ask of her neighbor, and any woman who lives in her house, for silver and gold jewelry, and for clothing. You shall put them on your sons and on your daughters. So you shall plunder the Egyptians" (3:21, 22).

Plundering the Egyptians would demonstrate many of God's perfections. It would prove that he keeps all his promises. Centuries before, when he made his covenant with Abraham, God specifically promised that his people would come out of their captivity "with great possessions" (Genesis 15:14). It would also show God's power. Ordinarily a defeated nation was plundered by mighty warriors. But in this case Egypt would be plundered by women—a complete triumph! Furthermore, claiming these trophies of war would demonstrate God's providence, for the silver and gold would eventually be used to build the tabernacle. Thus the Egyptians were plundered for the glory of God.

What is perhaps most important, however, is that plundering the Egyptians served to demonstrate divine justice. Scholars sometimes blame the Israelites for stealing. The King James Version contributes to this misunderstanding by stating that the Israelites would "borrow" treasure from the Egyptians, even though they had no intention of ever returning it. In fact, however, the Hebrew states that the Israelites simply asked the Egyptians for their treasures. This was God's way of making sure that his people got paid for all the work they did for Pharaoh, which was only fair! Umberto Cassuto writes:

> *The Hebrew slaves* who went forth from Egypt had already served their masters the number of years that Providence had predetermined, and consequently they were entitled to liberation, and upon liberation the bounty

> was also due to them. This was required by law—that is, absolute justice demanded it—and although no earthly court could compel the king of Egypt and his servants to fulfil their obligation, the Heavenly Court saw to it that the requirements of law and justice were carried out, and directed the course of events to this end.[5]

Later, when God gave his people the Law, he decreed that Hebrew slaves were never to be sent away empty-handed but always compensated for their labor: "If your brother, a Hebrew man or a Hebrew woman, is sold to you, he shall serve you six years, and in the seventh year you shall let him go free from you. And when you let him go free from you, you shall not let him go empty-handed. You shall furnish him liberally out of your flock, out of your threshing floor, and out of your winepress. As the Lord your God has blessed you, you shall give to him. You shall remember that you were a slave in the land of Egypt, and the Lord your God redeemed you" (Deuteronomy 15:12–15a). One of the deep principles of divine justice is that the redemption of a slave requires the payment of a gift. The same thing happened when the Israelites were freed from Babylon: They were given gold and silver for their return trip to Jerusalem (see Ezra 1).

There is an echo of this principle in the New Testament. When Jesus Christ liberated us from our bondage to sin, he lavished us with gifts—spiritual gifts to enrich our new life of freedom in Christ. As the Scripture says, "When he ascended on high he led a host of captives, and he gave gifts to men" (Ephesians 4:8). Jesus despoiled the devil through the cross, and now the gifts of the Holy Spirit serve as the bounty of our liberation.

## Special Signs

Obviously the messages that Moses was commissioned to take to the elders of Israel and to Pharaoh were full of valuable information about the God who saves. The Lord God of Abraham is a great God of miracles, power, and justice. Yet one wonders how carefully Moses was listening, because he was still worried about how he would be treated when he went back to the Israelites. Ignoring most of what God said, and returning to the initial instructions of 3:15 ("Say this to the people of Israel . . ."), "Then Moses answered, 'But behold, they will not believe me or listen to my voice, for they will say, "The Lord did not appear to you"'" (4:1).

Like the first two questions he asked ("Who am I?" and "Who are you?"), Moses' third question sounds almost reasonable. It is easy to see why he asked it. He was the only eyewitness to something that no one else had ever seen: the eternal Lord in a burning bush. Now he had to go back and persuade an entire nation that God had sent him to be their savior. Yet the last time he had spoken to them, they said, "Who made you a prince and a judge over us?" (2:14a). The only way they would listen to him now would be if they believed that God had actually appeared to him. But how would they ever believe that?

Moses' objection would be persuasive were it not for the fact that it was an explicit contradiction of God's word, a denial of divine revelation. Back in 3:18 God made this promise: "And they [the elders] will listen to your voice." When Moses came back with his protest ("Okay, but what if they don't?"), it was the height of impertinence. God not only promised that the elders would believe Moses, but he also promised that they would make his testimony their own. When they went to Pharaoh, they would say, "The LORD, the God of the Hebrews, has met with *us*" (3:18b). So by asking what would happen if the elders refused to listen to him, Moses was flatly rejecting God's promise.

This teaches us, by negative example, to believe the Word of God. When God makes a promise, we are not to contradict it the way Moses did but are simply to accept it. To give just one example, we are called to trust God's promise that he will save sinners by his grace. When it comes to evangelism—to sharing the gospel with family and friends—Christians are often tempted to ask the same question Moses asked: "What if they do not believe me or listen to me?" But God has promised to use his Word to save people from their sins: "So faith comes from hearing, and hearing through the word of Christ" (Romans 10:17). So we are called to keep sharing the good news about Jesus Christ and to leave the saving to God, who has promised to redeem his own.

## Miraculous Proof

As impertinent as it was, God graciously answered the question by giving Moses three signs or visible manifestations of divine power. God started with what was immediately at hand:

> The LORD said to him, "What is that in your hand?" He said, "A staff." And he said, "Throw it on the ground." So he threw it on the ground, and it became a serpent, and Moses ran from it. But the LORD said to Moses, "Put out your hand and catch it by the tail"—so he put out his hand and caught it, and it became a staff in his hand—"that they may believe that the LORD, the God of their fathers, the God of Abraham, the God of Isaac, and the God of Jacob, has appeared to you." (4:2–5)

It was a remarkable sign, especially because the staff was thoroughly ordinary. As a shepherd Moses had probably carried it around with him for years. Yet when God turned it into a snake—apparently poisonous—Moses was so frightened that he ran away from his own stick! It took faith to pick it back up again, especially because grabbing the snake's tail left him vulnerable to snakebite. The original Hebrew gives a hint how tentatively Moses reached for it. When God told him to take the serpent by the tail, he used a word that means to "take hold of" something firmly. But when the Bible describes what Moses actually did, it uses the word that means "to snatch at" or "to grab cautiously."[6]

There was a great deal to learn from that old shepherd's crook. There was a lesson in it for Moses, who was still having trouble believing he could do what God was calling him to do. God used the stick to show Moses how he can use something ordinary to accomplish his extraordinary purpose. By giving this sign, God was saying, "Look, Moses, if you have your doubts, let me show you what I can do. That stick there—let me show you what I can do with *that*!" Later God used Moses' staff to bring plagues on the Egyptians, to part the sea, and to bring water from a rock.

If God could do all that with a stick, imagine what he could do with Moses! And imagine what he might be able to do with you! In a wonderful sermon entitled "No Little People, No Little Places," Francis Schaeffer pointed out that in order for it to become an instrument of divine power, the staff of Moses had to become the rod of God (see 4:20, where it is called "the staff of God"). Schaeffer went on to say:

> Consider the mighty ways in which God used a dead stick of wood. "God so used a stick of wood" can be a banner cry for each of us. Though we are limited and weak in talent, physical energy, and psychological strength, we are not less than a stick of wood. But as the rod of Moses had to become the rod of God, so that which is *me* must become the *me* of God. Then I can become useful in God's hands. The Scripture emphasizes that much can come from little if the little is truly consecrated to God.[7]

What Moses learned from the stick was that in order to be used for God's glory, he had to place his life in God's hands. To use Schaeffer's expression, when we become the *we* of God in every aspect of our being, in every area of our lives, then God will use us for his great glory.

As we shall discover, the sign of the staff was also instructive for Israel. It would help convince the Israelites that God had spoken to Moses. It would help persuade them that God could lead them out of Egypt. The snake was a symbol of Egyptian power, for the Egyptians worshiped the serpent as a source of wisdom and healing. In doing so, ultimately they were worshiping that old serpent, the devil. But by changing a stick into a serpent and back again, God demonstrated his authority over the gods of Egypt, and over Satan himself. This symbolism would not have been lost on Moses or on the Israelites.

> The cobra represented in particular the national god of Lower Egypt and was the foremost symbol of Pharaoh, reflecting his claim to divine royalty, sovereignty, and power. Therefore, it constantly appears on his crown or helmet, as depicted in reliefs, paintings, and statues. His scepter is often a stylized cobra. Even the Egyptian gods are frequently depicted with a scepter in the form of a snake. We are safe in concluding that the transfor-

mation of the rod to a snake is a sign aimed precisely at the very symbol of Pharaoh's alleged power.[8]

The first sign was convincing enough, even for skeptics like Moses. Nevertheless, God gave a second sign. If he could use a stick, he could also use the hand that held it. "Again, the LORD said to him, 'Put your hand inside your cloak.' And he put his hand inside his cloak, and when he took it out, behold, his hand was leprous like snow. Then God said, 'Put your hand back inside your cloak.' So he put his hand back inside his cloak, and when he took it out, behold, it was restored like the rest of his flesh" (4:6, 7). The second sign was as impressive as the first. Leprosy was widespread in Egypt, and it was well known that the disease was highly infectious and completely incurable, thus requiring total seclusion (see Leviticus 13:45, 46). The sudden appearance of this dreadful disease would have been shocking to anyone who saw it, while its total disappearance would have been an unmistakable miracle.

The last sign would become the first of the plagues: "'If they will not believe you,' God said, 'or listen to the first sign, they may believe the latter sign. If they will not believe even these two signs or listen to your voice, you shall take some water from the Nile and pour it on the dry ground, and the water that you shall take from the Nile will become blood on the dry ground'" (4:8, 9). With this third sign, God dealt directly with Moses' fear that no one would believe him. Even if people did not believe the other miracles, at least they would believe Moses when he demonstrated God's power over the Nile, which the Egyptians considered the source of life.

Each of these signs verified Moses' credentials and authenticated his ministry as a true prophet. Like most Biblical miracles, the rod, the hand, and the blood served to confirm the truth of God's word. Whenever Moses performed these signs, he was proven to be a divinely empowered prophet. However incredible the report of his encounter with God may have sounded, his ability to perform miraculous signs would strengthen people's faith, convincing them to trust his testimony. In much the same way, the miracles of Jesus served to authenticate his teaching and to prove that he was the Christ.

Just as importantly, the signs of Moses demonstrated the true power of God, as miracles always do. Moses did not perform these miracles himself. He cast no spells and recited no incantations. In fact, he was as surprised as anyone when the miraculous signs appeared. But God was working through Moses, which is part of what the Lord meant when he promised, "I will be with you" (3:12). "For what Moses is able to do," writes John Durham, "he is enabled to do by God. The staff is Moses' staff, but what happens to the staff is clearly from Yahweh. The hand is Moses' hand, but what happens to that hand is also clearly from Yahweh. The water in the River Nile, which Yahweh will use to his purpose, also belongs to Yahweh, and what happens to it is the work of his power."[9] Together these three signs proved that the God of Israel was superior to the gods of Egypt.

Has God proved himself to you? Many people are looking for a sign from God. They want to know for certain that God is there, that he really is who the Bible says he is. They are willing to believe in him, but first they demand some sort of sign. They say, "God, if you're really there, show yourself to me! Then I will believe in you!"

The truth is that God has given a sign. It is a miraculous sign—the sign of the empty tomb (see Matthew 12:39, 40). Jesus of Nazareth, also called Christ, claimed to be God's Son. His earthly life ended on a wooden cross outside Jerusalem. The Bible says that his death paid the penalty for our sin. Then Jesus was buried. If he had remained in the tomb, there would be no sign that Jesus really is the Christ. But in order to prove that sin is forgiven through the cross and that we can have fellowship with God forever, Jesus was raised from the dead. His resurrection is the sign that Christianity is true—a sign recorded in Scripture and confirmed in historical accounts from many reliable eyewitnesses. Anyone who is unsure whether or not to believe in Jesus Christ and the sign of his resurrection should ask God for the gift of faith, and he will show his salvation.

# 9

# Here Am I . . . Send Someone Else

EXODUS 4:10–17

IN 1718 A NORWEGIAN PASTOR'S WIFE named Giertrud Rask received God's call to become a missionary. Her husband, Hans Egede, was preparing to leave their homeland and take the gospel to Greenland. But Giertrud was not ready to go, and with good reason. She was forty-five years old at the time, with four children to care for and the youngest barely a year old. It would be a dangerous journey for all of them, and Giertrud herself did not have a strong constitution.

The family's biographer reports that when Hans announced his plans, "His own and his wife's friends wrote to express their severest reprobation. . . . His mother-in-law further inflamed the feeling against him, and even his wife began to hint that she repented having attached herself to a man who by such plans was going to ruin himself and those belonging to him."[1] Giertrud must have felt much the same way that Moses felt when God called him to lead Israel out of Egypt. "Send someone else, Lord! Let somebody else do it . . . anybody but me!"

In this chapter we come to the end of Moses' encounter with the God of the burning bush. The prophet had received his basic instructions. God had called him to go back to Egypt and tell Pharaoh to let God's people go. Moses had also raised some questions: "Who am I? Who are you? How will they ever believe me?"

These were only the first three of what turned out to be five objections in all. As objections go, they were not altogether unreasonable, and in his patience God was willing to answer them. But the longer the conversation went on, the more obvious it became that Moses simply did not want to go. His final two objections show that when it came right down to it, he wanted God to send someone else.

## Moses' Speech Problem

Moses' fourth objection concerned his public speaking abilities: "Oh, my Lord, I am not eloquent, either in the past or since you have spoken to your servant, but I am slow of speech and of tongue" (4:10). The prophet recognized that the exodus was partly a diplomatic mission. Getting Israel out of Egypt required a public spokesperson with the oratorical abilities to persuade the world's most powerful leader to do something he had no intention of doing, and Moses doubted he was up to the task.

There has been a good deal of speculation as to what Moses meant when he complained about his inability to speak. What he literally said was something like this: "O Lord, I am not a man of words. . . . I am heavy of mouth." Perhaps his problem was psychological: he was too shy to speak in public. Possibly he lacked confidence because he had failed rhetoric back at Pharaoh University. Others have suggested that the prophet was inarticulate because he had a speech impediment. According to the Greek translation of the Old Testament known as the Septuagint, Moses stammered and stuttered. Still another possibility is that he was linguistically challenged. During his years as a shepherd he had lost his command of Egyptian, and he was worried that he would get tongue-tied when he went to the royal court.

Whatever his speech problem may have been, Moses told God that he was the wrong man for the job. In doing this he was not alone, for other Biblical prophets also doubted their ability to speak. When Isaiah was summoned to the throne room of God, he cried, "Woe is me! For I am lost; for I am a man of unclean lips, and I dwell in the midst of a people of unclean lips; for my eyes have seen the King, the LORD of hosts!" (Isaiah 6:5). When God's word came to Jeremiah, appointing him as a prophet to the nations, he said, "Ah, Lord GOD! Behold, I do not know how to speak, for I am only a youth" (Jeremiah 1:6). Although Moses may have been the first prophet to protest a lack of eloquence, he was by no means the last. Indeed, to this day many Christians hold back from sharing their faith for fear that they will not know what to say or how to say it.

For all we know, Moses may well have had a speech defect or struggled with some kind of language barrier. But what he had was not so much a speech problem as an obedience problem. God had given him a clear and unmistakable calling, but rather than trusting God to enable him to fulfill it, Moses was starting to make excuses.

The prophet's fourth objection was irrelevant. It did not matter how articulate Moses was because God had already told him exactly what to say—not only to Israel's elders, but also to Pharaoh. God practically dictated his speeches for him! Moses did not have to be an orator; he just had to be a reporter, faithfully repeating whatever God said to him. This was well within his capacities. Moses may have had some limitations when it came to public speaking, but at least he could talk, which is amply demonstrated by his conversation at the burning bush.

He seemed able to speak well enough when he wanted to argue with God! And if he could dialogue with the Great I Am, surely he could exchange a few words with the Pharaoh of Egypt.

God had also promised Moses that people would listen to him. This is a reminder that effectiveness in proclaiming God's Word does not depend on eloquence alone. Good speaking ability is useful, of course, but it is not essential to communicating the gospel. One thinks of the Apostle Paul, whose rhetorical abilities were often criticized. "His speech [is] of no account," some people said (2 Corinthians 10:10). But at least Paul had something to say! He proclaimed salvation in Christ through the cross and the empty tomb. Therefore, he was able to say to his critics, "Even if I am unskilled in speaking, I am not so in knowledge" (2 Corinthians 11:6a).

When it comes to proclaiming God's Word, the message is more important than the man. Indeed, in some mysterious way the very limitations of a preacher or a personal evangelist are often essential to the effective communication of the gospel. This is part of what the Scripture means when it says, "We have this treasure [the glorious knowledge of Christ] in jars of clay, to show that the surpassing power belongs to God and not to us" (2 Corinthians 4:7). From time to time, when a preacher stumbles around, the congregation is reminded that whatever effectiveness his preaching has comes from God and not from the man himself. Of course, this is not an excuse for evangelists to become anything less than the very best communicators they can become. But it helps to know that even our weaknesses can be used for God's glory.

Not only was Moses' objection *irrelevant* (because God was going to tell him what to say), but it was also *irreverent*. Notice the wording of his complaint: "I am not eloquent, either in the past or since you have spoken to your servant" (4:10). This comment was really a criticism. Moses was blaming God for not giving him the gift of utterance. When he said, "I am not eloquent, either in the past . . . " he was complaining about the way God made him. And when he said, "or since you have spoken," he was implying that if God really wanted him to go to Pharaoh, he would cure his impediment right then and there. It was as if to say, "Look, Lord, I've been standing here talking with you for fifteen whole minutes, and you *still* haven't done anything about my speech problem!"

By this reasoning it was God's fault that Moses couldn't do what God called him to do. How often we grow impatient with God, waiting for him to do something he has no intention of doing. And how often we complain that God is not giving us what we want, when the real problem is that we are not doing what he wants us to do.

## Who Gave You That Mouth Anyway?

God answered Moses by reminding him that he was fearfully and wonderfully made. Moses had been given exactly the gifts that God wanted him to have, and those gifts were to be used for God's glory: "Then the LORD said to him, 'Who has made man's mouth? Who makes him mute, or deaf, or seeing, or blind? Is it not I, the LORD?'" (4:11).

These rhetorical questions are a reminder that God made us exactly the way he wanted to make us. Who gave us our eyes, ears, and mouth? Obviously God did. If that is the case, then our abilities, inabilities, and even disabilities are ordained by him. God has equipped us with every talent we need to do his will. He made us the way that he made us for his glory.

People often wish they had someone else's abilities instead of their own. An example of this kind of covetous thinking comes from the movie *Amadeus*, which despite its historical inaccuracies makes a compelling spiritual point. The film is about the extraordinary musical talents of Wolfgang Amadeus Mozart (1756–1791), as viewed from the perspective of his fellow composer Antonio Salieri (1750–1825). Salieri was a fine musician in his own right, but he was no Mozart, and he knew it. Rather than using his own talents to glorify God, he envied the gift that God had given to Mozart. His resentment about Mozart led him to reject God, and in the end he became a bitter old man, the self-professed "patron saint of mediocrity."

If it is true that God made us exactly the way he wanted, then we cannot complain about our lack of ability without grumbling against God. When Moses said, "I don't know how to speak," God responded by saying, "Who has made man's mouth?" It was God's way of showing Moses that he was mouthing off. Every time we complain about our personal limitations, what we are actually doing is insulting the God who made us.

The thing to do instead is to serve God as well as we can. Even if our gifts are limited—as everyone's gifts are, in one respect or another—they should be used for God's glory. This is what Jesus taught in the parable of the talents (Matthew 25:14–30). A master went away on a long journey, leaving three servants in charge of his household. Each servant was given certain responsibilities, according to his ability, and when the master returned, each was called to give account. The servant with five silver talents had earned five more. Likewise, the servant with two talents had doubled his master's investment. Not surprisingly, both of these men were praised. But the servant with only one talent had buried it in the ground. That wicked servant was cast into the outer darkness not because he had failed to produce five talents, but because he had failed to use even his one talent to the best of his ability.

What talent has God given to you? Perhaps you have a penetrating intellect, a beautiful voice, or a strong body. Perhaps you have a practical gift such as the skill to care for the sick, to nurture small children, or to make money. Whatever ability you have been given, use it for God's glory.

Do the same thing with your disabilities, which can also be used to glorify God. God mentions blindness as well as sight in order to show that every human being is called to serve him. If God is the one who makes a person deaf or blind, then even these limitations can be used for his glory. There is a good example of this in the story of Jesus and a man who was born blind. The disciples were certain that someone was to blame for the man's deformity, so they wondered who had sinned—the man himself or his parents (John 9:1). Jesus contradicted them by saying, "It was not that this man sinned, or his parents, but that the works of God might be displayed in him" (John 9:3). The same is true for every child of God. We were made for God's glory, and we should not imagine that our personal limitations somehow place a limit on God's ability to glorify himself in our lives. However bright or dim we may be, if we have a mind, we can learn how to think Biblically. However strong or weak we may be, if we have a body, we can learn how to act Biblically. And if we can think and act Biblically, then we can live for God's glory.

A good example of how God can be glorified in someone's disability comes from the ministry of Donald Grey Barnhouse, the famous pastor of Philadelphia's Tenth Presbyterian Church. Barnhouse had been conducting a week of services in another church, and there had been a good deal of banter about the host minister, whose wife was expecting their first child to be born at any moment. On the last night of services, when the minister failed to arrive, Barnhouse knew what had happened.

What Barnhouse did not know, however, was that the child was born with Down syndrome. The minister was devastated. "Dr. Barnhouse," he said, "our child is a *mongoloid*. I haven't told my wife, and I don't know what I'm going to tell her."

Barnhouse replied, "My friend, this is of the Lord," and turning to the fourth chapter of Exodus, he read, "And the LORD said unto him, Who hath made man's mouth, or who maketh the dumb, or deaf, or the seeing, or the blind . . . have not I the LORD?" The minister demanded to see the passage for himself, and as he studied it Barnhouse said, "My friend, you know the promise in Romans 8 that all things, *including this mongoloid child*, work together for good to those who love the Lord."

The minister returned to the hospital, where his wife was beginning to worry that something was wrong with the baby. He was able to say to her, "My precious darling, the Lord has blessed us with a mongoloid child." After she was finished crying, she said, "Where did you get *that*?" and he proceeded to show her what the Scripture said. Later, when she called her mother to tell her the news, she said, "Mother, the Lord has blessed us with a mongoloid child. We don't know the nature of the blessing, but we do know it's a blessing." On the following Sunday, when more than seventy nurses from the hospital attended that man's church, thirty of them came to faith in Christ![2]

Another example of what it means to glorify God with a disability comes from the life of John Milton (1608–1674), the English poet who completed some of his greatest work in the years after he became blind. Like Moses, Milton was sometimes tempted to complain about his inability. He once wrote a sonnet titled "On His Blindness," in which he lamented his loss of sight. With light denied, his "one talent" seemed useless, and he feared that he would be unable to give a good account to his Maker. But as Milton struggled with his limitations, he came up with this answer:

> God doth not need
> Either man's work, or his own gifts; who best
> Bear his mild yoke, they serve him best: his state
> Is kingly; thousands at his bidding speed,
> And post o'er land and ocean without rest;
> They also serve who only stand and wait.

If the only thing we can do is stand and wait, then we are to do our standing and waiting to the glory of God.

As we stand and wait, we are called to remember that God is with us. We do not serve God on our own, working from our own strength, but rather exercise our gifts in the presence and with the assistance of God. Notice that God never evaluated Moses' speaking ability. He did not try to tell him that he was more eloquent than he thought he was. Nor did he admit that Moses really was slow of speech and tongue. Instead he told him the only thing that mattered, which was that God would be with him. Moses' objection had to do with himself: "*I* am not eloquent . . . *I* am slow of speech" (4:10). But God answered by pointing Moses back to himself: "Now therefore go, and *I* will be with your mouth and teach you what you shall speak" (4:12). Like Moses, we are prone to place far too much reliance on natural ability, and not nearly enough on supernatural assistance. If God is with us, then we will be able to do his will, even in spite of ourselves.

Remember that the "I" who promised to go with Moses—and who has promised to be with us forever—is the Great I Am, the eternal and all-powerful Lord. God reminded Moses of this at the end of verse 11, where he repeated his special divine name. What he literally said was: "Is it not I AM, the LORD, who gave you your mouth?" The God of the burning bush, the God of Abraham, Isaac, and Jacob, is the same God who made Moses' mouth. God had already promised to be with Moses (see 3:12). That general promise also included a very specific promise to be with Moses whenever he spoke. Jesus made a similar promise when he sent out his disciples: "When they deliver you over, do not be anxious how you are to speak or what you are to say, for what you are to say will be given to you in that hour. For it is not you who speak, but the Spirit of your Father speaking through you" (Matthew 10:19, 20). Jesus has not promised to put his words into our mouths, of course. That was a special promise for God's special messengers, the apostles. But he will help us whenever we speak for him, because he has promised to be with us always.

If God is with us, then whatever abilities or disabilities we have can be used for his glory. Even if we are tempted to complain about our lack of eloquence, as Moses was, at least we can testify that Jesus saves. And as we witness for the gospel, we can take encouragement from the third and fourth stanzas of William Cowper's hymn "There Is a Fountain Filled with Blood," which almost sound like Moses' testimony:

E'er since by faith I saw the stream
Your flowing wounds supply,
Redeeming love has been my theme,
And shall be till I die.

Then in a nobler, sweeter song
I'll sing your pow'r to save,
When this poor lisping, stamm'ring tongue
Lies silent in the grave.

## Send Someone Else!

As God patiently listened to all of Moses' objections, he never allowed himself to be distracted from his primary purpose. Throughout this conversation God kept returning to the basic issue: Moses was going to lead Israel out of Egypt. Four times he commanded Moses to go: "So now, *go*. I am sending you to Pharaoh" (3:10 NIV); "*Go* and gather the elders of Israel" (3:16); "You and the elders of Israel shall *go* to the king of Egypt" (3:18). God said it for the final time in 4:12: "Now therefore *go*, and I will be with your mouth and teach you what you shall speak."

By the time God had told Moses to "go . . . go . . . go . . . go," Moses had run out of excuses. He had asked all the questions he could think to ask and had raised all the objections it was reasonable to raise. In the end his true motivation was exposed in all its dreadful depravity: "Oh, my Lord, please send someone else" (4:13). This fifth and final objection exposed what was underneath all of Moses' excuses: a fundamental unwillingness to obey. The real issue was not that he lacked the stature to persuade Pharaoh, or that he was ignorant of God's name, or that the Israelites would not believe him, or that he was a poor public speaker. God had answered all of those objections. The real issue was that Moses refused to trust and obey.

At the very beginning of this encounter, when Moses first heard God's voice, he seemed ready to do as he was told. "Here I am," he said, expressing his willingness to serve (3:4). He even took off his sandals, indicating his status as God's slave. But the more he understood what God was asking him to do, the more reluctant he became, until finally he issued a flat refusal: "I'm still here, Lord, but you're going to have to find somebody else." Literally what Moses said was, "Lord, send anybody you want to send," with the unspecified implication, "as long as it isn't me." Moses was finished evaluating his call; now he was rejecting it.

The Bible does not say why Moses was unwilling to go. It probably had something to do with the issues he had already raised. If God's angry response in verses 14–16 is any indication, Moses was still worried about his speech problem. Very likely he felt inadequate and afraid. But whatever the reason was, it really didn't matter. Quite simply, he was refusing God's claim on his life.

There is a time when it is appropriate to ask the kinds of questions Moses had been asking: "Who am I, Lord?" "Are you really the God you say you are?" "Can I trust you to go with me and help me?" But once we know what God wants us to do, it is time to stop asking and start obeying. We are the only ones who can do what God has called us to do. So if you have been wrestling with God's claim on your life—trying to decide whether Jesus is the only way to God, for example, or evaluating some new opportunity for ministry—once you know the answer in your heart of hearts, you must follow God. Otherwise you are standing in rebellion against him.

Moses' rebellion is evident from the way he addressed God: "Oh, my Lord." This may sound respectful enough, but it lacked genuine reverence. Notice that *ord* in the word "Lord" are left uncapitalized. This is because Moses did not use the name that God had revealed to him, the special divine name *Yahweh* ("LORD"), and thus he failed to acknowledge God's full sovereignty and majesty. This shows how important it is to worship God properly. The God we praise is the God we serve. If we are not consistent and reverent in our worship, we will be inconstant and reckless in our obedience.

## Moses' Mouthpiece, Aaron

By this time God had heard enough out of Moses:

> Then the anger of the LORD was kindled against Moses and he said, "Is there not Aaron, your brother, the Levite? I know that he can speak well. Behold, he is coming out to meet you, and when he sees you, he will be glad in his heart. You shall speak to him and put the words in his mouth, and I will be with your mouth and with his mouth and will teach you both what to do. He shall speak for you to the people, and he shall be your mouth, and you shall be as God to him." (4:14–16)

The Bible teaches that God is slow to anger. In fact, when Moses later went back to Mount Sinai to receive God's law, God "passed before him and proclaimed, 'The LORD, the LORD, a God merciful and gracious, slow to anger, and abounding in steadfast love'" (34:6). The fact that God is "slow to anger" means that he is not easily angered, but it also means that he does get angry! He was angry with Moses at the burning bush—not in the sense that he lost his temper, for God cannot sin, but in the sense that he was filled with righteous indignation.

God had a right to be angry! He had patiently answered all Moses' questions and had dealt with all his objections. But when Moses refused to obey him, and thus to glorify him, it was right and good for God to be angry.

Recognizing God's anger helps us make sense of what he said about Aaron. Here we are introduced to Moses' brother. Since he is identified as a Levite, some have thought that perhaps the two men were half-brothers, but in any case Aaron was on his way to meet Moses. Possibly he was coming from Egypt to tell Moses that the Pharaoh who wanted to take his life was dead. God ordained Aaron to serve as Moses' spokesman. Unlike his brother, Aaron had the talent to handle public relations for the exodus. Moses would speak to Aaron, and then Aaron would speak to the people, repeating the words of God.

It almost sounds like God was giving in to Moses' demands, offering him a sort of compromise. But clearly, having Aaron speak for Moses was not God's first and best plan for the exodus. True, God was with Aaron, and he was a help to Moses in many ways. Their partnership helped them communicate effectively with Pharaoh, who was familiar with spokesmen because there was a high Egyptian official designated as "the mouth of the king" who spoke on Pharaoh's behalf, much as Aaron spoke for Moses.[3] The relationship between the two brothers was also a picture of the relationship between God and his prophets. In the same way that Moses spoke for God, Aaron spoke for Moses.

But Aaron's involvement would turn out to be a mixed blessing. His assistance did not relieve Moses from the responsibility to speak for God (4:15); but now Moses would have to share part of the honor with his brother. Furthermore, Aaron would later lead the people astray by making them a golden calf (32:1–4). By at first refusing to do what God called him to do, Moses missed out on part of God's blessing. No one is indispensable—not even Moses. God can always find someone else to do his will. But by refusing to do what God has called us to do, we will miss out on the fullness of God's blessing.

One woman who refused to miss out on the blessing was Queen Esther. In the providence of God, when the Jews were in mortal danger Esther was in a position to save them by interceding with the king. Her cousin Mordecai urged her to help, even though doing so would place her own life in danger. Mordecai knew that God would save his people one way or another, but he did not want Esther to miss God's blessing by rejecting her calling. He said to her, "For if you keep silent at this time, relief and deliverance will rise for the Jews from another place, but you and your father's house will perish" (Esther 4:14a). Through her courageous obedience, Esther not only saved her people, the Jews, but also received God's abundant blessing.

## A Prophet (Not) like Moses

The last thing God said to Moses was, "And take in your hand this staff, with which you shall do the signs" (4:17). God did not take no for an answer. In the end after all his questions and objections Moses had to do what God called him to do. By God's authority and with God's assistance—symbolized by the mighty staff—he went back to Egypt to rescue the children of Israel.

Moses proved to be a great leader, of course, but his reluctance to answer God's call is a reminder that there is only one perfect Savior. God promised that one day he would send his people a prophet "like [Moses]." He later said to Moses, "I will raise up for them a prophet like you from among their brothers. And I will put my words in his mouth, and he shall speak to them all that I command him" (Deuteronomy 18:18). Jesus Christ was that prophet, as Peter proved on the Day of Pentecost (see Acts 3:20–23). The Bible teaches that Jesus was "made like his brothers in every respect" (Hebrews 2:17), "yet without sin" (Hebrews 4:15). As God promised, Jesus was like Moses. He came to deliver us from our bondage to sin and to set us free from our captivity to death. God told us to "listen to him" (Matthew 17:5) because whenever we listen to him, we hear the very voice of God.

But for all the similarities between these two men, there are also some crucial ways that Jesus is *not* like Moses. One of the most obvious is that he was ready and willing to do God's will. He said to his Father, "Behold, I have come to do your will, O God" (Hebrews 10:7). True, Jesus agonized over the pains of the cross, but he did not refuse to endure them. He said to his Father, "Your will be done" (Matthew 26:42). And then he went out and freely offered his life for our salvation. He did not say, "Send someone else," for he knew that there was no one else! He and he alone could make perfect atonement for our sins.

If Christ is our Savior, then we must be ready and willing to serve him—to say, "Here am I, send *me*!" In the end this is what Giertrud Rask did. When her husband Hans received God's missionary call to go to Greenland, Giertrud was not willing to go. But her husband was a sensible man, sensitive to his wife's anxiety. Although he remained convinced that God was calling them to Greenland, he knew that Giertrud had to hear and answer the call for herself. So Hans did what he could "to make his wife see the will of God . . . and to regard it as their bounden duty to show a more resolute self-denial by leaving their home and going forth to preach the Gospel among the heathens."

By mutual agreement, Hans and Giertrud "laid the matter before God in prayer." God's Spirit worked in Giertrud's heart, and eventually she embraced the call to take the gospel to Greenland. Shortly before they were to set sail, however, Hans himself "was assailed by doubts as to whether he really had been justified in jeopardizing his and his family's welfare." Then it was Giertrud who proved her "great faith and constancy" by encouraging her husband to answer God's call. Together they traveled to Greenland, where they labored together in the gospel.[4] Of course, it is far better to answer God's call as soon as we receive it, but the most important thing is to be sure we answer it in the end.

# 10

# Back to Egypt

## EXODUS 4:18–31

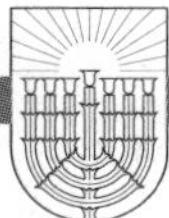

SO MOSES WENT BACK TO EGYPT. After all his questions and objections, after all his doubts and hesitations, and even after his outright refusal to go, the prophet answered God's call. His self-imposed exile was over.

After the encounter at the burning bush, the end of Exodus 4 comes as something of an anticlimax. These verses recount Moses' departure from Midian (4:18–23) and his arrival in Egypt (4:27–31), together with his near-death experience along the way (4:24–26). The key word in these somewhat miscellaneous verses—a word that is repeated over and over again—is "return" (*shuv*), also translated "go back." Moses was going back to the land of the pyramids, back to the slave camps of Pharaoh, and back to the people of God.

Moses was returning because God ordered him to return. Once he had fled from Egypt in fear and secrecy, but "the LORD said to Moses in Midian, 'Go back to Egypt, for all the men who were seeking your life are dead'" (4:19). This statement—a short summary of their long conversation at the burning bush—comes as a surprise. There is no question as to its truthfulness; we have already been informed that the Pharaoh who charged Moses with a capital offense was dead (2:23). What is less clear is why it mattered if his enemies were alive or dead. Perhaps God was just letting Moses know that he didn't have to worry about his death sentence anymore. But it sounds as if God was concerned about Moses' safety, as if he could only return when it was safe to go back. If so, then God's statement reminds us of the message Joseph received when he was in Egypt: "Rise, take the child [Jesus] and his mother [Mary] and go to the land of Israel, for those who sought the child's life are dead" (Matthew 2:20). But why would God be concerned about Moses' safety? He had promised to go with him on his journey, to help him and deliver him. With God's staff in his hand, Moses had nothing to fear. It seems better, therefore, to take the death of his enemies as a sign that the exodus had begun. Rather than reassuring Moses about his safety,

God's statement of Pharaoh's death serves as an announcement that the promise of deliverance was starting to come true.

## Moses Takes His Leave

Before returning to Egypt, Moses had some family business to take care of: "Moses went back to Jethro his father-in-law and said to him, 'Please let me go back to my brothers in Egypt to see whether they are still alive'" (4:18a).

Once Moses had received God's call, he went back to take leave of Jethro, the man who had given him a home in Midian. It is not hard to understand why Moses had to do this. Obviously he could not stay with Jethro any longer. He had a higher calling—a call to ministry that came from God himself. But he still needed to treat the man with respect. For one thing Jethro was his father-in-law, and in those patriarchal times family members needed permission from the head of the household before leaving. For another thing, Jethro was his employer, and Moses needed to return the sheep that he had taken to Mount Horeb.

In some ways Moses serves as an example for Christians who are trying to follow Christ and love their families at the same time. Our commitment to Christ comes first. Jesus said, "If anyone comes to me and does not hate his own father and mother and wife and children and brothers and sisters, yes, and even his own life, he cannot be my disciple" (Luke 14:26). Jesus meant that following him is a total life commitment. It demands an absolute allegiance that sometimes conflicts with family expectations. Even the people we love most should not prevent us from doing what God has called us to do. But Jesus did not mean that we should be hostile to our families, any more than he meant that we should take our own lives. On the contrary, Christians should treat their families with respect. This is especially important for Christians whose parents are not Christians. Because they do not share our commitment to Christ, they will not understand some of the choices we make. But even if we cannot compromise our calling, we still have a responsibility to love our parents, and that means discussing our plans with them patiently and respectfully.

What is puzzling is the excuse Moses gave for going back to Egypt. He said to Jethro, "Please let me go back to my brothers in Egypt to see whether they are still alive" (4:18a). This statement shows how thoroughly Moses had identified himself with God's people. He did not consider himself an Egyptian anymore but a Hebrew. It also gives a hint how long Moses had been away (forty years) and how badly the Egyptians had been treating the Israelites. The phrase "to see whether they are still alive" may have been an ancient expression for checking on someone's welfare, but it leaves open the question whether they were alive or dead.[1]

The problem with what Moses said is that it was not entirely truthful. He failed to mention anything about his encounter with God at the burning bush, and what he did say about his mission was misleading. He was not going back to see if his relatives were still alive—God had told him they were—but to rescue them from slavery!

Why didn't Moses tell the whole truth? Perhaps he was afraid that if he went into too much detail, his father-in-law would start raising questions about his trip. More likely, Moses still wasn't entirely sure himself whether everything God said was true. Like many people, he was wavering somewhere between faith and unbelief. But at least he was still walking down the path of obedience! Even if he lacked the courage to state his intentions, he was doing what God told him to do.

Moses left Midian with his father-in-law's blessing: "And Jethro said to Moses, 'Go in peace'" (4:18b). When Moses departed, the prophet took two things with him: his family and his God. The Bible says, "So Moses took his wife and his sons and had them ride on a donkey, and went back to the land of Egypt. And Moses took the staff of God in his hand" (4:20). Later Moses sent his family back to Midian, for Exodus 18 describes their eventual reunion. But when he first returned to Egypt, Moses brought his wife Zipporah and his sons Gershom and Eliezer with him. This shows that he was planning on leaving for good. It also serves as a reminder that his experiences as a husband and father were part of his preparation for ministry.

Not only did Moses have his family at his side, but he also had his staff in his hand. Except that it was no longer *his* staff at all—it was "the staff of God," the symbol of divine authority. Moses was going to deliver Israel by God's power. With God's staff he would perform miraculous signs to convince the Israelites that he was God's true prophet. Later God's staff would accomplish even greater wonders. It would bring disease and death upon the Egyptians, part the waves of the Red Sea, and draw life-giving water from a rock.

It is tempting to think of God's staff as a magic wand and to wish that we could have one ourselves. But what the staff represents *is* available to us! The staff was a visible sign of God's saving power, and now God's saving power comes through the cross. The place to find God's power is not in some supernatural wonder but in the message of the cross where Christ was crucified for sinners. The cross *is* God's sign. It is the sign of God's love—the sign that he loves us enough to die for us. It is the sign of God's mercy—the sign that our sins are forgiven. The Apostle Paul observed that whereas some people "demand signs . . . we preach Christ crucified . . . Christ the power of God" (1 Corinthians 1:22–24). It is through the cross of Christ that God has accomplished the greatest exodus of all, leading sinners out of bondage to sin and into relationship with him. The divine power represented by God's staff is available to everyone who lays hold of Jesus Christ.

## Pharaoh's Hard Heart

Moses did not have the message of the cross (at least in so many words), but he did have God's staff, and he was supposed to take the staff with him when he went to Pharaoh. "And the Lord said to Moses, 'When you go back to Egypt, see that you do before Pharaoh all the miracles that I have put in your power. But I will harden his heart, so that he will not let the people go'" (4:21).

This verse gives us two new pieces of information. One is that the signs and wonders were for the Egyptians as well as for the Israelites. Earlier God gave Moses three signs to perform for the elders of Israel, to help convince them that he was God's true prophet (4:1–9). Here God tells Moses to perform the same marvels for Pharaoh—not so he will let God's people go, but for exactly the opposite reason. Rather than making a believer out of Pharaoh, the signs would harden him in his unbelief. In his stubbornness he would refuse to let God's people go. The miracles of Jesus Christ had much the same effect: according to God's sovereign will, some believed and were saved, while others doubted and were condemned.

Moses already knew that Pharaoh's heart would be as hard as stone. Even if he did not know this from his own experience, which he probably did, God had said to him, "The king of Egypt will not let you go unless compelled by a mighty hand" (3:19). What is new in chapter 4—and this is the second new piece of information—is that God himself would harden Pharaoh's heart. In some mysterious way, Pharaoh's hardness of heart was part of God's saving plan.

The hardening of Pharaoh's heart is an important theme in the book of Exodus, and it has much to teach us about the sovereignty of God's will. We will encounter this theme again, because Exodus mentions Pharaoh's hardness of heart some twenty times, describing it in one of three different ways. Sometimes the Bible says that Pharaoh hardened his own heart: "But when Pharaoh saw that there was a respite, he hardened his heart and would not listen to them" (8:15). Other times the Bible says that Pharaoh's heart was hardened, without specifying who did the hardening: "Pharaoh's heart was hardened, and he would not listen" (7:13). There are also instances—like the one here in Exodus 4—where God identifies himself as the one who hardens Pharaoh's heart.

Taken together, what these statements show is that Pharaoh's heart was doubly hard. He hardened his own heart; nevertheless, God hardened his heart for him. Both of these statements are true, and there is no contradiction between them. Pharaoh's will was also God's will. God not only knew that Pharaoh would refuse to let his people go, but he actually ordained it. This is the paradox of divine sovereignty and human responsibility, which is not a puzzle to be solved but a mystery to be adored. As human beings made in the image of God, we make a real choice to accept or reject God, but even the choice we make is governed by God's sovereign and eternal will. The Old Testament scholar S. R. Driver rightly observed, "The means by which God hardens a man is not necessarily by any extraordinary intervention on His part; it may be by the ordinary experiences of life, operating through the principles and character of human nature, which are of His appointment."[2] The writer of Exodus understood this, which is why he described the hardening of Pharaoh's heart as both the will of Pharaoh and the will of God.

From beginning to end, the entire exodus was the result of God's sovereign decree. The whole agonizing and then exhilarating experience of slavery and freedom was part of his perfect will. It was God's will to bring his people out of Egypt. It was also his good pleasure to keep them there as long as he did, which is proved by his hardening of Pharaoh's heart. Peter Enns writes, "The deliverance of Israel from Egypt is entirely God's doing and under his complete control. The impending Exodus is a play in which God is author, producer, director, and principal actor."[3] Even when Pharaoh took his turn on stage, God received all the applause. Like everything else that God has ever done, the exodus was all for his glory.

## God's Firstborn Son

The sovereignty of God's will is such a great mystery that it causes some people to fear God—not simply to revere him, but actually to be afraid of him. However, God's people should never be afraid, because God's sovereignty includes our sonship. The reason God hardened Pharaoh's heart was to prove his love for his own children. God said to Moses, "Then you shall say to Pharaoh, 'Thus says the LORD, Israel is my firstborn son, and I say to you, "Let my son go that he may serve me." If you refuse to let him go, behold, I will kill your firstborn son'" (4:22, 23).

These two verses disclose the very heart of the exodus. They explain why God cared what happened to the Israelites, why out of all the nations in the world he went to the trouble of rescuing them from slavery. They had little to be proud of from a worldly point of view, and thus God seemingly had little reason to save them. But Israel was the son of God's choice. At the very deepest spiritual level, the exodus is a story about sonship, about a Father's love for his only son. Israel's deliverance is the true history of a loving Father who rescued his children so they could be together as a family. Thus it is not simply a story of *emancipation*—the release of a slave—but also of *repatriation*, the return of an only son to his father's loving care.[4] Later, when God reminisced about the exodus, he said, "When Israel was a child, I loved him, and out of Egypt I called my son" (Hosea 11:1).

Israel's status as God's firstborn son explains why God had a quarrel with Pharaoh. To Pharaoh the Hebrews were lowly slaves, but to God they were beloved sons. Thus the problem with Pharaoh was not simply that he was a slaveholder (although that was bad enough), but that he was preventing God's children from serving their Father. Instead of being free to call God "Father," the Israelites were forced to call Pharaoh "Master." So in order to reassert his claim on Israel, God said to Pharaoh, "Let my son go that he may serve me" (4:23a). God demanded that Israel be released from Pharaoh's bondage so that his son would be free to serve him once again. More specifically, he wanted the *worship* of his firstborn son. This is the grand theme of the exodus: God saving his sons from slavery so that they could serve him.

God's father-son relationship with Israel also helps explain why the judgments he executed on Egypt were so harsh. Exodus 4 (especially v. 23) foreshadows the tenth and final plague, which would claim the life of Pharaoh's heir, along with all the rest of the firstborn sons in Egypt. This calamity was necessary to persuade Pharaoh to give up his claim on God's son, Israel. His heart was so hard that getting him to let Israel go required nothing less than the death of his firstborn son. But this punishment was also a matter of strict justice. It was an eye for an eye, a son for a son. The Dutch Bible scholar Cornelis Houtman writes, "In the dispute about the question to whom Israel belongs and who is her legitimate ruler, Pharaoh or Yahweh, Yahweh at last will show that he has intimate emotional ties with Israel. Pharaoh had better know that to Yahweh Israel is not just his own people, they are also dear to him. . . . Pharaoh is going to be hit at his most sensitive spot, the spot where he has touched Yahweh himself, in the love for the firstborn."[5]

Sonship has its origins in the Old Testament, where God reveals himself as a father who desires a son to serve him. However, his son always proved a disappointment. This was true during the exodus, when Israel grumbled against Moses and complained about God's fatherly care. The Old Testament people of God never lived up to the demands of their sonship.

This is why God sent his only Son to be our Savior. The New Testament presents Jesus Christ as God's perfect Son, the one who served his Father with absolute devotion. Jesus was everything God had ever wanted in a Son, on one level accomplishing what Israel was supposed to accomplish. The Gospels make this connection explicit by describing the life of Christ as a new exodus. Not long after he was born, Jesus was sent down to Egypt, where he remained until the death of King Herod. His subsequent return to Israel reminded Matthew of the Old Testament promise: "Out of Egypt I called my son" (Matthew 2:15, quoting Hosea 11:1). It was Matthew's way of saying that Jesus is the true Israel, God's firstborn Son. This was confirmed when Jesus was baptized, and the Father said, "This is my beloved Son" (Matthew 3:17). The promise of sonship was fulfilled in Jesus Christ.

The amazing thing is that everyone who comes to Christ in faith becomes a true child of God. The work of Christ is to bring the slaves of sin into the liberty of sonship. Charles Spurgeon writes, "The Lord Jesus comes, identifies himself with the enslaved family, bears the curse, fulfils the law, and then on the ground of simple justice demands for them full and perfect liberty, having for them fulfilled the precept, and for them endured the penalty."[6] The Bible thus calls Jesus "the firstborn among many brothers" (Romans 8:29)—"many brothers" because every believer is a child of God. As the Bible also says, "In Christ Jesus you are all sons of God, through faith" (Galatians 3:26). To know Jesus as Savior is to know God as Father, and the exodus teaches us what kind of Father he is. He is not like human fathers, with all their failings. Rather, he is a good Father, always faithful to his children. In his tender compassion he cares for them and rescues them from every danger.

## A Matter of Life and Death

What happened next is a shocking reminder how strange the Old Testament can be. "At a lodging place on the way the Lord met *him* and sought to put him to death" (4:24). There is some question as to whether it was Moses who met with God or his son (presumably Gershom, his firstborn). Given the overall context, however, it seems much more natural for "him" to refer to Moses, especially since his son is not specifically introduced until verse 25.

What happened was this: while Moses was traveling back to Egypt, he stopped to camp for the night, and there in the wilderness God sought to slay him. Just when it seemed safe to return to Egypt, suddenly God became the prophet's adversary. The Bible does not say how God intended to kill him. Perhaps Moses had to wrestle with the angel of death, or perhaps he was afflicted with some deadly disease. However, the real question is not *how* God assaulted Moses but *why*. What possible reason could God have for attacking Moses, upon whom his whole plan for Israel's salvation depended? Moses was the one who was called to lead God's people out of Egypt. Moses was the one who would gather the elders, perform the miracles, and demand the release of God's firstborn son. Therefore, to subject his life to mortal danger was to jeopardize the entire exodus.

Depending on the situation, God might have many good reasons for taking someone's life, but in this particular case he seems to have been angry with Moses. The prophet was under God's wrath, apparently because he had not circumcised his son. The Bible does not say this in so many words, but it is a reasonable inference based on what follows: "Then Zipporah took a flint and cut off her son's foreskin and touched Moses' feet with it and said, 'Surely you are a bridegroom of blood to me!' So he let him alone. It was then that she said, 'A bridegroom of blood,' because of the circumcision" (4:25, 26).

These are some of the most enigmatic verses in the Old Testament, but we must try to understand them as well as we can. Once again it was a woman who came to the rescue. Acting courageously and decisively—possibly because Moses himself was too close to death to be able to respond—Zipporah severed her son's foreskin, touched it to Moses, and said, "You are a bridegroom of blood." The precise meaning of this technical term is uncertain, but it does not seem to mean that Zipporah was angry. Rather, as the editorial comment in verse 26 indicates, it had something to do with the rite of circumcision (and possibly also with Zipporah's inclusion in the covenant community). What saved

Moses' life was the circumcision of his son. But why was his son the one who was circumcised? If Moses was the guilty party, wouldn't it make more sense for the prophet himself to be circumcised? The simplest explanation is that God attacked Moses precisely because he had failed to circumcise his son, and therefore Gershom's circumcision was the only thing that could save his life.

This raises a more basic question: What was so important about circumcision? Consider this contrast: when Moses refused to go to Egypt, God patiently helped him on his way; but when he failed to circumcise his son, God threatened to take his very life. Peter Enns writes, "Moses can argue, pout, whine, and hold his breath about going to Egypt and God will deal patiently with him—but circumcision is another matter."[7] Quite literally, it was a matter of life and death. But why?

For one thing, circumcision was the distinguishing mark of God's people, a sign indicating membership in the covenant community, and thus it served as the proof of sonship in Israel, as Zipporah seems to have understood. Furthermore, circumcision was a covenant sign that went all the way back to the patriarchs (see Genesis 17). Therefore, if Moses intended to serve the God of Abraham, he had a covenant obligation to circumcise his sons. This was also an important part of his preparation for the exodus. Later, when the Israelites celebrated their first Passover, every male would be required to be circumcised (12:43–49). Moses had to set the example. If he was going to lead the people out of Egypt, he himself had to keep the covenant. How could he be Israel's prophet if he neglected his spiritual responsibility to his own family by failing to include them in God's salvation?

Moses' failure to keep the covenant of circumcision nearly cost him his life. His near-death experience teaches us at least two significant lessons about salvation in Christ. One is the spiritual importance of receiving the sign of the covenant, which for the Christian is baptism. There is a connection between the Old Testament sign of circumcision and the New Testament sacrament of baptism. As Paul wrote to the Colossians, "In him [Christ] also you were circumcised with a circumcision made without hands . . . by the circumcision of Christ, having been buried with him in baptism" (Colossians 2:11, 12). The example of Moses teaches us to regard baptism with the utmost seriousness. Although the sacrament itself does not save anyone, nevertheless believers (and their children!) are to be baptized.

The circumcision of Moses' son also shows that "without the shedding of blood there is no forgiveness of sins" (Hebrews 9:22). God used this encounter on the road back to Egypt to teach Moses the basic requirements of salvation. Although Moses passed through the shadow of death, God never actually intended to kill him. The whole experience was a test, like the one Abraham endured when he was told to kill his only son (Genesis 22), or like the one Jacob was given when he wrestled with the angel (Genesis 32:22–32). Rather than treating Moses with murderous intent, God was giving his prophet firsthand experience of salvation.

First God showed Moses the wages of sin by placing him under his divine wrath. But then God's deadly wrath was turned aside—or "propitiated," to use the proper term for it—by the blood of circumcision. Blood is mentioned specifically because in order to be delivered from death, Moses had to be touched by the blood of a sacrifice and thereby identified with it. It was not a full sacrifice, of course; nevertheless, that small portion of circumcised skin represented Gershom's entire person, offered in Moses' place. Moses was saved from God's wrath by the shed blood of a substitute.

As strange as this experience may sound, it reveals the one true way of salvation. Every human being is a sinner who stands under the wrath of God. Like Moses, we have failed to keep God's law and thus are subject to God's curse against our sin. The only way to be saved from eternal death is for God's wrath to be turned aside, which can only be done through an act of blood. This is exactly what Jesus provided on the cross: a perfect sacrifice for sin, offered through the shedding of his own blood. By dying in our place, Jesus turned aside the wrath of God against our sin. He is our substitute, the one "whom God put forward as a propitiation by his blood, to be received by faith" (Romans 3:25a). Everyone who believes in Jesus Christ will be saved from God's wrath through the vicarious sacrifice he offered on the cross. There is no other way to be saved.

## Back in Egypt

Once God's wrath against his sin had been turned aside, Moses continued on his way. The Bible offers a brief summary of the welcome he received from Aaron, from the elders, and from all the children of Israel:

> The Lord said to Aaron, "Go into the wilderness to meet Moses." So he went and met him at the mountain of God and kissed him. And Moses told Aaron all the words of the Lord with which he had sent him to speak, and all the signs that he had commanded him to do. Then Moses and Aaron went and gathered together all the elders of the people of Israel. Aaron spoke all the words that the Lord had spoken to Moses and did the signs in the sight of the people. And the people believed; and when they heard that the Lord had visited the people of Israel and that he had seen their affliction, they bowed their heads and worshiped. (4:27–31)

Everything went according to promise. Aaron went out to meet Moses on God's mountain, just as God had promised (4:14). Once the two brothers had embraced, Moses reported what had happened to him at the burning bush. Aaron agreed to help him, just as God had promised (4:15, 16). Together they returned to Egypt and gathered the elders of Israel. Aaron told them everything that Moses had seen and heard. Then he performed the sign of the snake, the sign of the leprous hand, and the sign of the blood. Once the people had witnessed these miracles, they believed the promise of salvation. It all happened just the way God had promised.

It is worth noticing how little space the Bible devotes to the meeting with the elders, especially when this is compared with the amount of time Moses spent worrying about the meeting beforehand. The prophet's fears turned out to be ill founded, as fears always are when they come from a failure to trust God's Word. In spite of all his misgivings, Moses had no trouble persuading the Israelites to believe the good news of their deliverance. There is a valuable lesson in this. Often the real struggle comes at the point of deciding whether or not to follow God. Once the decision to follow him has been made, everything falls into place, and we are able to glorify God, almost as a matter of course.

Exodus 4 ends with a doxology: "And when they heard that the Lord had visited the people of Israel and that he had seen their affliction, they bowed their heads and worshiped" (v. 31). This was the right response. Even while they were still waiting for their liberation, the Israelites began to give God the glory. Moved by divine compassion, they knelt in the sands of Egypt to praise the Lord. They understood that the God of Moses is a God to be worshiped and adored. He is a God who rules every heart by his sovereign will. He is a God who loves us the way a good father loves an only son. He is a God who gives what his justice demands: a perfect sacrifice for sin. He is a wonder-working God, a God who keeps every last promise of salvation. He is also our God who has seen our misery and is concerned about our suffering. Will you bow down and worship him?

# 11

# Who Is the Lord?

EXODUS 5:1–9

SO FAR, SO GOOD. Moses had returned to Egypt, and to his great relief—and probable amazement—everything had gone according to plan. On his way back to the Nile Delta the prophet had met his brother Aaron, who agreed to help him in his ministry. Together the two brothers went to the elders of Israel and performed their signs of miraculous power. Based on what they both heard and saw, the people believed the good news of salvation. So Exodus 4 closed with this remarkable scene: "And when they heard that the LORD had visited the people of Israel and that he had seen their affliction, they bowed their heads and worshiped" (4:31). The promise of the exodus was starting to come true. The children of Israel were beginning to worship the God of their salvation.

Now it was time for the two brothers to take their show to the palace. In the words of the old spiritual, the song of the African slaves:

> Go down, Moses,
> Way down in Egyptland,
> Tell old Pharaoh,
> "Let my people go."

Exodus 5 tells what happened when Moses went down to old Pharaoh. It is a story of courageous faith and rebellious unbelief.

## Let My People Go!

Moses and Aaron were God's ambassadors, sent to speak on God's behalf. They went to Pharaoh with a simple demand: "Thus says the LORD, the God of Israel, 'Let my people go, that they may hold a feast to me in the wilderness'" (5:1). The Israelites were God's own dear children. Rather than slaving away for Pharaoh, they needed to serve their Father, so God ordered Pharaoh to free his people from bondage.

The Bible does not indicate whether Moses and Aaron were accompanied by any of Israel's elders when they confronted Pharaoh. According to God's earlier instructions (3:18), the nation's spiritual leaders were supposed to accompany Moses and Aaron when they had their royal audience. Yet Exodus 5 fails to mention any elders, and it seems possible that they lost their nerve. Nor does the Bible indicate how the brothers managed to gain such ready access to the king. Perhaps this is a clue that Moses still had friends in high places, even after his long absence from the royal court. The Bible simply says that Moses and Aaron went to Pharaoh "afterward," meaning after they had gone to the Israelites. What is certain is that they approached Pharaoh with the strong confidence of a courageous faith. In the words of Hebrews, they went "not being afraid of the anger of the king" (Hebrews 11:27).

Courage is hardly what we have come to expect from Moses. We have seen him cover up a murder in the desert sand (2:12), run away from the Egyptian police (2:15), and refuse to deliver God's message for fear that no one would listen (4:1, 10, 13). Yet this time he walked up to the most powerful man in the world and demanded the release of his slaves. He spoke with the divine authority of a prophet: "Thus says the LORD!" We are compelled to ask, what happened to this man? What made the difference for Moses? What changed his life? What transformed him from a frightened fugitive into a bold spiritual leader?

The answer is that Moses had met the living God. Here is his personal testimony: "The God of the Hebrews has met with us" (5:3a; more literally, "The God of the Hebrews is on our side"). Moses had seen God's glory in the burning bush. He had heard the Great I Am announce the message of salvation. He had received God's call, accompanied by marvelous signs. And at first Moses had trouble believing that it was all true. But he did the right thing: he started to trust God's promises and obey God's commands. As he stepped out in faith, he discovered that God's word is indeed faithful and true, and that in spite of his many inadequacies he was supernaturally equipped to do what God had called him to do. From the first faltering steps of his pilgrimage, Moses' experience of God's presence made him confident to do God's will.

The same thing happened to the disciples of Jesus Christ. They were hardly the kind of men one would expect to change the world, coming as they did from humble and in some cases disreputable backgrounds. Apart from a few flashes of momentary insight, the Gospels portray the disciples as dim-witted, weak-willed glory seekers. When their Master came to the hour of his greatest need, they all betrayed him, first by falling asleep in the garden and then by scattering into the darkness. After the crucifixion we find them huddled together in a secret room, fearing that they would be discovered and executed. Yet only months later they went out into the streets of Jerusalem, fearlessly and openly broadcasting the good news of salvation in Jesus Christ. Even after enduring imprisonment, they risked death in order to fulfill God's calling. Again we are compelled to ask, what happened to these men? What transformed them from cowardly Jesus-groupies into death-defying apostles?

This is a question their enemies tried to answer. When the Jewish leaders who crucified Jesus tried to silence his disciples, they were amazed by the boldness of their faith. "Now when they saw the boldness of Peter and John, and perceived that they were uneducated, common men, they were astonished. And they recognized that they had been with Jesus" (Acts 4:13). That was the difference: They had been *with Jesus*. It was their life-changing encounter with Jesus Christ that made them bold to preach the gospel. They had heard his wise teaching, observed his perfect life, seen his divine miracles, and witnessed his atoning death and bodily resurrection. Once they had met the risen Christ, they were filled with such a courageous faith that nothing in the whole world could stop them from living for his glory.

The same thing happens to everyone who meets the living God. When we open our hearts to Jesus Christ, as he is offered to us in the gospel, God's Spirit changes us from the inside out. We believe God's promises and start to act upon them. We begin to love our family with the love that we have received from God. We start to speak to our neighbors openly and naturally about spiritual things. We refuse to compromise our Christian convictions in the workplace. When people wonder what has happened to us, there will be only one possible explanation: we have been with the God of Moses and with the Son, Jesus Christ.

If we continue to live by the courage of faith, God will bless our work and witness for him. When Charles Spurgeon preached on the life of Moses, he stated:

> I am persuaded that Moses, after he had got over his first little difficulties . . . was strong in faith. There he stood with the wondrous rod, turning waters into blood and slaying all their fish, covering the heavens with blackness, turning the dust into living creatures, bringing hail and . . . doing it all as calmly and quietly as he should do who feels that he is the voice of God. How steadily he kept at his work! With what diligence he persevered in it, till at last the tenth plague found Moses unmoved, ready to conduct the people away to the Red Sea and to bring them out into the wilderness. O servants of God, be calm and confident. Go on preaching the gospel. Go on teaching in the Sunday-school. Go on giving away the tracts. Go on with steady perseverance. Be ye sure of this, ye shall not labor in vain or spend your strength for naught. Do you still stutter? Are you still slow of speech? Nevertheless, go on. Have you been rebuked and rebuffed? Have you had little else than defeat? This is the way of success. . . . Toil on and believe on. Be steadfast in your confidence, for with a high hand and an outstretched arm the Lord will fetch out his own elect, and he will fetch some of them out by you. Only trust in the Lord and hold on the even tenor of your way.[1]

## Let Them Go, I Say!

Moses and Aaron went to Pharaoh in the courage of their faith, but in spite of their boldness—or perhaps because of it—Pharaoh refused to let God's people go. When he refused, the two brothers responded by repeating God's demand: "Then they said, 'The God of the Hebrews has met with us. Please let us go a three days' journey into the wilderness that we may sacrifice to the Lord our God, lest he fall upon us with pestilence or with the sword'" (5:3).

Some scholars have raised questions about the precise wording of this request. At first Moses and Aaron spoke of holding a feast in the desert (5:1). Strictly speaking—and this is one of the objections—God did not use the word "feast" when he gave his original instructions to Moses. Nevertheless, what Moses said was accurate, because a feast is exactly what God had in mind. He wanted his people to worship him with sacrifices and with feasting—in other words, to celebrate his goodness with a festival of praise. Thus the exodus had the same goal as the Christian life: to glorify and enjoy God.

Then there is the question of the three-day journey, which is an issue we discussed in connection with 3:18. If God was planning to get his people out of Egypt altogether, then why did Moses make the exodus sound like a short holiday? The question is whether this was entirely truthful, because the Israelites did not go away for three days but forever. For this reason, it is sometimes argued that Moses and Aaron negotiated in bad faith.

There are many ways to handle this objection. One is to suggest that dictators like Pharaoh have no right to the truth. Another is to point out that Moses and Aaron never said anything at all about returning to Egypt. But perhaps the best answer is that God was giving Pharaoh a test. His ultimate plan was to lead Israel out of Egypt altogether, but he began by giving his rival a simple opportunity to submit to his divine authority. Was Pharaoh willing to let Israel serve God for even three days or not?

Such a request was not without precedent. An ancient manuscript at the Louvre, dating to the time of Rameses II, indicates that Egyptian slaves were sometimes given time off to worship their gods.[2] There is also a limestone tablet from the same period listing the names of slaves, together with reasons for their absence from work, including the phrase, "Has sacrificed to the god."[3] What this proves is that the Pharaohs sometimes honored the kind of request that Moses and Aaron were making. Asking for three days of religious freedom was a reasonable demand that God used to expose the unbelief in Pharaoh's heart.

Still other questions have been raised about the way Moses and Aaron tried to reason with Pharaoh. Some scholars say that verse 3 sounds more like a polite request for permission than a bold demand for freedom. They suggest that once Pharaoh started to question God's authority, Moses and Aaron backed down. They became more apologetic, more timid. Instead of issuing divine commands, as they had in verse 1, they resorted to offering human excuses. By begging for a three-day vacation, the argument goes, they were bargaining with Pharaoh, trying to persuade him to change his mind. And by mentioning the plagues that God might inflict, they were appealing to Pharaoh's sympathies (as if he had any!) rather than challenging his authority.

Although this way of looking at verse 3 has some plausibility, the truth is that Moses and Aaron never backed down. Instead they were trying to reach Pharaoh by speaking to him in a way he could understand. In verse 2 Pharaoh asks, "Who is the LORD . . . ?" On the chance that it was an honest question, Moses and Aaron answered that he was "the God of the Hebrews." Then they explained what kind of feast they had in mind: a journey into the wilderness to offer sacrifices to their God. The two brothers also warned Pharaoh of the dire consequences of refusing to grant their request: death and disease. When they said, "lest he fall upon us with pestilence" (5:3), they were referring not only to themselves but also to Pharaoh. If God's people were not allowed to serve the Lord their God, the consequences would be devastating for Egypt as well as for Israel. In the end, of course, these words turned out to be prophetic, for the Egyptians were visited with ten dreadful plagues. But Pharaoh could hardly say that he hadn't been warned! Moses and Aaron used every means of persuasion to convince him that the God of Israel was not to be trifled with.

This dialogue is a model for bold Christian witness. Moses and Aaron began by telling Pharaoh exactly what he had to do. But they also took the time to explain who was making this demand and why and what would happen if it wasn't met. The God of Israel was demanding freedom for his people. He was making this demand so that he could be glorified in their worship, and if his demand was not met, he would respond with swift and terrible justice.

Christians ought to adopt a similar strategy in presenting the good news about Jesus Christ. The gospel is first of all a demand in which God commands sinners to repent and believe in his Son. But that demand requires some explanation. To *repent* is to be sorry for sin and turn away from it. To *believe* in God's Son is to trust in the crucifixion of Jesus Christ as the full payment for one's sin. Christians also need to be prepared to explain why God makes this demand. Very simply, it is because those who refuse to come to Christ will be lost in their sins and will suffer the eternal punishment of God's wrath. If you are not a Christian, consider yourself forewarned! Like Pharaoh, you have heard what God demands, as well as the consequences of refusing him.

## Pharaoh's Ignorance

Moses and Aaron approached Pharaoh with courageous faith. But no matter what they said to him or how they said it, he had not the slightest intention of letting God's people go. Whether God's word came to him in the form of a demand or a promise, he refused to allow the Israelites to go and worship their God. He was a man of rebellious unbelief.

It is not hard to understand why Pharaoh turned a deaf ear to God's demand. Just put yourself on his throne for a moment. You are the most powerful man in the world. Two foreign slaves come up—one of them a renegade and a murderer—and demand the release of your entire workforce. The very idea was so audacious, so preposterous, that Pharaoh must have laughed out loud when he heard it. Defying the threat of divine judgment, he said, "Who is the Lord, that I should obey his voice and let Israel go? I do not know the Lord, and moreover, I will not let Israel go" (5:2).

With these words, Pharaoh posed the central question of the exodus: Who is the Lord? Who is the one true God? Who is the supreme deity who alone has the right to demand praise from every creature?

God had revealed the correct answer to Pharaoh's question back at the burning bush. Who is the Lord? He is the God of Abraham, Isaac, and Jacob. He is Yahweh, the Great I Am, the eternal and self-existent Lord. He is the Father of Israel who knows and cares about the suffering of his dear children. As events continue to unfold, he will reveal himself as the Lord God of salvation. He will bring judgment on the house of Pharaoh, while leading his own people through the sea on dry land, until finally the Egyptians themselves will recognize his lordship. In the desperate moments before being lost at sea, they will say, "Let us flee from before Israel, for the Lord fights for them against the Egyptians" (14:25). By the time his army is swept away by God's infinite power, even Pharaoh will know who the Lord is!

The exodus was God's way of giving Pharaoh an education in theology, especially in the doctrine of God. This was something that ruler badly needed, for when he first heard about God's saving plan, he claimed that he did not even know who the Lord was. By his own admission, Pharaoh was an unbeliever. He was ignorant of God's identity, resistant to God's authority, and malevolent toward God's community. Pharaoh was an extreme case in many ways, yet these are the character traits of anyone who does not believe in the God of Moses.

First, the unbeliever is ignorant of God's identity. Pharaoh confessed his ignorance by raising a question. It was not an honest question but a rhetorical one, asked with sneering sarcasm: "Who is the Lord?" Far from seeking to find out who God really was, Pharaoh denied that God had any claim on his life: "I do not know the Lord." Spoken like a true unbeliever, for by definition an unbeliever is someone who does not know the Lord. In these post-Christian times, most people are unbelievers. They do not enjoy a personal relationship with Jesus Christ. Thus they are like the title character in a mercifully short-lived television program called *God, the Devil and Bob* who said, "You're supposed to be a benevolent God and look at the record. You're vague. You're unknowable. You're unreliable." The unbeliever is ignorant of God's true identity.

It was because of his ignorance that Pharaoh set himself up in the place of God. One of the basic principles of Egyptian religion was that the king was a god. As Henri Frankfort has shown, the Egyptians believed that "in the person of pharaoh, a super human being had taken charge of the affairs of man. And this great blessing, which insured the well-being of the nation, was not due to a fortunate accident, but had been foreseen in the divine plan. The monarchy then was as old as the world, for the creator himself had assumed kingly office on the day of creation. Pharaoh was his descendant and his successor."[4]

In this case Pharaoh's claim to be divine was evident from the way he treated the Israelites, asserting an absolute right to their work and worship. It is significant that the word Pharaoh uses for "work" (5:9) and the word God uses for "serve" (4:23) have the same Hebrew root: *abad*. Pharaoh considered the Hebrews to be his servants. His delusion of deity was also evident from the way that he spoke. When Moses and Aaron spoke on God's behalf, they said, "Thus says the LORD, the God of Israel . . ." (5:1). Similarly, when Pharaoh began to give his orders, he had his spokesmen say, "Thus says Pharaoh . . ." (5:10). In other words, Pharaoh put himself in the place of God. Both the Israelites and the Egyptians used the same vocabulary to claim the ultimate authority of their words. The words "Thus says Pharaoh" were an explicit attempt to usurp God's rightful place. Therefore the exodus was basically a theological argument, a disagreement about the identity of God. Göran Larsson writes, "The critical issue to be settled is nothing less than who is in charge, who has the authority over the people of Israel and ultimately over all nations and all of creation: the God of Israel or the gods of Egypt, manifest in Pharaoh."[5]

The only remedy for Pharaoh's ignorance was a direct, personal encounter with the God of Israel. This is what every unbeliever needs. Until we come to know and love the one true God, we remain on the throne of our own lives. This may give us the illusion of power, but it is guaranteed to end in disaster. Only the true God has the power and wisdom to govern our universe. We need to know him, and the place to meet him and discover his identity is in the pages of the Old and New Testaments. The best remedy for theological ignorance is always sound Biblical instruction.

Anyone who is still not sure who God is should start reading the Bible. Read the Psalms, which praise God for all his wonderful attributes, or read one of the Gospels, which introduce Jesus Christ as the Son of God and the Savior of the world. Learn from other Christians. Attend a church that teaches the Bible as the Word of God. Join a small-group Bible study. Read a basic book on the attributes of God, such as the ones written by A. W. Pink and A. W. Tozer.[6] Anyone who receives good, solid, Biblical teaching will not remain ignorant of God's identity for long.

## Pharaoh's Resistance

In the second place, Pharaoh was resistant to God's authority. Unbelief is not merely an intellectual problem but also a spiritual problem. It affects the heart as well as the mind. After Pharaoh admitted his ignorance (saying, "Who is the Lord?"), he went on to assert his defiance: "that I should obey his voice . . . ?" (5:2).

What is curious about Pharaoh's statement is that it was spoken in defiance of a God he said he didn't believe in! Even while he was casting doubt on God's existence—asking "Who is this God of yours?"—he was busy rebelling against him. He was saying something like, "I have no idea who this God of yours is, but whoever he is, I am not going to serve him." His professed ignorance of God's identity did not prevent him from resisting God's authority.

This is the contradiction that lies in every unbelieving heart. People who refuse to acknowledge the living God still defy him at every turn. The Apostle Paul wrote that the "wrath of God is revealed from heaven against all ungodliness and unrighteousness of men, who by their unrighteousness suppress the truth. For what can be known about God is plain to them, because God has shown it to them . . . although they knew God, they did not honor him as God or give thanks to him" (Romans 1:18, 19, 21a). What these verses show is that there is always something rebellious about unbelief. No one is completely ignorant of God's identity, for the reality of his divine being is written on every human heart. Even the most hardened unbeliever knows, somewhere deep down, that there is a God. But this knowledge is secretly subdued because the unbeliever wants to keep sinning. He is disobedient because he is ignorant, and he chooses to remain ignorant so that he can keep on being disobedient!

If someone is having trouble deciding whether or not to follow Jesus Christ, it is worth asking why. Perhaps the person's reservations are purely intellectual: Is the Bible true? Is Jesus of Nazareth the Son of God? Is the resurrection a fact of history? But the real difficulty may be moral. In reality, to quote the Apostle Paul, skeptics are "by their unrighteousness suppress[ing] the truth." Often what keeps people from God is their attachment to sin. It is hardly surprising for someone who is pursuing selfish ambition, indulging in sexual sin, or living for material gain to still have doubts about Jesus Christ. Disobedience has a way of perpetuating ignorance.

## Pharaoh's Malevolence

If ever a man suppressed the truth by his wickedness, it was Pharaoh, who said, "Who is the Lord, that I should obey his voice . . . ?" (5:2). Not only did Pharaoh reject God's will for his own life, he also refused to let anyone else follow God. "Who is the Lord," he asked, "that I should . . . let Israel go?" He was not willing to let the Israelites glorify God any more than he was willing to glorify God himself—especially since the Israelites were his slaves.

This brings us to a third characteristic of Pharaoh's unbelief: he was malevolent toward God's community. *Webster's* defines malevolence as "intense, often vicious ill will, spite, or hatred." This is precisely what Pharaoh demonstrated toward the people of God: intense, vicious, and spiteful hatred.

Pharaoh showed his hatred toward Moses and Aaron. As soon as he realized what they were demanding, he told them to get back to work: "But the king of Egypt said to them, 'Moses and Aaron, why do you take the people away from their work? Get back to your burdens.' And Pharaoh said, 'Behold, the people of the land are now many, and you make them rest from their burdens!'" (5:4, 5). Pharaoh had no concern for the welfare of others; all he cared about was what other people could do for him. No sooner had he sent Moses and Aaron back to the labor camps than he began to oppress the Israelites more ruthlessly than ever:

> The same day Pharaoh commanded the taskmasters of the people and their foremen, "You shall no longer give the people straw to make bricks, as in the past; let them go and gather straw for themselves. But the number of bricks that they made in the past you shall impose on them, you shall by no means reduce it, for they are idle. Therefore they cry, 'Let us go and offer sacrifice to our God.' Let heavier work be laid on the men that they may labor at it and pay no regard to lying words." (5:6–9)

Pharaoh's order was passed down the chain of command: "Keep making those bricks, you loafers! And while you're at it, find your own straw!" As a labor policy, this was completely irrational. How could the Hebrews keep meeting their quotas without the resources they needed to get the job done? And why would working harder prevent them from wanting to worship their God? But Pharaoh was a tyrant, and in their fury, tyrants are prone to making rash, self-destructive decisions. Inevitably the innocent are the ones who suffer most.

Although Pharaoh was an extreme case, his example shows that a man who opposes God ultimately oppresses God's people. Unbelief is partly an intellectual problem: the unbeliever does not know the Lord's name. It is partly a spiritual problem: the unbeliever refuses to obey the Lord's will. But often it is also a social problem: the unbeliever does not care for the Lord's people.

This explains why Christians often are persecuted. Jesus told his disciples to expect to be mistreated: "You will be hated by all for my name's sake. But the one who endures to the end will be saved" (Matthew 10:22). Sometimes persecution takes the form of brutal violence, such as Israel suffered in Egypt. But usually the attacks are more subtle: Christian ideas are excluded from public education. The church is misrepresented by the media. Christians are mocked by their coworkers in the marketplace. The underlying reason for all this malevolence is unbelief. What makes non-Christians uncomfortable is not so much Christians or even Christianity, but Christ.

When it comes to Christ, there are only two choices: courageous faith or rebellious unbelief. Either we will serve God as Moses did or we will serve ourselves, as Pharaoh did. What makes the difference is our relationship with Jesus Christ. Until we receive him as Lord, we will remain ignorant of God's identity, resistant to God's authority, and to some extent malevolent toward God's community. So the question is, who is the Lord? Or to make it personal, who is *your* Lord?

The difference between rebellious unbelief and courageous faith is knowing Jesus Christ as Lord. This was true for Thomas, the disciple who said that he would not believe in the resurrection until he saw the risen Christ with his own two eyes. For a brief time Thomas remained ignorant of Christ's true identity. But when he finally met Jesus and saw his resurrection body, he said, "My Lord and my God!" (John 20:28). The same thing was true for Paul the apostle, who had been a lot like Pharaoh—ignorant of God's true identity in Christ and malevolent in his persecution of the early church. But then Paul met Jesus and started to call him Lord (Acts 9:5).

Do you know Jesus as Lord? A woman once told me that she was unable to call Jesus Lord until she became a true child of God. She had grown up in the church and had long considered herself a Christian, but she did not have a personal relationship with Jesus Christ. As long as God remained a vague abstraction, she was able to refer to him as God, but she could never pray to him as her Lord. The very word made her squeamish. It was only when she received the gift of faith and surrendered her life to Christ that she was finally able to call him Lord, which is what everyone calls him who has this courageous faith.

# 12

# Bricks without Straw

## EXODUS 5:10–21

"OUT OF THE FRYING-PAN INTO THE FIRE." So reads the title of a chapter in J. R. R. Tolkien's wonderful adventure story, *The Hobbit*. The chapter describes how Bilbo Baggins and his friends (thirteen dwarves and the old wizard Gandalf) escaped from extreme peril, only to find themselves in an even worse predicament. The intrepid adventurers had been traveling through the tunnels under the Misty Mountains when they were beset by goblins. After a brief and bloody battle they escaped by the narrowest of margins. Bilbo himself was the last one out of the mountain. Stuck in the stone doorway that led to freedom, he only just managed to wriggle free, losing all his buttons in the process.

But even after Bilbo and his friends got out of the mountain, they were not out of danger, for as they hurried through the forest on foot, they were tracked and surrounded by a pack of hungry wolves. Although Bilbo and his companions managed to scramble up some trees, they were trapped. Soon the goblins tramped out of their mountain stronghold to take advantage of the predicament. The goblins stacked combustible materials at the foot of each tree, and soon there was a ring of fire all around the dwarves. The flames began to lick at their feet. "Smoke was in Bilbo's eyes, he could feel the heat of the flames; and through the reek he could see the goblins dancing round and round in a circle." Then they began to sing their terrible song: "Burn, burn tree and fern! / Shrivel and scorch! A fizzling torch / To light the night for our delight."[1] So it was that Bilbo and his friends escaped from one mortal danger only to find themselves in even more desperate straits. Out of the frying pan into the fire!

## Brick by Brick

The same expression could well be used to describe what happened to the children of Israel as they slaved away under the scorching desert sun. For just when it seemed that they were about to be saved—indeed, when God's chosen servant had gone to Pharaoh to demand their freedom—they were afflicted by an oppression more severe than any they had experienced previously.

The Hebrews had been living in the house of bondage for centuries, but then came the hopeful day when it seemed they would be delivered. Armed with the promises of God, Moses and Aaron went to the royal palace and said, "Thus says the LORD, the God of Israel, 'Let my people go,'" only to hear Pharaoh say, "Who is the LORD, that I should obey his voice . . . ?" (5:1, 2). Because he was ignorant of God's identity and resistant to God's authority, Pharaoh refused to let God's people go. Even worse, that day he issued a decree that tightened the chains of their captivity. The Israelites were already slaving away, building great cities for the glory of Pharaoh, brick by brick. But now in order to make those bricks, they would have to gather their own straw.

Pharaoh's word was law in Egypt, so the royal edict was passed quickly down the chain of command: "So the taskmasters and the foremen of the people went out and said to the people, 'Thus says Pharaoh, "I will not give you straw. Go and get your straw yourselves wherever you can find it, but your work will not be reduced in the least."' So the people were scattered throughout all the land of Egypt to gather stubble for straw. The taskmasters were urgent, saying, 'Complete your work, your daily task each day, as when there was straw'" (5:10–13). Verse 11, in which the taskmasters tell the Hebrews to go and get their own straw, is heavily ironic. God told Pharaoh to let his people go. Well, Pharaoh would let them go, all right—go and get their own straw! Their workload would be heavier than ever. Out of the frying pan and into the fire.

To understand what these verses teach, it helps to review our method for studying the book of Exodus. From the beginning our approach has been *Biblical*. The only way to understand Exodus is to study the book in its Biblical context. Our method is also *historical*. The book of Exodus contains the true history of Israel in Egypt. The more we know about the ancient Egyptians, the better we will understand the exodus. But Exodus is history with an agenda. As we study this book, God is teaching us about himself, about his plan of salvation, and about our place in that plan. Thus our method is *theological*: we seek to understand God's actions and attributes. At the same time, it is *Christological*; that is to say, it concerns the person and work of Jesus Christ, the Savior who was to come. Finally, our method is *practical*. Like everything else in the Bible, the exodus teaches us how to live for God's glory.

When we apply this method to Exodus 5, we notice immediately that the account is full of historical detail, especially concerning the making of bricks. Brick-making was an important industry in ancient Egypt. A relief from the tomb of Rekhmire at Thebes depicts workers in various stages of the process. Some are drawing water to mix with soil in order to make mud. Others are forming bricks in wooden molds and setting them out to dry in the sun. Still others are stacking the bricks and carrying them to a building site.[2] Straw was essential to the whole process because it reinforced the clay and helped each brick stay intact. In one papyrus an official filed the following complaint against his superiors: "I am staying at Kenkenento, unequipped, and there are neither men to make bricks nor straw in the neighborhood."[3] No straw, no bricks! One good place to see bricks with straw is the Field Museum in Chicago. Among the thousands of artifacts in the museum's collection of Egyptian antiquities are bricks from the city of Dashur, made during the reign of Sen-Wosret III, in which pieces of straw are clearly visible.

The Egyptians used bricks for all kinds of buildings. Their temples were generally made of stone, but their palaces, storehouses, military installations, administrative buildings, and official residences were all made of mud bricks. Thus it took millions of bricks to satisfy the architectural ambitions of the Pharaohs.[4] Egyptian officials discovered that the way to get slaves to make enough bricks was to establish daily quotas, a practice described in documents of the period. Fragments from Egyptian manuscripts indicate how many bricks were demanded, as well as how many were actually delivered.

In one ancient text an official claims, "They are making their quota of bricks daily."[5] However, the same could not be said of the Israelites. When they were forced to find their own straw, their supply was unable to keep pace with Pharaoh's demand: "And the foremen of the people of Israel, whom Pharaoh's taskmasters had set over them, were beaten and were asked, 'Why have you not done all your task of making bricks today and yesterday, as in the past?'" (5:14).

This conversation indicates how Pharaoh's labor force was organized.[6] As we know from other ancient sources, Semitic slaves were the ones who made Pharaoh's bricks, under the supervision of Egyptian slave drivers. But some of the slaves served on the job as foremen. Thus there was a top-down labor system: Egyptian bosses at the top, Hebrew managers in the middle, and the rest of the slaves at the bottom. Obviously Exodus 5 was written by someone who actually saw the brickfields along the Nile. Brevard Childs writes, "This section reflects a remarkably accurate historical knowledge of Egyptian slave-labor organization and its building techniques."[7] After reviewing the available evidence, James Hoffmeier concludes that it attests "to the very scenario portrayed in the Exodus narratives: a two-tiered administrative structure, the assignment of sometimes unattainable quotas, the problems of making bricks without straw, and the issue of allowing time off from work to worship one's deity."[8]

One further piece of historical research helps confirm the accuracy of the

Biblical text. Late nineteenth-century excavations at Tell el-Maskhutah (which some consider to be the city of Pithom mentioned in 1:11) revealed buildings made of brick without straw. One archaeologist commented, "I carefully examined round the chamber walls, and I noticed that some of the corners of the brickwork throughout were built of bricks *without straw*. I do not remember to have met anywhere in Egypt bricks so made."[9] These bricks may or may not have been made by the Israelites. Regardless, what the research shows is that the book of Exodus comes to us straight from the world of ancient Egypt. The story of the exodus is not fantasy but history. It is a true account of God's saving work in time and space. Like everything else in the Bible, it is accurate down to the last piece of straw.

Everyone who reads the Bible must decide whether it is, as it claims to be, the very Word of the only true God. Ultimately, accepting the authority of the Bible is a matter of faith, of believing that what God has said is true. As the apostle John wrote near the end of his Gospel, "These [things] are written so that you may believe that Jesus is the Christ, the Son of God, and that by believing you may have life in his name" (John 20:31). Taking God at his word requires faith; nevertheless, that faith is reasonable. It is not a leap in the dark or an ignorant prejudice that Christians hold in spite of the evidence. Rather, it is a conviction that is supported and defended by the historical record. Like everything else in the book of Exodus, chapter 5 agrees with what we know about ancient Egypt and thus strengthens our faith in God's infallible Word.

The Bible is so completely true that we can stake our salvation on it, right now and for all eternity. When President Andrew Jackson (1767–1845) was lying on his deathbed, he told a group of visitors, "Sirs, I am in the hands of a merciful God. I have full confidence in his goodness and mercy. . . . The Bible is true. . . . Upon that sacred volume I rest my hope for eternal salvation, through the merits and blood of our blessed Lord and Savior, Jesus Christ."[10]

## The Prison House of Sin

Our approach to the exodus is Biblical and historical, but the Bible is much more than a history book. We also study it for our spiritual benefit. And when we study Exodus 5, we find that the true story of bricks without straw is not only historically accurate, but also practically relevant.

The main thing this chapter teaches is that sin is a harsh taskmaster. Remember that the exodus from Egypt—the entire epic adventure from the baby in the basket to the glory in the tabernacle—reveals the pattern of salvation. God has given us the book of Exodus to help us understand his saving grace. As we study it, we discover that salvation means release from captivity, freedom from bondage, and deliverance from oppression. Exodus teaches that to be saved is to be rescued from slavery in order to serve the living God.

What a slavery it was! Back in chapter 1 we saw how Pharaoh used the

Israelites ruthlessly in all kinds of bitter labor. Howard Vos has summarized the harsh conditions that brickworkers had to endure:

> They worked out in the hot Egyptian sun all day (often in temperatures over 100°), driven to optimum production by their taskmasters. They had no hats to protect their heads and wore nothing but a brief kilt or apron on their bodies. . . . A wealthy Egyptian father talked with his son about the condition of their bricklayers. He observed that their "kidneys suffer because they are out in the sun . . . with no clothes on." Their hands are "torn to ribbons by the cruel work." And they have to "knead all sorts of muck." Certainly no one stood by to give the workers a drink every few minutes. It does not take much imagination to conclude that the severe "rigor" imposed on the Hebrews resulted in many of them dying of dehydration, heat prostration, heatstroke and the like.[11]

Just when things seemed as bad as they could get, Pharaoh made them worse, and they had to work harder than ever. By the end of Exodus 5 God's people were utterly desperate, facing impossible demands and then getting whipped for failing to meet them. We can almost hear the harsh voices of their slave drivers. Without so much as a word of explanation, they started yelling, "Go and get your straw yourselves" (5:11), and they "were urgent" (5:13): "Hurry, hurry, hurry! Work, work, work!" No doubt the masters derived perverse pleasure from abusing their slaves; bullies always enjoy making people suffer. How the Egyptians must have laughed to watch the Israelites scour the desert. Now that straw was no longer provided by the cartload, the Hebrews had to get it for themselves. But soon they ran out of straw and were reduced to using "stubble" (5:12). When they failed to meet their production targets—as was inevitable—they were beaten.

God's people suffered these things for God's glory. If they had only been in Egypt to see the pyramids, the exodus wouldn't be much of a story (or much of a salvation, for that matter). But it is a great story (and a great salvation) because the Israelites were in bitter bondage to the end of their time in Egypt. The Bible carefully records the details of their suffering to show their desperate need of salvation, and thus to prove the glory of God's grace. The good news of salvation means freedom for captives who thought that they would never be set free. After God saved them, he said, "I am the Lord your God, who brought you out of the land of Egypt, out of the house of slavery" (20:2).

This matters for us because everyone is born in captivity to sin. The Bible says that until Christ comes to set us free, we are slaves to sin, "which leads to death" (Romans 6:16; cf. 7:14). Even the parts of our bodies are "slaves to impurity and to lawlessness" (Romans 6:19). We are "disobedient, led astray, slaves to various passions and pleasures" (Titus 3:3). Like Simon, the man who wanted to pay cash for God's power, we are "in the bond of iniquity" (Acts

8:23), for the devil himself has taken us captive "to do his will" (2 Timothy 2:26). Over and over again the New Testament declares that we are in bondage to sin. Apart from the saving work of Jesus Christ, we are "slaves of corruption. For whatever overcomes a person, to that he is enslaved" (2 Peter 2:19), and we are enslaved by sin.

Consider a few examples: The angry man is mastered by his anger. When something makes him mad, he cannot control his temper. He always has to lash out. The lustful man is mastered by his lust. When temptation comes, he helplessly gives in to his craving for pleasure. The selfish woman is mastered by her selfishness. She spends all her time thinking about her own desires, and then pitying herself when they go unmet. She has no love left to give to anyone else. The gossip is mastered by her tongue. She cannot resist the urge to go tell somebody the latest news.

The problem, however, is not simply that we keep committing this or that sin; the problem is that we are sinners to the very core. Until we surrender to Jesus Christ, our entire orientation is sinful. A scene from one of George MacDonald's children's books—called *The Princess and Curdie*—illustrates this point. Early in the novel the young boy Curdie thoughtlessly shoots an arrow into a white pigeon. Suddenly overcome by remorse, he carries the wounded bird to an old, old princess to see if anything can be done to save it. But the woman is even more concerned about the boy than she is about the bird. Gently she tries to help Curdie recognize that his evil deed sprang from the all-pervasive wickedness of his heart. When finally he confesses his sinful condition, he says, "I see now that I have been doing wrong the whole day, and such a many days besides! Indeed, I don't know when I ever did right. . . . When I killed your bird I did not know I was doing wrong, just because I was always doing wrong, and the wrong had soaked all through me."[12]

As sinners we get so used to sinning that we scarcely recognize our bondage. Exodus gives us a powerful picture of what it really means to be enslaved. Just as the children of Israel were held prisoner in the house of bondage, so we too are incarcerated in the prison house of sin. In the same way that the Israelites had to take orders from Pharaoh, we have a fiendish slave driver who tries to get us to make bricks without straw. Sin is the harshest of taskmasters. It always demands more and more from us—while giving us less and less in return. The more the lustful man indulges his fantasies, the less happy he becomes, and the more sex he craves. The more the selfish woman gets, the less content she grows, and still she wants more. Satan never loosens his grip; he is always busy tightening the chains of our captivity. It is always more bricks and less straw, for it is the very nature of sin to seek to control the sinner's whole life: "Everyone who practices sin is a slave to sin" (John 8:34).

What we need is someone like Moses to set us free from bondage. What we need is a Savior—Jesus Christ, the Moses of our salvation. Here is where our method for understanding Exodus becomes *Christological*—in other words, where it focuses on the person and work of Christ. The Bible teaches that Jesus came to "deliver all those who through fear of death were subject to lifelong slavery" (Hebrews 2:15). Jesus is the mighty deliverer who rescues us from our captivity to Satan, the strong Savior who frees us from our bondage to death, and the great emancipator who liberates us from our slavery to sin. He does all this through the cross, which was the death of our sin, and also through the empty tomb, which is the guarantee of our release. It is through the crucifixion and resurrection of Jesus Christ that we pass from slavery into freedom. Everyone who trusts in Christ is released from the servitude of sin in order to live for the glory of God: "To him who loves us and has freed us from our sins by his blood . . . to him be glory and dominion forever and ever" (Revelation 1:5b, 6b).

## Pharaoh, Save Us!

Satan will not let us go without a fight. As soon as we come to Christ, the power of sin's hold on us is broken, with the result that we are becoming more and more liberated all the time. But there is something about a former slave that loves his bondage. Even when God's Spirit opens a doorway in our heart to freedom, it is tempting to remain in captivity to sin. This was true during the exodus. Even after the Israelites were free from slavery, they still longed to go back and serve as sharecroppers on Pharaoh's plantation (see 16:3; 17:3).

To see what a stranglehold Pharaoh had on his slaves, observe what the Israelite foremen did when they were beaten: "Then the foremen of the people of Israel came and cried to Pharaoh, 'Why do you treat your servants like this? No straw is given to your servants, yet they say to us, "Make bricks!" And behold, your servants are beaten; but the fault is in your own people'" (5:15, 16). Rather than praying for God to deliver them, they begged Pharaoh to make their bondage easier to bear.

It is easy to understand why the foremen did this. Although they were slaves themselves, they were used to being treated with some respect, and quota or no quota, they were shocked to receive a beating from their Egyptian overlords. As Peter Enns explains it, they went to Pharaoh "thinking, perhaps, that some mistake had been made, some breakdown in communication in the chain of command. They say, in effect, 'Why are you beating *us*? *Your* people are the ones who have stopped supplying us with straw. It's their fault. If anything, beat *them*.'"[13] It just wasn't fair! The foremen were "caught in the middle between the impossible orders given them by their Egyptian superiors and their own people who were unable to keep up their brick quotas and gather the straw necessary to their task. When they were whipped for a failure they had no power to prevent and interrogated about a command they knew could not be kept, they felt unjustly handled, and they took their protest straight to Pharaoh himself."[14]

If this had simply been a labor dispute, the foremen could be commended for taking their grievance to Pharaoh. There is nothing wrong with asking for better working conditions. Besides, it was always possible that the slave drivers had been abusing their authority, changing the rules without Pharaoh's permission. But remember that in this case the real conflict was spiritual. The central question of the book of Exodus was: Whom were the Israelites made to serve—God or Pharaoh? At the end of chapter 4, the Israelites bowed down to worship their God. But at the first sign of trouble, they ran right back to Pharaoh. Notice how they identified themselves. Throughout their royal audience, they kept calling themselves "your servants" (5:15, 16). The expression occurs three times in one short speech. That shows how much power Pharaoh still held over them. They were so used to being in bondage that they could not think of themselves as anything but slaves. Rather than seeking to be free, they went back to renegotiate the terms of their captivity.

They failed, of course. In mocking tones Pharaoh accused the Hebrew foremen of being slackers: "Lazy, that's what you are—lazy! That is why you keep saying, 'Let us go and sacrifice to the LORD.' Now get to work. You will not be given any straw, yet you must produce your full quota of bricks" (vv. 17, 18 NIV). This shows how twisted Pharaoh was. When his servants came to complain about being overworked, he assumed that they weren't working hard enough!

The foremen should have known better than to try to fix things on their own. God had chosen Moses and Aaron to serve as their representatives. By going to Pharaoh themselves, therefore, they were overstepping the bounds of their authority. The foremen also should have known better than to expect any sympathy from Pharaoh. He was the problem, not the solution. So what hope was there in appealing to him for salvation?

This failure shows the futility of asking one's master to be one's liberator. If we are mastered by sin, it is no use asking Satan to set us free! Sin is not our friend, but our enemy. Nor is there any possibility that somehow we will figure out our own way to escape from sin. It takes divine power to release someone from Satan's service. This was obviously true for the Israelites. The story of bricks without straw portrays Pharaoh as an impossible man whose heart was hardened beyond the power of any human being to change it. The only force capable of compelling him to let God's people go was God's own mighty hand.

In the same way, only God can deliver a sinner from sin. He alone has the power to change a sinner's heart and thus to bring freedom from sin and death. The way God does this is beautifully explained in one of the *Four Psalms* composed by Edvard Grieg (1843–1907):

> God's Son hath set me free from Satan's tyranny,
> from base desire, enslavement dire,
> from fear of death and hell's hot fire.
> Lord Christ did intercede, with God for me did plead;

he underwent my punishment, to torture, death, was sent.
I cannot fathom love so great however much I contemplate:
that he could be so merciful to me,
a sinner frail, whom naught could suit but tasting the forbidden fruit;
by day, by night, old Satan's might my soul had captured quite.

The psalm ends with these triumphant words: "O blessed sign! Christ's cross doth shine, makes bliss eternal mine. God's Son hath set me free!"

If Christ has set us free, we must not go back to the shackles of our former slavery. Christians are often tempted to do what the Hebrew foremen did, particularly when we first come to Christ. At first everything seems to go well. We make rapid spiritual progress and experience real victory over sin. But then we encounter some difficulty. Our first impulse is to go back to the old, sinful ways of coping with life. We return to self-pity, or to drugs and alcohol, or to secret sexual sin. In other words, there is a strong temptation to return to bondage. The only way to resist this temptation—and thus to remain free in Christ—is to hold on to the cross and trust in its power to save.

## On Eagles' Wings

Having failed to get any satisfaction from Pharaoh, the Israelite foremen left the palace in a foul mood. In the providence of God, while they were still smarting from their wounds, they happened to see Moses and Aaron. Talk about being in the wrong place at the wrong time! The Bible says, "The foremen of the people of Israel saw that they were in trouble when they said, 'You shall by no means reduce your number of bricks, your daily task each day.' They met Moses and Aaron, who were waiting for them, as they came out from Pharaoh" (5:19, 20). There is more than one way to translate these verses. One is to make the foremen the subject of the verb "waiting," so that instead of Moses and Aaron waiting for the foremen, it was the other way around: the foremen were waiting to pounce on their spiritual leaders.[15] "Pounce" may be just the word for it, because the word "met" can also be translated "attacked."

Wherever the foremen met Moses and Aaron, and whatever else they may have done, they assaulted their representatives with the following words: "The Lord look on you and judge, because you have made us stink in the sight of Pharaoh and his servants, and have put a sword in their hand to kill us" (5:21). Pharaoh's strategy of driving a wedge between Moses and his people seemed to have worked. The foremen were blaming their spiritual leaders for all their troubles. More than that, they were pronouncing a curse, calling down divine judgment on God's chosen servants. They were exaggerating, of course. The Israelites were already under the power of Egypt's sword, and Pharaoh had never cared very much for the way they smelled. But in their fear they vented their anger against Moses and Aaron.

This was a natural response. When people are mad, they usually find someone to yell at, whether or not it is the person with whom they are angry. It is also typical for people to blame their troubles on their spiritual leaders. In this case the foremen were right: it *was* all Moses' fault! Humanly speaking, his plan had completely backfired; his mission was a spectacular failure. Rather than delivering the Israelites, his pyramid diplomacy only served to harden their oppression.

But there was something else the Israelite foremen could have done in this situation, something else they *should* have done. They should have done what the Israelites did back at the end of chapter 2: "The people of Israel groaned because of their slavery and cried out for help. Their cry for rescue from slavery came up to God" (2:23). Or they should have done what Moses did in the very next verse: "Moses turned to the Lord and said, 'O Lord . . .'" (5:22). Rather than returning to Pharaoh or turning against Moses and Aaron, they should have turned back to God in prayer, for only he could save them.

And save them he would. At the beginning of this chapter we noted that the Israelites went out of the frying pan into the fire. We also left poor Bilbo and his friends up in the trees, about to be roasted by goblins. Fortunately, they managed to escape. At the last possible moment, giant eagles swooped down and carried them away to safety. This is exactly what God did for his people when they were slaves in Egypt. When their situation went from bad to worse, when their sufferings brought them to the limit of human endurance, they cried out to him and were saved. Afterward God said to them, "You yourselves have seen what I did to the Egyptians, and how I bore you on eagles' wings and brought you to myself" (19:4). Do not expect sin to release you from its own bondage. But if you want to be free, pray to God in the name of his Son Jesus Christ, and he will save you as on the wings of eagles.

# 13

# When Trouble Comes

## EXODUS 5:22—6:5

SOMETIMES THINGS DON'T WORK OUT the way we hope. In fact, sometimes we do exactly what we think God wants us to do and it turns out to be a complete disaster. For example, a young couple goes on the mission field, taking their small children with them. Despite constant opposition from their parents—who are not believers—they travel overseas to live in a remote village. Not long after they arrive, one of the children contracts a rare, life-threatening disease, and the missionaries are forced to go back home. Upon their return, their parents say, "See, we told you not to go!"

Or consider the employee who discovered corruption at his company. After agonizing over what to do, he decided that it was his duty as a Christian to report one of his coworkers for defrauding their customers. But the management wouldn't listen. Not only did they allow the corruption to continue, but the man who reported it was branded a troublemaker and was denied his promotion.

Then there was the woman who shared the gospel with her neighbor. The two women had been gradually getting to know one another, and eventually the Christian woman had an opportunity to share her testimony. Her friend listened politely, but she had no real interest in Christianity and soon changed the subject. Afterward, although they remained acquaintances, they never became close friends.

These kinds of things happen all the time. A woman refuses a man who is not a Christian; now she is still waiting for the right man, but no one ever calls. An employee refuses to work on Sundays and gets fired three months later. A mother does everything she can to raise her children right and then watches them squander her love by turning away from God. A pastor starts to teach the Bible, but rather than growing, his congregation starts to shrink. It happens often. A Christian does what God calls him to do, and it makes things worse!

Such developments make us start to wonder if we did the right thing, and maybe even to wonder if God cares what happens to us.

### From Bad to Worse

This is exactly what happened to Moses. Moses had done everything God commanded him to do. It took him a while to accept God's call, of course, but once he did, he was careful to do whatever God wanted him to do. From the moment he left the burning bush until the day he went to Pharaoh's palace, he did and said exactly what he was told to do and say.

Moses was at the center of God's will. So he was living the victorious spiritual life, right? Wrong! Things could hardly have gone worse than they did. Acting on God's instructions, Moses had told Pharaoh to let God's people go, but that turned out to be a complete fiasco. Not only had Pharaoh refused to let the Israelites go, but the demand made him so angry that he doubled their workload. Now the Israelites had to find their own straw to make Pharaoh's bricks. Not surprisingly, this setback made Moses Public Enemy Number 1. Now the only thing he had to show for following God was the contempt of his people, who said, "The Lord look on you and judge, because you have made us stink in the sight of Pharaoh" (5:21a). The more Moses obeyed, the worse things got, and his worst fears were starting to come true (see 4:1–17). He had been rejected by both the Hebrews and the Egyptians. So this is a story about what happens when we try to do things God's way and it only makes things worse. It is also a story about what to do when that happens. How should we respond when trouble comes for doing what is right?

To know what *not* to do, just look at the Israelite foremen. When they were in trouble—bloodied and beaten for failing to meet their quotas—they first appealed to Pharaoh. By doing so they were returning to the source of their bondage, foolishly hoping that their taskmaster would set them free. Then they took out their anger on Moses, trying to undermine his God-given authority. We are starting to see that Israel's opposition to Moses is a major theme in the book of Exodus. It is part of a broader Old Testament pattern in which the Israelites repeatedly reject God's prophets, until finally they crucify Christ himself (see Acts 7:51, 52). And it all started with their rejection of Moses. This is the way most people respond when trouble comes: they turn back to their sins and away from sound instruction, with the result that they are drawn ever deeper into spiritual bondage.

### Moses' Complaint

Moses did something different when he was in trouble. When, in spite of his willing obedience, things went from bad to worse, Moses took his troubles to the Lord: "Then Moses turned to the Lord and said, 'O Lord, why have you done evil to this people? Why did you ever send me? For since I came to Pharaoh to speak in your name, he has done evil to this people, and you have not delivered your people at all'" (5:22, 23).

It is not hard to understand why Moses felt so disappointed. Up until the end of chapter 4, everything was going beautifully. With Aaron's help, the prophet had performed miraculous signs, and the Israelites had responded by believing his message and worshiping God. Now, just a few days later, the exodus was in a shambles, and the people were letting Moses have it. As far as he could see, God's plan had backfired. Not only had Moses failed to rescue his people, but their deliverance seemed further away than ever.

Moses should not have been surprised when Pharaoh refused to let God's people go. He knew that Pharaoh would not give up his slaves without a fight, for God had said, "I know that the king of Egypt will not let you go unless compelled by a mighty hand" (3:19). God had also said, "I will harden his heart, so that he will not let the people go" (4:21b). But God had not said anything about the Israelites gathering their own straw or attacking their spiritual leaders. So Moses couldn't understand what was happening. He did exactly what God had told him to do, but things weren't turning out the way he expected.

In his frustration and confusion, Moses started to question his calling. "Why did you ever send me?" he asked. The prophet's question was more like an accusation. When Moses first heard God's call to lead the people out of Egypt, he said, "Oh, my Lord, please send someone else" (4:13). Now he was saying, "See, God, I told you to send someone else!" And given the way things turned out, he had a pretty good point! Anyone who has ever had trouble in ministry knows how Moses felt. Sometimes we do what we thought God is calling us to do and say what we think we are supposed to say, but things don't turn out the way we hope. It makes us wonder if we did the right thing at all.

When trouble comes, it also makes us wonder if God knows what he is doing. This is where it is easy to find fault with Moses, for his protest was not without sin. Moses was guilty of discontentment—of complaining about the ways and means of God. He was guilty of unbelief—of not trusting God to fulfill his promises. He was guilty of impatience—of not waiting on God to bring salvation in his own good time. Moses also came very near the sin of rebellion, for he accused God of being a troublemaker: "O Lord, why have you done evil to this people?" (5:22a). Notice how many times the prophet uses the word "you": "Why have you done evil?" "Why did you ever send me?" "You have not delivered your people." "You, you, you," Moses said reproachfully; "It's all *your* fault!"

In the same way that the foremen blamed Moses for their troubles, Moses blamed God, and he overstated his case in the process. Moses blamed God for two things in particular. One was causing trouble—the trouble of having to make bricks without straw. The other was breach of promise—failing to save his people. Moses had gone to Pharaoh, but so far God had done nothing at all to accomplish salvation. So Moses did what it is always tempting to do when trouble comes: he blamed God both for what he *was* doing and for what he *wasn't* doing. He said in effect, "Why did you get us into this mess, Lord, and why aren't you doing anything about it?"

All of this is a reminder that Moses was a man like us, a sinner in need of salvation. As we study Exodus, we are constantly evaluating this great prophet, trying to learn what he has to teach us about living for Christ. In some ways he is the perfect example, for his ministry reveals the pattern of salvation in Christ. But there are also times when his words and deeds are corrupted by sin. Thus we see him striving to follow God, but always in need of divine grace, just as we are.

### Any Questions?

Although it is easy to find fault with the complaint that Moses filed, there are at least two things to be said in his defense. One is that he did not raise this protest primarily for his own benefit, but on behalf of God's people. His concern was that *they* were still enslaved and thus in need of freedom.

This is one of the many ways that the ministry of Moses points us to the work of Christ. When God called Moses to lead his people, he was appointing him as their spiritual representative, a calling that included interceding for their salvation. This prepared the way for the coming of our spiritual representative, Jesus Christ, who intercedes for us at the throne of God's grace. Interceding for someone else is an act of selfless love. Moses was able to offer such intercession because God had begun to perform a work of grace in his life, filling his heart with love for God's people. This kind of love is essential for anyone in spiritual leadership. If anyone is under our spiritual care—a child, an employee, a member of a ministry or Bible study—we are called to pray that God will help us love that person more and more deeply.

The other thing to be said in Moses' defense—and this is the most important thing of all—is that he took his problems straight to God: "Moses turned to the LORD and said, "O Lord . . .'" (5:22a). There was a time when Moses scarcely dared to approach the God of the burning bush, but then God entered into a personal relationship with him and promised to be with him all the time (3:12). As that relationship deepened, and as Moses developed intimacy with God through prayer, he learned to take his troubles back to God. In moments of doubt and discouragement, his immediate impulse was to go and meet with God.

The Christian should have the same impulse. When trouble comes, we can turn our distresses over to God. He has entered into a personal relationship with us through Jesus Christ. By the presence of his Holy Spirit, Jesus has promised to be with us "always, to the end of the age" (Matthew 28:20b). This means that whenever trouble comes, God's help is never more than a prayer away.

The prayer that Moses offered when he was in trouble consisted primarily of questions (or perhaps two questions and a complaint): "What are you doing, Lord? Why am I here? Can't you see what's happening?" The prophet rightly sensed that it was okay to ask God questions, that there was room in their relationship to ask for some explanation. In *Letters to a Young Poet*, Rainer Maria Rilke has written, "Be patient toward all that is unsolved in your heart and try to love the *questions themselves* like locked rooms and like books that are written in a very foreign tongue."[1] When Moses had things that were unsolved in his heart, he took them to his God. One commentator writes, "Here is a pristine picture of an honest relationship with God, and of the triumph of faith. Not all his problems were solved or all his questions answered, but the crucial action was that Moses returned to where he belonged. He went to the only source of life and light . . . he returned to the Lord."[2]

This is what the great heroes of the faith have always done with their questions. When they couldn't understand what was happening, or when they were tempted to give up, they took their questions to the Lord. It is what Abraham did when God gave him the promise of the covenant. He asked, "O Lord GOD, what will you give me, for I continue childless . . . ?" (Genesis 15:2). It is what Job did when he lost everything he had. He said, "I will not restrain my mouth; I will speak in the anguish of my spirit" (Job 7:11); "Why do you hide your face and count me as your enemy?" (Job 13:24). It is what David did when he was surrounded by enemies: "Why, O LORD, do you stand far away? Why do you hide yourself in times of trouble?" (Psalm 10:1). It is what Jeremiah did when he was put in jail for preaching God's Word (Jeremiah 20:7–18), and what John the Baptist did when he was tempted to doubt whether Jesus was the Christ (Matthew 11:2, 3). And it is what Jesus himself did in the day of his trouble, when he was dying on the cross for our sins. "My God, my God," he asked, "why have you forsaken me?" (Matthew 27:46).

Such questions are not sinful, provided that they are asked honestly and faithfully. In his commentary on Exodus, Godfrey Ashby states:

> This is not atheism or even rejection of God, but a baring of the emotions to the Almighty and the taking of the complaint to "head office," simply because the power to respond lies right there, with God himself. Psalm 22, used by Jesus on the Cross, offers a prime example. Wherever this happens, it does not bring swift retaliation from Yahweh upon those who have dared to complain, but an assurance that their complaint has been heard and a promise given of action. It also provides a means of working through real emotions. This is the biblical way of dealing with anger and frustration, rather than suppressing it.[3]

If we have any questions about what God is doing, we should go ahead and ask! We should not ask impatiently or rebelliously, as Moses was tempted to do, but we should ask. It is much better to talk things out with God than to take them out on someone else. Whether or not God decides to answer our questions, he certainly is not afraid of them.

## God Remains in Control

In Moses' case God did provide an answer. The first part of that answer (6:1–5) contains two great truths about God, truths to hold on to whenever trouble comes: God always remains in control, and he remembers his covenant.

First, God always remains in control. Moses' complaint was that God wasn't doing what he had promised: "You have not delivered your people *at all*," he said (5:23). In other words, "You haven't even begun to set us free." But the truth was that God had everything under control, as he always does: "But the LORD said to Moses, 'Now you shall see what I will do to Pharaoh; for with a strong hand he will send them out, and with a strong hand he will drive them out of his land'" (6:1).

This may not have been the answer Moses was hoping for. God never exactly explained why he allowed his people to go through so much trouble or why Moses was still the right man for the job. God did not try to justify himself to Moses at all; he simply repeated his promise to glorify himself by defeating Pharaoh. Moses thought that things had gone from bad to worse, but as far as God was concerned, everything was going perfectly according to plan. John Durham writes, "What has appeared to Moses and the Israelites as a serious deterioration of an already bad situation has been instead a careful preparation for what is to come."[4] Even Pharaoh's hard-hearted refusal was part of the plan of salvation. God was setting things up so that Pharaoh would not only let God's people go but would help drive them out himself! The all-wise and all-powerful God had everything under control.

Theologians have a word to describe God's ability to keep things under control. The word is *sovereignty*. To say that God is sovereign means that he reigns supreme over the universe that he has made. He sits on his throne, ruling with what he calls his "strong hand" (cf. 6:1). As the *Westminster Confession of Faith* states, "God from all eternity, did, by the most wise and holy counsel of His own will, freely, and unchangeably ordain whatsoever comes to pass" (3.1). God is sovereign over all the affairs of humanity, working his plan.

If God is sovereign, then we may be sure that when trouble comes, he is still in control. Whether we understand it or not, he is working to accomplish some glorious purpose. Sometimes God allows our troubles to continue in order to prove that only he can save us. The story of the exodus is a perfect example. When Moses failed to change Pharaoh's mind, it became more obvious than ever that only God could set his people free. It was precisely when Moses despaired of providing deliverance himself that God said, "Now you shall see what I will do" (6:1). The lesson to apply is that when trouble comes, we are to trust in God alone for our salvation.

Sometimes God allows trouble to continue in order to teach us to be patient. Moses seemed to think that the exodus would commence the moment he started obeying God. But godliness does not guarantee immediate results, and God's plans often take a long time to develop, while he reveals his glory through the gradual unfolding of his purpose. In this case the Israelites had been waiting four hundred years for their salvation. Although God could have saved them at any moment, that was not his plan. In his commentary on these verses, John Calvin admits:

> It was, indeed, possible for God to overwhelm [Pharaoh] at once, by a single nod, so that he should even fall down dead at the very sight of Moses; but . . . He . . . chose more clearly to lay open His power; for if Pharaoh had either voluntarily yielded, or had been overcome without effort, the glory of the victory would not have been so illustrious. . . . [God] wished to accustom His servants in all ages to patience, lest they should faint in their minds, if He does not immediately answer their prayers, and, at every moment, relieve them from their distresses.[5]

Like Moses, we need to show a little patience by taking a long view and resisting the urge to quibble with God's timetable. We also need to be cautious about deciding whether something is God's will by looking at how it is turning out right at this moment. At the first sign of trouble Moses was ready to give up, but he needed to keep doing what he was called to do because God was still at work.

Things almost never turn out the way we expect, especially at first, and God loves to glorify himself in ways that go far beyond anything we anticipate. No successful ministry ever proceeds without difficulty. If Christians were to give up every time they ran into difficulty, God's work would never get done. So when trouble comes, remember that God is still in control. Trust his sovereignty, as Margaret Clarkson did in a wonderful verse from one of her hymns:

> O Father, you are sovereign in all affairs of man;
> No pow'rs of death or darkness can thwart your perfect plan.
> All chance and change transcending, supreme in time and space,
> You hold your trusting children secure in your embrace.

## God Remembers His Covenant

God's answer to Moses contained a second great truth—that God always remembers his covenant. "God spoke to Moses and said to him, 'I am the Lord. I appeared to Abraham, to Isaac, and to Jacob, as God Almighty, but by my name the Lord I did not make myself known to them. I also established my covenant with them to give them the land of Canaan, the land in which they lived as sojourners. Moreover, I have heard the groaning of the people of Israel whom the Egyptians hold as slaves, and I have remembered my covenant'" (6:2–5).

These are almost all things that God had said to Moses back in chapter 3: "My name is Yahweh"; "I am the God of your fathers"; "I will keep my covenant"; "I will bring you into the promised land"; "I know all about your suffering." When God repeats things like this, it is because we need to hear them more than once. So much of the Christian life consists of being reminded of what we already know, so we can apply it to each new situation in life. When trouble comes, we need to be reminded that God is still God. He is the God of history, the very same God who promised salvation to Abraham and brought Moses out of Egypt. Like Moses, we need to be reminded that God knows what we are going through and that he fully intends to keep every promise that he has ever made.

Verse 3 raises an obvious question. It seems to suggest that God never revealed his special name to the patriarchs, that he never called himself "Yahweh" until he spoke to Moses from the burning bush (3:14, 15). However, that special divine name—which expresses the active existence of the God who is—occurs more than one hundred times in the book of Genesis. A significant example is Genesis 4:26, which says that at the time Enosh was born, "people began to call upon the name of the LORD." Another important occurrence is Genesis 15:2, where Abraham addresses God with the title "Lord GOD." This shows that although the patriarchs ordinarily used God's other names—for example, *El Shaddai*, which means "God Almighty" (Genesis 17:1)—they were not unfamiliar with the special divine name "Yahweh."

Some scholars say that this is the kind of contradiction we should expect in a book written by more than one fallible human author. But this view is unacceptable to anyone who receives the Bible as God's inerrant Word. Another suggested possibility is that when the name "Lord" appears in Genesis, it is an anachronism. As Moses wrote the book of Genesis, he simply used God's later name to tell an earlier story. After all, he was still writing about the same God. Probably the best explanation, however, is that the patriarchs did not fully understand the *meaning* of God's proper name. There is a huge difference between simply knowing someone's name and actually knowing that person. What God said to Moses was this: "By my name the LORD [Yahweh] I did not make myself known to them." This does not mean that Abraham, Isaac, and Jacob had never heard God's name before. What it means is that they did not fully understand it because they did not know God in all his fullness.

Remember that although Abraham, Isaac, and Jacob knew the living God, they never witnessed his mighty work of salvation; they only received it by promise. This is the difference between Genesis and Exodus. Abraham knew God as a promise maker; Moses came to know him as a promise keeper. Whereas the patriarchs had to live by faith, therefore, the children of Israel also lived by sight. God was not simply making promises to them but was actually starting to keep them. In the exodus he was demonstrating the saving power behind his special name, revealing himself as the Lord of their salvation. Peter Enns thus offers this paraphrase: "I appeared to Abraham, Isaac, and Jacob, but only partially—in the capacity of El Shaddai. But who I am fully, which is what my name Yahweh captures, I did not make known to them. This is made known first only now, to you, the Exodus generation, who will witness my mighty saving power."[6]

The reason the exodus generation got to see this mighty saving power was because God remembered his covenant—his unbreakable promise of salvation. God never forgot that he had promised to make Abraham into a mighty nation and to give him a land to call his own (Genesis 15:18–21). Thus when Abraham's descendants were slaves in Egypt, God remembered that he had promised to bring them into Canaan. And he did it all for love. God told Moses, "I have heard the groaning of the people of Israel whom the Egyptians hold as slaves, and I have remembered my covenant" (6:5). This covenant was a love covenant. As God watched his people suffer, making bricks without straw and groaning under Pharaoh's whip, he was moved with compassion to rescue them—the compassion of his eternal covenant.

Fifteen hundred years later the same compassion moved God to send his Son to be our Savior. He saw that the people he loved were enslaved by the powers of sin, and he remembered his unbreakable promise of salvation. When Zechariah the priest heard what God was about to do he said:

> Blessed be the Lord God of Israel,
> for he has visited and redeemed his people
> and has raised up a horn of salvation for us . . .
> to remember his holy covenant,
> the oath that he swore to our father Abraham.
> (Luke 1:68, 69a, 72b, 73a)

God remembered his covenant in Jesus Christ. He remembered it on Christmas morning when Jesus was born to keep the covenant that we had failed to keep. He remembered it on Good Friday when Jesus died on the cross, suffering all the covenant curses against our sin so we could be forgiven. And he remembered it on Easter Sunday when he "brought again from the dead our Lord Jesus . . . by the blood of the eternal covenant" (Hebrews 13:20).

Now Jesus stands at the right hand of his Father in Heaven, ready to help us when trouble comes. When we commit a sin, Jesus intercedes for us, reminding his Father that all our sins have been washed away through the blood of his covenant. When things go from bad to worse—when in our suffering we are tempted to be discouraged—Jesus sends us the comfort and peace of his Spirit, the promised blessings of his covenant. God never goes back on a promise. He always keeps his word. As the psalmist wrote, "He remembers his covenant forever" (Psalm 105:8a). Therefore, he will remember his covenant to the end of the world, when Jesus comes to take his people to glory. God will remember his covenant on the day of judgment when he will forgive all our sins by his covenant mercy. And he will remember it forever after as he blesses us with his everlasting love.

# 14

# The Seven "I Wills" of Salvation

## EXODUS 6:6–12

BOB (PLAYED BY BILL MURRAY) is Dr. Marvin's lovable but troubled mental patient in the film *What About Bob?* He is so needy that he clings to Dr. Marvin at every turn—stopping by his office for unscheduled visits, telephoning him at home in the evening, showing up unannounced at his house, and generally making a nuisance of himself. As Dr. Marvin prepares to take a family vacation, he starts to wonder how he is ever going to get rid of Bob. Finally, in desperation, he tells his patient to do what he is doing himself and take a vacation. "A vacation from my problems," says Bob. "What a great idea!"

And it does sound like a great idea. We imagine getting in a car and driving away from our financial worries or hopping on a bus to escape all the troubles in our family. We imagine taking a train and leaving our health problems back at the station or buying an airline ticket to the other side of the world, where not even our employer can reach us. Sounds inviting, doesn't it?

The trouble is that problems generally do not take vacations. Even if we are able to get away from them for a few days, they are still there when we come back. Inevitably they have gotten worse, which is what happens in the film. Bob decides that if he is going to take a vacation from his problems, he might as well take it with his psychiatrist. To Dr. Marvin's dismay, Bob shows up at the family's resort and brings his problems right along with him.

Perhaps this is why the Bible never encourages us to take a vacation from our problems. It wouldn't help anyway, and the Bible is much too realistic about the difficulties of life in this fallen world to waste our time with hopeless solutions. So instead of running away from our problems, the Bible teaches us to bring them to the Lord.

## "I Am the Lord"

This is what Moses did with his problems: he took them straight to God. When the Israelites were making bricks for Pharaoh, and then blaming him for having to make them without straw, Moses took his problems back to God. And God answered him by repeating his promise of salvation. He assured Moses that no matter how desperate the situation became, he still had things under control (6:1), and he had not forgotten his covenant (6:2–5).

Of all the things that God said to Moses, the most important was this: "I am the LORD." We know this was important because God repeated it so often. "I am the LORD," he said again and again. God makes this statement more than a dozen times in the book of Exodus.[1] He first said it back at the burning bush: "I AM WHO I AM" (3:14, 15). Here in Exodus 6, when Moses gets into so much trouble that he starts to doubt God's plan of salvation, God says it repeatedly: "I am the LORD." He says it at the beginning, in the middle, and at the end, in verses 2, 6, 7, and 8. Brevard Childs writes, "The whole focus falls on God's revealing of himself in a majestic act of self-identification: I am Yahweh. . . . To know God's name is to know his purpose for all mankind from the beginning to the end."[2] Certainly God gave Moses plenty of other details about his plan of salvation. But the beginning, the middle, and the end of his message was, "I am the LORD."

God wanted his people to understand that the answer to all their problems was to be found in him. Every aspect of their salvation depended on his being and character. Salvation began with God because it all came from his grace, and it would end with God because it would all return to his glory. Whatever difficulties showed up in the meantime, God would be able to handle because he is the Lord! Rather than taking a vacation from our problems, therefore, the thing to do is to find rest and repose in the lordship of God. He is the answer to every difficulty.

Perhaps this is why God allowed Moses to fail the first time he went to Pharaoh. If Pharaoh had released the Israelites the first time they asked, they would have given Moses most of the credit. Instead the mission backfired, and he had to take all the blame. Then everyone knew that Moses was unable to lead God's people to the Promised Land. Only God could bring them out of Egypt, and the longer Moses and Pharaoh argued over the fate of Israel, the clearer this became. God was teaching his people to put all their trust in him. In this way they discovered that when all else failed, the one thing they could count on was the One who said, "I am the LORD" being able to save them.

Exodus is a God-centered book with a God-centered message that teaches us to have a God-centered life. Whatever problems we have, whatever difficulties we face, the most important thing is to know who God is. We are called to place our trust in the One who says, "I am the LORD." When there is trouble in the family, and we don't know how to bring peace, he says, "I am the LORD."

When a relationship is broken and cannot be mended, he says, "I am the Lord." When nothing seems to go right, and it is not certain how things will ever work out, even then he says, "I am the Lord."

## The God of All Salvation

The Lord who calls us to trust in him is the God of all salvation. In these verses he announces the seven "I wills" of salvation:

> Say therefore to the people of Israel, 'I am the Lord, and I *will* bring you out from under the burdens of the Egyptians, and I *will* deliver you from slavery to them, and I *will* redeem you with an outstretched arm and with great acts of judgment. I *will* take you to be my people, and I *will* be your God, and you shall know that I am the Lord your God, who has brought you out from under the burdens of the Egyptians. I *will* bring you into the land that I swore to give to Abraham, to Isaac, and to Jacob. I *will* give it to you for a possession. I am the Lord.'" (6:6–8)

One reason it is so helpful to turn problems over to the Lord is that he can actually do something about them. He doesn't just sit there. At the beginning of this conversation Moses pointed out that God didn't seem to be doing much of anything. "You have not delivered your people at all," he complained (5:23). But by the time the exodus was over, Moses saw God do absolutely everything necessary to rescue his people. When God said, "I am the Lord," what he meant was that he is the God of all salvation, the God who will do this, that, and everything else to save his people.

Although there are seven "I wills" in these verses, there are really only four basic promises. The first two "I wills" speak of *liberation*: "I will bring you out from under the burdens of the Egyptians, and I will deliver you from slavery to them" (6:6). At its most basic level, this is what salvation means: being freed from slavery or delivered from captivity. The main thing the Israelites needed was to be rescued from bondage, and when God said, "I am the Lord," he was promising to be their deliverer.

The second promise (the third "I will") is *redemption*: "I will redeem you with an outstretched arm and with great acts of judgment" (6:6b). Redemption is a financial term. In the ancient marketplace it was used to describe the release of a slave by the payment of a ransom. Later this became part of the Biblical law. If an Israelite had to sell himself into slavery in order to pay a debt, his own family members would redeem him by paying the price for his freedom (see Leviticus 25:47–53). But in the case of the exodus, the Egyptians were the ones who ended up paying the price! Israel was redeemed "with great acts of judgment," and God himself was the Redeemer, releasing his people "with an outstretched arm."

In Biblical times redemption was always the right of a near kinsman—that is to say, a family member or close relative. God was eligible to redeem the Israelites because of his kinship with them: "I will take you to be my people, and I will be your God" (6:7a). In this case the word "take" really means "to adopt," so the fourth and fifth "I wills" of salvation contain the promise of *adoption*.[3] This family promise is the heart of the covenant, in which God takes us to himself to be his people and gives himself to us to be our God. As God said when he made his covenant with Abraham, "I will . . . be God to you and to your offspring after you" (Genesis 17:7). In the exodus God proved his fatherly affection. As he warned Pharaoh, "Israel is my firstborn son" (4:22). So when he brought his son out of slavery, it was not simply a stroke of justice but also an act of love. God brought Israel out of Egypt into an intimate relationship of mutual affection.

The last two "I wills" concern what might be called the promise of *possession*. "I will bring you into the land that I swore to give to Abraham, to Isaac, and to Jacob. I will give it to you for a possession" (6:8). The land was another promise of the covenant, and by now we can see why God introduced the seven "I wills" of salvation with the word "moreover." The word "moreover" establishes a logical connection between the statement at the end of verse 5—"I have remembered my covenant"—and all the promises that follow. God saves because he has promised to save. The "I wills" of salvation are based on his everlasting covenant.

The promise of possession was first made in Genesis 12, when "the LORD appeared to Abram and said, 'To your offspring I will give this land'" (Genesis 12:7). When God made that promise, he now explained to Moses, he swore to honor it. The land was guaranteed by a promise, backed by the full faith and credit of Almighty God. Here in Exodus 6 God swore again, for when the prophet Ezekiel looked back on this great day he wrote: "Thus says the Lord GOD: On the day when I chose Israel, I swore to the offspring of the house of Jacob, making myself known to them in the land of Egypt; I swore to them, saying, I am the LORD your God" (Ezekiel 20:5, 6). The promise of possession—the promise of entering, conquering, and inhabiting the land of Canaan—was a solemn oath of the everlasting covenant.

These are the seven "I wills" of salvation, in which God proves that he is Lord by saving his people—liberating them, redeeming them, adopting them, and giving them a land to be their very own. Without getting lost in all the details, it is important not to miss the main point, which is that salvation belongs to the Lord. From beginning to end, every aspect of the exodus was accomplished by God, and by God alone. God promised to bring his people out of Egypt and to free them from bondage. He promised to take them to himself and make them his own. He promised to give them a land for their possession. The only thing left for the Israelites to do was to know him as their Savior and Lord, as God also promised they would: "You shall know that I am the LORD your God, who has brought you out from under the burdens of the Egyptians" (6:7). God saved the Israelites by his sovereign grace. He did all the saving so that he could keep all the glory.

The same is true with salvation in Jesus Christ, which is the greatest exodus of all. As we have seen, the book of Exodus is not simply the history of ancient Israel; it is also the story of our salvation. As we listen to Exodus, we hear the first strains of a melody that becomes a symphony in the Gospels. When Jesus said to his Father, "Behold, I have come to do your will, O God" (Hebrews 10:7), he was gathering up the "I wills" of salvation and making them his own. Jesus was saying, "I will save you. I will deliver you. I will redeem you. I will make you my own. I will give you a glorious inheritance."

Jesus is the liberator who "has freed us from our sins by his blood" (Revelation 1:5b). Jesus is the Redeemer who paid the costly price of our sin by suffering and dying on the cross: "In him we have redemption through his blood, the forgiveness of our trespasses" (Ephesians 1:7). It is also through Jesus that we are welcomed into the embrace of divine love, for it is to the church of Jesus Christ that God says, "I will be their God, and they shall be my people" (2 Corinthians 6:16). And at the end of all our days, Jesus is the one who will bring us to the land of glory. It is by his resurrection that we have "an inheritance that is imperishable, undefiled, and unfading, kept in heaven" for us (1 Peter 1:4). The Bible summarizes by saying that "all the promises of God find their Yes in him [Christ]" (2 Corinthians 1:20a). God made his promise long, long ago when he said, "I will save you." The way he kept his promise was by sending his Son to be and to do everything we need to be saved, so that from beginning to end we are saved by his grace.

All that is left for us is to know Jesus as our Savior and our Lord. Salvation is not about us doing something for God; it is about what God has done for us in Jesus Christ. All that is required is to trust in Jesus, believing that he has turned the "I wills" of salvation into the "I have done its" of the gospel.

## Israel's "I Won't"

What God said to Moses was such wonderful news that most people would have been happy to get it, but the sad truth is that when the Israelites heard the message of salvation by God's free grace, they wanted nothing to do with it. In verse 9 we turn from the "I wills" of salvation to the "I won't" of Israel: "Moses spoke thus to the people of Israel, but they did not listen to Moses, because of their broken spirit and harsh slavery."

"Well, that all sounds very exciting, Moses," the Israelites said, "but frankly, we're not interested." They were not impressed with God's mighty power or his ability to remember his covenant. They were unmoved by his promises of deliverance and conquest. They refused to believe that he was their Savior and their Lord. They didn't even care what his name was; they just wouldn't listen.

The same thing often happens when people first hear the message of salvation in Christ. Someone explains to them how they can receive forgiveness for their sins through the death and resurrection of Jesus Christ. They seem to be listening, but then very politely they change the subject, or they say that they already believe in God. They insist that while Jesus may be great for others, he is of no use to them, or they say flat out that they aren't interested. Christians are often surprised when this happens. How could anyone possibly reject the good news of salvation? All the pains of Hell can be avoided, all the blessings of Heaven are available, and the only thing a sinner needs to do is to believe in Jesus Christ. Yet even when this is explained, some people still aren't interested! Why not?

The Bible gives the answer: "They did not listen . . . because of their broken spirit and harsh slavery" (6:9). In other words, the Israelites were enslaved by their slavery. Their very chains were what prevented them from hearing the cry of freedom. As they slaved away for Pharaoh, making bricks without straw, they lost any hope of emancipation. The Bible says that they were discouraged. More literally, their spirits were broken—so broken that they would not listen to the promise of deliverance. What kept them in bondage was their bondage itself.

Sin is the same kind of bondage. The history of Israel in Egypt teaches the way of salvation, which begins with acknowledging that apart from the saving work of God's Spirit we are slaves to sin. No matter how much we try to stop, we always seem to keep on sinning, and often we commit the same sins over and over. We try to escape by trying a little harder to do a little better, but the next thing we know, we're right back into it. After a while it gets discouraging. The sinner gets so oppressed by sin that there seems to be no escape. The bonds of sin are so tight that they prevent the sinner from truly hearing the good news of the gospel. Theologians call this the doctrine of "total inability," which simply means that sinners cannot come to God on their own. In the words of the *Westminster Larger Catechism*, they are "utterly indisposed, disabled, and made opposite to all that is spiritually good" (A. 25). Sinners cannot save themselves because they cannot and will not come to God. This is perfectly illustrated by the Israelites, who would not listen to the promise of freedom exactly because they were enslaved.

One of the implications of the doctrine of total inability is that the only way a sinner ever comes to Christ is by divine intervention. God himself has to break the chains of sin, and he does this by his Holy Spirit, who opens hearts and minds to hear his gospel. Jesus said, "Truly, truly, I say to you, whoever hears my word and believes him who sent me has eternal life. He does not come into judgment, but has passed from death to life. Truly, truly, I say to you, an hour is coming, and is now here, when the dead will hear the voice of the Son of God, and those who hear will live" (John 5:24, 25).

## Total Recall

It took a long time for the Israelites to hear what God was saying to them, but in the meantime there was work to do: "So the LORD said to Moses, 'Go in, tell Pharaoh king of Egypt to let the people of Israel go out of his land'" (6:10, 11). Moses was part of God's plan for accomplishing the "I wills" of salvation. God told him to go back to Pharaoh and demand freedom for his people. If this sounds familiar, it is because God had sent Moses to Pharaoh before. That was the call; this was the recall.

By now the prophet's answer is all too predictable: "But Moses said to the LORD, 'Behold, the people of Israel have not listened to me. How then shall Pharaoh listen to me, for I am of uncircumcised lips?'" (6:12). Moses answered God's recall the same way he answered his call—by saying he did not have the gifts to do what God was calling him to do.

Some scholars have argued that there was really only one call, that Exodus 6 contains a shorter version of the same conversation that God had with Moses back in Exodus 3, 4. It is true that there are many similarities between the two narratives. The same two parties are talking—God and Moses. God gives the same promise of deliverance. In both cases Moses was sent to tell Pharaoh to let God's people go, and in both cases he refused because he was not a gifted speaker. The phrase "uncircumcised lips" may mean that he had some kind of speech impediment.

Yet for all the apparent duplication, there are also some crucial differences between these two accounts. One is location: God first called Moses at Mount Horeb, but this time he spoke to him in Egypt. Furthermore, on this occasion God did not appear to Moses in a burning bush. Nor did he give him any miraculous signs or say anything about Aaron. The response is different too. The first time Moses spoke to the Israelites they believed him, but this time they didn't even want to hear what he had to say. Given these significant differences, it is clear that Exodus 6 is not simply a rerun but a whole new episode.

It should not surprise us that Moses needed a recall, or even that he gave God the same lame excuse on two different occasions. God's servants often need to learn the same lesson twice (or more). This is one of the reasons there is so much repetition in Exodus. If we learned everything God wanted to teach us the first time, he wouldn't need to repeat himself. But the sad truth is that we are slow to understand, slow to believe, and slow to obey.

It is not hard to see why Moses hesitated. He had some legitimate reasons for thinking that he was not up to the task. Things hadn't gone all that well the first time. In fact, it had been a complete failure. The prophet had been rebuked by Pharaoh and rejected by his own people. Why would it be any different this time? Besides, if Moses couldn't get even his own people to listen, how was he ever going to persuade Pharaoh to let his slaves go free? It was only natural for the prophet to feel inadequate and incompetent, doubting his ability to do what God had called him to do.

Are you ever tempted to give up? Sometimes serving the Lord is so discouraging that it is tempting to stop doing something we know God has called us to do. A few problems emerge, and then all of the old fears and doubts return. We start to come up with some of the same old excuses: "I can't do it." "I'm not good at this." "I don't have time."

God is not interested in our excuses, as we shall see in his answer to Moses at the beginning of chapter 7. But the truth is that we already know the answer: "I am the LORD." This is always the answer. It was the answer when the Israelites were in slavery and had to make bricks without straw. It was the answer when Moses seemed to be failing and wasn't sure he could keep on serving God. And it is the answer for us whenever we face problems and are tempted to stop doing what God has called us to do. God says to us, "I am the LORD." If he is our Lord, then we must trust him and obey him.

One Christian who did this was John Calvin, the famous Reformation theologian. Calvin was first called to preach in Geneva in 1536. During the early years of his ministry, there were political and theological conflicts that eventually forced him out of the city. For several years Calvin lived in Strasbourg, where he enjoyed some of the happiest and most productive years of his life. But then God gave Calvin a recall. In 1540 the leaders of Geneva came and begged him to return to his pulpit ministry.

For his part, Calvin had no interest in going back to Geneva. He said, "Whenever I call to mind the wretchedness of my life there, how can it not be but that my very soul must shudder at any proposal for my return?" He also commented, "Rather would I submit to death a hundred times than to that cross on which I had to perish daily a thousand times over." Yet Calvin was willing to take up his cross, and finally he declared, "I am prepared to follow entirely the Lord's calling as soon as he shall have made it plain to me." Eventually God did make his calling plain to John Calvin, and Calvin answered the call. The Geneva *Register* for September 13, 1541, records his arrival there to serve Christ as a minister of the gospel.[4]

What is God calling you to do or to keep on doing? You may be having some problems. You may be discouraged. You may have your doubts about whether you can do it. But remember that you serve the Lord, who has promised to do everything to save you, from beginning to end.

# 15

# They Were the Levites

## EXODUS 6:13–27

GENEALOGIES MUST BE IMPORTANT because God has included so many of them in the Bible. Genesis is full of them: the account of Adam's line in chapter 5; the table of nations in chapter 10; the descendants of Jacob and Esau in chapters 35, 36; and so forth. The Book of Numbers carefully records the clans of Israel, while 1 Chronicles contains chapter after chapter listing the names of their descendants. These are just a few of the genealogies in the Old Testament, which seems to have a special fascination with the records of family history. Then, of course, there are the genealogies in the Gospels that culminate with the coming of Jesus Christ.

### More Than a List of Names

At first glance the biblical genealogies may not seem all that important. Consider the family record of Moses and Aaron:

> These are the heads of their fathers' houses: the sons of Reuben, the firstborn of Israel: Hanoch, Pallu, Hezron, and Carmi; these are the clans of Reuben. The sons of Simeon: Jemuel, Jamin, Ohad, Jachin, Zohar, and Shaul, the son of a Canaanite woman; these are the clans of Simeon. These are the names of the sons of Levi according to their generations: Gershon, Kohath, and Merari, the years of the life of Levi being 137 years. The sons of Gershon: Libni and Shimei, by their clans. The sons of Kohath: Amram, Izhar, Hebron, and Uzziel, the years of the life of Kohath being 133 years. The sons of Merari: Mahli and Mushi. These are the clans of the Levites according to their generations. Amram took as his wife Jochebed his father's sister, and she bore him Aaron and Moses, the years of the life of Amram being 137 years. The sons of Izhar: Korah, Nepheg, and Zichri. The sons of Uzziel: Mishael, Elzaphan, and Sithri. Aaron took as his wife Elisheba, the daughter of Amminadab and the sister of Nahshon, and she bore him

> Nadab, Abihu, Eleazar, and Ithamar. The sons of Korah: Assir, Elkanah, and Abiasaph; these are the clans of the Korahites. Eleazar, Aaron's son, took as his wife one of the daughters of Putiel, and she bore him Phinehas. These are the heads of the fathers' houses of the Levites by their clans. (6:14–25)

Such a passage does not make for very interesting reading. To us it is little more than a list of unfamiliar, strange-sounding names. Thus it is tempting to skim through these verses, or even to skip them altogether. Yet like everything else in the Bible, genealogies are "breathed out by God and profitable for teaching, for reproof, for correction, and for training in righteousness, that the man of God may be complete, equipped for every good work" (2 Timothy 3:16, 17). If the Biblical genealogies are supposed to be useful, what is the best way for us to make use of them?

From the beginning our method for studying Exodus has been Biblical (concentrating on what the Bible actually says), historical (setting the Bible in the context of ancient history), theological (learning about the character of God), Christological (relating the exodus to the person and work of Christ), and practical (applying the truth of Scripture to the Christian life). This is the right approach to take with the Biblical genealogies. Historically they are important because they help confirm the accuracy of the Biblical record. I once heard the story of a native tribe that was converted by a genealogy. A Western missionary had worked with them for many years and had often shared the good news about Jesus Christ, but with little result. Finally, he translated one of the Biblical genealogies that went all the way back to Adam. "Now we know that what you say is true," the natives said. "We recite the names of our ancestors, but we had forgotten the beginning. Now we know that your Bible is true." The natives repented of their sins and received Jesus Christ as the Son of David, the son of Adam, and the Son of God. The genealogy in Exodus 6 may not convert anyone, but it is historically significant because the ages given for Levi and his sons help confirm that Israel was in Egypt for more than four hundred years.[1]

Not only are the Biblical genealogies historically important, but they are also theologically instructive. Given careful study, they reveal significant insights about the character of God and the way of salvation. Many of them are Christ centered. They hold the promise of a Savior to come, and thus they help prove that Jesus of Nazareth is the Christ of God. They are also practical. The more we learn about the individuals mentioned, the more we learn about what it means to belong to the people of God.

## No "Little People"

One way to see the importance of a genealogy like the one we find in Exodus 6 is to answer this question: What if my name were Hezron? Or Uzziel? Or

Elisheba? To us it may not make much difference that "the sons of Merari: [were] Mahli and Mushi" (6:19), but to them it made all the difference in the world! It meant that they were included in the people of God, that God actually knew who they were. The Biblical genealogies show the importance of named individuality. God not only has a plan for the salvation of a people, but he has an intimate, personal relationship with every individual in his family. As far as God is concerned, there are no "little people" (Francis Schaeffer).

With a few notable exceptions, the Israelites were ordinary men and women. This is evident from their names, many of which tell us something about their personal traits. Pallu's parents must have been demanding, for his name means "extraordinary." Korah means "baldy," and we can surmise that he was hairless when he came out of his mother's womb. Nepheg means "clumsy," which is not very flattering, but then it is simply a fact that some people are less well coordinated than others. The Israelites were ordinary people. Even if we didn't know anything else about them, we would know that they were very much like us. They were men and women created in the image of God. They were fallen sinners in desperate need of God's grace. And like us, they were included in God's saving plan. Whether we know who they are is not nearly as important as whether God knows who they are. Carmi, Jachin, Zichri, Putiel, and all the rest of them prove the Biblical promise that "the Lord knows those who are his" (2 Timothy 2:19).

If anything distinguished these men and women, it was the way they looked to God for grace. This, too, is evident from the meanings of their names. Shaul must have been the answer to his parents' prayers because they named him "Prayer's Answer." Similarly, Eleazar means "God Has Aided," Elzaphan means "God Has Treasured," and Elkanah means "God Has Created." Apparently Jochebed's parents knew the chief end of man, for they named their daughter "God's glory." These Israelites received their children as gifts from God and gave them names that would serve as permanent reminders of his goodness and grace.

It is significant that this genealogy is organized by families. It begins by saying, "These are the heads of their fathers' houses" (6:14a). What the Bible means by "houses" is all the relatives gathered into one social group, united by the ties of common blood. In the Bible a family is an extended group of relatives living under the spiritual authority of one father. The important Biblical principle here is that ordinarily God extends his grace through the family. This does not mean that one has to be raised in a Christian family to be saved. One of the ways God often glorifies himself is by rescuing a sinner from spiritual ignorance and beginning a new work of grace that ultimately changes a family's destiny. Nor does it mean that children are saved by the faith of their parents. God calls every individual to serve him, and each child must make a personal decision to follow Jesus Christ.

What it does mean is that God holds fathers responsible for the spiritual well-being of their families. Reuben, Simeon, Levi, and the others were the heads of their households. It was their God-given responsibility to love their families by encouraging their wives in godliness and teaching their children to glorify God. God's best plan for the family is to show his love through the overflow of a father's heart. As Joshua would say to the Israelites many years later, "Choose this day whom you will serve. . . . But as for me and my house, we will serve the LORD" (Joshua 24:15). Joshua understood what it means to be the head of a family. Every good father makes a personal commitment to help his household serve the Lord.

## Aaron's Family Tree

The genealogy in Exodus 6 focuses on one family in particular: the family of Moses and Aaron. This fact helps answer a question that has puzzled many scholars—namely, what is this genealogy doing *here*?

A modern historian probably would have included these family records back in Exodus 2, in connection with Moses' birth. Here the genealogy seems to disrupt the flow of the narrative, and many Bible scholars consider it an interruption. However, ancient readers understood the importance of family history, and it is doubtful whether they would have seen it as an interruption at all. When we set aside our modern literary prejudices and study the passage in its context, what at first seems like a digression turns out to be carefully placed for a significant purpose.

The first thing to notice is how selective this genealogy is. Exodus began with a complete list of Jacob's sons, the tribes of Israel (1:1–5; cf. Numbers 26). Here in chapter 6 only three of the founding fathers are mentioned—Reuben, Simeon, and Levi—and of these three, Levi gets almost all the attention. Reuben and Simeon are given one verse each (6:14, 15), but there are ten verses for the sons and grandsons of Levi (6:16–25). So it appears that Reuben and Simeon are only mentioned to indicate Levi's place in the family as Jacob's third-eldest son.

Levi had three sons: Gershon, Kohath, and Merari. The genealogy lists each of these men, together with the names of their sons (6:16–19). However, special attention is given to the line of Kohath. Not only does the genealogy mention his sons—Amram, Izhar, Hebron, and Uzziel—but it proceeds to list *their* sons as well (6:20–22). In other words, out of all the great-grandsons of Levi, the genealogy is only interested in the grandsons of Kohath. The reason for this is fairly obvious: this genealogy is mainly about Aaron, who stands at its center (6:20). The first half of the genealogy traces Aaron's ancestry from Levi through Kohath to Amram. The second half lists Aaron's sons—Nadab and Abihu, Eleazar and Ithamar—ending with the birth of his grandson Phinehas (6:23, 25).

Notice that both of the women who are mentioned by name—Jochebed and Elisheba—were closely related to Aaron. Jochebed was Aaron's mother, and Elisheba was Aaron's wife. Also notice how little is said about Moses. His wife and children are not mentioned at all. This is because Moses has already been introduced. We already know about his birth, upbringing, training, and call to ministry. The only new information given here is the identity of his parents: "Amram took as his wife Jochebed his father's sister,[2] and she bore him Aaron and Moses" (6:20). But even this mainly serves to identify Aaron as Moses' brother. To summarize, what at first seems like a random list of names turns out to be a carefully organized presentation of the line of Aaron.

Aaron's importance is confirmed by the introduction and conclusion that enclose the genealogy. The introduction reads, "But the LORD spoke to Moses and Aaron and gave them a charge about the people of Israel and about Pharaoh king of Egypt: to bring the people of Israel out of the land of Egypt" (6:13). The conclusion is similar: "These are the Aaron and Moses to whom the LORD said: 'Bring out the people of Israel from the land of Egypt by their hosts.' It was they who spoke to Pharaoh king of Egypt about bringing out the people of Israel from Egypt, this Moses and this Aaron" (6:26, 27).

These skillful transitions make the genealogy part of Israel's story, reminding us that God's overarching plan was to rescue the Israelites from their bondage to Pharaoh. They also make it clear that the list of names that come in between is Moses' and Aaron's family tree. The genealogy thus establishes their pedigree as full-blooded Hebrews. The same Moses and Aaron who led Israel out of Egypt were true sons of Israel. But the genealogy is especially interested in the status of Aaron. Its purpose is to show that he is a legitimate leader in his own right, and thus a worthy partner for Moses. Up until now the focus has been on Moses, who as everyone knew was called to be Israel's prophet. But as the story resumes in Exodus 7, we are prepared for his older brother Aaron to take an increasingly prominent role.

## The Faithfulness of the Levites

Before seeing how God used Aaron to defeat the gods of Egypt—as we will do in the following chapter—it is worth pausing to ask what happened to the other members of his family. Earlier we noted that the Biblical genealogies are always practical. One of the most practical ways to study them is to see what kinds of examples these people set. As we leaf through the pages of Aaron's family album, we meet both saints and sinners. And like everything else in the Bible, their examples teach us, rebuke us, correct us, and train us in righteousness.

Gershon, Kohath, and Merari (see 6:16) teach us the meaning of faithful service to God. After the Israelites came out of Egypt, God gave detailed instructions for building a large, portable tent for worship. He put the tribe of Levi in charge of this tabernacle, as it was called. Out of all the tribes of Israel, the Levites were set apart for God's holy service. Since Gershon, Kohath, and Merari were sons of Levi, each of them had specific duties in the tabernacle, duties that were later shared by all their descendants.

The Levitical duties were all of a practical nature (see 1 Chronicles 9:14–32; 23:28–32). The Gershonites were in charge of the curtains. As the book of Numbers explains, "The guard duty of the sons of Gershon in the tent of meeting involved the tabernacle, the tent with its covering, the screen for the entrance of the tent of meeting, the hangings of the court, the screen for the door of the court that is around the tabernacle and the altar, and its cords—all the service connected with these" (Numbers 3:25, 26). The Kohathites were the interior designers. God put them in charge of the furnishings and utensils inside the tabernacle: "Their guard duty involved the ark, the table, the lampstand, the altars, the vessels of the sanctuary with which the priests minister, and the screen; all the service connected with these" (Numbers 3:31). The sons of Merari were the structural engineers; they did the heavy lifting: "The appointed guard duty of the sons of Merari involved the frames of the tabernacle, the bars, the pillars, the bases, and all their accessories; all the service connected with these; also the pillars around the court, with their bases and pegs and cords" (Numbers 3:36, 37). Each family had its own clearly-defined duties.

These tasks may sound mundane, but they were all essential to the worship of God, and thus the Levites held a position of great honor in Israel. It was one of the Kohathites who wrote,

> For a day in your courts is better
> than a thousand elsewhere.
> I would rather be a doorkeeper in the house of my God
> than dwell in the tents of wickedness. (Psalm 84:10)

Aaron's family treasured its rich legacy of glorifying God through practical service.

Today the Gershonites, Kohathites, and Merarites would serve as ushers and sextons. They would work on the support staff or serve as members of the building committee. On Saturday they would show up for the church work day, and on Sunday they would pass out the bulletins and prepare the elements for the Lord's Supper. The church's highest calling is to worship God, and the faithful servants who perform the practical tasks that enable the church to fulfill this high calling give great glory to God.

Many years later, when the Israelites folded up their tabernacle and began to worship at the temple, the Gershonites, Kohathites, and Merarites were still serving the Lord. They never stopped serving him in practical ways. There were Levites at the temple worshiping God and helping others to worship all day and all night (see 1 Chronicles 9:33). Pilgrims who traveled to Jerusalem for the great festivals would sing,

Come, bless the LORD, all you servants of the LORD,
who stand by night in the house of the LORD!
Lift up your hands to the holy place
and bless the LORD! (Psalm 134:1, 2)

The example of the Levites trains us to be faithful in our service and constant in our worship day and night. Charles Spurgeon wrote, "When night settles down on a church the Lord has his watchers and holy ones still guarding his truth, and these must not be discouraged, but must bless the Lord even when the darkest hours draw on."[3]

## The Zeal of Phinehas

It was during one of Israel's darkest hours that Phinehas took his stand. Phinehas is the last person mentioned in Aaron's genealogy (6:25). Apparently his mother Putiel was African, for Phinehas's name means "Ethiopian" or "black man."

The story of Phinehas and his righteous zeal is told in Numbers 25, which recounts a time when Moabite women were enticing Israelite men to commit sexual immorality and spiritual adultery. Not only did the Israelites of those days engage in extramarital intercourse, but they also worshiped the Moabite gods. The lawful punishment for idolatry was death, but Israel's judges could not bring themselves to execute capital justice. While they were still deciding what to do, a wicked man named Zimri brazenly brought his Midianite mistress (Cozbi) to the tabernacle, intending to have sex with her in God's very house. It was at this moment that Phinehas proved his worth: "When Phinehas the son of Eleazar, son of Aaron the priest, saw it, he rose and left the congregation and took a spear in his hand and went after the man of Israel into the chamber and pierced both of them, the man of Israel and the woman through her belly" (Numbers 25:7, 8a).

God was so pleased with what Phinehas had done that he removed his judgment against Israel. He said, "Phinehas the son of Eleazar, son of Aaron the priest, has turned back my wrath from the people of Israel, in that he was jealous with my jealousy among them, so that I did not consume the people of Israel in my jealousy. Therefore say, 'Behold, I give to him my covenant of peace, and it shall be to him and to his descendants after him the covenant of a perpetual priesthood, because he was jealous for his God and made atonement for the people of Israel'" (Numbers 25:11–13). By taking his stand against evil, Phinehas propitiated God's wrath. The Bible uses his zeal as an example of justifying faith, for in the Psalms we read that "Phinehas stood up and intervened, and the plague was stayed. And that was counted to him as righteousness from generation to generation forever" (Psalm 106:30, 31).

Phinehas went on to become a great leader in Israel. He served as a military commander during Israel's battle against the Midianites (Numbers 31:6). He remained faithful during all of Israel's wanderings in the wilderness, so that

God allowed him to enter the Promised Land (see Judges 20:28). Later, when civil war threatened to break out between the tribes of Israel, Phinehas helped keep the peace (see Joshua 22:32, 33). It was his descendants who became the high priests of Israel, which probably explains why Aaron's genealogy ends with him.

Phinehas was a great man, and what made him great was his zeal to serve God even when others were turning away. Something of his spirit is captured by a tablet in an old Yorkshire church, which contains the following inscription: "In the year 1652 when through England all things sacred were either profaned or neglected, this church was built by Sir Robert Shirley, whose special praise it is to have done the best of things in the worst of times and to have hoped them in the most calamitous."[4] Those words apply equally well to Phinehas, who did "the best of things in the worst of times."

These words also sound a rallying cry to everyone who lives for Christ. They challenge us to have the courage to defend God's honor when Biblical Christianity comes under attack, inside as well as outside the church. In these calamitous times, when sexual immorality has become commonplace and when Christians are divided against themselves, Christ calls us to be like Phinehas: zealous for God's glory and at the same time making peace within the church.

## Korah's Rebellion

Aaron had some relatives to be proud of. However, the Biblical genealogies are uncensored, and although most of his family members were faithful to God, not all of them were. There were a few skeletons in the family closet, as there are in most families.

Consider the tragic tale of Aaron's cousin Korah. In Numbers we read that "Korah the son of Izhar, son of Kohath, son of Levi . . . rose up before Moses" (Numbers 16:1a, 2a). Korah incited several hundred others to join him in challenging his cousins' spiritual authority: "They assembled themselves together against Moses and against Aaron and said to them, 'You have gone too far! For all in the congregation are holy, every one of them, and the LORD is among them. Why then do you exalt yourselves above the assembly of the LORD?'" (Numbers 16:3).

Korah was not content with his God-given place of ministry. He was ambitious. He wanted more recognition, and he thought that Moses was standing in his way. Yet by rebelling against Moses, Korah actually was rebelling against God, who had given Moses his authority in the first place. That is why Korah and his followers were destroyed. Moses pronounced God's judgment against them, and as soon as he was finished talking, "the ground under them split apart. And the earth opened its mouth and swallowed them up, with their households and all the people who belonged to Korah and all their goods. So they and all that belonged to them went down alive into Sheol, and the earth closed over them, and they perished from the midst of the assembly" (Numbers 16:31–33). Thus God showed his contempt for Korah's rebellion.

This tragedy is recorded in Scripture to rebuke us and correct us. In his first letter to the Corinthians, Paul recounts the calamities that the Israelites brought on themselves because of their sin. He does this to warn Christians not to come under judgment for committing the very same sins. Paul writes, "These things took place as examples for us, that we might not desire evil as they did . . . [do not] grumble, as some of them did and were destroyed by the Destroyer" (1 Corinthians 10:6, 10).

It is very dangerous to seek a higher position in the church than God has given us. Francis Schaeffer writes:

> Jesus commands Christians to seek consciously the lowest room. All of us—pastors, teachers, professional religious workers and nonprofessionals included—are tempted to say, "I will take the larger place because it will give me more influence for Jesus Christ." Both individual Christians and Christian organizations fall prey to the temptation of rationalizing this way as we build bigger and bigger empires. But according to the Scripture this is backwards: we should consciously take the lowest place unless the Lord Himself extrudes us into a greater one.
>
> The word *extrude* is important here. To be extruded is to be forced out under pressure into a desired shape. Picture a huge press jamming soft metal at high pressure through a die, so that the metal comes out in a certain shape. This is the way of the Christian: he should choose the lesser place until God extrudes him into a position of more responsibility and authority.[5]

As dangerous as it is to seek a higher position, it is even more dangerous to resent the spiritual leaders whom God has placed in authority over us. Christians are often tempted to think they deserve greater recognition. When they do not get what they think they deserve, they resent those who are in spiritual authority and start to think that they know better than their pastors and elders. Sometimes they do, for every spiritual leader is a fallen, fallible sinner. Nevertheless, God has given pastors, elders, and deacons their spiritual authority in the church. So be careful! Be content to receive whatever place of service God has given you until such time as God calls you—through the church—to a higher position.

## Nadab and Abihu's Folly

There is more than one cautionary tale in Aaron's genealogy. Two of the other black sheep in the family were Aaron's eldest sons, Nadab and Abihu (6:23). Like their father, these infamous men served in the tabernacle. One day they decided to try an experiment in creative worship. The Biblical principle for worship—sometimes called "the regulative principle"—is that God alone has the right to decide how he wants to be worshiped. We are not free to invent our own forms of worship, but only to worship in the way that he has commanded. In order to test this principle, "Now Nadab and Abihu, the sons of Aaron, each took his censer and put fire in it and laid incense on it and offered unauthorized fire before the LORD, which he had not commanded them" (Leviticus 10:1). Their experiment was not a success. "And fire came out from before the LORD and consumed them, and they died before the LORD" (Leviticus 10:2). Their cousins Mishael and Elzaphan had to drag them out of the tabernacle and carry them outside the camp.

The deaths of Nadab and Abihu corrects any temptation to offer un-Biblical worship. Christians must be careful to offer only such prayers and praises as God has ordained in his holy Word. Certainly this was the conclusion that Moses reached when he saw what happened to his nephews. He said to Aaron, "This is what the LORD has said: 'Among those who are near me I will be sanctified, and before all the people I will be glorified'" (Leviticus 10:3).

Worshiping God is serious business. The holy God demands to be worshiped in a holy way, and we must approach him with reverence and awe.

The deaths of Nadab and Abihu also rebukes those who count on their ministry to save them. Nadab and Abihu had a sacred office. In addition to serving in the tabernacle with the other Levites, it was their special privilege to accompany the seventy elders when they ascended Mount Sinai and saw the living God (24:1–9). However, despite their holy calling, they were not holy men, and thus they came to an unholy end. The sad truth is that some of the men and women who are ordained to the gospel ministry will never wear a crown of glory. Jesus said, "On that day many will say to me, 'Lord, Lord, did we not prophesy in your name, and cast out demons in your name, and do many mighty works in your name?' And then will I declare to them, 'I never knew you; depart from me, you workers of lawlessness'" (Matthew 7:22, 23). The only credential for gaining entrance to Heaven is faith in Jesus Christ.

Finally, this tragedy is a warning not to count on family connections for salvation. Nadab and Abihu came from the holiest tribe in Israel, and yet they perished in the flames of God's judgment. We cannot travel to Heaven on our parents' passport. If we want to escape the fires of Hell, we must repent of our sins and ask Jesus Christ to be our Savior.

## Our Great High Priest

The genealogy in Exodus 6 is full of practical instruction for Christian work and worship. The lives of the men and women in Aaron's family teach us to remain faithful in our worship day and night and to stand up for what is right even when everything seems to be going wrong. At the same time, the tragic deaths in the family warn us not to seek our own way in the work or worship of the church.

Imagine if your own name appeared in the Biblical genealogies. What would they say about you? Would they be able to say that you were faithful in your ministry, no matter how large or small it may have been? Would they be able to say that even when everyone else got caught up in sexual immorality and spiritual adultery, you were zealous for God's glory? Or would they say that you offered strange worship and rebelled against the church's spiritual authority?

These questions are interesting to think about, but the question that really matters is this: *What does God say about you?* Is your name written in his family record, the Book of Life? Do you belong to him by faith in Jesus Christ? For no matter how faithful we are, we can only be saved by the grace that God has shown through the death and resurrection of Jesus Christ.

There is a hint of this saving grace in Aaron's genealogy. Aaron married Elisheba, who was the daughter of Amminadab and the sister of Nahshon (6:23). Those names are significant because Amminadab and Nahshon were both ancestors of King David, and thus they are both included in the genealogy of Jesus Christ, the great High Priest (Matthew 1:4). Even in the days of Moses and Aaron, God was working out his plan to send a Savior to deliver his people from their sins.

# 16

# The Prophet's Prophet

## EXODUS 6:28—7:7

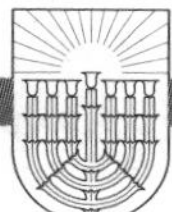

TO REVIEW, God had told Moses to go and tell old Pharaoh, "Let my people go!" But Moses didn't want to go because he didn't think Pharaoh would listen. The Lord God of Israel had commanded Moses and his brother Aaron to lead the Israelites out of Egypt, but in order to establish Aaron's credentials, the Bible took time to present his complete family history, from Levi to Phinehas (6:14–25). Since this genealogy was something of a digression, the story now resumes with a brief recap: "On the day when the LORD spoke to Moses in the land of Egypt . . ." (6:28) and so on.

### Moses' Faltering Lips

This portion of Exodus can be explained by using three body parts, starting with Moses and his faltering lips: "On the day when the LORD spoke to Moses in the land of Egypt, the LORD said to Moses, 'I am the LORD; tell Pharaoh king of Egypt all that I say to you.' But Moses said to the LORD, 'Behold, I am of uncircumcised lips. How will Pharaoh listen to me?'" (6:28–30).

For a man who complained that he couldn't speak, Moses sure had a lot to say! We have heard him raise this same objection before. He raised it back at the burning bush, when God first called him to be a prophet: "Moses said to the LORD, 'Oh, my Lord, I am not eloquent . . . I am slow of speech and of tongue'" (4:10). He said virtually the same thing at the beginning of chapter 6: "Behold, the people of Israel have not listened to me. How then shall Pharaoh listen to me, for I am of uncircumcised lips?" (6:12). Now he says it again, trying to convince God that he was the wrong man for the job. Pharaoh would never listen to him because he was not a gifted speaker.

Perhaps this was a summary of what Moses said earlier rather than a separate conversation. But it seems more likely that Moses was dragging up the same old excuses again. It is easy to grow impatient with Moses for this, but what he did is not uncommon. People often come up with excuses for not doing what God tells them to do. Like Moses, we tend to use the same objections over and over. It takes some Christians *years* to get past their tired old excuses for not giving, not going, not witnessing, or not serving. We need to discover what Moses discovered: God's call is always accompanied by God's gift.

God should not have had to put up with another speech from Moses about his faltering lips. For one thing, God made those lips in the first place, and he had already promised to teach his prophet whatever he needed to say and how to say it (4:11, 12). For another thing, God had guaranteed Moses that he would get help from his brother Aaron, who was a straight-A student in speech and thus had the rhetorical gifts to compensate for his brother's speech disability (see 4:14–16).

Furthermore, God was not asking Moses if he wanted to volunteer—he was ordering him to go. God said, "I am the Lord; tell Pharaoh king of Egypt all that I say to you" (6:29). Like all of God's commands, this imperative was based on the absolute lordship of God's sovereignty. God had the right to tell Moses what to do because he is Lord of Heaven and earth. His commands are not invitations to dialogue but orders to obey. Once God told him what to do, Moses simply needed to do as he was told, without arguing about whether it could be done.

## "God" to Pharaoh

At this point God had every right to say, "Listen, Moses, I don't need to give you a reason. I've told you what to do—now go and do it!" That is not what God said, however. He is a loving and gracious God who patiently teaches his servants how to serve. In this case he not only listened to Moses but also answered his question. Why would Pharaoh listen to a man with faltering lips? "And the Lord said to Moses, 'See, I have made you like God to Pharaoh, and your brother Aaron shall be your prophet. You shall speak all that I command you, and your brother Aaron shall tell Pharaoh to let the people of Israel go out of his land'" (7:1, 2).

God began by giving his prophet divine authority. Moses would be like God to Pharaoh. In fact, the Bible is even more emphatic. What the Hebrew literally says is not "I have made you *like* God to Pharaoh," but "I have made you *God* to Pharaoh." Moses was God's representative, his chosen prophet. So when he stood before Pharaoh's throne, he spoke with real divine authority. God himself was speaking and acting through Moses.

Here it is important to bear in mind that Pharaoh considered himself divine. One of the basic religious principles in ancient Egypt was that the Pharaohs were incarnations of the gods. So by making Moses God to Pharaoh, God was putting Pharaoh in his place (especially since Moses had been raised in Pharaoh's household). In his commentary on these verses, Peter Enns explains:

> In Egyptian royal ideology, the pharaoh was considered to be a divine being. So by calling Moses God, Yahweh is beating Pharaoh at his own game. It is not the king of Egypt who is god; rather, it is this shepherd and leader of slaves who is God. And this Moses-God defeats Pharaoh in a manner that leaves no doubt as to the true nature and source of his power: He controls the elements, bugs, livestock, fire from heaven, and the water of the sea; he even has authority over life and death. Moses is not simply *like* God to Pharaoh. He truly *is* God *to Pharaoh* in that God is acting through Moses.[1]

This does not mean, of course, that Moses was divine. There is only one God, and Moses was simply his prophet, a man of flesh and blood. Yet Moses did *represent* God. Here we encounter a great mystery: God has chosen human instruments to carry out his divine work. This was God's plan for the human race from the very beginning, when Adam and Eve were commissioned to rule over the world that God had made. Since our first parents were created in God's image, his deity was expressed in their humanity, and thus they were capable of representing God to the world. Moses had the same responsibility: He was not God, but he was "God" to Pharaoh.

This is one of the many ways that Moses prepared the way for the coming of Jesus Christ, who truly is divine. God's plan for using a human instrument to carry out his divine work was perfected in Jesus Christ, who is both God and man. Jesus is "the image of the invisible God" (Colossians 1:15), "the exact imprint of his nature" (Hebrews 1:3). God accomplished his great work of redemption through the man Jesus Christ, who died on the cross and was raised from the dead in a real body. But because of his divine nature, Jesus did these things not simply as a man but also as our God. By being God to Pharaoh, Moses points us to Jesus Christ, who is God to us because he is, in fact, God.

One way that Pharaoh would recognize Moses' divine authority was that he had his own prophet: "And the LORD said to Moses, 'See, I have made you like God to Pharaoh, and your brother Aaron shall be your prophet'" (7:1). When Moses told Pharaoh to let God's people go, Aaron would do the talking. He was the prophet's prophet. A prophet is someone who speaks on someone else's behalf, and Aaron spoke for Moses, just as Moses spoke for God. Earlier God had made Aaron a prophet to the Israelites. He said to Moses, "You shall speak to him [Aaron] and put the words in his mouth, and I will be with your mouth and with his mouth and will teach you both what to do. He shall speak for you to the people, and he shall be your mouth, and you shall be as God to him" (4:15, 16). Now, in addition to speaking to the Israelites, Aaron would speak to Pharaoh, who immediately would have understood what this meant. Pharaoh's own custom was to have spokesmen issue all of his commands. This preserved a sense of distance between himself and his people and thus reminded them of his supposedly divine status. So when Moses spoke to him through Aaron, he would have recognized that Moses was claiming divine authority.

We have already mentioned how mysterious it is that God is able to accomplish his divine work through mere human beings. Here is another aspect of that mystery: God communicates his divine message through human messengers. Aaron was the mouthpiece of Moses, who was the mouthpiece of God. When God had something to say to Pharaoh, he did not shout from Heaven but spoke through one of his servants on earth. This is the way God usually communicates. In the Old Testament he spoke through his servants, the prophets. Then when the time was right he sent the greatest prophet of all, Jesus Christ, who like Moses was "a prophet mighty in deed and word before God and all the people" (Luke 24:19). When Jesus ascended to Heaven, he passed this prophetic ministry on to his apostles, who were commissioned to proclaim his gospel to the nations (Matthew 28:18–20). The apostles said, "Therefore, we are ambassadors for Christ, God making his appeal through us" (2 Corinthians 5:20a).

Today God's message is communicated through the church. The words of the prophets, the apostles, and Christ himself are recorded in the pages of Scripture, but it is our responsibility to announce them to the world. This is what a preacher does. When he teaches the Bible faithfully, his voice is the voice of God. But Moses himself longed for the day when all God's people would be prophets (Numbers 11:29), and his longing is satisfied in the church of Jesus Christ. When God poured out his Holy Spirit on the early church, this fulfilled God's promise that "even on my male servants and female servants in those days I will pour out my Spirit, and they shall prophesy" (Acts 2:18; cf. Joel 2:28, 29). Theologians call this "the prophethood of all believers." It does not mean that every Christian is called to be a preacher. Still less does it mean that women should be ordained as pastors. What it does mean is that every believer is one of God's messengers. Every Christian man, woman, and child is called to share the gospel and to speak the truth of Scripture. Marcus Brownson, who served as pastor of Philadelphia's Tenth Presbyterian Church from 1897–1924, wrote:

> Our Lord has no eyes, no feet, no hands to use now but those of His people in His Church which is His body. Each member has a function and an obligation. . . . As it was in the Church of the early days of Christianity, when men, women and even children went everywhere talking of the Saviour and of redeeming love, so should it be today. Evangelism is the office of all believers. Every believer in Christ holds an office in the Church, the office of witnessing for Christ, and it is the highest, most honorable, most useful office in the world, "the office of all believers."[2]

This is a weighty responsibility. As Christians we carry Christ into the world. We may be the only genuine Christians that some of our friends and family members know. Their whole understanding of Christianity depends on our testimony. Therefore, we are Christ to them in the same way that Moses was God to Pharaoh.

In this prophetic ministry we are called to be faithful, as Moses and Aaron were. This section of Exodus closes with the statement that "Moses and Aaron did so; they did *just* [the Hebrew is emphatic] as the LORD commanded them. Now Moses was eighty years old, and Aaron eighty-three years old, when they spoke to Pharaoh" (7:6, 7). Up until now Moses had his doubts about God's saving plan, and about his own part in that plan. But from this moment until the very moment when the last Israelite set foot on the far side of the Red Sea, Moses was faithful in his calling. He went and told Pharaoh whatever God wanted him to say, no matter what the consequences, which is exactly what God calls every Christian to do in witnessing for Jesus Christ.

This example is a special encouragement to older Christians because Moses was a senior citizen. The Bible sometimes records a man's age when he is about to accomplish something great for God. Here we are told that Moses was eighty—well past the age that most Americans retire. In fact, Moses himself thought that eighty years was about the longest that a man could expect to live (see Psalm 90:10). The closer we get to eighty, the more tempting it is to think that our best years are behind us, that we have already accomplished our life's work. However, when Moses turned eighty, his work was just beginning! He had forty more years of service ahead of him, years in which he proved faithful to the very end. Dwight L. Moody observed that "Moses spent forty years in Pharaoh's court thinking he was somebody, forty years in the desert learning that he was nobody, and forty years showing what God can do with a somebody who found out he was a nobody."[3]

No matter how young or old we are, we should ask God how he wants us to serve him. As we grow older, God will open up new opportunities to glorify him through prayer, through sharing Christ with family members, or through offering spiritual wisdom to younger Christians. If we are afraid that we have nothing left to offer, we only need to ask God to show what he can do with somebody who is a nobody.

## Pharaoh's Hard Heart

So far we have been saying that there was no need for Moses to worry about his faltering lips. He was God to Pharaoh, so no matter how much he stammered and stuttered, he spoke with God's own authority through his prophet Aaron. But Pharaoh wasn't going to listen to him anyway! This brings us to the second body part in these verses: Pharaoh's hard heart. The Lord said to Moses, "But I will harden Pharaoh's heart, and though I multiply my signs and wonders in the land of Egypt, Pharaoh will not listen to you" (7:3, 4a).

No matter what Moses said, and no matter how many miracles he performed, Pharaoh wouldn't listen. The king was the very picture of an unbeliever—a man who was determined not to give in to God. This is exactly what Moses feared—that Pharaoh wouldn't listen. And with good reason! The last time he went to the palace on God's behalf, Pharaoh said he didn't even know who God was (5:2), and then he proceeded to double Israel's workload. No wonder Moses didn't want to speak with Pharaoh again!

What the prophet failed to understand was that Pharaoh's stubborn resistance was part of God's sovereign plan. Moses said, "It will never work, Lord. Pharaoh will never listen." God answered, "Right! That's exactly what I have in mind. I will harden his heart so that he will not listen to you." God used Pharaoh's rebellion to prove that God alone had the power to rescue his people.

The reason Moses had the wrong expectation was because he misunderstood his calling as a prophet. Moses was a pragmatist. He had a performance-based approach to prophetic ministry. He assumed that it was up to the prophet to get results. If people listened to him, then he was doing his job; if not, he should find some other line of work. This explains why Moses was always worrying about whether people would listen to him. "But behold, they will not believe me or listen to my voice . . ." he would say (4:1). Or, "How then shall Pharaoh listen to me?" (6:12, 30).

The problem with this approach to ministry is that spiritual results are always beyond human control. No matter how eloquent he is, and no matter how persuasive, there is nothing a prophet can do to make people believe God's Word. It takes faith for someone to believe, and faith is a gift of God's grace. The only thing that matters to God, therefore, is whether or not the prophet is faithful. The prophet is not responsible for the way the people respond to his message, but only for getting the message right. This is why he does not have the liberty to add anything to God's message or to leave anything out. As God said to Moses, "You shall speak all that I command you" (7:2). And as long as the prophet communicates God's message accurately, he is faithful in his calling, whatever the outcome.

This has obvious implications for preaching. The only good preacher is a faithful preacher. When Martin Luther studied Exodus, he wondered why God commanded Moses to do something that was doomed to fail. He wrote:

> The question is why God bids Moses preach although He Himself says: Pharaoh will not listen to you. Is it not foolish for someone to say to another: Friend, preach to Pharaoh, but be advised that he will not listen to you; for I intend to harden him? I would refuse such an assignment from anyone and would say: Preach yourself. But the answer is: We are bidden to preach, but we are not bidden to justify people and make them pious. This thought should comfort all preachers and Christians, and everybody should pursue his calling and faithfully perform its duties. Only the Word of God is entrusted to Moses, not the responsibility of making Pharaoh soft or hard by preaching. The Word is entrusted to him; this is God's will, and

> this Word he is to proclaim even though no one may want to listen to him. This is done for his consolation that he may not be frightened if nobody wants to follow and obey him. If I could be moved by the fact that my word and sermon are despised, I suppose I would stop preaching. But (says God) go on, Moses, preach![4]

This principle liberates us from a worldly standard of success, in which ministry is always measured in terms that people can quantify: How much? How many? How big? The primary thing that God demands from a minister is faithfulness to his gospel. God does not rank preachers by the number of their converts or the size of their churches. Rather, he judges them according to the accuracy of their Biblical exposition.

In the book *Liberating Ministry from the Success Syndrome*, Kent Hughes remembers a dark night of the soul when he almost left the pastoral ministry. With every expectation of success, having followed the advice of all the experts and accompanied by a strong nucleus of devoted Christians, he had planted a new church. But the church was failing. As their numbers started to dwindle, Hughes became despondent. He writes, "The focus of my resentment was God himself, the one who had called me to this. I had given *everything*—all my time, all my education, years of ministry and true Christian devotion (he knew!)—and now I was failing."

That pastor's wife tried to offer him some encouragement, pointing out that Noah had preached for 120 years without a single convert. "Yes," Hughes replied, "but there wasn't another Noah across town with people flowing into *his* ark!" He proceeded to express his true feelings of discouragement and despair, saying:

> Most people I know in the ministry are unhappy. They are failures in their own eyes. Mine as well. Why should I expect God to bless me when it appears he hasn't blessed them? . . . In cold statistics my chances of being a failure are overwhelming. Most pastors do little more than survive in the ministry in piddly little churches. . . . The ministry is asking too much of me. How can I go on giving all that I have without seeing results, especially when others are? . . . Those who really make it in the ministry are those with exceptional gifts. If I had a great personality or natural charisma, if I had celebrity status, a deep resonant voice, a merciless executive ability, a domineering personality that doesn't mind sacrificing people for success, I could make it to the top. Where is God in all of this? Just look at the great preachers today. Their success seems to have little to do with God's Spirit; they're just superior people! God has called me to do something he hasn't given me the gifts to accomplish. Therefore, God is not good.[5]

That is exactly what Moses thought, that God had called him to do something he wasn't qualified to do. Eventually Hughes came to understand that his real problem was his definition of success. As he and his wife studied the Scriptures, they discovered that God's servants are not called to be successful but to be faithful. In the words of the Apostle Paul, "This is how one should regard us, as servants of Christ and stewards of the mysteries of God. Moreover, it is required of stewards that they be found faithful" (1 Corinthians 4:1, 2).

What God said to Moses also gives us a whole new perspective on evangelism. Christians usually assume that the message of salvation is preached in order to turn people's hearts back to God. And so it is. One primary purpose of evangelism is the conversion of unbelievers to faith in Jesus Christ. But that is not evangelism's only purpose. One of the mysteries of God's sovereignty is that the gospel is also preached in order to confirm sinners in their unbelief. For example, when the prophet Isaiah was commissioned to announce the coming Messiah, God said to him,

> Make the heart of this people dull,
> and their ears heavy,
> and blind their eyes;
> lest they see with their eyes,
> and hear with their ears,
> and understand with their hearts,
> and turn and be healed. (Isaiah 6:10)

Jesus Christ repeated these words when his disciples asked him why his preaching was so hard for people to understand (Matthew 13:10–17). They assumed that Jesus was trying to convert everyone. If that had been his purpose, then we would virtually have to conclude that his preaching ministry was a failure, because at the time of his death Jesus had only a handful of followers. Most of the people who heard him preach rejected him.

However, the truth is that God's Word has a double effect. Some hearts are softened by it, while others are hardened. Some people believe the good news and are saved; others reject it and are lost forever. At the human level, the difference is a matter of personal choice, which is why the book of Exodus often states that Pharaoh hardened his own heart. But behind that choice is the sovereign will of God, who softens or hardens human hearts as he pleases. Before Pharaoh ever hardened his heart, God promised to harden it for him (4:21). Pharaoh is only one example of the universal principle that "[God] has mercy on whomever he wills, and he hardens whomever he wills" (Romans 9:18). God does this for his greater glory, for as he later said to Pharaoh, "For this very purpose I have raised you up, that I might show my power in you, and that my name might be proclaimed in all the earth" (Romans 9:17). One of the great mysteries of God's sovereignty is that the destiny of every human being rests on the eternal counsel of his will.

Not everyone believes in God's sovereignty. Pharaoh certainly didn't. He had too much invested in his own sovereignty. In his commentary on this passage, John Currid explains, "Ancient Egyptian texts teach that the heart is the essence of the person, the inner spiritual centre of the self. Pharaoh's heart was particularly important because the Egyptians believed it was the all-controlling factor in both history and society. It was further held that the hearts of the gods Ra and Horus were sovereign over everything. Because Pharaoh was the incarnation of those two gods, his heart was thought to be sovereign over creation."[6] Therefore, by hardening Pharaoh's heart, God was making a theological point. He was proving that he alone is sovereign over all things. Nothing is outside the purpose of his will, not even the heart of a king.

## God's Mighty Hand

Eventually God made a believer out of Pharaoh—not in the sense that the ruler repented of his oppression and embraced God with loving trust, but in the sense that he was forced to surrender to God's superior strength. This brings us to God's mighty hand (our third body part), which of course is only a manner of speaking because God does not have a body. The Lord said, "Then I will lay my hand on Egypt and bring my hosts, my people the children of Israel, out of the land of Egypt by great acts of judgment. The Egyptians shall know that I am the Lord, when I stretch out my hand against Egypt and bring out the people of Israel from among them" (7:4b, 5).

God intended to deal with Egypt in a completely different way than he dealt with Israel. The Israelites were God's own people. He had made a covenant to love them; so he was going to rescue them from Egypt. They would come out by "hosts." This military term means that rather than fleeing helter-skelter, the Israelites would march out of Egypt like an army arrayed for battle. But God's mighty hand of salvation was also a mighty hand of judgment, and at the same time that he saved the Israelites, he would punish the Egyptians. The word translated "judgment" here is actually the Hebrew word for "vindication" (*shaphat*), which suggests that the reason God had to judge Egypt was to protect his honor. Pharaoh was keeping God's people in bondage. He was even murdering their baby boys. So God vindicated his name by visiting Egypt with the plagues of his justice, especially the death of the firstborn.[7] In the exodus God used both sides of his hand. With his palm he gently led the Israelites out of bondage, while at the same time giving the back of his hand to the Egyptians.

God's salvation of Israel and his vindication against Egypt had the same purpose: to reveal his lordship. This was obviously God's purpose for saving Israel. Back at the beginning of chapter 6, he explained to Moses that he would deliver his people in order to prove that he is Lord. But that is also what he wanted to prove to the Egyptians: "Then I will lay my hand on Egypt . . . by great acts of judgment. The Egyptians shall know that I am the Lord" (7:4, 5). The plagues had an evangelistic purpose. As a result of these "great acts of judgment," some of the Egyptians would believe God's word (9:20). But even the ones who didn't—including Pharaoh—would be unable to deny God's power. There was a time when Pharaoh claimed that he had no idea who the Lord was at all (5:2). But the time would come when somewhere in his hard heart of hearts, he would know that the God of Israel is Lord of all. In short, the purpose of the exodus was the same purpose that God has for everything he does: to reveal his glory in both salvation and judgment.

God is doing the same thing through Jesus Christ: He is glorifying himself by demonstrating that Jesus is Lord. God does this in two ways. Some people receive Jesus as their Savior and Lord. They believe that he died on the cross for their sins, thereby rescuing them from the pains of Hell. They confess that God raised Jesus from the dead to make him the ruler of Heaven and earth, and they will live in his glorious presence forever and ever.

Others reject Jesus. They are not interested in the salvation he offers, and they are not willing to call him their Lord. But one day they will. Like the Egyptians, they will be judged for their sins, and then they will know that Jesus is Lord—not to their joy, but to their terror. The Bible promises that on the day of judgment "every knee [will] bow, in heaven and on earth and under the earth, and every tongue confess that Jesus Christ is Lord, to the glory of God the Father" (Philippians 2:10, 11). One way or another, whether you are a believer or an unbeliever, sooner or later you will be compelled to acknowledge that Jesus Christ is Lord and God. Why not make it sooner?

# 17

# The Staff That Swallowed the Snakes

## EXODUS 7:8–13

THE GREAT CONFRONTATION in Exodus was not simply a dispute between Moses and Pharaoh, or a conflict between Israel and Egypt, but a battle between God and Satan. In his exposition of the life of Moses, James Boice explained that this "battle pitted Jehovah, the true God, who moved Moses and Israel, against all the false gods of the Egyptian pantheon, backed by a host of fallen angels who had turned from God as a part of Lucifer's original rebellion."[1] Thus the exodus was another engagement in the invisible war that continually rages between Heaven and Hell.

In the first six chapters of Exodus, God positioned himself to strike his decisive blow against Satan's Pharaoh. First he allowed his people to be oppressed and enslaved. Then he raised up their deliverer, carefully sending Moses down the Nile in a basket, training him in Pharaoh's house, guiding him through the wilderness, and then meeting him at the burning bush. There God gave his prophet the signs and promises of salvation. Then he sent Moses to Pharaoh with this ultimatum: "Let my people go!" When Pharaoh refused, it was time for God to glorify himself by "execut[ing] judgments" not simply against Pharaoh, but "on all the gods of Egypt" (12:12; cf. Numbers 33:4).

God's judgment on Egypt and her gods came in the form of ten plagues: blood, frogs, gnats, flies, disease, boils, hail, locusts, darkness, and death. Although these calamities may have seemed like natural disasters, they were part of a supernatural struggle between God and Satan. God sent plagues against Egypt to free his people from the devil's power. Thus the prophet Moses would have agreed with the Apostle Paul that "we do not wrestle against flesh and blood, but against the rulers, against the authorities, against the cosmic powers over this present darkness, against the spiritual forces of evil in the heavenly places" (Ephesians 6:12).

## Prologue to the Plagues

The supernatural dimension of the struggle between Moses and Pharaoh becomes explicit in the story of the staff that swallowed the snakes. This brief episode serves as a preview of the plagues. It introduces nearly all the main themes of the next five chapters of Exodus: the obedience of Moses and Aaron, the counterfeit miracles of Satan and his servants, the superior power of God and his rod, and the perpetual hardening of Pharaoh's heart. Already in this prologue God announces his ultimate triumph. Just as Pharaoh's snakes are "swallowed" by Aaron's staff (7:12), so Pharaoh's army will be "swallowed" by the sea (15:12). The same word is used in both verses to establish the thematic connection.

God's warriors in this spiritual conflict were Moses and Aaron, the grandsons of Levi: "Then the LORD said to Moses and Aaron, 'When Pharaoh says to you, "Prove yourselves by working a miracle," then you shall say to Aaron, "Take your staff and cast it down before Pharaoh, that it may become a serpent"'" (7:8, 9). This was in keeping with God's plan, in which Moses was "God" to Pharaoh, and Aaron was his prophet. When Pharaoh demanded a sign, Moses would speak to Aaron, who would perform the sign that God first gave to Moses at the burning bush (4:2, 3). This is exactly what the brothers proceeded to do: "So Moses and Aaron went to Pharaoh and did just as the LORD commanded" (7:10a). This statement may seem rather matter-of-fact, but actually it represents a major spiritual victory. Prior to this, Moses had wanted to argue every time God told him what to do, but on this occasion he simply did as he was told. The prophet had finally reached the point of genuine submission to the will of God. This should be every Christian's goal: to be so obedient that doing God's will is our immediate and instinctive response.

As Moses and Aaron did what God commanded, they found that God equipped them to do it: "Aaron cast down his staff before Pharaoh and his servants, and it became a serpent" (7:10b). Moses had long agonized over his personal inadequacies for ministry. But as soon as he started to obey his calling, he discovered that God had given him everything he needed to fulfill it. God does the same thing for every one of his servants. As we answer God's call to ministry, he will provide all the gifts and resources that we need to serve him.

## The Sign of the Snake

There is some question as to whether Aaron's staff was the same staff that God had given to Moses back at the burning bush (4:17). Possibly Aaron had his own staff. Certainly God had the power to perform as many miracles with Aaron's staff as he could with the rod of Moses. However, it is also possible that Aaron used his brother's staff—the same staff that had already turned into a snake and that would later plague the Egyptians.

There is also some question as to what kind of snake it was. When Moses first threw his staff on the ground, it became a *nakash*, which means "serpent" (4:2, 3). However, when Aaron threw down his staff, it became a *tannin*, which is a more general term for any large reptile. Thus some scholars argue that Aaron's staff became a crocodile. Umberto Cassuto writes, "In place of the serpent (*nakash*), which is more suited to the desert, where the sign was given to Moses, we have here a *tannin*, that is, a crocodile, which is more in keeping with the Egyptian environment."[2] Indeed, some Egyptians worshiped the crocodile god Sobek as "the Ruler of the Nile."

It is true that the word *tannin* can be used to refer to crocodiles. It seems to be used that way in Ezekiel, where God says, "I am against you, Pharaoh king of Egypt, the great dragon [*tannin*] that lies in the midst of his streams, that says, 'My Nile is my own; I made it for myself'" (Ezekiel 29:3). However, the Bible also uses the term *tannin* to refer to large, venomous snakes. A good example is Deuteronomy 32:33, where "the cruel venom of asps [*tannin*]" is used as a synonym for "the poison of serpents" (cf. Psalm 91:13). Furthermore, the word *nakash* reappears in 7:15, where it refers to the same staff and the same reptile that Aaron threw down in front of Pharaoh. This leads us to conclude that what Aaron's staff became was a poisonous snake, probably a cobra. The term *tannin* is used either for the sake of variety or to make the theological point that even the great serpent Satan is under God's control.

The important fact here is not zoological but theological: The serpent (not the crocodile) was the symbol of Pharaoh's authority, and thus the staff that became a snake was a direct attack on his sovereignty. Pharaoh apparently sensed that some kind of challenge was coming because he asked Moses and Aaron to perform a miracle. They were claiming divine authority over him, so in order to check their credentials, Pharaoh demanded a sign.

Unbelievers often ask God to perform a miracle. They say they are willing to believe, if only he will show them some kind of sign. They are like the Pharisees who said to Jesus, "Teacher, we wish to see a sign from you" (Matthew 12:38). It was not wrong for Pharaoh to make such a request. Strangely enough, he seemed to understand the true purpose of divine miracles. God does not perform random acts of omnipotence but instead displays his miraculous power in order to confirm the truth of his Word. This was true of the Old Testament prophets, who performed signs and wonders to prove that they were men who spoke from God. In this particular case, Moses and Aaron claimed to be God's ambassadors, divinely commissioned to tell Pharaoh to let God's people go. The obvious way for them to authenticate their claim was to perform a miraculous sign.

This principle—that miracles confirm the truth of God's Word—explains why Jesus performed so many signs and wonders. His miracles helped prove his claim that he was the Son of God and the Savior of the world. This principle also explains why miracles have since become so rare. Although God may sometimes perform miraculous signs when the gospel first penetrates a culture, he has already given us the greatest sign of all in the resurrection of Jesus Christ. The Bible does not tell us to expect a miracle—not because God is unable to perform one, but because he doesn't need to. The resurrection is the last miracle we need to confirm the gospel truth that Jesus died to save sinners.

Of all the signs that God could have given to Pharaoh, he chose to turn Aaron's staff into a serpent. The more we know about the Egyptians and their snakes, the clearer it becomes that by doing this, God was waging war against Satan. The Egyptians were fascinated with snakes, partly because they were so afraid of them.[3] Many of them carried amulets to protect them from Apophis, the serpent-god who personified evil. Egyptian literature contains various spells and incantations to afford protection from snakebite. It was this fear of snakes that led Pharaoh to use the serpent as the symbol of his royal authority. His ceremonial headdress—like the famous death-mask of Tutankhamen—was crested with a fierce female cobra. The idea was that Pharaoh would terrorize his enemies the way a cobra strikes fear into her prey. This is how a relief at Karnak describes one of Shoshenk's victories in battle: "Thy war-mace, it struck down thy foes . . . thy serpent-crest was mighty among them."[4]

Despite their fear of snakes, the ancient Egyptians nevertheless were drawn to worship them. This is how Satan generally operates, using fear to gain power. Serpent worship was particularly strong in the Nile Delta, where the Hebrews lived. There the Egyptians built a temple in honor of the snake-goddess Wadjet, who was represented by the hieroglyphic sign of the cobra. Some of the Pharaohs believed that she had brought them to the throne and invested them with her divine powers. Others considered her to be their protector. In an inscription found at Tanis, Pharaoh Taharqa claimed, "I had taken the diadems of Re, and I had assumed the double serpent-crest . . . as the protection of my limbs."[5] According to another ancient text, "His gods are over him; His uraeus-serpents are over his head."[6] After surveying this and other evidence, John Currid concludes, "The serpent-crested diadem of Pharaoh symbolized all the power, sovereignty, and magic with which the gods endued the king."[7]

By finding his security in the serpent-god, Pharaoh was actually making an alliance with Satan. The ancient manuscripts are explicit about this. When Pharaoh first ascended the throne of Egypt, he would take the royal crown and say,

> O Great One, O Magician, O Fiery Snake!
> Let there be terror of me like the terror of thee.
> Let there be fear of me like the fear of thee.
> Let there be awe of me like the awe of thee.
> Let me rule, a leader of the living.
> Let me be powerful, a leader of spirits.[8]

With these words, Pharaoh offered his soul to the devil.

This background helps explain what Aaron was doing when he "cast down his staff before Pharaoh" (7:10). He was taking the symbol of the king's majesty and making it crawl in the dust. This was a direct assault on Pharaoh's sovereignty; indeed, it was an attack on Egypt's entire belief system. To draw a modern comparison, it would be like taking a bald eagle into the Oval Office and wringing its neck. When God confronts other gods he does not probe around, hoping to find a weakness. Instead he takes aim at his enemies' greatest strength and overwhelms it with superior force. In this case, he sent Moses and Aaron straight to Pharaoh's command center, where he proceeded to claim ultimate authority over all Egypt.

God's Spirit follows the same strategy when he wants to establish his throne in a sinner's heart. He makes his attack right at the source of the sinner's strength. If we crave power, God's Spirit will show us how weak we are. If we live for pleasure, he will make us so miserable that the more we get what we want, the unhappier we become. If we think life is all about making money, he will take away our financial security. Whatever gods we happen to worship, the Holy Spirit will confront them head-on. This strategy is useful to remember in evangelism. One of the best ways to convince people of their need for Christ is to find out what they are counting on and then show them why it cannot be trusted.

## Pharaoh's Magic Show

As soon as Pharaoh saw the emblem of his authority slithering across the floor, he called for backup. His assumption—and this was a common way to think in those days—was that the god with the most magic wins. So when his divine authority was challenged, "Pharaoh summoned the wise men and the sorcerers, and they, the magicians of Egypt, also did the same by their secret arts. For each man cast down his staff, and they became serpents" (7:11, 12a). Incidentally, the word used here for "magicians" (*kartom*) is of Egyptian derivation, providing further confirmation that the history of the exodus comes directly from the land of the pyramids.

Pharaoh's priests were a force to be reckoned with. Göran Larsson describes the role they played in Egyptian society:

> "Magic" was a main element in the Egyptian religion at this time, and those who mastered these powers were held in high esteem. The priests, belonging to the highest officials of Pharaoh, possessed secret knowledge and were skilled in all sorts of mysterious rites. By casting spells, they could allegedly overpower humans and control gods and thereby attain dominion over the world of nature and the world of the gods, realms which could not be separated since some animals were regarded as divine. Through magi-

> cal formulas, the magicians claimed to exercise the power of the gods. The master of magic therefore became a player in the world of the gods.[9]

The Bible makes it clear that Pharaoh's priests could put on quite a magic show. Aaron's demonstration had been fairly impressive, but they were able to duplicate it by showing the same sign. The question is, how did they do it? What does the Bible mean by "their secret arts"?

Some scholars think that Pharaoh's priests were magicians in the modern sense of the word—clever illusionists who performed parlor tricks by sleight of hand. In fact, turning a staff into a snake may have been a standard part of their repertoire. The Egyptians had a fascination with manipulation, and some ancient texts describe their efforts to turn ordinary objects into live animals. A famous account from the time of Cheops describes a priest making a wax crocodile and throwing it into a lake, where it came to life.[10]

Others say that Pharaoh's priests were snake charmers. The Egyptians were proud of their ability to handle venomous creatures, and there is a long history of snake-handling along the Nile. The nineteenth-century Bible scholar Ernst Hengstenberg witnessed the way that snake charmers induced catalepsy by pinching their snakes in the neck. He wrote, "When they wish to perform this operation, they spit in the throat of the animal, compel it to shut up its mouth, and lay it down upon the ground. Then, as if in order to give a last command, they lay their hand upon its head, and immediately the serpent, stiff and motionless, falls into a kind of torpor. They wake it up when they wish, seizing it by the tail, and rolling it roughly between the hands."[11] As recently as the 1960s, a tourist reported, "This is still done in Cairo today as a trick of magic. The Egyptian cobra can be paralyzed by putting pressure on a nerve in its neck. At a distance it is readily mistaken for a cane. When the magician throws it on the ground, the jolt causes it to recover, and it crawls away."[12]

These arguments have a certain plausibility, but rather than seeking some sort of natural explanation, it is better to concede that Pharaoh's priests performed their wonders by the power of Satan. When the Bible speaks of "secret arts," it refers specifically to demonic spells and incantations. This is a reminder of how powerful Satan is. Jesus called him "the ruler of this world" (John 12:31). He has the power to keep people in bondage to false gods, like the gods of Egypt.

The Bible often treats other gods as if they have no power at all. Comparatively speaking, this is true. False gods are unable to resist the power of the true God for even a single moment. Nevertheless, God permits demons to have spiritual power over their worshipers. Even if we decide not to worship God, we still have to worship something. I think of a man on an airplane who described to me his fabulous collection of baseball memorabilia. "Everybody has to have their thing," he said, "and my thing is baseball." The man was right: Everybody has their "thing," and their "thing" is their god. We are made to worship. If we do not worship the true God, we will worship some false god, and Satan will claim that worship for himself. This is why it is never safe to get involved with some religion other than the worship of the true God. Ultimately, every form of false worship is Satan-worship, and it always results in spiritual bondage. "When you did not know God," wrote the Apostle Paul, "you were enslaved to those that by nature are not gods" (Galatians 4:8).

In their enslavement to the gods of Egypt, Pharaoh's priests discovered that such alleged deities have real supernatural power. Whether they realized that they were serving Satan or not, they were controlled by "the spiritual forces of evil in the heavenly places" (Ephesians 6:12), evil forces that had at least enough power to perform a few miracles.

Notice, however, that the best they could do was to imitate what God did. Pharaoh's magicians simply repeated Aaron's sign. This is because Satan can only corrupt, never create. The Bible says that "the activity of Satan [is shown] with all power and false signs and wonders" (2 Thessalonians 2:9). Satan is always a counterfeiter, never an innovator. He is like the annoying little brother who never comes up with any ideas of his own but always copies his older siblings. This explains why every false religion has ethical principles or sacred rituals that seem vaguely similar to Christianity. Satan is a knockoff artist. Unable to make a religion that is truly unique, he is always borrowing something from God. To give just one example, a group of atheists in Irving, Texas, has established the North Texas Church of Freethought. The church meets once a month because, in the words of one member, "Nonbelievers, just like believers, need fellowship."[13] This is the kind of power Satan has today. He uses a false imitation of Christianity to keep people from serving the God of truth.

## Gulp!

No doubt Pharaoh's sorcerers were pleased with their little magic show: "For each man cast down his staff, and they became serpents" (7:12a). By their "secret arts," they were able to match God snake for snake. But then, to their complete disbelief and utter dismay, "Aaron's staff swallowed up their staffs" (7:12b). A few quick gulps, and there was only one serpent left in the palace.

This sign would have been especially impressive to the Egyptians, who believed that swallowing something was the way to acquire all its powers. By gobbling up their magic wands, Aaron's staff was not simply destroying their power and authority but was claiming that all their power and authority belonged to God. The obvious implication was that the God of Israel was also the Lord of Egypt. This is the great theme of Exodus: the Lord God is glorious above all other gods.

Perhaps it is not surprising that the magicians were the first Egyptians to confess God's power (see 8:19), for they confronted it firsthand. They could see that Aaron's sign was not a magic trick but a miracle. Aaron did not cast any spells or recite any incantations. All he did was take an ordinary staff and throw it to the ground. Thus it was Aaron's God who turned the staff into a snake. God has authority over everything that he has made, and he proved his supernatural power by making Aaron's staff gobble up all the others. In his summary of the exodus, the historian Josephus put the following words into Moses' mouth: "O king, I do not myself despise the wisdom of the Egyptians, but I say that what I do is so much superior to what these do by magic arts and tricks, as divine power exceeds the power of man: but I will demonstrate that what I do is not done by craft, or counterfeiting what is not really true, but that they appear by the providence and power of God."[14]

Aaron's victory over Pharaoh's magicians teaches us something important about spiritual warfare: Although Satan's power is real, it is not absolute. We have already seen that Satan has the power to perform counterfeit miracles that keep his servants in spiritual bondage. But he does not have the power to overrule the sovereign God. Satan can only do what God allows him to do; and whenever God decides to do something, there is nothing that Satan can do to stop him. Charles Spurgeon observed, "Whenever a divine thing is cast into the heart, or thrown upon the earth, it swallows up everything else, and though the devil may fashion a counterfeit, and produce swarms of opponents as sure as ever God is in the work, it will swallow up all its foes."[15] The limits of Pharaoh's satanic power will become even more obvious as the plagues continue. His magicians were able to mimic some of Aaron's miracles, but eventually their secret arts were swallowed up by the almighty power of God.

The exodus was God's triumph over Satan, but it was not his greatest triumph. God made his supreme demonstration of power over Satan through the crucifixion and resurrection of Jesus Christ. Satan opposed Jesus from the beginning, almost from the day he was born. He used the power of government, sending soldiers to kill him. He used the power of demons and even personally tempted Jesus in the wilderness. He used the power of religion, sending priests to accuse him. Finally, God allowed Satan to put Jesus to death, but that turned out to be Satan's biggest mistake of all because it was by dying for our sins that Jesus delivered us from the devil's power. Jesus disarmed Satan's authority and made a public spectacle of him, triumphing over him through the cross (Colossians 2:15). Then, in order to prove that he was not under Satan's power, Jesus was raised from the dead. Now we can say, "'Death is *swallowed up* in victory' . . . thanks be to God, who gives us the victory through our Lord Jesus Christ" (1 Corinthians 15:54, 57).

This is a promise for Christians to claim whenever we are tempted or fall under some other form of spiritual attack. Although Satan's power is real, it is not absolute. His power over sin was vanquished through the crucifixion. His power over death was swallowed up by the resurrection. When we feel so imprisoned by our sins that we fear we are still in spiritual bondage, all we need to do is hold on to Jesus, who defeated Satan through his cross and his empty tomb.

## The Hardest of Hearts

When Aaron's staff swallowed the other staffs, it was obvious that the God of Israel had supreme power over all the gods of Egypt. Obvious to everyone, that is, except Pharaoh: "Still Pharaoh's heart was hardened, and he would not listen to them, as the LORD had said" (7:13).

What Pharaoh should have done was to get down from his throne and begin to worship the one true God. He had heard God's word and seen God's sign, and the only proper response was to fall down at God's feet. The reason Pharaoh didn't do this was that spiritually he had a cardiac condition: his heart was hard. The verb used to describe this hardening (*hazaq*) appears in the perfect tense, which indicates completed action. In other words, Pharaoh's heart was not simply getting hard; it was hard already. Literally, it was "heavy." It was slow to grasp the truth. Utterly insensitive to true spiritual influences, it was not warmed by love for God. It was neither sorry for sin nor willing to change. Pharaoh's heart was hard all the way through.

God had predicted that this would happen. In fact, God had promised to *make* it happen. He had said, "I will harden Pharaoh's heart, and though I multiply my signs and wonders in the land of Egypt, Pharaoh will not listen to you" (7:3, 4a). One of the mysteries of God's sovereignty is that he hardens people in their sins, thereby condemning them to their own depravity, which is exactly what happened to Pharaoh.

If Pharaoh had realized how hard his heart was, he would have been terrified. The Egyptians believed that the heart was the essence of the person and thus the key to eternal life. Many of their temples and tombs depict a heart being weighed on the scales of justice. The meaning of this image is explained in "The Book of the Dead" found at the Palace of Anubis, in which a man named Ani enters the throne room of the gods for judgment. At the front stands the balance of truth on which the death-god Anubis will weigh the dead man's heart. Anubis is joined by Thoth, who will record the verdict, and by the goddess Amemit, who waits to devour the hearts of the damned.

Anubis calls for Ani's heart to be weighed against the feather of righteousness. His eternal destiny stands in the balance. If his heart is too heavy, he will be condemned for his sins and thrown to the voracious monster. But if his heart is as light as the feather, he will receive everlasting life. As John Currid explains, "Anyone whose heart was heavy-laden with misdeeds would be annihilated, while anyone whose heart was filled with integrity, truth, and good acts would be escorted to heavenly bliss."[16] The whole scene was so fearful that Ani cried out, "O my heart from my mother! O my heart from my mother! . . . Do not stand against me as a witness! . . . Do not be belligerent to me before the One who keeps the balance!"

Fortunately for Ani, his cries did not go unheard. Anubis announced, "His deeds are true in the Great Balance. No crime has been found in him. . . . No sin is found in him; he has no evil with which we might accuse him."[17]

Like every false form of worship, ancient Egyptian religion was based on the principle of works-righteousness, but it also contained echoes of Biblical truth. There will indeed be a final judgment, in which every human heart will be weighed against the righteousness of God. If that is true, then what will become of a hard-hearted man like Pharaoh? According to the Egyptians, such a man could never be saved. A man with a hard, heavy heart would be weighed in the balance and found wanting. The weight of his sins would drag him down to destruction.

Pharaoh's hardness of heart is a warning to anyone who has witnessed God's power but refuses to receive God's grace. Few men have ever seen the power of God the way Pharaoh did. He even had the opportunity to test that power by demanding a miracle. But even when God passed his test, Pharaoh still wouldn't believe. He was the kind of man who always acts as if God is the one who needs to be weighed in the balance, who has something to prove. He was like the atheist who was asked what he would say if he turned out to be wrong and really did have to meet God face-to-face for judgment. The man thought for a moment and then said, "I would say, 'Not enough evidence, Lord. Not enough evidence.'" In other words, the atheist would blame God for not providing sufficient evidence to make him a Christian.

The real issue is not the evidence, but what a person does with it. The Israelites were given the same signs that Pharaoh was given (see Exodus 4), and they believed and were saved. But Pharaoh later perished, which is what happens to everyone who follows Satan. After explaining that Satan's work is displayed "with all power and false signs and wonders," the Scripture goes on to say that those who are entranced by Satan will perish "because they refused to love the truth and so be saved. Therefore God sends them a strong delusion, so that they may believe what is false, in order that all may be condemned who did not believe the truth but had pleasure in unrighteousness" (2 Thessalonians 2:9–12). This serves as an apt description of Pharaoh: he was condemned to his own depravity because he did not believe in God's truth.

God has already provided more than enough evidence to persuade *anyone* to trust in him. The beauty of his glory is declared in the heavens. The gift of his grace is published in his Word. The power of his love is shown through his people. Anyone who has not yet believed in Jesus Christ cannot honestly say that God has provided insufficient evidence. The unbeliever's real problem is not intellectual but spiritual. What is needed is a change of heart. Hardness of heart is a cardiac condition that can only be treated by a complete transplant, in which the hard old heart is replaced with a soft new one that is made righteous by grace.

# 18

# River of Blood

EXODUS 7:14–24

IN SEPTEMBER 2000 Great Britain faced a serious fuel shortage. Angered by the high cost of gasoline—or petrol, as Britons call it—truckers conspired to blockade the nation's oil refineries. Within days the country was nearly at a standstill. There were long lines at the filling stations, where some owners charged as much as five times the former price of fuel. Reserves ran dangerously low, and Britain was within a day or two of a complete transportation shutdown: no planes, no trains, and no automobiles. It seemed that if the crisis lasted much longer, the whole British economy would collapse, taking the government down with it. It was all because of oil, the lifeblood of the modern state.

The British gas shortage shows how dependent a civilization is on the basic source of its economy, and thus it gives some idea what the Egyptians faced when their river turned to blood. The Nile meant everything to them. It was their mode of transportation, their source of nourishment, their standard for measurement, and even an object of worship. Therefore there was no better way for the God of Israel to show that he was also the Lord of Egypt than by turning the Nile into blood.

## God's Demand

The river of blood was the first of ten plagues that afflicted the Egyptians. Rather than calling them "plagues," the Bible prefers to call them "signs and wonders" (7:3). Nevertheless, the word *plague* expresses an important truth. The term comes from the Latin *plaga*, meaning "a blow or wound," which is exactly what the plagues were. God said, "I will stretch out my hand and strike Egypt with all the wonders that I will do in it" (3:20).

When he performed his miracles along the Nile, God struck ten mighty blows against not only the Egyptians but also their gods. This is how James Boice explains the religious significance of these miraculous signs and wonders:

> In order to understand these plagues we need to understand that they were directed against the gods and goddesses of Egypt and were intended to show the superiority of the God of Israel to the Egyptian gods. There were about eighty major deities in Egypt, all clustered about the three great natural forces of Egyptian life: the Nile river, the land, and the sky. It does not surprise us, therefore, that the plagues God sent against Egypt in this historic battle follow this three-force pattern. The first two plagues were against the gods of the Nile. The next four were against the land gods. The final four plagues were against the gods of the sky, culminating in the death of the firstborn.[1]

The story of the first mighty blow begins with God's demand: "Then the Lord said to Moses, 'Pharaoh's heart is hardened; he refuses to let the people go. Go to Pharaoh in the morning, as he is going out to the water. Stand on the bank of the Nile to meet him, and take in your hand the staff that turned into a serpent. And you shall say to him, "The Lord, the God of the Hebrews, sent me to you, saying, 'Let my people go, that they may serve me in the wilderness.' But so far, you have not obeyed"'" (7:14–16). Moses was speaking on behalf of the one true God, the Lord of Israel. God's basic demand had not changed: he wanted Pharaoh to let his people go! This was the commission he had given to Moses at the burning bush when he said, "Come, I will send you to Pharaoh that you may bring my people, the children of Israel, out of Egypt" (3:10). It is what God told the elders to demand when they first went with Moses to Pharaoh's palace (3:18). It is what Moses and Aaron said the first time that Pharaoh granted them an audience: "Let my people go" (5:1). Presumably it is also what they said the second time, when the staff swallowed the snakes. God insisted that Pharaoh let his people go, and he kept on demanding their release until it was finally granted.

The way God dealt with Pharaoh shows that his demands are nonnegotiable. Every time Pharaoh encountered God, he was confronted with the same God making the same demand. God never changed his terms or issued a counteroffer. This is because God never changes his terms: "The counsel of the Lord stands forever, the plans of his heart to all generations" (Psalm 33:11). What was true for Pharaoh during the exodus is true for sinners in salvation. God's terms remain unchanged. What God demands today is the same thing he demanded in the time of the apostles. When people asked what they had to do to be saved, the apostles said, "Believe in the Lord Jesus, and you will be saved" (Acts 16:31). God still requires sinners to repent of their sins and believe in Jesus Christ. We should not expect him to make us another offer. Jesus Christ is God's best and only bargain for eternity.

The reason God required Pharaoh to let his people go was very simple. Ultimately it was the same reason for everything that God requires. It was for his own glory. As God said to Pharaoh, speaking through his servant Moses, "Let my people go, that they may serve me" (7:16). The word translated "serve" (*abad*) is the same word that was used back in chapter 1 to describe Israel's slavery to the Egyptians (see 1:14), but the Israelites were not made to serve Pharaoh—they were made to serve the living God. Thus the goal of the exodus was the worship of God. God told Pharaoh to let his people go so they could give him the glory. And since God deserves all the glory, it would not have been right for him to demand anything less. The chief purpose of God's people and the ultimate end of all existence is to give praise to the glorious God.

As we have seen, Pharaoh was not interested in giving God the glory because he wanted it all for himself! So Pharaoh refused to give in to God's demand. Twice he rejected it, hardening his heart against God's will. As God said to Moses, "Pharaoh's heart is hardened; he refuses to let the people go" (7:14). Literally, his heart was heavy (*kabed*), weighed down with injustice and iniquity. And it was Pharaoh's obstinacy that brought the plagues down on Egypt. His example shows what happens to a man who sets himself up against God. Sooner or later he will be punished for his sins.

One of the reasons Pharaoh was so hard hearted was that his heart belonged to other gods. Notice that God told Moses to wait for Pharaoh on the banks of the Nile, where it was his custom to go every morning. The Bible does not say why Pharaoh went down by the riverside. Perhaps he went to the Nile to bathe, like his daughters (2:5), or he enjoyed taking an early-morning swim. But it seems likely that he also went there to pay homage to the gods of the Nile. It is easy to imagine Pharaoh blessing the waters in the name of Hapi, the god of the flood, or giving thanks every morning to Khnum, the guardian of the Nile. Perhaps he used the words of an ancient Egyptian hymn: "Hail to thee, Oh Nile, that issues from the earth and comes to keep Egypt alive!"[2]

In any case, it was on the very banks of the Nile that Moses confronted Pharaoh, saying, "Thus says the Lord, 'By this you shall know that I am the Lord: behold, with the staff that is in my hand I will strike the water that is in the Nile, and it shall turn into blood. The fish in the Nile shall die, and the Nile will stink, and the Egyptians will grow weary of drinking water from the Nile'" (7:17, 18). Moses made it clear that he was speaking in the name of the Lord. In his hand he held the rod of God, the symbol of divine authority. And to show that this was a pronouncement of divine judgment, he began with the solemn words, "Thus says the Lord."

Pharaoh needed to understand that this plague was God's work because God's purpose was to show the Egyptians who was Lord. He said, "By this you shall know that *I* am *the* Lord" (v. 17). The great purpose of the exodus was to demonstrate the lordship of God. God proved that he was Lord of Israel by delivering his people from slavery, and at the same time he proved that he was Lord of Egypt by punishing Pharaoh for his sins.

God often uses signs and wonders to prove that he is Lord. This was true of the ministry of Jesus Christ. One of the reasons Jesus performed so many miracles was to prove his lordship. When John the Baptist asked for proof that Jesus was the Christ, Jesus said, "Go and tell John what you hear and see: the blind receive their sight and the lame walk, lepers are cleansed and the deaf hear, and the dead are raised up" (Matthew 11:4, 5). The signs and wonders that Jesus performed—particularly the miracle of his resurrection from the dead—prove that he is Lord. But God proves his lordship through mighty acts of judgment as well as through miracles of grace. He often convinces people that he is Lord by causing them to suffer the consequences of their sins. So it was for Pharaoh and the Egyptians. It took an outpouring of divine wrath to convince them that the God of Israel was Lord over all the gods of Egypt.

## Egypt's Distress

The result of Pharaoh's failure to meet God's demand was great suffering in Egypt: "Moses and Aaron did as the LORD commanded. In the sight of Pharaoh and in the sight of his servants he lifted up the staff and struck the water in the Nile, and all the water in the Nile turned into blood. And the fish in the Nile died, and the Nile stank, so that the Egyptians could not drink water from the Nile. There was blood throughout all the land of Egypt" (7:20, 21). Divine judgment is not an idle threat. God always makes sure that his enemies get what they deserve.

In the case of the first plague, God executed his judgment through the obedience of Moses and Aaron, who were finally putting their faith into practice. In these verses God tells them to "go" (7:15), "say" (7:16), "take" and "stretch" (7:19). They did all these things just as God commanded. This shows how much God can accomplish through his people if only they will do as they are told.

Ultimately, however, it was God's power that turned the life-giving Nile into a blood-red river of death. There was blood everywhere: "And the LORD said to Moses, 'Say to Aaron, "Take your staff and stretch out your hand over the waters of Egypt, over their rivers, their canals, and their ponds, and all their pools of water, so that they may become blood, and there shall be blood throughout all the land of Egypt, even in vessels of wood and in vessels of stone"'" (7:19). The mention of Aaron's staff again raises the question as to how many staffs there were—one or two. But the important thing is that Pharaoh's entire water system was made bloody by the power of God. The river of blood started a chain reaction. The blood killed off the fish, and as they began to decompose, the whole river was putrefied. Not only was this disgusting, but if it had lasted much longer than a week (see 7:25), it would have been fatal.

Scholars have long debated the historicity of the plagues in Exodus. Some claim that they never happened at all, that they are merely symbolic literary inventions. Others have tried to find some sort of natural explanation for the plagues.[3] In the case of the first plague, it is sometimes suggested that the river did not actually turn into blood but merely resembled blood. Perhaps heavy rains in southern Egypt washed red soil into the Nile Delta. Perhaps the river was red with sediment from seasonal flooding, and the sediment led to an oxygen imbalance, which would account for the river's stench. Or perhaps the Nile was covered with a bloom of reddish algae or inundated with microorganisms. Whatever the precise explanation, some of these scholars admit that the plague was nevertheless an act of God. God judged Egypt by overruling his creation, using natural disasters to show his supernatural power.

There are several difficulties with these naturalistic explanations. One is that they have trouble accounting for the fatality of all the fish. Another is that they do not explain why there was blood throughout Egypt, and not simply in the Nile. Still another difficulty is explaining how the sediment or fungus or whatever it was appeared instantaneously when Moses struck the Nile with his staff. Then there is the plain language of Scripture, which clearly states that "the water in the Nile turned into blood" (7:20). The word "turned" (*haphac*) shows that a real transformation took place, while the word "blood" (*dam*) is generally used to refer not just to any thick red fluid but to blood, plain and simple.

The real problem with trying to explain away this miracle, however, is that a merely natural phenomenon would not have accomplished God's purpose, which was to prove that he was the Lord. If the Nile turned to blood every time there was a downpour somewhere upriver, this sign would have been meaningless. Pharaoh wouldn't have even bothered to call for his magicians. He would have said, "Big deal, Moses; this happens all the time." For all these reasons, it is right to believe and teach that the river of blood was a divine miracle, a supernatural demonstration that the Lord is God.

The historicity of the plagues finds further confirmation in the other Bible passages that treat these signs and wonders as real historical events.[4] The psalmist wrote, "He [God] turned their rivers to blood, so that they could not drink of their streams" (Psalm 78:44). Or again, "He turned their waters into blood and caused their fish to die" (Psalm 105:29). There may even be a reference to this plague in ancient Egyptian literature. According to a manuscript written around the time of the exodus (within a century or so of 1300 BC), "The River is blood. If one drinks of it, one rejects it as human and thirsts for water."[5]

To understand how distressing this was for the Egyptians, one has to appreciate how dependent they were on the Nile. The river was their lifeblood, the basis for their entire civilization. The Egyptians used the Nile for almost everything, and without it, their land would have become a desert. The river provided the transportation system that helped them move goods from place to place. It formed the irrigation system that enabled them to grow their crops. It was their water supply, and also their food supply, because fish was one of the staples of the Egyptian diet. The river's annual floods set their calendar and gave them fertile topsoil. In short, the land of Egypt was the gift of the Nile. The Greek historian Herodotus (c. 484–c. 425 BC) claimed that "even though a man has not before been told, he can at once see, if he have sense, that that Egypt to which Greeks sail is land acquired by the Egyptians, given them by the river."[6]

### The Nile's Deities

Since the Egyptians practically owed their existence to the Nile, it is not surprising that they worshiped the great river as their creator and sustainer. Donald Grey Barnhouse writes: "At certain seasons of the year the river overflowed its banks, and, when it retired to its accustomed bed, it left behind it an alluvial deposit of rich topsoil which made it possible for the land to bring forth in abundance. It was natural, therefore, that the Egyptians should have associated other of their gods with the fruitful soil which gave such abundance for such comparatively little labor."[7]

At least three Egyptian gods were associated with the Nile. One was the great Osiris, the god of the Nile, who was depicted with the river running through his bloodstream. Another was Nu, the god of life in the river. But the most important was Hapi, the god of the flood. Hapi was a fertility god who was portrayed as a bearded man with female breasts and a pregnant stomach. The idea was that the annual flooding of the Nile gave birth to Egypt and nursed its strength.

These were the river gods of the Egyptian—the gods they worshiped and served: Osiris, Nu, and especially Hapi. For centuries the Egyptians praised Hapi as "the giver of life," "the lord of sustenance," the one "who causes the whole land to live through his provisions."[8] They sang:

> Hail to your countenance, Hapi,
> Who goes up from the land, who comes to deliver Egypt . . .
> Who brings food, who is abundant of provisions,
> Who creates every sort of good thing . . .
> Who fills Upper and Lower Egypt. . . .
> Everything that has come into being is through his power.[9]

Then one day the river turned to blood. Moses struck the Nile with his staff, and blood flowed all over Egypt. In this way God demonstrated his power over the gods of Egypt and also punished the Egyptians for their idolatry. With one single blow he gave them a water and food shortage, a transportation shutdown, a financial disaster, and a spiritual crisis. He did it all by turning the river into blood, making the object of their worship a thing of horror. God's attack on the Nile was a direct attack on the Egyptians and their gods. It proved that

Osiris and Hapi did not have the power to meet their needs. Later, when the Israelites finally marched their way out of Egypt and Moses tried to summarize what God had done to Egypt, he proclaimed that "On their gods also the LORD executed judgments" (Numbers 33:4; cf. Exodus 12:12).

The gods of Egypt are specifically mentioned in Exodus 7:19: "There shall be blood throughout all the land of Egypt, even in vessels of wood and in vessels of stone." It is possible that this verse refers to stone and wooden vessels used for storing water. However, the Hebrew original says nothing about "vessels"; it simply states that there was blood "in the wood and in the stone." Ordinarily when the Old Testament refers to wood and stone, it is speaking of idols. A good example is Deuteronomy 29:17, where Moses warned the Israelites not to serve "detestable things . . . idols of wood and stone" like the Egyptians did. Umberto Cassuto claims that Egyptian priests washed their idols early every morning.[10] If that is true, then when they suffered their first plague, they had to wash their idols in blood. God turned the river into blood to show them how utterly worthless and contemptible it was to worship gods of wood and stone.

One day God will do the same thing to the gods of this age. The average American is not very different from an ancient Egyptian. We still worship the same gods—only the names have changed. What we count on, what we work for, what we play at, what we dream about—these are the gods that we worship. And what matters most to most of us is personal prosperity. We depend on our economy every bit as much as the Egyptians depended on theirs. They worshiped the Nile; we follow the NASDAQ—they are just two different names for the same god. Rather than trusting in God alone, we depend on economic growth, rapid transportation, and prepackaged foods. We even have our own creation myth. Believing in Darwinism is really just another way to worship Hapi. In much the same way that the Egyptians praised the river as their creator, many Americans believe that we have come from a random stream of genetic material.[11]

What would happen if all these things were taken away? Imagine what life in these United States would be like if the stock market collapsed, the price of gas rose to forty dollars a gallon, the supply of drinking water was contaminated, and grocery stores started running out of food. Can you imagine the utter chaos that would ensue? There would be rioting in the streets, death and destruction in every city. It could happen, and eventually it probably will. One day God will glorify himself in America the way he glorified himself in Egypt. He will triumph over every false god in order to prove that he alone is the Creator and the Provider, the giver and sustainer of life. If that happens—*when* it happens—it will show where we have placed our ultimate allegiance.

The practical application is very simple: We are to worship God by trusting in him alone for everything we need. If we trust in other gods for our peace and prosperity, we will be disappointed in the end. But if we place our confidence in

God alone as our Creator and Provider, then even when everything else is taken away, we will stand secure.

A good example of what it means to trust in the true God comes from a missionary. While she was traveling back to the Middle East, she met a man who had wrestled with the temptation to follow other gods. She writes:

> Someone prayed for me right before I boarded the airplane, that I should meet and speak of the Lord with my seat companion before the end of the ride. The man who sat next to me was on his way to Nigeria to minister the word to the Muslim militia. His goal was in fact to plant a church there. This pastor is a living example of Jonah. He told me that God had been urging him for some time to go back to his country and preach to the very rebels who had once attacked his own family. But he was unwilling. "The only way I will go," he said to the Lord, "is if you take away all of my comforts."
>
> He lost his job and was kicked out of his apartment a month later. So there he was on the plane next to me, smiling and praising God for all of his many blessings. And rejoicing (literally singing right there) in the work that God had planned for him in Nigeria.

That man's life was a testimony to God's triumph over the other gods in his life. When all his other comforts were taken away, he still had the one true God to worship and to serve.

## Pharaoh's Disobedience

It was different for Pharaoh and the Egyptians. When their gods were taken away, they hardened their hearts and refused to worship the God of Israel. The chapter ends with them returning to the power of Satan and struggling to make life work on their own terms: "But the magicians of Egypt did the same by their secret arts. So Pharaoh's heart remained hardened, and he would not listen to them, as the Lord had said. Pharaoh turned and went into his house, and he did not take even this to heart. And all the Egyptians dug along the Nile for water to drink, for they could not drink the water of the Nile" (7:22–24).

Once again Pharaoh's magicians were able to duplicate God's sign. Whether they did it by sleight of hand or by the power of demons, they performed a counterfeit miracle. Scholars have wondered where they got their water. The Bible doesn't say, but once we successfully get rid of the "vessels" in verse 19, it becomes possible that there was water stored somewhere at the palace. The irony is that rather than making the plague better, they made it worse! It would have made a great deal more sense for the magicians to undo the plague by turning the blood back to water, but they did not have the power to tamper with God's miracle. They could not reverse the disaster; they could only repeat it, adding plague upon plague. Thus God bent Satan's power to his own will.

What this shows is that Satan's power is self-defeating. Even his counterfeit signs and wonders ultimately serve the greater glory of God. The supreme example is the crucifixion of Jesus Christ. At the time it must have seemed like Satan's greatest triumph: the Son of God suffering, bleeding, and dying on a wooden cross. But what Satan didn't know was that as Jesus hung on that cross, he was turning away (or propitiating) God's wrath by atoning for the sins of his people. Three days later Jesus rose from the dead, and Satan discovered that his greatest triumph was actually his bitterest defeat. The death of Christ was the very thing that God used to grant sinners eternal life.

No matter how self-defeating it was to make more blood, Pharaoh seems to have been impressed. When he saw that his magicians could repeat God's sign by their own secret arts, he hardened his heart, turned his back, and returned to his palace. As the Scripture says, "He did not take even this to heart" (7:23). Of course he didn't. He couldn't! He had a hard heart, and a hard heart will continue to harden until it is broken by God's love. Pharaoh's cardiac condition prevented him from paying any attention to God, even when God judged him for his sins.

Exodus 7 closes with the pathetic picture of Pharaoh's servants digging feverishly for ground water: "And all the Egyptians dug along the Nile for water to drink, for they could not drink the water of the Nile" (7:24). When the great gods of the Nile failed, the Egyptians were left to their own resources. This is what always happens to people who worship false gods. Sooner or later their gods fail, and the people are left scrambling to make life work on their own. If we trust in our economy the way the Egyptians trusted in theirs, we should probably grab a shovel because eventually we will need it.

God has promised that his invisible war with Satan will end with the defeat of every false god. He has also promised that on the day of judgment water will turn to blood. The book of Revelation describes the seven angels who will pour out the seven bowls of God's wrath:

> The second angel poured out his bowl into the sea, and it became like the blood of a corpse, and every living thing died that was in the sea.
>
> The third angel poured out his bowl into the rivers and the springs of water, and they became blood. And I heard the angel in charge of the waters say,
>
> "Just are you, O Holy One, who is and who was,
> for you brought these judgments.
> For they have shed the blood of saints and prophets,
> and you have given them blood to drink.
> It is what they deserve!"
>
> And I heard the altar saying,
>
> "Yes, Lord God the Almighty,
> true and just are your judgments!" (Revelation 16:3–7)

This is an awesome and fearsome picture of divine judgment. In the same way that God punished the Egyptians for their worship of other gods, he is planning to punish unbelievers at the end of history. In his mercy he will give them one final opportunity to repent of their sins and believe in Jesus Christ. Will they turn back to God? No, for according to the Biblical prophecy, "They did not repent and give him glory" (Revelation 16:9). They had hardened and hardened their hearts until not even a river of blood could turn them away from their sins. If it teaches us nothing else, the book of Exodus teaches us not to trust in other gods because they will not save us.

# 19

# Why the Frogs Croaked

## EXODUS 7:25—8:15

"SEVEN FULL DAYS PASSED after the LORD had struck the Nile" (7:25). Seven *long* days—days when blood flowed through the river, down the streams, and into the ponds; days when the fish died and the river began to stink; days when the Egyptians had to dig for water on the banks of the Nile. During those seven long days the Lord God of Israel triumphed over the river gods of Egypt.

Then Moses went back to Pharaoh. Since the purposes of God's heart do not change, he was still making the same demand of freedom for his people: "Then the LORD said to Moses, 'Go in to Pharaoh and say to him, "Thus says the LORD, 'Let my people go, that they may serve me'"'" (8:1). What God demanded was nothing less than the unconditional release of his people. The Israelites were made for his glory, so rather than slaving away for Pharaoh, they needed to be free to serve him. The impetus for the exodus was the greater glory of God.

### Ribbit! Croak! Peep!

This time God's demand came with a solemn warning: If Pharaoh once again refused to let God's people go, Egypt would be plagued with frogs. The Lord said, "But if you refuse to let them go, behold, I will plague all your country with frogs. The Nile shall swarm with frogs that shall come up into your house and into your bedroom and on your bed and into the houses of your servants and your people, and into your ovens and your kneading bowls. The frogs shall come up on you and on your people and on all your servants" (8:2–4). On this occasion God specifically referred to the coming disaster as a "plague" (*nagap*), a term the Old Testament uses for striking a blow. God warned Pharaoh that he was about to smite Egypt in judgment.

In spite of this warning, God's demand met with the usual response, which was no response at all. Although the Bible does not record Pharaoh's exact answer, evidently he refused to let God's people go. And when he refused, God judged him for the sin of rebellion: "And the LORD said to Moses, 'Say to Aaron, "Stretch out your hand with your staff over the rivers, over the canals and over the pools, and make frogs come up on the land of Egypt!"' So Aaron stretched out his hand over the waters of Egypt, and the frogs came up and covered the land of Egypt" (8:5, 6).

When Moses promised that Egypt would swarm with frogs, he used the same word that God used on the fifth day of creation: "Let the waters swarm with swarms of living creatures" (Genesis 1:20). This is exactly what happened in Egypt. The frogs came from everywhere, perhaps not unlike the plague of frogs depicted in the 2000 film *Magnolia*. They came from the Nile and from all its streams, canals, and wetlands. The frogs also *went* everywhere, swarming all over the Nile Delta. As Weldon Kees wrote in his poem "The Coming of the Plague," "And one day in a field I saw / A swarm of frogs, swollen and hideous, / Hundreds upon hundreds, sitting on each other."[1] They hopped into people's living quarters—into every nook and cranny of their kitchens and bedrooms. They even went into their hot, dry ovens, which is about the last place one would expect to find a frog. At night their noisy croaking bothered everyone from the king down to the lowliest Egyptian slave. As the Scripture says, the frogs "covered the land" (8:6).

What caused this amphibious invasion? As with most of the plagues, various scholars have tried to come up with natural explanations. For example, Umberto Cassuto argues, "The episode of the frogs also corresponds to normal Egyptian phenomena. Every year after the inundation of the Nile, the number of frogs in the receding waters is enormous."[2] Others have tried to draw a connection between the proliferation of frogs and the river of blood that preceded it. Greta Hort hypothesized that the rotting fish were infected with anthrax, which in turn killed off the frogs that were driven from the river by the blood.[3]

Sometimes this hypothesis is developed into an elaborate theory that ties all of the plagues together into a natural sequence of seasonal changes. Among those who have attempted such a synthesis is Flinders Petrie, who writes:

> The river turned to blood, with the fish dying, was the unwholesome stagnant Nile just at the lowest before the inundation, when it is red and swarming with organisms. The Egyptians have to resort to wells and cisterns at this time in the early part of June. The frogs abound after the inundation has come in July. The plagues of insects, murrain, and boils, belong to the hot summer and damp unwholesome autumn. The hail and rain came in January. This is closely fixed by the effect on the crops. The barley must have been up early for the wheat to be yet "hidden" or hardly sprouting. This would show it was planted early in November, in ear by the middle of January, and ripe early in March. The flax has like seasons, and the wheat is a month later. The locusts come in the spring, over the green crops

> about February. The sand storms bring a thick darkness that may be felt, in March, at the break of the hot winds.[4]

This sequence has a certain plausibility. One of its advantages is that it connects the history of Exodus to the geography of Egypt. Yet there are a number of problems with it. One is that the Bible does not draw any connections among the various plagues. Each one is presented as a separate act of divine judgment. Thus the most that scholars can do is infer that one plague is somehow related to the next. In some instances—such as the plague of hail or the angel of death—this proves impossible. Nor are scholars able to agree on their explanations. Some say that the Nile was blood-red just before the annual flood; others say just after. In the case of the frogs, nearly everyone struggles to explain how a river that was lethal to marine life produced such an abundance of amphibians. Furthermore, the ten plagues took place on a scale far beyond anything that the Egyptians had experienced before, or since. As a result of these difficulties, we are led to conclude that the plagues were truly divine miracles. What brought the frogs up onto the land was the supernatural power of God, flowing through the staff of Aaron. In the words of the psalmist, "He [God] sent . . . frogs, which destroyed them" (Psalm 78:45).

This was one of God's funniest miracles ever. Frogs are not particularly dangerous, but they can be a nuisance, and the Biblical account includes some nice comic touches. Some of the frogs ended up in the "ovens and . . . kneading bowls" (8:3). We picture an Egyptian mother pulling out her mixing bowls and then screaming as she discovers a frog in the dough. The kids probably loved it—at least at first. The frogs even hopped into Pharaoh's royal chambers. The psalmist probably chuckled when he wrote, "Their land swarmed with frogs, even in the chambers of their kings" (Psalm 105:30). We imagine Pharaoh lying down for a nap and then leaping to his feet because something was croaking under his pillow. Some of the frogs had the audacity to jump on his royal person, for Moses said to Pharaoh, "The frogs shall come up on you" (8:4). In Great Britain it is considered a serious breach of protocol for a commoner to touch a member of the Royal Family. All the more so in Egypt, where the Pharaohs were considered to be gods. But frogs are no respecters of persons, and in this particular case they did not hesitate to hop up Pharaoh's leg.

This plague hit Pharaoh right where he lived. God did not allow the hard-hearted king to retreat into the privacy of his own palace but brought the frogs right into his bedroom. God's judgment affected Pharaoh so personally that he probably had to put his entire staff on amphibian patrol!

## The Frog-Goddess

God had a serious theological purpose for sending what seems to be such a silly plague. Once again he was demonstrating his power over the gods of Egypt. James Boice wrote:

> If we are to understand the full significance of this plague, we must recognize that a goddess of Egypt was involved in the judgment—the goddess Hekt [also Heqet], who was always pictured with the head and often the head and body of a frog. Since Hekt was embodied in the frog, the frog was sacred in Egypt. It could not be killed, and consequently there was nothing the Egyptians could do about this horrible and ironic proliferation of the goddess. They were forced to loathe the symbols of their depraved worship. But they could not kill them. And when the frogs died, their decaying bodies must have turned the towns and countryside into a stinking horror.[5]

Writing in a similar vein, Charles Spurgeon pointed out how appropriate it was for God to plague the Egyptians in this way:

> There was a suitableness in God's choosing the frogs to humble Egypt's kings, because frogs were worshipped by that nation as emblems of the Deity. Images of a certain frog-headed goddess were placed in the catacombs, and frogs themselves were preserved with sacred honors. These be thy gods, O Egypt! Thou shalt have enough of them! Pharaoh himself shall pay a new reverence to these reptiles. As the true God is everywhere present around us, in our bed-chambers and in our streets, so shall Pharaoh find every place filled with what he chooses to call divine. Is it not a just way of dealing with him?[6]

In the Egyptian pantheon, the frog-goddess Heqet was the spouse of the creator-god Khnum. The Egyptians believed that Khnum fashioned human bodies on his potter's wheel, and then Heqet breathed into them the breath of life.[7] She was the agent of life-giving power and also the symbol of fertility.

The Egyptians relied on Heqet for two things in particular. One was to control the frog population by protecting crocodiles, the frog's natural predators.[8] Obviously, when Egypt was overrun (or overhopped!) with frogs, Heqet was humiliated. This plague proved that she was powerless to resist the mighty strength of the Lord.

Heqet's other responsibility was to assist women in childbirth. Since she was the spirit who breathed life into the body, women turned to her for help when they were in the pains of labor. This suggests that there may be a connection between the second plague and Pharaoh's sin against the Hebrew midwives. Remember that the book of Exodus began with attempted infanticide. In his effort to exterminate the Israelites, Pharaoh commanded the Hebrew midwives to kill Israel's baby boys (1:15, 16). When his evil plan failed, he ordered the infants to be thrown into the Nile (1:22). Given that background, it seems significant that God's first two plagues struck blows against the gods of Egypt's river and the goddess of Egypt's midwives. It was a matter of strict justice: God was punishing the Egyptians for their sins. The very river that Pharaoh used as an instrument of genocide was turned to blood, and the first goddess to be humiliated was the one who governed labor and delivery. There was a connection between Pharaoh's crime and God's punishment.

What is equally important is the connection between Egypt's gods and our own postmodern deities. Our method for studying Exodus is practical, and one of the most practical ways to study the plagues is to recognize that we are tempted to serve the same idols. The question to ask about the second plague is this: In what ways are we tempted to worship Heqet?

To answer this question, we have to understand why the Egyptians worshiped Heqet in the first place. It was because they desperately wanted to gain control over childbirth. In the days of modern medical care it is easy to forget how dangerous it is to give birth—dangerous not only for the baby, but also for the mother. For most of human history, in most parts of the world, childbirth has been a potentially life-threatening experience. When an Egyptian woman went into labor, fearing both for her own life and for the life of her newborn child, her only comfort was to cry out to Heqet for the breath of life.

Childbirth is a spiritual matter, and the issues that surround it are among the most difficult spiritual issues most women ever face. Many single women long to share their love with a child. Some married women are unable to have children. Others lose children through miscarriage. Then there are all the anxieties that come with actually conceiving, bearing, and delivering a child. Surely the most difficult thing of all is to give birth, only to lose the child. These sufferings all find their ultimate cause in humanity's fall into sin. God said to Eve, "I will surely multiply your pain in childbearing; in pain you shall bring forth children" (Genesis 3:16a). This curse refers not only to the physical act of childbirth, but to all the losses and frustrations that are associated with it.

In times of discouragement it is tempting to turn to Heqet. Some couples make a sacrifice to the goddess of fertility by getting an abortion. When there are questions about how the fetus is developing, as there often are, they submit to the pressure to terminate the pregnancy. Other couples abuse various forms of birth control. While it is sometimes appropriate to regulate when a woman gives birth, birth control should never be used as a way of avoiding God's command to be fruitful and multiply. Eventually some couples will use the knowledge of the human genome to produce designer children whose genetic material is altered to prevent certain diseases or even to guarantee certain attributes or abilities. Others make the quest for a child an idolatrous obsession. This is not to say that some forms of fertility treatment, including various forms of medication, are un-Biblical. Nor is it to say that Christian parents should not pursue adoption, which is a beautiful picture of God's love for his lost children. But it is to say that couples should not place their supreme confidence in some course of treatment or in some adoption agency, but in God himself, for he alone is the giver of life. The birth of a child is not a human project but a divine gift from a sovereign Lord.

One reason not to trust in Heqet is that she does not have the power to comfort her worshipers. Only the true and living God is able to bring healing to the deepest hurts in a woman's heart. Some of the most courageous women I know have lost children before, during, or shortly after childbirth. In the bitter pain of their suffering, there were times when they were tempted to turn away from God. But in the end they were drawn closer to God as they experienced his mercy for their sorrow.

I think of my own mother-in-law, Elaine Maxwell, who lost her only son the day after he was born. During her pregnancy she was exposed to rubella, so Jack was born with a hole in his heart. It was the kind of loss that a mother never forgets, which probably explains why, when she walked into an art show twenty-five years later and saw a sculpture of a perfect baby boy, she burst into tears. It brought back the memory of such grief that she had to leave the exhibition. But when she returned she noticed that the baby was resting in two strong hands and that the sculpture bore the title, "In the Hands of God." Since this is where she had left her son—in God's hands—the sculpture is now displayed in her home.

It can take a long time to accept the will of God, and usually it takes even longer to understand it. Sometimes a woman never fully comprehends why everything surrounding childbirth brings such suffering. But the only way to experience true healing for life's deepest hurts is to place them in the hands of God. Those who worship Heqet will never experience the comfort God gives to everyone who trusts in him.

## Standing in the Need of Prayer

By the time frogs started showing up under his bedcovers, even Pharaoh was starting to have his doubts about Heqet's power. Once again he called for his magicians. Once again they were able to repeat God's miracle, this time by conjuring up some more frogs: "But the magicians did the same by their secret arts and made frogs come up on the land of Egypt" (8:7). Only this time Pharaoh wasn't all that impressed. He didn't want any more frogs than he already had! What he really wanted was for someone to get rid of them all; but rather than subtracting from the invasion, his magicians could only add to it, so that, again, even Satan's power was turned to God's glory.

The worse things got, the more desperate Pharaoh became, until finally he did the unthinkable: He ordered Moses and Aaron to return to the palace so he could share a prayer request. This was not a sign of Pharaoh's spirituality but only of his superstition. Many desperate people have called for a minister without ever really intending to call upon God. So it was that "Pharaoh called

Moses and Aaron and said, 'Plead with the LORD to take away the frogs from me and from my people, and I will let the people go to sacrifice to the LORD'" (8:8).

This is a remarkable request—remarkable because it shows how much Pharaoh had learned about the ways of God. For starters, he had learned God's name. The first time he encountered Moses, he said "Who is the LORD . . . ? . . . I do not know the LORD" (5:2). Now he was getting to know him after all—much better than he expected—just as God had promised. Pharaoh's speech to Moses and Aaron begins and ends with the special name of the Lord.

Pharaoh had also learned something about God's power. The reason he summoned Moses and Aaron was because he knew that this plague was a divine miracle. He knew that God had sent the frogs and that only God could take them away. By asking for their removal, he was admitting that the Lord God of Israel had power over all creation. Pharaoh even seems to have understood that the way to gain access to that power was through prayer. The word translated "plead" (*atar*) is the word for supplication, for making a humble entreaty. Somehow he knew that divine intervention would come through human intercession.

Pharaoh had learned what God requires. He ended his speech by making the first of many false concessions: "I will let the people go to sacrifice to the LORD" (8:8b). This turned out to be a lie, of course. People will promise God anything when they are in trouble, but the promise is soon forgotten. Nevertheless, Pharaoh's promise clearly shows that he understood what God demanded of him. At some level he knew that God's people were made for God's glory and that he needed to let the Israelites go and make sacrifices to their God.

What all this shows is how much a person can learn *about* God without ever coming to him for salvation. Pharaoh knew that God was both Creator and Judge. He recognized the power of God's name and believed that he could answer prayer. But he did not know God as his Savior and Lord. The proof is that he could not pray to God for himself; he had to ask Moses and Aaron to do the praying for him. He also made the wrong request. Rather than asking God to take away his sins, he asked God to take away the frogs. Pharaoh wanted relief from the punishment for his sin without being willing to repent of the sin itself. Quite literally, the man didn't have a prayer—at least not a proper prayer to call his own. Charles Spurgeon wrote, "There is a measure of faith which goes to increase a man's condemnation, since he ought to know that if what he believes is true, then the proper thing is to pray himself. It would have been a wonderfully good sign if Pharaoh had said, 'Join with me, O Moses and Aaron, while I pray unto Jehovah that he may take the frogs from me.' But, no, he had only a condemning faith, which contented itself with other men's prayers."[9]

Prayer is one of the best tests of a person's true spiritual condition. A life of prayer depends on a personal, saving relationship with God. There is a sense, of course, in which God listens to every prayer, even one offered in the name of Allah or Buddha. Because he is omniscient and omnipresent, God knows and hears every prayer that has ever been uttered. But the only prayers that have a claim on his fatherly heart are the ones that are offered to him through faith. In this era of the gospel, that means praying to God the Father through God the Holy Spirit in the name of God the Son, who is Jesus Christ. If people cannot pray for themselves, then asking a Christian to pray for them is better than nothing. But realize what this indicates about their spiritual condition: they must not be children of God, because unless we learn to pray for ourselves, we will never receive eternal life. Eternal life begins with a prayer. The only way to enter salvation is by speaking to God directly, telling him that we are sorry for our sins and that we want his Son to be our Savior.

## The Power of Prayer

Sadly, Pharaoh never became a child of God; so whenever he needed a prayer, he had to borrow one from someone else. What was curious in this case was his decision to put the prayer off until the following day. This is what happened:

> Moses said to Pharaoh, "Be pleased to command me when I am to plead for you and for your servants and for your people, that the frogs be cut off from you and your houses and be left only in the Nile." And he said, "Tomorrow." Moses said, "Be it as you say, so that you may know that there is no one like the LORD our God. The frogs shall go away from you and your houses and your servants and your people. They shall be left only in the Nile." (8:9–11)

What was Pharaoh thinking? Most Egyptians would have asked for the plague to stop right away. But Pharaoh said, "Just give me one more night with these frogs, Moses." Maybe he was fond of amphibians. Perhaps he still hoped they would hop away on their own, so he could avoid needing God's help. Or perhaps—and this seems more likely—he thought that even God would need at least twenty-four hours to get rid of so many frogs.

Whatever Pharaoh was thinking, it is not hard to guess what Moses had in mind. By letting Pharaoh decide when the frogs would croak (so to speak), he was showing his absolute confidence in the power of God. He was not just being polite—he was making a public statement of his faith. Whenever someone performs a miracle, there are always skeptics, so Moses gave Pharaoh the advantage of setting the time, which would prove that his power came from God. The next day, at Pharaoh's request, Moses made intercession for Egypt: "So Moses and Aaron went out from Pharaoh, and Moses cried to the LORD about the frogs, as he had agreed with Pharaoh. And the LORD did according to the word of Moses. The frogs died out in the houses, the courtyards, and the fields. And they gathered them together in heaps, and the land stank" (8:12–14).

The end of the plague was every bit as much a divine miracle as the plague itself. Some of the frogs hopped back into the Nile, where they belonged. The rest of them died all over Egypt. There were heaps and heaps of them. Their carcasses were stacked into giant piles, where they rotted under the hot African sun. This is the kind of detail that comes from someone who actually witnessed the events. No doubt it made Pharaoh wish he had been more specific about how he wanted the frogs removed! Even after massive cleanup efforts, he still had a public health crisis on his hands. This, too, was an act of divine judgment. The removal of the plague also turned out to be a curse, as God made the Egyptians face the consequences of their sins. Earlier the Hebrews had complained that Moses had made them "stink in the sight of Pharaoh" (5:21). Here the Bible uses the very same word to show that Egypt had become a stench before God!

Notice why the frogs croaked. They croaked because God answers prayer. Once he had promised that God would end the plague, Moses devoted himself to prayer. The Bible says that he "cried to the Lord" (8:12; cf. 17:4). His intercession was fervent, almost desperate. The verb "cry out" (*tsa'aq*) is used elsewhere in the book of Exodus to describe the way the Hebrews cried out against their slave drivers (5:15) and the way they cried out for salvation when they came to the Red Sea (14:15). Later Moses would cry out for his own salvation when the Israelites were ready to stone him (17:4). It may seem strange that on this occasion he cried out on behalf of Pharaoh, but Moses was not praying for Pharaoh's good as much as he was praying for God's glory. He had put God's reputation on the line by promising a miracle, so he pleaded for God to show his power by ending the plague.

One of the believer's great privileges is access to God through prayer, especially in times of disaster and distress. Sometimes we intercede on behalf of others, asking God to have mercy on those who suffer storms, famines, and earthquakes. On other occasions we are forced to plead for our own deliverance. But whenever we cry out, and for whatever reason, God will hear our prayers. Centuries later, when Solomon dedicated the temple in Jerusalem, he asked that if the Israelites ever had to be judged for their sins like the Egyptians, God would hear their cries for mercy. He prayed, "If there is famine in the land, if there is pestilence . . . whatever plague, whatever sickness there is, whatever prayer, whatever plea is made by any man or by all your people Israel, each knowing the affliction of his own heart and stretching out his hands toward this house, then hear in heaven your dwelling place" (1 Kings 8:37–39). This promise is still good. Whatever disaster may come, we may spread out our hands to God in prayer, and he will hear us from Heaven.

## A Little Breathing Room

Pharaoh promised that as soon as the frogs were gone, he would let God's people go. "But when Pharaoh saw that there was a respite, he hardened his heart and would not listen to them, as the Lord had said" (8:15). Moses prayed, God answered, and then Pharaoh broke his promise. It was the first time he went back on his word, but it wouldn't be the last. Pharaoh was the kind of man who says anything to get out of trouble, but as soon as his troubles are over, he goes right back to his old selfish ways.

The only thing that really mattered to Pharaoh was his own personal comfort. When he "saw that there was a respite," he once again hardened his heart against God. More literally, the Hebrew says, "when Pharaoh saw that there was room." He just wanted a little space, and as soon as he had enough space to get his life back on his own terms, he had no use for God. It was out sight, out of mind, because once the frogs were out of Pharaoh's sight, God was off his mind.

This shows what was wrong with Pharaoh's prayer in the first place. Like a lot of people, he only wanted God to take away the consequences of his sin; he never had any intention of getting rid of the sin itself. A better example of how to pray comes from John Newton's hymn "Come, My Soul, Thy Suit Prepare" (1779):

> With my burden I begin:
> "Lord, remove this load of sin;
> Let thy blood, for sinners spilt,
> Set my conscience free from guilt;
> Set my conscience free from guilt."

This is how Pharaoh should have begun his prayer—by asking God to take away his sins, not his frogs! But Pharaoh wasn't interested in having a relationship with God. He was motivated entirely by self-interest, and once he had a little breathing room, he reneged on his promise to live for God's glory.

Pharaoh's poor example shows the danger of making a temporary commitment to God that falls short of saving faith. One is reminded of Jesus' parable about two sons whose father asked them to work in the fields (Matthew 21:28–31). One of the sons told his father that he wouldn't go but ended up doing the job after all. The other son promised to do his chores but never went out to the fields. It was the first son who actually did his father's will. Pharaoh was like the second son, the one who went back on his promise. Jesus ended his parable with a warning that salvation is only for those who follow through by repenting and believing. A false promise of obedience will not lead to eternal life. It is not enough simply to say that we are Christians or that perhaps someday we will get saved. If we want God to save us, we must really and truly come to Jesus Christ.

Anyone who is still trying to decide whether to come to Christ or not should know that the plagues are coming again. In his revelation of the coming judgment, the apostle John wrote, "And I saw, coming out of the mouth of the dragon and out of the mouth of the beast and out of the mouth of the false prophet, three unclean spirits like frogs. For they are demonic spirits, performing signs, who go abroad to the kings of the whole world, to assemble them for battle on the great day of God the Almighty" (Revelation 16:13, 14). The only people who will be safe on that dreadful day are those who belong to Jesus Christ—not those who need to borrow a prayer from someone else, but those who have prayed for their own salvation.

# 20

# The Finger of God

## EXODUS 8:16–19

WHAT WOULD IT TAKE to persuade Pharaoh to let God's people go? More than a river of blood; more than an infestation of frogs. So God struck Egypt with another plague, a plague that came without any warning: "Then the Lord said to Moses, 'Say to Aaron, "Stretch out your staff and strike the dust of the earth, so that it may become gnats in all the land of Egypt."' And they did so. Aaron stretched out his hand with his staff and struck the dust of the earth, and there were gnats on man and beast. All the dust of the earth became gnats in all the land of Egypt" (8:16, 17).

### What Was Bugging Ol' Pharaoh?

There is some uncertainty as to exactly which insect afflicted the Egyptians. Before he became a world-famous cartoonist (*Peanuts*), the late Charles M. Schulz wrote a humorous book called *What Was Bugging Ol' Pharaoh?* In the case of the third plague, that is precisely the question: What kind of insect did God use to bug the Egyptians? The possibilities include gnats, fleas, lice, maggots, midges, sand flies, and mosquitoes. Take your pick!

In modern Hebrew the word *kinnim* means "lice," which is the way it is translated in the King James Version. The English Standard Version calls them gnats because this is the interpretation favored by the first Greek versions of the Old Testament. However, the Bible says that these insects "were . . . on man and beast" (8:17). In other words, they seem actually to have touched the Egyptians. Therefore, it seems more likely that they were lice or mosquitoes than gnats or fleas. Writing in the first century after Christ, Philo of Alexandria described these insects creeping up people's noses and into their ears.[1] However an entomologist would have classified them, they were nagging, annoying pests that swarmed all over Egypt, molesting every living, breathing creature.

The plague of bugs was the third of the ten plagues that afflicted the Egyptians. Bible scholars have made various attempts to organize these plagues into some sort of pattern. Umberto Cassuto divides them into pairs, based on the nature of the plagues themselves. The first two plagues (blood and frogs) affected the Nile; the next two (gnats and flies) involved insects; the fifth and sixth plagues (livestock and boils) were both diseases; the seventh and eighth plagues (hail and locusts) affected Egypt's crops; and the last two plagues (darkness and the death of the firstborn) involved different kinds of darkness.[2]

Many other scholars—going back to the early rabbis—have noticed that the first nine plagues come in three sets of three. Before the first plague in each cycle, Moses goes to Pharaoh early in the morning (plagues 1, 4, and 7; see 7:15, 8:20, and 9:13). Before the second plague in each cycle he confronts Pharaoh at his palace (plagues 2, 5, and 8; see 8:1–3; 9:1; and 10:1). The third and final plague in each group comes without any warning or confrontation at all (plagues 3, 6, and 9; see 8:16; 9:8; and 10:21). One advantage of grouping the plagues this way is that attention is drawn to the tenth and final plague, which stands alone as the deadly climax of God's judgment against the Egyptians and their gods.

As we have seen before, another way to organize the plagues is as a series of natural disasters, each one caused by the one that preceded it. In the case of the bugs, some scholars have suggested that they came from maggots brooding in the piles of rotting frogs. Alternatively, they were mosquitoes caused by seasonal flooding. Alan Cole writes: "If it is late autumn in Egypt, the fields are still flooded. Mosquitoes will breed in unbelievable numbers; when disturbed they rise in a black cloud, and the air is full of their shrill buzz."[3] Their numbers would have been especially great in this case, the argument goes, because there were no frogs to keep them in check.

The problem with these explanations is that they ignore the plain sense of the Scripture. God said, "Strike the dust of the earth, so that it may become gnats" (8:16). These insects did not come from the frogs or from the River Nile; they came from the dust of the ground, which Aaron struck with the rod of God. The Bible says further that "All the dust of the earth became gnats in all the land of Egypt" (8:17). The point is not so much that every single speck of dust became a bug, but that the whole land was covered with them. The word "dust" is used in a similar way in the book of Genesis. When God promised to make Abraham into a great nation, he said that his descendants would be "as the dust of the earth" (Genesis 13:16; cf. Genesis 28:14), meaning that he would have more offspring than he could count. The same was true with the insects that plagued Egypt—the sheer number of them was overwhelming.

Like the other nine disasters that afflicted the Egyptians, the plague of bugs was a genuine miracle. A miracle is a direct act of divine intervention in which God overrules his creation to display his glory. It is of the very essence of a miracle that it is supernatural; that is to say, it goes beyond the ordinary laws of nature. Louis Berkhof writes,

> The distinctive thing in the miraculous deed is that it results from the exercise of the supernatural power of God. And this means, of course, that it is not brought about by . . . the laws of nature. If it were, it would not be *supernatural* (above nature), that is, it would not be a miracle. If God in the performance of a miracle did sometimes utilize forces that were present in nature, He used them in a way that was out of the ordinary, to produce unexpected results, and it was exactly this that constituted the miracle.[4]

The plagues in Egypt were miracles in the true Biblical sense of the word. They were direct acts of divine intervention that superseded the causes of nature. One of the best defenses of the Biblical plagues as miracles comes from Joseph Free's book *Archaeology and Bible History*:

> Efforts have sometimes been made to explain away the plagues as natural phenomena in Egypt. It is quite true that unusual quantities of frogs and lice, unexpected darkness and the other serious heightenings of natural phenomena have been known in Egypt. An examination of the plagues shows, however, that they were miraculous in at least five different ways: (1) *Intensification*—frogs, insects, plagues on cattle, hail, and darkness were all known in Egypt, but now they are intensified far beyond the ordinary occurrence. (2) *Prediction*—the time was set for the coming of the flies ("tomorrow," 8:23), the death of cattle (9:5), the hail (9:18), and the locusts (10:4). The removal time was also set: e.g., frogs (8:10) and thunder (9:29). Modern science cannot accurately predict the cessation of natural phenomena such as hail. (3) *Discrimination*—in Goshen there were no flies (8:22), no death of cattle (9:4), no hail (9:26), and so forth. (4) *Orderliness*—the severity of the plagues increased until they ended with the death of Pharaoh's firstborn. (5) *Moral purpose*—the plagues were not just freaks of nature, but carried a moral purpose in these ways: (a) The gods of Egypt were discredited, a purpose indicated in Exodus 12:12; the Nile-god, frog-god, and sun-god were all shown to be powerless before God. (b) Pharaoh was made to know that the Lord is God, and to acknowledge him (9:27; 10:16). (c) God was revealed as Savior, in rescuing Israel from the hands of the Egyptians (14:30).[5]

Although God made use of natural phenomena like animals, diseases, and storms, these plagues went far beyond the ordinary course of nature. Whatever was bugging old Pharaoh was placed there by the finger of God; it was the product of his supernatural power.

## De-creation and Disorder

God could have chosen some other way to convince Pharaoh to let his people go. He could have written giant hieroglyphics in the sky, saying, "Let my people go! Sincerely, God." He could have given Moses the power to levitate one of the pyramids or sent a giant aircraft to transport his people to Palestine. Instead God took the ordinary forces of nature and overruled them by his supernatural power. The question is, why? Wouldn't it have been easier for God to give Pharaoh a sign that was completely outside of nature rather than a sign that turned nature against him?

One way to answer this question is to point out that most of the plagues were designed to defeat particular gods and goddesses in the Egyptian pantheon. We have already seen how God used the river of blood to conquer Hapi, Khnum, and Osiris, the gods of the Nile. We have also seen how the plague of frogs defeated Heqet, the goddess of fertility. The third plague may have been intended to humiliate the earth-god Geb. By turning the dust into bugs, God was claiming authority over the very soil of Egypt and thus over the god of the ground. God's strategy for gaining glory over the gods of Egypt was to defeat them one at a time by demonstrating his control over the creatures that the Egyptians worshiped.

God had another reason for using natural forces in a miraculous way, and that was to demonstrate his power over all creation. One of the striking things about the ten plagues is the way they disrupted the natural order. It was almost as if God was uncreating the world that he had made, at least in Egypt. Consider the following parallels that John Currid has noticed between the Exodus plagues and the six days of creation:

> When God created the world, he separated light from the darkness (Day 1; Gen. 1:1–5); but in the ninth plague light was blotted out (Exod. 10:21–29).
>
> When God created the world, he gathered the water into one place (Day 2; Gen. 1:6–8); but in the first plague the water was turned to blood (Exod. 7:15–25).
>
> When God created the world, he made vegetation grow on the land (Day 3; Gen. 1:9–13); but in the seventh and eighth plagues he destroyed Egypt's crops (Exod. 9:18–10:20).
>
> When God created the world, he put two great lights in the heavens (Day 4; Gen. 1:14–19); but with the ninth plague, the sun ceased to shine (Exod. 10:21–29).
>
> When God created the world, he made the waters swarm with creatures of the sea (Day 5; Gen. 1:20–23); but the first and second plagues ended with the death of fish and frogs (Exod. 7:15–8:15).
>
> When God created the world, he made land animals and people (Day 6; Gen. 1:24–31); but the third through sixth plagues afflicted both man and beast with pestilence and disease (Exod. 8:16–9:17), until God finally killed every first-born son in Egypt (Exod. 11–12).

The plagues brought such chaos that Currid concludes that God was "de-creating" Egypt.[6]

The plague of bugs was part of the de-creation. The Bible says that the insects came from "the dust of the earth." This calls to mind Genesis 2:7, where the Scripture says that "the LORD God formed the man of dust from the ground." In both cases God created something from the ground up, and in both cases he did it by the power of his word. In his summary of the plagues, the psalmist wrote: "He [God] spoke, and there came swarms of flies, and gnats throughout their country" (Psalm 105:31). The difference was that this time the animals had dominion over the people, and thus the order of creation was reversed.

By bringing chaos out of order, God was making another direct assault on the Egyptians and their gods. The Egyptians believed that Pharaoh had the power to maintain cosmic order, which they called *ma'at*. *Ma'at* was universal equilibrium, the "cosmic force of harmony, order, stability, and security."[7] It was Pharaoh's responsibility to maintain *ma'at* by controlling the climate, regulating the seasons, and generally preserving order in the world. A good example of the Egyptians' faith in Pharaoh to do this comes from an ancient text called "The Prophecy of Neferti." The text, which describes the accession of Amenemhet, promises that when the king begins to reign, "Then Order will come to its place, and Chaos will be driven out."[8]

The plagues attacked this faith at its very foundations. By striking the Egyptians with plague after plague, and thereby throwing their land into confusion, God was confronting their basic beliefs about order and balance in the universe. Pharaoh could not be the true God because he was unable to maintain *ma'at* in the world. Only the God of Israel had the power to control chaos in the cosmos.

One way to apply this lesson is to ask ourselves what our foundation is. What is the source of our equilibrium? Some people base their sense of security on their jobs or their investments. Others depend on their intelligence, charm, beauty, or physical stamina. But in the day of disaster, when chaos reigns, none of these things will be able to hold our world together. What happens when there is a correction in the market? Or when our department gets downsized and we have to send out our résumés? What happens when we go to university and start getting C's instead of A's, or when our parents file for divorce, or when we end up in the hospital? When our world gets turned upside down, we discover that our abilities and possessions cannot save us.

The Bible teaches that what brings true order and cohesion to the universe is the person and work of Jesus Christ: "For by him all things were created . . . and in him all things hold together" (Colossians 1:16, 17). Jesus Christ is the one who holds everything together. In the words of the old gospel song, "He's got the whole world in his hands." This is true not only cosmically but also personally. When your world seems to be out of control, the only stable foundation is faith in Jesus Christ.

## Satan Has His Limitations

When Pharaoh started to lose control, his magicians made one last desperate attempt to bring order out of chaos by their own powers. Up until now the performance of these sorcerers had been rather impressive. They had demonstrated their power to turn water into blood and to bring frogs out of water, so one might expect them to be able to bring bugs out of the dust. "The magicians tried by their secret arts to produce gnats, but they could not. So there were gnats on man and beast" (8:18).

The last phrase—"there were gnats on man and beast"—shows how miserably Pharaoh's magicians failed. Not only were they unable to produce any more bugs, but they were completely covered with them, and there was nothing they could do about it. It was utterly humiliating, especially because the religious leaders of Egypt prided themselves on their physical purity. Before performing their daily rituals, they bathed thoroughly and shaved off all their hair. Therefore, according to John J. Davis, it is "rather doubtful that the priesthood in Egypt could function very effectively having been polluted by the presence of these insects. They, like their worshipers, were inflicted with the pestilence of this occasion. Their prayers were made ineffective by their own personal impurity with the presence of gnats on their bodies."[9]

Since Pharaoh's magicians were servants of Satan, the plague of bugs clearly shows that Satan's power has its limits. Admittedly, the devil does have some power. The Bible says that his work is shown "with all power and false signs and wonders" (2 Thessalonians 2:9). As we have seen, whether by some clever trick or by some demonic enchantment, Pharaoh's magicians were able to duplicate the first two plagues. Either way, they performed their magic in opposition to God, and thus in service to Satan.

Satan has other powers as well. He has the power to rebel (Isaiah 14:12–14), to tempt (Matthew 4:1), to deceive (Revelation 20:10), and to accuse (Zechariah 3:1). He has the power to hold sinners captive in their iniquity (2 Timothy 2:26). On certain occasions he has the power to torment the elect with various afflictions (2 Corinthians 12:7), including disease (Job 2:1–7) and imprisonment (Revelation 2:10). The Bible describes Satan as the one "who has the power of death" (Hebrews 2:14). God even gave Satan the power to betray his one and only Son (Luke 22:3–5), a betrayal that resulted in our Lord's sufferings and death on the cross.

Satan is very powerful, but his powers are limited. Consider all the things he is unable to do or to be: He cannot create; he can only destroy. He cannot redeem; he can only be damned. He cannot love; he can only hate. He cannot be humble; he can only be proud. Most crushingly of all, he was unable to keep God's Son in the grave. God broke the devil's power by raising Jesus from the dead. The Bible says, "The reason the Son of God appeared was to destroy the works of the devil" (1 John 3:8b), and the way Jesus destroyed it was through his crucifixion and resurrection. In the end, Satan will be utterly vanquished. All his evil plans will come to nothing, and he himself will be "thrown into the lake of fire and sulfur," where he "will be tormented day and night forever and ever" (Revelation 20:10).

Satan should have seen it coming. Way back in Egypt, when his servants failed to turn dust into bugs, he should have realized that he would never be able to compete with the God of all power and glory.

We should remember Satan's limitations whenever we are tempted or face some form of spiritual opposition. He is potent but not omnipotent. If we are followers of Jesus Christ, then the God we serve is infinitely more powerful than our greatest enemy. God is able and willing to save us from the power of Satan. When we pray "deliver us from evil" (Matthew 6:13), he will hear our prayer. When we put on "the whole armor of God," he will enable us to "stand against the schemes of the devil" (Ephesians 6:11), for as the Scripture says, "resist the devil, and he will flee from you" (James 4:7). Among his many limitations, Satan is unable to withstand even a single Christian who trusts in God's mighty power to save.

## God's Finger

To their credit, Pharaoh's magicians realized that they were dealing with a higher power. What really impressed them was not the plague itself, but the fact that God had the power to prevent them from duplicating it. When they were unable to turn dust into bugs, "The magicians said to Pharaoh, 'This is the finger of God'" (8:19a).

At first, this sounds as if God had finally made believers out of these Egyptians. Pharaoh's priests seemed to confess their faith in the one true God. They acknowledged that the third plague was a divine miracle. They told Pharaoh that the land of the pyramids had been touched by the very finger of God. However, the term that they use for God (*Elohim*) is a general one, and there are several different ways to understand what they were saying.

Because *Elohim* occurs in the plural, Pharaoh's magicians may have been saying "This is the finger of the gods," meaning the gods of their own pantheon. According to Egyptian mythology, the two brothers Seth and Osiris constantly struggled for world domination with Horus, the god of Heaven. In their warfare Seth's finger constantly threatened to poke Horus's eye and thus to destroy it. The Egyptians also used the expression "finger of God" to describe an attack the moon-god Thoth made on Apophis the snake.[10] So when they spoke of "the finger of God," the magicians may have been attributing the plague of bugs to one of their own gods.

The other possibility is that when Pharaoh's priests spoke of "the finger of God," they really were admitting they were in the presence of the Supreme

Being. At first they thought that Moses and Aaron were magicians like themselves, but by the time the palace started crawling with insects, they were forced to surrender to the divine power of a superior God.

By giving some glory to God, the magicians were heading in the right direction spiritually. Yet they had not arrived at genuine saving faith, for although the magicians acknowledged God generally, they did not know him personally. We know this because they addressed God by his general name *Elohim*, not by his covenant name *Yahweh*, which means "Lord." Yet that was the entire purpose of the exodus. At the beginning of chapter 7, God said to Moses, "The Egyptians shall know that I am the Lord, when I stretch out my hand against Egypt and bring out the people of Israel from among them" (7:5). But the magicians still did not know that the God of Israel was Lord of all. In our last study we saw that Pharaoh knew a great deal about God without actually knowing God himself. The same was true of his magicians. They sensed they were in the presence of a cosmic force, a deity who was more powerful than any god they had ever worshipped, but they did not call him "Lord." This was because they lacked the one thing that is necessary for salvation: a personal relationship with almighty God.

Many people believe in God without ever coming to him for salvation. In fact, if the surveys are correct, *most* people believe in God. They acknowledge the existence of a Creator. They confess their need for "a Higher Power." They speak of "the Man Upstairs." When there is a natural disaster, they refer to it as "an act of God." They often use one of God's names when they curse. But the one thing they can never quite bring themselves to do is to confess Jesus as Lord. Yet that is exactly what God requires for salvation—not simply a general belief in God, but a personal faith in Jesus Christ as the true God and the only Savior: "If you confess with your mouth that Jesus is Lord and believe in your heart that God raised him from the dead, you will be saved. For with the heart one believes and is justified, and with the mouth one confesses and is saved" (Romans 10:9, 10). God does not merely hope that people will become more religious; he calls them to become Christians.

Everyone who has come to God through Christ, recognizing his lordship, is also able to look at what he has done and say, "This is the finger of God." King David saw the finger of God at work in creation. He wrote:

> When I look at your heavens, the work of your fingers,
> the moon and the stars, which you have set in place. . . . (Psalm 8:3)

David recognized that God has left his fingerprints on everything he has made. Moses saw the finger of God at work in revelation. When he met God on the mountain, Moses was given "the two tablets of the testimony, tablets of stone, written with the finger of God" (31:18). Many other people have seen the finger of God touching their lives in more ordinary ways: a prayer answered, a need met, a friendship restored, a sinner converted. When we see God at work in our lives, helping us because of his goodness and changing us by his grace, we are compelled to say, "This is the finger of God."

The very best place to see the finger of God is in the life and ministry of Jesus Christ. In fact, Jesus himself borrowed this line from Pharaoh's magicians after performing one of his miracles. The story is told in Luke 11. Jesus had driven a demon out of a man who was mute. The Bible says, "When the demon had gone out, the mute man spoke, and the people marveled. But some of them said, 'He casts out demons by Beelzebul, the prince of demons,' while others, to test him, kept seeking from him a sign from heaven" (Luke 11:14b–16).

Jesus responded with his famous teaching that a house divided against itself cannot stand. His point was that if he was driving out demons by the power of demons, then Satan's house was divided and would certainly fall. But of course Jesus was not driving out demons by Beelzebul; he was driving them out by his own divine power. In order to explain what he was doing, he said, "But if it is by the finger of God that I cast out demons, then the kingdom of God has come upon you" (Luke 11:20). It is easy to imagine Jesus lifting up his finger as he said this, because his finger *was* the finger of God. Whatever gesture he may have made, Jesus was making the same point that God made when he plagued Egypt with insects. He was showing that Satan has his limits. He was also showing that in order to defeat Satan, all he had to do was to lift his little finger.

Jesus Christ is the Moses of our salvation. He has defeated the power of Satan and opened the way to eternal life. When we hear the good news of his death and resurrection, we should say, "This is the finger of God." For it took the very power of God to atone for sin and to raise Jesus from the dead.

Once you see how the finger of God has touched the world through Jesus Christ, the thing to do is to receive Jesus as Savior. Do not do what Pharaoh did. The Bible says, "Pharaoh's heart was hardened, and he would not listen to them, as the Lord had said" (8:19b). Once again Pharaoh hardened his heart. Even when he was touched by the finger of God, he refused to give God the glory. This shows that what was really bugging him was God's superior power and might. If you have been touched by the finger of God, do not harden your heart to his salvation, but open your heart to Jesus.

# 21

# Lord of the Flies

## EXODUS 8:20–32

IN THE END Pharaoh was defeated by mighty forces like darkness and death. But long before the sky turned black over Egypt and the angel of death snatched his firstborn son, it was the little things that got to Pharaoh—little things like gnats and flies. One of the wonders of the exodus is that God used tiny insects to demonstrate his power over Pharaoh and his gods. This miracle led Charles Spurgeon to observe, "When it pleases God by his judgments to humble men, he is never at a loss for means: he can use lions or lice, famines or flies. In the armory of God there are weapons of every kind, from the stars in their courses down to caterpillars in their hosts."[1]

### Shoo, Fly, Shoo!

The first two plagues—the river of blood and the infestation of frogs—came by water. The third plague came from the earth: God turned the dust of the ground into gnats or perhaps lice. The Bible does not indicate when this plague ended, so it may have bugged the Egyptians for quite some time. But eventually the gnats disappeared, and God sent Moses back to Pharaoh to announce the fourth plague, which came by air: "Then the Lord said to Moses, 'Rise up early in the morning and present yourself to Pharaoh, as he goes out to the water, and say to him, "Thus says the Lord, 'Let my people go, that they may serve me. Or else, if you will not let my people go, behold, I will send swarms of flies on you and your servants and your people, and into your houses. And the houses of the Egyptians shall be filled with swarms of flies, and also the ground on which they stand'"'" (8:20, 21).

These verses mark the beginning of the second cycle of three plagues. By now the pattern is familiar: Moses went to meet Pharaoh early in the morning (cf. 7:15). He went down by the riverside, where he found Pharaoh still worshiping the same old gods. He went as God's chosen servant to bring a message from

Heaven. He was told to "present [himself] to Pharaoh"—literally, to "stand his ground"—and in the name of the God of Israel he said, "Let my people go, that they may serve me" (8:20).

That statement includes both God's demand and his people's destiny. God's demand was, "Let my people go." It was not right for Pharaoh to keep the Israelites in cruel bondage, forcing them to make heavy bricks under the hot, dry sun. They were not Pharaoh's people—they were God's people, and what God demanded was nothing less than their unconditional release. The reason he demanded freedom for his people was for his own glory. God said, "Let my people go, that they may serve me." God's people needed the liberty to go out into the wilderness, where they could worship their God and make atonement for their sins. This was the grand purpose of the exodus, in which God saved his people for his glory.

This is also the grand purpose of salvation in Jesus Christ. The exodus from Egypt reveals the pattern of his redemption. Until God's Spirit comes to set us free, we are held captive by Satan, who keeps us enslaved in our sins. But then—while we are still in bondage—we hear the gospel, in which God says to sin and to Satan, "Let my people go!" The good news about Jesus Christ is our emancipation proclamation. It declares that the death and resurrection of God's only Son have set us free from sin and death, and on that basis it demands our release from anger, lust, pride, and every other sinful desire. True spiritual freedom comes through faith in Jesus Christ. And God's ultimate purpose in bringing this liberation is to receive the glory of our praise. Once we have been released from our slavery to sin, we are free to worship God the way we were made to worship him. God's plan is to save us for his glory; to that end, he says, "Let my people go, that they may serve me."

Pharaoh turned a deaf ear to God's demand. This was the sixth time that Moses told him to let God's people go, and for the sixth time Pharaoh refused to give God the glory by giving the Israelites their freedom. In response God did exactly what he had said he would do. Verse 21 uses a play on words to say that if Pharaoh did not send the Israelites out, then God would "send" in the flies. The Scripture goes on to say, "And the LORD did so. There came great swarms of flies into the house of Pharaoh and into his servants' houses. Throughout all the land of Egypt the land was ruined by the swarms of flies" (8:24).

It was not the great things that overwhelmed Pharaoh but little things in very large quantities! There is some uncertainty as to precisely which insect afflicted the Egyptians. The Biblical term is not limited to houseflies and may in fact refer to several different kinds of flying insects. Perhaps they were mosquitoes or some other kind of biting, stinging insect. A number of ancient sources (such as the Septuagint, which was written in Egypt) indicate that they were "dog flies"—blood-sucking bugs that tormented both man and beast.[2]

Whatever they were, these insects swarmed all over Egypt. Literally, the

Bible says that they were "heavy" (*kabed*; 8:24), meaning that they were so numerous that they became a burden to the Egyptians. Flies are ugly, repulsive creatures with nasty, disgusting habits. Even one fly buzzing around a room can be a distraction. Ten flies are a nuisance. Fifty flies are a real annoyance, as I discovered once when I tried to study in a fly-infested house. But imagine a whole plague of them, an inundation so severe that flies covered every inch of ground and invaded every corner of every building. There were flies everywhere, buzzing in the ears of every Egyptian. The Bible says that they wreaked such havoc that the land was "ruined" (8:24). Psalm 78 further explains that God "sent among them swarms of flies, which devoured them" (Psalm 78:45a). The flies virtually ate the Egyptians alive (which suggests that they were, in fact, of the biting variety). This was all a testimony to the power of God, who is able to use even the smallest creatures with tremendous destructive force.

As we have been discovering, the plagues were designed to defeat the gods and goddesses of Egypt. The Lord God of Israel used these signs and wonders to demonstrate his power over Pharaoh's idols, sometimes in very specific ways. By turning the Nile into blood, God triumphed over the river god Hapi; the plague of frogs meant the demise of Heqet, the goddess of fertility; and so forth.

But what about the flies? How were they related to the Egyptian gods? John J. Davis connects the fourth plague to the ichneumon fly, which deposits its eggs on other living things, and which the Egyptians considered a manifestation of the god Uatchit.[3] Others argue that the flies were really flying beetles, also known as scarabs. Scarabs appeared frequently on Egyptian monuments, mummies, charms, and amulets. The scarab was sacred to the Egyptians. They had observed industrious beetles forming animal dung into round spheres that they then rolled back to their holes in the ground. As Donald Grey Barnhouse writes, "They soon made a connection in their minds between the spheres of dung and the sun in the sky and conceived the idea that a giant beetle rolled the sun from evening until morning through the underworld until the sunrise brought it back into the sky once more."[4] Thus the scarab became an emblem of the sun, which for the Egyptians represented eternity, the abiding life of the soul. Not surprisingly, the god of resurrection—who was called Khepre—was depicted as a beetle.

Another possibility is that the plague of flies was directed against Beelzebub (which means, "the lord of the flies"). Some Egyptians worshiped Beelzebub as their protector and guardian. Since his role was to protect their land from swarms of flies and other natural disasters, he functioned as a sort of insurance policy. But like the rest of Egypt's gods and goddesses, Beelzebub actually was a tool of the devil. This is confirmed by the Gospel of Luke, in which he is identified as the "prince of demons" (Luke 11:15; ESV: "Beelzebul"). Beelzebub was one representation of Satan's power over Egypt.

It is hard to determine the precise connection between the plague of flies and the religion of Egypt, but in one way or another God was demonstrating his power over Pharaoh's gods. The Egyptians trusted their gods for eternal life and physical protection, but the one true God overruled creation to show that the gods of Egypt were not in control. Beelzebub could not keep away the flies; Khepher could not raise the dead. While the Egyptians were busy trying to shoo away all the flies, they should have realized that the gods they worshiped did not have the power to save. The only God who has the power to grant eternal life is the God of Israel. Anyone who wants to be safe for all eternity must trust in him and in his Son, Jesus Christ, who alone has "the words of eternal life" (John 6:68).

## My People, Your People

It must have been awesome to see swarms of insects descend on Egypt and devour the land, but what was equally amazing was the complete absence of flies in Goshen. God said to Pharaoh, "But on that day I will set apart the land of Goshen, where my people dwell, so that no swarms of flies shall be there, that you may know that I am the LORD in the midst of the earth. Thus I will put a division between my people and your people. Tomorrow this sign shall happen" (8:22, 23).

These verses remind us that the plague of flies was a genuine miracle, a direct act of divine intervention in which God overruled his creation to display his glory. Insects are natural phenomena, of course, but these particular swarms of insects were a demonstration of God's supernatural power. Not only were there tremendous numbers of them, but Moses was able to announce beforehand the exact day on which they would appear. Furthermore, there were no flies in Goshen, and this preferential treatment was part of the miracle.

The land of Goshen seems to have been located somewhere on the Eastern Delta of the Nile. Israelites had made their home there since the days of Joseph. When Joseph had been reunited with his brothers in Egypt, he sent word back home to his father: "Come down to me; do not tarry. You shall dwell in the land of Goshen" (Genesis 45:9, 10; cf. Genesis 46:28, 29). Since the region of Goshen was right in the heart of Egypt, the fact that there were no flies there was truly miraculous. The absence of swarms in Goshen was as miraculous as their presence throughout the rest of Egypt. No merely natural explanation would suffice. The miracle in Goshen prevented the Egyptians or anyone else from trying to rationalize what God had done. The fourth plague was miraculous in its severity, miraculous in its timing, and miraculous in the absolute distinction it made between the Israelites and the Egyptians.

The book of Exodus makes it clear that in the plagues God treated his own people completely differently from the Egyptians. The Israelites did not lose their livestock, they were not afflicted with boils, their crops were not destroyed by hail and locusts, their sons were not taken by the angel of death, and they did not drown in the depths of the sea. However, the Egyptians *did* suffer all these disasters: Their cattle died of the plague, their bodies were covered with itching sores, their crops were lost, their sons died, and their army drowned. In order to show that he was sovereign over both nations, God discriminated between his people and Pharaoh's people. Exodus is the story of both the salvation of Israel and the condemnation of Egypt.

Why did God make this distinction? Obviously, Pharaoh got exactly what he deserved. The question is, what was it about the Israelites that secured their salvation? This is a difficult question because the Israelites were no better than the Egyptians. As we have seen, they were slow to embrace God's plan for their deliverance. At the first sign of difficulty, they blamed the God of Moses for all their troubles. As the story continues, we will discover that the Israelites were a fractious, rebellious, idolatrous people who deserved to be judged every bit as much as the Egyptians. So why did God save them? Why didn't he afflict the land of Goshen the same way he afflicted the land of Egypt?

The answer, very simply, is that although the Israelites were a sinful people, they were nevertheless God's people. God said it to Pharaoh over and over again: "Let *my people* go!" This statement partly shows what God demanded of Pharaoh (namely, the liberation of his slaves), but it also shows why God was making this demand. The Israelites were not someone else's property, but God's very own people. So when he sent the plague of flies God said to Pharaoh, "I will put a division between my people and your people" (8:23).

This distinction was introduced at the beginning of Exodus. In chapter 2 we read that when the Israelites prayed to be released from their captivity, "God heard their groaning, and God remembered his covenant with Abraham, with Isaac, and with Jacob. God saw the people of Israel—and God knew" (2:24, 25). The covenant was the guarantee of Israel's salvation. In the covenant God promised that they would be his people and that he would be their God. Among other things, this meant that when God's people got into difficulty and started praying for deliverance, God had a solemn obligation to save them.

This is what God was doing in his ten dreadful plagues—saving his people. The story of the flies is very specific about this. What God literally said to Pharaoh was not, "I will put a division between my people and your people" (8:23), but "I will set a redemption between my people and your people." This is the language of salvation. Redemption is the purchase price of freedom, the ransom payment for a slave. When the Israelites were enslaved in Egypt, they had no way of paying their own ransom, but God set a redemption between Israel and Egypt, between his people and Pharaoh's people. He intervened with saving power to deliver Israel from the hand of the oppressor. So when he struck Egypt with ten mighty blows, at the same time he preserved his own beloved people from the hand of judgment. The difference between living in Goshen and living anywhere else in Egypt was more than just a matter of good pest control. It was a matter of life and death, the difference between salvation and condemnation.

If we ask why God made this distinction, the answer is that this is one of the eternal mysteries of his sovereign plan. Later, when Moses tried to explain to the Israelites why God delivered them from Egypt, he said,

> It was not because you were more in number than any other people that the Lord set his love on you and chose you, for you were the fewest of all peoples, but it is because the Lord loves you and is keeping the oath that he swore to your fathers, that the Lord has brought you out with a mighty hand and redeemed you from the house of slavery, from the hand of Pharaoh king of Egypt. Know therefore that the Lord your God is God, the faithful God who keeps covenant and steadfast love. (Deuteronomy 7:7–9a; cf. Deuteronomy 10:14, 15)

In order to demonstrate his mercy and covenant love, God chose a people for himself. Out of all the nations he set them apart—a people who had nothing to commend them and thus no claim upon his grace. He chose them because he chose them, and he loved them simply in order to love them. Theologians call this "the doctrine of election." It means that God's grace is God's choice. The people of God are not saved through any merit of their own, but by the sovereign purpose of God's electing will. On the basis of his own choice, God makes an absolute distinction between his people and everyone else.

What was true for Israel in the days of Moses is true for the church of Jesus Christ. God has "set a redemption" for his chosen people. This redemption is found in Jesus Christ and nowhere else. When Jesus died on the cross, it was the greatest exodus of all. God took people who were in such bondage to sin that they were completely unable to deliver themselves. They were as hopeless and as helpless as the Israelites, but God did for them what he did for Israel: he set a redemption for them. He sent a Redeemer to rescue them from their slavery to sin by paying their ransom with his very own blood. Now his cross rightly discriminates between those who are God's people and those who are not. God's people are the ones who put their trust in Christ and in his cross, but anyone who does not believe in Jesus Christ remains outside the people of God.

This difference goes all the way back to eternity past, when God differentiated between those who *were* his people and those who were *not* his people: "He [God] chose us in him [Christ] before the foundation of the world" (Ephesians 1:4). The difference between being in Christ and being out of Christ lies in God's electing choice. It is a difference that makes all the difference in the world, because those who are in Christ receive every blessing of salvation, while those who are outside of Christ do not. Those who are chosen in Christ are born again by God's Spirit. When they hear the good news about Jesus Christ, they respond with faith and repentance, trusting in his cross and turning away from sin. On the basis of their faith, they are declared righteous in God's sight. Then, by the transforming work of God's Spirit, they become more and more holy, until finally in glory they become as perfect as Christ himself. All through life they rest secure in the knowledge that God is their loving Father who will help them in every difficulty and provide for their every need.

Those who do not believe in Jesus Christ remain outside the people of God and thus never experience any of these blessings. They are not called, regenerated, justified, sanctified, or adopted. But the saddest thing of all is that they will never be glorified, for in eternity the difference between the Christian and the non-Christian will be revealed as the difference between salvation and damnation. The Bible describes the final judgment as a permanent separation in which the sheep will be separated from the goats, the redeemed from the damned, and those who enter his presence from those who will remain outside it forever (see Matthew 25:31–46; Revelation 21:7, 8, 27).

The distinction between those who are God's people and those who are not has at least two practical implications. First, it shows the absolute necessity of coming to Christ in faith. Anyone who does not trust in Christ is outside salvation and will remain under God's wrath until repenting of sin. Yet even now God invites everyone to enter his salvation and to embrace the love that he has shown in Jesus Christ.

Second, the distinction between redemption and damnation shows the absolute necessity of missions and evangelism. God's mission was to bring Israel out of Egypt, setting his people apart from the world for salvation. Spurgeon said:

> God always puts a distinction between Israel and Egypt. He constantly speaks of the Israelites as "my people"; of the Egyptians, he speaks to Pharaoh as being "thy people." There is a continual and eternal distinction observed in the Word of God between the chosen seed of promise and the world. . . . The great object of God's interference with Egypt, was . . . the gathering out of his Israel from the midst of the Egyptians. Beloved, I have the conviction that this is just what God is doing with the world now. Perhaps, for many a year to come, God will gather out his elect from the nations of the earth as he gathered his Israel from the midst of the Egyptians. . . . Egypt is Egypt still, the world is the world still, and as worldly as it ever was, and God's purpose seems to be, through the ministry which he now exercises, to bring his chosen ones out. In fact, the Word which Jehovah is now speaking to the entire world with the solemn authority of an imperial mandate is this—"Thus saith the Lord, let my people go, that they may serve me."[5]

Since this is God's mission, then our commission—the Great Commission that we have received from Christ himself (Matthew 28:18–20)—is to go into all the world and preach the gospel. We proclaim the good news that the sinners of

Egypt can enter the Goshen of redemption, if only they will trust in Jesus Christ as their crucified and risen Lord.

### Without Compromise

Since Pharaoh did not live in the land of Goshen, he quickly discovered that he was not overly fond of flies. In fact, he didn't care for flies any more than he cared for frogs or gnats. And when he realized they were destroying his land, he decided that something had to be done. This time Pharaoh didn't even bother to call for his sorcerers and magicians. In the past he had relied on their devilry to replicate God's signs and wonders, but when they failed to reproduce the plague of gnats, he realized that his gods were defeated. He also realized that the only person who could do anything about the flies was Moses: "Then Pharaoh called Moses and Aaron and said, 'Go, sacrifice to your God within the land'" (8:25).

Pharaoh was a shrewd negotiator, and this was one of his cleverest ploys. It seemed like a reasonable compromise: He would permit the Israelites to offer their sacrifices, provided that they stayed in Egypt. They would not be allowed to go out into the wilderness (as God had demanded), but at least they would be able to make atonement for their sins.

It was a big enough concession that most people would have taken Pharaoh up on his offer. If Moses had been in a mood to compromise, it would have been easy to rationalize. "This is the best offer we're going to get," he might have said. "Why don't we take it? After all, the really important thing is that we offer our sacrifices to God, not where we do it." But Moses knew that what God had said to Pharaoh was not "Let my people sacrifice, on one condition," but "Let my people go, that they may hold a feast to me in the wilderness" (5:1). He also knew that God's plan was to bring Israel out of Egypt entirely (see 6:11). So he refused even to consider a partial compromise that fell short of full obedience to the revealed will of God. When Pharaoh tried to bargain with him, "Moses said, 'It would not be right to do so, for the offerings we shall sacrifice to the LORD our God are an abomination to the Egyptians. If we sacrifice offerings abominable to the Egyptians before their eyes, will they not stone us? We must go three days' journey into the wilderness and sacrifice to the LORD our God as he tells us'" (8:26, 27).

Moses' offer raises a number of questions. One concerns the request for a "three days' journey," which, given God's command to leave Egypt altogether, does not seem completely forthright. Answers to this objection were given back in chapter 8 of this commentary and need not be repeated here. However, scholars have also asked why Moses bothered to mention that the Egyptians would be offended by their sacrifices. Certainly his reasoning was correct: What was obligatory for the Israelites was objectionable to the Egyptians. The animals they intended to sacrifice—such as bulls and rams—were sacred in Egypt. Bulls were sacred to Apis, cows to Isis, calves to Hathor, rams to Amon, and so forth.

Once the Hebrews started sacrificing these representations of Pharaoh's gods, rioting would break out among the Egyptians, and human blood would also be shed (which perhaps is what Pharaoh secretly hoped). To draw a comparison, sacrificing bulls among the Egyptians would be like holding a pig roast at a synagogue or cooking burgers in front of a Hindu temple. In fact, Alan Cole reports that "The little Jewish colony at Yeb/Elephantine, on the Upper Nile, endured a pogrom at the hands of the Egyptians in the fifth century, for this very reason of animal sacrifice."[6] Thus Moses was making a pragmatic argument. He was trying to persuade Pharaoh that in addition to violating God's command, his compromise would be a political disaster.

Of course, the real issue was that staying in Egypt would violate God's command, which is why Moses went on to say, "We must go three days' journey into the wilderness and sacrifice to the LORD our God as he tells us" (8:27). On occasion it is appropriate to use a practical argument to persuade someone to do what is right, but the ultimate standard for right and wrong is the will of God. The reason Moses refused to compromise was because he had made a commitment to do exactly what God commanded. The prophet knew that one of the differences between God's people and Pharaoh's people was that God's people did what God said. Therefore, if God told them to make sacrifices out in the wilderness, then out into the wilderness they would go.

The example of Moses shows that when it comes to obeying God's commands, there can be no compromise. This is true at the beginning of the Christian life, when a sinner first comes to Christ. Just as God brought Israel out of the house of bondage, so he brings the church out of the prison house of sin—not halfway out but all the way! Some people are interested in getting religious without ever becoming Christians. They come to church on Sunday, but they are not willing to leave their sins behind the rest of the week. To put it in terms of Exodus 8, they are willing to make a few sacrifices, as long as they don't actually have to leave Egypt! But becoming a Christian means leaving sin behind to follow Christ. Spurgeon explained it like this:

> God's demand is not that his people should have some little liberty, some little rest in their sin, no, but that they should go right out of Egypt. . . . Christ did not come into the world merely to make our sin more tolerable, but to deliver us right away from it. He did not come to make hell less hot, or sin less damnable, or our lusts less mighty; but to put all these things far away from his people, and work out a full and complete deliverance. . . . Christ does not come to make people less sinful, but to make them leave off sin altogether—not to make them less miserable, but to put their miseries right away, and give them joy and peace in believing in him. The deliverance must be complete, or else there shall be no deliverance at all.[7]

Even after coming to Christ, Christians continue to struggle with the temptation to stay in Egypt. Every day we are confronted with opportunities to compromise our faith. Often there is a way to offer God partial obedience without disturbing the rest of our commitments. We are willing to call ourselves Christians as long as we do not have to take a moral stand in the workplace or give up part of our financial prosperity or speak with our neighbors about spiritual things or allow ourselves to be inconvenienced by the needs of others. Secretly we wish that we could offer sacrifices to God while remaining within the friendly confines of Egypt, but Moses teaches us not to settle for a partial compromise that falls short of full obedience. Everyone who claims to follow Jesus Christ must follow him without compromise. To quote again from Spurgeon,

> If Moses had thought that going a little way into the wilderness would have saved Israel, he would have let them go a little way into the wilderness, and there would have been an end of it. But Moses knew that nothing would do for God's Israel but to go clean away as far as ever they could, and put a deep Red Sea between them and Egypt. He knew that they were never to turn back again, come what might, and so Moses pushed for a going forth to a distance; as I would in God's name push for full committal to Christ with everybody who is tempted to a compromise.[8]

In her book *Out of Egypt*, Jeanette Howard applies the lessons of Exodus 8 to her struggle with homosexual sin. She writes:

> Compromising the word of God is always a backward step in our Christian walk. Moses had to face this problem in Egypt. God had clearly told him to take all of the Hebrew people into the desert so that they could offer sacrifices up to God. This action did not please Pharaoh, and he offered an alternative to God's command. . . . What do we hear today? The call to compromise reaches our ears: "Certainly, you can be a Christian. But you don't have to stop being a lesbian just because you want to worship God. Do both. Don't be so fanatical in your Christianity. After all, you're only doing what comes naturally, aren't you?"

Howard continues:

> [S]ome lesbians in a pang of conviction will walk away from their sin, but are loath to wander too far away. They stay in touch with gay friends, hold onto mementos, or continue to read gay books and magazines. These women stay close enough to return to their lesbian life once the fright of conviction is over. They vacillate between conviction and corruption, trying to maintain a precarious balance between the two. . . . But disaster comes when we worship God on Sunday and feed our lives with the influences of our past life during the rest of the week. If we are to break free from the bondage of lesbianism, we must follow God with our whole heart, mind and strength. We must be women who are wholly committed to God. . . . There is no place for compromise. God will not share your heart with the

> world and your flesh. Only a complete break with your past, leaving Egypt fully behind, will bring healing in your life.[9]

What is true of homosexuality is true of every sin: God does not desire partial obedience but an unconditional surrender to his grace.

## Say a Little Prayer for Me

Once he realized that Moses would never agree to a compromise, Pharaoh decided to let God's people go. He virtually had to, because he needed Moses and Aaron to say a little prayer for him. Yet even when he gave in, Pharaoh could not resist adding one last condition, namely, that the Israelites not go too far: "Pharaoh said, 'I will let you go to sacrifice to the LORD your God in the wilderness; only you must not go very far away. Plead for me'" (8:28). Pharaoh wanted the Israelites to stay close enough so his army could keep an eye on them. As it turned out, of course, he ended up sending his chariots out into the wilderness to track them down.

Since this restriction did not directly contradict God's command to let his people go, Moses accepted Pharaoh's offer:

> Then Moses said, "Behold, I am going out from you and I will plead with the LORD that the swarms of flies may depart from Pharaoh, from his servants, and from his people, tomorrow. Only let not Pharaoh cheat again by not letting the people go to sacrifice to the LORD." So Moses went out from Pharaoh and prayed to the LORD. And the LORD did as Moses asked, and removed the swarms of flies from Pharaoh, from his servants, and from his people; not one remained. (8:29–31)

The disappearance of the flies was another miracle. Although God sent ten plagues against the Egyptians, he performed more than ten miracles. In some cases the end of the plague was as miraculous as its beginning. The end of the fourth plague proved that Satan is not who he says he is after all. He claims to be Beelzebub, "the lord of the flies," but the truth is that not even flies are under his lordship. Jesus Christ is Lord of every winged and flying insect, flies included. In answer to the prayer of his prophet, God used his power over creation to remove every last fly from the land of Egypt.

Once the flies were gone, it was up to Pharaoh to keep his end of the bargain. Moses had specifically warned him not to be deceptive in this matter by refusing again to let God's people go. But of course that is precisely what Pharaoh did: "But Pharaoh hardened his heart this time also, and did not let the people go" (8:32). Once again, he "hardened his heart"; he failed to keep his word and refused to let God's people go.

What Pharaoh did seems very foolish. And indeed it was foolish, but that does not prevent many people from making the same mistake. Many people try to offer God some sort of compromise. When they need help, they start to negotiate with him. They promise that if only he will get them out of whatever trouble they happen to be in this time, they will start to follow him, but they never follow through. As soon as their troubles are over, they forget about God entirely. What makes this so foolish is that God cannot be mocked, nor can he be deceived. He draws a careful distinction between his people and those who are not his people. The dividing line is Jesus Christ. His cross is the redemption that God has set between faith and unbelief, between the hard-hearted and the born-again, between the redeemed and the damned. Given the choice, it is far better to live with the people of God than to stay in Egypt.

# 22

# A Plague on Your Livestock

EXODUS 9:1–7

IT WAS IN 1985 that English farmers first noticed they had a problem. Some of their cattle were sick, and as they weakened physically, they also deteriorated mentally. It was a strange disease. Infected cattle behaved erratically, becoming either fearful or aggressive. They seemed to be going mad, which is how the disease got the name mad cow disease, more properly known as bovine spongiform encephalopathy (BSE). The last stages of mad cow disease were frightening. Cattle staggered around the farm until finally they stumbled to the ground and died. But the disease became even more frightening in 1995 when doctors discovered that it had spread to humans. Individuals who had eaten contaminated beef lost their minds. Their brain tissue was gradually eaten away until it came to resemble a sponge.

Since there was no treatment and no cure, mad cow disease started a panic across Europe, becoming one of the most terrifying plagues of postmodern times. It naturally reminds us of one of the Biblical plagues. In the days of Moses, God struck Pharaoh with ten mighty blows. The fifth was a plague on Egypt's livestock. Much like mad cow disease, it was an infectious disease that spread from one cow to the next. It not only infected cattle, however, but also horses, donkeys, camels, sheep, and goats. The plague was a deadly contagion—epidemic in its onset and lethal in its outcome. The King James Version calls it "a very grievous murrain"; in the words of the Revised English Bible, it was "a devastating pestilence." The Hebrew original uses the same word that it often uses to describe Pharaoh's heart: *kabed* or "heavy." In other words, the plague was as hard as Pharaoh's hard, hard heart. It was a terrible pestilence that swept across Egypt like wildfire, infecting the beasts of burden on every farm until they fell down dead.

## The Fifth Miracle

By now the basic pattern of the Exodus plagues is becoming familiar. Like its predecessors, the fifth plague began with God's demand: "Then the LORD said to Moses, 'Go in to Pharaoh and say to him, "Thus says the LORD, the God of the Hebrews, 'Let my people go, that they may serve me'"'" (9:1).

With these words, God told Moses to go and seek another audience with the king of Egypt. Since he was God's representative, called to be God's ambassador to Egypt, Moses spoke to Pharaoh with true divine authority. He addressed him using the special name that God had revealed back at the burning bush. Moses spoke on behalf of Yahweh, the Great I Am, the Lord God of the Hebrews.

God's demand was very simple: "Let my people go, that they may serve me." For centuries the Israelites had been in bondage to the Egyptians. But they belonged to God by covenant, and God was not willing for them to remain enslaved any longer. They were *his* people, not Pharaoh's people, so he demanded their unconditional release. The reason the Israelites had to be set free was so they could worship their God—so they could "serve" him. The goal of the exodus was the glory of God. Israel's chief end was the same as man's chief end: to glorify and enjoy God.

God's demand came with a dire warning. Moses said to Pharaoh, "For if you refuse to let them go and still hold them, behold, the hand of the LORD will fall with a very severe plague upon your livestock that are in the field, the horses, the donkeys, the camels, the herds, and the flocks" (9:2, 3). This warning placed the blame squarely on Pharaoh's shoulders. He was the one holding God's people back by refusing to let them go. More literally, he was "making strength against them," tightening the grip of his oppression.

God was explicit about the consequences of Pharaoh's actions: If he persisted in his tyranny, the Egyptians would suffer a terrible plague. Their livestock—the domesticated animals on which they depended for milk, food, clothing, labor, and transportation—would get sick and die. John J. Davis explains, "Such a plague would have had grave economic consequences in the land of Egypt. Oxen were depended upon for heavy labor in agriculture. Camels, asses and horses were used largely for transportation. Cattle not only provided milk but were very much an integral part of worship in the land of Egypt. The economic losses on this occasion must have affected Pharaoh greatly because he kept large numbers of cattle under his control."[1] This suggests that the plagues gradually increased in their severity. Not only was the fifth plague the first to bring death, but it was also the first to destroy Pharaoh's personal property. This was only fair: If Pharaoh would not let go of God's property, then he would suffer the loss of his own. And his losses were mounting as his punishment became more intense. Whereas the plague of gnats was attributed merely to "the finger of God" (8:19), the plague on livestock was sent by "the hand of the LORD" (9:3).

Like the other plagues, the fifth plague was a genuine miracle. Some scholars have tried to draw a connection between this pestilence and one of the earlier plagues. For example, it has been suggested that the cattle contracted their disease from the piles of rotting frogs, which were contaminated by anthrax.[2] This may seem like an ingenious suggestion, but of course it is only a guess. What the Bible says is that this deadly plague was an act of God, a demonstration of his sovereign power over creation, sent by his very own hand. The plague was miraculous in itself, destroying all of Egypt's cattle. It was also miraculous in its timing: "And the LORD set a time, saying, 'Tomorrow the LORD will do this thing in the land'" (9:5). Moses was able to make this prediction not because he was a good guesser, but because God had revealed in advance the time of his intervention. John Currid summarizes by saying that "the miraculous nature of the pestilences is seen not only in their degree and intensity, but in their timing and duration."[3]

Furthermore, the fifth plague was miraculous in the careful distinction it drew between Israel and Egypt. God first made this distinction in the fourth plague, when flies swarmed all over Egypt—everywhere except in Goshen, where the Israelites lived. In the fifth plague God again discriminated between his people and Pharaoh's people. Moses said, "But the LORD will make a distinction between the livestock of Israel and the livestock of Egypt, so that nothing of all that belongs to the people of Israel shall die" (9:4). And of course that is exactly what happened: "And the next day the LORD did this thing. All the livestock of the Egyptians died, but not one of the livestock of the people of Israel died" (9:6). On the basis of his covenant, God set the Israelites apart, protecting them from the plagues and ultimately rescuing them from danger. But the Egyptians were not God's people, and thus they fell under his divine curse.

The distinction between God's cows and Pharaoh's cows was miraculous. Yet questions have often been raised about the precise wording of verse 6: "All the livestock of the Egyptians died, but not one of the livestock of the people of Israel died." The Hebrew is emphatic: "*All*" the Egyptian livestock died, but "*not one*" animal died in Goshen; literally, "not so much as one cow died." Some scholars have argued that this must be an exaggeration, or at least a hyperbole. Others have pointed out that there seems to be a discrepancy—if not an outright contradiction—between the fifth plague and the seventh plague, in which Moses explicitly instructed the Egyptians to bring their livestock in out of the hail (9:19). Obviously, if they still had animals to protect, then not all of their livestock had been destroyed.

This is the kind of question that Christians who believe in the inerrancy of the Bible must be prepared to answer. One possible explanation is that the plague only affected animals out in the field, not animals kept back at the barn. On a careful reading, verse 3 limits the plague to "livestock . . . in the field." This explanation is confirmed by our knowledge of Egyptian agriculture. Late in the year, as the floodwaters receded, farmers put their livestock out to pasture. However, since the recession was gradual, during the month of January the animals were divided between field and stable.[4] Another possible explanation is that the term "all" is used collectively rather than distributively. In other words, it means "all kinds" of animals rather than "each and every one." The great nineteenth-century German Bible scholars Keil and Delitzsch concluded, "All is not to be taken in an absolute sense, but according to popular usage as denoting such a quantity, that what remained was nothing in comparison; and according to verse 3 it must be entirely restricted to cattle in the field."[5] As is so often the case, there are reasonable answers for what may at first appear to be a difficulty in the Bible.

### Pharaoh's Sacred Cows

Like all the plagues, the pestilence on livestock demonstrated God's power over Pharaoh. Ancient Egyptian texts often referred to "the strong hand of Pharaoh," especially in the context of military conquest. But God's hand was stronger, which he proved by using it to bring this terrible plague.

By stretching his hand out against Pharaoh, God also proved his power over Pharaoh's gods. As we have seen, one of the keys to unlocking the spiritual meaning of the plagues is Numbers 33:4, which states that "On their gods also the LORD executed judgments." The God of Israel performed his signs and wonders in order to triumph over the gods of Egypt. This Biblically-based, divinely-ordained interpretation of Exodus encourages us to connect the plagues to the objects of Egyptian idolatry.

The symbolism of the fifth plague is especially potent because many of Egypt's gods and goddesses were depicted as livestock. Some Egyptians worshiped the bull, which they viewed as "a fertility figure, the great inseminator imbued with the potency and vitality of life."[6] Cults dedicated to the bull were common throughout Egypt. There was Buchis, the sacred bull of Hermonthis, and Mnevis, who was worshiped at Heliopolis. Sometimes bulls were considered to embody the gods Ptah and Ra. But the chief bull was Apis. At the temple in Memphis, priests maintained a sacred enclosure where they kept a live bull considered to be the incarnation of Apis. When the venerable bull died, he was given an elaborate burial. Archaeologists have discovered funeral niches for hundreds of these bulls near Memphis.[7]

Then there were the goddesses. Isis, the queen of the gods, was generally depicted with cow horns on her head. Similarly, the goddess Hathor was represented with the head of a cow, sometimes with the sun between her two horns. Hathor was a goddess of love and beauty, motherhood and fertility. One of her sacred functions was to protect Pharaoh, and on occasion she was depicted as a cow suckling the king for nourishment.[8] To summarize, like so many modern Hindus, the Egyptians loved their sacred cows. In fact, they seem to have worshiped the entire bovine family! Thus it is not surprising that when the Israelites later decided to rebel against the God of their salvation and return to the gods of Egypt, they made a golden calf (Exodus 32).

Since livestock were such an integral part of their religion, the Egyptians were devastated by God's plague on their livestock. Cattle lay dying on every farm and at every temple. Farmers anxiously watched their cattle get sick and grow weak. To their shame, priests saw their holy cows stagger around their sacred pens until they fell down dead. God was proving himself to the Egyptians on their own terms, exposing the cult of the cow as a false religion. Thus the fifth plague followed the pattern: when Pharaoh refused to meet God's demand, God sent a miraculous plague that demonstrated his power over Egypt's gods.

## Five Lessons from the Fifth Plague

In keeping with our practical method for studying Exodus, there are at least five lessons to learn from the plague on livestock. Most of these lessons were introduced in the earlier plagues, yet they are important enough to bear repeating.

First, we learn *the meaning of salvation*. In its most basic sense, salvation means deliverance. The fifth plague—in which God again commanded Pharaoh to let his people go—is a further reminder that God had come to set his people free. What was true for Israel under Moses is true for the believer in Jesus Christ. Jonathan Edwards taught that "Christ and his redemption are the subject of the whole Word of God."[9] This is especially true of the book of Exodus, in which salvation is displayed as deliverance from bondage. The exodus from Egypt prepared the way for the coming of Jesus Christ, the true exodus. By his sufferings and death on the cross, Jesus broke the power of sin and released sinners from its captivity. Now everyone who trusts in Christ and in his cross is delivered immediately from the guilt of sin, and ultimately from sin itself, for believers will be made perfect in Heaven. The gospel is the greater exodus, in which God says to Satan, "Let my people go! Release them from their slavery to sin. Allow them to come all the way out and find freedom in Christ."

Second, we learn *the purpose of life*, which is to glorify God. When God said, "Let my people go," he went on to say, "that they may serve me." The Israelites were saved for God's glory. This is our purpose as well—to give God the glory. Jesus Christ has set us free from sin and death so that we can serve the living God. He is both our Savior and our Lord. We turn to him not only to deliver us from our slavery to sin, but also for everything that follows—a whole life of fruitful work and worship for God. Like the Israelites, we are saved for God's glory.

Third, we learn *the folly of idolatry*. Pharaoh was such a proud man that in order to humble him, God had to humiliate his gods one by one. With the plague on livestock, God humiliated Apis, Hathor, and the rest of Egypt's sacred cows. Apis was a masculine god: he represented sexual prowess. Hathor was a feminine god: she represented glamor. Although we do not bow down before golden cows, we sometimes worship the very same gods and goddesses. We are tempted to gratify sexual desire outside the marriage covenant or to glamorize our outward appearance for the sake of our inward esteem. But this is utter folly. The idols of sex and beauty cannot save. They do not free us; they only bind us. The attractions they offer are temporary, and in the end those who lust after them will gain nothing but lonely, empty disappointment.

Fourth, we learn *the superiority of faith*. In the plague on livestock God differentiated between the Israelites and the Egyptians. This is the distinction he always makes—the distinction between the people of his choice, who receive all the blessings of his salvation, and the rest of fallen humanity, who remain under his curse. Just as protection from pestilence was only for those who trusted in the Lord God of Israel, so now the free gift of eternal life is only for those who trust in his Son, Jesus Christ. Believers have the unique privilege of knowing that God will keep them safe in his arms for all eternity. On the day of judgment, when rebellious sinners will face the fury of God's wrath, repentant sinners will be kept safe from the fires of Hell.

The superiority of faith is proved by a fifth lesson, which is *the consequence of rebellion*. It is true that God hardened Pharaoh's heart. This is one of the mysteries of sovereign predestination: God wills the choice of some for salvation, while he hardens others in their sins. But it is also true that Pharaoh hardened his own heart. The account of the plague on livestock is explicit about this. God said to Pharaoh, "If *you* refuse to let them go . . ." (9:2). Pharaoh was given every opportunity to meet God's demand. Yet he deliberately refused to let God's people go, choosing instead to keep Israel in bondage, thus rebelling against God's revealed will. Such defiance always brings divine judgment. As God's patience wore thin (to put it in human terms), he struck Pharaoh with the wrath of his hand.

Eventually everyone who rebels against God will suffer his holy wrath. It may not come in the form of frogs or pestilence, but it will come. It will come even if it is delayed until the final judgment. Many people doubt the reality of Hell. This is an age of "ignosticism." I refer not to agnostics, who are not sure whether God exists or not, but to "ignostics," who try to ignore God altogether. One of the main things they try to ignore is divine judgment. But the wrath of God is a reality that cannot be ignored forever. One day every human being will stand before God for judgment, and the plague on livestock is a sign that rebellion now will have dire consequences then.

## An Understanding Heart

These five lessons are taught again and again through the Biblical plagues. But there is a sixth and final lesson that is unique to the fifth plague, a lesson taught by a bad example: "And Pharaoh sent, and behold, not one of the livestock of

Israel was dead. But the heart of Pharaoh was hardened, and he did not let the people go" (9:7). From Pharaoh's response to the death of his cattle we learn *the necessity of an understanding heart*.

Pharaoh was a hardened skeptic. The man had a front-row seat for all God's signs and wonders in Egypt. Yet no matter how many miracles he saw, Pharaoh always found a way to ignore God's claim on his life. On those rare occasions when he hinted that he might give in to God's demand, doubt overcame belief, and he hardened his heart all over again. Still, Pharaoh was starting to get curious. Perhaps he knew that the land of Goshen somehow had managed to escape the plague of flies, or perhaps he overheard his officials whispering that the Hebrew cattle were still healthy. Whatever the reason, Pharaoh decided to investigate. He formed a blue-ribbon panel of agricultural experts and sent them on a fact-finding mission to Goshen. There is a subtle irony in the way the Bible describes this mission. Verse 7 begins with the words "Pharaoh sent," which is exactly what Moses had been demanding all along—for Pharaoh to send people away. But rather than sending Israel out of Egypt, Pharaoh sent a team of investigators to Goshen. What they discovered was that the Hebrew cattle were as healthy as ever. None of them had died—not one single cow.

It is not uncommon for skeptics to investigate God, as Pharaoh did. Skeptics thrive on their skepticism, so they need someone or something to be skeptical about. God seems like an easy target because he makes such absolute claims of power and authority. So the skeptic learns at least enough theology to criticize God and his Word. But even after studying God, the average skeptic refuses to come to God in faith. This was true of Pharaoh. He had more than enough facts to trust in God and obey his will. Not only had he witnessed miraculous signs and wonders, but he had also been warned of the consequences of refusing to respond in faith. He had also witnessed the miracle in Goshen, which provided further confirmation of God's power. Yet still he would not believe.

If Pharaoh's unbelief seems surprising, remember that God had promised to harden the man's heart. John Durham writes:

> That the epidemic should come with such sweeping devastation is one thing; that the livestock of Israel in Goshen should be spared is another; but that Pharaoh should still be heavy and dull of mind, in the face of such a double demonstration, is an enigma until we remember Yahweh's recurring prediction of Pharaoh's intransigence and Yahweh's continuing involvement in Pharaoh's reaction. Then we can understand why Pharaoh would send out those whom he had no need to send out, his factfinders to Goshen, and refuse to send out those whom Yahweh had commanded him to send out, the sons of Israel to their religious commitment.[10]

Not only did God harden Pharaoh's heart, but Pharaoh also hardened his own heart. The form of the Hebrew verb (a stative verb, to use the grammatical terminology) indicates that this was an ongoing condition. The heart is the spiritual center of the person, and Pharaoh's heart would not yield. He was an almost-believer whose hard heart was not willing to love what his mind knew to be true. What Pharaoh needed was an understanding heart.

There is a time and a place for investigating God. Before anyone can make a decision about following Jesus Christ, one has to answer some hard questions about who he is and what he has done. Can the Bible be trusted? What about the incarnation—was Jesus divine, or was he merely human? What about the crucifixion? When Jesus of Nazareth was crucified—as the historical records prove that he was—did he suffer the full price for sin? And what about the resurrection? Did Jesus rise from the dead on the third day, or was it all a hoax?

No one can make an honest appraisal of Christianity without answering these questions. However, there comes a time to stop investigating and start believing. Once someone has begun to consider that what the Bible says about Jesus Christ is true, then the only thing keeping that person from God is hardness of heart. Why is it that some people refuse to embrace Jesus Christ at the emotional level—even after they are convinced at the intellectual level that he is the true God and only Savior? The Bible answers, "They are darkened in their understanding, alienated from the life of God because of the ignorance that is in them, due to their hardness of heart" (Ephesians 4:18). What separates them from God is the same thing that prevented Pharaoh from doing God's will: hardness of heart.

Even Christians must be careful to avoid the danger of hard-heartedness. The writer to the Hebrews warns, "Take care, brothers, lest there be in any of you an evil, unbelieving heart, leading you to fall away from the living God" (Hebrews 3:12; cf. 1 Samuel 6:6). This is what Pharaoh had: an evil, unbelieving heart. His example warns us to embrace with our hearts what our minds know to be true. We know that Jesus Christ has come to deliver us from our slavery to sin and to enable us to glorify God. We must not only know this but also receive it with an understanding heart, "For with the heart one believes and is justified" (Romans 10:10a).

When I was a small boy I heard a sermon I will never forget. I had asked my father if I could go hear the baccalaureate—the sermon preached to the graduating class at Wheaton College. Every year I watched my father, Leland Ryken, don his academic regalia before setting off for the chapel, and I wondered what the service was like. So one year my mother took me to sit in the balcony. There I heard Dr. Hudson Armerding, then college president, preach to the graduates on "The Understanding Heart."

Dr. Armerding explained that in the Bible, the heart is more than an emotion; it is the spiritual center of the person that feels, thinks, and decides. He gave many Biblical examples—including that of Pharaoh himself—of men and women who could not understand God because of the hardness of their hearts. Then Dr. Armerding gave the students this warning:

> Many Christian college graduates do extraordinarily well in college. They accumulate a considerable body of knowledge and demonstrate that they can think logically and perceptively. But it is still possible for them to be graduated with a hardened heart, having all the information the disciples had, as well as the experience of observing supernatural things happen, and still determine not to accept the Word of God as normative or to acknowledge Jesus Christ as Lord.

He closed by saying, "We must recognize that Christian education is complete only when the result is an understanding heart" in which "the mind is informed by the authoritative statements of Holy Scripture; the emotions are moved to love the Lord with all the heart, soul, mind, and strength; and the will does acknowledge Jesus Christ as both Savior and Lord."[11]

When I heard those words I said, "That's what I want—an understanding heart!" It's what I still want. I want to believe and to love what my mind knows to be true about Jesus Christ. I want an understanding heart because I need an understanding heart. I need one as much as anyone, including Pharaoh himself. Anyone who wants an understanding heart should ask God, and he will surely give it.

# 23

# Can't Stand That Itch!

EXODUS 9:8–12

PROVERBS 27:22 partly comes from the palace kitchen, where women would make flour for bread by grinding grain between a mortar and a pestle, but it was also based on Solomon's experience with fools. The wise king had observed that no matter how often a fool is crushed by the consequences of his foolish mistakes, somehow his folly always manages to survive. Hence the proverb: "Crush a fool in a mortar with a pestle along with crushed grain, yet his folly will not depart from him."

When the old Jewish rabbis read Solomon's proverb, they naturally thought of Pharaoh, who was the biggest fool in the Old Testament—maybe the biggest fool ever. With each new plague, God was grinding Pharaoh between the mortar of his justice and the pestle of his wrath. Yet no matter how finely Egypt was ground, Pharaoh's folly remained. So the rabbis wrote, in one of their ancient commentaries:

> Of him [Pharaoh] and of all like him it is written: "Crush a fool in a mortar with a pestle along with crushed grain, but the folly will not be driven out," which means: if you crush and chastise the fool with the strikes of afflictions and plagues, and you give him alleviation by lifting up the pestle from the mortar, his foolishness will not depart from him, since he forgets all the plagues. Such was the evil Pharaoh. When he experienced alleviation between each plague . . . he forgot the plagues.[1]

First God turned the river into blood, but Pharaoh hardened his heart and would not listen to Moses. Then came all the frogs, and Pharaoh asked for prayer; but as soon as he got some relief, he hardened his heart once again. Next, insects swarmed all over Egypt. The magicians said it was the finger of God, but Pharaoh refused to listen. The fourth plague was flies, and Pharaoh finally decided to let God's people go; but as soon as the flies were gone, he changed his mind. Then all the livestock died, and yet Pharaoh's heart still refused to yield. Five plagues, and he was as big a fool as ever.

## Outbreak!

What was it going to take? Well, perhaps Pharaoh would relent if God afflicted his body. Physical suffering has a way of getting someone's attention in a way that nothing else can. So God sent a sixth plague, the plague of boils:

> And the LORD said to Moses and Aaron, "Take handfuls of soot from the kiln, and let Moses throw them in the air in the sight of Pharaoh. It shall become fine dust over all the land of Egypt, and become boils breaking out in sores on man and beast throughout all the land of Egypt." So they took soot from the kiln and stood before Pharaoh. And Moses threw it in the air, and it became boils breaking out in sores on man and beast. And the magicians could not stand before Moses because of the boils, for the boils came upon the magicians and upon all the Egyptians. (9:8–11)

Bible scholars—especially those who know something about medicine—have taken these symptoms and tried to deduce the precise disease that afflicted the Egyptians. The word translated "boils" (*shechin*) occurs a dozen times in the Old Testament and is used for a variety of infectious skin ailments. In Leviticus 13 it seems to refer to leprosy. That might also work for Exodus 9, especially since nothing is ever said about the disease going away; leprosy is incurable. Others have suggested that the Egyptians had smallpox.

But the most common suggestion is skin anthrax, which, as Greta Hort explains, "takes the form first of a big swelling of the affected part of the skin; after two to three days there appears a small bluish-red pustule with a central depression in the middle of the swelling; this depression dries up, and new boils shoot up; the tissue then swells into blains as if burnt, and finally peels off."[2] Hort argues that this disease was the natural result of the previous plagues. Flies (fourth plague) crawling in the carcasses of the livestock (fifth plague) would have picked up the pestilence and then transmitted it by biting both man and beast (sixth plague). She even goes so far as to identify the fly by its scientific name: *Stomoxys calcitrans*.[3]

Hort's argument is interesting but highly speculative. What is certain is that the Egyptians contracted a skin disease that was extremely unpleasant, if not actually life threatening. The Bible describes inflamed areas of skin, festering boils that broke out into blistering sores. The same ailment is described in Deuteronomy 28, where Moses warns the Israelites what would happen to them if they failed to keep God's law: "The LORD will strike you with the boils of Egypt, and with tumors and scabs and itch, of which you cannot be healed. . . . The LORD will strike you on the knees and on the legs with grievous boils of which you cannot be healed, from the sole of your foot to the crown of your head" (Deuteronomy 28:27, 35).

Things were starting to get personal. The first five plagues had been a real bother. The Egyptians had seen rivers of blood and had lost herds of livestock. Pharaoh himself had seen frogs jump in and out of his bed and had tried to shoo flies away from his royal person. But nothing drove them all crazy like this plague. The Egyptians were covered with painful, open sores from head to toe. This showed that the God of Israel had power over their bodies, and it should have warned them that their very lives were in danger.

Like the other plagues, the boils were a genuine miracle. No merely natural explanation is sufficient to account for all the details in this passage. The plague was miraculous in its *onset*. It came unannounced—a disaster without warning. The plague was miraculous in its *method*. Moses and Aaron scooped black soot from a furnace, and when they tossed it into the air, the soot was transubstantiated into "fine dust over all the land of Egypt" (9:9). What happened next was equally miraculous: The dust caused boils to break out, but only on the Egyptians. Verse 11 specifies that the boils were "upon all the Egyptians." As we have seen, God used the plagues to discriminate between his people and Pharaoh's people. Egypt was plagued, while Israel was protected. In this respect, as in all others, the outbreak of boils was a miraculous demonstration of God's infinite power over creation.

## Medics and Magicians

Like the first five blows that God struck against the Egyptians, the sixth plague had three results: first, Pharaoh's gods were humbled; second, Pharaoh's magicians were humiliated; and third, Pharaoh's heart was hardened.

Throughout our study of Exodus, we have seen that God's purpose was to glorify himself by defeating Pharaoh and his gods. The plague of boils was no exception. It proved that the gods and goddesses of Egypt could provide no protection from sickness and disease. The Egyptians—who were well-known for their interest in medicine—looked to their religion for healing. Many worshiped Amon Re, the creator-god whom one ancient text describes as "he who dissolves evils and dispels ailments; a physician who heals."[4] Others worshiped Thoth, who was the god of the healing arts. Still others worshiped Imhotep as the god of medicine, although he became more popular after the exodus. But the most common deity for dealing with disease was Sekhmet, whose priests formed one of the oldest medical fraternities in antiquity.[5] As John Davis explains, "[The] Egyptians were constantly aware of the possibility of infectious diseases and sores. This is reflected in the fact that Sekhmet, a lion-headed goddess, was supposed to have had the power of both creating epidemics and bringing them to an end. A special priesthood was devoted to her called *Sunu*. Amulets and other objects were employed by the Egyptians to ward off evil in their lives."[6]

The plague of boils was an attack on all the gods and goddesses that the Egyptians trusted for healing. When the Bible says that "On their gods also the Lord executed judgments" (Numbers 33:4), it is speaking comprehensively. God defeated the entire pantheon of Egypt—Amon, Thoth, Imhotep, Sekhmet, and all the rest. Perhaps this explains why God sent such a variety of plagues on the Egyptians: he wanted to expose the impotence of their idolatry by causing each and every idol to fail in its area of special expertise. When the Egyptians were covered with painful, oozing sores, they discovered that their gods could not heal.

Before dismissing the Egyptians for their folly, it is important to recognize that we are tempted to worship the same deities. This is an age of remarkable progress in medicine—the age of lasers and CAT scans, of antibiotics and anesthesia. During the twentieth century many diseases were virtually eradicated, diseases like polio and small pox. In the next hundred years scientists may well discover cures for killers like AIDS, cancer, BSE (mad cow disease), and the Ebola virus. Genetic research will develop new forms of treatment for hereditary diseases, including medicines that manipulate human DNA.

As a result of our advanced knowledge of the body and its various ailments, it is tempting to make medicine an object of faith. Most patients go to the hospital believing they will be cured. However, it doesn't always work out that way. Doctors and nurses sometimes make mistakes. They don't always make the right diagnosis or prescribe the right treatment. Besides, there is still no cure for death. So medicine has its limits. This is true not only of clinical medicine but also of alternative medicine, which uses the healing properties of vitamins and other naturally occurring substances. Despite all our skill at healing, we are not sovereign over the human body. This means that medical expertise must never become our source of ultimate confidence for physical well-being. Medicine makes a wonderful tool but a poor deity. Whenever we get a prescription filled or go in for surgery or start chemotherapy, we should remember that all healing comes from God and that Christ alone is Lord of the body.

At the same time that the God of Israel was humbling the gods of Egypt, he was humiliating Pharaoh's magicians. This had been going on for some time. Although the magicians had used their secret arts to imitate the plagues of blood and frogs, they were unable to replicate the plague of bugs. So, to their credit, they gave up and admitted that there was more power in God's little finger than in all their spells and incantations. The fourth and fifth plagues say nothing at all about the magicians. Presumably they were present, however—not to compete with God but simply to witness his power. Yet this plague was different. Not only were they powerless to prevent it and impotent to imitate it, but they themselves were afflicted by it.

To understand how completely God humiliated Pharaoh's magicians, it helps to know that by throwing ashes into the air, Moses was doing something that Egyptian priests often did. It was customary for Pharaoh's priests to take sacrificial ashes and cast them into the air as a sign of blessing. But God took that ritual act and turned it into a curse. This was a matter of justice, because the soot may well have come from a furnace for making bricks, like the bricks the Israelites baked for Pharaoh. If so, God was exacting strict justice, repaying the Egyptians for their sins. John Currid writes, "The type of furnace spoken of here was probably a kiln for burning bricks. The furnace, then, was a symbol of the oppression of the Hebrews, the sweat and tears they were shedding to make bricks for the Egyptians. Thus the very soot made by the enslaved people was now to inflict punishment on their oppressors."[7] God was making Israel's curse a blessing and was turning Egypt's blessing into a curse.

Another thing that made this plague humiliating was that infectious disease prevented the magicians from carrying out their religious duties. The Egyptians valued purity, so a priest covered with open sores would have been unable to perform his customary rituals. By thus denying their access to their deities, God made a mockery of Pharaoh's magicians. Their defeat was so complete, their humiliation so absolute, that the book of Exodus never mentions them again.

One more thing about the magicians needs to be mentioned. The Bible says that in contrast to Moses, who "stood before Pharaoh" (9:10), they "could not stand before Moses" (9:11). They just couldn't stand it; they had to go somewhere else and scratch! Perhaps the reason for this was medical; remember, the plague spread from their feet on up (Deuteronomy 28:35). But all this talk of standing may have a deeper spiritual significance. Pharaoh's evil magicians were unable to stand in the presence of God's holy prophet. Similarly, the Bible teaches that "the wicked will not stand in the judgment" (Psalm 1:5a).

This was true for Pharaoh's magicians, and it will be equally true for every sinner who refuses to trust in Jesus Christ for salvation. Unless we are covered with his righteousness by faith, we will never be able to stand before God. This is because the Bible prophesies a fresh outbreak of the very disease that plagued the Egyptians. Like many of the plagues in Exodus, the plague of boils will return at the final judgment. In his revelation of the end times, the apostle John saw that "the first angel went and poured out his bowl on the earth, and harmful and painful sores came upon the people who bore the mark of the beast and worshiped its image" (Revelation 16:2). The Bible does not answer all our questions about how and when this will happen. But what it does reveal is warning enough! A day is coming when everyone who rejects Jesus Christ as Savior and Lord will be plagued with the sore pains of God's wrath, before which no one can stand.

## Pharaoh's Heart Condition

Sadly, the plague of boils ended the same way all the other plagues ended—with the hardening of Pharaoh's heart. Even after his gods were humbled and his magicians were humiliated, Pharaoh's heart would not yield. And here, for the first time, the Bible explicitly says that *God* was the one who hardened Pharaoh's heart. After each of the first five plagues, the Scripture says "Pharaoh's heart remained hardened" (7:22), or he "hardened his heart" (8:15), or "the heart of Pharaoh was hardened" (9:7). However, this time it says that his heart was hard because God made it hard: "But the LORD hardened the heart of Pharaoh, and he did not listen to them, as the LORD had spoken to Moses" (9:12).

Pharaoh's hard heart confronts us with the mystery of divine sovereignty and human responsibility. Both of the following statements are true: Pharaoh hardened his heart; God hardened Pharaoh's heart. But how can these two statements be reconciled? What is the relationship between them?

Some scholars argue that God did not harden Pharaoh's heart until *after* Pharaoh hardened it himself. When God hardened Pharaoh's heart, he was simply confirming the decision that Pharaoh had already made. Thus the moral of the story is that "God hardens those who harden themselves."[8] This is often true. As a matter of justice, God sometimes hardens the hearts of those who have hardened themselves against him. However, in this case that explanation is less than fully adequate because even before Pharaoh hardened his heart, God promised to harden it for him. The Lord had told Moses, "I will harden his heart, so that he will not let the people go" (4:21b).

While it is true that Pharaoh hardened his own heart, the deeper truth is that even this was part of God's sovereign plan. The hardening of Pharaoh's heart was not God's response to Pharaoh, but his *purpose* for Pharaoh. God did this to demonstrate his justice. He also did it to demonstrate his power, as we will discover when we get to the seventh plague (9:16). And he did it to display his mercy. As God said to Moses, "I will harden Pharaoh's heart, and though I multiply my signs and wonders in the land of Egypt, Pharaoh will not listen to you. Then I will lay my hand on Egypt and bring my hosts, my people the children of Israel, out of the land of Egypt by great acts of judgment" (7:3, 4). God hardened Pharaoh's heart in order to multiply the plagues, which magnified the power of both his justice and his mercy.

Although it was perfectly just, and although God was glorified in it, there is still something sad about the hardening of Pharaoh's heart. A church member once wrote me the following note: "Pharaoh grieves me. He grieves me because his hardened heart and unwillingness to accept God's sovereignty remind me so much of my sister. Her heart is so hard towards Jesus and her will so unyielding to God's sovereignty. . . . She and Pharaoh have too much invested in sovereignty over their own lives. . . . Why doesn't she see that lasting peace comes only from knowing Jesus?"

## The Right Use of Serious Illness

That's a good question, and it raises a further question: What *should* Pharaoh have done? When he found himself covered with painful sores from head to toe, rather than hardening his heart, what would have been the right way for him to respond? One way to answer that question is to see what godly people have done in similar circumstances. The Bible contains many examples of men and women who dealt with serious illness not by hardening their hearts but by turning back to God.

The first to come to mind is Job, who had symptoms almost identical to Pharaoh's. Job was a righteous man who suffered many wrongs at the hands of Satan. He lost his livestock, his servants, and his children, yet he continued to praise God. This made Satan so angry that he "went out from the presence of the LORD and struck Job with loathsome sores from the sole of his foot to the crown of his head" (Job 2:7). This was excruciating. The Bible says that Job "took a piece of broken pottery with which to scrape himself while he sat in the ashes" (Job 2:8). He was so miserable that his wife recommended suicide, saying, "Curse God and die" (Job 2:9). But Job said to his wife, "You speak as one of the foolish women would speak. Shall we receive good from God, and shall we not receive evil?" (Job 2:10). The answer, of course, is "No!" Job understood that God is sovereign over sickness as well as over health. When we endure physical suffering, rather than hardening our hearts, we should accept God's will. Pharaoh should have done what Job did: instead of hardening his heart, he should have surrendered to God's sovereignty in his suffering.

Or Pharaoh could have followed the example of David. Like Pharaoh, David was a king, and like Pharaoh, he suffered for his sins. He said to God:

> There is no soundness in my flesh
> because of your indignation;
> there is no health in my bones
> because of my sin.
> For my iniquities have gone over my head;
> like a heavy burden, they are too heavy for me.
> My wounds stink and fester
> because of my foolishness. (Psalm 38:3–5)

David's condition was serious. He was suffering intense pain from a loathsome disease. Even worse, his illness was the direct consequence of his own sinful folly. It was an act of divine judgment. This is not true of every illness, but it is true of some. Some physical problems—lung cancer, for example, or syphilis—are the natural result of sinful choices. Other problems are caused by the sins of others, as is the case when someone is injured by a drunk driver. Then there are ailments that come for some other reason entirely. Job is the perfect example: he did not suffer because he was a sinner, but because he was righteous. Yet there are also times when sickness is an act of God's justice. Certainly this was true for the Egyptians. Later Moses warned the Israelites that if they were not careful, it would be true for them as well: "But if you will not obey the voice of the Lord your God or be careful to do all his commandments and his statutes . . . The Lord will make the pestilence stick to you until he has consumed you. . . . The Lord will strike you on the knees and on the legs with grievous boils of which you cannot be healed, from the sole of your foot to the crown of your head" (Deuteronomy 28:15, 21, 35).

Ordinarily it is impossible to know why God inflicts a particular disease on a particular person. However, every illness is an opportunity to renew our repentance. When we are sick we should examine ourselves, searching our hearts for unconfessed sin, which is what David did when he was sick. He said:

> For I am ready to fall,
> and my pain is ever before me.
> I confess my iniquity;
> I am sorry for my sin. (Psalm 38:17, 18)

By repenting of his sin, David used his poor health to good advantage. He took it as an opportunity for spiritual renewal. Pharaoh should have done what David did: rather than hardening his heart, he should have confessed his sin.

To take another example, Pharaoh should have done what Naaman did. Naaman was commander of the Syrian army. Like Pharaoh, he was a Gentile; and like Pharaoh, he had a serious skin condition. Naaman was a leper. Yet he had heard there was a prophet in Israel who could help him, so he gathered a small fortune to pay his medical bills and went off to find the cure. Eventually he found God's man Elisha, who told him to go jump in the Jordan River and wash himself seven times. Naaman thought the whole idea was preposterous, but eventually he did what Elisha told him to do, and when he came out of the river, "his flesh was restored like the flesh of a little child, and he was clean" (2 Kings 5:14). If Pharaoh had done what Naaman did, he would have been cured. Rather than hardening his heart, he should have turned to God for healing.

Now that God has given us his gospel, turning to him means turning to his Son, Jesus Christ. Although this is not something Pharaoh could have done, it *is* something we can do. There is a wonderful example in the Gospel of Mark, which tells of a woman who was so sick that she had been bleeding for twelve years. Her situation was desperate: "[She] had suffered much under many physicians, and had spent all that she had, and was no better but rather grew worse" (Mark 5:26). In her desperation she reached out to Jesus and held on for dear life. "For she said, 'If I touch even his garments, I will be made well.' And immediately the flow of blood dried up, and she felt in her body that she was healed of her disease" (Mark 5:28, 29). Then Jesus turned and explained that it was her faith that had made her well. He said, "Daughter, your faith has made you well; go in peace, and be healed of your disease" (Mark 5:34).

That is a beautiful promise: "Your faith has made you well . . . be healed of your disease." One day this promise will come true for every child of God. It does not always come true in this life, but it will and must come true in the life to come, when "death shall be no more, neither shall there be mourning, nor crying, nor pain anymore" (Revelation 21:4). The hope of Heaven reminds us, whenever we have physical problems, not to harden our hearts like foolish Pharaoh but to turn back to God. Like Job, we should accept our illness as the will of God. Our suffering is part of his sovereign plan. Like David, we should consider our infirmity an opportunity to confess our sin. Our illness may or may not be an act of divine judgment, but if it is, we certainly deserve it, so we should renew our repentance. Like Naaman, we should turn to God for healing, and that means holding on to Jesus by faith the way the bleeding woman did in the Gospels.

One Christian who often struggled with illness was the brilliant French philosopher and theologian Blaise Pascal (1623–1662), who was tormented by poor health until his death at the age of thirty-nine. Pascal was no fool, and through his many troubles he learned how to suffer like a Christian. Here is part of his prayer on "The Right Use of Serious Illness," which should become our prayer in every sickness:

> O Lord, whose spirit is so good and gracious in all things, and who art so merciful that not only the prosperities, but also the distresses which happen to Thine elect are the effects of Thy mercy, grant me grace not to act like a heathen in the state to which Thy justice has brought me; but that, like a true Christian, I may acknowledge Thee for my Father and my God, in whatsoever circumstances I am placed. . . .
>
> Thou gavest me health to be spent in serving Thee; and I perverted it to a use altogether profane. Now Thou hast sent me a sickness for my correction: O suffer me not to use this likewise to provoke Thee by my impatience. If my heart has been filled with the love of the world, while I was in possession of strength, destroy my vigor to promote my salvation. . . .
>
> O Lord, as at the instant of death I shall find myself separated from the world, stripped of all things, and standing alone in Thy presence, to answer to Thy justice for all the movements of my heart: grant that I may consider myself, in this disease, as in a kind of death, separated from the world, stripped of all the objects of my affections, placed alone in Thy presence, to implore of Thy mercy the conversion of my heart; and that thus I may enjoy great consolation in knowing that Thou art now sending me a sort of death, for the display of Thy mercy, before Thou sendest me death in reality, for the display of Thy justice.
>
> . . . Grant me grace, O Lord, to join Thy consolations to my sufferings, that I may suffer like a Christian. I pray not to be exempted from pain . . . but I pray that I may not be abandoned to the pains of nature without the comforts of Thy Spirit. Grant, O Lord, that . . . I may conform myself to

Thy will; and that being sick as I now am, I may glorify Thee in my sufferings. . . . Unite me to Thyself, fill me Thyself, and with Thy Holy Spirit. So that, being filled by Thee, it may be no longer I who live or suffer, but Thou, O my Saviour, who livest and sufferest in me; that having thus been a small partaker of Thy sufferings, Thou mayest fill me completely with . . . glory. . . . Amen.[9]

# 24

# The Worst Hailstorm Ever

## EXODUS 9:13–35

GOD STRUCK EGYPT with ten mighty blows. These plagues, as the Bible calls them, seem to have come in three sets of three, followed by the tenth and deadliest plague of all. One reason for thinking that the plagues are organized this way is that each group of three begins with Moses getting up early in the morning to confront Pharaoh (7:15; 8:20). This is also true of the seventh plague 9:13), which thus begins the final sequence.

The Bible gives the plague of hail the longest account so far. This leisurely approach allows the tension to mount. We are drawing toward the climax of the confrontation between the God of Israel and the gods of Egypt. By slowing down the story, the Bible heightens our suspense:

> Then the Lord said to Moses, "Rise up early in the morning and present yourself before Pharaoh and say to him, "Thus says the Lord, the God of the Hebrews, "Let my people go, that they may serve me. For this time I will send all my plagues on you yourself, and on your servants and your people, so that you may know that there is none like me in all the earth. For by now I could have put out my hand and struck you and your people with pestilence, and you would have been cut off from the earth. But for this purpose I have raised you up, to show you my power, so that my name may be proclaimed in all the earth. You are still exalting yourself against my people and will not let them go. Behold, about this time tomorrow I will cause very heavy hail to fall, such as never has been in Egypt from the day it was founded until now.""" (9:13–18)

With these words, God informed Pharaoh of something that should have been obvious to him already: The God of Israel had the power to wipe Egypt off the face of the earth. The first six plagues had caused enough hardship for Pharaoh to recognize God's power, but he hadn't seen anything yet! Speaking through his prophet Moses, God proceeded to warn Pharaoh that he was about to receive the hardest blow yet—what God called "all my plagues" (9:14).

We have seen that each plague was a supernatural demonstration of divine power. In a word, the plagues were miracles. One of the miraculous things about them is that they became increasingly more severe. They were miraculous in their intensification. Compared to the last four plagues, the first six plagues were little more than a nuisance. They began in the water and then moved onto land. However, with the seventh plague they started to rain down from the sky. Obviously things were getting worse. God was opening up the arsenal of judgment to pour out his deadly wrath on Egypt.

## The Purpose of the Plagues

Why did God do this? What was his purpose for plaguing Egypt? There are several ways to answer this question. One is to point out that God was punishing Egypt for Pharaoh's disobedience. Moses had told Pharaoh to let God's people go. When Pharaoh refused, his people had to suffer the consequences of his rebellion. Another answer, which we have repeated throughout our study of Exodus, is that God was saving his people for his glory. The plagues were part of his plan for bringing Israel out of bondage.

Here in chapter 9 God explains his intentions with even greater clarity by offering three purpose statements for the plagues. The first comes in verse 14: "This time I will send all my plagues on you yourself, and on your servants and your people, so that you may know that there is none like me in all the earth." God sent the plagues to demonstrate *the uniqueness of his omnipotence*.

In particular, the plagues showed that God was greater than Pharaoh. The precise wording of verse 14 is significant. Literally, what God said to Pharaoh was, "I will send the full force of my plagues *against your heart*." The Egyptians believed that Pharaoh's heart was the foundation of their society and the source of all human progress. Thus they considered Pharaoh to be their god, and Pharaoh agreed. This is confirmed by verse 17, in which God says to Pharaoh, "You are still exalting yourself against my people and will not let them go." By setting himself against Israel, Pharaoh was setting himself against God. He was exalting himself to the place of deity.

In order to confront this blasphemy, God sent the full force of his plagues against Pharaoh's heart. The purpose of the plagues was to demonstrate the Godness of God and thus to convince Pharaoh of the uniqueness of God's omnipotence. Before the plagues started, Pharaoh told Moses that he did not even know who God was (5:2). Well, now he knew! Pharaoh was getting a whole theological education, learning more about God than he had ever dreamed there was to know. One of the main lessons was this: there is no one like God in all the earth.

A second purpose for the plagues was to show *the universality of God's praise*. God said to Pharaoh, "But for this purpose I have raised you up, to show you my power, so that my name may be proclaimed in all the earth" (9:16). This verse proves that God was the one who put Pharaoh on his throne and allowed him to stay there. He did this for the specific purpose of showing Pharaoh his power. But this was not simply for Pharaoh's benefit. The plagues had global implications. God wanted to be worshiped around the world. And what better way to make that happen than to send the Egyptians plague after plague and by doing so to save his people?

History shows that the plagues have achieved God's missionary purpose. If there had been only one plague, it might have been forgotten. But *ten* plagues? Ten plagues were ten times more likely to be remembered. The Israelites recounted them to their children, saying, "We were Pharaoh's slaves in Egypt. And the LORD brought us out of Egypt with a mighty hand. And the LORD showed signs and wonders, great and grievous, against Egypt and against Pharaoh and all his household, before our eyes" (Deuteronomy 6:21, 22). The Israelites also recited the plagues in their psalms, singing:

> He destroyed their vines with hail
>   and their sycamores with frost.
> He gave over their cattle to the hail
>   and their flocks to thunderbolts. (Psalm 78:47, 48)

God's people never forgot God's triumph over Pharaoh through the plagues. But they weren't the only ones. Word of the plagues spread to the surrounding nations (see 15:14, 15). When the Gibeonites met with Joshua, they spoke of "the name of the LORD," saying, "We have heard a report of him, and all that he did in Egypt" (Joshua 9:9). Many years later, when the ark of the covenant entered their camp, the Philistines said, "Woe to us! For nothing like this has happened before. Woe to us! Who can deliver us from the power of these mighty gods? These are the gods who struck the Egyptians with every sort of plague in the wilderness" (1 Samuel 4:7b, 8). The plagues made God famous.

Since the exodus is the story of salvation, people later connected these events to the coming of Christ. When the Apostle Paul wanted to explain the sovereignty of God's grace, he quoted the words of Moses. He explained that salvation in Christ does not depend "on human will or exertion, but on God, who has mercy. For the Scripture says to Pharaoh, 'For this very purpose I have raised you up, that I might show my power in you, and that my name might be proclaimed in all the earth'" (Romans 9:16, 17). With these words Paul was praising God for the plaguing of Pharaoh. To this day, wherever Christ is preached, God is praised for his victory over Pharaoh. The plagues were part of God's missionary purpose to glorify his name in all the earth.

The third purpose statement comes in verse 29, which explains why God ended the plague of hail: "The thunder will cease, and there will be no more hail, so that you may know that the earth is the Lord's." Like the other purpose statements, this verse speaks of God's power. It emphasizes *his unlimited authority over all creation*. The plagues were supernatural demonstrations of God's power over the world that he created. There seems to be a special reference to this back in verse 22, which says that the storm struck "every plant of the field, in the land of Egypt." The Hebrew word used here for vegetation (*esheb*) is the same word that is used in Genesis 1:11, 12, where God told the land to "sprout vegetation." This verbal connection is a signal that when God sent his plagues against Egypt, he destroyed the very things that he had once created—every plant, every animal, and every person out in the fields.

Taken together, these three purpose statements explain why God plagued Pharaoh's Egypt. He did it to show his unique omnipotence, his universal praise, and his unlimited authority over all the earth. God accomplished the same purposes through the death and resurrection of Jesus Christ. By raising Jesus on the third day, God displayed his mighty power over sin and death. Now the good news of salvation in Christ is proclaimed around the world, so that God's name is praised in all the earth.

## Give Me Shelter!

The demonstration of God's praiseworthy power always demands a response, and really there are only two ways to respond. One is to believe that the Lord is God and to obey what he commands. The other is to doubt God's power, refusing to praise him, and then to wait and see what happens.

In order to show how Pharaoh would respond, God devised a test. Moses said to Pharaoh, "Now therefore send, get your livestock and all that you have in the field into safe shelter, for every man and beast that is in the field and is not brought home will die when the hail falls on them" (9:19). This was not the first time God had given Pharaoh advance warning. However, it was the first time he had given the Egyptians a chance to protect themselves. A killer hailstorm was on its way, but there was still time to seek shelter. Pharaoh had every reason to follow God's advice. He had already seen what God could do. He also had a huge cattle operation to consider, for his servants specialized in the cultivation of quality livestock. But Pharaoh was not about to take any orders from Moses, so he refused to bring his cattle in from the fields.

Pharaoh's refusal placed his staff in an awkward position. They had heard Moses' prophecy—which included hail in the forecast—and now they faced a choice. One option was to take their chances with the gods of Egypt. There were plenty to choose from, because many of the Egyptian gods and goddesses were personified in the elements of nature. Pharaoh's officials could trust in Shu, the god of the atmosphere, who held up the heavens. They could pray to Nut, the sky goddess, who represented the vaulting sky. They could depend on Tefnut, the goddess of moisture, or on Seth, who was present in the wind and storm. Maybe, just maybe there was something that one of their gods could do to save them. But frankly, some of Pharaoh's officials were starting to have their doubts. They didn't need ten plagues to convince them of God's power; six were more than enough! So as soon as they could leave the palace without being rude, they followed the safety instructions and ran for cover: "Then whoever feared the word of the LORD among the servants of Pharaoh hurried his slaves and his livestock into the houses" (9:20). They were listening, even if Pharaoh wasn't, and they decided to take God at his word.

The response of the officials who feared God shows that the plagues were starting to make believers out of the Egyptians. Their conversion process began with the third plague, when they first recognized "the finger of God" (8:19). It was complete by the time the Israelites left Egypt, because the Bible says that a "mixed multitude also went up with them" (12:38). Who were these people? Some of them may have been slaves from other ethnic groups, but at least some of them must have been Egyptians who put their faith in the God of Israel. Even when he was judging Pharaoh for his sins, God had a plan for Egypt's salvation. This plan can be traced throughout Scripture. Jeremiah prophesied Egypt's return to favor (Jeremiah 46:26). Ezekiel told of the nation's return from exile (Ezekiel 29:13–16). Isaiah promised a day when God would say, "Blessed be Egypt my people," and when the Egyptians would acknowledge him as Lord (Isaiah 19:19–25; cf. Psalm 87 NIV, margin). These promises were fulfilled on the Day of Pentecost, when the Holy Spirit was poured out on the church and Egyptians heard the apostles declare "the mighty works of God" in their own language (Acts 2:5–11).

The salvation of Egyptians started with the exodus, when God saved some of Egypt with Israel. The practical lesson to learn from their example is that salvation always comes in response to God's word. Some of Pharaoh's officials "feared the word of the LORD" (9:20). Here the Bible uses the word "feared" in its proper sense. Does it mean these men were afraid of what God said? You bet they were! They were scared enough to make sure that they did whatever they had to do to save their property. But they also feared God's word in the sense that they treated it with reverence and respect. They believed that what God said through his prophet Moses was true, and when they obeyed it, they were saved from the worst hailstorm ever.

This is how salvation always comes—by responding to God's Word with faith and obedience. God's Word tells us that we are needy sinners who will be lost forever unless we believe in Jesus Christ and his atoning death on the cross. This is a word to fear—in other words, a word to trust and obey—because it brings salvation.

## The Tempest

Some of Pharaoh's officials feared God's word, but not all of them. In fact, the great majority of them failed to heed God's warning. We know this because Moses later said to Pharaoh, "But as for you and your servants, I know that you do not yet fear the LORD God" (9:30), and also because at the end of this episode the same men hardened their hearts (9:34). They not only hardened their hearts, but they also deafened their ears. They "did not pay attention to the word of the LORD" (9:21); literally, they "did not set their hearts on God's word." Our response to God is always a matter of the heart. A heart that is not set on his word becomes dead set against his will.

Since they feared neither God nor his word, most of Pharaoh's officials decided to take their chances: "Whoever did not pay attention to the word of the LORD left his slaves and his livestock in the field" (9:21). This was a big mistake, because the storm came on schedule, striking with deadly violence:

> Then the LORD said to Moses, "Stretch out your hand toward heaven, so that there may be hail in all the land of Egypt, on man and beast and every plant of the field, in the land of Egypt." Then Moses stretched out his staff toward heaven, and the LORD sent thunder and hail, and fire ran down to the earth. And the LORD rained hail upon the land of Egypt. There was hail and fire flashing continually in the midst of the hail, very heavy hail, such as had never been in all the land of Egypt since it became a nation. The hail struck down everything that was in the field in all the land of Egypt, both man and beast. And the hail struck down every plant of the field and broke every tree of the field. (9:22–25)

It was the worst hailstorm ever. With the hail came rain, thunder, and lightning. Literally, there were "great balls of fire," rolling bolts of lightning flashing everywhere. It was a supernatural storm. God himself was present in power and glory, judging the Egyptians for their sins. As David would write on what must have been a similar occasion,

> He made darkness his covering, his canopy around him,
> thick clouds dark with water.
> Out of the brightness before him
> hailstones and coals of fire broke through his clouds.
> The LORD also thundered in the heavens,
> and the Most High uttered his voice. (Psalm 18:11–13; cf. Psalm 29)

By the time God was finished, the land was totally ruined. The only crops left standing were the seedlings of wheat: "The flax and the barley were struck down, for the barley was in the ear and the flax was in bud. But the wheat and the emmer were not struck down, for they are late in coming up" (9:31, 32). This comment explains why there was something left for the horde of locusts to devour when they came in the eighth plague. It also helps to confirm the historicity of Exodus and to date the plague of hail. Paintings from ancient Egypt show farmers simultaneously harvesting both flax and barley, as described in Exodus. This harvest generally took place in January, with the wheat harvested nearly two months later. This means that the plague of hail came at the beginning of the year, only months before the exodus itself, which occurred in April.[1] This time frame also fits what we know about cattle ranching in ancient Egypt: whatever livestock survived the pestilence of the fourth plague would have been left out-of-doors from the month of January on.

Although somehow the wheat managed to survive, the plague of hail destroyed everything else. The crops were beaten into the ground. The trees were stripped bare. Literally, they were smashed—blown apart by the sheer force of the tempest. There was also loss of life. The earlier plagues had caused real inconvenience, but as far as we know, they had not actually killed anyone. But the seventh plague brought death as well as discomfort, striking down everyone who was out working in the fields.

It was an awesome storm. The Egyptians had never seen anything like it. This is significant because whenever Pharaohs like Thutmose III wanted to boast about their accomplishments, they would say that they were doing "more than all the things that were in the country since it was founded."[2] Well, this was exactly the expression that God used to describe the seventh plague: It was "such as never has been in Egypt from the day it was founded until now" (Exodus 9:18). The nation of Egypt had been in existence for thousands of years, but this was the worst storm ever. This would have been especially impressive to the Egyptians because they believed that storms came from the gods. This particular storm was sent to prove God's power over the gods of Egypt.[3] It also proved God's justice, because in order to explain how bad the storm was, the Bible uses the same word that appears elsewhere to describe Pharaoh's heart—the word "heavy" (*kabed*). This shows that Pharaoh got exactly what he deserved—a storm that was every bit as bad as his heart!

The hailstorm of Exodus is a warning to pay careful attention to God's Word. There are basically two ways to respond to God: One is to fear his Word, and the other is to ignore it. Fearing God's Word means believing the good news about Jesus Christ, receiving him as Savior and Lord. Ignoring God's Word means doing nothing at all. But what will happen to those who do not take God's Word to heart? According to the book of Revelation, they will be crushed under the hail of God's wrath: "The seventh angel poured out his bowl into the air, and a loud voice came out of the temple, from the throne, saying, 'It is done!' And there were flashes of lightning, rumblings, peals of thunder. . . . And great hailstones, about one hundred pounds each, fell from heaven on people; and they cursed God for the plague of the hail, because the plague was so severe" (Revelation 16:17,

18a, 21). What Revelation describes really will be the worst storm ever—with not only lightning and thunder but also deadly hail.

The only way to be safe is to believe what God has said about his Son, Jesus Christ. God always saves those who trust in him. The seventh plague is a perfect example. Once again God discriminated between his people and Pharaoh's people: "Only in the land of Goshen, where the people of Israel were, was there no hail" (9:26). We can perhaps imagine the weather report: "Giant hail falls on Egypt—sunny skies over Goshen." By his supernatural and perhaps miraculous power, God protected his people from the mighty blows of his judgment. Some scholars have sought to explain this in terms of Egypt's geography, arguing that the hailstorm was confined to the Nile Valley. However, the real explanation is not so much geographical as it is theological. Israel was the object of God's affection, the choice of his electing love. The Israelites thus learned what is true for all God's children: they were safe in God's plans.

## False Confession

Enough was enough. When Pharaoh saw that the hail was destroying his country, he called for Moses and Aaron. Not only did he ask them to pray for him, but apparently he also began to confess his sins: "Then Pharaoh sent and called Moses and Aaron and said to them, 'This time I have sinned; the LORD is in the right, and I and my people are in the wrong. Plead with the LORD, for there has been enough of God's thunder and hail. I will let you go, and you shall stay no longer'" (9:27, 28).

There is something almost humorous about Pharaoh saying, "There has been enough of God's thunder and hail." No kidding. The Egyptians had *more* than enough! But what are we to make of Pharaoh's confession? Back in our study of the second plague, we criticized him for failing to say anything about his sins. However, this time—maybe for the first time in his whole life—he said, "I have sinned." In fact, this may have been the first time any Pharaoh had ever admitted that he was wrong. In those days, "individuals who approached Pharaoh were commanded to prostrate themselves, 'smelling the earth, crawling on the ground,' while 'invoking this perfect god and exalting his beauty.'"[4] Yet on this occasion, despite his delusions of deity, Pharaoh confessed that he was a sinner. Furthermore, he recognized the righteousness of God, saying, "The LORD is in the right, and I and my people are in the wrong" (9:27). Pharaoh used the language of justice, declaring both the righteousness of God and his own unrighteous sin.

Pharaoh's confession sounds good, but it fails to stand up to close scrutiny. Upon further review, it proves to be a false confession that falls short of true repentance. First, *Pharaoh did not confess his sins to God*. Notice that he was unable to pray for himself; he needed someone else to intercede for him. Like many people, he called for a minister when he was desperate, but he did not have his own personal relationship with the living God. Nevertheless, he believed in the power of prayer, and this actually served to increase his guilt. Charles Spurgeon explained it like this:

> In certain instances the man's hope in prayer is the result of *a condemning faith.* There is a justifying faith and a condemning faith. "What?" say you. "Does faith ever condemn men?" Yes, when men have faith enough to know that there is a God who sends judgments upon them, that nothing can remove those judgments but the hand that sent them, and that prayer moves that hand. There are persons who yet never pray themselves, but eagerly cry to friends, "Intreat the Lord for me." There is a measure of faith which goes to increase a man's condemnation, since he ought to know that if what he believes is true, then the proper thing is to pray himself.[5]

Pharaoh was such a man. Perhaps his unwillingness to pray explains why Moses was so skeptical about his confession. The prophet said, "As soon as I have gone out of the city, I will stretch out my hands to the Lord. The thunder will cease, and there will be no more hail, so that you may know that the earth is the Lord's. But as for you and your servants, I know that you do not yet fear the Lord God" (9:29, 30). Moses saw right through Pharaoh. He knew that Pharaoh's confession was false because he knew that when a man is truly sorry for his sins, he takes them straight to God. There is no repentance without the fear of God. We must recognize that more than anything else, sin is an offense against the holiness of God. A confession that acknowledges sin without fearing God is a false confession that falls short of true repentance.

Second, *Pharaoh did not confess* all *his sins*. His first words to Moses were, "*This time* I have sinned" (9:27). What Pharaoh said was true enough, but what about the other six times that he hardened his heart? What about his keeping the Israelites in bondage, forcing them to make bricks without straw? What about the baby boys he tried to drown in the Nile? By failing to confess his other transgressions, Pharaoh was minimizing his sin. He was willing to admit that he had made one or two mistakes, but he failed to recognize the depth of his depravity, the inherent rebellion of his whole nature. A confession that mentions one sin but forgets all the others is a false confession that falls short of true repentance.

Finally, *Pharaoh did not turn away from his sins*. He was very sorry that he was getting plagued with hail, but he was not truly sorry for his sins. The proof comes at the end of the passage: "So Moses went out of the city from Pharaoh and stretched out his hands to the Lord, and the thunder and the hail ceased, and the rain no longer poured upon the earth. But when Pharaoh saw that the rain and the hail and the thunder had ceased, he sinned yet again and hardened his heart, he and his servants. So the heart of Pharaoh was hardened, and he did not let the people of Israel go, just as the Lord had spoken through Moses" (9:33–35). As soon as Moses' prayers were answered and the storm was stilled, Pharaoh went right back to his sins. He was afraid of the plagues, but he did not fear God. To put this another way, he hated the consequences of sin without ever learning to hate the sin itself.

This is one of the differences between remorse and true repentance. Remorse is the sadness that comes from suffering God's judgment. Remorse is useful when it helps persuade sinners to repent. However, many people are filled with remorse for what is happening to them without ever truly repenting of their sins. The best way to tell is to see what happens *after* they confess their sins. True repentance is a complete change of heart that produces a total change of life. By that standard, Pharaoh's confession was false. It was only temporary. Once the storm stopped and the plague was over, his heart was as hard as ever. It turned out that he did not want a change of heart after all; he just wanted God to leave him alone. But a confession that does not lead to new obedience is a false confession that falls short of true repentance.

A close examination of Pharaoh's confession shows that he was an almost-believer whose repentance fell short of fearing God. His example thus reveals the deadly danger of partial repentance. If by God's Spirit we are able to admit that we are sinners, then we need to make a full confession. We must tell God that we are truly sorry for all our sins and then begin to walk in new obedience by his grace.

One man who truly did repent was Robinson Crusoe. Daniel Defoe's famous novel (the unabridged edition) by that name is really a story about repentance. The tale begins with young Robinson rebelling against his father and running away from home in order to pursue a life of sin. Things did not turn out quite as well as he had hoped, especially once he was shipwrecked. But he had only himself to blame, for as he later admitted, "I was . . . the willful Agent of all my own Miseries."

Robinson Crusoe was not delivered from his misery until he began to read his Bible and repent of his sin. In his diary he describes the happy day:

> I threw down the Book, and with my Heart as well as my Hands lifted up to Heaven, in a kind of Extasy of Joy, I cry'd out aloud, *Jesus, thou Son of David, Jesus, thou exalted Prince and Saviour, give me Repentance!*
>
> This was the first time that I could say, in the true Sense of the words, that I pray'd in all my Life; for now I pray'd with a Sense of my condition, and with a true Scripture View of Hope founded on the encouragement of the Word of God; and from this Time, I may say, I began to have hope.[6]

This was true repentance, and may God grant us the gift to offer it, for as the Scripture says, "Whoever conceals his transgressions will not prosper, but he who confesses and forsakes them will obtain mercy" (Proverbs 28:13).

# 25

# Something to Tell Your Grandchildren

EXODUS 10:1–20

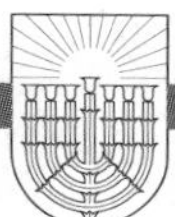

IN HER MEMOIRS OF HER LIFE as a young pioneer, Laura Ingalls Wilder recalls the day that a strange, dark cloud descended on the Minnesota prairie:

> Plunk! Something hit Laura's head and fell to the ground. She looked down and saw the largest grasshopper she had ever seen. Then huge brown grasshoppers were hitting the ground all around her, hitting her head and her face and her arms. They came thudding down like hail.
>
> The cloud was hailing grasshoppers. The cloud *was* grasshoppers. Their bodies hid the sun and made darkness. Their thin, large wings gleamed and glittered. The rasping whirring of their wings filled the whole air and they hit the ground and the house with the noise of a hailstorm.
>
> Laura tried to beat them off. Their claws clung to her skin and her dress. They looked at her with bulging eyes, turning their heads this way and that. Mary ran screaming into the house. Grasshoppers covered the ground, there was not one bare bit to step on. Laura had to step on grasshoppers and they smashed squirming and slimy under her feet. . . .
>
> Grasshoppers beat down from the sky and swarmed thick over the ground. Their long wings were folded and their strong legs took them hopping everywhere. The air whirred and the roof went on sounding like a roof in a hailstorm.
>
> Then Laura heard another sound, one big sound made of tiny nips and snips and gnawings. . . . The grasshoppers were eating. . . . You could hear the millions of jaws biting and chewing. . . . Day after day the grasshoppers kept on eating. They ate all the wheat and the oats. They ate every green thing—all the garden and all the prairie grass. . . . The whole prairie was bare and brown. Millions of brown grasshoppers whirred low over it. Not a green thing was in sight anywhere.[1]

Laura never forgot that dreadful day, or the hunger and hardship that followed as her family was brought to the edge of ruin. Naturally when she wrote about her childhood, she included the plague of grasshoppers. It was something to tell her grandchildren.

## Not Humbled but Hardened

For anyone who knows the history of the exodus, Laura's story calls to mind the eighth plague—the plague of locusts. The seventh plague was hail, and after the last hailstone melted, God repeated his ultimatum to Pharaoh, along with the consequences if he failed to surrender:

> So Moses and Aaron went in to Pharaoh and said to him, "Thus says the Lord, the God of the Hebrews, 'How long will you refuse to humble yourself before me? Let my people go, that they may serve me. For if you refuse to let my people go, behold, tomorrow I will bring locusts into your country, and they shall cover the face of the land, so that no one can see the land. And they shall eat what is left to you after the hail, and they shall eat every tree of yours that grows in the field, and they shall fill your houses and the houses of all your servants and of all the Egyptians, as neither your fathers nor your grandfathers have seen, from the day they came on earth to this day.'" Then he turned and went out from Pharaoh. (10:3–6)

God's demand was very simple: He told Pharaoh to set his people free so they could serve him. God's threat was simple too. If Pharaoh refused to submit, then his land would be destroyed. Moses prophesied total devastation. Locusts would cover the land, blanketing every visible surface and devouring every living plant. The Egyptians had already suffered the loss of their livestock and the damage of their crops. Now the locusts would consume what little was left.

When this terrible plague came, it was not a random act of nature but a deliberate act of divine justice. God was judging Pharaoh for his sinful pride. He asked, almost with a sense of astonishment, "How long will you refuse to humble yourself before me?" (10:3). It was a good question: How long was it going to take? Pharaoh had already suffered seven plagues, but he still hadn't made any real spiritual progress. Back in chapter 1, when Pharaoh made the Israelites his slaves, the Scripture says—literally—that he "humbled them with forced labor" (1:11). Now Pharaoh himself was about to be humbled, which of course was exactly what he needed. He had the opportunity to humble himself by letting God's people go, but if he continued to rebel, then eventually God would have to do the humbling for him. The choice was up to him: humility or humiliation.

Every human being faces the same choice. The Bible teaches that "God opposes the proud but gives grace to the humble" (1 Peter 5:5b). Then it goes on to make the obvious application: "Humble yourselves, therefore, under the mighty hand of God so that at the proper time he may exalt you" (1 Peter 5:6). The practical question for us is the one God posed to Pharaoh: "How long will you refuse to humble yourself before me?" There are other ways that we could put it: How long will you live such a sinful lifestyle? How long will you destroy yourself and the people you love? How long will you put off the day of repentance? Just how long will it be? When Charles Spurgeon preached on this passage, he said, "Forget Pharaoh, and only think of yourself; let the Lord Jesus Christ himself, with the thorn-crowned head and the pierced hand, stand by your pew, and looking right down into your soul, say in his matchless tone of music,—the music of the heart of love,—'How long wilt thou refuse to humble thyself before me?'"[2]

Pharaoh never did humble himself. He was unwilling and unable to do so because he was a hardened sinner, and yet in some mysterious way, even his hard heart was part of God's sovereign plan. Exodus 10 begins with these words: "Then the LORD said to Moses, 'Go in to Pharaoh, for I have hardened his heart and the heart of his servants, that I may show these signs of mine among them'" (10:1). Throughout our study of Exodus, we have seen that the plagues were part of God's plan. But here is a further mystery in the relationship between divine sovereignty and human responsibility. We sometimes think of the plagues as God's strategy for softening Pharaoh's heart. That is partly true. In the end the deadly plagues were what persuaded him to let God's people go. But there is another way to view the relationship between Pharaoh's hard heart and Egypt's terrible plagues. God hardened Pharaoh's heart in order to multiply the plagues. From the very beginning, God did not intend to send just one or two plagues but all ten of them. Hardening Pharaoh's heart was part of that plan. The harder his heart became, the more plagues God sent against Egypt, gaining more glory for himself.

## Story Time

God received this glory in the hearts and homes of his people. Why did God harden Pharaoh's heart? To perform miraculous signs in Egypt. And why did he perform these miraculous signs? God said to Moses, "That you may tell in the hearing of your son and of your grandson how I have dealt harshly with the Egyptians and what signs I have done among them, that you may know that I am the LORD" (10:2). The reason God plagued the Egyptians was so the Israelites would have something to tell their grandchildren.

Every child loves a good story, and this story was more entertaining than most. The whole exodus is an epic adventure. It had everything: a wicked tyrant, an unlikely hero, a bitter conflict, a daring rescue, a national triumph, a spiritual quest, and a happy ending, with lots of miracles for special effect. What a story! It even has its comic moments. Verse 2 hints at this when God describes how he dealt with Pharaoh. Literally, he did not say, "I have dealt harshly with the Egyptians," but "I made sport of the Egyptians." In sending his plagues against

Pharaoh, God was toying with the Egyptians. It was all part of his grand purpose, which was to give the Israelites something to tell their grandchildren.

As entertaining as this story was, it had the serious purpose of helping the Israelites know their God. "I am doing this," God said, "that you may tell in the hearing of your son and of your grandson . . . [and] that you may know that I am the LORD" (10:2). The exodus was not just any old story; it was *the* story, the story that shaped the Israelites into the people of God. It was the story of their salvation. It was a true story, a story based on the facts of history. It was a story that explained everything the children of God needed to know. It explained who they were: the people of God, delivered from slavery. It explained who God was: the Lord God of Israel, the God of all power and glory. It explained where they came from: out of Egypt. It told them where they were going: into the land of promise. And it explained what their purpose was: they were saved for God's glory. By sending his plagues against Pharaoh, God was giving his people a story that answered all the big questions: Who am I? Where did I come from? Where am I going? What is the meaning of life? Is there a God? If there is, how can I know him, and what does he want me to do?

The story was so important that God wanted all his children to know it. Moses was to be the chief storyteller. When God said, "tell in the hearing of your son and of your grandson" (10:2), he was speaking to Moses in the singular. As God's prophet, it was his responsibility to tell God's people the story of salvation. This was a responsibility that Moses took seriously. There is a good example in Exodus 18, when Moses met Jethro: "Moses told his father-in-law all that the LORD had done to Pharaoh and to the Egyptians for Israel's sake, all the hardship that had come upon them in the way, and how the LORD had delivered them" (18:8). Moses told Jethro the story of salvation, and the story accomplished its purpose: "And Jethro rejoiced for all the good that the LORD had done to Israel, in that he had delivered them out of the hand of the Egyptians. Jethro said, 'Blessed be the LORD, who has delivered you out of the hand of the Egyptians and out of the hand of Pharaoh and has delivered the people from under the hand of the Egyptians. Now I know that the LORD is greater than all gods, because in this affair they dealt arrogantly with the people'" (Exodus 18:9–11). It was the story that helped Jethro to know and glorify God. Moses did not stop with Jethro, of course, but recorded these events in the pages of Scripture. Now when we study the book of Exodus we sit at his feet, listening to our great-great-grandfather, so to speak, tell us the story of salvation.

Moses was not the only storyteller in Egypt. God's plan was for all the Israelites to glorify him by recounting their exodus from Egypt. When their children said, "Tell me a story!" (as children always do), they would tell them the story of their deliverance. And when their children wanted to know why they had to keep all God's rules, they would tell it to them again:

> When your son asks you in time to come, "What is the meaning of the testimonies and the statutes and the rules that the LORD our God has commanded you?" then you shall say to your son, "We were Pharaoh's slaves in Egypt. And the LORD brought us out of Egypt with a mighty hand. And the LORD showed signs and wonders, great and grievous, against Egypt and against Pharaoh and all his household, before our eyes. And he brought us out from there, that he might bring us in and give us the land that he swore to give to our fathers. And the LORD commanded us to do all these statutes, to fear the LORD our God, for our good always, that he might preserve us alive, as we are this day. And it will be righteousness for us, if we are careful to do all this commandment before the LORD our God, as he has commanded us." (Deuteronomy 6:20–25; cf. Deuteronomy 4:9, 10)

The story of salvation became the song of salvation. Many Hebrew psalms refer to the exodus in one way or another, and several of them—such as Psalm 78 (vv. 42–51) and Psalm 105 (vv. 26–36)—make specific mention of the plagues.

The purpose of all this storytelling was to enable the children of Israel to know God as their Lord and Savior. The Israelites passed down the story of the exodus not simply because it formed their national identity or because it was part of a good education, but because it promoted the knowledge of God. The history of their escape from Egypt shaped their theology and their spirituality. Children learned the story in order to know their God.

We, too, have a story. We have something to tell our children and our grandchildren. It is the story of Jesus Christ, the Moses of our salvation, who brought us out of the Egypt of our sin. It is a true story based on the facts of history: his virgin birth, his virtuous life, his vicarious atonement, and his victorious resurrection. What a story! It explains everything a child really needs to know. It explains who we are: the people of God. It explains where we came from: a life of sin and misery. It explains where we are going: to live with Christ in mansions of glory. It explains who God is: the Father of mercy and love. And it explains why we are here: to glorify God by living for Christ.

For those who know the story, there is no more important task than telling it to others. The storytelling starts at home, where fathers and mothers have a duty to instruct their children in Scriptural truth. Children should learn Bible stories not only at church, and perhaps also at school, but especially at home. Any father not personally engaged in the spiritual instruction of his children is not doing his duty. Fathers and mothers who teach their children Biblical theology are handing down a priceless treasure. By telling them the story that will shape their lives, they are passing on the legacy of salvation. The great Dutch theologian and statesman Abraham Kuyper (1837–1920) wrote, "A Church which does not teach her youth can never hope to retain a confession, but relinquishes it, cuts off all contact with the past, divorces herself from the fathers, and forms a new group. . . . If you desire to confess, you must learn."[3]

At Tenth Presbyterian Church in Philadelphia we assist parents in this task by providing a curriculum of memory work. On Sunday mornings children line up to recite their Bible verses and catechism questions. The minister also helps them prepare for worship by giving them a short preview of the sermon they will hear later. And of course we teach the Bible and its theology in our Sunday school classes. But all of this is intended merely to supplement what the children are learning at home, where their parents have the primary duty to train their minds and hearts in the gospel.

## Another Round of Negotiations

Pharaoh was in no mood for stories. He had suffered a series of supernatural disasters—everything from rivers of blood to invasions of insects and amphibians. He could sense that even though the Egyptians treated him like a god, the tide of public opinion was starting to turn against him. "Then Pharaoh's servants said to him, 'How long shall this man be a snare to us? Let the men go, that they may serve the LORD their God. Do you not yet understand that Egypt is ruined?'" (10:7).

Pharaoh's advisers were diplomats; so they couched their language in careful terms, identifying Moses as the main problem. But what they were really doing was blaming Pharaoh for Egypt's troubles. They asked the same question that Moses asked: "How long . . . ?" (10:3, 7). How long was it going to be before Pharaoh finally admitted that the God of Israel was the real deal and that any further attempt to resist his will was utter folly? The royal court wanted Pharaoh to rethink his policy on Israel. They practically begged him to let God's people go.

And Pharaoh was starting to weaken. Like most politicians, he was vulnerable to public pressure. So he agreed to meet with Moses one more time: "So Moses and Aaron were brought back to Pharaoh. And he said to them, 'Go, serve the LORD your God. But which ones are to go?'" (10:8). Obviously Pharaoh was suspicious. Moses had been asking for permission to go and worship God. He never actually came right out and said that once the Hebrews left, they were never coming back. However, that was the impression Pharaoh was starting to get. So before he granted any exit visas, he wanted to know just who would be going.

The answer, of course, was that they would *all* be going: "Moses said, 'We will go with our young and our old. We will go with our sons and daughters and with our flocks and herds, for we must hold a feast to the LORD'" (10:9). The prophet was emphatic: "We *will* go." And when they went, the Israelites would take everyone and everything—all their people and all their property.

As far as Pharaoh was concerned, this was totally unreasonable. Hence his sarcasm: "But he said to them, 'The LORD be with you, if ever I let you and your little ones go! Look, you have some evil purpose in mind'" (10:10). This was

Pharaoh's way of saying, "Look, Moses, I know what you're up to, and there's no way I'm going to fall for it!" If he let all the Israelites go, he was saying, then the Lord really would be with them (here Pharaoh's words were truer than he understood) because he was never going to do it! To show how opposed he was to freeing any slaves, he issued a threat: The words "evil purpose in mind" can also be translated, "evil is in store for you."

It was at this point that Pharaoh proposed a compromise: "'No! Go, the men among you, and serve the LORD, for that is what you are asking.' And they were driven out from Pharaoh's presence" (10:11). This was not the first time Pharaoh agreed to let God's people go, only to reconsider and then try to renegotiate. After the fourth plague he had said, "I will let you go to sacrifice to the LORD your God in the wilderness; only you must not go very far away" (8:28). This time he was willing to let them go as far as they wanted, provided they left behind their women and children. In effect, he would hold the women and children hostage in order to guarantee that their husbands and fathers would return to Egypt.

This seemed like a reasonable offer, but Pharaoh was making two false assumptions. One was that the women and children didn't count. Pharaoh assumed that when it came to performing religious duties, men were the only ones who mattered. If the Israelites wanted to worship, then why did everyone have to leave? Why not just let the men go and get it over with? Part of the answer, of course, was that God wanted freedom for all his people. From the very beginning he told Pharaoh, "Let my people go," and that meant everyone. God wanted to give the Israelites something to tell their grandchildren, which they could only do if they took their children with them. But there was also an important spiritual principle at stake: Worship is for the whole family, from the oldest to the youngest. God wants all his people to praise him. *The Westminster Shorter Catechism* says that "the chief end of man" is "to glorify God" (A. 1). This also happens to be the chief end of woman, and the chief end of children, which is why it is necessary for Christians to worship together—every man, woman, and child.

Pharaoh's other false assumption was that he could bargain with God. He assumed that he and God were on more or less equal terms, and therefore he could negotiate from a position of strength. But there would be no compromise. God does not discuss terms; he dictates them. What he demanded in this case was nothing less than Pharaoh's unconditional surrender. It was all or nothing, which is why God was not impressed with Pharaoh's offer to let the men of Israel go.

The practical lesson is that we must take God on his terms, not ours. Discipleship is not open to discussion. When we receive Jesus Christ as Savior, we do not make a few concessions here and there; we surrender our whole lives to the lordship of his will. And when God calls us to serve him—to stand up for Christ on the job, to exercise a ministry in the church, or even to become a missionary—he does not invite us to enter another round of negotiations. He commands us to go where we are sent and to do as we are told.

### The Coming of the Locusts

When Pharaoh realized that negotiations had broken down, he drove Moses and Aaron out of the palace. If he hadn't been such a fool, he would have braced himself for another plague.

> Then the LORD said to Moses, "Stretch out your hand over the land of Egypt for the locusts, so that they may come upon the land of Egypt and eat every plant in the land, all that the hail has left." So Moses stretched out his staff over the land of Egypt, and the LORD brought an east wind upon the land all that day and all that night. When it was morning, the east wind had brought the locusts. The locusts came up over all the land of Egypt and settled on the whole country of Egypt, such a dense swarm of locusts as had never been before, nor ever will be again. They covered the face of the whole land, so that the land was darkened, and they ate all the plants in the land and all the fruit of the trees that the hail had left. Not a green thing remained, neither tree nor plant of the field, through all the land of Egypt. (10:12–15)

This plague was really something to tell the grandchildren! Scientists report that the daily consumption of a locust equals its own weight. That may not sound like much. However, a full-scale swarm covers several hundred square miles, with between one hundred and two hundred million locusts per mile. John Davis writes, "The locust is perhaps nature's most awesome example of the collective destructive power of a species. An adult locust weighs at a maximum two grams and its combined destructive force can leave thousands of people with famine for years."[4] The Egyptians had never seen anything like this plague, and they will never see anything like it again. There have been other plagues, of course. Some are mentioned in the Bible, such as the invasion of locusts in the book of Joel.[5]

There have also been many locust plagues throughout history. In the 1920s and 1930s locusts swept across Africa and wiped out five million square miles, an area almost double the size of the United States.[6] In 1988 the *Chicago Tribune* reported: "Billions of locusts are moving across North Africa in the worst plague since 1954, blotting out the sun and settling on the land like a black, ravenous carpet to strip it clean of vegetation."[7] Then in 2001 an article from the *Times* in London stated: "Plagues of locusts are devastating crops from Central Asia to the American Mid-West, sending farmers to the book of Exodus for salvation. Not since the Egyptians incurred the wrath of God have so many locusts had their day. A billion-strong army is on the move, stretching far beyond the more normal swarming grounds of Africa and the Middle East."[8] The *Times* went on to report that in places the density of the infestation reached ten thousand locusts per ten square feet.

These descriptions help explain what happened to Egypt. The wind blew out of the east, a rare occurrence indicating God's direct intervention, his sovereign rule over nature. Borne by the wind, the locusts covered the land like a dark cloud, even hopping into people's homes. Their appetites were voracious. The crops had already been battered by the hail; so by the time the locusts were finished, there was nothing left. This would have caused an immediate food shortage, leading to famine and perhaps starvation. Since the Egyptians were dependent on their agriculture, the mass invasion of locusts jeopardized their entire future. Pharaoh himself called it "this death" (10:17).

It was another humiliation for Egypt's gods. The Egyptians worshiped Min, the patron of the crops. Min-worshipers held an annual harvest festival, which may well have coincided with the eighth plague. The Egyptians also worshiped Isis (the goddess of life, who prepared flax for clothing), Nepri (the god of grain), Anubis (the guardian of the fields), and Senehem (the divine protector against pests). They depended on all these gods to preserve their food supply. An inscription on the Tanis Stele, which dates from the reign of Taharqa, speaks of "a fine field, which the gods protected against grasshoppers."[9] But not this time. This time the gods failed, and the Egyptians learned not to trust them for their daily bread, which only the God of Israel can provide.

## The Rest of the Story

What happened next was completely predictable: "Then Pharaoh hastily called Moses and Aaron and said, 'I have sinned against the Lord your God, and against you. Now therefore, forgive my sin, please, only this once, and plead with the Lord your God only to remove this death from me'" (10:16, 17).

Pharaoh was up to his old tricks. Once again when things got desperate he called for a minister. Once again he admitted his wrongdoing. He confessed that he had sinned against God and also against Moses (not against Israel, however)—presumably by not listening to him or perhaps by previously throwing him out of the palace. But Pharaoh still wasn't ready to repent in the Biblical way. He did not confess his sins to God but asked Moses to intercede for him. He was still more concerned about the consequences of his sin than about the sin itself. His confession was a matter of practical expediency rather than deep spiritual conviction. It was a form of manipulation—another way of getting what he wanted. Pharaoh also seemed to think that this was the last time he would ever need to be forgiven. Literally, he said, "Forgive my sin only this once." He was still minimizing his sin, pretending that he had never sinned before and expecting never to sin again.

Pharaoh was a hardened sinner, and what he offered was a false confession that fell short of true repentance. It is not surprising, therefore, that the plague of locusts ended like all the other plagues: "But the LORD hardened Pharaoh's heart, and he did not let the people of Israel go" (10:20). This was the trouble with Pharaoh: he kept repenting of his repentance! All he really wanted was for God to side with him when he had a crisis. Who doesn't? But God is only on the side of those who actually turn away from their sin.

Pharaoh hardly deserved to have his request granted. Nevertheless, God took away the deadly plague: "So he [Moses] went out from Pharaoh and pleaded with the LORD. And the LORD turned the wind into a very strong west wind, which lifted the locusts and drove them into the Red Sea. Not a single locust was left in all the country of Egypt" (10:18, 19). The wind shifted, and the locusts were drowned in the sea. This was a preview of coming destruction, for soon Pharaoh's army would be destroyed in exactly the same way at exactly the same place (see 14:21–28).

The locusts were a warning to Pharaoh. They also stand as a warning to us because, like so many plagues from Exodus, they are a preview of the final tribulation:

> Then from the smoke came locusts on the earth, and they were given power like the power of scorpions of the earth. They were told not to harm the grass of the earth or any green plant or any tree, but only those people who do not have the seal of God on their foreheads. They were allowed to torment them for five months, but not to kill them, and their torment was like the torment of a scorpion when it stings someone. And in those days people will seek death and will not find it. They will long to die, but death will flee from them.
>
> In appearance the locusts were like horses prepared for battle: on their heads were what looked like crowns of gold; their faces were like human faces, their hair like women's hair, and their teeth like lions' teeth; they had breastplates like breastplates of iron, and the noise of their wings was like the noise of many chariots with horses rushing into battle. They have tails and stings like scorpions, and their power to hurt people for five months is in their tails. (Revelation 9:3–10)

That will be a locust plague to end all locust plagues. It will be even more terrible than the plague on Egypt because, rather than devouring plants, these locusts will torment everyone who does not belong to God. Is there any way to escape this terrible plague? Of course there is. The way to escape is to repent, humbling ourselves before God and praying for salvation in the name of Jesus Christ.

Everyone who truly prays for forgiveness will be protected from plague. King Solomon claimed this promise when he dedicated the temple and prayed:

> If there is famine in the land, if there is pestilence or blight or mildew or locust or caterpillar, if their enemy besieges them in the land at their

> gates, whatever plague, whatever sickness there is, whatever prayer, whatever plea is made by any man or by all your people Israel, each knowing the affliction of his own heart and stretching out his hands toward this house, then hear in heaven your dwelling place and forgive and act and render to each whose heart you know, according to all his ways (for you, you only, know the hearts of all the children of mankind), that they may fear you all the days that they live in the land that you gave to our fathers. (1 Kings 8:37–40)

A memorable example of deliverance comes from the childhood of Laura Ingalls Wilder. When Laura's family farm was devastated by grasshoppers, Pa headed back east to find work. He had to walk hundreds of miles, and he was gone for months. But during those difficult days, Ma continued to read the family Bible:

> One Sunday she read to them about the plague of locusts, long ago in Bible times. Locusts were grasshoppers. Ma read:
>
> "And the locusts went up over the land of Egypt, and rested in all the coasts of Egypt; very grievous were they.
>
> "For they covered the face of the whole earth, so that the land was darkened; and they did eat every herb of the land, and all the fruits of the trees which the hail had left; and there remained not any green thing on the trees, or in the herbs of the field, through all the land of Egypt."
>
> Laura knew how true that was. When she repeated those verses she thought, "through all the land of Minnesota."
>
> Then Ma read the promise that God made to good people, "to bring them out of that land to a good land and a large, unto a land flowing with milk and honey."[10]

The Ingalls family claimed that promise, praying that God would deliver them from famine. A few days later they saw a small cloud approach from the northwest. At first it seemed too small to do much good, but as it came nearer it grew larger and larger, until finally it rushed across the prairie and poured rain all over their house and their fields. It rained all day. By the next evening little shoots of grass started to come up. In a few days there was a green streak across the brown prairie, and the farm was saved. We all experience hardship in this fallen world, but in the scope of eternity, there are no deadly plagues for the righteous, but only the promise of a good land for them and their children.

# 26

# Heart of Darkness

EXODUS 10:21–29

ON AUGUST 1, 1914, Sir Ernest Shackleton (1874–1922) and his crew set sail from London aboard the ship *Endurance*. They were bound for Antarctica, where the famous explorer hoped to traverse the continent on foot. But Shackleton never made the trek because before the *Endurance* could reach land, the ship became hopelessly lodged in the ice pack. It was January 1915, and from this point their goal became simple survival.

The crew faced many hardships in the months that followed, including freezing temperatures and near starvation. But of all the frozen terrors they faced, none was more disheartening than the long polar night. The sailors grew uneasy as winter set in and the light began to fade. In early May the sun vanished altogether, not to be seen again until late July. Shackleton's biographer wrote, "In all the world there is no desolation more complete than the polar night. It is a return to the Ice Age—no warmth, no life, no movement. Only those who have experienced it can fully appreciate what it means to be without the sun day after day and week after week. Few men unaccustomed to it can fight off its effects altogether, and it has driven some men mad."[1]

## Sun Worshipers

Darkness drove Pharaoh mad too. God had already plagued him with blood, frogs, gnats, flies, pestilence, disease, hail, and locusts. But the ninth plague plunged Egypt into total darkness. For three whole days no one could see anything.

Days of darkness would frighten anyone, but they held a special terror for the Egyptians because they worshiped the sun. As Stephen Quirke notes in his study of ancient Egyptian religion, "We need to understand the place of the sun in Egyptian civilization before we can begin to know anything about ancient Egypt."[2] The Egyptians served Horus (the god of the sunrise), Aten (the god of the round, midday sun), and Atum (the god of the sunset). But the supreme deity in their national pantheon was Amon-Re, who said, "I am the great god who came into being of himself, He who created his names . . . he who has no opponent among the gods."[3] The Egyptians believed that this solar deity was their creator. "Unique God," they would sing in their great Hymn to the Sun-disk, "there is none besides him. / You mould the earth to your wish, you and you alone—/ All people, herds and flocks, / All on earth that walk on legs, / All on high that fly with their wings."[4] Every morning the rising of the sun in the east reaffirmed the life-giving power of Amon-Re. Sunset represented death and the underworld, but the rise of Amon-Re offered the hope of resurrection. For the Egyptians, it was a matter of faith that the eternally rising sun could never be destroyed.

Like most Egyptians, Pharaoh was a sun worshiper. More than that, he was regarded as the Son of Re, the personal embodiment of the solar deity. Egypt's king was Egypt's god, and as the incarnation of Amon-Re, he maintained the cosmic order. Stephen Quirke writes: "At the kernel of the civilization stands a special relation between the divine father figure of the sun god, ruler of creation, and his solitary offspring on earth, the reigning king of Egypt. . . . This establishes the key relationship in creation, between the sun god as the elder partner in the sky and his issue on earth, the junior partner. . . . Within the reign of each king, he alone appears as the living representative of the sun god on earth, and enjoys a unique sovereignty in the practical exercise of power."[5]

Many ancient texts identified Pharaoh with the gods of the sun. Pharaoh would pray, "Oh living Aten, who initiates life. . . . Oh sole god, without another beside him! You create the Earth according to your wish. . . . You are in my heart, and there is none who knows you except your son."[6] Or consider the following hymn of praise to the Pharaoh Ahmose:

> He is looked upon like Re when he rises,
> like the shining of Aten,
> like the rising of Khepri at the sight of his rays on high,
> like Atum in the eastern sky.[7]

Similarly, when the Pharaoh Merneptah ascended the throne of Egypt, his loyal subjects sang:

> Be joyful the entire land!
> Good times have come.
> The lord has ascended in all lands,
> and orderliness has gone down to its throne.
> The king of Upper and Lower Egypt, lord of millions of years,
> great in kingship just like . . . Re-Amun,
> who overwhelms Egypt with festivals,
> the Son of Re who is more excellent than any king,
> Merneptah.[8]

Here is yet another example of the kind of worship the Egyptians offered to Pharaoh as the god of the sun:

> Ra has placed the king on the earth of the living for ever and eternity,
> in order to judge humankind, to satisfy the gods,
> to make Right happen and to annihilate Wrong,
> such that he gives divine offerings to the gods,
> funerary offerings to the blessed dead.
> The name of the king is in the sky like that of Ra,
> he lives in joy like Ra-Horakhty.
> Nobles rejoice when they see him; the populace gives him praise
> in his role of "the Child."[9]

The Egyptians worshiped Pharaoh as their god. In school, children were instructed to "Worship [Pharaoh], living forever, within your bodies and associate with his majesty in your hearts. . . . He is Re, by whose beams one sees, he is one who illuminates the Two Lands more than the sun disc."[10] The Egyptians thus ascribed all majesty and eternity to Pharaoh. He was their illuminator, the lord of their hearts. Sometimes they even prayed to him, saying, "Attend to me, O rising sun that illuminates the Two Lands with his comeliness; O solar disk of mankind that dispels darkness from Egypt. Thy nature is like unto thy father Re who arises in heaven."[11]

These texts prove that Egyptian worship was deeply offensive, an affront to the honor of the Triune God. When the Egyptians identified Pharaoh as the son of Amon-Re, they were worshiping a mortal man as the eternal god. For his part, Pharaoh was claiming attributes and prerogatives that belong to God alone. He was an anti-Christ, a blasphemous impostor claiming to be the Son of God.

It is easy to assume that idolatry is a thing of the past, but how does the ninth plague apply to us today? In what ways are we tempted to worship Amon-Re? Almost no one worships the sun anymore, yet idolatry is still a real temptation. Somewhere the third-century theologian Origen wrote, "What each one honors before all else, what before all things he admires and loves, this for him is God." By Origen's definition, we too are idol-worshipers, because there are many things that we honor, admire, and love instead of God. The question is, what do we love most of all? Who is our supreme deity?

Like the ancient Egyptians, postmodern Americans have many gods, but our supreme deity seems to be Self. We honor, admire, and love ourselves more than anyone or anything else. For an example of this type of idolatry, consider Walt Whitman's famous "Song of Myself":

> I celebrate myself, and sing myself . . .
> the song of me rising from the bed and meeting the sun. . . .
> Divine am I inside and out, and I make holy whatever I touch. . . .
> If I worship one thing more than another it shall be . . . my own body.

Whitman is the most American of all our poets. We like to think of ourselves as a nation of rugged individualists. And it's true—we depend on our own abilities and admire our own accomplishments. We devote nearly all our attention to making our own plans, meeting our own needs, serving our own interests, and satisfying our own pleasures. We even complain about our own problems. It's all about us. We idolize ourselves.

### The Eclipse of Ra

Given the supremacy of the sun god, it was inevitable that before God was finished with Pharaoh, he would launch a direct attack on Amon-Re. God's purpose in all the plagues was to glorify himself by judging the gods of Egypt (see Numbers 33:4). Darkness was the penultimate plague, the ninth in a series of ten. In the first eight plagues God demonstrated his superiority over Hapi, Osiris, Heqet, Khepter, Apis, Isis, Sekhmet, and the rest of Egypt's lesser gods and goddesses. And this partly explains why there were so many plagues: God wanted to give his rivals a comprehensive defeat.

God saved the biggest deity for last. But Amon-Re was not difficult to defeat. All God had to do was to shut out the light: "Then the Lord said to Moses, 'Stretch out your hand toward heaven, that there may be darkness over the land of Egypt, a darkness to be felt.' So Moses stretched out his hand toward heaven, and there was pitch darkness in all the land of Egypt three days. They did not see one another, nor did anyone rise from his place for three days" (10:21–23a). Suddenly all was dark. The plague came unannounced, and for three long days the land of perpetual sunshine was smothered by what the Bible literally calls "a dark darkness." We can only imagine how dreadful this was for the Egyptians. When your god is the sun, and the sun gets blotted out, you are left with only emptiness and dread. It was so dark that the Egyptians couldn't even light their homes.

Scholars have suggested that the darkness had some natural cause. Some think it was a solar eclipse. Others say it was one of Arabia's sandstorms, commonly known as *khamsin*.[12] During these swirling, blinding storms, Egyptians are forced to stay indoors as part of their land is covered with a dense brown cloud of sand and dust. Perhaps this might explain what the Bible means by "a darkness to be felt" (10:21). However, these natural phenomena do not fully satisfy the details of the Biblical text. If the ninth plague was a common occurrence, then why was Pharaoh so troubled by it? And why doesn't the Bible just say it was a dust storm? What the Bible emphasizes instead is how dark it was. The darkness was palpable, and unlike a sandstorm, it was total. We conclude, therefore, that the darkness—like the rest of the plagues—was a supernatural miracle.

The plague of darkness proved God's absolute power over creation. God can unmake what he has made. This is something that all the plagues showed by reversing the six days of creation. The God who made the waters turned the Nile into blood. The God who made green things grow destroyed vegetation with hail and locusts. The God who made creatures swim in the sea and swarm on dry land brought death to fish and frogs. The God who made men and beasts sent them disease and even death. Finally, the God who brought light out of darkness made the light fade to black.

In short, the plagues were a kind of de-creation. To make this connection explicit, Exodus often uses key vocabulary from early Genesis. The point is that the sovereign God has the power to destroy as well as to create. Peter Enns writes:

> Creation is at God's command both to deliver his people and to destroy his enemies. The plagues are creation reversals: Animals harm rather than serve humanity; light ceases and darkness takes over; waters become a source of death rather than life; the climax of Genesis 1 is the creation of humans on the last day, whereas the climax of the plagues is the destruction of human beings in the last plague. The plagues do not run rampant, however. They eventually cease, and each cessation is another display of God's creative power. He once again restores order to chaos as he did "in the beginning": The waters are restored, the pesky insects and animals retreat. Each plague is a reminder of the supreme power of God who holds chaos at bay, but who, if he chooses, will step aside and allow chaos to plague his enemies.[13]

Darkness may not seem like much of a plague, especially compared to the death of men and cattle, but its spiritual significance would not have been lost on the Egyptians. God was adding insult to all their other injuries. As they groped around their homes, paralyzed by the darkness, they must have been stunned by the failure of Amon-Re and his son Pharaoh. The sun gods could not save them; even the light of day was controlled by the God of Moses.

God proved his supremacy in Egypt by blotting out the sun. What will it take for him to prove his sovereignty to us? In the same way that God defeated Amon-Re, he will expose our self-idolatry. If we trust in self, ultimately we will be disappointed. What will our self be able to do when we face financial ruin, when our family falls apart, or when we are diagnosed with a terminal illness? What will we do when we die and stand before God for judgment? Our self will not be able to save us. Sooner or later God will destroy every last trace of self-confidence in order to prove that he alone is God.

## The Shadow of Darkness

The darkness that fell over Egypt was physical, but it also had spiritual significance. In the Bible darkness signifies error, ignorance, sin, rebellion, and death—everything that is opposed to God. The Bible says, "The way of the wicked is like deep darkness" (Proverbs 4:19a). This is the result of sin, for as Jesus said, "People loved the darkness rather than the light because their works were evil" (John 3:19). Darkness dwells in the minds and hearts of sinners: "They are darkened in their understanding, alienated from the life of God because of the ignorance that is in them, due to their hardness of heart" (Ephesians 4:18). To disobey God is "walk in darkness" (1 John 1:6). The person who lives in darkness is destined to die in darkness: "He is thrust from light into darkness, and driven out of the world" (Job 18:18). Like all these other Biblical texts, the ninth plague symbolized spiritual darkness, the darkness that spread from Pharaoh's hardened, darkened heart.

The true condition of Pharaoh's heart was revealed at the end of Exodus 10, when he told Moses to get out of his face. But an earlier statement was just as telling: "Then Pharaoh called Moses and said, 'Go, serve the LORD; your little ones also may go with you; only let your flocks and your herds remain behind'" (10:24). This statement shows how much Pharaoh knew. He knew exactly what God wanted from him. He knew who had sent the darkness. He knew God's covenant name—Yahweh or "LORD." He knew that he was supposed to let God's people go. He even knew the purpose for their exodus: so the Israelites could go and worship God. Pharaoh knew all this, yet refused to give it all over to God. The heart of his darkness was his unwillingness to give God total control.

Gradually, grudgingly, Pharaoh had been making more and more concessions. After the fourth plague, he said, "Go, sacrifice to your God within the land" (8:25). Pharaoh was willing to let the Israelites worship God as long as they remained his own personal slaves. To put this in spiritual terms, he was trying to convince them that they could serve him and serve God at the same time. When Moses refused, Pharaoh said, "I will let you go to sacrifice to the LORD your God in the wilderness; only you must not go very far away" (8:28). This was another temptation: to follow God into freedom, but to stay close enough to run back into bondage. Pharaoh's next bargaining position was to allow the men to go, but not the women and children (10:10, 11), as if the men of Israel would have left their families in slavery! His final offer was to let all the Israelites go, provided that they left their flocks and herds behind. Pharaoh intended to hold their livestock hostage to guarantee Israel's return. He knew that they would not survive for long without food.

Pharaoh was always holding something back. By insisting on his right to hold on to God's livestock, he was refusing to give up his sovereignty. He wanted to deal with God on his own terms. He wanted to stay in control, so he only did what he absolutely had to do. But a heart that is not willing to go the whole way with God is a heart of darkness.

Like Pharaoh, many people bargain with God, trying to get him to lower his terms. They will say "The Sinner's Prayer" as long as they don't have to go to church every week. Or they will go to church as long as they don't have to get baptized. Or they will get baptized as long as they don't have to get involved. Or they will give some of their time as long as they don't have to give any of their money. Or they will give part of themselves to God as long as they don't have to give him everything. In short, they are willing to become Christians as long as they can still live for themselves. They imagine that there is some way for them to hold on to their sins and still get to Heaven. But anyone who thinks this way still has a heart of darkness. Salvation is only for those who walk by the light of God's Word.

## Down to the Last Hoof

The Israelites were not in the dark, and this was part of the miracle. As he had done in earlier plagues, God discriminated between his people and Pharaoh's people. The Bible states explicitly that "all the people of Israel had light where they lived" (10:23b), probably referring to the whole land of Goshen. The blackout only affected the Egyptians.

Like darkness, light has spiritual significance. It represents truth, beauty, and purity. This symbolism runs right through the Bible. The Bible says, "God is light, and in him is no darkness at all" (1 John 1:5). It also says that God's word is "a lamp shining in a dark place" (2 Peter 1:19). Therefore, when sinners are called to salvation, they are called "out of darkness into his marvelous light" (1 Peter 2:9). "At one time you were darkness," the Scripture says, "but now you are light in the Lord. Walk as children of light" (Ephesians 5:8).

The proof that the Israelites were children of light was their unwillingness to make even the smallest compromise in their commitment to God. It must have been tempting to take Pharaoh up on his offer. He was ready to give Moses almost everything he asked for. "But Moses said, 'You must also let us have sacrifices and burnt offerings, that we may sacrifice to the LORD our God. Our livestock also must go with us; not a hoof shall be left behind, for we must take of them to serve the LORD our God, and we do not know with what we must serve the LORD until we arrive there'" (10:25, 26).

Moses is sometimes criticized for being deceptive. His statement about not being sure how many animals they would need to sacrifice sounds disingenuous. After all, he had no intention of ever returning to Egypt. Some scholars think the prophet was trying to pull a fast one. However, this misses the spiritual significance of what he said. Moses understood that with God, it is all or nothing, so he insisted that Pharaoh meet his demands. Moses was not negotiating; he was giving orders. Literally, what he said to Pharaoh was, "You *will* allow us to offer sacrifices."

There could be no compromise. God had called Moses to lead Israel out of Egypt. It was not enough, therefore, for God's people to worship God while they stayed in Egypt. It was not enough for the men to go without taking their families with them. It was not even enough for the people to go without also taking their possessions. God commanded Moses to bring everyone and everything. This is what God always demands: everything we are and everything we have. The reason Moses insisted on offering God everything—including every single part of every last animal—was because he understood the demands of discipleship. Pharaoh would not get to keep so much as one hoof!

The heart of darkness tries to get God to lower his terms, but those who come into the light offer their hearts to God. They refuse to hold anything back, even without knowing in advance what God will demand from them. They say, "I do not know how much God will require me to give, what sacrifices he will ask me to make. I cannot tell what I will be called to give to the needs of the poor or the work of the church. I don't know how costly it will be to serve God in terms of my time, my talents, and my suffering. What I do know is this: I have surrendered everything to his service, so whatever God wants from me, he will have it. Jesus has given his life for my sins, and it is my joy to give my whole life for his glory."[14]

An example of what it means to follow Christ without compromise comes from Jeanette Howard's book *Out of Egypt*, which was quoted in chapter 21. As Howard describes her ongoing struggle with homosexual sin, she compares it with Israel's temptation to give in to Pharaoh. She writes:

> We are easily caught in a similar type of compromise. "No one is stopping you from going to church on Sunday!" say our gay friends. But disaster comes when we worship God on Sunday and feed our lives with the influences of our past life during the rest of the week. If we are to break free from the bondage of lesbianism, we must follow God with our whole heart, mind and strength. We must be women who are wholly committed to God. . . . [W]omen struggling with lesbianism tend to bargain with God. "OK, I'll give up having sex, but don't ask me to leave my (mutually dependent) friend." We tend to choose which sin we will or will not leave behind. There is no place for compromise. God will not share your heart with the world and your flesh. Only a complete break with your past, leaving Egypt fully behind, will bring healing in your life.[15]

The same principle applies to every aspect of the spiritual life. To come to Christ is to declare that there is no command we will not keep, no sin we will not forsake, no duty we will not perform, no talent we will not employ in our ambition to give all the glory to God.

## Come into the Light

The ninth plague shows the absolute difference between the darkness of sin and the brightness of God's glory. It is a terrible thing to live in darkness, and sadly, Pharaoh never came into the light. Exodus 10 ends with these words: "But the LORD hardened Pharaoh's heart, and he would not let them go. Then Pharaoh said to him, 'Get away from me; take care never to see my face again, for on the day you see my face you shall die.' Moses said, 'As you say! I will not see your face again'" (vv. 27–29).

Here was a complete breakdown of negotiations. Pharaoh was sick of seeing Moses' face. The prophet had brought him nothing but trouble. So in his rage Pharaoh threatened that Moses would die if he ever set foot in the palace again. This was just fine with Moses. He probably preferred never to see Pharaoh again, and he responded by saying, in effect, "I'm outta here!" As it turned out, these words—spoken in the heat of argument—may not have been prophetic because Moses may have seen Pharaoh again (12:31). However, by sending him away on this occasion, Pharaoh was squandering his last chance to leave the heart of darkness. Moses was God's prophet; he had the words of life. In fact, he was the only person who could help Pharaoh escape the darkness, but Pharaoh refused to listen. He sent Moses away.

Many people entertain the foolish notion that they can give their lives to God later. They assume that they will get another chance to get right with God. But people don't always get another chance. Sometimes God sends his message, giving an opportunity to respond, but then the moment passes and never comes again. Every salesman knows the importance of closing the deal. Once people walk out of the showroom without making a purchase, they almost never return. And that is what Pharaoh did. He entered into negotiations with God without ever closing the deal.

In Pharaoh's case, this was God's sovereign purpose. Instead of showing Pharaoh mercy, God hardened his heart. What is God's purpose for you? This is one of the mysteries of his divine will. But understand that darkness is coming again, when God will judge the world for its sin (see 2 Peter 2:17; Jude 13). In Revelation we read: "The fifth angel poured out his bowl on the throne of the beast, and its kingdom was plunged into darkness. People gnawed their tongues in anguish and cursed the God of heaven for their pain and sores. They did not repent of their deeds" (Revelation 16:10, 11). These verses serve as a reminder that the plagues in Exodus were a preview of the judgment to come.

The only way to escape the coming darkness is to trust in Jesus Christ, the Light of the World. When Jesus was born, it was true that "The people dwelling in darkness have seen a great light, and for those dwelling in the region and shadow of death, on them a light has dawned" (Matthew 4:16, quoting Isaiah 9:2). In order to bring us into his light, Jesus had to enter our darkness. The Bible explains that when Jesus was crucified, "there was darkness over the whole land" (Luke 23:44). This darkness was spiritually significant. It showed that Jesus had taken upon himself the guilt of all our sin, and therefore that he was under the dark curse God reserved for his enemies. Then Jesus went into the grave, where he remained in the deepest darkness for three days. But on the third day he was raised again, in a body dazzling with the light of God's glory. Now everyone who comes to Christ comes into the light of his salvation. "For God, who said, 'Let light shine out of darkness,' has shone in our hearts to give the light of the knowledge of the glory of God in the face of Jesus Christ" (2 Corinthians 4:6; cf. 1 John 2:8).

In one of his sermons from the book of Exodus, Charles Spurgeon emphasized the importance of coming into the light while there is still time. Spurgeon described a conversation between a minister and a young woman who, although she had heard the gospel many times, had never committed her life to Christ.

> At last he said to her, "Well, Hannah, do you intend to come to Christ one day?"
>
> "Yes, sir," she replied, "I do intend."
>
> "Well, now," he said, "will you give me a date when you will come to Christ? You are twenty now, will you come to the Lord Jesus Christ when you are thirty? Will you put that down as a definite promise?"
>
> The young lady answered, "Well, sir, I should not like to promise that, because I might be dead before I was thirty. Ten years is a long time. . . . I hope I shall know the Lord before that."
>
> "Well, Hannah," the good man said, "we will say nine years, then; that is to be the time that you fix when you will yield to the mercy of God."
>
> "Well, sir," she said, "I hope it will be before then."
>
> "No," he said, "the bargain is made; you will have to run risks for nine years, you know. You make the bargain that you will come to Christ in nine years' time; let it stand so, and you must run the risk."
>
> "Oh, sir!" she exclaimed, "it would be an awful thing, a dreadful thing, for me to say that I would wait nine years, because I might be lost in that time."
>
> The friend then said, "Well, suppose we say that you will serve the Lord in twelve months' time; will you just take this year, and spend it in the service of Satan, and then, when you have enjoyed yourself that way, give your heart to Christ?"
>
> Somehow, the young woman felt that it was a long . . . and very dangerous time. . . . She could not bear that thought; and as her minister pressed her to set a time, and brought it down by little and little, at last she said, "Oh, sir, it had better be to-night; it had better be to-night! Pray to God that I may now give my heart to the Lord Jesus Christ, for it is such a dreadful thing to be without a Savior. I would have Christ as mine this very night."[16]

Do not delay. God is calling us to leave the heart of darkness and give our hearts to him. Jesus said, "I am the light of the world. Whoever follows me will not walk in darkness, but will have the light of life" (John 8:12).

# 27

# The Deadliest Plague

EXODUS 11:1–10

THE PLAGUE OF DARKNESS proved once and for all that Pharaoh was not the Son of Light. Yet even after the God of Israel proved that he alone ruled both night and day, the King of Egypt continued to have delusions of deity. In his final audience with Moses he made the outrageous claim that he held the power of life and death, saying to God's prophet, "On the day you see my face you shall die" (10:28).

If these words sound familiar, it is because they were later spoken by the one true God. When Moses went up the mountain and asked to see God's glory, he was told, "You cannot see my face, for man shall not see me and live" (33:20). This was a danger the prophet seemed to have sensed instinctively, because back at the burning bush "Moses hid his face, for he was afraid to look at God" (3:6b). God is so awesome in his holiness that to see him is to perish. Thus for Pharaoh to assert the same power for his own countenance was an act of sheer arrogance. He was claiming a prerogative that belongs to God alone.

## Ten Mighty Blows

After all the wonders God had performed, Pharaoh still pretended to rule over life and death. So it was necessary for God to send another plague—the deadliest one of all. Exodus 11 is really a continuation of the conversation begun in chapter 10, Moses' last audience with Pharaoh. Verses 1–3 reiterate things God had already revealed to his prophet (see 3:21, 22; 4:21–23). Then in verses 4–8 Moses takes his parting shot, announcing the tenth and final plague: the death of Egypt's firstborn sons. It is only at the end of verse 8 that the prophet finally makes his dramatic exit: "And he went out from Pharaoh in hot anger." This is followed by a statement summarizing the plagues and their purpose in the plan of salvation (11:9, 10).

Chapter 11 is the place where the Bible finally uses the actual Hebrew word for "plague" (*nega*), meaning "strike" or "blow": "The LORD said to Moses, 'Yet one plague more I will bring upon Pharaoh and upon Egypt'" (11:1a). This statement, which announces that we are nearing the end of the plagues, marks a good place to summarize the main lessons to be learned from these wonders. What do the plagues teach about God's divine attributes?

First, the plagues teach that God is *almighty*, that he holds absolute power over everything he has made. The book of Genesis shows that God is the Creator, the God who made everything out of nothing and brought order out of chaos. The book of Exodus shows that God still rules over his creation. As we have seen, the plagues were creation reversals. God turned order into chaos and then brought it back into order again, miraculously revealing his power over the earth and sky. As Moses explained before the plague of hail, God performed these wonders so the Egyptians would "know that the earth is the LORD's" (9:29b). He is a mighty God.

Second, the plagues teach that God is *jealous*, that he will not share his glory with anyone else. The Egyptians turned away from God to put their confidence in gods of their own invention. They chose to idolize everything from beetles to cattle and to worship everyone from Hapi to Amon-Re. Words from the Apostle Paul describe the situation well: "Although they knew God, they did not honor him as God or give thanks to him, but they became futile in their thinking, and their foolish hearts were darkened. Claiming to be wise, they became fools, and exchanged the glory of the immortal God for images resembling mortal man and birds and animals and creeping things" (Romans 1:21–23). This is an exchange that God will not tolerate; so one by one he defeated Egypt's objects of worship. He is a jealous God.

Third, the plagues teach that God is *just*, that in his righteousness he deals with people according to their sins. Pharaoh was a cruel and wicked despot. In his rebellion against God he deliberately tried to destroy God's people. He stopped at nothing: slavery, servitude, slaughter. And for their part, the Egyptians willingly carried out Pharaoh's orders to oppress the Israelites. Therefore, when God afflicted them with rivers of blood, swarms of bugs, storms of hail, and days of darkness, he was giving them what they deserved. He is a God of justice.

Fourth, the plagues teach that God is *merciful*, that he saves the needy when they cry out for deliverance. The exodus was set in motion by the prayers of God's people: "The people of Israel groaned because of their slavery and cried out for help. Their cry for rescue from slavery came up to God. And God heard their groaning, and God remembered his covenant" (2:23b, 24a). The plagues were an answer to prayer because, by God's mercy, they finally led Israel out of Egypt.

Fifth, the plagues teach that God is *sovereign*, that his mercy and justice are his choice. The plagues discriminated between God's people and Pharaoh's people. The Egyptians suffered, while the Israelites were spared. Therefore the plagues teach the doctrine of election. God chose to place his special favor on the Israelites, even though they did not deserve it. At the same time, he chose to leave Pharaoh in his sins. So when Paul wanted to explain the mystery of God's sovereignty, he pointed back to the exodus and said,

> So then it depends not on human will or exertion, but on God, who has mercy. For the Scripture says to Pharaoh, "For this very purpose I have raised you up, that I might show my power in you, and that my name might be proclaimed in all the earth." So then he has mercy on whomever he wills, and he hardens whomever he wills. (Romans 9:16–18)

God's grace is God's choice because he is a sovereign God.

Each of these lessons has practical implications for daily life. The God who sent the plagues against Egypt still rules over Heaven and earth. Since he is almighty, he has the power to help us in every situation. Since he is jealous, we must not rob him of his glory by serving other gods. Since he is just, we can wait for him to judge his enemies. Since he is merciful, he will save us when we cry for help. Since he is sovereign, he is to be feared and worshiped.

## Lord of Life and Death

Effective education always involves repetition. So like any good teacher, God repeated these lessons in the last of the plagues, which was the climax. The first nine plagues were grouped in sets of three. Each set began with Moses going to Pharaoh and ended with a plague that came unannounced. But the tenth and deadliest plague stands alone.

The death of the firstborn obviously showed God's almighty power. It was another reversal of creation. On the sixth day of the world God breathed life into the man he made in his image, but the tenth plague brought death to the living. This was not simply the result of disease or some other natural occurrence. Rather, it was caused by divine intervention. The Bible is specific about this. God said, "Yet one plague more *I* will bring upon Pharaoh and upon Egypt" (11:1a); "About midnight *I* will go out in the midst of Egypt" (11:4).

God's direct involvement shows that the tenth plague was a real miracle. When some Bible scholars try to explain Exodus, they say the plagues should be viewed "as pure inventions or as natural events which were transformed by imagination into miracles."[1] But what natural event could possibly explain the death of Egypt's firstborn sons? What really happened was that God himself went out in the middle of the night to visit death on the Egyptians. As the psalmist wrote, "He it was who struck down the firstborn of Egypt, both of man and of beast" (Psalm 135:8; cf. 136:10). In the words of Nahum Sarna, "The tenth and final visitation upon the Pharaoh and his people is the one plague for which no rational explanation can be given. It belongs entirely to the category of the supernatural."[2] The deadly blow came from a supernatural source, revealing God's power over his creation. He is a mighty God.

The death of the firstborn also showed God's jealousy, which means his absolute refusal to share his glory with any other god—in this case, the god of death. The Egyptians were obsessed with death and the afterlife. Anyone who has ever studied Egyptian culture knows what elaborate arrangements they made to prepare for the life to come. According to *The Oxford Encyclopedia of Ancient Egypt*, the Egyptians invested a larger portion of their wealth in the afterlife than any other culture in the history of the world.[3] The Great Pyramids and the famous tombs in the Valley of the Kings stand as testimonies to their preoccupation with death and dying. To this day, there are mummies from ancient Egypt in museums all over the world.

The god of the dead was Osiris, whose name meant "the Mighty One; he who has sovereign power." His assistant was Anubis, the god of the underworld. Anubis supervised the embalming process and guided the dead during their passage to the afterlife. He came in canine form, which incidentally may partly explain the reference to dogs in verse 7a: "But not a dog shall growl against any of the people of Israel, either man or beast." The Israelites would remain untouched by death, thus proving that Anubis held no power over them. Meanwhile, the death of Egypt's sons would prove that Israel's God was the Lord of life and death.

The death of one individual was especially significant: "the firstborn of Pharaoh who sits on his throne" (11:5). Pharaoh's son was the prince of Egypt, the next in line to sit on Egypt's throne. More than that, the Egyptians believed that he was a successor to the gods. When his father died, he would become the son of Re and also the son of Osiris. Thus the Egyptians revered the life of the prince. But Moses told Pharaoh that his son would soon die. It would be the death of the next deity, the man who was expected to rule Egypt as god. The God of Israel is a jealous God. The God who says, "My glory I will not give to another" (Isaiah 48:11b) claimed the life of Pharaoh's son to prove that he is the one and only God, who alone deserves worship and praise.

## God of Justice

The one true God is also just, and like the rest of the plagues, the death of the firstborn was an act of divine justice. It is at this point that God is often criticized because some people question whether it was right for God to kill the sons of Egypt.

Certainly the tenth plague was dreadful in its severity. God said to Moses, "Every firstborn in the land of Egypt shall die, from the firstborn of Pharaoh who sits on his throne, even to the firstborn of the slave girl who is behind the handmill, and all the firstborn of the cattle. There shall be a great cry throughout all the land of Egypt, such as there has never been, nor ever will be again" (11:5,

6). No one would be unaffected. The slave grinding grain between two stones was the "the poorest of the poor,"[4] yet even she would suffer loss and grief. All the Egyptians would suffer, from Pharaoh down to the lowliest slave, and everyone else in between. A wail of anguish would go up from every house. The Egyptians had never suffered anything like it ever before, and they would never suffer anything like it again.

With this plague God would punish the Egyptians for their sins, and justly so. The death of the firstborn was an act of justice because Pharaoh had tried to exterminate the Israelites. Exodus began with attempted genocide, and it was only right for God to judge the Egyptians for their murderous intent. The wailing that went up from the Egyptians was fair punishment for the way they had made the Israelites wail for more than four hundred years. In both cases the Bible uses the same word to describe their lament (compare 3:7 and 11:6). According to God's perfect justice, it was Egypt's turn to cry out in distress.

The final plague was also just because the people whom Pharaoh oppressed were the children of God. When God first revealed his plan for plaguing the Egyptians, he told Moses to say to Pharaoh: "Israel is my firstborn son, and I say to you, 'Let my son go that he may serve me.' If you refuse to let him go, behold, I will kill your firstborn son" (4:22, 23). What God did to Pharaoh was a direct response to what Pharaoh had done to him.

But God's justice goes deeper. The Egyptians deserved to die because they were sinners by nature, and death has always been the wages of sin. Every last one of Egypt's sons was born in sin. Like everyone else, the Egyptians sinned in Adam and thus inherited from him a sinful nature. Then they compounded their guilt by committing many sins of their own: worshiping idols, oppressing their slaves, and so forth. God would have been justified in putting them all to death.

The Bible teaches that this is what everyone deserves. We are all sinners, and the proper punishment for sin is death: ". . . Sin came into the world through one man, and death through sin, and so death spread to all men because all sinned" (Romans 5:12). Thus when God chooses to claim a life, as he claimed the firstborn sons of Egypt, he is always justified in doing so. Really, given God's penalty against our sin, the question is not *if* we are going to die but *when*.

Nor can God be faulted for failing to give the Egyptians enough warning. They knew they were about to die. First God sent a series of dreadful plagues—nine of them in all!—to convince them of his divine power. Then finally he announced the deadliest plague of all. In the words of the old spiritual, he said, "Let my people go; If not I'll smite your first-born dead, let my people go." Yet still they refused to repent. Pharaoh knew that his doom was fast approaching, yet he failed to heed God's warning.

The lesson is obvious: When death is on its way—and with death, judgment for sin—it is absolutely necessary to make things right with God. As one anonymous poet wrote,

Before the journey that awaits us all
No man becomes so wise that he has not
Need to think out before his going hence,
What judgment will be given to his soul,
After his death, of evil or of good.

This is a reality that everyone must face because every human being stands under a death sentence inherited from Adam's sin. The Bible states that "it is appointed for man to die once, and after that comes judgment" (Hebrews 9:27).

Human beings have several basic ways of coping with death and its inevitability. The nihilist gives up entirely. He says, "I don't have anything to live for anyway, so I might as well destroy myself." The hedonist tries to distract himself so he doesn't have to think about death and eternity. "Eat, drink, and be merry," he says, "for tomorrow we die." The moralist tries to live the best life he can, hoping that perhaps God will accept him in the end. He says, "I've tried to be a good person. What more can God ask?"

What most people refuse to do is the one thing that God requires, and that is to be sorry for sin. This is a deadly mistake. Sin keeps us from God, and ultimately it will condemn us to Hell, unless we repent. There is a frightening prophecy about this in the book of Revelation, which contains many echoes from Exodus. The plagues are coming again: sores, blood, darkness, frogs, hail, and death (Revelation 16:1–21). What people ought to do when they are facing divine judgment is to repent of their sins and find safety in the mercy of God. Instead the Bible sadly tells how people "cursed the name of God who had power over these plagues. They did not repent and give him glory" (Revelation 16:9).

As an example, consider the fate of Timothy McVeigh, the terrorist who was sentenced to die for his 1995 bombing of the Alfred P. Murrah Building, a federal facility, in Oklahoma City. McVeigh was defiant to the end. Shortly before his execution on June 11, 2001, he said, "If I go to hell, I'm gonna have a lot of company." His last statement came from William Ernest Henley's (1849–1903) poem "Invictus," which reads in part:

It matters not how strait the gate,
How charged with punishments the scroll,
I am the master of my fate:
I am the captain of my soul.

McVeigh was as foolish as Pharaoh. Both men were warned of their deadly fate, yet refused to bow to God's authority, and thus they were struck down by God's justice.

## Plundering the Egyptians

There is a better way to face death, and that is to cry out to God, who gives mercy to sinners who repent. This is another perfection displayed in the last of the plagues: the mercy of God.

The death of the firstborn had the merciful purpose of delivering Israel from Egypt: "The LORD said to Moses, 'Yet one plague more I will bring upon Pharaoh and upon Egypt. Afterward he will let you go from here. When he lets you go, he will drive you away completely'" (11:1). Thus it was the deadliest plague that enabled the Israelites finally to escape, with all their belongings. God's act of justice against Pharaoh at the same time showed mercy to his people Israel. The psalmist made this connection when he wrote, "Give thanks to the LORD, for he is good, for *his steadfast love endures forever* . . . to him who struck down the firstborn of Egypt, for *his steadfast love endures forever*" (Psalm 136:1, 10).

As a further display of his mercy, God allowed the Israelites to plunder the Egyptians. He said to Moses, "Speak now in the hearing of the people, that they ask, every man of his neighbor and every woman of her neighbor, for silver and gold jewelry" (11:2; cf. 3:21, 22). Then the Bible adds this comment, by way of explanation: "And the LORD gave the people favor in the sight of the Egyptians. Moreover, the man Moses was very great in the land of Egypt, in the sight of Pharaoh's servants and in the sight of the people" (11:3).

Apparently some of the Egyptians had begun to fear God. They had a growing respect for his prophet Moses, whom they held in high esteem. They were coming to hold a favorable view of God's chosen people. To translate literally, God gave the Israelites *grace* in the eyes of the Egyptians. Soon they would even support the exodus. Moses told Pharaoh, "And all these your servants shall come down to me and bow down to me, saying, 'Get out, you and all the people who follow you.' And after that I will go out" (11:8). In the end the Egyptians would practically beg the Israelites to go. This was mainly because they wanted to escape God's judgment. The sooner the Israelites left, the better. The Egyptians would even make sure that they did not leave empty-handed. They would part with their jewelry and other valuables—anything to get rid of those plagues!

Commentators have wondered whether it was morally appropriate for the Israelites to plunder the Egyptians. Some have accused them of theft, of borrowing without ever returning. However, the Bible says nothing about borrowing, and no promise is ever made of return. This was a freewill offering! The Israelites simply asked for silver and gold, and the Egyptians handed it over because by this point they were glad to see God's people go, no matter what the cost.

Scholars have also tried to explain what the silver and gold represent. Some say they were Israel's wages. God wanted to make sure that his people got paid for all the work they did in Egypt. Others say it was the price of redemption, which was always required for release from slavery. Still others consider it a form of military tribute, which God made the Egyptians pay their conquerors. In any case, the silver and gold were a sign of divine favor. It would have been enough to escape from Egypt in one piece, but in his mercy God arranged to provide his people with what they needed for their journey (although, as we shall see, the plunder turned out to be a mixed blessing!). God often does this. In addition to spiritual salvation, he gives his people material blessings that go far beyond what they need or even ask.

When it comes to Israel's plunder, what is usually overlooked is what these gifts reveal about Egypt's spiritual condition. By his mercy God was turning some of his enemies into friends. Many of the Egyptians had begun to believe in the existence of the one true God. They acknowledged his power and honored his prophet. They recognized the importance of treating God's people with respect and generosity. They were making spiritual progress—so much progress, in fact, that when the Israelites finally left, some of the Egyptians actually went with them (12:38).

Sadly, however, most of the Egyptians stayed in Egypt. This too was part of God's sovereign plan. As he had done in the earlier plagues, he discriminated between his people and Pharaoh's people. While the Egyptians mourned their loss, not a son would be lost in Israel. God would do this so the Egyptians would "know that the Lord makes a distinction between Egypt and Israel" (11:7). By preserving his people from harm, God was teaching the Egyptians the doctrine of election. There is an absolute difference between those who are inside and those who are outside the family of God.

This distinction is drawn by the sovereign will of almighty God. Nevertheless—and this is one of theology's great mysteries—the Egyptians were responsible for their own choice to stay with their gods in Egypt. Tragically they became familiar with the God of Israel without ever giving their lives to his service. The same is true of many people who are interested in Christianity. They spend time at church and sometimes enjoy reading the Bible. They respect the minister and support Christian work. Yet they never give their lives to Jesus. While it is good to get acquainted with Christianity, that is never enough to get anyone into Heaven. What God requires is faith in Jesus Christ. Salvation comes by trusting in his death on the cross and his resurrection from the dead. In the same way that the Egyptians needed to get out of Egypt, sinners need to leave their bondage to sin and come to Jesus.

## Miracle Times Ten

There are many things to learn about God from his miracles in Egypt. He sent the plagues in order to demonstrate his power, jealousy, justice, mercy, and sovereignty. In a word, God did it to show his glory, which is the sum total of all his perfections. The history of the plagues thus ends with this summary: "Then the Lord said to Moses, 'Pharaoh will not listen to you, that my wonders may be multiplied in the land of Egypt.' Moses and Aaron did all these wonders before Pharaoh, and the LORD hardened Pharaoh's heart, and he did not let the people of Israel go out of his land" (11:9, 10).

The plagues were all part of God's plan to reveal his glory in the salvation of his people. Even Pharaoh's opposition was part of the plan. Each time he hardened his heart, God performed another miracle, so as to multiply his wonders. God did it all for his glory.

The same is true of everything that God has ever done—it is all for his glory. Why did God make the world? It was for his own glory: "The heavens declare the glory of God" (Psalm 19:1a). He made human beings for the same reason. God said, "Bring my sons from afar and my daughters from the end of the earth, everyone who is called by my name, whom I created for my glory" (Isaiah 43:6b, 7).

Knowing that we would fall into sin, God made a plan for our salvation, and this too was for his glory: "We have obtained an inheritance, having been predestined according to the purpose of him who works all things according to the counsel of his will, so that we . . . might be to the praise of his glory" (Ephesians 1:11, 12). To accomplish this saving plan, God sent his Son into the world. God the Son came to glorify God the Father in the salvation of sinners. When his work was almost finished, he said, "I glorified you on earth, having accomplished the work that you gave me to do" (John 17:4).

Now the message of salvation in Christ is spreading all over the world. It will not stop until God has declared "his glory among the nations, his marvelous works among all the peoples" (Psalm 96:3). Then all nations will give him the glory, saying:

> Blessed be the LORD, the God of Israel,
> who alone does wondrous things.
> Blessed be his glorious name forever;
> may the whole earth be filled with his glory! (Psalm 72:18, 19)

Jonathan Edwards identified the glory of God as "the ultimate end of God's works," "the last end for which he created the world."[5] If that is true—indeed, if it is true that everything God has ever done is for the praise of his glory—then we too were made to glorify God. In the face of death, and in view of God's mercy, the only satisfying way to live is for the glory of God.

# 28

# The First Passover

## EXODUS 12:1–13

IT IS NOT HARD to understand why God plagued the Egyptians. Their king was a cruel tyrant who tried to destroy the people of God. Pharaoh would not let them go, choosing instead to keep them enslaved in Egypt. And by refusing to let them depart, he was preventing them from giving glory to God the way that God intended. So God was justified in punishing the Egyptians with insects and amphibians, with disease and darkness.

By sending plague after plague—nine in all—God was showing his power over creation. What the Egyptians should have done in response was repent of their sins and join Moses in giving praise to the one true God. Yet the more Pharaoh suffered, the harder his heart became. This was because his heart was committed to serving other gods. So one by one God defeated the gods and goddesses of Egypt. The plague of blood defeated the river gods of the Nile, the locusts defeated the field gods of the harvest, the darkness defeated the gods of the sun and sky, and so forth.

Still Pharaoh refused to let God's people go. Finally God sent the tenth and deadliest plague of all: the death of the firstborn. This was a battle of the gods, a contest between the deities, and God was determined to win. He told Moses, "I will pass through the land of Egypt that night, and I will strike all the firstborn in the land of Egypt, both man and beast; and on all the gods of Egypt I will execute judgments: I am the LORD" (12:12; cf. Numbers 33:4). With this final plague God accomplished his objective—namely, to demonstrate his lordship over the Egyptians by defeating *all* their gods, together with the demonic powers they represented. With one deadly blow God achieved his conquest over Egypt's gods, and in doing so, he gave the Egyptians what they deserved. The last plague was a glorious act of his sovereign justice.

One Egyptian philosopher wrote, "There will come a time when it will be seen that in vain have the Egyptians honored the deity with heartfelt piety and assiduous service, and all our holy worship will be found bootless and ineffectual. . . . Oh Egypt, Egypt, of thy religion nothing will remain but an empty tale, which thine own children in time to come will not believe; nothing will be left but graven words, and only the stones will tell of thy piety."[1] Although these words were written after the time of Christ, they also serve as an apt commentary on the exodus, when God judged the Egyptians and their gods.

## The Wages of Sin

What God did to the Egyptians was no surprise, but what may seem surprising is the way he treated his people Israel. Like the Egyptians, the Israelites were under a sentence of death. The same night that God brought death to every house in Egypt, he also visited the home of every Israelite (12:13, 23), with the purpose of killing their firstborn sons. In his mercy, of course, God provided his people with a way to escape his wrath. But first we must reckon with the fact that "the destroyer," as God calls him (12:23), claimed the right to slay the children of Israel.

The Israelites must have been shocked to discover that their lives were in danger. All the previous plagues had left them unscathed because God had made a distinction between his people and Pharaoh's people. While chaos engulfed their oppressors, the Israelites had watched from the safety of Goshen. From this they learned that they were God's special people. This may have tempted them to believe that they were more righteous than the Egyptians, indeed, that they could do no wrong. But the truth was that they deserved to die every bit as much as their enemies. Indeed, if God had not provided a means for their salvation, they would have suffered the loss of every last one of their firstborn sons. The Israelites were as guilty as the Egyptians, and in the final plague God taught them about their sin and his salvation.

God's people had sinned in several ways. One was to reject the word of God's prophet. When Moses returned from his first audience with Pharaoh, the Israelites greeted him by saying, "The Lord look on you and judge, because you have made us stink in the sight of Pharaoh and his servants, and have put a sword in their hand to kill us" (5:21). Neither the Egyptians nor the Israelites would listen to God's word. Thus Alec Motyer writes that "when the wrath of God is applied in its essential reality, no one is safe. There were two nations in the land of Egypt, but they were both resistant to the word of God; and if God comes in judgment none will escape."[2]

The Israelites were also guilty of idolatry. That sin is not specifically mentioned here in Exodus, but it was remembered for years to come. When the Israelites renewed the covenant at Shechem, Joshua said, "Put away the gods that your fathers served beyond the River and in Egypt, and serve the Lord" (Joshua 24:14). Not surprisingly, during their long centuries of captivity, the Israelites grew to love the gods of Egypt. And for this sin God would have been justified in plaguing them, even to the death of their firstborn sons.

However, apart from any particular sin they may have committed, God's people were sinners by nature. The mere fact of their humanity meant that they participated in the guilt of Adam's race. The Bible teaches that "all have sinned and fall short of the glory of God" (Romans 3:23). The first Passover proved that fact by implicating Israel in Egypt's sin, thereby showing that "Jews and Gentiles alike are all under the power of sin" (Romans 3:9 NIV).

The reason the avenging angel visited the Israelites was because, like the Egyptians, they were sinners, and sin is a capital offense. The proper penalty for it is death, which has always been "the wages of sin" (Romans 6:23). When God planted Adam in the garden of Eden, he said, "Of the tree of the knowledge of good and evil you shall not eat, for in the day that you eat of it you shall surely die" (Genesis 2:17). Sadly, this is exactly what happened. As soon as our first parents ate the forbidden fruit, they became mortal, and so did all their children, down to the present generation. This fact would seem to demand some sort of explanation. In the entire history of our race, no generation has ever avoided going down to the grave. Why not? The Bible explains it like this: "Death spread to all men because all sinned" (Romans 5:12). The tenth plague was a sign of God's judgment against all humanity.

This is a reality that every individual must face. If all have sinned, that obviously includes us. And if death has come to all people, then we too can expect to die. It is as simple as that. We will never see our need of salvation until we accept that we are as guilty as everyone else, and that therefore our lives are forfeit to God.

One person who came to understand this was Major League baseball player Damion Easley. Easley was riding on an airplane when he overheard some teammates on the Angels talking about God. They were sitting several rows behind him, and he heard one of them ask, "If this plane were to crash right now, would you go to Heaven?" This made Easley uncomfortable because he wasn't sure. So he walked back and sat right behind his teammates, hoping to get some answers. He couldn't understand what they were talking about, however, so he started asking more questions: "What's the deal about God? What's this all about?" By the time the flight was over, Easley had given his life to Jesus Christ.[3] It all started with the recognition that, like Israel in Egypt, he was under the sentence of death for his sins.

## The Lamb of God

In his great mercy, God provided his people with a way to be safe. The reason he visited their homes was not to destroy them but to teach them about salvation. Like the Egyptians, the Israelites deserved divine judgment; but unlike the Egyptians, they would be saved by grace through faith.

What God's people needed was atonement, which God provided in the form of a lamb—a lamb offered as a sacrifice for sin. First he gave them careful instructions about how to choose, care for, and finally kill the lamb:

> The LORD said to Moses and Aaron in the land of Egypt, "This month shall be for you the beginning of months. It shall be the first month of the year for you. Tell all the congregation of Israel that on the tenth day of this month every man shall take a lamb according to their fathers' houses, a lamb for a household. And if the household is too small for a lamb, then he and his nearest neighbor shall take according to the number of persons; according to what each can eat you shall make your count for the lamb. Your lamb shall be without blemish, a male a year old. You may take it from the sheep or from the goats, and you shall keep it until the fourteenth day of this month, when the whole assembly of the congregation of Israel shall kill their lambs at twilight." (12:1–6)

Each household was to choose its own lamb, specifically a yearling. It had to be perfect. The lamb was destined to serve as a sacrifice for sin, and the only sacrifice acceptable to God is a perfect sacrifice; so the lamb had to be pure and spotless, whole and sound. As Moses later warned the Israelites, "You shall not offer anything that has a blemish, for it will not be acceptable for you. And when anyone offers a sacrifice . . . from the herd or from the flock, to be accepted it must be perfect; there shall be no blemish in it. Animals blind or disabled or mutilated or having a discharge or an itch or scabs you shall not offer to the LORD" (Leviticus 22:20–22a). Because God is holy, the only sacrifice that pleases him is the very best we have to offer.

God then proceeded to explain what to do with the lamb once it was slain:

> Then they shall take some of the blood and put it on the two doorposts and the lintel of the houses in which they eat it. They shall eat the flesh that night, roasted on the fire; with unleavened bread and bitter herbs they shall eat it. Do not eat any of it raw or boiled in water, but roasted, its head with its legs and its inner parts. And you shall let none of it remain until the morning; anything that remains until the morning you shall burn. In this manner you shall eat it: with your belt fastened, your sandals on your feet, and your staff in your hand. And you shall eat it in haste. It is the LORD's Passover. (12:7–11)

This meal was intended to serve as an annual reminder of what the Israelites suffered in Egypt. The bitter herbs would remind them how the Egyptians "made their lives bitter with hard service, in mortar and brick, and in all kinds of work in the field" (1:14). The unleavened bread would remind them how they had to flee in haste. They ate the first Passover standing up, ready to leave Egypt at a moment's notice. And there were no leftovers. Once it was roasted, the entire lamb had to be consumed. The Bible does not explain why, but presumably it was too sacred to be used for any other purpose. Perhaps eating the lamb also pointed forward to the coming of Christ, for as Jesus said, "Unless you eat the flesh of the Son of Man and drink his blood, you have no life in you" (John 6:53).

All these details are important, but the most important thing was killing the lamb. When God saw its blood on the doorpost, death would pass over, and the firstborn would be saved. What God required for salvation was the offering of a lamb. This is what he has always required. God required a lamb in the days of Adam and Eve. The Scripture says, "In the course of time Cain brought to the LORD an offering of the fruit of the ground, and Abel also brought of the firstborn of his flock and of their fat portions. And the LORD had regard for Abel and his offering, but for Cain and his offering he had no regard" (Genesis 4:3–5). Abel was the one who brought the lamb, and only his offering was accepted: God required a lamb.

In salvation God gives what God demands. So again and again through the history of redemption, God has always provided a lamb or other sacrificial animal to save his people. He provided a lamb in the days of Abraham. God told Abraham to go up and sacrifice his only son Isaac as a burnt offering. As the two of them went up the mountain, Isaac—who obviously was no dummy—realized that something was missing. "My father," he said, "Behold, the fire and the wood, but where is the lamb for a burnt offering?" (Genesis 22:7). Isaac knew what God required. Abraham knew it too, and his faithful answer explained the plan of salvation. Abraham said, "God will provide for himself the lamb for a burnt offering" (Genesis 22:8). That is precisely what happened. As Abraham took the knife to slay his son, he was interrupted by an angel, who said, "Do not lay your hand on the boy or do anything to him, for now I know that you fear God, seeing you have not withheld your son, your only son, from me" (Genesis 22:12). Then God provided a lamb for him to sacrifice instead: "Abraham lifted up his eyes and looked, and behold, behind him was a ram, caught in a thicket by his horns. And Abraham went and took the ram and offered it up as a burnt offering instead of his son" (Genesis 22:13). God provided what God required: a lamb to die in the place of Abraham's firstborn son.

Every year God provided a lamb or similar sacrifice for Israel. On the Day of Atonement, the high priest would bring an animal into God's presence and sacrifice it as a sin offering. These were his instructions: "Then he shall kill the goat of the sin offering that is for the people and bring its blood inside the veil . . . sprinkling it over the mercy seat and in front of the mercy seat. Thus he shall make atonement . . . because of the uncleannesses of the people of Israel and because of their transgressions, all their sins" (Leviticus 16:15, 16a). God provided what God required: a substitute sacrifice to die for his people.

There is an obvious progression here, with the lamb serving as a representative for larger and larger groups of people. At first God provided one lamb for one person. Thus Abraham offered a ram in place of his son Isaac. Next God provided one lamb for one household. This happened at the first Passover, when every family in the covenant community offered its own lamb to God. Then God provided one sacrifice for the whole nation. On the Day of Atonement, a single animal atoned for the sins of all Israel. Finally the day came when John the Baptist "saw Jesus coming toward him, and said, 'Behold, the Lamb of God, who takes away the sin of the world!'" (John 1:29; cf. John 11:50–52). God was planning this all along: one Lamb to die for one world. By his grace he has provided a lamb—the Lamb that was slain from the creation of the world (Revelation 13:8 NIV).

The consistent message of the Bible is that anyone who wants to meet God must come on the basis of the lamb that he has provided. All the other lambs prepared for the coming of Christ. A theologian would call them *types*. In other words, the lambs were signs pointing to salvation in Christ. As the famous Jonathan Edwards wrote in his *A History of the Work of Redemption*, "Christ and his redemption are the subject of the whole Word of God."[4] Clearly this was true of the first Passover, which, like everything else in Exodus, was about Christ and his redemption. To be sure we don't miss the connection, the New Testament says that "Christ, our Passover lamb, has been sacrificed" (1 Corinthians 5:7b).

For Jesus to be our Passover Lamb, he had to meet God's standard of perfection. Back during the exodus, the Passover Lamb had to be physically flawless. In the case of Jesus, the perfection God required was moral: Jesus had to be utterly sinless. The Bible is careful to show that this was indeed the case. By virtue of his virgin birth, his nature was free from the corruption of original sin. Nor did Jesus commit any actual transgressions. Peter said, "He committed no sin, neither was deceit found in his mouth" (1 Peter 2:22). The book of Hebrews says that he was "in every respect . . . tempted as we are, yet without sin" (Hebrews 4:15). Even Pontius Pilate said, "I find no guilt in him" (John 19:6b). Jesus was morally perfect. Therefore, when it came time for him to die, it was as an innocent victim—he "offered himself without blemish to God" (Hebrews 9:14). Hebrews uses the words "without blemish" because the writer was thinking of the kind of sacrifice that God required in the Old Testament: a perfect lamb, without spot or blemish.

It is theologically significant that Jesus was crucified right at the time of the Passover feast (see John 13:1; 18:28). This helps us see the connection between the first Passover and the final Passover—the Passion of Christ. The day that Jesus made his triumphal entry into Jerusalem was the very day that the Passover lambs were driven into the city, and when Jesus celebrated the Last Supper with his disciples, he was celebrating the Passover (Matthew 26:17). He said, "This is my body . . . this is my blood" (Matthew 26:26–28). His disciples didn't understand it at the time, but Jesus was really saying, "The Passover is all about me. I am the sacrificial lamb."

Then Christ was crucified. It was late in the afternoon on the eve of Passover. At twilight, lambs would be sacrificed by every household, according to the Law of Moses. All over the city fathers were getting ready to make the offering, gathering their families together and saying, "God has provided a lamb for us." Over at the temple the high priest was also preparing a lamb to present as an atonement for Israel's sin. Then there was Jesus, hanging on the cross, with the sacrificial blood flowing from his hands and side. He was the Lamb of God taking away the sins of the world.

## Nothing but the Blood

It is necessary to mention the blood of Jesus because the Passover regulations explicitly required a blood sacrifice. This is something that Steven Spielberg learned when he produced *The Prince of Egypt*, a film based on the life of Moses. The original script had God saying, "When I see the mark upon the doorframe." However, the religious leaders hired to consult with the film studio objected that this was not specific enough. They insisted that the mark had to be made of blood. So the line was changed to "When I see the blood."

There is blood spilling all over Exodus 12. The Israelites were commanded to slaughter their lambs (12:6), and of course there was no way to do this without shedding blood. Once the lamb was sacrificed, they were to take its blood and paint it on their doorframes. This too was absolutely essential, because God said, "The blood shall be a sign for you, on the houses where you are. And when I see the blood, I will pass over you" (12:13).

What was so important about the blood? It represented the taking of a life. Notice that this was a sign both to the Israelites and to their God. God said, "The blood shall be a sign for *you*. . . . And when *I* see the blood" (12:13). What the blood signified to the Israelites was that they had a substitute, that a lamb had died in their place. Their sin was a capital offense. God was coming in judgment, armed with a deadly plague. But when they looked up and saw the blood on the door, they knew they were covered. To use the technical term for it, the blood of the lamb was the *expiation* for their sins. While the book of Exodus does not draw an explicit connection between the blood of the lamb and the sin of God's people, this connection is plainly implied. In the words of the brilliant Dutch theologian Geerhardus Vos, "Wherever there is slaying and manipulation of blood there is expiation, and both these were present in the Passover."[5]

The importance of the lamb as a substitute would not have been lost on the firstborn son. Once the lamb was chosen, it was kept in the house for four days, during which time the family fed it, cared for it, and played with it. In that short time they would have identified with the lamb, so that it almost became part of the family. "This is our Passover lamb," they would say. Then it was slaughtered, which was a messy, bloody business. The head of the household took the lamb in his arms, pulled back its head, and slit its throat. Red blood spurted all over the lamb's pure white wool. "Why, Daddy?" the children would say. Their father would explain that the lamb was a substitute. The firstborn did not have to die because the lamb had died in his place.

On the first Passover the Israelites huddled in their homes, waiting for God to come in judgment. That night he would claim a life from every household in Egypt. All over the land they could hear the wailing of their enemies, who were mourning the death of their firstborn sons. But the children of God were saved by the blood of the lamb. Death passed over them. The reason death passed over them was because they were under the blood. When God came to the home of an Israelite, he could see the blood on the door. When he looked at it he said in effect, "Someone has died in this house. The penalty has been executed." To use the technical term for it, the blood was a *propitiation*—it turned away the wrath of God. The doorpost put blood between God and the sinner. When the people looked up, they saw that they had an expiation—a covering for their sin. When God looked down, he saw that they had made propitiation, and thus his wrath was turned aside.

Over the centuries this sacrifice was repeated millions of times. To give just one example, when King Josiah celebrated the Passover, he slaughtered more than thirty-seven thousand sheep (2 Chronicles 35). Imagine all those sheep and all that blood! According to Josephus, the ancient historian, several hundred thousand lambs were herded through the streets of Jerusalem every Passover.[6] Yet not even the blood of all those animals could atone for sin. In Hebrews we read that "it is impossible for the blood of bulls and goats to take away sins" (Hebrews 10:4). What was needed was a more efficacious sacrifice, the offering of a more precious blood.

What was needed was the blood of Jesus, our Passover Lamb. This is where some people start to get squeamish, including many contemporary theologians. They like to talk about Jesus as a Savior and Teacher, but they would rather not talk about his blood. Charles Spurgeon was responding to this attitude when he wrote:

> We do not subscribe to the lax theology which teaches that the Lord Jesus did something or other which, in some way or other, is in some degree or other, connected with the salvation of men. . . . We firmly believe . . . the doctrine of the atoning death of our great Substitute. . . . We stand to the literal substitution of Jesus Christ in the place of his people, and his real endurance of suffering and death in their stead, and from this distinct and definite ground we will not move an inch. Even the term "the blood," from which some shrink with the affectation of great delicacy, we shall not cease to use, whoever may take offense at it, for it brings out that fundamental truth which is the power of God unto salvation. We dwell beneath the blood mark, and rejoice that Jesus for us poured out his soul unto death.[7]

We believe in the doctrine of the substitutionary atonement: Jesus shed his own blood for our sins. The New Testament is very specific about this. When it explains the meaning of the crucifixion, it constantly draws attention to the blood of Jesus: "We have now been justified by his blood" (Romans 5:9). "In him we have redemption through his blood, the forgiveness of our trespasses" (Ephesians 1:7). "Jesus also suffered . . . to sanctify the people through his own blood" (Hebrews 13:12). "You were ransomed . . . with the precious blood of Christ, like that of a lamb without blemish or spot" (1 Peter 1:18, 19). "The blood of Jesus . . . cleanses us from all sin" (1 John 1:7).

The reason for all this talk about blood is very simple: "Without the shedding of blood there is no forgiveness of sins" (Hebrews 9:22; cf. Leviticus 17:11). Therefore, in order to be saved from death, we need the blood of a perfect substitute to interpose between our sin and God's holiness. The sign that we have a substitute is the blood of Christ. When we look up to the cross, we see that payment has been made for our sin. And what does God see when he looks down at the cross? He sees that it is stained with the blood of his very own firstborn Son. God does not have a substitute to offer in place of his Son; his Son *is* the Substitute! And when God sees the blood of his Son, he says, "It is enough. My justice has been satisfied. The price for sin is fully paid. Death will pass over you, and you will be safe forever."

The blood on the cross has the power to save because it is the blood of Jesus, who is the very Son of God. There is no more precious blood than this in all the universe. Unlike the blood of even the most perfect Passover lamb, it has infinite value. So the Bible says that Jesus "entered . . . not by means of the blood of goats and calves but by means of his own blood, thus securing an eternal redemption . . . how much more will the blood of Christ, who through the eternal Spirit offered himself without blemish to God, purify our conscience from dead works to serve the living God" (Hebrews 9:12, 14).

The only way to be saved from sin and delivered from death is by Jesus Christ, the Lamb of God. God calls everyone to trust in his blood. This is what the Israelites did at the first Passover: They trusted in the blood. Putting blood on the doorpost was an act of faith. In order to be delivered from death, they had to believe God's word, and that meant doing what Moses said. It was by faith that each family chose a perfect lamb, by faith that they took its life and roasted it with bitter herbs, and by faith that they spread its blood on the door. The blood was a public confession of their faith, a sign that they trusted in the atoning efficacy of the sacrificial lamb. Thus they were saved by grace through faith. God provided the lamb—that's grace—but the Israelites had to trust in the lamb, which is where faith comes in. "By faith," the Scripture says, "he [Moses] kept the Passover and sprinkled the blood, so that the Destroyer of the firstborn might not touch them" (Hebrews 11:28).

If you had been there for the first Passover, would you have sacrificed a lamb? Of course you would have! So, will you trust in the blood that Jesus shed on the cross? The Bible says that "God put forward [Jesus] as a propitiation by his blood, to be received by faith" (Romans 3:25a). God has provided the Lamb who takes away the sins of the world, and everyone who trusts in his blood will be saved.

# 29

# A Feast to Remember

## EXODUS 12:14–28

CHURCH HISTORIAN CLAIR DAVIS describes the Christian life as "a combination of amnesia and déjà vu." He says, "I know I've forgotten this before."[1] In other words, as we follow Christ we keep needing to learn the same lessons over and over because we keep forgetting them. And each time it happens, we suddenly remember that we have had to relearn these very same lessons before.

For example, we first come to God confessing that we cannot save ourselves—only Jesus can save us, and only by his cross. However, as we follow God we sometimes try to serve him in our own strength. We suffer from a kind of spiritual amnesia, forgetting that it is only by God's grace that we can do anything good. And when we forget, we fail. But then in his mercy God reminds us that we can do all things by the strength of his grace. All of a sudden we remember that this has happened to us before. We say, "Oh yes, I remember now! I can't make it on my own. Only Jesus can save me." So sometimes the Christian life is like a combination of amnesia and déjà vu, in which we keep learning what we keep forgetting.

It is because we are so forgetful that God so often commands us to remember: "Remember the Lord, who is great and awesome" (Nehemiah 4:14). "Remember also your Creator in the days of your youth" (Ecclesiastes 12:1). "Remember . . . I am God, and there is no other" (Isaiah 46:9). "Remember Jesus Christ, risen from the dead" (2 Timothy 2:8).

Of all the things that God wanted Israel to remember, the most important was their exodus from Egypt. The Lord God sent plague after plague against the Egyptians, culminating with the death of the firstborn, until finally Pharaoh agreed to let God's people go. It was a rescue to remember. So Moses said, "You shall remember that you were a slave in the land of Egypt, and the Lord your God brought you out from there with a mighty hand and an outstretched arm" (Deuteronomy 5:15). Later entire psalms would be written for the simple purpose of reminding the Israelites how God had delivered them from bondage (see Psalms 78, 106). The psalmist wrote, "Remember the wondrous works that he [God] has done, his miracles, and the judgments he uttered" (Psalm 105:5; 1 Chronicles 16:12).

## A Lasting Ordinance

To make sure that his people would never forget their salvation, God gave them a special memory aid: Passover, or the Feast of Unleavened Bread. This feast was meant to be an annual celebration. Three times God told Moses that he wanted Passover to become a permanent addition to Israel's calendar: "This day shall be for you a memorial day, and you shall keep it as a feast to the Lord; throughout your generations, as a statute forever" (12:14); "Therefore you shall observe this day, throughout your generations, as a statute forever" (12:17b); "You shall observe this rite as a statute for you and for your sons forever" (12:24).

The Israelites celebrated their first Passover in Egypt. They continued to celebrate it during the forty years they spent wandering in the wilderness (Numbers 9:1–5). Once they entered the Promised Land, they still kept the feast, for God said, "And when you come to the land that the Lord will give you, as he has promised, you shall keep this service" (12:25). No sooner had Joshua led the Israelites across the Jordan than they celebrated Passover in their new homeland (Joshua 5:10, 11).

Passover was a feast to remember. It was an annual reminder of God's saving grace, in which Israel's deliverance from Egypt was commemorated and celebrated. The exodus was not repeated, of course, but it was symbolically reenacted with blood and with bread. The feast God's people shared was something they could see, taste, touch, and smell. By reliving their escape from Egypt, they preserved the message of salvation in their collective memory. Passover was given so that future generations would know the salvation of their God.

In Exodus 12 the instructions for Passover are given twice, separated by instructions for the Feast of Unleavened Bread. Verses 1–13 concern the selection and slaughter of a perfect lamb. Once the lamb was slain, its blood was spread on the doorpost. The blood was a sign that a sacrifice had been made for sin, and thus it protected Israel's firstborn sons from the angel of death. Finally, the lamb was roasted and eaten, together with bitter herbs and bread without yeast. In verses 21–23 these instructions are repeated in a slightly different form:

> Then Moses called all the elders of Israel and said to them, "Go and select lambs for yourselves according to your clans, and kill the Passover lamb. Take a bunch of hyssop and dip it in the blood that is in the basin, and touch the lintel and the two doorposts with the blood that is in the basin. None of

> you shall go out of the door of his house until the morning. For the LORD will pass through to strike the Egyptians, and when he sees the blood on the lintel and on the two doorposts, the LORD will pass over the door and will not allow the destroyer to enter your houses to strike you."

What comes in between is a set of regulations for the Feast of Unleavened Bread (12:14–20), which was celebrated during the week that followed Passover. The way the chapter is organized has led some scholars to conclude that Passover and the Feast of Unleavened Bread were two separate celebrations. Some go so far as to argue that originally neither festival had any connection with the exodus at all. Sacrificing an animal, they say, was an ancient bedouin ritual, so Passover was a holdover from the days of Israel's wandering. And since the Feast of Unleavened Bread was associated with grain agriculture, it must have come later, when the Israelites settled in the Promised Land. One commentator writes, "Just as Passover has connections with a flock-animal sacrifice predating it, so also the ritual eating of unleavened bread cakes was first practiced in a setting having nothing to do with the exodus."[2]

The point of mentioning this scholarly argument is to defend the historicity of the exodus, and therefore the truthfulness of the Bible. There is no evidence that the Israelites borrowed Passover or the Feast of Unleavened Bread from anyone else. Of course, many ancient cultures sacrificed animals, and they all ate bread, but none of them celebrated these specific rituals. Nor is there any reason to doubt that the Feast of Unleavened Bread goes all the way back to Egypt. The Bible explains why the Israelites used bread without yeast. It was symbolic of their flight from Egypt: they left so quickly that they didn't even have time to let the dough rise. This is hinted at in verse 11, where God tells the Israelites to "eat . . . in haste," and it is made explicit in verse 39: "And they baked unleavened cakes of the dough that they had brought out of Egypt, for it was not leavened, because they were thrust out of Egypt and could not wait, nor had they prepared any provisions for themselves." No further explanation is needed. Eating unleavened bread was a historical happening that became a permanent part of Israel's annual religious ritual.

The truth is that God gave his people this feast when he brought them out of Egypt. As the Scripture says, "It is the LORD's Passover" (12:11). Furthermore, Passover and the Feast of Unleavened Bread go together. They are not two separate holidays but one week-long celebration. In the rest of the Old Testament this festival is sometimes called Passover and sometimes the Feast of Unleavened Bread, but either term can be used to refer to the whole celebration.

## Saved from Sin

There is another important reason for discussing how Exodus 12 is organized. Some scholars seem to think that the chapter doesn't quite fit together. They view it as a sort of hodgepodge, and they can't understand how the Feast of Unleavened Bread fits in. However, God's Spirit has given us the Bible exactly the way he intended. Therefore, rather than speculating about how these verses got here, we should receive them as Holy Scripture and study them to see what they teach.

When we consider how the Feast of Unleavened Bread is connected to Passover, we discover a very important truth about salvation—namely, that we are saved in order to be sanctified. Passover is about getting saved. It reminds us that we have been delivered from death by a perfect substitute whose blood was shed as a sacrifice for our sins. The Feast of Unleavened Bread reminds us what God wants us to do once we've been saved, and that is to live a sanctified life, becoming more and more free from sin.

First came the Day of Passover, which helped God's people remember how they were saved. God had brought them out of the land of Egypt, out of the house of bondage. They ate bitter herbs (lettuce, endive, and other garnishes), presumably to remind them of their bitter labor on Pharaoh's plantation. They also ate unleavened bread, which reminded them that when they escaped they had to flee for their very lives. But the most important thing they did was to slaughter a lamb, dipping a branch of hyssop (marjoram, a common plant with stalks that could hold liquid and thus serve as a sort of brush) into the blood and then sprinkling it on the door.

Every home had its own lamb. It is worth noting that Moses first gave these instructions to the elders of Israel. The head of each household—the father—was responsible for keeping the feast. When his children were curious to know what he was doing, he would explain, "It is the sacrifice of the LORD's Passover, for he passed over the houses of the people of Israel in Egypt, when he struck the Egyptians but spared our houses" (12:27a). God wanted to make sure that his people would never forget their great salvation. To this day, when Jews celebrate Passover they commemorate their national deliverance. They reaffirm their identity by remembering that God rescued them from slavery in Egypt.

Passover had an even deeper meaning, however. The lamb was called a "sacrifice" (12:27) because it was an offering for sin. Passover was not simply about deliverance from Egypt; it was also about salvation from sin. Like the Egyptians, the Israelites were sinners. Therefore, on the night that God plagued Egypt with death, he also claimed his right to Israel's firstborn sons. "The destroyer" (12:23) visited every house, but the blood on Israel's doorposts was a sign that a sacrifice had been paid for their sin. It was a sign both for God and for his people. When God looked down and saw the blood, he knew that his justice had been satisfied; when the people looked up and saw the blood, they knew their sins were covered.

The Israelites were reminded of this every year. When they celebrated Passover, they explained to their children how God had brought them out of Egypt and saved them from sin. In this way God was preparing his people for the coming of Christ. In fact, some Christians consider Passover to be a visual representation of the cross. Blood was smeared on the top and sides of the door. It may also have been spilled in the doorway, since the word "basin" (12:22) could also be translated "threshold." So perhaps the Passover lamb was slain in the doorway, in which case there was blood on all four sides of the door. Similarly, when Christ was crucified there was blood on top of the cross flowing from his wounded head, blood on both sides from his nailed hands, and blood at the bottom from his pierced feet.[3]

God may or may not have intended Passover to serve as a visual representation of the cross. What is certain is that he intended the feast to present the message of the cross. In the New Testament we read that "Christ, our Passover lamb, has been sacrificed" (1 Corinthians 5:7). This is a way of saying that Jesus is our substitute, the perfect lamb offered in our place, who suffered the penalty that we deserved for our sins. In the same way that the sons of Israel were covered by the blood on the doorposts, we are covered by the blood that Jesus shed on the cross.

Sometimes we forget this. We are prone to spiritual amnesia, so we forget that we are sinners in need of salvation. We forget that God sent his one and only Son to be our Savior. We forget that the Son shed his own blood on the cross for our sins. Thankfully, in order to bring us back to our senses, God has given us a feast to remember. It is called the Lord's Supper.

Jesus gave us this gospel feast when he celebrated Passover with his disciples for the last time. The Scripture states that it was the first day of the Feast of Unleavened Bread (Matthew 26:17), and then it goes on to describe the preparations the disciples made. But when Jesus kept the feast he did something more than celebrate Passover—he inaugurated a whole new sacrament. He gave his disciples bread and said, "This is my body" (Matthew 26:26). Then he gave them the cup and said, "This is my blood of the covenant" (Matthew 26:28). By doing this Jesus was announcing that he was the lamb sacrificed to take away their sins.

We remember his sacrifice every time we celebrate the sacrament of Communion. Passover was for the old covenant: It looked back to the exodus. The Lord's Supper is for the new covenant: It looks to the cross. We celebrate it by eating bread and drinking the cup. Why do we do this? Jesus said, "Do this in remembrance of me" (Luke 22:19). The Lord's Supper is a feast to remember. It helps make sure that we never forget that we are sinners saved by the body and blood of Christ.

## Making a Clean Sweep

Passover was followed by the Feast of Unleavened Bread, which lasted for an entire week. The regulations for this feast were very specific:

> Seven days you shall eat unleavened bread. On the first day you shall remove leaven out of your houses, for if anyone eats what is leavened, from the first day until the seventh day, that person shall be cut off from Israel. On the first day you shall hold a holy assembly, and on the seventh day a holy assembly. No work shall be done on those days. But what everyone needs to eat, that alone may be prepared by you. And you shall observe the Feast of Unleavened Bread, for on this very day I brought your hosts out of the land of Egypt. Therefore you shall observe this day, throughout your generations, as a statute forever. In the first month, from the fourteenth day of the month at evening, you shall eat unleavened bread until the twenty-first day of the month at evening. For seven days no leaven is to be found in your houses. If anyone eats what is leavened, that person will be cut off from the congregation of Israel, whether he is a sojourner or a native of the land. You shall eat nothing leavened; in all your dwelling places you shall eat unleavened bread. (12:15–20)

Not only were these instructions specific, but they were also strict. Four times the Israelites were told not to eat anything with yeast, and twice they were told that if they did, they would be "cut off from Israel"—in other words, they would be banished from the covenant community of God's people. They were not even allowed to have any yeast in their homes. Why not? Was it simply a matter of public hygiene? What was so important about yeast?

For one thing, as we have already seen, unleavened bread reminded the Israelites of their hasty departure. But getting rid of the yeast had another purpose. Although it is not explicitly stated in Exodus 12, Jewish teachers have always understood yeast to represent the corrupting power of sin. Unleavened bread symbolizes holiness. What makes this comparison suitable is that unleavened bread is made of pure wheat untouched by yeast. When God's people ate unleavened bread, therefore, they were reminded to keep themselves pure from sin, and especially from the evils of Egypt. To this day, when devout Jewish families celebrate Passover they search their homes for leaven and then sweep it out the door. This symbolic act shows that they have a commitment to lead a life free from sin.

Yeast is an appropriate symbol for sin because of the way it grows and spreads. As yeast ferments, it works its way all through the dough. Sin works the same way, which is why the Bible makes this comparison. Sin is always trying to extend its corrupting influence through a person's entire life. But God had something better in mind for his people. He was saving them to sanctify them, so before they left Egypt he wanted them to make a clean sweep.

Consider the way bread was made in those days. The Israelites didn't have yeast packets; they just used a pinch of the old dough. I remember something similar from my childhood. From time to time someone would give my mother instructions for making "friendship bread." She would start by mixing the ingredients. However, in order for the recipe to work, her friend had to give her some "starter"—a lump of dough with leaven in it. Once my mother added the starter, the dough would begin to rise. But that is exactly what God did *not* want the Israelites to do. In spiritual terms, the last thing he wanted them to do was to take a lump of dough from Egypt that would eventually fill them with the leaven of idolatry. Instead he wanted them to leave behind all of Egypt's gods and goddesses—the old life of sin. One commentator explains it like this:

> Unleavened bread was a symbol of discontinuity. Leaven was a bit of dough kept unbaked from the previous day's baking and added to the next day's batch of dough so that it would start the fermentation process there also. It was used in much the same way as yeast would be now. When a batch of bread was being baked a relatively small quantity of leaven or yeast is added, and it works its way through the dough and causes it to rise. The instruction to banish leaven from their houses and to take none of it with them from Egypt was a gesture that symbolised leaving behind all Egyptian influences that might work their way through their lives and corrupt them.[4]

God wanted to do something more than get his people out of Egypt; he wanted to get Egypt out of his people. He was saving them with a view to their sanctification, so he told them to make a clean sweep. He commanded them to get rid of every last bit of yeast, the old yeast of Egyptian idolatry. To further show that they were making a fresh start, God gave his people a new calendar. He said, "This month shall be for you the beginning of months. It shall be the first month of the year for you" (12:2). It was a new year to mark a new spiritual beginning.

How do we know this interpretation is correct? How can we be certain that Exodus uses yeast as a symbol for sin? We know this because it is what the New Testament teaches. When the New Testament comments on something from the Old Testament, it generally gives us the key to understanding it, especially as it relates to salvation in Christ. In the case of the Feast of Unleavened Bread, the New Testament teaching is perfectly clear. The Apostle Paul wrote to the Corinthians, "Do you not know that a little leaven leavens the whole lump? Cleanse out the old leaven that you may be a new lump, as you really are unleavened. For Christ, our Passover lamb, has been sacrificed. Let us therefore celebrate the festival, not with the old leaven, the leaven of malice and evil, but with the unleavened bread of sincerity and truth" (1 Corinthians 5:6–8).

These verses from the New Testament endorse the traditional interpretation of leaven. In them Paul is plainly referring to the Feast of Unleavened Bread, for he identifies Christ as the Passover Lamb and speaks of "celebrat[ing] the festival." When he talks about "cleans[ing] out" the old yeast, he is thinking of a ritual that no doubt went back to his childhood, when every year at Passover his family would sweep their home, searching for every last trace of yeast. Here the apostle explains that the old yeast represents the sins of the old life, sins like hatred, anger, and deceit. Jesus said something similar when he warned his disciples, "Beware of the leaven of the Pharisees, which is hypocrisy" (Luke 12:1). Both Jesus and Paul used yeast as a symbol for sin.

God wants us to remember that we are saved in order to be sanctified. It is good to remember our salvation, but we must also remember that we have been saved for God's glory, and that means getting rid of the sin in our lives. The Bible teaches that God "saved us and called us to a holy calling" (2 Timothy 1:9). Part of what it means to lead a holy life is to sweep away sin before it has a chance to grow.

Even a small sin is dangerous because, like yeast, it wants to spread. This is why God has a zero-tolerance policy when it comes to sin. Anyone who thinks that some sins can be tolerated misunderstands the whole meaning of salvation. God delivered us from our bondage so that we would make a clean sweep.

Every believer needs to apply this personally. Is there a sin that you have decided to tolerate? Are you nursing a private grudge or indulging a secret lust? Is there something you have decided is all right for you to take, even though it doesn't actually belong to you? Do you think that worry and impatience are not really sins but just bad habits? Is there some area of your personal life where you have decided that it is okay to be undisciplined?

Perhaps you think that it is only a small sin. Perhaps from time to time you tell yourself that you will start to do something about it once it starts to get out of control. If that is what you are doing, then you are in great spiritual danger because sin is like yeast: once it gets into your life, it will keep growing and spreading until it corrupts everything. Before that happens, God's Word has something very simple and very straightforward to say about that sin: "Get rid of it!"

## Worship and Obey

The Bible records what the Israelites did when they first received God's instructions for Passover and the Feast of Unleavened Bread: "And the people bowed their heads and worshiped. Then the people of Israel went and did so; as the Lord had commanded Moses and Aaron, so they did" (12:27b, 28). The people worshiped and obeyed. First they got down on their hands and knees to praise God, and then they got back up and did exactly what God told them to do, down to the last detail.

Their response is significant because it reminds us of the entire theme of Exodus. God's purpose in bringing Israel out of Egypt was to save a people for his glory, a people who would give him all the praise. Finally his people were starting to do that. The last we heard from them (5:21), they were so discouraged that they had given up any hope of salvation; but now they were starting to worship God, even before he actually saved them. All they had was the promise of salvation, although it is worth noting that God had already started to speak about their salvation in the past tense. He said, "You shall observe the Feast of Unleavened Bread, for on this very day I brought your hosts out of the land of Egypt" (12:17). A grammarian might call this a "perfect of confidence" or "prophetic perfect." God was so absolutely confident of his power to save that as far as he was concerned, Israel was as good as saved already. And because God's people believed this too, they started to give him the glory.

Their response is also significant because it shows us what to do whenever we recover from our spiritual amnesia. We are prone to forget. We forget the sinfulness of our sin and the grace of God in Christ. We forget that God wants us to stop sinning. Then we have another one of our déjà vu experiences. We say, "Oh, yes, I remember now. It's all coming back to me. The thing I need to remember about myself is that I am a sinner in need of salvation. And the thing I need to remember about God is that he has given me a glorious salvation in Jesus Christ." As soon as we remember all that, the proper way to respond is the way the Israelites responded—by getting down on our knees to worship God. Once we get back up on our feet, we need to remember what comes next. We are saved to be sanctified, so we should do whatever God tells us to do.

# 30

# Out of Egypt

## EXODUS 12:29–42

IT WAS THE DEAD OF NIGHT. Most people were in their homes, asleep. Families all over Egypt had gone down for the night. But then the visitor came, with a deadly purpose. He was a destroyer, the angel of death.

The visitor was on a mission from God. He swept across Egypt, calling on every house in Pharaoh's kingdom. It was obvious that he was looking for something, because as he came to each house he paused to inspect the doorway. In the land of Goshen, where the Israelites lived, he found what he was looking for. There was a mark of blood on the top and sides of every door. When the visitor saw the blood, he passed over the house, holding back his deadly blow because a sacrifice had been made for sin. The family inside had heard that they could be saved by the blood of a lamb, and the sign on the door was a public testimony of their faith in God's saving word.

The rest of the houses in Egypt were not marked with the sign of salvation. As the visitor traveled up and down the Nile, he came to entire towns and cities where not a single household had offered a lamb for their sins. The visitor did not pass by these houses but slipped inside to claim the life of the firstborn son. Thus a night that began in silence ended in suffering: "At midnight the LORD struck down all the firstborn in the land of Egypt, from the firstborn of Pharaoh who sat on his throne to the firstborn of the captive who was in the dungeon, and all the firstborn of the livestock. And Pharaoh rose up in the night, he and all his servants and all the Egyptians. And there was a great cry in Egypt, for there was not a house where someone was not dead" (12:29, 30).

### The Great Divide

The death of the firstborn was the final blow, the tenth and deadliest plague. By visiting death on the Egyptians, while at the same time protecting his people, God was declaring the basis for salvation. In one sense what happened that night will never happen again. The angel of death will never strike down the sons of Egypt again, and never again will the Israelites smear blood on their doorposts. But the distinction God made that night is the one that he always makes. It is the distinction between those who have faith in the blood of the sacrifice he provides and those who do not, and on that distinction rests the eternal destiny of every human being.

This distinction runs through the Bible from beginning to end. It was the difference between Cain and Abel. Cain brought God fruits and vegetables, but Abel offered a perfect lamb. God accepted Abel because he had faith in the blood of the sacrifice (Genesis 4:3–5). This is how people were saved all through the Old Testament. They received atonement by trusting in the blood of a lamb sacrificed as a substitute for their sins.

Jesus offers salvation on the same basis. "Truly, truly, I say to you," he said to his disciples, "unless you eat the flesh of the Son of Man and drink his blood, you have no life in you. Whoever feeds on my flesh and drinks my blood has eternal life, and I will raise him up on the last day" (John 6:53, 54). This may sound like a strange way to talk. Obviously Jesus was not speaking about people literally drinking his blood. Rather, he was looking forward to his crucifixion, when he shed his blood for our sins, and also to the Lord's Supper, in which Christians drink the cup that symbolizes his blood. Jesus was saying that eternal life depends on faith in the blood of the sacrifice he made on the cross. The power of his blood is proven at the end of the Bible, for when the book of Revelation draws back the curtain to give us a glimpse of glory, we see the saints enter Heaven by "the blood of the Lamb" (Revelation 7:14).

Sadly, the Egyptians did not have faith in the blood. They did not offer a sacrifice for their many sins against God and his people. They did not put blood on their doorposts, and therefore they were destined for destruction. Not one single family escaped. The Bible says "there was not a house where someone was not dead" (12:30). The terrible plague even came home to Pharaoh, because someone was dead at the royal palace. It was the prince of Egypt, the son born to be like god to his people. But there was also someone dead down in the dungeon: the firstborn son of Egypt's lowest criminal.

This indicates what things will be like at the final judgment. God has promised that one day he will judge the world. Revelation describes the coming judgment in great detail, including the return of the plagues. The angels of Heaven will pour out seven bowls of wrath, and people will be afflicted with rivers of blood, painful sores, darkness, disease, frogs, and hail (see Revelation 16)—the very plagues first suffered by the Egyptians. What Pharaoh suffered was only a premonition of the end of the world, when every human being who has ever lived will stand before God for judgment.

We will all be there: the high and the low, the rich and the poor, the sinners and the saints. From the dungeon to the throne, no one will escape. No one will be granted an exemption. No one will receive any special treatment. The rich may travel first-class all their lives, but when they get to the final judgment God will not examine their bank accounts. Nor will the poor have something coming to them simply because their lives were more difficult. God is no respecter of persons, and he will judge everyone by the same standard. He does not care what color we are, how much money we have, where we go to school, what company we work for, or even how good we are. What matters to God is whether we have faith in the sacrifice of his Son. Those who trust in the blood of Christ will receive eternal life. Those who do not hold on to him and to his cross will be finally and fatally lost. The great divide between salvation and damnation is marked in blood.

## Up All Night

The Israelites were saved by the blood. Most of them probably stayed up all night to see what would happen. Some of them may have heard loud cries of anguish coming from their neighbors—Egyptians mourning the loss of their sons. Whether they heard the wailing or not, as they huddled together in their homes they knew that death was in the air. But if they were afraid, all they had to do was look to the blood, which was the sign of their salvation. Believers in Jesus Christ have the same confidence. Whenever we are fearful or anxious, all we need to do is look to the cross, where we see the guarantee of our salvation marked in blood.

The most important thing, however, is that *God* sees the blood. God said to Moses, "When I see the blood, I will pass over you" (12:13). And God saw the blood. God always sees everything, of course. The Scripture says that "he who keeps Israel will neither slumber nor sleep" (Psalm 121:4). God is always looking to care for us, protect us, and deliver us. But the Scripture explicitly states that he kept a careful eye on his people the night of the tenth plague: "It was a night of watching by the LORD, to bring them out of the land of Egypt," and because he did, "this same night is a night of watching kept to the LORD by all the people of Israel throughout their generations" (12:42). God was up all night, standing guard. He was working the night shift of salvation in order to deliver his people from death.

God was watching to make sure that salvation came just the way he promised. God had promised to rescue his people Israel (3:8). He had promised that the Egyptians would not let them go until he struck them with all his wonders (3:20). He had promised that they would not leave empty-handed, but that the Egyptians would send them away with clothing and jewelry (3:21, 22). God had promised that when he saved his people, they would know that he was their God (6:6, 7), and that the Egyptians would know it too (7:5). He had promised that they would leave in a big hurry (12:11). And on the night of the deadliest plague, when the Israelites took their first steps to freedom, all of these promises came true.

God always sees to it that he keeps his promises. Everything he has ever promised us will come true: By faith we will persevere to the end of life, enter glory, be raised from the dead, and enjoy the pleasures of God for all eternity. God is keeping his vigil. He is watching to make sure that it all happens just the way he said it would.

### Unconditional Surrender

There are times when it seems like the day of salvation will never come. There were times when it must have seemed that way to the Israelites. For centuries they languished in captivity, bearing the bitter yoke of their slavery in Egypt. And when God finally decided to do something about it, things got worse instead of better because Pharaoh made them work even harder. Now, finally, Pharaoh seemed to be getting what he deserved. Still, the Israelites must have wondered how many plagues it was going to take. But while they waited, they had God's promise that his mighty hand would make Pharaoh drive Israel out of Egypt—not just let them go but actually drive them out (6:1; cf. 3:20). This is precisely what happened: "Then he [Pharaoh] summoned Moses and Aaron by night and said, 'Up, go out from among my people, both you and the people of Israel; and go, serve the LORD, as you have said. Take your flocks and your herds, as you have said, and be gone, and bless me also!'" (12:31, 32).

These verses are so heavy with irony that they almost fall through the Biblical page. Here is the most powerful man in the world being rudely awakened to face things totally out of his control, including the death of his eldest son. Pharaoh had told Moses that he never wanted to see his face again (10:28). How ironic, then, for him to summon God's prophet in the middle of the night, especially since Moses had told Pharaoh that one day his officials would come bow down at his feet and beg him to get out of Egypt (11:8). Pharaoh had treated the Israelites as his slaves, refusing to recognize their rights. But here he calls them "the people of Israel," thus recognizing their status as a free nation. How ironic! Pharaoh had refused to let the Israelites worship their God. In fact, he claimed that he didn't even know who their God was (5:2). How ironic, therefore, for him to tell the Israelites to "serve the LORD" (12:31). The word "serve" is another irony because the problem all along was Pharaoh insisting that the Israelites had to serve him.

How ironic as well for Pharaoh to command the Israelites to leave Egypt. He was not just letting them go; he was ordering them to depart! Pharaoh barked three short commands: "Up. . . . Leave. . . . Go" (NIV). It was like the children's book by Dr. Seuss, in which the narrator tries to get one Marvin K. Mooney to leave the room. Marvin stands his ground, stubbornly refusing to go. Finally, in exasperation, the narrator cries, "Marvin K. Mooney! I don't care HOW. Marvin

K. Mooney! Will you please GO NOW! I said GO and GO I meant."[1] This is the kind of summary dismissal that Pharaoh gave Moses: "Get up, get out, go!"

These details are important because they show how God fulfilled his promise of salvation. What makes them all so deliciously ironic is that they show a man who swore that he would never give in doing exactly what God wanted him to do. By the tenth plague Pharaoh was begging Moses to do the very thing that he had been asking to do all along. It was a total capitulation. There would be no more negotiations. Pharaoh gave in to all of Moses' demands, granting Israel's unconditional release. God's people could go. Their women and children could go. Their flocks and herds could go too, with no conditions set for the time of their return.

Pharaoh's little concession speech stands as a warning to anyone who chooses to resist God's will. For all his hardness of heart—all the times he told God no and all the times he said yes but never followed through—Pharaoh gained nothing. In the end he had to accept everything on God's terms anyway. So why not give in to God in the first place? It is much better not to resist his claim on your life but simply to accept his plan and his purpose.

Pharaoh's last words to Moses were totally pathetic. "And bless me also," he pleaded. Pharaoh had finally realized his mistake, but it was too little too late. Earlier he had asked God's prophet to pray for him. Now he was asking to receive a benediction. But what blessing could Moses possibly give to a man like Pharaoh? His request is reminiscent of a scene from *The Fiddler on the Roof*, in which a young Russian Jew asks the town rabbi if there is a blessing for the tsar. It is a tough question because the tsar is their oppressor, and yet surely God has some kind of blessing for everyone. The rabbi thinks about it for a moment, and then he says, "May the Lord bless the tsar and keep him . . . far away from us!"

There would be no blessing for Pharaoh, however—not even a mixed blessing. The man wanted God's favor without ever turning to him in faith and repentance. John Currid writes, "What we can say with certainty is that there was no real repentance on the part of the king. He gave no recognition of any personal responsibility—he wanted the blessing without the liability, the shame, or the consequences. He simply desired the plagues to be gone. We know this to be the case, because once the immediate shock following the final plague had subsided, the Egyptian king pursued the Hebrews in order to destroy them."[2] God will not bless a man who will not repent of his sin.

Almost everyone wants God's blessing. Even people who do not have a personal relationship with Jesus Christ sometimes seek the services of a Christian. They ask for prayer, they want spiritual advice, or they expect to get married or buried in a church. But God's blessing is for those who trust in the blood. In other words, it is for people who admit that they are sinners and who believe that God has paid for their sin with a perfect sacrifice. In the time of Moses, God only blessed people who were covered by the blood of the Passover lamb. Today

God blesses those who trust in Jesus Christ, believing in the sacrifice he offered for sin on the cross. If you do not come to God through faith in Jesus Christ, God will not bless you.

## The Gold of Egypt

When the Bible talks about being saved by the blood, it is talking about the real blood of a real sacrifice. Salvation is not merely an intellectual concept or a personal feeling; it is something that God has actually done in human history. The exodus from Egypt really happened in time and space.

In describing that exodus, the Bible gives the kind of details that a careful historian would include:

> The Egyptians were urgent with the people to send them out of the land in haste. For they said, "We shall all be dead." So the people took their dough before it was leavened, their kneading bowls being bound up in their cloaks on their shoulders. The people of Israel had also done as Moses told them, for they had asked the Egyptians for silver and gold jewelry and for clothing. And the LORD had given the people favor in the sight of the Egyptians, so that they let them have what they asked. Thus they plundered the Egyptians. (12:33–36)

These are the words of an eyewitness who saw the Israelites eat their unleavened bread. It was the original fast food. People didn't have grocery stores or burger joints in those days, so when they went on long trips they had to take their food with them. In this case the Israelites didn't have much time. All they could do was throw some dough into a bowl and carry it with them.

The Biblical historian also saw the Egyptians give the Israelites gold and silver as well as fine clothing. These gifts were important because they fulfilled God's promise to Abraham that his descendants would come out from slavery with "great possessions" (Genesis 15:13, 14). Through their sufferings the Egyptians had learned to fear the God of Israel. Perhaps giving their valuables was a sort of bribe, intended to make sure that the Israelites really left Egypt. Or perhaps they served as payment for all the work the Israelites had done—no hard feelings.

However, the word the Bible uses to describe these parting gifts is a military term: "plundered." This shows that the exodus was a victory for God's people. Similarly, the book of Numbers says that the Israelites "went out triumphantly in the sight of all the Egyptians, while the Egyptians were burying all their firstborn, whom the LORD had struck down among them. On their gods also the LORD executed judgments" (Numbers 33:3b, 4). The Israelites did not leave empty-handed. Though they had lived in Egypt as slaves, they left as conquerors, carrying the spoils of God's victory.

The plundering of the Egyptians has often been used to illustrate the relationship between Christianity and culture. Theologians of the early church, such as Origen, used this episode to defend their use of pagan learning.[3] They noted how the Israelites took precious metals and fine cloth from the Egyptians and used them to build God's house, the tabernacle. In the same way, they argued, Christians may borrow the best of human learning and dedicate it to God. Augustine reasoned that Christians may use the "Egyptian gold" of secular thought because all truth is God's truth. However, he cautioned that this learning must be tested against Scripture to determine whether or not it is genuine gold. Furthermore, Biblical truth is far more valuable than any form of merely human knowledge.[4]

There may be some truth to this interpretation. By God's common grace, even non-Christians can know and understand many things about the world that God has made, and Christians benefit from their insights. As Nigel Goodwin has stated, "God in His wisdom did not give all His gifts to Christians."[5] And perhaps the plundering of the Egyptians can be used to illustrate the way Christians can and should borrow truth from the secular world. However, what the subsequent experience of the Israelites also shows is how easy it is to misuse Egyptian gold. The gold was a gift from God. The Bible explicitly states that "the LORD had given the people favor in the sight of the Egyptians" (12:36). Nevertheless, the Israelites eventually used their jewelry to make the golden calf. This is the danger we always face: to abuse God's blessing by using his gifts for our own idolatrous purposes. So we become fascinated with the latest academic trends or pop icons. We are consumed by our work, our artwork, our hobbies, or our pleasures. How easily the things of this world become idols!

## Salvation in History

The Bible describes the exodus in careful detail. Nevertheless, it has often been challenged on historical grounds. Three of the standard objections concern information given in Exodus 12, and they deserve a response.

The first deals with the *route* of the exodus. The Bible says, "And the people of Israel journeyed from Rameses to Succoth" (12:37a). Rameses was a common name in ancient Egypt. This particular Rameses probably was the storage city mentioned in 1:11. It was located somewhere in the Nile Delta and is usually identified with modern-day Qantir. The location of Succoth is less certain. Archaeologists have concluded that the traditional site, Tel el Maskhuta, was not occupied until centuries later. Probably Succoth was somewhere along the Wadi Tumilat, some fifteen miles east of the land of Goshen.[6]

To this day, however, the location of these places remains uncertain. As we shall see, the same can be said for much of Israel's route through the Sinai Peninsula. But this does not cast any real doubt on the Bible's accuracy. Finding exact locations is a typical problem for ancient wilderness sites. Whether or not we can ever map out the entire exodus, it is clear from Exodus and also from Numbers that the Bible is referring to real places in the real world. As one scholar concludes, the Biblical itinerary "creates in the mind of even the most critical reader the impression of historical fact. . . . [T]he historian is absolute and specific." It is, he writes, "an impressive and credible piece of ancient historical writing."[7]

A second historical challenge concerns the *size* of the exodus. The Bible says, "And the people of Israel journeyed from Rameses to Succoth, about six hundred thousand men on foot, besides women and children. A mixed multitude also went up with them, and very much livestock, both flocks and herds" (12:37, 38). This account gives the kind of who, what, when, where, how information that a good historian is careful to include. But what about, how many? Can we really believe that God brought so many Israelites out of Egypt?

That's a good question. If there were six hundred thousand men, then there were perhaps two million Israelites in all, and this number presents a number of difficulties. If there were so many Israelites, then why aren't they mentioned in the annals of Egypt? They would have formed one of the largest populations anywhere in the world at that time. Could the land of Goshen have supported such a large population? And why can't we find any trace of them in the Sinai? Their exodus was one of the largest migrations in the history of the world. When they traveled, they must have formed a column more than ten miles long. These are the kinds of questions scholars have asked, with many concluding that whoever wrote the Bible must have inflated the numbers. S. R. Driver wrote that "tradition, in the course of years, greatly exaggerated the numbers of the Israelites at the Exodus."[8] N. H. Snaith calls the total figures "fantastic and incredible."[9]

There are two ways to handle this objection. One is to believe that the Bible does indeed mean to say that six hundred thousand Israelites (that is, men plus women and children) came out of Egypt, and therefore this is exactly how many people there actually were. Although some scholars think there are difficulties with that view, there are no impossibilities. The Israelites receive little mention in Egypt because they were only slaves there and because the manner of their departure was such a complete embarrassment to the Egyptians. Nor should we be surprised not to find much evidence for them in the Sinai. They were nomads after all, and their remains have been covered by three thousand years of sand. In addition, one good reason for accepting six hundred thousand as the right number is that it matches the statistics given elsewhere in Exodus (38:26) and also in the book of Numbers (see 1:46; 2:32; 26:51).

There is another possibility, however—one that may also be faithful to the Biblical text. The Hebrew word *eleph* can mean "thousand." However, early in the Old Testament it may also be used as an inexact term for a sizable cluster of people. Some scholars think it means something like "clan." Or it may be a military term for a fighting unit, like a platoon. Exodus 12:37 could then be read as follows: "There were about six hundred clans," or "There were about six hundred military units." On this reading, the total population of Israelites would have numbered in the tens of thousands, not in the millions.

One scholar who accepts this interpretation is James Hoffmeier, who writes, "The issue in Exodus 12:37 is an interpretive one. The word *eleph* can be translated 'thousand,' but it is also rendered in the Bible as 'clans' and 'military units.' When I look at the question as an Egyptologist, I know that there are thought to have been 20,000 in the entire Egyptian army at the height of Egypt's empire. And at the battle of Ai in Joshua 7, there was a severe military setback when 36 troops were killed. If you have an army of 600,000, that's not a large setback."[10] It is not a question of whether or not the Bible is true; it is a question of what the Bible means to say. What is certain is that God brought a great crowd of people out of Egypt. Indeed, as the Scripture says, "All the hosts of the Lord went out from the land of Egypt" (12:41).

The last historical question concerns the date of the exodus. The Bible concludes its account with these words: "The time that the people of Israel lived in Egypt was 430 years. At the end of 430 years, on that very day, all the hosts of the Lord went out from the land of Egypt" (12:40, 41). This number fits the prophecy God gave to Abraham: "Know for certain that your offspring will be sojourners in a land that is not theirs and will be servants there, and they will be afflicted for four hundred years" (Genesis 15:13; cf. Acts 7:6). The difference between the 400 in Genesis and the 430 in Exodus is relatively insignificant. Probably God was rounding things off when he made his prophecy to Abraham.

What is perhaps more significant is that there are two completely different versions of verse 41. The one that says the Israelites lived in Egypt for 430 years is the Hebrew text passed down to the Masoretes. However, the Greek Septuagint translation claims that Israel lived "in the land of Egypt *and the land of Canaan*" for 430 years. On this reading, the period of 430 years would also include the age of the patriarchs, from Abraham to Isaac (see also Galatians 3:16, 17). However this matter of dating is to be resolved (both readings are compatible with either an early or a late date for the exodus), the most important thing to know is that the Israelites left Egypt right on schedule, on the very day that God had planned.

The point of mentioning these historical objections is to defend the truth of Scripture. Even if it is not always certain which explanation is correct, it is clear that there are answers. Since it has become common for secular scholars to deny the historicity of the exodus, it is important for Christians to be able to defend this portion of the Bible. What is historically certain is that God brought Israel out of Egypt, leading every last Israelite from Rameses to Succoth, just as the Bible says.

The reason the history of the exodus matters is because it is part of the history of salvation. At stake is not simply the accuracy of the Bible but the factual basis for God's saving work in history. It is only because the Bible is absolutely true—not just in its spiritual parts but in all its particulars—that its message of salvation can be trusted. How can the Bible's promises be trusted if its memory is faulty? To put the question a different way, when the Israelites praised God for bringing them out of Egypt—sending the plagues, providing the lamb, parting the sea, and all the rest of it—were they praising him for something that he had actually done or were they simply making up a story about where they came from?

Some scholars seem to think that the book of Exodus is something like a James Michener novel: It accurately captures the feel of a general period of history, but its specific characters and events are fictional. Other people, like the carload of pilgrims described in Bruce Feiler's book *Walking the Bible*, deny that history even matters. When these visitors arrived at Marah, one of them said, "Who cares if the Israelites were actually here? We're here because it's biblical."[11] Such an attitude could hardly be more un-Biblical, because what the Bible presents is a real exodus that gives the real facts about Israel's salvation.

The importance of history becomes all the more evident when we consider the cross and the empty tomb. Did Jesus of Nazareth die on the cross or didn't he? Was he raised from the dead or not? Do we speak the historical truth when we say, in the words of the Apostles' Creed, "I believe . . . in Jesus Christ, his only Son, our Lord . . . [who] was crucified, dead, and was buried. . . . The third day he arose again"? These questions are absolutely crucial. The Apostle Paul reasoned it out like this: "If Christ has not been raised, your faith is futile and you are still in your sins" (1 Corinthians 15:17). What Paul said about the resurrection is equally true for the cross: If Christ was not crucified, your faith is futile; you are still in your sins. To believe the gospel is to believe that Jesus truly died on the cross for our very own sins.

To help people grapple with the historical basis for Christianity, Francis Schaeffer (1912–1984) used to ask this question: "Do you believe that if you had been there when Christ was crucified, you could have reached out to touch the cross and picked up a splinter in your finger?" Of course, what was really important was not just the wood but the blood that was staining it. And this brings us back to where we started, with the blood that marks the difference between those who are saved and those who will be lost forever. Do you believe that Jesus offered his life in your place as a sacrifice for your sins? To be specific, do you believe that if you had been at the crucifixion, you could have placed your hand on the cross and felt the warm blood of your Savior? That's how real it was—real enough to see and touch. And that is how real salvation is. It is something God has really done in time and space to bring us out of the Egypt of our sin.

# 31

# This Do in Remembrance of Me

EXODUS 12:43–51; 13:3–10

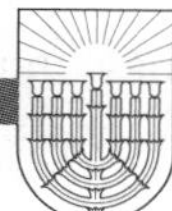

PASSOVER WAS A FEAST TO REMEMBER. It was a freedom festival—an annual reminder of the way God brought his people out of the land of Egypt, out of the house of bondage. To celebrate Passover was to recall God's great work of salvation. The Israelites ate bitter herbs to remember the bitterness of their captivity. They sacrificed a lamb to remember that God had provided a perfect sacrifice as a substitute for their sins. Then they took the lamb's blood and painted it on the door. When God saw the blood, he restrained his hand of judgment, and death passed over. The Israelites were saved by the blood of the lamb, the mark of distinction that separated the redeemed from the damned. For the next seven days they ate unleavened bread, which represented holiness and thus symbolized their decisive break with the old life of sin. Passover demonstrated what God had done in history to rescue his people from slavery, death, and sin.

At the same time, the feast pointed forward to the coming of Christ. Its details set the pattern for the salvation that God would accomplish through Christ's life, death, and resurrection. To use the technical term for it, Passover was a *type*. A type is a pattern, like the key on an old printing press that strikes a letter on the page. In the Bible, a type is a person, practice, or event from the Old Testament that sets the pattern for salvation in Christ. Charles Spurgeon said:

> It is our firm conviction and increasing belief, that the historical books of Scripture were intended to teach us by types and figures spiritual things. . . . We look upon the book of Exodus as being a book of types of the deliverances which God will give to his elect people: not only as a history of what he has done, in bringing them out of Egypt by smiting the firstborn, leading them through the Red Sea, and guiding them through the

> wilderness, but also as a picture of his faithful dealings with all his people, whom by the blood of Christ he separates from the Egyptians, and by his strong and mighty hand takes out of the house of their bondage and out of the land of their slavery.[1]

Passover is a type. It shows the pattern of salvation, in which the blood of a perfect sacrifice serves as a substitute for our sins. Just as the Israelites were delivered from death by looking to the blood on their doorposts, so we also are saved by looking to the blood that Jesus shed on the cross. And then, like the Israelites, we are called to sweep out the old leaven of sin and live in a way that is pure and pleasing to God. The Apostle Paul was referring to these "types" of salvation when he wrote, "Christ, our Passover lamb, has been sacrificed. Let us therefore celebrate the festival, not with the old leaven, the leaven of malice and evil, but with the unleavened bread of sincerity and truth" (1 Corinthians 5:7b, 8).

Yet beyond all this, there is still much more to learn because Passover has a rich depth of spiritual meaning. At the end of Exodus 12 God gives further instructions for Passover. Then at the beginning of chapter 13, Moses repeats some of the instructions that God had already given. While this information shows how important Passover was, the repetition may seem rather tedious. In fact, some scholars regard the end of chapter 12 as a sort of "appendix." They believe that these verses (12:43–49) were added by some later author. However, all the information is important. God wanted this feast to be celebrated properly, down to the last detail, because he wanted to give his people a full picture of salvation. Passover was a meal to share, a meal to eat, and a meal to explain.

## Sharing Passover

Passover was a meal to share with all God's people. God said to Moses, "All the congregation of Israel shall keep it" (12:47). This is something God had said from the beginning of his instructions for Passover: "Tell all the congregation of Israel that . . . every man shall take a lamb according to their fathers' houses" (12:3); "the whole assembly of the congregation of Israel shall kill their lambs at twilight" (12:6). This was partly a matter of public safety. The destroyer was coming, and the firstborn sons would only be safe if they were covered by the blood of a lamb. So God said, "None of you shall go out of the door of his house until the morning" (12:22b).

To be safe, all the Israelites needed to celebrate the first Passover. But even after death passed over, they all needed to keep the Feast of Unleavened Bread. God told them to "hold a holy assembly" (12:16), which meant the entire community was to gather for worship (see also Leviticus 23; Numbers 28, 29). If anyone refused to participate, he was cut off from Israel (12:15, 19). God also told his people that during Passover they all needed to stay up and keep watch:

"It was a night of watching by the LORD, to bring them out of the land of Egypt; so this same night is a night of watching kept to the LORD by all the people of Israel" (12:42). Passover was a meal to be shared, a celebration for the whole family of God.

The reason it was necessary for all God's people to celebrate Passover was because they were all rescued together. Exodus 12 closes with this summary: "All the people of Israel did just as the LORD commanded Moses and Aaron. And on that very day the LORD brought the people of Israel out of the land of Egypt by their hosts" (12:50, 51). Since salvation was something they shared, it was only right for them to join together for the feast that praised God for the grace they had all received.

In America most Christians think of salvation in individual terms. Evangelicals often talk about having a personal relationship with Jesus Christ. Christianity is about what God has done for *me*. However, we also believe in the communion of saints, which means that we all have something in common. In salvation God has joined us together with Jesus Christ.

This is why, when the New Testament explains the great doctrines of salvation, it almost always speaks in the plural. To give just one example, consider Paul's words to Titus: "But when the goodness and loving kindness of God our Savior appeared, he saved us, not because of works done by us in righteousness, but according to his own mercy, by the washing of regeneration and renewal of the Holy Spirit, whom he poured out on us richly through Jesus Christ our Savior, so that being justified by his grace we might become heirs according to the hope of eternal life" (Titus 3:4–7). Regeneration, justification, sanctification, glorification—together we share every aspect of salvation. We are all sinners in need of a Savior, we were all included with Christ when he died on the cross and rose from the grave, and one day we will all be transformed into his glorious image.

Since God wants to gather a people for his glory, corporate worship is an essential part of his saving plan. This explains why it is absolutely vital for Christians to be faithful in attending public worship. It is good to worship God in private. Every Christian should maintain some regular routine of personal prayer, praise, and Bible study. But we cannot be Christians on our own. It is of the very essence of our Christianity that we worship God together, praising him for the salvation we share in Christ. A Christian who decides that it is not necessary to attend church is in grave spiritual danger. As the Scripture says, "Let us consider how to stir up one another to love and good works, not neglecting to meet together, as is the habit of some, but encouraging one another" (Hebrews 10:24, 25).

Because it was a meal to share, Passover helped unite God's people into one community. All the Israelites kept the same feast at the same time in all their homes. We do something similar in the church whenever we celebrate the sacrament of Communion. Sharing the Lord's Supper is a powerful symbol of our unity and community in Christ. The Apostle Paul explained this to the Corinthians, who sometimes had trouble getting along with one another. He asked them, "The cup of blessing that we bless, is it not a participation in the blood of Christ? The bread that we break, is it not a participation in the body of Christ?" (1 Corinthians 10:16). The answer was "Yes!" In some mysterious way, by the power and presence of the Holy Spirit, Christians who eat the bread and drink the cup are spiritually connected to Christ. At the same time, we are also connected to one another. To have union with Christ is to have communion with his church. So Paul went on to say, "Because there is one bread, we who are many are one body, for we all partake of the one bread" (1 Corinthians 10:17). Like Passover, the Lord's Supper is a meal to be shared—a tangible demonstration of our community in Christ.

## A Place at the Table

Passover was a meal for all God's people to share. Everyone was included—every man, woman, and child in Israel. However, some people were excluded. Here again God's instructions were very specific: "And the LORD said to Moses and Aaron, 'This is the statute of the Passover: no foreigner shall eat of it. . . . No foreigner or hired worker may eat of it'" (12:43, 45). To be blunt, God discriminated. Passover was for his people, and for his people only.

The question about who was eligible for Passover came up almost immediately because the Israelites were not the only ones who left Egypt. The Bible says, "A mixed multitude also went up with them" (12:38). The term "mixed multitude" means that they came from a variety of ethnic backgrounds. Some of them may have been Egyptians who feared the God of Israel. Others undoubtedly came from other tribes—fellow-slaves who seized their opportunity to escape when they saw the Israelites walking into the desert. Thus the question naturally arose as to whether they were allowed to keep the feast.

The basic answer was no. Passover was exclusive. It was only for the people of God, and not for outsiders. Foreigners and migrant workers were not allowed to keep the feast. The reason was that they were not members of the covenant community. To use the contemporary term for it, they were not believers. This was not a matter of race but of grace. These outsiders had not yet put their faith in the God of Israel, and thus they had no right to receive the atonement that he provided through the Passover lamb. It was not appropriate for them to receive the sign of salvation because they were not trusting in the blood of the lamb.

The church maintains the same restriction at the Lord's Table. As we have seen, there is a connection between Passover and the Lord's Supper. Both sacraments are exclusive. Like Passover, the Lord's Supper is not for everyone. It is only for those who have come to faith in the Lord Jesus Christ. The Bible teaches that "whoever . . . eats the bread or drinks the cup of the Lord in an unworthy manner will be guilty concerning the body and blood of the Lord. Let a person examine himself, then, and so eat of the bread and drink of the cup. For anyone who eats and drinks without discerning the body eats and drinks judgment on himself" (1 Corinthians 11:27–29). At the very least, these verses mean that Communion is not for those who do not know Christ. It is inappropriate and even dangerous to participate in Communion without receiving Jesus Christ as Lord.

For this reason, it is necessary for ministers to warn some people not to receive the sacrament by saying something like this: "It is my duty to tell you that the Lord's Supper is for the people of God. It is for those—and for those only—who have confessed their sins, who have publicly professed their faith in Christ alone for their salvation, and who remain members in good standing of a gospel-preaching church." The old Scottish Presbyterians called this "fencing the table." The purpose of giving such a warning is not to keep people away from Christ, but to make it clear that the only way to receive salvation is by coming to him in faith. We cannot have communion with Christ unless we have faith in his blood. Telling people this helps clarify their spiritual condition. When a minister draws the line between those who are inside and those who are outside the church, it helps people who have not yet made a commitment to Christ to recognize that they are not yet saved.

There is a way to be saved, however, and that is to come to God in faith. The way people did that in the time of Moses was by receiving the sign of circumcision and thus joining the covenant community—the people of God. Once people were circumcised, whether they were Israelites or not, they were eligible to share Passover. God said, "Every slave that is bought for money may eat of it after you have circumcised him" (12:44).

The practice of circumcising slaves went all the way back to God's covenant with Abraham, to whom God said:

> This is my covenant, which you shall keep, between me and you and your offspring after you: Every male among you shall be circumcised. You shall be circumcised in the flesh of your foreskins, and it shall be a sign of the covenant between me and you. He who is eight days old among you shall be circumcised. Every male throughout your generations, whether born in your house or bought with your money from any foreigner who is not of your offspring, both he who is born in your house and he who is bought with your money, shall surely be circumcised. So shall my covenant be in your flesh an everlasting covenant. (Genesis 17:10–13)

Since the time of Abraham, God had allowed slaves to become members of the covenant community. Once they were circumcised, they were also eligible to share Passover.

Slaves were not the only non-Israelites who were allowed to join the covenant community, however. This privilege was also extended to "strangers," or foreigners who made their permanent home with God's people. The Old Testament granted aliens a number of important rights and protections. They were permitted to glean grain from the edges of a farmer's field (Leviticus 19:10; 23:22). They could seek safety in a city of refuge (Numbers 35:15). However, they were not allowed to celebrate Passover unless they were circumcised. God told Moses, "If a stranger shall sojourn with you and would keep the Passover to the Lord, let all his males be circumcised. Then he may come near and keep it; he shall be as a native of the land. But no uncircumcised person shall eat of it. There shall be one law for the native and for the stranger who sojourns among you" (12:48, 49). Circumcision was the prerequisite for Passover.

These regulations show that God has always offered salvation to everyone. No one has ever been excluded from coming to God simply on the basis of race. Even in the Old Testament, God provided a way for outsiders to come into his family and receive his saving grace. The way to come was by faith in the God of Israel, and circumcision was the public way of trusting in his promise of salvation. Already in the Old Testament God was declaring his glory to the nations. His people—both native-born Israelites and "a mixed multitude" of others—were saved by grace through faith.

Here again Passover helps explain what the Lord's Supper means for the church. Communion is an international feast, a meal to be shared by all nations. Jesus said, "I tell you, many will come from east and west and recline at table with Abraham, Isaac, and Jacob in the kingdom of heaven" (Matthew 8:11). This promise was about the way the gospel would gather the nations. Jesus was saying that those who were outside would come in to share God's feast. This promise is fulfilled whenever Christians from various tribes and nations sit down to share the Lord's Supper.

There is one requirement, however, and that is personal faith in Jesus Christ. This is absolutely essential. There is more to Communion than simply showing up at church and sitting down to receive the Lord's Supper. In order to receive it properly, a person must be baptized and make a public confession of faith in Christ. There was a similar requirement for resident aliens who lived in Israel during the time of the Old Testament. They derived many benefits from living with the people of God. However, salvation required something more than just living next door to an Israelite. It demanded a total personal commitment to God, signified by circumcision. Only aliens who had made this faith commitment were eligible to receive Passover, with all the benefits it symbolized: deliverance from death, atonement for sin, and strength for holiness. The same principle holds true for the church. There are many spiritual benefits to attending church, but salvation is not one of them. What God requires is faith in his Son, Jesus Christ, and only those who believe and are baptized are eligible fully to commune with God's people.

## The Passover Meal

Because Passover was a feast, obviously it was meant to be eaten. First the Israelites ate the lamb—the whole lamb. God had said to Moses, "Do not eat any of it raw or boiled in water, but roasted, its head with its legs and its inner parts. And you shall let none of it remain until the morning; anything that remains until the morning you shall burn" (12:9, 10). At the end of chapter 12 the Lord added, "It shall be eaten in one house; you shall not take any of the flesh outside the house, and you shall not break any of its bones" (12:46).

The Bible does not explain the reasoning behind these instructions, and scholars have struggled to understand what they mean. The instructions seem to emphasize the wholeness of the sacrifice. Passover was an undivided feast. One lamb was eaten by one family under one roof for one salvation. This served to strengthen their bonds of fellowship. Furthermore, the Israelites were not allowed to break off a bone and give it to a neighbor. Perhaps this was to ensure that no foreigner or alien would partake unless he had first been circumcised.

What is certain is that the command not to break any bones helps confirm that Jesus is the lamb of our salvation. Jesus and the two men who were crucified with him were nailed to their crosses the day before Passover. Some of the religious leaders wanted to make sure that their bodies were taken down before the holy feast, and in order to hasten death, they asked the Romans to break the legs of their victims. According to John, who witnessed these events, "The soldiers came and broke the legs of the first, and of the other who had been crucified with him. But when they came to Jesus and saw that he was already dead, they did not break his legs" (John 19:32, 33). Jesus' bones were left unbroken, and as John reflected on this, he recognized that "these things took place that the Scripture might be fulfilled: 'Not one of his bones will be broken'" (John 19:36). This assures us that Jesus really is the perfect sacrifice for our sin—unblemished and unbroken.

Once the Israelites finished eating the lamb, for the next seven days they ate unleavened bread. Again the instructions were detailed:

> Then Moses said to the people, "Remember this day in which you came out from Egypt, out of the house of slavery, for by a strong hand the LORD brought you out from this place. No leavened bread shall be eaten. Today, in the month of Abib, you are going out. And when the LORD brings you into the land of the Canaanites, the Hittites, the Amorites, the Hivites, and the Jebusites, which he swore to your fathers to give you, a land flowing with milk and honey, you shall keep this service in this month. Seven days you shall eat unleavened bread, and on the seventh day there shall be a feast to the LORD. Unleavened bread shall be eaten for seven days; no leavened bread shall be seen with you, and no leaven shall be seen with you in all your territory." (13:3–7)

This festival was to be observed even after the Israelites reached the Promised Land. Once they settled down, they would be able to eat bread with yeast because they would have plenty of time for the dough to rise. But every year at Passover they would eat bread without yeast as a testimony of their salvation. The bread would remind them how quickly they had to leave Egypt, and since the yeast represented sin, it would also remind them to lead holy lives. God did not want to find any trace of the old Egyptian sins in Israel.

To summarize, Passover was a meal. Both the lamb and the bread were meant to be eaten. But why? What was so important about having food for Passover? Why did God give his people an edible sign of salvation?

Having food was not unique to Passover. Eating and drinking run right through Scripture, from Melchizedek bringing out bread and wine for Abraham (Genesis 14:18) to "the marriage supper of the Lamb" (Revelation 19:9). Many Biblical worship services end with a meal. Moses and the elders of Israel ate and drank on the holy mountain (24:11). When Ezra and Nehemiah renewed the covenant, they told God's people to "eat the fat and drink sweet wine" (Nehemiah 8:10). Most Old Testament sacrifices were to be eaten, either by the people or the priests or both. Then Christ came to inaugurate a new covenant, and he gave his followers the bread and wine of Communion. God always presents the benefits of salvation to us in the form of a meal. Why is this?

God has many reasons for giving us something to eat and drink. It helps us understand the gospel by making salvation something we can see and touch, something so real we can taste it. Sharing a meal is also a form of fellowship. Eating brings people together. So when God invites us to sit down at his table, he is telling us that he wants to have a close relationship with us. Jesus said, "If anyone hears my voice and opens the door, I will come in to him and eat with him, and he with me" (Revelation 3:20).

Eating and drinking also identify us with Christ in his sacrifice for our sin. By eating the bread of his body and drinking the cup of his blood, we receive into our bodies tokens of salvation—covenant seals—that show our connection to Christ and his cross. At Passover the Israelites were identified with the sacrificial lamb. The blood on the doorpost showed a connection between the family inside and the lamb they had offered for their sins. *Eating* the lamb made the connection even closer. By ingesting the whole offering, they were making a total identification with the sacrifice that God had provided for their salvation. It was more than a symbol; it was a spiritual reality. In the same way, the sacrament of Communion makes a total identification between Christ and the Christian, sealing the covenant of grace. What Christ did on the cross is really ours. It is as much a part of us as what we eat and drink.

Finally, we eat the Lord's Supper for our nourishment. Whenever we take Communion, we are being fed something that is spiritually healthy for us. The Westminster Confession of Faith explains that those who partake of the bread and the cup by faith do "really and indeed, yet not carnally and corporally but spiritually, receive, and feed upon, Christ crucified, and all benefits of His death" (29.7). In other words, what happens in Communion is spiritual, not merely or even primarily physical. Nevertheless, by the presence of the Holy Spirit, it is real. In partaking of the Lord's Supper, we receive real spiritual nourishment to grow in grace. We are feeding upon Christ and the benefits of his salvation.

## Explaining Passover

The more we study Passover, the more we realize that this meal is a great mystery. Its presentation of the gospel is so profound that it would take a lifetime to learn everything it has to teach. For this reason, Passover was not simply a meal to share but also a meal to explain.

Whenever God's people celebrated Passover, they were supposed to talk about what it meant. Moses said, "You shall tell your son on that day, 'It is because of what the LORD did for me when I came out of Egypt.' And it shall be to you as a sign on your hand and as a memorial between your eyes, that the law of the LORD may be in your mouth. For with a strong hand the LORD has brought you out of Egypt. You shall therefore keep this statute at its appointed time from year to year" (13:8–10).

Many Jews have taken these words literally, not recognizing that Moses was using a figure of speech. To this day, in order to keep God's Word on their hands and foreheads, orthodox Jews write Scripture passages on scraps of paper, put them in little boxes, and tie them to their arms and heads with leather straps.[2] While it is easy to understand how this legalistic tradition got started, it is not what God intended, as Jesus pointed out to the Pharisees (see Matthew 23:5). What was supposed to function as the reminder was not a Bible verse in a box but Passover. The feast itself was the sign on the hand, the reminder on the forehead. In other words, Passover kept the message of salvation in front of God's people. But in order to do that, it had to be explained; otherwise it would simply become a meaningless ritual.

The ones who did the explaining were the parents. It was their responsibility to speak to their children about spiritual things. As a father prepared the lamb for the sacrifice, he would say to his son, "Do you remember why we do this every year?" Then he would give his testimony of faith in the God of Israel. He would say, "It is because of what the LORD did for me when I came out of Egypt" (13:8).

It made for a wonderful testimony. It was personal, given in the first person. Every Israelite needed to make a personal appropriation of the salvation God provided for all Israel. At the same time, it was a God-centered testimony. It was all about what God had done in history to save his people. Every Christian should be ready to give the same kind of testimony, one that is both personal and

Christ-centered. We should be ready to say, "I want to tell you what Jesus Christ has done for me. He died on the cross for my sins and gave me a whole new life."

By testifying to the meaning of Passover, God's people made sure they never forgot their salvation. What God did in rescuing them from slavery was so wonderful, so miraculous, that it needed to be remembered not just for a few years or even a few centuries but forever. Sadly, many Israelites did forget their salvation. But there were always some who remembered. One of them was Joshua, whose memory was absolutely essential because his entire generation perished in the wilderness. But because Joshua remembered, when the Israelites finished their wanderings and entered the Promised Land, almost the first thing he had them do was celebrate Passover (Joshua 5:10, 11). Kings like Hezekiah and Josiah remembered as well. They both ordered the nation of Israel to keep the feast (2 Chronicles 30, 35). Ezra and Nehemiah also remembered, celebrating Passover when Israel returned from exile (Ezra 6:19–22). And Jesus remembered too, for it was his usual custom to share the Passover with his disciples.

The way God's people remembered was very simple: They celebrated Passover the way their parents celebrated it, including the explanation. Each son learned the meaning of salvation from his father, who had learned it from his father, who in turn had learned it from his father, and so on, all the way back to Moses. Asaph had this educational process in mind when he wrote:

> We will . . . tell to the coming generation
> the glorious deeds of the LORD, and his might,
>     and the wonders that he has done . . .
> that the next generation might know them,
>     the children yet unborn,
> and arise and tell them to their children,
>     so that they should set their hope in God
> and not forget the works of God. (Psalm 78:4, 6, 7)

Many Israelites kept Asaph's promise, which helps explain why so many passages in the Old Testament refer back to the exodus (e.g. Psalm 105; Jeremiah 32:20, 21; Micah 6:4). Parents were always talking about it with their children.

This task has now been entrusted to Christian parents, and also to every adult in God's family, the church. It is our responsibility to teach children the Bible and its theology, to speak with them about spiritual things, to share with them our personal testimonies of faith in Christ, to explain to them the meaning of the Lord's Supper, and in every way to give them the gospel of God and his salvation.

It has often been observed that in any particular family, church, or nation, the gospel is only one generation away from extinction. It all depends on the next generation, so it all depends on parents teaching their children. This led Charles Spurgeon to remind his congregation:

> Children need to learn the doctrine of the cross that they may find immediate salvation. I thank God that . . . we believe in the salvation of children as children. . . . Go on . . . and believe that God will save your children. Be not content to sow principles in their minds which may possibly develop in after years; but be working for immediate conversion. . . . What a mercy it will be if our children are thoroughly grounded in the doctrine of redemption by Christ! . . . Some talk to children about being good boys and girls, and so on; that is to say, they preach the law to children, though they would preach the gospel to grown-up people! Is this honest? Is this wise? Children need the gospel, the whole gospel, the unadulterated gospel; they ought to have it, and if they are taught of the Spirit of God they are as capable of receiving it as persons of ripe years. Teach the little ones that Jesus died, the just for the unjust, to bring us to God.[3]

If this is what we teach our children—that Christ died for sinners—then that is what they will teach their children, and thus the message of the cross will be remembered long after we are gone, until the end of the world, and forever after.

# 32

# The Redemption of Sons

EXODUS 13:1, 2, 11–16

TO STUDY EXODUS is to learn the theology of salvation. The true story of Israel's escape from Egypt demonstrates many great doctrines of the Christian faith. It teaches about sin and judgment. When God sent his plagues against the Egyptians, he was judging them for their sins. The exodus teaches election: God rescued the Israelites because they were the people of his choice. It teaches substitutionary atonement: God's people were saved by the blood of a lamb offered in their place. This was also a propitiation because the blood turned aside God's deadly wrath. The exodus teaches the communion of saints. The Israelites shared Passover, and as they did, they remembered the God of their salvation. The exodus even teaches sanctification, because God told them to sweep away the yeast that represented their old life of sin. The exodus gave Israel nearly a complete theological education. Hardly a single major doctrine was left out.

Another pillar of soteriology is introduced in chapter 13—the doctrine of redemption. This chapter gives instructions for the redemption of sons. Like Passover and the Feast of Unleavened Bread, this ritual was to remind the Israelites how God saved them from Egypt. Their rescue was a redemption. In other words, it procured their release by the payment of a price.

Redemption helps complete our understanding of the exodus. It also helps us appreciate our own salvation, because this doctrine has many connections to the person and work of Christ. The Scripture says, "In him we have redemption through his blood, the forgiveness of our trespasses" (Ephesians 1:7; cf. Colossians 1:13, 14). As he reflected on this great truth, B. B. Warfield (1851–1921) concluded:

> There is no one of the titles of Christ which is more precious to Christian hearts than "Redeemer." . . . It gives expression not merely to our sense that

> we have received salvation from Him, but also to our appreciation of what it cost Him to procure this salvation for us. It is the name specifically of the Christ of the cross. Whenever we pronounce it, the cross is placarded before our eyes and our hearts are filled with loving remembrance not only that Christ has given us salvation, but that he paid a mighty price for it.[1]

## Who's Your Daddy?

The redemption described in Exodus 13 is the redemption of sons. This goes back to something Moses said to Pharaoh even before the plagues: "Thus says the LORD, Israel is my firstborn son, and I say to you, 'Let my son go that he may serve me.' If you refuse to let him go, behold, I will kill your firstborn son" (4:22, 23). The exodus from Egypt was the redemption of Israel, God's firstborn son (cf. Hosea 11:1).

To help his people remember their redemption, God gave them a special tradition. It began with the recognition that every son belongs to God: "The LORD said to Moses, 'Consecrate to me all the firstborn. Whatever is the first to open the womb among the people of Israel, both of man and of beast, is mine'" (13:1, 2; cf. 34:19, 20). God was claiming his right to Israel's offspring, as he would do again in 22:29: "The firstborn of your sons you shall give to me." God commanded the Israelites to dedicate their sons to him. The reason was that they belonged to him in the first place.

God's command specifically concerned Israel's *firstborn* sons. This obviously bears some connection to the tenth plague, in which God struck down the firstborn of Egypt. In case there is any doubt, this connection is made explicit in verse 15. In order to explain redemption, fathers were supposed to give their sons a history lesson: "When Pharaoh stubbornly refused to let us go, the LORD killed all the firstborn in the land of Egypt, both the firstborn of man and the firstborn of animals." It was not just Israel's firstborn that belonged to the Lord, but also the firstborn of Egypt, who were claimed by the angel of death.

Firstborn sons were important in the ancient world, as they are in many cultures today, because they "signified the center and future of the family."[2] The eldest son had special responsibilities and privileges, including the right of inheritance. But God was not showing favoritism. The point of consecrating the firstborn was really to show that the whole family belonged to God. The firstborn represented *all* the offspring, including the girls as well as the rest of the boys. The firstborn stood for the family as a part representing the whole—the way, for example, that a captain represents his team at the beginning of a football game or an executive represents his corporation at the bargaining table. The same principle applied when the Israelites brought their firstfruits to the Feast of Harvest (23:16, 19). They offered their first and their best to show that the whole harvest belonged to God. In the same way, the firstborn was the firstfruits of the family. To consecrate him was to consecrate everyone else who came from his mother's womb.

This helps explain why God was so angry with the Egyptians. Pharaoh had tried to kill Israel's sons by drowning them in the Nile (1:15, 16). Not only was this a vicious attempt at genocide, but it was also a rejection of God's paternal rights. Pharaoh was trying to take over God's prerogative. In the end he was punished with the death of his own firstborn son, just as God had warned him (4:23b). By afflicting the Egyptians with death, God was not being vindictive or throwing some kind of temper tantrum. On the contrary, he was rightly and justly defending his right to be a father to his sons.

God claims this same right over all his sons and daughters. He is our Father by virtue of creation. As our maker, he deserves our worship and our obedience. Near the end of his life, Moses asked, "Is not he your father, who created you, who made you and established you?" (Deuteronomy 32:6b). The answer is, "Yes!" Our Father-God is our Creator. We are his children by creation, which gives him the right to receive all our praise. But we also belong to God by salvation, which was the point of the ritual for redemption. God not only made us, but he also saves us. This gives us all the more reason to give our whole lives to his service. God is our rightful Father both by creation and by redemption.

## The Son's Substitute

At the time of the exodus, the Israelites acknowledged God's rightful ownership by dedicating their firstborn sons. But God wanted them to remember their salvation forever. So he had them continue this practice even after they reached the Promised Land: "When the Lord brings you into the land of the Canaanites, as he swore to you and your fathers, and shall give it to you, you shall set apart to the Lord all that first opens the womb. All the firstborn of your animals that are males shall be the Lord's. Every firstborn of a donkey you shall redeem with a lamb, or if you will not redeem it you shall break its neck. Every firstborn of man among your sons you shall redeem" (13:11–13; cf. 34:20).

The Israelites were commanded to give their offspring to God. They were to "set apart"—literally, to "pass over"—their firstborn. But what did this mean? Specifically, how were they to give their firstborn to God? In the case of animals, this meant offering the firstborn as a sacrifice. The instructions for this are given in the book of Numbers: "But the firstborn of a cow, or the firstborn of a sheep, or the firstborn of a goat, you shall not redeem; they are holy. You shall sprinkle their blood on the altar and shall burn their fat as a food offering, with a pleasing aroma to the Lord" (Numbers 18:17).

One exception to this was the donkey. The Israelites were allowed to use donkeys as pack animals, but they were not permitted to eat them or to offer them as sacrifices. God considered them ceremonially unclean and therefore unacceptable to use for a holy sacrifice. However, the firstborn donkey still belonged to the Lord, so he had to be given over somehow. How was this to be done? One option was simply to break the donkey's neck, but the owner could also redeem the donkey by offering a lamb in its place. To redeem is to buy back through the payment of a price. In this case the cost of redemption was the sacrifice of a lamb offered as the donkey's substitute.

What about firstborn sons? Believe it or not, they fell into the same category as donkeys![3] No sooner had Moses given the instructions for donkeys than he went on to say, "Every firstborn of man among your sons you shall redeem" (13:13b). This comparison is worth reflecting on for a moment. Donkeys were unclean. This was not so much a matter of hygiene as of spiritual principle. God had divided the animals between clean and unclean in order to teach his people how to distinguish between the sacred and the secular, the holy and the unholy. By setting certain things apart as holy to the Lord, the Israelites learned that they too were set apart for God's service. But here in Exodus 13 God places his people in the same category as donkeys. This showed them that they were sinners in need of salvation. In a word, they needed to be *redeemed*. Otherwise they would perish, as the donkeys did if they were unredeemed.

No matter how unclean they were, the sons of Israel belonged to God, and therefore they needed to be handed over to him. How was this done? Not, of course, by child sacrifice. Many ancient cultures did practice human sacrifice—usually by passing their children into the fire (see, for example, 2 Kings 16:3)—but this was strictly forbidden in Israel (Deuteronomy 18:10). Instead some Israelites gave their children to God by dedicating them to work and worship at the temple. This was done by the Levites, who were required to consecrate their sons to the priesthood, but it was done by others as well. The best example is Hannah, who vowed that if God ever gave her a son, she would "give him to the LORD all the days of his life" (1 Samuel 1:11). After her son Samuel was born, she took him to the tabernacle and said, "For this child I prayed, and the LORD has granted me my petition that I made to him. Therefore I have lent him to the LORD. As long as he lives, he is lent to the LORD" (1 Samuel 1:27, 28a).

Dedicating a child to priestly service was one way to give him to the Lord. However, God commanded the Israelites to *redeem* their firstborn sons, and that required the payment of a price. Exodus does not specify what the price was. Perhaps God assumed that his people would make the same offering they made for donkeys—a sacrificial lamb. If so, then this was a further example of salvation by substitution. The son was redeemed by a replacement—one who died in his place as a substitute for the unacceptable. Once again, Exodus points us to the cross of Christ, "who gave himself for us to redeem us from all lawlessness" (Titus 2:14). To say that Jesus is our Redeemer is to say that he died in our place. But if he is not our Redeemer, then we will perish like the donkeys that were broken at the neck.

Later God gave the priests more specific instructions for the redemption of sons. He said, "Every devoted thing in Israel shall be yours. Everything that opens the womb of all flesh, whether man or beast, which they offer to the LORD, shall be yours. Nevertheless, the firstborn of man you shall redeem, and the firstborn of unclean animals you shall redeem. And their redemption price (at a month old you shall redeem them) you shall fix at five shekels in silver, according to the shekel of the sanctuary, which is twenty gerahs" (Numbers 18:14–16). So the price of redemption was set at five shekels of silver, to be paid at the temple.

This helps explain what Mary and Joseph were doing when they took their firstborn son to Jerusalem. His name was Jesus, and they "brought him up to Jerusalem to present him to the Lord (as it is written in the Law of the Lord, 'Every male who first opens the womb shall be called holy to the Lord')" (Luke 2:22b, 23). Mary and Joseph were devout Jews who obviously knew what the law required. They were familiar with Exodus 13:1, which is the verse quoted in Luke's Gospel. Jesus did not need to be redeemed, of course, but it *was* necessary for him to fulfill all righteousness, so his parents kept the rite of redemption. Furthermore, his whole life was dedicated to serving God the Father. Jesus said, "I have come down from heaven, not to do my own will but the will of him who sent me" (John 6:38). How proper it was, then, for his earthly parents to give him over to his heavenly Father at the time of his birth. From beginning to end, from the manger to the cross, and then on to the empty tomb and the right hand of God, Jesus was dedicated to serving God in the salvation of sinners.

## Listen, Children

The act of dedicating and redeeming a son must have made a powerful impression on the child's parents. Here they were, just beginning to raise a family, and one of the first things they did was to consecrate their offspring to God. If God had simply taken their firstborn he would have been well within his rights. Instead he provided a way of redemption. By means of a substitute—through the payment of a price—the son that they offered up was given back for God's service.

The ritual of redemption helped parents understand that their children really did not belong to them at all; they belonged to God. One way Christian parents learn this same lesson is by presenting their children for baptism (or, in some churches, for dedication). As they hand their offspring into the arms of the church, they acknowledge their complete dependence on God's grace for their children's salvation. When they receive them back, it is not because they own them, but because they have been entrusted with them for the glory of God.

The problem with some of us is that sometimes we want to remake our children in our own image. Whether we realize we are doing it or not, we try to get our children to fulfill our own unsatisfied desires. But children do not exist for our benefit. We are to give them over to God.

One man who understood this was Abraham (Genesis 22). Indeed, it is hard to think of the redemption of sons and not think of his example. God told Abraham to take his son—his only son, Isaac, whom he loved—and sacrifice him as a burnt offering. Abraham did as he was told, and it was not until he raised his knife to slay his son that God intervened by providing a substitute.

Strange to say, this passage did not trouble me very much when I was growing up. It made perfect sense to me. As a son, I trusted my father and wanted him to do what was right before God. If God told Abraham to bind his son and offer him as a sacrifice, then of course that is what Abraham ought to do.

Then I became a father. My wife gave birth to our firstborn child, a son. I would look at him and say, "What a beautiful boy. That's my son!" Whenever I thought about Isaac and the sacrifice, I found the whole episode deeply disturbing. I knew I could never do what Abraham did. Are you kidding? Even if God stood right in front of me and told me to do it, I'm not sure I would. My problem was in making a false assumption about my son. "*My* son"—that was the problem right there. I assumed that he really belonged to me, and not to God. Apparently Abraham had a better understanding of what it means to be a father. He knew that Isaac was for God's pleasure, not for his own, and therefore he was willing to offer him up on God's altar.

The way the rest of the Israelites learned this lesson was by consecrating their children to God at birth. By redeeming their sons, parents learned that children are meant for God and for his glory. Then they had the responsibility to explain this principle to their children. Moses gave them this catechism:

> And when in time to come your son asks you, "What does this mean?" you shall say to him, "By a strong hand the LORD brought us out of Egypt, from the house of slavery. For when Pharaoh stubbornly refused to let us go, the LORD killed all the firstborn in the land of Egypt, both the firstborn of man and the firstborn of animals. Therefore I sacrifice to the LORD all the males that first open the womb, but all the firstborn of my sons I redeem." It shall be as a mark on your hand or frontlets between your eyes, for by a strong hand the LORD brought us out of Egypt. (13:14–16)

One reason God gave his people so many ways to commemorate the exodus—Passover, the Feast of Unleavened Bread, the consecration of the firstborn—was so they would have plenty of opportunities to give their children the facts of salvation. The redemption of sons was part of their national testimony. It pointed back to Israel's great escape, when the Egyptians paid for Israel's redemption at the cost of their firstborn sons.

The rite of redemption was a sign to the son that he had been saved by grace. It showed him that someone else had paid the price for his sins. It also made clear that he did not belong to his parents, or even to himself, but to God.

This was part of the meaning of the exodus, in which, as William J. Dumbrell explains:

> God intervenes as father to demand the return of his son from a tyrant who has enslaved him. As such he is a redeemer. Under the social regime of the Old Testament the enslaved son or relative thus delivered came under the complete power of the redeemer. . . . The understanding of the nature of Israel's Exodus redemption and thus of her covenant state is thus highlighted by the application of the redeemer concept. Israel had once been bond slaves in the land of Egypt. Now by redemption she had passed into the service of one whose service (slavery) was perfect freedom.[4]

If a son understood this, it would help shape his entire life. "Let me get this straight," he would say. "When I was little, you dedicated me to God. And in order to do it you had to pay the price, just like you would for a donkey?" The son would learn from this that he had a purpose in life, that someone had paid the price for his sins, and that now he belonged to God.

Today many children spend their lives struggling to get free from their parents. They are determined not to be controlled by their mothers and fathers but to live the way they want to live. Often they assume, wrongly, that they should own and operate themselves. But we were not made for our own pleasure—or our parents' pleasure, for that matter. We were made for God's pleasure, and we will not find joy until we commit our lives to him.

When it comes to deciding how to live, knowing whom we are made for makes all the difference. As we make choices about what to look at, how to use our bodies, with whom to spend time, and everything else, our primary concern is not to please ourselves, or our parents, but to please the God who saved us for his glory.

## Christ, the Firstborn

What was true for the sons of Israel is true for believers in Jesus Christ. We have been redeemed. Amazingly, we have been redeemed by the very Son of God—the Firstborn of the Father. The Bible calls Jesus "the firstborn of all creation" (Colossians 1:15), "the firstborn of the dead" (Revelation 1:5). This does not mean that God the Son is not eternal, as if somehow the Father gave birth to him. What it does mean is that Jesus is God's Number One Son, the first of all his sons and daughters, and the first to be raised from the dead.

The amazing thing is that in order to redeem us, God offered up *his* firstborn Son—not to be redeemed but to be the Redeemer. "He . . . did not spare his own Son but gave him up for us all" (Romans 8:32). Therefore, we have been redeemed at the greatest price. Redemption always requires the payment of a ransom, but in this case we have been redeemed by the blood of God's very own Son: "You were ransomed from the futile ways inherited from your forefathers, not with perishable things such as silver or gold, but with the precious blood of Christ, like that of a lamb without blemish or spot" (1 Peter 1:18, 19). When the New Testament speaks of redemption in Christ, it invariably emphasizes the costliness of its price.

One implication of this high-priced redemption is that we no longer belong to ourselves. Now we belong to God. In Exodus redemption was closely connected to consecration. The point of being redeemed was to be set apart for the service of God. The same is true with redemption in Christ. "You are not your own," the Bible says; "you were bought with a price" (1 Corinthians 6:19b, 20a). A great price has been paid for our redemption. It has been paid by God himself, in the person of his Son, and now we belong to him forever. Everything we are and have belongs to him: our time, money, bodies, talents—everything.

Redemption is very costly. It was costly to God, and in a way it is costly for us as well because it demands everything we have. But it is also the source of all our security and the basis for all our hope. In its opening question the *Heidelberg Catechism* asks, "What is your only comfort, in life and death?" The answer is this:

> That I belong—body and soul, in life and in death—not to myself but to my faithful Savior, Jesus Christ, who at the cost of his own blood has fully paid for all my sins and has completely freed me from the dominion of the devil; that he protects me so well that without the will of my Father in heaven not a hair can fall from my head; indeed, that everything must fit his purpose for my salvation. Therefore, by his Holy Spirit, he also assures me of eternal life, and makes me wholeheartedly willing and ready from now on to live for him.[5]

The doctrine of redemption has one further implication. The Bible says that Jesus is "the firstborn among many brothers" (Romans 8:29). It also describes God's people as "the assembly of the firstborn" (Hebrews 12:23). This means that everyone who has been redeemed in Jesus Christ belongs to the family of God. The purpose of redemption is to make us all God's sons and daughters, the children of the heavenly Father. There is no higher privilege than to be a child of God through the redemption of sons.

In one of his audiotapes Garrison Keillor tells the story of a hard-luck family from Lake Wobegon, Minnesota. In the story a nice, young Swedish woman runs off with a Scotsman, a stranger by the name of Campbell. They have three children together, but eventually the man leaves the woman, and she has to go back home in disgrace. She and her three children live in an old broken-down trailer, dependent on the charity of family and the pity of friends.

Yet they always dream of a better life. Then one day they get a letter asking for information about their family heritage, their connection to the Campbells. Soon someone writes again to inform them that they are direct lineal descendants of the House of Stuart, the ancient and royal family of Scotland, and that therefore they are rightful heirs to the throne. The letter closes with these words to the firstborn son:

> Your Royal Highness,
>
> Discovering you and your family has been the happiest accomplishment of my life. And if God, in his infinite wisdom, should deny me the opportunity to meet you face to face on this earth, I should still count myself the luckiest of men for this chance—however small—to restore Scotland to her former greatness. Please know that you are in my thoughts and prayers every day, and that I will work with every ounce of my being to restore you from your sad exile to the lands, the goods and the reverence to which you, by the will of God are entitled.

It must be wonderful to belong to royalty. We should know because we too have received a message from a far place, assuring us that by virtue of our redemption in Christ, we belong to the royal house of God. Jesus has a plan to elevate us all to greatness. We are in his thoughts and prayers every day, and he is working with every ounce of his being to restore us from our sad exile to the glory to which we are entitled by the grace of God.

# 33

# Between the Desert and the Sea

## EXODUS 13:17—14:14

LIKE ANY EPIC ADVENTURE, Exodus introduces a cast of memorable characters: kings and princes, masters and slaves. We have met Pharaoh, the seething tyrant whose mood could change without warning. We have met Shiphrah and Puah, the crafty midwives who saved the sons of Israel from infanticide. We have met Jochebed, the mother who put her baby in a basket, as well as the princess who found him there. We have met Aaron, who had a way with words, and his brother Moses, that mountain man of a prophet.

But there is a character in this true story who is more compelling than all the rest of them combined. He is infinitely amazing and endlessly fascinating—someone altogether unique. His name is Yahweh, and he is the Lord God of Israel. He is the God who hears, listening to the cries of the oppressed. He is the God who speaks, revealing his word to his servants. He is the God who acts, judging his enemies with plagues and rescuing his friends from bondage. Thus while there is something to learn from everyone in Exodus, the one who ought to command our full attention is the God of our salvation.

### Divine Guidance

God is not merely a character in the grand drama of redemption; he is the author, producer, and director. Never was this more obvious than on the day Pharaoh finally decided to let God's people go. What happened that day revealed several great truths about God. First, it showed that *God always knows which way is best*: "When Pharaoh let the people go, God did not lead them by way of the land of the Philistines, although that was near. For God said, 'Lest the people change their minds when they see war and return to Egypt.' But God led the people around by the way of the wilderness toward the Red Sea. And the people of Israel went up out of the land of Egypt equipped for battle" (13:17, 18).

God's people were starting down the road to freedom. They were bound for the Promised Land. That being the case, one would expect them to head north along the *Via Maris*, "the way of the sea." That coastal highway was the obvious escape route. One ancient Egyptian papyrus (Anastasi V) describes how two runaway slaves were caught trying to escape in that very direction. It was the most direct route. In fact, if the Israelites had headed straight for Canaan, they would have arrived there in less than two weeks (rather than the forty years it eventually took them!).

That would have been the shortest way, but it was not the best way because it was not God's way. God knew that if the Israelites stayed near the sea, they would face fierce resistance. Northern Sinai was a militarized zone in those days. The Egyptian army maintained a strong military presence in the region, protected by a series of fortresses and a long, wide, deep canal.[1] There were also the Philistines to consider. And then even if the Israelites somehow managed to fight their way through, they would still have to face the Canaanites when they reached the Promised Land.

God knew that the Israelites were in no shape to fight. They were not prepared to face such strong opposition, either spiritually or militarily. They were not actually "equipped for battle" (13:18), as the English Standard Version has it. What the verse actually says is that they left Egypt "in formation." They may have been fully equipped, but they were not ready to wage war. In fact, they would have turned and run back to Pharaoh at the first sign of danger. This was confirmed the following year when they finally reached Canaan. As soon as they saw how strong their enemies were, they were completely demoralized. They said, "Let us choose a leader and go back to Egypt" (Numbers 14:4).

Knowing all this, God changed course and led the Israelites in the exact opposite direction. He took them south, away from Canaan, into the wilderness. It was not the most obvious way. It was not the shortest way. It was not the most direct way. But it was the best way because it was God's way. God knew what his people could handle, and he knew that they needed to take the long way home.

As the Israelites traveled that long and winding road, they often doubted whether God's way really was the best way. But God knew what he was doing, as he always does. Whatever God happens to be doing right now, do you believe that it is all for the best? It may not seem that way, but it is, because the Bible says that "for those who love God all things work together for good, for those who are called according to his purpose" (Romans 8:28). Even when we are tempted to doubt whether God knows what he is doing, we are called to believe that his way is the best way.

A second great truth is that *God is always faithful to help his people*. We have already seen that the Israelites did not leave Egypt empty-handed but carried off loads of fancy clothes and shiny jewels. They carried something else as well: "Moses took the bones of Joseph with him, for Joseph had made the sons of Israel solemnly swear, saying, 'God will surely visit you, and you shall carry up my bones with you from here'" (13:19).

It may seem rather strange to carry around the remains of the dead—in this case a mummy embalmed by the Egyptian masters. However, this was something that the Israelites had promised to do centuries earlier, when "Joseph said to his brothers, 'I am about to die, but God will visit you and bring you up out of this land to the land that he swore to Abraham, to Isaac, and to Jacob.' Then Joseph made the sons of Israel swear, saying, 'God will surely visit you, and you shall carry up my bones from here.' So Joseph died, being 110 years old. They embalmed him, and he was put in a coffin in Egypt" (Genesis 50:24–26).

Joseph believed that God was faithful. The Bible says, "By faith Joseph, at the end of his life, made mention of the exodus of the Israelites and gave directions concerning his bones" (Hebrews 11:22). He had been told that his descendants would become slaves in Egypt, but he also knew that God would rescue them. Joseph knew this because God had promised it to Abraham by covenant. When God finally brought Israel out of Egypt, Joseph wanted to go along for the ride, so he made his brothers swear that they would bury his bones in the Promised Land. The Israelites kept their promise, carrying Joseph's bones all the way through the wilderness, until finally they were laid to rest in the family burial plot at Shechem (Joshua 24:32). What that interment proved was that Joseph trusted in the right God, the God who kept his promise to rescue Israel. Anyone who needs any kind of help should trust in the God of Abraham, Joseph, and Moses, because he is always faithful to help his people.

A third great truth is that *God is always present to guide his people*. Not only does he know which way is best, but he also goes along to make sure his people get there. The way God led his people out of Egypt was miraculous: "And they moved on from Succoth and encamped at Etham, on the edge of the wilderness. And the Lord went before them by day in a pillar of cloud to lead them along the way, and by night in a pillar of fire to give them light, that they might travel by day and by night. The pillar of cloud by day and the pillar of fire by night did not depart from before the people" (13:20–22).

Some scholars make it their business to try and come up with alternate explanations for the Biblical miracles. Sometimes their theories have a certain plausibility. However, it is hard to imagine what natural phenomenon could possibly explain God's fiery pillar of cloud. Was it a cloud of dust kicked up by the Israelites? A whirlwind? A smoke signal? Bad weather? A volcano? These are only some of the theories that have been put forward. According to one scholar,

> In Sinai when heavy weather is impending there is a most remarkable cloud formation—namely, a huge column of cumulus, black in the center with hard white edges. This column, which begins at the sky-line and is most impressive, extends to the zenith, constantly emitting lightning, and at night is an intermittent blaze of fire. This cloud . . . to the superstitious Israelites no doubt appeared to be a sign from the Almighty to show them the way. It also proved their salvation, as it heralded the heavy weather that accounted for the engulfing of the host.[2]

The trouble with these speculations is that the pillar traveled ahead of the Israelites, remaining with them day and night *for forty years*! The only sensible way to account for this is to accept the fiery, cloudy pillar as a genuine divine miracle. By day it was a bright column of protecting cloud; by night its radiance appeared like fire. This amazing cloud served as Israel's guidance system. It "went before them . . . to lead them along the way" (13:21). Wherever it moved, the people moved.

What the cloud represented was the very presence of God, who was in the cloud and fire to light the way. The Scripture states that "the LORD went before them by day in a pillar of cloud" (13:21). This showed that he was with his people all the time, day and night. The pillar was a visible manifestation of his personal presence. Theologians call this a theophany—a God-appearance. When God shows up this way, he appears in a fiery cloud of glory, sometimes called the *shekinah* (16:10; 40:34). It is an outward display of God's inward glory.

Sometimes we wish that God would give us the same kind of guidance today. If only a bright cloud would lead us directly to the school we should attend, the job we should take, or the person we should marry! Yet the truth is that God gives us all the divine guidance we need, and in a much better form. He has given us the fire of his Spirit, and now we have his glorious presence with us all day and all night. It is as if the column of cloud and the pillar of fire have come right inside us! Jesus said that the Holy Spirit "dwells with you and will be in you" (John 14:17). The Holy Spirit is the third person of the Trinity. Since he is divine, the Bible declares that "the Spirit of glory and of God rests upon you" (1 Peter 4:14). Now part of the Spirit's glorious work is to give us direction for life. Jesus promised that the Spirit would guide us into all truth (John 16:13a), and now by the power of his holy presence, God is always with us to guide us.

## Glory to God Alone

The God who brought Israel out of Egypt is a great God. He always knows which way is best. He is always faithful to help us. He is always with us to guide us. More than that, he is such a great God that he is able to work out everything for his own glory. This is the reason why God made the world in the beginning. It is also why he will save us in the end. He is doing it so that in both creation and salvation he will get all the glory.

If that is true—that God's grand purpose in everything he does is to display his glory—then it must be true of the exodus, and so it is. The theme of Exodus is "saved for God's glory." When God delivered Israel from Egypt, he did it in a way that guaranteed that he would receive all the credit: "Then the Lord said to Moses, 'Tell the people of Israel to turn back and encamp in front of Pi-hahiroth, between Migdol and the sea, in front of Baal-zephon; you shall encamp facing it, by the sea. For Pharaoh will say of the people of Israel, "They are wandering in the land; the wilderness has shut them in." And I will harden Pharaoh's heart, and he will pursue them, and I will get glory over Pharaoh and all his host, and the Egyptians shall know that I am the Lord.' And they did so" (14:1–4).

From the standpoint of military strategy, the detour God told the Israelites to take was sheer lunacy. They were already well on their way to freedom when God ordered them to turn around, go back, and camp between the desert and the sea. The precise location is uncertain. The sea, of course, is the Red Sea, although some scholars have called this into question (more on this in the next chapter). Migdol means "tower," so it was probably one of Egypt's forts. Most likely Pi-hahiroth was an opening in Egypt's canal system,[3] while Baal Zephon was named after one of the Canaanite gods. Beyond that, it is hard to be certain. Nevertheless, even though these places have long since been forgotten, it is obvious that they refer to real places located on a real map, if only we had an atlas of ancient Egypt.

Wherever they were, the Israelites were completely vulnerable. They were out on Egypt's frontier, surrounded by desert, with their backs to the sea. Why on earth would God put his people in this kind of position? Any military strategist would have recognized immediately that they were trapped, which is exactly what God wanted Pharaoh to think. The whole thing was a ruse. God was tricking the Egyptians into thinking that the Israelites had no idea what they were doing. This would entice them to press what seemed to be their strategic advantage. But once Pharaoh attacked, his army would be destroyed. Then it would be obvious to everyone that God had planned the whole thing. By putting his people between the desert and the sea, God would show both the Israelites and the Egyptians that he was Lord and that the glory of the victory belonged to him alone.

God wanted to gain this glory at Pharaoh's expense. He said, "I will get glory over Pharaoh and all his host" (14:4b). If this strategy seems familiar, it is because God used it again when he sent his Son to the cross. To Satan it must have seemed like Jesus had no idea what he was doing. He was God the Son; yet he allowed himself to be handed over to sinful men, who stripped him, beat him, and crucified him. On the cross he was so vulnerable that Satan thought he had the strategic advantage, and he pressed it to the death. But of course this was his fatal mistake, because the whole thing was a ruse. The cross was not a defeat for Jesus but a victory. By making atonement he was able to gain eternal victory over sin, death, and Satan. Thus the Bible says that "he disarmed the rulers and authorities and put them to open shame, by triumphing over them in him" (Colossians 2:15).

In order for God's brilliant strategy to work, Pharaoh had to pick up the chase. This takes us back to the palace, where Pharaoh was having another one of his infamous temper tantrums: "When the king of Egypt was told that the people had fled, the mind of Pharaoh and his servants was changed toward the people, and they said, 'What is this we have done, that we have let Israel go from serving us?'" (14:5). As soon as the Israelites left, Pharaoh realized that he had just lost most of his labor force. Who would complete his monuments? How would he ever complete his massive building projects? His cabinet officials were even more upset. Without slaves to do all their work for them, they would have to fend for themselves.

As they discussed all this, the Egyptians decided that they didn't want to let the Israelites go after all. There was not a moment to lose!

> So he [Pharaoh] made ready his chariot and took his army with him, and took six hundred chosen chariots and all the other chariots of Egypt with officers over all of them. And the LORD hardened the heart of Pharaoh king of Egypt, and he pursued the people of Israel while the people of Israel were going out defiantly. The Egyptians pursued them, all Pharaoh's horses and chariots and his horsemen and his army, and overtook them encamped at the sea, by Pi-hahiroth, in front of Baal-zephon. (14:6–9)[4]

Pharaoh's change of heart shows that he never truly repented of his sin. He had been given every opportunity to set his captives free. Time after time Moses had told him to let God's people go. First he refused. Then as the plagues started to come, he began to negotiate. He bargained and bickered. He asked for prayer, even begging Moses to give him God's blessing. But he never let go. When, finally, he said that he would do what God wanted, he immediately changed his mind and went right back to his sins.

Pharaoh's rebellion is a warning to anyone who never quite gets around to doing what God requires. By way of example, consider the fate of four fishermen whose boat suddenly overturned and spilled them into the sea. The men were out on the Delaware Bay, miles from shore, fighting for their lives in high waves. Only three of the men survived. Afterward one of them told a reporter about all the promises he made while he was struggling to stay afloat. "Let's just say that I'm going to church from now on," he said. Hopefully the man will keep his word. However, his was the same kind of promise that Pharaoh made, and more often than not, it is the kind of promise that gets broken. What God wants is a total commitment to him, right here, right now, and for the rest of our lives.

## Under Satanic Attack

Satan will not give us up without a fight, as the Israelites quickly discovered: "When Pharaoh drew near, the people of Israel lifted up their eyes, and behold, the Egyptians were marching after them" (14:10a). What the Israelites saw was the world's most powerful army, supported by the world's most advanced military technology—the chariot. In order to capture his runaway slaves Pharaoh quickly mobilized his forces and deployed his best battalion. They were in hot pursuit, and riding on horseback, they soon came within easy striking distance.

The Israelites were in a dangerous and desperate situation, trapped between Pharaoh and the deep blue sea. But instead of looking to God in all his grace and glory, they looked at their enemies and were afraid. What makes this so disappointing is that they had witnessed God's wonders, the plagues—all ten of them. Not to mention the fact that they had escaped from Egypt only the night before. The Scripture says that they marched out "defiantly" (14:8), meaning confidently. Yet at the first sign of danger, they panicked.

This is another place where Israel's exodus is a picture of our own deliverance from captivity to sin. The Bible says that "these things"—meaning the events in Exodus—"took place as examples" (1 Corinthians 10:6). This particular example shows what happens whenever God rescues his people from bondage: Satan tries to grab us before we can get away. No sooner do we make a commitment to follow Christ than we face doubt and discouragement. Satan is riding furiously after us, tempting us to give up and turn back. Jesus taught about this in the parable of the sower. He said that when some people hear the message of salvation, "the evil one comes and snatches away what has been sown" in their hearts (Matthew 13:19). Others fall away when they suffer persecution or when they are worried by the troubles of life.

It is a spiritual battle, and Satan never surrenders without a fight. This is not surprising because we were once his valuable servants, and he would like nothing better than to have us back under his employ. Like a slaveholder coming north to hunt for a runaway slave, Satan wants to drag us back to the plantation of sin. But there is no "fugitive slave law" in the kingdom of God. Once God has set us free, Satan has no right to take us back. So what should we do when he is chasing after us? Not what the Israelites did: "They feared greatly . . . [and] cried out to the LORD" (14:10b). True, the Israelites did cry out to God, and elsewhere the Scripture seems to view this in a positive light (see Joshua 24:6, 7; Nehemiah 9:9). However, this was not a pure cry of faith; it was also a fearful cry of desperation. The Israelites did not really believe that God would save them but fully expected to be destroyed.

The proof is that rather than waiting for God's answer, the Israelites immediately turned on his prophet. People often do this when they are under spiritual attack: they blame their spiritual leaders. In this case the Israelites said to Moses,

"Is it because there are no graves in Egypt that you have taken us away to die in the wilderness?" (14:11a). Thus began a long tradition of Jewish comedy! What gave their sarcasm its bite, of course, was that there were graves all over Egypt—like the Great Pyramids, to give just one example. They also said to Moses, "What have you done to us in bringing us out of Egypt? Is not this what we said to you in Egypt: 'Leave us alone that we may serve the Egyptians'?" (14:11b, 12a). In other words, "We told you so!" Maybe the Israelites did tell Moses to leave them alone, but if they did, the Bible does not mention it. Probably they were just sulking, the way people usually do when things don't go their way.

What was most alarming of all was their willingness to go right back into bondage. They told Moses, "It would have been better for us to serve the Egyptians than to die in the wilderness" (14:12b). The whole point of the exodus was for them to serve God, but here they were, wanting to go right back and serve Pharaoh. This was more than a loss of nerve—it was a lack of faith. By pledging their allegiance to Pharaoh they were denying the power of God. The psalmist put it bluntly when he said, "they . . . rebelled by the sea, at the Red Sea" (Psalm 106:7b).

We are often tempted to do the same thing. God wants to bring us all the way out of our sins. Our problem is that we only come out partway. We decide to follow Christ, but as soon as we start having problems we get scared and go right back to our old ways of coping: anger, addiction, depression, distraction. No matter how much we used to hate it, there was security in the way we used to live; so we return to the same old harmful friendships, the same old sinful attitudes, and the same old nasty habits.

## Making Our Stand

There is a way of escape. Consider that the Israelites were never in any real danger. Even though Pharaoh was coming after them, they were right where God wanted them, and he would rescue them. What was at stake was not simply their lives but God's glory, which he would protect at any cost. So what the Israelites should have done was to remember what kind of God they served—a God who always knows the best way, who is always faithful to help his people, and who always stays with them to guide them. More than that, they should have remembered his purpose—to work out everything according to his glorious plan.

Moses did remember all this, and thus he knew exactly what to do when he was caught between the desert and the sea: "And Moses said to the people, 'Fear not, stand firm, and see the salvation of the LORD, which he will work for you today. For the Egyptians whom you see today, you shall never see again. The LORD will fight for you, and you have only to be silent'" (14:13, 14). With these words Moses issued three commands: "Fear not, stand firm . . . be silent." "Fear not" is what grammarians call a *negative imperative*. It is "the strongest possible form of expressing negation in the Hebrew language."[5] Therefore, when Moses told the Israelites not to be afraid he was not comforting them—he was rebuking them.[6] He was telling them that they had no right to be afraid because they had no reason to fear. All they needed to do was stand their ground, quietly waiting to see what God would do.

In many military situations this would not be good advice, but what made it work in this case was that the Israelites had someone to do all the fighting for them. The Lord God was with them to save them. He was their warrior, and so all they needed to do was stand and see their salvation. In this battle they were not soldiers—they were only spectators.

The same principle holds true for our salvation from sin. Satan is pursuing us, but instead of running away, all we need to do is stand and see the salvation of our God. Christianity is not about something that we can do to become better people; it is about what Christ has done through the cross and the empty tomb. Jesus Christ has accomplished everything necessary for our salvation. He is the one who has atoned for sin, who has turned aside God's wrath, who offers perfect righteousness as the gift of faith, and who has gained entrance into resurrection life. When people ask, "What do we have to do to be saved?" the answer is that we don't have to do anything. Jesus has done it! We just need to look to him for our salvation.

Once we put our faith in Jesus, we need to stand our ground. We are in a spiritual battle, and in that battle the Bible gives us the same marching orders that Moses gave to Israel. "Therefore take up the whole armor of God, that you may be able to withstand in the evil day, and having done all, to stand firm" (Ephesians 6:13). In our struggle with Satan, we need to take our stand with Jesus, waiting for God to deliver us. Charles Spurgeon wrote:

> I dare say you will think it a very easy thing to *stand still*, but it is one of the postures which a Christian soldier learns not without years of teaching. I find that marching and quick marching are much easier to God's warriors than standing still. It is, perhaps, the first thing we learn in the drill of human armies, but it is one of the most difficult to learn under the Captain of our salvation. The apostle seems to hint at this difficulty when he says, "Stand fast, and having done all, still stand." To stand at ease in the midst of tribulation, shows a veteran spirit, long experience, and much grace.[7]

It is hard to be still and wait for God. Our temptation is to run away, cry out in fear, or try to fix things on our own. Instead God orders us to stand our ground. He is our defender, our champion. When we are caught between the desert and the sea, all we need to do is be still and look for his salvation.

# 34

# The Great Escape

EXODUS 14:15–31

ALL GOOD STORIES HAVE A CLIMAX, but the book of Exodus is such a great adventure that it has not one, but three. The first climax is Israel crossing the Red Sea in chapter 14, the second is God giving his Law at Mount Sinai in chapters 19 and following, and the third is the glory of the Lord filling the tabernacle at the end of chapter 40.

The first of these climactic moments may be the most famous event in the Old Testament. Anyone who knows anything about the Bible knows that the children of Israel passed through the sea. This miracle has been acclaimed by composers like George Frideric Handel, actors like Charlton Heston, preachers like Martin Luther King Jr., writers like Leon Uris, cartoonists like Charles Schulz, animators like Walt Disney, and even singers like Bob Marley: "Send us another brother Moses! From across the Red Sea . . . come to break down 'pression, rule inequality, wipe away transgression, set the captives free."

Given all this attention, it is not surprising that over the centuries a certain amount of misinformation has crept in about what exactly happened when Moses led God's people through the sea. This makes it all the more important to get the story straight. One way to do this is to approach Exodus 14 like a journalist, asking who, when, where, how, and especially why.

## Answers to Questions

*Who?* is an easy question. The people who crossed the sea were the Israelites. They were the people whom God had chosen to save, led by the prophet Moses. The people who were lost at sea were the Egyptians. For hundreds of years Pharaoh had kept God's people enslaved, but the miracle by the sea brought his bitter tyranny to an end. This was the final showdown in the battle between Israel's Lord and the gods of Egypt.

The *what?* is also well known: The sea was parted, and the Israelites walked through on dry land. But when the Egyptians tried to follow, riding on their chariots, the sea collapsed, and the army drowned. It was such a crushing defeat that Egypt did not threaten Israel again until sometime after the death of Solomon. Yet the Bible describes it all very matter-of-factly:

> The waters were divided. And the people of Israel went into the midst of the sea on dry ground, the waters being a wall to them on their right hand and on their left. The Egyptians pursued and went in after them into the midst of the sea, all Pharaoh's horses, his chariots, and his horsemen . . . the sea returned to its normal course when the morning appeared. And as the Egyptians fled into it, the LORD threw the Egyptians into the midst of the sea. The waters returned and covered the chariots and the horsemen; of all the host of Pharaoh that had followed them into the sea, not one of them remained. But the people of Israel walked on dry ground through the sea, the waters being a wall to them on their right hand and on their left. (14:21b–23, 27–29)

*When* did all this happen? Right at the time when everything seemed to be lost, when the Israelites were trapped between Pharaoh and the deep blue sea. God had told his people to reverse directions and make their camp by the sea. It was a terrible position, at least from the standpoint of military strategy, but it was all part of God's master plan for destroying Pharaoh. Even so, the Israelites understandably were terrified when they looked up and saw the Egyptians rushing after them in headlong pursuit. In desperation they cried out to God and his prophet. They were caught between an unconquerable army and an impassable sea.

It was just then that God saved his people, right when it was obvious there was nothing they could do to save themselves. First Moses told the Israelites not to be afraid, and rather than encouraging them to stand and fight, he told them to stand and wait to see what God would do. Once the prophet had delivered this message, "The LORD said to Moses, 'Why do you cry to me? Tell the people of Israel to go forward'" (14:15). This verse is puzzling because in it God seems to give his prophet a reprimand (the word "you" occurs in the singular, thereby referring to Moses). Yet Moses was hardly the one who needed to be rebuked! The Israelites were the ones who cried out in fear, not Moses, who for his part believed that God would deliver his people. So why did God rebuke him?

Probably the best way to understand this is to recognize that as Israel's prophet, Moses represented the people before God. He was their mediator in the covenant. The rebuke that God gave him, therefore, was really meant for all Israel. The hour of their salvation had come. This was no time for crying and complaining; it was time to move on. When Charles Spurgeon preached on this verse, he said, "Far be it from me ever to say a word in disparagement of the holy, happy, heavenly exercise of prayer. But, beloved, there are times when prayer is not enough—when prayer itself is out of season. . . . When we have prayed over a matter to a certain degree, it then becomes sinful to tarry any longer; our plain duty is to carry our desires into action, and having asked God's guidance, and having received divine power from on high, to go at once to our duty without any longer deliberation or delay."[1]

It was time for God's people to get up and get going. However, humanly speaking, what God told them to do was impossible. There was no way for them to move forward. It was the darkest hour before dawn, and they were up against the sea. But of course with God all things are possible (Matthew 19:26), even things that are impossible for mere human beings. This is especially the case in salvation. The constant message of the Bible is that we cannot save ourselves. Only God can save us.

When did the Israelites cross the sea? At a time when only God could open up the way to salvation. Today every sinner is in the same situation. There is nothing we can do to save ourselves. Until God's Spirit changes our minds and hearts, we will never come to Christ. Nevertheless, God commands us to repent and believe. If that seems impossible, the thing to do is to cry out to God for mercy, and he will save us.

## The Re(e)d Sea?

Before explaining how the Israelites crossed the sea, we need to ask *where?* Traditionally, both Jews and Christians have maintained that the Israelites crossed an arm of the Red Sea—the large body of water that separates Africa from the Middle East.

Recently, however, this identification has been challenged. The Bible calls the sea *yam suph*. The Hebrew word *suph*, which means "reeds," sometimes is used to refer to papyrus (e.g., 2:3). This fact was recognized by Luther and Calvin, as well as by many of the ancient Jewish commentators. Thus *yam suph* would seem to mean something like "the Sea of Reeds" or "the Papyrus Sea." The problem is that papyrus does not grow in the deep waters of the Red Sea; it only grows in the marshlands of northern Egypt. Thus many scholars have concluded that "Red Sea" is a mistranslation (first introduced by the Greek Septuagint in the third century BC) and that the Israelites actually crossed Lake Menzaleh, Lake Timsah, the Bitter Lakes, or some other large body of water in the eastern delta.

There are several problems with this view. One is that there are other places in the Bible where *yam suph* clearly *does* refer to the Red Sea.[2] This would explain why the Septuagint and some modern versions translate the phrase as "Red Sea." Bernard Batto has argued that *yam suph* does not mean "sea of reeds" at all, but "sea of the end." Thus it naturally refers to the Red Sea, which forms the southern border at the end of Egypt. The traditional view is that on their way to

Sinai and the south, the Israelites crossed the Gulf of Suez, the northwest arm of the Red Sea.

There is still another possibility, however, that perhaps best accounts for all the evidence. Recently James Hoffmeier has shown that in former days, when its water level was higher, the Red Sea used to extend farther north.[3] Indeed, there seem to have been times when the Gulf of Suez was connected to the Bitter Lakes in the north. If this is true, that would explain why the Bible identifies *yam suph* with the Red Sea. At the time of Moses, the Red Sea *was* the "Reed Sea" because there were in it places where papyrus grew. Perhaps, then, the Israelites crossed the Red Sea after all, only farther north than people used to think.

## The Hand of God

We may never know precisely where the exodus took place, but we do know *how* because the Bible tells us. To begin with, there was a mighty wind. A strong east wind blew all night long, and by morning the sea had turned to dry land (14:21).

Going back at least as far as Eusebius in the fourth century, scholars have tried to explain exactly how this happened. Late in the seventeenth century a scholar named Clericus wrote a lengthy treatise on the wind of Exodus.[4] More recent explanations have been more scientific. Umberto Cassuto claims that in order to understand the biblical account,

> we must bear in mind the natural conditions prevailing in the area. The following phenomenon is a common occurrence in the region of the Suez: at high tide, the waters of the Red Sea penetrate the sand, from under the surface, and suddenly the water begins to ooze up out of the sand, which had hitherto been dry; within a short time the sand turns to mud, but the water continues to rise and ultimately a deep layer of water is formed above the sand, the whole area becoming flooded. This was once experienced by Napoleon I, when he toured that neighbourhood; when he set out he passed, without difficulty, over dry land, but on his return he found the place covered with water, and his position became dangerous. . . . The reverse sometimes happens when the Red Sea is at low tide; the water covering the sand gradually diminishes and finally disappears, and in the part that, several hours earlier, was covered by water suddenly dry land appears.[5]

It is not hard to see how such phenomena might account for the exodus. First the wind and the tide emptied part of the sea, and the Israelites were able to make their escape. By the time the Egyptians tried to follow, however, the sea had turned to mud. Here is another, more sophisticated explanation:

> Oceanographer Dr. Doron Nof of Florida State University in Tallahassee and atmospheric scientist Dr. Nathan Paldor of the Hebrew University in Jerusalem proposed that at the shallow northernmost extremity of the Gulf of Suez winds of 40 knots (74 kilometers per hour) blowing steadily for ten

> to twelve hours might have pushed water a mile or two to the south, causing a 10-foot drop in sea level and exposing a large swath of sea floor over which the Israelites passed and on which Pharaoh's troops were drowned. "Our physical and mathematical analysis shows that both values for the drop in sea surface height and withdrawal distance for the water are more than sufficient to cause the calamity that befell the Egyptians."[6]

This kind of natural explanation is interesting, as far as it goes, but it does not go far enough. For one thing, the Bible states that "the people of Israel walked on dry ground through the sea, the waters being a wall to them on their right hand and on their left" (14:29; cf. Psalm 78:13). Most natural explanations fail to account for the two walls (the architectural term used here ordinarily is used for the walls of a city). For another thing, the Bible clearly states that the wind started when Moses took his staff and stretched his arm out over the sea. The prophet stretched it out once, and the seas parted; he stretched it out again, and the flood returned. In the words of the old spiritual, "Moses stood on the Red Sea shore, / Smotin' on the water with a two-by-four."

Moses' actions are mentioned four times. Twice God told him what to do, and twice he did it. God said, "Lift up your staff, and stretch out your hand over the sea and divide it, that the people of Israel may go through the sea on dry ground. . . . Then Moses stretched out his hand over the sea" (14:16, 21a). And again: "Then the Lord said to Moses, 'Stretch out your hand over the sea, that the water may come back upon the Egyptians, upon their chariots, and upon their horsemen.' So Moses stretched out his hand over the sea, and the sea returned to its normal course when the morning appeared" (14:26, 27). Israel crossed the Red Sea by the power of Moses and his mighty staff.

Yet even this explanation does not go far enough. There was wind, yes, and the strong arm of the prophet, but what brought Israel out of Egypt was the power of God. The whole chapter is full of divine activity. God was the one who told Moses to raise his staff, who hardened the hearts of the Egyptians so that they chased after the Israelites, and who protected the Israelites all night when they were between the desert and the sea. The Scripture describes how "the angel of God who was going before the host of Israel moved and went behind them, and the pillar of cloud moved from before them and stood behind them, coming between the host of Egypt and the host of Israel. And there was the cloud and the darkness. And it lit up the night without one coming near the other all night" (14:19, 20).

As we have seen, the pillar of cloud and fire was a theophany—a visible appearance of the invisible God. Here the cloud is identified as "the angel of God" (14:19), which means "the messenger of God." Somewhere the great Puritan theologian John Owen explained that the person who went behind the Israelites to protect them was "the Angel of the covenant, the great Angel of the presence of God, in whom was the name and nature of God." However, back in 13:21 the cloud was simply identified as "the LORD." And 14:24 says that "the LORD in the pillar of fire and of cloud looked down." To summarize, God himself was in the glorious cloud, but the cloud was also his messenger. Moses had experienced something similar back at the burning bush. What appeared to him there was "the angel of the LORD" (3:2), but the one who spoke to him was God himself. To make sense of all this, some Christians conclude that the person both in the bush and in the cloud was the pre-incarnate Son of God. God the Son is very God of very God; he is also God's messenger of salvation. So perhaps the glorious cloud represented the second person of the Trinity.

Whether this is right or not, God was certainly present with his people to protect them. When the prophet Isaiah looked back on this event, he wrote, "The angel of his presence saved them" (Isaiah 63:9). The cloud was their guard as well as their guide. It moved behind the Israelites to shield them from their enemies. The Egyptians were chomping at the bit, ready to attack, but all night long God kept them in the dark. Meanwhile, on the other side of this divine blockade, the children of God were in the light. This is what distinguishes God's people from the world: we are in the light, and God is always right where we need him to keep us safe.

God was doing something else that night too. He was parting the waters, virtually reversing creation by turning the sea back into dry land. Then, once his enemies had fallen into his trap and were stuck in the quagmire, God made the sea return and swept the Egyptians to their watery grave. He planned and executed the entire exodus. Isaiah asked:

> Was it not you who dried up the sea,
> the waters of the great deep,
> who made the depths of the sea a way
> for the redeemed to pass over? (Isaiah 51:10)

God was so actively involved that even the Egyptians knew he was there, fighting against them: "And in the morning watch the LORD in the pillar of fire and of cloud looked down on the Egyptian forces and threw the Egyptian forces into a panic, clogging their chariot wheels so that they drove heavily. And the Egyptians said, 'Let us flee from before Israel, for the LORD fights for them against the Egyptians'" (14:24, 25). By this point the wheels really were starting to come off! First God threw the Egyptians into a panic, possibly by sending a violent storm from his cloud (Psalm 77:17, 18). Then Pharaoh's chariots got bogged down in the mud, and the more they struggled, the more they got stuck. By the time they said, "Let's get out of here!" it was too late. And the Egyptians knew exactly who had derailed them. God had promised that one day they would know who was Lord. And that promise came true because when they finally went down to destruction, they went with God's name on their lips.

The Bible sums all this up by saying, "Thus the LORD saved Israel that day from the hand of the Egyptians, and Israel saw the Egyptians dead on the seashore" (14:30). How did the Israelites escape from Egypt? It was not just the wind and the tide. It was not simply poor strategy on the part of Pharaoh or an unexpected failure of military technology. It was not merely a sudden storm over the water. It was the power of God! He was the one who brought Israel out of Egypt.

Of course, God used the wind to drive back the sea. This simply shows that he is able to use creation in the service of redemption.[7] He also employed a human instrument. By faith Moses was able to perform the prophetic signs that accompanied salvation. The Scripture brings these three elements together—the natural, the human, and the divine—when it says, "Moses stretched out his hand over the sea, and the LORD drove the sea back by a strong east wind all night and made the sea dry land" (14:21). This is one of the mysteries of God's sovereignty. He is able to use the world that he has made, and even sinful human beings, to accomplish his saving purpose. Umberto Cassuto writes, "The miracle consisted in the fact that at the very moment when it was necessary, in just the manner conducive to the achievement of the desired goal, and on a scale that was abnormal, there occurred, in accordance with the Lord's will, phenomena that brought about Israel's salvation."[8]

No matter how one looks at it, crossing the Red Sea was a miracle. Donald Bridge tells the story of a liberal minister preaching in an old, Bible-believing, African-American church. At a certain point in his sermon the minister referred to the crossing of the Red Sea. "Praise the Lord," someone shouted. "Takin' all them children through the deep waters. What a mighty miracle!" However, the minister did not happen to believe in miracles. So he said, rather condescendingly, "It was not a miracle. They were in marsh-land, the tide was ebbing, and the children of Israel picked their way across in six inches of water." "Praise the Lord!" the man shouted again. "Drownin' all them Egyptians in six inches of water. What a mighty miracle!"[9]

## For His Own Glory

How did the Israelites make their great escape? By the hand of God, who saved them from the hands of their enemies (14:30, 31). The exodus had to come by God's hand in order for it to fulfill its divine intention. This brings us to the question of purpose: *Why* did God part the waters of the Red Sea? The answer is very simple—an answer that explains the whole exodus. Indeed, it is the answer that explains why God does everything that he has ever done, is doing right now, or will ever do. The answer is the glory of God. He did it all for his own glory.

God announced his intention to glorify himself before the Israelites even reached the sea. He said to Moses, "I will get glory over Pharaoh and all his host" (14:4). God accomplished this glorious purpose in two ways. One was by judging the Egyptians for their sins. He said, "I will harden the hearts of the Egyptians so that they shall go in after them, and I will get glory over Pharaoh and all his host, his chariots, and his horsemen. And the Egyptians shall know that I am the LORD, when I have gotten glory over Pharaoh, his chariots, and his horsemen" (14:17, 18).

This was all part of God's strategy. He lured the Egyptians into chasing Moses across the desert, and when they finally caught up, it was right at the spot where God planned for them to meet their watery doom. There were no survivors (cf. Psalm 106:11). A rushing wave swept over them, and the next thing anyone knew, their bodies were washing up on the seashore.[10] And God was glorified! Some may think it was harsh for God to drown an entire army, but it was right and just. Pharaoh and his soldiers were cruel men, bent on destroying God's people. Was it not right for God to punish evil men for killing innocent children? It was especially appropriate for them to die by drowning because they had once tried to drown the children of Israel in the Nile. What happened to them at the Red Sea was divine retribution. These men deserved to be punished for their sins. And God is glorified when he judges people for their sins because this displays his divine attribute of justice.

God was also judging Egypt's gods, and this too was for his glory. It is ironic that the Egyptians were defeated at daybreak because that is when their sun god was supposedly rising in the east. But Ra could not save them. Nor could Pharaoh save them, even though he too was revered as a god. According to one ancient Egyptian inscription, "He whom the king has loved will be a revered one, but there is no tomb for a rebel against his majesty, and his corpse is cast into the water."[11] This inscription was a threat to drown Pharaoh's enemies, but in the end the Egyptians were the ones who were lost at sea![12] And God did this for the praise of his justice.

Something similar will happen at the final judgment. Evil men will be destroyed, and God will be glorified. Revelation 18 tells how the city of Satan will be cast into the sea (Revelation 18:21a). This will be for the glory of God, because immediately afterward, the saints will sing a hallelujah chorus: "Hallelujah! Salvation and glory and power belong to our God, for his judgments are true and just" (Revelation 19:1b, 2a). God deserves our praise because he will do justice in the end.

God was doing something more than judging the Egyptians, however; he was also saving the Israelites, and this too was for his glory. What could be more glorious than God saving his people by bringing them through the sea? This is one of the most amazing things God has ever done. People are still talking about it. As Nehemiah said in one of his prayers, "You made a name for yourself, as it is to this day" (Nehemiah 9:10b; cf. Isaiah 63:12).

The crossing of the Red Sea brought glory to God by convincing the Israelites to believe in God, which may have been the greatest miracle of all. The Israelites must have had some faith already, because they were willing at least to follow God between two great walls of water. Indeed, Hebrews says, "By faith the people crossed the Red Sea as on dry land" (Hebrews 11:29a). But they made an even firmer faith commitment when it was all over. Exodus 14 ends on this triumphant note: "Israel saw the great power that the Lord used against the Egyptians, so the people feared the Lord, and they believed in the Lord and in his servant Moses" (14:31).

God was fulfilling his grand purpose of saving a people for his glory. For that to happen, his people had to trust him and worship him. Notice the order here: God did not wait for his people to trust in him before he would save them. If he had waited for that to happen, they never would have been saved! Instead God took the initiative. First the people saw their salvation (just as Moses had promised, 14:13); then they feared and believed. This is the pattern and the purpose of salvation. First God delivers us from danger, saving us when we cannot save ourselves. Then we respond in faith, trusting God and worshiping him.

## The Greatest Escape

As Christians, Israel's great escape is part of the history of our own salvation. However, we have experienced an even greater escape—the greatest escape of all. We have been saved from our bondage to sin through the death and resurrection of Jesus Christ. Here again we see the order of salvation, in which God takes the initiative. It is while we were still sinners that Christ died for us. God's saving work comes first, and then we are called to respond in faith.

It is noteworthy that the New Testament describes Christ's saving work in terms of the exodus. Not long after Jesus was born, his parents fled to Egypt. According to the Gospel of Matthew, their eventual return fulfilled the word of the prophet: "Out of Egypt I called my son" (Matthew 2:15b, quoting Hosea 11:1). Originally this prophecy referred to the exodus. However, there is a deep spiritual connection between what happened to Israel under Moses and what happened later in the person and work of Christ. Jesus is the perfect and ultimate Israel. One of the ways God showed this was by having Jesus recapitulate Israel's escape from Egypt. Later, as the crucifixion drew near, Jesus described his death as an "exodus" (Luke 9:31, literal translation). He was making another connection. Jesus is the new Moses—"worthy of more glory" (Hebrews 3:3)—who leads God's people out of their bondage to sin and into the promised land of eternal life.

The most significant connection in the present context is the one that the Apostle Paul made when he wrote, "I do not want you to be unaware, brothers, that our fathers were all under the cloud, and all passed through the sea, and all were baptized into Moses in the cloud and in the sea" (1 Corinthians 10:1,

2). Paul was making a connection between the exodus and baptism. For the Israelites, passing through the Red Sea was a type of baptism, and thus it was "a forecast of our final deliverance in Christ."[13] Once we were enslaved in the Egypt of sin, but now Christ has set us free. All of this is symbolized in the Red Sea event of baptism.

At this point some preachers would invite their congregations to identify their own "Red Sea" experiences and trust God to bring them through. One thinks of the scholar who wrote, "Every age has its Egypt, its force of oppression, just as every age has its children of Israel who long to be free."[14] However, this misses the point. Israel's passage through the sea is not primarily intended to teach us what to do when we are in spiritual trouble, any more than it serves as a how-to lesson on what to do when we come to a large body of water. Rather, it is meant to teach us about coming to God for salvation.

What happened at the Red Sea ought to help us clarify our relationship to Christ. The only "Red Sea experience" that really matters is the one that Jesus had when he passed through the walls of death and came out victorious on the other side. This means that baptized Christians have already had their "exodus experience." We had it at Calvary and in the garden tomb, because when Jesus died and rose again, he did it for us. We were included in these saving events when we were baptized into him, and now we are safe on the other side. All that remains for us to do is what the Israelites did: fear God and trust him as we go forward.

Sadly, those who have not yet come to Christ are still standing on the shores of the Red Sea. How will they ever escape? Only by looking to Jesus. When the Israelites saw what God had done for them, they put all their trust in him. God calls us to do the same thing. He calls us to see Jesus Christ, crucified and risen, and to believe in him. Jesus says, "Truly, truly, I say to you, whoever hears my word and believes . . . has passed from death to life" (John 5:24).

# 35

# The Song of Salvation

## EXODUS 15:1–21

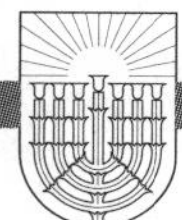

IN 1792 A GROUP OF SETTLERS traveled to Africa. There were more than a thousand of them, all of African descent. Some had worked as slaves on American plantations. Others had served as soldiers in the British army and then moved north to live in Canada. Together they planned to resettle what is now Sierra Leone, on land purchased as a Province of Freedom.

The settlers were all professing Christians. When they reached Africa, they marched ashore singing a hymn by William Hammond (1719–1783), the song "Awake, and Sing the Song":[1]

> Awake, and sing the song
> Of Moses and the Lamb!
> Wake every heart and every tongue,
> To praise the Saviour's Name. . . .
> Sing on your heavenly way!
> Ye ransomed sinners, sing!
> Sing on, rejoicing every day
> In Christ, the eternal King!

It was an appropriate hymn to sing. The settlers had been released from captivity, they had crossed the sea, and now they were entering the Promised Land. So they sang of the prophet Moses, who brought Israel out of Egypt. They also sang to Jesus Christ, the Lamb of God, who had set them free to serve God in a new land. God had done such a great thing for them that it called forth a song of praise.

### I Will Sing of My Redeemer

The phrase "the song of Moses and the Lamb" comes from the book of Revelation. When the Apostle John was taken up to Heaven, he heard the glorified saints singing "the song of Moses, the servant of God, and the song of the

Lamb" (Revelation 15:3a). As John must have realized, this was an echo from the exodus. After the children of Israel made their great escape, "Then Moses and the people of Israel sang this song to the LORD" (15:1a).

Some scholars have tried to argue that a song is out of place in Exodus 15. It doesn't add anything to the plot, they say, but rather interrupts the flow of the Biblical narrative, so it must have been added later. Certainly it could not have been written by Moses.

One way to answer this criticism is to prove the antiquity of the song from its grammar.[2] Brevard Childs concludes, "The cumulative evidence forms an impressive case for an early dating of the poem, particularly the tense system and the orthography."[3] But grammar aside, there is a deeper spiritual principle at work that helps explain how Exodus 15 is connected to what came before. Chapter 14 is the story of Israel's salvation: the flight from Egypt, the passage through the sea, and so on. But salvation always demands a response—a response of praise that is most suitably expressed in song. Therefore, the Song of Moses—the song of salvation—was not merely appropriate at this point in the exodus—it was mandatory.

Whenever God does something great, he deserves to be praised. Often this praise comes in the form of a song. There was singing at creation. The Bible says that when God made the world, "the morning stars sang together and all the sons of God shouted for joy" (Job 38:7). There is singing all through the Old Testament. Usually when God saved his people, they sang his praises. For example, when Israel defeated Jabin and Sisera, Deborah and Barak sang for joy (Judges 5). King David sang when God delivered him from his enemies (2 Samuel 22). This was the origin of many of his psalms. Perhaps the best example is Psalm 40, in which he describes how God lifted him out of the slimy pit and set his feet on the rock. Then David sang, "He put a new song in my mouth, a song of praise to our God" (Psalm 40:3a). When the Israelites came home from exile, they went singing on their way, as Isaiah prophesied: "The ransomed of the LORD shall return and come to Zion with singing" (Isaiah 51:11a; cf. Isaiah 44:23).

Then God sent his Son into the world, and all the angels sang for joy, with Mary, Zechariah, Simeon, and others joining the chorus (Luke 1, 2). Now in the church we are singing all the time, praising God for the life, death, and resurrection of Jesus Christ. The Scripture says, "Let the word of Christ dwell in you richly . . . singing psalms and hymns and spiritual songs, with thankfulness in your hearts to God" (Colossians 3:16). We are singing a song that will never end. To prove this, the Bible ends with "Holy, holy, holy," "Worthy is the Lamb," and other lyrics from Heaven's hymnal (Revelation 4, 5).

The history of salvation is sometimes described as a drama—the drama of redemption. However, this drama is actually a musical. It is impossible even to conceive of Biblical Christianity without songs of praise. Even though we do not have a soundtrack for the Bible, at least we have the libretto, including the song that Moses composed by the Red Sea ("The Song of the Sea," it is sometimes called).

Once we understand the essential role of music as a response to redemption, it becomes clear why Exodus 15 *has* to be a song. The Israelites had just been saved! Right at that moment they needed to praise God for delivering them. The Bible says, "*Then* Moses and the people of Israel sang this song to the Lord, saying, 'I will sing to the Lord, for he has triumphed gloriously'" (15:1a). The word "then" makes the connection between chapter 14 and chapter 15, between salvation and its song.

Salvation is what put the song into Israel's heart. As soon as the people were safe, they burst into song, offering God an exuberant doxology, a *Te Deum* of triumph. The psalmist wrote:

> He [God] rebuked the Red Sea, and it became dry,
> and he led them through the deep as through a desert.
> So he saved them from the hand of the foe
> and redeemed them from the power of the enemy.
> And the waters covered their adversaries;
> not one of them was left.
> Then they believed his words;
> they sang his praise. (Psalm 106:9–12)

Notice the order. First the Israelites saw God save them. Then they put their trust in him as their Savior. Finally, they sang to his glory, which of course was the entire purpose of the exodus. The Israelites were saved for the glory of God. The Song of Moses was their spontaneous, jubilant response to his grace.

In one of his last sermons, Dr. James Montgomery Boice described music as "a gift from God that allows us to express our deepest heart responses to God and his truth in meaningful and memorable ways. It is a case of our hearts joining with our minds to say, 'Yes! Yes! Yes!' to the truths we are embracing." This is what the Israelites were doing on the shores of the Red Sea: They were saying "Yes! Yes! Yes!" to the power and the glory of God, as it had been revealed in their salvation. A paraphrase of Exodus 15 by the poet Thomas Moore captures something of their exuberance:

> Sound the loud timbrel o'er Egypt's dark sea!
> Jehovah has triumphed—his people are free.
> Sing—for the pride of the tyrant is broken,
> His chariots, his horsemen, all splendid and brave—
> How vain was their boast, for the Lord hath but spoken,
> And chariots and horsemen are sunk in the wave.
> Sound the loud timbrel o'er Egypt's dark sea;
> Jehovah has triumphed—his people are free.[4]

The Song of Moses was for everyone. The whole nation joined in the music, forming a chorus of millions. The Bible makes a special point of mentioning the involvement of the women as well as the men:

> For when the horses of Pharaoh with his chariots and his horsemen went into the sea, the LORD brought back the waters of the sea upon them, but the people of Israel walked on dry ground in the midst of the sea. Then Miriam the prophetess, the sister of Aaron, took a tambourine in her hand, and all the women went out after her with tambourines and dancing. And Miriam sang to them:
>
> "Sing to the LORD, for he has triumphed gloriously;
> the horse and his rider he has thrown into the sea." (15:19–21)

This is the first time Miriam is mentioned by name, although she may well have been the young girl who looked after baby Moses in the basket (2:4–8). Possibly Miriam sang the entire Song of Moses. At the very least she sang the chorus, which was based on the first verse of Moses' song. It was an antiphon—a song with a call and a response. The Scripture literally says that Miriam "answered them." First Moses and the men sang to the Lord, then Miriam and the women answered by shaking their tambourines and dancing on the seashore.

The point is that the song of salvation is for all God's people. It was not enough for Moses to sing it, or even all the men of Israel. The women had seen the same salvation, and they were trusting in the same Savior, so they also needed to praise God for his victory at sea. The children were singing too, for they had been saved along with everyone else. One of the ancient rabbinical writings adds this comment: "Even the sucklings dropped their mothers' breasts to join in singing, yea, even the embryos in the womb joined the melody, and the angels' voice swelled the song."[5]

The whole church is called to offer the same kind of praise to God in the name of Jesus Christ. We have seen his salvation in our reading of the Gospels. By faith we have stood with the women at the cross, watching Jesus suffer and die for our sins. By faith we have looked over the shoulders of the apostles into the empty tomb, where Jesus rose again. Jesus has saved us from sin and death. Now every man, woman, and child in the church is called to join the choir and take up the song—the Song of the Savior.

## What God Has Done

It is difficult to determine how the Song of Moses is organized. Some Hebrew scholars think the break comes after verse 12. The first twelve verses are about Israel's past, while the rest of the song looks to Israel's future. Others see a transition at verse 6. The first five verses are *about* God, while the rest of the song is addressed *to* God. Still others divide the Song of Moses into three main stanzas:

verses 1–6, verses 7–11, and verses 12–16. There are grammatical reasons for this. For example, each of these three sections ends with the words "O Lord." However, in terms of theme and content, there is a good deal of overlap among the sections. Furthermore, the song does not follow a strict chronological order. Perhaps the best way to study the song, therefore, is to consider it as a whole and determine what it mainly emphasizes: what God has done and what this reveals about who God is.

The song's most obvious emphasis is on what God has done. Exodus 15 is rooted in the facts of history. It graphically portrays what God did to bring the Israelites across the sea and at the same time to destroy the Egyptians. It gives such specific details that we can almost see the exodus unfold before our very eyes.

Moses begins rather matter-of-factly. He gets straight to the point: "The horse and his rider he [God] has thrown into the sea" (15:1b). Then the prophet gives a more poetic description:

> Pharaoh's chariots and his host he cast into the sea,
>     and his chosen officers were sunk in the Red Sea.
> The floods covered them;
>     they went down into the depths like a stone. . . .
> At the blast of your nostrils the waters piled up;
>     the floods stood up in a heap;
>     the deeps congealed in the heart of the sea. (vv. 4, 5, 8)

This vivid imagery depicts what happened at the Red Sea. By the power of his wind, God piled up the seawater into two great walls. The Israelites went through on dry ground, but when Pharaoh and his elite forces tried to follow, they fell to the bottom of the sea.

To understand why God did this, one need only listen to Pharaoh:

> The enemy said, "I will pursue, I will overtake,
>     I will divide the spoil, my desire shall have its fill of them.
>     I will draw my sword; my hand shall destroy them." (v. 9)

These few, short, staccato lines capture the very essence of Pharaoh. The Egyptian monarch was thoroughly self-centered. Somehow he managed to refer to himself six times in only a single verse! Pharaoh was proud and boastful. He was also rash. He spat out these lines so rapidly that he hardly had time to take a breath. He was bloodthirsty and violent, bent on destruction. And he was greedy, lusting after the spoils of an unjust war.

But God is not mocked. So he humbled Pharaoh's pride by sending his army to a watery grave:

You blew with your wind; the sea covered them;
they sank like lead in the mighty waters. . . .
You stretched out your right hand;
the earth swallowed them. (15:10, 12)

This was all God's doing. God is the one who hurled the horse and rider into the sea (15:1, 4) and who threw down his enemies (15:7). It was his hand that shattered the enemy (15:6) and his breath that blew back the sea (15:8, 10). Moses praised God for what God had done.

We do the same thing whenever we sing a Christian hymn. We give glory to God for what he has done in and through Jesus Christ. There are some good examples from the New Testament—hymns of praise to Christ for his saving work. Philippians 2 praises him for his incarnation, crucifixion, and resurrection:

> And being found in human form, he [Jesus] humbled himself by becoming obedient to the point of death, even death on a cross. Therefore God has highly exalted him and bestowed on him the name that is above every name. (Philippians 2:8, 9)

Or consider the song that the saints and angels sing in glory: "Worthy is the Lamb who was slain, to receive power and wealth and wisdom and might and honor and glory and blessing!" (Revelation 5:12). These are some of the songs of salvation. They praise God for what he has done—specifically for what he has done in human history through the life, death, and resurrection of Jesus Christ.

This emphasis on what God has done should also characterize the hymns of the Christian church. Good hymns help us remember and recount God's saving work in history—the redemption that Christ accomplished through the cross and the empty tomb. As it says in the song of Moses and the Lamb, "Great and amazing are your deeds, O Lord God the Almighty!" (Revelation 15:3b).

## The Supreme Deity

What God has done shows who God is. His work always reveals something of his character. It is not surprising, then, that in his song Moses praised God for many of his divine perfections. He was not writing a systematic theology on the attributes of God; he was simply singing God's praises. Nevertheless, he found it impossible to do this without listing some of the things that make God so great.

Moses praised God for his *eternity*. He repeatedly called God by his special divine name, Yahweh. This is the name that God revealed to Moses at the burning bush. It means that God is the self-existent, eternal, and unchangeable Lord. The God who brought Israel out of Egypt is the God of the burning bush, the same God who first made his covenant with Abraham—"the Lord is his name" (15:3b).

Moses also praised God for his *power*. Given what happened at the Red Sea, this was one of his most obvious attributes: "Your right hand, O LORD, glorious in power . . ." (15:6a). God is omnipotent, all-powerful. He proved this at the Red Sea by overpowering his enemies.

Next the prophet praised God for his *wrath*:

> . . . your right hand, O LORD, shatters the enemy.
> In the greatness of your majesty you overthrow your adversaries;
> you send out your fury; it consumes them like stubble. (15:6b, 7)

Many people—including many Christians—find it difficult to praise God for his wrath. In fact, one of the ancient rabbis imagined that God must have been offended by this stanza from the Song of Moses: "The work of my hands are drowned in the sea, and you want to sing songs?"[6]

The answer is, "Yes!" God is so holy that it would not be right for him to tolerate sin, and thus he is to be praised for the justice of his wrath. Moses understood this. Realize that in this song he did not praise God for the exodus in general, but specifically for the death of the Egyptians as a demonstration of divine wrath. "The LORD is a man of war" (15:3a), Moses said, and God's war against Egypt was a holy war. It was holy in a way that no human war could ever be holy. It was holy because God is holy, and thus in his anger he does not sin.

Here it helps to understand how different divine wrath is from human anger. The main difference is that God's anger is always righteous. Divine wrath is holy hatred of sin and its perpetrators. As Mariano DiGangi explains, "This wrath of God is not a vehement, irrational, vindictive, arbitrary, capricious venting of some supernatural spleen. It is the manifestation of the repugnance of a holy God against all who defile, disrupt and destroy the world that He has made."[7] And, of course, this is exactly what the Egyptians had done—defiled, disrupted, and destroyed what God had made. Moses gives a significant reminder of their murderous slaveholding when he describes them as being "consume[d] . . . like stubble" (15:7). The word "stubble" echoes the beginning of Exodus, when Pharaoh made the Israelites "gather stubble for straw" (5:12). Repeating the word "stubble" was a way of hinting that God gave the Egyptians exactly what they deserved. His wrath was just, as it always is, and therefore he was to be praised. He will be praised this way again at the final judgment. As Jonathan Edwards wrote somewhere, "The future punishment of ungodly men . . . is to show the whole universe the glory of God's power."

Moses praised God for his *supremacy*. The eternal, just, and all-powerful God is superior not only to his enemies, but also to their gods. The prophet asked, "Who is like you, O LORD, among the gods?" (15:11a). The answer, of course, is that there is no one like God. He is utterly incomparable. As the plagues demonstrated, none of Egypt's gods had anything like the power of Israel's sovereign God.

In order to prove the supremacy of God's deity, Moses listed more of his superior traits:

> Who is like you, majestic in holiness,
> awesome in glorious deeds, doing wonders? (15:11b)

God alone is majestic in *holiness.* He is set apart, unique, perfectly and absolutely pure. God alone is awesome in glory, as the exodus was intended to demonstrate. He alone is able to work wonders like the plagues and the parting of the sea.

By this point Moses was positively gushing about God. The prophet identified him as holy, majestic, awesome, and glorious—the wonder-working God. Then there is his *love.*

> You have led in your steadfast love the people whom you have redeemed;
> you have guided them by your strength to your holy abode. (15:13)

By "steadfast love," Moses meant God's covenant-keeping love, his absolute loyalty to his people, and his faithfulness to his promise. God had proved his love to Israel over and over. Everything that had happened to this point in the book of Exodus was motivated by God's love. He had kept all of his love promises to Israel. In particular, he had kept his promise to redeem them, to buy them back from slavery.

Soon God would keep his promise to lead his people to the Promised Land. Moses looked to the future, confidently anticipating the days when God would lead his people to conquest. He traced the route that they would follow to Canaan. One by one, all their enemies would be defeated:

> The peoples have heard; they tremble;
> pangs have seized the inhabitants of Philistia.
> Now are the chiefs of Edom dismayed;
> trembling seizes the leaders of Moab;
> all the inhabitants of Canaan have melted away.
> Terror and dread fall upon them;
> because of the greatness of your arm, they are still as a stone.
> (vv. 14–16a)

This was a prophecy of victory, the fulfillment of which is documented in the book of Joshua. Moses was not describing random acts of violence but righteous acts of divine judgment that God would execute because of his great love for his people. Moses prophesied that God would keep judging the nations

till your people, O LORD, pass by,
 till the people pass by whom you have purchased.
You will bring them in and plant them on your own mountain,
 the place, O LORD, which you have made for your abode,
 the sanctuary, O Lord, which your hands have established.
 (15:16b, 17)

God does not keep his love to himself but shares it with his people. To that end, his grand purpose was to bring his people home to live with him. The "mountain" in verse 17 may refer to Mount Sinai, but more probably it refers to Mount Zion, the city of God in Jerusalem. It was there, in the holy sanctuary of his temple, that God made his earthly dwelling. The Old Testament is the story of God bringing his people to their home in the house of the Lord.

This is still God's plan for his people. The temple at Mount Zion was an earthly symbol of God's heavenly temple in the New Jerusalem. Every day God is bringing more and more children into his holy dwelling. Soon all God's people will be there to sing the song that will never end. So Moses ended his song with this chorus: "The LORD will reign for ever and ever" (15:18). This was the right note on which to end. After a long quarrel with Pharaoh, God had settled once and for all the question as to who was King. Moses praised God for his kingly rule not simply over Israel but over the whole creation, and not simply then, but now and forever.

What an amazing God! He is eternal and omnipotent, holy and just, loving and faithful. If anyone wonders whether this song is of any practical use, simply ask this question: What kind of God do we really need? Without question, the kind of God we need is the kind of God Moses considered worthy of song. We need a God who will be with us always. We need a God who has the power to save us, to triumph over sin in our lives. We need a God of wrath, who will see to it that justice is done in the end. We need a God of everlasting love, who will take us home to live with him forever. The God of Moses is everything that anyone could ever need or even want in a God.

## This Is My Story, This Is My Song

Whenever we describe the attributes of God, there is always the danger that his divine perfections may seem abstract or impersonal. If all we do is analyze them, we end up treating God like a philosophical proposition rather than as a friend. Therefore, it is absolutely necessary for us to praise God for his perfections as Moses did. The prophet not only wrote his song *about* God, but he also sang it *to* God. It is good to talk about the attributes of God, but it is even better to write them in poetic lines, set them to music, and sing them to God. Until we do this, we have not yet achieved the goal of theology, which is the worship of God. Tim Keller writes, "When we praise God, we are not discussing our enjoyment of

God, but the praising is the consummation and the completion of our worship as we glorify God."[8]

In order to worship God properly, we must have a personal relationship with him. We must come and claim him as our very own God. This is how the Song of Moses began, with the prophet's personal appropriation of God and his salvation. Moses sang:

> The LORD is my strength and my song,
> and he has become my salvation;
> this is my God, and I will praise him,
> my father's God, and I will exalt him. (15:2)

Moses had a personal relationship with God. He was able to say, "This God—the God whose praise I sing—is my God. He is my strength and my song. He is salvation itself to me. He is my praise and my exaltation. He is my God, as he was the God of my fathers before me."

The Song of Moses is theocentric; in other words, it is thoroughly God-centered. Moses gave all the glory to God. He did not say one single word about his own role in Israel's salvation. This distinguishes his hymn from the songs of the ancient pagans, which were unfailingly self-congratulatory. By contrast, the Song of Moses was written to the honor and praise of God alone.

Moses did want to mention, however, that the great and glorious God he praised was *his* God. He had found salvation in this God. He had come to know him by faith, and he wanted to set his personal testimony to music: "The LORD is my strength and my song, and he has become my salvation" (15:2). The prophet Isaiah sang the same tune: "The LORD GOD is my strength and my song, and he has become my salvation" (Isaiah 12:2b). The Christian gives the same testimony, only in slightly different words: "Jesus Christ is my strength and my song; he has become my salvation." To know God in a saving way is to know him in a personal way, and that means coming to him through faith in Jesus Christ.

Everyone who knows Jesus Christ will keep singing his praises until the end of the world. And then we will sing a new song. Whenever God does something great, he deserves to be praised. It will be a great day when Jesus comes again. God will bring every sin to judgment, and he will take his children home to live with him forever. It will be such a great day that it will require a song. The apostle John described it in his revelation of Heaven.

> I saw what appeared to be a sea of glass mingled with fire—and also those who had conquered the beast and its image and the number of its name, standing beside the sea of glass with harps of God in their hands. And they sing the song of Moses, the servant of God, and the song of the Lamb, saying,

"Great and amazing are your deeds,
O Lord God the Almighty!
Just and true are your ways,
O King of the nations!" (Revelation 15:2, 3)

John mentions the glassy sea to remind us of the exodus and the song that Moses sang by the shores of the sea. Then he tells us what he heard: a song of praise to God for who he is and what he has done. It will be the last number in the musical of redemption. As soon as we come to Christ, we join the chorus. Now, for the time being, we are still in rehearsal. We are preparing for the grand finale, when we will sing the everlasting song:

Awake, and sing the song
Of Moses and the Lamb!
Wake every heart and every tongue,
To praise the Saviour's Name. . . .

Soon shall ye hear Him say,
"Ye blessed children, come."
Soon will He call you hence away,
And take His wanderers home.

There shall our raptured tongue
His endless praise proclaim,
And sweeter voices swell the song
Of glory to the Lamb.[9]

# 36

# A Bitter Complaint

## EXODUS 15:22–27

EXODUS IS THE TRUE HISTORY of Israel's salvation. It also shows the pattern of salvation in Jesus Christ, which is why the New Testament describes the work of Christ in terms of the exodus. Once we were enslaved in the Egypt of our sin, but then Jesus came to set us free. He is our Passover Lamb who shed his blood on the cross as the sacrifice for our sins. He has also brought us through the Red Sea. In his burial Jesus passed through the deep waters of death, but by his resurrection he landed safe on the other side. All of this is signified in Christian baptism. The exodus from Egypt was a forecast of an even greater exodus: deliverance from sin through the death, burial, and resurrection of Jesus Christ.

Since the book of Exodus set the pattern for Christ, it is not surprising that it also sets the pattern for the Christian. The experience of Israel—living in slavery, trusting in the lamb, crossing from death to life, singing the song of salvation, embarking on a long pilgrimage, living by God's law, and finally reaching the Promised Land—is also the experience of God's new Israel, the church. Dietrich Bonhoeffer wrote:

> We, too, pass through the Red Sea, through the desert, across the Jordan into the promised land. With Israel we fall into doubt and unbelief and through punishment and repentance experience again God's help and faithfulness. All this is not mere reverie but holy, godly reality. We are torn out of our own existence and set down in the midst of the holy history of God on earth. There God dealt with us, and there He still deals with us, our needs and our sins, in judgment and grace.[1]

The New Testament explains the connection between the first exodus and the greater exodus like this: "Now these things happened to them as an example, but they were written down for our instruction, on whom the end of the ages has come" (1 Corinthians 10:11). In other words, Israel's experience was partly for our benefit. What happened to them teaches us how to live for Christ.

## Into the Wilderness

Keeping in mind this connection between the exodus and the gospel helps us understand what happened at the end of Exodus 15. Remember the scene: God had just brought his people through the sea, saving them from Pharaoh and his chariots. This miracle of grace brought the Israelites to saving faith. They saw, they believed, and they worshiped.

What comes next? To put the question in terms of the Christian life, what comes after saving faith? Once a sinner has turned to Christ for salvation, what happens next? The answer is sanctification—the long, hard, difficult process of being conformed to the holiness of God.

The Israelites made a decisive break with sin when they left Egypt, but a great deal of sanctification still needed to take place. This process began almost as soon as the music stopped. As the last chords of Miriam's song died away, "Then Moses made Israel set out from the Red Sea, and they went into the wilderness of Shur" (15:22a). God's people may well have expected to head straight for Canaan, going from grace right on to glory. Instead their triumph was followed by tribulation. God's plan did not call for any shortcuts. The Promised Land could only be reached by way of the wilderness.

The wilderness is a hard place. It is a place to meet with God, to be sure, and yet it is always a difficult place. It is barren and desolate. Thus the Israelites were setting out on a long and arduous journey. They had seen a great salvation, but for them it would not be "happily ever after." They still had a pilgrimage to make, a pilgrimage that was both spiritual and physical.

Going through the wilderness was not necessary for Israel's salvation, but it was necessary for their sanctification. John Mackay comments that

> it is God's normal way of working that entering into glory does not immediately follow salvation. Rather there is a time of preparation to make his people ready for the inheritance he will bestow on them. That was the method he followed in the case of the Israelites. Free they indeed were from the hand of Egyptian control, but they had still much to learn. For one thing their faith was still very weak, and it would take time for their trust in the LORD to develop so that they would be able to face every set of circumstances without hesitation. They were therefore led into times of difficulty and testing so that their spiritual faculties might be developed through use. It was one thing to sing the praises of their Deliverer, and quite another to live out that faith when confronted with the problems of ordinary living. Overcoming the latter challenge would bring them to a clearer understanding of themselves and of what it meant to have faith in the LORD.[2]

The lesson is easy to apply. The church is now living in the wilderness between the first and second comings of Christ. He came once to save us; he will come again to lead us home. In the meantime we are on a long and difficult pilgrimage, which God is using to make us holy. As the Scripture says, "Through many tribulations we must enter the kingdom of God" (Acts 14:22b). This does not mean our salvation is not secure. It *is* secure, and God *will* bring us to our journey's end. But the way is still hard. We will face disappointment and difficulty, discouragement and doubt.

All our problems and persecutions are meant to teach us to depend on God alone, to have absolute confidence in his faithfulness. It is important for us to know where we are in the Christian life. We have not yet reached the promised land. We are still in the wilderness, where God is sanctifying us. Knowing this keeps us from having the wrong expectations and also enables us to "count it all joy . . . when [we] meet trials of various kinds, for [we] know that the testing of [our] faith produces steadfastness" (James 1:2, 3).

## Israel Files a Complaint

Ready or not, the Israelites went into the wilderness of the northern Sinai. In those days the Desert of Shur stretched from Egypt almost all the way to Palestine. The Israelites did not find it very hospitable. The desert climate was semiarid, and its vegetation was sparse, insufficient to support a large group of refugees.

Although there were several watering holes in the desert—interspersed about a day's journey apart—the Israelites soon found themselves in real difficulty. Their crisis concerned the most basic of all physical needs: "They went three days in the wilderness and found no water. When they came to Marah, they could not drink the water of Marah because it was bitter; therefore it was named Marah. And the people grumbled against Moses, saying, 'What shall we drink?'" (15:22b–24).

We can only imagine the bitterness of Israel's disappointment. By the third day the people must have been getting desperate. It is hard to go much more than three days without water, especially in the desert. "If we don't find water soon," they must have said, "we will all die of thirst." Then, just when they were on the point of dehydration—praise God!—they saw an oasis on the horizon. They hurried to reach it, but when they bent down to take a drink, the water tasted brackish, and they had to spit it out. It was more than simply distasteful; it was unfit for human consumption. It tasted of salt, minerals, or perhaps even poison. "How can we drink this stuff?" they complained. Their oasis turned out to be a mirage of sorts. So they called the place Marah, which means "bitter." It is often identified with 'Ain Hawarah, where the waters are bitter to this day. More recently, Colin Humphreys has located the episode at Malha in Midian.[3]

Water is essential for life. So this was a real emergency; it was either drink or die. At this point the Israelites should have cried out to God for help, asking him to give them the water of life. Remember, they had every reason to believe that God would save them. They knew that God answered prayer because it was in response to their cries that he had rescued them from Egypt. They knew that he had power over creation because they had witnessed the plagues. In particular, they knew that God controlled the water supply. They had seen him turn the Nile to blood. They had also witnessed his wonders at the Red Sea, his mastery over the wind and the waves. The Israelites had witnessed God's mighty saving acts in history.

Furthermore, God himself had led the Israelites to this place. Even the bitter oasis was part of his providential plan. To be reminded of this, all they had to do was look up and see the pillar of cloud that had brought them to Marah. God was in the cloud to guard them and guide them. If necessary, he could send down rain to water their parched lips and thirsty throats. Thus they had nothing to complain about and every reason to believe that God would save them. All they needed to do was ask, and he would provide.

Instead, at the first sign of difficulty, the Israelites complained to God's prophet. "Okay, Moses," they said, "this whole trip was your idea. We're out of water. So what are you going to do about it?" It was not wrong for the people to approach the prophet with this kind of problem. They had a genuine physical need. Since Moses served as God's representative, it was appropriate for them to address their concerns to him. The problem was their attitude. To put it bluntly, they were whining.

## No Whining!

Whining always sounds childish. Consider the bumper sticker on which the word "Whining" is superimposed with a red circle slashed by a diagonal line—"No Whining!" It is not hard to guess who is inside the car (usually a minivan). Children are notorious for whining. To be guilty of this sin, as the Israelites were, is a sign of spiritual immaturity. One day the people were dancing on the beach, singing praises to God, but only a few days later they were on the verge of open rebellion. This is a clear sign that they were still in their spiritual infancy.

There are several ways to characterize Israel's sin. The people were *forgetful*. As the psalmist later wrote:

> Our fathers, when they were in Egypt,
> did not consider your wondrous works;
> they did not remember the abundance of your steadfast love,
> but rebelled by the sea, at the Red Sea. (Psalm 106:7)

Sure, God had delivered them from Pharaoh, but that was days ago. What had he done for them lately? The Israelites were also *selfish*. Their primary concern was what God could do for them. They were *ungrateful* and *immature*. But their deepest spiritual problem was *a lack of faith*. The Israelites simply did not believe that God would take care of them. They did not trust in the faithfulness of God.

This is a strong warning to anyone who has a complaining spirit. Remember, what happened to Israel is an example for God's new Israel, the church. Here the lesson is obvious: "[Do not] grumble, as some of them did" (1 Corinthians 10:10). It is not a sin for us to bring God our problems. He invites us to talk things over with him through prayer. What is a sin, however, is to have a complaining spirit that poisons our communion with Christ and thus robs us of the joy of serving God.

Sadly, grumbling is all too common. We live in a culture based on instant gratification. We do more than try to get what we want—we demand it. So we are always thinking about what we don't have and foolishly thinking that if only we had it, then we would be satisfied. But to do that is to locate the problem on the outside rather than on the inside. The real problem is our own dissatisfaction, the grumbling of a complaining heart.

Many Christians complain about the little things. We don't like the way a ministry is being handled, or we disagree with something in the worship service, or we have a problem with one of our spiritual leaders. So we grumble. We do the same thing at home. We complain about the brand of cereal our wife (or mom) bought or the jobs that have been left unfinished or the quality of the living room furniture. All of this complaining disturbs our relationships and hinders our witness.

Then there are the big things we complain about: poverty, disability, disappointment with children, dissatisfaction on the job, misfortune in love, chronic pain. These are the bitter places in our lives. Has something happened in your life—or not happened, for that matter—that has become a constant source of complaint? Is there something that has come between you and the Lord, something that hinders your prayers and limits your effectiveness in ministry?

A man from Philadelphia was ordained to the pastoral ministry. It was a remarkable occasion because only four years earlier he had almost dropped out of the church altogether. The man had dedicated his life to serving God. At the time he was working for the church, attending seminary, and preparing for the ministry. Then his newborn daughter was diagnosed with muscular dystrophy. As far as the man was concerned, this kind of suffering had never been part of the bargain. The deal was that he would serve God, and God would bless him. When God did not bless him, he was no longer willing to serve. It was not until he turned his bitterness over to God, trusting God to be faithful even in suffering, that he was restored to joy.

What we suffer may be bitter in itself, but however bitter it is, it does not need to make *us* bitter. The problem at Marah was not the water, bitter though it was, but the bitterness in the hearts of God's people. John Calvin pointed out that God "might have given them sweet water to drink at first, but He wished by the bitter to make prominent the bitterness which lurked in their hearts."[4] Bitterness does not come in the outward circumstance but in the inward response. We are called not to complain but to believe in the goodness of God, even when he leads us to the bitter waters.

## How Sweet It Is!

One reason to trust God is that he can turn what is bitter into something sweet, which is what happened at Marah: "And he [Moses] cried to the LORD, and the LORD showed him a log, and he threw it into the water, and the water became sweet" (15:25a).

When Moses was confronted with desperate physical need, he did not grumble. He did not turn around and bicker with the Israelites. Instead he took their troubles to the Lord in prayer. This was typical. Moses often cried out to God for help. He knew how to handle a difficult situation in a spiritual way. There was nothing that he could do to save God's people, but he knew that God could save them, and so he trusted in God. He exercised real dependence on God's promise to provide.

When Moses cried out to God, his one little prayer accomplished more than all the murmurings of the Israelites. It accomplished more because it was directed to God in faith. God answered by showing Moses a piece of wood—apparently a particular tree (literally, "the wood"). The word translated "showed" means "to direct or instruct." It suggests that God imparted some kind of knowledge about the tree to his prophet. When Moses threw it in, the water became pure, wholesome, and sweet. The people drank until they were satisfied, slaking their desperate thirst.

The question naturally arises as to whether this was a genuine miracle or whether in fact the wood had some kind of natural healing effect. Scholars have tried to determine whether any of the trees in Sinai has the inherent ability to purify water.[5] Perhaps there was a local remedy, some desert bush with the right chemical properties. However, no healing tree has been discovered. Besides, it is hard to see how one piece of wood could possibly purify so much water. We are bound to conclude that what happened at Marah was a genuinely supernatural miracle. The wood made the water sweet because it came from God's tree. This reminds us of some of the other trees in Scripture: the life-giving tree in the garden of Eden (Genesis 2:9); the tree of life in the New Jerusalem, with leaves for healing the nations (Revelation 22:2); and especially the tree on which Christ was crucified—the tree that heals our bitter, bitter sin. God seems to specialize in trees of healing.

What is remarkable is not that God was able to perform the miracle at Marah, but that he was willing to do it for such a bunch of malcontents. Calvin commented, "Herein shone forth the inestimable mercy of God, who deigned to change the nature of the water for the purpose of supplying such wicked, and rebellious, and ungrateful men."[6] God's grace is so amazing that he even provides for whiners, provided that we really are his children.

Why does God do this? He does it to show his mercy and grace. He also does it so that we learn to trust in him for the water of life. God wants us to have a deep dependence on his ability to provide. Often he teaches us this lesson by first leading us to taste bitter water. This was true for Israel. It was the bittersweet waters of Marah that increased their faith.

One sign of growing spiritual maturity is our ability to trust that God will provide, even when it is hard to see how. God has promised to give us "all things that pertain to life and godliness" (2 Peter 1:3a). This is a lesson that most Christians need to learn over and over, until we finally get to the point where we no longer question *if* God is going to provide, but only wonder *how* he will take care of us this time, waiting in faith until he does.

## Test Case

At Marah God turned what was bitter into streams of sweet, refreshing water. This powerful demonstration of his providence was also a teachable moment. Once his people had drunk their fill, God proceeded to teach them a vital spiritual lesson for the rest of their pilgrimage: "There the Lord made for them a statute and a rule, and there he tested them, saying, 'If you will diligently listen to the voice of the Lord your God, and do that which is right in his eyes, and give ear to his commandments and keep all his statutes, I will put none of the diseases on you that I put on the Egyptians, for I am the Lord, your healer'" (15:25b, 26).

The wilderness was Israel's teacher. Charles Spurgeon described it as "the Oxford and Cambridge for God's students. There they went to the University, and he taught and trained them, and they took their degree before they entered into the promised land."[7] Like most institutions of higher learning, Wilderness U. had an examination system. God tested his people Israel. At Marah he schooled them by making a small covenant, in which he set out the terms of their relationship. God gave his people a command with warnings and promises, blessings and curses.

Israel's command was to obey the word of their God. God told them to "diligently listen to the voice of the Lord your God, and do that which is right in his eyes, and give ear to his commandments and keep all his statutes" (15:26a). God's law was to be the absolute standard for their conduct. Usually we associate his law with the Ten Commandments given at Mount Sinai, but even before the Israelites reached the holy mountain, God required them to live for his glory. They were to listen to what he said, do what he wanted, attend to what he commanded, and keep what he decreed.

These requirements were *not* the basis for Israel's salvation. They were already saved! God had delivered them out of the land of Egypt, out of the house of bondage. He had brought them through the sea. But now it was time for their sanctification, so God gave them his law. He did not say, "Do this and I will save you." First he saved them, and then he said, "Now here are some things that I want you to do." If God had done it the other way around, then their salvation would have come by works. But as it is, salvation always comes by grace through faith.

If these commands were not for Israel's salvation, then what were they for? They were for Israel's sanctification. Genuine, saving faith is always followed by joyful good works. God wants us to do more than simply believe what he has done; he also wants us to obey what he has commanded. God gave Israel these instructions to help them live for his glory. Once we have been saved from sin, the way to experience the fullness of God's blessing is to trust and obey.

God gave his people these commands to see what their works would reveal about their relationship with him. Obedience was the test of their faith. But whether they obeyed or not, there would be consequences. This is the way a covenant always works. It contains promises and warnings, with blessings for obedience and curses for disobedience. God said "if you will diligently listen" and if you "do that which is right," *then* "I will put none of the diseases on you that I put on the Egyptians, for I am the Lord, your healer" (15:26b). The curse is implied: if God's people did not obey, they would suffer the same plagues they had witnessed in Egypt.

Yet God's desire was to bless and not to curse. He did not test his people so they would fail, but in the hope that they would learn to obey. Later Moses said to them, "God has come to test you, that the fear of him may be before you, that you may not sin" (20:20). Sadly, this was a test that the Israelites kept failing—not only at Marah, but throughout their wanderings in the wilderness. When they were thirsty, they did not trust and obey; they grumbled and complained. We often fail in the same way. Our need for provision is the testing of our faith. But when the time of testing comes, rather than waiting for God in quiet confidence, we get anxious and angry.

This is why we so desperately need Jesus, who *did* pass the test. In order to save us, Jesus had to keep the whole Law of God. Theologians call this "the active obedience of Christ," and it was necessary for our full salvation. Never was this obedience tested more severely than when God led Jesus into the wilderness to be tempted by the devil: "And after fasting forty days and forty nights, he was hungry. And the tempter came and said to him, 'If you are the Son of God, command these stones to become loaves of bread'" (Matthew 4:2, 3). The temptation was to get his own food in his own way, not trusting his Father to provide. But Jesus passed the test. He said, "It is written, 'Man shall not live by bread alone, but by every word that comes from the mouth of God'" (Matthew

4:4). Jesus did not complain about what God had failed to provide but trusted his Father to sustain him.

There is great blessing for those who learn to trust and obey. God's command at Marah came with a promise: If his people obeyed, he would not only spare them from the plagues but would also heal their diseases. Here God revealed another of his divine names. The Israelites already knew him as the Great I Am, the eternal and self-existent God. They had also come to trust him as the God who hears, the God who rescues, and the God who provides. Now God revealed himself as *Yahweh-rophe*, the God who heals. In the Old Testament *rophe* refers to wellness and soundness, both physically and spiritually. It means "to restore, to heal, to cure . . . not only in the physical sense but in the moral and spiritual sense also."[8] At Marah God demonstrated his healing power by curing the bitter waters. But this was intended to teach the Israelites to trust him for every kind of healing. Part of God's identity is wrapped up in his ability to heal. He is the God who forgives all our sins and heals all our diseases (Psalm 103:3).

The power to heal is another confirmation that Jesus is the Savior. Jesus was famous for his healing miracles. He went around "proclaiming the gospel of the kingdom and healing every disease and every affliction among the people" (Matthew 4:23). Everyone Jesus healed received a physical blessing. But this pointed to a deeper reality—namely, that Jesus is the remedy for everything that ails our sin-sick souls. He is the doctor of our salvation. Whatever healing we need—physical healing for disease and disability, spiritual healing for sin, or emotional healing for the wounds we receive from others—we are to look to Jesus. Some of our diseases will not be healed until the resurrection, but they will all be healed, because Jesus has promised to heal them.

## Palm Springs

Exodus 15 ends with God bringing his people to a healing place, an oasis along the way. After their bitter-sweet experience at Marah, they moved further into the wilderness. "Then they came to Elim, where there were twelve springs of water and seventy palm trees, and they encamped there by the water" (15:27; cf. Numbers 33:9).

We should be careful not to read too much into this verse. One of John Buchan's novels describes a Scottish minister who "preached for a year and six months on Exodus fifteen and twenty-seven, the twelve wells of water and three score and ten palm trees of Elim, a Sabbath to [each] well and [each] tree." The novel then comments that the minister "was never very strong in the intellectuals."[9] Indeed.

The Israelites learned more from the bitterness of Marah than they did from the sweetness of Elim; however, there is something to learn from these palm springs. Elim was a place of abundance. Usually it is identified with Wadi Gharandel, a lush oasis in northern Sinai. Wherever Elim was located, the presence of such large trees shows that it had a limitless supply of underground water. The numbers twelve and seventy are symbolic of fullness and blessing. There were a dozen wells, one for each tribe of Israel, and seventy trees, one for each of Israel's elders, so there was plenty for everyone. This shows that God's provision is abundant. It would be enough for God to give us what we need to survive, but ordinarily he gives enough to thrive. He satisfied Israel's thirst in the wilderness. Now from the everlasting fountain of his grace he showers his people with care, so that we flourish in every way.

God has made abundant provision for us by sending his Son to be our Savior. If we have Jesus, we have everything we need: "My God will supply every need of yours according to his riches in glory in Christ Jesus" (Philippians 4:19). Does that mean that God will meet all our material needs? Yes; he has promised to provide everything we truly need for daily existence. But more than that, he has promised to meet all our deepest spiritual needs, granting us forgiveness and giving us fellowship with him forever.

The Bible applies the lessons of Marah and Elim by describing Jesus as the water of life. Jesus said it himself: "If anyone thirsts, let him come to me and drink. Whoever believes in me, as the Scripture has said, 'Out of his heart will flow rivers of living water'" (John 7:37b, 38; cf. 4:13, 14). Jesus was speaking about the Holy Spirit, who is the refreshing source of all spiritual vitality. To come to Jesus is to receive the Holy Spirit, and with the Spirit, an everlasting supply of grace. Everyone who comes to Jesus discovers that he is deeply satisfying in every way. And everyone may come, for Jesus says, "Let the one who is thirsty come; let the one who desires take the water of life without price" (Revelation 22:17b).

# 37

# Bread from Heaven

## EXODUS 16:1–20

THE ISRAELITES CAMPED by the springs of Elim for several weeks, lingering under the palm trees and taking long drinks of cool water. Then it was time to move on. They were on a spiritual journey, a journey that reveals the pattern of the Christian life. Although there are times of refreshing, usually they do not last for long. Soon it is time to head back into the desert—the place of testing and spiritual growth.

### Israel's Protest

God's people headed south and east, deeper into the wilderness: "They set out from Elim, and all the congregation of the people of Israel came to the wilderness of Sin, which is between Elim and Sinai, on the fifteenth day of the second month after they had departed from the land of Egypt" (16:1). Soon the Israelites were tired and hungry, and once again they started to complain: "And the whole congregation of the people of Israel grumbled against Moses and Aaron in the wilderness, and the people of Israel said to them, 'Would that we had died by the hand of the LORD in the land of Egypt, when we sat by the meat pots and ate bread to the full, for you have brought us out into this wilderness to kill this whole assembly with hunger'" (16:2, 3).

Whining was Israel's besetting sin. It started when Moses first went to Pharaoh and the Israelites complained that he was making their job harder instead of easier. They grumbled at the Red Sea, where they accused Moses of bringing them out to die in the desert. They were even more bitter at Marah, but the complaining didn't stop there. The Israelites wandered for forty years, and they grumbled their way through most of it. By the time they reached the Desert of Sin, they were an entire nation of malcontents. Verse 2 says that "the whole congregation of the people of Israel grumbled." In verse 3 they complained about their meal plan. But what seems to have come first was the complaining itself, evidence of a grumbling spirit. Our complaints really are never caused by our outward circumstances. Instead they reveal the inward condition of our hearts. The Scripture says, "Rejoice in the Lord always; again I will say, rejoice" (Philippians 4:4). Our joy in the Lord should not be circumstantial but fundamental.

Really the Israelites had nothing to complain about. They were *not* running out of food. This is what they said, of course—"We're starving out here!"—but it simply wasn't true. In the next chapter they talk about needing water for their livestock (17:3). Obviously they still had the flocks and herds that they had brought out of Egypt. They could drink milk and make cheese; if necessary, they could even eat meat. So they were not starving. This is confirmed by Psalm 78, which speaks of "the food they craved" (Psalm 78:18, 30), not the food essential for their survival. The Israelites confused what they wanted with what they needed. This is often the source of our discontent—thinking that our greeds are really our needs.

The Israelites complained that their situation was worse than it actually was. They also did something else that complainers often do: They exaggerated the advantages of their former situation. "Remember the good old days?" they said. "Remember how stuffed we used to get?" They looked back with longing on their time in Egypt, when they used to belly up to Pharaoh's buffet. At least that's how they remembered it. In truth, it is doubtful whether Pharaoh fed them all the meat that they could eat. And if he did, it was only so they could work longer and harder. Nevertheless, the Israelites longed to go back, proving once again how much easier it was to get them out of Egypt than it was to get Egypt out of them.

The Israelites directed their complaint against their spiritual leaders, charging Moses and Aaron with attempted homicide, if not genocide. This was outrageous. These men had dedicated their lives to serving God's people. But the people impugned their motives, accusing them of trying to destroy Israel.

Israel's attitude is a warning against the great sin of complaining. It is always wrong to make the worst of things or to make baseless accusations against good people. But when the Israelites complained to Moses, what they were really doing was grumbling against God. "Yet they sinned still more against him," wrote the psalmist, "rebelling against the Most High in the desert" (Psalm 78:17). Moses and Aaron recognized this. So rather than getting defensive, they helped the people see what they were really doing: "For what are we, that you grumble against us? . . . what are we? Your grumbling is not against us but against the LORD" (16:7b, 8b).

The word "grumbling" hardly does the Israelites justice. The Hebrew word was "not designed to express a disgruntled complaint. Quite the contrary, it describe[d] an open rebellion."[1] When the people murmured against Moses, it was mutiny against Almighty God. They were repudiating their relationship with him. In fact, they wished that they were dead (16:3). The way they figured, if they were going to die anyway, it would have been better to die back in Egypt. Starving in the desert was a fate worse than death. In effect, they were saying that they wished they had never been saved.

Remember that the great question in Exodus concerned Israel's worship: Whom would they serve—God or Pharaoh? God wanted his people to serve him alone, but now the Israelites were saying, "We would rather serve Pharaoh." Patrick Henry's famous words were, "Give me liberty or give me death!" The Israelites said exactly the opposite: "Give us bondage or give us death!" Their complaining went far beyond griping about their menu. They were rebelling against God's plan for their salvation.

This is an important insight about the sin of complaining. All our dissatisfaction and discontent ultimately is directed against God. Usually we take out our frustrations on someone else, especially people who are close to us. A psychologist would call this *displacement*. In the case of the Israelites, although they were taking things out on Moses, they were really angry with God. This is why God always takes our complaints personally. He knows that when we grumble about our personal circumstances, our spiritual leaders, or anything else, what we are really doing is finding fault with him. We are complaining about what he has provided (or not provided, as the case may be). A complaining spirit always indicates a problem in our relationship with God.

## God's Provision

Amazingly, in spite of their whining, God listened to the Israelites and gave them what they asked for. Four times the Scripture says that God heard their grumbling (16:7, 8, 9, 12). God not only heard them, but he also provided for them: "And the LORD said to Moses, 'I have heard the grumbling of the people of Israel. Say to them, "At twilight you shall eat meat, and in the morning you shall be filled with bread. Then you shall know that I am the LORD your God"'" (16:11, 12).

The God of all grace was promising to provide for his people. His provision would be abundant. In verse 4 he told Moses, "I am about to rain bread from heaven." Then in verse 12 he promised that his people would be "filled with bread." Here God used the same word for being full that the Israelites used back in verse 3, when they were talking about how much food they used to eat. God promised to feed his people until they were satisfied. This was only by his infinite patience, because after all their grumbling, it was much more than Israel deserved.

God made good on his promise. He provided food that very night, and then again the following morning: "In the evening quail came up and covered the camp, and in the morning dew lay around the camp. And when the dew had gone up, there was on the face of the wilderness a fine, flake-like thing, fine as frost on the ground. When the people of Israel saw it, they said to one another, 'What is it?' For they did not know what it was. And Moses said to them, 'It is the bread that the Lord has given you to eat'" (16:13–15).

This was a genuine miracle—or actually, two miracles. The first was the miracle of the quail (*Coturnix coturnix*), a small game bird that is common in the Middle East. Quail are migratory. Each year they pass over Sinai in the spring and fall, flying low, carried along by the wind. When they stop, they roost on the ground. The Egyptians (who, according to Herodotus, considered quail a delicacy) trapped the birds with nets.[2] However, when quail are exhausted from their travels, they can also be captured by hand.

It is not surprising, then, that the Israelites found quail in the wilderness. Nevertheless, God's provision of quail was miraculous. The birds came that very evening, just at the time that God had promised. They also came in astonishing numbers, enough to feed a multitude of millions. According to the psalmist, "He rained meat on them like dust, winged birds like the sand of the seas" (Psalm 78:27). The quail came to the right place, at the right time, and in the right quantity. It was a miraculous providence, both in its timing and in its extent. God did not give his people quail every day. This miracle was repeated only one other time, after the Israelites left Sinai. The book of Numbers describes how "a wind from the Lord sprang up, and it brought quail from the sea and let them fall beside the camp, about a day's journey on this side and a day's journey on the other side, around the camp, and about two cubits above the ground" (Numbers 11:31).

What God did provide every day was bread in the form of manna, and this was the second miracle. The Bible says that manna "was like coriander seed, white, and the taste of it was like wafers made with honey" (16:31). This description has inspired a number of elaborate theories. Like the Israelites, scholars have asked, "What is it?" F. S. Bodenheimer claimed that the "liquid honeydew excretion of a number of cicadas, plant lice, and scale insects speedily solidifies by rapid evaporation. From remote times the resulting sticky and often times granular masses have been collected and called manna."[3] Another "widely accepted view is that the manna was identical with the lichen *Lecanora esculenta*. This lichen grows on rocks and produces pea-sized globules which are light enough to be blown about by the wind. They are well known for their sweetness and are often collected by the natives of central Asia."[4] But at present the most popular view associates manna with the tamarisk:

> Particularly in rainy years the tamarisk bush, indigenous to arid areas, is invaded by a species of plant louse. The insect sucks the sap and transforms its carbohydrates into a variety of high fructose products. These are secreted through the body and fall to the ground as small drops. There they crystallize into small white pellets, which can be consumed like sugar or honey. Since they melt in the sun, they have to be gathered

> early in the morning, just like the biblical manna. Still today the bedouins call them in Arabic *man*, which corresponds to the Hebrew word for "manna."[5]

There are some obvious problems with these theories. One is that the Israelites were mystified by the manna. They had never seen anything like it. If it was so common, then why did they go around asking what it was? Another problem is that none of the alternatives fits all of the Biblical data. These various excretions do not rot the way manna did; they all keep for several days. Then there are the quantities to consider. How many billion lice would it take to feed a nation for a day?

However, the biggest problem concerns how long the manna continued. The Bible says the Israelites "ate the manna forty years, till they came to a habitable land. They ate the manna till they came to the border of the land of Canaan" (16:35). Manna was not the only thing they ate, but it was one of the staples of their diet for forty years! The difficulty is that all of the plant and animal byproducts that scholars have mentioned are seasonal. They only occur for a few weeks out of the year.

A careful examination of the evidence thus shows that the manna in the wilderness was a genuine, divine miracle. This is the way the Bible consistently presents it. Moses called it "the bread that the LORD has given you to eat" (16:15). The psalmist spoke of it as "bread from heaven" (Psalm 105:40; cf. Psalm 78:24) and "the bread of the angels" (Psalm 78:25). Similarly, the Apostle Paul described it as "spiritual food" (1 Corinthians 10:3), meaning "supernatural food." Manna was the original wonder bread.

## More of His Glory

God did not perform this miracle simply because his people begged for it. He provided them bread for his own glory. God had announced this intention beforehand:

> So Moses and Aaron said to all the people of Israel, "At evening you shall know that it was the LORD who brought you out of the land of Egypt, and in the morning you shall see the glory of the LORD, because he has heard your grumbling against the LORD. . . . the LORD gives you in the evening meat to eat and in the morning bread to the full, because the LORD has heard your grumbling that you grumble against him." (16:6, 7a, 8a)

God gave his people bread to show that he was Lord. This was something that he had already proven to his enemies. He showed the Egyptians who was Lord by drowning them on their chariots in the sea. Now he was going to show his own people the same thing, only he would do it by meeting their needs. The meat and the bread would give them a personal, firsthand acquaintance with his lordship. The Israelites already knew that God was the Lord of Israel, but now they would learn it again by their own experience.

Another way to say this is that God would show Israel his glory. God's glory is his reputation. It is his honor, the weightiness of his character, the sum total of all his divine perfections. To know that he is the Lord, therefore, is to know him as the God of glory. To help his people see how glorious he is, God gave them a glimpse: "Then Moses said to Aaron, 'Say to the whole congregation of the people of Israel, "Come near before the LORD, for he has heard your grumbling."' And as soon as Aaron spoke to the whole congregation of the people of Israel, they looked toward the wilderness, and behold, the glory of the LORD appeared in the cloud" (16:9, 10).

Once again Aaron served as God's spokesman. He gathered the people into God's presence and then pointed them to God's glory. What the people saw was the *Shekinah*, the glorious cloud of God's presence and protection. God was glorified in the cloud, which was a visible manifestation of his invisible majesty. But God was also glorified in sending the manna and the quail. His miraculous provision added to his reputation as the God who hears and the God who cares. Every time God provides for his people, it is for the praise of his glory.

By this point in Exodus, we have come to expect God to do things for his own glory. If we learn nothing else from this book, we learn that we are saved for God's glory. At every stage of Israel's deliverance, God did what he did—and did it the way that he did—to receive all the glory and praise. However predictable it becomes, there is no more important lesson than this: God disposes all things for the ultimate good of his glory. Every time he provides, he adds a little more weight to his reputation.

God does the same thing for us. There is glory in the ordinary providence of God. Every time he takes care of our needs or spares us from danger, every time he enables us to repent of our sins or to believe in his promises, every time he works things out in a way that seemed impossible, we see a little bit more of his glory. Or at least we ought to. If we are not giving God the glory after all he has done for us, what more is it going to take?

## The Bread of Life

There are many things to learn from the manna and the quail, but the basic lesson is this: God provides for his people, giving us whatever we truly need. And since he is our all-sufficient provider, he himself is all we need.

God sent the bread to sanctify his people. Manna had the educational purpose of teaching them to depend on God for all their needs. Later Moses explained that although manna was a physical miracle, its purpose was to teach the spiritual lesson that God is the source of all our life. The prophet said, "He humbled you and let you hunger and fed you with manna, which you did not know, nor did your fathers know, that he might make you know that man does not live by bread alone, but man lives by every word that comes from the mouth of the LORD" (Deuteronomy 8:3).

These words immediately remind us of Jesus, who quoted them to Satan in the wilderness. Jesus had been fasting for forty days and forty nights. Like the Israelites, he was desperate for food, so the devil tempted him to turn the stones into bread. But Jesus answered, "It is written, 'Man shall not live by bread alone, but by every word that comes from the mouth of God'" (Matthew 4:4). Jesus knew that our deepest needs are not physical but spiritual. What we really need is God, and when we have him, we have everything we need.

This was something that Jesus often tried to teach his disciples. One time he was preaching to great crowds of people by the Sea of Galilee. Jesus knew they were starting to get hungry, so he performed the miracle of the loaves and fishes, the feeding of the five thousand. Afterward people *really* wanted to follow him! Yet Jesus knew that they were looking for the wrong thing, so he said, "Truly, truly, I say to you, you are seeking me, not because you saw signs, but because you ate your fill of the loaves. Do not work for the food that perishes, but for the food that endures to eternal life, which the Son of Man will give to you" (John 6:26, 27).

People were puzzled by this, so they asked Jesus to prove his credentials. Thinking back to the exodus, they asked, "Then what sign do you do, that we may see and believe you? What work do you perform? Our fathers ate the manna in the wilderness; as it is written, 'He gave them bread from heaven to eat'" (John 6:30, 31). The truth was that Jesus had already given them a sign. By feeding them bread he had demonstrated that he was the new and greater Moses. But the physical bread was not important. What was important was Jesus himself, who is the source of all spiritual life. So Jesus said to them, "Truly, truly, I say to you, it was not Moses who gave you the bread from heaven, but my Father gives you the true bread from heaven. For the bread of God is he who comes down from heaven and gives life to the world" (John 6:32, 33). He was talking about himself, obviously. Jesus could do much more than multiply the bread. He *was* the bread, the spiritual bread from Heaven that gives life to the world.

The people still weren't sure what Jesus was talking about, but at least they knew they wanted to sign up for his meal plan: "They said to him, 'Sir, give us this bread always.' Jesus said to them, 'I am the bread of life; whoever comes to me shall not hunger, and whoever believes in me shall never thirst'" (John 6:34, 35). The people were still looking for something physical, but Jesus was offering them something spiritual. When he said, "I am the bread of life," he meant that he was all they would ever need. He would provide for all their physical needs, of course; but more than that, he would meet all their deepest spiritual needs forever.

When the people heard this, they did exactly what the Israelites did in the wilderness: they grumbled and complained. They wanted God on their own terms, so they weren't interested in what Jesus had to offer. They didn't understand that this was a matter of life and death, that the difference between eternal salvation and everlasting damnation is faith in the Son of God. So Jesus explained it to them. He said:

> Truly, truly, I say to you, whoever believes has eternal life. I am the bread of life. Your fathers ate the manna in the wilderness, and they died. This is the bread that comes down from heaven, so that one may eat of it and not die. I am the living bread that came down from heaven. If anyone eats of this bread, he will live forever. And the bread that I will give for the life of the world is my flesh. (John 6:47–51)

Jesus was moving from the physical to the spiritual, from the temporal to the eternal, from the exodus to the cross. The manna in the wilderness was another *type*—something from the Old Testament that pointed to salvation in Christ. The manna taught Israel to depend on God for all their needs, but it had certain limitations. It was only bread; so it could only meet physical needs, and only for a little while. As Jesus pointed out, everyone who ate manna is now dead. Nevertheless, the bread taught people to look to God for their sustenance and salvation until he sent the true and living bread from Heaven. That bread came in the person and work of Jesus, who offered his body on the cross to give life to the world. The meaning of the manna is that all we need is Jesus.

Now God invites us to feed upon Jesus, who is the source of all our life. Jesus said:

> Truly, truly, I say to you, unless you eat the flesh of the Son of Man and drink his blood, you have no life in you. Whoever feeds on my flesh and drinks my blood has eternal life, and I will raise him up on the last day. For my flesh is true food, and my blood is true drink. Whoever feeds on my flesh and drinks my blood abides in me, and I in him. As the living Father sent me, and I live because of the Father, so whoever feeds on me, he also will live because of me. This is the bread that came down from heaven, not like the bread the fathers ate, and died. Whoever feeds on this bread will live forever. (John 6:53–58)

There are many ways to feed upon Jesus. We feed upon him as we study God's Word, which is all about our salvation in him. We feed upon Jesus as we have fellowship with him in prayer. And we feed upon him in the sacrament of the Lord's Supper—not physically but spiritually. The physical bread is a spiritual sign of the eternal life that Jesus gives to all who trust in him.

## This Is Only a Test

God has sent us bread from Heaven. This raises a practical question: Will we trust—really trust—that in Jesus, God will provide everything we truly need?

Whenever we need something, God is testing our faith, just as he tested the faith of Israel. Before he sent the manna and the quail, "the LORD said to Moses, 'Behold, I am about to rain bread from heaven for you, and the people shall go out and gather a day's portion every day, that I may test them, whether they will walk in my law or not. On the sixth day, when they prepare what they bring in, it will be twice as much as they gather daily'" (16:4, 5).

God gave his people some very specific instructions. Each day they were to go out and gather bread. They were only to gather as much as they needed for that day, except on the sixth day, when they could gather enough for the Sabbath. God was using this to test them (cf. Deuteronomy 8:16). The word "law" is the Hebrew word *torah*, which refers to God's law. God wanted to see if his people would keep his law, which obviously would require faith in his promise. Later Moses said, "Let no one leave any of it [the manna] over till the morning" (16:19). In other words, "No hoarding!" This meant that the people had to trust God for tomorrow as well as today. In this case, rather than storing up for the future (which God allows and even commands in many situations), they were called to believe that God would continue to provide what they needed on a daily basis. Every day God tested their faith in his providence. He was teaching them to trust him for their daily bread. Day by day, week by week, and year by year, they had to depend on him for everything.

God was faithful to provide what he promised. When the manna came down from Heaven, "Moses said to them, 'It is the bread that the LORD has given you to eat. This is what the LORD has commanded: "Gather of it, each one of you, as much as he can eat. You shall each take an omer, according to the number of the persons that each of you has in his tent."' And the people of Israel did so. They gathered, some more, some less. But when they measured it with an omer, whoever gathered much had nothing left over, and whoever gathered little had no lack. Each of them gathered as much as he could eat" (16:15b–18). The people did as they were told. An omer is about half a gallon—enough food for one day. As the people gathered the bread and then measured it out by the omer, they found that God provided exactly what they needed. It was never too much or too little, but always enough.

The Apostle Paul saw this as a lesson in fairness. When he challenged the Corinthians to care for the Christian poor, he wrote: "For I do not mean that others should be eased and you burdened, but that as a matter of fairness your abundance at the present time should supply their need, so that their abundance may supply your need, that there may be fairness. As it is written, 'Whoever gathered much had nothing left over, and whoever gathered little had no lack'" (2 Corinthians 8:13–15). Paul was quoting from Exodus 16:18 and was referring to the way Israel gathered manna in the wilderness. Apparently the reason they all had exactly what they needed was because they all shared. In the same way, as Christians we are called to share what we have with our brothers and sisters. God's plan for providing for his people around the world depends on our willingness to give what other Christians need.

Most of the Israelites were willing to trust God for their daily bread. "But [some] did not listen to Moses. Some left part of it till the morning, and it bred worms and stank. And Moses was angry with them" (16:20). Moses was right to be angry. Instead of only taking what they needed, some of the Israelites tried to make God's provision last an extra day. Not only was this unnecessary, but it showed a lack of faith in God's promise. These people failed God's test because they were worried about tomorrow. They also suffered the consequence: rotten, contaminated food.

This was partly a lesson about contentment. By giving everyone the same rations, God was teaching his people to be satisfied with their daily provision. How much is enough? We live in a culture of accumulation, where enough is never enough—we always want a little bit more. But all we really need is our daily bread, which God has promised to provide. As God sustains us from one day to the next, we are called to live in daily dependence upon his providence. Why does God tell us to trust him for our daily bread? Maxie Dunnam writes, "He does it for our sakes, that we may know the peace and strength that come from continual dependence upon Him, the joyful life that is ours when we trust Him and see the truth of our trusting. The happiest people I know are not people who don't have any needs, but people who experience the meeting of their needs by God."[6]

## Give Us This Day Our Daily Bread

Most of us are not living day-to-day. Right now we have enough food to last until tomorrow—probably enough to last until the end of the week. But what if we didn't?

One woman tells of a time when her family was almost out of food. She writes:

> Our broken, often discouraged single-parent family lived in the suburbs of Philadelphia. . . . As usual, bills accumulated and financial pressure intensified. . . . We had little food and no money to buy groceries. One Friday while I was home during a lunch break, I did what came easily: I sat on my bed and cried. During my crying and groaning the phone rang. . . .
>
> "I'm from the *Philadelphia Inquirer* Action Line, and I understand you could use a Thanksgiving dinner. . . . [W]e would like to know where you shop, so next Tuesday you can go to the store of your choice and pick up a gift certificate for $50. . . . We hope you have a wonderful Thanksgiving."
>
> My reaction was joy, relief, and excitement—plus guilt. I had neglected to trust the Lord, who remains faithful. Glancing at the clock, I rushed back to work and straight to a friend's office. Barbara had heard me

> exclaim many times that Jesus loves us. With great enthusiasm I told her what happened. She responded with a glint in her eye.
>
> "Ginny, I'll do one better than that. I have a turkey that was given to us in the freezer . . . I'll bring it to you on Monday, and you can spend the extra money on something else." . . .
>
> On Tuesday . . . [a]s we put the groceries away at home I was reflecting on how faithful God is even when our trust falters. Then, as I was about to shut the cabinet, the doorbell rang. . . . "Is your mother home? We are from the Church of the Open Door. . . . We have brought you your Thanksgiving dinner." . . . With my mouth still open we watched as they brought in seven bags of groceries—and a 21-pound turkey.
>
> We had to clear space for the groceries in the bathroom linen closet, the laundry room and under one bed. As we were preparing for bed that night, I received another phone call—Carol, a friend from church. "Ginny," she said excitedly, "John and I have just come from the market and we bought food for Thanksgiving. . . . We want you and the kids to come over. . . . We won't take no for an answer."[7]

Most people have never been in that exact situation. That's not important. God provides for each of his children in a different way. What is important is to know that if we were in that situation, it would be for the testing of our faith. All we would need to do is trust in Jesus, who for the sake of his glory will provide whatever we need.

# 38

# A Sabbath for Man

EXODUS 16:21–36

GOD'S PEOPLE WERE ON A SPIRITUAL JOURNEY. They had crossed the sea, and now they were in the wilderness, somewhere between the bondage of the past and the hope of the Promised Land.

The way was difficult. The Israelites confronted many physical dangers and suffered many spiritual doubts. But God was using these hardships—as he uses the problems in our own lives—to make his people holy. This part of their pilgrimage was about sanctification, as Christians have long recognized. Writing in the first century after Christ, Clement of Rome explained the spiritual purpose of Israel's wilderness experience:

> After this [Red Sea crossing], Moses, by the command of God, whose providence is over all, led out the people of the Hebrews into the wilderness; and, leaving the shortest road which leads from Egypt to Judaea, he led the people through long windings of the wilderness, that, by the discipline of forty years, the novelty of a changed manner of life might root out the evils which had clung to them by a long-continued familiarity with the customs of the Egyptians.[1]

## Bread for the Sabbath

Clement described the wilderness as "a changed manner of life," and was the change ever dramatic! The Israelites lived in desert tents, depending on God to send them manna from Heaven: "Morning by morning they gathered it, each as much as he could eat; but when the sun grew hot, it melted" (16:21). This kept God's people from getting lazy. If they wanted to eat, they had to get up and gather their daily bread. It also kept them from going hungry. Morning by morning they were sustained by God's mercy. This new lifestyle was a drastic change from their time in Egypt, when they lived in the houses and ate the bread that Pharaoh provided.

Exodus 16 introduces yet another change from the customs of Egypt. This change was an important part of living for God's glory. It was such a significant change, in fact, that Exodus describes it in four different places. Unlike Pharaoh, who made the Israelites work all the time, God gave them rest along the way. He graciously provided the gift of the Sabbath—one whole day in seven for worship.

This new rhythm of labor and leisure was reinforced by the manna: "On the sixth day they gathered twice as much bread, two omers each. And when all the leaders of the congregation came and told Moses . . ." (16:22). Apparently they were surprised to see how much manna there was. They were used to gathering what they needed, but on day six there seemed to be twice as much. However, if the leaders were surprised, they shouldn't have been, because God had already told them that this would happen. He had told Moses, "The people shall go out and gather a day's portion every day, that I may test them, whether they will walk in my law or not. On the sixth day, when they prepare what they bring in, it will be twice as much as they gather daily" (16:4b, 5).

On the sixth day of every week, God gave his people a two-day supply of bread. The seventh day—the Sabbath—was a day of rest (which is what the word *Sabbath* means—to cease or desist). By sending a double portion of manna the day before, God provided for his people seven days a week:

> He [Moses] said to them, "This is what the LORD has commanded: 'Tomorrow is a day of solemn rest, a holy Sabbath to the LORD; bake what you will bake and boil what you will boil, and all that is left over lay aside to be kept till the morning.'" So they laid it aside till the morning, as Moses commanded them, and it did not stink, and there were no worms in it. Moses said, "Eat it today, for today is a Sabbath to the LORD; today you will not find it in the field. Six days you shall gather it, but on the seventh day, which is a Sabbath, there will be none." (16:23–26)

This was all part of the miracle of the manna. Ordinarily manna did not keep for an extra day. It soon contaminated, as some of the Israelites unfortunately had discovered. However, this did not happen on the Sabbath. The manna was preserved. This seems to have been another divine miracle, although perhaps the preparations the Israelites made also had something to do with it. Moses told the people to boil and bake their manna (16:23). (Incidentally, none of the naturally-occurring substances alleged to be the "real explanation" for manna can be either baked or boiled, which further confirms that the manna was a miracle.)

By doing their boiling and baking on the sixth day of the week, God's people were preparing for the seventh day. Whatever they baked and boiled would be ready to eat on the Sabbath. They were only to bake what they needed, and whatever they didn't bake would go bad.

## The Origins of the Sabbath

What is remarkable about these instructions is that they were issued before God gave the Ten Commandments at Mount Sinai. Usually we associate the Sabbath with the fourth commandment:

> Remember the Sabbath day, to keep it holy. Six days you shall labor, and do all your work, but the seventh day is a Sabbath to the LORD your God. On it you shall not do any work, you, or your son, or your daughter, your male servant, or your female servant, or your livestock, or the sojourner who is within your gates. For in six days the LORD made heaven and earth, the sea, and all that is in them, and rested on the seventh day. Therefore the LORD blessed the Sabbath day and made it holy. (20:8–11)

The very wording of this commandment seems to assume that God's people already knew that God had divided their lives into weeks and that he wanted them to rest on the seventh day. How could they "remember the Sabbath day" unless they had heard about it before? The truth is that they were keeping the Sabbath even before they arrived at Mount Sinai. This was Israel's unique privilege. No other culture in the ancient world celebrated a weekly day of rest.

Most Christians say they believe in the Ten Commandments. However, some would be surprised to discover that the Sabbath is included. Many others would be inclined to view the fourth commandment as somehow less important than the others. Some even say that it is obsolete because it has been completely fulfilled in Christ. It is true that we find our ultimate rest in the finished work of Jesus Christ. Furthermore, the New Testament warns, "Let no one pass judgment on you in questions of food and drink, or with regard to a festival or a new moon or a Sabbath. These are a shadow of the things to come, but the substance belongs to Christ" (Colossians 2:16, 17).[2] Thus the question arises: Is the Sabbath obsolete, or is the gift of a weekly day of rest and worship still available to Christians today?

One good reason to be cautious about dismissing the fourth commandment is that its principle predates the giving of the Law at Mount Sinai. The Sabbath goes back to the wilderness, where God gave manna six days out of seven. But it goes back even farther than that, because it goes all the way back to the creation of the world. Genesis 2 begins with the assertion that "the heavens and the earth were finished, and all the host of them" (Genesis 2:1). Then it proceeds to reveal the Sabbath principle in the work and rest of God: "And on the seventh day God finished his work that he had done, and he rested on the seventh day from all his work that he had done. So God blessed the seventh day and made it holy, because on it God rested from all his work that he had done in creation"

(Genesis 2:2, 3). This account may explain why, when God mentioned the Sabbath to Moses, he used the past tense ("the Lord has given you the Sabbath," 16:29). It was something the Israelites had heard about before, something given with the creation.

The Sabbath is a special day, a holy day, set apart by God himself on the seventh day of the world. It is what theologians call a "creation ordinance." Therefore, keeping it is not something that is just for Jews—it is part of what it means to be a human being. God worked for six days and then rested on the seventh. This set the pattern for the people he made in his image. Keeping the Sabbath is one of the things that distinguishes us from every other creature. We alone are able to imitate our Creator by following his pattern of work and rest.

The way God first taught Israel to follow this pattern was by sending six days of manna, with enough on the sixth day to last through the Sabbath. God was following the pattern that he established at creation, providing for six days and then resting on the seventh. Peter Enns comments: "It is not simply that the Sabbath is 'observed' by the Israelites in that they refrain from gathering food. Rather, it is God who refrains from supplying the food. It is he who ceases working, so that no manna or quail is to be found."[3] When God rested, his people rested too. This rhythm of gathering and then not gathering engraved the Sabbath on the nation's heart.

## Breaking the Sabbath

Today many Christians struggle with keeping the Sabbath. There are many reasons for this. One is the pressure of our culture, which no longer recognizes Sunday as a special day for rest and worship. Another reason is that we generally prefer to follow our own agenda, so we would rather not have God tell us how to spend our hours and our days.

Then there is the fear of legalism. People who try to apply the Sabbath principle often make lists of rules about what we can and can't do—regulations concerning the conduct of commerce and the playing of sports, for example. There is a real danger that instead of being blessed by the law of God, we will be tyrannized by the laws of men. It was this issue that caused controversy between Jesus and the religious leaders of his day. The Pharisees, as they were called, had a complicated set of rules for keeping the Sabbath. They accused Jesus of breaking these rules by, for example, healing people on the Sabbath. But Jesus refused to acknowledge that their man-made regulations had anything to do with the heart of keeping God's law.

There is also the secret fear that keeping the Sabbath will be boring. Even Christians who believe that a weekly day of rest is binding for the church today can sympathize with Jonathan Edwards's daughter Esther, who once wrote in her journal, "O, I long for a Sabbath's frame of Mind. But instead of that my thoughts wander to the ends of the Earth. And in whatever duty I am engaged, I am as cold and Dead as a stone. My heart, I see, is on the World and not on God."

If we struggle with the Sabbath we are not alone, because the Israelites struggled with it too. From the very beginning, they found it difficult to understand and hard to obey. Moses told them not to expect any manna on the Sabbath. "On the seventh day some of the people went out to gather, but they found none" (16:27). These people were astonished to discover that God actually did what he said he would do and stopped sending the manna. Sending more manna was unnecessary because God had given them more than enough the day before. All the people needed to do was rely on what he had already provided.

The Israelites who went out on the seventh day were guilty of a treasonable offense. They broke the Sabbath, of course, but there was more to it than that: they did not trust God's word. The instructions Moses had given them were perfectly clear. They were to gather twice as much on the sixth day, but nothing at all on the seventh. This was as straightforward as the Sabbath command that God gave to us all at Mount Sinai. The problem was not that the people hadn't heard or couldn't understand, but that they wouldn't listen. They went out looking for manna because they trusted neither God nor his word.

One wonders if these Sabbath-breakers were the same people who earlier tried to hoard their manna and ended up with maggots. Probably they were, because in both cases they committed the same sin: they failed to trust what God said. When God told them to take only what they needed, they tried to save some extra. But when God told them to take twice as much, they said, "Oh no, we're not doing that again!" However, in this case keeping extra was not a sin but an act of faith. Sadly, some of the Israelites always had their own ideas about what God wanted, so they refused to submit to God's will. For the Christian, this is a reminder not only to study God's word, but also to do what it says in each and every situation.

## The Gift of the Sabbath

God was disappointed when the Israelites broke the Sabbath: "And the LORD said to Moses, 'How long will you refuse to keep my commandments and my laws?'" (16:28). This was a stinging rebuke because it echoed God's earlier words to Pharaoh. After sending the first seven plagues, God said, "How long will you refuse to humble yourself before me?" (10:3). Back then God wondered (so to speak—"How long?" is really a rhetorical question) when Pharaoh would ever let his people go. Now he was starting to wonder when his own people would ever learn to trust and obey.

Later, when God reminded his people what they had learned in the wilderness, he remembered how exasperated he was when they broke the Sabbath. Speaking through the prophet Ezekiel, he said:

> So I led them out of the land of Egypt and brought them into the wilderness. I gave them my statutes and made known to them my rules, by which, if a person does them, he shall live. Moreover, I gave them my Sabbaths, as a sign between me and them, that they might know that I am the LORD who sanctifies them. But the house of Israel rebelled against me in the wilderness. They did not walk in my statutes but rejected my rules, by which, if a person does them, he shall live; and my Sabbaths they greatly profaned. (Ezekiel 20:10–13a)

Why was God so frustrated? It was partly because of the dishonor done to his name. He had saved a people for his glory, but they were unwilling to serve him even one whole day out of seven. But God also grieved the damage his people were doing to themselves. He knew that keeping his commands brings life. In this case, keeping the Sabbath would bring spiritual life. So God said, "See! The LORD has given you the Sabbath; therefore on the sixth day he gives you bread for two days" (16:29a). God was reminding his people that the seventh day was for their benefit. He had *given* them the Sabbath. The Biblical view of the Sabbath starts with the recognition that it is a gift from God.

It's always nice to receive a gift, especially when it comes from someone who knows what you like and what you need. And who knows us better than God? No one, which is why we may be certain that the gift of the Sabbath is for our blessing. Jesus taught this truth to his disciples. They had aroused controversy by picking grain on the Sabbath. They simply had done what people usually did in those days when they got hungry: they picked a few stalks of wheat while they were walking through a field. Jesus defended their actions on the grounds that the Sabbath was God's gift to humanity. He said, "The Sabbath was made for man, not man for the Sabbath" (Mark 2:27). This principle is fundamental for a Christian understanding of the Sabbath. The day is not for God's benefit, but for our blessing.

The Sabbath contains many blessings, some of which we will consider when we get to the Ten Commandments (Exodus 20). The Sabbath is a day for worship and for mercy, but its primary purpose is mentioned here in chapter 16. God said to Moses, "Remain each of you in his place; let no one go out of his place on the seventh day" (16:29b). Then the Scripture adds this comment: "So the people rested on the seventh day" (16:30). The main blessing of the Sabbath is rest for the people of God. Even worship and mercy are forms of rest. To worship is to rest in God's grace, and to show mercy is to extend God's rest to those who are weary.

Resting on the Sabbath distinguished Israel from Egypt. The Israelites immediately would have seen that rest was one of the major differences between serving God and serving Pharaoh. Certainly the God of Israel recognized the importance of work. He is a working God who calls his people to work, but not all day and not all the time. So God gave his servants a Sabbath. The Egyptians, by contrast, generally did not believe in time off, especially for slaves. John Currid writes: "No concept of Sabbath rest has been found in ancient Egypt. That fact underscores the difference between Yahweh and Pharaoh: the God of the Old Testament is compassionate and caring towards his people. Pharaoh was merely a burdensome taskmaster."[4]

The difference between God and Pharaoh is further emphasized in Deuteronomy 5, the Bible's other version of the Ten Commandments. After telling God's people to "Observe the Sabbath day, to keep it holy" (Deuteronomy 5:12), the Scripture goes on to say, "Remember that you were a slave in the land of Egypt, and the Lord your God brought you out from there with a mighty hand and an outstretched arm. Therefore the Lord your God commanded you to keep the Sabbath day" (Deuteronomy 5:15). The gift of the Sabbath was for the remembrance of salvation. Every week, as the people rested in the goodness of their God, they were reminded of their redemption from slavery.

The gift of God's rest is still available today as one of the many blessings that God has given to his church. Several things have changed, however. One is the day. The Old Testament Sabbath was on the seventh day of the week. However, the New Testament day of worship and rest is the first day of the week (see 1 Corinthians 16:2), the day that Jesus rose from the dead. As a result of this change from Saturday to Sunday, the early church no longer called their day of rest "the Sabbath," but "the Lord's day" (Revelation 1:10).

There are also some changes in what the day means. The Old Testament Sabbath looked back to the exodus and back to creation, but it also looked forward. In the near future it looked forward to Canaan, the Promised Land of rest. At the same time the Sabbath anticipated the coming of a Savior. Jesus Christ is the fulfillment of all God's promises, including the promise of the Sabbath. When God's people rested on the seventh day, they were waiting in the hope of an everlasting rest. God fulfilled that promise by sending us Jesus, who said, "Come to me, all who labor and are heavy laden, and I will give you rest" (Matthew 11:28). When we come to Jesus in faith, we enter God's rest. We give up trying to work for our salvation. We also abandon the anxiety and the sheer exhaustion that go along with striving to be good enough for God. Instead we rest upon what Jesus did when he kept God's law, died on the cross, and rose from the dead on our behalf.

Today when we celebrate the Lord's Day, we are still looking backward and forward. We look back to creation, but we also look back to the resurrection as we rest in the finished work of Christ. Then we look forward to our everlasting rest. The Scripture says, "So then, there remains a Sabbath rest for the people of God, for whoever has entered God's rest has also rested from his works as God did from his. Let us therefore strive to enter that rest" (Hebrews 4:9–11a). Our weekly day of rest is both a day to remember and a day to wait in hope for the coming of Christ. According to theologian Richard Gaffin, "God wants us to view the final rest—the consummation order in store for God's redeemed children—as one grand, unending sabbath-rest. That suggests that the Sabbath day rest is an eschatological sign. In other words, our weekly Sabbath-rest is a recurrent pointer to that consummation. Weekly Sabbath keeping is a sign that points to the end of history and to the ultimate fulfillment of all God's purposes for his creation."[5]

In Christ the Sabbath has undergone a wonderful transformation to become the Lord's Day. In many ways the day's promise has been fulfilled. Therefore, if we regard the day in a legalistic way, merely treating it as an Old Testament Sabbath, we fail to recognize what God has done for us through the work of Jesus Christ. However, if we dismiss God's weekly gift of rest, we are failing to wait for our full and final rest, which we will not enjoy until Christ comes again. In one of his hymns John Newton rightly described Sunday as the "day of all the week the best, emblem of eternal rest."

### A Gift for Us

If ever a society badly needed the gift of God's rest, it is our own. We are always complaining about how tired and busy we are. As Christians, we grumble about not having enough time for Bible study, prayer, and ministry. Usually we blame these problems on our workload, but could it be that part of the problem is our own disobedience in not keeping a weekly day of worship and rest?

Observing the Lord's Day is increasingly out of step in America, even in the church. However, if we do not receive the gift of God's rest, then we are really still working for Pharaoh. Rushing around from one activity to the next, trying to get ahead in life, always working and never waiting (even on Sunday)—this lifestyle comes from the sinful nature. And according to the Bible, there is no peace or rest for the wicked (Isaiah 48:22). Therefore, as Christians we are called to stand against the strivings of the surrounding culture. The Lord's Day is a weekly opportunity for Christian witness. Keeping it holy ought to be one of the things that distinguishes the church from the world. Walter Brueggeman writes, "Sabbath means that there's enough bread, that we don't have to hustle every day of our lives. There's no record that Pharaoh ever took a day off. People who think their lives consist of struggling to get more and more can never slow down because they won't ever have enough."[6] To struggle this way is to go back to Egypt and all the drudgeries of slavery. This is unnecessary because God has given us the gift of his rest.

Keeping the Lord's Day holy is beneficial in every way. It is good physically; it helps our bodies recover from the wear and tear of our daily toil. It is good for the soul, helping us to lead spiritually-balanced lives. It even helps us work to the best of our ability. As a general rule, people who take the time to rest according to God's pattern are more productive in their labor.

Several years ago an article on Sabbath-keeping appeared in the pages of the in-flight magazine of United Airlines. The author began by identifying a common problem. "Not so long ago," she wrote, "I was just another harried working mom, rushing through the day with one thought always in mind: Why isn't there any time?" Eventually she found the time by enjoying a weekly day of rest:

> Now, if someone told you there was a way to stop the onslaught of everyday obligations, improve your social life, keep the house clean, revive your tired marriage, elevate spiritual awareness, and improve productivity at work—all overnight and without cost—you'd probably say the claim was absurd. I certainly did. But I was willing to see if some cosmic miracle cure might really work, and after a year of earnest research, I've discovered that adherence to a . . . Sabbath . . . yields a precious gift of time. . . . My personal life, my professional life, and my family life have all improved, and I plan to go on celebrating the Sabbath.[7]

As far as I know this woman was not a Christian. No doubt she would experience an even deeper rest if she set aside the works of her own righteousness to rest upon the grace that God offers in Jesus Christ. Nevertheless, she experienced God's blessing because she is made in God's image. Like everyone else, she needs a day of rest. Now she enjoys God's gift of a Sabbath—a gift that is still ours for the taking.

## Saving the Leftovers

The Sabbath was a day to remember. Each week, as God's people enjoyed their rest, they recalled God's mighty work in salvation. But the Sabbath was not the only memory aid that God had given them. He gave them the Passover to remember that they were saved by the blood of the Lamb. He gave them the Feast of Unleavened Bread to remember their exodus from Egypt. And he gave them the consecration of the firstborn to remember their adoption as sons.

God gave them something else to remember at the end of Exodus 16, in what at first seems like a miscellaneous list of editorial comments:

> Now the house of Israel called its name manna. It was like coriander seed, white, and the taste of it was like wafers made with honey. Moses said, "This is what the LORD has commanded: 'Let an omer of it be kept throughout your generations, so that they may see the bread with which I fed you in the wilderness, when I brought you out of the land of Egypt.'" And Moses said to Aaron, "Take a jar, and put an omer of manna in it, and place it before the LORD to be kept throughout your generations." As the LORD commanded Moses, so Aaron placed it before the testimony to be kept. The people of Israel ate the manna forty years, till they came to a habitable land. They ate the manna till they came to the border of the land of Canaan. (An omer is the tenth part of an ephah.) (16:31–36)

These verses provide additional information about the bread that God sent from Heaven. Manna looked something like seeds from *Coriandrum sativum*, a plant with small, gray, round seeds. And it was delicious! The manna tasted like honey, and thus it gave Israel a foretaste of Canaan, the land "flowing with milk and honey" (3:8). The goodness of the manna was also a sign of God's favor. The food that he provided for their daily rations was sweet to their taste.

God told Moses to save some of this tasty manna. The people were to keep it (16:32–34), preserving about two quarts in a jar. It is not certain when Moses did this. He may have done it some time later in their journey, but eventually the manna was put into "a golden urn" (see Hebrews 9:4) and kept in the Ark of the Covenant ("the testimony," as it is called here). By some divine miracle, this heavenly bread was kept from contamination and became one of Israel's national treasures. The manna served as a memorial. In addition to everything else that God wanted his people to remember—their atonement, their deliverance, their adoption—he wanted them to remember his provision. God wanted his people to remember how well he cared for them in the wilderness, giving them their daily bread for forty years, right up to the very day they entered the Promised Land (see Joshua 5:11, 12).

The people did remember. Passages throughout the Old Testament show that God's people never forgot the way God had provided for them. They told their children about the manna in the wilderness, and they praised God for it in song: "They asked, and he . . . gave them bread from heaven. . . . Praise the LORD!" (Psalm 105:40, 45b). Their remembrance was an encouragement to their faith. Recalling what God had done for them in the past helped them depend on him to provide for them in the present.

God has given us some things to remember as well. He has given us the Lord's Day to remember Jesus and his resurrection. He has also given us the bread of the Lord's Supper. This is a reminder of God's provision. More than that, it is a continual reminder of the cross where Jesus offered his body as a sacrifice for our sins. Here is God's promise to everyone who receives his gifts of rest and remembrance:

> If you . . . call the Sabbath a delight
> and the holy day of the LORD honorable;
> if you honor it, not going your own ways,
> or seeking your own pleasure, or talking idly;
> then you shall take delight in the LORD,
> and I will make you ride on the heights of the earth;
> I will feed you with the heritage of Jacob your father. (Isaiah 58:13, 14)

# 39

# That Rock Was Christ

EXODUS 17:1–7

THE WHOLE BIBLE IS ABOUT JESUS CHRIST. In the Old Testament his coming as Savior is expected. In the Gospels his glorious person and redeeming work are exhibited. In the Epistles his way of salvation by faith is explained. Then in the book of Revelation his majesty as King is exalted. From beginning to end it is all about Jesus.

We have encountered Christ throughout our study of Exodus. We saw him in the birth of Moses—the baby in the basket who was born to be the savior. We saw him at the burning bush, where Moses met the Great I Am. We also saw him in all of God's signs and wonders. The finger of God in the plague of gnats pointed us to Jesus and his miracles. The plague of darkness reminded us of the black hours he suffered on the cross. Then we saw Jesus at the Red Sea, where God's people were baptized from death into life. We saw Jesus in the wilderness too. The sweet desert springs refreshed us with his living water, and the manna tasted like the true bread from Heaven that gives life to the world. The history of Israel's deliverance is the story of our own salvation in Christ.

By this point we expect to meet Jesus at every turn. However, nothing has quite prepared us for the remarkable statement that the Apostle Paul makes in 1 Corinthians 10. Paul had been thinking through the connection between Israel and the church. Among other things, he recalled the events described in Exodus 17, when Moses struck his rod, and water flowed from the rock. When the Israelites drank in that miracle, they were drinking the same water that Christians enjoy today. As Paul explains it: "All drank the same spiritual drink. For they drank from the spiritual Rock that followed them, and *the Rock was Christ*" (1 Corinthians 10:3, 4).

This is a daring interpretation of the exodus. When the apostle studied Israel's experience at Meribah, he said, "Aha! I know who the rock was. That rock was Christ!" But what did Paul mean? How could the rock be Christ?

## The Crisis

To see Christ clearly in this passage, we need to study it carefully. This is what happened: "All the congregation of the people of Israel moved on from the wilderness of Sin by stages, according to the commandment of the Lord, and camped at Rephidim, but there was no water for the people to drink" (17:1). If this sounds familiar, it is because the Israelites had a similar experience back in chapter 15, when they reached the bitter waters of Marah. Once again they were out in the wilderness and out of water. For the purpose of their sanctification, God had led them away from the place of provision to a place where there was nothing to drink.

Rephidim means "resting place." As resting places go, it was a major disappointment. However, by now the Israelites ought to have known how to handle this kind of situation. They should have gathered for prayer and then waited for God to provide. Instead they did what they usually did, which was complain. It was so dry and hot that they were afraid of dying by dehydration. "Therefore the people quarreled with Moses and said, 'Give us water to drink'" (17:2a).

This was now the fourth time that God's people were guilty of grumbling (see 14:11, 12; 15:24; 16:2). Once again they found fault with Moses. They "quarreled" with him, a strong word suggesting that they had reached a new level of hostility. They were striving against Moses, revolting against his authority. Imperiously they demanded that the prophet provide water. Then they charged him—not for the first time (or the last)—with attempted homicide: "But the people thirsted there for water, and the people grumbled against Moses and said, 'Why did you bring us up out of Egypt, to kill us and our children and our livestock with thirst?'" (17:3).

Although the people picked a fight with Moses, their real argument was with God. Knowing this, "Moses said to them, 'Why do you quarrel with me? Why do you test the Lord?'" (17:2b). Moses was in a position of divinely appointed spiritual authority. He had led Israel to Rephidim not because he knew where the water was, but because that is where God told him to go. Therefore, the people could not reject him without also rebelling against God. What they were really doing was putting God to the test. This is confirmed by the psalmist, who wrote: "Today, if you hear his voice, do not harden your hearts, as at Meribah, as on the day at Massah in the wilderness, when your fathers put me to the test and put me to the proof" (Psalm 95:7b–9a; cf. 78:40, 41).

This is something else we have seen before: All our dissatisfaction shows that we are disappointed with God. To put it another way, all our complaints go straight to the top, where God rules the universe by his sovereign power. Whatever the reason for our discontent, what it really shows is that we are not satisfied with what God has given us. This is a great sin. It is not wrong to take our troubles to God, talking them over with him in prayer. In fact, the Bible encourages us to be honest about our doubts and difficulties. But God does not accept open revolt against his holy will or the refusal to trust in his perfect word.

## The Complaint

The Israelites made three statements to Moses, each of which represents a different kind of complaint. What they say is worth considering carefully because the Bible warns us not to "grumble, as some of them did" (1 Corinthians 10:10). So how did they grumble?

First they said, "Give us water to drink" (17:2a). The sin here is *demanding God's provision*—not asking for it or waiting for it, but insisting on it. They were telling God that he had to give them what they wanted or else there was no telling what they might do. In our rebellion we often do the same thing. We insist on having our own way. When God does not do for us what we think he ought to do, in the way we think he ought to do it, we complain about it. At home, at work, and in the church, we demand God's provision on our own terms.

The second thing the Israelites said was, "Why did you bring us up out of Egypt, to kill us and our children and our livestock with thirst?" (17:3). Here they were *denying God's protection*. The people assumed the worst, as they usually did, and thus they concluded that God had abandoned them, even to the point of death. Although their words were directed against God's prophet, they were really impugning God's motives. They were accusing him of trying to harm them. Again, we often commit the same sin. We complain that what God is doing in our lives—especially the suffering we must endure—is not good for us but actually harmful. This is to deny God's protection.

The third thing the Israelites did was to test God, saying, "Is the LORD among us or not?" (17:7). In this case, their sin was *doubting God's presence*. The lack of water made them wonder if God was really with them after all. Our own trials often raise the same question: "Are you really there, God? If you are, you sure don't seem to be blessing me very much right now!" When we adopt this attitude, we are guilty of denying God's presence.

We can understand the complaints that Israel made because we often make the same complaints ourselves. But really, we have nothing to complain about. None of our accusations are true. And if only the Israelites had taken the time to remember everything that God had done for them, they would have recognized this for themselves. God had done great things for his people. He had provided for them, turning bitter water into something sweet and feeding them in the wilderness: "They asked, and he brought quail, and gave them bread from heaven in abundance" (Psalm 105:40). The people also forgot God's protection, especially their deliverance from Pharaoh at the Red Sea. And they forgot his presence. They had seen his glory in the fiery pillar of cloud. How many times was God going to have to prove himself to these people? He was guiding them day and night, feeding them manna six days out of seven, and still they wondered whether he was there for them. Their unbelief was unbelievable!

God's people were suffering from a kind of spiritual amnesia. Their memory trouble made them forget the provision, the protection, and the presence of God. In the words of the psalmist, "They soon forgot his works" (Psalm 106:13a; cf. Psalm 95:9). And as a result of their forgetfulness, they committed the great sin of complaining.

This suggests one obvious remedy for our own discontent, which is to remember what God has done for us. When we are in need, we should recount all the ways that he has met our needs for food and shelter, for work and play, for love and friendship. We should rehearse the times when he protected us, sparing us from physical danger or from the consequences of our own folly. And we should revisit the places where he was close to us. God is our provider and protector, our ever-present help in trouble. If we remember this, we will be able to trust him without grumbling or complaining.

## The Court-Martial

Much of Israel's complaint at Meribah sounds familiar, but there is one very significant difference. This time the people actually brought God to trial. They initiated a legal proceeding against him, almost like a court-martial.

Rephidim was supposed to be a place of testing—not for God, but for his people. *They* were the ones on trial. God had been testing them all along. He tested them at Marah, where the water was bitter: "There the LORD . . . tested them" (15:25b). He tested them again when he sent manna from Heaven. He said, "The people shall go out and gather a day's portion every day, that I may test them, whether they will walk in my law or not" (16:4b). Then God tested his people once again at Meribah. As part of their ongoing spiritual education, he wanted to see if they would trust him to provide living water. But they were tired of being tested. They wanted to ask the questions, not answer them; so they charged God with breaking his covenant.

How can we tell that Israel was bringing God to trial? First, because twice this episode is called a "test" (17:2, 7), meaning a trial by ordeal. As Moses later reminded God's people, "You tested [him] at Massah, with [him] you quarreled at the waters of Meribah" (Deuteronomy 33:8). The Hebrew word used in these verses (*rib*) is the term for a covenant lawsuit. We also know that this was a trial because the people presented a list of their grievances, which were really accusations. As we have seen, they charged God with neglecting to provide for them, refusing to protect them, and failing to be present with them.

Furthermore, the alleged crime was a capital offense—namely, murder. The people said, "Why did you bring us up out of Egypt, to kill us and our children and our livestock with thirst?" (17:3b). Although they were pressing this charge against Moses, he, of course, was God's representative. They were really judging God *in absentia* for leading them into this wasteland. Not only were they rushing to reach a verdict, but they were also prepared to carry out the sentence. They figured that if they were going to die anyway, then at least Moses should be the first to go. So the prophet was compelled to cry out, "They are almost ready to stone me" (17:4b). Stoning was a conventional way to carry out the death penalty. Its mention here gives further evidence that the Israelites were conducting some kind of trial.

There is more. God said to Moses, "[Take] with you some of the elders of Israel" (17:5). In ancient times the assembly of elders passed judgment on disputed matters. Therefore, when Moses gathered them together, he was convening a court by forming a jury. Then he took up his staff to strike the rock. God had given Moses this staff back at the burning bush as the proof of his presence (see 4:1, 2). It represented God's power and authority as Judge. God called attention to this by saying to Moses, "Take in your hand the staff with which you struck the Nile" (17:5). Striking the Nile was an act of God's judgment against Egypt. For Moses to strike the rock, therefore, was another act of divine judgment.

Finally, there are the place names to consider: "And he [Moses] called the name of the place Massah and Meribah, because of the quarreling of the people of Israel, and because they tested the Lord" (17:7). Both Massah and Meribah are legal terms. Massah means "to test." Meribah means "to strive, to argue, to dispute, or to contend." It is a participle derived from the Hebrew word *rib*, the technical term for a covenant lawsuit. The famous Old Testament scholar Gerhard Von Rad thus concluded that the names Massah and Meribah "imply that legal cases were investigated and decided by ordeal there."[1]

When all the evidence is considered, the scene at Rephidim is easily recognized as a courtroom. It was more like the People's Court than the Supreme Court; nevertheless it was a court. The Israelites were instituting legal proceedings. What is significant is not so much the procedure as the attitude behind it. The people wanted to hold God responsible. They were not happy with the way things were going. Instead of trusting that God's plan was good and gracious, they wanted to bring him to judgment.

People often put God to the test this way. We want him to prove himself to us. So instead of starting with God and evaluating our experience from his point of view, we start with our own circumstances and judge him on that basis. When things go wrong, when life does not meet our expectations, we are quick to fix the blame squarely on his shoulders and to demand some kind of explanation. C. S. Lewis observed:

> The ancient man approached God as the accused person approaches his judge. For the modern man the roles are reversed. He is the judge: God is in the dock. He is quite a kindly judge: if God should have a reasonable

> defense for being the god who permits war, poverty and disease, he is ready to listen to it. The trial may even end in God's acquittal. But the important thing is that Man is on the Bench and God in the Dock.[2]

Lewis was right. People often claim the right to reach their own verdict about God. They demand some answers before they will even think about becoming Christians. Some of the questions are legitimate, such as "If God is good, then why does he allow evil?" or "If God is love, then why did he come up with such a narrow way of salvation?" It is not wrong to ask, but our motivation for asking makes all the difference. Are we asking from a genuine desire to know God, or are we raising objections that are really based on a refusal to believe in him? God loves to answer the questions of an honest seeker, but for those who expect God to meet their demands, his ways will forever remain a mystery.

To see how wrong it is to put God in the dock, consider that this was Satan's strategy. When the devil tempted Jesus in the wilderness, he tried to get Jesus to prove himself. Taking him to the highest point of the temple he said, "If you are the Son of God, throw yourself down, for it is written, 'He will command his angels concerning you,' and 'On their hands they will bear you up, lest you strike your foot against a stone'" (Matthew 4:6). Satan was putting Jesus in the dock. He was trying to get him to prove that he really was the Son of God. But Jesus refused to submit to the devil's trial, not because he couldn't pass, but because the trial itself was wrong. Thinking back to the exodus, Jesus said, "Again it is written, 'You shall not put the Lord your God to the test'" (Matthew 4:7; cf. Deuteronomy 6:16).

It is not our place to bring God to trial. The real question is not "What do we think about him?" but "What does he think about us?" It is not a matter of us reaching a verdict about him, but of him declaring his verdict on us. With reference to Israel's trial at Meribah, the Bible gives this warning: "Take care, brothers, lest there be in any of you an evil, unbelieving heart, leading you to fall away from the living God" (Hebrews 3:12).

## The Verdict

To our amazement, when Israel put God to the test—as wrong as that was—God went ahead and gave them the hearing they wanted. In order to teach them the way of salvation, he submitted himself to judgment—not their judgment, but his own!

God did this in response to the prayers of his prophet: "So Moses cried to the LORD, 'What shall I do with this people? They are almost ready to stone me'" (17:4). Before seeing how God answered this prayer, we should pause to notice how Moses himself had started to grumble. Admittedly, the prophet was in a difficult situation. He was surrounded by an angry, violent mob. The people were talking about stoning him, and as far as he could tell, they just might go ahead and do it!

In the face of this clear and present danger, Moses cried out for God's help. This was the right thing to do; however, as Calvin commented, there is "something in these words which sounds angry and obstreperous."[3] Apparently Israel's complaining was contagious, because now Moses was the one murmuring. He was complaining about his difficulties in ministry, as spiritual leaders often do, but he was grumbling against God. He was saying something like, "Just what do you expect me to do with these people? I didn't ask for this job, you know. Remember our little meeting back at the burning bush? You're the one who put me in charge here, God." Moses was afraid, and in his fear he complained against God.

In spite of his failings, at least Moses prayed to the right person, for God heard his cry and delivered his people: "And the LORD said to Moses, 'Pass on before the people, taking with you some of the elders of Israel, and take in your hand the staff with which you struck the Nile, and go. Behold, I will stand before you there on the rock at Horeb, and you shall strike the rock, and water shall come out of it, and the people will drink.' And Moses did so, in the sight of the elders of Israel" (17:5, 6).

This episode is not to be confused with a similar incident from the book of Numbers. In both cases water flowed from the rock. However, the incident recorded in Numbers 20 happened later in Israel's journey, after they had received the law at Mount Sinai. Furthermore, Moses handled that situation very differently. He struck the rock twice, not trusting God's power to provide, and for this he was prevented from reaching the Promised Land (Numbers 20:10–12).

Notice that God did not resolve the dispute between his prophet and his people—at least not directly. Instead he proved that he would provide, and thus he removed the cause of their conflict. In the words of Umberto Cassuto, God "does not intervene in the strife between the people and Moses, neither in regard to the people's allegations against Moses, nor in respect of his counter-charges against the people. His attitude is that of a father whose children are in distress, and in their distress an altercation breaks out between them; he pays no attention to the wrangling, but endeavours only to deliver his children from their trouble."[4]

God delivered his people by submitting to his own rod of judgment, taking the judgment in Moses' place. Here we encounter a mysterious and surprising detail in the Biblical text. Moses took the elders to "the rock at Horeb," not far from Mount Sinai. Horeb was the place where God had first appeared to Moses in the burning bush, and now God appeared there again. God said, "I will stand before you there on the rock" (17:6a). The Scripture does not say exactly what this looked like. Perhaps God appeared once again in the cloud of glory. Perhaps he was not even visible at all. But the New Testament makes such a close identification between the rock and Christ that what seems most likely is that

God was present in the person of his Son—the pre-incarnate Christ. However he appeared, God was standing there on the rock.

The elders gathered around to see what judgment God would give. Then Moses struck with his rod: "He [God] opened the rock, and water gushed out; it flowed through the desert like a river" (Psalm 105:41). Various attempts have been made to find some natural explanation for the water that flowed from the rock. Perhaps the rod released a spring that was just underneath the surface. Umberto Cassuto believes

> there was suddenly opened up a stream of running well water through the breaking of a thin layer of rock. Not long ago, too, an English officer saw with his own eyes, in a wady [*sic*] in the southern part of the Sinai Peninsula, a company of the Sudanese camel corps digging in the gravel heaped up by the side of a cliff in order to discover the source of the water that was dripping between the pebbles, when suddenly, after a hard knock with an axe that broke the outer face of the cliff, numerous cavities were revealed in the stone, from which an abundance of water began to gush.[5]

People often try to explain the Biblical miracles. This explanation is as plausible as any, but when it comes to miracles, it is better simply to believe them.

What did the water prove? It proved everything about God that the Israelites were calling into question. Remember, they were demanding his provision, denying his protection, and doubting his presence. But the water flowing from the rock proved all these things. Obviously it proved that God had the power to provide: "He split rocks in the wilderness and gave them drink abundantly as from the deep. He made streams come out of the rock and caused waters to flow down like rivers" (Psalm 78:15, 16). Not only was God their provider, but he was also their protector. Instead of judging his people for their sins—especially for their unbelief—he submitted himself to judgment so they could live. Finally, the rock was the proof of God's presence. The Israelites wanted to know if God was with them or not. Well, there he was—their Savior—standing on the rock.

## Christ the Rock

Has God proved himself to you?

In a sermon called "God on Trial," Ed Clowney describes a play about a group of people who put God to the test. They wanted to know who was responsible for the Holocaust—the destruction of millions of Jews and others in the Nazi concentration camps. Who was to blame?

The play is called *The Sign of Jonah*. It was written by Günter Rutenborn and was first performed in West Berlin shortly after World War II. The play not only asks the question, "Who's to blame?" but it also

> draws both the cast and the audience into the answer. No one is really to blame. A storm trooper merely followed orders. An industrialist merely kept up production. A citizen simply did not become involved. Yet in defending their own innocence each of the accused becomes an accuser. All are guilty. Some are guilty by words; others by silence. Some by what they did; others by what they did not. And suddenly the accused accusers all take up another cry. "We are to blame, yes, but we are not the *most* to blame. The real blame belongs much higher. *God* is to blame! *God must go on trial!*"

So that is what the people do: They put God on trial. In the play God is accused, prosecuted, convicted, and sentenced. What is the sentence? The characters decide that God must "become a human being, a wanderer on earth, deprived of his rights, homeless, hungry, thirsty. He himself shall die. And lose a son, and suffer the agonies of fatherhood. And when at last he dies, he shall be disgraced and ridiculed."[6]

Of course, that is exactly what happened. God sent his Son into the world, and people did to him what the Israelites wanted to do with Moses. The Son of God was a man without a home, a wanderer on earth. He was hungry and thirsty. And when his life was almost over, he was deprived of all his rights. He was stripped, mocked, beaten, and then condemned to die the most disgraceful and excruciating death—death on a cross. That rock was Christ.

The Bible often refers to God as a Rock. He is "the Stone of Israel" (Genesis 49:24; cf. Isaiah 30:29), "the Rock . . . [whose] work is perfect" (Deuteronomy 32:4), the Rock who is a "fortress" and a "refuge" (Psalm 18:2). He is "the rock of our salvation" (Psalm 95:1; cf. Deuteronomy 32:15). In keeping with this imagery, the rock that Moses struck with his rod was a symbol of God and his salvation. In particular, it showed how God would submit to the blow of his own justice so that out of him would flow life for his people.

God did this in the person of his own Son. The rock was Christ because like the rock, Christ was struck with divine judgment. This is what happened to him on the cross. Christ was bearing the curse for our sin, so God struck him with the rod of his justice. The Scripture says, "He was pierced for our transgressions; he was crushed for our iniquities; upon him was the chastisement that brought us peace, and with his wounds we are healed" (Isaiah 53:5). The judgment that Christ received on the cross is the proof of our protection. It shows that we will not suffer eternal death for our sins. God has taken the judgment of our guilt upon himself, and now we are safe for all eternity.

The rock was also Christ because it flowed with the water of life. Here we recall something significant from the crucifixion, something that John noticed as he stood near the cross. In his Gospel John records how, in order to confirm that Jesus was dead, "one of the soldiers pierced his side with a spear, and at once there came out blood and water" (John 19:34). The blood was the blood that he shed for our sins. But John also mentioned the water, not simply to prove that Jesus died on the cross, but also to show that by his death he gives life.

Jesus is the water of life. He said, "Whoever drinks of the water that I will give him will never be thirsty again" (John 4:14a). He is our provider as well as our protector. More than that, everyone who comes to Jesus by faith is filled with the Holy Spirit, and now his life flows within us. Jesus went on to say, "The water that I will give him will become in him a spring of water welling up to eternal life" (John 4:14b).

In Christ God is for us what he was for Israel—our provider, protector, and ever-present Lord. This is what Paul meant when he said "the Rock was Christ" (1 Corinthians 10:4). In the same way that God was with Israel at Horeb, he is with the church in Christ. Our Lord is our Rock, and we trust in his provision, his protection, and his presence.

# 40

# Lift Up Your Hands

## EXODUS 17:8–16

LESSONS FOR LIFE'S JOURNEY—that's what Israel was learning in the wilderness: "God saves." "No whining." "Trust your leaders." "God will guide you, protect you, and provide for you." "He will always be with you." These were the basic spiritual lessons that God's people learned during their long pilgrimage through the desert.

The next lesson had to do with prayer. There is an invisible war between the powers of darkness and the children of light. In the course of these hostilities, God's enemies often attack God's people, and the only way for us to prevail in this spiritual battle is by persevering in prayer.

### It's a Spiritual Battle

When the Israelites escaped from Egypt, the first enemies they faced were not external but internal. Their struggle was the war within—the battle that is waged in every human heart. The difficulties they encountered at Marah, in the Desert of Sin, and at Massah and Meribah were not caused by their outward circumstances, primarily, but by their own disbelief and discontent. They did not trust God to provide, and as a result they were divided and discouraged.

Then suddenly and unexpectedly they were attacked from the outside by an enemy: "Then Amalek came and fought with Israel at Rephidim" (17:8). This was the first military skirmish in Israel's long campaign to win the Promised Land. The Amalekites were nomads who traced their lineage back to Jacob's brother Esau (Genesis 36:12), and thus there were long-standing ethnic tensions between the two tribes. It is not certain why the Amalekites attacked the Israelites on this particular occasion. They may have felt threatened by Israel's sudden arrival in their territory, or they may have been trying to protect their water supply. Rephidim was an oasis, and the Amalekites must have been dismayed to watch so many people with so many animals come and drink "their" water.

Whatever the reason, the attack itself was cowardly. Moses later told God's people, "Remember what Amalek did to you on the way as you came out of Egypt, how he attacked you on the way when you were faint and weary, and cut off your tail, those who were lagging behind you, and he did not fear God" (Deuteronomy 25:17, 18). Not only was the attack unprovoked—it was targeted against the weak and the helpless, the stragglers at the back of the caravan. Rather than waging an honorable war for just cause, the Amalekites made a sneak attack on defenseless women and children. Hence Moses' comment: "He did not fear God."

It is obvious that the Amalekites were taking their orders from somewhere higher up, or rather from somewhere lower down. Since they were enemies of God, these soldiers were really in Satan's army, and Satan was determined to prevent the Israelites from ever reaching the Promised Land. For centuries he had kept them in bondage to Pharaoh. Now that tyranny was over, but Satan thought perhaps there was something else he could do to ambush the plan of salvation. So he enticed the Amalekites to attack the Israelites at Rephidim.

To see how this relates to our own spiritual experience, remember that the Israelites were already saved. They had been delivered from their bondage back at the Red Sea. On that occasion they had not taken up arms against their oppressors. This was because they had someone to fight for them. So Moses had given them these orders: "Fear not, stand firm, and see the salvation of the LORD, which he will work for you today. . . . The LORD will fight for you, and you have only to be silent" (14:13, 14). The God of Israel won their salvation all by himself, as he always does.

Israel's survival was at stake once again at Rephidim, only this time the Israelites *did* have to stand and fight. Not only were they fighting in self-defense, but they were also waging a holy war in which they were fighting for the glory of God. This was the first of many battles that God's people would fight before completing their conquest of Canaan. They had been saved out of Egypt by the strong arm of God. Now they were bound for the Promised Land, and they worked out their salvation by defeating the enemies they met along the way.

Israel's encounter with the Amalekites is a picture of the church in its spiritual warfare. This battle is another Old Testament *type*—a Biblical event that shows the pattern of our life in Christ. The attack was a historical event that pointed to a higher spiritual reality. We have been delivered from the Egypt of our sin, and now we are heading for the land of glory. Our ultimate victory is certain because Jesus won the crucial battle when he died on the cross. Speaking of his great enemy the devil and all the demons of Hell, Scripture says that God "disarmed the rulers and authorities and put them to open shame, by triumphing over them in him" (Colossians 2:15).

Now everyone who comes to faith in Christ is free from the powers of death and Hell. However, the enemies of Christ have not yet surrendered, so on our pilgrimage we continue to be ambushed by Satan. We are engaged in a constant spiritual struggle to resist temptation and carry on with the work of Christ and his gospel. The attacks we face are often sudden, but unlike the wars of the Old Testament, they are spiritual, not physical. The Scripture says that "we do not wrestle against flesh and blood, but against the rulers, against the authorities, against the cosmic powers over this present darkness, against the spiritual forces of evil in the heavenly places" (Ephesians 6:12). Charles Spurgeon wrote:

> The children of Israel were not under the power of Amalek—they were free men; and so we are not under the power of sin any longer. The yoke of sin has been broken by God's grace from off our necks, and now we have to fight not as slaves against a master, but as freemen against a foe. Moses never said to the children of Israel while they were in Egypt, "Go, fight with Pharaoh." Not at all; it is God's work to bring us out of Egypt and make us his people, but when we are delivered from bondage, although it is God's work to help us, we must be active in our cause. Now that we are alive from the dead we must wrestle with principalities and powers and spiritual wickedness if we are to overcome.[1]

There is a good deal of confusion in the church today about spiritual warfare. Part of the problem is that Christians think of spiritual warfare too much in physical terms. Often we assume that disease and depression, accidents and technical difficulties, natural disasters, warfare and terrorism are all direct attacks of Satan. It is true that God allows Satan to bring great evil into the world, and in truth, all our suffering can be traced back to the sin that he first tempted us to commit. But the real battle is not visible—it is invisible. The troubles we see in the world are only skirmishes in the cosmic spiritual strife between God and Satan.

The war is raging all around us, but more frightening is the way that it rages inside us. Our real enemy is not other people, whether outside or inside the church. If we see them as our spiritual opponents, then we will end up demonizing them, and we will also fail to sense our own great danger of falling into sin. Our real enemy is Satan himself, with all his unholy helpers. Even after we are saved, they keep attacking us in the hope that we will do something to dishonor God and thus rob him of his glory.

## The Prophet at Prayer

How can we fight back? How do we engage the enemy? We know that Jesus Christ must win the war, but what is our part in helping to wage it? We join the battle the same way that Moses did: through prayer. It is by persevering and prevailing in prayer that we are victorious on the battlefield of sin and temptation.

The Israelites fought their battle with real weapons. The next day they launched a counterattack: "So Moses said to Joshua, 'Choose for us men, and go out and fight with Amalek. Tomorrow I will stand on the top of the hill with the staff of God in my hand.' So Joshua did as Moses told him, and fought with Amalek, while Moses, Aaron, and Hur went up to the top of the hill" (17:9, 10). This is the first time Joshua has been mentioned. Appropriately enough, his name means "the Lord is salvation." Here he is introduced so matter-of-factly that the Bible seems to assume that we already know who he is. Joshua was Moses' aide-de-camp, and when the Israelites went into battle, he was their field commander.

First Joshua carefully selected Israel's bravest warriors, and then he went down into the valley to fight. And he fought with real weapons, for the Scripture says, "Joshua overwhelmed Amalek and his people with the sword" (17:13). It was necessary for Israel to fight; God required the proper use of means. However, the victory did not depend merely on Joshua and his weapons. Rather, it depended on prayer: "Whenever Moses held up his hand, Israel prevailed, and whenever he lowered his hand, Amalek prevailed" (17:11).

Before Israel's counterattack, Moses had taken up his position on the hillside overlooking the battlefield, where his only weapon was prayer. Admittedly, some scholars dispute this. They argue that when Moses lifted up the rod of God's power, he was doing something other than praying. For example, Nahum Sarna thinks that "Moses held up a standard bearing some conspicuous symbol that signified the presence of God in the Israelite camp."[2] This interpretation would explain why Moses built a victory altar called "The LORD Is My Banner" (17:15). Others think that Moses was performing some kind of magical ritual.[3] Even John Currid says there is "absolutely nothing in the text to support this idea" that "Moses' hands are raised for divine intervention."[4]

It is true that we do not know what Moses said while he was standing on the hillside. Nevertheless, his actions were an unmistakable sign of dependence upon God alone to win the battle. Moses was holding his staff, the instrument of divine power and the token of God's covenant promise. By holding it up to Heaven, he was appealing for God to defend his people.

Moses was also in the posture for prayer. He was standing with his arms raised up to God. The Israelites generally stood when they prayed, lifting their hands to offer their praises and their petitions up to God. For example, when God brought an end to the plague of hail, Moses said to Pharaoh, "I will stretch out my hands to the LORD" (9:29). Hannah and Jehoshaphat both stood at the temple to pray (1 Samuel 1:9–11; 2 Chronicles 20:5, 6). The psalmist said, "In your name I will lift up my hands" (Psalm 63:4b). This is still one appropriate posture for prayer in the church today, for God says, "I desire then that in every place the men should pray, lifting holy hands" (1 Timothy 2:8).

Whether we call it prayer or not, when Moses stood with his arms raised, he was appealing for God to show his power by saving his people. This interpretation seems to be confirmed at the end of the passage, when Moses says that "hands [literally, hand] were lifted up to the throne of the LORD" (17:16a NIV). This is a difficult verse, and giving the right translation depends on making a decision about three different words. The first is the word "throne." Some scholars amend the text to make it say "banner" instead of "throne" ("a hand upon the banner of the LORD").[5] What makes this interpretation plausible is the mention of the Lord as a banner in verse 15. However, it is better simply to take the text as it stands: "the throne of the LORD." Elsewhere the Bible describes prayer as coming to God's throne. On the basis of Jesus Christ and his saving work, we are invited "with confidence [to] draw near to the throne of grace, that we may receive mercy and find grace to help in time of need" (Hebrews 4:16).

The second question concerns the word "hand," which occurs here in the singular. Whose hand is it? Is it the hand of Moses, or is it perhaps the hand of God? The latter interpretation is possible, and it is adopted by, for example, the King James Version. On this view, God is raising his hand to swear vengeance against his enemies. This would tie in with the second half of the verse: "The LORD will have war with Amalek from generation to generation" (17:16b).

One problem with this interpretation is the preposition that comes before the word "throne." And this is the third word to consider: the Hebrew preposition *'al*, which usually means "up to" or "upon." Here it makes more sense for Moses to lift his hand up to the throne than it does for God to do so. However, there is still another possibility. The word *'al* can also mean "against." In that case the hand would belong to the Amalekites, who took up arms against God and thus rebelled against his sovereign throne. This interpretation also makes good sense. In the Old Testament the word "hand" is often used as a metaphor for military might. If it is used that way here, then the two parts of verse 16 fit together nicely. First the Amalekites lifted a hand against God's throne; then God waged war against them.

It is hard to say which interpretation is correct, although the English Standard Version seems to offer the best translation: "A hand upon the throne of the LORD!" But no matter how this verse is understood, each interpretation helps us understand the passage. The Amalekites *were* fighting against God, whether this is what verse 16 says or not, and God promised vengeance against them, whether or not he actually lifted his hand to swear an oath to that effect. For his part, Moses lifted his hands up to God's throne in prayer. Whatever words he used, by lifting his rod he was asking for divine intervention. He was appealing to God in a gesture of total dependence upon his power, the kind of dependence that we express today through prayer.

## The Power of Prayer

God answers prayer. Moses saw this firsthand as he watched the battle unfold. As Joshua closed with the enemy, Moses went up the hillside and raised his staff. At first everything went in Israel's favor. Things were going so well that prayer hardly seemed necessary, so Moses gradually lowered his staff. Then the fortunes of war seemed to turn. The Amalekites were gaining the upper hand. In desperation Moses lifted his staff even higher, appealing to God for victory. But soon his arms grew tired. When he lowered his staff, the same thing happened again. As the battle went back and forth, eventually Moses figured out that what happened down in the valley depended on what he was doing up on the hillside. When his hands were up, Israel was winning; when his hands went down, they started to lose. Their success in battle depended on prayer. People say that the pen is mightier than the sword, but in this case it was the *petition* that was mightier than the sword!

The same principle holds true for our own spiritual warfare. Our spiritual battles against the world, the flesh, and the devil are won and lost through the heavy artillery of prayer. This is why the Apostle Paul ended his famous teaching on "the whole armor of God" by commanding Christians to pray "at all times in the Spirit, with all prayer and supplication" (Ephesians 6:11, 18a).

What happens when we do not pray? It is very simple: We start losing the battle, even if we have put on the full armor of God. We may be wearing the belt of truth, the breastplate of righteousness, the shield of faith, the helmet of salvation, and the sword of the Spirit. However, if we do not ask God to save us, we will not be able to make our stand against the devil. Instead we will be led away from the truth into error. We will give in to temptation. We will be dragged down into doubt and discouragement.

This is true not only for individual Christians but also for the church. If we do not ask God to defend us, then our members will be divided, our leaders will fall into sin, our missionaries will fail to see any fruit, and the lost will not hear the gospel. Both individually and corporately, the neglect of prayer means the loss of spiritual warfare. Even if we fight like Joshua, we will not win the battle unless we pray like Moses.

Why does it all depend on prayer? Why is prayer such an effective spiritual weapon? Why does it make the difference between victory and defeat? The answer is that *God* is the difference between victory and defeat, and it is by prayer that we depend on him to win the battle. The victory depends on prayer because ultimately the victory depends on God.

There is a lot of talk these days about the power of prayer. Some Christians think that prayer itself is the important thing. If only we pray long enough, hard enough, or often enough, then God will do what we want him to do. The focus then becomes finding the right method for prayer. While it is good to pray early and often, the power of prayer is not the prayer itself, but the power of God. In prayer we acknowledge our absolute dependence on God to conquer the enemies of our faith.

This means that like everything else in the Christian life, prayer is for the glory of God. The way it glorifies God is by showing that the victory belongs to him alone. Perhaps this is why Moses went up on the hillside. By standing where everyone could see him, he was making sure that Israel learned the power of prayer. Imagine what would have happened if Moses had not done this. Undoubtedly the Israelites would have concluded that they had defeated the Amalekites in their own strength, and then they would have celebrated their own military prowess.

The same thing would happen to us if we were able to defeat our spiritual enemies without prayer. Imagine what we would be like if we had the power to resist temptation and overcome habitual sin in our own strength. We would become hopelessly self-righteous, claiming the glory for our own sanctification. But God brings us to our knees, where in our weakness we cry out to him as our only helper.

### Wherever Two or Three Are Gathered

Moses was a great man of prayer. Throughout the book of Exodus we hear him talking over his problems with God. It was also his privilege as prophet to intercede on behalf of Israel. He was the mediator, the one who presented their requests to God. So when he lifted his hands in prayer, he was elevating the entire nation before the throne of grace.

Moses received so many wonderful answers to prayer that God's people must have regarded him as a prayer warrior. However, what Exodus 17 reveals about his prayer life is not its strength but its weakness. The Scripture says "Moses' hands grew weary" (17:12). The prophet could not persevere in prayer. This points to our need for a better mediator, the Lord Jesus Christ, who "always lives to make intercession" for us (Hebrews 7:25), without ever needing anyone else to hold up his hands. But Moses was an old man by this point, and the work was too hard for him. He was exhausted. In his own strength he was unable to keep on praying. This is our struggle as well. Prayer can be wearisome work, and we often feel that the labor is too hard for us. As Jesus told his disciples, "The spirit indeed is willing, but the flesh is weak" (Matthew 26:41b).

The weakness of Moses served to magnify the glory of God. It showed that Israel was victorious not because Joshua was a military genius or because Moses was a man of prayer, but because God was their captain in the fight. John Calvin noted that even though Moses prayed, he could not "boastfully commend his own zeal in praying, but is rather the public witness and proclaimer of his weakness, that the glory might be entirely attributed to the gratuitous favor of God."[6] Moses was only a man, and when the Israelites recounted the day's events, they did not praise his power in prayer. Instead they said something like this: "Did you see old Moses up there today? Frankly, I wasn't sure he was going to make it. I don't know how much longer he would have been able to hold on. It's a good thing he had some help!"

The prophet did have some help: "But Moses' hands grew weary, so they took a stone and put it under him, and he sat on it, while Aaron and Hur held up his hands, one on one side, and the other on the other side. So his hands were steady until the going down of the sun" (17:12). People have offered creative interpretations of this verse. Some have seen it as a symbol of Calvary, the hill where Jesus Christ stretched out his arms to be crucified between two thieves. But Moses was not being offered for sin, and the men standing beside him were not criminals. Besides, there is a better interpretation. If lifting the staff was indeed an act of prayer, then the help of Aaron and Hur teaches our need to pray with others. It is a picture of corporate prayer.

We have met Aaron before. He was the brother of Moses who served as God's spokesman and Israel's priest. Hur came from a godly family. He was the son of Caleb and the grandfather of Bezalel (1 Chronicles 2:19, 20), who helped build the tabernacle (31:1–11). Hur later became a judge (24:14). Together these two good men assisted God's prophet in his ministry of intercession. Moses needed some support, so they helped him lift his hands up to the throne of grace.

We do the same thing in the church. From the very beginning, the Christian community has always believed in corporate prayer. In the book of Acts we often find the first Christians at prayer, usually in groups. They prayed in the upper room until they received the Holy Spirit (Acts 2:1–4). They met for prayer at the temple and in private homes (Acts 2:42–47). The apostles devoted themselves to prayer (Acts 6:4), not simply as private individuals, but as a team of spiritual leaders.

The first Christians met for special prayer whenever they came under attack. Consider the time when Peter was imprisoned for preaching the gospel. He was rescued in the middle of the night, and when he found his freedom, he said, "Now I am sure that the Lord has sent his angel and rescued me" (Acts 12:11). Immediately he went looking for his friends. What were they doing? They were having an all-night prayer meeting, of course. They were doing the same thing that Moses did in Exodus 17. Whenever the first Christians were under attack, they waged their warfare with the spiritual weapon of prayer. And as he had done in the days of Moses, God delivered them.

Prayer—especially corporate prayer—is our best defense against the evil one. We pray in our worship services, asking God to bless the ministry of the church and its missionaries. Before the service, the pastors and elders meet to pray that God would protect us from temptation and that his Spirit would be present in all his saving, sanctifying grace. Throughout the week we meet in small groups, lifting one another up in prayer. The pastors meet to pray for specific needs within the congregation. And we pray in our families, asking God to help us live for Christ. Why are we so committed to corporate prayer? It is partly because Jesus promised that wherever two or three gather in his name, he is right there with us (Matthew 18:20). But it is also because we know our weakness. Like Moses we need someone to help lift up our hands. While there is a place for private intercession, nothing strengthens our common life of prayer like praying for and with other Christians. That is how we prevail in prayer against the enemies of God and his church.

## The Banner of the Cross

Moses never forgot the way God answered his prayers, feeble though they were. To make sure that the rest of the Israelites remembered too, "the LORD said to Moses, 'Write this as a memorial in a book and recite it in the ears of Joshua, that I will utterly blot out the memory of Amalek from under heaven.' And Moses built an altar and called the name of it, The LORD Is My Banner, saying, 'A hand upon the throne of the LORD! The LORD will have war with Amalek from generation to generation'" (17:14–16).

The altar that Moses built was for God's honor. It was not designed for atonement but for thanksgiving. By the grace of God Israel had won the battle, and the only proper way to respond was by giving praise back to God. The Israelites had worshiped God for their salvation back at the Red Sea. Now they needed to worship him again, placing their thank offerings on Moses' altar. This time they were not praising God for the great victory of their salvation. It was only a small victory along the pilgrim road, but it was still worthy of worship. We too should praise God not only for our salvation in Christ, but for every victory in our perpetual struggle against sin and temptation.

The other thing that Moses did was to write a scroll of remembrance, which eventually became part of the first edition of the book of Exodus. He wrote a memorial inscription, a record of God's victory in battle. This was important for two reasons. One is because the Israelites would meet the Amalekites again. When they did, they would need to remember that these people were their mortal enemies and that God had promised to destroy them for attacking his chosen people.

Unfortunately, this was something the Israelites frequently managed to forget. Just two years later, when they reached the border of the Promised Land, they encountered the Amalekites again. Instead of praying for victory, they were afraid (Numbers 13:26–33), and as a result they spent the next thirty-eight years wandering in the wilderness (Numbers 13, 14). Meanwhile, the Amalekites lived to fight another day. Israel's next opportunity to defeat them came during the reign of King Saul, who was told to destroy the Amalekites completely (1 Samuel 15:1–3). However, Saul spared the life of their king, so it was left to Samuel (1 Samuel 15:32, 33) and later to David (1 Samuel 30) to finish the job.

There is another reason—a more important reason—why God had Moses record Israel's victory over the Amalekites. He wanted his people to remember what he did for them, so that whenever they came under attack, they would look to him for their salvation. Israel's warfare was not over. They would have to fight many battles—spiritual and otherwise—before they reached the Promised

Land, as well as within it. But if they remembered what happened at Rephidim, it would help them look to God for help.

"The Lord Is My Banner"—this is how Moses summarized what Israel learned from their fight with the Amalekites. In Hebrew it reads *Yahweh-Nissi*. Here is another one of the divine names that God revealed during the exodus: *Yahweh-Nissi*—the Lord is my Banner. A banner is a military standard, a piece of cloth bearing an army insignia and raised on a pole. Soldiers always look to their banner. It establishes their identity; it helps them know who they are. On the battlefield it also helps them keep their bearings and gives them courage and hope. As long as their banner is still flying, they know that the battle is not lost.

The Israelites had some practical experience with this. From time to time during the battle they would look up on the hillside. There they would see Moses holding up the staff that symbolized God's power. It was their banner, their military standard. Now Moses was pointing them to the real source of their courage and strength, which was not simply the staff but God himself. This was to be their rallying cry: "The Lord Is My Banner."

Everyone has a banner, something they look to for identity and security. Dante wrote about this in his classic work *Inferno*. In one of the outer circles of Hell, people were chasing back and forth after a banner. They could never reach it, but they never stopped chasing it either. Dante writes, "I saw a banner there upon the mist. Circling and circling, it seemed to scorn all pause. So it ran on, and still behind it pressed a never-ending rout of souls in pain."[7] Dante understood something important about human nature. People need a standard, something to look to for their identity and security. Some people spend their whole lives chasing after it, without ever reaching a place of rest.

What is your banner? What is the emblem of your hope? Where do you look for courage in times of difficulty and despair? Moses had the best answer. He said, "The Lord is my Banner. Whenever I am under attack I rally to his side."

The Lord is our banner too, but in a way that even Moses could hardly have imagined. The prophet Isaiah promised a day when "the root of Jesse . . . shall stand as a signal for the peoples—of him shall the nations inquire, and his resting place shall be glorious" (Isaiah 11:10). Isaiah's promise is now fulfilled in Jesus Christ. He is "the root of Jesse"—the son of David and the Son of God. Now he stands as a banner for God's people, who rally to him from every nation.

The Bible does not say that Jesus *has* a banner; it says that he *is* the banner. It is by looking to Jesus that we are saved—specifically by looking to his cross. Jesus said, "The Son of Man [must] be lifted up, that whoever believes in him may have eternal life" (John 3:14, 15). Jesus was lifted up on a cross to die for our sins. Now it is by looking to the crucified and risen Christ that we live. Our banner is the cross where he bled and died for our sins. Whenever we come under attack, Christ and his cross give us courage for the fight.

Christ the royal master
Leads against the foe;
Forward into battle,
See his banners go.
Onward, Christian soldiers,
Marching as to war,
With the cross of Jesus
Going on before.[8]

# 41

# Family Reunion

## EXODUS 18:1–12

EXODUS CONTAINS THE HISTORY of Israel's escape from Egypt. It moves from slavery under Pharaoh to the wanderings of the wilderness, the giving of God's law, and the building of his holy tabernacle. The exodus is also the story of the Christian life. There is a spiritual connection between the salvation of Israel and salvation in Jesus Christ. After a long bondage to sin, God has brought us through the deep waters of death. We have been saved by grace through faith in the greater exodus: the death and resurrection of Jesus Christ.

That was only the beginning of our spiritual pilgrimage, however. Now we are traveling through the wilderness, learning many of the same lessons that Israel learned. We are learning to sing praise to God, just as Israel sang the Song of Moses by the sea. Like Israel, we are trusting God to provide bread from Heaven and the water of life. Like Moses, we are lifting our hands up to God's throne, waging war against Satan through prayer.

The next spiritual lesson comes in the reunion of Moses and Jethro. Whereas the end of chapter 17 was about the necessity of prayer, the beginning of chapter 18 is about the duty of evangelism. We are called to bear witness to God's saving power.

### Reunited!

We begin with some family history. Moses' family has not been mentioned since chapter 4, when, after spending forty years on the family farm, the prophet went "to Jethro his father-in-law and said to him, 'Please let me go back to my brothers in Egypt to see whether they are still alive'" (4:18a). This was not entirely truthful (God had told Moses that his people *were* still alive), but it was respectful. Moses was asking permission to go back to Egypt. His father-in-law answered by sending him away with his blessing: "Jethro said to Moses, 'Go in peace'" (4:18b). Apparently the two men parted on friendly terms, and "Moses took his wife and his sons and had them ride on a donkey, and went back to the land of Egypt" (4: 20a).

Later Moses sent his wife and children back to Jethro. "Now Jethro, Moses' father-in-law, had taken Zipporah, Moses' wife, after he had sent her home, along with her two sons" (18:2, 3a). What we don't know is when this happened, or why. Many scholars assume that Moses sent his family away before the exodus, possibly for safekeeping. The other possibility is that he sent Zipporah to see her father after the Israelites reached Horeb, which was not far from where Jethro lived.

There is also some uncertainty about what kind of relationship Moses and Zipporah had. Many commentators assume they had a troubled marriage. This is partly because they think Zipporah was angry with Moses about the circumcision of their son (4:24–26). Furthermore, some of the ancient rabbis interpret 18:2 as a divorce. The Scripture says, "He [Moses] had sent her home," and the Hebrew verb for sending away (*shalach*) can be used as a technical term for obtaining a divorce.

This is all speculation, however. While the strange events surrounding Gershom's circumcision are difficult to interpret, nothing in the Bible indicates that Zipporah was angry with Moses. On the contrary, as we saw back in chapter 10 of this commentary, by circumcising her son she saved her husband's life. Nor did the couple get a divorce. Occasionally the verb *shalach* is used this way; however, that is not its usual sense. Divorce cannot be its meaning here because verses 5 and 6 both refer to Zipporah as Moses' wife. They were still married. Calvin, for one, is sure that Moses and Zipporah were never separated. He admits, "The greater number of commentators think that Zipporah, having been enraged on account of her son's circumcision, had turned back on their journey, and gone to live with her father." But then he goes on to say, "To me this does not seem probable. For Moses would never have allowed his sons to be deprived of the redemption of which he was the minister. . . . Besides, if he had deposited his wife and children in safety, and had advanced alone to the contest, he would have been deservedly suspected of deceit, or of excessive cowardice. Wherefore I have no doubt but that he underwent, together with his family, that miserable yoke of bondage by which they were long oppressed, and by this proof evidenced his faithfulness."[1]

In understanding how Moses related to his family, the names of his sons seem significant: "The name of the one was Gershom (for he said, 'I have been a sojourner in a foreign land'), and the name of the other, Eliezer (for he said, 'The God of my father was my help, and delivered me from the sword of Pharaoh')" (18:3, 4). When Moses named his sons, he was telling the story of his life. Gershom sounds like the Hebrew for "stranger there." The name expresses the alienation Moses felt after first leaving the land of his birth. He had killed an Egyptian; so he became a fugitive from Pharaoh's justice, finally ending up as a stranger in Midian (2:11–15). But he called his second son Eliezer, which means "God is my helper." Eventually Moses realized that his exile was also his salvation. God had delivered him from death by enabling him to escape from Egypt. Thus he gave his younger son a name that would serve as a living testimony of his faith in the God of Israel.

Together the names Gershom and Eliezer told the story of Moses' life: "I was a stranger there, but God is my helper." These two names also described what was happening to the nation of Israel. Like Moses, the Israelites were strangers in Egypt. But God was their helper; he saved them from Pharaoh's sword. We make the same transition when we come to faith in Jesus Christ. We move from sin—with all the alienation it brings—to salvation, in which we acknowledge God as our only help.

To summarize, there is no reason to think that Moses was estranged from his family or that he neglected his duties as a husband and father. What little evidence we have suggests the opposite, showing that salvation was being worked out in his own family the same way it was being worked out for Israel. All too often Christian leaders pursue their call to ministry at the expense of their families. But family life is also a divine calling, and God called Moses to lead both his household and his nation.

The Bible does not tell us what kind of husband and father Moses was. Here in Exodus 18 the most likely interpretation is that he sent his wife and kids off to see their grandparents when they were back in the neighborhood. What is certain is that after this visit the family was reunited: "Jethro, Moses' father-in-law, came with his sons and his wife to Moses in the wilderness where he was encamped at the mountain of God. And . . . he sent word to Moses, 'I, your father-in-law Jethro, am coming to you with your wife and her two sons with her'" (18:5, 6). Apparently word of Israel's triumph had started to spread. When Jethro heard that Moses was in the neighborhood, he wanted to hear the whole story, and thus he gave advance warning that he was coming for a visit.

## Evangelistic Opportunity

When Moses heard that Jethro was coming, there was one thought on his mind, and that was to give his father-in-law the gospel. *Gospel* is not an Old Testament word; it comes from the Greek New Testament. However, it is appropriate to use here because it means "good news"—the good news of salvation, which is exactly what Moses wanted to share.

Moses knew that Jethro had not yet come to faith in the true and living God. Presumably Moses had tried to evangelize him before. During the decades that they lived in the same tent, they must have spent at least some time talking about religion. After all, they lived in the Middle East! Surely Moses had told Jethro something about the God of Israel, the God of his fathers. Before going back to

Egypt, he may also have told his father-in-law something about his encounter with God at the burning bush.

But Jethro had never come to faith in the God of Israel. He was still "the priest of Midian" (18:1), the servant of a pagan god. His unbelief is confirmed in verse 11, where he says, "Now I know that the LORD is greater than all gods." Up until then he wasn't certain. He assumed that the God of Israel was only a tribal deity, like the rest of the gods he worshiped. Jethro had not yet come to believe in the one and only true God who provides the one and only true way of salvation. He was like many people today who think that all religions are more or less equal. They follow the creed of the title character in the film *Man Friday* who said, "Worship any way you like, as long as you mean it. God won't mind."

The trouble is that God *does* mind. He sent his one and only Son into the world to be the one and only Savior. The name of God's Son is Jesus Christ. Concerning him the Scripture says, "There is salvation in no one else, for there is no other name under heaven given among men by which we must be saved" (Acts 4:12). This is why Christians carry such a heavy burden for the salvation of their family members. We believe that Jesus is the only way to God and that unless we trust in him we will be separated from God forever. The decision people make about Jesus Christ marks the difference between life and death. So more than almost anything else in the whole world, we want our husbands and wives, our fathers and mothers, our brothers and sisters, and all our friends and relatives to know Jesus Christ, finding salvation in him.

Moses had a similar burden for his family, and his ministry to Jethro serves as a model for Christian witness. The prophet struck the right balance between two things that are essential for effective evangelism: love and truth. In his witness to Jethro, Moses lovingly and truthfully testified to God's saving work in history.

First, the prophet showed his love by treating Jethro with honor and deference: "Moses went out to meet his father-in-law and bowed down and kissed him. And they asked each other of their welfare and went into the tent" (18:7). By going out to meet Jethro, Moses was showing respect. Ordinarily a great man would wait in his tent to receive a guest, and make no mistake, Moses had become a great man. He was the leader of the mighty nation that triumphed over Egypt. Yet he humbled himself by going out to meet his father-in-law. And when Moses met Jethro, he bowed down, which was another sign of honor. Then he gave his father-in-law a warm, affectionate embrace. This was partly a matter of hospitality. In the ancient world it was customary for people to treat their visitors as honored guests. But Moses was also reaching out to his family in love. He knew how to love someone who was still outside the family of faith.

Some Christians reserve their warmest affection for other believers. Of course, we are called to love one another. We are united in love by the Holy Spirit. Thus we share a spiritual bond that is closer than the bond we share with anyone outside God's family, including our own flesh and blood. Yet often we fail to show the same kind of love to people who are outside God's family. Frankly, we do not always feel as comfortable with non-Christians. Even within our own families, it is possible to feel a profound sense of alienation from those who do not follow Christ. As a result, it is sometimes hard to treat them with the kind of costly love we are learning to give our spiritual brothers and sisters.

Sometimes the problem is our pride. Our desire to straighten people out spiritually gets in the way of our serving them with sacrificial love. This is especially true of new Christians. As soon as they discover the truth in Jesus Christ, they assume it is their job to correct everyone else's theology. This almost inevitably results in conflict, some of which is unnecessary. Often it takes years to repair the damage. Often it is better to do what a man from Philadelphia did when he first came to Christ. The man and his wife had never been religious. Then one day at work someone said something to the man about Jesus, and he said, "That's it! That's exactly what I need. I need Jesus." Within days he became a Christian. But he knew that if he told his wife about it, she would think he was out of his mind. So he said, "I don't know what to do, so I'm just going to love her with this new love that I have from God." This proved to be exactly the right thing to do. She noticed the difference almost immediately, and soon God opened her heart to receive the gospel.

God has called us to reach out to the lost, especially in our own families, with the love of Christ. Care for your husband or wife. Honor your parents. Serve your brothers and sisters. Show hospitality. Strengthen your family ties. Respect your family members, because your love for them is essential to effective evangelism. Unbelievers don't always know if we are telling them the truth. It takes the Holy Spirit to know God's Word, and without the Spirit they cannot know the truth about Jesus Christ. What they *do* know is whether or not we love them—really love them. Sometimes what turns people away from Christ is not his gospel but our failure to live by its love. The Bible says, "Love is patient and kind; love does not envy or boast; it is not arrogant or rude. It does not insist on its own way; it is not irritable or resentful; it does not rejoice at wrongdoing, but rejoices with the truth. Love bears all things, believes all things, hopes all things, endures all things. Love never ends" (1 Corinthians 13:4–8a). If you are still waiting for people in your family to be saved, reach out to them with that kind of love—the love of Christ—and see what God will do.

## To Tell the Truth

Moses did more than love Jethro—he also gave him the good news. In his witness he had the proper balance between love and truth. He did what the Apostle Paul called "speaking the truth in love" (Ephesians 4:15).

As we have seen, the prophet was careful to observe all the formalities. First he inquired after Jethro's welfare. Then, when the two men had exchanged pleasantries in the Middle-Eastern way, they got down to serious discussion: "And they asked each other of their welfare and went into the tent" (18:7b).

There Moses testified to his faith in the God of Israel. He shared the good news of Israel's salvation. Another way to say this is that he gave Jethro the gospel—the whole gospel. Exodus 18 begins with this summary: "Jethro, the priest of Midian, Moses' father-in-law, heard of all that God had done for Moses and for Israel his people, how the Lord had brought Israel out of Egypt" (18:1). The reason Jethro heard about "all" that God had done was because Moses told it to him: "Moses told his father-in-law all that the Lord had done to Pharaoh and to the Egyptians for Israel's sake, all the hardship that had come upon them in the way, and how the Lord had delivered them" (18:8). Here the word translated "told" is the Hebrew word for proclaiming. Moses was preaching the good news of salvation.

Moses' speech was not recorded; however, it is not hard to figure out what he said. He preached to Jethro the same message that he later set down in Scripture. First he reminded his father-in-law of the centuries of bondage that Israel had suffered in Egypt. He recounted what it was like to go back to Pharaoh and order him to let God's people go. He explained how at first this only made things worse because Pharaoh forced them to find their own straw to make bricks. Then Moses told how God delivered his people with mighty acts of judgment. He described the signs and wonders that God performed—rivers of blood, swarms of insects and amphibians, plagues of illness and disease, storms of hail and darkness. Moses reported how God struck down the firstborn of Egypt. He also spoke of redemption. He told his father-in-law about the Passover, how the sons of Israel were saved by the blood of a lamb. He described how God brought his people through the deep waters of the sea. Maybe he even sang Jethro the song of salvation.

Next Moses told Jethro about the wilderness. The Bible is specific about this. Verse 1 mentions "how the Lord had brought Israel out of Egypt," but verse 8 adds that Moses also spoke about "all the hardship that had come upon them in the way." God not only led Israel out of Egypt, but he also led his people through the wilderness. This too was part of the message of salvation. Moses reported how God had sent his people bread from Heaven and water from the rock. He gave an account of the battle of Rephidim, where hands were lifted up to God's throne and God defeated the Amalekites.

The most important thing about this proclamation is how thoroughly God-centered it was. After all, nothing Moses could have said about the Israelites would have been very flattering about either the prophet himself or his people. What had they contributed to their salvation? Nothing at all. At first they had doubted whether it was even possible, telling Moses to leave them alone so they could remain in their bondage. Then when the decisive moment came, and they were trapped between Pharaoh and the deep blue sea, all they did was stand and watch while God delivered them. Afterward, when they faced hardship in the wilderness, they constantly complained that they would be better off back in bondage. Thus the story that Moses told Jethro was not about how the Israelites found their way back to God. Instead it was a story about how God reached down and rescued them. There was something personal about his testimony, of course. Moses told Jethro what had happened in his life and in the lives of his people. But none of it was their doing. The exodus was all about what God had done—"how the LORD had brought Israel out of Egypt" (18:1) and "how the LORD had delivered them" (18:8)—so that God alone would receive all the glory.

Christians have a similar story to tell because our salvation is also based on what God has done in human history. The story starts with our bondage to sin. Our entire race sinned in Adam, and thus we have always been enslaved to sin. But after long centuries of captivity God sent a Savior to deliver us. It was his Son Jesus who saved us through his death on the cross. The Bible says that God the Son became a man "that through death he might destroy the one who has the power of death, that is, the devil, and deliver all those who through fear of death were subject to lifelong slavery" (Hebrews 2:14b, 15). This was our Red Sea crossing. The crucifixion—and with it, the resurrection—brought us from death to life, from bondage to freedom. But that is not the end of the story. In a way it is only the beginning. Now we are living for Christ, following him through the wasteland. As we walk this pilgrim road, we have a story to tell about how, in spite of our ongoing rebellion, God provides for us and delivers us from all our enemies.

A Christian testimony is always personal. My own testimony is the story of what God has done in my life to bring me to a saving knowledge of Jesus Christ. But the most important thing is to be sure that my testimony is God-centered. My testimony is not a story about how I found my way to God but about how God drew me to himself. It focuses first of all on what God has done in Christ, especially through his cross. Insofar as it touches on my own experience, it is only to show what God has done for me. The Apostle Paul wrote, "On my own behalf I will not boast, except of my weaknesses" (2 Corinthians 12:5b); "But far be it from me to boast except in the cross of our Lord Jesus Christ" (Galatians 6:14a).

The gospel story needs to be told. It is not enough to love the lost without also giving them the good news. It is our Christian duty to explain to people the truth of salvation in Christ. What they do with what we tell them is between them and God, but telling them is up to us.

One man who excelled at telling the gospel truth was Edward Studd, the father of C. T. Studd, the famous missionary to Africa. Studd was a wealthy Englishman who led a life of ease and entertainment until suddenly he was converted by the preaching of D. L. Moody. Edward's sons were away at school at the time, so they didn't know anything about what had happened to their father.

They were shocked when he arrived at Eton in the middle of the term and instead of taking them to the theater, as was his custom, took them to hear Moody preach. C. T. Studd later said:

> Before that time, I used to think that religion was a Sunday thing, like one's Sunday clothes, to be put away on Monday morning. We boys were brought up to go to church regularly, but, although we had a kind of religion, it didn't amount to much. . . . Then all at once I had the good fortune to meet a real live . . . Christian. It was my own father. But it did make one's hair stand on end. Everyone in the house had a dog's life of it until they were converted. I was not altogether pleased with him. He used to come into my room at night and ask if I was converted.[2]

One wonders whether Edward Studd had the kind of balance that Moses exemplified, but at least he was committed to the truth of the gospel, and eventually all his sons were saved.

## Now I Know!

Like C. T. Studd, Jethro got the message. When Moses told his father-in-law the story of salvation, the man put his trust in the God of Israel. In a word, he was saved.

There are three things to notice about Jethro's saving response to the gospel. The most important is his *faith*. Jethro came to a clear and certain conviction that the God of Israel was the one true and supreme deity. His faith is partly evident from his use of the divine name. When Jethro said, "Blessed be the LORD" (18:10), he called God by his covenant name, *Yahweh*. He had come to know the true God by his true name.

Then Jethro went on to say, "Now I know that the LORD is greater than all gods, because in this affair they dealt arrogantly with the people" (18:11). This was Jethro's testimony of his conversion. Like Moses, he focused on what God had done, on God's saving work in history. He understood the point of the exodus: God had saved Israel for his own glory. As Moses told him of the events surrounding the exodus, Jethro recognized that God had defeated all the gods of Egypt in order to vindicate his honor.

This triumph convinced Jethro of God's supremacy. The man had spent his entire life worshiping other gods, but now he knew the truth! Now his whole understanding of God was completely transformed, and he renounced his pagan past. Now it was clear to him that the God of Israel was infinitely superior. Obviously he was stronger than the gods of Egypt. By the sheer force of logic, then, he must also be stronger than the gods of Midian, who were weaker still. The true story of Israel's deliverance proved that the one true and living God is infinite in power and glory.

Do you have the kind of faith that Jethro had? Can you say, "Now I know that Jesus Christ is greater than all other gods"? To be a Christian is to know God's name, specifically the name of Jesus Christ. It is also to declare that Jesus is Lord, that he is the supreme God above all other gods. Jesus is superior in every way. He is superior in mercy: He grants forgiveness to sinners. He is superior in love: He gave his own life for our sins. He is superior in grace: He offers eternal life as a free gift. He is superior in power, because by his resurrection he has triumphed over death. And he is superior in glory, reigning supreme over Heaven and earth. No other god has ever even attempted to demonstrate the amazing love and grace that God has shown in Jesus Christ. To have faith is to believe that he is the one and only Savior, the one and only God of all grace and glory.

Jethro responded in faith. He also responded with *joy*: "Jethro rejoiced for all the good that the LORD had done to Israel, in that he had delivered them out of the hand of the Egyptians" (18:9). The Hebrew word translated "rejoiced" (*chadah*) is unusual. This rare word conveys an overwhelming sense of joy, the kind of happiness that penetrates to a person's very soul. Jethro did more than believe the good news about God. He celebrated it and rejoiced in it.

God gives the same joy to everyone who comes to Christ. There is great rejoicing in the knowledge that God has saved us and will love us forever and ever. One Christian witnessed this joy when he went to teach English in China. He lived in a college dormitory, where he often had opportunities to share his faith in Jesus Christ. One night he studied the Bible with the student next door. Together they read the Scriptures and discussed the meaning of salvation. Later that night the English teacher heard a strange noise coming from the student's room. It was a sound he had never heard before, a kind of gurgling sound from somewhere in the throat. When he went to investigate, he discovered that the student had come to faith in Jesus Christ. Now that student knew that there was love in the world and that there was a God in Heaven. He knew that his sins were forgiven and that he had received the free gift of eternal life. And in those first moments of salvation the student experienced such great joy that he simply had to give it utterance. The gurgling was coming from somewhere deep in his heart as he rejoiced in the knowledge of salvation. God gives great joy to everyone who comes to him in faith.

The third thing to notice is Jethro's *praise*: "Jethro said, 'Blessed be the LORD, who has delivered you out of the hand of the Egyptians and out of the hand of Pharaoh and has delivered the people from under the hand of the Egyptians'" (18:10). Whenever God brings people to saving faith, it is so they will bow down and worship him. So like Moses and like the Israelites, Jethro was saved for God's glory.

This is part of the purpose of evangelism. There are many reasons to share the gospel. It is the command of Christ, which is reason enough. It is also part of God's plan of salvation, his way of rescuing sinners from the wrath to come.

But the goal of all gospel ministry is the worship of God. We testify to the good news about Jesus Christ so that people will praise him. Our proclamation of the gospel is for the salvation of sinners, with a view to their celebration of God. Evangelism is for the glory of God.

As soon as Jethro got saved, he started giving God the glory, and he did this with other believers: "And Jethro, Moses' father-in-law, brought a burnt offering and sacrifices to God; and Aaron came with all the elders of Israel to eat bread with Moses' father-in-law before God" (18:12). Jethro became a member of a worshiping community, the communion of saints. This is what always happens when someone comes to faith in the living God. Evangelism leads first to worship and then to fellowship. In this case Jethro sat down with Moses and Aaron and all of Israel's elders to share communion. This has always been an important part of public worship—a sacred feast in the presence of God.

What makes this meal so remarkable is that Jethro was a Midianite and thus one of Israel's ancient enemies. It was the Midianites who brought Joseph into slavery (Genesis 37:28) and who later raided Israel in the days of Gideon (Judges 6, 7). In fact, God told the Israelites to "harass the Midianites and strike them down" (Numbers 25:17). But Jethro had come to saving faith in the God of Israel. Now he was welcomed into the fellowship of God's people. They had peace with one another in the presence of God.

The salvation of this man shows how God was working out his plan for the salvation of the world. This may be the most important lesson to learn from Jethro's conversion. This episode is much more than the story of the salvation of one man, or even of one family. The Bible tells this story because it reveals God's plan for the whole world. Salvation was never just for the Jews. From the very beginning, God intended to save people from all nations. This was even part of his plan for the exodus. God said to Pharaoh that he was bringing his people out of Egypt "to show you my power, so that my name may be proclaimed in all the earth" (9:16). A priest from Midian was virtually the first fulfillment of that promise, as Moses proclaimed salvation to Jethro.

God has given us a message to proclaim as well. It is the message of salvation in Christ: forgiveness through his cross and eternal life through his empty tomb. Each of us is called to do whatever we can to spread the word, so that all nations will come to worship God. We will keep spreading the word until we are gathered into glory. Then we will sing the song of Moses and the Lamb:

> Great and amazing are your deeds,
> O Lord God the Almighty! . . .
> All nations will come
> and worship you,
> for your righteous acts have been revealed. (Revelation 15:3a, 4b)

That will be a reunion to end all reunions—the best family reunion ever.

42

# Israel Gets Organized

EXODUS 18:13–27

BY DAY I SERVE AS A PASTOR. By night I sometimes also coach local youth sports teams. One night before soccer practice, as I was lacing up my cleats, one of the parents asked me about my work. "I heard that you're some kind of minister or something," she said. "Yes, that's right," I replied, and we began to talk about what kind of church I served, where it was located, and so forth. Then she asked, "Now, is that a full-time job?"

To tell the truth, I burst out laughing. As any faithful minister will tell you, the pastorate is always a full-time job and then some. Pastoral ministry takes as much time as it is allowed to take, especially in a large church. There are services to plan, sermons to prepare, talks to deliver, classes to teach, conflicts to resolve, letters to write, questions to answer, leaders to disciple, ministries to oversee, missionaries to send, and people to pray for. The work never ends. Indeed, for most ministers the work will not end until the minister dies or until Jesus comes again, whichever comes first.

## One-Man Show

If we take the pastoral burdens of a large congregation and multiply them by a thousand, we will get some idea of the challenges that Moses faced in leading Israel. The prophet governed a nation of one million people or more all by himself. The workload was staggering. When "Moses sat to judge the people . . . the people stood around Moses from morning till evening" (18:13). It was perhaps the world's first case of judicial backlog. Moses had no end of work to do.

When Moses' father-in-law Jethro saw the tremendous demands placed on God's prophet, he was shocked. The Bible gives us his reaction: "What is this that you are doing for the people? Why do you sit alone, and all the people stand around you from morning till evening?" (18:14). Loosely paraphrased, Jethro said, "Moses, what on earth do you think you're doing?"

Moses thought he knew what he was doing. He was declaring God's will for God's people. So he tried to justify himself: "Because the people come to me to inquire of God; when they have a dispute, they come to me and I decide between one person and another, and I make them know the statutes of God and his laws" (18:15, 16).

The work Moses was doing needed to be done. The prophet was helping the Israelites solve their problems. Like most people, they wanted to know God's will. They also wanted help resolving their disputes. So they brought all their troubles to Moses, looking to him for guidance. And Moses did two things to help them: He taught God's word, and he discerned God's will. The prophet served as both their counselor and their judge. Part of his work was educational. He taught the people God's word so they would know what God required. But he also helped them apply the truth of God's word in practical situations.

Moses was exercising such an important ministry—the explanation and application of God's word—that one might have expected his in-laws to be impressed. After all, until now the only thing Jethro had ever seen him do was tend sheep. Now Moses was the prophet for a nation, the most important man in Israel. He had people clamoring for his attention all day long. But Jethro was not impressed. On the contrary, he recognized that what Moses was doing eventually would prove destructive, not only to himself, but also to others: "What you are doing is not good. You and the people with you will certainly wear yourselves out, for the thing is too heavy for you. You are not able to do it alone" (18:17, 18).

There was no question about the sincerity of Moses' motives. The prophet was simply trying to be faithful to his calling. The people had spiritual needs, and he was graciously trying to meet them. Yet for all his willingness to serve, it was clear that Moses had taken on a burden that was too great for him to bear alone. Jethro had the wisdom to see that there was no way Moses could sustain this kind of pace. The workload was so overwhelming that soon Moses would be exhausted. He was headed for burnout. So Jethro was emphatic: What Moses was doing was "not good." In Hebrew these words express strong disapproval. Moses was taking on more work than he could handle, and it was a big mistake.

The principle here can be applied to almost any ministry situation. People never run out of needs; so when we take on the responsibility to help meet those needs, we will have as much work as we can handle. The problem comes when we try to carry burdens that are bigger than the ones that God has actually called us to bear. God never intends for us to do all the work ourselves. This is why he has placed us in the body of Christ, in which we are dependent on the help of others. It is utter folly for ministers or other spiritual leaders to think they can do it all by themselves. Christian ministry should never be a one-man (or one-woman) show. It is not good for us to try to do God's work all on our own. The Scripture says, "I say to everyone among you not to think of himself more highly than he ought . . . we, though many, are one body in Christ, and individually members one of another. Having gifts that differ according to the grace given to us . . ." (Romans 12:3, 5, 6). To use our gifts wisely, we need to know our limitations.

It is unwise to think that we can always handle more and more ministry. This is harmful to us, and in the end it will also be harmful to others. This was a significant part of Jethro's concern. Moses wasn't the only one who was getting tired; the people were tired too. Jethro said, "You *and the people* with you will certainly wear yourselves out" (18:18a). Since Moses was the only judge, the people had to wait all day to get his attention. There was always a long line of people waiting to see him.

Today people often face the same problem in the church. How can church members get the pastoral care they need? Is there a pastor who knows them well enough to really help? There are significant obstacles to effective pastoral care, especially in a large church. I once calculated that if I were to sit down for lunch every weekday with one of my parishioners, it would take me six years to meet with the entire congregation. By that time, of course, there would be hundreds of new members to meet. So how can a church provide the kind of pastoral care that its members need?

## A New Form of Government

Jethro had the solution. An army general would recognize it as the old military strategy of divide and conquer. An economist would call it the division of labor. The Bible has a word for it too. It is called *Presbyterianism*, the spiritual rule of God's people by a representative group of godly men, whom the Israelites called "elders." In the New Testament they are known as presbyters, from the Greek word *presbyteros* (e.g., Acts 20:17; Titus 1:5, 6; 1 Peter 5:1), which also means "elder." Hence the term *Presbyterianism*.

In his role as Israel's management consultant, Jethro proposed a new form of government. It was partly a judicial system, a way of deciding legal cases, with Moses serving as the chief justice. It was also a plan for providing pastoral care for the people of God.

Jethro started by preserving the role of the prophet. He said to Moses: "Now obey my voice; I will give you advice, and God be with you! You shall represent the people before God and bring their cases to God, and you shall warn them about the statutes and the laws, and make them know the way in which they must walk and what they must do" (18:19, 20). Jethro was not trying to take his son-in-law away from his calling. Moses would still be the prophet. He would continue to serve as the covenant mediator, standing between God and his people as Israel's representative. He would still teach God's law for daily life. He would show the people how to "walk." By the exposition of God's word and by the example of his own life, Moses would continue to lead the Israelites on their pilgrimage. None of that would change.

But Jethro also realized that Moses needed some help, so he presented a plan for governing Israel by the rule of elders. Here was his proposal:

> Moreover, look for able men from all the people, men who fear God, who are trustworthy and hate a bribe, and place such men over the people as chiefs of thousands, of hundreds, of fifties, and of tens. And let them judge the people at all times. Every great matter they shall bring to you, but any small matter they shall decide themselves. So it will be easier for you, and they will bear the burden with you. If you do this, God will direct you, you will be able to endure, and all this people also will go to their place in peace. (18:21–23)

Jethro's plan was a good one. It called for the selection of wise spiritual leaders who would help Moses govern the people. These men would answer everyday spiritual questions and adjudicate routine personal disputes. But whenever the elders needed help, they would consult with Moses, who would handle all the tough cases. This would preserve his prophetic authority, while at the same time giving him the help he needed to shepherd God's flock. As Maxie Dunnam explains, "It wasn't a matter of taking leadership from Moses; it was a matter of reordering and dispensing leadership in such a way that other people would share the load."[1]

## Spiritual Leadership

Jethro's proposal was based on three vital principles for spiritual leadership. First, spiritual leaders must be *mature*. Israel needed men who were able to handle the job, so Jethro told Moses to be choosy: "look for able men" (18:21). Here the word "look" has the connotation of insight or discernment. If God's people were to have wise leaders, they needed to be wisely chosen.

Specifically, what qualifications were needed? Jethro said nothing about the work experience of these men or about their educational background or about how much money they made. The qualifications he gave were not financial or intellectual but moral and spiritual. Moses was to select "men who fear God, who are trustworthy and hate a bribe" (18:21).

The first qualification concerned *a man's relationship to God.* A good elder is a man who fears God, who reveres him and seeks to honor him in all he does. Such a man has a holy zeal for God's name. Rather than pursuing his own agenda or fearing what people will think, his chief desire is to promote the glory of God. This means that he is willing, when necessary, to give people counsel they do not want to hear and to make judgments with which they do not agree. It takes a God-fearing man to do that. A man who fears God also knows the secret of all wisdom. The Scripture says, "The fear of the LORD is the beginning of wisdom" (Psalm 111:10a). Therefore, to find a wise spiritual leader, it is necessary to look for a man who fears God.

The other qualification concerned a man's relationship to others. A good elder is reliable. He is "trustworthy." He keeps his commitments. He is characterized by honesty and integrity. In particular, he is not greedy for personal gain. The reason for this is obvious. As one of Israel's elders worked to resolve various disputes, the opposing parties would try to persuade him to decide in their favor. Some would try to flatter him, while others might even resort to bribery. Only a man who hated dishonest gain could be trusted not to corrupt the course of justice.

The second main principle is that spiritual leadership must be *representative*. In other words, leaders must be drawn from across the spiritual community. Jethro told Moses to select "able men from all the people" (18:21). He should not choose elders from among his friends or from one particular group of Israelites, but from across the entire nation. Once these men were chosen, Moses was to "place such men over the people as chiefs of thousands, of hundreds, of fifties, and of tens" (18:21). In this practical way, the entire nation would be organized for spiritual care.

We learn more about this selection process from the book of Deuteronomy. Apparently the elders were not actually chosen until the Israelites left Mount Horeb, after God gave them the Ten Commandments. Moses began by telling the people, "Choose for your tribes wise, understanding, and experienced men, and I will appoint them as your heads" (Deuteronomy 1:13). In effect, the people were allowed to nominate their own elders. But it was the prophet, acting as God's representative, who delegated to them their positions of spiritual leadership. The final authority rested with Moses, who later said, "I took the heads of your tribes, wise and experienced men, and set them as heads over you" (Deuteronomy 1:15a).

Israel had a representative form of spiritual government, but it was not a democracy. We can only imagine how disastrous it would have been for the Israelites to be governed by the will of the people! Imagine what would have happened when they reached the Red Sea, or when they ran out of water, or when the Amalekites attacked them. In each case it would have been a complete disaster, and the Israelites never would have reached the Promised Land. This is because God's people are not capable of governing themselves. We have always needed divinely-appointed spiritual leadership—representatives called by God.

The third principle for spiritual leadership is that it must be *shared*. This was Jethro's main objective. There was far too much work for one man to do alone, but once the elders were selected, they could help Moses bear the burden. Together they would judge the people. In fact, since the elders were wise and godly men, they would handle most of the work themselves, which would solve the original problem. "So it will be easier for you," Jethro said, "and they will bear the burden with you" (18:22b).

Obviously what Jethro gave to Moses was sound advice for making his ministry more effective and more efficient. Yet some scholars have struggled with the fact that this plan for reorganizing Israel did not come straight from God, but through a mere human being (and a Midianite at that). However, this presents no real difficulty. There is always a place for practical prudence in the spiritual life. God has given us a great deal of freedom for life and ministry. Many of the decisions we face involve practical considerations that are not explicitly addressed in the Bible. Sometimes God uses other people—including our own in-laws—to help us know what to do. Sometimes we get good advice from new believers like Jethro, or even from people who are not believers at all.

The key is to test human wisdom against the perfect standard of God's Word. Is the advice people are giving us in agreement with Biblical principles? For his part, Jethro was careful not to give God's prophet any orders that would contradict the command of God. Instead he encouraged Moses to make sure that his advice was in keeping with God's will. He said, "Now obey my voice; I will give you advice, and God be with you!" (18:19). Jethro was submitting his counsel to God's blessing. He went on to say, "If you do this, God will direct you" (18:23). Some scholars treat this statement as a command. They translate the verse like this: "If you do this—God commands you."[2] But Jethro was in no position to give orders to God's prophet. Rather, he subjected his own practical advice to the perfect will of God.

God must have confirmed the wisdom of Jethro's counsel, because the Scripture says: "So Moses listened to the voice of his father-in-law and did all that he had said. Moses chose able men out of all Israel and made them heads over the people, chiefs of thousands, of hundreds, of fifties, and of tens. And they judged the people at all times. Any hard case they brought to Moses, but any small matter they decided themselves" (18:24–26). This shows that Moses was teachable. As part of his submission to God, he was willing to accept good practical advice for his ministry. After he received it, "Moses let his father-in-law depart, and he went away to his own country" (18:27). No doubt Moses always remembered this good man with profound gratitude, as his plan helped him endure the strain of ministry and thus satisfy the people of God.

## Church Government

The story of how Israel got organized raises an obvious practical question: How should God's people be governed today? Do the principles from this passage apply to the church? And if so, *how* do they apply?

The first thing to point out is one crucial difference: We no longer have a prophet like Moses. We no longer need one because God has sent his Son to be our Savior. First Jesus Christ died for our sins on the cross. Then God raised him from the dead. Now he is our Prophet, the one who reveals to us God's will. As God the Father said to the first disciples, "This is my beloved Son; listen to him" (Mark 9:7). This is a great advantage for us, because unlike Moses, Jesus never gets tired out. He has already carried the full weight of our sin, and now he is more than able to bear the daily burden of our spiritual needs.

The way Jesus teaches us God's will is not by some new revelation but by his Spirit speaking in Scripture. This is beautifully explained in the preface to *The Book of Church Order of the Presbyterian Church in America*, which announces: "Jesus, the Mediator, the sole Priest, Prophet, King, Saviour, and Head of the Church, contains in Himself, by way of eminency, all the offices in His Church. . . . He is present with the Church by His Word and Spirit, and the benefits of all His offices are effectually applied by the Holy Ghost."[3] This is the foundation of all church government: Jesus alone is the supreme Head of the church, and he exercises his authority by the Spirit and the Word.

But there is more. According to Scripture, Jesus Christ has called certain men to provide Biblical instruction and spiritual care on his behalf. *The Book of Church Order* explains, "It belongs to His Majesty from His throne of glory to rule and teach the Church through His Word and Spirit *by the ministry of men*; thus mediately exercising His own authority and enforcing His own laws, unto the edification and establishment of His Kingdom" (emphasis added). In other words, today Jesus exercises his authority through the church, specifically through its pastors and elders.

First there is the work of the minister, who in presbyterian churches is called a *teaching elder*. In many ways his work is analogous to that of Moses. His primary task is to teach the Bible, both in public and in private. But it is not enough simply to know what the Bible says; Christians must also do what God commands. So the minister shows God's people how to live, how to put what they are learning into practice.

If ministers tried to do this work all by themselves, they would soon have the same problem Moses had. They would be overwhelmed, which would be bad for them and bad for the church. But God has also provided godly men to share the work. In presbyterian churches these men are called *ruling elders*. In Romans 12:8 ruling (or leadership) is identified as one of the spiritual gifts. Then 1 Timothy 5:17 says, "Let the elders who rule well be considered worthy of double honor, especially those who labor in preaching and teaching." This verse teaches that elders are called to govern the church. It also seems to distinguish between pastors, who do most of the teaching, and the other elders, who share the burden of spiritual care.

This form of church government follows the same basic principles for spiritual leadership that Jethro commended to Moses. First, spiritual leadership must be *mature*. In 1 Timothy 3 and Titus 1, the New Testament carefully lists the qualifications of elders. These lists are longer than the one that Jethro gave to

Moses, but the emphasis is the same. Elders must be godly, trustworthy men. Therefore anyone who aspires to become an elder must learn to fear God instead of men and must demonstrate that he can be trusted to lead a ministry. Without such men, the church will fail to fulfill its calling to reach the world for Jesus Christ.

Second, spiritual leadership should be *representative*. Elders should be nominated by the people of God from across the congregation. In the end their qualifications must be confirmed by those who already serve as elders, but the congregation helps recognize their calling. Philadelphia's Tenth Presbyterian Church is divided into parishes that are organized geographically. Each parish nominates its own elders. We also desire to have elders who represent the ethnic and professional diversity of the congregation. Like the ancient Israelites, we want to have elders "from all the people" (18:21).

Third, spiritual leadership should be *shared*. Teaching and ruling elders are jointly responsible to provide spiritual care for the local church. Shared leadership is the heart of presbyterianism, which is the general form of church government taught in Scripture.

Church government may not seem like a very important topic. Admittedly, other aspects of Christianity are more central. It would be a mistake to give so much attention to the organization of the church that we neglect the saving work of Jesus Christ, which is the most important thing of all. But church government *is* important. It must be important because it is taught in the Bible, including Exodus 18. Why was this passage included in the Bible if not partly to teach basic principles of spiritual leadership and authority? Furthermore, sound church government is essential to the welfare of the church. Without the right leaders leading in the right way, the work of the gospel will falter.

Every Christian has a responsibility to promote good church government. Spiritual leaders do this by leading. Yet sadly, pastors and elders tend to commit one of two errors. Either they are too timid to exercise their true spiritual authority or they try to claim more authority for themselves than they have been given by Christ. Roger Beardmore writes:

> In evangelical circles today we are witnessing the abuse of ecclesiastical authority in two directions. There is, on the one hand, an abdication of church authority by some. Confronted with the individualistic, anti-law spirit of our time, cowardly church officers refuse to exercise the biblical oversight entrusted to them by Christ. In many circles authoritative preaching and corrective church discipline are conspicuously absent. Equally dangerous, however, is the tendency by others to overreact against such laxity. Church leaders lose sight of the fine line between the virtue of biblical counsel and guidance and the vice of usurping control over the conscience. . . . Counsel becomes control, control becomes coercion, and coercion becomes tyranny over the conscience.[4]

The way to avoid these errors is by exercising authority in a godly way. Elders who are timid should remember that they are called to promote the honor of Christ. Elders who love to rule should be careful to do so with gentleness, leading by persuasion and example.

Followers should follow. We should seek the instruction of our pastors and the wisdom of our elders. It is the duty of every church member to honor God by submitting to spiritual authority. Sadly, too many Christians are like the Israelites: We reserve the right to complain if we don't get our way. Sometimes we even rebel against spiritual authority in the church. We are called instead to honor God's plan for our spiritual care, which he has provided for our own benefit. Notice the appeal to self-interest at the end of the Bible's command: "Obey your leaders and submit to them, for they are keeping watch over your souls, as those who will have to give an account. Let them do this with joy and not with groaning, for that would be of no advantage to you" (Hebrews 13:17).

When the Bible says "obey . . . and submit," it means what it says. The Greek word translated "obey" (*peitho*) connotes persuasion. It means to have minds and hearts that are open and receptive to what our pastors and elders teach and counsel, so that what they say is fully persuasive to us. To submit is to yield. Our natural inclination is to resist authority, especially when we disagree. But God calls us to give up on having our own way, choosing instead to place ourselves under the direction of our spiritual leaders.

The Bible also commands us to love them. At the end of 1 Thessalonians, the Apostle Paul makes the following appeal: "We ask you, brothers, to respect those who labor among you and are over you in the Lord and admonish you, and to esteem them very highly in love because of their work. Be at peace among yourselves" (1 Thessalonians 5:12, 13). Some pastors and elders are hard to love; nevertheless, we have a responsibility before God to love them. The reason is because of their work: They are God's servants. Therefore we love and obey them, not because we have very much confidence in them, but because we have complete confidence in Jesus Christ. He is the Lord of the church, and thus we are willing to submit to his plan for its government.

Sometimes it is easier to criticize the church than to obey its leaders. Pastors and elders are as fallen as anyone else, and they have all the failings that are common to the rest of humanity. But whatever we say about the church, we should remember this: For all its weakness, it is the only institution that God has promised will last until the end of time (Matthew 16:18). This is because the church is the only organization in the world that is governed by God's very own Son.

# 43

# Kingdom of Priests

## EXODUS 19:1–6

UNDER THE LEADERSHIP of the prophet Moses, the Israelites came out of bondage, across the sea, and through the wilderness. Three months later they reached the mountain of God. Their arrival was the fulfillment of God's promise, for when God first revealed himself to Moses at the burning bush, he said, "I will be with you, and this shall be the sign for you, that I have sent you: when you have brought the people out of Egypt, you shall serve God on this mountain" (3:12). If any doubt remained as to whether or not Moses had been serving the right God, it was now settled. God had shown his people the sign. He had made good on his promise. He had brought them all to worship on his holy mountain.

### Up on God's Mountain

Israel's arrival at God's mountain is one of the high points of Exodus. It marks the achievement of God's plan to save a people for his glory. It also marks the beginning of a new stage in God's covenant relationship with his people. Thus Exodus 19 begins with a formal introduction that specifies the time and place: "On the third new moon after the people of Israel had gone out of the land of Egypt, on that day they came into the wilderness of Sinai. They set out from Rephidim and came into the wilderness of Sinai, and they encamped in the wilderness. There Israel encamped before the mountain" (19:1, 2).

Which mountain was it? Here the Bible simply says "*the* mountain." Later in the chapter it is identified as Mount Sinai. The trouble is that there are mountains scattered all over the Sinai Peninsula. Is it possible to make a more specific identification?

Some scholars think the mountain is somewhere in northwest Arabia, near the Gulf of Aqaba, in what was once called the land of Midian.[1] This location would seem to fit with the Apostle Paul's reference to "Mount Sinai in Arabia"

(Galatians 4:25). However, at the time Paul was writing, the Roman province of Arabia included nearly the whole Sinai Peninsula. Thus it still makes sense to look for God's mountain somewhere in the Sinai itself.

Perhaps the mountain was somewhere in the north, near Kadesh-Barnea. The mountain called Har Karkom is often suggested as a possibility, partly because it has a plateau on which Israel's elders might have worshiped. But the traditional site is far to the south, at an 8,000-foot mountain known to the nomads as Jebel Musa, the Mountain of Moses. Jebel Musa is where the pilgrims go. It is also where St. Catherine's Monastery is located (although, significantly, this was not built until sometime in the sixth century). Rising straight up from the desert floor, the mountain makes an impressive sight. In the words of one nineteenth-century visitor, "Among all the stupendous works of Nature, not a place can be selected more fitting for the exhibition of Almighty power."[2]

These are only some of many attempts to make a definitive identification. Yet to date there is no conclusive Biblical or archaeological evidence to resolve the dispute. Presumably if it were important for us to know, the Bible would have been more specific. What is indisputable is that Moses led God's people to a real mountain somewhere in the wilderness. There the Israelites pitched their tents and looked up at the rugged, rocky cliffs rising out of the desert. There they would remain for the rest of Exodus—first for the giving of the law, then for the building of the tabernacle.[3] And there, in that lonely place, they met the living God.

Moses met with him first. He had met God on this mountain before, and as soon as he arrived, he trekked up to meet with him again. The Scripture says, "Moses went up to God" (19:3). Moses had to go *up* because God is high and exalted. Indeed, a mountaintop is the most appropriate place to meet him. Mountains testify to God's transcendence, to his supreme majesty. The Scripture says that his "righteousness is like the mountains of God" (Psalm 36:6a).

## On the Wings of Eagles

While the mountain was a place for the people to meet with God, it was also a place for God to speak to his people. Moses was the mediator, the one who represented Israel before God. To communicate with his people, God spoke to his prophet: "Moses went up to God. The Lord called to him out of the mountain, saying, 'Thus you shall say to the house of Jacob, and tell the people of Israel . . .'" (19:3). This was a formal speech, as the style of language indicates. God addressed his people using their proper titles because he was setting forth the terms of their relationship. To use the Biblical term for it, he was renewing the covenant, his binding love commitment to his people.

The words that follow are sometimes described as the heart of the Old Testament. In them God described what he had done to save his people. He also told them what he expected from them, revealing his deepest desires for their ultimate destiny. God said:

> You yourselves have seen what I did to the Egyptians, and how I bore you on eagles' wings and brought you to myself. Now therefore, if you will indeed obey my voice and keep my covenant, you shall be my treasured possession among all peoples, for all the earth is mine; and you shall be to me a kingdom of priests and a holy nation. These are the words that you shall speak to the people of Israel. (19:4–6)

In this speech—which spanned the past, the present, and the future—God reminded Israel what he had done to deliver them. He also told them why he had done it and what plans he had for their future. Really everything else in the Old Testament—indeed, everything else in human history—can be explained in terms of the covenant relationship described in these verses.

God began by reminding his people what he had done for them: "You yourselves have seen what I did to the Egyptians, and how I bore you on eagles' wings and brought you to myself" (19:4). This summary of salvation mentions three separate stages in Israel's pilgrimage: a bringing out, a lifting up, and a drawing close.

First, there was what God did to Egypt. He humiliated Pharaoh's gods one by one, attacking them with ten terrible plagues. Then he drowned Pharaoh's army in the sea. In this way he brought his people out of slavery.

Next, God lifted his people up "on eagles' wings." This beautiful image is richly symbolic. The eagle is a fierce bird of prey; it attacks its enemies the way God attacked Egypt. It is also a bird of rescue. This is wonderfully portrayed in J. R. R. Tolkien's fantasy *The Hobbit*. At two different points in the story the heroes are rescued by eagles. The second time is near the end, when they are surrounded by hordes of goblins. Just at the moment when all seems to be lost, one of them "gave a great cry: he had seen a sight that made his heart leap, dark shapes small yet majestic against the distant glow. 'The Eagles! The Eagles!' he shouted. 'The Eagles are coming!'"[4]

The wings of eagles also depict God's protective nurture and tender care. The same image appears again in Deuteronomy 32, where Moses sings of God's love for his people. In that love song, it is clear that God is speaking of the way he cared for Israel in the wilderness:

> But the LORD's portion is his people,
> Jacob his allotted heritage.
> He found him in a desert land,
> and in the howling waste of the wilderness;
> he encircled him, he cared for him,
> he kept him as the apple of his eye.
> Like an eagle that stirs up its nest,

> that flutters over its young,
> spreading out its wings, catching them,
> bearing them on its pinions. (Deuteronomy 32:9–11)

The picture is of a mother eagle caring for her young. Eaglets are especially helpless, remaining in the nest for as many as one hundred days. Then, as one commentator explains, "When it is time for the young birds to leave the eyrie and learn to fly, the eagle stirs up the nest, but does not abandon her young. If they experience difficulties, the mother bird swoops down below them and lifts them on her wings back to safety."[5] This is precisely what God did for his people in the wilderness. They had been delivered from slavery, but they were vulnerable to starvation and to attack by their enemies. So God lifted them up on his mighty wings, providing them with food, water, and victory in battle.

The last thing God did for his people was to bring them to himself. He led them to his holy mountain, where they would worship him in all his majesty. The exodus was not just about getting Israel out of Egypt; it was about getting Israel close to God. This is always true in salvation. Salvation is never an end in itself. There is always something greater, and that is God himself, and our fellowship with him.

This was the history of God's relationship with his people Israel. He delivered them from Egypt, carried them through the wilderness, and saved them to himself. Since the Israelites had seen all this for themselves, God appealed to them as eyewitnesses: "You yourselves have seen what I did" (19:4).

What have you seen God do? Every Christian has seen God do essentially the same things that he did in the days of Moses, because Israel's salvation is the pattern for salvation in Jesus Christ. First God delivered us from our bondage to sin through the death and resurrection of Jesus Christ. Ever since then he has carried us on eagles' wings. He provides whatever we need, and whenever we are in danger of falling, he catches us and lifts us back up. All the while God is pulling us into the embrace of his love. God has brought us out, and now he is lifting us up and drawing us close, so that we will always be sure of his love.

## The Bond of Love

It is sometimes said that the past is only prologue. This is true in the Christian life. What God has done *for* us in history is the basis for what he expects *from* us today. His mighty work of salvation always demands a response. So after reminding his people how they were saved, God proceeded to set the terms for their relationship in the future: "Now therefore, if you will indeed obey my voice and keep my covenant . . ." (19:5a). What God demanded was nothing less than full obedience, the keeping of his covenant.

What is meant by "keep[ing] my covenant"? This is the first time that the Bible uses this exact expression. The covenant was God's unbreakable promise of love for his people. He made his covenant with Abraham, promising to give him a land and a people who would bless the whole world. He confirmed his covenant with Isaac and Jacob. Then, in order to make good on his promise (2:24; 6:4, 5), he brought his people out of Egypt. Exodus is the story of God remembering his covenant.

To this point, what the covenant mainly required of God's people was faith—faith in God's covenant promise. However, because it was a mutual relationship, it also required obedience—obedience to God's revealed will. Now God was about to unfold in fuller detail what the covenant demanded in terms of personal obedience. In chapter 20 he will give them his law in the form of the Ten Commandments. Then in the following chapters he will apply his commandments to various life situations. It is all part of keeping covenant with God.

Even before getting specific, God revealed to Moses the essence of what he required, which was full obedience. This is the main thing. Anyone who wants to enjoy fellowship with God must make a basic commitment to do everything God says. Once this commitment has been made, the rest is "just details." The decision to *do* what God demands has already been made; now it is simply a matter of learning what God demands. So God began with the basic commitment to do what he says: "If you will indeed obey my voice and keep my covenant . . ." (19:5a).

Realize that this statement was made to people who were already saved. The Israelites had been delivered from bondage and redeemed by the blood of the Passover lamb. This is crucial for understanding how God's law works in the Christian life. The order of the exodus is important: First God delivered his people from bondage, then he gave them his law. Imagine what would have happened if it had been the other way around. Suppose God had said to Moses, "Tell my people: 'If you obey me fully and keep my covenant, I will carry you away from Egypt on eagle's wings.'" In that case, there never would have been an exodus at all. God's people would still be in bondage due to their failure to keep covenant with God. But God is a God of grace. So he saved his people first, then he called them to obey his law. The history of the exodus thus helps us understand the function of the Law in the Christian life. First God rescues us from our sin; then he teaches us how to live for his glory. If personal obedience had to come first, we would never be saved. But as it is, God saves us *in* Christ before he calls us to live *for* Christ.

At the same time, however, we need to recognize that God's promise came with a condition. God said, "*If* you will indeed obey my voice . . . you shall be my treasured possession" (19:5). How are we to make sense of this? If Israel was saved by grace, then why did God make their destiny depend on their works? Could they lose their salvation?

One common way to answer this question is to say that although Israel's ultimate salvation was secure, in order for them to enjoy the fullness of God's blessing, they needed to keep the covenant. John Mackay writes: "The people have already been freed by divine grace and power. They are not given the law to save themselves, but so that they might continue to enjoy the salvation they have already been given."[6] There is some truth to this. The covenant is a love relationship, but how can anyone experience intimacy with God and at the same time break his law? Or to state the very nature of the case, we cannot enjoy fellowship with God while we are rebelling against him.

Yet we must take the covenant condition seriously. There is more at stake here than simply enjoying God's blessing. God really did *demand* Israel's full obedience. Here we need to remember that Exodus 19 is part of the Old Testament—that is to say, the old covenant. Thus there is a condition here that was not met until Christ came into the world. To be sure, even in the Old Testament salvation came by grace through faith. The exodus is the supreme example of the way salvation in Christ was written into Israel's history. But God also made it clear that full obedience—perfect covenant keeping—was required for salvation. As a matter of his eternal justice, God demanded nothing less than perfection. Therefore, in Exodus the law is presented in all its detail as the condition of the covenant.

Perfect obedience was a condition that God's people were unable to meet. Because of their sin, the Israelites never fulfilled their covenant obligations. But as they struggled and failed to keep God's law, they realized their need for grace all the more and looked for a Savior who *could* keep God's covenant. They were waiting for Jesus Christ, who is "the mediator of a new covenant . . . since a death has occurred that redeems them from the transgressions committed under the first covenant" (Hebrews 9:15). Jesus also died for us, for we too are covenant-breakers. But Christ has offered full obedience to God for us, and he has suffered the penalty that we deserved for our sins. God's covenant is unconditional for us only because Christ has kept its conditions. We have kept the covenant in Christ.

## A Precious People

The covenant that God made with his people at Mount Sinai came with a promise of blessing for those who fully obeyed him. God said, "Now therefore, if you will indeed obey my voice and keep my covenant, you shall be my treasured possession among all peoples, for all the earth is mine; and you shall be to me a kingdom of priests and a holy nation" (19:5, 6).

God had already told the Israelites who he was. He was the God of their salvation who saved them for himself. Now he was telling them who *they* were. This is the way the covenant always works. It is a mutual relationship in which God says, "I will be your God, and you will be my people." In Exodus 19 God started by telling the people what kind of God he was, and then he told them what kind of people they were supposed to be: a precious people with a special purpose.

They were a precious people, or as God put it, "my treasured possession" (19:5). God's treasure—this is one of the highest titles that anyone could possibly be given. The Hebrew word used here (*segulla*) indicates royal property. Indeed, it is the most prized possession in a king's personal treasury. The same word is used in 1 Chronicles 29 for the gift that King David gave for building the temple. He had already given some of his royal revenue for the project. However, more was needed. So David said, "I have a treasure of my own [*segulla*] of gold and silver, and because of my devotion to the house of my God I give it to the house of my God" (1 Chronicles 29:3).

The word David used to describe his private reserve of gold and silver and the word God used to describe his people are one and the same. Israel was God's royal property, his most prized possession. What made these people so precious? Were they especially gifted? Were they unusually talented? Did they have power and prestige? At the time the Israelites had none of these things, which led Ogden Nash to write his famous couplet, "How odd of God to choose the Jews."

What may seem like an oddity to some is really for the praise of God's sovereign grace. The Israelites were saved for no other reason than that they were the objects of God's covenant choice. This is explained in Deuteronomy 7, where Moses again speaks of royal treasure, saying to the Israelites, "The Lord your God has chosen you to be a people for his treasured possession, out of all the peoples who are on the face of the earth" (Deuteronomy 7:6b). Why did God make this choice? Moses went on: "It was not because you were more in number than any other people that the Lord set his love on you and chose you, for you were the fewest of all peoples, but it is because the Lord loves you" (Deuteronomy 7:7, 8a). What made God's people so precious was not their own intrinsic value; it was only the value placed on them by God's love. They were not precious because of who *they* were but because of who *God* was.

In one sense everyone belongs to God because we are all made in his image. God has showered many of his blessings on humanity in general. "All the earth is mine" (19:5b), he says, but in his heart God always reserves a special place for his own precious people. While we cannot deny his universal benevolence, it is not to be compared to the unique love that he has for his own people only. God placed his unique affection on Israel, saying, "You shall be my treasured possession among all peoples" (19:5a). The Israelites were God's "peculiar people" (Titus 2:14; 1 Peter 2:9, both KJV), his crown jewels among the nations.

This was Israel's identity. They were God's precious people. But what is our identity? Who are we? There may be times when we do not feel very precious. We struggle to make it from one day to the next. We are weighed down by on-the-job stress, or we spend all our time at home with small children. We never quite seem to succeed in business. We get discouraged by conflicts and difficulties in ministry. We struggle with illness and loneliness. Even when we seem to have it all together, there are still times when we feel unsatisfied and unfulfilled.

Whatever our struggles, we are God's treasure, for we have been drawn close to God through faith in Jesus Christ. The apostle Peter took the words of Moses and applied them directly to the church of Jesus Christ: "But you are a chosen race, a royal priesthood, a holy nation, a people for his own possession" (1 Peter 2:9a; cf. Revelation 1:5b, 6; 20:6). Every Christian is precious to God, loved with a unique and everlasting love. Do we deserve this? No, but God values us as equivalent with the infinitely precious blood of his very own Son. By the grace of his everlasting covenant, he loves us more deeply than we would ever dare to hope or imagine. We are his "treasured possession."

### A Special Purpose

God's precious people have a special purpose. We are called not simply to salvation but also to service. As God said to Israel, "You shall be to me a kingdom of priests and a holy nation" (19:6). But what is "a kingdom of priests"? This is the only place in the Old Testament where this phrase appears, so scholars have struggled to determine its precise interpretation.

"Kingdom of priests" seems to have a double meaning—one for Israel and one for the world. Within Israel, it meant that every single person in the kingdom was called to serve and worship God. Later God would designate the Levites to serve as Israel's official priests. The Levites had specific priestly duties. They offered sacrifices, led in worship, and looked after the tabernacle. But they were not the only Israelites who were called into God's service. God wanted "a *kingdom* of priests," a whole nation of people set apart to give him glory. Then Israel would be "a holy nation"—a people set apart for God and dedicated to serving him in all of life. This was a call God gave his people again and again, to be holy like him (see Leviticus 11:45; 19:1, 2; 20:7, 26).

The title "kingdom of priests" also had another meaning, one with global implications. As an entire nation, the Israelites were God's priests to the world. God chose Israel with the ultimate intention of saving the world. The English Standard Version captures the sense well here: "You shall be my treasured possession among all peoples, for all the earth is mine" (19:5b). This makes it clear that God's plan for Israel was part of his plan for the world. Israel was chosen not only *from* the nations, but also *for* the nations. This plan was first revealed to Abraham, to whom God said, "In you all the families of the earth shall be blessed" (Genesis 12:3b). The holy nation of Israel was part of the plan, for as Jesus himself said, "Salvation is from the Jews" (John 4:22). The Israelites were mediators of divine grace, serving as God's priests to the nations. As they worshiped God and as they lived in covenant holiness, they preserved the treasure of Biblical faith until the coming of the Savior brought salvation to the rest of the world.

When the Savior came, he was born the King of the Jews, but he did not just come to save the Jews. The Savior came to save the world, for God said, "I will make you as a light for the nations, that my salvation may reach to the end of the earth" (Isaiah 49:6b). The name of this Savior, of course, is Jesus Christ. He is the fulfillment of Israel's destiny to be a kingdom of priests for the nations.

## A Royal Priesthood

Now Jesus has given the church the same priestly task that God once gave to Israel. We have seen how the apostle Peter took Exodus 19 and applied it to us: "But you are a chosen race, a royal priesthood, a holy nation, a people for his own possession" (1 Peter 2:9a; cf. Revelation 1:6). We too are a precious people, saved out of all the nations. But for what purpose?

Peter went on to explain our special calling:

> But you are a chosen race, a royal priesthood, a holy nation, a people for his own possession, that you may proclaim the excellencies of him who called you out of darkness into his marvelous light. Once you were not a people, but now you are God's people; once you had not received mercy, but now you have received mercy.
>
> Beloved, I urge you as sojourners and exiles to abstain from the passions of the flesh, which wage war against your soul. Keep your conduct among the Gentiles honorable, so that when they speak against you as evildoers, they may see your good deeds and glorify God on the day of visitation. (1 Peter 2:9–12)

Like the Israelites, we are a kingdom of priests. Theologians call this *the priesthood of all believers*. God has made us his treasure, bringing us from slavery to royalty and setting us apart for his holy service. Since we are saved for God's glory, our service is to worship God, to glorify him by declaring his praises. But we also have a mission to the world—not to rule it, but to serve it. The way we serve is by leading holy lives. What distinguishes us from the rest of the world is our personal godliness. Or at least it ought to, because the way we live is part of God's plan for saving the world.

# 44

# Don't Touch!

EXODUS 19:7–15

SOME PERIODS OF CHURCH HISTORY have emphasized God's *transcendence*, meaning "his distance from his creatures because of his holiness and greatness."[1] To transcend means to go beyond. God's transcendence is his otherness and separateness from everything that he has made. When people see God as transcendent, they approach him with wonder and awe. This was true in the Middle Ages, when great cathedrals were built to the praise of God's lofty majesty.

At other times the church has emphasized God's *immanence*, which refers to "his nearness and relatedness to his creatures."[2] *Immanent* comes from a Latin verb meaning "to remain in." To speak of God's immanence, therefore, is to speak of his close personal involvement and interaction with his creation. When people see God as immanent, they approach him with confidence, expecting to experience the intimacy of his personal presence.

The truth is that God is both transcendent and immanent. He is exalted above all that he has made. At the same time he is intimately involved with everything that happens in his universe. Both of these things are true about God. The trouble is that the church usually tends to emphasize one at the expense of the other.

We live in an age of immanence, an age that sees God more as a personal friend than a supreme deity. Most Christians today feel more comfortable with a user-friendly God than with one who is holy and majestic. The result is a casual approach to worship. I refer not to the style of worship, primarily, but to the attitude of most worshipers. We come to church the way we would drop by someone's living room rather than the way we would enter the throne room of a king.

Is it possible that we are more comfortable worshiping God than we ought to be? In her book *Teaching a Stone to Talk*, Annie Dillard worries that we have forgotten how dangerous it is to come into the presence of the living God. She writes:

> On the whole, I do not find Christians, outside the catacombs, sufficiently sensible of the conditions. Does anyone have the foggiest idea what sort of power we so blithely invoke? Or, as I suspect, does no one believe a word of it? The churches are children playing on the floor with their chemistry sets, mixing up a batch of TNT to kill a Sunday morning. It is madness to wear ladies' straw hats and velvet hats to church; we should all be wearing crash helmets. Ushers should issue life preservers and signal flares; they should lash us to our pews.[3]

## God with Us

Exodus 19 began with the assurance of God's great love for his people. The Israelites had finally reached Mount Sinai, where they would meet with God. There God spoke to them, reminding them how he had carried them "on eagles' wings," like a mother bearing up her faltering young. He said, "I . . . brought you to myself" (19:4), showing that his goal for their salvation was fellowship with himself. God spoke tenderly to his people, assuring them that they had a special place in his heart. Out of all the nations, he chose Israel to be his royal possession, his crown jewel (19:5). This was an astonishing expression of intimacy. God was pledging his love for Israel, saying, "You will be my people, and I will be your God."

Israel responded in faith. First "Moses came and called the elders of the people and set before them all these words that the Lord had commanded him" (19:7). The elders were Israel's divinely appointed spiritual leaders, and they in turn communicated God's word to the rest of the nation. For their part, "All the people answered together and said, 'All that the Lord has spoken we will do.' And Moses reported the words of the people to the Lord" (19:8). With these words, the Israelites swore that they would keep their covenant with God. God had reached out to them in love, and they wanted to reciprocate.

God intended for this relationship to grow. So he told his people that he would come to visit them: "And the Lord said to Moses, 'Behold, I am coming to you in a thick cloud, that the people may hear when I speak with you, and may also believe you forever.' When Moses told the words of the people to the Lord . . ." (19:9). This was two-way communication. God was speaking to his people, and his people were speaking to him.

When God visited his people, they would actually see something of his glory. He promised to "come down on Mount Sinai in the sight of all the people" (19:11). This would be another theophany, another appearance of the divine presence in clouds of glory. Notice that God would have to come down to do this. God is not like the pagan gods who lived on Mount Olympus. He did not dwell on Mount Sinai; he only came down for a visit. Whenever God visits his people, it is always a comedown. The prophet Nehemiah would later say, "You came down on Mount Sinai and spoke with them from heaven" (Nehemiah 9:13a). This shows God's distance, or transcendence. He is separate and other. If he were not willing to stoop down and visit us, we would never be able to see him or talk to him.

But God is willing to stoop. He is immanent as well as transcendent. He says, "I dwell in the high and holy place, and also with him who is of a contrite and lowly spirit" (Isaiah 57:15). The whole story of redemption is about God stooping to save. In the beginning he walked and talked with Adam and Eve in the garden. Sadly, our first parents sinned, and thus they lost the immediacy of God's presence. Yet because of his great love, God has been reaching out ever since to restore our fellowship with him. This is why he sent his Son into the world, to come and be close to us. His name is Immanuel, "God with us" (Matthew 1:23).

## Too Close for Comfort

God was bringing his people close already at Mount Sinai. Yet the closer they came, the more clearly they saw the vast distance that still separated them from God. At the same time that God was revealing himself, he was also concealing himself. The more they experienced his immanence, the more they recognized his transcendence.

God kept his distance in several different ways. One was by hiding in the dark cloud of his glory: "And the Lord said to Moses, 'Behold, I am coming to you in a thick cloud'" (19:9). When God comes to his people, he is often covered with a thick, glorious cloud. There are several examples of this in the Bible. The psalmist wrote, "Clouds and thick darkness are all around him" (Psalm 97:2a). When Isaiah entered the throne room of Heaven, he saw God surrounded by smoke (Isaiah 6:4). At the transfiguration the disciples saw Jesus enveloped in a bright cloud (Matthew 17:5). The clouds that surround God's presence show his divine glory, but they also hide it. The clouds of glory "suggest both heavenly majesty and concealment of the divine from the scrutiny of mankind."[4] By keeping God shrouded in mystery, they are a sign of his transcendence. They show his otherness and separateness from his creatures. As Isaiah exclaimed, "Truly, you are a God who hides himself, O God of Israel, the Savior" (Isaiah 45:15). When God came down on Mount Sinai, he was both revealed and concealed by the glorious cloud of his presence.

God also kept his distance by telling Israel to stay off his holy mountain. God said to Moses, "And you shall set limits for the people all around, saying, 'Take care not to go up into the mountain or touch the edge of it'" (19:12a). In other words, "Don't touch that mountain!" When God descended on the mountain, the mountain itself was made holy by his presence, and thus it needed to be fenced off as a restricted area. To put this in contemporary terms, Moses and the elders marked out the boundary, put up the police tape, and posted the signs: "Keep Out!" "No Trespassing!" "Authorized Access Only." The Israelites were not allowed to go up the mountain until someone sounded the all-clear. God said, "When the trumpet sounds a long blast, they shall come up to the mountain" (19:13b).

In the meantime, the penalties for transgressing God's boundaries were severe. Violators were to be executed. The Israelites had orders to shoot on sight, for God said, "Whoever touches the mountain shall be put to death. No hand shall touch him, but he shall be stoned or shot; whether beast or man, he shall not live" (19:12b, 13a). The penalty for trespassing on God's holy mountain was death, and those who executed the death penalty were not even allowed to touch their victims. Otherwise they too would be contaminated with unholiness.

Why did God place all these restrictions on Israel? After all, he had told them that he wanted to draw them close. So why was he keeping them at arm's length?

It was partly to preserve his transcendence, his otherness and separateness, his eternal mystery. The Bible calls God "the blessed and only Sovereign, the King of kings and Lord of lords, who alone has immortality, who dwells in unapproachable light, whom no one has ever seen or can see" (1 Timothy 6:15, 16). We would like to know all the answers, to penetrate the mysteries of his deity, but there are some things that we are not meant to know. John Calvin wrote: "We know how great is men's natural curiosity, how frowardly they seek to penetrate the secrets of God, how daringly they indulge themselves, and how, by their irreverence, all religion and fear of God is extinguished in them; wherefore there was good cause why He should set these bounds, and restrain this perverse longing after unlawful knowledge."[5] It is not wrong to want to know God. What *is* wrong is to demand entrance into the secrets he has not chosen to reveal. It is part of the very godness of God to remain a mystery to mankind. On Mount Sinai God kept his mystery on the mountain.

The other reason God told his people to keep their distance was for their own protection. Having Moses place barricades around the mountain was a matter of public safety. God is dangerous! He is so perfectly and supremely holy that it is not safe to barge into his presence. On occasion sinners have been destroyed by the sheer holiness of God. It happened to Nadab and Abihu, who were burned by the fire from God's altar (Leviticus 10:1, 2). It also happened to Uzzah, who touched the Ark of God's Presence (1 Chronicles 13:10). God is so transcendent that coming into his holy presence can mean sudden death for sinners. As God would later say to Moses, "Man shall not see me and live" (33:20). When he brought the Israelites to himself, therefore, they were too close for comfort. God kept them off the mountain to keep them safe.

This is a warning not to be presumptuous in our worship. We are in the presence of a holy and transcendent God! Therefore, we should "offer to God acceptable worship, with reverence and awe, for our God is a consuming fire" (Hebrews 12:28b, 29).

## Consecrated to the King

So here was the awesome dilemma the Israelites faced: They were being drawn into a close personal relationship with a holy God who was too dangerous for them even to approach! What could they do to be safe?

God provided the answer. There were two things his people needed. The first was to prepare for his coming: "The LORD said to Moses, 'Go to the people and consecrate them today and tomorrow, and let them wash their garments and be ready for the third day. For on the third day the LORD will come down on Mount Sinai in the sight of all the people'" (19:10, 11).

To understand these preparations, it helps to understand that in Exodus 19 God is portrayed as a mighty King. The word *king* does not appear; however, this section of Exodus is structured like a treaty between a great king and one of his vassals.[6] Such treaties were common in the ancient world. For example, after the Hittites conquered one of their enemies, they would sign a treaty. And since they were the overlords, they were in the position to dictate its terms.

The treaty started with a formal introduction, known to scholars as the preamble. This was followed by a prologue giving the history of the relationship between the two nations, which usually culminated in some sort of battle. Next the overlord set the terms for their future relationship, including the vassal's obligation to provide allegiance, tribute, soldiers, and the like. These obligations were accompanied with blessings and curses. The vassal was told, in no uncertain terms, what the penalties were for failing to comply with the terms of the treaty. Two copies were made—one for each nation—and then the treaty was ratified in a covenant ceremony.

We find almost the same structure in Exodus 19 and following. As we read in a parallel passage, "The LORD made a covenant with the people of Israel, when they came out of the land of Egypt" (1 Kings 8:9b). Exodus 19:3 is the preamble, in which God the great King addresses his people Israel. Verse 4 is the historical prologue. It recounts what God had done for the Israelites, not to conquer them, but to deliver them. Their whole relationship was based on God's saving grace. Then in verse 5 God begins to set his basic terms, which are accompanied with a promise of blessing. The conditions of this covenant are stipulated in much more exhaustive detail in Exodus 20—23. Then finally in chapter 24 there is a covenant-making ceremony. Later we learn that two copies of the covenant were made—"the two tablets of the testimony" (32:15).

It is not surprising that there are so many similarities between the book of Exodus and the ancient treaties. God was speaking to his people in terms they could understand, terms familiar to them from their own cultural context. It should be emphasized that the Israelites were not simply borrowing from other civilizations. Their covenant was unique because it was the only one ever made by and with God himself. This was completely unprecedented. Other ancient treaties appealed to the gods as witnesses, but in no case did they involve a god making a covenant with men. This was a remarkable condescension—the transcendent God entering into a binding relationship with his people.

No wonder the people needed to get ready: The King was coming! And not just any king. He was *the* King, the Great King, "the King of the ages, immortal, invisible, the only God" (1 Timothy 1:17). The people of Israel were about to have a royal audience with His Majesty the King, who was coming to renew his covenant. Therefore, they needed to be consecrated, which means to be set apart as holy. After all, this was Israel's calling: to be a kingdom of priests, a holy nation, separated from the world for the worship and service of the Most High God.

The Israelites had three days to make their preparations. First they put on their Sabbath best. The King was coming, so they needed to wash their clothes. This was a sign of sanctification. In the Bible, clothing often serves as an outward symbol for someone's true spiritual condition. Here it indicates Israel's inward need for cleansing from sin before coming into the presence of the King.

The people also refrained from sexual intercourse (19:15b)—not because there is something wrong with sex, but as a form of fasting. Here Calvin makes the helpful comment that "although there is nothing polluting or contaminating in the marriage bed, yet the Israelites were to be reminded that all earthly cares were, as much as possible, to be renounced, and all carnal affections to be put away, that they might give their entire attention to the hearing of the Law."[7] According to the New Testament, the only reason to abstain from marital relations is for a spiritual purpose, and then only temporarily (see 1 Corinthians 7:5). What the Israelites did was in keeping with this principle: they abstained from intercourse for three days in order to give their undivided attention to their King and to his law.

These were the preparations that Israel made, but what about our own preparations? What was true for the Israelites is true, in a different way, for us: The King is coming. By virtue of his resurrection and ascension, Jesus Christ is now King. He came into the world once to be born in a manger and to die on a cross for sinners. Soon he will come again to judge the world. The King *is* coming. There is no question about that. The question is, are we ready to meet him?

Most people sense there is something we need to do to get ready to meet God. Bruce Feiler wrestled with this question when he visited Saint Catherine's Monastery on Jebel Musa, the traditional site of Mount Sinai. In his book *Walking the Bible*, Feiler describes going to the top of the mountain. Before going up he reminded his spiritual guide that in the Bible "Mount Sinai was so sacred—and so highly combustible—that no one was allowed to climb it, no less touch it, look at it, or sleep on it."

> "That's right," Father Justin said. "In the story, when the Israelites first came into contact with the mountain, they marked the whole area off. There was thunder and lightning and thick black clouds. Even the animals were not allowed to go up the mountain. And that's when they heard the sound of trumpets, as if the mountain was on fire. Everyone was terrified. And the people said to Moses, 'If we go up we will surely die, so you go up and speak to God for us.'"
>
> "If that's the case, then how do we justify walking up the mountain today?" I asked.
>
> Again he was serenely confident, even brotherly. "In ancient times," he explained, "a monk would be at the top of the path and he would hear a person's confession to make sure that he was spiritually prepared to be at the sacred place. That's how we justify it. You come to the monastery. You purify yourself. And then you ascend."[8]

Surely Father Justin was right about our need for personal purity. The Scripture says, "Let us cleanse ourselves from every defilement of body and spirit, bringing holiness to completion in the fear of God" (2 Corinthians 7:1). The reason we need to be pure is because only the pure can meet with God. David asked, "Who shall ascend the hill of the LORD? And who shall stand in his holy place?" (Psalm 24:3). His answer was, "He who has clean hands and a pure heart" (Psalm 24:4a). When it comes to meeting with God, we cannot come as we are because the Bible says that we need to "strive for . . . the holiness without which no one will see the Lord" (Hebrews 12:14).

The trouble is that we can never make ourselves holy enough for God. This is the problem with Father Justin's statement, "You purify yourself." We have been trying to purify ourselves since the day that sin first entered the world. Adam and Eve sewed fig leaves together in a desperate attempt to cover up their sin, and human beings have been trying to dress themselves up for God ever since. In one way or another, nearly every religion involves some form of self-purification. The world religions are all so many different ways to wash our own clothes as a way of getting ready for God. But we can never clean up well enough for God. He is perfect in holiness, and even our best efforts are stained with sin. As Isaiah said, "All our righteous deeds are like a polluted garment" (Isaiah 64:6). Therefore we are unable to purify ourselves.

## Moses the Mediator

To be ready for the coming of the King, we need something more than personal consecration. We need what Israel needed: a mediator. A mediator is a go-between, an intermediary, someone who bridges the gap between two parties who are at a distance. In this case what needed to be bridged was the distance between a holy, transcendent God and his finite, sinful people.

Moses had been serving as Israel's mediator ever since God called him to be a prophet at the burning bush. God gave Moses special access. It was his unique privilege to speak directly with God. Whenever God had something to say to his people, he spoke through his prophet. It was Moses who told them that God was going to rescue them, who gave them the regulations for Passover and the redemption of sons, and who told them how and when to gather the manna and the quail. In his role as mediator, Moses also represented the people before God. He cried out to God when the people needed water. He had to answer to God when the people grumbled in the wilderness. He also interceded for them before God's throne, raising his hands up in prayer during the time of battle.

On Mount Sinai Moses continued to carry out his mediatorial ministry. He spoke to God on behalf of the people, bringing their response to the terms of the treaty. God also spoke to Moses, and he did so in a way that confirmed his ministry as the mediator. He said to Moses, "I am coming to you in a thick cloud, that the people may hear when I speak with you, and may also believe you forever" (19:9). By speaking with an audible voice, God authenticated Moses as his prophet. Since the Israelites could hear the sound of God's voice for themselves, they knew that Moses was not simply inventing his own religion but was receiving revelation from God. To this day Moses is honored as God's faithful messenger, just as God promised.

As the mediator, Moses was a two-way messenger. It was his job to keep the lines of communication open. But there was something else that he did as well. The Scripture says, "So Moses went down from the mountain to the people and *consecrated the people*; and they washed their garments. And he said to the people, 'Be ready for the third day; do not go near a woman'" (19:14, 15). Before he repeated what God wanted him to say to the people, Moses "consecrated" them. Acting as the mediator, he set the Israelites apart as holy unto God.

How did Moses consecrate them? The Scripture does not specify, but apparently he performed some kind of consecrating act. He did something to make the Israelites holy. It was not enough for them to wash their clothes. They needed God to make them pure, which he did through the agency of his mediator. But what exactly did Moses do? What kind of action had the effect of making God's people holy?

The most likely explanation is that Moses performed some kind of sacrifice. This is what God has always required for holiness. Before we can be considered righteous in God's sight, a sacrifice must be made for our sins. This is what Adam and Eve needed when they failed in their attempt to cover up their sin. They needed the grace of God, who clothed them with the skins of animals offered in their place (Genesis 3:21).

The best way for Moses to consecrate the Israelites, therefore, was to offer a sacrifice for their sins. And he had a good precedent for this in his own experience. Before God brought Israel out of Egypt, he told Moses, "Consecrate to me all the firstborn" (13:2). How did Moses consecrate the firstborn of Israel? By offering an animal sacrifice, a substitute for their sins (13:11–15). Moses would do the same thing later, when it came time for him to set apart Aaron and his sons as Israel's priests. As part of their priestly consecration, Moses sacrificed a young bull and two rams as a sin offering (see Exodus 29). Although we cannot be certain, it seems probable that when Moses was told to consecrate the Israelites, he did it the only way he knew how, which was to offer a sacrifice. This was his role as the mediator—not simply to converse with God, but also to consecrate his people by making atonement for their sins.

This is what we need as well: a mediator, someone to cleanse us from sin and to consecrate us for God's holy service. By the grace of God, we do have such a mediator. The Bible says that he is a better mediator than Moses (see Hebrew 8:6), the best and only mediator we will ever need. His name, of course, is Jesus Christ. Jesus is the answer to the riddle of God's immanence and transcendence. He is God with us. Because he is truly divine, Jesus possesses all of God's kingly majesty. Because he is also a real human being, he shares in our humanity. He is the mediator who goes and speaks with God for us and who makes us pure enough for God. As the Scripture says, "We have been sanctified through the offering of the body of Jesus Christ once for all" (Hebrews 10:10).

In Jesus the transcendent God is immanent: "Veiled in flesh the Godhead see; / hail th' incarnate Deity, / pleased as man with men to dwell, / Jesus, our Emmanuel."[9] Without ever giving up his divine nature, Jesus took on our human nature and thus entered fully into our lost condition (yet remaining sinless). It was as a man that Jesus revealed God to us. It was as a man that he suffered all the indignities of life on this earth. And it was as a man that he suffered and died on the cross for our sins. The transcendent God is immanent through the person of his Son.

Now, for a time, Jesus has returned to Heaven, where he reigns in transcendent majesty. He is still with us by his Holy Spirit, of course, but we are waiting for the day when he will come and take us to be with him forever. On that day a loud voice from God's throne will say, "Behold, the dwelling place of God is with man. He will dwell with them" (Revelation 21:3a). God will be with us—and we will be with God—forever.

# 45

# Smoke on the Mountain

EXODUS 19:16–25

THE ISRAELITES WERE FINISHED with their preparations. Three days earlier the Lord God had told them that he would come and visit them at Mount Sinai, but before he came, his people needed to get ready. First they needed to be consecrated by Moses, the mediator, who probably offered a sacrifice for their sins. Then they needed to wash their clothes. This was a ceremonial symbol of sanctification, of their need for personal purity. They also abstained from sexual relations as a form of fasting.

Meanwhile, for reasons of public safety, Moses was marking out a perimeter around the mountain. When God descended, the whole mountain would become holy. It would not be safe for the people to ascend. Even touching the mountain would mean instant death. So as a precaution God told Moses to make a boundary that the people were not allowed to cross. This was symbolic of the vast distance between the Creator and the creature, between God's purity and our depravity.

## Fear and Trembling

By the third day the Israelites were as ready for God as they would ever be. Anxiously they awaited the coming of their King. From time to time they would look up at the mountain, wondering exactly what would happen when God stepped down from Heaven. He came right on schedule:

> On the morning of the third day there were thunders and lightnings and a thick cloud on the mountain and a very loud trumpet blast, so that all the people in the camp trembled. Then Moses brought the people out of the camp to meet God, and they took their stand at the foot of the mountain. Now Mount Sinai was wrapped in smoke because the LORD had descended on it in fire. The smoke of it went up like the smoke of a kiln, and the whole

> mountain trembled greatly. And as the sound of the trumpet grew louder and louder . . . (19:16–19a)

What the Israelites witnessed that day was one of the most awesomely terrifying displays of divine power that anyone has ever experienced. All the forces and powers of nature slammed against the mountainside: lightning, thunder, darkness, smoke, fire, and earthquake.

Understandably, the Israelites were overwhelmed with fear. The mountain *looked* scary. It was covered with a black and ominous cloud. Its peaks were charged with lightning. Its rocks were blazing with fire and belching smoke, which billowed like the smoke from a fiery hot furnace. The mountain also *sounded* scary. In addition to the constant blasts and booms of thunder, there was the incessant blowing of a trumpet. Possibly it was a giant *shofar*, made from a ram's horn. The sound of the trumpet grew louder and LOUDER and LOUDER as God came closer and closer. And Mount Sinai *felt* as scary as it looked and sounded. Acrid smoke was in the air, from a fire that radiated an intense, menacing heat. The whole mountain quaked and trembled; the ground underneath Israel's feet was moving and shaking.

Everything about this entire encounter was intended to inspire the fear of God. Franklin Delano Roosevelt said, "We have nothing to fear but fear itself." Well, that is what the Israelites had: fear itself! They were afraid because they were in the presence of a transcendent God in all his awesome power.

The Israelites were so terrified that they were physically shaking, for the Scripture says, "All the people in the camp trembled" (19:16b). This word is repeated in the following chapter: "Now when all the people saw the thunder and the flashes of lightning and the sound of the trumpet and the mountain smoking, the people were afraid and trembled" (20:18a). They were almost scared to death: "They stood far off and said to Moses, 'You speak to us, and we will listen; but do not let God speak to us, lest we die'" (20:18b, 19). Even Moses was scared. As brave as he was, the prophet was absolutely terrified when God came down on the mountain. We know this, not from Exodus, but from Hebrews, which tells us, "Indeed, so terrifying was the sight that Moses said, 'I tremble with fear'" (Hebrews 12:21; cf. Deuteronomy 9:19).

## Totally Awesome

There are many lessons to learn from the terrors on God's mountain. Calvin listed some of them in his commentary on the books of Moses, writing, "This terrible spectacle was partly to set the presence of God before their eyes, that His majesty might urge the beholders to obedience, and vindicate His doctrine from contempt, and partly to express the nature of the Law, which in itself produces nothing but mere terror."[1] The terrors of Mount Sinai teach about God, his law, and our sin.

The first and most obvious lesson is that God is totally awesome. Everything about the entire scene was designed to convey the supreme majesty and overwhelming power of Almighty God. The Israelites did not actually see God. All they saw were outward manifestations of his presence as revealed in nature. But the fire and the smoke communicated the "overpowering awe, mystery, and dramatic violent force of the actual presence of God."[2]

Another way to say this is that the mountain revealed God's glory. The whole purpose of the exodus was to reveal that God is "awesome in glorious deeds" (15:11). The Israelites had already seen the glory of God in their salvation. It was for his own glory that God delivered them from their bondage to Pharaoh. They had also seen God's glory in the wilderness, in the form of a fiery pillar of cloud. But at Mount Sinai they were given an even more dazzling display of the glory of God. There they saw him in all his glory.

Each of the natural phenomena revealed a different aspect of God's character. The thunder and the earthquake were signs of his power. The dark cloud was a sign of his mystery, showing that there are aspects of his being that we cannot penetrate. The fire was a sign of God's holiness, his bright and burning purity. Fire both attracts and repels. We are drawn to its warmth and beauty, but at the same time we are kept away by the danger of its burning. So, too, we are attracted to the beauty of God's holiness but at the same time repelled by its power to destroy us. The trumpet signified his sovereignty, for a trumpet signals the coming of a king. When God descended on Mount Sinai, he was given a royal fanfare to signify his kingly majesty. Together these spectacular signs displayed the glory of God, the sum total of his divine attributes. It must have been an amazing sight. The people who saw it could never forget that they had been in the presence of the living God in all his holiness and majesty.

We must realize that God still possesses this same glory *at this very moment*. Since God is invisible, we do not see his glory in its visible form. Yet if we were able to gaze upon God, to see him on his heavenly throne, we would behold the same glory that the Israelites saw at Mount Sinai. The prophet Isaiah was given the privilege of entering the throne room of the Most High God. There he saw the Lord exalted on his throne, and "the foundations of the thresholds shook . . . and the house was filled with smoke" (Isaiah 6:4). The apostle John saw the same thing. He too was granted a royal audience with God in Heaven. According to his eyewitness account, "From the throne came flashes of lightning, and rumblings and peals of thunder" (Revelation 4:5a). That is what we would see if we could see God right now. We would see and hear what Israel saw at Mount Sinai: thunder and lightning, fire and smoke—the glory of God.

The proper way to respond to God's glory is with reverence and awe, such as the angels have in Heaven. John heard them say, "Holy, holy, holy, is the Lord God Almighty, who was and is and is to come!" (Revelation 4:8b). John also heard the music of the saints in Heaven, the believers in Jesus Christ who have gone ahead to glory. They sing, "To him who sits on the throne and to the Lamb be blessing and honor and glory and might forever and ever!" (Revelation 5:13). If we could see God now we would be compelled to join them in giving God the glory. We would say, as Job said, "I had heard of you by the hearing of the ear, but now my eye sees you; therefore I despise myself, and repent in dust and ashes" (Job 42:5, 6). The God we serve is a great and glorious God, the very God who revealed his glory on the mountain.

Although we cannot see his glory now, we will certainly see it on the day of judgment. When God descends for the last time, to judge the earth, he will come in all his awesome glory. He will come with the same visible, audible signs of glory that the Israelites saw and heard on Mount Sinai. He will come with fire and earthquakes (2 Peter 3:10), with dark clouds and the sound of a great trumpet (Matthew 24:30, 31). The great Puritan poet John Milton described it well:

> With such a horrid clang
> As on Mount Sinai rang
> While the red fire and smould'ring clouds out brake;
> The aged Earth aghast
> With terror of that blast,
> Shall from the surface to the centre shake,
> When at the world's last session,
> The dreadful Judge in middle air shall spread his throne.[3]

And what will we think of God then?

We live at a time when most of our ideas about God are unworthy of his majesty. Most people think of God—if they think about him at all—as some kind of cosmic force or as a kindly old grandpa, "the man upstairs." They do not honor him as the totally awesome God who revealed his glory at Mount Sinai. But we may be sure that when the Israelites stood at the foot of Mount Sinai, they did not entertain any trivial notions about God. To borrow a famous title from Francis Schaeffer, what the Israelites experienced at Mount Sinai was *The God Who Is There*.[4] When they came into his presence, they worshiped him with reverence and awe, as we should worship him today, prostrating ourselves before him.

## He Is There and He Is Not Silent

The God of glory is a God who speaks, revealing his word to his people. God's primary purpose in coming down on Mount Sinai was to give his law. The spectacular signs that accompanied his coming—all the fire and smoke—were partly designed to prove that it was God who was speaking to them. Imagine how the Israelites would have responded to Moses if God had not displayed his glory on Mount Sinai. The prophet would have gone up the mountain and then come back down again with the Law. But how would the people know for certain that it was God's law and not simply the law of Moses?

Some scholars say that God spoke to Moses through some kind of inward, private inspiration. According to one interpretation, "The literal truth was that God spoke to the heart of Moses: the poetic truth was that He spoke in thunder and lightning from the crest of Sinai."[5] But in that case, how would the people have known that God was speaking to them? They would simply have had to take Moses' word for it, but of course his word didn't always count for much with them. So God performed miraculous signs to prove that the Law ultimately came from him.

Other scholars have tried to reinterpret what happened on Mount Sinai, explaining Exodus 19 simply in terms of various natural phenomena. There was an earthquake, they say, as well as a great storm on the mountain. And given all the fire and smoke, the mountain must have been a volcano. Then, based on this assumption, they have tried (generally unsuccessfully) to find an extinct volcano to identify as Mount Sinai.[6]

Critics have had more difficulty coming up with an explanation for the noises mentioned in verse 19: "And as the sound of the trumpet grew louder and louder, Moses spoke, and God answered him in thunder." What natural explanation can we offer for all this? These are supernatural phenomena that no naturalistic theory can explain.[7] Yet even the natural phenomena—the thunder and the lightning and all—were demonstrations of God's supernatural power. As he had done all through the exodus, God was using the forces of nature to prove his presence. And by proving his presence through outward signs, God confirmed that he was the one speaking to Moses. To use the title from another book by Schaeffer, *He Is There and He Is Not Silent*.[8]

The reason all this matters is because we need to know whether God has spoken to the human race or not. Has God given us his Word? Has he communicated with us in the form of true propositions that explain his work in human history? Has he proclaimed a message of salvation? Has he given authoritative commands to guide our daily conduct? If God did not speak to Moses, he has not spoken to us. For if ever God revealed his will for the human race, it was on the top of Mount Sinai. There God really did speak to Moses. The Bible says, "Moses spoke, and God answered him in thunder. The LORD came down on Mount Sinai, to the top of the mountain. And the LORD called Moses to the top of the mountain" (9:19b, 20a). What proved to the Israelites that God really was speaking to Moses were the miraculous signs that accompanied this revelation.

Furthermore, the people were able to hear the actual voice of God. To this day some scholars argue that the Law given at Mount Sinai was Moses' own invention, based on his experiences in Egypt and his study of other ancient legal codes. But this would make Moses the lawmaker, and not simply the lawyer. The way the people knew that the Law came from God was by hearing God's voice for themselves. As Moses later reminded them, "The LORD spoke with you face to face at the mountain, out of the midst of the fire" (Deuteronomy 5:4); "The LORD spoke to all your assembly at the mountain out of the midst of the fire, the cloud, and the thick darkness" (Deuteronomy 5:22a). The elders also testified, "Behold, the LORD our God has shown us his glory and greatness, and we have heard his voice out of the midst of the fire" (Deuteronomy 5:24a).

It was because *they* heard God's voice that *we* hear God's voice today. What was written in Exodus is the very word of God. This is true not simply for the writings of Moses, but for everything written on every page of the whole Bible. It all comes from God. As the Scripture says, "No prophecy was ever produced by the will of man, but men spoke from God" (2 Peter 1:21). Therefore, all the commands, warnings, and promises of the Bible are the commands, warnings, and promises of God. When the Bible offers eternal life through faith in Jesus Christ, the offer comes from God himself, backed by the full weight of his deity.

## Keep Your Distance!

God is there in all his awesome glory, and he is not silent. He speaks to us with all the authority of his divine sovereignty. Therefore we should be very careful how we approach him.

Moses had already warned the people that they could not simply barge into God's presence. He had placed limits around the mountain, warning them, "Whoever touches the mountain shall be put to death" (19:12b). Nevertheless, when Moses went up the mountain again, God found it necessary to repeat his earlier warnings: "And the LORD said to Moses, 'Go down and warn the people, lest they break through to the LORD to look and many of them perish. Also let the priests who come near to the LORD consecrate themselves, lest the LORD break out against them'" (19:21, 22). It is somewhat unclear who these priests were. Eventually Aaron and his descendants were anointed as Israel's priests, but that did not happen until chapter 28. Here in Exodus 19 the priesthood was not yet established. But perhaps at this time the firstborn in each family had a priestly function. Support for this suggestion comes from chapter 24: when the covenant was confirmed, the young men of Israel fulfilled the priestly function of offering sacrifices (24:5).

Whoever they were, the priests are mentioned here by way of comparison. When God spoke of the priests approaching him, he was not suggesting that they would be allowed to go up on Mount Sinai, but was referring instead to their routine priestly duties. Even though they were sometimes allowed to come into God's presence to perform certain religious rituals, they had to approach him in the right way. Unless they were properly consecrated, they would be destroyed. And if that was true for the priests, it was all the more true for ordinary Israelites. John Mackay writes, "The thought here is not that after due preparation the priests may come up the mountain, but that since it is only after rendering themselves cultically pure that the priests are able to offer sacrifice at the altar, how much greater is the barrier in the way of coming before the theophanic presence of God."[9] It was imperative for the Israelites to approach God in the right way, which in this case meant not touching his holy mountain at all.

It hardly seems necessary for God to have repeated this warning. One warning should have been enough. Once God had declared the mountain holy, who would have dared to risk sudden death by crossing the boundary to touch it? This was so obvious that Moses started to get impatient and told God, in effect, "We got the message the first time; you don't need to tell us again." "And Moses said to the LORD, 'The people cannot come up to Mount Sinai, for you yourself warned us, saying, "Set limits around the mountain and consecrate it"'" (9:23).

God responded by reiterating his warning, now for the third time. He said, "Do not let the priests and the people break through to come up to the LORD, lest he break out against them" (19:24b). Why did God keep repeating this warning? Weren't his earlier precautions adequate?

There are several plausible explanations for all this repetition. One is that an additional warning was needed every time Moses went up and down the mountain. Each time the people watched him cross the boundary, they might have been tempted to conclude that it was safe for them to go up the mountain as well. But it was not safe. It was only safe for Moses because he was the mediator, and the rest of the Israelites still needed to keep their distance.

Remember too that the Israelites generally were not very good at following directions. When Moses hinted that further warnings were unnecessary, he was really underestimating Israel's depravity. But God knew better. He knew that when it came to obeying the first time, or even the second time, his people often failed. Knowing this, and knowing the value of repetition, he gave them a triple warning. God repeated himself to make sure there wouldn't be any misunderstanding.

Whatever the reasons for it, Israel's warning to keep a distance is a sober reminder that God is dangerous. He is majestic and transcendent. He burns with a bright and blazing holiness. Therefore, as the Scripture says, "It is a fearful thing to fall into the hands of the living God" (Hebrews 10:31). The Israelites must have sensed this as they stood at the foot of Mount Sinai. They saw the smoke on the mountain, they heard the voice of God, and they did not dare to come any closer!

Yet God did provide a way for his people to approach. They could not go up the mountain themselves, but Moses could go up to meet with God for them. He was their mediator, the one who talked with God on their behalf. This was something the Israelites both needed and wanted. In chapter 20 we read, "Now when all the people saw the thunder and the flashes of lightning and the sound of the trumpet and the mountain smoking, the people were afraid and trembled, and they stood far off and said to Moses, 'You speak to us, and we will listen;

but do not let God speak to us, lest we die.' . . . The people stood far off, while Moses drew near to the thick darkness where God was" (20:18, 19, 21). Moses served as Israel's mediator, their go-between, their representative before God. When Moses later described his mediatorial work, he said, "I stood between the LORD and you at that time, to declare to you the word of the LORD. For you were afraid because of the fire, and you did not go up into the mountain" (Deuteronomy 5:5).

Moses also had someone to help him in this work because God said to him, "Go down, and come up bringing Aaron with you. . . . So Moses went down to the people and told them" (19:24a, 25). Aaron had already been serving as Moses' spokesman. Now God was preparing him for his ministry as high priest. With Moses, he was permitted to go up the holy mountain and meet with God. Later Aaron would do the same thing in the tabernacle. When the tabernacle was built, the people kept their distance, standing outside the boundaries of God's holy dwelling. But one man—the high priest—was permitted to enter the Holy of Holies and meet with God. Thus the tabernacle had the same spiritual structure, so to speak, as Mount Sinai: The people stood at a distance, while their mediator met with God.[10] In this way God's people learned what is required for coming into God's presence. We must be careful how we approach him. Only the mediator whom God has chosen can lead us to the most holy place.

## Have No Fear

God gave his people an extraordinary privilege when he met with them at Mount Sinai. Their privilege was unique. Moses once said, "For ask now . . . whether such a great thing as this has ever happened or was ever heard of. Did any people ever hear the voice of a god speaking out of the midst of the fire, as you have heard, and still live?" (Deuteronomy 4:32b, 33). The answer, of course, was no. No one else had ever experienced what Israel witnessed at Mount Sinai, where they learned how awesomely dangerous it is to approach the God who is there and is not silent.

As Christians we enjoy a far greater privilege. This privilege is explained in Hebrews 12, which draws a contrast between Mount Sinai and Mount Zion, between the terrors of the Law and the grace of the gospel. First the Scripture assures us that we no longer stand at the foot of Mount Sinai:

> For you have not come to what may be touched, a blazing fire and darkness and gloom and a tempest and the sound of a trumpet and a voice whose words made the hearers beg that no further messages be spoken to them. For they could not endure the order that was given, "If even a beast touches the mountain, it shall be stoned." Indeed, so terrifying was the sight that Moses said, "I tremble with fear." (Hebrews 12:18–21)

That is what Israel experienced, but it is *not* what we experience in the church. We have come to a different mountain, which Hebrews proceeds to describe:

> But you have come to Mount Zion and to the city of the living God, the heavenly Jerusalem, and to innumerable angels in festal gathering, and to the assembly of the firstborn who are enrolled in heaven, and to God, the judge of all, and to the spirits of the righteous made perfect, and to Jesus, the mediator of a new covenant, and to the sprinkled blood that speaks a better word than the blood of Abel. (Hebrews 12:22–24)

The contrast is absolute. It is the contrast between the Law and the gospel, between Mount Sinai and Mount Zion. One mountain was dark and stormy; the other is a city of bright and shining joy. One mountain was a place of fear and danger; the other is a place of peace and safety. On one mountain the angels blazed with fire and blasted with noise; on the other they form a welcoming party for a celebration. One mountain was designed to keep people away; the other was designed to draw them close.

What makes the difference? The difference does not lie in God himself. He is present on both mountains, and even on Mount Zion he sits in judgment: "You have come . . . to God," Hebrews says, "the judge of all" (Hebrews 12:22, 23). The difference is that when we come to Mount Zion we are on the right side of God's justice.[11] This is all because of Jesus Christ and the blood that he shed on the cross. In this passage the person and work of Jesus Christ stand in the climactic position. Hebrews lists all the things we come to at Mount Zion: the heavenly Jerusalem, the myriads of angels, the church of God. But the last thing is the most important: We come "to Jesus, the mediator of a new covenant, and to the sprinkled blood" (Hebrews 12:24).

In order to approach a holy and awesome God properly (and safely!), we need a mediator. Jesus is that mediator. He is the mediator who offered himself as the once-and-for-all sacrifice for our sins (Hebrews 7:27; 9:26; 10:10). By his crucifixion and resurrection he has delivered us from all the terrors of God's law and has granted us entrance to the glories of Heaven. Philip Hughes writes, "Such were the terrors of Sinai, the mount of God's law, where because of their sinfulness the people were unable to draw near to God's presence. How different are the circumstances of Zion, the mount of God's grace, where, thanks to the perfect law-keeping and the all-sufficient sacrifice of himself offered by the incarnate Son in our stead, we are invited to draw near with boldness into the heavenly holy of holies."[12]

We must decide where we would rather meet with God—Mount Sinai or Mount Zion. If we meet God on Mount Zion, then on the basis of what Jesus has done, we dare to approach him with as much confidence as reverence (see Hebrews 10:19–22). Peter Enns writes:

> This is not to say that we enter into his intimate presence casually, without reverence. But it does mean that, since the death and resurrection of Christ, we enter into that presence with a degree of joy, thanksgiving, and confidence, which were wholly lacking in Exodus 19, for we know that we are without sin before God and have been reconciled to God through Christ. As Moses consecrated the people in Exodus 19 to prepare their approach to God, we are consecrated by virtue of our relationship to the risen Christ.[13]

Now we are free to worship, free to love, and free to ask for whatever we need. In the words of John Newton's triumphant hymn:

> Let us love and sing and wonder,
> Let us praise the Savior's name!
> He has hushed the law's loud thunder,
> He has quenched Mount Sinai's flame:
> He has washed us in his blood.
> He has brought us nigh to God. . . .
>
> Let us wonder; grace and justice
> Join and point to mercy's store;
> When through grace in Christ our trust is,
> Justice smiles and asks no more:
> He who washed us with His blood
> Has secured our way to God.[14]

The only way to gain this kind of access to God is through faith in Jesus Christ. He is the Mediator, the one who brings us close to God. There is no other way to have a relationship with God except through Jesus. Hebrews 12 thus closes with a warning not to reject the salvation that God offers in Jesus Christ: "See that you do not refuse him who is speaking." Why not? Because God is coming again, in all his terrible, awesome majesty, to judge us for our sins: "For if they [the Israelites] did not escape when they refused him who warned them on earth [that is, at Mount Sinai], much less will we escape if we reject him who warns from heaven. At that time his voice shook the earth, but now he has promised, 'Yet once more I will shake not only the earth but also the heavens'" (Hebrews 12:25, 26).

These verses speak of the final judgment, warning us that if we reject Jesus now, we will not escape then but will be lost forever. God is there. He is not silent. And he is saying, "You must come to me through Jesus to be saved."

# 46

# Written in Stone

## EXODUS 20:1, 2a

IN THEIR BOOK *The Day America Told the Truth*, James Patterson and Peter Kim lay down the law for postmodern times. They observe that today there is "absolutely no moral consensus at all. . . . Everyone is making up their own personal moral codes—their own Ten Commandments." Patterson and Kim proceed to list what they call the "ten real commandments," the rules that according to their surveys people actually live by. These rules include the following:

- I don't see the point in observing the Sabbath;
- I will steal from those who won't really miss it;
- I will lie when it suits me, so long as it doesn't cause any real damage;
- I will cheat on my spouse—after all, given the chance, he or she will do the same;
- I will procrastinate at work and do absolutely nothing about one full day in every five.[1]

These new commandments are based on moral relativism, the belief that we are free to make up our own rules, based on our own personal preferences. The law is not something that comes from God, but something we come up with on our own. And our laws usually conflict with God's laws. It is not surprising that what Patterson and Kim call the "ten real commandments" generally violate the laws that God gave to Moses: Remember the Sabbath; six days shalt thou labor and do all thy work; thou shalt not commit adultery; thou shalt not steal; thou shalt not bear false witness; and so forth. We have become a law unto ourselves.

One would hope to find that the situation is somewhat better in the church. Surely God's own people honor the permanent, objective standard of God's law! Yet the church is full of worshipers who do not even know the Ten Commandments, let alone know how to keep them. This problem was documented in a recent report from The Princeton Religion Research Center. The headline read, "Religion Is Gaining Ground, but Morality Is Losing Ground," and the report showed how recent increases in church attendance and Bible reading have been offset by a simultaneous decline in morality.[2]

How is this possible? How can people be more interested in God and at the same time less willing to do what he says? The only explanation is that people do not know the God of the Bible, because if they did, they would recognize the absolute authority of his law. Respect for God always demands respect for his law. And whenever people have a low regard for God's law, as they do in our culture, it is ultimately because they have a low regard for God.

## The Lord Your God

If the Law comes from God, then the best place to begin understanding the Law is with God himself. This is precisely where the book of Exodus begins its presentation of the Ten Commandments, also known as the Decalogue, meaning "ten words": "And God spoke all these words" (20:1).

To get a sense of who God is, it helps to remember the setting. God was speaking to the Israelites as they were gathered at the foot of Mount Sinai. Exodus 19 described how God descended on the mountain in great power and glory, with thunder and lightning, fire and smoke. The Israelites were forbidden to come any closer, upon the pain of death. They had come into the presence of the awesome and almighty God, who lives in unapproachable holiness. Obviously, whatever such a God has to say demands our fullest and most careful attention. What we received from Mount Sinai was not simply the Law of Moses but the Law of *God*, spoken in the revelation of his glory. As Isaiah later wrote, "The LORD was pleased, for his righteousness' sake, to magnify his law and make it glorious" (Isaiah 42:21).

Although God revealed his glory in the fire and smoke on the mountain, he made a fuller disclosure of his deity when he began to speak. He said, "I am the LORD your God, who brought you out of the land of Egypt, out of the house of slavery" (20:2). This verse is sometimes called the preface or prologue to the Ten Commandments. In it God defends his authority as the lawgiver. What gives God the right to tell people what to do? In the words of the *Westminster Shorter Catechism*, "The preface to the ten commandments teaches us, That because God is the Lord, and our God, and Redeemer, therefore we are bound to keep all his commandments" (A. 44).

God is the Lord. Here he uses his special covenant name, *Yahweh*. He is the Great I Am, the sovereign and almighty Lord. He is the supreme, self-existent, eternal, and unchangeable God who bound himself to Abraham, Isaac, and Jacob with the unbreakable promise of his covenant. Furthermore, he is our very own God. "I am the LORD *your* God," he says. Somewhat surprisingly, he uses the second person singular, thus indicating that he has a personal relationship with each and every one of his people.[3] This personal relationship is also a saving relationship, for as God goes on to say, "I am the LORD your God, who brought you out of the land of Egypt, out of the house of slavery" (20:2). This was a summary of everything that had happened so far in Exodus. God was reminding the Israelites that he was not only their Lord and their God but also their Redeemer. And it was on this basis that he laid down his law for their lives. It was Israel's unique privilege to receive the Law straight from God.

What God said to Israel is essentially the same thing he says to every believer in Christ: "I am the Lord your God, who brought you out of the Egypt of your sin, out of your slavery to Satan." Through the saving work of Jesus Christ, crucified and risen, God is our sovereign Lord and very own Savior, and thus he has the right to claim legal authority over us. The Law comes from God, who is our Savior and our Lord.

## God and His Law

If the Law comes from God, then it must reflect his divine character. This is true of rules and regulations in general: They reveal something about the rule-maker. To give just one example, consider the extensive federal regulations that govern handicapped access to public buildings. What do these laws tell us about the society that made them? They tell us that Americans want to include the disabled in the ordinary events of public life.

The law always reveals the character of the lawgiver. This was especially true at Mount Sinai, where every one of the Ten Commandments was stamped with the being and attributes of Almighty God. So what does each law tell us about the God who gave it?

The *first* commandment is, "You shall have no other gods before me" (20:3). Obviously the God who gave this command is jealous; he will not share his glory with any other god. And rightly so, because he is the one and only true God. All the others are impostors. The first commandment announces the unique sovereignty of the God who alone is able to say, "I am the LORD, and there is no other" (Isaiah 45:18b). It also indicates his omnipresence because it tells us not to have any other gods "before him," meaning "in his presence" (this point is developed in chapter 49 of this book).

The *second* commandment is, "You shall not make for yourself a carved image, or any likeness of anything that is in heaven above, or that is in the earth beneath, or that is in the water under the earth" (20:4). This commandment is about worshipping the right God in the right way. God refuses to be worshiped by means of images. This shows that he is spirit, that he does not have a physical form. The mention of the heavens and the earth also shows that he is the Creator. One problem with idols is that they confuse the Creator with his creation. The commandment goes on to speak of God's mercy and justice: "You shall not bow down to them or serve them, for I the Lord your God am a jealous God, visiting the iniquity of the fathers on the children to the third and the fourth generation of those who hate me, but showing steadfast love to thousands of those who love me and keep my commandments" (20:5, 6). The God who gave the Law is a God who makes absolute moral distinctions. He punishes sinners while at the same time showing his love to generation after generation of the people he has chosen to save.

The *third* commandment is about honoring God's name: "You shall not take the name of the Lord your God in vain, for the Lord will not hold him guiltless who takes his name in vain" (20:7). The threat attached to this commandment shows that God expects to be obeyed. Those who break his law will be charged with guilt. The commandment itself shows that God is honorable, and that therefore he deserves to be treated with respect. Even his name is holy.

The *fourth* commandment is, "Remember the Sabbath day, to keep it holy. Six days you shall labor, and do all your work, but the seventh day is a Sabbath to the Lord your God" (20:8–10a). This commandment shows that God is sovereign over all the events of daily life. He is Lord every day of the week. It also makes an explicit connection between what is commanded and the one who commands it, between God and his law: "For in six days the Lord made heaven and earth, the sea, and all that is in them, and rested on the seventh day. Therefore the Lord blessed the Sabbath day and made it holy" (20:11). We are commanded to work and rest because we serve a working, resting God.

The first four commandments govern our relationship to God; the last six concern our relationships with one another. But even these commandments rest on various divine attributes. The *fifth* commandment is about respecting authority: "Honor your father and your mother, that your days may be long in the land that the Lord your God is giving you" (20:12). What stands behind this commandment is God's own authority as our Father. This is also the first command with a promise—the promise of long life in a good land, which shows how generous God is to provide for his people.

The *sixth* commandment is, "You shall not murder" (20:13). This reminds us that God is the Lord and the giver of life. He forbids the taking of innocent life because he is a life-giving God. Furthermore, this commandment preserves his sovereignty over life's end. He is Lord over death as well as over life.

The *seventh* commandment is the one that everyone knows: "You shall not commit adultery" (20:14). What does this tell us about God? It tells us that he is a God of purity and faithfulness, a God who expects covenants to be kept. It also tells us that he is a God of joy because this command preserves sex for the fellowship of marriage.

The *eighth* commandment is, "You shall not steal" (20:15). The God who gave this commandment is our Creator and Provider. To keep it is to recognize that ultimately everything belongs to him, and that therefore we do not have the right to take what he has given to someone else.

The *ninth* commandment is to tell the truth: "You shall not bear false witness against your neighbor" (20:16). This commandment comes from the God of truth, who is true in all he is, says, and does. As the Scripture says, "The Glory of Israel will not lie" (1 Samuel 15:29a).

The *tenth* commandment is about contentment: "You shall not covet . . ." (20:17a). Covetousness comes from a desire to possess what God has not given us. Like the eighth commandment, keeping this commandment requires faith in God's providence. God commands us not to covet because he can be trusted to give us everything we truly need. He is our provider.

One further divine attribute is revealed by the Ten Commandments as a whole, and this attribute is love. When Jesus summarized God's law he said, "You shall love the Lord your God with all your heart and with all your soul and with all your mind. This is the great and first commandment. And a second is like it: You shall love your neighbor as yourself" (Matthew 22:37–39; cf. Deuteronomy 6:5; Leviticus 19:18; Romans 13:9). In other words, the Ten Commandments can be reduced to two commandments: Love God and love your neighbor. So they are all about love. We love God by worshiping him and using his name properly. We love our parents by honoring them. We love our spouses by being faithful to them. We love our neighbors by protecting their lives, respecting their property, and telling them the truth. The God who gave these commandments is a God of love, who wants us to love him and to share his love with others. As Jesus said, "Whoever has my commandments and keeps them, he it is who loves me" (John 14:21a; cf. 1 John 5:3a). If this is true, then we cannot separate God's law from God's love.

To summarize, the Ten Commandments display the character of God. They reveal his sovereignty, jealousy, justice, holiness, honor, faithfulness, providence, truthfulness, and love.

When we see how God has poured himself into his law, it becomes obvious that he could not have given us any other commandments than the ones he gave. The Ten Commandments express God's will for our lives because they are based on his character. This helps answer an ancient dilemma, one that Plato posed in one of his famous dialogues: Does God command the law because the law is good, or is the law good because God commands it?[4] The answer is, both! The Law, with all its goodness, springs from the goodness of God's character. The Law is good because God is good, and his goodness penetrates every aspect of his law.

## It Will Never Pass Away

The fact that God's law expresses God's character has many implications. One is that when we break God's law we are making a direct assault on God himself. To worship another god is to deny God's sovereignty; to misuse his name is to deny his honor; to steal is to deny his providence; to lie is to deny his truthfulness; and so forth. Every violation of the Law is an offense against God's holy character.

Another implication of the relationship between our Lord and his law is that the Law is perpetually binding, that it remains in force for all persons in all places at all times. Sovereignty, justice, faithfulness, truthfulness, love—these are God's eternal attributes. He would have to un-God himself to set them aside. We should expect, therefore, that the Law that expresses his eternal attributes has eternal validity.

This perhaps explains why God set the Ten Commandments in stone, writing them out with his own finger (31:18; 32:16). A. W. Pink comments:

> Their uniqueness appears first in that this revelation of God at Sinai—which was to serve for all coming ages as the grand expression of His holiness and the summation of man's duty—was attended with such awe-inspiring phenomena that the very manner of their publication plainly showed that God Himself assigned to the Decalogue peculiar importance. The Ten Commandments were uttered by God in an audible voice, with the fearful adjuncts of clouds and darkness, thunders and lightnings and the sound of a trumpet, and they were the only parts of Divine Revelation so spoken—none of the ceremonial or civil precepts were thus distinguished. Those Ten Words, and they alone, were written by the finger of God upon tables of stone, and they alone were deposited in the holy ark for safe keeping. Thus, in the unique honor conferred upon the Decalogue itself we may perceive its paramount importance in the Divine government.[5]

The Ten Commandments were written in stone because they would remain in effect for as long as time endured. When would it ever be permissible to worship another god, to misuse God's name, to lie, murder, or steal? Never, because these things are contrary to God's very nature.

One way to prove that God's law is eternal is to show that it was in effect even before God wrote it down. Exodus 20 is sometimes described as "the giving of the law." However, these laws had already been given! The commandments God gave to Moses at Mount Sinai were not new; in fact, they were as old as the human race. We know this from the stories of the Bible, in which God often rebuked and punished people for breaking these very laws.

There are clear examples of commandment-breaking earlier in Exodus. The ten plagues God visited on Pharaoh were a direct punishment for Egypt's idolatry, which violated the first and second commandments (Numbers 33:4). Moses' own personal exodus was occasioned by his violation of the sixth commandment (2:11–15). At the burning bush God taught Moses to honor his name (3:1–15), very much in keeping with the third commandment. God revealed the Sabbath principle of the fourth commandment by giving manna six days out of seven, and those who failed to follow the appropriate instructions suffered for their disobedience (Exodus 16). So at various points the exodus presupposed the existence of God's law, even before the Israelites reached Mount Sinai.

We find the same principle at work in the book of Genesis, which contains many stories about people breaking God's law. Noah's son Ham was cursed for dishonoring his father (Genesis 9:18–27). Cain was condemned as a murderer (Genesis 4:10–12), the Sodomites as adulterers (Genesis 19:24, 25), Rachel as a thief (Genesis 31:19–32), Abraham as a liar (Genesis 20), and Lot's wife as a covetous woman (Genesis 19). God had always dealt with people on the basis of his law. Certain commandments had been revealed to them, and if they were written nowhere else, they were written on the tablets of their hearts (see Romans 2:14, 15).

God's moral law went all the way back to the garden of Eden, where (in addition to various other commands concerning sexuality, rest, and work) God told Adam and Eve not to eat from the tree of the knowledge of good and evil. Theologians argue about whether or not our first parents also knew any of the Ten Commandments. The Bible simply doesn't say. But whether or not God revealed any of its specific commands, Adam and Eve were ruled by its basic principles: love for God and love for one another. They were obligated to honor one another, to preserve life, and to tell the truth—the kind of conduct later mandated on Mount Sinai. And in their first sin, Adam and Eve managed to violate nearly all ten of God's basic rules. Taking the forbidden fruit was a theft, stimulated by a covetous desire, based on a lie about God's character. Eating it was a way of having another god. It was also tantamount to murder because it led to the death of the entire human race. From the beginning our first parents were bound by the basic principles of what theologians call the "law of creation" or "the law of nature."

So to summarize, God's law was in effect in various ways long before the Israelites ever reached Mount Sinai. What, then, were the Ten Commandments? Think of them as a fresh copy. They were a republication, in summary form, of God's will for humanity. As Peter Enns comments, "The 'giving' of the law at Sinai is not the first time Israel hears of God's laws, but is the codification and explicit promulgation of those laws."[6] This makes perfect sense when we remember that the Ten Commandments express the character of God, who does not change.

## The Law of Christ

Is the Law still binding today? This is a vital question. Do the Ten Commandments have any abiding relevance for Christians and the culture in which we live? Once we understand the relationship between our Lord and his law, this question is easy to answer: Yes, God's law is still binding today! His standard has not changed, any more than his character has changed. As ABC's Ted Koppel said in his now famous commencement address at Duke University, "What

Moses brought down from Mount Sinai were not the Ten Suggestions . . . they are commandments. *Are*, not were."[7]

Some people deny that God's law is still in effect today. This denial is obviously made by many non-Christians, who act as a law unto themselves. But even many people in the church pay little attention to God's law. This is partly because of the lawlessness of our surrounding culture, but it also comes from the way some Christians read the Bible. After all, the New Testament makes a number of statements that seem to set aside the Old Testament law. For example, according to John, "The law was given through Moses; grace and truth came through Jesus Christ" (John 1:17). Likewise, the Apostle Paul wrote, "You are not under law but under grace" (Romans 6:14), and "now that faith has come, we are no longer under a guardian" (Galatians 3:25; cf. Galatians 5:18). These and similar statements would seem to suggest that God's law has been superseded. On the other hand, the New Testament also seems to claim that the Law remains in effect. It claims that we are "under the law of Christ" (1 Corinthians 9:21), for example, or even that "it is easier for heaven and earth to pass away than for one dot of the Law to become void" (Luke 16:17).

This is not the place to give a full exposition of everything the Bible says about God's law. But it is vitally important to understand that one reason the New Testament talks about the Law in several different ways is because there are several different kinds of law. Here we should at least make a distinction between three types of law: the moral, the civil, and the ceremonial. These were all given in the Old Testament, sometimes interspersed. But in order to make sense of the Law—and ultimately of the gospel—they must be carefully distinguished as we see them through the clear lens of the person and work of Jesus Christ. "It is of the utmost importance," writes Ernest Reisinger, "to discern the differences between the ceremonial law, which pertained to the worship of Israel and prefigured Christ; the civil or judicial laws, which detailed the duties to Israel as a nation (having their roots in the moral law, particularly in the second table); and the moral law, by which the Creator governs the moral conduct of *all* creatures for *all* times."[8]

The *moral law* is summarized in the Ten Commandments. It is the righteous and eternal standard for our relationship with God and with others. The *civil law* consisted of the laws that governed Israel as a nation under God. These included guidelines for waging war, restrictions on land use, regulations for debt, and penalties for specific violations of Israel's legal code. The *ceremonial law* consisted of regulations for celebrating various religious festivals (e.g., 23:14–19) and for worshiping God in his sanctuary (e.g., Exodus 25—30). It included laws for clean and unclean foods, instructions for ritual purity, guidelines for the conduct of priests, and especially instructions for offering sacrifices—the whole sacrificial system (see Leviticus). God gave detailed regulations that covered specifics like who was supposed to cut which animal's throat and how and what was to be done with the blood.

The ceremonial law is no longer in effect; it has been abrogated. This is because all its regulations pointed forward to Jesus Christ. Concerning the Old Testament ceremonies, the Scripture says, "These are a shadow of the things to come, but the substance belongs to Christ" (Colossians 2:17; cf. Hebrews 10:1). This is most obviously true of the sacrifices. Now that Christ has offered himself as the once-and-for-all atonement for sin, no further sacrifice is needed. To continue to follow the old ceremonies would be to deny the sufficiency of his work on the cross. One of the errors of the theological perspective known as *dispensationalism* is to imagine that the old ceremonies and sacrifices will be reinstated in Israel.[9] But the sacrificial system has been superseded by Christ, and the only two ceremonies still in effect—baptism and the Lord's Supper—both look back to his cross.

The civil law has also expired, but for a slightly different reason: The church is not a state. We do have a king (namely, Christ), but his kingdom is spiritual. Therefore, although the civil laws of the Old Testament contain principles that are useful for governing nations today, God's people are no longer bound by their specific regulations. The basic error of the theological perspective known as *theonomy* (or "Christian reconstruction") is to imagine that civil laws from the time of Moses should still be enforced in America today. This is what some people mean when they talk about restoring a "Christian America." But as Calvin recognized, such a view is "perilous and seditious" because like the ceremonial law, the civic law has been superseded by Christ.[10] Today the people of God are governed instead by church discipline, which is based on the moral law, and which has spiritual rather than civil consequences.

The distinction between these three kinds of law—the moral, the civil, and the ceremonial—helps us understand what the New Testament teaches about God's law. The ceremonial law and the civil law were types and figures pointing forward to the cross and kingdom of Christ. Now that he has come, they have been set aside, which is why the New Testament sometimes seems so dismissive of the Law. As we have seen, what are now in effect are the sacraments and discipline of the church, which echo the ceremonial and the civil law respectively. The New Testament also completely rejects the idea that we can be justified by keeping the Law. It is in this sense especially that we are no longer "under law" (Romans 6:14; Galatians 5:18). Our salvation does not depend on our ability to keep the Law. As we shall learn in the next chapter, we are unable to keep it, and therefore we cannot be declared righteous by it (Romans 3:20). But since our natural inclination is to think that we *can* be saved by our own obedience, the Bible condemns any and every attempt to use the keeping of God's law as a way of justifying ourselves.

What the New Testament never does, however, is to declare an end to God's moral law as the standard for our lives. It is still, in the words of the *Westminster*

*Confession of Faith*, "a perfect rule of righteousness" (19.1), or as Calvin termed it, the "true and eternal rule of righteousness."[11] Similarly, Ernest Reisinger describes the moral law as "the eternal standard of right moral conduct—a fixed, objective standard of righteousness."[12] This makes sense when we remember the close relationship between the moral law and the character of the Lord who gave it. The Law is as eternal as God is.

Furthermore, the character of God is also the character of his Son Jesus Christ. The Bible teaches that Jesus "is the radiance of the glory of God and the exact imprint of his nature" (Hebrews 1:3a). Jesus is one and the same as the God who revealed his law to Moses; the Law expresses the character of the Son as well as of the Father. Therefore, to try and separate the God who gave the Law from the God who has shown his grace in the gospel would practically be to divide the Trinity. The Son is every bit as sovereign, jealous, life-giving, faithful, truthful, and loving as the Father revealed himself to be in the Ten Commandments.

Given the close relationship between God and his law, and between the Father and the Son, it is not surprising that Jesus warned us: "Do not think that I have come to abolish the Law or the Prophets; I have not come to abolish them but to fulfill them. For truly, I say to you, until heaven and earth pass away, not an iota, not a dot, will pass from the Law until all is accomplished" (Matthew 5:17, 18). Clearly Jesus was speaking about the moral law, at least in part, because he went on to say, "Whoever relaxes one of the least of these commandments and teaches others to do the same will be called least in the kingdom of heaven, but whoever does them and teaches them will be called great in the kingdom of heaven" (Matthew 5:19). The Law of Moses is not simply the Law of God; it is also the law of Christ.

## The Right Way to Live

Our focus throughout our study of Exodus 20 will be on God's moral law. One way to prove that this law is still binding is to show how, in one way or another, all ten of the original commandments are repeated in the New Testament, either by Jesus himself or in the teaching of his apostles.

When the New Testament lists the sins that lead to condemnation or the acts of obedience that are pleasing to God, it sometimes follows the outline of the Ten Commandments (e.g., Matthew 15:19; 19:17–19; Romans 7:8–10; 1 Corinthians 6:9, 10; 1 Timothy 1:9–11; Revelation 21:8). But the commandments are also treated individually. The *first* commandment tells us to have no other gods. Jesus made essentially the same claim about himself: "I am the way, and the truth, and the life. No one comes to the Father except through me" (John 14:6; cf. Acts 4:12). The *second* commandment forbids idolatry. John said, "Little children, keep yourselves from idols" (1 John 5:21). The *third* commandment tells us to honor God's name, which is exactly the way Jesus taught us to pray: "Hallowed be your name" (Matthew 6:9). The *fourth* commandment is about working and resting. As believers in Jesus Christ we are told that whatever we do, we should work at it with all our hearts (Colossians 3:23). We are also told that Jesus is Lord of the Sabbath (Matthew 12:8) and that there remains "a Sabbath rest for the people of God" (Hebrews 4:9).

The first four commands are about loving God, but what about loving our neighbor? In the *fifth* commandment we are bound to honor our parents. This command is repeated by the Apostle Paul: "Children, obey your parents in the Lord, for this is right. 'Honor your father and mother'" (Ephesians 6:1, 2a). Next, without in any way changing the *sixth* commandment, Jesus clarified its true spiritual purpose when he said, "You have heard that it was said to those of old, 'You shall not murder' . . . But I say to you that everyone who is angry with his brother will be liable to judgment" (Matthew 5:21, 22a). Jesus did the same thing with the *seventh* commandment: "But I say to you that everyone who looks at a woman with lustful intent has already committed adultery with her in his heart" (Matthew 5:28). As for the *eighth* commandment, the New Testament says, "Let the thief no longer steal, but rather let him labor" (Ephesians 4:28a). And with regard to the *ninth* commandment, the Scripture says, "Do not lie to one another" (Colossians 3:9a). Finally, the *tenth* commandment forbids coveting, which the apostle James condemns by saying, "You ask and do not receive, because you ask wrongly, to spend it on your passions" (James 4:3).

Is the Law still binding today? Of course it is! As the Bible demonstrates all the way through, the Ten Commandments show us the right way to live. They are based on the righteousness of God, which explains why even the New Testament has so many positive things to say about God's law. "Do we then overthrow the law . . . ?" asks the Apostle Paul. "By no means! On the contrary, we uphold the law" (Romans 3:31). Later he goes on to describe the commandments as "holy and righteous and good" (Romans 7:12) and to insist that he is "not . . . outside the law of God" but remains "under the law of Christ" (1 Corinthians 9:21).

So much for the Law. But what about the gospel? We will attempt to give a fuller answer to this question in the coming chapters. But the answer basically goes like this: It is our breaking of the Law that helps us see our need for the gospel. The more clearly we see what God's law requires, the more obvious it becomes that we cannot keep its commands, which is exactly why we need the gospel. We cannot be saved by our own keeping of the Law because we do not keep it. But Jesus did! He kept the whole Law on our behalf. Perfectly. Moreover, in his death on the cross he suffered the penalty we deserve for our failure to keep God's law. Now everyone who believes in Jesus Christ will be saved by *his* keeping of the Law and by *his* suffering of its curse.

As believers in Jesus Christ, do we still need to keep God's law? Yes. The moral law expresses God's perfect and righteous will for our lives. So Jesus commands us to keep it, not as a way of getting right with God, but as a way of pleasing the God who has made us right with him.

# 47

# A Multiuse Item

## EXODUS 20:2b

AMERICAN CONSUMERS have a fascination with multiuse items. Consider the extraordinary success of the Swiss army knife. In addition to an ordinary knife-blade, this handy gadget comes with a toothpick, tweezers, a pair of scissors, a couple of screwdrivers, a file, a saw blade, and a corkscrew. The tool is a knife, but it is also much more: an indispensable tool to perform seemingly any task.

Like an all-in-one tool, the Law of God is a multiuse item. This important truth helps explain why the Bible talks about the Law in so many different ways. God has more than one purpose for his law, and the important thing is to know how to use it. As the Apostle Paul observed, "Now we know that the law is good, if one uses it lawfully" (1 Timothy 1:8). In this chapter we consider three ways to use God's law: first, the Law teaches God's redeemed people how to live for God's glory; second, the Law restrains sin in society; and third, the Law shows sinners their need of a Savior.

### Teaching Us How to Live

It may be surprising to discover that Exodus 20 begins not with the Law but with the gospel: "And God spoke all these words, saying, 'I am the Lord your God, who brought you out of the land of Egypt, out of the house of slavery'" (20:1, 2). As we have seen, these verses teach that the Law comes from God—the great God of the covenant who revealed his glory on the mountain. And this great God is a God who saves!

At the beginning of chapter 20 God summarizes the whole epic adventure of the exodus in two short phrases: "who brought you out of the land of Egypt" and "out of the house of slavery." God was reminding his people of the good news of their salvation. For centuries they had languished in the prison house of Pharaoh. But by sending ten terrible plagues, by saving them through the blood of a lamb, by holding back the sea, and by providing bread in the wilderness, God delivered his people. Their liberation was *the* great saving event of the Old Testament.

Almost immediately after he set his people free, God gave them his law. The order is significant: first the gospel, then the Law. As the Dutch theologian Joachim Duma writes in his masterful exposition of Exodus 20, "The commandments follow the gospel of undeserved deliverance."[1]

Many Christians think that the Law is somehow opposed to the gospel. They assume that in the Old Testament salvation came by law, whereas in the New Testament salvation comes by grace. But the truth is that salvation has always come by grace, and that the Law and the gospel work together for salvation in *both* testaments. The grace of the gospel has never been opposed to the proper use of the Law.

We see the Law and the gospel working together in Exodus, which contains both the Old Testament's clearest example of salvation by grace and its fullest presentation of God's law. Significantly, God did not give Israel the Ten Commandments until chapter 20. Chapters 1—19 come first, and they tell the story of salvation by grace—God fulfilling his covenant promise by bringing Israel out of Egypt. Then comes chapter 20, in which God gives his people a law by which to live.

This law was for those who had already been redeemed. Here we need to remember the overarching theme of Exodus: God's people are saved for God's glory. The problem with Pharaoh and the Egyptians was not simply that it was wrong for them to hold slaves, but that they were preventing the Israelites from serving their God. With the exodus came a change of masters. God's people were released from their bondage to Pharaoh in order to serve the true and living God—not as captured slaves but as liberated sons and daughters. The law that God gave them at the time of their emancipation was not a new form of bondage, therefore, but a freedom charter. It was just because God's people had been saved by grace that they were now free to live by the law of his covenant community. They had been redeemed; *therefore*, they were not to have any other gods, make any idols, and so on. God did not set his people free so they could do whatever they wanted, but so they could live for him. This was the whole point of the exodus. And this is one of the Law's most important uses: to teach people who have been redeemed how to live for the glory of their God.

God's people always need to remember this connection between God's grace and God's law. In the book of Deuteronomy God gave Israel's parents these instructions:

> When your son asks you in time to come, "What is the meaning of the testimonies and the statutes and the rules that the LORD our God has commanded you?" then you shall say to your son, "We were Pharaoh's slaves

> in Egypt. And the LORD brought us out of Egypt with a mighty hand. And the LORD showed signs and wonders, great and grievous, against Egypt and against Pharaoh and all his household, before our eyes. And he brought us out from there, that he might bring us in and give us the land that he swore to give to our fathers. And the LORD commanded us to do all these statutes, to fear the LORD our God, for our good always, that he might preserve us alive, as we are this day." (Deuteronomy 6:20–24)

When the children of Israel asked why they had to keep God's law, their parents were supposed to tell them a story. The only way they could understand the meaning of the Law was by knowing its context, which was the experience of the exodus—the story of their salvation. First the gospel, then the Law.

The relationship between law and gospel in the exodus sets the pattern for (or "typifies") one purpose of the Law in the Christian life: The Law teaches God's redeemed people how to live. We too have a story to tell—the story of our redemption in Jesus Christ. The story begins with our slavery to sin. We were in such spiritual bondage that there was no way for us to escape. But God set us free from sin and from Satan through the saving work of Jesus Christ. His death and resurrection were our great exodus, our emancipation.

Now that we have received God's grace in the gospel, what comes next? Are we free to live as we please? Can we be saved and still lead a sinful life? Of course not! What we are free to do is to live in a way that is pleasing to God. Martin Luther once explained this principle to one of his students. He had been talking about God's free grace for sinners, how our salvation does not rest upon our own good works but upon the saving work of Jesus Christ. "If what you're saying is true," the student objected," then we may live as we want!" Luther replied, "Yes. Now what do you want?"[2]

What Luther said to his student was fully in keeping with Scripture. The apostle Peter said, "Live as people who are free, not using your freedom as a cover-up for evil, but living as servants of God" (1 Peter 2:16). It is just because we have been set free by God's grace that we are obligated to love and obey God. The Apostle Paul adds that we are also obligated to love our neighbor: "For you were called to freedom, brothers. Only do not use your freedom as an opportunity for the flesh, but through love serve one another" (Galatians 5:13). Notice what Peter and Paul are doing in these verses: They are telling us to love God and to love our neighbor, which is what the Ten Commandments are all about. Paul makes this connection explicit when he goes on to say, "For the whole law is fulfilled in one word: 'You shall love your neighbor as yourself'" (Galatians 5:14). But of course Peter and Paul were simply repeating what Jesus said when he summarized the Law in two great commandments: Love God and love your neighbor (Matthew 22:37–40). Jesus also said, "If you love me, you will keep my commandments" (John 14:15). The gospel of Jesus Christ obligates us to keep the Law of God.

As believers in Christ, we are called to live in a way that is pleasing to God, which means living according to his perfect standard. God's standard has not changed, as if somehow his grace has redefined his righteousness. On the contrary, as we saw in the previous chapter, the moral law expresses the very character of Christ. Now, under the skillful direction of the Holy Spirit, it is still our teacher and our guide. The Puritan Thomas Watson wrote, "The moral law is the copy of God's will, our spiritual directory; it shows us what sins to avoid, what duties to pursue."[3] Writing in a similar vein, the Anglican bishop J. C. Ryle argued, "There is no greater mistake than to suppose that a Christian has nothing to do with the law and the Ten Commandments, because he cannot be justified by keeping them. The same Holy Ghost who convinces the believer of sin by the law, and leads him to Christ for justification, will always lead him to a spiritual use of the law, as a friendly guide, in the pursuit of sanctification."[4] The Law is useful for instructing us in righteousness. It helps us to know what is pleasing to God. It shows us how to live.

### Restraining Sin in Society

A second use of the Law is also mentioned in Exodus 20. God uses his law to restrain sin in human society. The commandments of the Law, with their accusation of guilt and threat of punishment, discourage people from sinning against God. The Law does not keep people from sinning entirely, of course, because it cannot change our sinful nature. But to a certain extent the Law does serve to restrain our sin.

God intended his law to have this restraining effect on Israel. Once the people had received the Ten Commandments, they responded with fear and trembling. They were overawed by God and by the commanding power of his voice. But Moses assured them that God's law was ultimately for their benefit. He said, "Do not fear, for God has come to test you, that the fear of him may be before you, that you may not sin" (20:20). The Law was partly a deterrent. It had the preventive purpose of keeping God's people away from sin. The threat of the Law's penalty held their depravity in check. Calvin compared this use of the Law to the bridle that controls an unruly horse:

> The second office of the Law is, by means of its fearful denunciations and the consequent dread of punishment, to curb those who, unless forced, have no regard for rectitude and justice. Such persons are curbed, not because their mind is inwardly moved and affected, but because, as if a bridle were laid upon them, they refrain their hands from external acts, and internally check the depravity which would otherwise petulantly burst forth.[5]

The reason the Law is able to keep people from sinning is because, as we saw in the last chapter, it expresses many of the divine attributes of Almighty God, such as his sovereignty and justice. Therefore the Law has the power to encourage the fear of God, and at the same time to discourage any desire to sin against him. The Law teaches that there is a great and mighty God who punishes people for their sins. This inevitably has the effect of warning us not to sin against him.

The Law continues to have this restraining effect today, which is why many Christians are in favor of posting the Ten Commandments in the classroom and the courtroom. We live in an increasingly lawless society. The effects of this are seen at school, where teachers almost always deal with misbehavior and often with the real threat of violence. The effects are also seen at court, where juries are confronted with unspeakable crimes and judges struggle to know what justice requires. We need moral guidance, and what better guide than God's commandments, written in stone?

There are some reasons to be skeptical about how much good posting them will do. There is always the risk that putting God's law on a public building will trivialize it—much the way that God is trivialized when his name is plastered on American currency. Will simply posting the Ten Commandments make people respect God and his law? To some extent it will, but what people really need is not just the Law but the gospel. What good will it do for people to know what God requires unless the Holy Spirit makes them able to do it? Furthermore, as we shall see in a moment, one of the Law's main purposes is to prove that we are *not* able to keep it. Rather than keeping us from sin, therefore, what hanging the Ten Commandments on the wall mainly does is to show us how sinful we really are!

Nevertheless, and apart from any constitutional questions concerning the separation of church and state, posting the Ten Commandments is a good and godly idea. The commandments come from God's Word, which never fails to fulfill its purpose (Isaiah 55:11). Furthermore, it is good for people to be confronted with an objective standard of right and wrong, given by a God of truth and justice. The very existence of the Ten Commandments declares that we are accountable to God for what we do and for what we fail to do.

This no doubt explains why today there is so much opposition to posting the Ten Commandments. People feel uncomfortable having God tell them what to do; so they try to have his commandments taken down, and often they are successful. In *Stone v. Graham*, the United States Supreme Court rejected the idea that the Ten Commandments have any place in secular society. The Court reasoned:

> The preeminent purpose for posting the Ten Commandments on schoolroom walls is plainly religious in nature. The Ten Commandments is undeniably a sacred text . . . and no legislative recitation of a supposed secular purpose can blind us to that fact. The commandments do not confine themselves to arguably secular matters, such as honoring one's parents, killing or murder, adultery, stealing, false witness, and covetousness. Rather, the

> first part of the commandments concerns the religious duties of believers: Worshipping the Lord God alone, avoiding idolatry, not using the Lord's name in vain, and observing the sabbath day.[6]

Whether the justices reached the right decision on the constitutional question or not, they were exactly right about what the Ten Commandments do: They confront us with our duty to God as well as to our neighbor. And it is good for people to be confronted because God's law has the ability to restrain sin in society. Christians who want to post the Ten Commandments have the right instinct. Although by itself the Law cannot save, it does help promote a just society. God's law informs the conscience, so that someone who reads the Ten Commandments has a heightened sense of what God requires and what God forbids. This knowledge of God and his law can keep people from sin. And as God's law—with all its threats and punishments—works its way into the law of the land, it deters people from committing especially destructive sins.

### Revealing Our Need for a Savior

So far we have considered what the Law is able to do. It teaches God's redeemed people how to live for God's glory, and it restrains sin in society. But there is one thing the Law is not able to do, and that is to bring full and final salvation. The Law is powerless in this regard because it is weakened by the sinful nature (see Romans 8:3). Yet even in its powerlessness the Law turns out to be useful, because it proves that we need someone else to save us. This is perhaps the Law's most important use: to show sinners their need of a Savior.

To see how the Law does this, it is necessary to understand that Israel was obligated to keep the Law perfectly. There are several indications of this in Exodus. One comes in chapter 24, where the Israelites promise to obey God's law. After Moses read the Book of the Covenant, the people said, "All that the LORD has spoken we will do, and we will be obedient" (24:7). The Israelites were bound by their own promise to keep the whole Law of God. Another way to say this is that they were required to keep God's covenant. Moses later told them, "He [God] declared to you his covenant, which he commanded you to perform, that is, the Ten Commandments, and he wrote them on two tablets of stone" (Deuteronomy 4:13).

The Israelites were bound to keep God's law not simply because that is what they promised, but because that is what their salvation required: perfect obedience to the revealed will of God. In one sense, of course, the Israelites were already saved. They had been delivered from Egypt. However, this was not their full and final salvation. It was only an earthly deliverance, and God was planning for them to spend an eternity with him in Heaven. But in order for them to reach their destiny, they had to fully meet the righteous requirements of God's law. As Moses later reminded them, "The LORD commanded us to do all these statutes. . . . And it will be righteousness for us, if we are careful to do all this commandment before the LORD our God, as he has commanded us" (Deuteronomy 6:24a, 25). Or again he said to them, "You shall therefore keep my statutes and my rules; if a person does them, he shall live by them" (Leviticus 18:5). Jesus later made much the same claim: "If you would enter life, keep the commandments" (Matthew 19:17b). To be righteous before God, the Israelites had to keep his law; and if they did so, they would be saved forever.

The trouble was that they couldn't keep it! In fact, no sooner had God told them not to have any other gods or make any idols than they made a golden calf (Exodus 32). This shows that for all its usefulness in teaching us how to live, the Law does not have the power to transform our sinful nature. Instead, like a mirror that shows every spot on someone's face, it shows how sinful we truly are.

Even worse, the Law has a way of actually provoking our sin. The Apostle Paul discussed this in Romans 7. First he made the point that we have just been making, namely, that the Law reveals our sin: "Yet if it had not been for the law, I would not have known sin" (Romans 7:7b). Then, using the tenth commandment as an example, he went on to explain that in some ways the Law actually serves to stimulate sin: "For I would not have known what it is to covet if the law had not said, 'You shall not covet.' But sin, seizing an opportunity through the commandment, produced in me all kinds of covetousness" (Romans 7:7c, 8a).

It is bad enough that the Law provokes sin, but the situation gets even worse because sin leads to death. Paul continued: "For apart from the law, sin lies dead. I was once alive apart from the law, but when the commandment came, sin came alive and I died. The very commandment that promised life proved to be death to me. For sin, seizing an opportunity through the commandment, deceived me and through it killed me" (Romans 7:8b–11). Breaking the Law leads to death. This would be bad enough, but believe it or not, the situation gets even worse, because those who sin and die are under God's curse. As the Scripture says, "Cursed be everyone who does not abide by all things written in the Book of the Law, and do them" (Galatians 3:10).

So here was the situation: God's people were bound to keep a law that they could not obey. Rather than bringing them full and final salvation, therefore, the Law exposed their sin, subjecting them to death and finally to the wrath and curse of God. John Calvin wrote that while the Law "shows God's righteousness, that is, the righteousness alone acceptable to God, it warns, informs, convicts, and lastly condemns, every man of his own unrighteousness."[7]

So why did God give his people the Law? Why did he give them something that would not simply command them but also condemn them? The answer is that he gave them his law so they would believe his gospel. All the great theologians have understood this. Augustine said, "The usefulness of the law lies in convicting man of his infirmity and moving him to call upon the remedy of grace which is in Christ."[8] Martin Luther explained it like this: "Therefore we do not abolish the Law; but we show its true function and use, namely, that it is a most useful servant impelling us to Christ. After the Law has humbled, terrified, and completely crushed you, so that you are on the brink of despair, then see to it that you know how to use the Law correctly; for its function and use is not only to disclose the sin and wrath of God but also to drive us to Christ."[9] John Calvin put it more simply, saying, "Moses had no other intention than to invite all men to go straight to Christ."[10] And Charles Spurgeon said, "As the sharp needle prepares the way for the thread, so the piercing law makes a way for the bright silver thread of divine grace."[11]

God's plan was to send his people a Savior. But first he gave them the Law in the form of a covenant of works—a covenant they could not keep. By revealing their sin, this law showed them that they needed an everlasting Savior, and thus it made them long for the coming of Christ. Like us, the Israelites were saved by grace through faith. The primary difference is that their faith was in the Savior to come, whereas ours is in the Savior God has already sent. But how would the Israelites ever have seen their need of a Savior unless their sin was first exposed and cursed by the Law of God? This is why they needed the Law. They needed it to help them believe in the gospel, and in this way God's law ultimately served to glorify God's grace. Paul explained it like this: "Now the law came in to increase the trespass, but where sin increased, grace abounded all the more, so that, as sin reigned in death, grace also might reign through righteousness leading to eternal life through Jesus Christ our Lord" (Romans 5:20, 21).

## Using the Law Today

As a multiuse item, God's law is as useful now as ever. It shows God's redeemed people how to live for God's glory, and it restrains sin in society. But there is one thing the Law cannot do, which is to make us right with God. We cannot be justified by our own keeping of the Law.

If we were able to keep God's law perfectly, then it *would* be able to save us. According to God's own Word, the person who obeys the commandments will live by them (Romans 10:5; Galatians 3:12). The trouble is that we can't keep them. As the Scripture says, "No one living is righteous before you [God]" (Psalm 143:2b). And what proves that we are unrighteous is the law of God: "For by works of the law no human being will be justified in his [God's] sight, since through the law comes knowledge of sin" (Romans 3:20). And because sin leads to judgment, the Law therefore shows us that we are condemned by God and that apart from his grace we will be lost forever.

In one of his many Exodus-related drawings, the cartoonist Baloo depicts Moses giving Israel the Ten Commandments. With a look of dismay, the people say, "We were hoping to be accepted as we are."[12] This is what we often hope, that God will let us come as we are. But because God is holy, he cannot accept us as we are, and we need to know this. It is absolutely essential for us to know.

We need to see ourselves as we really are, which is why we still need God's law—not to save us, but to show us how much we need a Savior. According to Martin Luther, "The true function and the chief and proper use of the Law is to reveal to man his sin, blindness, misery, wickedness, ignorance, hate and contempt of God, death, hell, judgment, and the well-deserved wrath of God."[13]

The Law shows us these things so that we will start looking for a Savior. Donald Grey Barnhouse explained it like this: "The law of God is like a mirror. Now the purpose of a mirror is to reveal to you that your face is dirty, but the purpose of a mirror is not to wash your face. When you look in a mirror and find that your face is dirty, you do not then reach to take the mirror off the wall and attempt to rub it on your face as a cleansing agent. The purpose of the mirror is to drive you to the water."[14] This is how the Law helps us: not by saving us, but by showing us our need for a Savior. And it does this for Christians as much as for non-Christians. The Law shows us our sin to remind us to praise God for saving us through Christ.

Sadly, God's law has fallen out of favor in the contemporary church. It is no longer preached as the eternal standard of God's righteousness or applied in its full relationship to the gospel. No doubt this is because the Law is not very seeker friendly. In fact, sometimes it makes people mad. However, preaching the Law is absolutely essential for reaching the lost. It is only by hearing God's law that sinners are convicted of their sin and thus see their need for the gospel. One minister who understood this was Archibald Alexander, one of the founding professors of Princeton Seminary. When Dr. Alexander's son was ordained to the pastoral ministry, he gave him this advice:

> Let the law be faithfully proclaimed, as binding on every creature, and as cursing every impenitent sinner, and let the utter inability of man to satisfy its demands be clearly set forth, not as an excuse, but as a fault; and then let the riches of grace in Christ Jesus be fully exhibited and freely offered, and let all—however great their guilt—be urged to accept of unmerited pardon, and complete salvation.[15]

This is the right place to end this chapter on the right use of the Law, with the riches of grace that God offers in Jesus Christ. The more we look into the mirror of God's law, the more clearly we see that we are sinners who need a Savior. Once we see this, we need to look to Jesus, who has fully met the requirements of God's law and has suffered the penalty that we deserve for our sin. There is pardon for every lawbreaker and forgiveness for every sinner who trusts in Jesus Christ.

48

# Interpreting God's Law

EXODUS 20:3–17

ONE CARTOON DEPICTS MOSES standing on top of God's mountain, holding the two tablets of the Ten Commandments. The prophet is beaming. "Hey, these are great," he says enthusiastically. "From now on, nobody will have trouble distinguishing right from wrong."[1]

What makes the cartoon funny is that obviously we still *do* have trouble distinguishing right from wrong, the Ten Commandments notwithstanding. The problem is not the commandments themselves. As we have seen, God's law provides an objective moral standard that clearly distinguishes between good and evil. The problem is with us. In our fallen condition, sin often deceives us into thinking that what is wrong is right and that what is right is wrong. We also live in a fallen world. Sin has such a corrupting influence on human society that we don't always know the right thing to do. As sinful people living in a sinful world, we face real moral dilemmas that make it hard for us to distinguish right from wrong. The Ten Commandments do not clarify everything.

There is another reason why the Ten Commandments don't immediately answer all our ethical questions: They are not as simple as they look. At first they seem thoroughly straightforward. There are only ten of them—one for each finger—so they are relatively easy to remember. They are not very long either. It takes only a minute or so to recite them. They are so simple, in fact, that the Bible refers to them as "the ten words" (literal translation of 34:28). God has given us ten short rules that apply to all people in all places. What could be simpler?

When these apparently simple commandments are studied carefully, however, they turn out to have amazing depth. The Ten Commandments are profound in what they reveal about God and about living for his glory. The commandments are also broad. When they are properly understood, they turn out to be relevant for any and every situation—one law for all of life. To make full and proper use of this law, therefore, we need to know how to apply it. And if there is any doubt as to the importance of having the right interpretation, one need only think of the Pharisees, who despite all their efforts to keep God's law often violated it. This was partly because they did not know how to interpret the Decalogue according to its true intention and proper application.

## In All the Scriptures

The first rule of interpretation is *the Biblical rule*: Every commandment must be understood in the context of the entire Bible. This is simply the Reformation principle that Scripture interprets Scripture. The way to know the full and true meaning of any Bible passage is to know what the rest of the Bible says on the same theme. And this is true of the Ten Commandments. To understand the full implications of each commandment, we need to know what the whole Bible teaches about it, including the teaching of Jesus and his apostles.

To take just one example, consider the second commandment, which says, "You shall not make for yourself a carved image, or any likeness of anything that is in heaven above, or that is in the earth beneath, or that is in the water under the earth. You shall not bow down to them or serve them" (20:4, 5a). This command sounds so simple that further explanation hardly seems necessary. Yet our understanding of the second commandment is greatly expanded when we know what the rest of the Bible says about worship in general and about idolatry in particular. We need to know what the prophet Isaiah said about the folly of making images with our own hands and then bowing down to worship them (Isaiah 44:6–23), what Jesus said about worshiping God in spirit and in truth (John 4:24), and what the Apostle Paul said about greed as a form of idolatry (see Ephesians 5:5; Colossians 3:5). In addition to studying the second commandment on its own terms, we need to study what is taught on the subject elsewhere in Scripture.

What makes this method of interpretation valid is that everything in the Bible comes from the mind of God, as breathed out by his Holy Spirit. What God says in one place agrees with what he says somewhere else because God cannot disagree with himself! Furthermore, all the prophets and apostles accepted the abiding authority of God's moral law. They did not set it aside but in various ways interpreted and explained it. And because their teaching is also authoritative, whatever they have to say about the Law also applies to us.

The same is true of what Jesus Christ said about the Law. Some people refer to Jesus as the new Moses who gave God's people a new law. It is not hard to understand why. Like Moses, Jesus went up the mountain to teach God's people how to live. There he addressed some of the same issues that God dealt with in the Ten Commandments. Jesus said, "You have heard that it was said to those of old, 'You shall not murder; and whoever murders will be liable to judgment.' But I say to you that everyone who is angry with his brother will be liable to judgment" (Matthew 5:21, 22a). Jesus said something similar about adultery. It almost sounded as if he were giving a whole new law.

This was not what Jesus was doing, however. When he said, "You have heard that it was said," he was not correcting Moses but was contradicting the Pharisees for their false interpretation of Moses. As John Calvin explained, rather than adding to the Law, Christ "only restored it to its integrity, in that he freed and cleansed it when it had been obscured by falsehood." Calvin thus referred to Jesus as the Law's "best interpreter."[2] Similarly, the great Swiss theologian Francis Turretin said, "[Jesus] does not act as a new lawgiver, but only as an interpreter and vindicator of the law given by Moses."[3] If we want to understand the Ten Commandments properly, therefore, we need to know how Jesus interpreted them. This is in keeping with our first rule of interpretation—namely, that the Law must be understood in the context of the whole Bible.

## Inside and Out

The second rule is *the inside/outside rule*: The Ten Commandments are internal as well as external. They demand inward integrity as well as outward conformity. Another way to say this is the way the Apostle Paul said it: "The law is spiritual" (Romans 7:14). In other words, it deals with our souls as well as our bodies. This distinguishes God's law from any human law. According to an old Puritan proverb, "Man's law binds the hands only, God's law binds the heart."[4]

This guideline for interpretation is in keeping with the being and character of God. God himself is spirit. He is omniscient and omnipresent. Nothing escapes his attention. He is immediately aware of everything we think as well as everything we say or do. He knows our inward intentions as well as our outward actions. As the Scripture says, "Man looks on the outward appearance, but the LORD looks on the heart" (1 Samuel 16:7b). Therefore, God holds us accountable not only for the sins we commit with our bodies, but also for the sins we commit in the privacy of our own hearts, minds, and wills. Remember too that each of the Ten Commandments was given in the singular. When God holds us accountable to keep his law, he holds us personally accountable—inside as well as out.

The spirituality of God's law is made most explicit by the tenth commandment. On the surface at least, the first nine commandments only deal with outward conduct. They govern observable actions like bowing down before idols, cursing, killing, and stealing. But the tenth commandment deals exclusively with the heart: "You shall not covet your neighbor's house; you shall not covet your neighbor's wife, or his male servant, or his female servant, or his ox, or his donkey, or anything that is your neighbor's" (20:17).

The tenth commandment does not address an action at all but only an affection. According to the Jewish scholar Umberto Cassuto, this kind of commandment was completely unprecedented in the ancient world.[5] All the other legal codes governed outward sins like stealing. But only Israel's God presumed to rule a person's thoughts and desires.

What was made explicit in the tenth commandment is equally true of all the others. The Ten Commandments are spiritual; they require inward as well as outward obedience. This is one of the things that Jesus clarified in his Sermon on the Mount. One might think that the seventh commandment—which outlaws adultery—only deals with how we use our bodies. But Jesus said, "I say to you that everyone who looks at a woman with lustful intent has already committed adultery with her in his heart" (Matthew 5:28). What the seventh commandment forbids is not just inappropriate sexual activity but also sinful desires. Jesus handled the sixth commandment the same way, teaching that it condemned anger and hatred as well as murder (Matthew 5:21, 22; cf. 1 John 3:15a). As Jesus later said, "Out of the heart come evil thoughts, murder, adultery, sexual immorality, theft, false witness, slander" (Matthew 15:19).

Now we begin to see how demanding God is, and how thoroughly his law exposes our sin. If we thought that somehow we could get by on good behavior, we were mistaken. Since the Law is spiritual, we must apply the Ten Commandments to our inward affections as well as to our outward actions. And now we can sympathize with the tribal chieftain who said, "I would rather have the 7777 commandments and prohibitions of the Towanda Adapt than the Ten Commandments of the Christians, for the Ten Commandments demand my whole heart, whereas the 7777 ancestral commands and prohibitions leave room for a lot of freedom."[6]

## Both Sides of the Law

Like the second rule, the third rule of interpretation widens our application of the Ten Commandments. It is *the two-sided rule*. It could also be called the law of opposites, the law of contraries, or the law of contrapositives. Whatever it is called, what it means is very simple: Every commandment is both positive and negative. Where a sin is forbidden, the corresponding duty is required; and where a duty is required, the corresponding sin is forbidden.

People usually think of the Ten Commandments as a list of don'ts: Don't make other gods, don't steal, don't lie, and so forth. It is true that most of the commandments are worded as don'ts rather than dos. The only completely positive commandment is the fifth: "Honor your father and your mother" (20:12). Even the fourth commandment, which tells us to "Remember the Sabbath," also tells us not to work (20:8–10).

All these "thou shalt not's" can sound rather negative. However, when we interpret the Ten Commandments properly, we find that they are both positive and negative. There is a flip side to every commandment. Each one condemns a particular vice, while at the same time it commands a particular virtue. For example, the third commandment forbids the misuse of God's name. We may not dishonor God by abusing his name. However, by sheer force of logic, this command also requires us to use God's name honorably and reverently. To give another example, the commandment that forbids murder simultaneously requires the preservation of life. Similarly, while the eighth commandment rules out theft, it also demands that we give generously to people in need. The true intent of each commandment is to tell us what *to* do as well as what *not* to do.

The commandments that are stated positively need to be interpreted the same way. Where a duty is commanded, the corresponding sin is forbidden. Consider the fourth commandment, which reads in part, "Six days you shall labor, and do all your work" (20:9). The command to work promotes the virtue of industry. At the same time, it forbids all the sins that hinder our work, such as time-wasting and other forms of laziness. The same commandment also tells us to "remember the Sabbath." This very positive command also forbids us to do something—namely, to break the Sabbath.

Every commandment is both positive and negative. This "law of opposites" helps keep us from following the letter of the Law while avoiding its full application. We can't just say, "Well, at least I don't shoplift" while failing to give to the poor and still think that we are really keeping the eighth commandment. This rule also makes the Ten Commandments at least twice as hard to keep as most people think! In order to keep the first commandment, for example, we must not only stay away from false religions, but we must enthrone the one and only true God as our supreme Lord. And in order to keep the ninth commandment, it is not enough simply to avoid telling any lies; we must also use our words to encourage and to bless. As we shall see, these principles make the Ten Commandments much more impossible to obey than most people have ever imagined.

## Categories

When the Ten Commandments are interpreted properly, they are comprehensive. They deal with areas of sin that are discussed all through the Scriptures. They command both the body and the soul. They not only forbid disobedience, but they also require obedience. To those guidelines we can now add a fourth, *the rule of categories*: Each commandment stands for a whole category of sins. It governs not only the specific sin that is mentioned, but all the sins that lead up to it, and all the supposedly lesser sins of the same kind. *The Westminster Larger Catechism* states this rule formally: "That under one sin or duty, all of the same kind are forbidden or commanded; together with all the causes, means, occasions, and appearances thereof, and provocations thereunto" (A. 99.6).

The easiest way to explain what this means is to give some examples. Consider the sixth commandment: "You shall not murder." Taken literally, this is a commandment that relatively few people break (although as Jesus explained, since the Law is spiritual, it also condemns very common sins such as hatred).

But in addition to outright murder, the sixth commandment forbids any form of physical violence. It even condemns fistfights, bodily injury, and domestic violence. It also condemns neglecting our personal health. And it includes everything that leads up to these sins, such as fits of anger, reckless driving, or even playing violent video games. What God forbids is not simply murder but everything that harms the body, threatens physical well-being, or inures us to the dangers of violence.

To take another example, consider the seventh commandment, which forbids adultery. In its most literal sense, what the seventh commandment forbids is extramarital intercourse. If this is the only sin it covers, then it is a (relatively) easy law to keep. However, according to our fourth rule of interpretation, each commandment stands for a whole category of sin. So the seventh commandment includes not simply the act of adultery but every form of sexual misconduct. Premarital sex, the use of pornography, self-stimulation—all of these sins are forbidden. Also forbidden are all the sins that lead up to adultery. God calls husbands and wives to nurture their fellowship with one another. It is unlawful for a couple to grow apart from one another physically, spiritually, emotionally, or sexually. It is also wrong for a husband or wife to have intimate relationships with other men or women, even if those relationships are not sexual (at least not yet)—adultery begins long before two people get in bed together. These are only a few examples of the many sins included under the category of the seventh commandment.

These examples help us understand that the Ten Commandments generally forbid the most extreme example of a particular kind of sin. Bowing down in front of an idol is the worst form of false worship, misusing God's sacred divine name is the worst form of blasphemy, murder is the worst form of violence, adultery is the most destructive act of sexual sin, and so forth. But this approach is not intended to make us think that the big sins are the only ones that matter. Rather, it shows us that God considers every sin in that category to be as sinful as the most heinous form of that particular sin. So, for example, every kind of poor stewardship is as culpable as stealing, every kind of dishonesty is as reprehensible as lying under legal oath, and so on.

The rule of categories also warns us not to commit lesser sins that by their very nature are bound to lead us into greater sins. People generally do not start out with grand larceny; they start with petty theft. Similarly, it is by telling little white lies that people learn how to pull off grand deceptions. But God rules out the little sins to help prevent the big ones. Turretin explained the principle this way:

> What are most base and capital in each species of sin are forbidden, under which all the others are included, either because they flow thence or because they lead at length to it; or because what appear the smallest to men

> are in the most accurate judgment of God rated more severely. This is not done, therefore, to excuse or exclude lesser sins, but that a greater detestation of sin may be impressed upon our minds.[7]

## My Brother's Keeper

It was Cain who asked the famous question, "Am I my brother's keeper?" (Genesis 4:9b). The next guideline for interpreting and applying God's law answers in the affirmative. In addition to keeping the Ten Commandments ourselves, we are required to help others keep them. According to *the brother's keeper rule*, we are not allowed to encourage someone else to do what God has told us not to do. To put it more positively, we must do everything in our power to help other people keep God's law. Ernest Reisinger writes, "Whatever is forbidden or commanded of us, we are bound, according to our position, to discourage or encourage in others according to the duty of their positions."[8]

Reisinger uses the word "position" because our station in life often gives us spiritual influence over others. Parents shape their children's morals, both for evil and for good. The Ten Commandments thus require fathers and mothers to teach their children how to put God first, how to keep the Sabbath, how to tell the truth, and so forth. The same principle applies to the classroom, and also to the workplace. Employers set the moral standard for their employees. They have a responsibility not only to keep God's law but also to create an environment in which their workers are encouraged to keep God's law too.

If we fail to help others keep God's law—or worse, if we fail to hinder them from breaking it—then in some way we share in the guilt of their sin. In his commentary on the Ten Commandments, the Puritan Thomas Watson listed some of the many ways we can become an accessory to someone else's sin.[9] One is by telling people to do something that God forbids—for example, when Aaron told the Israelites to give him their jewelry to make a golden calf (Exodus 32). Few Christians actually tell other people to sin, the way Aaron did. But this is not the only way to share in the guilt of others. Another way to participate in their iniquity is by encouraging them to sin. The Bible says, "Woe to him who makes his neighbors drink—you pour out your wrath and make them drunk" (Habakkuk 2:15). Anyone who has ever been to school knows that some kids have a way of coming up with the ideas that get other kids in trouble, without ever getting caught themselves. But according to God's law, they are still guilty.

Then there are the sins we help cause by setting a bad example. Our own failure to keep God's law has a way of encouraging others to break it too. This is an area where spiritual leaders need to be especially careful. As Jesus said to his disciples, "Temptations to sin are sure to come, but woe to the one through whom they come! It would be better for him if a millstone were hung around his neck and he were cast into the sea than that he should cause one of these little ones to sin. Pay attention to yourselves!" (Luke 17:1–3a).

A more subtle way to promote sin is by failing to prevent it. The failure to stop a sin, when it lies within our power to do so, is as culpable as committing the sin itself. This is one of the ways that parents often share in the sins of their children. By failing to rebuke and punish them, they actually condone their disobedience. This is why God judged Eli so harshly. He said, "I declare to him that I am about to punish his house forever, for the iniquity that he knew, because his sons were blaspheming God, and he did not restrain them" (1 Samuel 3:13). Like Eli, those who fail to punish offenders share in their offense.

Yet another way to become an accessory to sin is by endorsing someone else's violation of the Law. A clear Biblical example is what Saul did at the stoning of Stephen. The Bible says that the people who carried out this murderous act "laid down their garments at the feet of a young man named Saul" (Acts 7:58). Saul didn't even lift a stone; all he did was run the coat check! Yet by agreeing with his heart, he too had a hand in Stephen's death. The Bible thus condemns him with these words: "And Saul approved of his execution" (Acts 8:1). As far as God is concerned, we are as guilty for the sins that have our consent as we are for the sins that we commit.

There are many ways to share in someone else's sin. In their widest application, what the Ten Commandments require is not merely our own obedience but also our refusal to participate in the sins of others. More than this, we are called to do everything we can to help others respect and obey God's law.

## The Demands of the Law

These are some of the rules for interpreting God's moral law. There are others. One is *the law of the tables*, which states that the first table of the Law always takes precedence over the second. In other words, our duty to God in the first four commandments always governs our duty to one another in the last six commandments; our love for our neighbor is subject to our love for God. So if a parent tells a child to worship a false god, the child is bound by the first commandment ("no other gods") rather than the fifth commandment ("Honor your father and your mother"). This is the principle Peter was applying when he said to the Sanhedrin, "We must obey God rather than men" (Acts 5:29).

There is also *the all-at-once rule*. Obviously we cannot perform every positive duty simultaneously. So the *Westminster Larger Catechism* teaches "that what God forbids, is at no time to be done; what he commands, is always our duty; and yet every particular duty is not to be done at all times" (A. 99.5). Then there is *the rule of love*, which states that the purpose of every commandment is to show love, especially love for God. As the Scripture says, "Love is the fulfilling of the law" (Romans 13:10b). Even the commandments that require love for our neighbor promote love for God. We do not love and serve our neighbor simply for the sake of our neighbor, but ultimately for the sake of God.[10]

As we begin to use these interpretive principles to apply the Ten Commandments, we quickly discover that these laws are not so simple after all. They cover everything. They rule us inside as well as outside. They are positive as well as negative. Each of them governs a whole category of sins and duties. They apply not only to our own conduct but also to our influence over the conduct of others.

Using these principles, even the simplest commandment places overwhelming demands on our obedience. To take just one example, consider the ninth commandment: "You shall not bear false witness against your neighbor" (20:16). In other words, "Don't lie." This sounds simple enough, until we understand the full implications of the commandment, as explained in the *Westminster Larger Catechism*:

> The sins forbidden in the ninth commandment are, all prejudicing the truth, and the good name of our neighbours, as well as our own, especially in public judicature; giving false evidence, suborning false witnesses, wittingly appearing and pleading for an evil cause, out-facing and over-bearing the truth; passing unjust sentence, calling evil good, and good evil; rewarding the wicked according to the work of the righteous, and the righteous according to the work of the wicked; forgery, concealing the truth, undue silence in a just cause, and holding our peace when iniquity calleth for either a reproof from ourselves, or complaint to others; speaking the truth unseasonably, or maliciously to a wrong end, or perverting it to a wrong meaning, or in doubtful or equivocal expressions, to the prejudice of truth or justice; speaking untruth, lying, slandering, backbiting, detracting, tale-bearing, whispering, scoffing, reviling, rash, harsh, and partial censuring; misconstructing intentions, words, and actions; flattering, vain-glorious boasting, thinking or speaking too highly or too meanly of ourselves or others; denying the gifts and graces of God; aggravating smaller faults; hiding, excusing, or extenuating of sins, when called to a free confession; unnecessary discovering of infirmities; raising false rumours, receiving and countenancing evil reports, and stopping our ears against just defence; evil suspicion; envying or grieving at the deserved credit of any, endeavouring or desiring to impair it, rejoicing in their disgrace and infamy; scornful contempt, fond admiration; breach of lawful promises; neglecting such things as are of good report, and practising, or not avoiding ourselves, or not hindering what we can in others, such things as procure an ill name. (A. 145)

And this is only what is forbidden! The catechism also explains what the ninth commandment requires in similar detail. Now we see that if somehow we thought that we were not guilty of breaking the ninth commandment, it was only because we didn't have much idea what it required. The truth is that we are liars.

This is bad news because God requires perfect obedience. To quote again from the *Larger Catechism*, "The law is perfect, and bindeth every one to full conformity in the whole man unto the righteousness thereof, and unto entire obedience for ever; so as to require the utmost perfection of every duty, and to forbid the least degree of every sin" (A. 99.1). And if we break even one commandment we are guilty before God. As the apostle James wrote, "Whoever keeps the whole law but fails in one point has become accountable for all of it" (James 2:10). Even worse, everyone who breaks the Law is subject to the wrath and curse of God.

## The Curse of the Law

Some people—including some Christians—might think that interpreting the Law too carefully is legalistic. We have enough trouble keeping the easy commandments, so what is the point of looking at God's law in exhaustive detail? Isn't that legalistic?

On the contrary, it is when we have a limited understanding of the Law that we are most tempted to legalism, because then we think that we can keep it. If all God commanded us to do was to avoid murdering someone, we might be able to obey him. But we need to interpret the sixth commandment in the context of the whole Bible, with everything it says about murderous intentions. Since the Law is spiritual, it condemns unrighteous anger as well as murder. Since it is positive as well as negative, it requires the active preservation of life. And since it represents a whole category of sins, we are forbidden to harm people in any way or to allow others to do so.

Is this a legalistic way of thinking? Not at all. This kind of Biblical reasoning rescues us from legalism by preventing us from lowering God's standard. God's standard is only maintained when we recognize what his righteousness truly requires. And when we know what God requires, in all its fullness, we also see the full extent of our sin. It is only a full understanding of God's law that reveals our full need for the gospel. In the words of J. Gresham Machen, "A low view of law always brings legalism in religion; a high view of law makes a man a seeker after grace."[11]

Here we need to recall how to use God's law. As we have seen, the Ten Commandments are a multiuse item. One of their primary purposes is to show us our sin, so that we will see our need for a Savior. The Law points us to Jesus Christ, whom the Scriptures identify as "the end of the law" (Romans 10:4), meaning that he is the goal or true purpose of the Law. The more clearly and thoroughly we understand what God's law requires, the more clearly and thoroughly we understand the grace that God has provided for us in Jesus Christ.

What does the moral law, summarized in the Ten Commandments and rightly interpreted, reveal about the person and work of Jesus Christ? It reveals the full extent of his perfect obedience. The Bible assures us that although Jesus was "born under the law" (Galatians 4:4), he "fulfill[ed] all righteousness" (Matthew 3:15) and "committed no sin" (1 Peter 2:22). This was no small accomplishment! The Law of God searches to the very soul. It is utterly exhaustive in the righteousness it requires. We are not capable of keeping even a single commandment with perfect integrity. But Jesus kept them all, down to the last detail, and he did it on our behalf. If we are joined to him by faith, then God regards us as if we had kept his whole law perfectly. Christ was crucified "in order that the righteous requirement of the law might be fulfilled in us" (Romans 8:4a). Therefore, the Law shows us what perfect righteousness we have in Christ. To put this in more technical terms, when we know what the Law requires, we can understand the doctrine of justification.

The moral law also reveals the full extent of Christ's atonement. The Bible teaches that Jesus Christ died on the cross for our sins. If we have a narrow understanding of God's law, we might imagine that we did not have very many sins to die for. But a full interpretation of the Ten Commandments reveals the full extent of our sin, and thus it reveals the full extent of the atonement. Christ died for all our sins. He died for our sins against God and our sins against humanity. He died for our idolatry, profanity, and adultery. He died for our lying, stealing, and murder. He died for our sins both inside and out. He died for all the sins we commit in every category of God's command. He even died for all the sins we committed by sharing in the sins of others. Christ died for *all our sins*, suffering the full penalty that our guilt deserved. The more thoroughly we understand the implications of God's law, the more truly grateful we are for the grace of God in the atoning death of Jesus Christ. When we know what the Law requires, we can understand the cross.

Finally, for those who have put their faith in Jesus Christ, the moral law reveals the full duty of the Christian life. This is another use of God's law. It shows God's redeemed people how to live for God's glory. When we give the Law its full interpretation, we gain a better grasp of God's righteous standard in all its perfection, and thus we have a better idea of how to please him. To put this in theological terms, when we know what the Law requires, we can understand the doctrine of sanctification. This is why we study God's law: to understand our great need for Christ and his gospel and to learn how many ways we can glorify God for his grace.

# 49

# The First Commandment: No Other Gods

EXODUS 20:3

ONE OF THE FIRST LESSONS parents try to teach their children is how to share. Fathers and mothers are forever reminding their sons and daughters to share their space, share their toys, and share their food. "You have to share," they say.

As important as it is to learn how to share, it is also important to realize that some things are not meant to be shared. A bite-sized candy bar, for example. Or a unicycle. Or a piece of confidential information, like the answers to a test. Or, to take an even more serious example, the sexual love between a husband and wife. These things were never intended to be shared with someone else. In order to be used properly at all, they have to be kept exclusive.

If some things were never meant to be shared, then it is not surprising to learn that there are times when even God refuses to share. He is a loving and merciful God who loves to pour out his mercy and grace on his people. But there are some things that he will not share. This is especially true when it comes to the prerogatives of his deity. God will not share his glory with any other god. So he has given us this command: "You shall have no other gods before me" (20:3).

This is the fundamental commandment, the one that comes before all the others and lays the foundation for them. Before we learn anything else about what God demands, we need to know who he is and who we are in relationship to him. "Now get this straight," God is saying, "I am the one and only God. And since I am the only God, I refuse to share my worship with anyone or anything else." God will not share the stage with any other performers. He refuses to have any colleagues. He will not even acknowledge that he has any genuine rivals. God does not simply lay claim to one part of our life and worship; he demands that we dedicate all we are and all we have to his service and praise. Thus the

Ten Commandments begin by asserting the great theological principle of *soli Deo gloria*: glory to God alone.

## Other Gods in Egypt

In order to understand the first commandment, it helps to know the context in which it was given. The Israelites had just come out of Egypt, where they had lived in one of the most polytheistic cultures ever. *Polytheism* is simply the worship of many gods, and in this the Egyptians were unsurpassed. They worshiped the gods of fields and rivers, light and darkness, sun and storm. Swearing their allegiance to the gods and goddesses of love and war, they bowed down to worship idols in the form of men and beasts.

The Israelites worshiped these gods too. Over the long centuries of their captivity, they had gradually given in to the temptation to worship strange gods. God told them, "Cast away the detestable things your eyes feast on, every one of you, and do not defile yourselves with the idols of Egypt; I am the LORD your God. But," he lamented, "they rebelled against me and were not willing to listen to me. None of them cast away the detestable things their eyes feasted on, nor did they forsake the idols of Egypt" (Ezekiel 20:7, 8a). Like the Egyptians, the Israelites worshiped many gods.

As for God, he has always been a monotheist; he has only ever believed in one God. So in the first commandment he took his stand against the gods of Egypt and against every other false deity—past, present, and future. He said, "You shall have no other gods before me" (20:3). In other words, "I am to be your one and only God." This command was without precedent. None of the other nations in the ancient world prohibited the worship of other gods. They simply assumed that every nation would serve its own deities. But on this issue the God of Israel was completely intolerant. He refused to acknowledge the legitimacy of any other god.

What gives God the right to make this kind of demand? He's God! Remember how the first commandment is introduced. God said, "I am the LORD your God, who brought you out of the land of Egypt, out of the house of slavery. You shall have no other gods before me" (20:2, 3). What God commanded was based on who he was and what he had done. God had saved his people for his glory, and now he was saying to them, "As the sovereign Lord of Heaven and earth, it is my right to rule over you. But more than this, I am your very own God. We are bound together by my covenant promise. And I have redeemed you. I have released you from your bondage to Pharaoh. With ten mighty plagues I have defeated all the deities of Egypt, showing that I am the one and only true God. And now I claim my right to all your worship and all your praise. Because of who I am and on the basis of what I have done, I will not share my glory with any other god."

If God is the only God, then why does he speak of "other gods" as if they had any real existence? The Bible insists that there is only one God and that every other deity is a fraud. As God said through his prophet Isaiah, "There is no other god besides me, a righteous God and a Savior; there is none besides me" (Isaiah 45:21b). "We know that 'an idol has no real existence,'" wrote the Apostle Paul, "and that 'there is no God but one'" (1 Corinthians 8:4b). If this is true, then what is the point in telling us not to have any other gods? If there aren't any other gods to begin with, then how *could* we have another one?

The answer is that even false gods hold a kind of spiritual power over their worshipers. "People worship powerful forces within creation as if these were deities. They are not gods, but only so-called gods; still, they are very real powers, able to enslave a person totally."[1] As Paul reminded the Galatians, "Formerly, when you did not know God, you were enslaved to those that by nature are not gods" (Galatians 4:8). The reason false gods have this enslaving power is ultimately because demonic forces use them to gain mastery over their worshipers. Thus the gods of Egypt held real spiritual power over the minds and hearts of the Egyptians, and also the Israelites. This is why God took the trouble to defeat them, one by one. It was to break their spiritual influence and thereby to show that he alone was worthy of worship.

## Before My Face

The first commandment comes from the God who is our Lord and Savior. But what about the commandment itself? What can we learn from the way it is worded—specifically from its last phrase? God said, "You shall have no other gods *before me*" (20:3). This does not mean that it is permissible to worship other deities, as long as we put God first. When God says, "before me," he is not trying to tell us where he falls in the rankings! But what is he trying to say?

The words "before me" mean "before my face." Sometimes they are used in a spatial sense. In that case, the commandment would mean something like this: "You shall have no other gods 'in front of me' or 'in my presence.'" Taken literally, this would forbid people from bringing foreign idols into the place where God is worshiped. But since God is everywhere, it really forbids us from worshiping false gods anywhere. Any time we serve any other god, we are doing it in the presence of God. The word "before" can also be used to describe two things that are in opposition to one another. In that case, the commandment would read, "You shall not have any gods over against me." Here the picture is that of putting one thing in the face of another. In other words, setting up a false deity is like insulting God to his face.[2] Obviously "before" is a flexible word, and although it is hard to decide how it is used here, both of the possible meanings are Biblically correct. No matter where we do it, we are not allowed to serve anyone or anything besides God. To do such a thing is to set ourselves against him and against his commandment.

The point is that when it comes to worshiping God, it is all or nothing. This is the way it has always been. It was this way on Mount Sinai, when God first gave Moses the Law. It was this way when Joshua renewed the covenant and said, "Put away the gods that your fathers served . . . in Egypt, and serve the Lord . . . choose this day whom you will serve" (Joshua 24:14b, 15a). This is the way it was on Mount Carmel, when Elijah liberated the Israelites from their bondage to Baal. He said, "If the Lord is God, follow him; but if Baal, then follow him" (1 Kings 18:21b). And it is the same way with Jesus Christ, who says, "No one can serve two masters . . . You cannot serve God and money" (Matthew 6:24). God's people have always faced a choice. Religious pluralism is not a recent development. There have always been plenty of other gods clamoring for our attention, and God has always demanded our exclusive loyalty.

When God commands us to reject false gods, he is also commanding us to choose him as the true God, enthroning him as our only Lord. John Calvin said that the first commandment requires us "to contemplate, fear and worship his majesty; to participate in his blessings; to seek his help at all times; to recognize, and by praises to celebrate, the greatness of his works—as the only goal of all the activities of life."[3] So the command tells us whom to worship as well as whom not to worship. It is positive as well as negative. For its positive statement, consider the creed that most Israelites recited every day: "Hear, O Israel: The Lord our God, the Lord is one. You shall love the Lord your God with all your heart and with all your soul and with all your might" (Deuteronomy 6:4, 5).

"Love" is the right word to use because the first commandment solidifies the covenant relationship between God and his people. Notice that in this commandment God speaks to us in the singular. God says, "*You* [individually] shall have no other gods before *me* [personally]." We do not worship *a* god but *the* God, and he wants to have an exclusive love relationship with each one of his people. Obviously in order for this relationship to work, it is essential for us not to share our love with any other god. We must be faithful to the only true God. We must give him our total allegiance, honoring, adoring, and revering him as our Lord and Savior.

## A Royal Folly

The first commandment is, "You shall have no other gods before me." But what happens when we break it? There is a story about violating the first commandment in the Bible. It is the story of the tragic downfall of a great king. He was one of the greatest kings in the ancient world. He was powerful, the most powerful king his nation had ever seen. He had horses and chariots by the thousands. He crushed his enemies, expanding his kingdom until it stretched from the mountains to the sea. He was also the wealthiest king his nation had ever seen. His palace was filled with gold but not with silver, which during his reign was considered too common for royal use. The name of this rich and powerful king was Solomon.

The most remarkable thing about Solomon was that he possessed true spiritual wisdom. In the early days of his reign, God appeared to him in a dream and said, "Ask what I shall give you" (1 Kings 3:5). It was the opportunity of a lifetime! The king could ask for anything he wanted. His answer would reveal what god he wanted to serve: If he served riches, he would ask for gold; if he served power, he would ask for death to his enemies; if he served pleasure, he would ask for beautiful women. But Solomon wanted to serve the one and only true God, so he asked for the wisdom to rule his people in righteousness.

God granted the king's request. Solomon was recognized as the wisest man in the ancient world. People came from all over to test his knowledge. The Bible tells how he judged between right and wrong and how he served as a counselor to kings and queens. In his wisdom Solomon did many great things for God. He was generous: he built a temple in God's honor. He was also a man of prayer. The magnificent prayer he offered at the dedication of the temple could only have come from a man who knew the Scriptures and understood the character of God (2 Chronicles 6). And God answered Solomon's prayer by descending on his temple in power and glory. There has never been a man more greatly blessed than King Solomon. He had everything a person could possibly want, including the opportunity to do great things for God.

If only Solomon had kept the first commandment! God said to him, "And as for you, if you will walk before me, as David your father walked, with integrity of heart and uprightness, doing according to all that I have commanded you, and keeping my statutes and my rules, then I will establish your royal throne over Israel forever. . . . But if you turn aside from following me . . . and do not keep my commandments and my statutes that I have set before you, but go and serve other gods and worship them, then I will cut off Israel from the land that I have given them, and the house that I have consecrated for my name I will cast out of my sight" (1 Kings 9:4–7a). It was very simple: All Solomon had to do was to give God the glory. In particular, he had to obey the first commandment by refusing to serve any other gods.

Sadly, Solomon failed to keep God's law: He served other gods. The Scripture tells how "Solomon went after Ashtoreth the goddess of the Sidonians, and after Milcom the abomination of the Ammonites" (1 Kings 11:5). It also tells how God responded: "And the Lord was angry with Solomon, because his heart had turned away from the Lord, the God of Israel, who had appeared to him twice and had commanded him concerning this thing, that he should not go after other gods. But he did not keep what the Lord commanded. Therefore the Lord said to Solomon, 'Since this has been your practice and you have not kept my covenant and my statutes that I have commanded you, I will surely tear the kingdom from you'" (1 Kings 11:9–11). King Solomon was condemned specifically for violating the first commandment.

## A Real Tragedy

Most people are surprised by what happened to Solomon. The collapse of his kingdom comes as a real shock. How could a man who was so wise be so stupid? Yet if we look at Solomon's life carefully, we see that his heart started to turn away from God long before he ever bowed down in front of any idols. Solomon started well, but gradually he drifted away until finally he was worshiping completely different deities. The same thing happens to many Christians. Although we never intend to break the first commandment, our hearts are lured away by the temptation to follow other gods.

What is so tragic about King Solomon is that he ended up serving the very gods he had once rejected. He did not ask God for gold, yet in time he started serving the god of wealth. The best example of this comes in 1 Kings 7, which describes how he built his palace. Chapter 6 tells how Solomon built a house for God and ends by saying that he "was seven years in building it" (1 Kings 6:38b). Then the king built a house for himself. Chapter 7 begins with words that can only be interpreted as a reproach: "Solomon was building his own house thirteen years, and he finished his entire house" (7:1). Once the king had done something for God, he decided it was time to do something for himself, and he took almost twice as long doing it! This shows how dangerous it is to be rich. Money brings many temptations, and even if we resist them at the beginning, they may come back to destroy us in the end.

Solomon also began to worship power. Again this was not something he asked for, but in time he started serving the god of military strength. God had specifically forbidden the Israelites to build up a cavalry (see Deuteronomy 17:16); yet Solomon amassed an entire army of horses and chariots (1 Kings 10:26–29).

He made the same mistake when it came to women. God said, "[The king] shall not acquire many wives for himself, lest his heart turn away" (Deuteronomy 17:17a). Sadly, Solomon failed to heed God's warning. Although at the beginning he did not ask for pleasure, he started serving the goddess of sex, and this was his downfall. "Now King Solomon loved many foreign women, along with the daughter of Pharaoh: Moabite, Ammonite, Edomite, Sidonian, and Hittite women, from the nations concerning which the LORD had said to the people of Israel, 'You shall not enter into marriage with them, neither shall they with you, for surely they will turn away your heart after their gods.' Solomon clung to these in love. He had 700 wives, who were princesses, and 300 concubines. And his wives turned away his heart" (1 Kings 11:1–3). Some of these wives were acquired to satisfy his political ambitions; they helped him form strategic alliances. But most of them were acquired to satisfy his sexual addiction. Solomon had the wealth and power to pursue pleasure to its limits. All the while he was following after other gods, until finally he suffered the ultimate spiritual degradation: he bowed down to blocks of wood and stone.

God punished Solomon by tearing apart his kingdom, but that was not the real tragedy. The real tragedy was not the punishment but the sin itself—the sin of breaking the first commandment. Solomon discovered to his own dismay how empty life is for those who follow other gods. Later, when he looked back on what he had done, he remarked, "I said in my heart, 'Come now, I will test you with pleasure; enjoy yourself'" (Ecclesiastes 2:1a). Then he described his royal projects: "I built houses and planted vineyards for myself. I made myself gardens and parks, and planted in them all kinds of fruit trees. I made myself pools from which to water the forest of growing trees. I bought male and female slaves, and had slaves who were born in my house. I had also great possessions of herds and flocks, more than any who had been before me in Jerusalem. I also gathered for myself silver and gold and the treasure of kings and provinces. I got singers, both men and women, and many concubines, the delight of the sons of man" (Ecclesiastes 2:4b–8). Solomon had it all.

This was Solomon's grand experiment: the pursuit of other gods. He summed it all up by saying, "Whatever my eyes desired I did not keep from them. I kept my heart from no pleasure" (Ecclesiastes 2:10a). What was the result? Was he satisfied? Did he get what he wanted? Was it worth it? No; his pursuit of power, pleasure, and prosperity led him into emptiness and despair. He said, "I considered all that my hands had done and the toil I had expended in doing it, and behold, all was vanity and a striving after wind, and there was nothing to be gained under the sun. . . . So I hated life, because what is done under the sun was grievous to me" (Ecclesiastes 2:11, 17a).

This is what happens to everyone who breaks the first commandment. In the end, of course, those who follow other gods will be judged for their sins, as Solomon was. But long before judgment there is emptiness and despair. The desire to have more and more is insatiable. But the shiny new products and exciting new experiences cannot quiet the nagging doubt. Is this all there is? Isn't there something more to life? When we break the first commandment we discover that other gods do not satisfy and cannot save. "How weak the gods of this world are," wrote Elizabeth Barrett Browning in a poem called "Idols"—"And weaker yet their worship made me!"

## Two Tests for Idolatry

The story of Solomon is a warning to everyone who has made a decision to follow God but is gradually coming under the influence of other gods. Many people assume that idolatry is a thing of the past. Who would ever bow down to a figure made of wood or stone? It sounds so primitive! But the truth is that the spirit of Solomon is alive and well today. We may not worship Ashtoreth anymore, or

Milcom, but we do worship other deities. And in many cases we serve exactly the same gods that Solomon served: money, sex, and power.

How do we identify our own private idolatries? There are two tests that we can use to determine which gods we are tempted to worship. One is *the love test*: What do we love? Back in chapter 26 we quoted Origen, the third-century theologian who observed that the first commandment has to do with what we love. Origen wrote, "What each one honors before all else, what before all things he admires and loves, this for him is God." It only makes sense: we are called to love God with all our hearts and all our minds, but if instead we give our love to someone or something else, then we are serving some other god.

So what do you love? Or to ask the same question a different way, what do you desire? When your mind is free to roam, what do you think about? How do you spend your money? What do you get excited about? A false god can be any good thing that we focus on to the exclusion of God. It could be a sport or recreation. It could be a hobby or personal interest. It could be an appetite for the finer things in life. It could be a career ambition. It could be personal health and fitness. It could even be a ministry in the church. Certainly we are allowed to enjoy the good things in life, but we must not allow them to replace God as the object of our affections.

Another test is *the trust test*: What do you trust? Where do you turn in times of trouble? Martin Luther said, "Whatever thy heart clings to and relies upon, that is properly thy God."[4] Similarly, the Puritan Thomas Watson said, "To trust in any thing more than God, is to make it a god."[5] This makes sense too. We are called to trust in God alone for our salvation, but if we put our trust in someone or something else, we are serving some other god.

So what do you trust? Some people trust their addictions. When they are in trouble—when they are lonely or discouraged—they count on drugs and alcohol or sex or shopping or some other obsession to pull them through. Other people trust things that are good in themselves but that nevertheless have a way of replacing our confidence in God. Some trust their jobs, their insurance policies, or their pension plans for their security. Some put their faith in the government and its control of the economy. Some trust their families or their social position. Some people trust science and medicine. God can use all of these things to care and provide for us, but we are to place our ultimate confidence in him alone.

The truth is that we are tempted to love and to trust many things other than God. The Puritan Matthew Henry said, "Pride makes a god of self, covetousness makes a god of money, sensuality makes a god of the belly; whatever is esteemed or loved, feared or served, delighted in or depended on, more than God, that (whatever it is) we do in effect make a god of."[6] There are many examples of this kind of reasoning in the Bible. Job said, "If I have made gold my trust or called fine gold my confidence . . . this also would be an iniquity to be punished by the judges, for I would have been false to God above" (Job 31:24, 28). The prophet Habakkuk described God's enemies as people "whose own might is their god!" (Habakkuk 1:11). The Apostle Paul was even more blunt, saying of the enemies of Christ, "Their god is their belly" (Philippians 3:19). Whether it's money, power, or even your own belly, the world is full of God substitutes and God additives—things that take the place of God in daily life. The reason we have trouble recognizing our own private idolatries is not because we don't have any false gods anymore but because we have so many!

Behind all the lesser idols we serve is the god or goddess of self, the supreme deity of these postmodern times. In his famous study of American religion, Robert Bellah recounted an interview with a woman named Sheila Larson. Sheila was the ultimate individualist. She said, "I believe in God. I'm not a religious fanatic. I can't remember the last time I went to church. My faith has carried me a long way. It's Sheilaism. Just my own little voice." Bellah comments, "This suggests the logical possibility of over 220 million American religions, one for each of us."[7] What do we love? We are infatuated with ourselves. Whom do we trust? We believe in ourselves.

Christians are as prone to this kind of false worship as anyone else. We say that we want to serve God, but we spend most of our time thinking about our own needs, plans, problems, and desires. We have discovered, as Oscar Wilde famously wrote, that to "love oneself is the beginning of a life-long romance."[8]

## No God but Christ

What can deliver us from the worship of self and all the other gods we are tempted to serve? *Rolling Stone* magazine asked this question back in December 1992. "Thou shalt not worship false idols," the editors wrote, slightly misquoting the Scripture, "but who else is there?"

The only answer is to fall passionately and deeply in love with God, specifically by trusting in his Son, Jesus Christ. The only thing that can tear our hearts away from all our other affections is true love for God. And the only thing that can replace all the other things we trust is a total faith commitment to the Lord Jesus Christ.

The Bible teaches that there is one God in three persons—Father, Son, and Holy Spirit. Jesus is God the Son, and since there is only one God, he is one with the Father (John 10:30), "God over all" (Romans 9:5). Therefore, to worship Jesus is not to worship some other god but to worship "the only Son from the Father" (John 1:14). Jesus makes the same claim on us that God has always made: "I am the Lord; that is my name; my glory I give to no other" (Isaiah 42:8); "You know no God but me, and besides me there is no savior" (Hosea 13:4b). Jesus calls us to turn away from everything else we are tempted to worship and to give glory to him alone.

It is becoming increasingly common for people to claim that there are many ways to God. Pluralism has come to America, where there are now more than six hundred non-Christian religions. With so many options, people say it doesn't really matter which religion we choose, as long as our faith is right for us. It is fine to follow Christ, but only if we recognize that he is not the only god. Even in the church there are some people who say that Jesus is *a* Savior but not *the* Savior.

This pluralistic approach to religion is a direct attack on the first commandment, in which we are commanded to worship God alone. God is as intolerant today as ever. To deny that Jesus is the only way is to say that there are other gods. But there are no other gods! This false theology must be rejected both for the honor of Christ and for the keeping of the first commandment. Jesus claims exclusive rights to our worship. He is not simply one among many prophets. He is the only way, the only truth, and the only life (John 14:6). He is the only incarnate Son of God. He alone kept the whole law for God's people, offered a perfect sacrifice for our sins, and was raised from the dead to open the way to eternal life, so he alone deserves our praise.

It is not simply our duty to worship Christ as the only God but also our privilege. He alone is our Savior and our Lord. So we make it our aim to please him in all our work and play, in all we do. We worship him and adore him; we trust him and thank him. For he says to us, "I am the Lord your God, who brought you out of your bondage to sin, out of your slavery to Satan. You shall have no other gods before me."

# 50

# The Second Commandment: The Right God, the Right Way

EXODUS 20:4–6

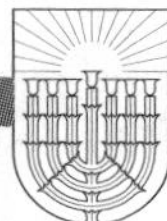

WHENEVER I HAVE A CHANCE to show Roman Catholics the interior of Tenth Presbyterian Church in Philadelphia, I ask them what's missing. "Do you notice anything strange about this sanctuary?" I ask. "Yes," they invariably reply, "there's no crucifix! Why not? Where is it?"

My standard answer is that the cross is in our message. Every week we preach that Jesus Christ was crucified for sinners. This is something that we announce from the Scriptures, but it is not something that we hang on our walls. There is an important Biblical and theological reason for this: a visual representation of Christ on the cross can easily become an object of worship and thus violate the second commandment.

## Two Different Commandments

One reason Roman Catholics have trouble accepting this is because they divide the Ten Commandments differently. According to Catholics, and also to Lutherans, Exodus 20:3–6 is a single commandment. The prohibition against making idols is part of the commandment not to have any other gods (the way they make up the difference is by dividing coveting into two commandments).

This raises an important question: Are Reformed Protestants correct in recognizing 20:4 as the beginning of a new commandment? The answer is yes. Having other gods and not making idols are two different regulations. The first commandment has to do with worshiping the right God. We must reject every false god in order to worship the true God, who alone is our Lord and Savior. The second commandment has to do with worshiping the right God in the right way. We may not worship him in the form of any man-made idol. Whereas the first commandment forbids us to worship false gods, the second commandment forbids us to worship the true God falsely. *How* we worship matters nearly as much to God as *whom* we worship. We may not worship him any way we like, but only the way that he has commanded. In the words of the *Westminster Shorter Catechism*, "The second commandment forbiddeth the worshipping of God by images, or any other way not appointed in his word" (A. 51).

A good illustration of the difference between the first and second commandments comes from the life of King Jehu. The Bible praises Jehu for eliminating Baal worship from Israel, which he did by putting the wicked Queen Jezebel to death (2 Kings 9:30–37) and by destroying the ministers of Baal (2 Kings 10:18–27). The account of Jehu's victory ends with this commendation: "Thus Jehu wiped out Baal from Israel" (2 Kings 10:28).

So far, so good. Jehu refused to worship other gods. But the Bible goes on to say, "But Jehu did not turn aside from the sins of Jeroboam the son of Nebat, which he made Israel to sin—that is, the golden calves that were in Bethel and in Dan" (2 Kings 10:29). If Jehu got rid of Baal worship, then what were these sacred cows still doing in Israel? The answer is that although Jehu enforced the first commandment, he allowed his people to break the second commandment. The golden calves did not represent other gods; they were intended to represent the God of Israel. But this is precisely what the second commandment forbids: worshiping God with an idol. Whereas the first commandment forbids false gods, the second forbids false worship.

## Idolatry Explained

The second commandment is one of the longest: "You shall not make for yourself a carved image, or any likeness of anything that is in heaven above, or that is in the earth beneath, or that is in the water under the earth. You shall not bow down to them or serve them, for I the Lord your God am a jealous God, visiting the iniquity of the fathers on the children to the third and the fourth generation of those who hate me, but showing steadfast love to thousands of those who love me and keep my commandments" (20:4–6).

There are four parts to this commandment: the rule, the reason, the warning, and the promise. *The rule* is very simple: "Don't make any carved images" (v. 4a; see also Leviticus 26:1). This translation comes close to the original meaning. An idol was something crafted by a tool. Whether it was carved out of wood, chiseled out of stone, or engraved in metal, it was cut and shaped by human hands. It was a man-made representation of some divine being.

This did not mean that the Israelites were forbidden to use tools. Nor did it mean that they were not allowed to produce artwork. Later, when it was time to build the tabernacle, God sent the Israelites his Spirit "to devise artistic designs, to work in gold, silver, and bronze, in cutting stones for setting, and in carving wood, to work in every craft" (31:4, 5). So what the second commandment ruled out was not making things, but making things to serve as objects of worship. This is clarified in the second part of the rule: "You shall not bow down to them or serve them" (20:5a). The Israelites were strictly forbidden to make images of God to use in worship. Although God appreciates artistry, he will not tolerate idolatry.

This rule is clarified with a list of the kinds of idols God forbids: "You shall not make for yourself a carved image, or any likeness of anything that is in heaven above, or that is in the earth beneath, or that is in the water under the earth" (20:4). That pretty much covers it: nothing in the sky, nothing on the ground, and nothing in the sea! In other words, the Israelites were not allowed to represent God in the form of anything in all creation. Remember that the Israelites had been living with the Egyptians, who worshiped many gods, nearly all of which they represented in the form of animals. The god Horus had the head of a falcon, the god Anubis had the head of a jackal, and so on. When it came to the Egyptians and their idols, any animal was fair game! But the God of Israel refused to be represented in the image of any of his creatures.

There are many good reasons for this rule, but the one God specifically mentions is his love: "You shall not make for yourself a carved image . . . for I the LORD your God am a jealous God" (20:4a, 5b). This is *the reason* for the rule. God forbids idolatry because of his jealousy. To use a more positive and also a more accurate word, it is because of his zeal—the burning passion of his love.

Jealousy doesn't get much positive publicity these days. When people talk about it they generally mean something more like envy, the desire to get something that does not belong to you. However, when something really does belong to you, there are times when it needs to be protected. A holy jealousy is one that guards someone's rightful possession. The most obvious example is the love between a husband and wife. No husband who truly loves his wife could possibly endure seeing her in the arms of another man. It would make him intensely jealous, and rightly so!

God feels the same way about his people. His commitment to us is total. His love is exclusive, passionate, intense—in a word, jealous. As one commentator explains, "Godly jealousy is not the insecure, insane, and possessive human jealousy that we often interpret this word to mean. Rather, it is an intensely caring devotion to the objects of His love, like a mother's jealous protection of her children, a father's jealous guarding of his home."[1]

If this is what jealousy means, then God *has* to be jealous. He loves us too much not to be! In fact, jealousy is one of his divine perfections. As Christopher Wright has written:

> A God who was not jealous . . . would be as contemptible as a husband who didn't care whether or not his wife was faithful to him. Part of our

> problem with this profound covenantal reality is that we have come to regard religion, like everything else, as a matter of 'consumer choice.' . . . We resent monopolies. But the unique and incomparable, only living God makes necessarily exclusive claims and has the right to a monopoly on our love. . . . Jealousy is God's love protecting itself.[2]

What God so jealously protects in the second commandment is the honor of his love. God not only loves us, but he also wants us to love him in return. Among other things, this means worshiping him in a way that is worthy of his honor. God has the right to tell us how he wants to be worshiped, and he has commanded us not to spurn his love by turning him into an idol.

## The Sins of the Fathers

God's jealousy explains why the second commandment ends with a warning ("visiting the iniquity of the fathers on the children to the third and the fourth generation of those who hate me," 20:5b) and a promise ("but showing steadfast love to thousands of those who love me and keep my commandments," 20:6). God shows his zeal to be glorified in our worship by cursing those who break the second commandment and blessing those who keep it.

*The warning* is that children will be punished for the sins of their fathers. The word for "iniquity" refers to something twisted. It suggests that idolatry is a kind of perversion, a turning against God. It may seem very religious to worship idols, but since God hates idolatry (Deuteronomy 16:22), it is really a way of showing hatred for him, and it is not at all surprising that God threatens to punish those who do such a hateful thing. What some people wonder, however, is whether God's curse is just. How can God judge a person for someone else's sin? Is it really fair to punish children for the sins of their fathers?

Many scholars do not think it is fair, so they try to find some other way to explain this verse. Some interpret it sociologically. They point out that a father's sin has consequences that can last for generations. They also point out that because children imitate their parents, sin tends to run in the family. One generation sets the spiritual tone for the next. So perhaps the second commandment is based on universal truths about family relationships.

The commandment says something more, however. It says that God punishes children for the sin of their fathers. What a father passes on to his children is not simply a bad example but the guilt of his sin. The principle here is covenant solidarity: God holds families responsible for their conduct as families. The Israelites were in covenant with God, and when the covenant head of any family sinned against God, his whole family was judged. To give just one example, all seventy of Ahab's sons were killed for their father's idolatry (2 Kings 10:1–17).

This is not to deny individual responsibility. God holds each one of us accountable for our own sin. The Bible says, "The soul who sins shall die. The son shall not suffer for the iniquity of the father, nor the father suffer for the iniquity of the son" (Ezekiel 18:20a). God never condemns the innocent but only the guilty. Here it is important to notice something in the second commandment that is often overlooked—namely, how the threat ends. God says that he will punish three or four generations "of those who hate me" (20:5). It is not only the fathers who hate God but also their children. People who struggle with the fairness of this commandment usually assume that although the father is guilty, his children are innocent. But the children hate God as much as their father did (which, given the way they were raised, is not surprising). Therefore, it is fair and just for God to punish them for their sin and for their father's sin.

God also promises to show mercy to those who love him and keep his commandment not to serve idols. *The promise* is more powerful than the warning because its blessing lasts not just for three or four generations but for a thousand; in other words, it will last forever. This was God's promise going all the way back to Abraham: "I will establish my covenant between me and you and your offspring after you throughout their generations for an everlasting covenant, to be God to you and to your offspring after you" (Genesis 17:7). All we have to do is respond to the God who loves us by loving him in return.

God's threat in the second commandment may seem discouraging to someone who comes from a family that does not honor God, but God's blessing triumphs over God's curse, and God often intervenes in the history of a family to turn their hatred into love and worship. He does what he did for Abraham: He calls a family to leave its idols behind and follow him. And when God does this, he establishes a lasting legacy. His grace rests on a family from one generation to the next. This is not some kind of automatic guarantee, because children are free to turn away from the God of their fathers and mothers. But it is a promise to receive by faith.

What is God doing in your family? As parents plan for the future, they should be more concerned about the second commandment than they are about their financial portfolio. This commandment contains a solemn warning for fathers. When a man refuses to love God passionately and to worship God properly, the consequences of his sin will last for generations. The guilt of a man who treasures idols in his heart will corrupt his entire family, and in the end they will all be punished. But a man who loves God supremely—a man who bows before him in genuine worship and serves him with true praise—will see the blessing of God rest on his household forever. What kind of life are you leading? What kind of worship are you giving? What kind of legacy will you leave?

## Idolatry Illustrated

There is a story in the Bible that shows what's wrong with idols. It is set in Athens—the story of Paul and the philosophers. Athens was a great city in those days, the intellectual capital of the world. High on the Acropolis stood the Parthenon, the showpiece of Greek architecture. The streets bustled with commerce. There was also a great deal of traffic in the marketplace of ideas. As the Scripture reports, "All the Athenians and the foreigners who lived there would spend their time in nothing except telling or hearing something new" (Acts 17:21).

Athens was also full of idols. There were images of all shapes and sizes, made of wood and stone, gold and silver. They represented all the gods and goddesses in the Greek pantheon. There were so many idols that one Roman writer joked that it was easier to find a god in Athens than a man![3] And towering over them all was the great goddess Athena, whose statue could be seen forty miles away.[4] Athens held perhaps the most spectacular display of idols that the world has ever seen.

When the Apostle Paul saw all these graven images, he was provoked almost to anger. The Bible says that "his spirit was provoked within him as he saw that the city was full of idols" (Acts 17:16). He was disheartened and dismayed to see so many people worshiping so many idols and thus denying God his glory. For days he reasoned with the Athenians, trying to persuade them to turn away from all their false gods in order to worship the one and only true and living God. He preached the gospel, the good news about Jesus and the resurrection.

Eventually Paul came into contact with members of the Areopagus, the famous philosophical society that met on Mars Hill. These men were the censors who controlled the religious lectures given in Athens. Their society also served as a kind of think tank, something like the Brookings Institution or the American Enterprise Institute. The Areopagus included some of the most learned men of the ancient world, men who loved to argue about philosophy and religion. Wanting to learn more about what Paul was saying, they invited him to address their assembly.

One might have expected Paul to tell the philosophers that they were worshiping the wrong gods. All of their idols represented false deities; so he might have said, "You shall have no other gods," addressing them on the basis of the first commandment. This is not what Paul said, however. It was one of the implications of what he said, but it is not where he placed his emphasis. Instead, he addressed them on the basis of the *second* commandment. He told them that God cannot be worshiped by way of idols. Their problem was not simply that they were serving the wrong gods, but that they were worshiping the wrong way altogether.

Paul began by establishing a point of contact. He stood up and said, "Men of Athens, I perceive that in every way you are very religious. For as I passed along and observed the objects of your worship, I found also an altar with this inscription, 'To the unknown god.' What therefore you worship as unknown, this I proclaim to you" (Acts 17:22b, 23). This was a clever rhetorical strategy. By making an idol to an unknown god, the Athenians were trying to cover all their bases. But they were also admitting that there was at least one thing about religion that they didn't know. So the apostle told them that he was there to explain it.

Next Paul said that the Creator God is a living spirit who cannot be put in a box: "The God who made the world and everything in it, being Lord of heaven and earth, does not live in temples made by man, nor is he served by human hands, as though he needed anything, since he himself gives to all mankind life and breath and everything" (Acts 17:24, 25). Paul was clarifying the relationship between the Creator and the creature. We do not make God; he made us. We do not give life to God; he gives life to us. To strengthen this point, Paul proceeded to quote from one of their own Greek poets, who said, "For we are indeed his offspring" (Acts 17:28b).

This brief doctrine of God had one very obvious implication. If God is the Creator and Giver of Life, then he cannot be squeezed into some man-made idol. How could the transcendent God possibly be reduced to a mere object? Hence Paul's conclusion: "Being then God's offspring, we ought not to think that the divine being is like gold or silver or stone, an image formed by the art and imagination of man. The times of ignorance God overlooked, but now he commands all people everywhere to repent" (Acts 17:29, 30). Paul was saying something very important about the second commandment. He was saying that when we use idols, we are not worshiping the true God but are constructing a false god—a god made in our own image. As Paul later explained to the Romans, "They exchanged the truth about God for a lie and worshiped and served the creature rather than the Creator" (Romans 1:25).

This was the problem with idolatry all along: It created a false image of God that was inadequate to his deity and unworthy of his majesty. God is infinite and invisible. He is omnipotent and omnipresent. He is a living spirit. Therefore, to carve him into a piece of wood or stone is to deny his attributes, the essential characteristics of his divine being. An idol makes the infinite God finite, the invisible God visible, the omnipotent God impotent, the all-present God local, the living God dead, and the spiritual God material. In short, it makes him the exact opposite of what he actually is. Thus the whole idea of idolatry rests on the absurdity of human beings trying to make their own image of God. An idol is not the truth but a lie. It is a god who cannot see, know, act, love, or save.

## Idolatry Applied

It is tempting to think of idol worship as a thing of the past. Unless we go overseas to serve as missionaries, the only place we are likely to see traditional idols is in a museum. We certainly don't have any idols in the church, do we?

Maybe not, if an idol is only something we can see and touch. But like the rest of God's law, the second commandment is spiritual: It applies to the heart. And in our hearts we are always busy fashioning God in our image. John Calvin said the human heart is "a perpetual factory of idols."[5] Rather than worshiping God "in spirit and truth" (John 4:24), we reshape and remake him until he is safely under our control. What are some of the ways we manufacture our own gods?

We make an idol whenever we worship an image rather than listening to the Word. One of the problems with physical images of God is that they keep us from hearing God's voice. This is why God did not reveal himself in a physical form on Mount Sinai. Moses said to the Israelites, "Since you saw no form on the day that the Lord spoke to you at Horeb out of the midst of the fire, beware lest you act corruptly by making a carved image for yourselves" (Deuteronomy 4:15, 16a). The way God revealed himself at Mount Sinai was not through a visible image but through an audible word. This tells us something about the way he wants to be worshiped. He does not want us to look but to listen. Nahum Sarna comments:

> In the Israelite view any symbolic representation of God must necessarily be both inadequate and a distortion, for an image becomes identified with what it represents and is soon looked upon as the place and presence of the Deity. In the end the image itself will become the locus of reverence and an object of worship, all of which constitutes the complete nullification of the singular essence of Israelite monotheism.[6]

We are living in a visual age. Everywhere we go we see images flickering across the screen. Some Christian leaders say that the church needs to adapt by becoming more visual in its presentation of the gospel. Instead of simply talking about God, we need to show people something. But this impulse is idolatrous. In his influential book *Amusing Ourselves to Death*, Neil Postman writes:

> In studying the Bible as a young man, I found intimations of the idea that forms of media favor particular kinds of content and therefore are capable of taking command of a culture. I refer specifically to the Decalogue, the Second Commandment of which prohibits the Israelites from making concrete images of anything. . . . The God of the Jews was to exist in the Word and through the Word, an unprecedented conception requiring the highest order of abstract thinking. Iconography thus became blasphemy so that a new kind of God could enter a culture. People like ourselves who are in the process of converting their culture from word-centered to image-centered might profit by reflecting on this Mosaic injunction.[7]

Indeed. What the image always wants to do in worship is to distract us from hearing the Word. The crucifix, the icon, the drama, and the dance—these things are not aids to worship but make true worship all but impossible. In a visual age we need to be all the more careful not to look at the image but to listen to the Word.

We also make an idol whenever we turn God into something that we can manipulate. This was the whole point of pagan idolatry. The Egyptians did not think that the gods actually lived in their idols, but they did think that idols gave them the kind of spiritual contact that would enable them to control their gods. So much contemporary spirituality tries to do the same thing. People are always looking for a more user-friendly god, a god who can be adapted to suit their purposes. They say, "If I do this, then God will do that." If I touch the minister, then I will be healed. If I fulfill my vow, then God will make me rich. If I say the right prayer every day, I will have the key to unlock God's blessing. If I follow the right parenting method, then my kids will grow up to be godly. As long as we approach God the right way, we will get what we want. But God will not be manipulated. When he commands us not to make idols, he is saying he "will not be captured, contained, assigned or managed by anyone or anything, for any purpose."[8] God wants us to trust him and obey him, not use him.

We also make an idol whenever we choose to worship God for some of his attributes but not others. The old liberal church wanted a God of love without justice, so they denied fundamental doctrines like the wrath of God and the substitutionary atonement. Now many evangelicals are downplaying the same doctrines. Nearly half of the students at evangelical colleges and seminaries say that talking about divine judgment is bad manners.[9] Feminist theologians deny the fatherhood of God. They prefer a god more in the image of woman. Open theists deny the foreknowledge of God. Although they say that God knows some things about the future, since he does not know what human beings will decide to do, he does not know everything. In effect these theologians are advocating a deity who thinks more the way they do, a god who is trying to figure things out as he goes along. But all these new theologies are really forms of idolatry. When people say, "I like to think of God as . . ." they are usually remaking God in their image.

We too are tempted to worship God the way we want him to be rather than the way he actually is. We tend to emphasize the things about God that we like and minimize the rest. We place a higher priority on knowing the Bible than on loving God. We think that God is more concerned with private morality than with social justice. And since we are legalists at heart, we are motivated more by a sense of duty than by a deep gratitude for God's grace. When we do all this, we end up with a deity without the love, compassion, or grace of God.

How can we worship God the right way? What can save us from our own private idolatries? The answer is very simple: Rather than remaking God into *our* image, we need to be remade into *his* image. God does this by bringing us into a personal, saving relationship with his Son Jesus Christ.

Here is a deep mystery. When God first created the world, he made men and women in his image (Genesis 1:26, 27). We were made to be like God, to reflect his glory. And this is another reason why God tells us not to make images. He already has an image! *We* are God's image. As Calvin said, "God cannot be represented by a picture or sculpture, since He has intended His likeness to appear in us."[10] Or as Christopher Wright has written: "The only legitimate image of God . . . is the image of God created in his own likeness—the living, thinking, working, speaking, breathing, relating human being (not even a statue will do, but only the human person)."[11] We are not allowed to make God's image but only to *be* God's image.

Our ability to do this was badly damaged by our fall into sin. The image of God in us has been defaced, like so much graffiti on a mirror. In our fallen and sinful condition, we are no longer able to reflect God's glory as he intended. But God has sent his Son Jesus Christ into the world to repair his image in us. Jesus is the true image, "the image of the invisible God" (Colossians 1:15; cf. 2 Corinthians 4:4), "the exact imprint of his nature" (Hebrews 1:3). This is why Jesus could say that anyone who sees him has seen God (John 14:9). He is the point of contact. In order to come to God in true worship, we don't need to make some kind of idol; all we need to do is come to him through Jesus Christ. And when we come to Christ, then God lives in us by his Holy Spirit. He works in us to repair his image, so that we can live for his glory.

# 51

# The Third Commandment: Name above All Names

EXODUS 20:7

ONE OF THE FIRST DUTIES OF PARENTS is to name their children. This can be a difficult task. The parents make lists. They read baby name books and field suggestions from family members. They try various combinations and say them out loud to see how they sound. They consider all the possible nicknames, and then they check to see what the initials spell. Even after all this, they may still end up at the hospital not having reached agreement about what to call the child!

The one thing that is certain in all of this is that the parents will do the naming. Human beings do not name themselves. Our full names are given, not chosen, which shows that naming is an act of authority. I remember holding each of my newborn children in my arms, calling them by name, and telling them that I was their daddy. Naming a child is the first way that parents exercise their God-given authority.

By contrast, one of the remarkable things about God is that no one ever named him. Admittedly, from time to time people have come up with various false names for God. But God's true name is chosen and revealed by God himself. We do not tell God who he is; he tells us. God has his own naming rights, and this is a sign of his sovereign authority. God's name comes before all other names.

## What's in a Name?

The third commandment defends the honor of God's great name: "You shall not take the name of the Lord your God in vain, for the Lord will not hold him guiltless who takes his name in vain" (20:7). Unlike the first two commandments, here God refers to himself in the third person. There is a special reason for this.

First God said, "You shall have no other gods before me" (20:3), speaking in the first person. But here he refers to himself more indirectly. Rather than saying, "You shall not misuse my name," he says, "You shall not take the name of the LORD your God in vain." He does this to call attention to his special covenant name *Yahweh*, or Lord.

This was a name God revealed long before the Israelites even reached Mount Sinai. Back at the burning bush Moses asked for God's name, and because of his great love for his people, God gave it to him:

> God said to Moses, "I AM WHO I AM." And he said, "Say this to the people of Israel, 'I AM has sent me to you.'" God also said to Moses, "Say this to the people of Israel, 'The LORD, the God of your fathers, the God of Abraham, the God of Isaac, and the God of Jacob, has sent me to you.' This is my name forever, and thus I am to be remembered throughout all generations." (3:14, 15)

The name that God revealed was his personal name *Yahweh*, sometimes called the *tetragrammaton* because in Hebrew it consists of four letters: YHWH. Literally God's name means "I am who I am" or "I will be who I will be." It speaks of God's self-existence, self-sufficiency, and supreme sovereignty. As the events of the exodus unfolded, it also testified to his saving power. The Israelites learned from their deliverance that the God who revealed his name to Moses is a God who saves.

As we start unpacking the meaning of God's name, it quickly becomes obvious that *Yahweh*, or "LORD," is much more than a name. It is God's identity. This was the whole Hebrew understanding of names. For us a name is a label; it is something we have, not something we are. But for the Hebrews the name was inseparable from the person. It expressed a person's inward identity. When we use the name of God, therefore, we are referring to the essence of his divine being.

His supreme name was simply *Yahweh*, the Lord God. This name is much more than a convenient way to address God. It represents God's entire reputation. The literary term for this manner of speech, in which one part stands for the whole, is *synecdoche*. For example, when someone says, "There were a lot of new faces at the meeting," this does not imply that their faces were somehow disconnected from the rest of their bodies. A face is part of a whole, and thus it can stand for the entire person. Similarly, God's name represents his whole identity.

God's name is used this way elsewhere in the Old Testament. David sang, "O LORD, our Lord, how majestic is your name in all the earth!" (Psalm 8:1a). He was praising God not simply for his name, but for being the God who made all things for his own glory. God has made a name for himself in creation, and also in redemption. This was the whole point of the exodus. God was saving a people for his glory. Or as the psalmist put it, referring specifically to the rescue at the Red Sea, "he saved them for his name's sake, that he might make known his mighty power" (Psalm 106:8; cf. Psalm 111:9). God brought Israel out of Egypt for the honor of his name. Therefore, by the time the Israelites reached Mount Sinai, they should have known that God's name was much more than a name. It communicated God's glory in creation and redemption, and thus it deserved as much reverence and respect as God himself.

## Misusing God's Name

Like the rest of God's moral law, the third commandment is both negative and positive. In its negative form it forbids the misuse of God's name. To quote the old King James Version, "Thou shalt not take the name of the LORD thy God in vain." Or to give a more literal translation, "You shall not lift up the name of the Lord your God for nothingness."[1]

What does it mean to "lift up" God's name? This term had a fairly technical meaning. It was used in legal situations to refer to the taking of an oath.[2] When witnesses needed to confirm their testimony, instead of swearing on a Bible, they lifted a hand and swore by God's name. However, the term was also used more broadly for other situations when people took God's name on their lips. His name was "lifted up" in worship and whenever else people talked about him.

God's people were not forbidden to use God's name. Many orthodox Jews take this commandment more strictly than God intended, refusing to use God's special divine name at all, for fear of misusing it. But God *wants* us to use his name! This is proven by the Old Testament, where God's sacred divine name is used all over the place—almost 7,000 occurrences in all. God gave us his name so that we would be able to address him personally. Calling him by name strengthens our love relationship with him.

What God forbids is not the use of his name, then, but its *mis*use. To be specific, we are not to use it in a vain or empty way. The specific misuse that God has in mind is speaking about him carelessly, thoughtlessly, or even flippantly, as if he didn't matter or really didn't exist at all. God's name has deep spiritual significance. So to treat it like something worthless is profanity in the truest sense of the word: It is to treat something holy and sacred as common and secular. To dishonor God's name in any way is to denigrate his holiness. It is a way of saying that God himself is worthless.

In his careful study of the Ten Commandments, the Dutch scholar Jochem Douma mentions three ways that God's name was commonly profaned in Old Testament times: in sorcery, in false prophecy, and in the taking of false oaths.[3]

Sorcery has to do with the occult. In the ancient world many people believed they could gain access to supernatural power by using divine names in magical incantations. They called upon their gods to heal their bodies, to tell the future, and to give them victory in battle. The Egyptians specialized in this kind of thing. But God refuses to be manipulated, so he commanded his people not to use his name for the casting of spells. Later he said, "There shall not be found among you anyone who . . . practices divination or tells fortunes or interprets omens, or a sorcerer or a charmer or a medium or a necromancer or one who inquires of the dead, for whoever does these things is an abomination to the LORD" (Deuteronomy 18:10–12a).

God's name was also misused in connection with false prophecy. The prophets always said, "Thus saith the Lord." However, when a false prophet tried to quote God this way, it was a lie and therefore an abuse of God's holy name. As God said on one occasion, "The prophets are prophesying lies in my name. . . . Therefore thus says the LORD concerning the prophets who prophesy in my name although I did not send them . . ." (Jeremiah 14:14a, 15a). False prophecy was an attempt to use God's special divine name to advance a prophet's own agenda. There are many examples of this from church history. People often try to boost their own credibility by claiming that God is on their side. His name has been used to endorse everything from the Crusades to the slave trade, from political parties to social causes, and the results are almost always disastrous.

The third common misuse of God's name was in swearing false oaths. To persuade others that they were telling the truth—in court, for example, or in connection with a business deal—people often said something like, "As the LORD lives" (Jeremiah 5:2). By lifting up God's name they were trying to prove that what they were saying was true. In effect they were calling God as their witness. The problem came when people took an oath in God's name and then proceeded to lie. This was perjury—a direct violation of the third commandment. It was using God's name to confirm what was false rather than what was true. So God said, "You shall not swear by my name falsely, and so profane the name of your God: I am the LORD" (Leviticus 19:12).

These are some of the ways that God's sacred name was misused in Old Testament times. In each case people tried to use his name for their own advantage. But God said, "You shall not take the name of the LORD your God in vain" (20:7a).

He also said that anyone who breaks the third commandment will be held accountable: "The LORD will not hold him guiltless who takes his name in vain" (20:7b). The precise punishment is left unspecified. In fact, the threat seems almost understated: The lawbreaker simply is said not to be without guilt. However, this expression is what grammarians call a *meiosis*, in which less is said, but much more is intended.[4] For example, when people in authority say, "I wouldn't do that if I were you," they are not simply offering a casual opinion but are issuing a stern warning. So when God says that he will not hold us guiltless, what he means is that he will condemn us. We will not be innocent but guilty—reckoned unrighteous by Almighty God.

The reason God will condemn us is because misusing his name is a very great sin. It is a direct attack on his honor and glory, and anyone who makes such an attack deserves to be condemned. Here God's justice can be defended by means of an analogy:

> One way for a modern American to begin to understand this commandment is to treat God's name as a trademarked property. In order to gain widespread distribution for His copyrighted repair manual—the Bible—and also to capture greater market share for His authorized franchise—the Church—God has graciously licensed the use of His name to anyone who will use it according to His written instructions. It needs to be understood, however, that God's name has not been released into the public domain. God retains legal control over His name and threatens serious penalties against the unauthorized misuse of this supremely valuable property. All trademark violations will be prosecuted to the full limits of the law. The prosecutor, judge, jury, and enforcer is God.[5]

When people break the third or any other commandment, they are guilty before God, and ultimately they will be judged for their sins. There are many examples in the Bible. Perhaps the most shocking occurs in Leviticus 24. A dispute broke out between two Israelites, one of whom was part Egyptian. As they fought, the man of mixed descent blurted out a curse against God. The Scripture says that he "blasphemed the Name, and cursed" (Leviticus 24:11a). The bystanders were appalled at what the man said, so they seized him and brought him to stand trial before Moses.

The Lord did not hold the man guiltless but said, "Bring out of the camp the one who cursed, and let all who heard him lay their hands on his head, and let all the congregation stone him. And speak to the people of Israel, saying, Whoever curses his God shall bear his sin. Whoever blasphemes the name of the Lord shall surely be put to death" (Leviticus 24:13–16a). When God says that anyone who misuses his name will be held responsible, we should take him at his word!

## His Name Is Wonderful

Like the rest of the moral law, the third commandment is positive as well as negative. At the same time that it forbids the misuse of God's name, threatening us with guilt, it also commands us to use his name properly. Instead of taking his name in vain, we should take it in all seriousness. According to John Calvin:

> The purpose of this commandment is: God wills that we hallow the majesty of his name. Therefore, it means in brief that we are not to profane his name by treating it contemptuously and irreverently. To this prohibition duly corresponds the commandment that we should be zealous and careful to honor his name with godly reverence. Therefore we ought to be so disposed in mind and speech that we neither think nor say anything concern-

> ing God and his mysteries, without reverence and much soberness; that in estimating his works we conceive nothing but what is honorable to him.[6]

Calvin's use of the word "hallow" brings to mind the first petition of the Lord's prayer: "hallowed be your name" (Matthew 6:9b). To hallow is to consecrate, to set apart for a sacred purpose. And this is what God wants us to do with his name: to preserve it for the purpose of worship and praise.

There are many ways to use God's name properly. His name can be praised, honored, blessed, and celebrated. It can be lifted on high and exalted. It can be worshiped and adored. To honor God's name, wrote Martin Luther, is to "use that very name in every time of need to call on, pray to, praise, and give thanks to God."[7] But one of the best places to learn the proper use of God's name is the book of Psalms. Many of the Biblical psalms show us how to honor God's name: "Ascribe to the LORD the glory due his name" (Psalm 29:2a; Psalm 96:8a); "Sing the glory of his name; give to him glorious praise!" (Psalm 66:2); "Blessed be his glorious name forever" (Psalm 72:19a); "Bless the LORD, O my soul, and all that is within me, bless his holy name!" (Psalm 103:1). Elsewhere the Bible instructs us to "call upon the name of the LORD" (Genesis 4:26), to prophesy in the name of the Lord (Deuteronomy 18:19), to "trust in the name of the LORD" (Isaiah 50:10), and in every way to "fear this glorious and awesome name, the LORD your God" (Deuteronomy 28:58).

By telling us to honor God's name, the third commandment helps us honor God himself, giving him the same reverence and respect that we give to his holy name. The Apostle Paul gave perhaps the fullest, most positive statement of this command in his letter to the Colossians: "And whatever you do, in word or deed, do everything in the name of the Lord Jesus, giving thanks to God the Father through him" (Colossians 3:17).

## A Terrible Beating

Mentioning "the name of the Lord Jesus" brings to mind a Bible story about breaking and keeping the third commandment. It is the story of the seven sons of Sceva, whom the Apostle Paul met on his first mission to Ephesus. It had been an extraordinary visit. Shortly after arriving, Paul baptized some of the Ephesians, and they received the Holy Spirit. He then spent three months in the synagogue, arguing with the Jews about the kingdom of God. After this he preached to the Greeks daily for two years at the public lecture hall. During these years he performed many signs and wonders: "And God was doing extraordinary miracles by the hands of Paul, so that even handkerchiefs or aprons that had touched his skin were carried away to the sick, and their diseases left them and the evil spirits came out of them" (Acts 19:11, 12).

Now there was one group of men who were watching Paul's ministry very carefully, and they noticed that whenever he performed a miracle, he always did it in the name of Jesus. Paul did everything in Jesus' name. Baptizing, preaching, healing—it was all in the name of Jesus. Eventually they realized that there was something powerful about this name, and they reasoned that if this fellow Paul could use it, they could use it too. They wanted to use the name of Jesus Christ—the very name of God—to work their own wonders. However, things didn't work out quite the way they had hoped:

> Then some of the itinerant Jewish exorcists undertook to invoke the name of the Lord Jesus over those who had evil spirits, saying, "I adjure you by the Jesus whom Paul proclaims." Seven sons of a Jewish high priest named Sceva were doing this. But the evil spirit answered them, "Jesus I know, and Paul I recognize, but who are you?" And the man in whom was the evil spirit leaped on them, mastered all of them and overpowered them, so that they fled out of that house naked and wounded. (Acts 19:13–16)

To understand this story, all we need to know is the third commandment, which says, "You shall not take the name of the LORD your God in vain, for the LORD will not hold him guiltless who takes his name in vain" (20:7). The seven sons of Sceva misused God's name, employing it to perform magic tricks for their own personal advantage. And God did not hold them guiltless but allowed them to get the beating they deserved.

Perhaps the most significant part of the story is what happened next: "And this became known to all the residents of Ephesus, both Jews and Greeks. And fear fell upon them all, and the name of the Lord Jesus was extolled" (Acts 19:17). God preserved the honor of his name. By refusing to allow anyone to manipulate him, God demonstrated his supreme and sovereign authority. He showed that he was nothing like the pagan gods, who could be controlled. He alone would decide when to perform a miracle, and he would only do it through his chosen servants.

What happened to the seven sons of Sceva only served to enhance God's reputation. The Ephesians understood what it meant: Jesus Christ was Lord over every other god; his was the name above all names. They also saw how dangerous it was to dabble in the occult: "Also many of those who were now believers came, confessing and divulging their practices. And a number of those who had practiced magic arts brought their books together and burned them in the sight of all. And they counted the value of them and found it came to fifty thousand pieces of silver" (Acts 19:18, 19). The story ends with this thrilling conclusion: "So the word of the Lord continued to increase and prevail mightily" (Acts 19:20). When God's name is honored, his kingdom grows.

## For the Honor of His Name

As the story shows, there is a clear connection between honoring God's name and spreading the gospel. When the name of Jesus Christ is lifted up and exalted, people come to him for their salvation. Therefore, keeping the third commandment is doubly important. Not only is it the lawful thing to do, but when we do it, sinners believe and are saved. The application is obvious: as servants of the Lord Jesus Christ, we should do everything we can to honor God's name.

Since we are Christians, we bear the very name of Christ. It was by calling on his name that we were saved in the first place (Acts 4:12; Romans 10:13; 1 John 5:13). We received his name upon entering the church, when we were baptized "in the name of the Father and of the Son and of the Holy Spirit" (Matthew 28:19). Since we always carry the name of Christ, God has a personal stake in our ongoing spiritual progress. The Bible says, "You were washed, you were sanctified, you were justified in the name of the Lord Jesus Christ" (1 Corinthians 6:11). Now the very name of Christ is associated with everything we do. Our reputation is a reflection on his reputation, so we should always make it our aim to honor his name.

We must confess that we are sometimes tempted to dishonor God's name. The most obvious temptation is to use it as a swear word. This is what people usually think the third commandment is mainly about. Today many people call down divine damnation on whatever (or whoever) happens to be a source of frustration. Or they use the name Jesus Christ as a kind of exclamation point. All of the bad language on television and at the movies shows how godless our culture has become. But it also shows that we can never get away from God. People can't seem to swear without using God's name. Why is this? What does it tell us about the human condition? I think it proves the existence of God. Like everything else people say, cursing comes from the heart. When non-Christians use God's name—even in vain—it shows that deep down they know there really is a God. Their rage is direct rebellion against his honor.

As Christians, we need to watch our language. Most Christians try not to curse—at least not out loud (or at least not when anyone else is listening)—but it is not uncommon for churchgoing people to use mild oaths: "Gosh darn it!" "Oh, my God!" "What the heck?" "Good Lord!" "I swear to God." Some people think these are manners of expression, but they are really just a more polite way to swear. They may also be a better indication of our true spiritual condition than what we say in church.

We also have a responsibility to remind others to watch their language. There are good and gracious ways to do this. In his book on the Ten Commandments, Rob Schenck tells how he confronted two men for breaking the third commandment:

> Some years ago, after a long speaking itinerary in the midwest, I boarded a late-night flight to return home. I was tired and looking forward to a rest. Sitting behind me in the airplane were two salesman whose conversation was peppered with profanity. I had finally had it when they began running

> the Lord's name into the gutter. I raised myself up from my seat and turned around so that I was looking down on them from my perch. Then I asked, "Are either of you in the ministry?"
>
> The one in the aisle seat raised his eyebrows incredulously and said, "What the . . . would ever make you think that?"
>
> "Well, I am in the ministry," I said with a smile. "And I am amazed at your communication skills. You just said God, damn, hell, and Jesus Christ in one sentence. I can't get all of that into a whole sermon!" They both blushed, and I didn't hear another word from them for the remainder of the flight![8]

God's Spirit can use this kind of godly response to convict someone who swears of how sinful it is to take God's name in vain.

A more serious way to break the third commandment is by using God's name to advance our own agenda. Some Christians say, "The Lord told me to do this." Or worse, they say, "The Lord told me to tell *you* to do this." This is false prophecy! God has already said whatever he needs to say to us in his Word. Of course, there is also an inward leading of the Holy Spirit. But this is only an inward leading, and it should not be misrepresented as an authoritative word from God.

Most Christians don't actually claim to hear God's voice. What we are often tempted to do, however, is to misinterpret Scripture for our own purposes. How easy it is to take one idea from Scripture—or even one verse—lift it out of context, and then use it to support our own personal opinions. We become so certain that God is on our side that we refuse to listen to other believers or to submit to spiritual authority in the church.

Sometimes we use God to endorse our political views, so that he becomes a sort of party mascot. Sometimes we use him to prop up our position so that other people will have to do what we say. Sometimes we fix his stamp of approval to our ministry or to our plans for the church. But whenever we confuse what we want with what God wants, we take his name in vain. Stephen Carter makes this point in a book on the role of religion in public life, a book suitably called *God's Name in Vain*:

> In truth, there is probably no country in the Western world where people use God's name quite as much, or quite as publicly, or for quite as many purposes, as we Americans do—the Third Commandment notwithstanding. Few candidates for office are able to end their speeches without asking God to bless their audience, or the nation, or the great work we are undertaking, but everybody is sure that the other side is insincere. . . . Athletes thank God, often on television, after scoring the winning touchdown, because, like politicians, they like to think God is on their side. Churches erect huge billboards and take out ads in the paper. . . . God's will is cited as a reason to be against gay rights. And a reason to be for them. God is said

> not to tolerate poverty. Or abortion. Or nuclear weapons. . . . Everybody who wants to change America, and everybody who wants not to, understands the nation's love affair with God's name, which is why everybody invokes it.[9]

There are many other ways to take God's name in vain. We do it when we say, "Praise the Lord!" or use some other Christian cliché without really meaning it. We do it when we slap God's name on a T-shirt or bumper sticker or use it as a slogan to boost sales. We do it when we use his Word to make jokes or when we write Christian songs with trite lyrics.

These are all serious violations of the third commandment, but the subtlest and perhaps most common way we break it is by being careless in our worship. As we look at the church today, it is tempting to wonder whatever happened to God. There seems to be so little reverence and awe, so little trembling before his majesty. Instead we take God lightly. David Wells calls this "the weightlessness of God."[10] Others have described it as "the trivialization of God."[11] Such a trivial view of God comes from trivial talk about him. We do not recognize his true glory when we come into his presence for worship. Our thoughts wander when we pray. Our eyes pass over the pages of Scripture, but our minds are not open to God's Word. And when we sing, our hearts are not in tune with our voices. We are like Shakespeare's Hamlet, who said, "My words fly up, my thoughts remain below; words without thoughts never to heaven go!"[12] Our worship is casual, careless, and insincere, and in this way we dishonor God's name.

## At the Name of Jesus

God has said that if we confess these sins, he will forgive them (1 John 1:9). He will do this because Christ was crucified for all our sins, including our violations of the third commandment. We need to confess our misuse of God's name because God has said that he will not hold us guiltless. We will discover this for ourselves at the final judgment, when what we do with God's name will determine what God does with us.

Some people will keep using God's name in vain right up until the day of judgment. Jesus said,

> Not everyone who says to me, "Lord, Lord," will enter the kingdom of heaven, but the one who does the will of my Father who is in heaven. On that day many will say to me, "Lord, Lord, did we not prophesy in your name, and cast out demons in your name, and do many mighty works in your name?" And then will I declare to them, "I never knew you; depart from me, you workers of lawlessness." (Matthew 7:21–23)

What a shock! At the final judgment there will be people who think they know Jesus but will be lost forever. There will be professing Christians—even people involved in Christian ministry—who will be condemned to Hell. The reason is because they were taking God's name in vain all along. Although it was often on their lips, it was never in their hearts.

There is something else that will happen at the final judgment: The name of Jesus Christ will be truly praised. The Bible says that Jesus obeyed God to his very death on the cross, where he paid for all our violations of God's law. Then it says that "God has highly exalted him and bestowed on him the name that is above every name" (Philippians 2:9). What name is this? What name is above every name? The Bible continues: "That at the name of Jesus every knee should bow, in heaven and on earth and under the earth, and every tongue confess that Jesus Christ is Lord" (Philippians 2:10, 11a). The name that is above every name is not "Jesus" but "Lord." The Son of God was given the name "Jesus" at the time of his incarnation. But his exalted name—the name that demonstrates his deity by identifying him as the Lord God—is "Lord." The day is coming when Jesus Christ will be revealed as the God of Moses, and everyone will give him the glory that his special divine name deserves.

If that is the honor that Jesus will receive at the end of history, it is also the honor that he deserves right now, and we should give it to him. Don't take the name of the Lord Jesus Christ in vain!

# 52

# The Fourth Commandment: Work and Leisure

EXODUS 20:8–11

A FEW YEARS AGO a friend telephoned with an urgent request. "Phil," he said, "I'm calling to ask a favor. I need the most precious thing you have."

Can you guess what he needed? He was asking for my time, of course. As the pastor of a large church—not to mention the father of a growing family—few things are more precious to me than my time. I need time to work, worship, rest, and play. I need time to spend with the Lord. I need time to prepare sermons and give people spiritual counsel. I also need time to love my family. It all takes a great deal of time, and there never seems to be quite enough.

Many people have the same frustration. We often feel rushed. We never seem to have time for work and leisure, for family and ministry. So we complain, "If only I had one extra day this week; then I could get all my work done." Or we say, "You know, I could really use some time off." Or, "If only I had more time to study the Bible and serve the Lord." In these and many other ways we grumble about being overtired and overworked. It is all part of the frustration of living as finite creatures in a fallen world.

Out of his great mercy, God has provided a remedy: one whole day out of seven to rest in his grace. He has given us a rhythm of work and rest, with six days for labor and one day for leisure. And he grants us our leisure specifically for the purpose of his praise. The Sabbath is a day for worship, a day for mercy, and a day for rest.

## Remembering the Sabbath

Keeping the Sabbath holy may not seem very productive. In fact, sometimes it even keeps people away from Christ. They would rather do something else—anything else—than go to church on Sunday. When billionaire Bill Gates was asked why he didn't believe in God, he said, "Just in terms of allocation of time resources, religion is not very efficient. There's a lot more I could be doing on a Sunday morning."[1]

Even if devoting a whole day to God may not seem very efficient, it must be important, because God has commanded it:

> Remember the Sabbath day, to keep it holy. Six days you shall labor, and do all your work, but the seventh day is a Sabbath to the LORD your God. On it you shall not do any work, you, or your son, or your daughter, your male servant, or your female servant, or your livestock, or the sojourner who is within your gates. For in six days the LORD made heaven and earth, the sea, and all that is in them, and rested on the seventh day. Therefore the LORD blessed the Sabbath day and made it holy. (20:8–11)

This is the longest commandment, and it comes in three parts. Verse 8 tells us *what* to do, verses 9, 10 specify *how* we are to do it, and verse 11 explains *why*.

*What* God wants us to do is to "remember the Sabbath day, to keep it holy" (v. 8). The word "remember" has a double meaning. For the Israelites, it was a reminder that they had heard about the Sabbath before. On their journey to Mount Sinai, God provided manna six days out of seven. The seventh day was meant to be "a day of solemn rest, a holy Sabbath to the LORD" (16:23a). So when they reached Mount Sinai, God commanded them to "remember" the Sabbath.

This was something they needed to remember not just once, but every week. It is something we need to remember too, so the fourth commandment calls us to a weekly remembrance of the Sabbath. We are prone to forget the great work of God in creation and redemption. And when we forget, we fail to praise him for making us and saving us. But the fourth commandment is a reminder. It is God's memorandum to his people, reminding us to give him glory for his grace.

Remembering involves more than just our memories; it demands the total engagement of our whole person in the service of God. Remembering the Sabbath is like remembering one's anniversary. It is not enough to say, "Oh, yes, I remember—it's our anniversary!" It takes dinner and flowers—maybe even jewelry—and a romantic evening for two. In much the same way, remembering the Sabbath means using the day to show our love for God in a special way. It means "keep[ing] it holy." Literally, we are to "sanctify it," setting it apart for sacred use.

## Keeping the Sabbath Wholly

*How* are we to do this? The fourth commandment gives explicit instructions for keeping the Sabbath holy. God begins by telling us what he wants us to do with the rest of our week: "Six days you shall labor, and do all your work" (20:9).

Although this part of the fourth commandment is often overlooked, it is our duty to work. This does not mean that we have to work all day every day. But it does mean that God governs our work as well as our rest. He has given us six whole days to fulfill our earthly calling.

People generally have a negative attitude about work. At best, work is treated as a necessary evil, and in fact sometimes it is thought that work is the result of sin. In a column for *Time* magazine, Lance Morrow claimed, "When God foreclosed on Eden, he condemned Adam and Eve to go to work. From the beginning, the Lord's word said that work was something bad: a punishment, the great stone of mortality and toil laid upon a human spirit that might otherwise soar in the infinite, weightless playfulness of grace."[2] This is completely false. Work is a divine gift that goes back before the fall, when "The LORD God took the man and put him in the garden of Eden to work it and keep it" (Genesis 2:15). We were made to work. The trouble is that our work has been cursed by our sin. It was only after Adam had sinned that God said, "Cursed is the ground because of you; in pain you shall eat of it all the days of your life" (Genesis 3:17b). But it was not that way from the beginning. The fourth commandment reminds us to honor God by doing an honest week's worth of work. We find God's blessing in doing what he has called us to do.

According to the Puritan Thomas Watson, having six days to work is a divine concession, and thus a sign of God's favor. God would have been well within his rights to make *every* day a Sabbath. Instead he has given us six days to do all our work. Watson thus imagined God saying,

> I am not a hard master, I do not grudge thee time to look after thy calling, and to get an estate. I have given thee six days, to do all thy work in, and have taken but one day for myself. I might have reserved six days for myself, and allowed thee but one; but I have given thee six days for the works of thy calling, and have taken but one day for my own service. It is just and rational, therefore, that thou shouldest set this day in a special manner apart for my worship.[3]

Watson was right: six days are for work, but the seventh day is for worship. How do we keep the fourth commandment? By worshiping the Lord on his day. To keep something holy in the Biblical sense is to dedicate it exclusively for worship. Whereas the other six days of the week are for us and our work, the Sabbath is for God and his worship. This is the positive aspect of the fourth commandment: "The seventh day is a Sabbath *to* the LORD your God" (20:10a). Elsewhere God refers to the seventh day as *his* Sabbath—the day that belongs to him: "You shall keep my Sabbaths: I am the LORD your God" (Leviticus 19:3b). The commandment was worded this way to remind the Israelites that their relationship with God was special. No other nation could claim that the Lord was their God, so no other nation kept the Sabbath. There were other ancient civilizations that divided their time into periods of seven days. However, they generally associated the seventh day with misfortune.[4] Only the Israelites kept the Sabbath as a day for worshiping the one true God as their Savior and Lord.

To keep a Sabbath "to the LORD" is to give the day over to God, setting it apart for him and his glory (which, remember, was the whole point of the exodus). The book of Leviticus calls the Sabbath "a holy convocation" (Leviticus 23:3), meaning corporate worship. Jesus endorsed this practice by attending weekly Sabbath services at the synagogue (Luke 4:16). This focus on worship led the Puritans to refer to the Sabbath as "the market-day of the soul."[5] Whereas the other six days of the week are for ordinary commerce, this is the day on which we transact our spiritual business, trading in the currency of Heaven. "This day a Christian is in the altitudes," wrote Thomas Watson. "He walks with God, and takes as it were a turn with him in heaven."[6] We meet with God by prayer and the ministry of the Word, by singing his praises and presenting our offerings to him, by celebrating the sacraments and sharing Christian fellowship. The result, according to Watson, is that "The heart, which all the week was frozen, on the Sabbath melts with the word."[7]

The Sabbath is not only a day for worship but also a day of rest. It is a day for ceasing from work, and especially from common labor. Here we need to notice that the fourth commandment is stated both positively and negatively. It is the only commandment to do so explicitly. The positive requirement comes first: "Remember the Sabbath day, to keep it holy" (20:8). Then there is the absolute prohibition: "On it you shall not do any work" (20:10).

The word translated "Sabbath" comes from the Hebrew word meaning "to cease or to rest." It is not a day for business as usual. Rather, it is a day for relaxation and recuperation, a day to step back from life's ordinary routines in order to rediscover God's goodness and grace. To quote again from Thomas Watson, "To do servile work on the Sabbath shows an irreligious heart, and greatly offends God. To do secular work on this day is to follow the devil's plough; it is to debase the soul. God made this day on purpose to raise the heart to heaven, to converse with him, to do angels' work; and to be employed in earthly work is to degrade the soul of its honour."[8]

To see how strict this command was under the Law of Moses, consider the man who gathered wood on the Sabbath (Numbers 15:32–36). He was stoned to death. Or to take a positive example, consider the women who wanted to prepare the body of Christ for burial: "Then they returned and prepared spices and ointments. On the Sabbath they rested according to the commandment" (Luke 23:56b). Gathering wood was such a small thing to do; what was the harm in doing it on the Sabbath? Taking spices to the tomb of Christ was a noble act of piety. So why not go ahead and do it? The answer was, because God had commanded a day of rest.

This rest was for everyone to enjoy: "On it you shall not do any work, you, or your son, or your daughter, your male servant, or your female servant, or your livestock, or the sojourner who is within your gates" (20:10b). Here we see that the fourth commandment has profound implications for the wider community. When it comes to work and leisure, parents are to set the agenda by teaching their children how to worship and rest. The Sabbath really is a day to spend with the family.

By including servants, the commandment also teaches that employers have a responsibility to care for their workers. Some commentators have thus described the fourth commandment as the world's first workers' bill of rights. In the ancient world there was a sharp division between masters and slaves. But here is a new social order, in which work and leisure are not divided along class lines. Everyone should work, and everyone should rest, because everyone should be free to worship God. This law extended this right to the gates of the city, including everyone in the whole community. It even applied to beasts of burden. God wanted all his creatures to get some relief from their labor. Now imagine what the world would be like if everyone kept this commandment in the Biblical way. Imagine the whole creation at rest. Once a week people all over the world would stop striving and turn back to God.

What are we commanded to do? To keep the Sabbath holy. How do we do this? By working six days and then dedicating a day to the Lord for worship and rest. This is all summarized in Leviticus: "Six days shall work be done, but on the seventh day is a Sabbath of solemn rest, a holy convocation. You shall do no work. It is a Sabbath to the LORD in all your dwelling places" (Leviticus 23:3).

## God's Work, God's Rest

The reason for this commandment is very simple. We are called to work and rest because we serve a working, resting God. *Why* should we remember the Sabbath? Because "in six days the LORD made heaven and earth, the sea, and all that is in them, and rested on the seventh day. Therefore the LORD blessed the Sabbath day and made it holy" (20:11). Keeping the Sabbath may be the oldest of the Ten Commandments, because it goes all the way back to the creation of the world.

There are many additional reasons for keeping the Sabbath (today, the Lord's Day) holy. It promotes the worship of God. It restores us both spiritually and physically, so it is for our benefit. As Jesus said, "The Sabbath was made for man" (Mark 2:27). It is good for children and workers; it can even be good for animals. But our fundamental reason for obeying the fourth commandment is not practical but theological: God made the world in six days, and then he rested. His activity in creation thus sets the pattern for our own work and leisure.

We serve a working God who has been at work from the beginning. The Scripture says, "And on the seventh day God finished his work that he had done"

(Genesis 2:2a). Part of the dignity of our work comes from the fact that God is a worker. We work because we are made in the image of a working God.

We also serve a resting God. Once his creative work was done, God took his divine leisure. The Scripture says, "He rested on the seventh day from all his work" (Genesis 2:2b). To mark the occasion, "God blessed the seventh day and made it holy, because on it God rested from all his work that he had done in creation" (Genesis 2:3). The first time that God blessed anything, he blessed a day for us to share in his rest. We keep the Sabbath because God made it holy. Like work, leisure is "something that God put into the very fabric of human well being in this world."[9]

There is one further reason for keeping a day of rest. Although it is not mentioned here in Exodus, it is mentioned in Deuteronomy, where the Ten Commandments are repeated. There the first part of the commandment is virtually identical (Deuteronomy 5:12–14), but the reason is different: "You shall remember that you were a slave in the land of Egypt, and the LORD your God brought you out from there with a mighty hand and an outstretched arm. Therefore the LORD your God commanded you to keep the Sabbath day" (Deuteronomy 5:15). There is no contradiction here. The Sabbath looked back not only to creation but also to redemption. It reminded God's people that they had been delivered from slavery in Egypt. One of the benefits of their rescue was that now they didn't have to work all the time. Back in Egypt they had to work seven days a week, fifty-two weeks a year, without ever getting a vacation. But now they were set free. The Sabbath was not a form of bondage to them but a day of freedom. It was a day to celebrate their liberation by giving glory to God.

### Business as Usual

Sadly, the Israelites often forgot to remember the Sabbath. And when they did, they inevitably fell back into spiritual bondage. There is a story about this in the book of Nehemiah—the story of the governor and the salesmen.

God's people had returned from their captivity in Babylon to rebuild the city of Jerusalem. Under Nehemiah's leadership, the whole community was restored. They rebuilt the city walls, reestablished their homes, and started gathering again for public worship. They read the Law and kept the feasts; they repented of their sins and promised to keep covenant with God. They also reestablished the priesthood. The Levites were serving, the choirs were singing, and God was blessing the holy city.

Then the governor went back to Babylon for a short time. Sadly, on his return to Jerusalem, Nehemiah found that the Israelites were failing to keep God's covenant. In particular, they were breaking the Sabbath by using it as a day to conduct commerce. They had promised that "if the peoples of the land bring in goods or any grain on the Sabbath day to sell, we will not buy from them on the

Sabbath or on a holy day" (Nehemiah 10:31a). Yet here is what Nehemiah said was happening:

> In those days I saw in Judah people treading winepresses on the Sabbath, and bringing in heaps of grain and loading them on donkeys, and also wine, grapes, figs, and all kinds of loads, which they brought into Jerusalem on the Sabbath day. And I warned them on the day when they sold food. Tyrians also, who lived in the city, brought in fish and all kinds of goods and sold them on the Sabbath to the people of Judah, in Jerusalem itself! (Nehemiah 13:15, 16)

These businessmen were not residents of Jerusalem but traveling salesmen. To them, one day was no different from the next, so they assumed that the Sabbath was a day for business as usual. This proved to be a source of temptation for the people of God. Many of the people in Jerusalem were genuine believers. They attended public worship and supported God's work with their tithes and offerings. They knew God's law, including all ten of the commandments (see Nehemiah 9:14, 15). Yet they were breaking the Sabbath. Frankly, they were like many Christians today. Although basically they were committed to following God, under pressure from the surrounding culture they treated the Sabbath pretty much like the rest of the week.

Nehemiah needed to take strong action. First he spoke out against Israel's sin: "Then I confronted the nobles of Judah and said to them, 'What is this evil thing that you are doing, profaning the Sabbath day? Did not your fathers act in this way, and did not our God bring all this disaster on us and on this city? Now you are bringing more wrath on Israel by profaning the Sabbath'" (13:17, 18). Nehemiah had a good point. When God explained why he sent his people into captivity, he often mentioned their failure to keep the Sabbath holy (see Jeremiah 17:19–27; Ezekiel 20:12, 13). As the city's governor, Nehemiah knew that keeping the fourth commandment was a matter of public safety.

Nehemiah did more than preach, however. The governor also enforced public laws for keeping the Sabbath special: "As soon as it began to grow dark at the gates of Jerusalem before the Sabbath, I commanded that the doors should be shut and gave orders that they should not be opened until after the Sabbath. And I stationed some of my servants at the gates, that no load might be brought in on the Sabbath day" (Nehemiah 13:19). It didn't take long for the salesmen to take the hint: "Then the merchants and sellers of all kinds of wares lodged outside Jerusalem once or twice. But I warned them and said to them, 'Why do you lodge outside the wall? If you do so again, I will lay hands on you.' From that time on they did not come on the Sabbath. Then I commanded the Levites that they should purify themselves and come and guard the gates, to keep the Sabbath day holy" (Nehemiah 13:20–22a).

We need to be careful how we follow Nehemiah's example. God is not calling us to establish the Sabbath by force. However, there is a principle here that we can apply. In order to preserve a day of worship and rest, we need to bar the gates against the clamor of our culture. Otherwise we will end up mixing the business of this world with the pleasure of spending time with God.

## The Lord's Day

What does the fourth commandment mean for the Christian? Like the Israelites, we are made in the image of a working, resting God. We still need to work, we still need our rest, and we can still receive the creation blessing of God's holy day. The main thing that has changed is that we have received a new and greater deliverance. We no longer look back to the old exodus for our salvation; we look to Jesus Christ, who accomplished a greater exodus by dying for our sins and rising again. Jesus is the fulfillment of the fourth commandment, as he is of all the others. The Old Testament Sabbath pointed to the full and final rest that can only be found in him.

Jesus gives a whole new meaning to work and a whole new meaning to rest. He came into the world to finish the work of his Father (John 4:34), and on the basis of that work, he is able to give rest to our souls (Matthew 11:29). There is no need to strive for our salvation. All we need to do is repose in the finished work of Jesus Christ. David said, "For God alone my soul waits in silence; from him comes my salvation" (Psalm 62:1). The way for us to find this rest is by trusting in Christ alone for our salvation, depending on his work rather than our own. The Scripture assures us that in Christ, "there remains a Sabbath rest for the people of God, for whoever has entered God's rest has also rested from his works as God did from his" (Hebrews 4:9, 10). This is the primary fulfillment of the fourth commandment. As Martin Luther wrote: "The spiritual rest which God especially intends in this commandment is that we not only cease from our labor and trade but much more—that we let God alone work in us and that in all our powers we do nothing of our own."[10]

Christ's saving work has transformed the weekly Sabbath. It is no longer the seventh day of the week but the first, and it is no longer called the Sabbath but the Lord's Day. This is because the apostles observed their day of worship and rest on the day that Jesus rose from the dead (John 20:19; Acts 20:7; 1 Corinthians 16:2). Already by the end of the first century, Ignatius was able to write that Christians "no longer observe the Sabbath, but direct their lives toward the Lord's day, on which our life is refreshed by Him and by His death."[11] B. B. Warfield explained it like this: "Christ took the Sabbath into the grave with him and brought the Lord's Day out of the grave with him on the resurrection morn."[12]

Keeping the Lord's Day holy preserves the Sabbath principle of resting one whole day out of seven. Although the specific day was provisional—a sign of Israel's coming salvation—the commandment is perpetual. Like the rest of the Ten Commandments, it was written in stone. Back in chapter 47 we drew a distinction between three types of law: the moral, the civil, and the ceremonial. The Old Testament teaching on the Sabbath included aspects of all three. As a nation, Israel executed strict civil penalties for Sabbath-breaking. Since these are no longer in effect, to a certain extent the fourth commandment has been made less strict. There was also a ceremonial aspect to the Sabbath. The rest it provided was a sign pointing to salvation, and its observance on the seventh day was part of the whole Old Testament system that found its fulfillment in Christ (see Colossians 2:17). But even if the fourth commandment has found its primary fulfillment in Christ, there remains an obligation—based on the eternal standard of God's law—to rest one whole day in seven.

To summarize, the civil aspect of the command has expired, the ceremonial aspect has been fulfilled, but the moral aspect remains. In the words of the *Westminster Confession of Faith*, Sabbath-keeping is "a positive, moral, and perpetual commandment" (XXI.7). Frankly, it takes a commandment to make us rest. In the words of Eugene Peterson, "Nothing less than a command has the power to intervene in the vicious, accelerating, self-perpetuating cycle of faithless and graceless busy-ness."[13]

## Rest Assured

God is honored when Christians celebrate the Lord's Day. However, we need to be on our guard against legalism in all its forms. We do not base our standing before God on what we do on Sunday. We do not judge others for the way they keep—or fail to keep—the Lord's Day holy (see Romans 14:5, 6a; Colossians 2:16). And we do not have a set of man-made regulations for keeping the Sabbath. This is what the Pharisees did, and Jesus condemned them. When they heard that they couldn't work on the Sabbath, the Pharisees wanted to know exactly what counted as work and what didn't, so they developed their own guidelines. Eventually these became so elaborate that the true purpose of the Sabbath was lost entirely.

The way to avoid all this legalism is to remember that the Lord's Day is for celebrating the freedom that we have in Christ. Jesus said, "The Sabbath was made for man, not man for the Sabbath" (Mark 2:27). This does not mean that anything goes. A call to freedom, like the one we are given in the fourth commandment, is never an excuse for seeking our own pleasure (see Isaiah 58:13). However, the freedom we have in Christ does mean that for the Christian, the Sabbath is not a straitjacket.

Keeping the Lord's Day holy begins with working hard the rest of the week. In America we usually work at our play and play at our work, but God has given us six days for the ordinary business of life, and we are called to use them for his glory. Christians ought to be the most faithful and diligent workers. Our industry is an important part of our piety, while sloth is a very great sin. To waste our time is to squander one of the most precious resources that God has given us.

The duty to work is for everyone, not just for people who get paid. It is for housewives, for retired people, for the disabled and the unemployed—all of us are called to do something useful with our time. Even if we don't need to earn an income, we need to glorify God in whatever work we do. Today many Americans assume that they will work for the first sixty years of their lives and then take the rest of their lives off. This is not the Biblical view of work and leisure, because the Bible calls all of us to maintain the rhythm of work and rest that is essential to our humanity.

The week begins with the Lord's Day. This is not a day for inactivity but a day for worship, mercy, and rest. One of the best summaries of how to keep the day holy comes from the *Westminster Confession of Faith*: "This Sabbath is then kept holy unto the Lord, when men, after a due preparing of their hearts, and ordering of their common affairs before-hand, do not only observe an holy rest, all the day, from their own works, words, and thoughts about their worldly employments and recreations, but also are taken up, the whole time, in the public and private exercises of His worship, and in the duties of necessity and mercy" (XXI.8). The choice of the word "recreations" is unfortunate, because one purpose of the Lord's Day is to refresh us in the joy of our Creator. It is a day to "catch our breath," which can include God-centered recreation. But the Confession is right that this is not a day for "worldly . . . recreations."

The Lord's Day is for worship. It is a day for attending corporate worship, for enjoying fellowship with the people of God, for catching up on our spiritual reading, and for spending the whole day in ways that really make it the *Lord's* Day. In order to worship well, we need to be prepared. Thus keeping the Lord's Day holy also means getting ready the night before. Thomas Watson wrote, "When Saturday evening approaches, sound a retreat; call your minds off from the world and summon your thoughts together, to think of the great work of the approaching day. . . . Evening preparation will be like the tuning of an instrument, it will fit the heart better for the duties of the ensuing Sabbath."[14]

The Lord's Day is for mercy. This is what the Pharisees failed to understand. Some maintained "that if a wall fell on top of someone on the Sabbath, only enough rubble could be removed to find out how badly the person was injured. If he was not injured too badly, then he must be left until the Sabbath ended, when the rescue could be completed."[15] But Jesus said the day was for mercy, which is why he performed so many miracles on it. He was not violating the fourth commandment—as the Pharisees thought—but was fulfilling its true purpose. We follow his example whenever we use the Lord's Day to welcome the stranger, feed the poor, or visit the sick.

Finally, the Lord's Day is for rest, for ceasing from our labor. The fourth commandment teaches us to have a leisure ethic as well as a work ethic.[16] Keeping the Lord's Day holy is the Biblical answer to workaholism. The businessman should rest from his business, the housewife from her housework, the student from his studies. Of course, Christians have always recognized that some work is necessary. Workers who provide medical care or preserve public safety need to do their jobs, as do ministers in the church. People who do such work are wise to set aside another day of the week for rest, if not for public worship. There are also some basic daily chores that need to be done. But this is a day to close the calendar, go off the clock, and put away the "to do" list. It is a day to step out of the frenzy, stop buying and selling, and quit worrying about the profit margin. In a culture that increasingly treats Sunday like any other day of the week, thereby turning what is sacred into something secular, we need to resist the tendency to let our work enslave us. This too requires us to plan ahead, ordering our daily work so that there is time for our weekly rest.

At this point many Christians still want to know what they can and cannot do on the Sabbath. Can I watch TV? Can I play Frisbee? Can I go to a restaurant? Can I catch a flight back home? Can I play Monopoly, or do I have to stick to Bible trivia games? The danger in making universal applications is that we are prone to Pharisaism; it is easy for us to slip back into legalism. In keeping the fourth commandment there is room for Christian freedom and the wise exercise of godly judgment. For example, even the Puritans recognized there were times when it might be appropriate or even necessary to dine at a public inn.[17] However, when we start asking these kinds of questions, it is usually because we want to know what we can get away with. We want to know how far we can go without actually breaking the fourth commandment. But if we are looking for a loophole in the Lord's Day, then we are missing the whole point of that commandment. God is calling us away from our own business to transact the most important business of all, which is to glorify him in our worship. And when we try to make as much roomas we can for our own pleasures, then we miss the greatest pleasure of all, which is fellowship with the living God.

Our problem is that we find it so hard to take genuine delight in the sanctified pleasures of God. Dare I say it? God bores us. We are willing to spend some time worshiping him, but then we feel like we need a break, and so we go right back to the world's lesser pleasures. But the more we learn to delight in God, the more willing we are to keep his day holy. And then we discover that we are able to answer the questions that once seemed so vexing: Can I take a job that will require me to work on Sundays? Is it okay to catch up on my work? Should we let our kids play Little League baseball on Sunday? Is it a good day for watching commercial television? Most of the practical applications are easy when we want to honor the Lord on his day. The strain and struggle come when we want to use it to do our own thing.

Dr. Robert Rayburn once told the story of a man who was approached by a beggar on the street.[18] The man reached into his pocket to see what he had.

Finding seven dollars and feeling somewhat sorry for the beggar, he held out six bills and said, "Here you go." Not only did the beggar take the six dollars, but with his other hand he struck his benefactor across the face and grabbed the seventh dollar too.

What do you think of the beggar? Don't you think he was a scoundrel? Then what do you think of a sinner, saved by the grace of Jesus Christ, who insists on taking seven days a week—or even six and a half—for himself? The way to avoid this scandal is to remember the Lord's Day by keeping it holy.

# 53

# The Fifth Commandment: Respect Authority

EXODUS 20:12

MANY HISTORIANS BELIEVE THAT a significant shift in American attitudes toward authority took place during the 1960s. It was the decade of the antiestablishment. Young people were antibusiness, anti-government, antimilitary, and antischool. But of all the institutions that came under attack, perhaps the most significant was the family.

Annie Gottlieb is one of many participants who identify "the Sixties" as "the generation that destroyed the American family." She writes, "We might not have been able to tear down the state, but the family was closer. We could get our hands on it. And . . . we believed that the family was the foundation of the state, as well as the collective state of mind. . . . We truly believed that the family had to be torn apart to free love, which alone could heal the damage done when the atom was split to release energy. And the first step was to tear ourselves free from our parents."[1]

What makes Gottlieb's analysis so chilling is the connection she draws between the family and the state. She's right: the way to destroy a nation is to destroy the family, and the way children can destroy the family is by disobeying their parents.

## Charity Begins at Home

God's plan for preserving the family calls for keeping the fifth commandment: "Honor your father and your mother, that your days may be long in the land that the LORD your God is giving you" (20:12). The placement of this commandment shows the special importance of the family. When God gave his law, he wrote it down on two tablets (31:18). Perhaps this means that he provided Moses with two copies. This was customary in ancient times whenever two parties established a covenant. Or perhaps the Law was divided into two parts. Traditionally the first four commandments are distinguished from the last six. The first table of the Law consists of the four commandments that govern our response to God. The second table consists of the six commandments that govern the way we treat one another. Obviously our human relationships cannot be separated from our relationship to God, but there is a distinction: The first four commandments teach us to love God, while the last six teach us to love our neighbor.

Love for God must come first. We cannot truly love one another unless we love God. If we do not respect God, we will not respect one another. So we can hardly begin to keep the last six commandments until we learn how to keep the first four. According to John Calvin, "The first foundation of righteousness is the worship of God. When this is overthrown, all the remaining parts of righteousness, like the pieces of a shattered and fallen building, are mangled and scattered. . . . [A]part from the fear of God men do not preserve equity and love among themselves. Therefore we call the worship of God the beginning and foundation of righteousness."[2]

If we analyze the Ten Commandments this way, then the second table of the Law would begin with the fifth commandment. This is significant. In telling us how to treat one another, God starts with our families. Loving our neighbor starts at home:

> Just as the relationship with Yahweh is the beginning of the covenant, so this relationship [i.e., between parents and children] is the beginning of society, the inevitable point of departure for every human relationship. The first relationship beyond the relationship with Yahweh, who according to the OT is the giver of life, is the relationship to father and to mother, who together are channels of Yahweh's gift of life. No other human relationship is so fundamental, and none is more important.[3]

Augustine emphasized the importance of the fifth commandment by posing a rhetorical question: "If anyone fails to honor his parents, is there anyone he will spare?"[4] Presumably not, because the relationship between parent and child is the first and primary relationship, the beginning of all human society. Under ordinary circumstances, the first people a child knows are his parents. God intends the family to be our first hospital, first school, first government, first church.[5] If we do not respect authority at home, we will not respect it anywhere. Charity really does begin at home!

### Honor Your Father and Your Mother

Like the rest of God's law, the fifth commandment needs to be studied carefully. The first word is "honor." This is a heavy word—literally. The word is *kaved*, which is Hebrew for "heavy" or "weighty." It is the word the Old Testament uses for the glory of God, for the weightiness of his divine majesty. To honor one's parents, therefore, is to give due weight to their position. It is to give them the recognition they deserve for their God-given authority. To honor is to respect, esteem, value, and prize fathers and mothers as gifts from God.

The opposite of honor is dishonor. Just as the fifth commandment requires respect for parents, so it forbids showing them any disrespect. If parents are weighty, then they should not be treated lightly, as if the fifth commandment doesn't even matter. Sadly, rebelling against parents has become a common sin. The cover of one magazine for teenage girls asked, "Do you really hate your parents? Like, who doesn't?" The magazine proceeded to offer advice on "how to deal with your detestables."

The Bible has a deep revulsion to this kind of disrespect, treating it almost with a kind of horror. When I was a youth pastor, I once took my high school students through the Biblical passages that deal with disobedience to parents. We discovered that some of the most frightening curses in the Old Testament are reserved for children who rebel against their parents. Here are two examples:

> For anyone who curses his father or his mother shall surely be put to death; he has cursed his father or his mother; his blood is upon him. (Leviticus 20:9)

> If a man has a stubborn and rebellious son who will not obey the voice of his father or the voice of his mother, and, though they discipline him, will not listen to them, then his father and his mother shall take hold of him and bring him out to the elders of his city at the gate of the place where he lives . . . Then all the men of the city shall stone him to death with stones. So you shall purge the evil from your midst, and all Israel shall hear, and fear. (Deuteronomy 21:18, 19, 21)

Not surprisingly, by the time I finished reading these and many similar passages, the kids in my youth group were very quiet. Like most young people, they had always assumed that breaking the fifth commandment was part of their job, an ordinary part of growing up. God obviously considers dishonoring one's parents to be one of the worst sins that anyone can possibly commit. This is true even if the Old Testament penalties for breaking this commandment are no longer in effect. In the New Testament, disobedience to parents is listed as one of the signs that we are living in the "times of difficulty" of "the last days" (2 Timothy 3:1, 2).

Notice that the commandment includes both fathers and mothers: "Honor your father *and* your mother." Elsewhere the Bible makes it clear that fathers have a unique responsibility for the spiritual leadership of their families. However, this does not mean that mothers deserve any less honor. The Scripture says, "My son, keep your father's commandment, and forsake not your mother's teaching" (Proverbs 6:20). In fact, Leviticus 19:3 mentions mothers first: "Every one of you shall revere his mother and his father." God commands children not to try to take advantage of their mothers but to give them equal respect.

This commandment was without parallel in the ancient world. Although today the Bible is often considered patriarchal—especially in the Old Testament—it always strikes the proper balance, confronting every culture's structures of sin. Here the Bible insists that mothers should receive as much honor as fathers (this part of the fifth commandment obviously rules out same-sex parents). Unless a parent is removed by death, every child is expected to honor both a father and a mother. This is God's pattern for all people in all places. Where there are exceptions—as in the case of orphans, for example, or when one parent dies—they are just that—exceptions to the Biblical rule.

### Live Long and Prosper

Why should children respect their parents? For many reasons. Parents deserve to be honored for the many sacrifices they make on behalf of their children. They deserve to be listened to because of their wealth of life experience. There is also the simple fact that keeping the fifth commandment glorifies God, which is reason enough. The Bible says, "Children, obey your parents in everything, for this pleases the Lord" (Colossians 3:20). It also says that honoring one's parents is the right thing to do: "Children, obey your parents in the Lord, for this is right" (Ephesians 6:1).

These are all good reasons to keep the fifth commandment, but the reason given in the commandment itself is that honoring our parents serves our own best interest: "Honor your father and your mother, that your days may be long in the land that the LORD your God is giving you" (20:12). The Apostle Paul said this was "the first commandment with a promise" (Ephesians 6:2), and the promise is intended to give special encouragement to children. God knows how hard it is to obey our parents. He also knows that children find it easier to obey when they are promised a reward, so the fifth commandment comes with the promise of long life in God's land.

This promise had special meaning for the Israelites. They had just been brought out of the land of slavery, and God had promised to lead them to a new and better country. One way they could ensure they would keep living in the Promised Land was to honor their fathers and mothers in the faith.

This general promise should not be taken as an automatic guarantee that children who obey their parents will live to be ninety. Nor does it necessarily mean that someone who dies young is guilty of breaking the fifth commandment. For reasons of his greater glory, God sometimes allows people to meet what we consider an untimely end, even if they almost always obeyed their parents. Many providences determine the length of a person's life. But the promise still stands: Children who honor their parents receive the gift of life.

Here it helps to know that when the Bible talks about living long in the land, it is not simply talking about how old people are when they die. The expression "be long in the land" is a Hebrew phrase for the fullness of God's blessing. It means to have an abundant life. This is confirmed by the New Testament, which says, "'Honor your father and mother' . . . 'that it may go well with you and that you may live long in the land'" (Ephesians 6:2, 3). Anyone who wants to live long and prosper should honor his mother and father.

There is one more reason to keep the fifth commandment, and it may be the most important reason of all: Parents have a God-given responsibility to teach their children how to know and serve God. But children will not learn those lessons if they do not respect their parents, so keeping the fifth commandment is essential to God's plan for passing down the faith. Of all the ways children honor their parents, the most important is listening to what they say about God and the way of salvation.

Spiritual instruction is a responsibility for both fathers and mothers. Solomon said, "Hear, my son, your father's instruction, and forsake not your mother's teaching" (Proverbs 1:8), and "My son, do not forget my teaching, but let your heart keep my commandments, for length of days and years of life and peace they will add to you" (Proverbs 3:1, 2). These words are a commentary on the fifth commandment. Solomon repeats the promise of long life and prosperity and ties it specifically to Biblical teaching in the home. This is the heart of the fifth commandment: receiving the gift of life by respecting our parents in the faith. Today God commands us to honor our fathers and mothers because this is how many people first come to know Jesus Christ.

Learning God's plan for the family sometimes brings sadness and disappointment to people who never had a good family background. Is a person who was not raised in a Christian home at a spiritual disadvantage? In a way, yes. We are always damaged by the sins of others, including the sin of parents in not raising their children "in the discipline and instruction of the Lord" (Ephesians 6:4). But God is gracious, and by the saving work of his Spirit he adopts orphan sinners into the best and most important family of all: the family of God. The Bible gives every child of God this precious promise: "For my father and my mother have forsaken me, but the LORD will take me in" (Psalm 27:10).

## Honor to Whom Honor Is Due

In order to make the fullest and best use of the fifth commandment, we need to understand that it is not just for children, but it really applies to everyone. According to the *Westminster Shorter Catechism*, "The fifth commandment requireth the preserving the honour, and performing the duties, belonging to everyone in their several places and relations, as superiors, inferiors, or equals"

(A. 64). In other words, respecting authority applies to every person in every relationship.

Here we need to remember one of our rules for interpreting the Ten Commandments. According to "the rule of categories" (see chapter 48), every commandment stands for a whole category of sins and duties. By implication, when God tells us to respect our parents, he is telling us to respect anyone who has legitimate authority over us. This is something the Israelites would have readily understood because they often used the term *father* in relationships outside the home. For example, the Israelites referred to the king as their father (e.g., 1 Samuel 24:11). On occasion they used the same title for the prophets. Elisha called out to Elijah, "My father, my father!" (2 Kings 2:12). Similarly, Israel's elders were honored as the fathers of their people (see Acts 7:2). So the Israelites naturally would have applied the fifth commandment to other relationships that involved authority.

We should do the same. The fifth commandment rules our relationship to the government. The Bible says, "Be subject for the Lord's sake to every human institution. . . . Honor everyone. . . . Fear God. Honor the emperor" (1 Peter 2:13, 17). Today honoring the king means respecting officers of the law and representatives of the state. It means praying for politicians. It means obeying the laws of the government and paying our taxes. In all these ways we are called to "be subject to the governing authorities. For there is no authority except from God" (Romans 13:1).

The fifth commandment also regulates our work. We are to respect our bosses and show honor to our employers. After telling children to obey their parents, Paul proceeded to tell slaves (employees in our culture) to serve their masters (i.e., employers). It was all part of respecting authority. He wrote: "Bondservants, obey your earthly masters with fear and trembling, with a sincere heart . . . knowing that whatever good anyone does, this he will receive back from the Lord" (Ephesians 6:5, 8). Keeping the fifth commandment on the job means working hard and speaking well of the management.

The fifth commandment also requires respect for our leaders in the church. Specifically, it requires submission to our pastors, elders, and deacons—the leaders who serve as our spiritual fathers in the household of God. The Scripture says, "Let the elders who rule well be considered worthy of double honor, especially those who labor in preaching and teaching" (1 Timothy 5:17). To honor our elders is to pray for them, encourage them, and assist them in their efforts for our spiritual progress. It is to accept their counsel and discipline with humility, for as the Scripture says, "Obey your leaders and submit to them" (Hebrews 13:17a).

In all of these relationships, "we should look up to those whom God has placed over us, and should treat them with honor, obedience, and gratefulness."[6] We should do this even when those in authority don't seem to deserve our respect. *The Heidelberg Catechism* is right when it says that the fifth commandment requires "that I show honor, love, and faithfulness to my father and mother and to all who are set in authority over me; that I submit myself with respectful obedience to all their careful instruction and discipline; *and that I also bear patiently their failures, since it is God's will to govern us by their hand*" (A. 104, italics added). Respect for those who are in authority is respect for God because all authority comes from him. Our respect is not based on their personal qualities or professional qualifications, but on the position they have been given by God.

There is another side to all this, which is that people in authority have a responsibility to exercise it in ways that are pleasing to God. We may not abuse our authority by using it harshly or by overstepping our bounds. Nor may we fail to do our duty. Leaders in government are called to protect their citizens. Pastors and elders are called to serve God's people in the church, not to abuse them. And people in management are called to care for the people who work for them.

The fifth commandment has special relevance for fathers and mothers. Our family duties are reciprocal. If children are supposed to obey their parents, then obviously parents are supposed to give them proper discipline. The New Testament makes this explicit when it attaches these words to the fifth commandment: "Fathers, do not provoke your children to anger, but bring them up in the discipline and instruction of the Lord" (Ephesians 6:4; cf. Colossians 3:21). When parents place unreasonable demands on their children, when they correct them in anger rather than in love, or when they stunt their growth by stifling their freedom, they abuse their authority.

Parents are called to give their children many other things besides proper discipline. We are called to pray for them, encourage them, counsel them, protect them, and provide for their daily needs. We are called to set a godly example, for although children don't always listen to their parents, they never fail to imitate them. We are called to educate our children, preparing them for their life's work, including marriage and parenthood, according to the providence of God. Most important of all, if children are commanded to listen to their parents, then we are commanded to teach them the Scriptures and lead them in the worship of God.

## God Save the King

It is not always easy to respect authority, and there is a story about this in the Bible—the story of two best friends, David and Jonathan. These brave young men were spiritual brothers, bound by a covenant of friendship. Both were mighty warriors, both had a courageous faith in the God of Israel, and both had proven themselves in battle. David is well known for killing Goliath, but Jonathan was just as brave. On one occasion the Israelites faced the Philistines without any weapons. Only Jonathan had a sword. Yet he said, "It may be that the Lord will work for us, for nothing can hinder the Lord from saving by many or by few" (1 Samuel 14:6b). With those words he launched a one-man attack, killing twenty Philistines and sending the rest of their army into a panic.

The only person who gave David and Jonathan more trouble than the Philistines was Jonathan's father, King Saul. God had anointed Saul king over Israel; yet he was an angry, impetuous, ill-tempered man who often made rash threats against his own people. During one battle Saul swore an oath cursing any soldier who had anything to eat before he could avenge his enemies. Unfortunately, Jonathan didn't hear his father's oath; so when he saw honey oozing on the ground, he went ahead and dipped his staff into the honeycomb and tasted it. When Saul eventually learned what had happened, he said to his son, "God do so to me and more also; you shall surely die, Jonathan" (1 Samuel 14:44). The other soldiers intervened to spare Jonathan's life, but the episode showed what kind of man Saul was—the kind who would do violence to his own son over a mouthful of food.

Saul treated David even worse. At first he was pleased with David because he loved to hear him play the harp. Then after David killed Goliath, Saul welcomed him into his own house and gave him a high rank in the army. David excelled in everything the king asked him to do. However, he soon became more famous than Saul, which aroused the king's jealousy. One day, in a fit of anger, the king hurled his spear, trying to pin David to the wall. David escaped, but this only added to Saul's anger. Next Saul tried to get rid of David by having him killed in battle. He promised David his daughter's hand in marriage if only he would kill one hundred Philistines. Saul's secret hope was that the young warrior would die at the hands of his enemies. But David killed two hundred Philistines without getting a scratch.

Saul could see from all this that David had God's blessing, which of course made him angrier than ever. Swearing eternal enmity, the king ordered his soldiers—including his son Jonathan—to kill David. This put Jonathan in a bad position. He knew he was supposed to honor his father, but he also knew that murder was wrong. So Jonathan did the right thing: He honored God by disobeying his father. First he warned David what his father was planning to do so he had a chance to escape. Then he interceded with his father, saying, "Why then will you sin against innocent blood by killing David without cause?" (1 Samuel 19:5b). By doing this, Jonathan was not dishonoring his father but preserving his honor. On this occasion Saul listened to his son. He repented of his anger and welcomed David back into his home. Their truce didn't last for long, however. David had more success in battle, Saul became more jealous, and once again he hurled his spear in anger.

The point of telling this unhappy story is that if ever there was a father who failed to deserve the respect of his son, or a king who failed to deserve the respect of his subjects, it was Saul. And yet David and Jonathan both honored the king. They respected his God-given authority, honoring him because they honored God.

The way David honored Saul was by refusing to take his life. After the king had his last blowup, David left for good. Saul chased him into the hills, where on two separate occasions he had an easy opportunity to take the king's life. Once Saul came alone into the very cave where David was hiding. David's men told him to seize his chance: "Here is the day of which the LORD said to you, 'Behold, I will give your enemy into your hand, and you shall do to him as it shall seem good to you'" (1 Samuel 24:4a). But David decided not to kill Saul. Instead he sneaked up and cut off the corner of the king's robe. Yet afterward David was sorry for what he had done. Even after everything Saul had done to him, his conscience told him that it was dishonorable for him to show disrespect to Israel's king. David said, "The LORD forbid that I should do this thing to my lord, the LORD's anointed, to put out my hand against him, seeing he is the LORD's anointed" (1 Samuel 24:6). Notice David's reasoning. His repentance was not based on how Saul had treated him. He said nothing about what kind of king Saul was. The only thing that mattered was that his kingship came from God and therefore demanded his respect. So after Saul left, David stepped out of the cave and cried, "My lord the king!" Then he said, "See, my father, see the corner of your robe in my hand. For by the fact that I cut off the corner of your robe and did not kill you . . ." (1 Samuel 24:8, 11a). David called Saul "father" as a sign of respect for his kingly authority.

Jonathan honored Saul too, and he did so by trying to stop him from sinning against David. This put a tremendous strain on his relationship with his father. On one occasion Saul was so angry with Jonathan for siding with David that he hurled a spear at him and said, "You son of a perverse, rebellious woman" (1 Samuel 20:30–33). Naturally this made Jonathan angry.

It also grieved him because he loved his friend David. But even after all the violent outbursts, Jonathan remained loyal to his father. Although he was not blind to the man's faults, he still loved him as his father. The last we see of Jonathan, he is at his father's side, desperately trying to defend him from the Philistines. Jonathan was an honorable son who died fighting to save his father (1 Samuel 31:1–6).

Obviously Saul is not a very good model of the proper exercise of authority. There were times when David and Jonathan had to disobey him. In doing so they did not break the fifth commandment but kept it by honoring their higher commitment to obey their Father in Heaven. There were also times when David and Jonathan had to protect themselves. Submitting to authority never means subjecting ourselves to violence, domestic or otherwise. Perhaps this point needs to be emphasized: When there is physical abuse, the duty to preserve life takes precedence over the duty to obey one's parents. But the difficulties these friends faced make their example all the more remarkable. David and Jonathan understood that there is something sacred about authority. Because it comes from God, it demands our highest respect.

## A Lifetime of Respect

There are many ways to honor God by honoring our parents. The fifth commandment is for young children. God wants boys and girls to speak respectfully to their parents, using good manners. He wants them to obey their parents all the time, doing everything they ask with a good attitude. The Puritans said, "A child should be the parents' echo; when the father speaks, the child should echo back obedience."[7]

The fifth commandment is for teenagers. Many high school students are amazed at how out of touch their parents are—how little they seem to know about life. Most parents deserve more credit than this, of course, but even the ones who don't still ought to be obeyed. Honoring father and mother means speaking well of them to friends. It means listening to what they say, including their warnings about spending time with the wrong friends or experimenting with things that can cause permanent physical and spiritual damage. It also means talking to parents, letting them know what's happening. I once heard a mother say that her son went through his entire senior year of high school doing nothing more than grunting at her. He dishonored his parents, although apparently he did know how to use words because within several years he could once again carry on intelligent conversations with his parents in English!

The fifth commandment is also for young adults. Often around age twenty sons and daughters finally recognize that their parents are gifts from God. One recent college graduate told me that he was pleased (and a little surprised) that he was starting to have a better relationship with his parents. I said, "You know, it's amazing how much your parents have matured in the last couple of years!" Young adults have major decisions to make about education, career, and sometimes marriage. Children honor their fathers and mothers by seeking their counsel. The decisions are theirs to make, especially once they leave the home, but it is wise to get whatever help and blessing their parents have to offer.

Here we need to consider what children should do when their parents fail to give them godly advice. Remember, the Israelites were told to honor their parents so they could learn to know God. But what if someone's parents don't know God? What if they aren't Christians? And what if they try to stop their children from doing what God is calling them to do? What does it mean to honor your father and mother then?

This situation is not uncommon. Some parents find it very hard to accept their children putting Christ first in decisions about education, career, family, and ministry. Where there is faith, Jesus brings families together; but where there is unbelief, he drives them apart. Christians can never let honoring their parents get in the way of following Christ. This is what Jesus meant when he said, "Whoever loves father or mother more than me is not worthy of me, and whoever loves son or daughter more than me is not worthy of me" (Matthew 10:37). If it comes down to a choice, the Christian's true Father is in Heaven, and it is *his* will that we must follow. This is one of the reasons the Bible tells us to obey our parents "in the Lord" (Ephesians 6:1; cf. Colossians 3:20). This is an important qualification. The honor we owe our parents can never come at the expense of the honor we owe to God.

When Christians who need guidance cannot rely on their parents for godly counsel, they should turn to the church, which after all is our primary family. But even when we cannot accept our parents' advice, we still need to show them honor and respect. This means listening to what they say, caring for their needs, and strengthening the family ties in any way we can.

The fifth commandment remains in force even after children grow up and move out on their own. Honoring father and mother means giving them a certain precedence in life, making them a priority. It means loving them and appreciating them. It means caring for them to the very end of their lives. The Scripture says, "Listen to your father who gave you life, and do not despise your mother when she is old" (Proverbs 23:22). One ancient writer expanded on this by saying, "My child, support your father in his old age, do not grieve him during his life. Even if his mind should fail, show him sympathy, do not despise him in your health and strength."[8] Yet this is precisely what many people do: They despise their parents. Barely half of Americans think that children have a responsibility to care for elderly parents.[9] Many children abandon their parents, or worse, try to help them die. This shows flagrant contempt for God's law.

When Jesus saw some of the Pharisees refusing to provide for their parents in old age, he accused them of violating the fifth commandment: "For God commanded, 'Honor your father and your mother,' and, 'Whoever reviles father or mother must surely die.' But you say, 'If anyone tells his father or his mother, "What you would have gained from me is given to God," he need not honor his father.' So for the sake of your tradition you have made void the word of God" (Matthew 15:4–6). Instead of taking care of their parents, the Pharisees were keeping their money for themselves and then claiming they had dedicated it to God. But children have a responsibility to make sure that their parents get all the physical, medical, spiritual, and emotional care they need. To honor one's father and mother in these ways is to honor God. For the Scripture says, "You shall stand up before the gray head and honor the face of an old man, and you shall fear your God: I am the Lord" (Leviticus 19:32).

## The Perfect Child

It is good to ask ourselves whether we are keeping the fifth commandment. Does our relationship with our father or mother bring glory to God? The truth is that it is hard for children to honor their parents. One man complained: "Youth today love luxury. They have bad manners, contempt for authority, no respect for older people, and talk nonsense when they should work. Young people do not stand up any longer when adults enter the room. They contradict their parents, talk too much in company, guzzle their food, lay their legs on the table, and tyrannize their elders."[10] Who was this man? It was Socrates, the philosopher who lived four hundred years before Christ! His words describe what young people are still like today because they describe what young people are always like.

Like the rest of God's law, the fifth commandment is impossible for us to keep. Here are some questions for self-examination: Do you ever talk back to your parents? Do you ever hide anything from them? Do you ever silently curse them? Do you speak well of your parents? Are you taking the time to strengthen your relationship with them? Are you giving them the care they need and the honor they deserve for their position in life? We all fail somewhere. The fifth commandment is part of God's Law, and like the rest of God's law, we have broken it. No one is the perfect child.

Except Jesus. When Jesus died on the cross, he paid the penalty for our breaking the fifth commandment as much as for any other sin. But Jesus has done more than that: He has also kept the fifth commandment in our behalf. It was not enough for Jesus to pay the price for our sin—he also had to offer God the obedience that his law demands. And Jesus did that. He honored his parents. The Bible says explicitly that Jesus "went down with them and came to Nazareth and was submissive to them" (Luke 2:51a). The only times their relationship was strained were when Jesus stayed behind at the temple in Jerusalem (Luke 2:41–50) and when he kept preaching instead of stopping to visit with his family (Luke 8:19–21). But even then he kept the fifth commandment by honoring his higher commitment to his Father in Heaven. And Jesus honored his earthly parents right to the very end of his life. He was not able personally to care for his mother in her old age, but he provided for her in his dying moments by asking his friend John to be like a son to her (John 19:26, 27).

From the manger to the cross, Jesus was an obedient son who brought honor to his earthly parents and his heavenly Father. In respecting his parents' authority he is more than our example: He is the perfect child God demands that we should be. Everyone who trusts in Jesus has perfect obedience to the fifth commandment, because when Jesus obeyed his parents, he was keeping God's law on our behalf.

To illustrate this, consider the way I once chastised my son for failing to clean his room. "You didn't clean your room," I said. "I told you to clean your room, and you didn't do it." After hearing my son's excuse—which although carefully developed nevertheless was thoroughly unpersuasive—I said, "I don't care what happened. I told you to clean your room, and you didn't do it." Then, trying to help him understand the gospel, I said, "You know, you like to think you're a pretty good boy. But the truth is that you're not a good boy. Actually, you're a bad boy. God wants you to obey me all the time, but sometimes you don't. How can God accept you if you keep disobeying your parents?"

My son wasn't sure, but his father was a pastor, so of course he knew that the answer was probably Jesus. And he was right: Jesus *is* the answer. God does not accept us on the basis of what we have done but on the basis of what Jesus has done. And one of the things Jesus has done is to keep the fifth commandment. So instead of looking at what we have done—all the times we dishonored and disobeyed our parents—God looks at what Jesus did when he obeyed his parents perfectly. It is almost as if Jesus cleaned our room for us and then did everything else a child is supposed to do. One of the reasons he is the perfect Savior is because he was the perfect child.

# 54

# The Sixth Commandment: Live and Let Live

EXODUS 20:13

APPARENTLY SOME AMERICANS consider the Ten Commandments dangerous. Put them up—at work, in the classroom, or at the courthouse—and someone will try to make you take them down. Hence the recent cartoon depicting two public school administrators watching a line of students pass through a metal detector. "It's the latest in school safety devices," one of them explains. "That light and horn go off if a student tries to smuggle in a gun, knife, bomb or a copy of the ten commandments!"[1]

Which commandments cause the controversy? Almost all of them. People strongly object to the first commandment, which rules out other gods. They don't really see the point of the fourth commandment, which requires a weekly day of rest. They enjoy indulging in a little sexual sin every now and then, so they don't care for the seventh commandment.

Just about the only commandment everyone still seems to accept is number six. No one approves of murder. It is so contrary to the law of nature that every culture has some sort of prohibition against it. Even in America, homicide is still a criminal act. However, when we study the sixth commandment carefully and come to understand its full implications, we find that no commandment is more blatantly or brutally violated.

## Lawful and Unlawful Killing

The sixth commandment is one of the shortest. It is just two words in the original: *lo ratzach*, or "Don't kill." But what kind of killing does the Bible have in mind? The Hebrew language has at least eight different words for killing, and the one used here has been chosen carefully. The word *ratzach* is never used in the legal system or in the military. There are other Hebrew words for the execution of a death sentence or for the kind of killing that a soldier does in mortal combat. Nor is the word *ratzach* ever used for hunting and killing animals. So the King James Version, which says, "Thou shalt not kill" (20:13), is somewhat imprecise. What the commandment forbids is not killing, but the *unlawful* killing of a human being.

The English Standard Version comes closer to the truth when it says, "You shall not murder." Murder is what the sixth commandment mainly has in mind: the premeditated taking of an innocent life, the deliberate killing of a personal enemy. However, even "murder" is somewhat imprecise because *ratzach* can be used for any form of wrongful death. It is used for voluntary manslaughter, a crime of passion. It is also used for involuntary manslaughter. Some accidental deaths, although unintentional, are nevertheless culpable, which is why God's law includes legal sanctions for a person who "kills his neighbor unintentionally, without being at enmity with him in time past" (Deuteronomy 4:42).

To summarize, what the sixth commandment forbids is the unjust taking of a legally innocent life. It applies to "murder in cold blood, manslaughter with passionate rage, [and] negligent homicide resulting from recklessness or carelessness."[2] Perhaps the best translation is, "You shall not kill unlawfully."

God's people have always recognized that there are some situations where taking a life is not only permitted but actually warranted. One such situation is self-defense, the protection of one's self and one's family from violent attack. To extend the principle, we may also kill in the defense of our nation. As Stephen Carter explains, "War is horrible and should be fought rarely, and only to avoid greater horrors."[3] But this view has increasingly come under attack. After the horrific attack on the World Trade Center in New York City, some people said, "If we kill as a response to this great tragedy, we are no better than the terrorists who launched this awful offensive. Killing is killing, and killing is wrong."[4] This is not the Biblical position. The Bible teaches that it is not unlawful to kill enemies in wartime, provided that the war is just. Of course, the justice of a war needs to be considered carefully, especially by nations as heavily armed as the United States. Christians have long believed that a war is just only if it is waged by a legitimate government, for a worthy cause, with force proportional to the attack, against men who are soldiers, not civilians.

Another situation where killing is lawful is the execution of a death sentence. It is always wrong for us to take the law into our own hands. If justice is to be done, the plaintiff may not serve as the jury, the judge, and the executioner. This is what Moses did when he killed the Egyptian taskmaster (see 2:11–15), and it was wrong. However, the Bible makes a distinction between private individuals and the state. Capital punishment—when it is justly administered by the governing authorities—is one lawful form of killing. For a public official "to kill an offender is not murder, but justice."[5] This is taught not only in the Old Testament, but also in the New. Paul told the Romans, who were then under imperial authority, that the government "does not bear the sword in vain" because the one who governs "is the servant of God, an avenger who carries out God's wrath on the wrongdoer" (Romans 13:4b). Although it is always wrong to avenge ourselves (see Romans 12:19), the government has a God-given responsibility of vengeance.

These examples show that not all killing is morally wrong. But why does God permit some forms of killing? What makes them lawful? The answer is that their goal is not the destruction of life but its preservation. This is obviously true in the case of self-defense. Sometimes it is necessary to take a life in order to save a life. In the case of a just war, the same principle applies on a larger scale. The purpose of having an army is not to kill people but to keep a country's citizens safe.

The same life-preserving principle even holds true for capital punishment. The execution of a murderer stops him from killing again and deters other would-be criminals from doing the same. His execution is also a matter of justice. The Bible says, "Whoever sheds the blood of man, by man shall his blood be shed, for God made man in his own image" (Genesis 9:6). This is the Biblical logic behind capital punishment. It is precisely *because* life is precious that someone who takes it unlawfully must be put to death. What makes life so precious is that every human being is made in God's image. God has put his stamp on every one of us the way a great artist signs his name to a work of art. Therefore, to damage a life is to deface one of God's masterpieces. Calvin wrote, "Our neighbor bears the image of God: to use him, abuse, or misuse him is to do violence to the person of God who images himself in every human soul."[6]

The sixth commandment preserves the sanctity of human life. It also preserves God's sovereignty over life and death. Jesus Christ is the Lord of life. He is its author and inventor, its ruler and sustainer. Since he is the giver of life, it is also his prerogative to take it, and to do so at his own time, in his own way. The sovereignty of God is always at stake in matters of life and death. Yes, God has delegated his authority so that in some situations it is lawful for one person to take another person's life. But this can only be done according to God's will. To take a life unlawfully is to violate God's sovereignty over life and death.

It is also to rob God of his glory. God has given us life and breath so that we might live for his praise. The psalmist wrote, "I shall not die, but I shall live, and recount the deeds of the LORD" (Psalm 118:17). Life is not given for its own sake but for God's glory, and for this reason it may not be taken unlawfully. One theologian has observed, "A person may not be killed for this reason, that he is, either actually or potentially, someone who declares God's praise, and therefore anybody who kills another person thereby robs God."[7]

## The Unsanctity of Life

The sixth commandment has important implications for contemporary society. We like to think of America as a civilized country, but we are living in angry, violent times, when murder in all its forms is very common. There is such a callous disregard for human life that many people say we are now living in what Pope John Paul II rightly called a "culture of death." There is death in the city. In places like Philadelphia there is a shooting almost every day of the year; hundreds of people die. There is death at school. There has been a rash of shootings from Kentucky to Columbine, and teachers have to watch out for students who carry weapons. Little League parents want to kill the ump, and sometimes they do. There is death on the highway, where motorists get into a rage or drive under the influence of alcohol. There is even violence at home, where parents violate their sacred trust by striking in anger.

Where does all this violence come from? From evil hearts that have turned away from God. But the rapid spread of brutality in America has been accelerated by violence in the media, where an entire industry promotes the breaking of the sixth commandment. According to the American Psychological Association, by the time the average child finishes elementary school, he or she will have watched eight thousand televised murders and one hundred thousand acts of on-screen violence. And things are getting worse. The *New York Times* comments, "If you have the impression that movies today are bloodier and more brutal than ever in the past, and that their body counts are skyrocketing, you are absolutely right. Inflation has hit the action-adventure movie with a big slimy splat."[8]

Something else is happening too. Movies are not just getting more violent—they are also treating violence as a form of humorous entertainment. Movie critic Michael Medved writes:

> The current tendency is to make mayhem a subject of mirth. As the on-screen mutilation and dismemberment become progressively more grotesque and horrible, film makers make light of their characters' pain by introducing sadistic humor as an indispensable element of entertainment. . . . [I]t's the violence itself that's supposed to be hilarious, and that leaves audiences howling with laughter. . . . The nightmarish mix of comedy and carnage demonstrates more clearly than anything else that the brutality in today's films is different in kind, not just extent, from the screen violence of the past.[9]

What is so disturbing about all of this is that it affects the way people live. In 1998 the American College of Forensic Psychiatry conducted a comprehensive review of scientific studies on the relationship between violence on the screen and violence in real life. Out of 1,000 studies, more than 980 established a definite link between violence on the screen and violence in real life.[10] According to the best estimates, media violence has doubled America's homicide rate. David Grossman is not surprised. A retired military psychologist, Lt. Col. Grossman is an expert on teaching people to overcome their natural reluctance to kill. He was shocked to realize that children who watch TV and play violent video games are subjected to the same methods—the conditioning and the desensitization—that the Army uses to train soldiers. We are teaching our children how to kill, and we should not be surprised when they do.[11]

Not all forms of murder are violent. Sometimes death carries a clipboard and wears a lab coat. In a recent book called *Culture of Death*, Wesley J. Smith argues that "a small but influential group of philosophers and health-care policy makers" actively seek to persuade our culture that "killing is beneficent, suicide is rational, natural death is undignified, and caring properly and compassionately for people who are elderly, prematurely born, disabled, despairing, or dying is a burden that wastes emotional and financial resources."[12] This kind of thinking is a direct assault on the Biblical view of personhood. Often the assault is intentional. In the words of one medical professor:

> We can no longer base our ethics on the idea that human beings are a special form of creation made in the image of God, singled out from all other animals and alone possessing an immortal soul. Once this religious mumbo-jumbo has been stripped away, we may continue to see normal members of our species as possessing greater capacities of rationality, self-consciousness, communication, etc. than members of other species, but we will not regard as sacrosanct the life of each and every member of our species.[13]

This kind of rhetoric has convinced many Americans that some lives are less worth living than others, that in fact some lives are not worth living at all. The result is that abortion, infanticide, euthanasia, and assisted suicide are exceedingly common. In some cases they have legal protection, but they are all forms of murder—violations of the sixth commandment.

Christians have always believed that an unborn child is a person made in the very likeness of God. To cite just one example, Calvin insisted that "the *foetus*, though enclosed in the womb of its mother, is already a human being, and it is almost a monstrous crime to rob it of the life which it has not yet begun to enjoy."[14] This is what Christians have always believed because it is what the Bible teaches. "For you formed my inward parts," wrote the psalmist; "you knitted me together in my mother's womb. . . . My frame was not hidden from you, when I was being made in secret, intricately woven in the depths of the earth. Your eyes saw my unformed substance" (Psalm 139:13, 15, 16a). A child in the womb is a living human being who has a relationship with God and with its mother. Therefore, to kill such a child is as great an evil as Pharaoh committed when he tried to drown Israel's baby boys in the Nile.

What is true of the unborn is true of all God's children. The young and the helpless, the elderly and the infirm, the diseased and the disabled—we are all made in the image and likeness of God. Every life is precious in his sight. None can be discarded; all must be preserved.

This means that as Christians we have a duty to oppose euthanasia. God alone is the Lord of life, and he alone has the right to determine when it is time for someone to die. The difficulty is that we now have the medical capacity to keep a body functioning long after that time has come. This raises many more ethical questions than we can address here. But briefly, although we always have a duty to provide basic nourishment, we do not always have a duty to provide extraordinary measures like artificial respiration. There is a legitimate moral distinction between killing and allowing someone who is terminally ill to die. In other words, there is a difference between terminating life—which is never permissible—and terminating treatment—which can be a way of turning life (and thus also death) back over to God. But this calls for constant vigilance, because many people (including many health professionals) don't know the difference, and thus they often cross the line that should never be crossed.

We also have a duty to oppose suicide. God has not given us the right to kill ourselves. To commit suicide is to claim lordship over our own lives. Physician-assisted suicide, in which a doctor becomes an accessory to his patient's self-murder, is especially dangerous. Such voluntary euthanasia is wrong in itself, but there is another danger: Voluntary euthanasia almost always becomes involuntary. This has been the experience in the Netherlands, where thousands of medical patients are killed every year. What is especially frightening is that most of the requests for these so-called mercy killings do not come from the patients themselves but from their families, who frankly are trying to get rid of them.

These are only some of the many signs that we are living in a culture of death. People also commit murder by sheer recklessness. One thinks of all the deaths that result each year from the abuse of drugs and alcohol and from other irresponsibly risky behaviors. The "two-sided rule" teaches us to look for the positive side of each commandment (see chapter 48). When it comes to the sixth commandment, this means that we have a duty to preserve both our own lives and the lives of our neighbors. Tragically, when this ceases to be a concern, the results are deadly.

We are not the only ones who are living in a culture of death. Such is the hatred of the human heart that people are killing one another all over the world. There is ethnic violence in Europe, attempted genocide in Africa, religious warfare in the Middle East. Communists persecute Christians in China, and there is a threat of terror wherever militant Islam confronts the West. Even if we do not personally face these terrors ourselves, the sixth commandment demands a global perspective. John Calvin rightly said, "The purpose of this commandment is: the Lord has bound mankind together by a certain unity; hence each man ought to concern himself with the safety of all."[15]

## The Pro-Life Samaritan

Many Bible stories illustrate the sixth commandment. Perhaps the most obvious is the story of Cain and Abel—the first murderer and his victim. There is also the story of Lamech, who performed the original gangsta rap:

> Adah and Zillah, hear my voice;
>   you wives of Lamech, listen to what I say:
> I have killed a man for wounding me,
>   a young man for striking me.
> If Cain's revenge is sevenfold,
>   then Lamech's is seventy-sevenfold. (Genesis 4:23, 24)

And these examples come from only the first few chapters of Genesis. The rest of the Bible contains so many acts of violence that it is hard to know which to choose.

However, one story hits closer to home than almost any other. It is a story Jesus told about a man who got mugged and what happened to him afterward. It began like this: "A man was going down from Jerusalem to Jericho, and he fell among robbers, who stripped him and beat him and departed, leaving him half dead" (Luke 10:30). It was a terrible crime, and if there were any justice in the world, the men who committed it would be punished for violating the sixth commandment. Although they did not actually kill the man, they almost did, and God forbids any form of lawless violence.

But the robbers were not the only men who broke the sixth commandment that day. There were two fine, upstanding citizens who also broke the Law—not by killing, but by leaving a man to die. Jesus continued: "Now by chance a priest was going down that road, and when he saw him he passed by on the other side. So likewise a Levite, when he came to the place and saw him, passed by on the other side" (vv. 31, 32).

Like many of the stories Jesus told, this one was intended to shock and offend. The priest and the Levite were respected religious leaders. Think of them as pastors, elders, or deacons. They both saw that the man was in need, but neither of them did anything to help. It's not hard to imagine reasons why. Maybe they were late for worship. Maybe they told themselves he was already dead. Maybe they just didn't want to get involved. But whatever the reason, they both made a deliberate choice not to save the dying man. The priest and the Levite saw that he was in need, yet they made a conscious decision to avoid him. They looked the other way, pretending not to notice, and they went to the other side of the road. It was a shocking thing for men in their position to do. In a way, the worst thing that happened to the victim that day was not getting mugged, but getting rejected by his spiritual leaders, who were too busy to save his life.

What this story shows is that sometimes all it takes to break the sixth commandment is to do nothing at all. Martin Luther said,

> This commandment is violated not only when a person actually does evil, but also when he fails to do good to his neighbor, or, though he has the opportunity, fails to prevent, protect, and save him from suffering bodily harm or injury. If you send a person away naked when you could clothe him, you have let him freeze to death. If you see anyone suffer hunger and do not feed him, you have let him starve. Likewise, if you see anyone condemned to death or in similar peril and do not save him although you know ways and means to do so, you have killed him. It will do you no good to plead that you did not contribute to his death by word and deed, for you have withheld your love from him and robbed him of the service by which his life might have been saved.[16]

These are sobering words for Christians who live in a culture of death. Media violence, homicide, rape, abortion, euthanasia, assisted suicide, warfare, terrorism—the evils are so overwhelming that it is tempting to do nothing at all. But we must at least do what we can. We can teach our children how to resolve conflict without resorting to violence. We can pray for peace in the troubled parts of the world. We can intercede on behalf of the unborn, the disabled, and the elderly. We can help save children through adoption and foster care. We can care for the sick and the dying. We can send relief to those who are oppressed. We can work to make laws that bring justice and promote life.

This is the positive side to keeping the sixth commandment. At the same time God forbids us to take life unjustly, he commands us to guard it carefully. We are called to protect life, one life at a time. In other words, we are called to be like the hero of Jesus' story, the Good Samaritan. Here is how that story ends:

> But a Samaritan, as he journeyed, came to where he was, and when he saw him, he had compassion. He went to him and bound up his wounds, pouring on oil and wine. Then he set him on his own animal and brought him to an inn and took care of him. And the next day he took out two denarii and gave them to the innkeeper, saying, "Take care of him, and whatever more you spend, I will repay you when I come back." (Luke 10:33–35)

There is more to keeping the sixth commandment than not mugging people. The Samaritan took the time to see what the man needed, and when he saw the need, he was filled with compassion. Rather than closing off his emotions, he opened his heart to be touched by someone else's suffering. He got involved, even when things were messy. He invested his own valuable time and money to provide what was needed. And he followed through, making sure that the victim was fully restored. But what is most remarkable of all is that he did all this for someone outside his own people group. In those days Jews did not associate with Samaritans, but rather than giving in to that kind of ethnic hatred, the Good Samaritan treated his enemy the same way he would treat a friend.

Jesus told the story of the pro-life Samaritan to a man who wanted to know who counted as his neighbor. The man knew that he was supposed to love his neighbor, but that seemed awfully open-ended. It might include anyone! Hoping to find some way to limit his obligations, he asked Jesus, "And who is my neighbor?" (v. 29). In response Jesus told his story about the man who got mugged on the Jericho road. When he had finished, Jesus asked, "Which of these three, do you think, proved to be a neighbor to the man who fell among the robbers?" (v. 36). The answer was obvious. The man questioning Jesus replied, "The one who showed him mercy." Then seizing the opportunity to drive his point home, Jesus said, "You go, and do likewise" (v. 37).

Jesus says the same thing to us. Keeping the sixth commandment means more than not murdering anyone. It means loving our neighbor. It means showing kindness to strangers and mercy to our enemies. *The Heidelberg Catechism* says it well: "Is it enough then, if we do not kill our neighbor in any such way?" (A. 107). The answer is "No; for when God condemns envy, hatred, and anger, he requires us to love our neighbor as ourselves, to show patience, gentleness, mercy, and friendliness toward him, to prevent injury to him as much as we can, and also to do good to our enemies."

## Murder of the Heart

Like the rest of God's law, the sixth commandment is a lot harder to keep than it seems at first. Most people don't think of themselves as murderers. Sometimes even murderers don't think of themselves that way. Back in 1931 one of "America's most wanted" was Two-Gun Crowley. Two-Gun was charged with a string of brutal homicides, including a cop-killing. That spring he was finally captured after a fierce gun battle in his girlfriend's apartment. When the police searched him, they found a blood-spattered note that read, "Under my coat is a weary heart, but a kind one, one that would do nobody any harm."[17]

Two-Gun was wrong. His heart *was* unkind; he *did* want to do somebody harm. But we are all guilty of the same kind of self-deception. We like to think of the sixth commandment as one of the few we actually keep. At least we haven't murdered anyone! But Jesus said, "You have heard that it was said to those of old, 'You shall not murder; and whoever murders will be liable to judgment.' But I say to you that everyone who is angry with his brother will be liable to judgment" (Matthew 5:21, 22).

Here we need to remember one of our rules for interpreting the Ten Commandments. According to the "inside/outside" rule (see chapter 48), each commandment covers inward attitudes as well as outward actions. *The Heidelberg Catechism* explains it like this: "I am not to dishonor, hate, injure, or kill my neighbor by thoughts, words, or gestures, and much less by deeds" (A. 105). So instead of being one of the easiest commandments to keep, "You shall not murder" actually is one of the hardest, because even if we do not kill one another with our deeds, we often dishonor one another with our words and in our thoughts.

How easy it is to commit what Calvin called "murder of the heart"![18] By this standard, it is as wrong to hate those who carry out abortions as it is for them to perform them in the first place. To quote again from the *Heidelberg Catechism*, "By forbidding murder God teaches us that He hates the root of murder, such as envy, hatred, anger, and desire of revenge, and that He regards all these as murder" (A. 106). But these are the kinds of homicide we have all committed. Envy in the Biblical sense is not simply the desire to have what someone else has, but to take it away from them so that they are harmed in the process. Hatred is a settled resentment, a permanent and vindictive grudge, the desire to get back at someone. It is really a way of wishing someone were dead, for as the Bible says, "Everyone who hates his brother is a murderer" (1 John 3:15; cf. Leviticus 19:17). Anger is a more sudden and more violent passion. Sometimes we say, "If looks could kill . . ." The point Jesus was trying to make was that sometimes they can. There is almost always something murderous about our anger. There is a place for righteous anger, of course, but we are not very righteous, and our unrighteousness usually shows up in our anger.

We also break the sixth commandment with our words. Jesus said, "Out of the abundance of the heart the mouth speaks" (Matthew 12:34b). This means that when we use angry words—when we put people down, when we whisper about their reputations, when we make racist or sexist remarks—we reveal that there is murder in our hearts. According to Proverbs, "rash words are like sword thrusts" (12:18), which is another way of saying that our words can be used as murder weapons. What we say can be deadly at home, on the job, and in the church.

Are you a murderer? Do you ever say anything to hurt someone? Do you ever take secret satisfaction in another's misfortune? Do you have an enemy—someone you are out to get? Do you want to make somebody pay for what they've done? Do you ever get so angry that you're out of control? There are many ways to break the sixth commandment, and we are all guilty of some of them, if not all of them.

This is a real problem because the Bible explicitly excludes murderers from the kingdom of God. When the book of Revelation lists the kinds of sinners who will be sent into "the lake that burns with fire and sulfur" (Revelation 21:8), murderers are specifically mentioned. Elsewhere the Bible says that anyone who is guilty of "enmity, strife . . . fits of anger . . . [and] envy . . . will not inherit the kingdom of God" (Galatians 5:20, 21). So if we commit murder—even if only in our hearts—then we deserve to go to Hell. If there is no way for murderers to be saved, there is no way for anyone to be saved. We all need a Savior.

It's a good thing Jesus kept God's law, including the law that said, "You shall not kill unlawfully." The Bible says that Jesus was "oppressed, and he was afflicted . . . although he had done no violence" (Isaiah 53:7a, 9). It says further that "like a lamb that is led to the slaughter . . . he opened not his mouth" (Isaiah 53:7b). In other words, Jesus was peaceable even when he was provoked, and in this way he offered perfect obedience to the sixth commandment.

It's a good thing, too, that when Jesus died on the cross, he died for murderers as much as for anyone else. We know this because he offered forgiveness to the very people who murdered him (Luke 23:34). Afterward, when Jesus had ascended into Heaven, the apostle Peter preached in Jerusalem to the same people who had called for Christ to be crucified. He basically accused them of murder, of killing the one who came to be their Savior. When they realized what they had done, they desperately wanted to know what they could do about it. Peter said, "Repent and be baptized every one of you in the name of Jesus Christ for the forgiveness of your sins" (Acts 2:38a). There was a way for their murderous sin to be forgiven. The very death that they were guilty of demanding—Christ's death on the cross—was the death that atoned for their sin.

If you're the kind of person who breaks the sixth commandment, then there is hope for you in the cross of Christ. If you are prone to get angry, if there is someone you secretly resent, if there is murder in your heart—or if you have ever committed any other kind of murder in thought, word, or deed (including abortion, infanticide, or euthanasia)—then repent and believe in Jesus Christ for the forgiveness of your sins. Save a life (your own!) by trusting in him.

# 55

# The Seventh Commandment: The Joy of Sex

## EXODUS 20:14

IN ONE OF THE MORE embarrassing experiences of my adolescence, my father's name appeared on the cover of *Christianity Today*. Why was this an embarrassment? Because the title of his cover article—which was printed in bold white letters against a black background—was "The Puritans and Sex."

Although it offended my teenage sensibilities, the article's title had the kind of frankness that many Puritans might have appreciated. Prior to the Reformation the church generally regarded sex—even within marriage—as a necessary evil. Tertullian regarded the extinction of the human race as preferable to procreation. Ambrose said that married couples ought to be ashamed of their sexuality. Augustine was willing to admit that intercourse might be lawful but taught that sexual passion was always a sin. Many priests counseled couples to abstain from sex altogether. The Catholic Church gradually began to prohibit sex on certain holy days, so that by the time of Martin Luther, the list had grown to 183 days a year.[1]

Thank God for the Reformation, which began to restore sexual sanity by celebrating the physical act of lovemaking within marriage. According to my father, "The Puritan doctrine of sex was a watershed in the cultural history of the West. The Puritans devalued celibacy, glorified companionate marriage, affirmed married sex as both necessary and pure, established the ideal of wedded romantic love, and exalted the role of the wife."[2] In other words, they promoted a more Biblical view of human sexuality.

## The Gift of Sex

The Biblical view of sex begins with acknowledging our sexuality as a gift from God. After all, the physical union between a husband and wife was God's idea in the first place. It was part of the goodness of his creation. God told Adam to cleave to his wife so that they could be fruitful and multiply (Genesis 1:28a). And it is by the inspiration of God's Spirit that the Bible includes the following duet between the lover and his beloved:

> Let him kiss me with the kisses of his mouth!
>     For your love is better than wine . . .
> Draw me after you; let us run.
>     The king has brought me into his chambers. (Song of Solomon 1:2, 4a)
>
> Behold, you are beautiful, my love;
>     behold, you are beautiful;
>     your eyes are doves.
> Behold, you are beautiful, my beloved, truly delightful.
> Our couch is green. (1:15, 16)
>
> How beautiful is your love, my sister, my bride!
>     How much better is your love than wine,
>     and the fragrance of your oils than any spice!
> Your lips drip nectar, my bride;
>     honey and milk are under your tongue. (4:10, 11a)
>
> I slept, but my heart was awake.
> A sound! My beloved is knocking.
> "Open to me, my sister, my love,
>     my dove, my perfect one,
> for my head is wet with dew,
>     my locks with the drops of the night."
> I had put off my garment;
>     how could I put it on?
> I had bathed my feet;
>     how could I soil them?
> My beloved put his hand to the latch,
>     and my heart was thrilled within me.
> I arose to open to my beloved,
>     and my hands dripped with myrrh,
> my fingers with liquid myrrh,
>     on the handles of the bolt. (5:2–5)

It doesn't take much imagination to understand what kind of sexual intimacy the Holy Spirit has in mind. Although God's Word is never pornographic, it is unashamedly erotic. If this comes as an embarrassment to some Christians, it is only because we are more prudish than God is. The Bible celebrates the sexual act of love—exclusively within marriage (see Proverbs 5:15–19)—as a gift from God.

The traditional Roman Catholic view of sex was utilitarian. Intercourse was only for procreation, the propagation of the human race. The Biblical view is that sex is not merely procreational but also relational, and even recreational. Sex is for love, for pleasure, and for joy. And it is in order to protect this joy that God has given us the seventh commandment: "You shall not commit adultery" (20:14).

## Eros Defiled

What does it mean to commit adultery? The simplest answer is that adultery is marital infidelity. It is sexual intercourse that breaks the bonds of a marriage covenant. So the primary purpose of this commandment is to protect marriage. Adultery is the greatest sexual sin because it violates the trust between a husband and wife. It breaks the marriage covenant, a promise made before God. For this reason, adultery does more damage than other forms of sexual sin, such as having sex before marriage. The Bible confirms this by making the penalty for adultery so severe: "If a man commits adultery with the wife of his neighbor, both the adulterer and the adulteress shall surely be put to death" (Leviticus 20:10). Was this punishment just? Douglas Wilson comments: "Certainly an adulterer is worthy of death; a man who will betray his wife will betray anyone and anything. Adultery is treason against the family, and God hates it."[3]

Having sex is not the only way to commit adultery, however. As we have seen, the Ten Commandments generally rule out the most extreme form of every kind of sin, but by implication they also rule out all the lesser sins that lead up to it. In the case of the seventh commandment, what is forbidden is everything that causes adultery. Most adulterous relationships don't start with sex; they start with inappropriate intimacy. The seventh commandment thus forbids a married man to flirt with a woman who is not his wife, or a single man to get close to someone else's wife. In order to forestall temptation, a certain social distance needs to be maintained. The commandment also forbids a married woman to seek emotional support from some other man, whether at work, at church, or in an Internet chat room. To put things more positively, the seventh commandment requires husbands and wives to nurture their love for one another emotionally and spiritually as well as sexually.

Furthermore, committing adultery is not the only way to break the seventh commandment. According to the rule of categories, each commandment applies to every sin of the same kind. So the seventh commandment rules out any form of sexual immorality, or what the Greek New Testament calls *porneia*. "You shall not commit adultery" also means, to use the proper terminology, "you shall not fornicate." Fornication is sexual intercourse in a relationship outside the covenant commitment of marriage. It refers most specifically to premarital sex, which is a violation of the seventh commandment.

Couples that are dating often wonder how far they can go. The Bible doesn't say where the line is. Certainly any form of genital stimulation is ruled out. Until a man and a woman are actually married, they do not have the right to enjoy the sexual parts of one another's bodies. But the real problem is the question itself. Instead of wondering what they can get away with, couples ought to be asking questions like "How can I protect my sexual purity?" and "How can I preserve the joy of the person I love?" As Christians we are called to purity, not because we are sexually repressed, but because we are unwilling to settle for illicit pleasures that rob the joy of marital intercourse.

What else is ruled out? Prostitution is forbidden on the same grounds as adultery and fornication. Homosexual intercourse is ruled out because the Biblical pattern calls for sex to be shared only between a husband and wife. Also forbidden is sexual violence, including rape, pedophilia, incest, or any form of sexual abuse within a marriage. In short, the seventh commandment forbids any sexual activity that violates the covenant of marriage. Period. There are no exceptions and no loopholes.

Why is adultery, in all its forms, forbidden? Not because sex is bad, but because it is designed to be such a powerful force for good. Sex is like superglue. When used properly, intercourse seals the bond of matrimony. It is the glue—the "covenant cement," as New York City pastor Tim Keller calls it—that helps hold a marriage secure. This is why husbands and wives are required to have sexual relations. The Bible says, "The husband should give to his wife her conjugal rights, and likewise the wife to her husband. . . . Do not deprive one another" (1 Corinthians 7:3, 5a; cf. Hebrews 13:4). God has made us sexual beings to seal the love between a husband and wife. Their sexual union cements their total spiritual communion.

Whenever sexual intercourse is divorced from this total life commitment, it loses its true purpose and its highest joy. According to C. S. Lewis,

> The Christian idea of marriage is based on Christ's words that a man and wife are to be regarded as a single organism. . . . [T]he male and the female were made to be combined together in pairs, not simply on a sexual level, but totally combined. The monstrosity of sexual intercourse outside marriage is that those who indulge in it are trying to isolate one kind of union (the sexual) from all the other kinds of union which were intended to go along with it and make up the total union. The Christian attitude does not mean that there is anything wrong about sexual pleasure, any more than about the pleasure of eating. It means that you must not isolate that pleasure and try to get it by itself, any more than you ought to try to get the pleasures of taste without swallowing and digesting, by chewing things and spitting them out again.[4]

Whenever people try to isolate the pleasures of sex, they always end up harming themselves and others. Since sex is like superglue, squeezing it out at the wrong time or in the wrong place always creates an awful mess. The wrong things get joined together, and getting them unstuck again tears at the soul. This is why adultery is forbidden. It is because sex is a great force for good, but only when it is used to join one man and one woman for life.

Another reason God forbids adultery is because there is a close connection between our sexuality and our spirituality. The union between a husband and wife is intended to exemplify the exclusive relationship between God and his people. There is something transcendent about our sexuality. In the same way that husbands and wives give themselves to one another—holding nothing back—God gives himself to us and wants us to give ourselves to him. In the Old Testament God often compared his relationship with his people to the romance between a husband and wife. When his people were unfaithful—when they broke their love covenant with him—they were guilty of committing spiritual adultery (e.g., Jeremiah 3:1–10; 5:7–11; Hosea 2; Malachi 2:10–16).

The New Testament deepens the mystery by defining marriage in terms of our relationship to Jesus Christ. Paul quotes from Genesis: "'Therefore a man shall leave his father and mother and hold fast to his wife, and the two shall become one flesh'" (Ephesians 5:31). Then he adds this comment: "This mystery is profound, and I am saying that it refers to Christ and the church" (v. 32). In other words, the union between husband and wife exemplifies the union between Christ and his church.

This has major implications for our sexuality. For the Christian, every act of sexual immorality is a kind of spiritual desecration. It is an offense against God the Son. "The body is not meant for sexual immorality," Paul told the Corinthians, "but for the Lord, and the Lord for the body. . . . Do you not know that your bodies are members of Christ?" (1 Corinthians 6:13b, 15a). If this is true—if our bodies are in Christ and for Christ—then sexual immorality is a sin against God the Son. Paul continues: "Shall I then take the members of Christ and make them members of a prostitute? Never! Or do you not know that he who is joined to a prostitute becomes one body with her? For, as it is written, 'The two will become one flesh.' But he who is joined to the Lord becomes one spirit with him" (vv. 15b–17). For Christians to have sex with someone who is not a spouse is to violate the holiness of their union with Christ. We show our covenant loyalty to God by maintaining our sexual fidelity to our spouse (or our future spouse).

Sexual sin also dishonors the Holy Spirit. Paul goes on to say this: "Flee from sexual immorality. Every other sin a person commits is outside the body, but the sexually immoral person sins against his own body. Or do you not know that your body is a temple of the Holy Spirit within you, whom you have from God? You are not your own, for you were bought with a price. So glorify God in your body" (vv. 18–20). Our bodies were purchased for God when Christ died on the cross. Now they are inhabited by God's Spirit. This means that whatever we do with our bodies is directly related to our fellowship with the triune God. In addition to damaging ourselves and others, committing adultery dishonors the Father, the Son, and the Holy Spirit.

### The Deadly Sin of Lust

Sexual immorality is common in our culture. People are looking for love, but they are settling for sex. Consider the casual sex on the college campus, the aggressive promotion of homosexuality as a lifestyle, and all the sexual material on television. With all the encounters and innuendoes, the average American views sexual material more than ten thousand times a year.[5] And by a ratio of more than ten to one, the couplings on television involve sex outside of marriage. This is because, as one TV producer explained, "married or celibate characters aren't as much fun."[6] Consider as well the vast pornography industry: the video stores, the strip clubs, the phone lines, and the cable channels. And consider the way that sex is used to sell—the soft pornography of the advertising industry. Then consider the personal consequences of all this sexual immorality: divorce, disease, and the sexual abuse of children.

It is tempting to think that our hypersexed culture is the problem, but of course sexual immorality is nearly as common in the church. Christians, including pastors and other spiritual leaders, get caught up in all the same kinds of sexual sin. On any given Sunday there are people sitting in church who only the night before watched a pornographic video or had sex outside of marriage. This shows that the problem is not our culture, even for all its temptations; the problem is our own sinful hearts.

Jesus said, "You have heard that it was said, 'You shall not commit adultery.' But I say to you that everyone who looks at a woman with lustful intent has already committed adultery with her in his heart" (Matthew 5:27, 28; cf. 15:19). When Jesus spoke these famous words, he was using the inside/outside rule for interpreting the Ten Commandments: The Law governs our inward thoughts as well as our outward actions. It covers both the desires of the heart and the deeds of the body. For the seventh commandment, this means that we are forbidden to lust.

To lust is to look at a woman—or a man, for that matter—and to imagine the sexual possibilities. Jesus told his disciples not to look at anyone *lustfully*. Looking is not the problem. The problem is looking at someone in a way that leads to sexual arousal. Whenever we look at someone that way, viewing a person as an object to satisfy our desire, we are lusting after sin. This sin is compounded when our lust leads to sexual self-gratification (i.e., masturbation), which is an act of self-worship.

There are many other ways to commit inward adultery. Martin Luther said, "[T]his commandment applies to every form of unchastity, however it is called.

Not only is the external act forbidden, but also every kind of cause, motive, and means. Your heart, your lips, and your whole body are to be chaste and to afford no occasion, aid, or encouragement to unchastity."[7] *The Westminster Shorter Catechism* states the matter more simply: "The Seventh Commandment requireth the preservation of our own and our neighbor's chastity, in heart, speech, and behavior" (A. 71). To apply these principles, we break the seventh commandment by reading sexual literature, such as most romance novels. We break it by fantasizing about relationships that include sexual intimacy. We also break it by what we say, by making suggestive comments or telling dirty jokes. The Bible says, "But sexual immorality . . . must not even be named among you, as is proper among saints. Let there be no filthiness nor foolish talk nor crude joking, which are out of place" (Ephesians 5:3, 4). These are all ways of breaking the seventh commandment in the heart.

Most people have a higher tolerance for their inward sins than they do for their outward sins. We're less concerned about the sins of our hearts because no one else knows about them (or so we think). But our inward flaws are just as fatal. This is true of lust, which the medieval church rightly listed as one of the seven deadly sins. No doubt there are more than seven, but however many there are, lust certainly belongs on the list!

Lust has many unhappy consequences. It's expensive. It will cost a man his money, and maybe even his life: "Do not desire her beauty in your heart, and do not let her capture you with her eyelashes; for the price of a prostitute is only a loaf of bread, but a married woman hunts down a precious life" (Proverbs 6:25, 26). Giving in to lust is like playing with fire. Solomon asked, "Can a man carry fire next to his chest and his clothes not be burned?" (Proverbs 6:27). Lust leads men and women into shame and disgrace (Proverbs 6:32, 33). But worst of all, sexual sin brings us under the wrath of God: "Or do you not know that the unrighteous will not inherit the kingdom of God? Do not be deceived: neither the sexually immoral, nor idolaters, nor adulterers, nor men who practice homosexuality, . . . will inherit the kingdom of God" (1 Corinthians 6:9, 10). "Let marriage be held in honor among all, and let the marriage bed be undefiled, for God will judge the sexually immoral and adulterous" (Hebrews 13:4).

Thankfully, God gives grace to sinners who repent of their lust and come to faith in Jesus Christ. Having listed the various kinds of people who are excluded from eternal life, Paul goes on to say, "And such were some of you. But you were washed, you were sanctified, you were justified in the name of the Lord Jesus Christ and by the Spirit of our God" (1 Corinthians 6:11). Through the death and resurrection of Jesus Christ, God offers forgiveness to lusty sinners.

But God offers something more than forgiveness. By his Spirit he gives grace in the time of temptation. He has also provided a practical way to preserve our chastity. It's called marriage. Admittedly there are some Christians who have the gift of continence, or celibacy. For some physical or spiritual reason, they have a special capacity for refraining from sexual sin. However, most Christians do not have that gift, and obviously it would be good for them to get married. The Apostle Paul said, "But each has his own gift from God, one of one kind and one of another. To the unmarried and the widows I say that it is good for them to remain single as I am. But if they cannot exercise self-control, they should marry. For it is better to marry than to burn with passion" (1 Corinthians 7:7b–9).

Every unmarried single Christian is called to sexual purity. As we shall see, there are practical ways to live out this calling. God gives grace to those who seek to honor him by preserving their chastity. However, anyone who struggles with sexual self-control should make spiritual preparations for marriage. For men, this means learning to live for others, practicing the self-sacrificing love of Christ. For women, this means learning to serve others, living in submission to Christ. Unfortunately, many Christian men are too self-centered to get outside themselves and love others. Often they get caught up in secret sexual sin, including pornography and masturbation. Relationally broken, they settle for the false intimacy and false acceptance of self-fulfillment without ever learning how to love a woman. The sad result is that many good Christian women suffer for the want of a good Christian man. It would be better for all concerned if these men (and also these women) made spiritual preparations for marriage, and the best way to do this is to grow in submission and sacrifice.

Submission and sacrifice are the virtues that marriage demands, and not surprisingly they also prove to be the virtues that bring joy to sex. Our culture places far too much emphasis on technique, trying to turn lovemaking into some kind of scientific skill. But husbands and wives are called to do more than "have sex"; they are called to find joy in the sexual love that they share. When couples are not finding satisfaction, usually the problem is not sexual but relational, and therefore spiritual. Often there is a lot of blame-shifting, with husbands and wives criticizing one another for their shortcomings. What is the answer?

At the risk of oversimplifying, the answer is for husbands to love their wives in sacrificial ways. The husband's spiritual leadership is fundamental for everything that happens in a marriage, including what happens in bed. Of course, wives also have an obligation to their husbands, including a sexual obligation. As mentioned earlier, "The husband should give to his wife her conjugal rights, and likewise the wife to her husband" (1 Corinthians 7:3). Interestingly, here is one place where the Bible teaches mutual submission: "For the wife does not have authority over her own body, but the husband does. Likewise the husband does not have authority over his own body, but the wife does" (v. 4). So husbands and wives must offer themselves to one another in what the Puritans called "the mutual communication of bodies." This is their marital duty. But it will always be a chore if a wife is not cherished by her husband. The key to a happy marriage, sexually and otherwise, is, "Husbands, love your wives, as Christ loved the church and gave himself up for her" (Ephesians 5:25).

## David's Folly

The poet Wendell Berry once defined sexual love as "the power that joins a couple together" and marriage as "the way we protect the possibility that sexual love can become a story."[8] Berry is right: When a man and a woman are joined together in marriage, their love becomes a story. However, when their love is betrayed, the story turns into a tragedy, as in the story of David and Bathsheba.

David was the king of Israel, and the Bible tells how one night he "arose from his couch and was walking on the roof of the king's house" (2 Samuel 11:2a). That warm spring evening David had everything a man could ever want. He had conquered his enemies and established his kingdom. He was living in royal luxury. He was famous and handsome. Moreover, he was righteous, a man after God's own heart. He wrote beautiful hymns of praise to the God who had promised him an eternal kingdom. As he strolled around the roof, David was the master of all that he surveyed. There was nothing more for him to gain . . . but he still had everything to lose.

Tragically, David had exposed himself to temptation. Walking around the roof seems innocent enough, but David had no business being there at all. He should have been out defending his people in battle. Instead he was walking back and forth, going nowhere, killing time. The story of his tragic downfall begins with these ominous words: "In the spring of the year, the time when kings go out to battle, David sent Joab, and his servants with him, and all Israel. And they ravaged the Ammonites and besieged Rabbah. But David remained at Jerusalem" (2 Samuel 11:1).

This verse does more than simply tell us where David was; it tells us where he should have been and what he should have been doing. His nation was still at war, and as the king it was his duty to lead his armies into battle. Instead David decided to take it easy. When the Bible tells us that he "remained at Jerusalem," this is meant as a reproach. The king had stopped serving, sacrificing, and giving his life away for others. It is not at all surprising that it was at this time that he indulged in sexual sin.

Committing adultery is sometimes considered a masculine thing to do. "That's just the way men are," people say. But David's example shows that the real truth is just the opposite: Sexual sin is a failure of godly manliness. Elsewhere the Bible says that to break the seventh commandment is to "give your honor to others" (Proverbs 5:9). The man of God does not live for himself but for others, and this enables him to keep his sexual desire under the power of love. But when a man turns inward, he is vulnerable to all kinds of sexual temptation.

This is a key insight for anyone who struggles with sins against the seventh commandment. Sexual sin is never just about sex; it is always connected to the rest of life. David never would have committed adultery if he had been doing what God had called him to do. Instead he abdicated his royal responsibility and retreated to his palace. There, in his idleness and isolation, he gave in to temptation. This shows how vulnerable we are to sexual sin when we are living for ourselves and not for others. What we do with our bodies is not just physical but also spiritual. It comes from the deepest desires of the heart. One way to gain victory over sexual sin is to live self-sacrificially rather than self-indulgently, and to do so in every area of life. Godliness in one area promotes godliness in others.

David made a strategic blunder when he stopped giving himself away in love. Then he made a serious tactical mistake: "He saw from the roof a woman bathing" (2 Samuel 11:2). If David had simply caught a glimpse of the woman, he would not have been guilty, but he did more than this. His glance became a gaze. He ogled the woman, looking her up and down, thinking about what he'd like to do with her.

This gives us a further insight into sexual temptation and how to avoid it. The eye is a window to sinful desire. One way to gain victory over sexual sin, therefore, is to turn away our lusty gaze. And godly women have always understood that this requires modesty in the way they dress. Godly men have always understood that preserving sexual purity means being careful what we keep looking at. The apostle Peter wisely warned against having "eyes full of adultery" (2 Peter 2:14; cf. 1 John 2:16). Job's remedy was this: "I have made a covenant with my eyes; how then could I gaze at a virgin?" (Job 31:1).

Being careful what we see has never been more important than it is today, when there are sexual images almost everywhere we look. Porn has become the norm, and the greatest danger of all is the Internet, which is the most powerful purveyor of pornography in the history of the world. What makes the Internet so dangerous is that it is anonymous, accessible, and affordable.[9] Anyone with a computer can download pornography in complete privacy. And the stream of sexual material is endless. Other forms of pornography eventually lose their appeal because the images have all been seen before. But on the Internet there is always something new. According to one popular men's magazine,

> What makes sex online far more compelling than any shrink-wrapped smut [is] instant gratification in endless variety—you never get to the end of the magazine and have to start looking at the same pictures again. With old porn, once you view it, you've consumed it. You've chewed the flavor out of the gum. This can't be done on the Net. The gum never runs out of flavor. A new piece of flesh waits behind every old one, and expectation bids you to go further. Much further. Because as long as there's more to come, you'll keep looking. This is all so new. No stimulus like this ever existed before.[10]

As long as there is more to see, some people will keep looking, including some Christians. One Internet expert wrote the following letter to his pastor:

> I'm deeply concerned about the avenues for decadent content that have been opened into the home.
>
> I'm fortunate to have many good Christian male friends that I can confide in and talk openly with about their faith and areas in their life where they are struggling. What has been alarming to me is that out of a dozen or so close friends that I have talked to, all but one has admitted that they struggle in this area and frequently fail. All of these friends are very committed followers of Christ, many involved in full time Christian service. What I see is that Christians who would have never even considered going into an adult store, renting an R/X rated movie, or dialing a 900 number, are now continually failing in this area because of the anonymity and free and easy access to this type of content on the Internet. What is worse, is seeing the grip and pull it has on people once they start down this path.
>
> Based on my experience, the Internet has become Satan's number one tool in the 21st century and it seems to be a more silent infection into the body of believers because it typically only involves the user and [his or her] computer.[11]

The silent infection of pornography in the church is deadly. It denigrates women, damages relationships, and destroys a man's spiritual ability to lead. The Puritan Thomas Watson rightly said that pornographic pictures "secretly convey poison to the heart."[12]

To see how deadly lust is, look what happened to David. The more he looked at the woman, the more he wanted her. Sin was starting to take control, and as David began to fantasize, he found himself unable to turn away. Rather than fleeing from temptation (see Genesis 39:12; Proverbs 5:8; 2 Timothy 2:22), he began to "make . . . provision for the flesh, to gratify its desires" (Romans 13:14). He toyed with the possibilities: "The woman was very beautiful. And David sent and inquired about the woman. And one said, 'Is not this Bathsheba, the daughter of Eliam, the wife of Uriah the Hittite?'" (2 Samuel 11:2b, 3).

The whole matter should have ended right there. Bathsheba was a married woman. Giving her any further thought was out of the question for a man of God, but David felt like he had to have her. Bathsheba had become an obsession. This is the way lust works. It takes on a power of its own, pulling us in deeper and deeper until we feel powerless to resist. And since David was the king, he could do what most men can only dream of doing. If he wanted a woman, he could take her, and so he did: "So David sent messengers and took her, and she came to him, and he lay with her" (v. 4a).

It seemed like such a small thing—only a moment of weakness, that's all. But soon Bathsheba discovered that she was pregnant, and the cover-up started. By the time David was finished, Bathsheba's husband was dead, and the king was guilty not only of adultery but also of lying, stealing, and murder. And for a while it seemed like he would get away with it all, too. Sure, he had to scramble a little bit to make it happen, but everything went according to plan. Except for this: "The thing that David had done displeased the LORD" (2 Samuel 11:27b).

Like David, Christians often seem to think they can sin with impunity. We engage in a little sexual fantasy. Why not? Then we look at some pornography. Who doesn't? At first it doesn't seem all that harmful. We can still carry out our ministry as effectively as ever. No one will ever know. But God always knows. Solomon said, "Why should you be intoxicated, my son, with a forbidden woman and embrace the bosom of an adulteress? For a man's ways are before the eyes of the LORD, and he ponders all his paths" (Proverbs 5:20, 21). God sees everything we do with our bodies. He knows what we look at, think about, desire, and touch, and he will hold us accountable.

God certainly held David accountable! From the moment the king decided to act on his lust, his life became a tragic series of disappointments. He lost almost everything he had worked so hard to obtain. Bathsheba's son died. David's family was torn apart by rape, incest, and fratricide. His kingdom was divided. His beloved son rebelled against him, even having sex with David's wives on top of the palace, bringing shame to his father's house. And all for the sake of a few minutes in bed.

Do you think it was worth it? If not, then what about your own sexual sins? What do you really gain, and what are you willing to lose?

## Eros Redeemed

In this whole sordid affair there was only one thing that David did right: He admitted his sin. God loved David, and out of his marvelous mercy and amazing grace, he sent his prophet Nathan to confront him. Once his sin was exposed, David knew that he was guilty. Even more, he knew that what he had done was worthy of death. So he did the only thing a guilty sinner can do, and that is to cry out to God for mercy. He said, "I have sinned against the LORD" (2 Samuel 12:13a).

There are many lessons to learn from David's interview with Nathan. We learn that we cannot hide our sin from God. We learn that sin always has consequences. We learn that because sexual immorality thrives on secrecy, we need the open assistance of other believers—especially pastors—to help us turn away from sin. But we also learn this: when we sin, we should go straight back to God and confess it.

David's full confession is recorded in Psalm 51. He began by crying out for God to forgive him:

> Have mercy on me, O God,
> according to your steadfast love;

according to your abundant mercy
  blot out my transgressions.
Wash me thoroughly from my iniquity,
  and cleanse me from my sin! (Psalm 51:1, 2)

David made his appeal for forgiveness on the basis of an atoning sacrifice, the blood of a lamb applied to the guilt of his sin:

Purge me with hyssop, and I shall be clean;
  wash me, and I shall be whiter than snow. (Psalm 51:7)

Then he prayed for God's ongoing work of sanctification in his life:

Create in me a clean heart, O God,
  and renew a right spirit within me.
Cast me not away from your presence,
  and take not your Holy Spirit from me.
Restore to me the joy of your salvation,
  and uphold me with a willing spirit. (Psalm 51:10–12)

David got it right at last. He made a full and open confession, and God had mercy on him, as he does on every sinner who truly repents. Nathan said to David, "The Lord also has put away your sin; you shall not die" (2 Samuel 12:13b). To be sure, David still had to face the consequences of his sin. But his sin was forgiven, his guilt was taken away.

So often when we break the seventh commandment, we feel so guilty that it is all we can do to drag ourselves back to the cross, when what we ought to do instead is to run back to the cross and confess our sin. At the cross we can find a sacrifice for our sin, with cleansing for our guilt and the power to start living again for Christ.

When God confronts us with the guilt of sexual sin we have a choice. If we keep hiding our sin, we may be sure that it will destroy us in the end. But if we repent of our sin, God will have mercy. In a sermon on adultery, Martyn Lloyd-Jones said, "Even adultery is not the unforgivable sin. It is a terrible sin, but God forbid that there should be anyone who feels that he or she has sinned himself or herself outside the love of God or outside His kingdom because of adultery. No; if you truly repent and realize the enormity of your sin and cast yourself upon the boundless love and mercy and grace of God, you can be forgiven and I assure you of pardon."

Lloyd-Jones could have stopped there, but he added this comment: "But hear the words of our blessed Lord: 'Go, and sin no more.'"[13] These were Jesus' words to the woman caught in adultery, and they are also his words to us, for the Bible says:

> For this is the will of God, your sanctification: that you abstain from sexual immorality; that each one of you know how to control his own body in holiness and honor, not in the passion of lust like the Gentiles who do not know God; that no one transgress and wrong his brother in this matter, because the Lord is an avenger in all these things, as we told you beforehand and solemnly warned you. For God has not called us for impurity, but in holiness. Therefore whoever disregards this, disregards not man but God, who gives his Holy Spirit to you. (1 Thessalonians 4:3–8)

# 56

# The Eighth Commandment: What's Mine Is God's

EXODUS 20:15

IN HIS BOOK ON THE TEN COMMANDMENTS, Cecil Myers describes a picture by Norman Rockwell. The well-known painting, which first appeared on the cover of *The Saturday Evening Post*, shows a woman buying a turkey for Thanksgiving dinner. The turkey is being weighed on the scale to determine the price. Behind the counter is the jolly butcher, with his apron stretched tightly over his ample belly and his pencil tucked neatly behind one ear. His customer is a respectable-looking woman of perhaps sixty. Like the butcher, she looks pleased. The two of them exchange a knowing smile, almost as if they are sharing a joke, but the joke is really on them because the painting shows what they are secretly doing. The butcher is pressing the scale down with his big fat thumb, to raise the price. At the same time, the woman is trying to get a better deal by pushing the scale up with her forefinger. The reason both of them look pleased is that neither is aware of what the other is doing!

In typical Rockwell style, the painting is a charming scene from American life that makes us laugh at our own foibles. But really what the butcher and his customer were doing was violating the eighth commandment. Myers comments: "Both the butcher and the lovely lady would resent being called thieves. The lovely lady would never rob a bank or steal a car. The butcher would be indignant if anyone accused him of stealing; and if a customer gave him a bad check, he would call the police, but neither saw anything wrong with a little deception that would make a few cents for one or save a few cents for the other."[1] In a word, they were stealing.

## On the Take

Everyone knows that stealing is wrong. Even people who don't read the Bible know the eighth commandment, which says, "You shall not steal" (20:15). To steal is to take something that doesn't belong to you. The Hebrew word for stealing (*ganaf*) literally means to carry something away, as if by stealth. To give a more technical definition, to steal is to appropriate someone else's property unlawfully.

What the eighth commandment forbids seems very simple. However, most people fail to understand its full meaning. Like the rest of God's law, the prohibition on stealing is comprehensive:

> *Ganaf*—stealing—covers all conventional types of theft: burglary (breaking into a home or building to commit theft); robbery (taking property directly from another using violence or intimidation); larceny (taking something without permission and not returning it); hijacking (using force to take goods in transit or seizing control of a bus, truck, plane, etc.); shoplifting (taking items from a store during business hours without paying for them); and pickpocketing and purse-snatching. The term *ganaf* also covers a wide range of exotic and complex thefts . . . [such as] embezzlement (the fraudulent taking of money or other goods entrusted to one's care). There is extortion (getting money from someone by means of threats or misuses of authority), and racketeering (obtaining money by any illegal means).[2]

This is only a partial list of the countless ways people violate the eighth commandment. They pilfer public property, stealing supplies from hospitals, building sites, and churches. In fact, one hotel reported in its first year of business having to replace 38,000 spoons, 18,000 tiles, 355 coffee pots . . . and 100 Bibles![3]

Citizens steal from the government by underpaying their taxes or making false claims for disability and Social Security. The government steals too. With its huge bureaucracy, the federal government commits theft on a national scale by wasting public money and by accumulating debt without fully planning to repay. Deficit spending is really a way of stealing from future citizens.

There is also theft at work. Employees fill in false time cards and call in sick when they want a day off. They help themselves to office supplies, make long-distance phone calls, and pad their expense accounts. Sometimes they go so far as to embezzle, but a more common workplace theft is simply failing to put in a full day's work. Instead workers idle away their time, sitting in their offices and surfing the Internet, sending e-mail to friends—even playing computer games. Whenever we give anything less than our best effort, we are robbing our employer of the productivity we owe.

These are not victimless crimes. Employee theft of time and property costs American businesses and their investors more than 200 billion dollars a year.

This affects all of us. According to some estimates, as much as one-third of a product's cost goes to cover the various forms of stealing that occur on its way to the marketplace. This "theft surcharge," as analysts call it, is a drag on our whole economy.

For their part, employers often steal from their workers. They demand longer hours than contracts allow. They downsize their workforce to improve their profits, and then the workers who still have jobs end up doing all their own work plus the work that used to be done by the people who were laid off! This is just a sophisticated way for companies to steal from their best employees.

Large corporations steal from the general public. They keep some of their transactions off the books. They hide their losses in offshore accounts. They manipulate securities by providing false information. One of the worst offenders in recent history was Enron, the vast energy company whose spectacular collapse in 2001 injured the whole US economy and cost some people their life savings. Enron's fall was quickly followed by a series of others, as Arthur Andersen, WorldCom, Adelphia, Rite-Aid, and other well-known corporations were caught cheating the public. The nefarious executives from these companies knew all the tricks, but this is hardly a recent phenomenon.

Martin Luther identified certain men of his day as "gentlemen swindlers or big operators. Far from being picklocks and sneak-thieves who loot a cash box, they sit in office chairs and are called great lords and honorable, good citizens, and yet with a great show of legality they rob and steal."[4] And John Calvin said, "It follows, therefore, that not only are those thieves who secretly steal the property of others, but those also who seek gain from the loss of others, accumulate wealth by unlawful practices and are more devoted to their private advantage than to equity."[5]

Many common business practices are immoral, even if technically they are not illegal. This is especially true in marketing. What many business people consider good salesmanship actually violates the eighth commandment. There is price gouging, in which the laws of supply and demand are used to take advantage of helpless consumers. There is false advertising and deceptive packaging, which is designed to make a product look bigger and better than it actually is. Salesmen exaggerate the value of their products, trying to sell people things they really don't need. Before the sale, every car is touted as the finest vehicle in automotive history, but once the sale is made, and it's time to talk about a service contract, suddenly the car is going to need all kinds of repairs that ought to be paid for in advance! And so it goes.

These practices are all violations of the eighth commandment. Calvin was right when he said, "Let us remember that all those arts whereby we acquire the possessions and money of our neighbors—when such devices depart from sincere affection to a desire to cheat or in some manner to harm—are to be considered as thefts."[6] Similarly, Luther said that we break the eighth commandment whenever we "tak[e] advantage of our neighbor in any sort of dealing that results in loss to him."[7] How much business fails to measure up to this simple standard? Much of it falls into what Scott Adams aptly terms the Weasel Zone—that "gigantic gray area between good moral behavior and outright felonious activities."[8]

Then there is all the theft that is tied up with credit. There is usury, the lending of money at exorbitant rates of interest in order to make unjust profits. Today the most blatant offenders are credit card companies that charge interest at nearly 20 percent or more. The same sin is committed on a larger scale by international banks that hold debtor nations in fiscal bondage. This is only one small aspect of a much wider problem, which is that a small minority uses the vast majority of the world's resources—and does everything they can to protect their advantage. But the Bible teaches that the poor need our help and that they should receive loans free of interest, at least within the community of God's people (Leviticus 25:35–38; Deuteronomy 15:7, 8). There is another side to this, of course, which is that some people buy on credit without ever intending to repay. No doubt this helps explain why in recent decades credit card debt has risen from 5 billion to more than 500 billion dollars.

The list goes on. There is insurance fraud, the filing of false claims. There are the deliberate cost overruns that make up the difference between the estimate and the final price whenever work is contracted. There is the theft of intellectual property and the violation of copyrights, including the unlawful duplication of music and videos. There is plagiarism, the misappropriation of someone else's work. Then there is identity theft, in which personal information is stolen off the Internet and used to run up outrageous charges.

There are countless ways to steal. *The Heidelberg Catechism* summarizes by saying that in the eighth commandment, "God forbids not only outright theft and robbery, but also such wicked schemes and devices as false weights and measures, deceptive merchandising, counterfeit money, and usury; we must not defraud our neighbor in any way, whether by force or by show of right. In addition God forbids all greed and all abuse or squandering of his gifts" (A. 110). The trouble is that when it comes to stealing, nearly everyone is doing it. Yet nearly 90 percent of evangelical Christians claim that they never break the eighth commandment.[9] This statistic is hardly encouraging. What it shows is that Christians have forgotten what stealing really means. The truth is that theft is pervasive at every level of American society, and like everyone else, we are in on the take. But this is not just an American problem. The whole human race is a band of thieves, and we all suffer the loss. Martin Luther said, "If we look at mankind in all its conditions, it is nothing but a vast, wide stable full of great thieves."[10] He also speculated what would happen if we were all brought to justice. "It is the smallest part of the thieves that are hung," he said. "If we're to hang them all, where shall we get rope enough? We must make all our belts and straps into halters."[11]

## God's Providence, Our Stewardship

What's wrong with stealing anyway? Like the rest of God's law, the eighth commandment has deep spiritual significance. Whenever we take something that doesn't belong to us—however we do it—we sin against God as well as against our neighbor.

Stealing is a sin against God in at least two ways. First, every theft is a failure to trust in his provision. Whenever we take something that doesn't belong to us, we deny that God has given us or is able to give us everything we truly need. Therefore, keeping the eighth commandment is a practical exercise of our faith in God's providence.

Every theft is also an assault on God's providence for others. This is a second way that stealing is a sin against God: It robs what he has provided for someone else. Here it is important to understand that the eighth commandment assumes a right of ownership. By saying, "You shall not steal," God indicated that people have a right to own their private property. Otherwise, the whole concept of stealing would fail to make any sense. Only something that belongs to someone can be stolen from them. But the reason that anything belongs to anyone is because it comes from God, and we do not have the right to take for ourselves what God has given to others.

This brings us to the positive side of the eighth commandment. What the Bible means by ownership is not possessing things to use for our own purposes, but receiving things from God to use for his glory. So at the same time that we are forbidden to take things that don't belong to us, we are required to use what we have in ways that are pleasing to our God. To put it very simply, the eighth commandment isn't just about stealing—it's also about stewardship.

A steward is someone who cares for someone else's property. He is not free to use it however he pleases, but only to manage it in accordance with his master's intentions. This is our situation exactly. Whatever we possess is God's property, and he has given us the sacred trust of looking after it. This is the way it has been since the beginning. Adam did not own any property, he just managed it: "The Lord God took the man and put him in the garden of Eden to work it and keep it" (Genesis 2:15). As Calvin explained,

> [T]he custody of the garden was given in charge to Adam, to show that we possess the things which God has committed to our hands, on the condition, that being content with a frugal and moderate use of them, we should take care of what shall remain. . . . [T]hat this economy, and this diligence, with respect to those good things which God has given us to enjoy, may flourish among us; let every one regard himself as the steward of God in all

> things which he possesses. Then he will neither conduct himself dissolutely, nor corrupt by abuse those things which God requires to be preserved.[12]

Like Adam, we are called to be good stewards of God's world.

Good stewardship means taking care of what we have been given, not letting things fall into disrepair. It means not being wasteful. Whenever we squander money that could be better spent on something else, we are guilty of a kind of theft. This is one of the problems with gambling, which has become one of the most common ways of breaking the eighth commandment. Each year Americans spend more money on various forms of gambling than they do on food or clothing. "What's wrong with that?" some may ask. The Southern Baptist Convention has provided an excellent answer:

> While the Bible contains no "thou shalt not" in regard to gambling, it does contain many insights and principles which indicate that gambling is wrong. The Bible emphasizes the sovereignty of God in the direction of human events (see Matthew 10:29–30); gambling looks to chance and good luck. The Bible indicates that man is to work creatively and use his possessions for the good of others (see Ephesians 4:28); gambling fosters a something-for-nothing attitude. The Bible calls for careful stewardship; gambling calls for reckless abandon. The Bible condemns covetousness and materialism (see Matthew 6:24–34); gambling has both at its heart. The moral thrust of the Bible is love for God and neighbor (Matthew 22:37–40); gambling seeks personal gain and pleasure at another person's loss and pain.[13]

Good stewardship also means working hard. The Bible is very specific about this. The book of Proverbs teaches that laziness leads to poverty (6:10, 11). This is not the only cause of poverty, of course, but it is one of them. Poverty, in turn, brings the temptation to steal (Proverbs 30:8, 9). One obvious way to avoid this temptation is to work hard for honest gain, with the goal of becoming financially independent (see 1 Thessalonians 4:11, 12). The Bible says, "Let the thief no longer steal, but rather let him labor, doing honest work with his own hands, so that he may have something to share with anyone in need" (Ephesians 4:28). In other words, the burglar must become a benefactor, as Zacchaeus did when he made restitution for his many sins against the eighth commandment (Luke 19:8). As soon as we realize what we have stolen, it is our responsibility to pay back what we owe, and then some.

This brings us to the last aspect of good stewardship, which is giving away what God has given to us so that other people will have what they need. Jerry Bridges has observed that there are three basic attitudes we can take toward possessions. The first says, "What's yours is mine; I'll take it." This is the attitude of the thief. The second says, "What's mine is mine; I'll keep it." Since we are selfish by nature, this is the attitude that most people have most of the time. The third attitude—the godly attitude—says, "What's mine is God's; I'll share it."[14]

Christians are called to live generously. We do not work simply to satisfy our own desires, but also to provide for others. This is not to say that we can never enjoy what God has given us. After all, enjoying God's gifts is one aspect of good stewardship. But Christians who are as wealthy as we are should always be thinking about what we can give to someone else. It is only in this way that money loses its power over us. As Kent Hughes has said, "Every time I give, I declare that money does not control me. Perpetual generosity is a perpetual dedeification of money."[15]

Good stewardship starts with meeting the needs of our families. Then it extends to the church and to the global work of the gospel. Finally, it reaches out to the poor in our own community and around the world. The Bible says, "You shall give to him freely, and your heart shall not be grudging when you give to him, because for this the Lord your God will bless you in all your work and in all that you undertake" (Deuteronomy 15:10). The consequences of such generosity will last forever. As A. W. Tozer once explained, "Any temporal possession can be turned into everlasting wealth. Whatever is given to Christ is immediately touched with immortality."[16] To put this another way, the only money we can count on ever seeing again is the money we invest in the kingdom of God. Jesus said, "Do not lay up for yourselves treasures on earth, where moth and rust destroy and where thieves break in and steal, but lay up for yourselves treasures in heaven, where neither moth nor rust destroys and where thieves do not break in and steal. For where your treasure is, there your heart will be also" (Matthew 6:19–21).

If we fail to make this investment, we are guilty of breaking the eighth commandment. The famous fourth-century preacher Chrysostom served a wealthy congregation in the great city of Constantinople. Chrysostom was well known for challenging his people not to be stingy. On one occasion he said,

> This also is theft, not to share one's possessions. Perhaps this statement seems surprising to you, but do not be surprised. . . . Just as an official in the imperial treasury, if he neglects to distribute where he is ordered, but spends instead for his own indolence, pays the penalty and is put to death, so also the rich man is a kind of steward of the money which is owed for distribution to the poor. He is directed to distribute it to his fellow servants who are in want. So if he spends more on himself than his needs require, he will pay the harshest penalty hereafter. For his own goods are not his own, but belong to his own fellow servants. . . . I beg you remember this without fail, that not to share our own wealth with the poor is theft from the poor and deprivation of their means of life; we do not possess our own wealth but theirs.[17]

## The Tent of Thieves

There are many thieves in the stories of the Bible, but the most audacious was probably Achan. Achan was a soldier in Israel's army. He fought in the battle of Jericho, when the Israelites marched around the city until the walls fell down.

On the morning of that famous victory, General Joshua gave his troops the order of the day. He commanded them,

> Shout, for the LORD has given you the city. And the city and all that is within it shall be devoted to the LORD for destruction. . . . . But you, keep yourselves from the things devoted to destruction, lest when you have devoted them you take any of the devoted things and make the camp of Israel a thing for destruction and bring trouble upon it. But all silver and gold, and every vessel of bronze and iron, are holy to the LORD; they shall go into the treasury of the LORD." (Joshua 6:16b, 17a, 18, 19)

This was holy war. The Israelites were not fighting for their own advantage but for the glory of God. They were agents of his divine justice, and as such they were not allowed to claim the spoils of battle. Everything was to be devoted to the Lord, upon the pain of death.

In the battle everything went according to plan. The people cried out, the walls collapsed, and the Israelites conquered the Canaanites: "Then they devoted all in the city to destruction, both men and women, young and old, oxen, sheep, and donkeys, with the edge of the sword. . . . And they burned the city with fire, and everything in it. Only the silver and gold, and the vessels of bronze and of iron, they put into the treasury of the house of the LORD" (Joshua 6:21, 24). The soldiers did everything that Joshua commanded.

Except for Achan. In the aftermath of the battle, as he rummaged through the wreckage, Achan's heart was captured by the city's treasure: gold, silver, and fancy clothes with designer labels. "There's so much stuff here," he must have said to himself, "that if I took something, no one would ever notice it was missing." The more treasure he saw, the more he wanted some of it for himself. "After all," Achan reasoned, "I'm a soldier in this army, and I deserve some kind of reward for fighting!"

Achan started thinking about how he could smuggle some of the treasure back to his tent. As his mind worked through the possibilities, he decided to go for it. He "saw among the spoil a beautiful cloak from Shinar, and 200 shekels of silver, and a bar of gold weighing 50 shekels" (Joshua 7:21a). He coveted them, he stole them, and then he hurried back to his tent. When he arrived—breathless—he dug a hole in the ground to hide all his loot. It would be their little family secret.

As robberies go, Achan didn't take much. In today's market it would amount to something like a five hundred dollar suit, a few hundred dollars of silver, and several thousand dollars' worth of gold. Yet that one modest theft brought death and destruction on Israel. The defeat came quickly. After his great success against Jericho, Joshua was eager to attack the next city. The general sent his scouts to spy out the region, and soon they returned to say that their next target would be easy pickings. Joshua didn't even need to send out his whole army; several thousand soldiers would be more than enough. Yet to their shock and dismay, the Israelites were badly beaten.

To Joshua this seemed like a military crisis. After he had managed to retreat, he threw himself down on the ground and complained to God. But the Lord said to him:

> Get up! Why have you fallen on your face? Israel has sinned; they have transgressed my covenant that I commanded them; they have taken some of the devoted things; they have stolen and lied and put them among their own belongings. Therefore the people of Israel cannot stand before their enemies. They turn their backs before their enemies, because they have become devoted for destruction. I will be with you no more, unless you destroy the devoted things from among you. (Joshua 7:10–12)

The problem was that someone had violated the eighth commandment. So God proceeded to give instructions for identifying and then executing the thief.

The next morning the whole nation was brought before Joshua for judgment. Achan was there, at first wondering what it was all about, and then desperately hoping that his sin would remain undiscovered. He probably said to himself, *Come on, with a million people here, how could the general ever find out?* The tribes were called forward, Judah was taken by lot, and Achan's heart jumped into his throat. Judah! Why, that was *his* tribe. What were the chances of that! Then all the clans of Judah stepped forward, and the descendants of Zerah were taken, and guess whose grandfather that was! Achan's, of course, and the blood drained from his face. The Zerahites came forward, and the family of Zimri was taken. Then Achan knew that he was a dead man, because Zimri was his father. One by one every member of the family went forward, until finally Joshua came to Achan, the thief.

Shortly before he died, Moses had told the Israelites that if they obeyed God he would give them the Promised Land. But he also warned them, "[I]f you will not do so [keep their oath before God], behold, you have sinned against the LORD, and be sure your sin will find you out" (Numbers 32:23). This is exactly what happened to Achan: His sin found him out, which is not surprising because it was such a stupid sin to commit in the first place. It's one thing to hide stolen property, but to really gain anything by his theft, Achan would have to use what he had taken. Think about it: When would he ever be able to wear his fancy robe or show off his cache of precious metals?

Achan never got the chance, and in the end he lost everything. Joshua forced him to confess his crime in front of the whole nation. Then messengers were sent to look for the stolen goods. Sure enough, they were buried in the thief's tent. The messengers brought everything back where everyone could see it. "And Joshua and all Israel with him took Achan the son of Zerah, and the silver and the cloak and the bar of gold . . . and all that he had. And they brought them up to the Valley of Achor. And Joshua said, 'Why did you bring trouble on us? The LORD brings trouble on you today.' And all Israel stoned him with stones" (Joshua 7:24, 25). Achan lost everything—including his life—and all for the sake of ill-gotten booty.

Why did God treat Achan so harshly? It was partly to make an example of Achan, so that everyone would know that God is holy and that he wants his people to be holy too. What better way to deter other would-be thieves from even thinking about taking something that belonged to God? But it was also a matter of justice. Achan was guilty of breaking the eighth commandment. He had broken it, not just by stealing from Jericho, but by stealing from God. This is what made his crime so heinous. All the spoils of battle belonged to God. They were designated for his house, where they would be dedicated to his praise. What Achan took belonged to God, and thus he was guilty of the greatest of all thefts: robbing God of his glory.

### Between Two Thieves

Achan's sin and its punishment stand as a warning to anyone who steals anything that belongs to God. There are many ways to do this. One of the most obvious is to use our money for ourselves rather than giving generously back to God. Everything we have belongs to God. While he gives us the freedom to use what we need, he also calls us to give for the work of his gospel, and to neglect this duty is to rob God.

Most Christians would deny that they are stealing from God. They would deny it the way the Israelites denied it in the days of Malachi. When that faithful prophet told them they were robbing God, they were deeply offended. "How have we robbed [God]?" they asked. God answered by saying, "In your tithes and contributions. You are cursed with a curse, for you are robbing me, the whole nation of you. Bring the full tithe into the storehouse, that there may be food in my house. And thereby put me to the test . . . if I will not open the windows of heaven for you and pour down for you a blessing until there is no more need" (Malachi 3:8–10). A tithe is 10 percent, and this is a useful guideline for Christian giving, but God does not operate on a percentage basis. How much we give to the church is a matter of Christian freedom. However, we should always try to give more and more, and to give less than we can is spiritual theft.

Another way to rob God is to fail to give him the best of our time and our talents. All our abilities and opportunities come from God, and they are all to be used for his glory. The Bible says, "Whatever you do, work heartily, as for the

Lord and not for men" (Colossians 3:23). When we waste our time, or fail to develop our gifts to their highest potential, we are robbing God.

Still another way to rob God is to break his law, and thus to deny him our obedience. Every violation of the Ten Commandments involves some form of theft. Bowing down to idols steals God's worship. Desecrating the Sabbath steals his holy day. Murder steals life; adultery steals purity; lying steals the truth. But the real theft is that every sin we commit dishonors God, and thus steals the glory that our lives ought to give him.

Are you a thief? One of the benefits of studying the Ten Commandments is that they confront us with our sin. When we explore their full implications, we discover we are not able to keep a single commandment in all its integrity. So the Law condemns us. It declares, "You are the idolater. You are the foul-mouthed sinner. You are the Sabbath-breaker and the rebel. You are the murderer, the adulterer, and the thief." The Law says all this to show that we are guilty sinners who need the gospel.

The gospel is the good news that Jesus died on the cross and rose again to give salvation to everyone who believes in him. Jesus died on the cross in the place of sinners—specifically, in the place of thieves. The Bible says that when Jesus was crucified, "two robbers were crucified with him, one on the right and one on the left" (Matthew 27:38), thus fulfilling the prophecy that the Savior would be "numbered with the transgressors" (Isaiah 53:12). In his crucifixion, Jesus was considered a thief. Martin Luther explained the situation like this:

> Christ is innocent so far as His own Person is concerned; therefore He should not have been hanged from the tree. But because, according to the Law, every thief should have been hanged, therefore, according to the Law of Moses, Christ Himself should have been hanged; for He bore the person of a sinner and a thief—and not of one but of all sinners and thieves. For we are sinners and thieves, and therefore we are worthy of death and eternal damnation. But Christ took all our sins upon Himself, and for them He died on the cross. Therefore it was appropriate for Him to become a thief and, as Isaiah says (53:12), to be "numbered among the thieves."[18]

It is well known that Christ was crucified between two thieves. But as far as God's justice was concerned, there were really *three* thieves on the cross that day: two who died for their own crimes and one who took our sins upon himself. Luther gave this illustration:

> [A] magistrate regards someone as a criminal and punishes him if he catches him among thieves, even though the man has never committed anything evil or worthy of death. Christ was not only found among sinners; but of His own free will and by the will of the Father He wanted to be an associate of sinners, having assumed the flesh and blood of those who were sinners and thieves and who were immersed in all sorts of sin. Therefore

> when the Law found Him among thieves, it condemned and executed Him as a thief.[19]

This is a great comfort to everyone who has ever broken the eighth commandment. When Christ died on the cross he died for thieves, so that every thief who trusts in him will be saved. The first thief to be saved was the one hanging next to him on the cross, the one who said, "Jesus, remember me when you come into your kingdom" (Luke 23:42). Jesus gave him the answer he gives to every lawbreaker who turns to him in repentance and faith: "[Y]ou will be with me in Paradise" (v. 43).

# 57

# The Ninth Commandment: To Tell the Truth

## EXODUS 20:16

IN DECEMBER 2001 George O'Leary was on top of the world. He had just been named head football coach at the University of Notre Dame—the Fighting Irish. It was the dream of a lifetime. O'Leary was in charge of one of the most prestigious sports programs in the world.

Then two days later, at the end of his first day on the job, the call came. A reporter had been trying to contact some of the guys who had played college football with O'Leary back at New Hampshire. The strange thing was, nobody could remember anyone named George O'Leary. So Notre Dame's sports information director telephoned to find out what it was all about. O'Leary reluctantly admitted that he hadn't actually *played* football at New Hampshire. Let's see, he had a knee injury one year, then he had mono . . . someone must have made a mistake.

Indeed, someone *had* made a mistake, and the next day the reporter called to say that he had documentation. Years before, when O'Leary applied for a job at Syracuse, he had been asked for information about his athletic background. Some of what he provided was true, like the high school football championships, but somehow it didn't look impressive enough, so the applicant decided to improve his résumé. There it was twenty-one years later, in his own handwriting: "College—Univ. of New Hampshire—3 yr. lettered." It was just a small lie, really, but it was big enough to turn O'Leary's dream into a nightmare, costing him not only his job, but also his reputation.

Perhaps the most telling response came from the coach's brother, who said, "Is anyone trying to tell me that résumés are truthful? In the America we live in, the willingness to lie on a résumé is an indication of how much you want the job."[1] Sadly, this attitude is all too typical. According to a survey of nearly three million job applicants, nearly 50 percent of American résumés contain one or more falsehoods.[2]

We all know that lying is wrong. Yet we are so used to massaging the truth for personal advantage that we have trouble holding the line against falsehood. A columnist for *Time* magazine wrote: "The injunction against bearing false witness, branded in stone and brought down by Moses from the mountaintop, has always provoked ambivalent, conflicting emotions. On the one hand, nearly everybody condemns lying. On the other, nearly everyone does it every day." Then he asked this question: "How many of the Ten Commandments can be broken so easily and with so little risk of detection over the telephone?"[3]

## Nothing but the Truth

Long before anyone ever lied over the phone, God gave his people the ninth commandment: "You shall not bear false witness against your neighbor" (20:16). The immediate context for this commandment is a court of law, so it governs the legal testimony that a witness gives in a public trial before a jury. The word "neighbor" suggests a trial that takes place within the covenant community (see Leviticus 19:18), but it is not limited to this. After all, Jesus taught that everyone is our neighbor (see Luke 10:25–37). Therefore, what God most specifically condemns in the ninth commandment is a lying witness, someone who testifies falsely against anyone accused of a crime.

To understand this commandment it helps to know more about the justice system in the ancient world. In those days people who were charged with a crime had little protection. They were not presumed innocent until proven guilty, but presumed guilty until proven innocent. There were few standards for the presentation of evidence, and sometimes the accused didn't even get the chance to mount a defense. Furthermore, most ancient courts were willing to convict someone on the strength of a single witness.

Obviously this whole legal system was subject to abuse, which explains why God stated the ninth commandment the way that he did: "You shall not bear false witness against your neighbor" (20:16). In the days before forensic evidence, almost everything depended on the witness. Usually it came down to one person's word against another's, and since many crimes were treated as capital offenses, often the defendant's life was at stake. The words of a false witness could be fatal.

In the wisdom and providence of God, the situation was different in Israel. When a member of the covenant community was put on trial, he appeared before a jury of elders. There had to be more than one witness, for as God said in his law, "A single witness shall not suffice against a person for any crime or for any wrong in connection with any offense that he has committed. Only on the evidence of two witnesses or of three witnesses shall a charge be established"

(Deuteronomy 19:15). This was especially important in a trial for a capital offense: no one could be put to death by a single witness (Numbers 35:30; Deuteronomy 17:6).

Another protection concerned the execution of judgment. When someone was sentenced to die, his accuser had to throw the first stone (Deuteronomy 17:7; cf. John 8:7). This was a significant safeguard because it is one thing to accuse someone, but quite another to put him to death. Furthermore, if the allegations proved to be false, the accuser was punished: "The judges shall inquire diligently, and if the witness is a false witness and has accused his brother falsely, then you shall do to him as he had meant to do to his brother" (Deuteronomy 19:18, 19a). These legal safeguards were designed to protect the innocent from injustice. God's people were not allowed to bear false witness against one another. As the prophet Zechariah was later to say: "Speak the truth to one another; render in your gates judgments that are true and make for peace" (Zechariah 8:16b).

These principles are still relevant for trials today, whether civil or ecclesiastical. Many people have lost confidence in public justice, and it can only be restored by the rejection of every form of falsehood. Where there is no truth, there can be no justice. Jochem Douma states that when we consider the ninth commandment,

> we must always include reference to the significance of the system of justice. Past interpreters of the ninth commandment never hesitated to mention various persons who have a role in administering justice. These interpreters would demand of a *judge* that he be incorruptible and not judge rashly. . . . They required of the *accuser* that he never accuse somebody unnecessarily, out of antipathy or revenge. They expected the *witness* to tell the truth and nothing but the truth. The *lawyer* was forbidden to call black white and white black, even when he had the valuable function of coming to the aid of the accused and demanding that proof of guilt—if there was any—be airtight. These interpreters required the *accused* to confess his guilt where such guilt was proved.[4]

In other words, everyone involved in the entire legal process has an obligation to maintain the truth, the whole truth, and nothing but the truth.

## Liar! Liar!

A courtroom is not the only place where someone can give false testimony. Remember how the Ten Commandments work. What they forbid is the most extreme form of any particular sin. Murder is the worst kind of hatred, adultery is the most destructive sexual sin, and so on. Similarly, the ninth commandment forbids the deadliest lie: one that condemns an innocent man for a crime he did not commit.

According to "the rule of categories" (see chapter 48), each commandment also applies to lesser sins of the same kind. In the case of the ninth commandment, the underlying principle is that God forbids every form of falsehood. This is confirmed by the prophet Hosea, who accused the Israelites of "swearing, lying, murder, stealing, and committing adultery" (Hosea 4:2a). Hosea was clearly referring to the Ten Commandments, but rather than using the Hebrew term for false testimony (*shaqar*), he used a more general word that refers to any kind of lying (*kachash*). The ninth commandment means "You shall not lie." It is not just about the false testimony that people give in court, but also about the lies they tell their neighbors over the backyard fence and the rumors they whisper between the pews at church.

There are many different ways to lie. *Roget's Thesaurus* offers an impressive list of synonyms. A falsehood can be described as an invention, an equivocation, a falsification, a fabrication, or a prevarication. Dishonesty also comes in all different sizes. There are the big lies—the whoppers and the grand deceptions. Then there are all the little lies we tell—the half-truths, the flatteries, and the fibs. What we say may be true, as far as it goes, but we leave out the details that might put us at a disadvantage. Or we say something that is technically true, yet nevertheless intended to deceive. We overstate our accomplishments, putting ourselves in the best possible light. At the same time we exaggerate other people's failings, thinking and saying the worst about others. We mislead, misquote, and misinterpret. We twist people's words, taking things out of context. In these and many other ways, we exchange the truth for a lie.

The most blatant violation of the ninth commandment is any lie that harms someone else. What is especially forbidden is falsehood *against* our neighbor. God has given us the capacity to speak so that we can use our words to praise him and to bless others. However, our speech is corrupted by our sin, so it has the power to do great damage. The apostle James described the tongue as "staining the whole body, setting on fire the entire course of life, and [is] set on fire by hell" (James 3:6). Like a massive forest fire set by a single careless individual, a lying tongue consumes everything in its path. James also said, "No human being can tame the tongue. It is a restless evil, full of deadly poison" (3:8). Truly the tongue is the most dangerous part of the body!

Given how dangerous words can be, it is not surprising that when the New Testament lists the sins we need to avoid, it often tells us to watch what we say. The Apostle Paul warned the Corinthians about "quarreling . . . slander, gossip" (2 Corinthians 12:20). He told the Galatians that "strife" and "dissensions" were acts of the sinful nature (Galatians 5:19, 20). He told the Ephesians to get rid of "slander" and "malice" (Ephesians 4:31). These sins of speech all violate the ninth commandment, because rather than being used to build people up, words are used to tear them down.

When the Bible condemns gossip, it means something more than just casual talk about other people's business. Gossip is talking about people in a way that damages their reputation with others. Reputations are important. The Bible says, "A good name is to be chosen rather than great riches, and favor is better than silver or gold" (Proverbs 22:1). One problem with gossip is that it tries to steal this treasure. When this is done in speech, it is called slander; when it appears in print, it is called libel. Either way the victims of gossip never get to defend themselves. They never have a chance to explain their circumstances, clarify their motives, or correct the misconceptions people have about them. Instead they are charged, tried, and convicted in the court of private opinion.

Most gossip contains a fair amount of misinformation. People who gossip trade in hearsay, rumor, innuendo, and other notoriously unreliable forms of communication. However, even true words can violate the ninth commandment. Sometimes what a gossip reports is true, but it is said to the wrong person or for the wrong reason, to the injury of others. The words may contain some version of the truth, but the testimony is false because it is malicious. Jochem Douma comments:

> Perhaps the one spreading gossip is not lying, but he or she is being untruthful: saying things that are true, but in the context of slander, is deceitful. The neighbor's mistakes, faults, and shortcomings are discussed in minute detail. People realize this kind of chatter gets them an attentive audience. For it is a universal phenomenon that we would rather hear something bad about our neighbor than something good. And something dirty always sticks long after the conversation has died. As Martin Luther put it in his Large Catechism, reputation is something quickly stolen, but not quickly returned.[5]

Gossip is such a common sin that we forget how ungodly it is, but before we open our mouths and start talking about someone else, we need to ask ourselves some hard questions: Is what I am about to say true? If so, does it really need to be said to this person in this conversation? Would I put it this way if the person I'm talking about were here to listen? If our words fail these simple tests, then it would be better for us not to speak at all.

There is another side to this too. As wrong as it is to gossip, it is just as wrong to listen to gossip. This too is injurious to the truth. According to an old rabbinic saying, slander "kills three: the one who speaks it, the one who listens to it, and the one about whom it is spoken."[6] The Puritan Thomas Watson made a similar point when he said, "He that raises a slander, carries the devil in his tongue; and he that receives it, carries the devil in his ear."[7] Watson was right: Whenever we listen to gossip, we become implicated in its sin. We get drawn into making judgments about others when it is not our place to judge. The problem is that most of us like to hear a little gossip. We have an appetite for it, especially if it's juicy. According to Proverbs, "The words of a whisperer are like delicious morsels; they go down into the inner parts of the body" (Proverbs 18:8). But no matter how tasty it is, gossip is still poison.

What should we do when someone tries to tell us something we know we shouldn't hear? Interrupt! We should say, "You know, this is starting to sound like gossip; we need to talk about something else." Or we should say, "Wait, before you say anything more, why don't we stop and pray about this?" Then, after bringing the matter before the Lord, we can say, "Now, what was it you wanted to talk about?" Or we should say, "I'm sorry, I'm not sure I can listen to any more of this. Tell me, have you gone and spoken about it to the people involved? Because if you haven't, it wouldn't be right for us to talk about it."

All too often, people who like to complain about others are unwilling to do the spiritual hard work of helping them grow in godliness. But the Bible is very clear about the right way to deal with the sins of others. First, before talking with anyone else, we need to go directly to them and discuss it (Matthew 18:15). If they are not willing to confess their sin, there are appropriate ways to involve other people from the church in addressing the issue. But the only time we can talk about someone else's sin is when it is our God-given responsibility to give them spiritual help. Otherwise, it is none of our business. If only everyone would follow these simple guidelines, there would be no one left for gossips to talk to!

### The Best Policy

According to "the two-sided rule" (see chapter 48), there is something that each commandment forbids and also something that it requires. For the ninth commandment this rule is easy to apply. If lying is forbidden, then what is required is telling the truth.

It is not easy to stand up for the truth. George Orwell said, "In a time of universal deceit, telling the truth is a revolutionary act."[8] If this is true, then Christians are called to be revolutionaries, because we are certainly living in a time of universal deceit, when everyone seems to be lying. As we saw in the previous chapter, there are the lies that businesspeople tell—all the ways they economize on the truth. There are the lies that academics tell. These days the biggest lie on campus is that there is no universal truth, only different versions of reality. This is part of what some scholars call postmodernism. It is the big lie that makes it possible for academics to tell all sorts of other lies. Then there are all the lies that politicians tell, especially during campaign season. After all the attack ads and broken promises, voters are more cynical than ever. We often find ourselves asking the question *Time* magazine asked before a recent presidential election: "Is anyone telling the truth in this campaign?"[9] There are also the lies that journalists tell. When the story is more important than the truth, the line between fact and fiction gets blurry. With all the lies going around, it is hardly surprising to learn that fewer than half of Christian young people believe there is an objective standard of truth.[10]

In a culture of lies—what Charles Colson has termed a "Post-Truth Society"[11]—we are called to be people of the truth. If we are scholars, we are called to be careful with our quotations and fair with our criticisms. If we are politicians, we are called to be honest about our record, as well as that of our opponents. If we are in business, we are called to deal honestly with people. If we are journalists, we are called to get the story straight. These are only examples, of course. Every discipline has its own deceptions, but whatever lies people tell in our line of work, we are called to tell the truth.

The reason we are called to be people of the truth is because we serve a truth-telling God. God the Father is true. The Bible says, "Let God be true though every one were a liar" (Romans 3:4). God the Son is true. The Bible says that he came "from the Father, full of grace and truth" (John 1:14), and "there was no deceit in his mouth" (Isaiah 53:9), for he is truth personified. Jesus said, "I am . . . the truth" (John 14:6) and "Everyone who is of the truth listens to my voice" (John 18:37). God the Holy Spirit is also true. In fact, the Bible calls him "the Spirit of truth" (1 John 4:6). If God is true—Father, Son, and Holy Spirit—then he must be true to his word. And so he is. Everything that God has ever said—including every word on every page of the Bible—is absolutely, unmistakably, and entirely true. Therefore, we can always take God at his word: "Your word is truth" (John 17:17a).

If God is true to us, then we must be true to him, and also to one another. The Scripture says, "You . . . shall not deal falsely; you shall not lie to one another. You shall not swear by my name falsely, and so profane the name of your God: I am the LORD" (Leviticus 19:11, 12). It also says, "Therefore, having put away falsehood, let each one of you speak the truth with his neighbor, for we are members one of another" (Ephesians 4:25). John Calvin summarized the Biblical teaching as follows: "The purpose of this commandment is: since God (who is truth) abhors a lie, we must practice truth without deceit toward one another."[12] Honesty really is the best policy, not simply because it helps us get along with other people, but because our interpersonal communication ought to be grounded in the character of God.

Telling the truth means thinking and saying the best about people. Rather than being suspicious of their motives, we should put the best construction on what they have said or done. Telling the truth also means defending people when they are unfairly attacked. All too often, people stand by in silence, but as William Barclay writes, "It is an important principle that a cowardly or careless and irresponsible silence can be as senseless a crime as false and lying speech. The sin of silence is as real as the sin of speech."[13]

Sometimes sin needs to be confronted, and in those cases keeping the ninth commandment means "speaking the truth *in love*" (Ephesians 4:15). Unfortunately, the love is usually what's missing. Some Christians are more than willing to "tell it like it is," but there is something brutal about their honesty. Understand that keeping the ninth commandment does *not* mean saying whatever comes to mind. There are many situations in life when it is better to say nothing at all. What the ninth commandment means is saying the honest thing—when it is our duty to say it—in a loving way.

People sometimes wonder whether there is ever a time when it is permissible to lie. What about telling a tall tale for comic effect, or pulling someone's leg? Provided they are told with affection, these kinds of jokes really do not violate the ninth commandment because ultimately there is no intention to deceive. However, it is always wrong to use humor to damage someone else's dignity.

What about times of warfare or persecution? Is it okay to lie then? Going back to Augustine, many theologians have said no. However, there were a number of incidents in the Bible when deception was not condemned. There were the Hebrew midwives, Shiphrah and Puah, who deceived Pharaoh in order to avert genocide. There was Rahab, who deceived the Canaanites in order to save Joshua's spies. There was Gideon, who used concealment as a stratagem of war. The Bible does not condemn these falsehoods. However, each of those untruths was told to prevent evil men from committing even greater sins, such as murder. We should not use these extreme cases to justify falsehood when we are in a tight spot or when we think the end justifies our means. Even in those rare cases when a lie seems necessary to protect others, it is still wrong in itself.

## The Drop-Dead Lie

There are lots of liars in the Bible. There was the Serpent who lied to Eve in the garden of Eden. There was Jacob, who tricked his brother into selling his birthright. There were the men Jezebel bribed to testify against Naboth. There were the lying prophets who criticized Jeremiah. And of course there were all the lies that people told about Jesus Christ. But the most terrifying story of deception comes from the early church. It's the story of a husband and wife and their drop-dead lie.

Ananias and Sapphira were members of the first church in Jerusalem. It was an exciting time to be a Christian. Jesus had returned to Heaven and had poured his Spirit out on the church. The apostles were preaching the gospel and performing miraculous signs and wonders. People were coming to faith in Christ every day!

Almost as remarkable was the way the first Christians cared for one another's practical needs. The Bible says: "Now the full number of those who believed were of one heart and soul, and no one said that any of the things that belonged to him was his own, but they had everything in common. . . . There was not a needy person among them, for as many as were owners of lands or houses sold them and brought the proceeds of what was sold and laid it at the apostles' feet, and it was distributed to each as any had need" (Acts 4:32, 34, 35; cf. 2:44, 45). When the first Christians did this, they were saying something significant. They were testifying that since they had found their treasure in Jesus Christ, they were willing to give everything they had for the work of his kingdom. When they sold their property and gave it all back to God, it was a public gesture of total commitment to Christ.

One of the people who did this was a man from Cyprus named Joseph. The Bible says that he "sold a field that belonged to him and brought the money and laid it at the apostles' feet" (Acts 4:36, 37). Joseph wasn't even from Jerusalem, yet he gave to God's work in that great city. It was such a generous offering that the apostles gave him a new nickname. They called him Barnabas, which means "Son of Encouragement."

Ananias and Sapphira saw what Barnabas did. They also noticed how his offering enhanced his reputation in the church. The couple realized that if they wanted to get the kind of attention they thought they deserved, they needed to make a major donation to the apostles, and so they did: "But a man named Ananias, with his wife Sapphira, sold a piece of property, and with his wife's knowledge he kept back for himself some of the proceeds and brought only a part of it and laid it at the apostles' feet" (Acts 5:1, 2). "No one will ever know," they must have thought to themselves.

Understand that Ananias and Sapphira had the right to use their property any way they wanted. They were not required—by God or by anyone else—to sell their field. And once they sold it, they were not obligated to give all their money to God. It was a matter of stewardship, and they had the freedom to use what they had however they chose. God would have accepted them if they had given only some of it to the church, or even none at all, as long as ultimately they did it for his glory.

The problem was not what Ananias and Sapphira did, but what they said. They said they were paying God full price when in fact they were taking a discount. It's not entirely clear how Ananias said this. Maybe he said it out loud, or maybe it was simply implied by the act of putting money at the apostles' feet. But however he did it, Ananias lied. He acted like he had done something totally for God when in fact he had done it partly for God and partly for himself.

Somehow Peter knew what Ananias had done, because no sooner had he received the offering than he gave this stinging rebuke: "Ananias, why has Satan filled your heart to lie to the Holy Spirit and to keep back for yourself part of the proceeds of the land? While it remained unsold, did it not remain your own? And after it was sold, was it not at your disposal? Why is it that you have contrived this deed in your heart? You have not lied to man but to God" (vv. 3, 4).

Peter said three important things to Ananias. First, he told Ananias what his sin was. It was not a sin of theft, primarily, or even of covetousness, but of deception. What he broke was the ninth commandment, not just the eighth and the tenth commandments.

Second, Peter told Ananias where his sin came from. It came from a heart infected by the poison of demonic deception. Satan is the one who filled Ananias's heart with lies, which is not surprising because Satan was a liar from the very beginning. Jesus called him "a liar and the father of lies" (John 8:44). Ultimately every lie comes from Satan. This helps us understand why lying is so despicable, and why God hates it so much (see Proverbs 6:16–19; Zechariah 8:17). Whereas ultimately every truth comes from our Father in Heaven, every lie comes from the devil himself.

The third thing Peter did was to tell Ananias whom he had sinned against. He had not sinned primarily against Peter and his apostolic authority, or even against the church, but against God first and foremost. Peter said that Ananias "lie[d] to the Holy Spirit" (Acts 5:3). Then he said, "You have not lied to man but to God" (v. 4). This is what lying really is: a sin against the God of all truth.

Here again—as with so many other commandments—we are confronted with the absolute folly of sin. How can anyone lie to God and expect to get away with it? And of course he didn't get away with it: "When Ananias heard these words, he fell down and breathed his last. And great fear came upon all who heard of it. The young men rose and wrapped him up and carried him out and buried him" (vv. 5, 6). End of story, except that for some reason Sapphira didn't hear about it: "After an interval of about three hours his wife came in, not knowing what had happened" (v. 7). Peter gave her a chance to repent of her sin. He said, "Tell me whether you sold the land for so much" (v. 8a). The price Peter mentioned was not the full price of the sale; it was only the amount of the offering, as Sapphira well knew, but she said, "Yes, for so much" (v. 8b).

Whenever we lie, there is always the danger that we will get trapped in the web of our own deception. But in this case Sapphira never saw it coming. First Peter accused her of deception: "How is it that you have agreed together to test the Spirit of the Lord?" he asked (v. 9a). Then with the impeccable timing of God's justice, he said, "Behold, the feet of those who have buried your husband are at the door, and they will carry you out" (v. 9b). No sooner had the men stepped across the threshold than they had to turn around and go back to the burial ground, because "Immediately she fell down at his feet and breathed her last. When the young men came in they found her dead, and they carried her out and buried her beside her husband" (v. 10).

## The Truth about Us

Are you shocked by what God did to Ananias and Sapphira? Imagine what it would be like if this happened at your church. Imagine a well-respected couple dropping dead at the pastor's feet for what most people would consider a trivial deception—a little white lie about how much they put in the offering plate. Everyone would be amazed . . . and afraid, which is exactly how people responded in Jerusalem. The Bible says, "Great fear came upon the whole church and upon all who heard of these things" (v. 11). No kidding!

The whole episode sent a chill down their collective spine. The punishment was so severe and so sudden. One day Ananias and Sapphira were in church, singing hymns and going to Bible study. The next day they were dead! Within a matter of hours they were both dragged off and buried. Was it really fair for God to do this?

Of course it was fair! It was fair because lying is a deadly sin. King David said, "You destroy those who speak lies" (Psalm 5:6a), and when Ananias and Sapphira dropped dead, his words came true. David also asked this question: "O LORD, who shall sojourn in your tent? Who shall dwell on your holy hill?" (Psalm 15:1). The king answered, "He who . . . speaks truth in his heart; who does not slander with his tongue" (vv. 2, 3). The implication is that the only people who are worthy to enter the kingdom of God are people who keep the ninth commandment. But what about people who break it? Jesus said that the place where liars belong is "in the lake that burns with fire and sulfur" (Revelation 21:8), and that "everyone who loves and practices falsehood" will be shut out from his eternal city forever (Revelation 22:15). Every liar deserves to die, and after that, to suffer God's eternal wrath against sin.

No wonder everyone was scared: What happened to Ananias and Sapphira was a preview of the judgment to come. They were scared because they knew they were liars too. They realized that what Ananias and Sapphira had done was no worse than many of the lies they had told. It was just an exaggeration, that's all—an error in mathematics. If God killed people for something like that, then they deserved to die too, and pretty soon there wouldn't be any church left! No doubt for weeks afterward they were very careful not to claim that they had done anything more for God than they actually had!

If there is one thing God hates, it is the lies that Christians tell to make themselves look more righteous than they really are. Our testimony is that we are unrighteous, that there is no way we could ever be saved apart from the grace of God in Jesus Christ. The real truth about us is that we are so guilty that the very Son of God had to be crucified to pay for our sins. If this is true, then why would we ever pretend to be anything more than sinners saved by grace? To act like we have it spiritually together is a lie. But even more it is a denial of the grace of God, which alone has the power to save us.

At a local church meeting another pastor confronted me. He rebuked me for being a legalist, for not demonstrating God's grace. Frankly, he was a little forward, and I'm not sure his rebuke was fair. But what could I say? He was right, of course. I am a Pharisee at heart. And that's not the worst of it either. I am a lawbreaker who likes to follow other gods. Even though I have a sacred ministry, I profane God's name. I am guilty of murderous intentions, lustful thoughts, covetous desires. And yet I am able to cover most of this up most of the time (or at least I think I can). But that's the real truth about me, the truth that people would be able to see if it weren't covered up with so many lies.

What's the truth about you? What lies have you been telling? What are the lies you tell yourself? What are the lies you try to sell to others? The biggest lie is the one we live with every day, the lie we work so hard to maintain. It is the lie that we are on the inside what we pretend to be on the outside. But Jesus said, "Woe to you, . . . hypocrites! . . . you also outwardly appear righteous to others, but within you are full of hypocrisy and lawlessness" (Matthew 23:27, 28).

Something wonderful happens when we're willing to confess the real truth about ourselves and all our sin. What happens is that we are able to see the real truth about Jesus and what he has done for our salvation. It is only when we tell the truth about our sin that we are able to see how much we need a Savior—the Savior who said, "You will know the truth, and the truth will set you free" (John 8:32).

# 58

# The Tenth Commandment: Being Content

EXODUS 20:17

JESUS SAID MANY THINGS that stand directly at odds with the way most people live. He said, "Blessed are the meek, for they shall inherit the earth" (Matthew 5:5), and "Love your enemies, do good to those who hate you" (Luke 6:27). But of all the things that Jesus said, none contradicts the values of our consumer culture more directly than this: "Take care, and be on your guard against all covetousness, for one's life does not consist in the abundance of his possessions" (Luke 12:15).

But of course today most Americans seem to believe that life *does* consist in the abundance of our possessions. We are always trying to get more for less, always spending but never satisfied. One pastor confessed,

> I belong to the Cult of the Next Thing. It's dangerously easy to get enlisted. It happens by default—not by choosing the cult, but by failing to resist it. The Cult of the Next Thing is consumerism cast in religious terms. It has its own litany of sacred words: *more, you deserve it, new, faster, cleaner, brighter*. It has its own deep-rooted liturgy: *charge it, instant credit, no down-payment, deferred payment, no interest for three months*. It has its own preachers, evangelists, prophets, and apostles: ad men, pitchmen, and celebrity sponsors. It has, of course, its own shrines, chapels, temples, meccas: malls, superstores, club warehouses. It has its own sacraments: credit and debit cards. It has its own ecstatic experience: the spending spree. The Cult of the Next Thing's central message proclaims, "Crave and spend, for the Kingdom of Stuff is here."[1]

Why are we so tempted to belong to the Cult of the Next Thing? It is because our hearts are full of sinful desire. Rather than being satisfied with what we have, we always crave something else. Instead of being content, we covet.

## Unholy Desire

Coveting is strictly forbidden by the tenth commandment: "You shall not covet your neighbor's house; you shall not covet your neighbor's wife, or his male servant, or his female servant, or his ox, or his donkey, or anything that is your neighbor's" (20:17).

What does it mean to covet? To covet is to crave, to yearn for, to hanker after something that belongs to someone else. We covet whenever we set our hearts on anything that is not rightfully ours. John Mackay calls coveting "a consuming desire to possess in a wrong way something belonging to another."[2] It's not simply wanting something we don't have; it's wanting something that someone else has. Since coveting has to do with wanting, it is a sin of desire. The Puritan Thomas Watson defined it as "an insatiable desire of getting the world."[3] By "the world" he meant any of the things that this world has to offer, as opposed to the spiritual things that can only come from God. A more recent commentator has described coveting as "an inordinate, ungoverned, selfish desire for something."[4]

Not all desires are selfish, of course. God made us to be creatures of desire. Our desire for food reminds us to eat. Our desire to do something useful motivates us to work. Our desire for friendship draws us into community. Our desire for intimacy—including sexual intimacy—may drive us to get married. We have many healthy desires, including the deepest of all desires, which is to know God. But like everything else about us, our desires are corrupted by sin. We often want the wrong thing, in the wrong way, at the wrong time, and for the wrong reason, and this is what the tenth commandment rules out. According to the *Westminster Shorter Catechism*, "The tenth commandment forbiddeth all discontentment with our own estate, envying or grieving at the good of our neighbor, and all inordinate motions and affections to anything that is his" (A. 81).

There is always something envious about coveting. This goes all the way back to the garden of Eden. Before Eve took the forbidden fruit, she coveted it (Genesis 3:6). This was not because she admired it as a piece of fruit, but because Satan tempted her to envy by telling her that if she ate it, she would be like God. Eve took the fruit to gain something she was not intended to have.

We have been sinning this way ever since. One good place to see it is in a nursery full of toddlers. Nothing arouses a child's interest in a toy like seeing it in the hands of another child, and the transition from coveting to stealing is almost instantaneous. Adults are more subtle, but we are guilty of the same sin. Coveting is what causes that little twinge of disappointment whenever someone else gets what we want. It's how we react when a coworker gets the promotion, when our roommate finds romance and we are still single, or when a friend goes where we can only dream of going for vacation. We are always comparing ourselves to others, and frankly we resent it when we don't get what they have.

The apostle James asked, "What causes quarrels and what causes fights among you? Is it not this, that your passions are at war within you? You desire and do not have, so you murder. You covet and cannot obtain, so you fight and quarrel" (James 4:1, 2a).

There are all kinds of things to covet. Usually we associate coveting with material possessions, and rightly so. The tenth commandment mentions various forms of property, such as houses, servants, and livestock. Today most people are less interested in donkeys and oxen than they were back then, but the commandment still stands. We covet things like bigger houses, faster cars, and better entertainment. We also covet clothes with designer labels, appliances with more features, gadgets from mail-order catalogs, trinkets from shopping networks, and a million other trivial products.

Consumption has become our way of life. No matter how much we have, we always want more, and our desire for newer and better things is almost insatiable. This is what makes advertising so successful: our inability to keep the tenth commandment. Has there ever been a more covetous country than the United States of America? The quintessential American writer Ralph Waldo Emerson said, "Things are in the saddle and ride mankind." We usually call it "chasing the American dream," but the Bible calls it coveting.

What else do we covet? The tenth commandment mentions "your neighbor's wife" (20:17). This is a reminder that sex can be one of our most unruly desires. Whenever we engage in sexual fantasy, we are guilty of a kind of coveting. We are feeding a sinful desire that soon will demand to be gratified.

To summarize, the tenth commandment lists several things that we are tempted to covet. However, the list is not meant to be complete because it ends by saying, "or anything that is your neighbor's." This closes any last loophole. The items listed are not exhaustive; they are only suggestive. What we are forbidden to covet is anything at all. We may not covet other people's attributes: age, looks, brains, or talents. We may not covet their situation in life: marriage, singleness, children. We may not covet spiritual attainments, like a more prominent place of ministry in the church or wider recognition of our spiritual gifts. We are not allowed to covet anything at all. God's law rules out every unlawful desire.

## Deadly Desire

Most people think of coveting as a relatively minor sin. Somehow it doesn't seem to be in the same league with "big" sins like murder and adultery. As one commentator confessed, "It has occurred to me that whoever approved the final order of these commandments didn't have much of a sense of suspense or climax. He put all of those dramatic, intriguing sins like stealing, adultery, and murder, first. Then he ended with coveting. It would have seemed more logical to begin with the bland, throw-away sin like coveting, and then work up to the big stuff."[5]

Whenever we are tempted to minimize the evil of coveting, however, we need to remember that God included it in the Ten Commandments. Furthermore, coveting is condemned everywhere else in the Bible. Jesus listed it right up there with theft, murder, and adultery (Mark 7:21, 22). The apostle Paul claimed that people who covet will not inherit the kingdom of God (1 Corinthians 6:9, 10). He also said, "For you may be sure of this, that everyone who is sexually immoral or impure, or who is covetous (that is, an idolater), has no inheritance in the kingdom of Christ and God" (Ephesians 5:5; cf. Colossians 3:5). The Puritan Thomas Watson gave a vivid illustration. He said, "As a ferryman takes in so many passengers to increase his fare, that he sinks his boat; so a covetous man takes in so much gold to increase his estate, that he drowns himself in perdition."[6] Coveting can sink us down to Hell as fast as any other sin.

Another reason coveting is evil is because it causes many other sins. It is such an intense desire that almost inevitably it leads people to break other commandments. The person who covets goes beyond simply wanting something to plotting how to get it. A good example is Achan, the thief we encountered when we studied the eighth commandment. The Bible says that before Achan stole treasure from Jericho, he "coveted" it (Joshua 7:21). This means something more than that he admired it. It means that he wanted it so badly that he started scheming how to get it. And once he came up with a workable plan, he went ahead and committed the sin. The sinful desire that Achan treasured in his heart took control of his will, until he couldn't keep his hands off someone else's stuff.

This is how sinful deeds always start—with sinful desire. First we see something we want. Then we start thinking about how much we want it, and why. Soon it starts to dominate our thoughts, until finally it becomes an obsession. By the time we reach this point, sin will have its way with us. The Apostle James explained that "each person is tempted when he is lured and enticed by his own desire. Then desire when it has conceived gives birth to sin, and sin when it is fully grown brings forth death" (James 1:14, 15). Evil desire gives birth to sin and finally to death.

This is why God included coveting in the Ten Commandments: Unholy desires quickly turn into deadly desires. As the Scripture says, "But those who desire to be rich fall into temptation, into a snare, into many senseless and harmful desires that plunge people into ruin and destruction" (1 Timothy 6:9). Coveting can be just as fatal as any other sin, which should cause us to ask a very practical question: What does my heart desire, and where will that desire lead me in the end?

## The Heart of the Matter

There is something unusual about the tenth commandment that distinguishes it from the rest of the Decalogue: It goes straight to the heart. The other nine commandments explicitly condemn outward actions like making idols, working on the Sabbath, and killing innocent victims. As we have seen, these commandments also forbid sins of the heart like hatred and lust. According to our "inside/outside rule" (see chapter 48), each commandment governs inward attitudes as well as outward actions. But the first nine commandments generally start on the outside and then work their way in as we learn how to apply them.

What is different about the tenth commandment is that it starts on the inside. The commandment about coveting is not concerned with what we do, in the first instance, but with what we *want* to do. It governs our internal desires. This has led some commentators to wonder if perhaps the tenth commandment might be superfluous. Isn't coveting really included in the eighth commandment? If God's law against stealing condemns our greedy hearts as well as our thieving hands, then why do we need the tenth commandment?

The answer is that the tenth commandment makes explicit what the other commandments only imply—namely, that God requires inward as well as outward obedience. If God had not given us the tenth commandment, we might be tempted to think that outward obedience is all we need to offer. But the tenth commandment proves that God judges the heart. In case anyone misses the point, the command against coveting shows that God's law is spiritual.

Michael Horton tells of the rabbi who said to him, "You know, one of the greatest differences between our two religions is this idea that you've committed a sin just by desiring or thinking it. We believe you have to actually commit the physical act before it's really sin. Otherwise, we'd be sinning all the time!"[7] The rabbi was right: If God judges us for what is inside as well as for what is outside, then we are all sinning all the time. This is *precisely* what the tenth commandment is intended to teach. Martin Luther said, "This last commandment, then, is addressed not to those whom the world considers wicked rogues, but precisely to the most upright—to people who wish to be commended as honest and virtuous because they have not offended against the preceding commandments."[8] As Luther recognized, this commandment—more than any other—convinces us we are sinners. It does this for the gracious purpose of showing us that we need a Savior.

The tenth commandment seems to have had this effect in the life of the Apostle Paul. Paul went through the first part of his life assuming that he could measure up to the perfect standard of God's law. He did not murder; he did not commit adultery; he did not steal; he did not lie—at least not outwardly. Then Paul came to the tenth commandment, and the Law exposed his sin. Here is how he described his experience: "Yet if it had not been for the law, I would not have known sin. For I would not have known what it is to covet if the law had not said, 'You shall not covet.' But sin, seizing an opportunity through the commandment, produced in me all kinds of covetousness" (Romans 7:7, 8a).

Far from being an anticlimax, therefore, God's law against coveting is what convinces us that we are sinners in need of salvation. The tenth commandment disabuses us of any notion that we are able to keep God's law. As Francis Schaeffer wrote:

> "Thou shalt not covet" is the internal commandment which shows the man who thinks himself to be moral that he really needs a Savior. The average such "moral" man, who has lived comparing himself to other men and comparing himself to a rather easy list of rules, can feel, like Paul, that he is getting along all right. But suddenly, when he is confronted with the inward command not to covet, he is brought to his knees.[9]

## Grapes of Wrath

Of all the Bible stories about coveting, the juiciest is the story of Ahab and the grapes of wrath. The Bible describes how "Naboth the Jezreelite had a vineyard in Jezreel." Then it goes on to explain that the vineyard was "beside the palace of Ahab king of Samaria" (1 Kings 21:1). This was the perfect setup for a story about coveting: two men, but only one piece of choice property.

The incident began with nothing more than a desire. King Ahab noticed how nice Naboth's vineyard was, and how close it was to the royal palace. And the more he thought about it, the more he wanted it. It was a vineyard fit for a king, or at least that's how it looked to him! Naturally Ahab started thinking about how he would develop the land if he owned it. However nice it was as a vineyard, it would be even nicer as a vegetable garden—especially one that belonged to him. Ahab's mouth started to water; he could practically taste the parsnips and the rutabagas.

So the king decided to make a business proposition: "Ahab said to Naboth, 'Give me your vineyard, that I may have it for a vegetable garden, because it is near my house, and I will give you a better vineyard for it; or, if it seems good to you, I will give you its value in money'" (v. 2). It seemed like a fair offer. Ahab would give Naboth a vineyard at least as good as the one near the palace. Or if he preferred to get out of the grape industry altogether, Ahab would pay him whatever the land was worth.

Naboth immediately declined, saying, "The LORD forbid that I should give you the inheritance of my fathers" (v. 3). The reason Naboth turned Ahab down was because he knew his Bible. According to the Law of Moses, the children of Israel were not permitted to sell their property. God had said, "The land shall not be sold in perpetuity, for the land is mine. For you are strangers and sojourners with me" (Leviticus 25:23); "every one of the people of Israel shall hold on to the inheritance of the tribe of his fathers" (Numbers 36:7). Since the land belonged to God, the vineyard could not be sold. Naboth was the kind of man who served God rather than money. If it meant violating the Law of God, he would not sell the family farm, even if it were to his financial advantage. What was merely a luxury to Ahab was a matter of piety to Naboth. God forbid that he should part with the inheritance of his fathers, a vineyard belonging to the Lord!

Naboth is a good example of what Jesus was talking about when he said, "Where your treasure is, there your heart will be also" (Matthew 6:21). He had found his treasure in the promises of God. By contrast, Ahab's heart was in the wrong place altogether. When he saw that his little real estate venture was slipping through his fingers, he did what any little kid does when he doesn't get his way—he pouted. "And Ahab went into his house vexed and sullen because of what Naboth the Jezreelite had said to him, for he had said, 'I will not give you the inheritance of my fathers.' And he lay down on his bed and turned away his face and would eat no food" (1 Kings 21:4).

Poor Ahab! What had started as an idle notion had become a sinful obsession. His desire had degenerated into out-and-out coveting. He just *had* to have that vineyard! And when he couldn't get it, he was full of sour grapes. In his commentary on this passage, F. B. Meyer treats the covetous king with delicious sarcasm:

> In a room of the palace, Ahab, King of Israel, lies upon his couch, his face towards the wall, refusing to eat. What has taken place? Has disaster befallen the royal arms? Have the priests of Baal been again massacred? Is his royal consort dead? No; the soldiers are still flushed with their recent victories over Syria. The worship of Baal has quite recovered from the terrible disaster of Carmel; Jezebel—resolute, crafty, cruel, and beautiful—is now standing by his side, anxiously seeking the cause of this sadness.[10]

The portrait of Jezebel's concern is almost touching. She could tell that something was wrong: her husband wouldn't even come to dinner!

As soon as Jezebel figured out what was eating Ahab, she immediately took charge. She was hardly the kind of woman to let little things like God's law stand in the way of what she wanted. She said to her husband, "Do you now govern Israel? Arise and eat bread and let your heart be cheerful; I will give you the vineyard of Naboth the Jezreelite" (v. 7). And so she did. Jezebel bribed some unscrupulous men to accuse Naboth of blasphemy. Since there were two witnesses, the people immediately took Naboth out and stoned him to death, thus clearing the way for Ahab to plant his precious vegetables. This wicked plot proves that "the love of money is a root of all kinds of evils" (1 Timothy 6:10a), for what started out as a covetous desire led to false witness, murder, and stealing.

But God is not mocked, and in the end breaking God's law led to Ahab's destruction. As soon as Jezebel told him that Naboth was dead, Ahab "arose to go down to the vineyard of Naboth the Jezreelite, to take possession of it" (1 Kings 21:16). When the king got there, God's prophet Elijah was waiting to meet him and to speak the words that chilled the king right down to his soul: "Thus says the LORD, 'Have you killed and also taken possession?' . . . 'In the place where dogs licked up the blood of Naboth shall dogs lick your own blood'" (v. 19). Ahab's wife received the same sentence. Later the king and the queen were both thrown to the dogs.

If there is one thing we learn from the stories of the Bible, it is that things do not turn out well for people who break the Ten Commandments. They always get what they deserve in the end.

## If Only . . .

Ahab's downfall started with his discontent. The king had most of the finer things in life, but rather than giving thanks to God for what he had, he became obsessed with the one thing he didn't have: a vegetable garden next to the palace. This is how the whole thing started. Ahab wanted something that didn't belong to him, and then he wanted it more and more badly until finally he coveted it. It all came from not being content.

So much of our frustration in life comes from wanting things that God has not given us. In our covetous desire, we concentrate on what we don't have rather than on what we do have. Ahab said, in essence, "If only I had Naboth's vineyard, then I would be happy." The Israelites said this too. They said it when God led them out into the wilderness: "Would that we had died by the hand of the LORD in the land of Egypt" (Exodus 16:3a); "Oh that we had meat to eat!" (Numbers 11:4). All our discontent comes from the same kind of reasoning. If only . . .

Sometimes we say "if only" about our material possessions: "If only I made a little more money." "If only I had a bigger place in which to live." Once we start thinking this way, there is no end to our discontent. The story is often told of the reporter who asked the billionaire Nelson Rockefeller how much money it takes to be happy. Rockefeller answered, "Just a little bit more." The Scripture rightly says, "He who loves money will not be satisfied with money, nor he who loves wealth with his income" (Ecclesiastes 5:10). This is true of both the poor and the rich. Coveting is not limited to a particular tax bracket.

Sometimes we are discontent with our physical attributes: "If only I had a different body type, people would like me better." "If only I didn't have this disability; then I would be able to serve the Lord more effectively." On other occasions we are discontent with our place of service in the church: "If only people would recognize how important my ministry is." "If only they would give me the chance to use my gifts the way they ought to be used."

Then there are all the times when we are discontent with our situation in life. Singles are discontent with their singleness: "If only I could find someone to marry, it would make all the difference." Then we get married, and we are discontent with that, too. "If only my spouse would do a better job of meeting my needs." If only . . .

As long as we base our sense of contentment on anything in the world, we will always find some excuse to make ourselves miserable. Our problem is not on the outside—it's on the inside, and therefore it will never be solved by getting more of what we think we want. If we do not learn to be satisfied right now in our present situation—whatever it is—we will never be satisfied at all. I once heard Charles Swindoll quote the following poem:

> It was Spring, but it was Summer I wanted:
> The warm days and the great outdoors.
>
> It was Summer, but it was Fall I wanted:
> The colorful leaves and the cool, dry air.
>
> It was Fall, but it was Winter I wanted:
> The beautiful snow and the joy of the holiday season.
>
> It was Winter, but it was Spring I wanted:
> The warmth and the blossoming of nature.
>
> I was a child, and it was adulthood I wanted:
> The freedom and the respect.
>
> I was 20, but it was 30 I wanted:
> To be mature and sophisticated.
>
> I was middle-aged, but it was 20 I wanted:
> The youth and the free spirit.
>
> I was retired, but it was middle-aged I wanted:
> The presence of mind without limitations.
>
> My life was over,
> and I never got what I wanted.

## The Secret of Being Content

The truth is that if God wanted us to have more right now, we would have it. If we needed different gifts to enable us to glorify him, he would provide them. If we were ready for the job or the ministry we want, he would put us into it. If we were supposed to be in a different situation in life, we would be in it. Instead of always saying, "If only this" and "If only that," God calls us to glorify him to the fullest right now, whatever situation we are in.

The word for this is *contentment*. Contentment is the positive side of the last commandment; it is the remedy for covetous desire. *The Westminster Shorter Catechism* says, "The tenth commandment requireth full contentment with our own condition, with a right and charitable frame of spirit toward our neighbor and all that is his" (A. 80). This emphasis on contentment is thoroughly Biblical. "Godliness with contentment is great gain" (1 Timothy 6:6). "Keep your life free from love of money, and be content with what you have" (Hebrews 13:5a).

Contentment means wanting what God wants for us rather than what *we* want for us. The secret to enjoying this kind of contentment is to be so satisfied with God that we are able to accept whatever he has or has not provided. To put this another way, coveting is a theological issue: Ultimately, it concerns our relationship with God. Therefore, the way to get rid of any covetous desire is to be completely satisfied with God and what he provides. In a wonderful book called *The Rare Jewel of Christian Contentment*, the Puritan Jeremiah Burroughs explained what we ought to say to ourselves whenever we are tempted to be discontent: "I find a sufficiency of satisfaction in my own heart, through the grace of Christ that is in me. Though I have not outward comforts and worldly conveniences to supply my necessities, yet I have a sufficient portion between Christ and my soul abundantly to satisfy me in every condition."[11]

Godly people have always known this secret. Asaph knew it. True, there was a time in his life when Asaph was disappointed with God. He saw wicked men prosper, while he himself had nothing to show for his godliness. It made him angry with God and bitter about what life didn't seem to offer. But then Asaph learned the secret of being content, and he was able to say to the Lord, "Whom have I in heaven but you? And there is nothing on earth that I desire besides you" (Psalm 73:25).

The Apostle Paul knew the secret, too. He said, "I have learned in whatever situation I am to be content. I know how to be brought low, and I know how to abound. In any and every circumstance, I have learned the secret of facing plenty and hunger, abundance and need" (Philippians 4:11b, 12). In other words, Paul had learned that contentment is not circumstantial; it does not depend on our situation in life. So what's the secret? Paul said, "I can do all things through him who strengthens me" (Philippians 4:13).

God is all we need, and therefore all we ought to desire. To be even more specific, all we need is Jesus. God does not offer us his Son as a better way of getting what we want. No; God gives us Jesus and says, "Even if you don't realize it, he is all you really need." When we come to Jesus, we receive the forgiveness of our sins through his death and resurrection. We receive the promise of eternal life with God. We receive the promise that he will never leave us or forsake us, that he will help us through all the trials of life. What else do we need?

And as for everything else—all the things that we spend so much time coveting—God says, "Trust me. I will provide everything you truly need." Faith is always the answer to our discontent. Michael Horton writes: "It is not poverty or wealth that leads us to contentment and trust in the Lord, but the confidence that if God provided so richly for our salvation by choosing, redeeming, calling, adopting, and justifying us, and by sending His Spirit to cause us to grow up into Christ's likeness, then surely we can count on Him for the less essential matters of daily existence."[12]

Jesus said it even more plainly: "But seek first the kingdom of God and his righteousness, and all these things will be added to you" (Matthew 6:33). The first thing, the main thing, the only thing that really matters is to trust in Jesus. He is enough for us. Really, he is.

# 59

# The End of the Law

## EXODUS 20:18–21

JOHN BUNYAN'S FAMOUS BOOK *Pilgrim's Progress* tells of Christian's long spiritual journey from the City of Destruction to the Celestial City. The story begins with Christian weighed down by the great burden of his sin and fearful of the judgment to come. But Evangelist comes to tell him how to enter the narrow way of salvation, where his burden can be taken away.

Not long after Christian began his pilgrimage, he met a man who informed him of a faster way to get rid of his burden. All Christian needed to do was go and see a gentleman named Legality, who lived in the village of Morality. To put this in spiritual terms, he could get rid of his sins simply by keeping God's law. Christian was intrigued by this possibility. Obviously he didn't want to make his journey any more difficult than necessary. Could Mr. Legality help him get rid of his burden?

When Christian went ahead and asked the way to Morality, the man answered by pointing to a high mountain and saying, "By that hill you must go." Christian followed the man's directions.

> [He] turned out of his way to go to Mr. Legality's house for help; but behold, when he was got now hard by the hill, it seemed so high, and also that side of it that was next the wayside did hang so much over that Christian was afraid to venture further, lest the hill should fall on his head. Wherefore there he stood still, and [knew] not what to do. Also his burden, now, seemed heavier to him than while he was in his way. There came also flashes of fire out of the hill that made Christian afraid that he should be burned; here therefore he sweat, and did quake for fear.[1]

John Bunyan did not mention this hill by name, but it is not hard to guess which one he had in mind. It was a hill of fire and smoke—Sinai, the mountain of God's law. Far from removing Christian's burden, that great hill only made him more afraid. This is because the Law does not have the power to save but only to threaten us with judgment, and thus to show us our need of salvation.

## The Terrors of Law and of God

When the children of Israel stood at Mount Sinai, they felt the way Christian did. They were terrified. The Bible says, "Now when all the people saw the thunder and the flashes of lightning and the sound of the trumpet and the mountain smoking, the people were afraid and trembled, and they stood far off" (20:18). It was an awesome sight. Smoke billowed from the mountain, and great balls of fire blazed from peak to peak. The sounds were awesome too. There were great claps of thunder and mighty blasts from a trumpet, and the ground shook under Israel's feet. These natural and supernatural phenomena were first mentioned back in Exodus 19, where the Scripture explained the reason for such awesome sights and sounds. It was "because the LORD had descended on it [Mount Sinai] in fire" (v. 18). What the Israelites saw were visible manifestations of the glory of the invisible God.

Some scholars have wondered why the description of Mount Sinai is repeated in chapter 20. Why does the Bible describe thunder and lightning both before and after the giving of the Ten Commandments? The answer is that these awesome sights and sounds continued during the whole time that God was giving his law. They are mentioned again in chapter 20 simply to show how the Israelites responded. Umberto Cassuto writes: "This concluding paragraph does not merely come to relate what occurred after the proclamation of the *Decalogue*, but to describe the reaction of the people to the Revelation as a whole."[2] Back in chapter 19 God set limits around the mountain and warned his people not to break through the boundary; otherwise they would be destroyed. By the time he was finished giving his law, those precautions hardly seemed necessary! The people were trembling with fear; they were shaking in their sandals. The Bible says that "they stood far off" (20:18), which implies that they kept well behind the safety perimeter that Moses set around the mountain.

Why were the Israelites so frightened?

One thing the Israelites feared was the Law itself. God had just given them his righteous requirements in the form of the Ten Commandments. They could see that God was demanding their total allegiance in every aspect of life. He required them to worship him alone and to love one another in everything they did and said.

The Israelites probably didn't realize the full extent of God's law. Undoubtedly there were some things about the Ten Commandments that they didn't yet understand: how each commandment is both positive and negative, or how it governs inward attitudes as well as outward actions, or how it represents a whole category of sin and duty. But surely they understood that God was making an absolute claim on their worship, time, relationships, possessions, bodies, speech, and desires. So the first time they heard the Ten Commandments—even before they learned them all by heart—the Israelites knew that God was giving them one righteous standard for all of life. He wanted them to obey all of them, all the time, and this terrified them. Back in chapter 19 they had promised they would do whatever God said (v. 8), but as soon as they found out what was included, they panicked. They were frightened by the total demand of God's law.

The Israelites were also frightened by the threat of God's judgment, and perhaps this was the main reason they were afraid. Fire and smoke, thunder and lightning, the loud blast of a trumpet—whether the Israelites knew it or not, these signs will all reappear at the final judgment. The people had come into the very presence of the great and terrible judge of all sin. They were guilty sinners before a holy God, and they could sense that this was a life-threatening encounter. Indeed, in the smoke on the mountain they caught a glimpse of the wrath to come. In a sermon on Israel at Sinai, Charles Spurgeon said:

> This terrible grandeur may also have been intended to suggest to the people the condemning force of the law. Not with sweet sound of harp, nor with the song of angels, was the law given; but with an awful voice from amid a terrible burning. . . . [B]y reason of man's sinfulness, the law worketh wrath; and to indicate this, it was made public with accompaniments of fear and death: the battalions of Omnipotence marshaled upon the scene; the dread artillery of God, with awful salvos, adding emphasis to every syllable. The tremendous scene at Sinai was also in some respects a prophecy, if not a rehearsal, of the Day of Judgment.[3]

No wonder the Israelites were terrified! When they looked upon Mount Sinai, they were confronted with the condemning power of a law-giving God who will judge the world on the Last Day.

## The Mediator

One of the first things people do when they get into trouble with the law is to hire a lawyer. This is exactly what the Israelites did at Mount Sinai. As soon as they heard the demands of God's law, they asked Moses to be their legal advocate, their mediator. They said to him, "You speak to us, and we will listen; but do not let God speak to us, lest we die" (20:19). The Israelites were afraid to deal with God directly, for obvious reasons. They had heard the commandments of his law, they had seen the fire and the smoke of his glory, and it was all too much for them to bear. So they begged Moses to do the talking: "We don't want to talk to God; *you* talk to him!" And the "you" in verse 19 is emphatic: "*You* speak to us."

Many people claim that they want to have an unmediated experience of God. "If only God would speak to me directly," they say. "If only he would show himself to me, then I would believe." People who make such demands really have no idea what they are asking, because anyone who has ever caught even the slightest glimpse of God's true glory has been filled with fear. He is an awesome and all-powerful God, whose holiness is a terror to sinners.

This means that the Israelites were right to ask for a mediator. They needed one! A mediator is someone who stands in the gap to bring two parties together. And this is what the Israelites needed: someone to stand between Heaven and earth, to bridge the gap between God's deity and their humanity. They needed someone to represent them before God and to represent God before them. They needed someone to be God's spokesman because they could not bear the sound of God's voice. And even if they didn't realize it, what they needed most of all was someone to protect them from God's curse against their sin, the penalty of his law.

When the Israelites asked Moses to be their mediator, they were asking for something that God had already provided. God made Moses the mediator back at the burning bush, and the prophet had been speaking for God ever since. But when God revealed his law, the Israelites finally understood for themselves their need for a mediator. In their fear they begged Moses to be their go-between with God.

No sooner had the Israelites made their request than Moses began to serve as their mediator, doing two things that a mediator is called to do. First, he spoke to them for God: "Moses said to the people, 'Do not fear, for God has come to test you, that the fear of him may be before you, that you may not sin'" (v. 20). Later, when Moses looked back on this experience, he said, "I stood between the LORD and you at that time, to declare to you the word of the LORD. For you were afraid because of the fire, and you did not go up into the mountain" (Deuteronomy 5:5).

When Moses spoke to the people, it was partly to explain the purpose of God's law. As we saw back in chapter 47 of this commentary, God's law is a multiuse item. It has three primary purposes. One is to restrain our sin by threatening us with punishment. The Law fulfills this function in human society. Its penalties act as a deterrent, keeping people away from sin. Another use of the Law is to reveal our sin by proving that we cannot live up to God's perfect standard. Later, after we have been saved by grace, the Law shows us how to live in a way that brings glory to God. While continuing to restrain us from sin and to show us our need for grace, it also instructs us in righteousness.

When Moses explained the purpose of God's law, which of its three main uses did he have in mind? At first, it may seem that Moses was talking about the civic use of the Law, its ability to restrain sin in society. After all, he said to the Israelites, ". . . that the fear of him may be before you, that you may not sin" (20:20b). Certainly the Israelites were afraid, for they had heard God's voice from the mountain. Thus it would make sense for Moses to say that this experience would help them not to sin. Whenever they were tempted to break any of God's commandments, they would remember his terrible voice, and this would remind them not to break his law. Moses also described Israel's encounter with God as a test. He said, "God has come to test you" (20:20a). The Hebrew word for "test" (*nasa*) is used elsewhere in Exodus. God tested the Israelites by the bitter waters at Marah (15:25). He tested them again by telling them not to gather more manna than they needed for each day (16:4). In both cases, the test was a trial of Israel's obedience. God gave his people another test at Mount Sinai. His law was a test of their obedience. Did they pass the test? No; they sinned against God. So there is at least a hint here of a second use of the Law: its function is to show God's people their sin.

God also wanted his people to keep his law, however, and this was a third use of the Law. The Law was given for their obedience, and it was the mediator's job to encourage them in this. The first thing he told them was not to be afraid. It was not God's intention to destroy them but to save them. So rather than cringing in fear, terrified by God's law, they were called to live for God in joy and obedience. Moses told them that the fear of the Lord would be with them—not fear simply in the sense of abject terror, but also in the sense of reverence and respect. Their experience of God on Mount Sinai would remain with them in order to help them obey. Reverence would lead to obedience.

The point is that the Israelites needed a mediator to tell them all this. They needed a representative from God to tell them not to be afraid and to explain to them what the Law was for—its three primary purposes. Moses was the mediator. He spoke to the people for God, so that they could hear and obey.

There was a second thing that Moses did for the Israelites. As their mediator, he went for them to God: "The people stood far off, while Moses drew near to the thick darkness where God was" (20:21). "The thick darkness where God was"—this evocative phrase is sometimes taken as a word of comfort for believers in difficult circumstances. But the darkness Moses approached was not the darkness of personal difficulty; it was the mysterious darkness of God's own being. In the fire and smoke on Mount Sinai, God preserved the infinite mystery of his eternal deity. Who would dare to approach? Who could stand to enter the thick darkness where God was?

Only the mediator. This is what a mediator does: He enters God's presence on behalf of God's people. He draws near to God as their representative. To put it another way, he boldly goes where no one else would dare to go. And Moses did that. While everyone else in Israel was trembling with fear, he alone went up to meet with God, to talk with God and receive the rest of his law. He did this on behalf of God's people so they would know God's will for their lives. Moses spoke for God to the people and went for the people to God. He was the mediator God chose to lead them in the way of salvation.

There are many other things a mediator does, and as the rest of Exodus shows, Moses did most of them as well. A mediator makes atonement for sin, which Moses did too. After sacrifices were offered unto God, he sprinkled the people with the saving blood (24:5, 6, 8). A mediator intercedes for God's people, and Moses did that too. He pleaded with God not to destroy them when they sinned (32:9–14). A mediator lays down his life for the people he serves, and Moses was even willing to do that. When the Israelites broke God's law by worshiping a golden calf, he prayed, "Now, if you will forgive their sin—but if not, please blot me out of your book that you have written" (32:32). God did not just give his people his law and then leave them to suffer the consequences of breaking it. He gave them Moses, the mediator, to lead them in the way of salvation.

## The Limits of the Law

The reason the mediatorial work of Moses matters is because we need a lawyer too. Earlier I quoted Charles Spurgeon, who described the giving of the Law at Mount Sinai as a dress rehearsal for the Day of Judgment. Spurgeon went on to ask this provocative question: "If the giving of the law, while it was yet unbroken, was attended with such a display of awe-inspiring power, what will that day be when the Lord shall, with flaming fire, take vengeance on those who have willfully broken His law?"[4]

That's a good question: If simply hearing the Law was such a frightening experience, then how terrifying will it be to meet God after breaking it? This is an especially good question to ask after studying the Ten Commandments. Many people think that God will accept them because they generally play by the rules. Ironically, most of them would have trouble even naming the Ten Commandments, let alone keeping them. Nevertheless, they assume that because they have never murdered anyone, or committed perjury, God will be pleased enough to let them into Heaven.

Anyone who thinks that he or she can keep God's law should go ahead and try! But what we soon discover—provided we know what God's law really requires—is how impossible it is for us to keep the Ten Commandments. We are sinners by nature, and thus we are unable to obey God in everything. And if there is one thing we learn from the Ten Commandments, it is that we are not able to keep them. Frankly, we are the kind of people who like to serve other gods, use bad language, resist authority, lust after sexual pleasure, take other people's stuff, and say things to tear people down. So we know from experience that the *Westminster Shorter Catechism* is right when it says: "No mere man, since the fall, is able in this life perfectly to keep the commandments of God, but doth daily break them, in thought, word, and deed" (A. 82).

If we cannot keep God's law, then it is a threat to us, a deadly threat. The famous American missionary David Brainerd remembered a time in his life when the terrors of the Law kept him away from God. The Law made him angry because it was so strict. Brainerd wrote:

> I found it was impossible for me, after my utmost pains, to answer its demands. I often made new resolutions, and as often broke them. I imputed the whole to carelessness and the want of being more watchful, and used to call myself a fool for my negligence. But when, upon a stronger resolution, and greater endeavors, and close application to fasting and prayer, I found all attempts fail; then I quarreled with the law of God, as unreasonably rigid. I thought if it extended only to my outward actions and behaviors, I could bear with it; but I found it condemned me for my evil thoughts and sins of my years, which I could not possibly prevent.[5]

As Brainerd discovered, if we try to keep God's law on our own, we are doomed to failure and frustration. The Scripture says, "By works of the law no human being will be justified in his sight, since through the law comes knowledge of sin" (Romans 3:20). It says further that "whoever keeps the whole law but fails in one point has become accountable for all of it" (James 2:10). The Law cannot save us; it can only show us our sin. John Murray wrote:

> Law can do nothing to justify the person who in any particular has violated its sanctity and come under its curse. Law, as law, has no expiatory provision; it exercises no forgiving grace; and it has no power of enablement to the fulfillment of its own demand. It knows no clemency for the remission of guilt; it provides no righteousness to meet our iniquity; it exerts no constraining power to reclaim our waywardness; it knows no mercy to melt our hearts in penitence and new obedience. It can do nothing to relieve the bondage of sin; it accentuates and confirms the bondage.[6]

We know what we have to do—that's not the problem. God has told us what to do in his law. The problem is that we can't do it! If we were able to keep the Law, we could be saved by it. But since we cannot keep it, we can only be condemned by it. Like the Israelites, we should be standing at a distance, trembling with fear.

## A Better Mediator

What we need is a good lawyer! And this is how the Law leads us to the gospel: It condemns us for our sin, so that we start looking for some kind of legal remedy, and then we discover that God has provided one for us in Jesus Christ. Jesus can do what the Law cannot do, and that is to save us: "For God has done what the law, weakened by the flesh, could not do. By sending his own Son . . ." (Romans 8:3a).

The New Testament teaches that the Son of God is our mediator. In fact, he is the only mediator we will ever need: "For there is one God, and there is one mediator between God and men, the man Christ Jesus, who gave himself as a ransom for all, which is the testimony given at the proper time" (1 Timothy 2:5, 6). The book of Hebrews describes Christ's mediatorial work by drawing a comparison with Moses. Moses was a great mediator—the greatest in the Old Testament. But "Jesus has been counted worthy of more glory than Moses" (Hebrews 3:3a). He is a superior mediator (Hebrews 8:6), the mediator of a new and better covenant (Hebrews 9:15). As we saw back in chapter 45, the book of Hebrews goes on to assure us that we do not have to go through what the Israelites went through when they met God at Mount Sinai. The Bible says to the Christian: "For you have not come to what may be touched, a blazing fire and darkness and gloom and a tempest and the sound of a trumpet and a voice whose words made the hearers beg that no further messages be spoken to them. For they could not endure the order that was given" (Hebrews 12:18–20a). In other words, as believers in Christ we are not back in Exodus 20. But if we are not at Mount Sinai, where are we? The Bible says, "You have come . . . to Jesus, the mediator of a new covenant" (Hebrews 12:22–24). Things are different for us because we have a better mediator—the Lord Jesus Christ.

Jesus does everything a mediator is supposed to do. He goes to God for us. He is our go-between, the one who approaches the thick darkness where God is. He is able to do this much more effectively than Moses ever did because he is God as well as man. Jesus has both a divine nature and a human nature; therefore he is uniquely capable to represent us before God. And as he approaches God on our behalf, Jesus does something that Moses could never do: He offers perfect obedience to the Law. Whatever mediation Moses offered was limited by the fact that he was himself a lawbreaker. He was not able to offer perfect obedience to the Ten Commandments. But Jesus could do it. When he presented himself to God, Jesus said, "Behold, I have come to do your will, O God" (Hebrews 10:7), and then he did it. Perfectly. Jesus worshiped God alone, honored God's name, kept the Sabbath holy, obeyed his parents, loved his enemies, told the truth, and did everything else God commanded him to do.

This is the kind of mediator we need: someone to keep God's law for us. We are idolaters, rebels, liars, and cheats, and thus we could never be saved by our own obedience. But everything Jesus ever did counts for everyone who trusts in him. By faith in Christ we offer perfect obedience to God's law. Martin Luther said, "[T]he Christ who is grasped by faith and who lives in the heart is the true Christian righteousness, on account of which God counts us righteous and grants us eternal life."[7] All we have to do is trust in Jesus, and this is absolutely necessary because the Day of Judgment is coming. Since we are in trouble with the Law, we will need a lawyer. If we don't have one, we will have to face the justice of God's wrath all on our own, and what will happen to us then? But in his mercy God has provided a mediator, and like the Israelites, we should cry out for him to save us.

Once we come to Jesus there is something else that he does as our mediator, which is to teach us God's law. As the Scripture says, we are "not . . . outside the law of God but [are] under the law of Christ" (1 Corinthians 9:21). Earlier we saw how Moses explained the Law to the Israelites. Jesus does the same thing for us. First, like Moses, he tells us not to be afraid. This is because the Law holds no terror for those who are safe in Christ. Jesus has suffered the penalty that we deserved for our sin, and the Law can frighten us no longer. "There is therefore now no condemnation for those who are in Christ Jesus" (Romans 8:1).

What the Law can still do is teach us how to live. As the Puritan Thomas Watson explained, "Though a Christian is not under the condemning power of the law, yet he is under its commanding power."[8] To that end, part of Christ's mediatorial work is to teach us God's law all over again. He does not teach us the ceremonial law, which he fulfilled in his life and through his sacrificial death. Nor does he teach us the civil law, which was especially for the Old Testament nation of Israel. But Jesus does teach us the requirements of the moral law—the eternal standard of God's righteousness. Jesus said, "Do not think that I have come to abolish the Law or the Prophets; I have not come to abolish them but to fulfill them. For truly, I say to you, until heaven and earth pass away, not an iota, not a dot, will pass from the Law until all is accomplished" (Matthew 5:17, 18).

More than anyone else, Jesus is the one who teaches us to obey the will of God. He explains God's law and applies it to our hearts so that we can live in a way that is pleasing to him. To put it another way, Jesus takes the Law that once drove us to him for salvation and gives it back to us. The Puritan Samuel Bolton put it this way: "The law sends us to the gospel that we may be justified; and the gospel sends us to the law again to inquire what is our duty as those who are justified. . . . The law sends us to the gospel for our justification; the gospel sends us to the law to frame our way of life."[9] So as Christians we now keep the Ten Commandments—not so much because we have to, but because we get to! And because in Christ we are able to! We obey, not to justify ourselves, but to show our gratitude to the Savior who justified us.

Everything we have said about the Law and the gospel in relation to Christ has been helpfully summarized by Ernest Reisinger, who says of Jesus, "He explained the law's meaning, He expressed its character, He embodied its duties, and He endured its penalty."[10] Thomas Ascol offers a fuller explanation:

> The law was given to teach sinners their sin. When a sinner sees the law in all its strictness and spirituality, he thereby comes to understand the spiritual bankruptcy and grave danger of his condition. The law, able to condemn but unable to save, sends the convicted sinner looking for salvation in the only place it can be found. It sends him to Jesus Christ who, in His perfect law-fulfilling life and perfect law-fulfilling death, gave Himself to redeem helpless sinners. When Christ receives repentant, believing men and women, He forgives them, grants them His righteousness, and gives them His Spirit. He writes His law on their new hearts and empowers them to follow Him in obedient discipleship. As the One

> who perfectly kept the law Himself, He then leads His disciples to obey the commandments.[11]

And obey the commandments we do. All of them. By the grace of God, we keep what James called "the perfect law, the law of liberty" (James 1:25). We have been liberated from our service to other gods, and now we are free to worship God alone with reverence and joy, taking his name in earnest. We have been justified by faith, not by works, and now we are free to rest in God's grace. We have come to know God the Father through Jesus the Son, and now we are free to give honor where honor is due. By the love of God we have been delivered from murderous hate, and now we are free to forgive. We have found real pleasure in Christ, and now by the purity of his Spirit we are free to be chaste. All our lies have been exposed, and now we are free to tell the truth. And since we have the provision of Christ, there is no longer any need for us to steal or even to covet.

We do not keep God's law in order to be saved. We have been saved by grace alone through faith alone in Christ alone. But why were we saved? To glorify God, which we do by keeping his commandments. Jesus said, "If you love me, you will keep my commandments" (John 14:15).

# 60

# The Altar of God

## EXODUS 20:22–26

DID GOD GIVE ISRAEL HIS LAW? The Bible says that in the days of Moses, God descended on Mount Sinai with fire and smoke, and that with a loud voice he issued the Ten Commandments. But is it really true? Does Exodus 19, 20 provide an accurate account of something that actually happened in human history?

Today many scholars deny that this is the case. They argue that the story of the exodus is not fact but fiction—a story the Israelites made up to explain where they came from. In the words of one popular rabbi, "The story of the Exodus did not happen the way the Bible depicts it, if it happened at all. . . . Archaeology and biblical history have demonstrated that the Bible is not intended to be taken as literal history. It is a spiritual history, and that is the way modern [people] ought to relate to the biblical text."[1]

### A Voice from Heaven

If the critics are right, and Exodus is a fairy tale, then this overturns God's law. Either God spoke to Israel from Mount Sinai or he didn't. If he didn't, then the Ten Commandments do not come from him at all. They are merely the product of human legislation, written with the pen of Moses rather than by the finger of God. And in that case whatever obedience we offer is a matter of personal preference rather than holy obligation to the sovereign will of Almighty God.

The question is, did God give Israel his law? Did he really speak to his people from the mountain? This question may perplex some scholars, but it would not have posed any difficulties for the Israelites, who knew what they had seen and heard. The Israelites were given both visible and audible signs of the presence of God. They saw his mysterious glory and heard his mighty voice. Did God really give them the Law? Of course he did! No one who was there at Mount Sinai could ever deny that the Law came from God.

God reminded his people of this when he said to Moses, "Thus you shall say to the people of Israel: 'You have seen for yourselves that I have talked with you from heaven'" (20:22). From this point on, Moses would do the talking. He was the mediator—the man who spoke for God. So whenever God had something to say to Israel, he would do it through his prophet Moses. In the chapters that follow, Moses applies God's law to various life situations. But the first thing God wanted his prophet to do was to remind the people about who spoke to them on the mountain: It was the great God of the covenant. From this point on, everything Moses said was based on this great fact, that God had spoken to his people. The Law did not come from earth; it came from Heaven, and for this reason the Israelites were obligated to obey.

People sometimes wonder whether God has spoken to us. Perhaps he spoke to Moses, but does he still speak today? The answer is yes! He speaks to us in and through the Scriptures of the Old and New Testaments. The Ten Commandments were not just for the Israelites back then; they are for us right now. Sometimes we are tempted to doubt this because we were not there. We did not see what Israel saw on the mountain or hear what they heard. But we do have the Bible, which contains an exact record of what God said at Mount Sinai, as well as a complete account of everything else he has done for our salvation.

There are many good reasons to believe that what the Bible says is true. It is an ancient book, preserved in reliable manuscripts, which explains in a straightforward way what people experienced when they met with God. History and archaeology generally confirm the historical accuracy of the Bible. But of course the divine origin of Scripture cannot be proven. While it is reasonable to believe that what the Bible says is true, it still takes faith to receive it as the Word of God.

Here we have an advantage over the Israelites. Usually we think they had all the advantages. After all, they were eyewitnesses, and they heard God's voice for themselves. But we have God's Holy Spirit. He is the one who inspired the Scriptures in the first place. Now he testifies that the Bible really is the Word of God. Theologians call this the inward witness of the Holy Spirit. It is God confirming his own Word in the mind and heart of every believer. This is how God communicates with us: by the Holy Spirit speaking in Scripture.

The *Westminster Confession of Faith* helps explain this aspect of the Spirit's work. First the *Confession* lists some reasons to believe that the Bible is the Word of God: "We may be moved and induced by the testimony of the Church to an high and reverend esteem of the Holy Scripture. And the heavenliness of the matter, the efficacy of the doctrine, the majesty of the style, the consent of all the parts, the scope of the whole (which is, to give all glory to God), the full discovery it makes of the only way of man's salvation, the many other incomparable excellencies, and the entire perfection thereof, are arguments whereby it doth abundantly evidence itself to be the Word of God" (I.v). These are some of the many reasons for thinking that the Bible comes from God. Its reputation, theology, style, consistency—these things all confirm that God is the one who speaks to us in Scripture.

However, reason can only take us so far. Accepting the Bible as the Word of God is not simply a matter of the intellect; it is also a matter of the heart. It takes faith to hear God's voice, and this faith is the gift of God's Spirit. Thus the *Westminster Confession* goes on to say that "our full persuasion and assurance of the infallible truth and divine authority [of the Bible], is from the inward work of the Holy Spirit bearing witness by and with the Word in our hearts" (I.v).

When we accept the Ten Commandments as the Law of God, therefore, we are not simply taking Moses' word for it: We are taking the Spirit's word for it! God himself testifies to the truth of his own Word. He says to us today what he said to his people at the mountain: "'You have seen for yourselves that I have talked with you from heaven'" (20:22). God has spoken to us as clearly as he spoke to Israel. We do not regard the Ten Commandments as a cultural relic, a legal code from the ancient past. On the contrary, we receive them as God's living Word, believing that we too are commanded to serve God and love our neighbor.

## No Other Gods

People say that seeing is believing. This was true for the Israelites. God reminded them of what they had seen so they would take him at his word. But for the people of God, seeing is never just believing—it is also worshiping. Getting a clear sight of God always brings us to the point of praise. We have observed this pattern throughout our studies in Exodus: God's people are saved for God's glory. Whenever the Israelites had some new experience of God's saving grace, they always responded in praise. So after reminding his people of what they had seen, God proceeded to give them further instructions pertaining to worship.

The first instruction concerned idolatry: "'You shall not make gods of silver to be with me, nor shall you make for yourselves gods of gold'" (v. 23). This verse sounds familiar because it restates the first and second commandments. The Decalogue began with God commanding the Israelites not to have any other gods and not to make any idols. Here these commandments are virtually repeated. It is tempting to skip over them, on the assumption that we already know all about idolatry. But rather than ignoring things the Bible repeats, we ought to give them special attention. Obviously, God thought it was important to warn the Israelites against the great sin of idolatry more than once!

We need to hear this warning again because we, too, are tempted to worship false gods. Or to put it another way, we are tempted to let other things fill up the space in our lives that God ought to occupy. To identify our own idols, it helps to ask ourselves questions like these: What am I hoping for? What am I counting on? What gives my life meaning? Where do I get my personal sense of worth? What am I thinking about? What am I working for? What makes me feel good? Where do I turn when I need comfort? These are questions we need to keep asking because it is so easy for us to manufacture other gods, the lesser deities we love and serve.

The truth is that God alone deserves all the glory. One cartoon depicts Moses standing on the mountain and saying, "No other gods before You?—That's going to make us look pretty intolerant."[2] And of course it *is* intolerant! God will not tolerate any other god. He refuses to share his glory. If other gods deserved any glory, it would be wrong for God to be so intolerant. But there are no other gods, so God commands us again and again not to act as if there were.

Certain aspects of God's instructions about idolatry here are new. One is the mention of silver and gold. The second commandment focused on what idols are supposed to represent. Ancient idols were made in the form of things up in the heavens, down on the earth, and under the sea. They represented various celestial objects, as well as birds, animals, and fish. But here the emphasis falls not on what idols represent but on how they are made. In those days most idols were made of silver and gold. Some were cast entirely of some precious metal; for others, a thin overlay of metal was pressed down over a wooden figure. Either way, the precious metal was part of the attraction. Idols were something to look at; they had a visual appeal.

This is true in our day as well. People are attracted to the glamour and the glitz. What catches our eye is the colorful image, the flickering screen—what essayist John Seabrook calls "Buzz." To explain what he means by this, Seabrook describes his experience of living and working in New York City:

> The air was fuzzy with the weird yellow tornado light of Times Square by day, a blend of sunlight and wattage, the real and the mediated—the color of Buzz. Buzz is the collective stream of consciousness . . . a shapeless substance into which politics and gossip, art and pornography, virtue and money, the fame of heroes and the celebrity of murderers, all bleed. In Times Square you could see the buzz that you felt going through your mind. I found it soothing just to stand there on my way to and from work and let the yellow light run into my synapses. In that moment the worlds outside and inside my skull became one.[3]

Usually we are tempted to laugh at the ancient pagans for their primitive worship. We wonder how anyone could ever bow to an idol made of silver and gold. But is it any less ridiculous to spend our time staring at computers and compulsively watching television? When we get caught up in the Buzz, our spiritual life suffers. We find it hard to devote ourselves to prayer and the study of God's Word. We have trouble concentrating on spiritual things. We lose our appetite for communion with Christ. We would rather be entertained than worship. So it is for our own spiritual good that God says, "You shall not make gods of silver to be with me, nor shall you make for yourselves gods of gold" (20:23).

An important theological principle lies behind this command: God is not the kind of deity who can be adequately represented in the form of an idol. He is the God who speaks from Heaven. The Israelites met him on the mountain in fire and smoke. They experienced his splendor and glory. How can anything we are tempted to look at—no matter how precious it is, or how shiny, or how well made—ever compare with the real beauty and majesty of God? The things of earth cannot compete with the glories of Heaven. What is immanent cannot rival what is transcendent. Therefore, rather than getting caught up in all the Buzz, we are called to turn back to the living God.

## True Worship

Having reissued his commands against idolatry, God gave Moses a second set of instructions about worship. This time he did not restate the Law but told the Israelites what to do when they broke it. They were to make a sacrifice for their sins. God said to Moses:

> An altar of earth you shall make for me and sacrifice on it your burnt offerings and your peace offerings, your sheep and your oxen. In every place where I cause my name to be remembered I will come to you and bless you. If you make me an altar of stone, you shall not build it of hewn stones, for if you wield your tool on it you profane it. And you shall not go up by steps to my altar, that your nakedness be not exposed on it. (vv. 24–26)

Some of these instructions may seem rather strange. Why did God insist on having an altar made of earth and rough stones rather than one crafted by using tools? And what was wrong with raising an altar up on steps?

The answer is that God wanted to keep his people from worshiping like pagans. Making altars out of square blocks, building step pyramids, worshiping naked—these practices were common in Mesopotamia. When the Canaanites worshiped idols, they did it on altars of finished stone, built high for show, as archaeologists have discovered. We also know that Canaanite worship was obscene, combining idolatry with ritual prostitution and other forms of indecent exposure. But God wanted his people to worship him rightly, and this meant avoiding the appearance of idolatry. It meant making altars from the earth and stone that he created. It also meant staying fully clothed. In fact, God later instructed his priests to wear linen undergarments (28:42), to preserve their modesty.

True Biblical worship is characterized by simplicity and purity. In keeping with these priorities, God told his people to build plain altars of earth and stone. John Mackay comments:

> "Dressed stones" were used by the people of Canaan to construct their altars, because they were building materials of the highest quality from which all roughness had been chiselled away. An altar made from such costly and aesthetically pleasing stone would be a tribute to human craftsmanship, but it would be defiled from the Lord's point of view because it distracted attention from him and his goodness. The restriction to natural stone would have emphasised that it was a God-given provision and not an act of human conception.[4]

Although we no longer build altars for sacrifice (more on this in a moment), there are principles here for us to apply. One is that God alone has the right to determine how he wants to be worshiped. The Israelites were not allowed to build any old altar; they had to build it according to God's instructions. We are under a similar obligation to worship God the way *he* wants, not the way we want. Often this means that what we do in church is different from what everyone else does. Far too much of our thinking about worship and evangelism begins with the opposite assumption, namely, that we should try to fit in with our culture as well as we can. But in the same way that God told the Israelites not to worship like Canaanites, he tells us not to pattern our worship after the values of the surrounding culture.

God's instructions also teach us something about the simple beauty that always characterizes true Biblical worship. God did not want his people to build a fancy altar that might distract them from offering real praise. All he asked was a simple altar made from the good earth and rough stone that he created. Our worship should be simple too. What God requires is for us to worship him in the ordinary acts of singing songs and hymns, saying prayers and petitions, celebrating the sacraments of baptism and the Lord's Supper, giving tithes and offerings, and reading and hearing God's Word. Nothing should be done for show.

This principle can be illustrated from the life of an inmate preparing for pastoral ministry. He described his pulpit at a Texas prison like this: "Given the circumstances, we as inmates come together to hold service and we rotate to preach and teach. I'm given the opportunity to teach 2 to 3 times a month. . . . I praise the Lord, we meet in recreation on one section of bleacher on a baseball field and use a commercial trash can as our pulpit and pick stones from the ground to hold the pages of the Bible for the person teaching that morning." This is the kind of pulpit God honors—one where the plain teaching of his Word is what matters.

The instructions in 20:24–26 contain many other principles to apply. These verses show the absolute necessity for those who lead worship to be sexually pure. When ministers are caught in sexual sin, it always causes a scandal, and rightly so! The purity of God's worship demands the decency of his ministers. These verses also teach us something important about the location of worship. God said, "In every place where I cause my name to be remembered I will come to you and bless you" (v. 24b). This meant that the Israelites did not have to stay at Sinai forever, as if a particular mountain were the only place on earth where God would meet with his people. There would be other places for them to worship—especially the tabernacle—and God would be present there as well. And eventually God would send his Holy Spirit, and then God would be worshiped all over the world. As Jesus said, "Where two or three are gathered in my name, there am I among them" (Matthew 18:20).

## Two Kinds of Sacrifice

The foregoing principles for worship are all important. The Israelites needed to be careful what kind of altar they constructed. Its size, its materials, and its location were governed by God's command. They also needed to be careful what they wore when they approached the altar. But the most important thing of all was what happened *on* the altar. The word translated as "altar" comes from the Hebrew word for slaughter (*zabach*), so the altar was a place to make sacrifice for sin.

The book of Leviticus describes Israel's sacrificial system in detail. There were many kinds of sacrifices, all carefully regulated by God's command. But here in Exodus 20 God mentions two of the most important sacrifices.

The first was the *'olah*, or burnt offering (see Leviticus 1). Sometimes this is called "the whole burnt offering" because the entire sacrifice was burned with fire. The burnt offering was a sacrifice of atonement; it paid for sin. This was always necessary because the altar was the place where God met with his people. Anyone who approached the altar was coming into his holy presence. But we are all sinners, and God hates sin. So before anyone could meet with God, something had to be done about his sin. Hence the need for a burnt offering, in which a perfect animal was placed on the altar and then consumed with fire. The word *'olah* means "to rise up," and the idea was that the smoke of the offering would rise to Heaven, where God would recognize that a sacrifice had been made for sin.

In his book *Immanuel in Our Place*, Tremper Longman shows what the Old Testament sacrifices teach about salvation in Christ. His explanation of burnt offerings is worth quoting at length:

> First . . . the worshiper laid hands on the head of the animal. It is with this act that we get at the heart of the significance of the *'olah* sacrifice. . . . It was not a magical transference between the one offering sacrifice and the animal, but rather a symbolic identification. This step was crucial because when the animal was sacrificed, clearly the death of the animal occurred in place of the death of the worshiper. The assumption behind this was that the worshiper was a sinner coming into the presence of a holy Lord. As a sinner, the human participant deserved death, but the animal stood in his or her place. The worshiper then slaughtered the animal, the verb implying

> the slitting of the animal's throat. After the death of the animal, the blood was collected and sprinkled against the side of the altar. . . . Then the entire animal was placed on the altar by the priests and burned completely, the smoke rising to the Lord.[5]

The one who really deserved to die was the sinner who offered the sacrifice. But instead the sacrificial animal—usually a lamb or a goat—died in the sinner's place, and God accepted this as atonement for sin.

The second kind of sacrifice God mentioned to Moses was the *shelamim*, or fellowship offering (see Leviticus 3). Sometimes this is called the peace offering because its name comes from *shalom*, the Hebrew word for peace. The fellowship offering also dealt with sin, but it had a different emphasis. It showed what kind of relationship God had with his people once atonement had been made for their sin. Fellowship offerings were given on various occasions, sometimes to thank God for a special blessing or a specific answer to prayer and sometimes for no particular reason at all, other than to praise God for his glory. Whatever the reason, the fellowship offering was a tangible reminder that the people were no longer separated from God but had fellowship with him.

In recognition of God's reconciliation with his people, the fellowship offering was not consumed by fire. This was the main difference between the burnt offering and the fellowship offering. The burnt offering was burned to a crisp, as its name implies, but with the fellowship offering, only the fat was burned. In other words, the choicest part of the animal was offered to God. The rest was cooked until tender and then eaten by the worshipers as a way of celebrating God and his grace. The fellowship offering was a feast to the glory of God. Longman writes: "*Shalom*, after all, refers to the condition that results from being in covenant with God. Sin disrupts *shalom*, and so *shelamim* describes the condition that results once that breach has been resolved. As we will see, the sacrifice was a joyous celebration, a kind of religious party, where priests and worshipers enjoyed a sumptuous meal in the presence of God."[6]

What is significant is that God mentions these sacrifices almost immediately after giving his law. God gave his people Ten Commandments for all of life, ordering them to obey. However, he also knew that they would disobey him. So he provided a way for them to atone for their sins and come back into fellowship with him. Both the burnt offering and the fellowship offering were for sinners in need of salvation.

By providing a way to make atonement, God gave his people everything they needed for their salvation. First he brought them out of their bondage in Egypt. Then he told them how he wanted them to live. He sent a mediator to make sure that they understood well enough to obey. But God knew that his people would break his law, so he also gave them sacrifices to pay for sin and reconcile them to himself.

## God's Sacrifice . . . and Ours

God has always provided his people with atonement for their sin. He did it in the garden of Eden. After Adam and Eve had sinned, God clothed them with the skins of animals—a sacrifice was made for their sin. There was an altar again after the great flood. The world had been judged for its wickedness, but Noah was saved, and when he set foot on dry land he made a sacrifice to God. The patriarchs all built altars, as did Moses, and then David. There was always an altar where God's people could make atonement for sin.

This was all preparing the way for Jesus to make atonement once and for all. The Bible says that "God put forward [Jesus] as a propitiation by his blood, to be received by faith" (Romans 3:25a). As we saw in the previous chapter, Christ was the mediator who suffered the Law's penalty in our place. Here we discover another way to describe his work. When Jesus was crucified, he made an atoning sacrifice on the altar of God. In fact, the Bible goes so far as to refer to Jesus as our "altar" (Hebrews 13:10). He is the burnt offering that made atonement for our sins, as well as the fellowship offering that reconciled us to God.

Everyone who has ever been saved has accepted Jesus as a sacrifice for sin. Whatever sins we have committed—whatever blatant violations of the Ten Commandments, and whatever inward sins of a loveless, idolatrous, covetous heart—Jesus died on the cross to save our kind of sinner. No one is excluded. There is salvation for every sinner who comes to Christ. In describing Christ's work on the cross, Martin Luther said:

> All the prophets saw this, that Christ was to become the greatest thief, murderer, adulterer, robber, desecrator, blasphemer, etc., there has ever been anywhere in the world. He is not acting in His own Person now. Now He is not the Son of God, born of the Virgin. But He is a sinner, who has and bears the sin of Paul, the former blasphemer, persecutor, and assaulter; of Peter, who denied Christ; of David, who was an adulterer and a murderer, and who caused the Gentiles to blaspheme the name of the Lord. In short, He has and bears all the sins of all men in His body—not in the sense that He has committed them but in the sense that He took these sins, committed by us, upon His own body, in order to make satisfaction for them with His own blood.[7]

This explains why we no longer need to make God an altar. The sacrifice has been offered. Atonement has been made. Fellowship has been restored. And it is all through Jesus and his death on the cross.

If there is any sacrifice left to offer, it is only the sacrifice of living for the glory of God. The Bible says, "I appeal to you therefore, brothers, by the mercies of God, to present your bodies as a living sacrifice, holy and acceptable to God, which is your spiritual worship" (Romans 12:1). Jesus has offered himself as the sacrifice for our sins. Now it is our privilege and joy to offer ourselves for his service: "Through him then let us continually offer up a sacrifice of praise to God, that is, the fruit of lips that acknowledge his name. Do not neglect to do good and to share what you have, for such sacrifices are pleasing to God" (Hebrews 13:15, 16).

# 61

# Bound for Freedom

## EXODUS 21:1–11

THE FIRST TWENTY CHAPTERS of Exodus tell the story of an epic adventure, in which a people enslaved by their enemies make a daring escape into the wilderness. The next three chapters are somewhat less entertaining. God said to Moses, "Now these are the rules that you shall set before them" (21:1). Then he proceeded to issue a long list of rules for everyday life—regulations covering everything from what to do in the case of wrongful death to how to put up collateral for a loan. When God was finished, Moses "came and told the people all the words of the LORD and all the rules" (24:3a).

This section of Exodus—which the Bible calls "the Book of the Covenant" (24:7a)—does not make for very exciting reading (unless one happens to be a lawyer). Frankly, it's one part of Exodus that preachers usually skip. As one Bible scholar describes it, "Boredom seems to set in at this point, relieved only by the golden calf incident narrated in chapter 32. . . . The impression is given that the writer of Exodus has now inserted into a brilliant narrative a series of rules and regulations that are of interest only to historians."[1]

Whether or not we find it very interesting, the Book of the Covenant is important. The mere fact that it is in the Bible means that it merits our attention. But the Book of the Covenant also teaches us how to live for God day by day. First God gave Israel his moral law in the form of the Ten Commandments. Then he showed them how to apply his law in various life situations. This is where the Book of the Covenant comes in. It is "an application of the Decalogue to the specific social context of Israel as a nation."[2]

The Book of the Covenant was revealed by God, just as were the Ten Commandments. Some scholars say the Israelites borrowed most of their laws from other civilizations. It is true that by the time of Moses other laws had been written, such as Hammurabi's famous code (c. 1700 BC). It is also true that some of the laws in Exodus are similar to ones archaeologists have discovered elsewhere.

This is not surprising. Most cultures have laws to prohibit murder, stealing, and other common crimes. Yet for all the similarities, the differences are more striking. For example, the Book of the Covenant afforded legal protections for women and the poor that were unavailable anywhere else in the ancient world. But the biggest difference was that no other nation had ever entered into a covenant with Almighty God. Whereas all the other nations came up with their laws on their own, the Israelites received them straight from God.

This means that the regulations in the Book of the Covenant are as fully authoritative as the Ten Commandments. However, there are some things that make them different. This part of Exodus was not written directly by the finger of God, but with the pen of Moses—not in stone, but on parchment (24:4a). The implication is that they do not bind with the same eternal force; somehow they are less fundamental. This explains why we do not continue to keep these laws down to the very letter. While the Book of the Covenant contains principles that we can still apply today, its specific civil pronouncements and penalties were for the nation of Israel and thus are no longer binding on the church or the state.

We must also understand that even in the days of Moses, the Book of the Covenant was never intended to address every possible situation. It was more a guide to cases than a statutory code. Whereas the Ten Commandments were expressed as universal absolutes, the laws in the Book of the Covenant dealt with specific situations. They provided a series of legal precedents that wise elders could use in settling disputes. While these case laws could not possibly cover every new situation that might arise, they illustrated basic legal principles for living in community with the people of God.

Truly, this was exciting. The Book of the Covenant showed the Israelites how the Law applied to daily life. Regulations about livestock grazing in a field may seem mundane. However, this is where most of us live most of the time—at the level of ordinary existence. Thankfully, God is as interested in this part of our lives as he is in anything else that happens in his world. The Book of the Covenant is about living for God, not just when we are standing at the foot of the mountain and gazing at his awesome glory, but when our neighbor borrows a video and fails to give it back, when someone is spreading rumors, or when an argument turns into a fistfight. In other words, it is about real life.

### Manservants

At first the Book of the Covenant may seem somewhat disorganized, a hodgepodge of unrelated rules. Yet there are clear signs of organization, including important connections to the Ten Commandments. Various sections of the covenant seem to be tied to particular commandments.

The Book of the Covenant starts with slavery, which in fact is the way the Ten Commandments begin. Before God gave his people the Law, he reminded them how he brought them "out of the land of Egypt, out of the house of slavery" (20:2). How appropriate, then, for God to begin the Book of the Covenant with the same topic. The Israelites were former slaves, and now that they were free, it would be unthinkable for them to treat one another the way Pharaoh had once treated them. Thus God began his Book of the Covenant by regulating the relationship between masters and servants.

We might have expected God to abolish slavery altogether. What he did instead was to allow for certain forms of servitude, with safeguards to protect the welfare and dignity of those who served. This is consistent with what the Bible teaches elsewhere. Without ever defending the practice of slavery, the Bible assumes that some form of servitude will continue. Yet it transforms the institution by carefully regulating the relationship between master and slave in ways that eliminate abuse and ultimately cause slavery (at least as we know it) to disappear.

This is hard for us to understand. In America we struggle with the Biblical teaching about masters and slaves because our painful national experience with slavery makes it hard for us to appreciate the very different social and economic circumstances of the ancient Near East. When we hear the word *slavery*, we think of the Civil War and everything that led up to it. But there were crucial differences between that kind of slavery and servitude in Israel.

In Israel servitude was voluntary (at least for Israelites). People hired themselves into the service of others. Usually this was because they were poor, and they recognized that the best way to meet their needs while at the same time paying off their debts was to become someone's servant. *Servant* is the proper word for it. They were not *slaves*, as we usually think of the term, but something more like apprentices, hired hands, or indentured laborers. They lived in their master's home, where they worked hard in exchange for room, board, and an honest wage.

Involuntary slavery was forbidden. Only a few verses later the Law demands the death penalty for slave traders: "Whoever steals a man and sells him, and anyone found in possession of him, shall be put to death" (21:16). This verse rules out the whole institution of slavery as it was practiced in Africa and the West, and as it is still practiced in some parts of the world today. The Bible condemns the sin of man-stealing. Whenever people try to defend slavery on Biblical grounds, this is something they generally overlook. But the Bible passages dealing with masters and servants have little to do with slavery in America because that form of slave trading was a flagrant violation of the Law of God.

Another difference between servitude in Israel and most other forms of slavery is that in Israel servanthood was temporary. God gave his people this law: "When you buy a Hebrew slave, he shall serve six years, and in the seventh he shall go out free, for nothing" (v. 2). Here again we see the Sabbath principle at work. Just as God's people had the freedom to rest one whole day in seven, Hebrew slaves were set free in their sabbatical year. Once they had served their time, they had a chance to start over, and this prevented them from remaining in perpetual servitude.

When Hebrew slaves were set free in the seventh year, they were not sent away empty-handed. Instead, their masters were required to give them everything they needed to make a new start in life:

> If your brother, a Hebrew man or a Hebrew woman, is sold to you, he shall serve you six years, and in the seventh year you shall let him go free from you. And when you let him go free from you, you shall not let him go empty-handed. You shall furnish him liberally out of your flock, out of your threshing floor, and out of your winepress. As the LORD your God has blessed you, you shall give to him. You shall remember that you were a slave in the land of Egypt, and the LORD your God redeemed you; therefore I command you this today. (Deuteronomy 15:12–15)

Masters had a responsibility to set their former slaves up in business. In effect, they gave them what some folks talked about giving American slaves after the Civil War, but the government never delivered: the proverbial "forty acres and a mule." God is gracious, and he wanted his people to treat one another with the same kind of grace they had received when they were delivered from Egypt and went out loaded with silver and gold (12:35, 36).

This proves that the Biblical form of slavery had a constructive purpose. It was for the benefit of the servant as well as of the master. This is not the way slavery usually works. Ordinarily it is for the master's advantage: He gets his work done at his slave's expense. But the purpose of slavery in Israel was to train men and women to become productive members of society. The reason they had to become servants in the first place was because they were in debt, sometimes through their own negligence and sometimes to make restitution for a theft. In such cases their servitude was made necessary by their sin. But rather than being condemned to a life of perpetual poverty, they had a chance to improve their situation. Slavery was God's way of training irresponsible men to manage their own affairs.[3]

By selling themselves to other members of the covenant community, debtors became members of stable households, where their needs were met and where they could get on-the-job training. They learned how to work in the context of a family. This was all in preparation for their ultimate freedom. Thus slavery had a redemptive purpose. Its goal was not perpetual bondage but responsible independence. The Hebrew servant was bound for freedom.

Here again we see how different things were in Israel, where even slavery was for the good of humanity and the glory of God. The relationship between the master and the servant is always subject to abuse. Taking advantage of others is part of our sinful nature, and whenever we have power, we tend to abuse it. But God wanted his people to care for one another. To that end, he regulated this relationship so that it would be mutually beneficial. Voluntary, temporary slavery was as much for the servant's benefit as for his master's.

A final difference between conventional and Biblical slavery concerned marriage. In America, slavery had a devastating effect on black families. Slave owners bought and sold human beings as they pleased, with the result that husbands and wives were often separated. But the Bible—even in its regulations for slavery—preserves the sanctity of marriage. Consider what happened when a slave was set free: "If he comes in single, he shall go out single; if he comes in married, then his wife shall go out with him" (21:3). In other words, a former slave returned to his former station in life. If he was single, he stayed single. If he was married, he stayed married.

Things got more complicated, however, when the man married another slave. In this case, although he was set free, his wife and children remained with their master: "If his master gives him a wife and she bears him sons or daughters, the wife and her children shall be her master's, and he shall go out alone" (v. 4). Certainly this law cannot be faulted for a lack of fairness. If the wife and children belonged to the master to begin with, they were his property, and he had a right to keep them. Furthermore, the Law allowed slaves in this situation to choose to stay with their families, as we shall see (vv. 5, 6). Yet most commentators still have trouble accepting a law that let a man go free while his family remained in bondage. "A cruel inconsistency," they call it.[4] The law hardly seems like a good way to strengthen a marriage. What was God doing?

It is at least possible that this law actually was for the protection of women and children. Remember that the husband and father in this case was a former debtor. If his servitude had served its purpose, he was now ready to become a productive member of the covenant community. Soon he would be able to buy his family's freedom (see Leviticus 25:47–55), and they would all be united under one roof—his roof. But if he had failed to learn his lesson, he would soon be back in debt, and this time his wife and children would also have to suffer the consequences. For the time being, then, the safest thing would be for them to remain under the care of their master. They were still a family, but the woman and her children would remain in their master's household until their husband and father could take full responsibility for them in a God-honoring way.[5]

What practical application do these laws have for today? The question we always need to ask about the Book of the Covenant is this: "If that was what was required back then with their particular set of circumstances, then how do we put the same basic principles into operation today when we are faced with this different set of circumstances?"[6] Here the answer is that employers should not exploit their employees but should seek to promote their welfare, even to the point of helping them advance their careers. When people are in debt, they should be given an opportunity to pay back what they owe, in a context where they can learn how to be responsible citizens. The lack of such opportunities is a major problem in America today. Debtors should not be given handouts, of course; they need to learn how to work. But this requires the personal involvement of people who are willing to take the time to show them how.

### Maidservants

Servanthood in Israel was supposed to be very different from conventional slavery. It was voluntary, it was temporary, and its purpose was to lead people into freedom. God's slave laws were also designed to protect the family, especially women and children. This was true not only of the laws for menservants, but also of the laws for maidservants, which began as follows: "When a man sells his daughter as a slave, she shall not go out as the male slaves do" (21:7).

At first this law seems unfair, and thus it raises some obvious questions: Why did God allow his people to sell their daughters into slavery? And why didn't he allow maidservants to go free in the same way that menservants could? It doesn't seem right! In fact, at first it seems like God treated the men better than the women. Not surprisingly, this is one of the passages people use to criticize the Bible for being sexist.

To understand these laws, it is necessary to know the cultural context. While we do not have all the details we might like, we know enough to recognize that these laws had a benevolent purpose. The man who sold his daughter was not trying to get rid of her but to improve her prospects in life. What this verse describes was really a form of arranged marriage, which, however strange it may sound to most Americans, has been common in many parts of the world for most of human history. A poor man would send his daughter to a rich man in the hope that she would become a permanent member of his household. She entered into a conditional form of servitude, hoping that eventually she might marry the master's son.

Obviously, this arrangement was subject to abuse. A bad master might take advantage of a maidservant by treating her harshly, selling her to slave traders, or even releasing her from servitude. Such freedom may sound ideal. However, in the ancient world a woman who did not belong to a household was vulnerable to all kinds of danger; it was not safe for her to go free. In order to flourish, she needed to live within the community of a family. So by not allowing maidservants to go free, God was not seeking to restrict them but actually to protect them. He knew that even within the covenant community, men would try to take advantage of servant girls.

God's law afforded maidservants three specific protections. The first concerned a master who decided that he didn't want her service after all. For whatever reason, he was displeased with her. In this case he was not allowed to treat her any way he pleased. Instead he was obligated to let her return to her own family: "If she does not please her master, who has designated her for himself, then he shall let her be redeemed. He shall have no right to sell her to a foreign people, since he has broken faith with her" (v. 8). There was a probationary period for the maidservant to prove her worth. But notice that if things didn't work out, the maidservant was not to blame. The master was the one at fault, not she; so the right and honorable thing was to allow her family to ransom her. They had the right to purchase her redemption.

The second situation involved a master who was pleased with his maidservant—so pleased in fact that he wanted her to marry his son. In this case, "If he designates her for his son, he shall deal with her as with a daughter" (v. 9). Apparently at this point the maidservant was only engaged, not married. Yet she was welcomed as a full member of the family, with all the privileges of a daughter. This was really a form of adoption. Here again we see that God's law had the woman's best interests at heart: A maidservant could gain her freedom by being betrothed to the master's son. As a married woman, she would have the full rights of a free citizen.

Sometimes engagements get broken, and—even more sadly—sometimes marriages end in divorce. When this happened to a maidservant, what would become of her? This question is important because in those days when a woman was married she received bride money from her husband. This was a form of security. It ensured that in the event something happened to her husband, or to their marriage, she would have enough to live on.

A maidservant did not have this protection. She was already treated as a member of the family, so no one paid her the price of a bride. But this left her without any insurance if her fiancé changed his mind or if her husband later decided to take another wife. So the law stated, "If he takes another wife to himself, he shall not diminish her food, her clothing, or her marital rights. And if he does not do these three things for her, she shall go out for nothing, without payment of money" (vv. 10, 11). No matter what happened, there were three things a husband had to provide for his wife: food (literally, meat), clothing (meaning shelter, which is a form of physical protection), and marital rights (which probably refers here to sexual intimacy). If a man failed to provide these things for a maidservant, she was released from her servitude. This prevented masters from taking advantage of their servant girls.

Critics sometimes say that the Bible has a negative attitude about women. Even some Christians secretly suspect that they ought to be embarrassed about the Old Testament attitude toward women, or that it is hard to defend God against the charge of chauvinism. But the truth is that God has always loved his daughters. If the Biblical teaching about men and women challenges our preconceptions, it is because our own thinking is distorted by sin. This is true of everyone and in every culture. Gender relationships always need to be transformed by the life-changing power of God's Word, so we should expect that some of our attitudes about what it means to be male and female need to be changed. But we should never doubt the goodness of God, who loves his daughters as much as his sons and has always given them the care and protection they need to flourish.

In practical terms, the Law for maidservants helps set the agenda for Christian marriage. What does a wife need? She needs to eat, so it is a husband's responsibility to provide. She needs shelter, so she ought to find protection in his care. She also needs intimacy, at every level. Sex is never just about what people do with their bodies. It is an expression of the total love commitment between a husband and wife. These are all areas where a woman contributes to the marriage as an equal partner. But her husband has the responsibility before God to make sure that she gets what she needs. A husband who fails to care for his wife in any of these areas—provision, protection, or the physical expression of love—violates the law of God.

## Servants for Life

Even though we are not bound to follow the Old Testament slave laws today, they teach us practical principles to apply at home and at work. They also provide wonderful pictures of our salvation in Christ.

The Book of the Covenant showed how a servant living with a bad master could be redeemed and go back home. It also showed how a slave without any prospects could gain her freedom by marrying her master's son. These narratives ought to sound familiar because they are both part of the gospel story. We were born as slaves to sin, tyrannized by the cruel mastery of the devil. But when Christ was crucified, he paid the price to redeem us, and now we are free to go back home to God. To tell the same story a different way, we were all alone, living without hope. But when we came to God, he engaged us to marry his one and only Son. Thus the Bible describes the Church as the bride of Christ. We are married to the Master's Son. These are two examples of how the Law of Moses points us to salvation in Christ.

But perhaps the most beautiful picture of the gospel comes from the Law's special provision for a slave who wanted to enter his master's permanent service. God said: "But if the slave plainly says, 'I love my master, my wife, and my children; I will not go out free,' then his master shall bring him to God, and he shall bring him to the door or the doorpost. And his master shall bore his ear through with an awl, and he shall be his slave forever" (21:5, 6).

It must have been a remarkable occasion. After six years of labor, a slave decided that rather than going free, he wanted to continue to serve his master. Some masters might take advantage of this law by forcing their slaves to keep working. In order to prevent this, there had to be a public ceremony. First the slave went before the elders to make a formal declaration of his desire to keep serving. The Bible literally says that the slave must be taken "before God," meaning in this case his representatives among the spiritual leaders of the covenant community. Today we would say that the slave made his declaration "before God and these witnesses." The declaration had to be emphatic. The Hebrew idiom could be translated like this: "If the servant *truly* declares . . ." There could be no doubt as to the man's intentions.

Once the servant had made his declaration, everyone went to the doorpost of the master's house, where a sharp object was driven through the slave's ear. This was symbolic. The ear is the most important part of a servant's body. He has to hear before he can obey. By having his ear pierced, therefore, the servant was making a public commitment to do what his master said. The doorpost was also symbolic. Not only did it serve as a place for driving the awl, but it also showed that the servant was now attached to his master's household. The doorpost was marked with the blood of a covenant between master and slave.

This form of servitude was totally voluntary. Anyone who saw the servant's earring would know that he had chosen to serve. But why would anyone make this choice? What could persuade a man to renounce his freedom and remain bound to his master? The answer is love. The slave who had his ear pierced swore an oath of allegiance: "I love my master" (21:5). His servitude was not a form of tyranny, but a voluntary act of love.

This raises a further question: What kind of master would deserve so much love? The master who deserved to be loved was a good master. He took care of all his servant's needs. He was also a kind master, one who treated his servant like a friend. And he was a generous master: He had his servant's best interests at heart. In a word, he was a *loving* master, and thus it was only natural for his servant to love him in return. Rather than looking for freedom somewhere else, the servant had found it in his master's house.

This special provision of the Law has much to teach us about our relationship to God. David wrote about it in one of his psalms:

> Sacrifice and offering you did not desire,
>     but my ears you have pierced;
> burnt offerings and sin offerings
>     you did not require.
> Then I said, "Here I am, I have come—
>     it is written about me in the scroll.
> I desire to do your will, O my God;
>     your law is within my heart." (Psalm 40:6–8 NIV)

According to David, pleasing God means more than simply offering a sacrifice for sin. It also means doing what God says, obeying him the way a servant obeys the master he loves. To illustrate this, David referred to the ancient custom and compared himself to a servant who had his ear pierced. He had learned to hear and obey, offering himself in loving service to God.

This is the only way for us to find true freedom: not by serving ourselves, but by choosing to become servants of God. "I will run in the way of your commandments," wrote the psalmist, "when you enlarge my heart!" (Psalm 119:32). We are loved by the best Master of all. He takes care of all our needs. He does not treat us like slaves, but more like friends. He always has our best interests at heart. If all this is true, then why would we want to serve anyone else?

But there is more. We serve a Master who has made himself our slave, taking on the very nature of a servant (Philippians 2:7). This is the story of our salvation, that the Son of God "came not to be served but to serve, and to give his life as a ransom for many" (Mark 10:45). This means that the words of David are really the words of Jesus. David was standing in for the Messiah, who lived in a way that said to his Father, "My ears you have pierced. . . . 'Here I am, I have come—it is written about me in the scroll. I desire to do your will, O my God; your law is within my heart'" (Psalm 40:6–8 NIV). Jesus always chose to do his Father's will. We could even say that he is the servant who declared, "I love my master, my wife, and my children; I will not go out free" (21:5). Out of his great love for his Father—and for us as his bride, his sons, and his daughters—Jesus bound himself to God's will, even when it meant suffering and dying for our sins. The greatest service of all was his death on the cross.

If a servant loves a master who takes care of him and treats him like a friend, imagine what a servant would do for a master who saved him, and at the cost of his own life! We are loved by such a Master. Why would we ever want to serve anyone else, least of all ourselves? What we ought to do is give ourselves entirely to his service. We ought to make a public declaration of our allegiance to Christ. We ought to listen to his Word and obey his voice. We ought to say, "I love my Master, and I want my heart to be bound to him forever." Service to such a gracious master is not bondage but freedom. As Ambrose rightly said, "That man is truly free . . . who is entirely God's."[7]

The story is told of a visit Abraham Lincoln once made to a slave auction, where he was appalled to see the buying and selling of human beings.

> His heart was especially drawn to a young woman on the block whose story seemed to be told in her eyes. She looked with hatred and contempt on everyone around her. She had been used and abused all her life, and this time was but one more cruel humiliation. The bidding began, and Lincoln offered a bid. As other amounts were bid, he counter-bid with larger amounts until he won. When he paid the auctioneer the money and took title to the young woman, she stared at him with vicious contempt. She asked him what he was going to do next with her, and he said, "I'm going to set you free."
>
> "Free?" she asked. "Free for what?"
>
> "Just free," Lincoln answered. "Completely free."
>
> "Free to do whatever I want to do?"
>
> "Yes," he said. "Free to do whatever you want to do."
>
> "Free to say whatever I want to say?"
>
> "Yes, free to say whatever you want to say."

> "Free to go wherever I want to go?" she added with skepticism. Lincoln answered, "You are free to go anywhere you want to go."
>
> "Then I'm going with you!" she said with a smile.[8]

Whether this story is fact or fiction, it shows us what it means to follow Jesus Christ. Anyone who trusts in Christ for salvation has been delivered from sin and death. Now we are free. Free for what? Free to say, "Jesus, I'm going with you!"

# 62

# An Eye for an Eye

## EXODUS 21:12–36

CONSIDER THE FOLLOWING news items:

> A man strangles a woman in her city apartment.
>
> A young girl vanishes from her home during the night, apparently abducted by a stranger.
>
> A homeowner is startled by an intruder, who in the ensuing scuffle strikes a fatal blow.
>
> A woman loses control of her ferocious dogs, and they maul a neighbor to death.

Stories like these are in the news every day. Each of them raises serious questions about justice: Does a murderer deserve the death penalty? What is the proper sentence for a kidnapper? How much responsibility does someone have for an accidental death or an unintended injury? When does negligence become criminal?

It is hard to find agreement on these questions. Just listen to the talk shows, where everyone has a different opinion. Although we all want justice, we don't always agree what justice requires. Not even our legal system has all the answers. A jury reaches a verdict, but the judge throws it out on a technicality. A judge makes a decision, only to have it overturned on appeal. In the end, we are left wondering whether justice has really been done.

The Bible can help. It does not give us a complete code with regulations for every situation that might arise in every culture. However, it does provide a set of cases to help us understand the basic principles of divine justice. These legal cases are contained in the Book of the Covenant that God gave to Moses. Each case consists of both a crime and a punishment. The punishments God gave to Israel as a nation under his direct divine rule do not always apply today. Yet they still help us understand how to seek justice in an unjust world.

## Capital Crimes

The Book of the Covenant began with slave laws (21:1–11). The next section deals with three different kinds of crimes: capital crimes (vv. 12–17), personal injuries (vv. 18–27), and criminal negligence (vv. 28–36). There seems to be a general progression from greater crimes to lesser crimes. Every crime is a sin against God and thus deserves his displeasure. But some crimes do more damage than others, and it is only right for them to be punished more severely. God's law teaches us to have a sense of proportion, so that the punishment fits the crime.

The most serious offenses are capital crimes—crimes that demand the death penalty. The Book of the Covenant mentions three such crimes, each of which is based on a different commandment from the Decalogue. First comes murder, a crime against the sixth commandment: "Whoever strikes a man so that he dies shall be put to death" (v. 12). In this case justice demands strict retribution: a life for a life. Anyone who takes someone else's life in cold blood no longer deserves to live but should be put to death by an act of public justice.

Some people think that the death penalty itself violates the sixth commandment. If God has commanded us not to kill, they argue, then we do not have the right to execute someone. This is a serious misunderstanding. When the sixth commandment says we must not kill, it is talking about murder, not about the judicial use of deadly force. The Hebrew language has several different words for killing, and the word used in the sixth commandment is the word for homicide, not the word for execution. God's law does not rule out the death penalty but in fact requires it! In the case of murder, death is the only penalty that preserves the value of human life. Any other punishment is inadequate.

Death for murder is one penalty that still applies today. God established this legal principle long before he ever gave his law to Moses. After the great flood, God said to Noah, "From his fellow man I will require a reckoning for the life of man. 'Whoever sheds the blood of man, by man shall his blood be shed, for God made man in his own image'" (Genesis 9:5b, 6). Every human being is made in God's image. The murder of another human being, therefore, is an attack against God. When someone commits such an assault on his divine sovereignty, the perpetrator's life is forfeit. Nothing less than death can pay for murder.

Once the death penalty has been carried out, it can never be undone. This means that no one should ever be executed unless guilt is certain. God's law gave careful safeguards to protect the innocent from being put to death. For example, no one could be executed on the testimony of a single witness (Deuteronomy 17:6, 7). This has implications for justice today. In the case of homicide, the Bible calls for the death penalty. However, in order for that penalty to be just, it must be administered justly. This means having fair trials that reach correct verdicts in a legal system that is free from racial bias and other forms of injustice.

Since it is hard to find perfect justice in an imperfect world, there are times when it is necessary for Christians to oppose the death penalty, even though they agree with it as a matter of principle.

Sometimes people get killed by accident, and this calls for a different measure of justice. God's law made a distinction between intentional and unintentional crimes: "But if he did not lie in wait for him, but God let him fall into his hand, then I will appoint for you a place to which he may flee. But if a man willfully attacks another to kill him by cunning, you shall take him from my altar, that he may die" (21:13, 14).

What is in view here is a crime of passion. In the heat of argument, or perhaps in self-defense, one man killed another. This was not a case of premeditated murder, a crime committed "with malice aforethought." Rather, it was unintentional—a form of involuntary manslaughter. To say, "God let it happen" is to say that it was beyond human control. Nevertheless, a life had been lost. What did justice demand?

In most ancient cultures the perpetrator would have been killed by the victim's relatives. But rather than resorting to revenge, God provided a better way for justice to be done. As soon as the killer realized what he had done, he ran to a divinely appointed place of safety. Later, when the Israelites entered the land, God designated six towns as cities of refuge (Numbers 35:6–15; cf. Deuteronomy 19:1–13). When the killer reached a city of refuge, he would run to the sanctuary and put his hands on the altar of God. He could not be touched until the authorities had a chance to investigate his crime properly. If after due process they judged that the crime was indeed an accident, the perpetrator was allowed to live. But if the man's crime was deliberate, not even the altar could save him. There is a notable example of this from Israel's history. Joab sought protection from Solomon by seizing the horns of God's altar. But Joab had shed innocent blood, so the king's men hauled him off and justly put him to death (1 Kings 2:28–34).

The second capital crime may seem surprising. According to God's law, "Whoever strikes his father or his mother shall be put to death" (21:15), and "Whoever curses his father or his mother shall be put to death" (v. 17). Notice that these laws applied to mothers as well as fathers. This is one of the many places where women received equal protection under God's law.

Notice as well that although these cases did not involve murder, in Old Testament Israel they still demanded the death penalty. To understand why, it helps to know what kind of attack the Bible has in mind. The Hebrew used here (*naka*) refers to a vicious assault, virtually an attempted murder. Ordinarily such a violent attack only required the death penalty if someone actually got killed. But this crime was aggravated by its assault on parental authority. The fifth commandment said, "Honor your father and your mother" (20:12). If someone so dishonored his parents as to strike them with the intent to kill, he deserved to die. While this law may seem harsh, it was for the preservation of the family, and thus for the protection of the nation.

The death penalty also applied when someone cursed his parents. What is in view here is not a single act of disrespect but a total repudiation of their parental authority. The man who cursed his father and mother disowned them. To be more specific, he treated them with such utter contempt that he refused to care for them in their old age. This is the way Jesus understood the law when he challenged the Pharisees:

> And why do you break the commandment of God for the sake of your tradition? For God commanded, "Honor your father and your mother," and, "Whoever reviles father or mother must surely die." But you say, "If anyone tells his father or his mother, 'What you would have gained from me is given to God,' he need not honor his father." So for the sake of your tradition you have made void the word of God. (Matthew 15:3–6)

This law reminds us to honor our parents. If we speak against them—or even worse, if we strike them—we are guilty of a great sin against God. And if we fail to care for our parents, we curse them and thus violate the Law of God.

The third capital crime is one we encountered in our study of slavery: "Whoever steals a man and sells him, and anyone found in possession of him, shall be put to death" (21:16; cf. Deuteronomy 24:7; 1 Timothy 1:10). This law forbids any kind of kidnapping, but what it mainly has in mind is the slave trade. It rules out the evil sin of man-stealing, which violates the eighth commandment. To give a Biblical example, this was the sin that Joseph's brothers committed when they sold him to the Midianites (Genesis 37:28).

As far as God is concerned, such a sin demands the death penalty. God does not tolerate free men to be turned into slaves against their will. What is surprising about this law is that it applied to everyone. In Hammurabi's Code, the prohibition against kidnapping only applied to the upper class. Common people could be captured without breaking the law. But every person is made in the image of God, and therefore in Israel it was illegal to kidnap anyone—rich or poor—upon the pain of death.

## Personal Injury

Some acts of violence do not lead to death. This brings us to a second category of crimes: nonfatal cases of bodily injury. People injure one another in many different ways. Obviously, not every case is covered here. But the cases that are listed provide basic principles for doing justice when someone gets hurt. If there is anything they have in common, it is this: People who injure others should provide their victims with some form of compensation. They should pay for what they have done. To use the proper legal term, they should make restitution. And since the payment came out of the perpetrator's own pocket, it was also a form of retribution—a punishment for the crime.

The principle of restitution is clearly spelled out in the first case: "When men quarrel and one strikes the other with a stone or with his fist and the man does not die but takes to his bed, then if the man rises again and walks outdoors with his staff, he who struck him shall be clear; only he shall pay for the loss of his time, and shall have him thoroughly healed" (21:18, 19).

In this case, a man tried to settle an argument by resorting to physical violence. He clenched his fist, grabbed a rock, or used whatever else was handy and struck his opponent in such a way as to cause serious injury. If the victim died, the laws for a capital crime applied. If he survived, there was no charge of manslaughter. However, if the victim was disabled, the man who caused the injury obviously had a responsibility to help. According to God's law, he had to pay for his crime—both by compensating the victim for his loss of income and by making sure that he received adequate medical care. To put this in contemporary terms, the man who committed the crime had to pay workmen's compensation and take care of his victim's medical bills.

This law reminds us not to resort to violence. Arguments have a way of escalating, and once we get angry, there is no telling what we might do. But there is never any excuse for fistfighting. Of course, if our lives are in danger we have the right of self-defense. Yet even then it is usually wiser to turn and run rather than stand and fight. But we are never justified in using physical force to settle a personal dispute. If we break this law, we must take full responsibility for whatever damage we cause. The right thing to do is make restitution.

The next case also involves injury, except the person injured is a slave: "When a man strikes his slave, male or female, with a rod and the slave dies under his hand, he shall be avenged. But if the slave survives a day or two, he is not to be avenged, for the slave is his money" (vv. 20, 21). Similarly, "When a man strikes the eye of his slave, male or female, and destroys it, he shall let the slave go free because of his eye. If he knocks out the tooth of his slave, male or female, he shall let the slave go free because of his tooth" (vv. 26, 27).

Obviously these regulations assumed that a master had the right to administer corporal punishment. If a slave refused to obey, then he could be beaten, preferably on his hindquarters. However, a master did not have the right to injure his slave in any way. If the slave died, the master was guilty of murder. Killing a slave was a capital crime. If the slave lived, there was no need for compensation because the slave worked for the master. It was the master's loss, so no further payment was necessary. Nor did anything need to be said about medical care because it was in the master's own best interest to help his slave heal and get back to work.

But what if the slave was permanently injured? In that case—whether the injury was as serious as losing an eye or as minor as losing a tooth—the slave was set free. This was a major difference between slavery in Israel and slavery anywhere else. If a master so much as knocked out a tooth, his slave would be set free. The master had failed in his God-given duty to protect his servant, so he was released from his servitude. This law was intended to eradicate the physical abuse of slaves. Such a law was unparalleled. We know of no other statute from the ancient world that provided similar protection for slaves. But this law is in the Bible because everyone (slaves included) is made in the image of God and thus has a right to his fatherly care.

Sometimes the person who gets hurt is an innocent bystander. Here the Law considers an unusual case of injury to a third party: "When men strive together and hit a pregnant woman, so that her children come out, but there is no harm, the one who hit her shall surely be fined, as the woman's husband shall impose on him, and he shall pay as the judges determine" (v. 22).

When a pregnant woman was struck in a way that induced labor, there was an obvious risk of injury or even death to both mother and child. If there was a serious injury to either one of them, then the man who caused it would deserve strict justice—an eye for an eye, and so on. But even if the mother and her child survived, the man still needed to pay a fine, as determined by the elders. His rash and violent act had threatened two of the most vulnerable people in society: a mother and her unborn child. The Law demanded a fine to show that the weak deserve special care.

This case has many practical implications. It shows that God holds us responsible even when the damage we do is unintentional. Presumably the men who were fighting never intended to cause a miscarriage. As far as they were concerned, it was just an accident. Yet they were out of control, and when that happens, other people can get hurt. And when they get hurt, the person who hurt them is guilty before God. Today this principle would apply to a drunk who gets behind the wheel of an automobile or to a father who loses his temper and strikes his children in anger. "I didn't mean it!" people usually say. But the Law says, "Whether you meant it or not, you did it, and you have to make things right."

Another implication of this case is that a fetus is a person who deserves special protection. The Law of God imposed strict penalties on anyone who harmed an unborn child. It treated the injury of an unborn child the same way it treated the injury of any other human being. By this standard, performing an abortion is an act of murder, for which the proper penalty is "life for life" (v. 23). To put it bluntly, abortionists deserve the death penalty. It should be emphasized that this is a sentence no private individual ever has the right to execute. Killing a doctor who performs abortions is also murder, because only the proper authorities have the right to use deadly force. Nevertheless, the proper legal category for abortion is murder, with all the penalties that apply—never in a private vendetta, but as a matter of public justice.

What these laws show is that people who don't count to us still count to

God. The innocent bystander who is struck with a violent blow, the child ripped from his mother's womb, the slave beaten by his master—all of these people deserve special care. The fetus is not a mass of tissue. The slave is not a piece of property. We are all made in the image of God. Since we all need protection, we all need to protect one another. And whenever anyone is harmed, justice should be done.

## Criminal Negligence

There is a third category of bodily injury. The first dealt with deliberate acts of violence that deserve the death penalty. The second concerned accidents and injuries that require restitution. The third category deals with negligence. Sometimes people get hurt or even killed because someone else failed to be careful.

The laws for negligence in Exodus 21 mainly have to do with animals. Animals are unpredictable, and sometimes they attack without warning: "When an ox gores a man or a woman to death, the ox shall be stoned, and its flesh shall not be eaten, but the owner of the ox shall not be liable" (v. 28). This case is fairly straightforward. An animal that kills someone has to die: a life for a life. But the animal's owner should not be punished (except for the loss of his animal, which is no longer fit for human consumption). How could the owner have known what would happen? Since he didn't know, he couldn't be held responsible.

However, the situation was different when the animal was a known offender:

> But if the ox has been accustomed to gore in the past, and its owner has been warned but has not kept it in, and it kills a man or a woman, the ox shall be stoned, and its owner also shall be put to death. If a ransom is imposed on him, then he shall give for the redemption of his life whatever is imposed on him. If it gores a man's son or daughter, he shall be dealt with according to this same rule. If the ox gores a slave, male or female, the owner shall give to their master thirty shekels of silver, and the ox shall be stoned. (vv. 29–32)

In each of these cases, the owner was held accountable because his animal had a history. The owner knew this; in fact, he had been notified that the animal was dangerous. Thus it was his responsibility to keep the beast penned up. By failing to keep his animal under control, he became liable for wrongful death, even though he never intended to commit murder.

The most obvious way to apply this law is to say that our animals are our responsibility. If they cause an injury, it's our fault. But there is a deeper principle here: We are responsible for the injuries we should have prevented as well as for the ones we actually cause. When an accident happens, people usually say, "It's not my fault! I didn't do it!" But according to the Law of God, if we reasonably could have prevented an accident, then we bear responsibility for it when it happens. Legal liability—both at home and at work—is a Biblical principle.

According to God's law, when criminal negligence led to a deadly accident, strict justice demanded the death penalty. However, the Law allowed a victim's family to show mercy by demanding restitution instead of retribution. Rather than executing the death penalty, they could demand a ransom, apparently set by the town's elders. The ransom was blood money, or what today we would call a death indemnity. Obviously, no one could bring the family member back to life, and no price could ever equal the value of even one precious life. However, the payment of a ransom would at least acknowledge that the family had suffered a great loss.

This law shows how right it is for the families of victims to receive compensation after an accident, especially when it was caused by someone's negligence. Usually victims' families are criticized for being greedy, and sometimes they are. As we shall see, there need to be limits for damages. But the demand for payment meets the Biblical standard for justice.

In most of the ancient world the right of compensation only extended to men who owned property. However, in Israel this right also applied to sons and daughters, and even to slaves. There was equal justice for all. Here again we see God honoring the dignity of every person made in his image—male and female, slave and free. The only difference was that in the case of a slave, the owner of the ox had to pay the slave's owner an extra thirty shekels, which was the average price for a slave. This figure is significant because it was quoted again when Judas betrayed Jesus for thirty pieces of silver (Matthew 26:15). The Son of God was sold for the price of a slave gored by an ox and left to die. This was the price that Judas was paid. But the price *Jesus* paid was the one that measured his true worth. When he died on the cross for our sins, the blood that Jesus shed was the infinitely precious blood of God the eternal Son—the price that paid for our salvation.

The last two laws in Exodus 21 deal with injuries to animals:

> When a man opens a pit, or when a man digs a pit and does not cover it, and an ox or a donkey falls into it, the owner of the pit shall make restoration. He shall give money to its owner, and the dead beast shall be his. When one man's ox butts another's, so that it dies, then they shall sell the live ox and share its price, and the dead beast also they shall share. Or if it is known that the ox has been accustomed to gore in the past, and its owner has not kept it in, he shall repay ox for ox, and the dead beast shall be his. (vv. 33–36)

By now these principles of justice ought to be familiar. We are responsible not only for what we do, but also for what we fail to do. A man who digs the pit for a cistern is obligated to cover it with a stone. If he fails to do this, and an animal falls into his pit, he is responsible for its death and must make restitution.

Whenever our carelessness results in someone else's loss, we have to make good for it, even if it was never our intention to hurt anyone.

Applying this law requires wisdom. Today some people try to get rich by making false claims about someone else's negligence. When this happens, a wise judge will throw out the case. But sometimes negligence really is criminal, in which case whoever was negligent should be required to pay the damages. If everyone followed this simple, Biblical principle for justice, the world would be a much better place.

### *Lex Talionis*

It is easy to get lost in the details of the laws for personal injury. But the basic principle is that the punishment has to fit the crime. This comes through clearly in the most famous verses from the passage: "But if there is harm, then you shall pay life for life, eye for eye, tooth for tooth, hand for hand, foot for foot, burn for burn, wound for wound, stripe for stripe" (vv. 23–25).

These summary verses are famous because Jesus referred to them in his Sermon on the Mount: "You have heard that it was said, 'An eye for an eye and a tooth for a tooth.' But I say to you, Do not resist the one who is evil. But if anyone slaps you on the right cheek, turn to him the other also" (Matthew 5:38, 39). At first it seems like Jesus is contradicting Moses. Is he saying that the Book of the Covenant no longer applies? This cannot be the right interpretation, because earlier in the same sermon Jesus said that he did not come to abolish the Law but to fulfill it (Matthew 5:17). So what did Jesus mean?

It helps to know what the original law meant. "Eye for eye, tooth for tooth" is usually known as the law of retaliation (*lex talionis*). But its primary purpose was to stop people from taking their own revenge. The law of retribution was for the elders to apply as Israel's divinely appointed judges. This means that private citizens did not have the right to carry out vengeance against people who hurt them. Only the authorities had this right. Furthermore, in a case of personal injury, penalties were not allowed to be excessive. Usually when people get hurt, they want the person who injured them to suffer more than they did. But God's law did not allow the violence to escalate. The punishment had to fit the crime.

How was this law carried out? In the case of premeditated murder it was very simple: "life for life." So the murderer was stoned. But what about "eye for eye" and all the rest of it? To us it seems barbaric. Did God really intend for his people to be mutilated?

The Jewish rabbis believed that these were only the maximum penalties, and that ordinarily cases of personal injury would be settled by giving the victim financial compensation.[1] The rabbis may be right. The ESV rendering is: "you shall *pay* . . . eye for eye," and it can also be translated, "you are to *give* eye for eye." The same word appears in verse 22, where it is translated "determine" and refers to the payment of a fine. So rather than having his body parts taken away, the person who committed the crime could pay his victim some money. The phrase "eye for eye" may support this interpretation, because the word "for" can mean "as compensation for."[2]

The context also needs to be considered. With the exception of the death penalty, the legal remedies in Exodus 21 are financial rather than physical. If the penalties in verses 23–25 also allow for fines, then they fit the context well. Finally, this interpretation finds added confirmation in Numbers, where the law says, "You shall accept no ransom for the life of a murderer, who is guilty of death, but he shall be put to death" (35:31). The implication is that although ransom could not be accepted in the case of murder, it *could* be accepted for lesser crimes. Therefore, *lex talionis* was not so much a law of retaliation as it was a law of compensation. Whenever pain was inflicted, damages were awarded.

At the time of Jesus, this interpretation was being challenged. Some Jewish leaders were saying that the Law required strict justice, without any room for mercy. "An eye for an eye," they said, "that's all there is to it." As far as they were concerned, this was the minimum penalty, not the maximum. Furthermore, some people were using the law of retaliation as an excuse for taking private revenge. Their attitude was, "If you hurt me, I have the right to hurt you." Whenever they were harmed, they wanted to make someone pay. It was measure for measure, tit for tat.

Jesus corrected the religious leaders not by overruling the Law but by correcting their interpretation of it. As we saw in our study of the Ten Commandments, this is what Jesus always did with the Law of Moses: He explained it for people who had forgotten what it truly required. When it came to personal injury, Jesus said, "But if anyone slaps you on the right cheek, turn to him the other also" (Matthew 5:39). A blow on the right cheek was much more than an injury. It was also an insult, because such a blow was struck with the back of the right hand. Most people would fight back. Some of them would justify it by saying, "An eye for an eye, a tooth for a tooth." But according to Jesus, this is not what the Law meant at all. The Law was actually about making things right when we hurt someone else; it was not about getting what we have coming to us when someone else harms us.

Strangely enough, we do not usually quote the law of "eye for eye" and "tooth for tooth" when we are in the wrong. We tend to quote it only when we think someone else needs to be punished for what they did to us. Jesus was saying that we have it backwards. When we are in the wrong, we need to make things right, and we ought to do everything justice requires. But when someone does us wrong, we do not have to insist on strict justice. Instead we have an opportunity to offer mercy.

Commentators usually surround this verse with a thousand qualifications. Jesus did not mean that soldiers do not have the right to defend their country in a just war, they insist. Nor did he mean that society should not bring criminals to justice. Such qualifications are necessary because what Jesus said here has to be compared with the rest of Scripture. But the problem with making all kinds of qualifications is that we usually end up missing the point. Here the point is that when we are wronged, rather than seeking revenge or even demanding perfect justice, we should be willing to suffer injury so that we can show mercy.

This is what Jesus calls us to do because it is what he did. Jesus suffered all kinds of insults and injuries on his way to the cross. Did he demand wound for wound and bruise for bruise? No. He said, "I gave my back to those who strike, and my cheeks to those who pull out the beard; I hid not my face from disgrace and spitting" (Isaiah 50:6). And when he died on the cross for our sins he prayed, "Father, forgive them" (Luke 23:34).

Therefore, when Jesus asks us to do what seems impossible—namely, giving up our right to make people pay for what they've done to us—he is only asking us to do what he did. And when he asks us to show mercy, he is only asking us to give what he has given to us! Rather than exacting strict justice down to the last tooth, God has shown us his mercy. He has forgiven our sins and granted us the free gift of eternal life through faith in Jesus Christ.

This has profound implications for the conflicts we have with one another. When someone hurts us, what should we do? Now that mercy has triumphed over judgment, should we seek vengeance, or will we show mercy? If everyone demanded an eye for an eye and a tooth for a tooth, the world would be full of blind, toothless, wounded cripples without hands or feet! But God has been merciful to us so that we can show his mercy to others.

# 63

# Property Law

## EXODUS 22:1–15

IN 2001 AND 2002 American investors were stunned to watch a series of businesses falter after being exposed for fraudulent criminal activity. They were all major corporations—energy companies, accounting firms, pharmaceutical distributors, telecommunications companies. These corporations had some of the best reputations in the business. Yet they were all caught breaking the law, and they all suffered the consequences.

As federal investigators examined these companies, they discovered they were setting up false accounts, cheating on taxes, inflating their profits, lying about their losses, and generally violating the ethical standards of fair business. Alan Greenspan—then serving as the chairman of the Federal Reserve Board—rightly observed that "an infectious greed seemed to grip much of our business community," with a resulting "outsized increase in opportunities for avarice."[1] In almost every case the corruption went right to the top. The ones guilty of committing the corporate crime turned out to be leading executives, and most Americans took a certain amount of satisfaction from seeing them get what they deserved. The pictures were on the evening news. Consumers watched as the crooks were arrested in their luxury apartments, escorted to unmarked cars, and taken in for questioning. In some cases they had to go to jail.

The reputations of these men were destroyed, but was justice really done? Most of their victims never got their money back. In one notorious case, employees who held stock in their own company were denied access to their retirement accounts. By the time they were allowed to sell, it was too late: The company had collapsed, the stock was almost worthless, and their life savings had all but disappeared. Meanwhile, the company's top executives had been selling off their private holdings of company stock for a huge profit.

When something like this happens, what does justice require? How should the victims be compensated? Should the wrongdoers simply be put in jail, or is there something else they should do to make things right?

## Restitution Required

The laws in Exodus 22 help us understand what justice demands when people lose their property. At first these regulations may not seem very relevant to life in the twenty-first century. They deal with issues most Americans don't face, such as stolen sheep, lost donkeys, and livestock grazing in the wrong field. But like everything else in Scripture, these laws are "profitable for teaching, for reproof, for correction, and for training in righteousness" (2 Timothy 3:16). So we need to know what they teach.

Exodus 22 helps us know what to do when someone gets ripped off. The property laws in this chapter deal with four basic situations. The first category involves cases of outright theft:

> If a man steals an ox or a sheep, and kills it or sells it, he shall repay five oxen for an ox, and four sheep for a sheep. If a thief is found breaking in and is struck so that he dies, there shall be no bloodguilt for him, but if the sun has risen on him, there shall be bloodguilt for him. He shall surely pay. If he has nothing, then he shall be sold for his theft. If the stolen beast is found alive in his possession, whether it is an ox or a donkey or a sheep, he shall pay double. (vv. 1–4)

These are specific applications of the eighth commandment: "You shall not steal" (20:15). To put it another way, they are civil laws based on the moral law. The cases mentioned all involve animals, which in the ancient world were people's primary source of wealth. But the Biblical principles apply to any kind of property. The Bible assumes that people have a God-given right to own private property, which is to be used for God's glory, and therefore it is wrong to take it away from them.

But what if something does get stolen? In a case of theft, the victim was to be compensated, with the amount depending on what was stolen and what happened to it afterward. For example, "If a man steals an ox or a sheep, and kills it or sells it, he shall repay five oxen for an ox, and four sheep for a sheep" (22:1). A man's ox was the most valuable tool of his trade. It took years to train a good beast of burden, and its loss was hard to replace. By way of comparison, consider the plight of a Philadelphia contractor who had all his tools stolen from his truck. Understandably, the workman was distraught because his tools were his livelihood. The theft of an ox was the same kind of evil. If a stolen ox (or a sheep, for that matter) was sold or slaughtered, there was no way it could be recovered. What justice required in this case was four- or fivefold restitution. The thief had to pay punitive damages that were quadruple or even quintuple what he had taken.

Less compensation was required if the animal was still alive: "If the stolen beast is found alive in his possession, whether it is an ox or a donkey or a sheep, he shall pay double" (v. 4). The reason for the difference is obvious. If the animal was still alive, then the owner didn't have to go out and find a replacement; he got his own property back. But the thief still had to pay his victim back double. That is to say, in addition to giving back what he had stolen, the thief had to give him an additional animal. According to God's law, he had to give back what he had stolen plus something extra.

The laws about theft also included instructions about breaking and entering: "If a thief is found breaking in and is struck so that he dies, there shall be no bloodguilt for him, but if the sun has risen on him, there shall be bloodguilt for him" (vv. 2, 3a; cf. 21:12, 13). Some scholars think this law is out of place here because it doesn't have anything to do with compensation. It does have to do with theft, however, so this is as good a place for it as any.

Most buildings were made of mud bricks in those days. So if a thief wanted to break into someone's house, he went right through the wall. If somebody tried to do this in the middle of the night, a homeowner had the right to defend his property. There was no telling what the intruder intended to do or how heavily he was armed. The homeowner didn't have time to ask questions; he had to defend himself. If the thief happened to get killed in the process, the homeowner could not be charged with murder. However, the situation was different in broad daylight. If a criminal broke in during the daytime, he could not be killed outright. Presumably, the homeowner could see whether he was a murderer or simply a burglar, in which case he was to be brought before the proper authorities. The Law did not allow vigilante justice. Even thieves had a right to live.

The second legal category in Exodus 22 involved cases of negligence that led to the loss of property: "If a man causes a field or vineyard to be grazed over, or lets his beast loose and it feeds in another man's field, he shall make restitution from the best in his own field and in his own vineyard. If fire breaks out and catches in thorns so that the stacked grain or the standing grain or the field is consumed, he who started the fire shall make full restitution" (vv. 5, 6).

Both of these cases were accidents. In the first, a man was careless with his flocks and herds. There was no barbed wire in those days, so it was hard for people to keep their animals where they belonged. Sometimes livestock would venture into a neighbor's field and eat their neighbor's grass—a precious resource in the ancient Near East. When this happened, it was not enough to say, "Sorry! It was an accident." The right thing to do was to make restitution by allowing the neighbor's animals to eat one's own best produce. Even if it was an accident, God's justice required things to work out for the neighbor's advantage.

The same was true in the case of a wildfire. This too was common. Farmers often set their fields on fire to clear the ground. But there was always the danger that the thorns along the edge of a field would start on fire, and then a neighbor's field would catch fire as well. This was not a case of arson; the man who started the fire never intended it to spread. But whether through carelessness or some unexpected gust of wind, his actions had the indirect consequence of harming his neighbor. According to the Law of God, the man who started the fire had to make restitution for whatever his neighbor lost. Legal liability is a thoroughly Biblical principle, even in the case of an accident. God expects us to take full responsibility for our actions, whether we intended to damage someone else's property or not.

### Borrowers and Lenders

So far we have considered cases of theft and negligence. The third set of laws involved property given to someone for safekeeping, which was a common practice in the ancient world. There were no banks in those days—no safe-deposit boxes or secure storage facilities. When people traveled, ordinarily they couldn't take all their stuff with them. Thus it was customary for them to leave their most valuable possessions with a neighbor.

If the belongings were still there when they returned, all was well and good. But what if something "happened" to them while they were gone? God had laws to cover this situation. First, "If a man gives to his neighbor money or goods to keep safe, and it is stolen from the man's house, then, if the thief is found, he shall pay double" (v. 7). This case simply follows the principle already established—namely, a thief had to pay double for his crime.

Unfortunately, criminals don't always get caught. So the Law stipulated what should happen when a crime went unsolved: "If the thief is not found, the owner of the house shall come near to God to show whether or not he has put his hand to his neighbor's property" (v. 8). This is the kind of situation that naturally arouses suspicion. A man goes away on business and leaves his valuables with a trusted friend. When he comes back, the money is gone. His friend *says* that a robber came in the middle of the night, but is he telling the truth? In Israel the way to resolve such a dispute was by taking it to the elders, who were supposed to make a careful investigation. If the friend turned out to be the one who took the money, then he was the thief who had to make double restitution. If he was telling the truth, then apparently the original owner was out of luck. The friend who had been taking care of his property didn't owe a thing.

The same rules applied when livestock was involved: "If a man gives to his neighbor a donkey or an ox or a sheep or any beast to keep safe, and it dies or is injured or is driven away, without anyone seeing it, an oath by the LORD shall be between them both to see whether or not he has put his hand to his neighbor's property. The owner shall accept the oath, and he shall not make restitution" (vv. 10, 11). Here again, property under safekeeping was lost or damaged—a situation that could easily lead to resentment. If the animal disappeared, then all the neighbor had to do was swear before God that it was not his fault. The man who suffered the loss had to take his friend at his word, and no restitution was required.

The situation was different if it was a known case of theft or if the animal was killed by a predator: "But if it is stolen from him, he shall make restitution to its owner. If it is torn by beasts, let him bring it as evidence. He shall not make restitution for what has been torn" (vv. 12, 13). The Law does not say why the neighbor had to make restitution for a stolen animal. However, there may be a clue in the wording of verse 12, which literally says, "If the animal was certainly stolen." The man who was looking after his neighbor's property knew that the animal was stolen, presumably because he had watched it happen. But in that case he should have done something to stop it! Due to his negligence, he was required to make restitution. This was not required if the livestock was attacked by a wild animal. Here all that the neighbor had to do to prove his case was produce part of the carcass as evidence.

The last category of cases involved borrowed property. Anyone who has ever lent something to a neighbor knows how easy it is for borrowing to go bad. As Shakespeare famously wrote in *Hamlet*, "Neither a borrower nor a lender be." However, this advice came from a character (Polonius) who wasn't nearly as wise as he thought he was. The truth is that people often need to borrow something. The Bible recognizes this and also helps us know what to do when this leads to a dispute: "If a man borrows anything of his neighbor, and it is injured or dies, the owner not being with it, he shall make full restitution. If the owner was with it, he shall not make restitution; if it was hired, it came for its hiring fee" (vv. 14, 15).

In the case of safekeeping, the person who asked his friend to watch his things assumed the risk. When it came to borrowing, however, the borrower had to take full responsibility. If something happened to borrowed property—even if it was only an accident—the borrower had to make full restitution. No penalties were involved because the borrower was innocent of wrongdoing, but he still had to make up the owner's loss. There were some exceptions. If the owner happened to be present when the accident or injury happened, then the owner had to take responsibility for his own property. It was up to him to make sure that everything possible was done to save the animal. The owner also had to take responsibility if the animal was hired rather than borrowed. In this case the rental price was supposed to cover the loss, so it was up to the owner to calculate the risk of hiring out his animal and factor it into his price.

These laws were never intended to cover every case. Instead they were examples of the kinds of situations that arise when people ask their friends to look after their property. Whenever God's people had a property dispute that wasn't covered by one of these rules, they were to take their case before the judges. The Law came with this catch-all provision: "For every breach of trust, whether it is for an ox, for a donkey, for a sheep, for a cloak, or for any kind of lost thing, of which one says, 'This is it,' the case of both parties shall come before God. The one whom God condemns shall pay double to his neighbor" (v. 9). The judges' decision was final. People who had stolen property in their possession—no matter how they obtained it—had to pay double. In other words, the Bible does not teach "finders keepers." Whoever owned a piece of property in the first place was supposed to get it back in the end. Whatever was theirs was still theirs.

## Making Things Right

When we take the time to study these laws carefully, we see how sensible they are. For some reason, the Old Testament has the reputation of being harsh. Probably this is because most people don't want anyone telling them what to do, as God does in his law. But the Law is for our benefit, and God's laws about property are a good example. These regulations were a blessing because they taught God's people how to live in community. The Law taught the people to respect one another's property. It gave guidelines for settling disputes. By demanding double compensation, it deterred would-be criminals, who knew that if they got caught they would have to pay back double what they had stolen. Through the irony of God's justice, they would lose exactly what they hoped to gain. Rather than being enriched, they would be impoverished. This kind of restitution also satisfied the victim. Not only did he get his property back, but he got double for his time and trouble. When these laws were properly carried out, they helped bring harmony to the community of faith. They dealt with sin in a way that restored relationships.

In addition to protecting property, these laws also protected life—the life of the thief. Other ancient laws generally put thieves to death. A famous example is Hammurabi's Code, which said, "If a seignior made a breach in a house, they shall put him to death in front of that breach and wall him in. If a seignior committed robbery and has been caught, that seignior shall be put to death."[2] God's law was less harsh and more righteous because it protected property without destroying life. The Law said, "He shall surely pay. If he has nothing, then he shall be sold for his theft" (22:3b). As far as God was concerned, putting a thief to death was unjust. If he was unable to make restitution, he was supposed to work until he could pay off his debts. So there was justice all the way around. The thief got what he deserved, and the victim got back what was rightfully his.

There was another difference between God's law and the laws of the pagans. In other ancient cultures, the penalty for theft was based on the social status of the victim. The justice system discriminated on the basis of class, determining a thief's punishment not by what he took, but by the person from whom he took it. Here again Hammurabi's Code provides an example when it

> imposes penalties on theft that vary with the status of the victim, depending on whether the ox was stolen from the king, temple, a man of middle

> station, a slave, etc. The sliding scale of penalties ranged from death at one end to tenfold at the other with thirtyfold in the middle for good measure. If the thief could not pay the penalty it was death. Several scholars have pointed out that one of the crucial differences between the Torah and the Babylonian codex is the fact that the former makes no distinction between rich and poor, king or priest.[3]

Israel's law was different because the Israelites served a just God, who offers equal protection under his law. God is not on the side of the rich but also defends the poor.

The more we study the legal cases in Exodus, the clearer it becomes that God's law is right and good. In fact, the Biblical principles of property law would help our own society. We are no longer bound by the specific details of the civil law given to Israel as a nation under God. These laws are not the law of our land. However, we are wise to follow their general principles for justice. When it comes to theft, our own justice system demands incarceration, but it doesn't always provide restitution. Sometimes thieves are thrown in jail, but they don't always have to pay what they owe. Or if they do, the fines are sometimes paid to the state rather than straight to the victim, as the Law of Moses required. Corporate fraud is the perfect example. Even when crooked executives are found guilty—which isn't often—their victims almost never get back what they've lost. But God's property law is different. It doesn't demand jail time at all, but it does require thieves to pay back everything they owe.

God's law also requires restitution when people are negligent. The wildfire in the farmer's field is an interesting example because the same thing sometimes happens in America. Every summer firefighters are busy putting out forest fires all over the West. Most of these fires are started by lightning, but some are caused by careless human beings. The infamous Hayman fire is a good example. In the summer of 2002, a Forest Ranger started a huge fire in Colorado when she carelessly burned a letter near open brush. By the time the fire was contained, tens of thousands of acres were destroyed, and many people lost their homes. The woman who started the fire said it was an accident, but what did justice require? Whether she meant to start the fire or not, she started it, and therefore she needed to do everything in her power to make restitution.

The Hayman fire is a dramatic example of a principle we need to apply at home, at work, at school, and in the church. Whenever we do something that damages someone else's property—whether we meant to do it or not—we need to rectify the damage. It is not enough to say, "Sorry! It was an accident" and then expect other people to pay for what we've done. An apology is a good start, but justice demands that we make things right.

Consider some examples. If your dog digs up your neighbor's prize begonias, you need to replace them. If you are visiting a friend and knock over an antique vase, you need to pay for it. If you swing late on a fastball and the ball sails through a car window, you need to pay the repair bill. If you borrow a friend's computer game and accidentally break it, you need to buy a new one. These are only examples. The thing to remember is that it is our responsibility to repair whatever damage we do, *whether we meant to do it or not*.

Sometimes victims demand too much. Everyone has heard stories about outrageous lawsuits, like the man who sued the fast-food restaurants for causing his heart disease. However, it is right for genuine victims to have their true losses restored. If people would simply follow this basic Biblical principle for restitution, it would solve many problems in personal relationships.

The other property laws can be applied in similar ways. We should be careful to take good care of anything we borrow—better than if it belonged to us. And if anything happens to what we borrow, we should be prepared to make full restitution. Anyone who has stolen anything should give it back, and then some. In most situations this means giving back twice as much as we took. To apply this personally, ask the following questions: Have I helped myself to something that wasn't really mine? Have I taken advantage of a client in a business deal? Is there anything in my home that doesn't belong to me? Even if it's something that was stolen a long time ago, it needs to be given back. To be right with God, we need to make things right with another, which means giving back anything that doesn't belong to us.

## What Zacchaeus Did

To this point we've been considering the righteous requirements of the Law, but what about the grace of the gospel? The Old Testament property law is useful for helping us get along with one another. Everyone ought to know these regulations and put their principles into practice. Of course, keeping them cannot bring salvation. Nevertheless, they have something to do with salvation because the whole Bible is about Jesus Christ and the salvation he brings. The question is, how does the property law help us understand the gospel?

One way to answer this question is to consider the story of a man from the New Testament who applied one of these regulations. The man was a crook who had spent most of his life stealing other people's money. He was in a good position to do this because he was the chief tax collector in Jericho, which in those days was one of Israel's three major centers for collecting Roman taxes. The thief, whose name was Zacchaeus, was "the kingpin of the Jericho tax cartel."[4] His strongmen would go out and force the Jews to pay their taxes. Then they would bring the money back to Zacchaeus, who would send it on to Rome.

Not surprisingly, along the way a good deal of revenue ended up sticking to his own pockets. Tax collectors were despised in those days because, as everyone knew, they were lying, cheating swindlers. And Zacchaeus was worse than most. He knew all the tricks. He knew how to overcharge and then underreport, how to skim a percentage off the top, and how to keep two sets of books—one for the government and one for himself.

How do we know Zacchaeus was a thief? Partly because he was so wealthy (Luke 19:2) and partly because everyone called him "a sinner" (v. 7), but mainly because once he met Jesus, he made restitution for everything he had ever stolen. The story is well-known. As Jesus was passing through Jericho, Zacchaeus wanted to see him. He had heard something about Jesus, his curiosity was aroused, and he was determined to see the man for himself. But the crowds were so large and he was such a wee little man that he couldn't get a good look at Jesus. So the scheming little tax collector ran ahead and climbed up a sycamore tree.

This would be the end of the story except that Jesus, who had come "to seek and to save the lost" (v. 10), was always on the lookout for low-life sinners like Zacchaeus. The Bible says, "And when Jesus came to the place, he looked up and said to him, 'Zacchaeus, hurry and come down, for I must stay at your house today'" (v. 5). When he heard this, Zacchaeus practically fell out of the tree. There was Jesus, inviting himself right into the sinner's life. And Zacchaeus responded with the obedience of faith. He jumped down and "received" Jesus (v. 6), welcoming him not only into his home, but also into his heart.

There was something Zacchaeus still needed to do, however. If he wanted to follow Jesus, he had to turn away from his sin. In a word, he had to *repent*, for repentance is when "a sinner, out of the sight and sense . . . of the filthiness and odiousness of his sins . . . so grieves for, and hates his sins as to turn from them all unto God."[5] For Zacchaeus, turning away from sin meant making things right with all the people he had cheated. The tax collector promised to do this. He confessed his sin, saying, "If I have defrauded anyone of anything, I restore it fourfold" (v. 8). Zacchaeus must have known his Bible, because the idea of making restitution comes right out of Exodus 22. The wee little man recognized that he had broken the Law of God, and now that he had entered into a personal relationship with Jesus Christ, he wanted to do what was right and just.

There is something significant about the promise Zacchaeus made. He told Jesus he would pay back four times as much as he had taken, which is more than the Law required. According to the book of Leviticus, if a man confessed a theft on his own initiative, he only had to give back what he had stolen plus one-fifth of its value. The Law said, "If he has sinned and has realized his guilt and will restore what he took by robbery or what he got by oppression or the deposit that was committed to him or the lost thing that he found or anything about which he has sworn falsely, he shall restore it in full and shall add a fifth to it, and give it to him to whom it belongs on the day he realizes his guilt" (Leviticus 6:4, 5). The regulations in Exodus 22 were only for people who got caught stealing, not for people who came forward to confess what they had done (which shows that people who admit their sin should be treated more leniently).

What Zacchaeus did, therefore, was much more than the Law required. He was paying back 400 percent when all he owed was 120 percent. By doing this, he was putting himself into the very worst category of thieves, counting himself as the chief of swindlers. He knew that he was as wicked as the most despicable sinner, like a sheep stealer or a cattle rustler. This is what happens when sinners come to Jesus. As soon as we see Jesus as he truly is—in all his beauty—we see ourselves as we truly are, in all our sin.

Then Zacchaeus went one step further. He was not content simply to make up for the sins of the past—he wanted to serve God right away, and he wanted to do it with his money—in the one area of life where he was such a sinner. So he started emptying his pockets and said to Jesus, "Behold, Lord, the half of my goods I give to the poor" (Luke 19:8a). This is what happens when a sinner comes to Jesus. Out of gratitude to God for his wonderful grace, we want to do far more than simply meet the minimum requirements of the Law. We respond to the gospel by offering everything we are and everything we have for God's service.

God sent his Son Jesus Christ to be our Savior. Jesus offered his own life for our sins, dying on the cross to save us. If God has done all this for us, then what will we do for him? At the very least, we will give back what we have stolen and restore what we have damaged. But even more, we will give as much as we can to meet the needs of the poor and to spread the gospel around the world. It is good to stop stealing and better to pay back what we owe, but best of all to give away what is ours for Jesus.

64

# Good Laws from a Great God

EXODUS 22:16–31

MOST BOOK LOVERS have a favorite spot to do their leisure reading. They like to read while lying on the beach, for example, or sitting at a sidewalk cafe. But almost no one does their leisure reading at a law library—not even lawyers. The shelves are weighed down with massive volumes, richly bound and embossed in gold. Lift one from the shelf, and one finds countless pages of legal regulations and judicial opinions, all printed in small type and carefully indexed. They are books people read when they have to, not because they want to.

No doubt a lawyer would protest that the law has a beauty all its own. But an honest lawyer will admit that sometimes the law can be tedious. People often feel this way about the laws in the Bible. As legal codes go, the Old Testament Law is relatively brief. The whole Law can be bound in a slim paperback. But when most people read through it, they find it hard to concentrate. They get so little out of the Law that they wonder whether it's really worth the trouble.

But there are many good reasons to study the Old Testament Law. It teaches us what God expects. It guides us into godliness. It exposes our sin and thus shows us our need for the gospel. But the Law does something else that is very exciting: It reveals God's character. This makes the Old Testament Law different from any law code or book of court decisions. The Law reveals the Lawgiver. We do not study it to find out what we have to do, but to know our God. And as we study and apply his law, we are conformed to his character.

## Premarital Sex

The laws at the end of Exodus 22 deal with a wide range of issues. At first they may seem somewhat disorganized. However, every law on the list teaches us something about God, and together these laws show us how to live for his glory.

The first law has to do with premarital sex and thus serves as a specific application of the seventh commandment: "If a man seduces a virgin who is not betrothed and lies with her, he shall give the bride-price for her and make her his wife. If her father utterly refuses to give her to him, he shall pay money equal to the bride-price for virgins" (vv. 16, 17).

This law is often misunderstood because people don't know the social context behind it. This was not a case of rape. If it had been, then the man who committed the crime would have been punishable by death (see Deuteronomy 22:25–27). But in this case the couple's intercourse was consensual. It was a seduction in the true sense of the word. The woman was receptive to the man's advances, for when the Bible says the man "seduces" (22:16), it means "he persuades the girl and she consents."[1] Nor was the woman being bought and sold, although that is the way these verses often are taken. Some people think that the laws about seduction were part of the property law, like the scholar who said, "Underlining these rules is the thought that a virgin through sexual intercourse has been transferred from the ownership of the father to that of the seducer."[2] Even though this interpretation is incorrect, it has a certain plausibility. The term "bride-price" naturally suggests that brides were bought and sold.

Notice, however, that the Bible does not indicate who received the bride-price (*mohar*). It may have been paid to the woman's family, but even then it was not really a purchase. The renowned Old Testament scholar Roland de Vaux wrote:

> This obligation to pay a sum of money, or its equivalent, to the girl's family obviously gives the Israelite marriage the outward appearance of a purchase. But the *mohar* seems to be not so much the price paid for the woman as a compensation given to the family, and, in spite of the apparent resemblance, in law this is a different consideration. The future husband thereby acquires a right over the woman, but the woman herself is not bought and sold. The difference becomes clear if we compare the *mohar* marriage with another type of union, which really was a purchase: A girl could be sold by her father to another man who intended her to be his own, or his son's, concubine; she was a slave, and could be re-sold, though not to an alien.[3]

There is another possible interpretation. Perhaps the bride-price was paid to the woman rather than to her father. In this case, the payment was the wife's guarantee of support in the event that something happened to her husband or to their marriage.[4] There seem to be examples of this in Genesis, such as Rebekah, who received silver and gold from Isaac (Genesis 24:53). Rather than calling this kind of payment a "bride-price," it would be better to call it a "wedding-price." It was not intended to protect the property rights of the father, but to provide for his daughter.

A bride was not a commodity. In fact, rather than treating a woman as a piece of property, these laws were for her protection. There are always men around who would like to have the pleasures of sex without the responsibilities of marriage. Given the chance, they will take advantage of a young woman. But sex should never be separated from a covenant commitment. So in Israel a man couldn't just sleep around. If he seduced a girl, he had to do the right thing, which was to marry her.

There was one exception. Even after a seduction, a father could refuse to allow a man to marry his daughter. By itself, the act of intercourse did not establish a marriage, as if the couple were "married in the sight of God." No; if they were to be married at all, they had to be married properly, which included having the father's blessing. In most cases he would probably consent, partly to protect his daughter's reputation. But if he thought that the man was unsuitable, he had the right of refusal. This provided a strong incentive for a man who wanted to get married to conduct himself in an honorable way. If he went ahead and had sex with a girl, he was really pushing his luck! He still had to get her father's permission, only now his character was in question.

Furthermore, if her father did refuse, then the man still had to pay the wedding-price! He had robbed the woman of her virginity, which would make it harder for her to get married. Some people would probably treat her as "damaged goods." However, if she had her wedding-price, then at least she would have some means of support. This might also make it easier for another man to marry her, because he wouldn't have to pay the wedding-price.

These laws were designed to promote godly patterns of courtship, marriage, and sex—in that order. Although the cultural context has changed, many of the same basic principles still apply. Ordinarily a couple who has shared intercourse should get married, but this is not automatic. It is better to avoid a bad marriage. And when it comes to marriage, fathers have a duty to look after their daughters. Under ordinary circumstances, when a couple (especially a young couple) wants to get married, they should seek the permission and blessing of the woman's father.

Sex is for marriage, and not just for personal pleasure. Therefore, single men are called to sexual purity, and they bear full responsibility before God for any misconduct. This is not to say that women don't have to answer to God for their own sin. But there is a Biblical principle of male leadership that is designed to protect women. These days most women have to look out for themselves, which puts them in an extremely vulnerable position. Things ought to be different in the church. A real man of God can be trusted to preserve his own chastity and to protect the purity of women. When a man fails to do this he causes real damage, and God will hold him accountable. This may seem old-fashioned to some, but it is in keeping with the character of God. Because he is holy and pure, he wants us to preserve the purity of our sexuality.

## Three Capital Crimes

The laws about seduction are followed by laws against three crimes so heinous that they demanded the death penalty: witchcraft, bestiality, and sacrifices made to pagan gods. The Law said, "You shall not permit a sorceress to live. Whoever lies with an animal shall be put to death. Whoever sacrifices to any god, other than the LORD alone, shall be devoted to destruction" (22:18–20).

Each of these crimes involved false worship. This is obvious in the case of witchcraft. A sorceress was a woman who tried to gain spiritual power through demonic influence, "who claimed supernatural knowledge or power which was used to influence the gods or to cast magic spells."[5] Possibly the Bible refers to a woman here because using religious magic is more of a temptation for women. However, sorcery was also forbidden for men, such as the magicians in Pharaoh's court (see 7:11). As God said to Moses on another occasion, "A man or a woman who is a medium or a necromancer shall surely be put to death" (Leviticus 20:27a).

Sorcerers told fortunes, communicated with the dead, and generally practiced the rituals of the occult. All of these activities were absolutely forbidden in Israel (see Deuteronomy 18:9–14). Other ancient cultures tried to make a distinction between black magic and white magic, which supposedly was used for good rather than evil. But white magic is as much a tool of the devil as black magic. Any attempt to know God's will apart from his revelation or to prevail over his will by using satanic powers is an evil attack on his sovereignty. Sorcery is a sin because God wants to be trusted, not manipulated.

The next crime is another abomination: bestiality, or sexual intercourse with animals. This disgusting form of deviancy violated the natural order. As John Mackay comments, "In Scripture this is condemned as 'perversion' because it is a flagrant disregard of the structure and order that God has endowed on creation. Crossing or blurring the divine boundary between the human and the animal in such an unholy and unnatural manner constitutes an act of rebellion against the authority of the covenant king."[6] Such intercourse lowers people to the level of animals. It is also dangerous, as the spread of diseases has shown.

This law was not just about sex, however. It was also about worship. Some pagans portrayed their deities as having sex with animals. This was true of the Canaanites, who depicted Baal having intercourse with a cow. Sometimes bestiality became a ritual part of pagan worship. People tried to unite with their gods through physical union with the animals that represented them. But this was absolutely forbidden in Israel, upon the pain of death. God did not want his people to be contaminated by the filthy practices of people who worshiped false gods. As he said to Moses, "You shall not lie with any animal and so make yourself unclean with it, neither shall any woman give herself to an animal to lie with it: it is perversion. Do not make yourselves unclean by any of these things, for by all these the nations I am driving out before you have become unclean" (Leviticus 18:23, 24).

The third capital crime was idolatry, the offering of a sacrifice to a pagan god. Anyone who committed such an open act of rebellion against the God of Israel was to be destroyed. The Hebrew word used here for destruction (*charam*) means "the surrendering of something to God for the purpose of utter and complete destruction."[7] This sacred act of judgment was a consecration to destruction involving not only the death of the sinner, but also the destruction of his property. God is jealous of his glory, refusing to share his worship with any other god.

These three sins—witchcraft, bestiality, and idolatry—are so ungodly that it is almost embarrassing to mention them. Yet they are all too common in the twenty-first century, when many people are fascinated by witchcraft. Half a million Americans identify themselves as Wiccans. It is easy to find a fortune-teller, visit a spirit shop, or tune in to a psychic hotline. Popular television programs—including shows for children—feature witches as main characters. Children are also exposed to supernatural powers through role-playing games like *Pokémon* or *Magic: The Gathering*, or even through some of the toys based on the Harry Potter books by J. K. Rowling. Dabbling in the occult has become so common that most Americans, including many Christians, hardly even notice.

To some extent this is also true of bestiality. It is such a vile sin that we almost wonder why it has to be forbidden. Yet at the movies and even on television it is increasingly common to hear rude jokes about people having sexual intercourse with animals. One well-known celebrity was quoted in *Time* magazine as saying she wanted to make a pornographic film about "seven girls, two guys, and a dog."[8] When something so vulgar is considered suitable for publication, there is no telling what degrading things people will actually do. Finally, there is idolatry. Even if most people do not actually offer sacrifices to pagan deities, they are worshiping more and more false gods all the time.

Sorcery, bestiality, and idolatry are heinous because they are contrary to God's character. God is sovereign and good, so we must not use dark powers to control his world. He is holy and pure, so we must not violate the sanctity of his image in us by behaving like animals. He is the only God, so we must not worship anyone else.

If these sins are so ungodly, then what should be done about them? Remember that it is not our place to put anyone to death for breaking the Old Testament Law. The laws in Exodus 22 and elsewhere were given to Israel as a nation under God, but their punishments are not for all people in all places. When the church forgets this, the results are always disastrous. One thinks of the infamous Salem witch trials. Possibly there really were witches in Salem, but the Bible said nothing about throwing women into the water to find out!

So what can we do? Remember that these laws were given to protect the purity of worship in the community of faith. The way we apply them today is by making sure that none of them are broken in the church. God always gives grace to sinners who repent, no matter what they have done. But someone who claims to be a Christian and practices sorcery, bestiality, or out-and-out idolatry must suffer the penalty. The "death penalty" Christ has given his people today is excommunication, by which unrepentant sinners are put out of the church. In cases of scandalous sin, the honor of God demands the faithful exercise of church discipline.

## The God Who Cares

God's law reveals God's character. What we learn from the next set of laws is that God is full of compassion, because these laws were meant to protect the disadvantaged and the defenseless. Usually the weakest members of any society get treated the worst. One college football team wore T-shirts that read "TRAMPLE THE DEAD, HURDLE THE WEAK."[9] Things were supposed to be different in Israel, where God said, "You shall not wrong a sojourner or oppress him, for you were sojourners in the land of Egypt. You shall not mistreat any widow or fatherless child" (22:21, 22).

These laws deal with the weakest members of society: strangers, widows, and orphans. First comes the stranger, or the sojourner. Foreigners are always at a disadvantage because they don't know the language, don't know the rules, and don't have any connections. But the people of God were not allowed to take advantage of outsiders. Here God appealed to their own experience. The Israelites knew what it was like to be strangers in a strange land and to suffer mistreatment because they had been slaves in Egypt. In fact, the word used here for oppression is the same Hebrew word (*lachats*) used earlier to describe what Pharaoh did to them (see 3:9).

Most ancient cultures were like Egypt: People could treat outsiders any way they wanted. But the people of God had a responsibility to welcome strangers, and even to love them. This is because they served a loving, welcoming God, who said, "You shall treat the stranger who sojourns with you as the native among you, and you shall love him as yourself, for you were strangers in the land of Egypt: I am the Lord your God" (Leviticus 19:34). As Alan Cole comments, "Love for the resident-alien is not based on mere humanitarianism, but on a fellow-feeling which comes from a deep personal experience of God's saving grace, when in a like situation."[10]

God also wanted his people to take good care of widows and orphans. They too were at a disadvantage. In those days widows suffered not only the loss of a lover, but also the loss of their livelihood. Without someone to support them, widows often struggled to survive. The same was true of orphans, or more literally, children without fathers. There was no one to protect them from injustice except God. So God himself became a husband to the widow and a father to the orphan. He established laws to protect them and provide for them. And if his people failed to keep these laws, they would be severely punished. God said, "You shall not mistreat any widow or fatherless child. If you do mistreat them, and they cry out to me, I will surely hear their cry, and my wrath will burn, and I will kill you with the sword, and your wives shall become widows and your children fatherless" (22:22–24). It makes God very angry when widows and orphans are neglected. If the Israelites were guilty of such neglect, they would suffer divine retribution. They would end up as widows and orphans themselves, just like the Egyptians after the Red Sea.

The practical application is obvious. If we claim to follow God, then we must show his compassion by caring for strangers, widows, and orphans. The Bible says, "He executes justice for the fatherless and the widow, and loves the sojourner, giving him food and clothing" (Deuteronomy 10:18). Then it says this: "Love the sojourner, therefore, for you were sojourners in the land of Egypt" (v. 19).

Christians in America have an extraordinary opportunity to reach the world by loving internationals. People still immigrate to the United States, and every year hundreds of thousands of internationals come here to study. In fact, one out of every ten students involved in higher education comes from overseas. Most of them will return to their own countries, where they will serve as the world's political, economic, and intellectual leaders for the next generation. Yet only one in seven will have any meaningful contact with Christians while they are here.[11] Some Christians are unaware of the opportunity, while others assume that reaching out to internationals is somebody else's responsibility.

What makes this so unfortunate is that for many international students, their time in America is the best chance they will ever have to hear the gospel. One missionary wrote, "Never in the history of the Christian church has a generation of Christians had a greater opportunity to reach the nations of the world than we in North America have today." Then he posed this question: "Can we consistently claim that we are concerned about world evangelism when we are largely ignoring the transplanted foreign mission field which God has brought to us?"[12]

Internationals who are welcomed by the church often come to know Jesus Christ as Savior and Lord. An effective evangelistic outreach to internationals includes not only friendship but also practical help with housing, shopping, transportation, local customs, and the English language. The way we welcome internationals into the church—no matter where they come from, what they look like, or how well they can communicate—ought to be the proof of God's love. As one Japanese girl said to the woman who helped bring her to Christ, "You built a bridge to me through friendship, and then Jesus came walking over the bridge."

It is just as important for us to care for widows and orphans, who have a special place in God's heart and thus a special claim on our love. Church leaders should know the widows in their congregations, and they should be quick to provide whatever friendship and practical help are needed. Whether married or single, men and women should go out of their way to start friendships with boys and girls who don't have a father or mother at home. This is the way we should live because this is the kind of God we serve—"Father of the fatherless and protector of widows" (Psalm 68:5).

## As We Forgive Our Debtors

Another group of people who deserve our compassion are the poor: "If you lend money to any of my people with you who is poor, you shall not be like a moneylender to him, and you shall not exact interest from him. If ever you take your neighbor's cloak in pledge, you shall return it to him before the sun goes down, for that is his only covering, and it is his cloak for his body; in what else shall he sleep? And if he cries to me, I will hear, for I am compassionate" (22:25–27). Here the Law forbids taking advantage of someone else's misfortune, the way a moneylender would. To be specific, if the Israelites lent money to the poor, they were not allowed to charge interest. There were several situations in which God did allow money to be lent at interest, especially to foreigners (e.g., Deuteronomy 23:20). Likewise, Jesus seems to have allowed people to collect interest on business loans (see Matthew 25:27). But God never allowed his people to make money off the poor, especially within the community of faith. God wanted to protect his people from the terrible burden of debt. So he said, "You shall not charge interest on loans to your brother, interest on money, interest on food, interest on anything that is lent for interest" (Deuteronomy 23:19).

Sometimes poor people needed money, and when a loan was made, it was customary for the lender to receive some collateral. The Law considers the case of a man so destitute that all he has to offer is his cloak—a heavy outer garment used for sleeping on the ground. A coat may not seem very valuable as collateral, but at least it would prevent the poor man from taking out a second loan from someone else![13] In this situation it might be tempting for the lender to keep the coat. What better way to remind the debtor what he owed than to make him shiver outside in the cold every night? But God has compassion on the poor, so he made the creditor give back the coat at nightfall. He wanted to make sure that even the poorest man in Israel got tucked in for a good night's sleep.

These laws may seem to lose some of their relevance in the era of big government and modern banking, when poor people seldom ask for large personal loans. But the principle still stands. When a believer who has fallen on hard times needs help, a brother or sister in Christ should provide an interest-free loan. The Law shows that the Lawgiver has a special concern for the poor—especially in the church. So we are called to care for them too.

Jesus took this one step further. Rather than sticking to the letter of the Law, he taught his disciples to show grace to the poor and needy. He said, "If you lend to those from whom you expect to receive, what credit is that to you? Even sinners lend to sinners, to get back the same amount. But love your enemies, and do good, and lend, expecting nothing in return" (Luke 6:34, 35a). Jesus was saying that it is good to loan people money, but even better simply to give it away—not only to friends, but also to enemies. Many people think the poor should look after themselves. Even Christians who actually help the poor can sometimes be harsh, but Jesus calls us to show compassion. If someone needs money, we should make it a gift, not just a loan. This is not to deny that there are times when it is more merciful not to give anything at all, such as when the recipient will use the money to feed a self-destructive addiction. But we are called—whenever possible—to do something more than simply pass up the interest. When people need our help, we are called to let them keep the principal too!

This may not be a very good way to run a business, but it's a wonderful way to show God's love. Jesus went on to make this promise to Christians who open their hearts to the poor: "Your reward will be great, and you will be sons of the Most High, for he is kind to the ungrateful and the evil. Be merciful, even as your Father is merciful" (Luke 6:35b, 36).

Jesus was saying that we need to show people mercy because this is what God wants to show them. Even more, it is what God has shown to us! These laws remind us of the gospel because they come from the same God who sent his Son to be our Savior. We were strangers in the world, alienated from God by our rebellion. We were widows and orphans, outside the family of God. We were debtors, impoverished by the stinginess of our own sinful hearts. But God loved us in Jesus Christ. Jesus became a man—a real human being—to end our estrangement. Everyone who believes in Jesus is welcomed into God's family. We are no longer widows: The Bible describes the church as a beautiful bride for Christ (e.g., Revelation 21:2). We are no longer orphans, because through faith in Christ we have been adopted as sons and daughters of God the Father. God has even paid the debt that we owe for sin by sending Jesus to die on the cross.

Now we should treat others the way God has treated us. If we are strong, we should notice the weak, and our hearts should go out to them. Who is an outsider? Who is alone? Who is unprotected? Who is poor? If we belong to God, then these people are our responsibility. What are we doing to help them? And if we are weak—if we find ourselves among the strangers, the widows, the orphans, or the poor—then we have the promise of God's protection. We should not go around demanding help; we should cry out to God. He will hear us when we pray, because as far as he's concerned, we're family!

## Giving to God What Is God's

What we owe to one another is compassion. But what do we owe to God? What should we render to him for all his kindness and compassion? Exodus 22 ends with a short list of our duties to God—simple ways we can respond to his grace.

First, "You shall not revile God, nor curse a ruler of your people" (v. 28). To "revile," as the word is used here, is not to curse God but to take him lightly. It is to dishonor his name by failing to acknowledge the full weight of his majesty. To treat God with such disrespect is a sin against the third commandment, a way of taking his name in vain.

This is closely related to a sin against the fifth commandment—namely, cursing the ruler of God's people. This law referred to Moses, Aaron, and all of Israel's kings and high priests. Notice the way that cursing God and cursing his earthly representatives are put into the same category. There is a close connection between divine and human authority. To speak out against one of our leaders is to make an attack against God himself. Today this law applies to both civil and spiritual authority, to preachers as well as politicians. Every leader is God's representative and therefore demands our respect. As the Scripture says, "Whoever resists the authorities resists what God has appointed, and those who resist will incur judgment" (Romans 13:2).

It is not uncommon for Christians to speak disrespectfully about their political leaders, and sometimes even their pastors. This is more than simply bad manners: It is an offense against divine authority. We are to show our leaders honor not because they are always right, but because they have been given to us by God. A notable example comes from the life of the Apostle Paul. Paul was on trial before the Sanhedrin, falsely accused of violating God's law. While he was making his defense, one of the priests ordered Paul to be struck on the mouth. The apostle responded angrily, saying, "God is going to strike you, you whitewashed wall!" (Acts 23:3a). Then someone informed him that he had insulted the high priest. Paul remembered the law from Exodus, and he recognized that he had sinned against God by dishonoring someone in authority (even though the high priest was behaving badly). The apostle said, "I did not know, brothers, that he was the high priest, for it is written, 'You shall not speak evil of a ruler of your people'" (v. 5). One of the ways we give God the honor he deserves is by respecting the authority he has placed over us in the church and the state.

What else do we owe to God? We owe him our gifts and tithes: "You shall not delay to offer from the fullness of your harvest and from the outflow of your presses" (22:29a). According to the Law, the Israelites had to bring God the first and best of their grain and grapes. Everything we have belongs to God, and the proper way for us to acknowledge this is to give some of our very best back to him. Our second-best is never good enough for God. How much should we give to his work? As much as we can, and more and more all the time.

We also owe God our families and our flocks: "The firstborn of your sons you shall give to me. You shall do the same with your oxen and with your sheep: seven days it shall be with its mother; on the eighth day you shall give it to me" (vv. 29b, 30). As we learned when we studied the rite of redemption in Exodus 13, every firstborn son in Israel was consecrated to God with an animal sacrifice.

This was a way of showing that the whole family belonged to God. Animals also belonged to God, so firstborn cattle and sheep were to be sacrificed to him in praise. God is our rightful owner, and therefore all our property is really his property.

The last regulation seems the strangest: "You shall be consecrated to me. Therefore you shall not eat any flesh that is torn by beasts in the field; you shall throw it to the dogs" (22:31). To put this in contemporary terms, the Israelites were not allowed to eat any roadkill. Why not? Was it a matter of public health? Of personal hygiene? No; it was a matter of ritual purity. In order to teach his people how important it was for them to remain separated from sin, God distinguished between clean and unclean animals. A carcass lying in an open field had been torn apart by predators and scavengers that were ceremonially unclean. Such an animal was unfit for human consumption. This restriction was not just for priests, who had to offer pure sacrifices, but for everyone in Israel. This law was a symbol of God's plan for Israel, which was for the whole nation to be holy, "a kingdom of priests" (19:6). God wanted all his people to be holy, even in the little things.

This is what God wants from us as well: comprehensive holiness. We have been set apart to serve God. God wants us to be like him, so that our whole lives are stamped with his character. What we do with our bodies, the way we care for the needy, the way we handle our money—in all these things, both large and small, we are called to holiness because we serve a holy God. The Scripture says, "As he who called you is holy, you also be holy in all your conduct, since it is written, 'You shall be holy, for I am holy'" (1 Peter 1:15, 16).

# 65

# The People's Court

EXODUS 23:1–13

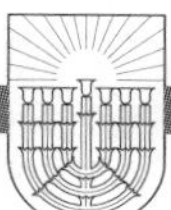

ON THE LAST DAY OF THE 2001 BASEBALL SEASON, Barry Bonds of the San Francisco Giants hit a towering fly ball to right field. When the ball landed on the far side of the outfield wall it would be home run number 73—a Major League record. It would also be worth one or two million dollars to the lucky fan who caught it. That fan may have been Alex Popov. But then again, maybe not. It's hard to say, because the baseball fell into a mob of frenzied fans, all trying to grab a piece of sporting history. By the time Security arrived to sort things out, the man holding the ball was little Patrick Hayashi.

What really happened? It depends whom you ask. Alex Popov says he caught the ball, only to have it violently torn from his grasp. Kathryn Sorenson agrees. She says Popov caught the ball and fell to the ground, where he was mauled by a pile of grabbing, grasping humanity. Jim Callahan says it wasn't like that at all, that people were saying things like "Sorry" and "Excuse me" as they scrambled for the ball. Callahan also claims that the ball he saw in Popov's glove wasn't the one Bonds hit. Doug Yarris disagrees. He landed right next to Popov, saw the ball, and recognized it as the real thing. Jeff Hacker and Paul Castro claim that Popov told them he had the real ball but lost it when he tried to switch it with the ball in his pocket.

When the officials arrived, they started pulling people off the pile. By the time they got down to Popov, everyone expected him to have the home run ball. He had a ball all right, but it wasn't the one that Bonds hit. "This isn't it!" he cried in dismay. Right behind him was a little man holding up a baseball and saying, "I got it." It was Patrick Hayashi, who claims he just saw the ball lying on the cement and grabbed it.[1] It was hard to tell who deserved to be the ball's rightful owner. It was locked up in a California vault as lawyers prepared to go to trial.

This strange story shows what often happens when there's a dispute. Sometimes it seems almost impossible to know the truth with any certainty, which makes it hard to see that justice gets done.

## False Witness

Truth and justice were just as hard to find in the days of Moses, but the Israelites served a righteous God, who in the interest of justice wanted them to guard the truth. Therefore he gave his people basic laws for truth and justice. These laws were included in the Book of the Covenant—the part of God's law that applied the Ten Commandments to various life situations.

The first law was a direct application of the ninth commandment: "You shall not spread a false report. You shall not join hands with a wicked man to be a malicious witness" (23:1). The verse begins with a general prohibition on any kind of gossip. Then it gives a specific command for someone called to give evidence in a formal trial. "A wicked man" is someone who is guilty. "A malicious witness" is someone who causes trouble by deliberately lying in court. So what is in view here is a conspiracy in which a witness gives false testimony in order to get someone who is guilty declared innocent.

This command is for everyone, not just witnesses who pervert the course of justice. In order to apply it to our own lives, we need to know what it means to "spread a false report." A false report could be one that is untrue. There are countless ways to say something that isn't true, as we learned when we studied the ninth commandment. The most obvious is to say what we know to be false, but most of our lies are more subtle. Sometimes we tell only one side of the story, leaving out the details that don't fit our interpretation. Sometimes we take what people say out of context. Sometimes we only hear what we want to hear. Then when it comes time to tell someone else what we heard, we are not really telling them what was said. Whenever we fail to tell the truth, the whole truth, and nothing but the truth, we are spreading false reports.

However, there is another meaning of the word "false." A false report can also be one that is unfounded. To be "false" in this sense is to be "empty" or "worthless."[2] In other words, the report does not have a firmly established basis in fact. It may or may not be true. Usually it turns out to be false, but not always. But whether it's true or not, the person spreading it doesn't know for certain, and this is the problem. The report is based on an unreliable combination of hearsay and conjecture, usually with a little bit of prejudice mixed in for good measure. Even if some of it may prove to be true, it is not well-founded, and thus it should not be spread.

A great deal of trouble could be avoided if people would only follow this simple command. Thankfully in most churches it is rare for someone to tell an out-and-out lie. Yet sadly it is not uncommon for people to spread the kind of false reports that God forbids. As a pastor I often try to help people resolve personal disputes. Usually both parties are fully convinced of the truth and justice of their own position, yet no one is telling the full story. Invariably, what we think we know to be true is tainted by self-interest and tarnished by the unjustified conclusions we have reached about other people's motives.

Most people would deny ever spreading false reports, but we should know ourselves better than this. We ought to be more savvy about our own depravity. We tend to believe what we want to believe and repeat what we want other people to hear. We tend to be overconfident about the accuracy of our judgments concerning others. We also tend to put too much confidence in what we heard about who said what to whom. Therefore, it is very easy for us to spread false reports, sometimes without even fully realizing what we are doing.

The trouble is, false reports are terribly destructive. They are prejudicial to the truth. They stir up controversy. They damage relationships. Even a rumor can destroy a reputation, and once a false report gets repeated, it tends to take on a life of its own. Although we may try not to be influenced by what we've heard, it's hard to put it out of our minds. In these and many other ways gossip poisons the well of any community. When it happens in the church, it brings dishonor to Christ. So God has given us this command: "You shall not spread a false report."

How can we avoid spreading such reports? By not listening to unfounded rumors in the first place. If someone tries to tell us something that is none of our business, we shouldn't even listen. If it is our business, then we should go back to the people involved and make sure that we have the story straight. We should be careful not to believe everything we hear, especially from someone who is angry or has an ax to grind. We should also be careful not to repeat everything we hear. We should only say what we certainly know to be true. Even then, we should only say it if it is our place to say it, if it is said out of true love for others, and if it will advance God's work in the world. If our words are unable to pass these simple tests, it would be better for us not to say anything at all!

### Minority Rules

Another temptation witnesses sometimes face is to tell people what they want to hear. We are easily influenced by the opinions of others. We want others to like us, and as a result we often stretch and squeeze the truth to make it fit our audience. But God says, "You shall not fall in with the many to do evil, nor shall you bear witness in a lawsuit, siding with the many, so as to pervert justice, nor shall you be partial to a poor man in his lawsuit" (23:2, 3).

Once again these laws regulate the testimony given in a public trial. This time the witness honestly intends to tell the truth but finds it hard not to be influenced by the verdict that has already been reached in the court of public opinion. The courtroom is not the only place this happens. Every day we feel pressure to play to the crowd. So the Bible commands us to say only what is true, even when we know it will be unpopular and unwelcome. This law deserves special attention because it is so hard to obey. Even though the majority is often wrong, we are so used to going along with the crowd that we join right in. But the Bible says, "You shall not fall in with the many to do evil" (v. 2a). Rather than letting the majority rule, we are called to follow Jesus Christ, and often this means going in the opposite direction.

This is the law to remember when everyone at school is making fun of the kid that nobody likes or in college when everyone wants to go out drinking on Friday night. It is the law to remember when your company is cheating or when everyone on the board wants to approve something immoral. These are only the pressures we face from our peers. Add to them all the pressures we face from the culture around us. What does the crowd tell us? It tells us to get as much as we can, to prize outward beauty more than inward piety, to go ahead and gratify our sinful desires, and not to let ourselves be inconvenienced by other people's needs. Before we know it, we are not only dressing the way other people dress and buying what other people buy, but thinking the way they think and doing what they do. But God has called us to be different. He says, "Do not follow the crowd in doing what is wrong. You belong to Jesus, and you need to follow him."

Strange to say, sometimes there is pressure to side with someone who is poor, and even this temptation needs to be resisted. The poor man is the one who has everyone's sympathy. He's the underdog, the little guy going up against the big establishment, so the special-interest groups shout for so-called justice. Since the poor man is a victim, they argue, he ought to have the verdict go in his favor. There is even a school of theology based on this principle. Liberation theology teaches that in the Bible there is a "preferential option for the poor." God is always for the poor and against the rich, they claim.

It is true that God is on the side of the poor against injustice. However, God also knows that the poor are as sinful as everyone else. In a legal situation this means that a poor man is as likely to be guilty as anyone else. God loves the poor, but he is not sentimental about the virtues of poverty, and he will not allow financial need to become an excuse for injustice. If a poor man is guilty, he should be condemned.

The opposite prejudice is equally unjust and probably more common. The rich often add to their wealth at the expense of the poor. However, it is as wrong to favor the rich as it is to prefer the poor. God said, "You shall not pervert the justice due to your poor in his lawsuit. Keep far from a false charge, and do not kill the innocent and righteous, for I will not acquit the wicked" (23:6, 7). Whereas the laws in verses 1–3 were for witnesses, these laws are especially for judges. Judges have a responsibility to make sure that poor people get a fair trial, which includes getting competent counsel. Rich people have more resources, and this gives them a tremendous advantage when it comes to legal matters. It is up to judges to protect the powerless, making sure that the poor get what they deserve.

Here, as always, the Bible strikes the perfect balance. The poor are not always right, nor are the rich always in the wrong. Thus there should be neither bias toward the rich nor prejudice for the poor, but everyone should receive equal justice. This principle is repeated in Leviticus, which says, "You shall do no injustice in court. You shall not be partial to the poor or defer to the great, but in righteousness shall you judge your neighbor" (19:15). Today in law and politics there is a good deal of talk about favoring this group or that group, but there is nothing like this in the Bible. Favoritism leads to injustice, and ultimately to resentment and revenge.

Judges and juries face other temptations as well. One is to entertain charges they know to be false. Another is to condemn a man they know to be innocent, maybe even to death. But the Law says, "Keep far from a false charge, and do not kill the innocent and righteous, for I will not acquit the wicked" (23:7). This is the flip side of verse 1, where the injustice was to help the guilty go free. Here the injustice is to treat the innocent as if they were guilty.

God's law also ruled out any form of bribery: "And you shall take no bribe, for a bribe blinds the clear-sighted and subverts the cause of those who are in the right" (v. 8). Justice can never be for sale. Whether it comes in cash, in a gift, or in some other form of *quid pro quo*, bribery always corrupts the course of justice. It closes a judge's eyes to the truth and thus leads to blind injustice. It is also contrary to the character of God: "For the LORD your God is God of gods and Lord of lords, the great, the mighty, and the awesome God, who is not partial and takes no bribe" (Deuteronomy 10:17).

Then there is the temptation to deny justice to outsiders. The Law said, "You shall not oppress a sojourner. You know the heart of a sojourner, for you were sojourners in the land of Egypt" (23:9). God told his people to show kindness to strangers back in chapter 22. Here the same command is repeated, only this time in the context of public justice. In legal matters, as in everything else, the people of God were not allowed to take advantage of foreigners.

These regulations have special relevance for anyone involved in a public trial. Witnesses should tell the truth. Judges should be fair. Juries should make sure that justice is done. The same principles apply to the disputes we have at home, at work, at school, and in the church. As followers of the Lord Jesus Christ, we are always called to be truthful, impartial, and fair.

We need to be careful to do what is just because God himself is just, and he wants us to be like him. But whether we act justly or not, God will see to it that justice gets done in the end. One poet wrote:

Though the heel of the strong oppressor
May grind the weak to dust,
And the voice of fame with loud acclaim
May call him great and just,
Let those who applaud take warning,
And keep this motto in sight:

> "No question is ever settled
> Until it is settled right."[3]

In a sinful world some questions never do get "settled right," but there will be justice in the end. God assures us of this when he says, "I will not acquit the wicked" (23:7). God has promised that one day he will judge the world in righteousness. When the day of judgment comes, the guilty will get exactly what they deserve, whether or not they were ever brought to justice here on earth.

How, then, can anyone be saved? The more we study the Law, the more we see how guilty we are. But God has said that he will not acquit the guilty. So how can we be saved? Only by trusting in Jesus Christ. Jesus died on the cross to pay the penalty for all our guilty sins. Now that he has met the Law's demand, we can be declared innocent—not because of what we have done, but because of what *he* has done. This is something we could never deserve, which is why the Bible calls it grace.

### Love Your Enemies

The next set of laws also has to do with grace—the grace we ought to show our enemies. Usually people hurt their enemies. This is what an enemy is—someone we hate, and therefore someone we think it's okay to abuse. But God holds us to a higher standard. Rather than hurting our enemies, we should help them: "If you meet your enemy's ox or his donkey going astray, you shall bring it back to him. If you see the donkey of one who hates you lying down under its burden, you shall refrain from leaving him with it; you shall rescue it with him" (vv. 4, 5).

These case laws come in the middle of the rules for witnesses and judges, and it is hard to know exactly how they fit in. Possibly the kind of enemy God has in mind is a legal adversary, someone on the other side of the courtroom. But the Law applies more broadly to any situation in which we have trouble getting along with others. If we have the chance, we should help them out.

The Law gives two examples. One is a situation where a man chances upon one of his enemy's animals. It would be tempting to do nothing at all and let the animal wander off. After all, no one would ever know. But the right thing to do is to catch the animal and take it back to its rightful owner. The second situation involves an actual encounter with the enemy. A man is walking along (probably thinking about how right he is and how wrong his enemy is), when suddenly he sees his adversary struggling with his donkey. It has fallen, and it can't get up. When something like this happens, it's hard not to enjoy it. But the Scripture says, "Do not rejoice when your enemy falls, and let not your heart be glad when he stumbles" (Proverbs 24:17). Instead God calls us to rush to our enemy's side and lend him a helping hand. Clement of Alexandria commented: "The Lord tells us to relieve and lighten the burden of beasts of burden, even when they belong to our enemies. He is teaching us at a distance not to take pleasure in the misfortunes of others and not to laugh at our enemies."[4]

Another way to say this is that God wants us to treat our enemies as we treat our friends. And when we treat them this way, that is what they become—our friends. It is hard to hold onto a grudge at the same time we're holding onto our enemy's donkey. Something happens in our hearts that turns cruelty into kindness. It is also hard for an enemy to keep hating someone who comes to help him. Compassion triumphs over aggression.

Do you have any enemies? Has anyone mistreated you? Is there someone who antagonizes you? Are there people you secretly try to avoid? Is there anyone who arouses your animosity? If there is, then this is the person you are called to love. The Bible says, "If your enemy is hungry, give him bread to eat, and if he is thirsty, give him water to drink" (Proverbs 25:21). One of the distinguishing marks of the followers of Jesus Christ is that they do good to those who hate them. Jesus said, "You have heard that it was said, 'You shall love your neighbor and hate your enemy.' But I say to you, Love your enemies and pray for those who persecute you, so that you may be sons of your Father who is in heaven" (Matthew 5:43–45a).

When I think of loving enemies, I think of a man who lost the better part of his inheritance. The man's cousin had conned his aging parents into a foolhardy investment scheme that cost them hundreds of thousands of dollars. Needless to say, it put a strain on family relationships. But when the man's parents died, the cousin went ahead and showed up at the funeral. And as soon as the man saw his cousin—the man who had cost him thousands—he went over and greeted him warmly. "I'm glad you're here," he said. "Thank you so much for coming."

Or I think of a woman whose husband was murdered on the job. He was a traveling salesman, and one day a man posing as a prospective customer killed him in cold blood. It was a wicked crime, the kind only an enemy would commit. But the woman was a Christian who knew that she was supposed to love her enemies. So as her spiritual and emotional wounds began to heal, she asked God for the grace to forgive. Some years later, when her husband's killer was on death row, she was able to write to him in prison. She offered him full forgiveness and encouraged him to put his faith in Jesus Christ.

Did the condemned man ever receive Christ as his Savior and Lord? Only God knows. What is certain is that someone showed him the love of God. This is what we are called to do as an ordinary part of our Christianity: love our enemies. This is the kind of love we give because it is the kind of love we have been given—a love that treats enemies like friends. It's the love that Jesus showed us when he died on the cross. The Bible says, "While we were enemies we were reconciled to God by the death of his Son" (Romans 5:10). Now, having been reconciled to God, we can reconcile our enemies by reaching out to them in practical deeds of love.

## Sabbath Mercy

The next set of laws may not seem to have very much to do with justice or mercy. These laws are about keeping the Sabbath, which most people associate with worship. For this reason, many scholars group the Sabbath commands in verses 10–12 with the laws about religious festivals that follow. It is true that the Old Testament Sabbath was for worship. We learned this when we studied the fourth commandment. However, if we read the laws in Exodus 23 carefully, we discover that they are more about mercy than ceremony.

The first law was for the Sabbath year: "For six years you shall sow your land and gather in its yield, but the seventh year you shall let it rest and lie fallow, that the poor of your people may eat; and what they leave the beasts of the field may eat. You shall do likewise with your vineyard, and with your olive orchard" (vv. 10, 11). At the time this law was given, the Israelites were preparing to enter the Promised Land. When they arrived, they were supposed to let their fields lie fallow every seventh year. This was good agriculture. A good farmer rotates his crops so that his fields get a chance to rest. As Wendell Berry has written, "Make your land recall / In workdays of the fields / The sabbath of the woods."[5]

Although the Sabbath rest was good for the land, this was not its stated purpose. The Sabbath was mainly for the people and the animals who depended on the land for food. In the seventh year the orchards, fields, and vineyards were left to grow on their own—"unpruned, unguarded, and unharvested."[6] There is some question as to whether the whole land of Israel rested in the same year, or whether the rest was staggered field by field (the latter would seem most beneficial to the poor). However it was timed, the Sabbath year was one of the ways God provided for the hungry, and also for the animals that he created. Plenty of food was left for wild animals and the poor, who were free to gather whatever they needed.

Like the Sabbath year, the Sabbath day was intended to bless the poor and the hungry: "Six days you shall do your work, but on the seventh day you shall rest; that your ox and your donkey may have rest, and the son of your servant woman, and the alien, may be refreshed" (v. 12). The word *Sabbath* comes from the Hebrew word for "cease." It was a day for cessation from ordinary work. As a day of rest for both man and beast, it was really a form of social justice. The Sabbath was God's guarantee that workers and livestock would get a day off.

By being kind to animals, these Sabbath laws teach us to care for the environment. Many conservative Christians are suspicious of environmentalism, sometimes with good reason. Some people seem to worship the environment. This is to mistake the creation for its Creator. Others treat animals as if they were more important than people, which overturns the divinely ordained order of nature. Still others make vegetarianism a moral imperative, even though God has given us certain animals for food. Nevertheless, caring for the creation is one of the ways we glorify God. Taking care of plants and being kind to animals are important parts of being a Christian, and so is giving rest to the land. Sadly, today many farms are run more like factories. We squeeze everything we can out of our fields and then pump them with fertilizer to make them stay fruitful. We confine animals and feed them to the point of obesity. But this was not God's plan. When God gave us the creation for food, he wanted us to receive it as a gift that requires the best of our care. The whole creation bears the effects of God's curse against our sin, and it is only right for us to work for its redemption.

These Sabbath laws also teach us something about caring for the poor. The *Sabbath year* reminds us that the poor need to eat. Under the Biblical workfare system, the poor were expected to gather what they needed from the Sabbath fields. But in order for this system to work, people with means had to obey God's law by giving their fields a rest. The *Sabbath day* reminds us that workers need to rest too. The Sabbath was not just something the people owed to God, but also something they owed to one another. When they were slaves in Egypt, the Israelites never had a chance to rest. However, God did not want that sin to be repeated in Israel. Workers, including household servants, needed to be refreshed by celebrating a weekly Sabbath.

We can apply this principle today by making sure that we do not cause others to perform unnecessary work on the Lord's Day. One place to exercise such caution is at home. To give a simple example, our family stopped having a big dinner after church on Sundays when I realized how much it was interfering with my wife's day of rest. The same principle also applies in the workplace. Here a notable example is the Chick-fil-A corporation, which always stays closed on Sundays. This costs the company as much as 20 percent in projected annual sales.[7] But Truett Cathy, who founded the company, wanted to be sure that his employees had a day for worship and rest. By keeping the Lord's Day holy, Mr. Cathy not only glorifies God but also loves his neighbor.

## Whatever God Says

The Sabbath laws are followed by a verse that seems to serve as the conclusion for this whole section of Exodus. At the beginning of chapter 21 God said to Moses, "Now these are the rules that you shall set before them" (v. 1). The next three chapters, which are usually called the Book of the Covenant, contain a long list of regulations. These laws deal with work, slavery, injury, property, sex, money, poverty, and justice. Then at the end of it all God said, "Pay attention to all that I have said to you, and make no mention of the names of other gods, nor let it be heard on your lips" (23:13).

God is not interested in partial obedience. He has not given us the freedom to choose which laws we want to keep and which ones we want to disobey. He is the only God, the sole and supreme deity who rules over Heaven and earth.

Therefore, he rightfully demands our total obedience. There is one God, we have one life to give him, and he wants it all to be used for his glory.

At this point many preachers would reassure their congregations that it is impossible to obey God's law perfectly. They would say that one of the Law's primary purposes is to convince us that we are sinners who need a Savior. And of course this is true. We cannot be saved by keeping the Law because we are lawbreakers. We can only be saved by trusting in Jesus Christ. By his perfect obedience to the Law of God, Jesus has fulfilled all righteousness; and by his death on the cross, Jesus has paid the penalty for all our disobedience.

All this is true. Nevertheless, God still commands us to be very careful to do everything he has said. In order to help us do that—not perfectly, of course, for we will not be perfect until we get to glory—he has sent us his Holy Spirit. Part of the Spirit's work is to help us do what is pleasing to God. The Law shows us what to do, and the Spirit helps us do it.

So what does God want us to do? He wants us to keep people safe from injury, protect their property, practice sexual purity, show kindness to strangers, care for the poor, tell the truth, pursue justice, love our enemies, take care of his good earth, and do all the other things required in his law. Some of these things are really hard to do—even for Christians—because they are so contrary to the sinful nature. Nevertheless, God commands us to do them. He not only commands us to do them but enables us to do them, and we will enjoy his pleasure when we do.

# 66

# Three Pilgrim Feasts

EXODUS 23:14–19

WHEN IN APRIL the sweet showers fall / And pierce the drought of March to the root, and all / . . . Then people long to go on pilgrimages."[1] These lines come from "The Prologue" to one of the most famous poems in the English language, *The Canterbury Tales* by Geoffrey Chaucer. The poem tells how a group of "nine and twenty" travelers from all walks of life—"sundry folk," as Chaucer called them—gathered south of London and set off riding to Canterbury Cathedral. They were on a pilgrimage—a physical journey that marks progress toward a spiritual goal.

People have always longed to go on pilgrimages. Augustine said that our hearts are restless until we find our rest in God. And as long as we remain restless, we keep traveling here and there, searching for God. The idea of making a pilgrimage to find him goes all the way back to the Bible. God said to his people Israel, "Three times in the year you shall keep a feast to me" (23:14). This was the fulfillment of God's grand purpose for the exodus. God had told Pharaoh to let his people go out and hold a feast in his honor (5:1; 10:9). This was not just a one-time event; it was supposed to be done three times a year. Curiously, the Hebrew word for "times" also means "foot." This is fitting because when the Israelites reached the Promised Land, they celebrated these festivals at the temple in Jerusalem, and they had to travel on foot to get there. In other words, they went on a pilgrimage.

## The Feast of Unleavened Bread

There were three pilgrim feasts in the Hebrew calendar. The first came in the springtime: "You shall keep the Feast of Unleavened Bread. As I commanded you, you shall eat unleavened bread for seven days at the appointed time in the month of Abib, for in it you came out of Egypt" (23:15a).

Fuller instructions for observing the Feast of Unleavened Bread are given elsewhere, almost always with instructions for the Feast of Passover (e.g., 12:43–13:10). The two feasts were connected. Passover is when every household in Israel offered a sacrificial lamb. This was to commemorate the night back in Egypt when they put blood on their doorposts and the angel of death passed over them. Passover was immediately followed by the Feast of Unleavened Bread, when—as the name implies—the people ate bread without yeast. For seven days they celebrated by eating unleavened bread.

What were they celebrating? Since the feast coincided with the start of the barley harvest, some scholars think that originally it was some kind of harvest festival. However, the Biblical explanation is theological, not agricultural. The Feast of Unleavened Bread was a commemoration of Israel's salvation. It looked back to the exodus, when God brought his people out of bondage. For centuries they had served as slaves in Egypt, but God delivered them. He sent ten plagues against the Egyptians, culminating in the death of the firstborn. On the night that Pharaoh finally let God's people go, the Israelites had to leave in such a hurry that they didn't even have time to let their bread rise (12:11). To remind them of this, God gave his people a feast of remembrance. Every year when they ate their unleavened bread, the festival would call to mind their exodus from Egypt. This was to be a lasting ordinance. As it says in one of the liturgies for Jewish Passover, "In every generation it is everyone's duty to look upon himself as if he came out of Egypt."[2]

The Feast of Unleavened Bread was a liberation celebration. It was a time to remember God's mighty saving work in history. The feast was similar in this respect to Good Friday or Easter. Christians are not Biblically required to observe these days. But when we do, we look back to the crucifixion and resurrection of Jesus Christ. We remember God's mighty saving work in history. In the same way, the Feast of Unleavened Bread was a commemoration of salvation.

## The Feast of Harvest

The second feast came a month or two later, in early summer. This festival was also tied to the agricultural cycle: "You shall keep the Feast of Harvest, of the firstfruits of your labor, of what you sow in the field" (23:16a). This feast—also known as the Feast of Firstfruits—was carefully timed. When the grain was ready for harvest, the Israelites would take the first sheaf of wheat and wave it before the Lord (Leviticus 23:9–11) as a way of acknowledging that the whole harvest came from him. This was done on the day after a Sabbath, but it was only the beginning. Next the Israelites would count off seven full weeks, which explains why the celebration had yet another name: the Feast of Weeks. Then on the fiftieth day the people would bring an offering to their God.

The main thing the Israelites offered was bread—not unleavened bread this time, but leavened bread, representing the fullness of the harvest. They also made sacrifices, as the Law required:

> You shall bring from your dwelling places two loaves of bread to be waved, made of two tenths of an ephah. They shall be of fine flour, and they shall be baked with leaven, as firstfruits to the LORD. And you shall present with the bread seven lambs a year old without blemish, and one bull from the herd and two rams. They shall be a burnt offering to the LORD, with their grain offering and their drink offerings, a food offering with a pleasing aroma to the LORD. And you shall offer one male goat for a sin offering, and two male lambs a year old as a sacrifice of peace offerings. And the priest shall wave them with the bread of the firstfruits as a wave offering before the LORD, with the two lambs. They shall be holy to the LORD for the priest. And you shall make a proclamation on the same day. You shall hold a holy convocation. You shall not do any ordinary work. It is a statute forever in all your dwelling places throughout your generations. (Leviticus 23:17–21; cf. Numbers 28:26–31)

The Feast of Harvest was a time of joyful celebration. The Israelites offered rich sacrifices unto God. They rested from all their work. And they gathered for public worship, praising God as their provider and thanking him for their daily bread.

## The Feast of Ingathering

The third feast was also connected to the harvest, except it came in the autumn, seven months after Passover, when all the crops were safely gathered in. God said, "You shall keep the Feast of Ingathering at the end of the year, when you gather in from the field the fruit of your labor" (23:16b). Like American Thanksgiving, this was the feast of "harvest home." It took place after the final harvest, when every stalk of grain from the field had been threshed, every olive in the orchard had been pressed, and every grape in the vineyard had been squeezed.

The Feast of Ingathering lasted a full week, during which the Israelites lived in makeshift booths made of leaves and branches. This is why the festival was also called the Feast of Booths or the Feast of Tabernacles. God said to Moses, "You shall celebrate it as a feast to the LORD for seven days in the year. It is a statute forever throughout your generations; you shall celebrate it in the seventh month. You shall dwell in booths for seven days. All native Israelites shall dwell in booths, that your generations may know that I made the people of Israel dwell in booths when I brought them out of the land of Egypt: I am the LORD your God" (Leviticus 23:41–43).

Like the Feast of Unleavened Bread, the Feast of Ingathering looked back to God's saving work in history. The people camped out to remind them of the story of their salvation. After their escape from Egypt, the Israelites went out into the wilderness, where they lived in tents. By living in temporary living quarters for a week-long festival, they would reenact part of the exodus every year. By doing this, each new generation would enter into the exodus experience.

They would become pilgrims all over again, and this would strengthen their assurance of salvation. The God who saved his people through the wilderness would continue to guide them on their way.

The Feast of Ingathering was a time of great celebration. For months the people worked hard to gather their crops in from the fields. Once their work was done, it was time to rest, and also to play. God said, "You shall rejoice in your feast, you and your son and your daughter, your male servant and your female servant, the Levite, the sojourner, the fatherless, and the widow who are within your towns. For seven days you shall keep the feast to the LORD your God at the place that the LORD will choose, because the LORD your God will bless you in all your produce and in all the work of your hands, so that you will be altogether joyful" (Deuteronomy 16:14, 15).

As a tangible expression of their joy, this was the time of year that the people brought their tithes. As God said in his law, "None shall appear before me empty-handed" (23:15b). The Feast of Ingathering was the best time of year for tithing because it occurred when God had given his people the most, and thus they had the most to give back to him. The Law said, "Every man shall give as he is able, according to the blessing of the LORD your God that he has given you" (Deuteronomy 16:17).

## The Lamb's High Feast

So the Israelites kept three pilgrim feasts—Unleavened Bread, Harvest, and Ingathering. Each annual festival testified to the grace of God. Unleavened Bread reminded God's people of the night they left Egypt, and thus it spoke of their salvation. Harvest and Ingathering both celebrated the bounty of God's provision: The God who saves is a God who provides. There seems to be a progression. The worship year began with unleavened bread and ended with lavish feasting. This says something about God and his grace. Salvation is always getting bigger and better as God piles one blessing on top of another. But these three festivals were only the beginning. God was just starting to show his people what salvation was all about. He was giving them experiences that would teach them to look to him in faith for their full and final salvation—the salvation he ultimately provided in Jesus Christ.

One of the amazing things about Israel's pilgrim feasts is that each of them contained seeds of the gospel story. Consider the Feast of Unleavened Bread, which was always linked to Passover. In the Bible yeast represents growth and maturation.[3] Often it is connected with the growth of evil or the spread of sin. This was its symbolic meaning during the Feast of Unleavened Bread. Whenever the Israelites celebrated this feast, they swept the yeast out of their homes. This was supposed to symbolize holiness. God's people were making a clean sweep, getting rid of the old life of sin.

We do the same thing when we come to Jesus Christ. Once we trust in him for our salvation, we have to leave behind the old life of sin. So the Scripture says, "Cleanse out the old leaven that you may be a new lump, as you really are unleavened. For Christ, our Passover Lamb, has been sacrificed. Let us therefore celebrate the festival, not with the old leaven, the leaven of malice and evil, but with the unleavened bread of sincerity and truth" (1 Corinthians 5:7, 8). The Feast of Unleavened Bread thus helps us understand the gospel. Jesus Christ is our Passover Lamb, the sacrifice for our sins. Now we need to make a clean sweep, getting rid of all our wicked ways and living in true holiness. The Feast of Unleavened Bread gives us a picture of what it means to be sanctified in Christ.

Or consider the Feast of Harvest. It too has important connections with the gospel. To begin with, it teaches us about the resurrection. The New Testament describes Jesus as "the firstfruits of those who have fallen asleep" (1 Corinthians 15:20). This is a clear reference to the Feast of Harvest, which started when the first sheaf of grain was waved before God. That first sheaf of grain was part of the harvest, but it also held the promise of much more to come. The same is true of the resurrection. Jesus was the first to be raised, but only the first: "For as in Adam all die, so also in Christ shall all be made alive. But each in his own order: Christ the firstfruits, then at his coming those who belong to Christ" (1 Corinthians 15:22, 23). The Old Testament Feast of Firstfruits helps us understand the gospel by giving us a picture of both the first and the final resurrection.

The Feast of Harvest also helps us understand the final judgment. Here it helps to know that the New Testament term for this festival was *Pentecost*, which comes from the Greek word for "fifty" (remember, the timing of this festival was counted to the fiftieth day). The story of Pentecost is told in the second chapter of Acts. It was fifty days after Passover, and Jerusalem was crammed with people. As usual, Jews from all over the world had made their pilgrimage for the Feast of Harvest, only that year something special had happened. At the time of Passover, Christ was crucified—the Lamb of God who takes away the sins of the world. So something special happened at Pentecost too. God fulfilled the promise Jesus had made and poured out his Spirit on the church. With a great rush of wind and fire, "they were all filled with the Holy Spirit and began to speak in other tongues as the Spirit gave them utterance" (Acts 2:4). People from all over the world heard the good news about Jesus Christ in their own language, repented of their sin, and trusted in him for their salvation.

How appropriate it was for all this to happen at Pentecost! In the Old Testament the Feast of Harvest was not directly connected to the story of salvation. It was simply a way for people to give thanks to God for meeting their needs. But the feast finds its fulfillment in the New Testament, where we discover that the Old Testament grain harvest was preparing the way for God's great harvest of souls. Jesus often described his saving work in terms of the harvest. He described the world as a field, his people as wheat, his enemies as weeds, and the final judgment as the great harvest when the wheat will be harvested and the weeds will be burned forever (Matthew 13:24–30, 36–43). Jesus also said, "Look, I tell you, lift up your eyes, and see that the fields are white for harvest. Already the one who reaps is receiving wages and gathering fruit for eternal life, so that sower and reaper may rejoice together" (John 4:35b, 36). This great spiritual harvest began at Pentecost, the Feast of Harvest. What God sowed in Jesus Christ, he started to reap from the nations. By the power of his Holy Spirit, he gathered people from every tribe and tongue.

Then consider the Feast of Ingathering, which was such a grand celebration that by the time of Christ it was simply known as "*the* Feast." Ingathering reached its climax on the eighth and final day. On that day, in addition to all the other closing ceremonies, a grand procession drew water from the Pool of Siloam and poured it out at the temple. This libation was the context for a well-known incident from the Gospels: "On the last day of the feast, the great day, Jesus stood up and cried out, 'If anyone thirsts, let him come to me and drink. Whoever believes in me, as the Scripture has said, "Out of his heart will flow rivers of living water"'" (John 7:37, 38). Jesus was identifying himself as the water of life, the fulfillment of the Festival.

The Feast of Ingathering also anticipated the gospel in all its sacrifices. Each pilgrim festival called for animal offerings, but Ingathering had by far the most.

> The opening day and the post-festival eighth day involved the same number of sacrifices and were each called a "sacred assembly," requiring the cessation of all work. But the seven days of the festival involved an astonishing number of sacrifices, as indicated by the list in Numbers 29:12–40. The sacrifices for each day are enumerated there. Each day young bulls, two rams, and fourteen one-year old male lambs were offered. With these were also offered a *minhah* [tribute offering] and a drink offering. Finally, a male goat was offered as a *hattat* [sin offering]. With this was the regular daily *'olah* (burnt offering), as well as its accompanying grain offering and drink offering.
>
> The sacrifice of young bulls was the one offering that varied in number from day to day. On the first day, thirteen young bulls were offered; on the second, twelve; on the third, eleven; all the way down to the seventh day, when only seven young bulls were offered! . . . The total number of animal sacrifices on these eight days was 192.[4]

By making all these sacrifices, the Israelites were learning something important about the sinfulness of their sin. They were also learning about the Savior who would deal with their sin by his own perfect sacrifice. They were learning to look for Jesus, who has now "appeared once for all at the end of the ages to put away sin by the sacrifice of himself" (Hebrews 9:26b).

The three major Old Testament feasts were rich in their teaching about salvation. Jesus Christ is the Savior God always planned to send, so already in the Old Testament he gave his people experiences that would help them (and us) understand the meaning of their salvation. Jesus is the source of our sanctification, the firstfruits of our resurrection, the Lord of the harvest, the water of life, and the sacrifice for our sin. This is the gospel according to Moses, as recorded in Exodus 23.

We no longer celebrate the pilgrim feasts of Exodus. There is still a place for feasting, of course, and for celebrating salvation in Jesus Christ. But as Christians we are not required to go to Jerusalem three times a year for the Feasts of Unleavened Bread, Harvest, and Ingathering. These three big feasts were all part of the ceremonial law, and thus they all found their fulfillment in the saving work of Jesus Christ.

The one feast that Jesus has ordained for the church is the sacrament of the Lord's Supper. Every other festival on the Christian calendar is strictly optional, but the Lord's Supper is to be observed frequently until Christ returns. This sacrament celebrates many of the same things as the Old Testament festivals. The bread comes from the bounty of God's provision and reminds us that, among other things, he takes care of our daily needs. The cup represents the blood of Christ's sacrifice. It announces that God has provided what he promised through the old sacrifices—full atonement for sin. The festival we are called to keep is the Lamb's high feast.

## Living Sacrifices

Even though we no longer keep the pilgrim feasts, they teach us important things about our salvation. They also teach us how to respond to our salvation by giving ourselves to God. The Israelites were required to present themselves before God three times a year. Now, in view of the mercy God has shown us in Jesus Christ, we are to offer ourselves to God as living sacrifices (Romans 12:1). Since Jesus has made the once-and-for-all sacrifice for sin, we no longer need to bring God sacrifices of bread and animals. But what we can give him is a *living* sacrifice—a life offered up for his service.

The regulations for the pilgrim feasts help us know what kind of sacrifice is pleasing to God. After listing the annual festivals, God gave important instructions about how they were to be observed: "Three times in the year shall all your males appear before the Lord God. You shall not offer the blood of my sacrifice with anything leavened, or let the fat of my feast remain until the morning. The best of the firstfruits of your ground you shall bring into the house of the Lord your God. You shall not boil a young goat in its mother's milk" (23:17–19).

The last regulation is perhaps the best place to begin because it is the most difficult to understand. The end of verse 19 is obscure, and Bible scholars have long struggled to know what it means, with some concluding that it is simply "a garbled piece of irrelevance."[5] Orthodox Jews take it as a dietary law—a general prohibition on mixing meat products with dairy products. This is not what the verse says, however. The only thing forbidden is cooking a young goat in its *own* mother's milk.

If there is a general principle here, it is pro-life: The source of life should never become the cause of death. A young goat is supposed to be nourished by its mother's milk, not boiled in it. And so, in the words of the ancient Jewish scholar Philo, God considered it "grossly improper that the substance which fed the living animal should be used to season and flavor the same after its death."[6] But there is another reason this practice was forbidden. Boiling a young goat in its mother's milk was a ritual part of Canaanite worship.[7] Therefore, this command was a safeguard against idolatry. When the Israelites celebrated their harvest festivals, they were not allowed to adopt pagan practices.

Instead they were to offer themselves to God alone. They were to be people "in whose heart[s] are the highways to Zion" (Psalm 84:5). But what do we do when we find him? The proper thing to do is to present ourselves for his service. The Law said, "Three times in the year shall all your males appear before the Lord God" (23:17; cf. Deuteronomy 16:16). The Bible says "males" because men were the spiritual heads of their households, but elsewhere the Bible makes it clear that women and children were included (Deuteronomy 16:11). Everyone in Israel was required to appear before God. It was a solemn assembly, a roll call of the faithful—the people who belonged to God. Therefore, all the Israelites were to present themselves to their one and only Savior and God. As their sovereign Lord, God claimed exclusive rights to their service. Their worship and their obedience belonged to him alone, and not to any other deity. The same is true for every believer in Jesus Christ: we are called to offer ourselves to God, and to God alone.

How are we to do this? First, by offering ourselves to God *continually*. God commanded his people to make a pilgrimage not just once, but three times a year. The Israelites presented themselves to God repeatedly. This helps us understand something important about the Christian life. Some Christians think that surrendering to Jesus Christ is something they only do at the beginning of the Christian life. Once they make a decision for Christ, they can get back to living their lives the way they planned. But if we claim to follow Christ, we need to keep giving ourselves over to God—not just three times a year, but all the time. Offering ourselves as living sacrifices is not just a one-time thing. This is one reason it is so necessary for us to attend weekly public worship. Every time we gather with God's people, we present ourselves to our Sovereign Lord and offer ourselves for his service all over again.

We are also called to offer ourselves to God *righteously*. That is to say, we are called to be holy in all our ways. God said, "You shall not offer the blood of my sacrifice with anything leavened" (23:18a). This regulation was associated with the Feast of Unleavened Bread (see also 34:25); however, it applied to other sacrifices as well. The Law said, "No grain offering that you bring to the LORD shall be made with leaven, for you shall burn no leaven nor any honey as a food offering to the LORD" (Leviticus 2:11). The only exception was the Feast of Ingathering, when two loaves of bread baked with yeast were "to be waved . . . as firstfruits to the LORD" (Leviticus 23:17). The mention of a sacrifice reminds us that we can only come to God on the basis of a blood offering, which is what we do every time we worship in the name of Jesus Christ. By his death on the cross, Jesus has made the atoning sacrifice for our sin.

But what about the yeast? Why were the Israelites forbidden to offer a sacrifice that included any form of yeast? As we have seen, the Bible uses yeast as a symbol of growth, and especially for the spread of spiritual corruption. Thus, keeping yeast away from the sacrifice was a symbol of separation from sin. It would not be right for the people to present themselves to God—no matter how regularly—and then return to their old patterns of sin. They were called to put away all unrighteousness, and this was symbolized by making unleavened offerings.

The application for us is that whatever we offer to God must be undefiled by our immorality. This principle is especially important for spiritual leaders. Whatever ministry we perform in the name of Jesus Christ must be purged of every proud ambition, fleshly lust, and greedy desire. But this ought to be true of *every* Christian. God wants us to lead holy lives. We offer him our best and purest service when we are careful to be righteous in all our ways. The best servant is a holy servant. If we are living in unconfessed and unrestrained sin, our witness is compromised, and our ministry loses its spiritual power.

Then we are called to offer ourselves to God *wholeheartedly*. As God said in his law, "You shall not . . . let the fat of my feast remain until the morning" (23:18). This regulation was not about keeping the kitchen clean; it had an important spiritual purpose. Today fat is usually considered unhealthy, but in the ancient world it was the choicest, juiciest part of the animal. The temptation would have been to leave some fat on the altar and then come back to get it the next morning.

We face the same temptation in the Christian life—to offer ourselves to God, but at the same time to hold back. We are willing to serve God, but we want to keep something for ourselves. So we worship him on Sundays, but not in our daily work. We praise him in our worship, but we don't talk about him with our friends. We try to please him in our ministry, but not in our use of entertainment. We are willing to help the needy, but not to give up the comforts of home. But God says, "Don't leave any fat on the altar. I want everything you have to offer, all the time."

God also wants the best we have to offer. This too is part of what it means to serve him wholeheartedly. God said to the Israelites, with reference to the Feast of Harvest, "The best of the firstfruits of your ground you shall bring into the house of the Lord your God" (23:19a). In other words, God wants the best of our very best. He wants the best of our time and talents, the best of our work and worship, the best of our minds and hearts. He wants us to be living sacrifices, continually offering ourselves to him for righteous, wholehearted service.

One woman who offered herself to God in this way was Betty Stam, a missionary to China who was martyred for her faith in Jesus Christ. Betty was forced to watch as the Communists brutally beheaded her husband, and then she herself was murdered in the same way. Yet God used her life and death to bring many people to a saving knowledge of Jesus Christ. It all started when she was a young woman and offered herself to God as a living sacrifice. Here is her prayer—a prayer for pilgrims who have found God and want to give themselves wholeheartedly to him: "Lord, I give up all my own plans and purposes, all my own desires and hopes, and accept thy will for my life. I give myself, my life, my all utterly to thee, to be thine forever. Fill me and seal me with thy Holy Spirit. Use me as thou wilt. Send me where thou wilt, and work out thy whole will in my life at any cost, now and forever."[8]

# 67

# Guardian Angel

## EXODUS 23:20–33

EVEN PEOPLE WHO DON'T BELIEVE IN GOD like to believe in angels. It is comforting to think that there is someone watching out for us—someone with supernatural power and special access to God. So angels continue to fascinate people. There are angels on TV and angels at the bookstore. There is even an entire magazine devoted to them, called *Angels on Earth*.

There is always a danger in giving angels more attention than they deserve. Naturally we are curious about these supernatural beings. However, our fascination quickly becomes unprofitable. The angels do not desire to call attention to themselves but to point us to God. Therefore, the Bible warns us not to worship them (Colossians 2:18). The apostle John found this out when he tried to bow down to one. "You must not do that!" the angel said. "I am a fellow servant with you and your brothers who hold to the testimony of Jesus. Worship God" (Revelation 19:10).

As wrong as it is to worship the angels, it is just as wrong to doubt their existence or to deny their proper place in God's plan. God has made beautiful spiritual beings to serve him in Heaven and to carry out his will on earth. These angels exist for the glory of God and the good of his people. It is their happy privilege to protect us, watch over us, and help us along in our pilgrimage. As the psalmist said, "He [God] will command his angels concerning you to guard you in all your ways" (Psalm 91:11).

### The Angel of God

There is an angel in Exodus. He is mentioned near the end of chapter 23, when God was giving Moses the laws of his covenant. Typically an ancient covenant ended with blessings and curses. These described in careful detail what would happen if the covenant was kept or broken. The Book of the Covenant was no exception. After telling his people what to do, God told them what would happen if they did it or failed to do it.

God began his warnings and promises with the announcement that he was sending Israel an angel: "Behold, I send an angel before you to guard you on the way and to bring you to the place that I have prepared. Pay careful attention to him and obey his voice; do not rebel against him, for he will not pardon your transgression, for my name is in him" (vv. 20, 21).

The first thing to resolve about these verses is the identity of the angel. Some scholars think the angel was the glory cloud that led the Israelites day and night, because like the cloud, the angel was with the Israelites all the way through the wilderness. However, a cloud is an inanimate object, whereas this angel is described as a living, moving, speaking person. Others think the angel "stands only for the guidance and help of the Lord."[1] Yet God clearly distinguished himself from the angel. "I send an angel," he said.

Another suggestion is that the angel was a human being. Since the Hebrew word for "angel" simply means "messenger," it need not necessarily refer to a glorious angel from Heaven. Some scholars think Moses was the messenger. Certainly Moses spoke for God. However, the obvious difficulty is that the angel was sent to conquer the Promised Land, which Moses never entered. The man who did lead God's people there was Joshua, so many fine commentators have argued that he was the messenger. Writing sometime around AD 200, Tertullian commented that "Joshua was to introduce the people into the land of promise, not Moses. Now he [God] called him an angel on account of the magnitude of the mighty deeds which he was to achieve (which mighty deeds Joshua the son of Nun did, as you can yourselves read) and on account of his office of prophet announcing the divine will."[2]

Augustine took this interpretation a step further by noting that Joshua is the Hebrew name for Jesus. This gives new significance to verse 21, in which God said, "My name is in him." God gave the messenger his divine name. On this interpretation the messenger would be Joshua, which is another name for Jesus. "It follows," said Augustine, "that he who said, 'My name is in him' is the true Jesus, the leader who brings his people into the inheritance of eternal life, according to the New Testament, of which the Old was a figure. No event or action could have a more distinctly prophetical character than this, where the very name is itself a prediction."[3]

Of course, the angel could be exactly that—an angel, in the usual sense of the word. If so, then it was a guardian angel sent to keep the Israelites safe on their way to Canaan. As Scripture says, "The angel of the LORD encamps around those who fear him, and delivers them" (Psalm 34:7). The angel went ahead to guide the people on their way, just like he did when the Israelites were camped by the sea (14:19). It was like playing Follow the Leader: The angel led, and the people followed. The angel also served as God's representative. He spoke for

God, and when he did, the people had to listen to what he said. Moreover, they had to give him their absolute obedience. To listen to the angel was to listen to God, and to rebel against him was to rebel against God. In this connection it is worth noting that the word used in verse 21 for "rebel" is generally used elsewhere in the Old Testament for opposition to the Almighty.[4]

By now we are getting the distinct impression that this messenger was more than an angel. He was so closely associated with God as to be identified with him. This is confirmed by the angel's power to forgive or not to forgive sin. God said, "Do not rebel against him, for he will not pardon your transgression." But the Scripture also says, "Who can forgive sins but God alone?" (Mark 2:7). So who was this guiding, guarding angel who acted for God, spoke for God, and held the power of forgiveness?

Whoever he was, he bore God's very name, for God said, "My name is in him" (23:21). God's name is always more than a name. It indicates his special presence and refers to his divine being. According to John Mackay, the Name is a "revelation of the character and attributes of God," which means that "[h]ere we have a unique dignity accorded to the angel as manifesting all that God has made known regarding himself. That is why the angel can command complete obedience and trust: his presence is the equivalent of the presence of the Lord himself."[5]

To summarize, this messenger was distinguished from God, yet at the same time had uniquely divine attributes. Therefore, many Christians have identified him as the second person of the Trinity, the preincarnate Son of God. We have encountered this phenomenon before, back at the burning bush and at the place where the water came from the rock. Long before his incarnation, long before he was born in Bethlehem, Christ was with his people on their way to salvation. Mackay concludes: "Christian interpreters have generally identified the angel mentioned here and the angel of the Lord found throughout the Pentateuch as the one phenomenon, which is a temporary preincarnate appearance of the second person of the Trinity to give encouragement to the people of God. He is the one who goes before his people to protect them and bring them to the place he has prepared for them."[6]

Whether this is the right interpretation or not, the angel of the exodus certainly points us to Christ. This is one of the many places where the Old Testament reveals what kind of Savior God was promising to send. Like Israel's angel, Jesus is our guardian along the way. By the presence of his Holy Spirit, he is always with us to save us. He says, "And behold, I am with you always, to the end of the age" (Matthew 28:20). Like Israel's angel, Jesus is our guide. When his disciples wanted to know the way to glory, Jesus simply said, "I am the way" (John 14:6). Now we are called to follow him every step of the road, until we reach the promised land.

Like Israel's angel, Jesus speaks to us for God. He is the messenger God sent to bring us the good news of salvation. The Father said, "This is my Son, my Chosen One; listen to him!" (Luke 9:35). And if we refuse to listen to him, we do so at our own peril. It is only by trusting in Jesus that our sins can be forgiven. So if we rebel against him, how can we be forgiven? There is no one else to save us from our sins. And like Israel's angel, Jesus bears the very name of God. He is God the Son. Everything that is true of God is true of him. He has the same character and attributes. He is "the radiance of the glory of God and the exact imprint of his nature" (Hebrews 1:3). Thus the New Testament everywhere identifies Jesus as our Lord and our God. In all these ways the angel of the exodus points us to the messenger of our salvation. Jesus Christ is our guardian and guide, our teacher, Savior, and Lord.

This should encourage us in our spiritual pilgrimage. Like the Israelites, we have received salvation. We have crossed from death to life through the crucifixion and resurrection of Jesus Christ. But we have not yet reached the promised land, and the way is long and hard. We must endure many hard trials and suffer many painful sorrows in the journey of our faith. But God has given us a Guardian Savior who will lead us where we need to go. Jesus will protect us from danger along the way. If we listen to his Word, he will tell us everything we need to know. And in the end he will lead us home to God.

## God Victorious

The angel of the exodus did many things to save Israel, but what is promised at the end of Exodus 23 is the conquest of Canaan. When God brought his people out of Egypt, he also promised to lead them to the Promised Land. This meant driving out the people who lived there—God's enemies—and this was the special responsibility of Israel's guardian angel.

The angel's conquest teaches us at least three important lessons about God's plan for our salvation. They are lessons God taught his people in the days of Moses, but each of them has implications for God's new people in Christ. Concerning Israel's pilgrimage from Egypt to Canaan, the Bible says, "Now these things happened to them as an example, but they were written down for our instruction, on whom the end of the ages has come" (1 Corinthians 10:11). In other words, Exodus was written for the edification of the church.

To see how something that happened back then can help us today, it is useful to remember where the Israelites were in the story of salvation. They were somewhere between Egypt and Canaan. That is to say, although they were already saved, their salvation was not complete. They had been baptized into salvation through the waters of the Red Sea, and they were on their way to the Promised Land. But in order to enter their full and final salvation, they still had enemies to conquer.

We are in the same position, spiritually speaking. We can map out the story of Israel's salvation somewhere in the spiritual geography of our own souls. God has won a great victory for us. We have been baptized into salvation through the death and resurrection of Jesus Christ. Now we are on our way to the promised land—the glorious Heaven that God has prepared for all his friends. But we still have enemies to face. The victory that Jesus won is not yet complete. We are still striving to be sanctified, struggling against the attacks of Satan. What can Israel's angel teach us about the conquest and the fight?

The first thing the angel shows is that the victory belongs to God. God said, "But if you carefully obey his voice and do all that I say, then I will be an enemy to your enemies and an adversary to your adversaries. When my angel goes before you and brings you to the Amorites and the Hittites and the Perizzites and the Canaanites, the Hivites and the Jebusites, and I blot them out . . ." (23:22, 23). These verses seem to confirm the angel's identity as the second person of the Trinity. Notice how God moves back and forth between what *he* will do and what the *angel* will do, establishing the closest connection between his own work and the work of his messenger. This ought to remind us of something Jesus said to his disciples: "Whatever the Father does, that the Son does likewise" (John 5:19).

What the angel would do—what God would do—was to drive out all of Israel's enemies. This was a holy war in which God would do the fighting. He made the same promise a few verses later: "I will send my terror before you and will throw into confusion all the people against whom you shall come, and I will make all your enemies turn their backs to you. And I will send hornets before you, which shall drive out the Hivites, the Canaanites, and the Hittites from before you" (23:27, 28). Usually ancient treaties ended with the overlord reminding his subjects of their duties. God did this in his Book of the Covenant, but he also undertook some obligations of his own. He established a mutual defense pact in which Israel's enemies became his enemies. This meant that he would be the one to do the conquering, the handing over, and the driving out. God would terrify the Hittites, confuse the Canaanites, and make the Hivites run for cover.

When God and his conquering angel went ahead to enter the Promised Land, Israel's enemies would be overcome with dread. They would panic the way people do when they get buzzed by a bee. First they are paralyzed, and then they run, even if no one gets stung. The same thing would happen to the Canaanites. It is hard to know what the Hebrew word translated "hornets" (v. 28, *hatsir'ah*) actually means. It may refer to a plague of stinging insects, which could be either literal or figurative. If it is figurative, then it might be a reference to Egypt, because the Pharaohs used the hornet as one of their royal symbols.[7] Possibly God would send Pharaoh's army to attack Canaan shortly before the Israelites arrived, with the Egyptian attack preparing the way for his victory. In any case, God promised to be the ultimate intimidator. When the Captain of his angelic armies led Israel into battle, the courage of the Canaanites would melt away. All God had to do was come close, and the rout was on.

This is exactly what happened. When Israelite spies made their first foray into Canaan, they met a woman named Rahab. She said:

> I know that the Lord has given you the land, and that the fear of you has fallen upon us, and that all the inhabitants of the land melt away before you. For we have heard how the Lord dried up the water of the Red Sea before you when you came out of Egypt, and what you did to the two kings of the Amorites who were beyond the Jordan, to Sihon and Og, whom you devoted to destruction. And as soon as we heard it, our hearts melted, and there was no spirit left in any man because of you, for the Lord your God, he is God in the heavens above and on the earth beneath. (Joshua 2:9–11; cf. Exodus 15:14–16)

God still has this effect on his enemies today. Our warfare is not physical but spiritual. This is one of the major differences between the Old Testament and the New Testament. Spiritual warfare can still be frightening. Some Christians are fearful of Satan and what he might do to them. However, we are not the ones who ought to be afraid. The Bible says that when the demons think about God, they shudder (James 2:19). And well they should! God has the power to destroy them with fire, and he has promised that one day soon he will do it.

In the meantime, we should trust God to win the victory. Many Christians take the wrong approach to spiritual warfare. The emphasis is all on technique. If we repeat the right prayer, claim the right promise, apply the right kind of oil, or exorcise the right demon, then we will win a spiritual victory. Certainly there are some things God calls us to do. This was true for the Israelites. God said, "*I* will give the inhabitants of the land into your hand, and *you* shall drive them out before you" (23:31b). When it comes to spiritual warfare, we are not passive observers. We are called to watch, to pray, to believe, and to study God's Word. However, the main thing we are called to do is "be strong in the Lord and in the strength of his might" (Ephesians 6:10). The battle and the victory belong to God, and we should not struggle for the victories he has promised to win.

This is especially true when it comes to our progress in holiness. Many Christians seem to believe in sanctification by self-effort. They think that God did his part by bringing us to salvation in Christ, and now the rest is up to us. It is true that we are called to pursue godliness. Unlike justification, sanctification is not by faith *alone*. God has work for us to do. The same thing was true for the Israelites when they conquered the Promised Land. They had to do more than just cross the Jordan River. They had to pray, march, and even fight. But ultimately the victory belonged to God. So it is in the Christian life. The Scripture says, "Work out your own salvation with fear and trembling, for it is God who works in you, both to will and to work for his good pleasure" (Philippians 2:12b,

13). Do not be discouraged in your ongoing struggle with sin, but trust the Holy Spirit to use the Word, sacraments, and prayer to help you grow in grace.

## Little by Little

The second thing the angel shows is that often the victory does not come all at once but little by little. Although eventually it will be total, right now the victory is gradual. God said, "I will not drive them out from before you in one year, lest the land become desolate and the wild beasts multiply against you. Little by little I will drive them out from before you, until you have increased and possess the land" (23:29, 30).

No doubt the Israelites wanted the victory to come right away. They wanted to march in one day, watch their enemies march out the next, and then take over the Promised Land. However, that was not God's plan, and for the very practical reason that the Israelites were not ready to take full possession. If their enemies left right away, the fields would grow wild, predators would take over, and the land would become desolate. So God, in his infinite wisdom and mercy, ordained that the "process of occupation and colonization was to be a progressive one in order that they might maintain complete control over that land."[8]

Eventually the whole land would be theirs. God said, "I will set your border from the Red Sea to the Sea of the Philistines, and from the wilderness to the Euphrates" (v. 31a). This was a huge territory, and God's promise was not fulfilled until the reign of Solomon, when the kingdom of Israel extended to its widest boundaries (see 1 Kings 4:21). But that was centuries later. So the conquest came—as God had promised—little by little.

This teaches us something important about the Christian life. It is not always God's plan to give us instant and total victory. Usually our spiritual progress comes little by little. However, even this can be for our benefit. We would prefer to be sanctified right away, without any struggle. But for many merciful reasons, God does not allow this to happen. He wants us to learn how to depend on him in ways we never would unless we had to persevere through the gradual conquest of our sin.

This is true for the church generally. If he had wanted, God could have taken his people to glory right after Jesus rose from the dead. But God had a better plan, one that was for both our good and his glory. He wanted to work out salvation through long centuries of human history so he could save a vast host of souls. The kingdom of God has been spreading the way Jesus said it would, like the yeast in a lump of dough, or like a tiny seed that slowly grows into a large tree (Matthew 13:31–33). Little by little God is working out his purpose until all his people are saved.

The same principle holds true for individual Christians. God does not give us the victory all at once. We do not go to Heaven the moment we trust in Christ. To put this in theological terms, we do not go immediately from regeneration to glorification. Usually there is a long, slow process of sanctification that comes in between. This too is for our good and for God's glory. It teaches us to depend on God's grace, it drives us to our knees in prayer, and it refines our character in more perfect detail.

Knowing that God works little by little helps us to gain perspective on some of our frustrations. Sometimes we struggle so hard with a particular sin that we wish God would just take it away. We are tempted to give up, and perhaps even to doubt whether the Holy Spirit has the power to change us. But God is working little by little to make us holy. Sometimes we get frustrated in ministry. We long to see more fruit, or perhaps we wonder when God will give us the opportunity to serve him the way we have always dreamed. Yet God is at work. Little by little his Spirit is preparing people to trust in Christ for their salvation, and at the same time he is preparing us for a wider field of ministry. Sometimes we despair of ever seeing the people we love—our children, for example—reach spiritual maturity. Sometimes they seem to be going backward rather than forward. But God is working little by little. The victory belongs to him, and he will see it through to the very end.

## No Room for Compromise

In the meantime there is no room for us to make any compromise with ungodliness. This is the third and final lesson to learn from Israel's angel and the conquest of Canaan: Don't compromise. While we are waiting for God to win the full and final victory, we must do everything we can to separate ourselves from sin.

This was hard for the Israelites to do. They faced a strong temptation to make their peace with the Canaanites and to worship their gods—especially since the conquest came little by little. Rather than taking the trouble to drive their enemies all the way out, why not live in peaceful coexistence? But God said, "You shall not bow down to their gods nor serve them, nor do as they do, but you shall utterly overthrow them and break their pillars in pieces" (23:24). He also said, "You shall make no covenant with them and their gods. They shall not dwell in your land, lest they make you sin against me; for if you serve their gods, it will surely be a snare to you" (vv. 32, 33).

Obviously the Israelites were not allowed to worship the gods of Canaan. They were to worship the God of Israel, and to serve him only. But God knew how tempting it would be for his people to worship false gods. To help them avoid even the possibility of this temptation, he told them to smash Canaan's idols to pieces. Their "gods" were idols of wood and precious metal. Their sacred pillars stood ten feet tall. All these idols were to be destroyed. Godfrey Ashby writes, "There is to be no apostasy, no worship given to any other gods, no lapsing into the cults of neighboring peoples, but only absolute loyalty to Yahweh alone."[9]

The Israelites were also forbidden to make a covenant, or peace treaty, with the Canaanites. In those days covenants were sealed with sacred rituals in which nations sacrificed to their gods. So the Israelites could not make a treaty with the Canaanites without in some way acknowledging their gods. This they were absolutely forbidden to do. There is only one supreme and sovereign deity, and the Israelites were called to worship him alone. The whole point of the Book of the Covenant was that they were entering into an exclusive relationship with the only true God.

The other problem with granting amnesty to the Canaanites was that the longer they stayed around, the more likely the Israelites were to be led astray. It is always easier to be influenced than to influence. In the words of one commentator, "Given the sinful propensities of the human heart, it is far easier for the false and debased to degrade the true than for the pure to elevate the corrupt."[10] If the Canaanites wanted to turn away from their idols to serve the true and living God, that was one thing. But if they kept practicing their pagan rituals, they would inevitably cause the Israelites to stumble. So God adopted a zero tolerance policy toward the Canaanites and their gods. Their worship was vulgar. It involved sexual promiscuity, child sacrifice, and the worship of wood and stone. The Canaanites deserved to be punished for these sins, and God was well within his rights to say that they could not live in his land—the place where he was establishing a people for himself as part of his plan for saving the world.

If the Israelites let the Canaanites stay, they would get lured or trapped into false worship. Verse 33 describes idolatry as "a snare," like a trap set for a small animal, and of course this is exactly what it turned out to be. God's warning proved to be all too necessary. The Israelites never totally got rid of the Canaanites, and throughout the rest of their history they kept getting ensnared by pagan deities again and again.

Things would have gone much better for the Israelites if they had obeyed. Then God would have blessed them the way he promised: "You shall serve the Lord your God, and he will bless your bread and your water, and I will take sickness away from among you. None shall miscarry or be barren in your land; I will fulfill the number of your days" (23:25, 26). If God's people did what God told them to do, they would have plenty of food and water. They would have good health. They would have large families and grow to old age.

This does not mean that people who obey God never get sick. Still less does it mean that people who are starving or childless or who die young have been disobedient. These promises were for the Old Testament people of God, given at a time when God was using material blessings to teach spiritual truths. Therefore, we need to be careful not to apply these blessings and curses too literally. Our Savior was a suffering servant, and like him we must pass through suffering to enter glory. Only then will we be delivered from hunger, pain, and death. But even if the suffering church may not receive the material blessings God promised to Israel, the principle still holds true: obedience is the pathway to blessing.

Sadly, the Israelites missed out on God's blessing because they compromised with the Canaanites. This warns us of the danger of settling for a partial victory that stops short of full obedience to Christ. God is winning the victory—usually little by little—but if we compromise with sin, our victory will turn into defeat.

We are tempted to think that since our salvation is secure, it will not harm us to be exposed to sin, at least in small quantities. We tell ourselves that it is okay to indulge in a little self-pity, especially since life is so discouraging. We think that it's all right for us to look at pornography because we still have things "under control." Or we say, "I don't really have a drinking problem; I just get drunk sometimes." We cut a few corners at work; no one will ever know. We enjoy a juicy morsel of gossip. Or we shade the truth. We don't lie, exactly, but if someone gets the wrong impression and it works to our advantage, we don't take the trouble to correct them. These are the kinds of little compromises that trap Christians every day, and they inevitably lead to bigger and bigger sins.

When it comes to sin and its little compromises, we need to adopt a policy of zero tolerance. There are things we need to get rid of entirely, so as to remove any temptation. There are places we should not go, things we should not see, friends we should not meet, ideas we should not entertain, conversations we should not start, and desires we should not indulge. If we claim to follow Jesus Christ, we need to get rid of anything and everything that can become a snare.

Here are some questions every Christian needs to ask: What do I need to get rid of? What temptations do I need to avoid? What is keeping me from total obedience to Christ? If we don't get rid of these things, we'll be trapped. We need to remember that as Christians we are on the way to glory land. We are under the watchful care of our Guardian Savior—Jesus Christ—who has won the victory and whose kingdom is advancing little by little. There is no room for compromise. So don't settle for a partial victory that falls short of full obedience to Christ!

68

# The Blood of the Covenant

EXODUS 24:1–8

WHEN WE FIRST EMBARKED on our long journey through Exodus, we described the book as an epic adventure. As in any epic, there have been many dramatic moments: the burning bush, the ten plagues, the crossing of the Red Sea, and the Ten Commandments, to name only a few. But no scene is more dramatic than the one described in chapter 24, in which God confirms his covenant with Israel.

For three chapters God has been giving his people his law for their lives in the form of a covenant, such as was common in those days. First he gave them a history lesson recounting how he had saved them out of Egypt. This was to remind them that they owed him their very lives and thus also their obedience. God had the right to tell them not to serve other gods, make idols, dishonor his name, murder, steal, or break any of his other commandments. He was Israel's Savior, so the Israelites had to honor him as their Lord. He was their God; they were his people. This is what the Bible means by covenant: a sacred relationship, established by God, in which God belongs to his people and his people belong to him.

## Approaching God

In order for any covenant to be properly established, it has to be confirmed. This is what happens in Exodus 24. Whereas chapters 20—23 set forth the terms of the covenant, chapter 24 describes how it was ratified.

The Israelites had gathered at the foot of Mount Sinai. To this point God had been speaking to the nation generally, but now he spoke directly to his prophet Moses, calling him to come and worship: "Come up to the Lord, you and Aaron, Nadab, and Abihu, and seventy of the elders of Israel, and worship from afar.

Moses alone shall come near to the LORD, but the others shall not come near, and the people shall not come up with him" (24:1, 2).

The confirmation of a covenant was a solemn occasion, in which everything needed to be done "decently and in order" (1 Corinthians 14:40). First Moses went up to meet with God. This was not the first time he had done this. In fact, it is difficult to keep track of all the times Moses went up and down the mountain. But this was his job. Moses was the mediator, the man who walked between Heaven and earth, going between a holy God and his sinful people.

Whenever Moses went up the mountain, he represented the people before God. This time he had some company. His brother Aaron was with him, as the father of Israel's priests. Aaron's sons were also there—Nadab and Abihu, who were later destroyed for offering unholy fire on God's altar (Leviticus 10). They were joined by seventy of Israel's elders, presumably men chosen back in chapter 18 when Moses appointed elders to help him govern Israel. These seventy men represented the various tribes of Israel.

Together these men approached God for worship; however, they were not allowed to get too close. God made it clear that it was an awesome thing to enter his holy presence. Most of the people were not allowed to go up the mountain at all. Their priests and elders were allowed to go partway up, but even they had limited access. God told them to keep their distance. Only Moses, the mediator, was permitted to draw near. By setting these boundaries God was teaching his people to honor his holiness. He is a great and awesome God, perfect in righteousness. We can only come close if we come the way he has appointed. Back then the people approached God through their priests, and especially through his prophet Moses. Today we come through the one and only "mediator between God and men, the man Christ Jesus" (1 Timothy 2:5). Through Jesus we gain access to God. No one else can or needs to go to God for us. We meet with him in Christ.

To speak of meeting with God is really to speak of worshiping God. To worship God is to come into his presence with praise. And whenever we come into his presence, we need to bow down and worship. This is what Israel's priests and the elders did. God told them to "worship," which in Hebrew specifically means to bow low before someone. So Exodus 24 is the story of a worship service, the first one fully described in the Bible. It contains nearly all the basic elements of a public service, and thus it sets the pattern for Biblical worship. There was a call to worship, the reading of God's Word, a confession of faith, and the sharing of a sacramental meal. This was all done under the oversight of Israel's elders and by the servant appointed to lead public worship. And it was all done in the presence of a holy and glorious God. This is what worship is: meeting with God. And this is why God saved the Israelites—so they could worship him. Exodus 24 is a fulfillment of that promise. In order to confirm the covenant, God's people gathered for a solemn assembly. They met at the mountain to worship God and behold his glory.

## Reading the Law

Moses was the worship leader, and as such he had some important responsibilities. The first was to read God's law. The Scripture says, "Moses came and told the people all the words of the LORD and all the rules" (24:3a). The phrase "words . . . and . . . rules" is significant. "Words" refers specifically to the Ten Commandments, which the Bible introduces by saying, "And God spoke all these *words*" (*dbarym*, 20:1). There were ten "words" in all—the categorical commands of God.

The word "rules" does not refer to the Ten Commandments, but to the case laws that follow. God had earlier said to Moses, "Now these are the *rules* that you shall set before them" (*mishpatym*, 21:1). Then he proceeded to give detailed regulations about everyday situations involving things like slavery, personal injury, the loss of property, and social justice. So Moses read the Law as it had been revealed to him on the mountain. He read both the Ten Commandments (20) and the Book of the Covenant (21—23)—"all the words of the LORD and all the rules" (24:3).

"And Moses wrote down all the words of the LORD" (24:4a). This was important because ancient covenants were always written down. As John Mackay explains, "It was customary when overlords entered into treaties with their vassals for there to be a formal, authoritative text detailing what was involved in the agreement. Once the terms had been set out and accepted, they were written down and not subject to further change. That is what Moses as the covenant mediator does here."[1] This verse is also important for showing how we got our Bible. Presumably what Moses wrote down included everything from Exodus 19—23. This was the first draft (so to speak) of the Old Testament. The Israelites did not simply rely on oral tradition but wrote things down. Thus they had the Word of God, written. Whenever God said something important, they put it in writing so that it would never be forgotten, which is why we still have these words today.

Next Moses read the Law again. The Bible says that after offering sacrifices (more on this in a moment), Moses "took the Book of the Covenant and read it in the hearing of the people" (24:7a). This is the verse that gives the Book of the Covenant its name. It is also a verse to which some scholars object, on the grounds that it is redundant. If Moses read "all the words of the LORD and all the rules" in verse 3, why did he do it again in verse 7?

There are at least two good answers. One is that reading the Law was a necessary part of the ceremony for confirming the covenant. Moses read God's law the first time so the people would know what they were getting into. As soon as the Israelites heard what God wanted, they decided to accept his terms:

"Moses came and told the people all the words of the LORD and all the rules. And all the people answered with one voice and said, 'All the words that the LORD has spoken we will do'" (v. 3). But even after they decided to accept God's covenant, they needed to hear the Law again to *confirm* the covenant. The second reading of the Law was part of the ceremony. The Law was read once to help the people understand what God demanded; it was read a second time so they could promise to do it.

Something similar happens in a wedding. At the beginning of the ceremony the bride and the groom are asked to declare their intent. The minister says, "Will you have this person as your lawful wedded spouse?" If they say, "I will," it means they are willing to enter into the covenant of matrimony. But they are not actually married until they say their marriage vows. Something similar happened when God established his covenant with Israel. First the Israelites declared their intent (v. 3); then they took their vows (v. 7).

Another good reason for Moses to reread the law was that the people needed to hear it more than once. It is not enough to listen to God every now and then; we need to hear his voice again and again. This is especially important when it comes to public worship. The covenant was confirmed in a worship service, a central part of which was the public reading of God's Word. This is still true today. God is not properly worshiped unless his Word is read (and also explained). We need to hear what God has to say every time we meet for worship.

Whenever God's Word is read, it always calls for a response. And the Israelites responded to the reading of the Law by promising to do whatever God said. They made it unanimous. The first time Moses read the law, "all the people answered with one voice and said, 'All the words that the LORD has spoken we will do'" (v. 3b; cf. 19:8). They made the same promise the second time Moses read the Law, only this time they were even more emphatic: "And they said, 'All that the LORD has spoken we will do, and we will be obedient'" (24:7b).

This was a daring promise. The people had just heard God's law—all of it. Moses "told the people *all* the words of the LORD and all the rules" (v. 3). They had heard God say that they couldn't have any other gods, couldn't make any idols, couldn't lie, steal, or covet. They had also heard God's regulations for property and injury. They had heard all of the Law's commands, as well as many of its applications. They had heard the Law in all its righteousness. They knew what perfect obedience God was demanding in every area of life. Yet when Moses finished reading the Law, the whole community said in essence, "Let's do it! Yes, Lord, we will obey every last word of your covenant."

Apparently they were optimists. What else can explain their decision to make such a rash promise? They were natural-born sinners, but God's law demanded perfect obedience. There was not a man, woman, or child anywhere in Israel who was able to keep God's law. And it wasn't simply that they failed here and there. They were unable to keep even a single command in perfect integrity.

Nevertheless, they agreed to keep the whole Law of God. And really, how could they have done otherwise? God is the Creator and Redeemer, so he has the right to demand whatever he pleases. He is also holy and just; so what he demands is always righteous. Therefore, when God gave his people the terms of his covenant, the only thing they could do was to accept. Whether they were able to do it or not, keeping God's law was the right way for them to live.

## Sprinkling the Blood

To show his people how serious he was in demanding their obedience, God sealed this covenant relationship with blood. This was the second main thing Moses had to do. After reading the Law, he made sacrifices and then sprinkled the blood as a confirmation of the covenant:

> He rose early in the morning and built an altar at the foot of the mountain, and twelve pillars, according to the twelve tribes of Israel. And he sent young men of the people of Israel, who offered burnt offerings and sacrificed peace offerings of oxen to the LORD. And Moses took half of the blood and put it in basins, and half of the blood he threw against the altar. (vv. 4b–6)

Following the second reading of the Law, "Moses took the blood and threw it on the people and said, 'Behold the blood of the covenant that the LORD has made with you in accordance with all these words'" (v. 8).

As Moses did these things, he was careful to follow God's instructions. He was engaged in a solemn ritual. Moses also followed God's instructions promptly. He sealed the covenant as quickly as he could, starting first thing the next morning. There is a practical lesson in this. When it comes to entering into a relationship with God, it is important not to delay. Some people spend a long time studying Jesus Christ without ever trusting in him for their salvation. But anyone who is trying to decide whether or not to become a Christian should seal the deal as soon as possible. Then salvation will be secure forever.

Moses started by building an altar, presumably according to the instructions given in 20:24–26. The altar, which represented God's presence, was a place for making sacrifices. This was essential because sinners can only worship a holy God on the basis of a sacrifice. People worshiped God long before there was a temple, or even a tabernacle, but they never worshiped him without an altar. When Noah and the patriarchs worshiped God, they always started by building an altar.

The altar Moses built was used for more than one kind of sacrifice. Initially these various sacrifices were offered by Israel's young men, who served as a temporary priesthood until God appointed priests. One sacrifice was the burnt offering, in which an entire animal was consumed by fire (cf. Leviticus 1). Nothing was left; the whole offering was given over to God. This costly sacrifice represented full atonement for sin and total dedication to God.

The other sacrifice mentioned in these verses represented peace with God, and thus it was called the peace offering (cf. Leviticus 3). Unlike the burnt offering, the peace offering was not consigned to the flames but was grilled until tender and then served for dinner. But before any of this could be done, the blood had to be drained. Blood from the fellowship offerings was carefully collected in large bowls and then sprinkled. This was the most important part of the ceremony. Moses took half the blood and sprinkled it on the altar. Then, after reading the Book of the Covenant, he took the other half and sprinkled it on the people. Why did he do this? It sounds primitive, almost barbaric. What purpose did it serve to splatter the people with blood?

The Bible does not provide an explanation but expects us to understand this ritual from its context and from the rest of Scripture. Not surprisingly, not everyone agrees what the ceremony signified. Some scholars say the blood symbolized kinship, making God and his people something like blood brothers.[2] Others say it was a form of consecration. God sprinkled his people to set them apart as holy.[3] However, there was more to the ceremony than this. The blood showed that the covenant was a matter of life or death. In the ancient world a covenant typically was sealed in blood to show what would happen if either party failed to comply. This was the symbolism, remember, of the covenant that God made with Abraham (Genesis 15). God told Abraham to carve up sacrifices, separating the pieces into two rows. Then God, in the form of a burning torch, passed between the pieces. This was part of the custom. When people made a covenant (or "cut" a covenant, as they said in those days), the parties passed between the severed animals. It was a way of saying that if they failed to keep the covenant they deserved to be dismembered, just like the animals they had sacrificed.

The blood of God's covenant with Israel meant something similar. In the words of O. Palmer Robertson, "The same pledge-to-death which played such a prominent role in the inauguration of the Abrahamic covenant manifested itself in the inauguration of the Mosaic covenant."[4] Animals were sacrificed. Then their blood was sprinkled on the people, and also on God, represented by his altar. Both parties were undertaking a covenant commitment. This covenant was not signed but was sealed in blood, which showed that the whole arrangement was a matter of life and death: "Keeping the covenant meant that life would ensue; breaking it led to the spilling of blood and to death."[5] The blood of the covenant held the threat of divine judgment for everyone who broke God's law.

At the same time, the blood was a sign of God's mercy. God was not simply showing his people what would happen if they failed; he was also showing that there was a way for them to remain in his favor, even after they sinned. To put this another way, although the relationship God established with his people under Moses had a legal basis, it was a covenant of grace. This was shown by the sprinkling of the blood. First Moses sprinkled it on the altar of God, which showed that the people's sins were forgiven. This is what a bloody altar always signifies: the forgiveness of sins. Atonement has been made; God has accepted a sacrifice as payment for sin. The blood was also a propitiation: It turned aside God's wrath. Then the blood was sprinkled on the people. This showed that God had accepted their sacrifice and that they were now included in the covenant through the forgiveness of their sins. The blood—and therefore its benefits—was applied directly to them.

God's relationship with his people was maintained on the basis of a sacrifice. Since there were two sides to this relationship, the blood was sprinkled on both parties, tying them together. The covenant was a blood relationship, "a bond in blood" between God and his people.[6] It is significant that the blood was put on God's altar first. For the people to have any kind of relationship with God at all, God had to accept the sacrifice they made for their sins. Notice as well the way Moses describes this relationship: "the covenant that the Lord has made with you" (24:8). There were two sides to the relationship, but it all started with God. The Israelites did not go to God and say, "Look, Lord, we'd really like to have a relationship with you." On the contrary, the whole arrangement was his idea in the first place. Peter Enns thus notes that "this covenant is essentially not a matter of a mutual agreement or pact made between God and the Israelites. It is, as we read, 'the covenant that the Lord has made with you.' It is by his initiative. He is the instigator. What the Israelites are to do is to accept and agree to live by the terms of the covenant that God and God alone has stipulated."[7]

It was only after the blood was sprinkled on God's altar that it could also be sprinkled on God's people. Alec Motyer explains this side of the covenant:

> The blood moves first Godward in propitiation, but then, secondly, manward. "And he took the book of the covenant, and read it in the hearing of the people: and they said, 'All that the Lord has spoken will we do, and be obedient.' And Moses took the blood, and sprinkled it on the people." On what people did he sprinkle it? At what precise moment did that sprinkling of blood occur? At the moment when they committed themselves to a life of obedience. First comes the commitment to obedience according to the Lord God, "All that the Lord has said we will do, and we will be obedient," then the sprinkling of the blood manward. And what does that mean? It means that just as the blood of the covenant on the one hand establishes the relationship of peace with God by propitiation, so on the other hand the blood of the covenant maintains the relationship of peace with God for a people who are committed to walk in obedience. God knows that the people are professing beyond their strength. . . . "Very well," says God, "I will make provision for them." The same blood which has made peace with God will keep peace with God. As they walk in the way of obedience, the blood is available for a people committed to obey. As they stumble and fall, so the covenant blood will be available for them.[8]

This is the covenant God made with his people. By the blood they were bound to keep God's law, and by the same blood their sins were forgiven.

## The New Covenant

What is the value in making such careful study of the covenant that God made with Israel? Simply this: Israel's experience at Mount Sinai shows us how to have a right relationship with God. Like the Israelites, we stand in the presence of a holy God who calls us to worship him. Like the Israelites, we are obligated to keep God's law, upon the pain of death. Unfortunately, we cannot keep it any better than they did. But like them, we can belong to God on the basis of blood.

Blood has always been the basis for a relationship with God. The Old Testament sacrifices—including the ones that confirmed the covenant—taught God's people to look for salvation to come by blood. This was preparing the way for Jesus, who showed the full significance of the old sacrifices when he shed his blood on the cross for our sins. When the New Testament talks about Christ, it often describes his saving work in terms of blood: "God put forward [Jesus] as a propitiation by his blood, to be received by faith" (Romans 3:25a); "We have now been justified by his blood" (Romans 5:9); "In him we have redemption through his blood, the forgiveness of our trespasses" (Ephesians 1:7); "You . . . have been brought near by the blood of Christ" (Ephesians 2:13); "Through him to reconcile to himself all things, whether on earth or in heaven, making peace by the blood of his cross" (Colossians 1:19, 20); "To him who loves us and has freed us from our sins by his blood" (Revelation 1:5b). It is by the blood of Jesus that we are justified, redeemed, reconciled, forgiven, and released. We are saved by the blood—the blood of the covenant.

Sometimes the New Testament describes salvation specifically in terms of *sprinkling* (e.g., 1 Peter 1:2). This is especially true of Hebrews, which says that Jesus "entered once for all into the holy places . . . by means of his own blood, thus securing an eternal redemption" (9:12) and then goes on to make a comparison between the Old Testament sacrifices and the blood of Christ: "For if the blood of goats and bulls, and the sprinkling of defiled persons with the ashes of a heifer, sanctify for the purification of the flesh, how much more will the blood of Christ, who through the eternal Spirit offered himself without blemish to God, purify our conscience from dead works to serve the living God" (9:13, 14). Anyone who has a guilty conscience—as every sinner does—can come clean by trusting in the blood of Christ. Like the Israelites, we can be saved by the sprinkling of blood.

The writer to the Hebrews was obviously thinking about Exodus 24, because he went on to describe the covenant God made with Israel: "For when every commandment of the law had been declared by Moses to all the people, he took the blood of calves and goats, with water and scarlet wool and hyssop, and sprinkled both the book itself and all the people, saying, 'This is the blood of the covenant that God commanded for you'" (9:19, 20). The Mosaic covenant was established on the basis of blood. As it says in verse 18, "Not even the first covenant was inaugurated without blood." Why was it made in blood? Because "without the shedding of blood there is no forgiveness of sins" (v. 22).

If all this is true, then for us to find forgiveness and have a relationship with God, some kind of sacrifice has to be made for our sins. This is exactly what Jesus provided on the cross: "But as it is, he [Jesus] has appeared once for all at the end of the ages to put away sin by the sacrifice of himself" (Hebrews 9:26b; cf. v. 28b). God has made a covenant with us in Christ. To be a proper covenant, the bond had to be established in blood. And so it was! Just as Moses sprinkled blood on the altar, so Christ shed his blood on the cross. The cross is where blood was sprinkled, atonement was made, and sins were forgiven. Therefore, the cross is where we have to go to find salvation. As Hebrews goes on to say, "You have come . . . to Jesus, the mediator of a new covenant, and to the sprinkled blood" (12:22–24).

In the old covenant, blood was sprinkled on the people as well as on the altar. Is there any equivalent for this in the new covenant? We enter into a covenant relationship with God simply by trusting in Jesus Christ and in his blood. Salvation comes by grace through faith. But we *do* get sprinkled, because the outward symbol of belonging to God by covenant is Christian baptism. Baptism is the formal act by which we become part of the covenant community. And in baptism we are sprinkled. With blood? No, because Jesus has made the one and only sacrifice for our sins. No other blood can be shed, and no other blood can be sprinkled. But God has given us the sprinkling with water in baptism as a sign of his covenant. This was promised already in the Old Testament, when God promised to send a Savior who would "sprinkle many nations" (Isaiah 52:15). Scholars debate whether the sprinkling Isaiah had in mind involved water or blood. Possibly both. Jesus saved the nations through the blood he sprinkled on the cross, and the nations are joined to God in covenant through the sprinkling of water baptism (whether by immersion, affusion, or simple sprinkling).

## The Eternal Covenant

The covenant draws us into the deepest mysteries of the Christian faith. What happened in Exodus 24 shows what it means for anyone to have a relationship with God. But it goes even deeper, because the covenant lies at the heart of the universe, right at the center of God's plan for humanity. We see this at the end of Hebrews, where Christ's blood is described as "the blood of the eternal covenant" (13:20).

What does the Scripture mean by this? What is "the blood of the eternal covenant"? The eternal covenant goes back before the beginning of time. This refers to the covenant of redemption God made among the persons of his own triune being. Somewhere in eternity past, the Father, the Son, and the Holy Spirit made a covenant for the salvation of sinners. Charles Spurgeon imagined how this may have happened. He envisioned the Father, the Son, and the Holy Spirit making their covenant. The first to speak is the Father, who vows to save a people whom he will love forever:

> I, the Most High Jehovah, do hereby give unto my only begotten and well-beloved Son, a people, countless beyond the number of the stars, who shall be by him washed from sin, by him preserved, and kept, and led, and by him, at last presented before my throne, without spot, or wrinkle, or any such thing. I covenant by oath, and swear by myself, because I can swear by no greater, that these whom I now give to Christ shall be for ever the objects of my eternal love. Them will I forgive through the merits of his blood. To these will I give a perfect righteousness; these will I adopt and make my sons and daughters, and these shall reign with me through Christ eternally.

Then it is the Holy Spirit's turn to speak. For his part, the Spirit promises to bring sinners to a knowledge of salvation:

> I hereby covenant that all whom the Father giveth to the Son, I will in due time quicken. I will show them their need of redemption; I will cut off from them all groundless hope, and destroy their refuge of lies. I will bring them to the blood of sprinkling; I will give them faith whereby this blood shall be applied to them; I will work in them every grace; I will keep their faith alive; I will cleanse them and drive out all depravity from them, and they shall be presented at last spotless and faultless.

Finally it is time for the Son of God to make his covenant commitment:

> My Father, on my part I covenant that in the fullness of time I will become man. I will take upon myself the form and nature of the fallen race. I will live in their wretched world, and for my people I will keep the law perfectly. I will work out a spotless righteousness, which shall be acceptable to the demands of thy just and holy law. In due time I will bear the sins of all my people. Thou shalt exact their debts on me; the chastisement of their peace I will endure, and by my stripes they shall be healed. My Father, I covenant and promise that I will be obedient unto death, even the death of the cross. I will magnify thy law, and make it honorable. I will suffer all they ought to have suffered. I will endure the curse of thy law, and all the vials of thy wrath shall be emptied and spent upon my head. I will then rise again; I will ascend into heaven; I will intercede for them at thy right hand; and I will make myself responsible for every one of them, that not one of those whom thou hast given me shall ever be lost, but I will bring all my sheep of whom, by thy blood, thou hast constituted me the shepherd—I will bring every one safe to thee at last.[9]

This is the covenant made from all eternity among the three persons of the Godhead. To be a proper covenant, of course, it had to be sealed in blood. And so it was! The eternal covenant was ratified with the blood of the very Son of God. When Moses sprinkled blood on the people, he said, "Behold the blood of the covenant" (24:8). But when Jesus came to offer himself on the cross, he said, "This is *my* blood of the covenant, which is poured out for many for the forgiveness of sins" (Matthew 26:28). What Jesus offered was not just *the* blood, but *his* blood—the blood of God.

Now we can see why the cross must be at the center of our salvation. It is only by the blood Jesus shed on the cross that we are able to have a covenant relationship with God. And it is by the same blood that God established his eternal covenant. When Jesus died on the cross, he sealed the deal that the Triune God made in eternity past.

The application is very simple. The only way to be saved—that is, to be forgiven, to have a right relationship with God, and ultimately to get to Heaven—is by the blood of Jesus Christ. If ever we are to be saved, we are going to have to deal with Jesus. His atoning work must be applied directly to our sins. We must be "sprinkled with the blood" (Hebrews 9:21), for it is only by trusting in the blood that he shed on the cross that anyone ever gets saved.

Everyone who believes in Jesus has the strongest reason for confidence. We do not need to be plagued with guilt, as if somehow our sin could keep us away from God. We don't need to keep our distance, as if we were unworthy to come into God's presence. God has made a relationship with us by the blood of his very own Son. Nothing could possibly establish a more certain basis for our salvation! There is no way to get *un*sprinkled. "Therefore, brothers, since we have . . . the blood of Jesus, . . . let us draw near with a true heart in full assurance of faith, with our hearts sprinkled clean from an evil conscience" (Hebrews 10:19, 22).

# 69

# They Saw God

## EXODUS 24:9–18

WHEN MY DAUGHTER KATHRYN WAS A BABY, her closest bond was with her mother, who fed her and stayed with her almost all the time. But Kathryn seemed to get the most delight from seeing her daddy. Whenever she saw me enter the room, she started babbling to get my attention. And when she caught my glance, she broke into a broad smile. Her greatest joy was to gaze into her father's eyes.

The day my daughter was baptized I realized how deeply spiritual her joy was. When I presented her in church, the minister took her in his arms and asked for her name. I said, "Kathryn," and she looked up expectantly. To me, she was the most beautiful baby in the world. Then the minister pronounced a blessing based on her name. He said, "This is Kathryn, the Greek word that means 'pure.' May our Lord fulfill his promise from Matthew 5: 'Blessed are the pure in heart, for they will see God.'"

When the minister quoted this verse, it struck a sympathetic chord in my heart. Gazing upon God is the most wonderful experience that any person could possibly have. We come into the world with a deep spiritual longing for the knowledge of God. We want to know him as he is—in a word, to see him. Our highest aspiration is to behold the person of God in the glorious face of his Son. So Kathryn was given the best of all blessings: a prayer that one day she would get to see God.

### Going Up to See God

We catch a glimpse of this blessing in Exodus 24. The chapter began with God inviting Moses to come and meet him. First the prophet confirmed God's covenant with his people. Then he climbed God's holy mountain: "Then Moses and Aaron, Nadab, and Abihu, and seventy of the elders of Israel went up, and they saw the God of Israel. There was under his feet as it were a pavement of sapphire stone, like the very heaven for clearness. And he did not lay his hand on the chief men of the people of Israel; they beheld God, and ate and drank" (vv. 9–11).

This episode—what one scholar calls a "scene of peaceful majesty and bright grandeur"[1]—is one of the most surprising in the whole Bible. It is surprising because looking at God was supposed to be fatal. Later God said to Moses, "Man shall not see me and live" (33:20). Yet here we are told—twice—that the leaders of Israel saw God and then lived to tell about it. This makes some Bible scholars uncomfortable, and there is a long history of trying to "fix" these verses to make them say something else. When the Old Testament was translated into Greek (the version known as the Septuagint), words were added to make the text read, "They saw the place where the God of Israel stood." Some ancient rabbis claimed that the elders did not see God but "the glory of God."[2] Similarly, the great medieval scholar Moses Maimonides said that seeing "must be understood as intellectual perception, but in no way as a real perceiving with the eye."[3]

The problem with trying to evade what the Bible says is that the text is perfectly clear. It simply reads, "They saw . . . God." They looked at him. They beheld him. And as John Currid writes, "The verb translated 'beheld' is not the normal Hebrew word meaning 'to see.' It is a stronger, more intense term."[4] These men fixed their gaze upon God.

The Bible is well aware of the difficulties this raises because it adds the following editorial comment: "And he did not lay his hand on the chief men of the people of Israel" (24:11). The raising of God's hand implies divine judgment through some disastrous display of supernatural power. By saying that this *didn't* happen, the Bible implies that it certainly could have happened, and would have under normal circumstances. Israel's leaders were in real danger. A visual encounter with Almighty God put them in jeopardy of sudden death. Yet the Bible indicates, almost with a sense of surprise, that they did not die. By acknowledging the danger, the Bible confirms that these men really did see God.

What, exactly, did they see? Strangely enough, the Bible does not describe their vision of God at all. Nothing is said about his divine appearance. The Bible only mentions his surroundings, especially what was under his feet. And even this was hard to put into words. Moses says it resembled "a pavement of sapphire stone" (v. 10). The Hebrew word for "pavement" refers to flooring made of brick or tile. The word "sapphire" probably means lapis lazuli, a brilliant blue stone that is usually opaque but on this occasion was as clear as the blue sky.

Why doesn't the Bible say more about what God looked like? Maybe because the elders never looked much higher than the bottom of God's feet! They seem to have become most intimately acquainted with the floor, which suggests that they fell on their faces to worship. They took one look at God and immediately they lowered their gaze. As John Durham explains it, "The group was not given permission to lift their faces toward God and so could describe only what they actually did see, the 'pavement' beneath him, before which they were prostrate in reverential awe."[5] This is the posture we should take every time we come into God's presence. He is a great God, and we bow before him in humble adoration.

Another possibility is that Moses and the elders were not on the pavement at all. Rather, they were looking up at God from somewhere underneath. This interpretation comes from comparing Exodus 24 to Ezekiel's vision of God. Ezekiel said, "There was the likeness of an expanse, shining like awe-inspiring crystal, spread out above their heads" (Ezekiel 1:22). This was probably the same pavement that Moses saw, a flawless sheet of ice-blue glass. Through it Ezekiel could see God, way above the sky:

> And above the expanse over their heads there was the likeness of a throne, in appearance like sapphire; and seated above the likeness of a throne was a likeness with a human appearance. And upward from what had the appearance of his waist I saw as it were gleaming metal, like the appearance of fire enclosed all around. And downward from what had the appearance of his waist I saw as it were the appearance of fire, and there was brightness around him. Like the appearance of the bow that is in the cloud on the day of rain, so was the appearance of the brightness all around. Such was the appearance of the likeness of the glory of the LORD. (vv. 26–28a)

Although Ezekiel provided more detail, he seems to have seen the same thing as Moses and the others. He looked up and saw a man shining with the glory of God. It was a vision of the second person of the Trinity, the preincarnate Son of God. This might explain why Moses did not say that he saw "the LORD," which would refer to the Father, but simply "God."

Like Moses, Ezekiel struggled to put what he saw into words. He kept using phrases like "as it were," "their appearance was like," and "the likeness of." What he saw could not be fully explained, even under the inspiration of the Holy Spirit. Perhaps this is why Moses did not try to describe the appearance of God. What words would be adequate to explain such a vision? Even the floor under God's feet defied description! It was the most spectacular thing any of them had ever seen. All Moses could say was that it was a "likeness," something like something else. What, then, could he say about seeing God himself? It went beyond the boundaries of human language. Keil and Delitzsch wisely give this warning: "We must not go beyond the limits drawn in [Scripture] in our conceptions of what constituted the sight . . . of God; at the same time we must regard it as a vision of God in some form of manifestation which rendered a divine nature discernible to the human eye. Nothing is said as to the form in which God manifested himself."[6] Moses and the elders of Israel were given some direct apprehension of the divine being in visible form. More than this the Bible does not say, so we should be careful not to speculate.

This is the opposite of what the ancient pagans tried to do. People like the

Canaanites and the Egyptians were always making images of God to look at, reducing him to the form of men and beasts. Sadly, in just a few short weeks the Israelites would do exactly the same thing, fashioning a god into the form of a golden calf (32). They were not content with the distant glory on the mountain; they wanted a god they could lay their eyes on. Rather than waiting for God to reveal himself, they wanted to see him right away. But this was not God's plan. God wanted to keep himself hidden from their view, as he often does.

Skeptics often say, "If only I could see God, then I would believe in him." But the skeptics have it backward. God has revealed enough of himself in his Word and in creation for us to know him and love him. But his existence still has to be taken on faith, and the gift of seeing him is only given to those who believe. When it comes to religion, people often say, "I have to see it to believe it." But God says, "You won't see it *unless* you believe it. If you believe, then you'll see! You'll see me in the person of my Son, when he comes in glory at the end of days."

Israel's elders were granted the exceptional privilege of seeing that glory in advance. God gave them a sneak preview—a glimpse of his majesty. This was to show them what it means to be saved. The events of Exodus 24 tell the story of salvation. Moses and the elders started at a distance. They were separated from God by their sin. But then God invited them to come into his presence. He gave them his word. He atoned for their sin through the blood of his covenant. Then he brought them into his presence, where they could gaze upon his glory. It was a foretaste of Heaven.

What happened to Moses and the elders is also the story of our own salvation. There was a time when we were separated from God by our sin. Like the Israelites, we were lawbreakers. But God atoned for our sin through the blood of his covenant—the blood that Jesus sprinkled on the cross. Soon he will welcome us into his glorious presence. Then the longing of our hearts will be satisfied, and we will see God face-to-face.

## Eating and Drinking

Moses and Aaron, Nadab and Abihu, and the seventy elders of Israel went up and saw God. It was the most glorious thing they had ever seen or ever would see. The famous Puritan theologian John Owen rightly described seeing God as "one of the greatest Privileges and Advancements that Believers are capable of."[7] To catch even a single glimpse of God is to behold a beauty that is dazzling beyond all imagination and perfect beyond all thought. Therefore, seeing God was all that these men could ever want. However, they were given a further privilege: "They beheld God, and ate and drank" (24:11).

The Bible does not indicate what Israel's leaders ate and drank, any more than it tells us what they saw. Perhaps they consumed what was left of the peace offerings they had sacrificed to the Lord (v. 5). Or perhaps they shared bread and water together, or maybe bread and wine. But whatever they ate and drank, it was a meal of covenant fellowship. In those days it was not uncommon for people making a covenant to sit down and share a meal together afterward. For example, when Isaac made a covenant with Abimelech and his army, he "made them a feast, and they ate and drank" (Genesis 26:30). Jacob and Laban shared the same kind of meal when they were reconciled after Jacob's escape (Genesis 31:46). Breaking bread was a symbolic act of friendship. So Israel's leaders eating and drinking on the mountain showed that they had fellowship with God.

Few things establish a greater sense of fellowship than sharing a meal. There is something about eating and drinking with other people that fosters friendship. The power of a meal to bring people together is vividly portrayed in *Babette's Feast*, a film set around a dinner table. In the film a master chef living as an exile from Paris in a small Danish fishing village spends her fortune to prepare an elaborate feast. Although her guests are generally cantankerous and unkind, the feast forms the context for the restoration of old friendships, the rekindling of old loves, and the reconciliation of old enemies. Meals have a way of bringing people together. Any gathering is more intimate when people share food. This is why it is so important for households to make the dinner table a central part of their daily routine. This is also why Thanksgiving dinner holds such a prominent place in American culture. Sharing a meal is a powerful symbol of belonging.

Consider how significant it is, therefore, that the prophet, the priests, and the elders of Israel ate and drank with God, and furthermore that this happened in the context of public worship. Remember, Exodus 24 is a covenant worship service. The service included a call to worship, the reading of God's Word, a confession of faith, and the sprinkling of sacrificial blood. Then the whole thing concluded with a sacramental meal—the sharing of food and drink that symbolized communion with God. First God invited the leaders of Israel to worship. He spoke to them through his word, and they responded in faith, promising to obey. But their obedience could never be perfect, so God provided a sacrifice for their sin. Finally, God invited Israel's representatives to sit down for a meal of covenant friendship. Atonement had been made for their sin, and now the way was clear for them to have table fellowship. They not only saw God, but they also ate and drank with him.

The theme of eating and drinking with God runs all the way through Scripture. The Bible often describes our relationship with God in terms of sharing a meal. The idea is present already in the patriarchs. The earliest example is Abraham, who welcomed a divine angel to his tents for dinner (Genesis 18). King David said, "You prepare a table before me" (Psalm 23:5a). Isaiah promised that one day God would sit down with his people at a great banquet: "On this mountain the Lord of hosts will make for all peoples a feast of rich food, a feast of well-aged wine, of rich food full of marrow, of aged wine well refined"

(Isaiah 25:6). This prophecy was about the coming of God's kingdom, when people from every nation would find a place at God's table.

Then Jesus came to be the King, and he described his kingdom in terms of eating and drinking. He said that it was like a great banquet: "Many will come from east and west and recline at table with Abraham, Isaac, and Jacob in the kingdom of heaven" (Matthew 8:11). Jesus was saying that the prophecy had come true: There is a place for everyone at his table. He is not only the King of Israel—he came to rule the world. So his covenant meal isn't just for Moses and the elders anymore, or even for the Israelites. It's for people all over the world.

God is always busy handing out invitations to his feast. Every time the gospel is preached, people are invited to eat and drink with God. God is getting ready to throw the last and longest banquet of all, what the book of Revelation calls "the marriage supper of the Lamb" (Revelation 19:9). The way to RSVP for that great banquet is to believe in Jesus Christ for salvation. One day God will welcome everyone who trusts in Jesus to sit down at the feast that will never end.

Even now the final preparations are being made. While we are waiting for the announcement that dinner is ready, God has given us a special meal to remind us that we belong to him by covenant. This meal is the sacrament of the Lord's Supper.

The worship service in Exodus 24 included the ministry of both word and sacrament. This has implications for Christian worship, and especially for our celebration of the Lord's Supper. In much the same way that sprinkling the covenant blood pointed to baptism, sharing a covenant meal pointed to Communion. Both sacraments are connected to the covenant. "For Christians, the sacraments serve as 'signs and seals of the covenant'—they are sacred ceremonies that substantiate and confirm the covenant relationship between God and his people."[8] Baptism marks our entrance into the covenant community through faith in the atoning work of Jesus Christ. The Lord's Supper marks our continuance in the covenant. We eat and drink around the table to show that we have fellowship with God. By establishing a new covenant in Christ's blood, he has welcomed us into his love.

What all the covenant feasts (Moses and the meal on God's mountain, the Lord's Supper, and the Marriage Supper of the Lamb) show us is that God wants to have a relationship with us. He invites us to sit down with him and share a meal. He offers us the kind of intimate fellowship we have with our closest family and friends when we sit down together around the dinner table.

Is this the kind of relationship that you have with God? Do you have such a close friendship that it's like sitting down to eat and drink with God? The way to have this kind of relationship with God is simply by trusting in Jesus Christ. Jesus said, "Behold, I stand at the door and knock. If anyone hears my voice and opens the door, I will come in to him and eat with him, and he with me" (Revelation 3:20). Jesus is ready and waiting to sit down with us at the table. All we need to do is invite him into our hearts.

## The Two Tablets

The Bible does not indicate how the meal on the mountain ended—whether Moses and his men had dessert, or whether they pronounced some kind of benediction, or whether their repast ended some other way. But eventually the men who saw God were finished eating and drinking with him. Some time after this, God invited his prophet alone to come even closer: "The Lord said to Moses, 'Come up to me on the mountain and wait there'" (24:12a).

Before joining Moses for his final ascent, there are several things to notice. One concerns what God intended to give Moses when he reached the summit of Mount Sinai. He said to Moses, "I [will] give you the tablets of stone, with the law and the commandment, which I have written for their instruction'" (v. 12b).

What was written on these tablets? At the beginning of this chapter Moses had told the people "all the words of the Lord and all the rules" (v. 3). As we have seen, the phrase "words . . . and . . . rules" included both the Ten Commandments and the Book of the Covenant. However, here at the end of the chapter the wording is slightly different. God speaks of his "law and the commandment" (v. 12). This refers specifically to the Ten Commandments. We know this because Moses later said, "He declared to you his covenant, which he commanded you to perform, that is, the Ten Commandments, and he wrote them on two tablets of stone" (Deuteronomy 4:13). These were the same tablets that Moses angrily dashed to the ground when he saw the Israelites dancing around the golden calf (32:19).

Later these stone tablets were rewritten (34:1, 27, 28). There were two of them, not because there wasn't enough room for the whole Decalogue on one tablet or because the Law was divided into two parts (such as love for God and love for one's neighbor), but because Israel was given two complete copies. Remember the context: God was making a covenant with his people. Since a covenant is a legally binding relationship, it needs to be written down. According to the ancient custom, two copies were prepared—one for each party.[9] In this case God allowed his people to keep both the original and the duplicate: two copies to remind the Israelites that they were bound to God by covenant.

The two tablets of the covenant were written in stone. As it says later in Exodus, there were "two tablets of the testimony, tablets of stone, written with the finger of God" (31:18). So the words on these tablets were not words that Moses put into God's mouth. Rather, they were commands that he received from God. This is important because it shows that the Law comes from God, and not from any man. Liberal scholars often attack the book of Exodus at precisely this point. They say that the Mosaic Law was collected from the wisdom of the ancient world. If this were true, then we would be free to go ahead and live any way we like. There would be no divine law for us to obey. But, of course, this line of reasoning is false. The Law comes from God, as the Bible says.

This passage tells us two different things about how the Law was written, and both of them are true. Near the beginning of the passage, the Bible says that "Moses wrote down all the words of the LORD" (24:4a)—specifically his "words . . . and . . . rules" (v. 3). Later God gave Moses what he called "the law and the commandment, which I have written for their instruction" (v. 12). There is no contradiction here. The Bible was revealed to men like Moses. What they wrote was not the product of their own invention, but "men spoke from God as they were carried along by the Holy Spirit" (2 Peter 1:21). This is precisely what we see in Exodus 24, where Moses wrote what God said, and then later God wrote part of it down again. Taken as a whole, this passage confirms the divine authority of Scripture as communicated to mortal men.

## Who's in Charge?

The prophet had one last thing to do before making his final assault on the mountain: "So Moses rose with his assistant Joshua, and Moses went up into the mountain of God. And he said to the elders, 'Wait here for us until we return to you. And behold, Aaron and Hur are with you. Whoever has a dispute, let him go to them'" (24:13, 14). Moses seems to have said this back at the base of the mountain. As we have noted before, it is hard to keep track of all his trips up and down the mountain. But apparently Moses and the elders descended after they ate and drank with God. We know from chapter 32 that Aaron at least was not up on the mountain during Moses' subsequent absence, but down with the people.

This time Moses took only one companion: Joshua, who went only partway up the mountain. Although Joshua is a minor figure in Exodus, he becomes more important when he leads Israel into the Promised Land. But this period of his life was very important. Joshua was learning valuable lessons in ministry by serving his master in practical ways. He was Moses' assistant—literally, his minister. On this occasion he served as his porter, almost like the famous Sherpas who help people climb Mount Everest. This is God's pattern for developing spiritual leadership. We learn to lead by serving at someone else's side.

One of a leader's most important tasks is delegating responsibility to others in his absence. In case there are any difficulties or disagreements, people need to know who's in charge. And the people in charge had better be trustworthy. With this in mind, when Moses went up the mountain he appointed his brother Aaron and his friend Hur to be the leaders. At the time it seemed like a good choice. After all, these men had helped defeat the Amalekites by lifting up the prophet's hands during battle (17:8–16). So Moses was leaving things in good hands, or so he thought. Unfortunately, a lot can go wrong in forty days, as Moses learned when he came back down the mountain and discovered what Aaron had decided to do in his absence.

## Farther Up and Farther In

Exodus 24 is one of the most important chapters in the whole Old Testament. It lays out the Biblical pattern for worship. It establishes God's covenant with his people on the basis of blood. It tells how God gave his law. It shows how mortal men met their Maker face-to-face . . . and lived to tell about it. But the climax comes at the end, when Moses entered into glory:

> Then Moses went up on the mountain, and the cloud covered the mountain. The glory of the LORD dwelt on Mount Sinai, and the cloud covered it six days. And on the seventh day he called to Moses out of the midst of the cloud. Now the appearance of the glory of the LORD was like a devouring fire on the top of the mountain in the sight of the people of Israel. Moses entered the cloud and went up on the mountain. And Moses was on the mountain forty days and forty nights. (vv. 15–18)

Moses had been getting closer and closer to God ever since the exodus started. He met with God at the burning bush. He spoke with God on the mountain and heard his voice from the glorious cloud. With the rest of Israel's leaders, he saw God and shared a covenant meal with him. He was the mediator, the man who represented the people before God, and now God was inviting him to enter his glory.

We have mentioned glory many times in our study of Exodus. God's glory is his reputation—the majesty of who he is and what he does. It is the weight of his divine being and the wealth of his saving grace. God's glory was revealed in everything he did to save Israel out of Egypt. It was glorious for him to remember his covenant, have compassion on Israel's suffering, plague the Egyptians, lead his people through the sea, guide them through the wilderness, and give them his law. Exodus is the story of God doing one glorious thing after another. And this was God's plan: He was saving his people for his glory. As he promised Moses near the beginning of the whole adventure, "I will get glory" (14:4).

God is always glorious. However, on special occasions he expresses his glory in visible form. To help people appreciate his awesome majesty, he reveals himself in burning, dazzling light. This is what Exodus means when it speaks of "the glory of the LORD": an outward and visible manifestation of God's inner divine beauty.

God revealed his glory many times during the exodus. He showed it to his prophet back at the burning bush. What Moses saw in those unquenchable flames taught him about God's self-existence and self-sufficiency. God revealed his glory again when the Israelites escaped from Egypt. He led them in a fiery pillar of cloud, which was another visible manifestation of his invisible glory. He revealed his glory yet again when they reached his holy mountain. God descended in fire and smoke, and "the glory of the LORD dwelt on Mount Sinai" (24:16). When the people looked up, they saw what "was like a devouring fire on the top of the mountain" (v. 17). God was there, indwelling and inhabiting the cloud of his glory. In the exodus God revealed glory upon glory.

Chapter 24 ends at the climactic moment when Moses entered God's cloud of glory. It was his unique privilege not simply to see glory or merely to admire it but actually to enter it. He was drawn closer and closer to the glory of God, until finally he was swallowed up inside. A passage in *The Last Battle* by C. S. Lewis may help us understand what happened to Moses. The book ends with the old land of Narnia passing away and all true Narnians entering the new Narnia. This is a picture of Heaven, in which the old passes away and all things become new. There is a tremendous sense of excitement as the subjects of that new and glorious kingdom begin to explore. They leap over hills and cascade down waterfalls. Each new thing they encounter is more amazing than anything they have ever seen before. They don't stop; they keep moving faster and faster. Everyone shouts, "farther up and farther in," and then they rush off to see more wonders in their new land.[10]

This was Moses' experience on Mount Sinai. He went farther up and farther in. God called him up the mountain. There the prophet saw God's glory, heard God's voice, and ate and drank with him. Then he entered into glory. He kept going farther up and farther in until finally he was enveloped by the luminous, radiant presence of God.

This is also the story of our own salvation, which Exodus 24 reveals from beginning to end. First God calls us to worship him, speaking to us by his Word. But we are separated from God by our sin. Therefore, we have to keep our distance until God provides a sacrifice of atonement through the blood of his covenant. Then, once our sins are covered, we can have fellowship with God. We can sit down to feast at his banquet. But how does the story end? It ends with our entrance into glory. This is the goal of our salvation: not just to see God and to sit down with him but to participate in his glory. What happened to Moses will happen to us: God will come down and lift us up into glory.

God has come to us in the person of his Son, Jesus Christ, who was sent to be our Savior. Jesus came down from Heaven to reveal the glory of God. The apostle John said, "We have seen his glory, glory as of the only Son from the Father, full of grace and truth. . . . No one has ever seen God; the only God, who is at the Father's side, he has made him known" (John 1:14b, 18). John was talking about Jesus, of course. His point was that Jesus reveals the glory of God in his very person. Since he was the divine Son of God, he was the full expression of God's glory. As Jesus said, "Whoever has seen me has seen the Father" (John 14:9). Like the bright cloud that settled on the mountain, Jesus came down to reveal the glory of God.

Jesus came down so that one day we could be lifted up. What happened to Moses is a picture of what will happen to everyone who comes to God through faith in Jesus Christ. Glory is in our destiny. The Bible says, "Behold, he is coming with the clouds, and every eye will see him" (Revelation 1:7a). It also says, "We who are alive . . . will be caught up together with them in the clouds to meet the Lord in the air, and so we will always be with the Lord" (1 Thessalonians 4:17). We will go farther up and farther in. Like Moses, we will be surrounded by the radiance of God's glory.

This is all so foreign to our experience that it is hard for us even to imagine. We live in a world that is inglorious—a world that for all its beauty is tragically marred by sin. In our mundane existence we are surrounded by everything trashy and tawdry. If nothing else, we continually have to live with the ugliness of our own sin. But there is something better in our destiny. We have been saved for the glory of God, and one day everyone who trusts in Jesus Christ will be lifted up into the brightness of his glory. We believe this because we have God's Word on it: "'What no eye has seen, nor ear heard, nor the heart of man imagined, what God has prepared for those who love him'—these things God has revealed to us through the Spirit" (1 Corinthians 2:9, 10).

# 70

# Freewill Offering

EXODUS 25:1–8

IN EXODUS 24 God confirmed his covenant with Israel in a public worship service. This service included a call to worship, a confession of faith, a reading from God's word, and a celebration of communion. This was all done in the glorious presence of God, on the basis of a blood covenant. It was a complete worship service. Virtually the only thing the Israelites didn't do was take an offering! However, this omission gets rectified in chapter 25. Moses went up God's mountain, where he waited six days for God to tell him what to do next. Then on the seventh day, when the prophet entered into glory, God spoke to him. The first thing he told Moses to do was to collect an offering for the tabernacle, the holy sanctuary where God would dwell with his people. To put it in contemporary terms, it was time to pass the plate.

Giving to God is an important sign of our commitment to Christ. Our willingness to give back some of what we own is one of the leading indicators of our spiritual health. Generosity is one of the vital signs of real Christianity, and a Christian who isn't giving probably isn't growing. How unfortunate, then, that today there is so little sound teaching on stewardship.

Some ministers are obsessed with money. They spend all their time talking about it. One thinks of the televangelists who preach the prosperity gospel. They seem unable to talk for more than five minutes without mentioning how important it is to support their ministry financially. Once I watched a minister who was desperate for pledges say to his television audience, "Just pick up the [profanity deleted] phone and call!"

On the other hand, some Christians are too embarrassed to talk about money at all. They view their finances as a private matter—it's none of the church's business. One minister received the following letter: "I was never so disappointed in a service as I was Sunday. I have an unbelieving friend that I got to come with me, and what were you preaching about? *Money!* I can assure you she was not impressed! And why money, when there are so many beautiful things to say? You'd better reconsider such messages in the future. Leave money to God, and he will handle everything, believe me. I love this church and usually like the sermons, but that was terrible." The letter was signed, "A Christian who loves to go to church to hear the Word."[1]

Well, sooner or later anyone who wants to hear God's Word will hear a sermon on giving, because it's an important Biblical theme. More than four hundred Bible passages talk specifically about money, as well as many others that teach general principles for Christian stewardship. Exodus 25 is one of those passages. The instructions God gave to Moses teach us to give our very best to God—from the heart—for his holy work.

## Giving to God

An offering is something we give to God: "The LORD said to Moses, 'Speak to the people of Israel, that they take for me a contribution'" (25:1, 2a). The people were not giving to enrich Moses. Their offerings were not for the personal benefit of Aaron and the other priests or for the elders. This offering was for God. It was an act of holy worship. Whatever the people brought was for the glory of God.

Christians sometimes speak of giving "to the church." Talking this way makes a certain amount of sense. Most of our giving does indeed go to the church. When we put money in the offering plate, we usually do it in church. And when we write a check, we normally make it out in the church's name. But what we are really doing is giving part of what we own back to God. God has commissioned the church to do his work in the world. So when we give to the church, we are really giving to God. This explains why we collect an offering during the worship service. Giving to God is an act of worship. We're not handing over the price of admission or paying our dues; we're offering something to God as an expression of our adoration and praise. As the Scripture says, "Ascribe to the LORD the glory due his name; bring an offering, and come into his courts!" (Psalm 96:8).

Bringing an offering is one of the best ways that we can do something for God. What is remarkable is that God is willing to receive our offerings as an act of worship. Everything we have belongs to him already, and he would be well within his rights to take it back. Instead God allows us to offer it to him as an act of worship. It's like a father who gives his children money to buy him a birthday present. When he opens the gift, he is getting back his own. But the giving of the gift is significant for their relationship. It's not about the money or where it came from—it's about the affection that the children have for their father. So a wise father gives his children the wherewithal to show him their love in a tangible way.

God does the same thing with his children. If he had wanted to, God could have performed a miracle and sent his people a whole tabernacle, ready-built.

Instead he gave them an opportunity to contribute to its construction. This is the way God usually works: He gives us an opportunity to participate. Although we can never repay him, we can offer ourselves for his service. Note that all of the things the Israelites brought were things they had received from God. They brought gold, silver, and precious gems—the plunder God provided at the expense of the Egyptians (see 12:35, 36). They brought wood from trees God planted on the earth. They brought cloth that came from animals he put in their flocks. There was nothing they could bring that did not come from God to begin with. This was a nation of slaves, a people without money or power. Unless God gave them something to bring, they would have nothing to offer. But out of the riches of his grace, he provided something for them to give.

The same is true of everything we offer to God. God has given us the resources to respond to his grace. Whenever we bring an offering we are simply giving back to God part of what he has given to us. As it says in one of the old hymns, "We give thee but thine own, whate'er the gift may be; all that we have is thine alone, a trust, O Lord, from thee."[2]

## Straight from the Heart

Whatever we give to God should come from the heart. God did not impose a tax on the Israelites, something they had to pay whether they liked it or not. This was a freewill offering. God said, "From every man whose heart moves him you shall receive the contribution for me" (25:2b). Their contributions were not compulsory but voluntary. John Currid explains it like this: "God makes giving to the building of the tabernacle a voluntary gesture! He does not demand, or command, how much a person is to give, or even that a person must give. He leaves it to the heart of the individual member of the covenant community."[3]

This is why an offering is called an *offering*! It's not something God takes from us, but something we freely give. As Paul told the Corinthians, "Each one must give as he has decided in his heart, not reluctantly or under compulsion, for God loves a cheerful giver" (2 Corinthians 9:7). The apostle was saying the same thing that Moses said and that God says to us now. Giving comes from the heart. We should never give grudgingly but always joyfully. And how much we give should not be based on a requirement imposed by others, but from the overflow of our hearts. What is more important to God than the amount we give is our attitude in giving it.

There were some times when God *did* specify the amount his people should give. This was known as tithing, which literally means to give one tenth. For example, when the Israelites entered the Promised Land they were required to give 10 percent of their gross produce back to God. The Law said, "Every tithe of the land, whether of the seed of the land or of the fruit of the trees, is the LORD's; it is holy to the LORD" (Leviticus 27:30). This tithe was used to support the Levites, who did not have any land of their own but were scattered around the country. A second tithe went to support temple worship in Jerusalem (Deuteronomy 12:17ff.). God expected his people to give regularly and faithfully to his worship and work. Also special occasions—such as the building of the tabernacle—called for special offerings.

We follow the same general pattern in the church today. The New Testament does not specify a tithe or any other amount that Christians ought to give. Nevertheless, many Christians find that 10 percent serves as a useful guideline. Since it's a percentage, it varies according to our income, and thus can help guide our giving whether we are rich or poor. Christians who are not tithing should rearrange their finances and ask God to enable them to give at least 10 percent of their gross income to Christian work as soon as possible. Christians who are tithing should pray that God will allow them to give even more as they grow in the grace of generosity.

No matter how much we give, the Bible encourages us to follow a regular plan for giving. Paul counseled the Corinthians, "On the first day of every week, each of you is to put something aside and store it up, as he may prosper" (1 Corinthians 16:2). Since tithes are part of our worship, it makes sense that we should bring them to God every week. Beyond that, we should look for special opportunities to give to God, like the Israelites did when God told them to build a tabernacle. We should give God as much as we can as often as we can.

## Giving Out of Gratitude

Freewill offerings raise an obvious question. If God does not impose a tax, how will his kingdom ever get enough money? By way of comparison, imagine how much trouble the IRS would have if paying federal income tax were strictly voluntary! If how much we give is up to us, how will the church get what it needs to do God's work?

The answer is that when our hearts are touched by God's grace, we feel compelled to give. What God said to Moses is significant: "From every man whose heart moves him you shall receive the contribution for me" (25:2b). The word "moves" is hardly strong enough to convey the meaning. More literally, Moses was to collect an offering from "every man 'whose heart makes him vow.'"[4] Those who gave felt *compelled* to give. Something had happened in their hearts that bound them to be generous.

What had happened, of course, was that they had been saved by grace. God had rescued them from slavery. He had showered them with treasure. He had delivered them from their enemies. He had led them through the wilderness. He had provided water to drink and food to eat. He had given them his law and shown them his glory. He had provided atonement for their sins through the blood of his covenant. Out of the rich abundance of his grace, he had done everything necessary for their salvation. And when they reflected on what God had done, their hearts swelled with gratitude. They were compelled by grace to give something back to God.

Their example helps us know how to respond when we have an opportunity to give to Christian work. Every time a ministry asks for financial help, we have a choice to make: Will we give or not? Usually our decision is based on how much money we have and how committed we are to the ministry. But it should also be based on our experience of God's grace. We should consider what God has done for us.

And what *has* God done for us? He has met our needs for food and shelter. He has given us his Word. Best of all, he has offered his Son to be our Savior. The Bible says, "In him we have redemption through his blood, the forgiveness of our trespasses, according to the riches of his grace, which he lavished upon us, in all wisdom and insight" (Ephesians 1:7, 8). This is the generosity of God's grace—grace that compels our gratitude. If God has done all this for us, what can we do for him? The least we can do is offer back to him a portion of what we have. If we do this from the heart, which is the center of our entire being, we are really offering our whole selves to God.

There is a wonderful example of generous giving in the New Testament. When poor Christians in Macedonia heard that the church in Jerusalem was in need, they sent an offering to help. Paul described it like this: "In a severe test of affliction, their abundance of joy and their extreme poverty have overflowed in a wealth of generosity on their part. For they gave according to their means, as I can testify, and beyond their means, of their own accord, begging us earnestly for the favor of taking part in the relief of the saints" (2 Corinthians 8:2–4). The Macedonians gave because their hearts had been touched by the grace of God.

Is giving to God something we ought to do? Of course it is, but duty aside, we *want* to bring an offering. There is something about giving to God that makes the heart sing. Furthermore, it is the best use of our money that we can possibly make. Of course, there are some other things we need. But the best investment is one that will last for eternity, and nothing else we buy can accomplish this goal. What we pay for housing, what we use for food and clothing, what we spend on entertainment, even what we invest for education or retirement—none of these things will last. But Jesus said, "Sell your possessions, and give to the needy. Provide yourselves with moneybags that do not grow old, with a treasure in the heavens that does not fail, where no thief approaches and no moth destroys. For where your treasure is, there will your heart be also" (Luke 12:33, 34). And where our hearts are, that is where we will put our treasure.

If all this is true—as we know it is—then why do we spend so much money on other things? Why do we shortchange God? It is because our hearts are hard. Often the choice is between spending money on ourselves or using it for God. One woman unexpectedly gave a large sum of money to her church—a tithe from her inheritance. But her decision to give did not come easy. After her death, someone found the following entry in her diary next to the date she made her contribution: "Quick, quick, before my heart gets hard!"[5]

The woman obviously faced the temptation we all face—namely, to keep what we have to ourselves. This is a matter of the heart. Anytime we have the impulse to give, we should obey it. The impulse comes from the Holy Spirit, who is trying to teach us to be more generous. We should give as much as we can, as soon as we can, with the hope that someday soon we will be able to give even more. This is an excellent way to test our spiritual progress, because what we do with our money shows where our priorities lie. Am I becoming more generous? If not, it is a sign of my spiritual poverty.

## Giving Our Very Best

Whenever we give something to God, we should bring him the best we have to offer. This is what giving from the heart means. When we put our heart into something, we give it our best effort. And when it comes to giving, this means offering God our very best.

God had a long list of items he wanted: "And this is the contribution that you shall receive from them: gold, silver, and bronze, blue and purple and scarlet yarns and fine twined linen, goats' hair, tanned rams' skins, goatskins, acacia wood, oil for the lamps, spices for the anointing oil and for the fragrant incense, onyx stones, and stones for setting, for the ephod and for the breastpiece" (25:3–7). This list sounds like the notices that sometimes appear in church bulletins the month before Vacation Bible School: "The VBS needs the following items for craft time." However, this was no ordinary craft. God had a major project in mind: a tabernacle to serve as his holy dwelling. The tabernacle was a portable structure—a giant tent—that represented God's presence with his people.

The construction of the tabernacle dominates the last sixteen chapters of Exodus. The first step was to take up a collection. All the items listed at the beginning of chapter 25 were needed: animal skins for the tent and the fence around it, wood for the poles, fabric for the curtains, gemstones for the priestly vestments, and precious metals for the holy objects used in worship.

Many of these items were costly. God told his people to bring the gold, silver, and bronze that they had plundered from the Egyptians (11:2). The colored fabrics they brought were nearly as valuable. "The first stuff," writes Umberto Cassuto, "is . . . wool dyed the colour of . . . a dye extracted from a species of shell-fish found in abundance in the sea, by the coasts of the Mediterranean, and especially by the shores of Phoenicia and the Land of Israel. The dyers used to prise open the shell-fish whilst they were still alive, and the transparent liquid secreted from their glands acquired in sunlight a *deep violet* colour."[6] It took thousands of shells to collect enough dye for even a single robe, and thus the process was extremely expensive.[7] The other yarns—the purple and the scarlet, which was collected from a type of worm—were less costly, but no less opulent.

The Israelites also brought fine linen (an Egyptian specialty), as well as expensive spices and perfumes. Then there were the gemstones that studded the robes of the high priest (cf. 28:17–20). These materials were not everyday items; they were treasures. The Israelites brought their finest and rarest possessions to build a sanctuary that was good enough for God, who always deserves our very best.

Not everyone had pure gold, fine linen, and precious gems to contribute. Happily, some of the items God needed were less expensive. The Israelites could bring olive oil for lighting sacred lamps. Or they could offer the strong hides of the sea cows (dugongs) that swam in the Red Sea. God also accepted acacia wood—a hard, durable wood that was perfect for a portable structure. If a poor man's heart prompted him to give, all he had to do was to go out and cut down one of the trees that was common to that region. Or he could bring goat hair and ram skins from his flock. As Petrus Dathenus comments, "In the construction of the tabernacle of the Lord, the poor people who donated goat skins or hair were as welcome to God as those who donated gold, silver or gems."[8]

Everyone in Israel was invited to give. The important thing was for people to bring the most valuable thing they had, whatever that happened to be. If they had gold, then they needed to bring gold. Some people didn't have very much gold, so it was up to the people who did to bring it. Otherwise, there wouldn't be any gold for God's tabernacle. But if all people had was goat hair and olive oil, then God would accept that, because that was the best they had to offer.

This was an extraordinary opportunity. God was building a home for his glory, and the Israelites had a chance to participate. Theirs was the high privilege of offering the gifts that went into the tabernacle. What would you have given? What contribution would you have made? No doubt you would have offered whatever you could. If so, then you should do the same thing today. Every time we go to church we have an opportunity to give something to God. We can make a donation to support the work of the local church. We can contribute to the worldwide work of missions. We can give to the poor and needy. When the offering is collected, we should give whatever we can.

Rich Christians who give large quantities of their wealth to Christian work make an extraordinary difference for Christ. This is why God has made them rich—so his servants would have the resources they need to spread the gospel. If we have gold we should give it, because not everyone does, and we need to give God the best that we have to offer. But what poor Christians give is equally valuable. This is why God has always had spiritual leaders collect offerings from all his people. When we do our giving together, we can give far more than any one person is able to give. Whether our gifts happen to be large or small, they glorify God, who deserves the best we have to offer.

## Giving for God's Holy Work

God does not hoard what we give him but employs it for some spiritual purpose. When we give our best to God—from the heart—he uses it to do his holy work.

The Israelites contributed to the holy work of building God's tabernacle. God said to Moses, "And let them make me a sanctuary, that I may dwell in their midst" (25:8). The chapters that follow describe the structure and symbolism of this sacred space in careful detail. For now it is sufficient to say that the tabernacle was a portable sanctuary representing God's presence with his people. Basically it was a giant tent. Since the tabernacle was similar to the tents they lived in, it showed how close God was. This was the blessing of the covenant: God was with his people, and they were with their God. At the same time, since the tabernacle was so elaborate, it reminded them that God was separated from them by his holy majesty.

These two aspects of God's relationship with his people—his closeness and his holiness (or to use more technical terms, his immanence and transcendence)—are reflected in two names God gave the structure. First he called it "a sanctuary" (25:8, *miqdash*). This means "holy place," or more literally, "separated place"—a place set apart for sacred use. God's dwelling was set apart from the community to show that he is holy. Next God called it a "tabernacle" (v. 9, *mishkan*), a term that means "dwelling place." This did not mean that God lived within the four walls of a tent, as if he had physical limitations. God is infinite in his omnipresence. Not even the universe can contain him! As God said through his prophet Isaiah,

> Heaven is my throne,
>     and the earth is my footstool;
> what is the house that you would build for me,
>     and what is the place of my rest? (Isaiah 66:1)

Nevertheless, God promised to be present with his people in a special way—not for his benefit, but for theirs. And to make his presence known, he told them to build a tabernacle. To summarize,

> When they looked at the Tabernacle in the Wilderness, the Israelites saw a movable structure like their own tent dwellings, which pointed to the nearness of God. But at the same time they were aware that God's tent was something far more costly and grand than their own. The precious metals used in its construction, the gorgeous colours of the hangings and draperies, the careful attention to the symmetry of the various items in the Tabernacle and in its whole layout, the beautiful and splendid clothing of the high priest—all pointed to the majesty and glory of the God who was pleased to dwell with them.[9]

The Israelites were called to the holy task of building a dwelling place for

God. They first participated by bringing their offerings. When God said, "You shall receive the contribution" (v. 2), it is clear that he was not speaking to Moses alone because the word "you" occurs in the plural. This indicates that Moses was joined by Israel's elders in receiving the offering and then disbursing it as the tabernacle was built. It was a communal offering used to do a common work.

What holy work has God given us to do, and how can we contribute? The construction of the tabernacle has some obvious implications for church building projects. Of course, God does not live in a local church. Today our property has a different purpose. God does not descend in a cloud of glory every time a church dedicates a building. However, a church *is* God's house in the sense that God meets his people there in worship. It is the place where God's people gather to hear God's Word. It is where we meet for fellowship. A church building is also useful for ministry, providing a base for reaching out into the surrounding community.

If church buildings are used for such holy work, then God's people should bring offerings to support them. Some Christians think that building funds are unspiritual. They say, for example, that the money could better be spent on missions. But a building that provides a place for preaching, worship, and ministry is part of God's holy work. And we participate in his work by giving.

Sometime around the year 2000, the trustees at Tenth Presbyterian Church in Philadelphia began to recognize the need for a new roof. The old roof, which was made of copper sometime in the late 1800s and was built to last a hundred years, was finally starting to wear out. Various solutions were proposed, including some temporary measures to patch the roof. But the leadership of the church agreed that the right thing to do (if at all possible) was to install a roof that would last another century.

Churches always face hard choices about priorities. Certainly it is sensible to do things as economically as possible. However, the cheap solution often turns out to be poor stewardship in the long run. It can also be a poor testimony. Christians should be exemplary in the care of their property. This is part of being a good neighbor. A church that takes poor care of its property brings dishonor to Christ. According to the resources that God provides, we should aspire to build beautiful buildings and keep them well maintained.

There are other ways to participate in God's work by giving as well. Some of our tithes and offerings support the local church. They provide for the pastor who preaches God's Word. They pay for the staff who teach, provide spiritual care, lead ministries, and help meet people's practical needs. Our giving also supports the worldwide work of missions. It funds evangelists to preach the gospel, pastors to plant churches, teachers to witness to their students, and doctors to heal physical and spiritual wounds.

We participate in this holy work by doing what the Israelites did. We place our offerings in the hands of our spiritual leaders to be used for spiritual work.

And we do it for this reason: so that God will come and live in people's hearts. The Bible says that in Christ "you also are being built together into a dwelling place for God by the Spirit" (Ephesians 2:22). As amazing as the tabernacle was, God is doing something much more amazing through his church. Back in the days of Moses, God came down to dwell with his people. But today, by the life-transforming presence of the Holy Spirit, he dwells *in* his people. "Do you not know that you are God's temple and that God's Spirit dwells in you?" (1 Corinthians 3:16). Whenever someone comes to faith in Jesus Christ, the holy presence of God comes right inside.

Earlier I asked what you would have given to build the tabernacle. Now consider this question: What would you give to have God descend and dwell in the hearts of lost and dying sinners? Jesus gave his very life. Since eternity past, God the Son had enjoyed all the glories of Heaven. But he gave it all up by coming into the world, becoming a man, and finally dying on the cross. And he did it for this reason: to live in us. After he was raised from the dead, Jesus sent his Holy Spirit to make a dwelling place for God in our hearts. We help complete this work by spreading the gospel. We preach Jesus Christ as the Savior who died on the cross for sinners and the Lord who rose from the dead. When people believe in Jesus, God the Holy Spirit comes to live in them forever. This is why we bring our offerings. This is why we support the ministry of God's Word through the local church and give to the global work of the gospel. It is so the living God will dwell in people's hearts through faith (cf. Ephesians 3:17). What will you give to accomplish this?

## Pennies for God

A wonderful story about what happens when we give our very best for God's holy work comes from the city of Philadelphia. In 1886 a little girl named Hattie May Wiatt was sitting outside Grace Baptist Church on Broad Street. She was crying because the church was already filled to capacity; there was no way for her to get in. The preaching of the pastor—Dr. Russell H. Conwell—was so renowned that the little church was packed every week.

When Dr. Conwell arrived at the church that morning, he recognized Hattie May's problem, lifted her up onto his shoulders, carried her inside, put her down on the platform, and told her she could sit there during the service. That day Dr. Conwell told his congregation that he hoped someday they could build a new church. Hattie May took him seriously and began saving her pennies. Sadly, in the providence of God, she became ill and died just a few months later. After the little girl's funeral, her parents came to Dr. Conwell, handed him fifty-seven pennies, and told him they were for the new church. It was the first contribution to the building fund.

At the time there were no serious plans for a new building; it was simply a possibility for the future. But when Dr. Conwell told the church's trustees what had happened, they decided it was time to buy some property. They found a lot on Broad Street and began to negotiate. The owner was not a Christian, but when he heard about Hattie May Wiatt, he agreed to take her fifty-seven cents as the down payment and to let the balance stand on a 5 percent mortgage. It was a generous offer, but the congregation did the trustees one better. When they heard about Hattie May and her pennies, they raised the full amount for the land and presented it to their pastor as a gift. Within a few years Philadelphia's famous Baptist Temple was built.

The best thing about this story is not the building itself, but what it was used for. In Dr. Conwell's own words, "The mission of the church is to save the souls of men. That is its true mission. . . . We are here to save the souls of dying sinners; we are here for no other purpose."[10] Dr. Conwell was right: The purpose of the church is to save dying sinners by preaching the death and resurrection of Jesus Christ. We are sinners saved by grace, and our hearts compel us to give our very best for this holy work.

# 71

# The Ark of the Covenant

## EXODUS 25:9–22

DOWN THROUGH THE MILLENNIA human beings have constructed many remarkable buildings. One thinks of the Great Pyramids, the palace at Machu Picchu, the Parthenon, the Taj Mahal, the World Trade Center. But the most important structure ever built was the tabernacle of God.

The tabernacle was not very large. The whole thing would have fit inside any decent-sized church building. Nor was it especially ornate. Although it was beautiful, it was not dazzling. Nevertheless, the tabernacle was the only building ever designed by Almighty God and constructed according to his plan. Furthermore, it was laid out in such a way as to teach the way of salvation. M. R. DeHaan writes:

> The only building ever constructed upon this earth which was perfect from its very beginning and outset in every detail, and never again needed attention, addition or alteration, was the tabernacle in the wilderness. The blueprint, the pattern and the plan, the design, and all of its specifications, were minutely made in heaven, committed unto Moses for the children of Israel, while he was in the mountain, shortly after their deliverance from Egypt. Every single detail was designed by Almighty God, every part had a prophetic, redemptive, and typical significance. There is no portion of Scripture richer in meaning, more perfect in its teaching of the plan of redemption, than this divinely designed building. God Himself was the architect, and every detail points to some aspect of the character and work of the person of His Son, Jesus Christ, and, in its complete form, it is probably the most comprehensive, detailed revelation of Jesus the Son of God, and the plan of salvation in the entire Old Testament.[1]

## God's Blueprint

A building always starts with a plan, and the tabernacle was no exception. God said to Moses, "Exactly as I show you concerning the pattern of the tabernacle, and of all its furniture, so you shall make it" (25:9). If Moses was going to build something for God, it had to be done right, down to the last detail. So God showed Moses his plans, possibly in the form of some kind of blueprint. However, the word "pattern" suggests something more like a three-dimensional model. God revealed the prototype for the tabernacle, so Moses could build a full-scale replica.

This didn't happen overnight; it took some time. Commentators have long observed that whereas it took God only six days to create the world, it took him forty days to explain how to build the tabernacle![2] Obviously God wanted his holy dwelling to be put together exactly the way it was designed. He said to Moses, "See that you make everything according to the pattern that was shown you on the mountain" (Hebrews 8:5). The reason God was so attentive to detail was that this building was designed to teach something about his character and about what it means to have a relationship with him. Furthermore, the tabernacle was used for his holy worship, and God always has the right to determine exactly how he wants to be worshipped.

The tabernacle was a tent approximately fifteen feet wide by forty-five feet long. It was surrounded by a tall fence enclosing an area of a little more than 10,000 square feet. In the courtyard outside the tabernacle stood a bronze altar for making sacrifices and a large basin for ceremonial cleansing. The tabernacle was divided into two rooms. The outer room, which was called "the Holy Place," was furnished with a golden lampstand, an altar for incense, and a table of bread. The inner room was called "the Most Holy Place" or "the Holy of Holies." This was the sacred space that housed the ark of the covenant.

The general meaning of the tabernacle is fairly obvious: God was coming to live with his people. As they wandered through the wilderness, they were not alone. God was with them on their way to the Promised Land. He said to Moses, "And let them make me a sanctuary, that I may dwell in their midst" (25:8). This fulfilled the promise of the covenant, in which God declared that he would be with his people to be their God. What better way to show that he was with them than to pitch his tent right in the middle of their camp. If the Israelites ever wondered whether God was still with them, all they had to do was look over and see his campsite. Thus the tabernacle was their way of connecting with God. It represented his presence at the center of their community. And whenever they moved, God moved with them. In the words of Tremper Longman, the tabernacle was "sacred space for the long haul."[3]

The question to ask as we study the tabernacle is, how can *we* connect with God? What does it take for us to get close to him? The Israelites met God at the tabernacle, but how can we gain access to God? The answer is that he has come to live with us in the person of his Son, Jesus Christ. This was the purpose of his incarnation. According to the Gospel of John, "The Word became flesh and dwelt among us" (John 1:14a).

The word John uses for "dwelt" is central to our whole understanding of Exodus. It is the Greek word for tabernacle (*skene*). Thus the Bible makes an explicit connection between the tabernacle in Exodus and the coming of Christ. Jesus Christ is the tabernacle of God. God gave us his Son, just as he gave Israel the tabernacle, so that he could come and live with us. Only this time he didn't just pitch his tent—he took on our own flesh and blood! The old tabernacle was a visual aid to show what kind of relationship God wants to have with his people. But the greater reality is the person of Jesus Christ, who gives us direct access to God. The way to meet with God is to believe in his Son Jesus Christ.

## Building the Ark

The first piece of furniture God told Moses to build was the ark of the covenant. Why did the ark come first? Out of all the things that went inside the tabernacle, why begin with the ark? And why start with a piece of furniture rather than the tent itself?

The answer is that the ark of the covenant was the most important thing in the whole tabernacle. It was the exact place where God descended to dwell with his people, which of course was the purpose of the building. The very center of God's presence was the ark of the covenant, which was located in the Holy of Holies—the innermost tent in the tabernacle. By starting with the ark, God was working from the inside out. He was also putting first things first, beginning with the holy place for his dwelling.

God not only told Moses what to build, but he also told him how to build it, giving technical specifications for assembling the ark:

> They shall make an ark of acacia wood. Two cubits and a half shall be its length, a cubit and a half its breadth, and a cubit and a half its height. You shall overlay it with pure gold, inside and outside shall you overlay it, and you shall make on it a molding of gold around it. You shall cast four rings of gold for it and put them on its four feet, two rings on the one side of it, and two rings on the other side of it. You shall make poles of acacia wood and overlay them with gold. And you shall put the poles into the rings on the sides of the ark to carry the ark by them. The poles shall remain in the rings of the ark; they shall not be taken from it. (25:10–15)

Sometimes the ark of the covenant is compared to Noah's ark (Genesis 6:14), or even to the little ark or basket that saved baby Moses from drowning (2:3). However, the Hebrew word used in those passages is not the one used here; there is no linguistic connection. Basically, the ark of the covenant was a plain wooden box that measured two and a half by one and a half by one and a half cubits. A cubit was a general unit of measure in the ancient world. It was the distance between a man's elbow and the tip of his fingers—somewhere between fifteen and twenty inches, or about a foot and a half. So the ark was an ordinary rectangular box, a little smaller than four feet by three feet.

Although the ark's basic design was simple, it had some ornamentation. There was molding around the top. The whole thing was also covered with gold fit for a king: pure gold refined to remove any impurities. Perhaps this royal covering came in thin sheets of gold leaf that were pressed into the wood. More likely the ark was covered with thick golden plates that were nailed into place in the Egyptian fashion.[4] Then at the bottom of the ark were four feet (not "corners," as some translations have it) to keep it from resting directly on the ground. Gold rings were soldered to these feet—two on each side of the ark. These rings were for the poles used to move the ark, one on each side. Whenever the Israelites were on the move, the priests lifted the poles onto their shoulders and carried the ark.

These poles were never to be removed (25:15). This may seem like a minor detail, but like all the details surrounding the tabernacle, it was important. Some of the other furnishings also had carrying poles, but only the ones for the ark were permanent. The reason was very simple: To touch the ark was to die. Remember, the ark represented the holy presence of God. It was sacred, not because it was some kind of magic box (as in the movie *Raiders of the Lost Ark*, starring Harrison Ford as Indiana Jones), but because it was the place where God was. In order to teach his people to revere his majesty, God had designated the ark as the special place of his earthly presence. Therefore, it was not to be touched! When it needed to be moved, the priests were supposed to use the poles, being very careful not to touch the ark itself. Therefore, the poles needed to stay in place all the time.

To see how serious God was about these regulations, we only need to consider the tragic death of Uzzah, the man who touched the ark. King David had decided to bring the ark up to Jerusalem. Rather than carrying it properly—on their shoulders—the priests had loaded the ark onto an ox cart: "And when they came to the threshing floor of Nacon, Uzzah put out his hand to the ark of God and took hold of it, for the oxen stumbled. And the anger of the Lord was kindled against Uzzah, and God struck him down there because of his error, and he died there beside the ark of God" (2 Samuel 6:6, 7; cf. 1 Chronicles 13:9, 10).

The shocking story of Uzzah's sudden death shows how holy the ark was, and thus it teaches us not to trifle with the holy things of God. Everything associated with God is holy: his name, his Word, and his worship. We must be very careful not to treat such holy things carelessly. We are in the presence of God. We should honor his name. We should hear his Word. We should revere his worship.

We should also remember that we ourselves are called to be holy. The Bible says, "Or do you not know that your body is a temple of the Holy Spirit within you, whom you have from God? You are not your own, for you were bought with a price. So glorify God in your body" (1 Corinthians 6:19, 20). In the context, the Bible is referring specifically to sexual immorality, which violates the sanctity of God's Spirit within us. But the principle applies to any sin we commit with our bodies. By the indwelling presence of the Holy Spirit, our bodies have become holy sanctuaries—tabernacles for God. To use them for any sinful purpose is to desecrate God's holy presence within us.

## The Cherubim and the Testimony

There was something that went inside the ark of the covenant and also something on top of it. So having told Moses how to build this box, God proceeded to give instructions for what to put into it and how to make the lid:

> And you shall put into the ark the testimony that I shall give you. You shall make a mercy seat of pure gold. Two cubits and a half shall be its length, and a cubit and a half its breadth. And you shall make two cherubim of gold; of hammered work shall you make them, on the two ends of the mercy seat. Make one cherub on the one end, and one cherub on the other end. Of one piece with the mercy seat shall you make the cherubim on its two ends. The cherubim shall spread out their wings above, overshadowing the mercy seat with their wings, their faces one to another; toward the mercy seat shall the faces of the cherubim be. And you shall put the mercy seat on the top of the ark, and in the ark you shall put the testimony that I shall give you. There I will meet with you, and from above the mercy seat, from between the two cherubim that are on the ark of the testimony, I will speak with you about all that I will give you in commandment for the people of Israel. (25:16–22)

Cherubim are special angels mentioned almost one hundred times in the Old Testament. They are first mentioned in Genesis 3, where they were charged with guarding the way to the tree of life. This seems to show their function. Unlike some of the other angels, the cherubim are not messengers but remain in God's presence to deny access by anything unholy. They are the palace guards for the King of kings—"guardians of the sacred and throne attendants of the Almighty."[5]

Today cherubs are usually rendered as chubby little creatures with jolly faces. But this is not the way the Bible portrays them. Cherubim are serious angels, which is only appropriate for supernatural beings who live in the holy presence of God. The prophet Ezekiel described them like this:

> And from the midst of it came the likeness of four living creatures. And this was their appearance: they had a human likeness, but each had four faces,

> and each of them had four wings. Their legs were straight, and the soles of their feet were like the sole of a calf's foot. And they sparkled like burnished bronze. Under their wings on their four sides they had human hands. And the four had their faces and their wings thus: their wings touched one another. Each one of them went straight forward, without turning as they went. As for the likeness of their faces, each had a human face. The four had the face of a lion on the right side, the four had the face of an ox on the left side, and the four had the face of an eagle. Such were their faces. And their wings were spread out above. Each creature had two wings, each of which touched the wing of another, while two covered their bodies. . . . As for the likeness of the living creatures, their appearance was like burning coals of fire, like the appearance of torches moving to and fro among the living creatures. And the fire was bright, and out of the fire went forth lightning. (Ezekiel 1:5–11, 13)

Later Ezekiel says, "These were the living creatures that I saw underneath the God of Israel . . . and I knew that they were cherubim" (Ezekiel 10:20).

Ezekiel's vision helps us understand the ark of the covenant. Some scholars say the Israelites borrowed their cherubim from other ancient symbols, like Egypt's Giant Sphinx, which was part man and part beast. But cherubim are *not* imaginary creatures. If Heaven were to open so that we could see God on his glorious throne today, we would see him enthroned above the cherubim. The psalmist wrote, "The Lord reigns; let the peoples tremble! He sits enthroned upon the cherubim" (Psalm 99:1; cf. 80:1; Revelation 11:19). Similarly, King Hezekiah prayed, "O Lord, the God of Israel, enthroned above the cherubim, you are the God, you alone, of all the kingdoms of the earth" (2 Kings 19:15). This is one of God's holy titles: he is the one who sits enthroned between the cherubim.

This means that the ark of the covenant was an earthly symbol of a heavenly reality. Its cover was a three-dimensional picture of a scene from Heaven, where God is surrounded by his holy angels. The cherubim on the ark represented the burning angels beneath God's throne. They were not borrowed from some other culture but were revealed by Almighty God. God seems not to have told Moses exactly what they looked like, except that they had faces and wings, which they spread protectively over the ark. Above these cherubim—whom Hebrews calls "the cherubim of glory" (Hebrews 9:5a)—was the holy presence of God. No doubt this explains why the cherubim lowered their gaze, looking down on the ark rather than up to God. They were bowing in God's presence to worship him with reverence and awe.

The space above the cherubim was empty. God did not tell Moses to make any representation of his divine being. Any such representation would have been a graven image, an idol of a false god. Instead the space between the cherubim was left empty, only to be filled with the living presence of God.

This is where Moses met with God and received his commands. Another name for the tabernacle was "the tent of meeting" (see 29:42; 30:36). The specific place where Moses went to meet with God was the ark of the covenant in the Holy of Holies. There, between the cherubim, was the glorious presence of God. The Bible says, "And when Moses went into the tent of meeting to speak with the Lord, he heard the voice speaking to him from above the mercy seat that was on the ark of the testimony, from between the two cherubim; and it spoke to him" (Numbers 7:89). This is what the tabernacle was all about: gaining access to God, who sits enthroned above the cherubim.

There was also something under the cherubim. Inside the ark Moses deposited "the testimony"—that is to say, the two tablets containing the words of the Ten Commandments (see 31:18). This explains why the ark was called "the ark of the covenant." It held the terms of God's relationship with Israel: two complete copies of his law for their lives.

In effect, these tablets were placed under God's feet. If the top of the ark was God's throne, then the ark itself was God's footstool, and the Bible sometimes describes it this way. When the pilgrims went up to worship God in Jerusalem, they sang, "'Let us go to his dwelling place; let us worship at his footstool!' Arise, O Lord, and go to your resting place, you and the ark of your might" (Psalm 132:7, 8). This is where Moses deposited the covenant: in the footstool of God.

Placing the Law under God's feet was significant because it related to the way covenants were established in the ancient world. Umberto Cassuto writes:

> It was the custom in the ancient East to deposit the deeds of a covenant made between human kings in the sanctuaries of the gods, in the footstool of the idols that symbolized the deity, so that the godhead should be a witness to the covenant and see that it was observed. . . . This custom makes it clear why the testimony to the covenant made between the Lord and Israel was enshrined in the ark. Among the Israelites there was no image to symbolize the God of Israel, but there was His footstool, and therein the testimony of the covenant was placed and preserved.[6]

Thus the covenant always remained in God's presence.

## The Mercy Seat

There was one problem with this arrangement. God was above the ark, enthroned between the cherubim. The Law was under his feet, written in stone. But God's people were not able to keep the terms of that covenant—not perfectly. The more we get to know the Israelites, the more we see how completely they broke God's law. They were the kind of people who liked to serve other gods, worship idols they made with their own hands, forget the Sabbath, take things that didn't belong to them, and generally break the commandments of God. Therefore, what was in the ark could not save them; it could only condemn them. The Law deposited in the ark condemned their sin, and God was right on top of it!

This is why the lid to the ark was so important. Some modern translations call it "an atonement cover." Other versions call it "the mercy seat," a term first used by Martin Luther and then picked up by William Tyndale when he translated the Bible into English. Here the word "seat" does not refer to some kind of chair or throne. It simply means "location," as in the phrase "the seat of power." Thus the mercy seat was the place where mercy was found—the mercy of forgiveness for sin.

The mercy seat was used only once a year, on the Day of Atonement. This is reflected in its name, which in Hebrew is *kapporet*, a term derived from the word that means "to make atonement."[7] The ark's cover was used in making atonement for sin. First the high priest offered a sacrifice for his own sins. The Law said, "Aaron shall present the bull as a sin offering for himself, and shall make atonement for himself and for his house. He shall kill the bull as a sin offering for himself. . . . And he shall take some of the blood of the bull and sprinkle it with his finger on the front of the mercy seat on the east side, and in front of the mercy seat he shall sprinkle some of the blood with his finger seven times" (Leviticus 16:11, 14).

After he made atonement for his own sins, the priest offered a sacrifice for the nation of Israel: "Then he shall kill the goat of the sin offering that is for the people and bring its blood inside the veil and do with its blood as he did with the blood of the bull, sprinkling it over the mercy seat and in front of the mercy seat. Thus he shall make atonement for the Holy Place, because of the uncleannesses of the people of Israel and because of their transgressions, all their sins. . . . [H]e comes out and has made atonement for himself and for his house and for all the assembly of Israel" (Leviticus 16:15, 16a, 17b).

When the high priest sprinkled blood on the mercy seat, this showed that sin was forgiven, that atonement had been made. To put it another way, the people were covered. The sacrificial blood protected them from the wrath of God. As John Mackay writes, "The position of the atonement cover above the tables of the law makes clear that what is being covered is the penalty that is demanded for infringements of the sovereign commands of the covenant King."[8] Thus the location of the blood was significant. Above it was God, in all his holiness. Underneath was the Law that exposed Israel's sin. In between came the blood of the atoning sacrifice that covered transgression and turned away wrath, reconciling the people to God. The blood on the ark thus provided safety from judgment. When God came down to dwell with his people, he would not see the Law that they had broken, first of all, but the saving blood of an atoning sacrifice.

Atonement really means "at-one-ment" (indeed, this is the meaning of the word, which was coined by Tyndale). Parties that were separated have now become one. What accomplished this reconciliation for Israel was the blood on the mercy seat. Mackay comments: "It was not merely the presence of the atonement cover that effected atonement for the sinner. It indicated the divine provision of a facility for implementing reconciliation, but it was only when the payment that divine justice regarded as sufficient to cover the sinner's debt was made that atonement was actually effected. The beautiful atonement cover on its own was not sufficient; it had to be sprinkled with the blood of the sacrifice."[9]

Some people get turned off by all this talk about blood. Why take the time to study such a gory Old Testament ritual? Really, what is the point in taking a beautiful golden ark and splattering it all over with blood? The answer is that "without the shedding of blood there is no forgiveness of sins" (Hebrews 9:22). There is no mercy unless there is blood on the mercy seat. God is up above, enthroned in majesty. We are down below, breaking his law. If we are to be saved, something has to come between his perfect holiness and our unholy sin—namely, the blood of a sacrifice acceptable to God.

This is precisely what Jesus was doing on the cross: He was offering himself as a sacrifice acceptable unto God. It was a sacrifice in blood—his own blood, poured out for sinners. The Bible says, "But when Christ appeared . . . through the greater and more perfect tent (not made with hands, that is, not of this creation) he entered once for all into the holy places, not by means of the blood of goats and calves but by means of his own blood, thus securing an eternal redemption" (Hebrews 9:11, 12). Our mercy seat—the place where atonement was made and where we can be reconciled to God—is the cross where Jesus shed his own blood for our sins.

The New Testament often describes the saving work of Jesus Christ in terms of the mercy seat. It says that Jesus came "to make propitiation for the sins of the people" (Hebrews 2:17). It says, "God put forward [Jesus] as a propitiation by his blood, to be received by faith" (Romans 3:25). It says, "In this is love, not that we have loved God but that he loved us and sent his Son to be the propitiation for our sins" (1 John 4:10). The word that the Bible uses in each of these verses (*hilasterion*) refers specifically to a sacrifice poured on the mercy seat. The cross of Christ is our mercy seat. It is the place where the blood of an atoning sacrifice reconciles us to God by coming between his holiness and our sin. The cross is the place where sinners can find mercy.

## Mercy for Sinners

Jesus told a wonderful story about a man who found mercy. The man was a sinner—a tax collector by trade—who had swindled many people out of their money. He was such a notorious thief that really he did not entertain much hope that God would ever forgive him. But he was searching for God—looking for grace, so he went to the temple to pray. There he stood in the shadows, not even daring to look up to Heaven, but lowered his eyes and said, "God, be merciful to me, a sinner!" (Luke 18:13). Or more literally, "God, have mercy on me, *the* sinner," as if he were the only sinner in all the world.

To put it even more literally, he said, "God, be mercy-seated to me, the sinner." The man was standing in the temple, not far from the ark of the covenant. Apparently he understood what the ark symbolized. He started his prayer with God, who is enthroned above in holiness. He ended his prayer with himself, the sinner who had broken God's law. But if there was any hope that he would find forgiveness, something needed to come in between. That something was the mercy of God, granted on the basis of an atoning sacrifice. So he prayed, "God, have mercy on me, the sinner." These words have come to exercise a profound influence on my own relationship to God. In the morning I generally try to pray as soon as I am conscious of being awake. The first sentence that most often forms in my mind is this: "God, have mercy on me, the sinner."

Beginning the day this way puts life into proper perspective. I acknowledge who God is: my merciful Father in Heaven. And I acknowledge who I am in relationship to him: a sinner who is under his mercy. Then, once I have God in his place and me in mine, I can talk with him about everything else on my mind and heart. But first I need to come asking God to have mercy on me through Jesus Christ. Thank God there is mercy for sinners, if we trust in the blood of Jesus to cover all our sin.

# 72

# The Bread of the Presence

## EXODUS 25:23–30

GOD SHOWED REMARKABLE FAVOR to his people Israel. He heard their cries for mercy and rescued them from slavery. He defeated their enemies. He led them through the wilderness and provided for their daily needs. He taught them how to behave by giving them his law. Then he came down to live with them and be their God. This was the primary meaning of the tabernacle—the house that Moses built. The living God had come to dwell with his people.

Another way to say all this is that God was fulfilling his covenant with Israel. The covenant was God's unbreakable promise to love and save his people. At the heart of that covenant was his commitment to be with his people. He said, "I will turn to you and make you fruitful and multiply you and will confirm my covenant with you. . . . I will make my dwelling among you. . . . And I will walk among you and will be your God, and you shall be my people. I am the LORD your God, who brought you out of the land of Egypt, that you should not be their slaves. And I have broken the bars of your yoke and made you walk erect" (Leviticus 26:9, 11–13).

The construction of the tabernacle was in fulfillment of God's covenant. God was making good on his promise to be with his people by pitching his tent in the middle of their camp. This was all in preparation for the time when God would send his Son to be our Savior. The tabernacle of the exodus was an amazing new step in the plan of salvation, as God came down to live with his people and be their God. But the ultimate tabernacle is Jesus Christ, for "the Word became flesh and dwelt among us" (John 1:14a). This is the gospel according to the tabernacle.

## Details, Details

As we study the tabernacle, it's important not to lose sight of the big picture: God coming down to live with his people. However, we also need to pay close attention to the details, so as not to miss their spiritual significance. The Bible describes the tabernacle carefully because every part of the building has something to teach about God and his salvation in Jesus Christ. The purpose of the tabernacle was partly pedagogical.

Some scholars say this means that the details aren't all that important. They claim that Moses simply borrowed his building plans from the Egyptians or from the religion of some other ancient culture. Or they claim that the tabernacle furnishings were primarily functional. For example, someone has said that the altar of incense was designed to keep away flies, like a giant citronella candle.[1] However, we need to remember that the tabernacle was planned from top to bottom by Almighty God. It was the house that Moses built, but its designer and architect was God, and whatever symbolism it held was *his* symbolism. Therefore, we should expect to find his Spirit in the details.

The problem is that the Bible doesn't explain all the details, so it isn't always easy to know how to understand them. Thus there is a long history of interpreting, misinterpreting, and reinterpreting the tabernacle. The ancient Jewish commentator Philo said its structure represented the universe. The seven branches on the lampstand stood for the seven planets; the four basic materials used to build the tabernacle stood for the four elements of earth, air, fire, and water; the twelve stones on the priest's breastplate stood for the twelve signs of the zodiac; and so on.[2]

Sometimes attention is given to the metals used in the tabernacle. Origen claimed that "faith compared to gold, the preached word to silver, patience to bronze."[3] Other commentators have found special symbolism in its colors. For example, white linen is said to represent the righteousness of Christ, whereas the red ram skins portray his sufferings and death on the cross.[4]

Often two people look at the same symbol and interpret it two different ways. Consider the sacred ark of the covenant. Gregory the Great said, "What is symbolized by the ark but the holy church? The orders are that it is to be provided with four rings of gold in the four corners—obviously because, being extended to the four parts of the world, it is declared to be equipped with the four books of the holy Gospels."[5] Others, however, have seen the ark as a symbol of the incarnation: "The ark was made of acacia wood overlaid with gold within and without. Wood speaks of His incorruptible humanity, and gold His Divinity. Two materials, yet one ark; two natures yet one person, the God-man."[6]

At first most of these interpretations seem plausible, but the problem is that some of them are arbitrary. Rather than drawing meaning out of the tabernacle, some interpreters read into it. For example, how do we know that the four golden rings stand for the four Gospels? What is the connection, other than the number four? And if these really are the plain meanings of the symbols, why do different commentators interpret them different ways?

Given these difficulties, we can sympathize with scholars who have given up trying to figure out what the details mean at all. They are impatient with people who try to "find Jesus" in every detail. With reference to the shape of the Holy of Holies and its possible interpretation, one exasperated commentator finally asked, "In what sense can Christ be square?"[7] Not surprisingly, some scholars have concluded that "all the numerous and varied proposals that have been advanced with a view to interpreting the construction of the Tabernacle allegorically have no value in so far as the plain meaning of the Scriptural passages is concerned."[8]

While it may be true that we can't find Jesus everywhere, it nevertheless remains true that the tabernacle is a revelation of his glory. Jesus *is* in many of the details. He is there because God put him there. So rather than giving up any hope of finding him, or coming up with our own fanciful interpretations, we need reliable principles for interpreting the tabernacle.

One of these principles is to *use the New Testament as the key to unlock the Old Testament*. A number of New Testament passages explain what the tabernacle meant. The book of Hebrews calls the tabernacle "a copy and shadow of the heavenly things" (Hebrews 8:5). It also calls the tabernacle "symbolic" (Hebrews 9:9) of "the greater and more perfect tent" (Hebrews 9:11). To make sure we understand what it was supposed to illustrate, Hebrews goes on to explain how the tabernacle is connected to Christ, and especially the access to God that we now have through his sacrificial blood.

Another reliable principle of interpretation is to *study the way a detail is used in its original context*. If something has a symbolic function in the Old Testament, then in all likelihood it is connected to the Bible's main story of salvation and is intended to point us to Christ. However, if something does not have a spiritual meaning in its Old Testament context, we should be careful not to give it one and then make some sort of arbitrary connection to Christ.

A few examples may help explain what I mean. Consider the wooden crossbars that were used to hold up the tabernacle (26:26–29). They were in the shape of a cross. So are they intended to teach us something about the cross of Christ? No, because they don't have any symbolic significance in the Old Testament. They are not connected in any specific way to meeting with God or to making atonement with sin. All they do is hold up the tabernacle. Or consider the ram skins that were dyed red and used to cover the tabernacle. Does the Old Testament draw any connection between them and the offering of a sacrifice?[9] It does not seem to do so. So if we connect the red cloth to the sacrifice of Jesus Christ, we are in danger of stretching things. Or does the Bible attach any special significance to the colors of yarn used in the tabernacle? Apparently not, so we should be careful what significance we attach to them.

What about the acacia wood and the gold? Is this a symbol of the incarnation, with the gold representing Christ's deity and the wood his humanity? While this is an attractive interpretation, again the answer is probably no. The New Testament is silent about this feature of the ark. Nor does the Old Testament give any clue that acacia wood has symbolic significance or that there is special meaning in combining wood with gold. Besides, the ark of the covenant was not the only piece of furniture made of wood and covered with gold. Was the table for the showbread also a symbol of Jesus and his incarnation? What about the carrying poles? They too were made of wood covered with gold. But it's hard to see how they have any connection to the union of deity and humanity in Christ. Although it is important to see how Christ is taught in all the Scriptures, we shouldn't try to find him in places he doesn't actually appear. The foregoing examples teach us to be careful.

When something from the Old Testament *does* have a symbolic meaning, we need to consider how it is connected to Christ. We saw this when we studied the ark of the covenant. The cherubim on the ark clearly represented the glorious cherubim in Heaven. The Old Testament describes God as "enthroned upon the cherubim," which means that the space above the ark symbolically represented his throne. The lid is called "the mercy seat," which connects it to the whole Old Testament system of sacrifice, especially the sin offerings made on the Day of Atonement. Then the ark itself is described as God's footstool, symbolizing his rule and authority. These symbols are all present in the Old Testament. They teach us about the glory of God and our need to have our sins covered by the blood of an atoning sacrifice. Once we understand the true symbolism of the ark, we can see how it relates to Jesus Christ and the way his blood covers our sin and brings us to God's throne. This symbolism finds further confirmation in the New Testament, which describes the ark as "symbolic for the present age" (Hebrews 9:9), when Christ has opened the way to God through the sacrifice of his blood.

To summarize, there are at least two valid principles we can use to interpret the full meaning of the tabernacle and at the same time keep our interpretation under control. One is to use the New Testament as the key to unlock the meaning of the Old Testament. We use Scripture to interpret Scripture, allowing the Bible to explain its own symbolism. The other principle is to pay careful attention to the Old Testament to see whether a particular detail has any symbolic meaning in its original context. If it does, then we should ask how this meaning relates to the person and work of Jesus Christ. If it doesn't, we should be careful not to invent a meaning of our own. We should not read into the Old Testament anything we are not able to read out of it.

## The Table

With these basic principles for interpreting what went into the tabernacle, we are ready to study the next piece of furniture. The first thing God told Moses to make was the ark of the covenant. This was the most important object in the tabernacle—the place where God was. Then God moved out to the Holy Place just outside the Holy of Holies. He said to Moses:

> You shall make a table of acacia wood. Two cubits shall be its length, a cubit its breadth, and a cubit and a half its height. You shall overlay it with pure gold and make a molding of gold around it. And you shall make a rim around it a handbreadth wide, and a molding of gold around the rim. And you shall make for it four rings of gold, and fasten the rings to the four corners at its four legs. Close to the frame the rings shall lie, as holders for the poles to carry the table. You shall make the poles of acacia wood, and overlay them with gold, and the table shall be carried with these. And you shall make its plates and dishes for incense, and its flagons and bowls with which to pour drink offerings; you shall make them of pure gold. And you shall set the bread of the Presence on the table before me regularly. (25:23–30)

There are some obvious similarities between the way the table was built and the way the ark was built. Both were made of acacia wood, both were covered with gold, and both were crowned with molding. Both pieces of furniture had rings and poles for carrying. The difference was that unlike the ark, the carrying poles for the table were removable. Although the table was holy, it was not as holy as the ark.

Like most of the tabernacle furnishings, the table for the bread was not large. This helps us realize that the tabernacle was not built on a grand scale. The building's true magnificence was its message, not how massive it was. This was also true of the table, which was roughly the size of a coffee table: three feet long, a foot and a half wide, less than three feet tall. The table was encircled by a wide rim. If this rim was at the top, then presumably it was intended to keep what was on the table from falling off. However, the rim may have been lower down, circling the four legs of the table. This is the way the table is depicted in the famous Arch of Titus, which shows some of the sacred items (replicas, not the originals) that the Romans plundered from Herod's Temple when they captured Jerusalem in AD 70.[10]

The Bible gives the table several different names. Here in Exodus it is simply called "the table" (25:27, 30). Numbers calls it "the table of the bread of the Presence" (4:7). In Leviticus it is called "the table of pure gold" (24:6), or more literally, "the pure table." But the most elaborate title comes from 1 Kings, which describes it as "the golden table for the bread of the Presence" (7:48).

This title identifies the most important thing about the table—namely, what was on it. The table in the Holy Place held twelve loaves of sacred bread as well as various plates, dishes, pitchers, and bowls. Presumably the plates were for holding the bread. Although it is not stated here, the dishes were for holding incense (see Leviticus 24:7). The pitchers and bowls were "to pour drink offerings" (25:29). However, these offerings were not made in the Holy Place; they were made on the altar in the courtyard outside. So why were the pitchers and bowls kept in the Holy Place? Perhaps the priests set these sacred utensils in the Holy Place for safekeeping and then simply carried them out whenever they made a drink offering to God.

Nothing is said here about how the bread was used, but we get more information from Leviticus:

> You shall take fine flour and bake twelve loaves from it; two tenths of an ephah shall be in each loaf. And you shall set them in two piles, six in a pile, on the table of pure gold before the LORD. And you shall put pure frankincense on each pile, that it may go with the bread as a memorial portion as a food offering to the LORD. Every Sabbath day Aaron shall arrange it before the LORD regularly; it is from the people of Israel as a covenant forever. And it shall be for Aaron and his sons, and they shall eat it in a holy place, since it is for him a most holy portion out of the LORD's food offerings, a perpetual due. (Leviticus 24:5–9)

The showbread—or "shewbread," as William Tyndale called it when he translated the Bible into English—was baked the day before the Sabbath. Then on the Sabbath the priests ate the old bread and set the new bread on the table in twelve loaves (see 1 Samuel 21:6; 1 Chronicles 9:32). These were not loaves in the modern sense but more like large round cakes. The bread "was made of fine wheat flour, doubtless unleavened, but beaten up light, baked in twelve loaves, containing each one fifth of an ephah of flour (or about four quarts) . . . probably . . . twelve inches in diameter and four inches thick—still a large family loaf."[11] Most modern translations say the bread was lined up in two rows, but it may have been stacked in two piles. This was the bread of the Presence on the golden table in the tabernacle.

### The Holy Bread

What did all this mean? What was its spiritual significance? Most of the instructions God gave for the table were not symbolic but functional. There is nothing especially significant about acacia wood, the rim, the four golden rings, or even the dishes. These details are not given any symbolic significance, either in their original context or in the New Testament. So we should not look for any hidden meanings.

The one thing that clearly *was* symbolic was the bread of the Presence. In fact, the reason there was a table at all was to provide a place for putting the bread. It was "the table for the showbread" (2 Chronicles 29:18). The bread was the important thing, not the table.

So what did the bread represent? Some scholars say the Israelites borrowed this ritual from other religions, in which people put food out for their gods—like leaving a plate of cookies for Santa Claus on Christmas Eve. The gods never actually ate anything, but people liked to feed them:

> In Mesopotamia they would arrange on the table the foods that had been prepared as a meal for the gods, such as boiled or roasted flesh, placed in dishes or plates, loaves of bread, jars of wine, milk and honey, and various kinds of fruit, recalling the tables set before kings. . . . The practice was based on the belief that the gods, who, like human beings, also needed food, actually ate and drank, in some traditionary manner, the foods and the drinks that were put before them, like a king who eats and drinks of the repast that his servants have set before him on his table.[12]

It goes without saying that this is *not* what the Israelites were doing. There is not the slightest hint anywhere in this passage that the bread was for God's sustenance. In fact, this idea is idolatrous. Feeding bread to God makes him in our image and thus contradicts everything the Bible teaches about his divine character. The true and living God does not need our help. As the Apostle Paul wrote, "Nor is he served by human hands, as though he needed anything, since he himself gives to all mankind life and breath and everything" (Acts 17:25). God is eternally self-sufficient and self-existent. He never gets hungry or thirsty. There is nothing we need to do or even can do to keep him going. He does not depend on us to provide for him.

The truth is quite the opposite: We are utterly dependent on God for everything we need. And this is what the bread signified. Bread is basic food. It is what we need to survive. According to the psalmist, it is what sustains the heart of man (Psalm 104:15). Therefore, bread represents God's providential care. When Jesus prayed, "Give us this day our daily bread" (Matthew 6:11), he was teaching us to ask God to meet our daily needs. The bread at the tabernacle represented the same thing. It stood for God's provision: "He provides food for those who fear him; he remembers his covenant forever" (Psalm 111:5).

It is worth noting that there were twelve loaves of bread—one loaf for each of the twelve tribes of Israel; every tribe had a place at the table. It is also significant that the bread was in God's presence. This is why it was called "the bread of the Presence"—literally, it was "before God's face" (25:30). And it was *always* there. As soon as one set of loaves started to grow stale, it was replaced with fresh bread. This was a perpetual reminder of God's providential care. The people brought the bread right into God's holy presence—not for his benefit, as if he might forget what they needed, but for *their* benefit. The showbread symbolized God's constant awareness of their daily needs. In case they were ever tempted to doubt his providence, it reminded them that their needs were ever before him. God saw what they needed. Their needs were always on his mind.

God not only saw what they needed, but he also provided it. The Israelites knew this from their own experience. God had been with them every step of the way to meet all their needs. He watched over them in Egypt, growing them into a mighty nation. He sustained them in the desert, caring for them along the way by sending bread from Heaven and water from the rock. The bread in the tabernacle was a continuous reminder of God's constant care. Moses said, "Every Sabbath day Aaron shall arrange it before the LORD regularly; it is from the people of Israel as a covenant forever" (Leviticus 24:8). And all through the long centuries, God provided what he promised: daily bread. Week after week, month after month, year after year, and century after century the bread of the Presence was a sign of God's providence.

There was something else the bread of the Presence symbolized: God's fellowship with his people. Back in chapter 24, Moses and the elders had fellowship with God around his table. They "beheld God, and ate and drank" (24:11). Later this privilege was extended to Israel's priests. At the end of every week they baked twelve new loaves of bread. Then they ate the holy bread from the previous week. All week long the bread was in God's presence, symbolizing his fellowship with his people. It stood as a perpetual thank offering to God for all the blessings of his providence.[13] Then when the priests ate the bread, they were eating in the presence of God, gathering around his table. Vern Poythress writes, "In the ancient Near East sharing a special meal together was an act of friendship and personal communion. The host undertook solemn responsibility to serve and protect his guest while they enjoyed the meal. Thus God invites Israel to share a meal with Him and enjoy His protection."[14]

This was all in preparation for the day when God would invite his people to sit down at his table—not just the elders and the priests, but all the children of God. We have all been invited to the great supper of God. We have fellowship around his table whenever we share the Lord's Supper. As M. R. DeHaan has written, "The table in the tabernacle pointed to the Lord Jesus, our Sustainer, and the bread on the table was symbolic of His own body."[15]

## The Bread of Life

God still provides for his people today. The lesson we learn from the bread of the Presence is as practical as it is simple: God knows what we need and can be trusted to provide it. This is one of the great themes of the Bible and one of the great truths of the Christian life. Whatever we need, God will provide.

The bread in the tabernacle encourages us to believe that God always knows what we need. Our needs are ever before his face. He never overlooks our concerns or neglects to provide for them. Whether it is meeting a basic material need, granting wisdom for a major decision, sustaining us through a serious illness, comforting us in a painful sorrow, or providing friendship in a time of loneliness, God never fails to provide what we truly need. Whatever difficulties we may encounter, we can trust him to sustain us along the way.

Often, in order to confirm how thoroughly he knows our situation, God provides *exactly* what we need. In their book *Common Sense Parenting*, Kent and Barbara Hughes describe how God provided for their family when their first child was born. At the time Kent was a full-time college student and a full-time factory worker. Times were tight. As Barbara's due date approached, the Hugheses calculated that they would have only 160 dollars to pay their medical bills. Unfortunately, the doctor's fee was 250 dollars, and the hospital bill was another 250 dollars. All they could do was pray.

Then, during Barbara's last checkup, the doctor happened to notice that Kent was planning to go to seminary. Although he was not a churchgoing man, the doctor casually observed that deliveries for clergy were free of charge. This took care of half the bill, but the other half still had to be paid. On the day Barbara and her new baby girl were released from the hospital, Kent walked up to the cashier with only 163 dollars in his pocket. When the cashier handed him the bill, he was shocked. Since Barbara had been admitted in the middle of the night, the hospital had knocked one full day off their charges. The total came to 160 dollars. It only took Kent a few moments to realize what the extra three dollars were for: God had provided just enough money for him to buy Barbara some flowers![16]

God knows what we need and can always be trusted to provide it. And by giving us our daily bread, God is teaching us a deeper lesson. He wants us to learn that what we really need is himself. As God meets our daily needs, he is teaching us that he is all we need.

Eventually most Christians learn to trust God for their daily needs. As we go through life, we have specific experiences of God's providing care. God uses our times of need to teach us that we can count on him to provide. It happens again and again. We need shelter, and God provides a home. We need work, and God provides a job. We need food, and God provides a meal. Even if we are not very good at inductive reasoning, eventually we figure out that God can always be trusted to provide whatever we truly need.

What some Christians still need to learn is that our real need is for God himself. It is true that we need God to provide for us. But our deepest need is to have fellowship with the living God. More than needing God to feed us, we need to feed on God. Eventually Moses figured this out. Years later, when he looked back on all the things God had done to provide for his people, he said to them, "He humbled you and let you hunger and fed you with manna, which you did not know, nor did your fathers know, that he might make you know that man does not live by bread alone, but man lives by every word that comes from the mouth of the Lord" (Deuteronomy 8:3). Why did God provide his people with bread? Was it to teach them to trust him for their daily needs? Yes, but the bread had a deeper purpose. God sent it to teach his people to feed upon his Word, placing their total dependence upon his divine grace.

Have you learned to feed upon God? Are you drawing spiritual nourishment from his Word and his sacraments? Do you have a growing appetite for spending time alone with God in prayer? God is not some kind of cosmic vending machine: Just pull the lever and out pops a job or a car or whatever else we happen to need. Of course, these are all things that God provides, but what he is trying to teach us is our total need for himself. Our relationship with God is need-based. And our needs are not merely physical but also spiritual; they are not simply temporal but also eternal. So what we need is not only for God to do this or that for us, but for him to be our God. This is something we will need long after all our material needs have been met. We will still need God the way a beggar needs bread. He is the food for our soul.

This is not an easy lesson to learn. It is easier for us to ask God to do something for us than it is to crave God himself. People had the same problem in Jesus' day. The best example is what happened after Jesus fed the five thousand. The next day everyone was looking for him, but they were missing the point because all they wanted was more bread. They only wanted Jesus for what he could do for them, not for who he was in himself. Jesus could see what their motivation was. He said to them, "Truly, truly, I say to you, you are seeking me, not because you saw signs, but because you ate your fill of the loaves" (John 6:26).

What the people really needed was Jesus—not the bread he could provide, but Jesus himself. Only Jesus could forgive their sins. Only Jesus could satisfy their souls. Only Jesus could bring them into a relationship with God. Only Jesus could give them eternal life. So he said:

> Truly, truly, I say to you, it was not Moses who gave you the bread from heaven, but my Father gives you the true bread from heaven. For the bread of God is he who comes down from heaven and gives life to the world. . . . I am the bread of life; whoever comes to me shall not hunger, and whoever believes in me shall never thirst. . . . I am the living bread that came down from heaven. If anyone eats of this bread, he will live forever. And the bread that I will give for the life of the world is my flesh. (John 6:32, 33, 35, 51)

When Jesus talked about the true and living bread that came down from Heaven, he was talking about himself. He was referring specifically to the body he offered on the cross to save sinners. His message was very simple: "All you really need is me. I am the bread. I am the eternal source of life. I am the one who can satisfy the hunger in your soul. And if you believe in me, you will live forever."

# 73

# The Golden Lampstand

EXODUS 25:31–40

THE TABERNACLE OF GOD was a tent four layers thick. Its inner lining was made of fine linen, covered with cloth woven from goat's hair. These two layers, in turn, were covered with ram skins. Over the top went a waterproof tarp made from the thick hides of sea cows.

Imagine how dark it must have been underneath all these layers. There were no windows, so a priest entering the Holy Place of God was swallowed in darkness. No light could penetrate. It would have been utterly and completely black, unless God made his light to shine in the darkness. But God, who never leaves his people in the dark, set up a light in his dwelling place—the golden lampstand.

## The Light in God's House

The golden lampstand stood in the Holy Place, opposite the table for the bread of the Presence. As with all the other furnishings in the tabernacle, God gave Moses careful instructions for its fabrication:

> You shall make a lampstand of pure gold. The lampstand shall be made of hammered work: its base, its stem, its cups, its calyxes, and its flowers shall be of one piece with it. And there shall be six branches going out of its sides, three branches of the lampstand out of one side of it and three branches of the lampstand out of the other side of it; three cups made like almond blossoms, each with calyx and flower, on one branch, and three cups made like almond blossoms, each with calyx and flower, on the other branch—so for the six branches going out of the lampstand. And on the lampstand itself there shall be four cups made like almond blossoms, with their calyxes and flowers, and a calyx of one piece with it under each pair of the six branches going out from the lampstand. Their calyxes and their branches shall be of one piece with it, the whole of it a single piece of hammered work of pure gold. (25:31–36)

Based on this description, it would be hard to make an exact reproduction of the lampstand—especially since God did not provide Moses with any measurements—but we get a good idea what it looked like. Anyone who has ever seen a *menorah*, which to this day remains a prominent symbol of Judaism, has the basic picture.

The lampstand had one central shaft, which broadened out at the bottom to form a base. Six branches spread out from the main lampstand—three on each side, probably reaching up in pairs about as high as the central shaft. This is the way the lampstand is depicted on the famous Arch of Titus in Rome. The lampstand shown on the arch came from the temple in Jerusalem and was crafted long after the time of Moses, but the tradition for what it looked like may well have gone back to the prophet himself. What the Bible clearly says is that there were seven lamps in all.

The lampstand was beaten out of pure gold. In the craftsmanship of that day, the gold was set against a wooden mold and then hammered into shape. According to verse 39, the whole thing was made from a single talent of solid gold, which in today's measurements would weigh roughly seventy-five pounds. The base and branches were not assembled but were made all of one piece, and when the lampstand was finished it stood perhaps five feet tall.

The lampstand was ornate. It was not pounded roughly into shape but was carefully crafted and elaborately festooned with flowers. Each branch had three golden decorations of almond buds, blossoms, and fruit. The central shaft had four of these decorations. Presumably three of them anchored the places where pairs of branches intersected the central lampstand, and there was one more decoration at the top.[1] As John Durham describes it, "Each of these branches ended in a leafy base of a bud, from which opened the petals of an almond flower, and into this receptacle was fixed a lampholder or cup. This bud-and-bloom motif was repeated along both the trunk or shaft of the Lampstand and also along the six branches extending from it, four times on the trunk and three times on each branch."[2]

The flowery cup at the top of each branch was designed to hold a lamp. God said to Moses, "You shall make seven lamps for it. And the lamps shall be set up so as to give light on the space in front of it. Its tongs and their trays shall be of pure gold. It shall be made, with all these utensils, out of a talent of pure gold. And see that you make them after the pattern for them, which is being shown you on the mountain" (vv. 37–40).

This kind of lighting system was common in those days. In order to illuminate a room, oil lamps were placed on top of a stand. The lamps were removable bowls or saucers, usually made of pottery, but in this case possibly gold. Each little bowl was filled with oil to provide fuel for the light. Then a wick was set on the rim of the lamp, usually in a place where the bowl was pinched so as to hold the wick in place. This was the kind of lamp that was set into each cup atop the golden lampstand. Once they were lit, the lamps were turned toward the table of the showbread to provide light, not only for the table, but also for the rest of the room.

We read about this again in Numbers: "Now the Lord spoke to Moses, saying, 'Speak to Aaron and say to him, When you set up the lamps, the seven lamps shall give light in front of the lampstand.' And Aaron did so: he set up its lamps in front of the lampstand, as the Lord commanded Moses. And this was the workmanship of the lampstand, hammered work of gold. From its base to its flowers, it was hammered work; according to the pattern that the Lord had shown Moses, so he made the lampstand" (Numbers 8:1–4).

Several utensils were needed to tend these lamps. One was a pair of tongs for trimming the wicks, a task the priests performed both morning and evening (see 27:20, 21). As the wicks were trimmed, the discarded ends were put on a tray and then carried out of the tabernacle. Like everything else in the Holy Place, the tray and the tongs were made of gold, to convey a sense of God's royal majesty.

This was all done according to God's plan, in keeping with "the pattern" he showed to Moses (25:40). The things in the tabernacle were used in the holy worship of God, so everything had to be done right. To this end, God showed Moses the prototype for the lampstand on the mountain. Then when the prophet came back down he was able to make it exactly the way God said.

## Tree of Life, Tree of Light

The golden lampstand had an obvious practical function, which was to shed light on the tabernacle's interior. Every home needs light, and God's holy dwelling place was no exception. His golden lampstand illuminated the Holy Place, enabling the priests to see what they were doing as they carried out their service to God.

But what symbolic significance did the lampstand have for the people of God? There are two ways to answer this question. One is to see if the New Testament has anything specific to say about the lampstand; the other is to see how it was used in its original context. By these methods we discover that the golden lampstand represented the life and light God gives to his people.

The lampstand may have other meanings as well. Some commentators associate it with the rod of power that God gave to Aaron. Their reason for making this connection is that when Aaron's staff blossomed, it was with flowers from the almond tree, just like the ones on the lampstand (Numbers 17:8). So there may have been a connection between the staff, which represented the Levites, and the lampstand that gave light to the place where they served. But the more obvious and important purpose of the lampstand was to show that in God's presence there is light and life.

The lampstand stood for life because it was made in the shape of a tree. Its central shaft formed the trunk, from which branches spread that were covered with beautiful buds, blossoms, and fruit. This botanical motif was not merely decorative but also symbolic. As the lampstand branched out, it was budding, blooming, and ripening with fruit. In other words, the three stages in the life cycle of a tree were occurring simultaneously.[3] This made the lampstand a potent symbol of God's life-giving power.

The Bible doesn't fully explain the symbolism of the tree; so there is some mystery here. The white almond flowers may have been a symbol of hope, because (like crocuses and daffodils) they were the first to appear in the springtime, and thus their early blossoms held the promise of the growing season. But as a "stylized tree of life,"[4] the golden lampstand was also an echo from Eden. "It signifies life," writes John Currid, "continued existence and productivity for the people of God as they stand before him. In one sense, then, the lampstand is a metaphor for the tree of life that was in the garden of Eden. God gives life to his people."[5] When God first planted Adam and Eve in the garden, he gave them a tree of life (Genesis 2:9), which taught them to look to him as the source of all their vitality. But once they fell into sin, our first parents were cut off from the tree of life. The wages of their sin was death. But all was not lost. God had a plan for giving his people new life, like almond blossoms in springtime. The golden lampstand stood as a permanent reminder that God is the life-giver. The life we lost through sin is regained wherever he is present. As King David wrote, "With you is the fountain of life" (Psalm 36:9a).

In the same verse David went on to say, "In your light do we see light." This, too, was part of the lampstand's original meaning. The presence of God is shining with light as well as growing with life. He is the light-giver as well as the life-giver.

One purpose of the golden lampstand was to light the Holy Place (see 25:37). In the words of one commentator, it served as "a welcome sign that someone is home."[6] The tabernacle meant that God was at home with his people, and the lampstand helped to show this. But it provided something more than a friendly glow. The deeper meaning of the lampstand is that God himself *is* the light; there is no darkness where God is. As the Scripture says, "God is light, and in him is no darkness at all" (1 John 1:5b). The lamp in the tabernacle showed that as the people approached God, they were coming into the light. God gives light to his people. The light is where God is. He is our light and our salvation (see Psalm 27:1).

Like the tree of life, the lights on the lampstand looked back to creation, when God said, "'Let there be light,' and there was light" (Genesis 1:3), and when he put lights in the sky to "be for signs and for seasons, and for days and years" (Genesis 1:14). There were seven lights on the lampstand. In the Bible seven is a number of completion—the perfection of the light. Some commentators also see the seven lights as representing the sun, the moon, and the five visible planets.[7] On this reading, the Holy Place represents the visible heavens, with the Holy of Holies representing Heaven itself.[8] Whether this is the case or not—and the Bible does not state that it is—the lampstand showed that God is the source of all light.

This is true not only in creation but also in redemption. As the psalmist prayed, "Send out your light and your truth; let them lead me; let them bring me to your holy hill and to your dwelling!" (Psalm 43:3). This was a summary of Israel's experience. God led his people out of slavery and into freedom by the presence of his glorious light. As John Mackay writes, "There is to be no darkness in the presence of the Creator who has redeemed his people. Just as he gave light to the original creation to bring order into the realm he had made, so now he provides for light in the miniature representation of the realm of his restored fellowship with his people."[9]

## Light and Life to All He Brings

The lampstand showed Israel that God alone is the source of all life and light. Now God's promise to give his people life and light has been fulfilled in Jesus Christ. At the beginning of his Gospel, as the apostle John described what it meant for the Son of God to come into the world and "tabernacle" among us, he wrote, "In him was life, and the life was the light of men" (John 1:4). The golden lampstand taught the Israelites to look to God for life and light. Now we look to Jesus Christ, who is the life and the light of God. As Charles Wesley wrote in his famous hymn on the incarnation ("Hark! the Herald Angels Sing"), "Light and life to all he brings."[10]

Jesus Christ is the *life*. The Bible says, "Whoever believes in him may have eternal life" (John 3:15). It also tells us, "The Son gives life to whom he will" (John 5:21b). "Everyone who looks on the Son and believes in him should have eternal life" (John 6:40). "I came," Jesus said, "that they may have life and have it abundantly" (John 10:10b). He said, "I give them eternal life, and they will never perish" (John 10:28). He said, "I am the resurrection and the life. Whoever believes in me, though he die, yet shall he live" (John 11:25). And he said, "This is eternal life, that they know you the only true God, and Jesus Christ whom you have sent" (John 17:3). Jesus Christ *is* the life. "He is the true God and eternal life" (1 John 5:20b). To know him is to live. And we should never forget that the way he became the life-giver was by dying for our sins on the cross and rising from the dead to justify us before God. This was the promise of the Old Testament: "Out of the anguish of his soul he shall see and be satisfied" (Isaiah 53:11a).

Jesus Christ is also the *light*. This was another great promise from the Old Testament. As the prophet Isaiah looked forward to the coming Savior, he said, "The people who walked in darkness have seen a great light; those who dwelt in a land of deep darkness, on them has light shone" (Isaiah 9:2). The light Isaiah promised was not for the priests only but for the whole human race. God said to his Servant, "I will make you as a light for the nations, that my salvation may reach to the end of the earth" (Isaiah 49:6b). Then the Savior finally came: "The true light, which gives light to everyone, was coming into the world" (John 1:9). His name was Jesus, and to explain his identity, all he had to say was, "I am the light of the world" (John 9:5b). Jesus Christ is the brightness of his Father's glory—the radiance of God (see Hebrews 1:3).

If Jesus is the life of God and the light of the world, then anyone who does not have a personal saving relationship with him is still living in death and darkness. Every person born into this world has natural life, but what about spiritual life? The Bible says that apart from Jesus Christ, we are "dead in [our] trespasses and sins" (Ephesians 2:1; cf. Romans 6:23). We are not alive to the voice of God speaking in Scripture. We do not have the living and active work of God's Spirit in our lives. And worst of all, those who die outside of Christ will not inherit eternal life. Instead they will come under the everlasting judgment of God, which the Bible describes as a Hell of fire. The Bible says, "God gave us eternal life, and this life is in his Son. Whoever has the Son has life; whoever does not have the Son of God does not have life" (1 John 5:11, 12). Outside of Christ, we're dead.

We're also in the dark. The Bible describes our spiritual condition without Christ as wandering in the darkness: "The light has come into the world, and people loved the darkness rather than the light because their works were evil" (John 3:19; cf. John 1:5). The Bible says that "the way of the wicked is like deep darkness" (Proverbs 4:19a). It says, "they became futile in their thinking, and their foolish hearts were darkened" (Romans 1:21). And without the light of Jesus Christ, even the Bible remains dim: "The light shines in the darkness, and the darkness has not overcome it" (John 1:5). People read the Bible, and at a certain level they understand it, but it does not shine for them with the truth of God. Only the Spirit of Christ can illuminate our minds and hearts so that the Bible becomes a lamp to our feet and a light for our path (Psalm 119:105).

This is why life is such a spiritual struggle for people who have not received Jesus as their Savior and Lord. They do not see things clearly, and they will keep stumbling around in the darkness until they come into the light of Jesus Christ. As the Bible says, "They are darkened in their understanding, alienated from the life of God because of the ignorance that is in them, due to their hardness of heart" (Ephesians 4:18). The only way to have the life and the light of God is to come to faith in Jesus Christ, who said, "I am the light of the world. Whoever follows me will not walk in darkness, but will have the light of life" (John 8:12). And whoever follows Jesus has been called "out of darkness into his marvelous light" (1 Peter 2:9; cf. Ephesians 5:8; 2 Corinthians 4:6).

The life and the light symbolized by the golden lampstand are now embodied in Jesus Christ, God's true tabernacle. The life and light he gives are eternal. So these themes of life and light are carried right through to the end of the Bible. The end of Revelation promises that there is a tree of life growing in Heaven (Revelation 22:2) and that everyone who believes in Jesus has the right to eat from it and live forever (Revelation 22:14). But one thing Heaven does not have and does not need is a lampstand. According to Revelation, God's heavenly city "has no need of sun or moon to shine on it, for the glory of God gives it light, and its lamp is the Lamb" (21:23). The Lamb is Jesus Christ, who offered himself as a sacrifice for our sin. He is the lamp of Heaven. So when the priests entered the Holy Place to trim the golden lampstand—that shining tree of lights—they were glimpsing the glorious destiny of the children of God. Anyone who comes to Jesus Christ in faith will never go down to darkness and death but will live forever in his light.

## Let Your Light Shine

That's the end of the story. However, we have not yet reached the final chapter. One day we will live in the very presence of God's light. But in the meantime we are called to live for Christ and shine for Christ in the world. God has made us "alive together with Christ" (Ephesians 2:5). This means that his life flows into our lives. Jesus described this in a way that may remind us of the lampstand in the tabernacle. He said, "I am the vine; you are the branches. Whoever abides in me and I in him, he it is that bears much fruit" (John 15:5). By faith we are joined to Jesus as the source of our spiritual life. As his life flows into us, we blossom and become fruitful, and this in turn helps bring other people to life as well. When they see how alive we are in Christ, they want to experience this new life for themselves.

We also shine as God's lights in the world. Jesus said, "As long as I am in the world, I am the light of the world" (John 9:5). But Jesus is no longer in the world. He has returned to Heaven, where he is waiting for the great day when he will be revealed in all his glory. But in the meantime he has left his light in the world to keep it from being plunged back into darkness. We are called to "shine as lights in the world" as we "[hold] fast to the word of life" (Philippians 2:15b, 16a). Significantly, the book of Revelation compares us to lampstands (see Revelation 2:1). We are the lights shining for Jesus in the world. If people are going to see him, they will see him in and through us. The same Jesus who said that *he* was the light of the world also said, "*You* are the light of the world . . . let your light shine before others, so that they may see your good works and give glory to your Father who is in heaven" (Matthew 5:14a, 16; cf. 1 John 1:7). As M. R. DeHaan has written, "The world has no light other than the light which we shed abroad, by holding aloft the lamp of the Word and lifting the Lord Jesus Christ and letting Him shine through us."[11]

J. B. Phillips has written a wonderful story about Christians shining for Christ. His parable begins with a senior angel showing a very young angel "the splendors and glories of the universe." Finally the two angels came to our own galaxy:

> As the two of them drew near to the star which we call our sun and to its circling planets, the senior angel pointed to a small and rather insignificant sphere turning very slowly on its axis. It looked as dull as a dirty tennis ball to the little angel whose mind was filled with the size and glory of what he had seen.
>
> "I want you to watch that one particularly," said the senior angel, pointing with his finger.
>
> "Well, it looks very small and rather dirty to me," said the little angel. "What's special about that one?"
>
> "That," replied his senior solemnly, "is the Visited Planet."
>
> "'Visited'?" said the little one. "You don't mean visited by—"
>
> "Indeed I do. That ball, which I have no doubt looks to you small and insignificant and not perhaps overclean, has been visited by our Prince of Glory."

This was beyond the little angel's comprehension. So to help him understand, the senior angel took him back in human history:

> While . . . the two of them moved nearer to the spinning ball, it stopped its spinning, spun backward quite fast for a while, and then slowly resumed its usual rotation.
>
> "Now look!" and as the little angel did as he was told, there appeared here and there on the dull surface of the globe little flashes of light, some merely momentary and some persisting for quite a time.
>
> "What am I seeing now?" queried the little angel.
>
> "You are watching this little world as it was some thousands of years ago," returned his companion. "Every flash and glow of light that you see is something of the Father's knowledge and wisdom breaking into the minds and hearts of people who live upon the earth. Not many people, you see, can hear His Voice or understand what He says, even though He is speaking gently and quietly to them all the time."
>
> "Why are they so blind and deaf and stupid?" asked the junior angel rather crossly.
>
> "It is not for us to judge them. We who live in the Splendor have no idea what it is like to live in the dark. . . . But watch, for in a moment you will see something truly wonderful."
>
> The Earth went on turning and circling round the sun, and then, quite suddenly, in the upper half of the globe there appeared a light, tiny, but so bright in its intensity that both angels hid their eyes.
>
> "I think I can guess," said the little angel in a low voice. "That was the Visit, wasn't it?"
>
> "Yes, that was the Visit. The Light Himself went down there and lived among them. . . . Open your eyes now; the dazzling light has gone. The Prince has returned to His Home of Light. But watch the Earth now."

> As they looked, in place of the dazzling light there was a bright glow which throbbed and pulsated. And then as the Earth turned many times, little points of light spread out. A few flickered and died, but for the most part the lights burned steadily, and as they continued to watch, in many parts of the globe there was a glow. . . .
>
> "You see what is happening?" asked the senior angel. "The bright glow is the company of loyal men and women He left behind, and with His help they spread the glow, and now lights begin to shine all over the Earth."[12]

What J. B. Phillips described in his parable is our privilege as Christians. God has given us new life, and now that we are alive in Christ, we are called to shine for Jesus, giving a glowing testimony of his saving grace. We shine for Jesus when we go out of our way to show special kindness. We shine for Jesus when we do our work cheerfully, without complaining. We shine for Jesus when we give generously to help those in need. And we shine brightest of all when we share the gospel, telling people what God has done to save us through the death and resurrection of Jesus Christ.

An old children's hymn that speaks about being a radiant Christian gives us a strong challenge to shine for Jesus:

> Be a light for Jesus, brightly shine each day;
> Radiate the Savior, in the home, at play.
> Others soon will see it, as you onward go;
> Keep on burning brightly, with a steady glow.
>
> Never let it flicker, never let it dim;
> Trim your lamp for Jesus, let it shine for Him.
> Shine on thru the darkness, precious in God's sight,
> Are His own dear children, walking in His light.[13]

This should be our prayer: never to flicker or grow dim, but to keep shining brightly for Jesus.

# 74

# The Tabernacle of God

EXODUS 26:1–37

RONALD REAGAN WAS KNOWN AS "The Great Communicator." As President of the United States, Reagan delivered many memorable speeches. One of the most moving was the one he gave after the Space Shuttle *Challenger* disaster in 1986. Only minutes after takeoff, the spaceship had exploded in a great ball of fire, killing all seven astronauts on board. As the President struggled to put a nation's grief into words, he quoted a line from a poem by the World War II aviator John Gillespie Magee. Our astronauts, Mr. Reagan said, had "slipped the surly bonds of earth to touch the face of God."[1]

This line of poetry expresses one of our deepest longings. We were made for friendship and fellowship with God. This is the way God designed us. So we are seeking a relationship with him. We want to see him and know him. We are searching for the place where earth touches Heaven, the place where we can go and meet with God. We need guidance. We need direction. We need security and stability in a mixed-up, crazy world. What we need, very simply, is God and the kind of relationship with him that provides direction and meaning for life. But how can we connect with him?

## Setting Up God's Tent

At first Exodus 26 may seem like an unlikely place to have a close encounter with the living God. This chapter contains detailed instructions for setting up God's tent—the tabernacle in the wilderness. Frankly, it is the kind of Bible passage that most people skim (if they read it at all). Architectural plans may be necessary for a building project, but they don't make for the most interesting reading.

However, this was no ordinary building. It was the tabernacle of God. It was the place where earth touched Heaven—the first earthly residence for Heaven's mighty king. The Hebrew word for tabernacle (*mishkan*) comes from the

Hebrew word that means to dwell (*shakan*). So the tabernacle was the tent where God lived, and thus its construction revealed his divine character. The tabernacle also showed what was required for sinners to meet with a holy God. This is why its plans were so important, and why to this day they deserve careful study.

God started showing Moses the design for the tabernacle back in chapter 25, where he told him what went inside: the ark, the table, and the lampstand. Then in chapter 26 we finally get a description of the tabernacle itself—not the whole complex, but the main tent that housed the Holy Place and the Most Holy Place. As God gave his instructions for the building, he worked from the inside out. He started with the ark of the covenant, which went inside the Holy of Holies—the place of his glorious presence. Then he worked his way out to the furniture in the Holy Place. Only then did he tell Moses how to build the tent where these things were housed.

To understand the tabernacle, we need to learn as much as we can about how it was built. This requires patience. We take the Bible as it comes, and in this case it comes in the form of detailed instructions for fabricating and erecting a large portable sanctuary. Like everything else in Scripture, these instructions are "breathed out by God and profitable" (2 Timothy 3:16). So rather than skimming over them, we should study them with diligence and faith.

First God told Moses how to make the tabernacle proper, the tent of his dwelling:

> Moreover, you shall make the tabernacle with ten curtains of fine twined linen and blue and purple and scarlet yarns; you shall make them with cherubim skillfully worked into them. The length of each curtain shall be twenty-eight cubits, and the breadth of each curtain four cubits; all the curtains shall be the same size. Five curtains shall be coupled to one another, and the other five curtains shall be coupled to one another. And you shall make loops of blue on the edge of the outermost curtain in the first set. Likewise you shall make loops on the edge of the outermost curtain in the second set. Fifty loops you shall make on the one curtain, and fifty loops you shall make on the edge of the curtain that is in the second set; the loops shall be opposite one another. And you shall make fifty clasps of gold, and couple the curtains one to the other with the clasps, so that the tabernacle may be a single whole. (26:1–6)

This was the innermost layer of the tabernacle. It was made with ten sheets of fabric, each measuring approximately six feet by forty-two feet. These sheets were sewn together in sets of five to make two enormous curtains, which were then joined by fifty golden clasps. These tapestries were draped over a frame to make the roof and sides of the tabernacle. They were made of fine linen—a superior white or off-white fabric. They were also adorned with colorful blue, purple, and scarlet yarn. Either woven into or embroidered onto these tapestries were images of cherubim, representing the angels who guard God's heavenly throne.

The linen was covered with a layer of wool, which in turn was covered with two protective layers of animal skins:

> You shall also make curtains of goats' hair for a tent over the tabernacle; eleven curtains shall you make. The length of each curtain shall be thirty cubits, and the breadth of each curtain four cubits. The eleven curtains shall be the same size. You shall couple five curtains by themselves, and six curtains by themselves, and the sixth curtain you shall double over at the front of the tent. You shall make fifty loops on the edge of the curtain that is outermost in one set, and fifty loops on the edge of the curtain that is outermost in the second set. You shall make fifty clasps of bronze, and put the clasps into the loops, and couple the tent together that it may be a single whole. And the part that remains of the curtains of the tent, the half curtain that remains, shall hang over the back of the tabernacle. And the extra that remains in the length of the curtains, the cubit on the one side, and the cubit on the other side, shall hang over the sides of the tabernacle, on this side and that side, to cover it. And you shall make for the tent a covering of tanned rams' skins and a covering of goatskins on top. (vv. 7–14)

The second layer of curtains was made of goat hair, a sturdy fabric that Middle Eastern nomads use to this day in making tents.[2] These woolen curtains were slightly larger than the ones underneath, measuring perhaps six feet by forty-four feet. Thus they covered the curtains of linen, completely concealing what was inside. Then two more layers were put on top to protect everything underneath from the elements, almost like a tarp. These outer tents were made of leather: ram skins and the weather-resistant hides of goats.

Every good desert tent needs poles, and the tabernacle was no exception. God told Moses to construct the kind of sturdy frame that was common in those days:

> You shall make upright frames for the tabernacle of acacia wood. Ten cubits shall be the length of a frame, and a cubit and a half the breadth of each frame. There shall be two tenons in each frame, for fitting together. So shall you do for all the frames of the tabernacle. You shall make the frames for the tabernacle: twenty frames for the south side; and forty bases of silver you shall make under the twenty frames, two bases under one frame for its two tenons, and two bases under the next frame for its two tenons; and for the second side of the tabernacle, on the north side twenty frames, and their forty bases of silver, two bases under one frame, and two bases under the next frame. And for the rear of the tabernacle westward you shall make six frames. And you shall make two frames for corners of the tabernacle in the rear; they shall be separate beneath, but joined at the top, at the first ring. Thus shall it be with both of them; they shall form the two corners. And there shall be eight frames, with their bases of silver, sixteen bases; two

> bases under one frame, and two bases under another frame. You shall make bars of acacia wood, five for the frames of the one side of the tabernacle, and five bars for the frames of the other side of the tabernacle, and five bars for the frames of the side of the tabernacle at the rear westward. The middle bar, halfway up the frames, shall run from end to end. You shall overlay the frames with gold and shall make their rings of gold for holders for the bars, and you shall overlay the bars with gold. (vv. 15–29)

The "upright frames" for the tabernacle were nearly fifty pillars or columns made of wood, covered with gold, and measuring perhaps fifteen feet tall. For support, these columns rested on silver pedestals, two per column, for a total of almost one hundred. For stability, the pillars were connected by golden crossbars, with double columns at the corners. It was over this interlocking framework that the tent curtains were draped. Although its roof was flat rather than pitched or peaked, the tabernacle was not unlike a circus tent. It consisted of fabric stretched over a frame and pegged to the ground. And like a circus tent, it could be moved from place to place.

Once Moses knew how to make the main tent, God told him what to put inside:

> And you shall make a veil of blue and purple and scarlet yarns and fine twined linen. It shall be made with cherubim skillfully worked into it. And you shall hang it on four pillars of acacia overlaid with gold, with hooks of gold, on four bases of silver. And you shall hang the veil from the clasps, and bring the ark of the testimony in there within the veil. And the veil shall separate for you the Holy Place from the Most Holy. You shall put the mercy seat on the ark of the testimony in the Most Holy Place. And you shall set the table outside the veil, and the lampstand on the south side of the tabernacle opposite the table, and you shall put the table on the north side. (vv. 31–35)

The veil described in these verses divided the tabernacle into two rooms, sealing off the Most Holy Place from the Holy Place. The whole tabernacle measured approximately fifteen feet wide by forty-five feet long. The Holy Place was a rectangle fifteen feet by thirty feet. The Most Holy Place, or Holy of Holies, was only half as long, and thus it formed a perfect cube measuring fifteen feet by fifteen feet by fifteen feet. Separating these two rooms was a heavy screen suspended by golden clasps—what Exodus later calls "the veil of the screen" (39:34; 40:21). Inside the Most Holy Place was the ark of the covenant; in the Holy Place outside were the lampstand and the table (as well as the altar of incense).

Finally, God told Moses how to make the flap that covered the doorway: "You shall make a screen for the entrance of the tent, of blue and purple and scarlet yarns and fine twined linen, embroidered with needlework. And you shall make for the screen five pillars of acacia, and overlay them with gold. Their hooks shall be of gold, and you shall cast five bases of bronze for them" (26:36, 37). Like the inside of the tabernacle, the curtain that hung across the entrance was made of fine linen with blue, purple, and scarlet thread.

These instructions give us a fair idea what the tabernacle looked like, but they do not answer all our questions. Anyone who has ever compared pictures of the tabernacle knows that no two drawings are quite the same. This is partly because some of the details were left to the craftsmen. It is also because Moses is the only person who ever saw the original model. Before assembling something, it always helps to see a diagram, which is exactly what God provided for his prophet. He said to Moses, "Then you shall erect the tabernacle according to the plan for it that you were shown on the mountain" (26:30). Presumably what God showed his prophet was the prototype for the tabernacle, and seeing it helped him make sense of all the instructions.

## Limited Access

The reason we study the tabernacle today is not so we can draw pictures of it or build an exact replica (although this can be helpful), but to learn what the tabernacle teaches us about knowing God. The question is, what did the tabernacle mean? Why did God tell Moses to set up a tent, and why did he tell him to do it this way?

There are two ways to answer these questions. One is to see what the New Testament says about the tabernacle and how it is connected to Christ. But before we do that, we need to study the Old Testament to see what the tabernacle meant in its original context. In his book *The Shadow of Christ in the Law of Moses*, Vern Poythress writes: "We must try to understand the law of Moses within its original historical context, as God gave it to the Israelites. . . . We ought to place ourselves in the position of an Israelite in the time of Moses, or in the position of Moses himself. What would they think about the tabernacle? What could they have legitimately discerned about its significance?"[3] So we begin by studying the tabernacle on its own terms, the way the Israelites did.

One of the main things God wanted his people to see was that the tabernacle was a piece of Heaven on earth. This was obvious from the very fact of God's presence. God had said to Moses, "And let them make me a sanctuary, that I may dwell in their midst" (25:8). Heaven is where God is; so when God came to live with his people, he brought Heaven down with him. This is confirmed by the way the tabernacle was made. As we saw when we studied Exodus 25, the ark of the covenant in the Holy of Holies represented God's throne. The figures on its cover represented the cherubim—God's royal attendants—the mysterious winged creatures who stand guard in the throne room of Heaven. There were more cherubim on the curtains, their images skillfully woven into the walls and veil of the tabernacle. So when the high priest entered the Holy of Holies—

God's sanctuary on earth—he caught a glimpse of Heaven, where God sits enthroned above the cherubim.

This explains why God took such great care to make sure that Moses built the tabernacle according to his exact specifications. Although the structure was made of wood, metal, and cloth, it was a copy of something in Heaven. The book of Hebrews calls it "a copy and shadow of the heavenly things. For when Moses was about to erect the tent, he was instructed by God, saying, 'See that you make everything according to the pattern that was shown you on the mountain'" (Hebrews 8:5). As the cherubim helped to show, the tabernacle was an earthly building designed to teach heavenly realities.

The tabernacle was a microcosm of the universe. Inside was Heaven, and outside was earth, with God at the center of it all. The heart of the tabernacle was the Holy of Holies, where God reigned in glory. The tabernacle, in turn, was at the heart of Israel, with all twelve tribes surrounding it. And Israel was the heart of the world, the centerpiece in God's plan for saving the nations. The tabernacle was the most important place in the world, a little bit of Heaven on earth. The point was not that somehow God could be contained within the four walls of a tent. No; the tabernacle was set up like Heaven to show that God rules over both Heaven and earth.

As the Israelites thought about the tabernacle and its meaning, they were confronted with a hard reality: Most of them were never allowed to go inside. They could see it from a distance, and they knew that God had his dwelling there, but they never even had a chance to see past the door, let alone go inside and meet with God. Everything was concealed under layers of fabric. John Mackay writes, "The description of the Tabernacle leaves one lasting impression: that of the number of coverings and entrance curtains. Though Israel had this tremendous privilege of the divine presence in their midst, there was to be no doubt that he is the Holy One, and that access to him was no easy matter, even though his palace and temple was right there at the centre of their camp."[4]

The tabernacle was the one place in the entire world where people could enter God's presence. God had come down to live with his people. However, there was almost no way for them to get in! The facility had limited access. Most Israelites only saw the curtains and other furnishings when the priests moved the tabernacle from place to place. But they never got to tour the place. Only the priests could enter, and only when they had some priestly duty to perform. And as soon as they entered, they were confronted with another curtain—the veil that separated the Holy Place from the Most Holy Place! According to the Jewish Talmud, this veil was four inches thick and took more than a hundred priests to move.[5]

Nothing symbolized Israel's limited access more clearly than the cherubim. The first time cherubim are mentioned in Scripture is Genesis 3. After Adam fell into sin, he had to be prevented from eating from the tree of life: "Therefore the LORD God sent him out from the garden of Eden to work the ground from which he was taken. He drove out the man, and at the east of the garden of Eden he placed the cherubim and a flaming sword that turned every way to guard the way to the tree of life" (vv. 23, 24). These cherubim blocked the entrance back to Eden. The cherubim on the tapestries in the tabernacle represented something similar. In a symbolic manner, they guarded the way to God.

This was all designed to show the supreme holiness of God. God is pure in his majesty and pristine in his righteousness. He is also just, which means that his holiness requires him to punish sin. Therefore, we need to be careful how we approach him. The Israelites knew this because they had seen God in action. They had seen what he did to the Egyptians back at the Red Sea, and they had heard his law from the mountain. They knew that he was a holy God who demanded perfect obedience. But they also knew they were sinners. So they understood perfectly well why, even when God came close, they still had to be separated from him. Probably they were relieved that they didn't have to go into the tabernacle, and thus that the way to God was almost closed.

*Almost* closed because there *was* one way to enter. The curtains in the tabernacle were doorways, after all, so they were designed to let God's people in. The way they could enter God's presence was to send a representative to go for them—first Moses, and later the high priest. And the way their representative penetrated the veil was by carrying an atoning sacrifice for sin—his sin as well as the sins of his people. This was the only way. The tabernacle did not have a back door. The only way for unholy sinners to enter the presence of a holy God was by means of a blood sacrifice.

## The True Tabernacle

The God who lived in the tabernacle is the same God who rules today. He is still the great King who sits enthroned above the cherubim. He is still the Lord of all the earth, and his character has not changed. He is still the holy God who demands perfect obedience and the just God who punishes sin. He is as awesome today as he was in the days of Moses.

And we are still separated from God by our sin. Sometimes people wonder why they don't have a closer relationship with God. They are on a spiritual quest, but they are never quite able to find God. They cry out to God when they're in trouble, but they're never quite sure whether God is listening when they pray. If he's there at all, God seems distant. And what causes the distance, keeping us away from God, is our sin.

One man who wanted to get closer to God was King David. He asked, "O Lord, who shall sojourn in your tent?" (Psalm 15:1). In other words, he wanted to know who could enter God's holy tabernacle. Here was the answer:

He who walks blamelessly and does what is right
 and speaks truth in his heart;
who does not slander with his tongue
 and does no evil to his neighbor,
 nor takes up a reproach against his friend;
in whose eyes a vile person is despised,
 but who honors those who fear the LORD;
who swears to his own hurt and does not change;
who does not put out his money at interest
 and does not take a bribe against the innocent.
He who does these things shall never be moved. (vv. 2–5)

This is all there is to it. If we want to meet with God—if we want to slip "the surly bonds of earth to touch the face of God"—all we have to do is lead a perfect life. The problem is that we're sinners. We *don't* always do what is righteous. We stretch the truth. We say things to cut other people down. We only keep our word as long as it's in our best interest; then we break it. We use our money to serve ourselves rather than to help others. These and all our other sins keep us from entering the holy place where God is. And this is why we need Jesus.

Remember that we have two strategies for interpreting the tabernacle. One is to study Exodus to learn what the tabernacle meant in its original context. The other is to see what the New Testament teaches about the tabernacle, especially as it relates to the person and work of Christ. One of the most important verses for understanding the tabernacle comes from the Gospel of John: "And the Word became flesh and dwelt among us" (1:14). This verse is important because the word translated "dwelt"—the Greek word *eskenosen*—comes from the Greek word for tabernacle (*skene*). So the verse means this: "The Word became flesh and *tabernacled* among us." God the Son became a man so he could come down to dwell with us. This is the interpretation of the incarnation: Jesus Christ is the tabernacle of God.

Consider the marvelous construction of the incarnate Son of God. We have seen how carefully God designed the tabernacle in the wilderness. But what intricate design was required for the Son of God to become a man and thus to live as one person with two natures—a divine nature and a human nature! Consider the mysteries of his virgin birth. Consider the secret entrance of the Holy Spirit into Mary's womb. Consider the miraculous conception of Jesus Christ—God becoming flesh. Consider the way his deity was joined to humanity as he took on not only a human body but also a human mind, heart, and will.

Jesus Christ is the true tabernacle of God. He is the sacred space where Heaven comes down to earth so we can touch the face of God. Unlike the first tabernacle, he is not made of silver and gold, linen and wool, skins and hides stretched on a wooden frame. Rather, he is made of flesh and blood, skin and bone, sinew and tendon. And all this is joined to the divine nature, because despite his humanity, Jesus retains his deity as God the very Son.

It was as the God-man that Christ was crucified, his body torn by the hard nails of our hatred and sin. And as Jesus hung on the cross, suffering and dying to pay the fair price for our sin, something miraculous happened at the temple in Jerusalem. The curtain that separated the Holy Place from the Most Holy Place was torn in two. It was rent asunder by the almighty power of God, for the Bible says: "And Jesus cried out again with a loud voice and yielded up his spirit. And behold, the curtain of the temple was torn in two, from top to bottom" (Matthew 27:50, 51a; cf. Mark 15:37, 38).

Make no mistake: This *was* a miracle. If the curtain had been only a bedsheet, someone might have been able to rip it in two. But the curtain was much too thick for anyone to tear. Furthermore, it was torn from top to bottom. Recall that the curtain was fifteen feet high, so no one could reach the top without a ladder. But imagine what would have happened if a priest had climbed up and started tampering with the curtain to the Holy of Holies! The other priests would have taken him out to stone him. All things considered, the only reasonable explanation for the rending of the veil is that it was a genuine divine miracle. The curtain was torn by the hand of Almighty God.

Imagine how shocked the priests must have been when they saw this! There they stood, outside the Holy of Holies, gazing in on the ark of the covenant. The sacred place of God's holy presence was open for all to see. What could they do? Sew it back together?

Something monumental had happened in human history. The veil that for more than a millennium had separated God's people from God's presence had parted. Now the way was open for the priests and indeed for the whole human race to meet with God in the Most Holy Place. It is not surprising to learn from the book of Acts that after Jesus ascended to Heaven, "a great many of the priests became obedient to the faith" (Acts 6:7). This is not surprising because the priests had witnessed the miracle confirming that the way was now open to God. God opened the curtain and invited them in. And once the curtain was torn, it was no longer a barrier but a gateway. It was an open door to fellowship with God.

The way is still open today. There is a way for sinners on earth to touch the face of God. The only way we can approach God is on the basis of a sacrifice. But that is what Jesus has provided. By his death on the cross, he has paid the price for our sins once and for all. In making this sacrifice Jesus has gone ahead of us into the Most Holy Place. He has entered the Holy of Holies in Heaven. According to Hebrews, "He entered once for all into the holy places, not by means of the blood of goats and calves but by means of his own blood, thus securing an eternal redemption. . . . For Christ has entered, not into holy places made with hands, which are copies of the true things, but into heaven itself, now to appear in the presence of God on our behalf" (9:12, 24). In other words, when Jesus made his sacrifice, he took it into the very throne room of God in Heaven, and not into some earthly tabernacle. And once Jesus presented his sacrifice in Heaven, the way was open for everyone who trusts in him to go and meet with God. As Hebrews goes on to say, "Therefore . . . we have confidence to enter the holy places by the blood of Jesus, by the new and living way that he opened for us through the curtain, that is, through his flesh" (10:19, 20).

This is how we gain access to God. It is through Jesus Christ and by faith in him. This is the way we gain access when we come to God for the first time. For anyone who is on a spiritual quest or who wonders how to get connected to God, the answer is, through Jesus Christ. We must confess that we are separated from God by our sin. We must trust that Jesus made the sacrifice for our sins when he died on the cross. And when we trust in Jesus, we come into a relationship with God.

This is also how we gain access to God afterward. Sometimes as Christians we drift away from God. We feel distant from him. We no longer have the same sense of access to God in prayer. We find it hard to concentrate on the truth of Scripture. We are not warm to God in worship. When this happens, we often feel like we have to work our way back to God. We assume that it is only when we return to worship and start having devotions and spending more time in prayer that God will accept us. We operate as if our relationship with God—which started by faith in Christ—must be maintained by works.

The truth is that we *always* have immediate access to God through Jesus Christ. All we need to do is turn to him. Do we need forgiveness for our sins? Peace through the stress and trials of life? Comfort in our loss? Guidance for a major decision? Provision for our material needs? Healing for either body or soul? Hope to face the future? Strength to make it through life's daily duties and difficulties? Whenever we come to God through faith in Jesus Christ, we find that he is all we need.

# 75

# The Altar in the Courtyard

EXODUS 27:1–19

THE HIGH KING OF HEAVEN came down to earth to live with his people. This was the meaning of the tabernacle in the wilderness—the tent that Moses built. The tabernacle was a place to worship God, to enter his presence, and to behold his glory. It was a place for the sons and daughters of earth to meet the Lord of Heaven.

To accomplish this purpose, the tabernacle was carefully constructed. God designed it in such a way as to reveal deep spiritual truths about his divine character. He made the tabernacle to communicate his supreme holiness, as well as his covenant love for his people. In his excellent book on the law of Moses, Vern Poythress explains what the Israelites learned when they looked at the tabernacle:

> They saw a tent with two inner rooms and a yard outside. In the yard was the Israelite equivalent of a stove, namely, a place where meat could be roasted on a fire. A tent means very little to us, but Israelites knew all about tents because they were living in tents themselves. Then God told them to make a tent for Him, a tent where God Himself would dwell and meet with them. His tent had rooms and a yard and a fireplace like their own. Yet it was also unlike their own. It was majestic, covered with gold and blue. It was beautiful, because of the symmetry of its dimensions and the artistry of its construction. Do you see? God was saying that he was majestic and beautiful. But He would not simply remain in heaven and let Israel go its way. He would come right down among them. They were living in tents. He too would be in a tent, side by side with their own tents.[1]

## The Altar of Bronze

God's stove—as Poythress calls it—was an altar for making sacrifices. Here is how God told Moses to make it:

> You shall make the altar of acacia wood, five cubits long and five cubits broad. The altar shall be square, and its height shall be three cubits. And you shall make horns for it on its four corners; its horns shall be of one piece with it, and you shall overlay it with bronze. You shall make pots for it to receive its ashes, and shovels and basins and forks and fire pans. You shall make all its utensils of bronze. You shall also make for it a grating, a network of bronze, and on the net you shall make four bronze rings at its four corners. And you shall set it under the ledge of the altar so that the net extends halfway down the altar. And you shall make poles for the altar, poles of acacia wood, and overlay them with bronze. And the poles shall be put through the rings, so that the poles are on the two sides of the altar when it is carried. You shall make it hollow, with boards. As it has been shown you on the mountain, so shall it be made. (27:1–8)

The altar was the biggest piece of furniture in the tabernacle, measuring more than seven feet wide, seven feet long, and four feet high. Its shape was square, with horn-like projections at each of the four corners. This style of altar was common in those days, and archaeologists have discovered similar specimens at Arad, Beersheba, and Dan.[2]

It is not entirely clear what the horns were for. They may simply have been ornamental. Or they may have been used for the practical purpose of tying down animals. Then again, the horns may have been symbolic, representing the horns of the animals that were slain there. In the ancient world, the horn was a symbol of strength, and it is sometimes used this way in the Bible. David said, "The LORD is . . . the horn of my salvation" (Psalm 18:2). Perhaps this is also what the horns mean here in Exodus: The altar was the place of salvation. In later times people held on to the horns of the altar for safety. When accused criminals were pursued by justice, they sometimes came to the altar and grabbed its horns for protection (e.g. 1 Kings 1:50, 51; 2:28). But whatever the horns symbolized, they must have been important, because the priests sprinkled the blood of their sacrifices on them (29:12).

The altar was made of wood overlaid with bronze (copper mixed with tin). Up to this point, all the tabernacle furnishings had been made of gold, but the altar was made of bronze. There were good practical reasons for this. Bronze is more durable and heat resistant than most metals, so it was the right material to use for an altar. There was also a good spiritual reason to use bronze: The altar stood in the courtyard outside the Tent of Meeting. All the furnishings mentioned so far went inside the tabernacle, in the place where God was, and thus they were covered with gold. God is the King of kings; thus it is only fitting for his throne to be surrounded with splendor. So the ark, the table, and the lampstand were all golden. Even the clasps that joined the innermost tents were made of gold. It must have been an amazing sight, especially for a wilderness people like the Israelites. When the priests entered the Holy Place, they were dazzled with treasures fit for a king. "I wish you could see what it's like in there," they must have told their friends. "Everything's made of gold!" This splendor would remind the Israelites that their God was the great King.

The tabernacle was only gold on the inside, where God was. The pedestals that held up the tent posts were made of silver because they rested where Heaven met earth, where the tabernacle touched the ground. And in the courtyard outside the tabernacle, where people first approached God's presence, everything was made of bronze. Gold, silver, and bronze: The closer the Israelites were to God, the more precious the metal, with gold reserved for his royal presence. As Vern Poythress explains it:

> All the furnishings in the rooms are covered with gold, signifying the royal splendor of heaven. Outside in the courtyard, the altar is made of bronze, a less expensive metal, and common Israelite worshipers may enter. The courtyard is more earthy in character. The relations between the two would doubtless suggest to Israelites their own earthiness in contrast to God's heavenly character. Israelites are on earth and God is in heaven.[3]

Since the altar was out in the courtyard, it was made of bronze, as were its utensils. There were shovels and pots for removing ashes from the stove. There were bowls for collecting and sprinkling sacrificial blood. There were long forks for turning meat over the flame. This was for the sacrifices that the people and priests were allowed to eat. And there were fire pans for scooping up live coals when the tabernacle was transported from place to place.

Halfway up the altar was a grate, also made of bronze, that was held up by rings at the four corners. Some scholars think the grating went around the outside of the altar, perhaps for decoration, or possibly to catch anything that fell off. But it seems more likely that the grate went inside the altar. Essentially the altar was a large grill. The spaces in the grillwork allowed a steady flow of oxygen from underneath. As the grill held the sacrifice above the flames, it also allowed the fat to drip down.

Like everything else in the tabernacle, the altar was designed to be portable. Not only did it come with carrying poles, but it was also hollow (see 27:8). In other words, it was an empty frame. The four sides of the altar were solid, but there was nothing inside except the grate. This helps us reconcile the instructions given here with God's prior command to make his altar out of earth and stone (20:24, 25). Since it was hollow, the bronze altar allowed the Israelites to keep this commandment. Whenever they traveled to a new place, they set up the frame and then built an altar of earth and stone inside.[4]

## God's Courtyard

Before explaining what kinds of sacrifices were made on this altar and what they teach us about salvation in Christ, something needs to be said about the courtyard where the altar stood. The tabernacle was not simply a free-standing tent; it was surrounded by a fence. The bronze altar was outside the tent, but it was inside the perimeter of the fence, in the middle of the yard.

God wanted this enclosure to be made in a particular way. He said to Moses:

> You shall make the court of the tabernacle. On the south side the court shall have hangings of fine twined linen a hundred cubits long for one side. Its twenty pillars and their twenty bases shall be of bronze, but the hooks of the pillars and their fillets shall be of silver. And likewise for its length on the north side there shall be hangings a hundred cubits long, its pillars twenty and their bases twenty, of bronze, but the hooks of the pillars and their fillets shall be of silver. And for the breadth of the court on the west side there shall be hangings for fifty cubits, with ten pillars and ten bases. The breadth of the court on the front to the east shall be fifty cubits. The hangings for the one side of the gate shall be fifteen cubits, with their three pillars and three bases. On the other side the hangings shall be fifteen cubits, with their three pillars and three bases. (27:9–15)

This fence marked the tabernacle's outer boundary. It measured approximately 75 feet by 150 feet, for a total area of more than 10,000 square feet. By way of comparison, this is roughly the size of four tennis courts. The Tent of Meeting took up less than 1,000 square feet; so there was plenty of open area. The courtyard fence consisted of sixty pillars set into sixty bases and joined by white linen curtains. The fence was nearly 8 feet tall, which permitted the Israelites to see the top of the tabernacle and the smoke rising from the altar, but not what was happening inside.

There was one way into the courtyard, however, and God gave instructions for this as well:

> For the gate of the court there shall be a screen twenty cubits long, of blue and purple and scarlet yarns and fine twined linen, embroidered with needlework. It shall have four pillars and with them four bases. All the pillars around the court shall be filleted with silver. Their hooks shall be of silver, and their bases of bronze. The length of the court shall be a hundred cubits, the breadth fifty, and the height five cubits, with hangings of fine twined linen and bases of bronze. All the utensils of the tabernacle for every use, and all its pegs and all the pegs of the court, shall be of bronze. (vv. 16–19)

The entrance was made of the same cloth that adorned the inside of the tabernacle: white linen embroidered with blue, purple, and scarlet thread. This established a connection between the entrance to the tabernacle and what went on inside. It was the gateway to the Holy Place where God was.

Many scholars have tried to determine what the colors in the fabric may have meant. Some say they signify the four Gospels.[5] Others say they represent different aspects of the saving work of Jesus Christ. In the words of one Bible teacher, "Blue stands for Christ's heavenly origin; scarlet for His sacrificial death; purple for His royal character and His regal nature; and white, His sinless righteousness and perfection."[6] One scholar goes so far as to say that we should read these colors the way we read a code, and that when we do, they reveal this message: "Heaven's Royal Blood Purchases Purity."[7] This is all true, as far as Christ is concerned, but the Bible does not say what these colors were supposed to symbolize. Patrick Fairbairn's comments on this subject are worth quoting at length:

> We therefore discard . . . the meanings derived . . . from the . . . distinctive colors employed in the several fabrics. They are here out of place. The question is not, whether such things *might* not have been used so as to convey certain ideas of a moral and religious nature, but whether they actually were so employed here; and neither the occasion of their employment, nor the manner in which this was done, in our opinion, gives the least warrant for the supposition. . . . A symbolical use of certain colors we undoubtedly find, such as of white, in expressing the idea of purity, or of red, in expressing that of guilt; but when so used, the particular color must be rendered prominent, and connected also with an occasion plainly calling for such a symbol. This was not the case in either respect with the colors in the tabernacle. The colors there, for the most part, appeared in a combined form; and if it had been possible to single them out, and give to each a distinctive value, there was nothing to indicate how the ideas symbolized were to be viewed, whether in reference to God or to His worshippers.[8]

The colors in the tabernacle may simply have been chosen for their beauty, and seeing any added significance in them runs the risk of being arbitrary. The same must be said of various attempts to interpret the size of the entrance, which is sometimes taken as a symbol of the wideness of God's mercy. Again, this is a Biblical truth: God loves to welcome people into the arms of his grace. But the question is whether the tabernacle teaches this truth. Given all the people who had to make sacrifices, and all the animals they needed to bring, the width of the entrance was more a practical necessity than a lesson in theology.

What is perhaps more significant is that the pillars around the courtyard, like the altar and all its utensils, were made of bronze. As we have seen, everything inside the tabernacle was covered with gold, which is a universal symbol of royalty. Since the Holy of Holies represented the throne room of God, everything inside was golden. But the courtyard belonged to the earth, and thus it was made of bronze instead of gold. The tabernacle complex was a microcosm of the universe, with God at the center, ruling over Heaven and earth. The progressively more precious metals that surrounded his presence symbolized his grandeur.

The three main sections of the tabernacle—the courtyard, the Holy Place, and the Most Holy Place—separated three different kinds of worshipers. We encountered a similar situation back at Mount Sinai. Only Moses was allowed to go up the mountain and meet with God. He was the mediator, the man who represented the people before God. The elders were allowed to approach God, and even to commune with him, but they could only go halfway up. Then down at the bottom were the rest of God's people, who were not allowed to approach him at all but had to stay off God's holy mountain.

The tabernacle was structured in a similar way. Only the high priest could enter the Holy of Holies. He was the mediator, the man who represented the people before God. The rest of the priests were allowed to go halfway; they could enter the Holy Place, but not the Most Holy Place. The people were kept outside. They could go into the courtyard, but they were not allowed to enter the Tent of Meeting. Perhaps one more group of people should be mentioned. Gentiles generally were not allowed to enter at all (although they *could* enter if they bound themselves in faith to the God of Israel, receiving the covenant sign of circumcision; see Leviticus 17:8, 9 and 22:18, 19). The tabernacle was set off from the camp of Israel, and Israel was set apart from the world.

Later, when Solomon replaced the tabernacle with the temple in Jerusalem, there were two courtyards: an inner courtyard and an outer courtyard. The temple of Herod's day had four courts. In those days only the priests were allowed to enter the innermost court. Outside was the court for the men of Israel, and then beyond that, the court for women. The outermost court was for the Gentiles. According to Josephus, this courtyard was separated from the inner courts by a stone wall "with an inscription, which forbade any foreigner to go in under pain of death."[9]

Not all of these courtyards were in keeping with God's law. God never said anything about keeping the women out. But access to God *was* limited. This was intended to teach the Israelites that they were separated from the holy presence of God by their sin. And as we saw in the previous chapter, this was one of the reasons that Jesus came to do his saving work. By his death and resurrection, Jesus tore the veil that kept sinners out of the Most Holy Place. He opened the way back to God.

Now the way is wide open, not only for Jews, but also for Gentiles. Through his death on the cross, Jesus "has made us both one and has broken down in his flesh the dividing wall of hostility" (Ephesians 2:14). When the Bible speaks of "the dividing wall," it may refer explicitly to the temple wall that kept out the Gentiles. But Jesus came to make sure the Gentiles could get in: "For there is no distinction between Jew and Greek; for the same Lord is Lord of all, bestowing his riches on all who call on him. For 'everyone who calls on the name of the Lord will be saved'" (Romans 10:12, 13).

Jesus did the same thing for women, so that everyone could have direct access to God: "There is neither Jew nor Greek, there is neither slave nor free, there is no male and female, for you are all one in Christ Jesus" (Galatians 3:28).

Whenever someone tries to keep people away from God on the basis of their ethnicity or gender, this is not Biblical Christianity. A person doesn't have to be Jewish or male to go and meet with God. Any sinner in need of grace can have access to God through faith in Jesus Christ.

## By the Blood

In the Old Testament, the only place to gain access to God was the tabernacle, and later the temple. The first step was to walk through the entrance into the courtyard. This was always a busy place, full of people, priests, and animals. And it was a place where the Israelites loved to go. They wrote poetry about how wonderful it was to walk in God's courtyard:

> When iniquities prevail against me,
>     you atone for our transgressions.
> Blessed is the one you choose and bring near,
>     to dwell in your courts!
> We shall be satisfied with the goodness of your house,
>     the holiness of your temple! (Psalm 65:3, 4)
>
> My soul longs, yes, faints
>     for the courts of the Lord;
> my heart and flesh sing for joy
>     to the living God. (Psalm 84:2)
>
> For a day in your courts is better
>     than a thousand elsewhere.
> I would rather be a doorkeeper in the house of my God
>     than dwell in the tents of wickedness. (Psalm 84:10)
>
> Enter his gates with thanksgiving,
>     and his courts with praise!
>     Give thanks to him; bless his name! (Psalm 100:4)

We should have the same feelings of exuberance when we go to worship with God's people. Drawing near to God is a blessing to the soul. Our hearts cry out for him. And when we get close to God in worship, he fills us with good things. This is why it is better to be in church—even just standing in the doorway—than anywhere else in the world.

There were many reasons why the Israelites loved to enter God's courts. But the most important reason—the one that put the song in their hearts—was that in the courtyard they received forgiveness. Standing in the center was the altar where they offered sacrifices to atone for their sins. This was the first thing they encountered. As soon as the Israelites entered the courtyard, they saw a flaming altar, and the first thing they did was to make a sacrifice for their sins.

Consider how significant this is for our understanding of what it means to have a relationship with God. Many people say they want to know God. Usually what they really mean is that they want God to bless them. They're not interested in God as much as they are in what he can do for them. They have a long list of questions they'd like him to answer, problems they'd like him to solve, and blessings they'd like him to bestow. But this is not how God operates. Before anything else happens, something has to be done about our sin. God is holy; we're not. And until this is dealt with, there is no way for us to have a relationship with him. First things first: a sacrifice has to be made so that our sins can be forgiven and we can be reconciled to God.

The tabernacle was designed to show this. The most prominent part of its structure was the Tent of Meeting—the place where God was. But standing between the worshiper and the presence of God was the largest piece of furniture at the tabernacle: an altar of bronze. The altar was a place of blood and death where animals were slashed and burned. In the words of A. W. Pink, "It was at the Brazen-altar that the holiness and righteousness of God were displayed: His hatred of sin, and His justice in punishing it."[10] The only way to approach this righteous, holy God was through a blood sacrifice for sin. This is what God's justice requires, "for the wages of sin is death" (Romans 6:23a), and "without the shedding of blood there is no forgiveness of sins" (Hebrews 9:22).

Many of us find this rather unpleasant. We would rather not talk about sin, let alone about paying its price in blood. We hope to find some other way to God. Usually we want to reach him by climbing the ladder of our own obedience. We think that somehow we can make ourselves good enough for God. Or we want God to accept us as we are, without ever repenting of our sin. We hope to find a loophole in the terms of salvation. We assume there is a back door to Heaven. We want to find a way around the bloody, smoky altar of sacrifice.

But there is no other way. Sinners cannot come into the presence of a holy God unless atonement has been made for their sin. We see this all the way through the Bible. At every stage of salvation, God's people needed to bring a sacrifice for their sins. This was true for Adam and Eve. It was true for Cain and Abel. It was true for Noah and his family. It was true for Abraham, Isaac, and Jacob.

It was also true for Moses, as we have seen throughout Exodus. Before Israel could get out of Egypt, the nation had to celebrate Passover. This meant that every household had to sacrifice a perfect lamb and paint its blood on the door. This is what had to be done before Israel could go and meet with God in the wilderness (see 3:18). The people offered more sacrifices at Mount Sinai. There Moses built an altar, offered sacrifices, and then sprinkled blood on both the altar and the people of God (24:5, 6, 8). This had to be done. Whenever God establishes a relationship with people, atonement has to be made for sin. This is what God has always required.

This forces each of us to ask a serious question: Has atonement been made for *my* sin? If a blood sacrifice is what God requires, then a blood sacrifice is what we need. And, of course, this is why we need Jesus. If there is any way for us to meet with God, if we are ever going to find forgiveness, then we need some kind of sacrifice. And God has provided one. The Bible says, "God put forward [Jesus] as a propitiation by his blood, to be received by faith" (Romans 3:25a). If we trust in Jesus, then a sacrifice has been made for our sin, and we have a relationship with the living God.

## The Altar of God

To fully understand what God has done for us through Christ and his cross, it helps to know more about the sacrifices that the Israelites made on their altar. There was one altar for the entire nation, and it was in almost constant use.

The five main kinds of required sacrifices are described in the opening chapters of Leviticus. First there was the *burnt offering* (Leviticus 1)—a general sacrifice for sin, in which an entire animal was burned on the altar. This represented not only atonement for sin but also a complete surrender—total consecration to God. At least two burnt offerings were made every day, in the morning and in the evening (see 29:38–41; cf. Numbers 28:3–8). There was also the *grain offering* (Leviticus 2), in which part of the harvest was dedicated to God with thanksgiving for all his blessings. Part of the grain offering was burned on the altar, and part of it was given to the priests. Then there was the *peace offering* (Leviticus 3), in which part of an animal was sacrificed to God and the rest was eaten by the worshiper. This symbolized reconciliation with God on the basis of atonement for sin.

Finally, there was the *sin offering* (Leviticus 4:1—5:13) and also the *guilt offering* (Leviticus 5), in which atonement was made for sin—either for an individual or for the nation, whether the sin was deliberate or not. To show that the price had been paid, blood from the sacrifice was sprinkled on the altar. Since blood signifies life, this showed that an animal had died and that the value of its death had been applied to the sinner. Vern Poythress explains the procedure:

> In a typical case the process begins with the worshiper who brings an animal without defect to the priest. The worshiper has raised the animal himself or paid for it with his earnings, so that the animal represents a "sacrifice" in the modern sense of the word. It costs something to the worshiper, and a portion of the worshiper's own life is identified with it. The worshiper lays his hand on the head of the animal, signifying his identification with it. He then kills the animal at the entranceway into the courtyard, signifying that the animal dies as a substitute for the worshiper.
>
> From that point onward the priest takes over in performing the sacrificial actions. The intervention of the priest indicates that a specially holy person must perform the actions necessary to present the worshiper before God, even after the death of the animal. The priest takes some of the blood

> and sprinkles it on the sides of the bronze altar or on the horns of the altar . . . depending on the particular type of sacrifice. . . . All of these actions constitute the permanent marking of the altar as testimony to the fact that the animal has died.[11]

God carried out his wrath against the animal. It died in place of the sinner, a life for a life. This was in keeping with the strictest demands of God's justice. God said, "For the life of the flesh is in the blood, and I have given it for you on the altar to make atonement for your souls, for it is the blood that makes atonement by the life" (Leviticus 17:11).

After a while, the description of these offerings can start to get monotonous. It is hard for us to keep all the details straight. When were people supposed to bring a grain offering? How was the fellowship offering prepared? What was the difference between the sin offering and the guilt offering? But if reading about all these sacrifices gets tedious, it must have been far more tedious actually to offer them. The Israelites had to sacrifice many animals on many occasions for many reasons.

No doubt this explains why the bronze altar was always burning. God said, "The fire on the altar shall be kept burning on it; it shall not go out. The priest shall burn wood on it every morning, and he shall arrange the burnt offering on it and shall burn on it the fat of the peace offerings. Fire shall be kept burning on the altar continually; it shall not go out" (Leviticus 6:12, 13). The priests had a responsibility to make sure that the fire was never extinguished. A. W. Pink comments: "There it stood: ever smoking, ever blood-stained, ever open to any guilty Hebrew that might wish to approach it. The sinner, having forfeited his life by sin, another life—an innocent life—must be given in his stead."[12]

This was a powerful witness to the totality of Israel's depravity. The altar was always ready to receive another sacrifice. Imagine how many sacrifices must have been made on that altar! At least two burnt offerings were sacrificed every day for more than one thousand years. Fellowship offerings were made whenever people were grateful to God. Then there were all the sin offerings and guilt offerings. Think of all the bulls, goats, lambs, and pigeons that must have been required to atone for the sins of a million people. Then imagine continuing to make those sacrifices every day for a millennium.

But it still wasn't enough! The people were always committing more sins, so there were always more sacrifices to make. It was a messy, bloody business. And if we think we get bored by all the sacrifices—what about God? Imagine how many sacrifices he must have seen on Israel's altar. And this was exactly the point. The Old Testament sacrifices were intended to overwhelm. The people could keep on offering animal sacrifices forever, but it still wouldn't deal adequately with the problem of their sin. As the Scripture says, "It is impossible for the blood of bulls and goats to take away sins" (Hebrews 10:4).

What people need is a perfect sacrifice, one that does away with sin once and for all. And of course this is what Jesus offered on the cross: one perfect sacrifice to atone for sin forever. Jesus didn't make his sacrifice on the bronze altar at the tabernacle. He did it by suffering and dying on the cross, shedding his own blood—the very blood of God. And when he did this, Jesus was making atonement for our sins. He was serving as our substitute, dying in our place so that we could have forgiveness and come into a right relationship with God. The Bible says:

> For Christ has entered, not into holy places made with hands, which are copies of the true things, but into heaven itself, now to appear in the presence of God on our behalf. Nor was it to offer himself repeatedly, as the high priest enters the holy places every year with blood not his own, for then he would have had to suffer repeatedly since the foundation of the world. But as it is, he has appeared once for all at the end of the ages to put away sin by the sacrifice of himself. (Hebrews 9:24–26)

When we approach God today, we come by way of the cross. Jesus is the only altar we need. He is the atoning sacrifice. His blood has paid the price of our sin. As the great Puritan theologian John Owen said, "The altar which we now have is *Christ alone*, and his sacrifice. For he was both priest, altar, and sacrifice, all in himself."[13] We come to God through Jesus, and through the cross where he died. If we trust in him, then we have an atoning sacrifice, and our sins are forgiven.

No more sacrifice for sin is needed: "Now when sins have been forgiven, there is no need to offer any more sacrifices" (Hebrews 10:18, NLT). However, there is one sacrifice that we *can* still make, which is to offer ourselves for God's service. Now that Jesus has paid the price of our sin, God no longer commands us to *bring* a sacrifice, but he does want us to *become* one! He says, "Present your bodies as a living sacrifice, holy and acceptable to God, which is your spiritual worship" (Romans 12:1). This is the sacrifice we make, not on an altar of bronze, but on the altar of our own minds and hearts.

# 76

# A Priest before God

EXODUS 27:20—28:14

THE TABERNACLE IS WHERE the people of God transacted their spiritual business. It was the place they brought their thank offerings, made atonement for their sins, and entered the presence of the living God. But they did not do these things on their own. The tabernacle was not self-service. Rather, its sacred duties were performed by holy men with a holy calling. These men served in the tabernacle as priests before God. Theirs was the high privilege of entering the Holy Place where God was.

## The Eternal Flame

Up to this point in Exodus, God has said relatively little about the priests and their duties. First he told Moses how he wanted the tabernacle constructed, and only then did he explain what was supposed to happen inside. But we already have a good idea what the priests did from the way the tabernacle was furnished. The priests made holy bread and put it on the table of showbread. They offered sacrifices on the altar in the courtyard. They took care of the sacred objects used to pour drink offerings, sprinkle sacrificial blood, and tend the fire on the altar. And the priests took down, carried, and set up the tabernacle whenever God and his people were on the move.

The priests also kept the lights burning on the golden lampstand. This was the first sacred duty that God explicitly demanded: "You shall command the people of Israel that they bring to you pure beaten olive oil for the light, that a lamp may regularly be set up to burn. In the tent of meeting, outside the veil that is before the testimony, Aaron and his sons shall tend it from evening to morning before the Lord. It shall be a statute forever to be observed throughout their generations by the people of Israel" (27:20, 21).

As we saw in Exodus 25, the lampstand stood in the Holy Place. Part of its purpose was to light the tabernacle, dispelling the darkness. It was also a symbol of light and life. It was made in the shape of a tree—the tree of life. As a lampstand, it was also a tree of light. Thus it symbolized God's life-giving, light-spreading power.

To keep the light shining, God commanded his people to bring oil to the tabernacle, specifically "pure beaten olive oil" (27:20). This was oil of the finest quality—lightly beaten, but not crushed, so as to avoid contaminating the oil with pulp from the olive. Such pure oil would burn almost smoke-free, with a clean, pure light.

This light was always shining. Verse 20 implies that the golden lampstand was to be kept burning all the time. But according to verse 21, the priests only had to keep it burning through the night. In effect, the lampstand was the night-light in God's house. However, the words "from evening to morning" may simply mean that the priests performed their duty in shifts, so that some of them were on duty all night. This is how the priests interpreted God's command (at least in later times), because according to Josephus, they kept the light burning during the day as well as all through the night.[1]

Either way, the meaning of the light was the same. Whether it burned all the time or all night, every night, it represented the eternal presence of God. His light was shining for his people as a symbol of his constant and watchful care. In the words of Aaron's famous benediction, "The LORD bless you and keep you; the LORD make his face to shine upon you and be gracious to you" (Numbers 6:24, 25).

At the same time, the light showed that God deserves everlasting praise. The light on the lampstand was an eternal flame, for God said to Moses, "It shall be a statute forever to be observed throughout their generations by the people of Israel" (27:21b). But in order for this to happen, a priest always had to be in the tabernacle to tend the flame. This ensured that someone was always worshiping God in his holy sanctuary—not just by day, but all through the night.

Knowing this filled God's people with great joy. They sang, "Come, bless the LORD, all you servants of the LORD, who stand by night in the house of the LORD! Lift up your hands to the holy place and bless the LORD!" (Psalm 134:1, 2). With these words, the people encouraged the priests in their sacred calling. They knew that their priests were representing them before God, staying up all night to keep the fire burning, and that by doing this they were offering God perpetual praise.

The lampstand was a little bit of Heaven on earth. Heaven is the place where God is glorified by all the saints who have gone to glory, the place where he has received praise since the moment the angels began singing for joy. The perpetual flame on the golden lampstand was a symbol of the heavenly worship that never ends. What God deserves is nothing less than everlasting praise. Sadly, because of our weakness and sin, we are not able to give it to him. But whenever we praise God here on earth we join the everlasting song. As we wait for the day when we will enter glory, we declare that to our God belongs eternal praise.

## The High Priest and His Garments

The men who tended the eternal flame were the priests. Before explaining the rest of their duties, God told Moses who should serve. He said, "Then bring near to you Aaron your brother, and his sons with him, from among the people of Israel, to serve me as priests—Aaron and Aaron's sons, Nadab and Abihu, Eleazar and Ithamar" (28:1).

Aaron was Moses' brother. He had been a leader in Israel since Moses first told Pharaoh to let God's people go. Aaron had served as Moses' spokesman. He had performed miraculous signs. He had held the prophet's hands up in prayer. He had gone up the mountain to see God. Now God was calling Aaron and his sons to serve as priests in his holy tabernacle. Aaron was the father of the priesthood, the first in a long line of priests before God.

It is significant that Aaron and his sons did not claim this office for themselves. Their calling came from God. There was no such thing as a self-appointed priest. The same principle holds true in the church. There are no self-appointed pastors, elders, or deacons. When God calls someone to public service in the church, he gives an inward sense of calling. But if the call to sacred ministry really comes from God, then it will also come through those who hold spiritual authority in the church. This principle is illustrated by the call of Aaron, who did not volunteer to become high priest. He was appointed by God, speaking through his servant Moses. As God later said, "Did I choose [Aaron] out of all the tribes of Israel to be my priest, to go up to my altar, to burn incense, to wear an ephod before me?" (1 Samuel 2:28a).

The mention of the ephod indicates that God had special clothes for his priests to wear—especially the high priest. God said to Moses,

> And you shall make holy garments for Aaron your brother, for glory and for beauty. You shall speak to all the skillful, whom I have filled with a spirit of skill, that they make Aaron's garments to consecrate him for my priesthood. These are the garments that they shall make: a breastpiece, an ephod, a robe, a coat of checker work, a turban, and a sash. They shall make holy garments for Aaron your brother and his sons to serve me as priests. They shall receive gold, blue and purple and scarlet yarns, and fine twined linen. (28:2–5)

These articles of clothing are described more fully later in Exodus. They were carefully made by men with a God-given gift for craftsmanship. First came the breastpiece, adorned with gemstones, which went over the high priest's chest. This was attached to the ephod—a long, sleeveless vest something like an apron. The ephod was suspended by shoulder straps, almost like overalls, and tied around the priest's waist with a belt. These were Aaron's outer garments. Underneath he wore a robe, a tunic, and linen underclothes. To top it all off, he had a turban for his head.

These were the ceremonial robes the high priest wore as he performed the sacred duties of his office. The Bible uses three important words to describe his garments: "holy," glory," and "beauty." The Hebrew word for holiness comes at the beginning of verse 2: "Make holy garments." These clothes were *qodesh*, which means "sacred" or "set apart." Obviously, they were not for everyday use. In fact, apart from the high priest, no one has ever worn anything like them. These garments were set apart for sacred duty: holy clothes for a holy calling. What the high priest wore showed that what he did—whether it was lighting the lampstand or offering sacrifices on the altar—was holy before God.

The high-priestly garments were also glorious and beautiful. These words come at the end of verse 2: "And you shall make holy garments for Aaron your brother, for glory and for beauty." The word translated "glory" is *kavod*. More literally, it means "weighty," and thus it refers to the gravity of the priestly office. There was something glorious about the high priest's calling, and this was displayed by the special grandeur of his clothes. The last word is *tipara*, which is one of the Hebrew words for beauty. And the high-priestly garments *were* beautiful. They were designed with an obvious appreciation for fashion and style. The high priest was the best-dressed man in Israel. His robes were made of pure white linen, decorated with colorful yarn in gold, blue, purple, and scarlet.

These were the same colors used in making the tabernacle. The furniture in the Tent of Meeting was made of gold. Its white linen curtains were embroidered with blue, purple, and scarlet. What the high priest wore, therefore, was made of the same material. It was almost as if the high priest "embodied the tabernacle."[2] Anyone who saw him immediately recognized that he belonged there. The holiness, glory, and beauty of his apparel associated him with God's sacred space.

The priest and the tabernacle both pointed to God. The words used to describe the high-priestly garments could just as well be used to describe God's divine nature, and in fact this is the way the Bible generally employs them. God is holy, set apart in his purity. God is glorious, working all things for his glory. Glory is "the uncovering of God's character—the disclosure of who God is."[3] And God is glorious *in* his holiness: "Holy, holy, holy is the Lord of hosts; the whole earth is full of his glory!" (Isaiah 6:3). God is also beautiful. Nothing is more beautiful to the soul than to contemplate his divine perfections. King David said, "One thing have I asked of the Lord, that will I seek after: that I may dwell in the house of the Lord all the days of my life, to gaze upon the beauty of the Lord and to inquire in his temple" (Psalm 27:4). Israel's holy sanctuary was full of God's beauty.

Holiness, glory, beauty—these are essential attributes of God: "Give unto the LORD the glory due unto his name; worship the LORD in the beauty of holiness" (Psalm 29:2 KJV). If this is what God is like—beautiful in his holiness and glorious in his splendor—then the only way to approach him is to be adorned with holiness, glory, and beauty, the way the high priest of Israel was dressed when he put on his sacred robes and entered the Most Holy Place.

## The Ephod

The grandeur of these garments was important not only for the high priest but also for the nation of Israel. Whenever the priest performed his sacred duties, he represented God's people. He did not act for himself alone, but for all the people before God. What he wore, therefore, was as important to them as it was to him.

The priest's role as representative was symbolized by the ephod. *Ephod* is a strange word, and scholars are not entirely certain what the garment looked like. Here is how God described it:

> And they shall make the ephod of gold, of blue and purple and scarlet yarns, and of fine twined linen, skillfully worked. It shall have two shoulder pieces attached to its two edges, so that it may be joined together. And the skillfully woven band on it shall be made like it and be of one piece with it, of gold, blue and purple and scarlet yarns, and fine twined linen. (28:6–8)

Like everything else in the tabernacle, the ephod was made of fine linen adorned with richly colored thread. It seems to have been a long, sleeveless apron or vest, with two straps or suspenders that went over the priest's shoulders. God gave Moses special instructions for putting these together:

> You shall take two onyx stones, and engrave on them the names of the sons of Israel, six of their names on the one stone, and the names of the remaining six on the other stone, in the order of their birth. As a jeweler engraves signets, so shall you engrave the two stones with the names of the sons of Israel. You shall enclose them in settings of gold filigree. And you shall set the two stones on the shoulder pieces of the ephod, as stones of remembrance for the sons of Israel. And Aaron shall bear their names before the LORD on his two shoulders for remembrance. You shall make settings of gold filigree, and two chains of pure gold, twisted like cords; and you shall attach the corded chains to the settings. (vv. 9–14)

To finish the ephod, craftsmen took two semiprecious stones and mounted them in ornate settings made with golden wire (according to *Webster's 11th New Collegiate Dictionary*, filigree is "ornamental openwork of delicate or intricate design"). The stones were then attached to the shoulder pieces of the ephod. Two chains of golden braid hung down like ropes, presumably to hold up the breastpiece.

The most important thing about the ephod was what was written on it. Inscribed on the two stones were twelve names. These were names of the sons of Jacob, later called Israel. The names on one stone were Reuben, Simeon, Judah, Dan, Naphtali, and Gad; the names on the other were Asher, Issachar, Zebulun, Ephraim, Manasseh, and Benjamin.[4] These were the twelve tribes of Israel.

Consider the spiritual significance of these inscriptions. The twelve tribes of Israel were camping in the wilderness, living in a giant city of tents organized by tribes, with three tribes camping at each of the four points of the compass. At the center of it all was the tabernacle—the tent where God was. And when the high priest entered that Holy Place, he wore the tribal names of Israel on his shoulders. This showed that the high priest represented the people before God. As God said to Moses, "Aaron shall bear their names before the LORD on his two shoulders for remembrance" (28:12b).

Whenever the high priest put on his ceremonial robes, he lifted the people onto his shoulders and carried them into the presence of God. Back at Mount Sinai, God had said, "Now therefore, if you will indeed obey my voice and keep my covenant, you shall be my treasured possession among all peoples, for all the earth is mine; and you shall be to me a kingdom of priests and a holy nation" (19:5, 6a). These great spiritual realities—that Israel belonged to God as a treasure and was called to serve him as a holy kingdom of priests—were symbolically reenacted every time the high priest went before God. His clothes made a fashion statement. They said, "Here we are, Lord, all twelve tribes of us—your precious kingdom of priests."

The priest wore these clothes when he first made atonement for sin.[5] God said to Aaron, "Draw near to the altar and offer your sin offering and your burnt offering and make atonement for yourself and for the people, and bring the offering of the people and make atonement for them, as the LORD has commanded" (Leviticus 9:7). As Aaron offered this sacrifice, he was carrying Israel on his shoulders, representing the people before God. Through the priestly act of this one man, atonement was made for all the sin of God's people.

## Our Great High Priest

There was only one problem with this arrangement: The high priest himself was a sinner. No matter how magnificent his clothes were—how holy, glorious, or beautiful they were—they could not hide the sin in his heart. The clothes did not make the man. So the sacrifices the high priest offered were neither perfect nor permanent. He had to keep going back into the tabernacle over and over to make atonement, both for his own sin and for the sins of God's people.

To enter the glorious presence of God requires perfect holiness, and the high priest didn't have it. The stories in the Bible prove this time and again. None of Israel's high priests ever lived up to God's standard. Aaron sinned by leading the people in false worship: He made the golden calf (32). His sons Nadab and

Abihu sinned by offering unholy fire on God's altar; for that they were destroyed (Leviticus 10:1, 2). Eli sinned by failing to discipline his sons. They were also priests, but they were such wicked men that God struck them both down on the same day (1 Samuel 2:12–25).

As we read on through the prophets, we discover that as much as anything else, it was the corruption of the priests that led Israel into exile. Eventually the priesthood broke down altogether. From Hosea we learn that "the children of Israel shall dwell many days without king or prince, without sacrifice or pillar, without ephod or household gods" (Hosea 3:4). This was a chilling prophecy. It meant that when the people of God fell under judgment, they would live without a royal king or a holy priest. There would be no one to wear the ephod, no one to bear the tribal names as a memorial before God, and no one to offer a sacrifice for their sins—and this went on for centuries.

God's people needed a perfect priest. They needed a holy priest who was uncorrupted by his own sin. They needed a glorious priest who would shine forever in God's light. They needed a beautiful priest who would offer his pure life to God. In a word, they needed Jesus, because the great message of the gospel is that God has provided the perfect priest in the person of his own Son.

Seeing this helps us understand how the Old Testament and the New Testament fit together. Theologians have long recognized that there were three main offices in Old Testament Israel: prophet, priest, and king. The prophet was the man who spoke God's word. The priest was the man who went into God's presence to make atonement for sin. The king was the man who ruled with God's authority.

All three of these offices were vitally important to the success of the nation. God's people flourished whenever they had faithful prophets, holy priests, and godly kings. Unfortunately, this didn't happen very often. Usually a faithful prophet had to deal with an ungodly king, or the authority of a godly king was undermined by an immoral priesthood. The results were always disastrous. Again and again the Old Testament confronts us with Israel's desperate need for these offices to come together. God finally supplied the need by sending his Son to do the work of all three offices. God sent Jesus Christ to be our faithful prophet, holy priest, and godly king. The more we learn about these three offices from the Old Testament, the more clearly we understand the person and work of Christ.

We learn about Christ's priestly ministry by studying the tabernacle. Whatever the high priest did for Israel in that holy place, Jesus has done for us in Heaven itself. This is the main argument of the book of Hebrews, which says, "We have a great high priest who has passed through the heavens, Jesus, the Son of God" (4:14). But in order for Jesus to serve as our high priest, he had to meet the qualifications. He had to be able to enter God's glorious presence in the beauty of holiness.

In the Old Testament, the high priest made himself presentable by wearing special clothes—"holy garments . . . for glory and for beauty" (28:2). Unfortunately, the inward reality of the priest's life never matched the outward splendor of his appearance. Enter Jesus. The writer to the Hebrews asks, "Now if perfection had been attainable through the Levitical priesthood . . . what further need would there have been for another priest to arise?" (7:11). The obvious answer is that perfection could *not* be attained through Israel's priesthood; it could only come through a greater priest. So the Scripture goes on to say, concerning Jesus and his priestly ministry:

> For it was indeed fitting that we should have such a high priest, holy, innocent, unstained, separated from sinners, and exalted above the heavens. He has no need, like those high priests, to offer sacrifices daily, first for his own sins and then for those of the people, since he did this once for all when he offered up himself. For the law appoints men in their weakness as high priests, but the word of the oath, which came later than the law, appoints a Son who has been made perfect forever. (Hebrews 7:26–28)

Jesus is a priest without sin. He is holiness incarnate—perfectly righteous in his own person. He is also glorious. As the Scripture says, "He is the radiance of the glory of God and the exact imprint of his nature, and he upholds the universe by the word of his power. After making purification for sins, he sat down at the right hand of the Majesty on high" (Hebrews 1:3). Jesus is pristine in his holiness, magnificent in his glory, and sublime in his beauty.

This means that when he performed the great work of his priesthood—which was to offer himself as the sacrifice for our sins by dying on the cross—he did not need to wear any of the high priest's clothes. He did not wear the ephod. He did not have precious stones on his shoulders or a breastpiece over his chest. He did not wear the robe or the tunic, the turban or the sash. Jesus did not wear any of these things but suffered for our sins in naked glory. He did not need any outward splendor but had a splendor all his own. It was the glorious holiness of his own beautiful person that made his offering acceptable unto God. And when God the Father saw Jesus making atonement for sin, he said, "Now here is a sacrifice that will pay for sin once and for all. The priest who offers it is perfectly holy, without any spot or blemish of sin. And he is more beautiful than anything in all creation because he shines with the glory of my own divine nature. This great high priest is my own beloved Son."

Now here is the amazing thing: This is not simply how the Father looks at his Son but how he views everyone who trusts in his Son, because Jesus is our great High Priest before God. Sometimes people wonder how they can ever approach God. They get so weighed down by their sins that they find it hard to believe that God will accept them. But the truth is that God has promised to accept anyone and everyone who comes to him in the name of Jesus Christ.

When he died on the cross, Jesus was carrying us on his shoulders, taking our sin upon himself in order to deal with it in the presence of God. Our names have been written on God incarnate, for as God said through the prophet Isaiah, "Behold, I have engraved you on the palms of my hands" (Isaiah 49:16a). And Jesus stands as our representative before God to this very day. To quote again from the book of Hebrews, "Now the point in what we are saying is this: we have such a high priest, one who is seated at the right hand of the throne of the Majesty in heaven, a minister in the holy places, in the true tent that the Lord set up, not man" (8:1, 2).

The tabernacle was the place of God's presence. Now the true tabernacle is in Heaven—the place where God is. And our great High Priest is in the tabernacle. Just as the Israelites looked to their high priest, so we look to Jesus: "Therefore, holy brothers, you who share in a heavenly calling, consider Jesus, the apostle and high priest of our confession" (Hebrews 3:1). And as we look to Jesus, in all the beauty of his holiness, we find the assurance of our salvation. We know that just as God has accepted our great High Priest, so he will accept us: "We have this as a sure and steadfast anchor of the soul, a hope that enters into the inner place behind the curtain, where Jesus has gone as a forerunner on our behalf" (Hebrews 6:19, 20a).

# 77

# Knowing God's Will

## EXODUS 28:15–30

HAVE YOU EVER WANTED TO KNOW exactly what God wanted you to do? Decision making can be difficult, and when it's time to make an important life choice, people often wish that God would come right out and tell them what he wants them to do. What college should I go to? Which job should I take? What church should I attend? Is God calling me to be a missionary? Is it time to relocate? Whom should I marry? Which medical treatment should I choose? Life is full of decisions, and when it comes to the tough ones, it would be nice to know exactly what God has in mind.

When I was a child, kids in my neighborhood tried to figure out the future by consulting a plastic toy known as The Magic 8-Ball. The toy looked like a large, black billiard ball. It was filled with liquid, with a flat window on one side. This is where the answers to life's questions would appear, as if by magic. A kid would ask a question and shake the ball. Everyone else would crowd around to see what answer would show up in the window: "Yes." "No." "Maybe." "Ask again."

There are times when we want to know God's will for our future, when we wish he would give us something like The Magic 8-Ball. Am I supposed to go here or there? Is it this or is it that? Should I stay or should I go? Tell me, Lord: Is it maybe, yes, or no?

In his infinite wisdom, God has not provided a guidance system to shake and then wait for his divine will to appear. However, God did give his people a way to make decisions in the Old Testament. Israel's high priest carried the tools for knowing God's will in his front pocket—the Urim and Thummim. By studying these strange devices in their total Biblical context, we can come to a better understanding of how God guides his people today.

## The Breastpiece

To review, the high priest served in the tabernacle—the Holy Place where God was. It was his responsibility to make atoning sacrifices and offer fervent prayers on behalf of God's people. As the high priest carried out these duties, he wore special clothes. These sacred garments, which were made of the same stuff as the tabernacle, were designed to make him presentable to God. They were holy, glorious, and beautiful—just like God. This showed what it takes for sinners to come into the presence of a holy God. We must be gloriously and beautifully holy . . . or else represented by someone who is. This is what the high priest did for Israel: He represented them before God. The people were not allowed to go into the Most Holy Place and meet with God. They were separated from his holiness by their sin. But they did have a mediator to meet with God for them—the high priest, dressed in righteous robes.

The most important garment the high priest wore was the ephod—the long, sleeveless vest that hung over the priest's shoulders. Attached to the front of the ephod was a breastpiece, which God told Moses to make as follows:

> You shall make a breastpiece of judgment, in skilled work. In the style of the ephod you shall make it—of gold, blue and purple and scarlet yarns, and fine twined linen shall you make it. It shall be square and doubled, a span its length and a span its breadth. You shall set in it four rows of stones. A row of sardius, topaz, and carbuncle shall be the first row; and the second row an emerald, a sapphire, and a diamond; and the third row a jacinth, an agate, and an amethyst; and the fourth row a beryl, an onyx, and a jasper. They shall be set in gold filigree. There shall be twelve stones with their names according to the names of the sons of Israel. They shall be like signets, each engraved with its name, for the twelve tribes. (28:15–21)

The breastpiece is sometimes called the breastplate, which makes it sound like a piece of armor. However, it was made of fabric, not metal, and it wasn't very large. It measured the breadth of a man's hand from thumb tip to fingertip, or roughly nine inches square. The most striking feature of the breastpiece was its beautiful collection of gems. These were arranged in four rows, with three precious or semiprecious stones in each row. The translation of some of the Hebrew words for these stones is uncertain, so it is impossible to know which gems God had in mind or what color they were. But the breastpiece presented a dazzling array of colorful stones.

Nearly all these gemstones were found in the garden of Eden (see Ezekiel 28:13). We will see them again in Heaven, where they decorate the foundations of God's city (Revelation 21:19, 20). This is a hint that what God was doing with Israel at the tabernacle was part of his plan for the world—a plan that stretches from creation to glory.

These gemstones represented the people of God. There were twelve stones—one for each of the twelve tribes of Israel. Each stone was engraved with the name of a tribe. This was a vivid reminder of what God said when his people first arrived at Mount Sinai: "Now therefore, if you will indeed obey my voice and keep my covenant, you shall be my treasured possession among all peoples, for all the earth is mine; and you shall be to me a kingdom of priests and a holy nation" (19:5, 6a; cf. 1 Peter 2:9). God's promise was displayed on the breastpiece. As the high priest went about his sacred duties, he represented the holy nation of God's people—a kingdom of priests. By their inscriptions, the ruby, topaz, and emerald signified that these people were God's treasure. The gemstones declared that Israel was precious unto God.

The breastpiece was securely fastened to the ephod:

> You shall make for the breastpiece twisted chains like cords, of pure gold. And you shall make for the breastpiece two rings of gold, and put the two rings on the two edges of the breastpiece. And you shall put the two cords of gold in the two rings at the edges of the breastpiece. The two ends of the two cords you shall attach to the two settings of filigree, and so attach it in front to the shoulder pieces of the ephod. You shall make two rings of gold, and put them at the two ends of the breastpiece, on its inside edge next to the ephod. And you shall make two rings of gold, and attach them in front to the lower part of the two shoulder pieces of the ephod, at its seam above the skillfully woven band of the ephod. And they shall bind the breastpiece by its rings to the rings of the ephod with a lace of blue, so that it may lie on the skillfully woven band of the ephod, so that the breastpiece shall not come loose from the ephod. (28:22–28)

These instructions were given for the practical purpose of keeping the breastpiece where it belonged. There were four rings on the breastpiece—one for each corner. The top two rings were attached to the shoulder pieces of the ephod with golden chains. The bottom two rings were attached to both the ephod and the high priest's belt with blue cords.

## Close to the Heart

The rings on the breastpiece, with their cords and chains, prevented the breastpiece from coming loose. This was important because it kept the tribes of Israel close to the mediator's heart. We have seen how the high priest represented the people before God. The stones on his shoulders were inscribed with the names of the tribes of Israel—six tribes on each shoulder. This showed that he carried God's people on his shoulders, especially when he made atonement for their sins. The names of the tribes were also written on the high priest's breastpiece, which showed that he carried the people close to his heart. God said, "So Aaron shall bear the names of the sons of Israel in the breastpiece of judgment on his heart, when he goes into the Holy Place, to bring them to regular remembrance before the LORD" (v. 29).

A memorial calls something to remembrance. In this case, the breastpiece served as a memorial to God. It put the tribes of Israel front and center, reminding God of his people. Not that he ever forgets. God always knows his people and their needs. In fact, the whole epic adventure of the exodus started with him remembering his covenant with Israel (2:24). Nevertheless, the breastpiece was a "remembrance." As the high priest went about his intercessory work, his clothing was a reminder that he served on behalf of God's people. This was something God knew already, of course, but then again, this is the way prayer works. When we pray, we tell God what he already knows, and often we ask for what he has already promised.

The breastpiece was also a memorial for the high priest, who wore it close to his heart as he interceded for God's people. The phrase "on Aaron's heart" is repeated three times in verses 29, 30. This draws attention to Israel's place near the high priest's heart. It was his responsibility not only to bear the people's burdens on his shoulders but also to have their interests at heart. The heart is the center of the person, the seat of love and affection. And it was there that the people of God were tied to their high priest. They were bound to him with cords of love and affection, the way the stones on his breastpiece were tied to the ephod—close to his heart.

Carrying people close to the heart is the responsibility of any spiritual leader. The story is told of a rabbi who was asked how he could remember all the burdens that his people brought to him for prayer. People want their spiritual leaders to pray for them, but sometimes it is hard to remember all their requests. So how did the rabbi keep track? He said:

> I do not need to enumerate them. When somebody comes to me and tells me about his troubles, I feel so deeply with that person that his ordeal gives me a wound in my heart. When later I stand before God in prayer, I only have to open my heart and cry out to our Father in heaven, "See!" And when he looks into my heart he can read every little detail about the people who have shared their sorrows and burdens with me.[1]

The rabbi's answer may sound pious, but it is not very reassuring. It almost sounds like a way of saying that he *doesn't* pray for the needs of his people, at least not explicitly. But the leader has a responsibility to actually *pray* for God's people, not simply to let God read their needs in the wounds of his heart!

There is someone who really does take our needs to heart, however, and that is the Lord Jesus Christ. Jesus is our great High Priest—the only priest we need before God. He is the one who bears our burdens on his shoulders, especially the heavy weight of our guilt, which he bore when he died for our sins on the cross. Now Jesus continues to carry our concerns close to his heart. One of his High-Priestly duties is to pray to God on our behalf. The Bible says that Jesus "always lives to make intercession" for us (Hebrews 7:25). He is uniquely qualified to do this because he holds our needs so close to his heart. As the Bible assures us, "We do not have a high priest who is unable to sympathize with our weaknesses" (Hebrews 4:15a). Rather, we have a High Priest who always has us on his heart and in his mind. Our names are engraved, so to speak, on the gemstones that cover his breastpiece. He has bound us to himself with the cords of his everlasting love, making us secure forever in a place close to his heart.

Anyone who wants to be loved with this kind of love should pray to receive Jesus as Savior and Lord, making the request that King Solomon made: "Set me as a seal upon your heart" (Song 8:6a). Here is how one Bible teacher explained what the breastpiece in Exodus teaches us about salvation in Christ:

> The names of God's people [are] borne upon the heart of the priest, shining out in all the sparkling lustre and beauty of the stones on which they are engraven. This symbolises the fact that believers are before God in all the acceptance of Christ. When God looks upon the great High Priest, He beholds His people upon His heart, as well as upon His shoulders, adorned with all the beauty of the One on whom His eye ever rests with perfect delight. . . . And with what joy does He so present them before God! For they are those for whom He has died, and whom He has cleansed with His own most precious blood, those whom He has made the objects of His own love, and whom finally He will bring to be forever with Him; and He pleads for them before God according to all the strength of these ties.[2]

Those who belong to God through faith in Christ are regarded as his treasured possession. We are close to God's heart, like the sapphire on the breastpiece of the high priest. Jesus has our needs and concerns at heart. If we need forgiveness, he will pardon our sin. If we need work, he will give us a calling. If we need a home, he will give us shelter. If we have a question, he will provide the answer. If we have a problem, he will come up with the solution. If we need fellowship, he will be our friend. If we need healing, he will bind up the wounds of our souls as well as our bodies.

## The Urim and Thummim

But what if we need guidance? Will God provide this as well? And if so, how will he do it? It is wonderful to know that God loves us from the heart, but what plan does he have for our lives?

The Israelites received divine guidance through the breastpiece of the high priest. When God gave Moses the instructions for making it, he called it "a breastpiece of judgment" (28:15a) or "a breastpiece for making decisions" (NIV). He said, "And in the breastpiece of judgment you shall put the Urim and the Thummim, and they shall be on Aaron's heart, when he goes in before the LORD. Thus Aaron shall bear the judgment of the people of Israel on his heart before the LORD regularly" (v. 30; cf. Leviticus 8:8).

The breastpiece was folded double to make an elaborate pocket or pouch. Inside went special objects known as the Urim and Thummim. Apparently the Israelites knew how these were made and used. However, we do not know because the Bible does not describe them. This is probably just as well, because it keeps us from trying to use them today, which is not God's plan.

The Hebrew words *urim* and *thummim* mean "light" and "perfection," which isn't much to go on. They seem to have been thrown to determine God's will, like some kind of holy dice. Some scholars speculate that they were made of stone; others say they were precious gems, like the ones on the breastpiece. We simply don't know.

There are also many opinions about how the Urim and Thummim were used.[3] Some scholars think they were letters that spelled out answers, since the words *urim* and *thummim* begin with the first and last letters of the Hebrew alphabet. Others think they had numbers on them, odd and even, or that they had two sides—one that said "yes" and one that said "no." According to John Mackay, "The most plausible idea is that they were stones of different colours, probably black and white. In situations of public uncertainty, it seems to have been the right of the leader of Israel to put a question to the high priest who would draw out a selected number of stones and according to which colour predominated, the answer would be yes or no. The precise stones brought out of the pouch were viewed as being divinely determined, so that the answer given was from the Lord."[4]

What is certain is that the Israelites used these decision-making tools to get direct guidance from God. Whatever the high priest did with the Urim and Thummim, the Israelites understood that God was using them to declare his will. As the Scripture says, "The lot is cast into the lap, but its every decision is from the Lord" (Proverbs 16:33). The Israelites trusted God to reveal his will through the breastpiece of the high priest. And this was its primary purpose. The breastpiece was for making decisions under the sovereign direction of Almighty God.

Several episodes from the Old Testament show how "the breastpiece of judgment" was used. When Joshua was appointed to succeed Moses, he was given the right to consult the Urim and Thummim. God said, "And he shall stand before Eleazar the priest, who shall inquire for him by the judgment of the Urim before the Lord. At his word they shall go out, and at his word they shall come in, both he and all the people of Israel with him, the whole congregation" (Numbers 27:21). Joshua told the Israelites when to stay and when to go, and the way he knew was by consulting the Urim and Thummim.

Another man who consulted the breastpiece of judgment was King Saul. When the Philistines mobilized their forces, Saul was afraid and wanted to know the outcome of the battle. He consulted the Urim and Thummim, but he did not get the answer he was looking for (1 Samuel 28:6). It was not "yes" or "no," but "maybe." By contrast, when David asked God if he should attack the Philistines, God said, "Go and attack the Philistines" (1 Samuel 23:1, 2). David later received the same answer when he used the ephod to learn if he should attack the Amalekites (1 Samuel 30:1–8).

The Urim and Thummim were used again in the days when Nehemiah rebuilt Jerusalem. As the Israelites tried to rebuild their city, a question arose as to whether certain men were eligible to serve as priests. Since their family records had been lost, there was no way to determine whether they were descendants of Levi. This was exactly the kind of question the breastpiece of judgment was supposed to answer. Unfortunately, it wasn't yet back in service. So Nehemiah ordered the men whose status was in doubt "not to partake of the most holy food until a priest with Urim and Thummim should arise" (Nehemiah 7:65; cf. Ezra 2:63).

The Israelites probably used the breastpiece of judgment on other occasions when they consulted the Lord as well, even though it is not specifically mentioned. The high priest cast lots between two goats on the Day of Atonement (Leviticus 16:8). After Joshua died, the Israelites asked God which tribe should lead them into battle against the Canaanites (Judges 1:1, 2; cf. 20:18–28). King Saul drew lots to determine who had violated his order not to eat or drink on the day of battle (1 Samuel 14:41, 42). David asked the Lord if he should go up to Judah (2 Samuel 2:1), and if he should attack the Philistines (2 Samuel 5:18, 19). Most of these passages do not refer to the Urim and Thummim explicitly, but they were probably used on some or all of these occasions.

What do we learn from these examples? On the basis of the Biblical evidence, the Jewish scholar Umberto Cassuto has written an excellent summary of the way the Urim and Thummim were used. According to Cassuto, we know:

> 1) That permission to inquire of the Lord through the priest by means of the Urim and Thummim in the pouch of the ephod was granted only to the person standing at the head of the people and only on matters of public concern;
> 2) That the inquiry related to matters that human beings could not possibly know, for instance an issue dependent on the conscience of an individual or something belonging to the future;
> 3) That the question had to be so formulated as to make only one of two answers possible: yes or no; the first matter or the second;
> 4) That two or more inquiries could not be made simultaneously; the answer was given to one question only;
> 5) That the reply was given by lot, as the expressions "casting" and "taking" indicate; this was based on the belief that the lot was not a matter of chance, but that God made his "judgment" known thereby, namely, His decision or verdict.[5]

The first of those statements is the most important. The breastpiece of judgment could only be consulted by Israel's leader, and only for things that really mattered. The Urim and Thummim were not used by ordinary people in making ordinary decisions. People did not go to the high priest every time they wondered what outfit to wear or what they should eat for dinner. They did not even use them to resolve more serious questions, like what job to choose or whom to marry. Like us, when it came to practical decisions for daily living, as well as to personal choices that affected the future, the Israelites had to rely on sanctified common sense.

### Divine Guidance

All of this raises important questions about knowing God's will. Obviously, if God had wanted to, he could have given every single Israelite his own personal set of Urim and Thummim. Then his people always would have known exactly what he wanted them to do.

God could have done the same thing for us. He could have given us holy dice to carry around in little pouches. Then anytime we wondered what to do, we could take them out and roll them on the table: "Should I go to Pennsylvania Tech? Should I marry Genevieve? Should I take the job in Schenectady? Should I become a missionary to Indonesia? Yes or no? Just lay it out for me, Lord, and I'll do it."

This is the kind of guidance most people want, which explains why there is always such a large market for psychics, dream analysts, fortune-tellers, and other dubious characters who claim to know the future. People want to know what's going to happen and what they ought to do. However, God, in his infinite wisdom, has not chosen to give us a direct means of divine guidance for specific decisions.

This is partly because God has already told us the most important thing we need to know. He has told us that salvation is through his Son, Jesus Christ, who died on the cross to pay for sin and rose from the dead to give eternal life. From time to time God gave direct guidance to Israel because he was still working out his plan of salvation. He needed to preserve his people so the Messiah could come. But now that salvation is here, God has said everything that needs to be said. The Bible says, "Long ago, at many times and in many ways, God spoke to our fathers by the prophets, but in these last days he has spoken to us by his Son" (Hebrews 1:1, 2a). When God's people were in their infancy, they needed things like the Urim and Thummim to guide them. But now salvation has reached its full maturity, and God has said it all in Jesus. Today the most important decision we have to make is whether or not we will trust in him for our salvation.

There are some other things we need to decide, of course, and God gives guidance for those decisions as well. He mainly does this through the Bible—the one Word he has given us for all of life. The Bible does not contain private information about each person's destiny, but it does reveal God's will for our lives.

It says, "For this is the will of God, your sanctification: that you abstain from sexual immorality; that each one of you know how to control his own body in holiness and honor, not in the passion of lust like the Gentiles who do not know God" (1 Thessalonians 4:3–5). Or again, it says, "Rejoice always, pray without ceasing, give thanks in all circumstances; for this is the will of God in Christ Jesus for you" (1 Thessalonians 5:16–18). The Bible, with all its promises and commands, is sufficient to guide our conduct. It tells us what to do and what not to do.

This means that knowing God's will starts with reading, studying, and obeying God's Word. What we need more than anything else—even more than knowing what to *do*—is a deeper and more personal knowledge of God through the study of his Word. Guidance for life's decisions comes through getting to know the Guide. And when we know the Bible and do what it says, then whatever specific decisions we make will be in keeping with God's revealed will. The *Westminster Shorter Catechism* asks, "What rule hath God given to direct us how we may glorify and enjoy him?" The answer is: "The word of God, which is contained in the scriptures of the Old and New Testaments, is the only rule to direct us how we may glorify and enjoy him." Knowing God's Word helps us to know the godly thing to do in all the situations we face.

To help us understand his Word, God has also given us his Spirit, whose inward leading helps guide us in the right path. God has not given us a pair of decision-making dice to carry in our front pocket. He has given us something better. He has given us his very own Spirit to come and dwell within us, much the way he made his dwelling place in the tabernacle. And part of the Spirit's work in us is to help us to know and to do God's will. As Jesus promised his disciples, "the Helper, the Holy Spirit, whom the Father will send in my name, he will teach you all things and bring to your remembrance all that I have said to you" (John 14:26). This does not mean that the Holy Spirit gives us direct revelation of God's will, so that we are able to say, "God told me to do thus and so." His leading is much subtler. He is living within us, shaping our minds and hearts, helping us make good choices, and giving us inward peace when we finally arrive at the right decision.

Sinclair Ferguson says that knowing God's will "comes through a combination of the study of God's word (where we learn the great principles of his will), a heart which is submitted to the Lord of the word, and the help of the Spirit who illuminates the word and leads us into a true application of its principles *to our own situation*" (emphasis his).[6] Whenever we are uncertain what to do, we should pray that the Spirit would use the Word to show us the way. And God will answer our prayers, for the Bible says, "If any of you lacks wisdom, let him ask God, who gives generously to all without reproach, and it will be given him" (James 1:5).

## Trusting God for Guidance

Finally, God directs us through the working of his providence. When we face difficult decisions, we should pray for God to use our circumstances to clarify his calling. What gifts has God given us? What desires has he placed on our hearts? What opportunities has he set before us? What needs are we able to meet? God uses all these things to guide us. We should ask God for the discernment to know what our gifts are, the contentment to want what he wants, and the compassion to give our lives for the sake of others. At the same time, we should pray for God to close the doors that need to be closed and to open the doors he wants us to walk through. And then we should use the freedom he has given us to make the best choice we can. This is the way God leads us. To quote again from Dr. Ferguson, "His leading is not usually a direct assurance, a revelation, but his sovereign controlling of the circumstances of our lives, with the word of God as our rule."[7]

If it is true that God uses the circumstances of life to show us his will, and if we are uncertain as to what God is calling us to do, then we are called to wait upon the Lord. As far as we know God's will, we should do it. But where the way is not yet clear, we should quietly wait for God to work, trusting that he will guide us in and through our circumstances in his own good time. As the Scripture says, "Wait for the LORD; be strong, and let your heart take courage; wait for the LORD!" (Psalm 27:14).

In a letter to a friend, the great Puritan preacher and hymn writer John Newton asked the same question that we have been asking in this chapter: "But how then may the Lord's guidance be expected?" Newton's wise answer summarizes everything that we have been saying about divine guidance:

> In general, he guides and directs his people, by affording them, in answer to prayer, the light of his Holy Spirit, which enables them to understand and to love the Scriptures. The word of God . . . is to furnish us with just principles, right apprehensions to regulate our judgements and affections, and thereby influence and direct our conduct. They who study the Scriptures, in an humble dependence upon divine teaching . . . are gradually formed into a spirit of submission to the will of God, [and] discover the nature and duties of their several situations and relations in life. . . . By treasuring up the doctrines, precepts, promises, examples, and exhortations of Scripture, in their minds, and daily comparing themselves with the rule by which they walk, they grow into an habitual frame of spiritual wisdom. . . . And they are seldom mistaken, because they are influenced by the love of Christ, which rules in their hearts, and a regard to the glory of God, which is the great object they have in view. In particular cases, the Lord opens and shuts for them, breaks down walls of difficulty which obstruct their path, or hedges up their way with thorns, when they are in danger of going wrong, by the dispensations of his providence. They know that their concernments are in his hands; they are willing to follow

> whither and when he leads; but are afraid of going before him. Therefore they are not impatient: because they believe, they will not make haste, but wait daily upon him in prayer. . . . [A]nd the Lord, whom they serve, does not disappoint their expectations. He leads them by a right way, preserves them from a thousand snares, and satisfies them that he is and will be their guide even unto death.[8]

Perhaps you are facing a difficult life decision right now. If so, then you may have hoped that this chapter would answer all your questions. It hasn't, of course, which may come as a disappointment. But this is the way God usually works. He does not put the decision in our pockets or write our future in the sky. He calls us to walk with him by faith, trusting him for tomorrow as well as for today.

If you are a believer in the Lord Jesus Christ, then his guidance will never fail you. You are his treasured possession. He always carries you close to his heart. If you follow him, he will not let you wander off in the wrong direction. By the teaching of his perfect Word, by the leading of his Holy Spirit, and by the guidance of his daily providence, he will direct you in the way that you should go.

# 78

# Fit for a Priest

## EXODUS 28:31–43

WHILE STUDYING FOR THE Roman Catholic priesthood, Donald Smarto performed the role of the cardinal in a religious play. To help him look the part, his monastery arranged for him to borrow ornate robes from the cardinal of his diocese. "I was excited by this," Smarto writes in his autobiography, "and when they arrived, I went to my room, locked the door and carefully removed the red cassock with matching sash and scarlet cape from the suit bag."[1]

Smarto's clothes were fit for a priest, but as he wore them, they became an obsession:

> Though each evening the play began at eight o'clock, I found myself putting the cardinal's robes on earlier and earlier. It only took about half an hour to fasten all the buttons, but by the last days of the performance, I was dressing by two o'clock in the afternoon, five hours before the beginning of the play. I would strut back and forth in front of a full-length mirror, and as I did, a feeling would come over me. I stood for the longest time looking at my reflection, and I liked what I saw. . . . I had a sense that I was holy—and not only because I was imitating my superiors. I simply didn't think I was a sinner; I felt confident that my works pleased God.[2]

Not long afterward, Smarto's false confidence was shattered, and he saw what the person under the robes was really like. It happened at the movies:

> The film was a satire of priests and nuns in Rome. They were wearing elaborate, if not garish, garments. In the film, an amused audience was mesmerized as the clerics strutted around in garments lit by flashing neon tubing. . . . Then a bishop came on the stage in the movie. Dressed in a beautiful vestment studded with sparkling gems, he walked out slowly from behind a curtain. As he walked, however, a large gust of wind ripped open his vestment, revealing a rotted skeleton underneath.

> In an instant, my mind said, *That's me*. . . . I immediately blocked out the thought. . . . "That's not me!" I said with the intensity with which Peter denied Christ. . . . I wanted to push the film images out of my mind, but it didn't work. . . . I kept talking to myself and to God to try to make myself feel better. "Make this feeling go away," I said to God. "I am *not* a hypocrite. I am *not* an actor. I'm a *good person*!" I kept thinking of all the good things I did. . . . Yet, these thoughts didn't bring consolation.[3]

We all try to dress ourselves up for God. But somewhere deep down, Don Smarto was starting to discover something we all need to learn: even if we wear clothes fit for a priest, we are not good enough to stand before God.

## The Rest of the High Priest's Outfit

If ever a man needed to be good enough to stand before God, it was the high priest of Israel. He had the awesome responsibility of entering the tabernacle to meet with God. In order to do this properly, the high priest had to wear the clothes God told him to wear. He had to wear the ephod with the names of the twelve tribes of Israel on his shoulders. He had to wear the breastpiece of judgment that kept God's precious people close to his heart. The high priest also had to wear a robe:

> You shall make the robe of the ephod all of blue. It shall have an opening for the head in the middle of it, with a woven binding around the opening, like the opening in a garment, so that it may not tear. On its hem you shall make pomegranates of blue and purple and scarlet yarns, around its hem, with bells of gold between them, a golden bell and a pomegranate, a golden bell and a pomegranate, around the hem of the robe. And it shall be on Aaron when he ministers, and its sound shall be heard when he goes into the Holy Place before the LORD, and when he comes out, so that he does not die. (28:31–35; cf. Leviticus 8:7)

The robe was made of blue or violet—the same color used for the entrance curtain and the veil that concealed the Most Holy Place. It was a seamless garment that went under the ephod and hung down to at least the knees. Since the high priest pulled it over his head like a poncho, God told Moses to make the collar extra sturdy.

The hem was fringed with bells and pomegranates. The little bells made a tinkling sound whenever the high priest moved (more on this in a moment). The pomegranate is a roundish, reddish fruit filled with large seeds. Here it may serve as a symbol of fruitfulness, like an echo from Eden. Or it may simply connote beauty. In the ancient Near East pomegranates were often used for decoration, much the way that pineapples were used in colonial America.

Then the high priest's outfit was topped off with a turban:

> You shall make a plate of pure gold and engrave on it, like the engraving of a signet, "Holy to the LORD." And you shall fasten it on the turban by a cord of blue. It shall be on the front of the turban. It shall be on Aaron's forehead, and Aaron shall bear any guilt from the holy things that the people of Israel consecrate as their holy gifts. It shall regularly be on his forehead, that they may be accepted before the LORD. (28:36–38)

The turban was made of linen and twirled around the high priest's head. Josephus, the ancient Jewish historian who knew about these things because he served temporarily as a temple priest, left the following description:

> Upon his head he wears a cap, not brought to a conic form nor encircling the whole head, but still covering more than half of it . . . and its make is such that it seems to be a crown, being made of thick swathes, but the contexture is of linen; and it is double rounded many times, and sewed together: besides which, a piece of fine linen covers the whole cap from the upper part, and reaches down to the forehead, and hides the seams of the swathes, which would otherwise appear indecently: this adheres closely upon the solid part of the head, and is thereto so firmly fixed that it may not fall off during the sacred service about the sacrifices.[4]

The most important part of the turban was the golden plate or crown (more literally, the "flower")[5] that was fixed to the front and rested on the high priest's forehead. This diadem was made of gold, suitable for entering the throne room of God, and it was engraved with the words "Holy to the LORD." This inscription marked the high priest as belonging to his Majesty's sacred service. It meant that the people he represented were a holy nation, a royal priesthood (see 19:5, 6).

Underneath his other clothes, the high priest wore a tunic—a long-sleeved garment that went down to the ground. God said: "You shall weave the coat in checker work of fine linen, and you shall make a turban of fine linen, and you shall make a sash embroidered with needlework. For Aaron's sons you shall make coats and sashes and caps. You shall make them for glory and beauty. And you shall put them on Aaron your brother, and on his sons with him, and shall anoint them and ordain them and consecrate them, that they may serve me as priests" (28:39–41).

What the other priests wore was similar to the high priest, only simpler. Since they did not represent the whole nation of Israel, they did not wear crowns that said, "Holy to the LORD." Nor did they wear all the extra garments that the high priest wore. But the tunic underneath was the same. God clothed all his priests with "glory and beauty." The coat was the sacred garment they wore when they were set apart for sacred service—when they were anointed, consecrated, and ordained to the priestly ministry, as described in Exodus 29.

God's final instructions concerned their undergarments. These breeches were something like long boxer shorts. God said, "You shall make for them linen undergarments to cover their naked flesh. They shall reach from the hips to the thighs; and they shall be on Aaron and on his sons when they go into the tent of meeting or when they come near the altar to minister in the Holy Place, lest they bear guilt and die. This shall be a statute forever for him and for his offspring after him" (28:42, 43).

Like the coat, this linen underwear was for all the priests, not just the high priest. Its purpose was to preserve their modesty. Unlike pagan priests, who wore next to nothing, God wanted his servants to dress decently as they performed their sacred duties in his holy presence (cf. 20:26). To that end, he told them what he wanted them to wear—all the way down to their underclothes! Aaron and his sons wore clothes fit for a priest to make them fit for the holy service of God.

### Danger!

Exodus 28 gives such a careful description of the priestly garments that it's easy to get lost in all the details. What is unmistakable is that the whole elaborate ensemble conveyed a sense of the sacred. The high priest was adorned with holy majesty. To get an idea how the Israelites felt when they saw him, consider the following description from a letter written in the second century before Christ: "Their appearance makes one awestruck and dumbfounded: a man would think he had come out of this world into another one. I emphatically assert that every man who comes near the spectacle of what I have described will experience astonishment and amazement beyond words, his very being transformed by the hallowed arrangement of every single detail."[6]

The high priest wore such magnificent clothes because his ministry was so important. His special outfit was symbolic of his sacred calling, which was to stand for the people before God. God is holy in his majesty and glorious in his beauty. Therefore, whoever approaches him must be dressed with dignity and honor. This was especially important when the high priest atoned for Israel's sin. His clothes were connected to this crucial priestly function, for God said, "It [the seal inscribed as "Holy to the Lord"] shall be on Aaron's forehead, and Aaron shall bear any guilt from the holy things that the people of Israel consecrate as their holy gifts. It shall regularly be on his forehead, that they may be accepted before the Lord" (v. 38).

The high priest entered God's holy sanctuary to bear the guilt for Israel's sin. Whenever the people sinned, they brought their "holy gifts" (meaning their offerings and sacrifices) to the tabernacle, and then the high priest presented them to God. God would only accept them on the basis of a sacrifice, and for the sacrifice to be accepted, it had to be offered by a holy priest. This is why the statement on the high priest's headband was so important: It confirmed that God regarded him as holy, and thus it gave assurance that the Lord would accept his people's sacrifice. The high priest was holy on behalf of the people. Their salvation depended on the representative righteousness stamped on his forehead. When the people saw the inscription, they knew that God would accept them, considering them to be holy in his sight.

The Scotsman Robert Murray M'Cheyne made a famous comment about pastoral ministry that has served as a moral compass for many ministers. He said, "My people's greatest need is my personal holiness." M'Cheyne's point was that a holy calling demands a holy life, which is true, but of course M'Cheyne was exaggerating. A church's greatest need is not the personal holiness of its minister, but the perfect righteousness of Jesus Christ. However, if Israel's high priest had said what M'Cheyne said, it would *not* have been an exaggeration. His people's greatest need *was* his personal holiness! God can only accept what is suitable to his own nature and character. Since he is a holy God, he can only accept a holy sacrifice offered by a holy representative.

We sometimes fail to appreciate how dangerous this was. Coming into God's presence can be fatal! He is a God of such supreme holiness that it is dangerous even to approach him. We have sensed this danger all the way through Exodus. When God appeared to Moses, it was in a burning, flaming bush. When God visited Egypt as an avenging angel, the people were only safe if they had blood on their doorposts. When the Israelites reached Sinai, not only were they forbidden to go up and meet with God, but they weren't even allowed to touch his holy mountain. It wasn't safe! The only person who was allowed to approach God was the mediator, and only if he was dressed in holiness.

The high priest had the most dangerous job in Israel. His life was in jeopardy every time he served in the tabernacle. Even his clothes gave off a warning. The little bells on his robe, which jingled as he walked, were necessary to protect his very life. God said, "Its sound shall be heard when he goes into the Holy Place before the LORD, and when he comes out, so that he does not die" (28:35b).

Some scholars think that these bells were for the benefit of the priests, or for the people of Israel. As the high priest did his work behind the tabernacle curtains, the jingling of his bells would let people know that he was okay. (He did not wear his bells into the Holy of Holies; he only entered there on the Day of Atonement, and then he only wore his tunic—see Leviticus 16:4.) Even when they couldn't see him, they would know that he was still alive. But what is more likely is that he wore his bells for God. The sound of their ringing announced that he was coming into God's royal presence. People don't barge in on a king. It simply isn't done. This was especially true in the ancient Near East, where "a person always appeared before the king dressed in finery and was announced before entering."[7] What announced the coming of the high priest were his golden bells. They indicated that he was holy, that he was doing God's work in God's way, and thus they kept him safe in God's presence. The high priest had to tread carefully. He needed to wear his bells or else he would die.

Another warning comes at the end of the chapter, in the instructions about the undergarments. God said, "They shall be on Aaron and on his sons when they go into the tent of meeting or when they come near the altar to minister in the Holy Place, lest they bear guilt and die" (v. 43a). Here again we see how dangerous it was to enter God's presence. So dangerous that a priest could be destroyed for wearing the wrong kind of underwear. If there is any doubt as to whether God was serious about this, it is dispelled in Leviticus 10. There we read of the tragic fate of Nadab and Abihu, the sons of Aaron whom God destroyed for unholiness in his tabernacle (vv. 1–7).

Coming into God's presence was a matter of life and death. This was true not only for the high priest, but also for the nation of Israel. Their salvation depended on whether or not God accepted their priest. If God did not accept him, they would die in their sins. The same is true for all of us. Coming into God's presence is always a matter of life and death. Will God accept us or reject us? Will he condemn us for our sins, or will he accept us on the basis of a holy sacrifice offered by a holy priest? This question will be answered once and for all on the day of judgment, when every person will stand before God. Then only the holy will survive, for as the Scripture says, without holiness "no one will see the Lord" (Hebrews 12:14). How, then, can anyone be saved?

## The Dirtiest Laundry

One man who can tell us the answer is the prophet Zechariah, who saw a vision that helps connect Exodus to the gospel. Zechariah saw "Joshua the high priest standing before the angel of the Lord" (Zechariah 3:1). It was not uncommon for the high priest to stand before God. It happened once every year, on the Day of Atonement, when the high priest offered a sacrifice for the sins of God's people. However, this particular high priest had a serious problem. He was supposed to wear clothes fit for a priest. Since he was in the presence of God, he was required to wear the white linen tunic that represented his righteousness. A. W. Pink comments that on the Day of Atonement, the high priest "was robed only in spotless white, foreshadowing the personal righteousness and holiness of the Lord Jesus, which fitted Him to undertake the stupendous work of putting away the sins of His people."[8] But here was the problem: "Joshua was standing before the angel, clothed with filthy garments" (Zechariah 3:3).

The word used to describe the condition of these clothes is almost vulgar. According to the best Hebrew lexicon, it means "filth, specifically human excrement."[9] There are one or two similar words in the English language—four-letter words that are not used in polite conversation. I won't use them here, but maybe I should, because nothing is more obscene than the filthiness of our sin.

What Zechariah saw was a picture of our sinfulness before God. We are inclined to minimize our sin. We compare ourselves to others who are more sinful than we are (or so it seems). We excuse our sin, claiming that there were extenuating circumstances. Or we simply get used to it, much the way a hog farmer gets used to the smell of slop. But we are covered with the excrement of our depravity. Our pride, our lust, and our greed—our self-indulgence, self-advancement, and self-pity—these sins are filthy in God's sight. Indeed, they are a stench to his holy nostrils.

This is what God wanted Zechariah to see, if not actually to smell. He took Joshua the high priest—the man generally considered to be the holiest man in the world—and showed Zechariah what the man looked like next to the holiness of God. As the prophet (Zechariah) could plainly see, the high priest (Joshua) looked like he was spattered with excrement. He was supposed to be adorned with righteousness from his turban down to his undershorts. Instead he was covered with sin.

It gets worse. Not only was the high priest stained with his filthy sin, but Satan was standing there to accuse him before God (Zechariah 3:1). Anyone who has read Exodus 28 and knows what kind of clothes the high priest was supposed to wear—not to mention how dangerous it was to enter God's sanctuary—immediately recognizes that Joshua was a dead man. There was no way for a priest who looked and smelled like this to survive the holiness of God, especially with Satan standing there to accuse him. It gets even worse, because the high priest represented the people before God. If he was covered with filth, then they were covered with filth too. If he was guilty, they were guilty. If he was dead, they were dead. Therefore, what Zechariah saw was a vision of humanity lost in sin, of dying sinners guilty before God.

This is where the story gets amazing, because God did not destroy the high priest after all. Instead he demonstrated his grace for sinners. God did this by replacing Joshua's filthy clothes with righteous robes: "And the angel said to those who were standing before him, 'Remove the filthy garments from him'" (v. 4a). So they stripped the high priest down to his bare skin. As he stood there, trembling and naked with fear, the Lord said, "Behold, I have taken your iniquity away from you, and I will clothe you with pure vestments" (v. 4b). There was nothing Joshua could do to save himself. It was all grace. God took away his sin. God made him holy and acceptable in his sight. And when God did this, the high priest no longer stood covered with the odious filthiness of his sin but clothed with God's own righteousness. He was holy to the Lord—not because of his own holiness, but by the holiness given to him by God.

It was at this point that Zechariah chimed in. As he witnessed this remarkable scene, there was something he desperately wanted to say—something he *needed* to say—so he just blurted it right out. Sometimes this happens in dreams or visions. The person dreaming starts to participate in what's happening. In this case Zechariah said, "Let them put a clean turban on his head" (v. 5a).

Why did Zechariah say this? He said it because his salvation depended on it. Remember, the turban is what declared that the people whom the high priest represented were "Holy to the Lord." The prophet knew his Bible. He knew that the high priest's outfit was not complete unless it was topped off with a turban. He also knew what the turban said. He knew that the words "Holy to the LORD" were fastened to the high priest's forehead so that God would accept his people (28:38). So Zechariah called for the turban. By doing so, he was acknowledging his own need for righteousness before God. He was saying, "I'm a sinner, and I need someone to stand for me before God—someone who is holy from head to toe."

God answered Zechariah's prayers. As the prophet watched, the angels clothed the high priest in spotless robes, complete with turban. Then both the priest and the people he represented were able to say, "I will greatly rejoice in the LORD; my soul shall exult in my God, for he has clothed me with the garments of salvation; he has covered me with the robe of righteousness" (Isaiah 61:10).

## Our Holy Priest

Zechariah's vision was about the forgiveness of sin. It was about justification. It was about how God declares sinners righteous by imputing to them his righteousness. In other words, it was about the gospel. This is clear from the rest of Zechariah's prophecy. The prophet went on to say that what he saw was "a sign," that it concerned the Savior whom God was planning to send, who would remove his people's sin in a single day (Zechariah 3:8, 9). In other words, it was about Jesus and the salvation of sinners through his death on the cross.

What the Old Testament says about the priesthood points us to Jesus Christ, whom God has appointed to be our great High Priest. The commentator John Mackay has noticed something significant about the way the Old Testament does this. He writes:

> Perhaps the most remarkable feature of the Old Testament institution of the priesthood is its concentration on the office of High Priest. The existence of many others who were priests is indeed acknowledged, and provision is made for them. But the essence of the priesthood focuses on the person of one man, and in this it foreshadows Christ as the great High Priest to come. He is the divinely recognised mediator who "is selected from among men and is appointed to represent them in matters related to God, to offer gifts and sacrifices for sins" (Heb. 5:1).[10]

Jesus Christ is the one man whom God has appointed to be our great High Priest forever. The apostle John hints at this near the end of his Gospel. According to John, "When the soldiers had crucified Jesus, they took his garments and divided them into four parts, one part for each soldier; also his tunic." Then John tells us something significant about this tunic: it was "seamless, woven in one piece from top to bottom" (John 19:23). Earlier he had described the garment as "a purple robe" (John 19:2). John included these details not because he was interested in fashion but because they connected to the Old Testament. For one thing they confirmed the prophecy of Psalm 22 that people would gamble for the Messiah's clothes. But they also pointed to Jesus' identity as priest. Who was the man in the Old Testament who wore a seamless robe, woven with purple? It was the high priest, whose robe was made of a single piece, with an opening for his head. By mentioning the seamless robe, John hinted that when Jesus died on the cross, he was doing the high-priestly work of bearing our sin.

The high priest was the symbol; Jesus is the reality. He does all the things for us that the high priest did for Israel. He bears the burden of our sin on his shoulders. He carries our concerns close to his heart. He represents us before God. And as he does this priestly work, he stands in perfect holiness, so that we are holy to the Lord.

Holiness is not something Jesus puts on like a robe or writes on his forehead. It is who he is! The Bible says that Jesus is "holy, innocent, unstained, separated from sinners" (Hebrews 7:26). It also says that he is our "sanctification" (1 Corinthians 1:30). In other words, he is holy for us, so that we can be holy to God. The Bible says further that if we sin, "we have an advocate with the Father, Jesus Christ the righteous" (1 John 2:1). So if we look to Jesus in faith—the way the Israelites looked to their high priest—we will be holy to the Lord.

So often we try to cover up our sin, dressing ourselves up to be good enough for God. What we ought to do instead is to confess our sin and look to Jesus for our salvation. In the words of one old commentator:

> The great object which men propose to themselves, is to quieten their own consciences, and to stand well with their neighbors. To this end they invent a religion. But as soon as we have to do with God, the conscience is convicted, and the guilt and shame which before were quieted, spring up within, and nothing can still the restless uneasiness of the heart. We become aware that all things are naked and opened to the eyes of Him with whom we have to do. The soul in vain attempts concealment. The still, small voice of God sounds within, and drags the culprit out to stand before Him. It is here that a righteousness not our own becomes unspeakably precious to the soul. A covering that both blots out all sin, and forever clothes the sinner with spotless purity, which conceals from the searching eye of God all iniquity, and in so doing completely justifies the sinner before Him.[11]

It is the righteousness of our holy priest—Jesus Christ—that enables us to stand before God.

This chapter began with the shocking discovery of Don Smarto's sin. God used a film to show the aspiring young priest that underneath the proud robes of his own righteousness he was dead in sin. But there is more to the story. As Smarto returned to his monastery that night, he struggled to justify himself before God. He walked out into the surrounding cornfields to walk in the moonlight. Soon the moon was covered with clouds, and the night turned black. As Smarto stumbled around in the darkness, with his heart pounding, he cried out to God, "Tell me I am doing the right thing. Tell me that everything I do pleases you. Speak to me clearly!"

When he was almost in despair, Smarto heard a strange humming sound and walked toward it. He reached out in the darkness and touched a solid piece of wood. It was only a telephone pole. But as he looked up, the clouds began to part, and he could see the crossbar that held up the phone lines. There, silhouetted against the moonlight, was the form of a cross. Don Smarto was standing at the foot of the cross, looking to Jesus for his salvation. He writes:

> Now I knew, I really knew, that Christ had died for me. It was coupled with the more important revelation that I was a sinner, that I was *not* the good person I had thought I was a moment before. All at once I embraced the telephone pole and began to cry. I must have hugged that piece of wood for nearly an hour. I could imagine Jesus nailed to this pole, blood dripping from his wounds. I felt as if the blood were dripping over me, cleansing me of my sin and unworthiness.[12]

I am not the good person I would like to think that I am either. And neither are you. We are all covered with the filth of our sin. What we need is someone to stand for us before God in perfect holiness. So we look to our holy priest—the Lord Jesus Christ—and hold on to the cross where he died for our sins.

# 79

# The Ordination of Priests

EXODUS 29:1–21

ORDINATION TO THE GOSPEL MINISTRY is an unforgettable experience, as any pastor can testify. In most churches ordination comes after years of spiritual preparation. The process generally goes something like this: First God brings a man to saving faith in Jesus Christ. Then he works in the man's life to give him an irrepressible desire to preach the gospel. The candidate devotes himself to studying the Bible, preferably in the original languages, and to learning theology in a systematic way. At the same time, he serves in the church, so that his gifts for teaching and shepherding can be tested and developed.

Finally, the man stands in front of the church to be ordained. He affirms his trust in the Bible as the Word of God. He confesses his faith in orthodox Christian theology. He vows submission to the church. He promises to defend the gospel against all opposition. He commits himself to being faithful in all his duties as a Christian and a minister. Then as he kneels before God, the elders ordain him with prayer and the laying on of hands. In the same way that the apostles commissioned the first pastors in the early church, the elders set the man apart for holy service. And when he rises to his feet, he has a new calling as a minister of the gospel.

## Getting Ready

Moses did something similar but even more dramatic for Aaron and his sons. Remember that the priests—especially the high priest—represented the people before God. The spiritual welfare of the entire nation depended on their ability to enter God's presence with prayer and sacrifice. It was their sacred duty to enter the holy tabernacle. But in order to do this, they had to be completely holy. So God told Moses to consecrate Aaron and his sons as priests.

Ordaining these men to their sacred office involved an elaborate ritual. First, God told Moses to gather what was needed: "Now this is what you shall do to them to consecrate them, that they may serve me as priests. Take one bull of the herd and two rams without blemish, and unleavened bread, unleavened cakes mixed with oil, and unleavened wafers smeared with oil. You shall make them of fine wheat flour. You shall put them in one basket and bring them in the basket, and bring the bull and the two rams" (29:1–3). The animals had to be perfect, in the prime of life. Together with the unleavened bread they were presented to God as sacrifices (more about these in a moment).

Next came the men to be ordained. Moses escorted Aaron and the other priests to the doorway of the tabernacle. But before they could enter God's holy presence, they had to be washed from head to toe. God said, "You shall bring Aaron and his sons to the entrance of the tent of meeting and wash them with water" (v. 4). This bath was symbolic of spiritual purification. The priests were not allowed to go in and handle anything in the Holy Place until they had been cleansed.

Once they were washed, the priests were dressed. God said, "Then you shall take the garments, and put on Aaron the coat and the robe of the ephod, and the ephod, and the breastpiece, and gird him with the skillfully woven band of the ephod. And you shall set the turban on his head and put the holy crown on the turban" (vv. 5, 6). To perform his sacred office, the high priest needed to don his sacred vestments. The technical term for this is *investiture*. Moses clothed Aaron with the white linen tunic that represented righteousness, the jeweled breastpiece that represented the twelve tribes of Israel, and the ephod used for making decisions. Then to top it all off he put on the golden diadem that said, "Holy to the LORD."

Finally, Aaron was ready to be ordained. God said, "You shall take the anointing oil and pour it on his head and anoint him" (v. 7). Anointing with oil was the performative act that set a man apart for public office, whether kingly or priestly. In this case, Moses used a special blend of oil and spice prepared specifically for the occasion (see 30:22–33). This anointing oil was poured over the high priest's head and ran down onto his garments. The psalmist described it as "precious oil on the head, running down on the beard, on the beard of Aaron, running down on the collar of his robes!" (Psalm 133:2). This anointing with oil showed that the high priest was holy, that God had poured out his Spirit on the man.

Only the high priest was anointed this way. Later Moses would call Aaron "chief among his brothers, on whose head the anointing oil is poured and who has been consecrated to wear the garments" (Leviticus 21:10). But the other priests were also ordained. God said: "Then you shall bring his sons and put coats on them, and you shall gird Aaron and his sons with sashes and bind caps on them. And the priesthood shall be theirs by a statute forever. Thus you shall ordain Aaron and his sons" (29:8, 9). This was to be done in perpetuity. Generation after generation the Israelites ordained their priests by washing with water, donning with vestments, and anointing with oil.

To appreciate how holy these things were, consider what happened to Nadab and Abihu—the sons of Aaron who were destroyed for offering unholy worship in the tabernacle. Nadab and Abihu were burned alive, consumed by the fire of God's judgment (see Leviticus 10:2). Strangely, when their corpses were carried outside the camp, men were able to lift the bodies of Nadab and Abihu by their coats (Leviticus 10:5), which were still intact. Although the priests themselves were destroyed with fire, their garments went unscathed! The clothes were still holy to God, even though the men who wore them were profane.[1]

## Three Holy Sacrifices

So far, so good. The priests looked good, and they smelled nice. However, they were still sinners. There was a gap between their outward appearance and their inward spiritual condition. Yet in order to serve God in his tabernacle, they had to be holy all the way through. Therefore, something had to be done about their guilt, and the priests were not fully consecrated until sacrifices were made for their sins.

There were three kinds of sacrifices, spread out over seven days. The first was the most important because it made atonement for sin. It was also the biggest. God said to Moses:

> Then you shall bring the bull before the tent of meeting. Aaron and his sons shall lay their hands on the head of the bull. Then you shall kill the bull before the Lord at the entrance of the tent of meeting, and shall take part of the blood of the bull and put it on the horns of the altar with your finger, and the rest of the blood you shall pour out at the base of the altar. And you shall take all the fat that covers the entrails, and the long lobe of the liver, and the two kidneys with the fat that is on them, and burn them on the altar. But the flesh of the bull and its skin and its dung you shall burn with fire outside the camp; it is a sin offering. (29:10–14)

The bull for the sin offering was sacrificed in the courtyard outside the tabernacle, and its blood was sprinkled on the horns of the altar. This sanctified the altar, making it holy unto God (see Leviticus 8:15). It also showed that God would receive whatever sacrifices were offered there as payment for sin. The unclean parts of the bull were taken outside the camp and burned. But the rest of the animal was placed on the altar and offered as an atoning sacrifice. God said, "The life of the flesh is in the blood, and I have given it for you on the altar to make atonement for your souls, for it is the blood that makes atonement by the life" (Leviticus 17:11).

The significance of the sin offering was powerfully demonstrated by the action of the priests. Before Moses killed the bull, the priests gathered around to lay their hands on its head. This identified them with the sacrifice, imputing sin from the priests to the bull. According to John Currid, "What we see is a case of *transference*, in which the unholiness and impure nature of the priesthood are transferred to the animal. The animal is then sacrificed, thus making atonement for those men."[2] What happened to the sacrifice is what should have happened to each sinner. As the priests watched the bull burn on the altar—the bull on which they had lain their own sinful hands—they realized they were the ones who deserved to die. God was executing his death penalty against their sin. But in his mercy he allowed the bull to serve as their substitute, dying in their place.

The sin offering had to come first. Before the priests could proceed to ordination, something had to be done about their sin. Significantly, this is the first time that the term *sin offering* is used in the Bible, which shows that the priests needed their sins to be forgiven as much as anyone else.

The next sacrifice involved the first of the two rams. God said,

> Then you shall take one of the rams, and Aaron and his sons shall lay their hands on the head of the ram, and you shall kill the ram and shall take its blood and throw it against the sides of the altar. Then you shall cut the ram into pieces, and wash its entrails and its legs, and put them with its pieces and its head, and burn the whole ram on the altar. It is a burnt offering to the LORD. It is a pleasing aroma, a food offering to the LORD. (29:15–18)

Once again the priests placed their hands on the sacrifice. Once again blood was smeared on the altar, only this time it was sprinkled on the sides, not on the horns. Then the entire ram was committed to the flames. Nothing was left. This was a whole burnt offering, symbolizing total dedication to God. In the same way that the ram was offered to God, the priests offered themselves for God's service. They, too, were totally dedicated to God.

Finally, Moses offered the second ram, which was the third sacrifice. God said:

> You shall take the other ram, and Aaron and his sons shall lay their hands on the head of the ram, and you shall kill the ram and take part of its blood and put it on the tip of the right ear of Aaron and on the tips of the right ears of his sons, and on the thumbs of their right hands and on the great toes of their right feet, and throw the rest of the blood against the sides of the altar. Then you shall take part of the blood that is on the altar, and of the anointing oil, and sprinkle it on Aaron and his garments, and on his sons and his sons' garments with him. He and his garments shall be holy, and his sons and his sons' garments with him. (vv. 19–21)

This sacrifice was only for the priests. Everyone in Israel needed sin offerings and burnt offerings, but the ram of ordination was unique to the priesthood. Because it was a blood sacrifice, it may have symbolized atonement. However, its main function was to sanctify the priests for their sacred duties. This is why the blood was sprinkled directly on their bodies and their sacred garments. The blood shed on the altar was for their justification as sinners. But the blood sprinkled on them was for their sanctification as priests.

By the time the last ram was slaughtered, there was blood everywhere. There was blood on the altar from the earlier sacrifices. There was also blood all over the priests. It was smeared on their earlobes, their right thumbs, and their right big toes. It was also spattered on their garments. This set the priests apart for God's service. It showed that what they did in the tabernacle was holy unto God. As it says in Hebrews, "Under the law almost everything is purified with blood" (9:22). This included the priests, whom God dedicated for his service. They were washed with water. They were robed in righteousness. They were anointed with oil. They were sprinkled with sacrificial blood. They were purified, sanctified, anointed, and justified, and in this way they were consecrated for the holy service of God. In a word, they were ordained.

## Jesus Christ Ordained as Priest

The ordination of the priests is important because it reveals deep spiritual truths about Christ and Christian service. In one way or another, everything at the tabernacle was connected to Christ. The tabernacle itself pointed to Christ's dwelling with his people. It was symbolic of his incarnation, in which the Word became flesh and "tabernacled" among us (John 1:14, literal translation). The golden lampstand symbolized Jesus as the light of the world. The bread of the presence symbolized him as the bread of life. Even the curtain that separated the Holy Place from the Most Holy Place symbolized how his bodily death opened the way to God. The tabernacle in the wilderness was a revelation of Jesus Christ.

Christ was also revealed in the ordination of the priests. The sacrifices that consecrated them to God pointed to the sacrifice he made for us on the cross. Jesus Christ is the sin offering that atoned for our sins. When we lay our hands on him by faith, he becomes our substitute, dying in our place. As the Scripture says, "For our sake he made him to be sin who knew no sin, so that in him we might become the righteousness of God" (2 Corinthians 5:21). By his blood we are also purified for the holy service of God. In the words of Bede, the venerable theologian from the early Middle Ages: "Who does not know that the sacrifice of those animals and their blood designate the death of our Lord and the sprinkling of his blood, through which we are set free from sins and strengthened for good works?"[3]

There is a special connection between the sufferings of Christ and the sacrifice of a bull as a sin offering for the priests. As we have seen, the skin and offal of the bull were carried off and burned outside the camp. This was symbolic of the death of Christ, who was crucified "outside the camp." That is, he was crucified outside the holy city of Jerusalem. The Scripture says, "For the bodies of those animals whose blood is brought into the holy places by the high priest as a sacrifice for sin are burned outside the camp. So Jesus also suffered outside the gate in order to sanctify the people through his own blood" (Hebrews 13:11, 12). To make atonement, Jesus was taken out to the place of disease and death, there to suffer God's curse against our sin.

Jesus is not simply the sacrifice, however; he is also the priest. This is another way the tabernacle points us to Christ. Jesus Christ is the priest who enters God's presence on our behalf. The book of Hebrews calls him "a merciful and faithful high priest in the service of God" (2:17); the "high priest of our confession" (3:1); "a great high priest" (4:14); "a high priest forever" (6:20); "a high priest of the good things that have come" (9:11); "a great priest over the house of God" (10:21). As our great High Priest, Jesus presents our prayers to God, interceding on our behalf. He also stands before God in perfect righteousness, so that we can be accepted in God's sight.

If Jesus is our priest, then presumably he must have been ordained to the priesthood. And so he was. This is part of the meaning of his baptism. Jesus' public ministry began when he entered the Jordan River to be baptized. Remember, washing with water was the first step in the ordination of a priest. So Jesus was washed not because he was unclean, but so he could be set apart as a priest for sinners. His baptism was part of his ordination to priestly ministry.

His baptism was also an anointing. God sent Jesus to be the Messiah, which means "the Anointed One." The actual anointing took place at his baptism. The Bible says that when Jesus was baptized, "the heavens were opened, and the Holy Spirit descended on him in bodily form, like a dove" (Luke 3:21b, 22a). In the Old Testament priests were anointed with oil. This was symbolic of the Spirit setting them apart for God's service. But Jesus was anointed with the Spirit himself. Later, when the apostle Peter wanted to explain who Jesus was, he said, "God anointed Jesus of Nazareth with the Holy Spirit and with power" (Acts 10:38a). Jesus was ordained for his ministry as our priest by the anointing of the Holy Spirit, who came upon him in all the fullness of his divine power.

This explains why Jesus is such a wonderful priest. He has been anointed with the third person of the Trinity! It was by the Spirit that Jesus performed miracles, by the Spirit that he taught God's Word, by the Spirit that he offered his life for our sins, and by the Spirit that he was raised from the dead. Now it is by the Spirit that he works in our lives and hears our prayers. Whatever we need from God—protection, provision, peace, healing, comfort, guidance, forgiveness, victory over sin, or any other form of divine assistance—we are invited to ask for it in the name of Jesus Christ. He is our priest, the priest so perfect that we will never need any other. Jesus has made the only sacrifice we need by dying on the cross for our sins. And now he intercedes for us in Heaven, giving us direct access to God's grace.

## The Consecration of the Christian

The ordination of the Old Testament priests points us to Christ and to his perfect priesthood. It also shows what it means to be consecrated by Christ. It does this by telling the story of our salvation. There were four main stages in the ordination of a priest. Aaron and his sons were washed with water, robed in righteousness, anointed with oil, and sprinkled with blood. Each part of their ordination service relates to a different aspect of our salvation in Christ.

First there is the washing with water. Naturally this reminds us of Christian baptism, which signifies the washing away of our sins. Sin makes us dirty. Our angry thoughts, our profane language, our sexual immorality, our selfish ambitions, our greedy strategies—these things make us unclean. If we are to have any kind of relationship with God at all, something has to be done about the filthiness of our sin.

We can only be clean if God makes us clean. This is symbolized in Christian baptism, the sacrament in which we were sprinkled with water. But the real cleansing is what God does on the inside to wash away our sin—what the New Testament calls "the washing of regeneration and renewal of the Holy Spirit, whom he poured out on us richly through Jesus Christ our Savior" (Titus 3:5, 6; cf. 1 Corinthians 6:11). God makes us clean when we are born again by his Spirit. Then the Spirit continues to cleanse us, as often as we are stained by sin. Our sins make us feel dirty (or at least they ought to), but God can make us clean. He has promised that "if we confess our sins, he is faithful and just to forgive us our sins and to cleanse us from all unrighteousness" (1 John 1:9). Therefore, "let us draw near with a true heart in full assurance of faith, with our hearts sprinkled clean from an evil conscience and our bodies washed with pure water" (Hebrews 10:22).

Next comes our robing in righteousness. God does something more than simply wash away our sin; he also clothes us with the perfect righteousness of Jesus Christ. The Bible says, "For as many of you as were baptized into Christ have put on Christ" (Galatians 3:27). The Old Testament priests were dressed in sacred garments symbolizing their holiness before God. It takes holiness to stand before God, and the priests could not enter his holy sanctuary unless they were suitably dressed. But we have the most righteous robes of all. Every believer has put on Jesus Christ and thus is dressed with the perfect righteousness of Christ's obedience to God. We do not stand on our own merits, which would never be good enough for God. Instead God accepts us on the basis of what Jesus has done. We are clothed with Christ.

God has washed us by his Spirit and clothed us with his Son. He has also anointed us for his service. This was the third step in the ordination of the high priest. Aaron was anointed with oil, which consecrated him for God's service. We too have been anointed—not with oil but with the Holy Spirit. The Bible says that we have "been anointed by the Holy One" (1 John 2:20). To be specific, God "anointed us, . . . and [gave] us his Spirit in our hearts" (2 Corinthians 1:21, 22). God the Holy Spirit has set us apart for sacred service.

Finally, there were sacrifices. There was a sin offering—a sacrifice of atonement pointing to the propitiation Jesus made on the cross for our sins. There was a burnt offering—a sacrifice of dedication in which a whole animal was offered to God. Then there was the offering that was only for priests—a sacrifice of purification that consecrated them for God. Each of these offerings began with the priests laying their hands on the head of the sacrifice. They identified themselves with the animal, which then died in their place. The sacrifice was their substitute.

We too have a substitute. A sacrifice has died in our place to make atonement for our sin. This substitutionary sacrifice has been made by the Lord Jesus Christ, who is the Son of God and the Savior of sinners. To receive forgiveness, all we need to do is lay our hands on him by faith. When we do, God imputes all our sin to him.

One man who received forgiveness through the substitutionary work of Jesus Christ was Charles Simeon, the great preacher at Holy Trinity Church in Cambridge, England. When Simeon began university he was not yet a Christian. This explains why he was so alarmed to receive—shortly after his arrival—a summons from the head of his college requiring him to take Holy Communion in three weeks' time. Simeon panicked. "The thought rushed into my mind," he later wrote, "that Satan himself was as fit to attend there as I; and that if I must attend, I must prepare for my attendance."

Desperate for help, Simeon bought a Christian book called *The Whole Duty of Man*. As he read it, he began to cry out to God for mercy. Eventually Simeon began to feel the first glimmerings of hope. In his own words,

> It was an indistinct kind of hope, founded on God's mercy to real penitents. But in Passion week as I was reading Bishop Wilson on the Lord's Supper, I met with an expression to this effect: "That the Jews knew what they did when they transferred their sin to the head of their offering." The thought rushed into my mind, What! May I transfer all my guilt to another? Has God provided an offering for me, that I may lay my sins on his head? Then, God willing, I will not bear them on my own soul one moment longer. Accordingly I sought to lay my sins on the sacred head of Jesus; and on the Wednesday began to have a hope of mercy; on the Thursday that hope increased; on the Friday and Saturday it became more strong; and on the Sunday morning (Easter Day) I awoke early with those words upon my heart and lips, "Jesus Christ is risen to-day! Hallelujah! Hallelujah!" From that hour peace flowed in rich abundance into my soul; and . . . I had the sweetest access to God through my blessed Saviour.[4]

The mercy that Charles Simeon received—forgiveness, peace, joy, and access to God—come to everyone who trusts in Jesus Christ for salvation.

## The Priesthood of All Believers

God has provided full salvation in Christ. He has washed us clean, robed us in righteousness, anointed us with his Spirit, and atoned for our sins. When God did all these things in Exodus 29, it was for the ordination of the priests. So why has he done it all for us? For one very important purpose: to ordain us as priests.

The New Testament takes the word *priest* and applies it to *everyone* who has been saved from sin by the atoning work of Jesus Christ. We are "a royal priesthood" (1 Peter 2:9). We are "a kingdom, priests to his God and Father" (Revelation 1:6). We are "priests of God and of Christ" (Revelation 20:6). Martin Luther called this "the priesthood of all believers." He said, "We are all priests, as many of us as are Christians."[5]

This means that God has important work for us to do. We have been called into his holy service. Many Christians still think of ministry as something that is primarily or even exclusively for ministers and missionaries. It is true that ministers and missionaries are called to serve. Like the Old Testament priests, men ordained to gospel ministry have been consecrated for holy service to God. But God has given all of us a sacred calling. We are priests of the living God, and we have a holy obligation to serve him. We no longer serve him in the tabernacle but in his holy sanctuary the church, and also in the world. We serve him by praising his name. We serve him by giving generously to the church. We serve him by binding up the wounds of the brokenhearted and embracing the outcasts of society. We serve him by loving those who are hard to love with the same merciful love that we have received from God in Christ. We serve him by telling people to trust in Jesus and by doing whatever we do for his glory.

When the Old Testament priests were ordained, they were marked with blood in three places: their earlobes, their thumbs, and their big toes. This meant that they belonged to God from head to toe. As John J. Davis explains it: "This act implied the complete dedication of life and ability to the service of God. Symbolically the blood put on the right ear sanctified that organ to hear the word of God; that which was put on the right hand set the hands apart in their performance of mediatorial work. The right foot spoke of the sanctified walk of the life of the priest as an example to others."[6]

God has made the same claim on everyone who belongs to him through faith in Jesus Christ. We have been marked with the blood of the very Son of God. The Bible says, "For if the blood of goats and bulls, and the sprinkling of defiled persons with the ashes of a heifer, sanctify for the purification of the flesh, how much more will the blood of Christ, who through the eternal Spirit offered himself without blemish to God, purify our conscience from dead works to serve the living God" (Hebrews 9:13, 14).

We have been set apart to serve. Our ears belong to God. He wants us to listen to his Word. Our thumbs belong to God, too, along with the rest of our hands. God wants us to serve him with all our strength. Even our big toes belong to God, which is something to think about every time we put on our socks! God wants us to walk with him as we make our way through the world. We have a high and holy calling. We have been ordained as priests to serve the living God.

# 80

# The Big Picture

EXODUS 29:22–46

ONE OF THE TRUE MASTERPIECES AT THE Art Institute in Chicago is a massive painting by Georges Seurat called *Sunday Afternoon on the Island of La Grande Jatte* (1884–1886). When standing close to the picture, an observer can only see tiny dots—millions of them. Seurat pioneered the artistic technique known as *pointillism*, in which tiny points of color are applied to canvas with the tip of a brush. From a foot away, all anyone can see are the beautiful colors. But from a distance, a picturesque scene emerges. Parisians are sitting in the park on a Sunday afternoon, or strolling with their parasols, gazing serenely at the River Seine. From the proper vantage point, Seurat's little points of color become part of a bigger picture.

Something similar happens at the end of Exodus 29. Since the beginning of chapter 25, God has been giving Moses the plans for constructing his holy sanctuary, the tabernacle. God showed his prophet how to build the frame and sew together the tent. He told him what pieces of furniture to put inside and what equipment to arrange outside in the courtyard. Then God turned his attention to the priests who served in the tabernacle—what they should wear and how they were to be ordained.

We get still more details at the end of Exodus 29. We find out what the priests did with the meat from their sacrifices. We discover how many bulls were offered to atone for their sin and what kind of sacrifices they had to offer each day on God's altar. By this point it would be easy to get lost in all the details, but God steps back to reveal the big picture. At the end of the chapter he explains how the tabernacle achieves his ultimate purpose of bringing glory to his name by saving and sanctifying his people.

In his lectures on Old Testament theology, the British scholar Alec Motyer explains: "God's tabernacle is the climax of redemption; he brought them out of Egypt for this very purpose that he might dwell among them. Don't weary over all those tedious details to do with the tabernacle; they are describing to you the climax of God's redemptive covenant programme for his people."[1] Up close, the seemingly mundane details of the tabernacle may seem like little points of color swimming on a large canvas. But when we step back, a beautiful picture emerges—one that takes us right to the heart of God's plan for his people, the covenant of his grace.

## Providing for the Priests

Before God reveals the big picture, he provides more details. Although we shouldn't weary over them, we should study them because they are part of what God has revealed for our benefit. The first of these details concerns the final sacrifice. We have seen how Aaron and his sons were cleansed, clothed, and consecrated for the holy service of God. Their ordination was a step-by-step process. The priests were washed with water, robed in righteousness, anointed with oil, and sprinkled with sacrificial blood.

Three kinds of sacrifices were made for the priests, the last of which was known as "the ram of ordination," or more literally, "the ram of filling." The term *filling* comes from an ancient custom. In Biblical times when someone was appointed as a king or priest, an official would come forward to "fill his hand." This was the term used for an ordination or installation. Scholars are not altogether certain what it means. It may mean that a symbol of office was placed in the man's hand. For example, a royal staff might have been placed in the hand of a king. But the expression may indicate that the hand of the new official was filled with some form of tribute. As long as he held office, he had the right to receive revenue; the people "filled his hand." Given what the Bible says about the ordination of priests, the latter explanation seems more likely. God said to Moses:

> You shall also take the fat from the ram and the fat tail and the fat that covers the entrails, and the long lobe of the liver and the two kidneys with the fat that is on them, and the right thigh (for it is a ram of ordination), and one loaf of bread and one cake of bread made with oil, and one wafer out of the basket of unleavened bread that is before the Lord. You shall put all these on the palms of Aaron and on the palms of his sons, and wave them for a wave offering before the Lord. Then you shall take them from their hands and burn them on the altar on top of the burnt offering, as a pleasing aroma before the Lord. It is a food offering to the Lord. (29:22–25)

Several important things happen in these verses. One is that the fat and innards were offered to the Lord with fire. In other words, the best parts of the animal were given back to God. They might not be the parts that we would choose for this purpose, but the priests gave what they considered the fattest, juiciest parts of their sacrifice as an offering unto God.

The priests also made various offerings of bread. Together with the inner parts of the animal sacrifice, these offerings were waved before the Lord and then burned on the altar. It is not certain how this waving was done. The priests may have waved their offerings back and forth as a symbolic way of calling them to God's attention. Or they may simply have lifted their offerings up to God as an act of worship, elevating them to declare that what they offered belonged to him. But however they waved their offerings, the priests did not come empty-handed. Their hands were filled with good things to offer back to God.

Moses had something in his hand too. God said, "You shall take the breast of the ram of Aaron's ordination and wave it for a wave offering before the Lord, and it shall be your portion" (v. 26). By making the ordination sacrifices, in effect Moses served as Aaron's priest. As the priest, he had the right to receive a portion of the sacrifice for his nourishment. So the ram's breast belonged to Moses, who waved it before the Lord and then ate it.

From then on, the privilege of eating from the sacrifice would belong to Aaron and his sons because they would make all the sacrifices. God clarified this by saying, "And you shall consecrate the breast of the wave offering that is waved and the thigh of the priests' portion that is contributed from the ram of ordination, from what was Aaron's and his sons'. It shall be for Aaron and his sons as a perpetual due from the people of Israel, for it is a contribution. It shall be a contribution from the people of Israel from their peace offerings, their contribution to the Lord" (vv. 27, 28; cf. Leviticus 7:31–34). This was God's permanent provision for the priesthood. The people brought their offerings to God, and God in turn gave the priests their share.

This brings us to an important point of application. God does not expect his people to serve him for nothing but promises to provide for their (our) needs. In the Old Testament, he provided for his priests by giving them a portion from the sacrifice. Something similar happens in the church. We give our tithes and offerings to the church, and part of our giving goes to those who minister in his name. As the Scripture says, referring specifically to the work of the pastor, "The laborer deserves his wages" (1 Timothy 5:18). Unfortunately, some Christians feel it is God's responsibility—not theirs—to provide for ministers and other Christian workers. Others assume that because people in full-time ministry are more godly, they can live with less! There are several problems with this line of reasoning, but according to the Bible, a generous share of what we give to God rightfully belongs to those who minister in his name. Participating in this ancient practice brings joy to God's people.

This blessing is not just for ministers, however. There is a wider principle here. The church is a royal priesthood, in which every believer has the priestly duty to serve the living God. Therefore, God's provision for Aaron and his sons encourages us to believe that he will provide for us as well. The God who gave his priests nice, juicy pieces of meat will graciously supply whatever we need.

## Details, Details

The next detail has to do with the high priest's clothes: "The holy garments of Aaron shall be for his sons after him; they shall be anointed in them and ordained in them. The son who succeeds him as priest, who comes into the tent of meeting to minister in the Holy Place, shall wear them seven days" (29:29, 30).

We have seen that Aaron wore special clothes for his ordination as high priest. Here we learn that these clothes were not just for him, but for a whole succession of priests. After Aaron died, his sons were to fill his office after him, and so his brand-new robes would eventually become hand-me-downs. In fact, the Bible describes how the sacred priestly garments were stripped from Aaron shortly before he died and were then put on his son Eleazar (Numbers 20:22–29).

Down through the centuries, the priestly office was passed from one generation to the next. Each new high priest was ordained with the ceremony described in Exodus 29. To this day, Jews who bear the name of "priest"—that is, the name Cohen, with all its variations—are able to trace their genetic heritage back to a single ancestor. The succession of Aaron's priestly line was preserved as a living testimony to the truth of Scripture. But what is more important is that God has provided an eternal priest for his people. The sons of Aaron only served as high priests until God sent his Son to be our Savior. Now the Lord Jesus Christ is our great High Priest before God. There were priests who came before him, but none will come after. Jesus has offered the one and only sacrifice to atone for our sins, and he will be our High Priest forever.

Here are more details—more points of color to apply to our canvas as we seek to understand the Old Testament priesthood. After the ram of ordination was properly sacrificed, the priests sat down to eat its meat in the presence of God. First the fat and innards were burned as a special offering to God. Then Moses claimed the breastpiece that belonged to him. But everything else was given to the priests. God said,

> You shall take the ram of ordination and boil its flesh in a holy place. And Aaron and his sons shall eat the flesh of the ram and the bread that is in the basket in the entrance of the tent of meeting. They shall eat those things with which atonement was made at their ordination and consecration, but an outsider shall not eat of them, because they are holy. And if any of the flesh for the ordination or of the bread remain until the morning, then you shall burn the remainder with fire. It shall not be eaten, because it is holy. (29:31–34)

This sacred meal was the next stage in the ordination of priests. After the priests were washed with water, robed in righteousness, anointed with oil, and sprinkled with sacrificial blood, they sat down to eat a covenant meal. Just as Israel's elders ate and drank with God on the mountain (see 24:11), so Israel's priests ate with God at the tabernacle during the seven days of their ordination. The meal they shared showed that they had fellowship with the living God, that they were bound to him in the covenant. The priests were feasting upon his grace.

We have seen how each stage of ordination symbolizes a different aspect of our salvation in Christ. Washing with water points to our regeneration and baptism by the Holy Spirit. Robing in righteousness points to the holiness that is ours in Christ. Anointing with oil points to the blessing of God's Spirit. Sprinkling the sacrificial blood points to our consecration through the cross. Eating the ram of ordination also points us to the gospel. Once we come to God through faith in Jesus Christ, we are invited to eat at his Table, communing with him in the Lord's Supper.

After a while we get so comfortable celebrating Communion that we forget what a sacred privilege it is to sit down for a meal with the living God. The nineteenth-century missionary John Paton was reminded of this when he first served the Lord's Supper to the natives of New Hebrides. Paton had left Scotland to evangelize tribes of cannibals. After years of patient witness, they finally came to Christ. Here is how Paton describes their first celebration of Communion:

> For years we had toiled and prayed and taught for this. At the moment when I put the bread and wine into those dark hands, once stained with the blood of cannibalism but now stretched out to receive and partake the emblems and seals of the Redeemer's love, I had a foretaste of the joy of glory that well-nigh broke my heart to pieces. I shall never taste a deeper bliss till I gaze on the glorified face of Jesus himself.[2]

This glorious joy belongs to every Christian who eats at the Lord's Table. We have fellowship with God through the saving work of Jesus Christ, and this is a foretaste of Heaven.

## Seven Days, Seven Bulls

The next detail helps us appreciate how elaborate the ordination ritual was. God said, "Thus you shall do to Aaron and to his sons, according to all that I have commanded you. Through seven days shall you ordain them, and every day you shall offer a bull as a sin offering for atonement. Also you shall purify the altar, when you make atonement for it, and shall anoint it to consecrate it. Seven days you shall make atonement for the altar and consecrate it, and the altar shall be most holy. Whatever touches the altar shall become holy" (29:35–37).

It took one whole week to ordain the priests, and on each day of the week a fresh bull was sacrificed on God's altar. This made atonement for the altar itself, purifying it and consecrating it. The altar was set apart for God. It was the place where he accepted sacrifices for his people's sin. Therefore, it had to be made holy, and this was done by sprinkling it with the blood of seven perfect sacrifices.

These sacrifices were also for the priests, because they too needed atonement. There was never any doubt as to whether or not these men were sinners. Certainly they had been chosen to serve in God's holy tabernacle. But as far as their own righteousness was concerned, they were no better than anyone else. So before they could offer holy service to God, atonement had to be made for their sin. Nor was one sacrifice enough. *Seven bulls* had to be offered for their sins—one for each day of the week! As the priests witnessed these sacrifices, day after day and bull after bull, they saw the grace of God in taking away their sin.

The same is true for us. We need a sacrifice for our sin, and God has provided one through Christ's death on the cross. By the blood of his very own Son, God has set us apart to serve. Talking about blood like this has a way of making people squeamish, including some who call themselves Christians. They prefer to think that God will accept them on some basis other than a sacrifice for sin. One thinks, for example, of John Shelby Spong, the infamous Anglican bishop who denies the need for atonement. Spong complains about Christians who are always talking about the blood that Jesus shed on the cross. He writes, "I would choose to loathe rather than to worship a deity who required the sacrifice of his son."[3] But this is what it takes to make someone holy for the service of God: the blood of a perfect sacrifice.

John Currid recounts the story of a rabbi's son who asked his father, "What is it that makes atonement for the soul?" The rabbi answered, "It is the blood," and then to prove his point he quoted Leviticus 17:11: "Because the life of the flesh is in the blood. And I have given it for you on the altar for atonement for your souls." The boy responded with a further question: "Then why are there no blood sacrifices in our synagogues?" The rabbi sadly explained that this was impossible. The only place to offer a lawful sacrifice was at the temple in Jerusalem, but this was destroyed almost two thousand years ago. "Then," said the boy, "we have no atonement."[4]

In a way, the boy was right: no blood, no atonement. But he was also wrong, because we *do* have an atonement. God has provided one for both Jews and Gentiles through the saving work of Jesus Christ. Everyone who believes in him will be saved, because his blood was shed to take away our sin.

Once they had received atonement for their own sins, the priests had to make sacrifices for the sins of others. After explaining what was required for their ordination, God gave additional information about their priestly duties:

> Now this is what you shall offer on the altar: two lambs a year old day by day regularly. One lamb you shall offer in the morning, and the other lamb you shall offer at twilight. And with the first lamb a tenth measure of fine flour mingled with a fourth of a hin of beaten oil, and a fourth of a hin of wine for a drink offering. The other lamb you shall offer at twilight, and shall offer with it a grain offering and its drink offering, as in the morning, for a pleasing aroma, a food offering to the Lord. It shall be a regular burnt

> offering throughout your generations at the entrance of the tent of meeting before the LORD. (29:38–42a)

Once they were ordained, the priests would offer these sacrifices every day. They would offer a lamb both morning and evening. These daily sacrifices, which were combined with grain, oil, and wine, were a sign of Israel's devotion to God. As the sacrifices burned, their smoke wafted up to Heaven. Thus every day began and ended with an aroma pleasing to God.

Like the other offerings in the Old Testament, these sacrifices are connected to Christ and the Christian life. One application is obvious: In the same way that the Israelites opened and closed the day with sacrifices, we are called to begin and end every day with God. But there is something deeper at work here. The Apostle Paul alluded to it when he wrote, "Therefore be imitators of God, as beloved children. And walk in love, as Christ loved us and gave himself up for us, a fragrant offering and sacrifice to God" (Ephesians 5:1, 2). The words "fragrant offering and sacrifice" refer explicitly to the twice-daily sacrifices that the Israelites offered in the tabernacle and later at the temple. As Paul reflected on the meaning of the crucifixion, he saw that the cross was connected with the offerings God's people had been making every day for centuries. When Jesus made the atoning sacrifice for our sins, it filled Heaven and earth with the perfume of his love.

Now we are called to live with the same kind of sacrificial love. When we give to others—when we place a higher priority on them than we do on ourselves, giving ourselves away for Jesus—then our lives are like fragrant perfume that brings joy to the heart of God.

## Seeing the Big Picture

Every detail of the tabernacle is full of beauty. In Exodus 29 we see how God provides for his people, how Jesus fulfills the promise of an eternal priesthood, how God welcomes us into the fellowship of his Table, how the blood of Jesus atones for our sin, and how a life of sacrifice rises to Heaven like sweet perfume.

We should not lose sight of the big picture, however. At the end of the chapter, God steps back to remind Moses why he was building this tabernacle. He said:

> There I will meet with the people of Israel, and it shall be sanctified by my glory. I will consecrate the tent of meeting and the altar. Aaron also and his sons I will consecrate to serve me as priests. I will dwell among the people of Israel and will be their God. And they shall know that I am the LORD their God, who brought them out of the land of Egypt that I might dwell among them. I am the LORD their God. (vv. 43–46)

The last phrase—"I am the LORD their God"—places God's signature on this entire section of Exodus.[5] Here God is explaining what the tabernacle was all about. And what *was* it all about? It was about the God of Heaven making a place to dwell on earth. It was about God building a place where he could meet with his prophet and his people, establishing a point of contact where he could speak to them. It was about God consecrating a place by his presence. It was about God making his people holy to serve him. It was about God revealing himself so that he would be known as their God. It was about God being his people's God and the people becoming his people. It was about God completing the work of salvation that he had begun when he brought Israel out of Egypt.

The tabernacle was about all of these things, and all for this grand purpose: so God could reveal his glory. Remember, this was the whole purpose of the exodus: God was saving his people for his glory. And the tabernacle was central to his plan of salvation. It was the place where God would come down in glory.

As we study the tabernacle, we cannot help but be impressed with the extraordinary pains God took to get everything ready. Before he descended in glory, everything was made holy. God made the tent holy—consecrating it with holy sacrifices. He made the furniture holy. Each piece was carefully crafted to reveal something about his divine character. He made the priests holy. He washed them, dressed them, anointed them, and sprinkled them with consecrating blood. He even put a label on their foreheads that said, "Holy to the LORD." It was all holy, for as God said, "I will consecrate the tent of meeting and the altar. Aaron also and his sons I will consecrate to serve me as priests" (v. 44).

What would happen then? God said that when everything was holy, "I will dwell among the people of Israel and will be their God. And they shall know that I am the LORD their God, who brought them out of the land of Egypt that I might dwell among them. I am the LORD their God" (vv. 45, 46). This is why God took so much trouble to sanctify the tabernacle and everything in it. He did it to consecrate a place for the presence of his glory. He did it to live with his people and be their God. He did it so that they would understand the meaning of their salvation.

This was something that God had long promised. When Moses first went to Pharaoh, and things seemed to be going very badly, God reassured his people with this promise: "I will take you to be my people, and I will be your God, and you shall know that I am the LORD your God, who has brought you out from under the burdens of the Egyptians" (6:7). This was the great promise of the covenant. No greater promise has ever been given. What greater promise could God make to mere mortals than to say that he would be their God and they would be his people? The tabernacle was one fulfillment of that promise. It was the place where the Israelites met God in all his glory and came to know him as their God.

When we see what God was doing with the tabernacle, we can see more clearly than ever what wonderful things he has done for us. The Bible describes the church as a tabernacle or temple for God. It says, "Do you not know that you are God's temple and that God's Spirit dwells in you?" (1 Corinthians 3:16). It describes the individual Christian the same way, as "a temple of the Holy Spirit" (1 Corinthians 6:19). How amazing this is, that the living God would come and live with his sinful people! But this is what God has done. By the inward presence of his Holy Spirit, he has come to dwell in us.

In order for this to happen, God first had to make us holy. He did it in much the same way that he made the priests holy in the Old Testament. He washed us, robed us, anointed us, and sprinkled us with the saving blood of his Son. And he did this so we would make a suitable dwelling for his Spirit. God has come to live in us forever, so that we would know him as our God who saved us from our sins through the death and resurrection of Jesus Christ.

This is the big picture—the ultimate purpose for what God is doing in this world. With all the difficulties and distractions of daily life, it is easy for us to get lost in the details. We are so busy toiling at our work, worrying about our finances, struggling with our limitations, enjoying our entertainments, pursuing our pleasures, and grasping our ambitions that we forget to step back and see what God is doing. So take a look: God is making a holy place for his dwelling, so that our lives will display his glory.

# 81

# Sweet Altar of Prayer

EXODUS 30:1–10, 34–38

THE PUNGENT SPICE of burning leaves on a crisp afternoon in autumn. The savory aroma of Thanksgiving turkey roasting in the oven. The leathery smell of a brand-new baseball glove. The narcotic aroma of fresh dittoes from the duplicating machine. The musty smell of a cabin in the woods. The pleasing scent of box hedges lining an English rose garden. The fragrant perfume of my first and only true love. These are a few of my favorite smells. Each one immediately calls to remembrance significant personal experiences. The sense of smell adds spice to life.

If there was one smell that Israel's priests could never forget, it was the smell of burning incense. Their service in the tabernacle was a complete sensory experience. There were things to touch, like fine linen fabric, cool water, and the hairy skins of sacrificial animals. There were beautiful things to see: bright lights, golden furniture, and colorful curtains. There were good things to taste: fresh bread, fine wine, and juicy meat. There were pleasing things to hear, such as the bells on the high priest's robe. But there were also some things the priests could smell. Outside in the courtyard they sniffed the savory aroma of burning sacrifices, but inside the Holy Place they smelled something more fragrant. It was the pungent scent of sweet, spicy incense rising from a golden altar.

## The Altar of Incense

The altar of incense was the last piece of furniture God put in the tabernacle. Back in Exodus 25, he described the other furnishings that went inside his holy tent: the ark of the covenant, the table of showbread, and the golden lampstand. Then he gave Moses instructions for building the tabernacle itself, for landscaping its courtyard, and for ordaining its priests. Only then did God install the altar of incense.

The question naturally arises as to why God waited. Wouldn't it have made more sense to put the altar of incense with the rest of the furniture back in chapter 25? Scholars who are critical of the Bible see this as a later revision. It wasn't part of the original text, they say, but was added later, almost like an appendix.

There are a number of problems with this kind of criticism. One is the sheer absence of any manuscript evidence to support it. The only edition of Exodus we know is the one we have in our Bibles. Another problem is historical. Formerly some scholars said that altars for incense were a late innovation. But archaeologists have discovered that by the time of Moses, people had been using them for almost a thousand years![1] There is also a logical problem with this kind of criticism. If an editor added the altar of incense to the Bible's original text, why did he put it here? Some explanation is still needed. According to the critics, it would have made more sense to put it back in chapter 25 with the rest of the furniture. So the person who tried to rewrite the Bible must have been a bad editor!

The answer, of course, is that the altar of incense is in the Bible right where God wanted it to be, after the ordination of the priests. Perhaps God put it here because he is starting to focus on the worship offered in his sanctuary. Once he had explained how the priests were ordained, he could then begin to describe their duties. The altar of incense was not mentioned until there was a priest to burn incense on it.

How was this altar made? God told Moses:

> You shall make an altar on which to burn incense; you shall make it of acacia wood. A cubit shall be its length, and a cubit its breadth. It shall be square, and two cubits shall be its height. Its horns shall be of one piece with it. You shall overlay it with pure gold, its top and around its sides and its horns. And you shall make a molding of gold around it. And you shall make two golden rings for it. Under its molding on two opposite sides of it you shall make them, and they shall be holders for poles with which to carry it. You shall make the poles of acacia wood and overlay them with gold. (30:1–5)

The altar of incense wasn't very large. It was about a foot and a half square and no more than three feet high. In its craftsmanship and design, it was similar to the other furniture in the tabernacle. Like the table of showbread, it was made of acacia wood covered with gold, rimmed with a golden border. It had to be gold because it was in the royal chamber—the holy place where God was. Like the great bronze altar in the courtyard, the altar of incense had horns on its top four corners. And like everything else in the tabernacle, it was designed to be portable. There were rings on two sides of the altar, allowing it to be lifted up on a pair of staves and carried wherever God would lead.

Where was the altar of incense located? God told Moses, "And you shall put it in front of the veil that is above the ark of the testimony, in front of the mercy seat that is above the testimony, where I will meet with you" (v. 6). So the altar of incense went in the middle of the Holy Place, between the table of showbread and the golden lampstand. It was placed right next to the veil that separated the Holy Place from the Most Holy Place. In other words, it was placed directly in front of the ark of the covenant, God's royal throne on earth. There was a thick curtain that separated the altar of incense from the presence of God, but the altar was oriented in that direction. It was close to the mercy seat—so close that even though it went in the Holy Place, in Solomon's day it was called the "altar that belonged to the inner sanctuary" (1 Kings 6:22; cf. Hebrews 9:3, 4), meaning the Holy of Holies.

This means that when the priests stood at the altar of incense, they were standing right in front of God. With the exception of the high priest, who was allowed to enter the Holy of Holies once a year, this was the closest they would ever get to the glorious presence of God. And what did the priests do there? God said, "And Aaron shall burn fragrant incense on it. Every morning when he dresses the lamps he shall burn it, and when Aaron sets up the lamps at twilight, he shall burn it, a regular incense offering before the LORD throughout your generations. You shall not offer unauthorized incense on it, or a burnt offering, or a grain offering, and you shall not pour a drink offering on it" (30:7–9).

Burning incense on the golden altar was part of the priests' daily routine. Every morning they tended the golden lampstand, trimming the wicks and replenishing the oil. At the same time they would burn fragrant incense on the altar. This routine was repeated at nightfall, when the priests relit their lamps and made a fresh offering of incense. This was a perpetual part of priestly worship, something the priests did morning by morning and evening after evening, from generation to generation.

The priests were not free to use this altar any way they wanted. Like everything else in the tabernacle, the altar of incense came with specific instructions. It was never to be used for burnt offerings, grain offerings, or drink offerings. It was only for incense. And the only incense the priests were allowed to use was the special blend of spices described at the end of the chapter:

> The LORD said to Moses, "Take sweet spices, stacte, and onycha, and galbanum, sweet spices with pure frankincense (of each shall there be an equal part), and make an incense blended as by the perfumer, seasoned with salt, pure and holy. You shall beat some of it very small, and put part of it before the testimony in the tent of meeting where I shall meet with you. It shall be most holy for you. And the incense that you shall make according to its composition, you shall not make for yourselves. It shall be for you holy to the LORD. Whoever makes any like it to use as perfume shall be cut off from his people." (vv. 34–38)

Not all of these spices can be precisely identified, so we are not able to reproduce the sacred mixture. The spices used were mixed in equal proportions and then pulverized. This aromatic incense was for God, and not for anyone else. Since it was holy to the Lord, it was not to be used for any other purpose or in any other place. It may have been burned directly on the golden altar. More likely the ingredients were first put into some kind of bowl or pan—a brazier with burning coals. In this way, holy incense was burned before a holy God. And to see how holy, we only need to remember Nadab and Abihu, who were struck dead for their failure to follow God's instructions for the altar of incense (Leviticus 10).

## An Altar for Prayer

The important question to ask about the altar of incense is what it symbolized. As the fragrance of the incense permeated the tabernacle, with its smoke rising toward Heaven, what was this supposed to signify?

Scholars have answered this question in different ways. Some think the incense was a form of tribute—a pleasing aroma for God. Some say it is a sign of his holy presence.[2] Others see it as a symbol of royalty, because ancient Near-Eastern kings often burned incense in their royal chambers. Still others think the incense was an air freshener to hide the stench of sacrifice. Tremper Longman says, "The altar of incense had one very practical purpose. With all the slaughtering of sacrifices and the manipulation of blood, the odor would have been overpowering without incense."[3] Still others think the incense was a form of protection, that its smoke concealed the curtain to the Holy of Holies and thus shielded the priests from the holy presence of God.[4]

None of these suggestions is fully satisfactory. The incense may have made the tabernacle smell nice, but it must have had some symbolic significance as well. It was not primarily a sign of the divine presence; the way God was present at the tabernacle was in the cloud of glory. Nor did the smoke protect the priests from the Holy of Holies—this is what the veil was for. As we consider the various possibilities, with their weaknesses, we can sympathize with the commentator who said, "Of all the purposes that have been proposed for the burning of incense . . . none provides a satisfactory explanation."[5]

However, there is one more possibility to consider—namely, that the altar of incense was an altar for prayer. This interpretation finds support in the altar's location. Remember that the altar of incense was in the middle of the tabernacle, next to the veil that separated the Holy Place from the Most Holy Place. In other words, it was in front of the ark of the covenant, separated from it only by a thick curtain. So when a priest offered incense on the golden altar, he was approaching the mercy seat. He was coming before the throne of grace—the place where God answers prayer.

The book of Leviticus seems to confirm this when it describes the altar of incense as "the altar that is before the LORD" (16:18). It was a place for coming before God, specifically for prayer. The Bible teacher C. W. Slemming explains this by using a modern analogy. He writes:

> I have sometimes thought of this little piece of furniture standing before the veil as an electric plug such as we use to tap the electric power laid behind our walls. Behind the veil of the tabernacle was the Shekinah Glory of the presence of the Lord, and behind the veil of the sky are all the resources of the great triune God. By putting in the plug of prayer with the hand of faith, we are able to tap those resources and find that "prayer changes things." Great things happen at the hour of prayer when incense is being offered.[6]

Exodus 30 gives at least some indication that the altar of incense was for prayer, but the real proof comes from other passages in the Bible. The safest way to interpret Scripture is by comparing it with other Scripture. In this case, the place to begin is with Psalm 141, in which David writes:

> O Lord, I call upon you; hasten to me!
>   Give ear to my voice when I call to you!
> Let my prayer be counted as incense before you,
>   and the lifting up of my hands as the evening sacrifice! (vv. 1, 2)

David was referring to the daily ritual for worship in the tabernacle, in which incense was burned before the Lord. As David cried out for help, he asked God to hear his prayers. Even though he was not a priest and therefore did not have the right to burn incense on God's altar, he asked God to receive his prayers all the same, just as he received the incense of prayer in the tabernacle.

Another passage connecting incense to prayer comes in the Gospel of Luke. It concerns a priest named Zechariah, who was visited by an angel proclaiming good news about the coming of Christ. Here is how that Gospel describes the scene:

> Now while he was serving as priest before God when his division was on duty, according to the custom of the priesthood, he was chosen by lot to enter the temple of the Lord and burn incense. And the whole multitude of the people were praying outside at the hour of incense. And there appeared to him an angel of the Lord standing on the right side of the altar of incense. (1:8–11)

Zechariah was on duty at the temple. In the providence of God, it was his turn to burn incense on the golden altar. As Zechariah prepared to make his offering, a crowd of people gathered outside to pray. This happened at the temple every day, morning and evening. At the same time that incense was offered in the Holy Place, people met for prayer out in the courtyard. The priest was praying too. We know this because when the angel appeared to Zechariah, he said, "Do not be afraid, Zechariah, for your prayer has been heard" (v. 13a). The time for offering incense was a time for intercession. As the people prayed, and as the priest prayed for the people, the incense symbolized their prayers ascending to the throne of God.

The book of Revelation uses the same symbolism. In his vision of glory, the apostle John saw twenty-four elders worshiping God on his heavenly throne. He also saw what they were doing: "Each [held] a harp, and golden bowls full of incense, which are the prayers of the saints" (5:8b). Here the Bible explains its own symbolism: Incense represents the prayers of God's people. The same connection is made three chapters later. There John writes, "And another angel came and stood at the altar with a golden censer, and he was given much incense to offer with the prayers of all the saints on the golden altar before the throne, and the smoke of the incense, with the prayers of the saints, rose before God from the hand of the angel" (8:3, 4). The prayers of God's people are joined to the incense they offer, and together both their incense and their prayers rise up to God.

These passages all connect the offering of incense with the life of prayer. They help us understand what the priests did at the golden altar. Prayer was an important part of their ministry. The priests offered prayers for God's people every day, and this was symbolized by the smoking incense. According to David Levy, "The priest took a censer full of burning coals from the brazen altar in one hand and specially prepared sweet incense in the other hand and ignited the incense by sprinkling it over the burning coals. A thick cloud of smoke curled upward filling the Tabernacle, symbolic of Israel's prayers to God."[7]

## Why God Hears Our Prayers

Before any incense could be offered, something very important had to happen first: Atonement had to be made for sin. The altar of incense—that sweet altar of prayer—had to be consecrated with sacrificial blood. God said to Moses, "Aaron shall make atonement on its horns once a year. With the blood of the sin offering of atonement he shall make atonement for it once in the year throughout your generations. It is most holy to the LORD" (30:10).

The sin offering was the blood sacrifice of an animal to atone for sin. Once a year—on the Day of Atonement—this offering was made for all God's people on the great bronze altar in the courtyard. When the animal was sacrificed, its blood was carefully collected in a bowl and then carried inside the tabernacle. Some of it was sprinkled on the mercy seat in the Holy of Holies, but some was also sprinkled on the altar of incense.

The book of Leviticus explains how this was done. First the high priest sprinkled blood on the mercy seat, showing that Israel's sins were covered. "Then," God said, "he shall go out to the altar that is before the LORD and make atonement for it, and shall take some of the blood of the bull and some of the blood of the goat, and put it on the horns of the altar all around. And he shall sprinkle some of the blood on it with his finger seven times, and cleanse it and consecrate it from the uncleannesses of the people of Israel" (16:18, 19). This action showed that not even our prayers are acceptable to God unless our sins are forgiven. Before the altar could be used for prayer, it had to be consecrated with sacrificial blood. This demonstrated that the basis for access to God through prayer was the blood that made atonement for sin.

The sacrifice that made it possible for Israel to use the sweet altar of prayer was made once a year, on the Day of Atonement. However, the connection between prayer and sacrifice was also made in a more subtle way every day. One of the curious things about the altar of incense was that it was even called an altar. An altar is a place for making sacrifices, but no sacrifice was ever made on this altar. It was only for incense—the special blend that God gave to Moses. So why was it called an altar?

The answer is that by calling it an altar, God was making a connection between what happened on the great bronze altar out in the courtyard and what happened on the little golden altar inside the tabernacle. Both altars were square, and both had horns rising up on their corners. So there was something similar about their shape. Also, they were both used at the same time of day. Remember that the priests offered incense at dawn and at dusk. Something else important was happening at the same time, both morning and evening: Priests were out in the courtyard offering a sacrificial lamb. These daily religious rituals were synchronized. Thus there was a close connection between the two altars, in both their design and their function.

The connection between the two altars served as a daily reminder that the life of prayer depends on having a sacrifice for sin. What secures a place for us before the throne of God's grace is the atoning blood that was shed for our sins. This is why God hears our prayers. In his classic study of Old Testament typology, Patrick Fairbairn explained what the altar of incense teaches us about prayer and sacrifice:

> That this altar, from its very position, stood in a close relation to the mercy-seat or propitiatory on the one hand, and by the live coals that ever burned in its golden vials, stood in an equally close relation to the altar of burnt-offering on the other, tells us, that all acceptable prayer must have its foundation in the manifested grace of a redeeming God,—must draw its breath of life, in a manner, from that work of propitiation which He has in His own person accomplished for the sinful.[8]

M. R. DeHaan makes a similar point in his study of the tabernacle, connecting its sacred altars directly to the work of Christ:

> At the brazen altar Christ died for us, shed His blood, reconciled us to God, and made us forever secure in Him. But at the golden altar He lives in

> heaven to intercede for those for whom He has already died, and who are already saved. The brazen altar speaks of the death of Christ; the golden altar speaks of the living, resurrected, ascended Lord Jesus Christ. The two altars, therefore, speak of the death and the resurrection, and constitute the full message of the Gospel.[9]

## Praying through Our Priest

Seeing the sacrificial basis for prayer helps us answer a question people often ask: Does God hear the prayers of the ungodly, or does he only listen to Christians? To put the question another way, does God pay any attention to Muslims, Jews, Hindus, and others who do not call on him in the name of Jesus Christ?

There is a sense in which God hears everyone's prayers. He is omniscient (all-knowing). Therefore, nothing that anyone ever says escapes his notice. Not one cry for help, not one desperate plea, not one invocation of his divine name (whether in blessing or as a curse) ever goes unnoticed. God hears everything. Of course he does! However, that really is not the question. The question is whether or not he receives every prayer with the same fatherly concern. What does it take for God to accept someone's prayers?

To answer this question, we need to remember that access to God in prayer depends on having atonement for our sins. Sin separates us from God. We cannot have fellowship with a holy God in prayer unless something is done about the penalty we deserve for our sin. We need forgiveness through the blood of a sacrifice.

So where is our sacrifice? The Israelites offered their sacrifice on the Day of Atonement. But the only sacrifice available for us today is the one that Jesus offered when he suffered and died for our sins on the cross. The Scripture says, "We have confidence to enter the holy places by the blood of Jesus, by the new and living way that he opened for us through the curtain, that is, through his flesh" (Hebrews 10:19, 20). When Jesus died on the cross, he was opening the way for us to come to God in prayer.

This explains why Christians always pray "in Jesus' name." This is not simply a way of signing off, like "Sincerely yours." Rather, it establishes the basis for our praying to God at all. Jesus Christ has atoned for our sins through his death on the cross; therefore we are able to come to God in prayer. It is the blood of his sacrifice that sprinkles the sweet altar of our prayers.

John Newton wrote about this in one of his famous hymns. The hymn begins with an invitation to prayer, based on what the priests used to do in the tabernacle:

> Approach, my soul, the mercy seat
> Where Jesus answers prayer;
> There humbly fall before his feet,
> For none can perish there.

But what gives us the right to come to God in prayer? Only the atonement that Jesus made for our sins by dying on the cross. So Newton ends by praising Christ for his saving work:

O wondrous love! to bleed and die,
To bear the cross and shame,
That guilty sinners, such as I,
Might plead thy gracious name!

God accepts our prayers when we approach him in the name of Jesus Christ, claiming his atoning death as the basis for our access to his throne of grace. When we come to God in Christ, he will hear all our prayers!

As we come to God in prayer, it is important to realize that Jesus is no longer on the cross. He was raised from the dead, he ascended into Heaven, and now he sits at God's right hand, where he presents our prayers to God. One of the most important things we learn from the tabernacle in the wilderness is that Jesus is our great High Priest. If the Israelites wanted a relationship with God, they had to go through Aaron. But now that God has sent Jesus to be our priest, we deal with God directly, and we do not need any other priest.

This has special importance when we pray because it means that our prayers go straight to God. One of the priestly duties Jesus performs for us is to present our prayers to God. He is always interceding for us (Hebrews 7:25), constantly appearing for us in God's presence (Hebrews 9:24). What, exactly, does Jesus do there?

One thing he does is to claim that we have forgiveness for our sins. The Bible says, "If anyone does sin, we have an advocate with the Father, Jesus Christ the righteous. He is the propitiation for our sins" (1 John 2:1b, 2a). Jesus serves as our advocate, our defense attorney. Whenever we sin, he speaks on our behalf, securing our forgiveness on the basis of his sacrifice. It is only by the merits of Christ that God receives our prayers. In her book *Gold by Moonlight*, Amy Carmichael writes:

> I did not fully understand the Divine simplicity of the words "And the smoke of the incense, which came with the prayers of the saints, ascended up before God out of the angel's hand," till I saw incense used, as it has been from time immemorial in India, in simple household ways. You throw a few grains on burning charcoal and a column of smoke rises straight up. Anyone coming into the room notices the fragrance long after the smoke has disappeared. It fills the room, floats out through the open doors and windows, and for an hour or so, if the air be still, you are still aware of it about the house. I never watch that white column of smoke, laden with its own peculiar fragrance, without a grateful thought of that of which it is the figure. There is nothing in our prayers that would cause them to rise. But

> they are cleansed and perfumed and lifted. It is all of Him who ever liveth to make intercession for us.[10]

By his intercession Jesus ensures that God hears our prayers. When we come to God through Christ, all our praises and petitions go straight to his throne of grace. Ultimately, this is what the altar of incense was intended to signify. As A. W. Pink has written, the altar portrays "the ministrations of our great High Priest in the heavenly sanctuary. Though He is now seated at the right hand of the Majesty on high, yet He is not inactive. He is constantly engaged before God on behalf of His redeemed, presenting to the Father—in the sweet fragrance of His own perfections—both the petitions and worship of His people."[11]

By way of example, consider what the intercession of Christ means for the petitions we offer in the Lord's Prayer. When we pray the way Jesus taught us to pray, all our petitions go straight to God. As soon as we say, "Our Father," we are talking directly with the God of the universe. When we ask for his name to be hallowed, we are asking the thrice-holy God who is adored by angels. When we ask for his kingdom to come, we are asking the God who rules over every authority in Heaven and on earth. When we ask for his will to be done, we are asking the God "who works all things according to the counsel of his will" (Ephesians 1:11). When we ask for our daily bread, we are asking the God of all providence. When we ask for our debts to be forgiven, we are asking the God who sent his Son to pay for our sins. When we ask him to deliver us from the evil one, we are asking the God who "will soon crush Satan under [our] feet" (Romans 16:20a).

This is a lot to ask for! Nevertheless, it all goes from our mouths to God's ear, because Jesus has opened up the way. When we approach the throne of grace on the basis of the blood that Jesus shed on the cross for our sins, God hears all our prayers.

## Going to the Altar

Most Israelites would have given anything to offer their prayers straight to God, yet this privilege was only given to the priests. They alone could enter the Holy Place and make petitions at the sweet altar of prayer. Everyone else had to pray through them. How the Israelites must have envied the priests for having this privilege! How they must have longed to have direct access to God through prayer! If only they had been allowed to enter the Holy Place and offer the incense of prayer, they would have used the golden altar every day, both morning and evening.

As believers in Jesus Christ, we have been given an even greater privilege. Through the atoning sacrifice that Jesus made on the cross, we have been granted immediate access to the throne room of Almighty God. We are able to approach him at any time, day or night, for any reason. We can ask him to establish his kingdom by advancing the work and witness of his church around the world. We can ask him to do his will in our lives in any and every way that will bring him glory. We can ask him to supply our needs. We can ask him to forgive our sins. We can ask him to protect us from spiritual attack. What an amazing opportunity! Who would neglect to take advantage of this extraordinary privilege?

Sadly, countless Christians neglect the privilege of prayer every day. We do not pray for God's kingdom to come. We do not ask for his will to be done. We do not ask him for daily provision, protection, and pardon. To put it bluntly, by our neglect we despise the sweet altar of prayer. And in doing this, we really despise the cross of Christ, because our privilege to pray was purchased by his blood.

We ought to pray all the time. The Israelites used the altar of incense every day, both morning and evening. Smoke was always rising from the altar of incense (see 30:8). We should be equally constant in prayer. We should go to the altar; we should approach the mercy seat, we should come to God in prayer. The Bible tells us to pray without ceasing. It says, "Rejoice always, pray without ceasing, give thanks in all circumstances; for this is the will of God in Christ Jesus for you" (1 Thessalonians 5:16–18). At the very least, we should pray to God every morning and every evening. His glory and grace should be our first thought when we rise in the morning and our last petition before we sleep.

Do not neglect the sweet altar of prayer. Have you been using it today? Did you use it yesterday? Will you use it tomorrow? In his comments on the altar of incense, Patrick Fairbairn wrote, "Pray without ceasing; the spirit of devotion is the element of your spiritual being, the indispensable condition of health and fruitfulness; all, from first to last, must be sanctified by prayer; and if this be neglected, nothing in the work and service of God can be expected to go well with you."[12]

If we neglect the sweet altar of prayer, we should not expect things to go well for us in ministry, or in anything else. But when we pray, our petitions rise to Heaven like sweet incense, and God is pleased to bestow his blessing on us.

# 82

# Bought with a Price

EXODUS 30:11–33

*THE PRICE OF A CHILD,* by the Philadelphia writer Lorene Cary, is a story of liberation and redemption.[1] In the novel a black woman named Ginnie Pryor travels north with her white master—a Virginia planter. While they are staying in Philadelphia, Ginnie seizes her chance to run away, taking her older children with her. Yet sadly, her baby Bennie is back in Virginia, still enslaved. There is an ache in Ginnie's heart whenever she thinks of her little boy. She knows that unless something is done to save him, he will grow up suffering the degradations of slavery.

At the end of the novel, Ginnie and her children travel farther north. Before they board a steamship going to New York, a friend hands Ginnie an envelope. Inside she finds a note with the names of two men who help former slaves find and recover their lost relatives. Attached to the note are five one-hundred-dollar bills—the buying price for a child Bennie's age. Thus the novel ends with the hope of redemption. There is money for the ransom.

## Head Count

Redemption is a rich Biblical theme. The Bible often describes salvation as the rescue of a life through the payment of a ransom. There is a striking example in the story of the tabernacle:

> The Lord said to Moses, "When you take the census of the people of Israel, then each shall give a ransom for his life to the Lord when you number them, that there be no plague among them when you number them. Each one who is numbered in the census shall give this: half a shekel according to the shekel of the sanctuary (the shekel is twenty gerahs), half a shekel as an offering to the Lord. Everyone who is numbered in the census, from twenty years old and upward, shall give the Lord's offering." (30:11–14)

It is not uncommon to take a census. Sooner or later most nations decide to count how many people they have. In the United States we do it every decade, and God expected his people to do it as well. Literally, he told them to take "a head count," because the Hebrew phrase for taking a census means "to lift up the head."

The Israelites took their first head count out in the wilderness. The results are carefully recorded in the book of Numbers, which begins with God telling Moses, "Take a census of all the congregation of the people of Israel, by clans, by fathers' houses, according to the number of names, every male, head by head" (1:2). The Israelites probably did this on other occasions as well.[2] The Hebrew word translated "to count" or "to number" has military connotations. It means "to muster for battle." Significantly, the only people counted were males twenty years old and up (30:14). In other words, the Israelites were counting men old enough to fight. (This is one place where the Scripture indicates that only men should serve as military combatants.) The military context of census taking is also confirmed in the book of Numbers, where God says to Moses, "From twenty years old and upward, all in Israel who are able to go to war, you and Aaron shall list them, company by company" (1:3). As the Israelites prepared for battle, they numbered their troops.

Whenever the Israelites took a census, and for whatever reason, God wanted it done in a particular way. All the men of Israel were to gather in one place. As they numbered off, one by one, they crossed over to the other side, moving from the group that hadn't been counted to the group that had. On their way over, they paid half a shekel, probably made of silver. In those days a shekel was not a coin but a unit of measure. Its size varied throughout the ancient world, but in this case it was measured against the standard weight of a sanctuary shekel. A shekel was small, and a half-shekel was even smaller—much less than an ounce.

All the half-shekels added up, however, and by the time Moses finished counting, there was a huge pile of silver. This money belonged to God; so all the proceeds went for the construction of his holy sanctuary, the tabernacle. God said to Moses: "You shall take the atonement money from the people of Israel and shall give it for the service of the tent of meeting, that it may bring the people of Israel to remembrance before the LORD, so as to make atonement for your lives" (30:16). Some of this money may have been used for the ongoing maintenance of the tabernacle, but it was mainly used for the foundations that held up its posts. These foundations were made of silver (see 26:18, 19), and whenever the Israelites saw them, they would remember that their house of worship rested on the price that was paid for their redemption.

The punishment for failing to pay the ransom price was severe. Any man who failed to make a contribution was afflicted with one of the very plagues that God had sent against Pharaoh—deadly disease. Taking a census was a risky business; doing it properly was a matter of life and death.

A famous example of the dangers of census taking comes from the life of King David, who once decided to count his fighting men. This was over the strenuous objections of his general, Joab, who said, "May the Lord your God add to the people a hundred times as many as they are, while the eyes of my lord the king still see it, but why does my lord the king delight in this thing?" (2 Samuel 24:3). Joab wanted David to have a big army, but he didn't want him to figure out how big it was. Why not? Because he knew how dangerous it was to take a census.

Yet David was undeterred; he went ahead with his census. Unfortunately, he didn't do it the way God commanded. He numbered his troops without having them each pay a half shekel as a ransom price. And God judged the Israelites for David's sin: "So the Lord sent a pestilence on Israel from the morning until the appointed time. And there died of the people from Dan to Beersheba 70,000 men" (2 Samuel 24:15). This was in keeping with what God had said to Moses, that taking a census without paying a ransom would bring a deadly plague on the people of God.

### Atonement Money

All of this raises an obvious question: Why was it so dangerous to take a census? To understand Israel's peril, it helps to understand that numbering things is an act of authority. Who has the right to take inventory? Only the person who owns whatever is being counted. We only have the authority to count things that are rightfully ours. We can't put our numbers on other people's stuff.

So who had the right to number the Israelites? Only God. They were his people, so he alone had the authority to count them. A. W. Pink comments: "When God numbers or orders anything to be numbered, taking the sum of them denotes that they belong to Him, and that He has the sovereign right to do with them as He pleases. The action itself says of the things numbered, 'These are Mine, and I assign them their place as I will.'"[3] Therefore, the only proper way to count the Israelites was for the glory of God alone.

Whenever the Israelites took a census, they were in serious danger of forgetting this. After all, they were the ones doing the counting. Thus they would be tempted to think that their great numbers were a credit to them rather than to God. And although it was not a sin to take a census, it was a sin to rob God of his glory. This was David's downfall. He started saying, "Wow, look how many troops we have! I wonder just how large our army is. I can't even begin to guess. What do you think, Joab? How big is my army? You know, we ought to count how many soldiers we have, just so we know. I think we may have the biggest army in the world!" David got caught up in the numbers game. He wanted to boast in the size of his army.

This kind of boasting is a temptation for everyone. It's a temptation for churches. Pastors always want to see the latest attendance figures. Such information can be useful, of course, but the temptation is to use it as a way of keeping score. Individuals face the same temptation. We base our self-worth on our grade point average, our scoring statistics, our sales performance, or the size of our portfolio. If there is anything we can count, we keep checking it to see how we're doing. When we're doing well, we use the numbers to boost our sense of importance. On the other hand, when the totals don't add up, we make excuses or get angry and discouraged. But either way we're always keeping score.

We should never keep this kind of score at all. The truth is that everything we are and everything we have belongs to God. To make sure that the Israelites remembered this—especially when they were taking a census and might be tempted to forget—God required a ransom from every man in Israel. By paying a half shekel, they were acknowledging that they did not belong to themselves but to God.

The payment of this price did not atone for sin. As we have seen throughout Exodus, atonement for sin only comes through a sacrifice of blood. Everyone in Israel had already received atonement through the sin offering made on the altar of sacrifice. Salvation from sin is always a free gift of God's grace—a gift that comes "without money and without price" (Isaiah 55:1b). There is no payment we can make for our sins. Nevertheless, the ransom paid during the census was called "the atonement money." And although it did not atone for the people's sins, according to God it "made atonement for their lives."[4] It rescued them from the particular punishment of the plague, reminding them that they belonged to God and not to themselves.

Israel's atonement money should remind us of the price that was paid for our redemption. The Bible says, "You are not your own, for you were bought with a price" (1 Corinthians 6:19b, 20a; cf. 7:23). And what a costly price it was! The Bible also says, "You were ransomed from the futile ways inherited from your forefathers, not with perishable things such as silver or gold, but with the precious blood of Christ, like that of a lamb without blemish or spot" (1 Peter 1:18, 19). The Israelites were ransomed with a sliver of silver, which was precious enough, but we have been redeemed by the blood of the Lamb. Jesus Christ paid for our sins through his death on the cross.

This means that God now has a purchase on us. We belong to him not only by creation, but also by redemption. We owe our lives to him, now and forever. Rather than taking any credit for ourselves or claiming the right to live the way we please, we must always remember that we belong to God. Our true worth is the price he paid to redeem us. This is not a value we set on ourselves, but the value God placed on us through the death of his Son. Whenever we are tempted to feel worthless, we should remember the great price that God paid for our redemption. People sometimes ask, "How could God ever love someone like me?"

Truthfully, we don't know how. All we know is that God loves us; he has proved it by sending his very own Son to be our Savior.

Jesus paid the same price for all of us, showing that we are all of equal worth to God. The ransom price for the census made a powerful statement about this. God said to Moses, "The rich shall not give more, and the poor shall not give less, than the half shekel, when you give the LORD's offering to make atonement for your lives" (30:15). Every Israelite was equal in the sight of God. Whether he was rich or poor, each man had to pay the same half shekel. No one was worth any more or any less than anyone else. Everyone stood before God on equal terms.

What value has God placed on us? Jesus died on the cross to pay the price for sin. Everyone who trusts in him is ransomed by his redemption. Whether we are male or female, young or old, black or white, the same price was paid for all of us. The blood of God's Son is the true basis for the full equality of every member of the church.

## Wash or Die

The payment of a ransom is a wonderful picture of salvation. However, there is more to salvation in Christ than being bought with a price. The Bible uses many images to describe God's saving work, each of which teaches us something essential. We have been ransomed, redeemed, rescued, and reborn. We have been elected, enlightened, delivered, justified, adopted, and raised to life from the dead. Each of these Biblical images tells the same story of our salvation in a different way.

The next image of salvation in Exodus 30 is washing with water:

> The LORD said to Moses, "You shall also make a basin of bronze, with its stand of bronze, for washing. You shall put it between the tent of meeting and the altar, and you shall put water in it, with which Aaron and his sons shall wash their hands and their feet. When they go into the tent of meeting, or when they come near the altar to minister, to burn a food offering to the LORD, they shall wash with water, so that they may not die. They shall wash their hands and their feet, so that they may not die. It shall be a statute forever to them, even to him and to his offspring throughout their generations." (vv. 17–21)

The basin was the last piece of furniture for the tabernacle. It went in the courtyard, between the altar of sacrifice and the doorway to the Tent of Meeting. Like everything else in the courtyard, this laver was made of bronze. We are not certain what size or shape it was. Presumably it was round, and large enough to hold sufficient water for the priests to wash. One thing we know is that the bronze laver came in two parts. The basin itself was set on top of a stand or pedestal and then filled with water.

This washbasin was in almost constant use. Before a priest went inside the Tent of Meeting to perform his sacred duties, he had to stop at the bronze basin. It was located in front of the tent to remind the priests to wash before entering. They washed their hands and their feet—the body parts they used to serve God. The priests also had to wash up before they made any kind of sacrifice on the great bronze altar. As the priests came and went, they were always stopping at the basin for cleansing.

Like almost everything else the priests did, this was a matter of life or death. Some households allow people to come inside without wiping their feet or to sit down for dinner without washing their hands. But that's not how things worked in God's household, where cleanliness really *was* next to godliness! The priests had to either wash or die. As David once asked, "Who shall ascend the hill of the Lord? And who shall stand in his holy place?" (Psalm 24:3). The answer is: "He who has clean hands and a pure heart" (v. 4a).

Washing up was partly a matter of respect. When the priests entered the tabernacle, they were coming to God in worship. It was only right for them to go through some kind of ceremonial purification, especially if they were bloody from all the sacrifices they offered. Washing their hands and feet was part of their spiritual preparation for service. The physical washing was a sign of spiritual cleansing. It was symbolic of their sanctification, which was something they needed not just once but every time they served.

The priests had already received a once-and-for-all cleansing from sin at their ordination. Before they were ever allowed to set foot in the courtyard to the tabernacle, they were washed from head to toe. This was their baptism, their consecration to the priestly service of God. At their ordination the priests also received atonement for their sins; seven bulls were sacrificed to pay the debt they owed to God.

So why did the priests need to keep washing? If they had already received cleansing and atonement from sin, why did they continue to use the bronze basin? The answer is that they needed to be sanctified for their service to God. Even after they were forgiven for what they had done, they still needed God to make them holy. The layout of the tabernacle helps to show this. The first thing the priests encountered when they entered was the great bronze altar of sacrifice. This was the place where atonement was made for their sins. The altar was symbolic of their *justification*. They were accepted by God on the basis of a sacrifice.

The next thing the priests encountered was the bronze washbasin, which was symbolic of their *sanctification*. The guilt of their sin had been taken away on the altar of sacrifice. Their sins were forgiven. But they were still sinners, and in order to cleanse themselves from the corruption of ongoing sin in their lives, the priests had to wash their hands and feet. This ritual cleansing was symbolic of their progress in holiness. Even the priests—as holy as they were—had to be sanctified before they could enter the Holy Place and serve a holy God.

We need the same thing as Christians. Here again we can use the layout of the tabernacle to trace the geography of our Christian experience. As soon as we come to God through faith in Christ, we receive full forgiveness for all our sins through his death on the cross. But this does not mean that we are perfectly holy. We continue to sin, and therefore we need constant cleansing from the corruption of sin. Just as the bronze altar is a symbol of our justification, so the bronze washbasin is a symbol of our sanctification. According to John J. Davis, the basin

> provided for a type of cleansing which served to maintain fitness for a spiritual ministry. The priests' guilt because of sin was dealt with at the altar of sacrifice, yet something else was required for effective fellowship and worship in the tabernacle. This had to do with the defilement of sin, that effect of sin which the blood did not remove. Before one could enter the presence of a holy God this had to be cared for. It followed the sacrifice at the altar and was based upon the merit of it but was a definite separate act. So it is with the believer in Christ today. He is freed from the guilt of sin and its penalty by the application of the blood, yet there remains defilement of sin that comes through daily living. This is cared for by continuous washing of the water which is the Word of God. The Holy Spirit also plays a significant role in the application of that Word of God, thus producing a cleansing effect. There is a sanctification which is complete and final through the blood of Christ, but there is also a sanctification which is continuous and practical. It paves the way for continued effective fellowship with God.[5]

Some people think that once they pray to receive Christ, they'll never have to deal with sin again. As far as our guilt is concerned, this is true. God has forgiven us once and for all in Christ. But we still have to face the reality of indwelling sin in our lives. As we serve God, we continually need him to purify us, sanctify us, and make us clean. As the Bible says, "Let us cleanse ourselves from every defilement of body and spirit, bringing holiness to completion in the fear of God" (2 Corinthians 7:1).

By way of personal testimony, this is something I experience nearly every Sunday morning, when my day begins with a special season of repentance—not as some kind of chore or duty but as a spontaneous gift of God's Spirit, who is preparing me to lead God's people in worship. If we are to continue serving God, we need an ongoing work of his cleansing grace.

There is a powerful illustration of this truth in John 13, the chapter in which Jesus washes the feet of his disciples. When Peter saw what Jesus was doing, he said, "You shall never wash my feet." But Jesus answered, "If I do not wash you, you have no share with me" (v. 8). With his typical flair for excess, Peter said, "Lord, not my feet only but also my hands and my head!" (v. 9). But Jesus refused, saying to Peter, "The one who has bathed does not need to wash, except for his feet, but is completely clean. And you are clean" (v. 10).

Jesus was distinguishing between two kinds of cleansing. One is the total cleansing that comes at the beginning of the Christian life and washes away the guilt of our sin. Another is the ongoing cleansing that is needed throughout the Christian life. This cleansing washes away the corruption of sin and purifies us for service to God. And this is what Peter needed—not the kind of cleansing that would save him, but the kind that would purify him for the service of God. David Levy comments: "By washing the disciples' feet, the Lord taught that we who have been thoroughly cleansed through His blood must still be cleansed in our daily walk with Him. Daily sins must be confessed to God in order to maintain an unbroken communion and fellowship with Him."[6]

How does God do this cleansing, sanctifying work in our lives? He does it by the power of his Holy Spirit, who makes us holy through his Word. The Bible says that Jesus cleanses us "by the washing of water with the word" (Ephesians 5:26; cf. John 17:17). God's Spirit uses God's Word to produce real spiritual change in our lives. If we want to make progress in holiness, we need to spend time in God's Word—both publicly and privately—asking God's Spirit to sanctify us all the way through.

## Anointed with Oil

Once they were clean, the priests were able to serve God in his holy sanctuary. Exodus 30 ends by reminding us how holy it was. Everything in, on, and around the tabernacle was anointed with sacred oil, and in this way it was set apart for God's service.

First the oil had to be carefully prepared: "The Lord said to Moses, 'Take the finest spices: of liquid myrrh 500 shekels, and of sweet-smelling cinnamon half as much, that is, 250, and 250 of aromatic cane, and 500 of cassia, according to the shekel of the sanctuary, and a hin of olive oil. And you shall make of these a sacred anointing oil blended as by the perfumer; it shall be a holy anointing oil'" (vv. 22–25).

This special blend of spices weighed almost forty pounds. It featured expensive ingredients from all over the world: liquid myrrh, cinnamon bark, and other rare imports from India, Arabia, and Lebanon. These fine ingredients were carefully distilled in olive oil, which served as the base for the sacred mixture. The process was complex:

> A 'perfumer' 'mixed' spices and oils to create ointments and scents. Ancient sources show that they practised their art by steeping the spices in the oil, possibly heating the mixture, so that the oil absorbed the aroma of the spices. . . . The oil was subsequently pressed out of the mixture, and as it

> retained the fragrance of the spices, the relatively small amount of oil became the sacred anointing oil, specially reserved for the Lord.[7]

Once the sacred oil was ready, it was applied directly to the tabernacle and all its sacred furnishings. God said: "With it you shall anoint the tent of meeting and the ark of the testimony, and the table and all its utensils, and the lampstand and its utensils, and the altar of incense, and the altar of burnt offering with all its utensils and the basin and its stand. You shall consecrate them, that they may be most holy. Whatever touches them will become holy" (vv. 26–29).

The oil was not smeared on the tabernacle but sprinkled—a few drops on every curtain, every piece of furniture, and every holy utensil. Everything was set apart from its ordinary use and dedicated to the service of God. From then on, anything or anyone that touched these items also had to be holy. The point of verse 29 was not that anything that touched the tabernacle would become holy (as if holiness were contagious), but that in order for anything to touch the tabernacle, it had to be holy. Otherwise—and this is only implied—it had to be destroyed.

Today anointing with oil has become an evangelical fad. Churches take a few drops of oil and anoint their sanctuary, their worship instruments, or even local buildings as a way of dedicating them to God. This practice has no basis in Scripture. Although God commanded the Israelites to anoint the tabernacle, he has given no similar command to the church. The only exception is anointing the sick, which is a ministry of the elders (James 5:14). Rather than anointing things with oil, which smacks of superstition, we should simply trust in the power of prayer. It is by praying that we invoke the ministry of the Holy Spirit, which Israel's sacred oil was intended to signify.

In addition to anointing their tabernacle, the Israelites also anointed their priests. God said to Moses: "You shall anoint Aaron and his sons, and consecrate them, that they may serve me as priests. And you shall say to the people of Israel, 'This shall be my holy anointing oil throughout your generations. It shall not be poured on the body of an ordinary person, and you shall make no other like it in composition. It is holy, and it shall be holy to you. Whoever compounds any like it or whoever puts any of it on an outsider shall be cut off from his people'" (30:30–33).

The anointing oil was sacred. It was for the priests, and only for the priests. No one else was allowed to wear it. Nor were the priests allowed to keep it for personal use. The penalty for violating this command was excommunication, possibly even death. Anyone who tried to market God's holy perfume was cut off from Israel.

This shows how sacred it is to be anointed for God's service. This is true for ministers; a call to gospel ministry is a sacred gift that only God can give. But ministers are not the only people anointed to serve God. The Bible says that

God "anointed us . . . and [has] given us his Spirit in our hearts" (2 Corinthians 1:21b, 22b). In other words, every believer has been set apart for God's service. Our lives are sacred. By the anointing of the Holy Spirit, we have a high and holy calling to do God's work in the world.

Now we belong entirely to the Lord. After all, we were bought with a price, so we no longer belong to ourselves but to God. This has staggering implications for everything we do and everything we have. It means that our possessions no longer belong to us; they belong to God and are to be used for his service. Our work belongs to God too. Whether we work at home or in the marketplace, in sacred or secular work, all our energies are ultimately directed toward his glory. The same is true of our free time, which ought to be sanctified with a desire to please God. Then there is our situation in life. Our singleness belongs to God, as if we were married to Christ. Our marriages belong to God as well, for God intends marriage to be a display of his divine love. Even our children belong to God. They do not live for us, or even for themselves, but for God. The seasons of life belong to God too. Younger Christians have a lifetime ahead of them, and it all belongs to God. Imagine what God can do with a whole life dedicated to his service! Older Christians may feel they have less time to give, but whatever time we have left is for God and his glory.

What service have you been anointed to perform? There is not one single part of who we are or what we have that belongs to us. In the same way that the whole tabernacle was anointed with holy oil, we too have been set apart for God, body and soul. Jesus Christ has paid the costly price of our salvation, and now we are called to give all our best back in service to him.

John Currid illustrates this exchange from the life of the famous British general Charles George Gordon (1833–1885), who was also known as "Chinese Gordon" for putting down the rebellion at Taiping. As Currid explains,

> [T]he government wanted to reward him with money and titles, but he refused all those honours. He was finally persuaded to accept a medal inscribed with his various military engagements. After his death, this medal could not be found. He had had it melted down and the proceeds given to the poor children of Manchester during a particularly severe famine. He wrote in his diary the following words, "The last and only thing I have in this world that I value I have given over to the Lord Jesus Christ."[8]

What do you have that is of any value? You have time and talent, money and possessions, labor and leisure. Whatever you have belongs to Jesus—who bought you by his blood—and it should be consecrated for his service. Will you take the last and only things you have in this world and use them for his glory?

# 83

# Art for God's Sake

EXODUS 31:1–11

IT ISN'T EASY TO BE AN ARTIST. It never has been. While every calling has its own unique trials and tribulations, the life of the artist is especially hard. There is the difficulty of the art itself—of creating, executing, and perfecting a design. It is always costly, in personal terms, to produce a work of art. Then once the work is produced, it is often undervalued. People fail to grasp its message or appreciate its artistry. To be an artist is to be misunderstood. There is also the inescapable fact that most artists are underpaid. They aren't called "starving artists" for nothing!

Things are even more difficult for Christian artists. Some churches do not consider art a serious way to serve God. Others deny that it is a legitimate calling at all. As a result, Christian artists often have to justify their existence. Rather than providing a community of support, the church surrounds them with a climate of suspicion.

These tensions were exposed in an article from the student newspaper at Wheaton College. The article featured a senior art student who reveled in her calling as an artist. "God made me to be an artist," she said. "He gave me that talent. . . . That's my response to God, to his world, to his message of salvation. When you see something that's so wonderful, you want to join." Unfortunately, as the artist learned, not everyone wants to join after all. "By the end of her sophomore year," the paper said, "she was sick of her peers' indifference to her calling. She was fed up with comments that suggested art is a waste of time, a field for slackers and weirdos." She wrote in her journal, "I felt I had to justify myself. . . . That is a terrible thing. I am a child of God. God made me a person who sees the world in a manner that is different from most perceptions. He gave me the urge to create."[1]

## Art and the Church

There are many reasons why some churches have a negative view of the arts. Art trades in images, and images easily lend themselves to idolatry—especially when objects of art are brought into the church for religious worship. At various times in church history, such as during the iconoclastic movement of the eighth century or the Protestant Reformation in Europe, church leaders have tried to smash this form of idolatry by taking statues and other works of art out of the church and destroying them. They were not opposed to the use of art, only its abuse. However, some Christians failed to understand the difference, and there was a lingering suspicion about the visual arts.

More recently many Christians have objected to art on the grounds that it is dominated by an anti-Christian view of the world. During the last century art has suffered a tragic loss of beauty. So much modern and postmodern art has been attracted instead to absurdity and ugliness. Anyone who doubts this should attend the senior exhibition at nearly any art school in America. So much contemporary art is the art of alienation, which if it is true at all, is only true about the disorder of a world damaged by our depravity. As a general rule, such art does not point us to the redemptive possibilities of a world that, although fallen, has been visited by God and is destined for his glory.

Yet even Christians who dismiss art continue to produce it. This is inescapable. Every time we build a sanctuary, arrange furniture in a room, or produce a brochure, we are making artistic decisions. The question is not whether we will be artists, but whether we will aspire to high aesthetic standards. All too often Christians settle for something that is functional but not beautiful. Sometimes what we produce can only be described as *kitsch*—tacky artwork of poor quality that appeals to low tastes. The average Christian bookstore is full of the stuff, as the real artists will tell us, if only we will listen.

Ultimately this kind of art undermines our message. Art has the power to shape culture. What is happening in the arts today is prophetic of what will happen in our culture tomorrow. So when Christians abandon the artistic community, the church loses a significant opportunity to speak the gospel into our culture. What we need to recover—or possibly discover for the first time—is a full Biblical understanding of the arts—not for art's sake, but for God's sake. Then we will be able to produce good art that testifies to the truth about God and his world. This is important not just for artists, but for everyone made in God's image and redeemed by his grace.

## The Artist's Calling

One of the best places to begin constructing a Biblical view of art is Exodus 31, where God calls two men to be artists. This passage teaches at least four fundamental principles for a Christian theology of the arts: (1) the artist's call and gift come from God; (2) God loves all kinds of art; (3) God maintains high standards for goodness, truth, and beauty; and (4) art is for the glory of God. To fully understand these principles, we need to see what they tell us about the character of God and the artistry he displayed in the crucifixion and resurrection of Jesus Christ.

Exodus 31 begins with God's calling two men to be his official artists and granting them the gifts they needed to fulfill their calling: "The Lord said to Moses, 'See, I have called by name Bezalel the son of Uri, son of Hur, of the tribe of Judah, and I have filled him with the Spirit of God, with ability and intelligence, with knowledge and all craftsmanship. . . . And behold, I have appointed with him Oholiab, the son of Ahisamach, of the tribe of Dan. And I have given to all able men ability, that they may make all that I have commanded you'" (vv. 1–3, 6).

By this point in Exodus, God had given complete instructions for the tabernacle and everything that went inside it. There was an extraordinary amount of work to be done: sawing, building, sewing, cabinetmaking, casting, metalworking, stonecutting, and engraving. Furthermore, God indicated that this work had to be done skillfully (see, e.g., 26:1; 28:3). So it was no job for Moses, even though he was the one writing down all the instructions. It wasn't his job because it wasn't his gift. Moses was a prophet, but the tabernacle needed an artist. In order to fulfill its divine function, God's holy dwelling had to be made by the best artisans, as well as with the finest materials.

So God called two men to serve as his holy artists—Bezalel and Oholiab, the master craftsman and his top assistant. These men were not selected by a jury of fellow artists but were appointed by the sovereign and electing choice of God. What the Scripture literally says is that they were called by name (31:2, 6). Bezalel and Oholiab were God's personal choice for this job. And their calling as artists was so sacred that their names were preserved for posterity. Bezalel means "in the shadow of God." It's a good name for an artist working under divine direction, with God as the patron of his art.[2] The meaning of Oholiab's name was even more appropriate: "my tent is the Father-God."[3] Oholiab's job was to build God's dwelling on earth, and his name explained what that holy tent was designed to show—namely, that God is the shelter for his people.

Bezalel and Oholiab were not just called—they were also gifted. God gave Bezalel the "ability and intelligence, with knowledge" to do all kinds of artwork (31:3). Different scholars define these terms in different ways. According to John Durham, Bezalel was "specially endowed for his assignment by an infilling of the divine spirit, which adds to his native ability three qualities that suit him ideally for the task at hand: wisdom, the gift to understand what is needed to fulfill Yahweh's instructions; discernment, the talent for solving the inevitable problems involved in the creation of so complex a series of objects and materials; and skill, the experienced hand needed to guide and accomplish the labor itself."[4] No matter how these words are defined, they show that an artist needs spiritual insight as well as practical skill. Taken together, "ability and intelligence, with knowledge" refer to what the artist is thinking in his mind and feeling in his heart as well as to what he is making with his hands. Bezalel and Oholiab were artists, and thus their work came from their whole persons.

The artistic gifts these men possessed all came from God. To be specific, they came from God the Holy Spirit. Presumably Bezalel and Oholiab already had some natural talent for the arts and crafts (which also came from God). However, they were being given a special commission, and with that commission came special gifts. They alone were called to build God's holy tabernacle, and in order to do this work they were inspired in the true sense of the word: they were filled with the Holy Spirit.

This is the first time such language is used in the Bible, which shows how central the tabernacle was to God's plan. The same Spirit who created the world equipped these men with the skill they needed to build the tabernacle. This also teaches us something about the arts. If he had wanted to, God could have built the tabernacle all by himself, without using Bezalel or Oholiab or anyone else to do it. But God called a community of artists to make the tabernacle; and to make sure that they did it right, he equipped them with every kind of artistic skill. By doing this, God was putting his blessing on both the arts and the artists.

No one else has ever received the special gifts that Bezalel and Oholiab were given. However, their example shows that God will equip us to do whatever he calls us to do. Neither Bezalel nor Oholiab had ever built a tabernacle before. Nevertheless, God called them to build it, and when he called them, he also equipped them. The same is true for everyone who serves God. When God calls us to do something, we should trust that he will also give us whatever we need to fulfill that calling.

The example of Bezalel and Oholiab shows that God chooses some men and women to be artists. Their calling legitimates the calling of every artist. In the same way that Moses teaches us what it means to be a minister, these men teach us what it means to be an artist. And what was true for them in a special way is true in a general way for every artist. Artists are called and gifted—personally, as if by name—to make things for the glory of God.

This call should be pursued, no matter what sacrifices are required. Most artists face difficult decisions about meeting their practical needs. Often they have to supplement their income, sometimes by doing something not directly related to their artwork. This, too, can be part of God's plan. But the one thing artists should never do is abandon their calling. If you are called to be an artist, be an artist! God's gifts are never to be hidden; his calling is never to be denied. Even if sometimes, for reasons of practical necessity, art becomes an avocation rather than a vocation, it should still be pursued with deep joy and a strong sense of purpose.

## All Kinds of Art

A second principle for a Christian theology of art is that God loves all kinds of art. In Exodus 31 he proves this in several ways. One is by giving Bezalel the full range of artistic gifts. God said, "I have filled him with the Spirit of God, with ability and intelligence, with knowledge and all craftsmanship, to devise artistic designs, to work in gold, silver, and bronze, in cutting stones for setting, and in carving wood, to work in every craft" (vv. 3–5).

Bezalel was able to work in a wide variety of artistic media. He was a metalworker, stonecutter, and woodworker, with the skill to work in "every craft." Oholiab was equally versatile. Later we learn that in addition to helping Bezalel with his other work, Oholiab served as "an engraver and designer and embroiderer in blue and purple and scarlet yarns and fine twined linen" (38:23). Most artists do their best work in a narrow specialty, but like Michelangelo or Leonardo da Vinci, these men had the rare ability to work with equal skill in various media.

In granting them this gift, God placed his seal of approval on the flourishing of the arts. Some artists have the gift of making things out of wood, others out of paper. There are different kinds of painting. Some artists work in oil, others with watercolors. There are different kinds of drawings: sketches and line drawings in pencil, ink, and charcoal. Many things can be done with thread or yarn, from knitting to macrame. There are various techniques for making sculptures in wood, clay, stone, or metal. The forms of artistic expression are seemingly infinite, from the origamist who makes tropical birds by folding paper to the cake decorator who makes fruit out of marzipan. Then there are the nonvisual arts, such as drama and music. In Exodus 31 God sanctifies the wide spectrum of artistic gifts by blessing all kinds of craftsmanship. Most arts and crafts—like animation, for example, or découpage—are not explicitly mentioned here or anywhere else in the Bible. But Exodus 31 shows that God blesses all kinds of art.

The reason Bezalel and Oholiab needed to work in so many different media was that the tabernacle had so many different parts. These men and their helpers were called to employ their varied skills to make many things. God said:

> And I have given to all able men ability, that they may make all that I have commanded you: the tent of meeting, and the ark of the testimony, and the mercy seat that is on it, and all the furnishings of the tent, the table and its utensils, and the pure lampstand with all its utensils, and the altar of incense, and the altar of burnt offering with all its utensils, and the basin and its stand, and the finely worked garments, the holy garments for Aaron the priest and the garments of his sons, for their service as priests, and the anointing oil and the fragrant incense for the Holy Place. According to all that I have commanded you, they shall do. (vv. 6b–11)

This list summarizes what went into the tabernacle. Israel's artists were called to make the tent itself, along with all its furnishings and utensils. God took whole chapters of Scripture to explain what to make and how to make it. But it was up to Bezalel, Oholiab, and the rest of Israel's artistic community to execute God's design.

Some commentators think that all the artists had to do was copy God's pattern. According to one scholar, "the works they were to produce had been described in detail already to Moses. No room is left for creative variations on the plans Yahweh had given."[5] It is true that God gave Moses plenty of instructions, yet he left many things unspecified (which is why we don't know exactly what the tabernacle looked like). God did not explain how the cherubim were supposed to appear. He didn't describe the decorative molding that went around the rim of the table of showbread. He didn't provide a pattern for weaving the colorful threads in the high priest's robe, or tell Moses what script to use for the inscription on his turban. These things were left up to the artists' imagination.

This is what usually happens when an artist receives a commission. Whoever commissions the work has some idea what the finished product will look like. However, the artist has the freedom to create the work of art. To give just one example, the architects who submitted plans for rebuilding the World Trade Center in New York City had to meet certain requirements in terms of location and square footage. But they were free to decide what the buildings would look like. God's plans for the tabernacle were much more specific. This is because the tabernacle was for God, who has the right to tell us how he wants to be worshiped. But even in the tabernacle, some things were left up to the artists, who were free to exercise their creativity within the bounds of obedience to God.

We should notice how many different kinds of art they produced. In his excellent book *The Liberated Imagination*, Leland Ryken points out that Bezalel and Oholiab produced three major kinds of visual art: symbolic, representational, and nonrepresentational (or abstract) art.[6] Symbolic art (which can be either representational or nonrepresentational) uses a physical form to stand for a spiritual reality. So, for example, the ark symbolized atonement, and the lampstand symbolized the light of God's glory and grace. Representational art imitates life by portraying a recognizable object from the physical universe. A good example is the pomegranates on the robe of the high priest. Nonrepresentational or abstract art is pure form. There are examples of this, too, such as the colors of the curtains in the Holy Place or the shapes of the physical spaces that made up the tabernacle complex.

Some Christians still think that certain forms of art are more godly than others. Usually symbolic art is prized, especially if its symbolism is religious. Representational art is also prized because it imitates the world that God has made. But what Christians tend to criticize is abstract art, especially as it has come to expression in modern art. Yet abstraction has God's blessing as much as any other art form. God loves all kinds of art, in all kinds of media and all kinds of styles. As John Calvin said, "All the arts come from God and are to be respected as divine inventions."[7] Therefore, as Christians we are not limited to crosses, flannelgraphs, and calligraphy. God wants all the arts to flourish in all the fullness of their artistic potential.

## The Good, the True, and the Beautiful

This does not mean that anything goes. God has high standards for art, as he does for everything else. Using Exodus 31 as a guide—and this is our third principle—God's aesthetic standards include goodness, truth, and beauty.

Goodness is both an ethical and an aesthetic standard. Obviously Bezalel and Oholiab were not allowed to make anything that violated the Ten Commandments—especially the second commandment, which outlawed idolatry. Similarly, Christian artists are not allowed to make anything that is immoral or will be used as an object of religious worship. But goodness is also an aesthetic category. Israel's artists were called to make good art—art that was excellent. At the end of his instructions, God said that Bezalel and Oholiab were to make everything according to his specifications (v. 11), and in the preceding chapters we have discovered just how specific God can be. His careful instructions for building the tabernacle give the impression that he is a perfectionist. Actually, he's not a perfectionist—he's just perfect, that's all! And his perfection sets the standard for whatever we do in his name. Israel's artists were obligated to give God their very best. Whatever we happen to make—not only in the visual arts, but in all the arts—we should make it as well as we can.

To be pleasing to God, art must be true as well as good. Truth has always been an important criterion for art. Art is an incarnation of truth. It penetrates beneath the surface of things to portray them the way they really are. The tabernacle is a good example. The whole building was designed to communicate truth about God and his relationship with his people. And in order to fulfill this purpose, the artistry that went into the tabernacle had to be true. It had to be true to nature. When it represented something in creation—like flowers, for example, or pomegranates—it had to be true to what God made. It also had to be true to who God is. Each part of the tabernacle said something about God. The ark symbolized his throne, the basin signified his power to wash away sin, and so forth. In order to communicate these truths, the tabernacle had to tell the truth. Its art was in service to its truth.

The kind of art that glorifies God is good, true, and also beautiful. Today it seems like the art world is struggling to overcome an aesthetic of ugliness. Beauty used to be one of the artist's highest priorities; now for many artists it is one of the lowest, if it is a priority at all. But God is a great lover of beauty, as we can see from the collection of his work that hangs in the gallery of the universe. Form is as important to him as function. Thus it was not enough for the tabernacle to be laid out in the right way; it also had to be beautiful. There was beauty in the color of its fabrics, the sparkle of its gems, the shape of its objects, and the symmetry of its proportions. The tabernacle was a thing of beauty. God made sure of this by taking the unprecedented step of endowing its artists with the gift of his Spirit.

Beauty and truth belong together. As the poet John Keats said in his famous "Ode on a Grecian Urn," "Beauty is truth, truth beauty—that is all ye need to know." This is an exaggeration, but truth and beauty *are* connected. The problem with a good deal of modern and postmodern art is that it offers truth without beauty. It only tells the truth about ugliness and alienation, leaving out the beauty of creation and redemption. So-called Christian art tends to have the opposite problem. It tries to show beauty without admitting the truth about sin, and to that extent it is false. Think of all the bright, sentimental scenes that portray an ideal world unaffected by the fall. Such a world may be nice to look at, but it is not the world God sent his Son to save.

So what kind of art is able to meet God's standard? Not art that is bad, false, or ugly, but art that incarnates the good, the true, and the beautiful. This does not mean that Christian artists never portray anything ugly. We have to tell the truth about ugliness in a world spoiled by sin. But we are always drawn to the beauty that endures. In a world that has been uglified by sin, the Christian artist shows the plausibility of redemption by producing good work that is true in its beauty.

## Art for the Glory of God

A fourth principle for a Christian theology of the arts is that art is for God's sake. Artists often talk about art for art's sake. Sometimes what they mean is that art has intrinsic worth: It has value in and of itself, apart from any utility. This needs to be said because there are always some people who wonder why we need art, on the assumption that in order to be a legitimate calling it must perform some practical function. But in the words of Ralph Waldo Emerson, "Beauty is its own excuse for being."[8] The artistry of the tabernacle proves the truth of this statement. Some of its features—the gold molding on the ark of the covenant, for example—were purely decorative. When Bible scholars try to find a spiritual meaning for every detail, they are missing the point. Some of the artistry in the tabernacle was art for art's sake, in the full and proper sense of the expression.

The problem is that artistry easily becomes idolatry. And when this happens, art only exists for its own sake, and not for any higher purpose. Rather than dedicating their work to God, some artists produce it for their own glory. For example, when Henri Matisse (1869–1954) completed his masterful paintings in the Chapel of the Rosary at Venice, he stepped back and proclaimed, "I did it for myself." One of the Catholic sisters overheard him and immediately objected, "But you told me you were doing it for God." "Yes," Matisse replied, "but I am God."[9]

Matisse is hardly the only artist ever to have delusions of deity. There is a reason for this: Art is such a wonderful gift that those who love it sometimes forget to praise its Giver. Anyone who doubts the tendency of artistry to become idolatry only needs to read Exodus 32, where Aaron makes the golden calf. That sordid episode shows what happens when people pursue art for their own purposes: They end up worshiping art rather than God. It is only when we create things for God's sake that our artwork promotes his glory rather than competing with it.

Art for God's sake—this is what the tabernacle was all about. Every detail in that sacred building was for the praise of God's glory. The altar and the mercy seat testified to his grace. The table of the showbread proclaimed his providence. The lampstand spread his light. But even the things that were not symbolic were for God. This is why the tabernacle was made so carefully, with such fine materials and fancy decorations: it was all for the glory of God.

The same should be true of everything we create. It should all be for God's glory. This does *not* mean that all our art has to be evangelistic in the sense that it explicitly invites people to believe in Christ. To give an example from another calling, the way a Christian who makes cars glorifies God is not by painting "John 3:16" on the hoods. Rather, he glorifies God by making a good car. Similarly, the artist glorifies God by making good art, whether or not it contains an explicit gospel message.

Another way to say this is that art can be Christian without serving as a vehicle for evangelism. A creation always reveals something about its creator. What artists make tells us how they view the world. Thus the art of a Christian should be consistent with a life of faith in Christ. Johann Sebastian Bach is famous for signing his works with the letters "sDg," meaning *soli Deo gloria*—to God alone be the glory. This was a pious act. However, the important thing was not the letters Bach added to his music, but the notes themselves, which were a testimony to his faith in God. In the same way, every artist whose talents are under the lordship of Jesus Christ will produce art for God's sake.

## Beautiful Savior

So this is the Christian view of art: The artist is called and gifted by God—who loves all kinds of art, who maintains high aesthetic standards for goodness, truth, and beauty, and whose glory is art's highest goal. We accept these principles because they are Biblical, and also because they are true to God's character. What we believe about art is based on what we believe about him. Art is what it is because God is who he is.

Each of our principles reveals something about his divine being and attributes. Why does God call people to be artists? Because he is the Artist, and we are made in his image. When we first meet the God of the Bible, he is busy making things and calling them good (see Genesis 1). Thus it is only natural for him to take some of the people he has made and call them to be artists.

Why does God love all kinds of art? Because he is infinite in his perfections and has made a universe that is vast in its beauty. To serve such a God, in such a world, the arts must flourish in all their variety. And they should be measured against the standards of goodness, truth, and beauty. These are God's standards because they are essential attributes of his being. He is a good, true, and beautiful God. As Jonathan Edwards said, "All the beauty to be found throughout the whole creation, is but the reflection of the diffused beams of that Being who hath an infinite fullness of brightness and glory; God . . . is the foundation and fountain of all being and all beauty."[10] And since God is so infinitely beautiful, all our art is rightly dedicated to his glory. Art comes from God and should return to his praise.

If God has such a passion for the arts, then we should expect him to reveal his artistry in the plan of salvation. But here we come up against a shocking reality—namely, that the center of God's masterpiece of salvation was an event of appalling ugliness and degradation. This masterpiece was the cross where Christ was crucified for sin, and there was nothing beautiful about it. The crucifixion was an ugly, ugly obscenity—a twisting, bleeding body of pain. As Isaiah wrote concerning the crucified Christ:

> He had no form or majesty that we should look at him,
> and no beauty that we should desire him.
> He was despised and rejected by men;
> a man of sorrows, and acquainted with grief;
> and as one from whom men hide their faces
> he was despised, and we esteemed him not.
> Surely he has borne our griefs
> and carried our sorrows;
> yet we esteemed him stricken,
> smitten by God, and afflicted. (Isaiah 53:2b–4)

God sent his Son to be our Savior: That was the plan. But what God sent him to do was grotesque. How can we explain this? Why would the God of all glory and beauty do something so ugly, and then make us look to it for our salvation? The cross shouts against all the sensibilities of his divine aesthetic!

God did this because it was the only way he could save us. Sin had brought ugliness and death into the world. In order to save his lost creation, God sent his Son right into all the absurdity and alienation. There Jesus took our sin upon himself, dying to pay the price that justice demanded. It was so ugly that people had to turn away. Not even God himself could bear to see it, as we know from the darkness that descended over the cross (Matthew 27:45) and from the Son's cry of dereliction: "My God, my God, why have you forsaken me?" (Matthew 27:46).

This is not how the story ends, however. God did not just leave his Son in death and decay. He's much too good an artist for that. His design was to transform ugliness into beauty. He did it first with the body of his Son, raising Jesus from the dead and giving him a glorious resurrection body more beautiful than anything we can imagine. That body still bears the marks of the crucifixion. We know this because Jesus invited his disciples to touch the places where he was pierced. But those ugly wounds have been transformed into glory. The hymn-writer Matthew Bridges described it well: "Behold his hands and side, rich wounds, yet visible above, in beauty glorified."[11] For all eternity the body of Jesus will bear reminders of the suffering he endured for sin—but now it is transformed into glorious beauty.

God will do the same thing with everyone who has faith in Jesus Christ. Whenever we get discouraged by the ugliness of our sin, we need to remember that we are still works in progress. One day the best of artists will take everything that has been disfigured by our depravity and by his grace will transform us into works of beauty that will be a joy forever. Our salvation is directed by a redemptive aesthetic.

What kind of art would be worthy of such a God? Only good art—art that represents the goodness of his creation. Only true art—art that tells the truth about our fallen condition. Only beautiful art—art that incarnates the beauty of our redemption. And only glorious art—art that anticipates the coming of his glory.

In his wonderful little book *Art and the Bible*, Francis Schaeffer describes a mural in the art museum at Neuchâtel, painted by the Swiss artist Paul Robert. Schaeffer writes:

> In the background of this mural he pictured Neuchatel, the lake on which it is situated and even the art museum which contains the mural. In the foreground near the bottom is a great dragon wounded to the death. Underneath the dragon is the vile and the ugly—the pornographic and the rebellious. Near the top Jesus is seen coming in the sky with his endless hosts. On the left side is a beautiful stairway, and on the stairway are young and beautiful men and women carrying the symbols of the various forms of art—architecture, music and so forth. And as they are carrying them up and away from the dragon to present them to Christ, Christ is coming down to accept them.[12]

What Robert's mural represents is the triumph of beauty and the redemption of the arts. Schaeffer comments that this future reality should shape the present, for "if these things are to be carried up to the praise of God and the Lordship of Christ at the Second Coming, then we should be offering them to God now."[13] Indeed, we should. We are living in a fallen and broken world, yet for all its ugliness, this world was made by God and will be saved by his grace. Therefore, we should devote all our skill to making art for the glory of God and for the sake of his Son—our beautiful Savior, Jesus Christ.

# 84

# God's Holy Day

EXODUS 31:12–18

IT IS HARD TO SAY which of God's commandments gets broken most frequently. Is it the commandment that forbids lying or the one that outlaws idolatry? Is it God's law against lust or his law against murderous anger? Such questions are impossible to answer because people seem to break all the commandments all the time.

What is perhaps easier to determine is which commandment is the most likely to get ignored altogether. Nearly everyone knows that it is wrong to lie, curse, or steal. But how many people know that God has given us a holy day of rest, when we may cease from our regular labor and offer ourselves to God in worship? Most secular people don't know this commandment at all, which is why the old Sunday restrictions have all but disappeared. Sunday has become a day for shopping and sporting events, just like the rest of the week, only more so.

The situation is not all that different in the church. Most Christians still go to church on Sunday mornings. However, they do not dedicate the whole day to God. Historian Benton Johnson has traced the decline of Sabbath observance in the Presbyterian church during the nineteenth and twentieth centuries. Already by 1950 most Presbyterians had abandoned their historic commitment to keeping the Lord's day holy. According to Johnson, this change has led to a loss of spiritual vitality and a decline in church membership.[1]

Today some Christians do not think they need to honor God's holy day at all. And even the ones who do keep the Sabbath consider this commandment less important than the rest of God's law. Is this really the way God wants us to treat his holy day?

## What's New?

Remembering the Sabbath is clearly important to God. In Exodus he mentions it no less than five times. The first was when he sent manna six days a week and told his people that the seventh day was "a day of solemn rest, a holy Sabbath to the Lord" (16:23). The second time, of course, was when he gave Moses the fourth commandment:

> Remember the Sabbath day, to keep it holy. Six days you shall labor, and do all your work, but the seventh day is a Sabbath to the Lord your God. On it you shall not do any work, you, or your son, or your daughter, your male servant, or your female servant, or your livestock, or the sojourner who is within your gates. For in six days the Lord made heaven and earth, the sea, and all that is in them, and rested on the seventh day. Therefore the Lord blessed the Sabbath day and made it holy. (20:8–11)

This commandment is repeated in the Book of the Covenant, where God uses it to promote social and ecological justice: "Six days you shall do your work, but on the seventh day you shall rest; that your ox and your donkey may have rest, and the son of your servant woman, and the alien, may be refreshed" (23:12). By this point the Israelites should have known that God wanted them to keep his day holy. Yet the commandment is repeated two more times, once at the end of chapter 31 and then again at the beginning of chapter 35. Obviously God thought that Sabbath-keeping was very important. It was central—not peripheral—to his plans for his people.

These five passages may seem repetitive, but they are not redundant. Each one provides a slightly different perspective on the Sabbath, so that we get the full picture of God's purposes for the day. What God says in chapter 31 is similar to what he said in chapter 20, but at least three things are new.

One is that keeping the Sabbath comes in *a new position*. Earlier it was part of the Ten Commandments. Here it is reiterated in the context of the tabernacle. After giving his building instructions, "the Lord said to Moses, 'You are to speak to the people of Israel and say, "Above all you shall keep my Sabbaths"'" (31:12, 13a). By "Sabbaths" the Bible means the weekly Sabbath. God refers to them as *his* Sabbaths because they follow his example and are given at his command.

As usual, there are scholars who think this command is out of place. How can we answer them? Why did God put the Sabbath in this position? The commandment is put here to remind Bezalel, Oholiab, and the rest of Israel's artists that they did not have to work on the tabernacle all the time. They were serving the Lord, making the most important building in the world. Nevertheless, they still needed to keep the Sabbath. They could not use their sacred calling as an excuse not to take their holy rest. This is emphasized by the grammar of verse 13, where the Hebrew word translated "above all" (*'akh*) functions as a restrictive adverb.[2] It makes an exception to what has just been said. God has been telling his artists to make the tabernacle; however, they were restricted from working on the Sabbath.

This reminds us not to use our service to God as an excuse for breaking his law. More specifically, it warns us not to come up with reasons why it is okay for us to break the Sabbath. If anyone had a good excuse, it was Bezalel and Oholiab. But even they had to honor God's holy day. Of course, there are some kinds of work that must be done on Sunday: works of ministry, such as preaching the gospel; works of mercy, such as feeding the homeless; and works of necessity, such as putting out fires or performing emergency surgery. But the rule is to honor God on his holy day, and we should be slow to grant ourselves exceptions, even for what may seem like good reasons.

## What Else Is New?

Another thing that is new in Exodus 31 is that the Sabbath has *a new purpose*: "And the Lord said to Moses, 'You are to speak to the people of Israel and say, "Above all you shall keep my Sabbaths, for this is a sign between me and you throughout your generations, that you may know that I, the Lord, sanctify you"'" (vv. 12, 13). Here God makes explicit what to this point had only been implied—namely, that the weekly Sabbath was designed to promote the knowledge of God.

God had entered into a relationship with his people, a covenant relationship in which they were to know him as their God. To that end, he decreed that they should set apart one whole day in seven to rest in his grace. God had already told them to set aside some sacred space: the tabernacle where he promised to dwell. But he also knew that building a relationship takes time. His people needed more than a place to worship. They needed holy time to meet with their God. The Sabbath was "a tabernacle in time," as Göran Larsson calls it.[3] It was God's way of making sure that his people would take the time to get to know him.

Together the tabernacle and the Sabbath put God at the center of Israel's time and space. The Sabbath looked back to creation, when God made the world in six days and rested on the seventh. Peter Enns develops this point by showing how Exodus uses the phrase "Then the Lord said" to echo the story of creation, when God said certain things and they were so (Genesis 1). By using this phrase, the Bible is presenting Israel as God's new creation. In several translations, the words "Then the Lord said" appear seven times in 25—31. The first six times all relate to building the tabernacle (25:1; 30:11, 17, 22, 34; 31:1). The seventh comes in 31:12, where God tells his people to rest. So Exodus repeats the creation pattern: There are "six days" to build the tabernacle, and then it is time to rest.[4]

The Sabbath also looked forward to full redemption, when God's people would enter their rest in the Promised Land. But for the present it was a time to grow deeper in the knowledge of God. By spending time in prayer and praise, God's people would come to know him as their God. And in the process they would become holy, like him. God gave them the Sabbath so that they would know him as "the LORD" who sanctifies them (31:13). Their covenant relationship with God was a sanctifying relationship, and the Sabbath was part of the process. As the people set apart a day for worship and rest, God set them apart for his service. In other words, he sanctified them. Jesus said, "The Sabbath was made for man" (Mark 2:27), and one way the Sabbath is *for* us is that it helps us grow in the knowledge of God. When we sanctify God's holy day, God uses it to sanctify us.

A third thing that is new about the Sabbath command in Exodus 31 is the punishment of those who break it. There is *a new penalty*: "You shall keep the Sabbath, because it is holy for you. Everyone who profanes it shall be put to death. Whoever does any work on it, that soul shall be cut off from among his people. Six days shall work be done, but the seventh day is a Sabbath of solemn rest, holy to the LORD. Whoever does any work on the Sabbath day shall be put to death" (vv. 14, 15).

The prohibition was absolute. The word *Sabbath* means to cease, and on the Sabbath the Israelites were not allowed to do regular work of any kind. As Michael Horton comments, the day did not require "cessation from activity but cessation from a particular kind of activity—namely, the six-day labor that is intrinsically good but has suffered the curse after the fall."[5] It was not a day for business as usual, or for people to "do their own thing." If they did, they would suffer the penalty. Verse 14 speaks of "profan[ing]" the Sabbath, and there is some question as to what falls under this category. Does it refer to any work at all, or only to certain kinds of heavy labor? Similarly, there is some question as to what is meant by the phrase "cut off from among his people." Does this refer to the death penalty or to some form of excommunication? If the account in Numbers 15 is any indication, the answer is that all work was forbidden under the strictest pains of death, because there we read about a man who was executed for gathering firewood on the Sabbath (Numbers 15:32–36).

This penalty no longer applies. Remember that there were three types of Old Testament law: moral, civil, and ceremonial. The moral law is God's universal and eternal will for all people in all places. The civil law was for Old Testament Israel as a nation under the direct rule of God; its judicial sanctions are no longer binding. The ceremonial law governed the rituals of religious worship, such as the system of sacrifice. This law has been fulfilled in Christ.

So where does the command to keep the Sabbath fit in? What kind of law is it? In its essential requirement, it is part of the moral law, which is why it is included in the Ten Commandments. God demands that once a week we cease from our regular work to worship him. Certain aspects of this law were ceremonial, such as the day it was celebrated (Saturday) and the addition of other Sabbath days to Israel's festival calendar (such as Passover). There were also penalties for breaking the Sabbath, which were part of Israel's civil law. But these sanctions were not part of the Ten Commandments, and they are no longer binding.

Yet the punishment still seems severe. Why did Sabbath breaking demand the death penalty? Remember that the commandment's purpose was to protect and preserve God's relationship with his people. Peter Enns comments, "This penalty seems harsh, but not when we realize what the Sabbath was intended to do. By not keeping the Sabbath, the Israelite was showing that he or she was not interested in knowing [God]."[6] Breaking the Sabbath was an act of defiant rebellion. It was a repudiation of the covenant. It was a way of saying to God, "My relationship with you isn't important to me. You're not worth the time it would take to get to know you." When people say that, they really are cutting themselves off from God, and it is only right for them to be cut off from their people.

This is why keeping the Lord's day holy ought to be important to us: We want to know God. We want to grow in our relationship with him and make progress in holiness. So rather than treating every day the same, we honor God's holy day. It is not just holy to him; it is holy to us.

## Sabbath Keeping Today

The question many Christians ask today is whether or not we still have to keep the Sabbath. And this is the way people usually ask the question: Do we *have* to? It's as if six days are not enough for us! We want to claim all seven, so we begrudge God his holy day.

Sabbath keeping is a matter on which Christians often disagree. Some believe that the Sabbath has been so fulfilled in Christ that we are no longer obligated to rest one whole day in seven. As we rest in Christ, trusting in his work for our salvation, we find the true rest that God has promised. The Sabbath was "a shadow of the things to come, but the substance belongs to Christ" (Colossians 2:17). Now every day is equally holy to God.

One problem with this view is that keeping the Sabbath is one of the Ten Commandments, which were written in stone as a testimony of their abiding authority. Exodus 31 ends by saying, "And he gave to Moses, when he had finished speaking with him on Mount Sinai, the two tablets of the testimony, tablets of stone, written with the finger of God" (v. 18). What was written on these two tablets was the Decalogue, including the fourth commandment. Therefore, setting aside a day for rest and worship was not just God's law for Israel—it was his will for all people.

Furthermore, the basis for Sabbath keeping went all the way back to creation. In Exodus 31 the commandment is given as a sign of God's covenant with his people. But it is also rooted in creation because "in six days the LORD made heaven and earth, and on the seventh day he rested and was refreshed" (v. 17). The Sabbath is one of the world's original institutions, going back to the week the world was made.

As we have seen, certain aspects of Sabbath keeping—such as the death penalty—were only for Old Testament Israel. The Sabbath also had unique significance for Israel as a sign of the covenant. There was already a Sabbath, but now it was given added significance as a sign of their relationship with God. God said, "Therefore the people of Israel shall keep the Sabbath, observing the Sabbath throughout their generations, as a covenant forever. It is a sign forever between me and the people of Israel that in six days the LORD made heaven and earth, and on the seventh day he rested and was refreshed" (vv. 16, 17).

These verses emphasize the Sabbath's abiding significance. God's holy day is to be kept in perpetuity. To understand how this applies to us, we need to remember that in the New Testament the church is called "the Israel of God" (Galatians 6:16). God's promises to his people Israel are fulfilled in the church of Jesus Christ. Where do Jews come to salvation today? Not outside the church, but within it; not apart from Christ, but in him as their Messiah. So where will God's holy day be honored? Also in the church.

When we turn to the New Testament, we find that the early church cherished Sunday as a day of rest and worship. It was on the first day of the week that the Holy Spirit was poured out on the church (Acts 2:1–4; Pentecost came fifty days after Passover—the first day of the week). It was on "the first day of the week" that Christians "gathered together to break bread" (Acts 20:7a), and also to present their tithes and offerings (1 Corinthians 16:2). Sunday was their Sabbath. But rather than calling it "the Sabbath," the apostles referred to it as "the Lord's day" (e.g., Revelation 1:10) to show that it had come under the lordship of Jesus Christ.

Why did the early church celebrate God's holy day on Sunday rather than Saturday? What gave the apostles the right to change the day? The answer is that they didn't change it—Jesus did! The only thing that could change the day of God's command was something as significant as the creation itself: the resurrection of Jesus Christ. God transformed his holy day from Sabbath to Lord's Day by raising Jesus from the dead. He accomplished this new exodus on Sunday, the first day of the week. From then on the people of God—both Jews and Gentiles—observed Sunday as a day of rest and worship. The Old Testament people of God were looking forward to salvation. It was only right for them to have their special day of worship at the end of the week, in anticipation of the coming of their Savior. But now that Christ has come, we begin our week by worshiping God on the day of resurrection. We do not keep the Jewish Sabbath in all its particulars, with all its penalties, but we do honor the Lord's Day by ceasing from our regular work and devoting the day to the pleasures of knowing God.

Sunday worship was the practice of the apostolic church. This is not discussed in the New Testament; it is simply mentioned in passing (see the passages above). But the practice is explained by the early church fathers. The *Epistle of Barnabas*, written around AD 120, said of Christians, "They keep the eighth day with joyfulness, the day in which Jesus rose from the dead." Similarly, Justin Martyr said, "Sunday is the day on which we all hold our communion assembly because Jesus Christ, our Savior, on the same day arose from the dead." And in AD 194 Clement of Alexandria praised a fellow believer because "he, in fulfillment of the precept according to the Gospel keeps the Lord's Day."[7] Sunday was celebrated as the Lord's Day throughout the early church.

The Lord's Day is a day for looking back. We look back to creation, when God made the world in six days and then rested. We also look back to Easter, when God gave us life by raising Jesus from the dead. But we also look forward to our everlasting rest. The Scripture says, "So then, there remains a Sabbath rest for the people of God" (Hebrews 4:9). We find our rest in Jesus, who has done all the work of our salvation: He kept the Law; he died for our sins; he rose from the dead. Now, by trusting in what Jesus has done, "the believer has ceased from his 'work' (in the sense of trying to earn his own salvation) and entered into that spiritual rest and peace of heart that comes to those who know themselves to be already accepted and justified by God."[8] One day we will enter our full and final rest. In the meantime we rest in Jesus—especially on his holy day.

## Keeping the Sabbath Wholly

Do we have to keep the Lord's Day holy? Ask the question this way and the answer is, "Yes, we do." But a more positive way to say it is that we *get* to keep the day. The benefits of Sabbath-keeping are still available to us as believers in Christ.

In keeping God's holy day, we are simply following the example of Jesus himself. First Jesus had to rescue the Sabbath from legalism, of course, but he honored the day itself. He loved to be in the synagogue for Sabbath worship (e.g., Mark 1:21; Luke 4:16). He also loved to use the day for showing mercy by healing the sick (e.g., Matthew 12:9–14). Jesus Christ is the Lord of the Sabbath (Mark 2:28), and one of the ways we experience the joy of his lordship is by keeping God's day holy.

The Lord's day is not an obligation but a privilege, not a chore but a gift, not a burden but a delight (see Isaiah 58:13). Here Christians can learn something from the Jews and their Sabbath prayers: "Come, let us welcome the Sabbath in joy and peace! Like a bride, radiant and joyous, comes the Sabbath. It brings blessings to our hearts; workday thoughts and cares are put aside. The brightness of the Sabbath light shines forth to tell that the divine spirit of love abides within our home. In that light all our blessings are enriched, all our griefs and trials are softened."[9] Who would not welcome such a day?

Christians welcome God's holy day as a weekly opportunity to experience life's highest pleasures. What are the blessings of this day?

First, there is the blessing of *spiritual refreshment*. Here we are simply following the example of God himself. The Bible says that "on the seventh day he rested and was refreshed" (31:17), or more literally, he stopped "to catch his breath." This is what we do on the Lord's day: We take a spiritual breather. And as we do, the Lord refreshes our souls and renews our spirits.

The Lord's Day is a vacation for the soul. It is a day to revel in the wonders of God and the mysteries of his Word. It is a day to regain perspective. Before we launch out into another week, with all the difficulties and distractions of daily life, we take a day to remember who God is and who we are in relationship to him. Calvin said:

> The Sabbath should be to us a tower whereon we should mount aloft to contemplate afar the works of God, when we are not occupied nor hindered by any thing besides, from stretching forth all our faculties in considering the gifts and graces which He has bestowed on us. And if we properly apply ourselves to do this on the Sabbath, it is certain that we shall be no strangers to it during the rest of our time and that this meditation shall have so formed our minds, that on Monday, and the other days of the week, we shall abide in the grateful remembrance of our God.[10]

One of the day's primary purposes is to help us know God. To that end, the Lord's Day is for worship, especially public worship. Nothing we do makes a bigger difference in who we become than worshiping with the people of God every week. Of course, we need to spend time with God every day. Daily Bible reading and prayer sustain our spiritual vitality. But meeting weekly with God in corporate worship provides an anchor for our whole spiritual existence. Praise God that we can set aside a day to do this!

And it is a day, not just a morning. As in any relationship, developing deeper intimacy with God cannot be rushed. It takes time to develop—more than just a couple of hours on a Sunday morning. This is why some churches still hold worship services also on Sunday evening. If we are able, we should attend. A pastor once remarked that he had never known anyone who was faithful in attending evening worship (in addition to the morning) to leave the faith or fall into scandalous sin. No doubt there are exceptions, but as a general rule, someone who is faithful in attending public worship will grow in grace. This makes sense when we remember what God said to Moses: "Above all you shall keep my Sabbaths . . . that you may know that I, the Lord, sanctify you" (31:13). God uses the Sabbath to sanctify us. When we keep it, it has a way of keeping us—away from sin and close to God.

Another blessing of God's holy day is *physical rest*. This is important because the last thing most people need is another day of work. We are living in an accelerated culture, where everything is moving faster and faster. Yet for all our labor-saving devices and time-saving products we do more work and have less time to spare than ever. Two British theologians comment:

> Like visitors to an art gallery who arrive 20 minutes before closing time we rush from exhibit to exhibit, fearful that we shall miss something worthwhile. The horizon of our own finitude haunts us, and we rush to cram as much as we possibly can into the available space, travelling ever faster and further, seeing and tasting more, trying out as many options as we can while we have the time and, ironically, as a consequence having time for very little at all. Has there ever been a generation with so little time actually to take time and enjoy the world? Always craving the next thing we so often fail to savour the moment offered to us.[11]

God's holy day offers us a weekly opportunity to savor the moment. It is a day to show by our actions that there is more to life than just work. By getting some rest we are following God's example. The Scripture says that on the seventh day God stopped and "rested" (31:17). We do the same thing on the Lord's Day. We stop working and instead rest in God's peace. We stop producing and rest in God's provision. We stop accomplishing and rest in our identity in Christ. We stop acquiring and rest in God's care. We stop worrying and rest in God's sovereignty.[12]

People who refuse to do this, writes Leonard Doohan, "are those who trust in their own strength rather than God's grace."[13] By contrast, those who keep the Sabbath are resting in God and his grace. At the outset of her exceptional book on keeping the Sabbath, Marva Dawn writes:

> We will consider many aspects of Sabbath ceasing—to cease not only from work itself, but also from the need to accomplish and be productive, from the worry and tension that accompany our modern criterion of efficiency, from our efforts to be in control of our lives as if we were God, from our possessiveness and enculturation, and, finally, from the humdrum and meaninglessness that result when life is pursued without the Lord at the center of it all. In all these dimensions we will recognize the great healing that can take place in our lives when we get into the rhythm of setting aside every seventh day all of our efforts to provide for ourselves and make our way in the world. A great benefit of Sabbath keeping is that we learn to let God take care of us—not by becoming passive and lazy, but in the freedom of giving up our feeble attempts to be God in our own lives.[14]

This does not mean that we should spend the Lord's Day doing nothing. God has called us to worship with his people. Sunday is also a day for works of mercy, works of necessity, and works of ministry. But it is primarily a day of rest. This is the way God made us. Today companies talk about working 24/7: twenty-four hours a day, seven days a week. God's numbers are a little different. Since the week that he made the world they have been 6 and 1: six days of work and one day of rest. Do we think that somehow our work is more important than his?[15] We function best when we stop working one day a week to enjoy the kind of rest and recreation that bring physical renewal. And strangely enough, when we get the rest we need, we become more productive and also more likely to receive as a gift all the things we are struggling so hard to obtain.

Here are some questions we can use for self-examination as we seek to find God's rest: Am I honoring God by getting enough rest? Am I taking advantage of the Lord's Day as an opportunity to grow in my relationship with God? Is Sunday a day of rest for me, or am I letting my work get in the way? J. C. Penney observed, "If a man's business requires so much of his time that he cannot attend the Sunday morning and evening services, and Wednesday night prayer meeting, then that man has more business than God intended him to have."[16] Many Christians need to learn how to follow Penney's example. Like nature, work abhors a vacuum: It will expand to fill as much time as we give it. God has given us six full days a week for work. When Sunday comes, he doesn't want us to keep working away; he wants us to stop and rest, keeping our work within the boundaries of obedience to him.

A third blessing of the Lord's Day is *evangelistic witness*. Honoring God's holy day is one of the things that ought to distinguish us from the world. Outwardly we are like our neighbors in many ways. But the Sabbath is a clear sign that we belong to the covenant community of God's people. Simply by attending worship on the Lord's Day we are making a public confession of our faith in Christ. When our neighbors see us in our Sunday best, they know we are going to church, and this provides the spiritual context for our relationship with them. We also make a statement whenever we tell people that we can't do something on Sunday, like work an extra shift or show up for baseball practice. Sometimes this invites opposition or even ridicule. This is to be expected. But it also gives us an opportunity to explain that nothing is more important to us than honoring Jesus Christ.

Sunday also gives us opportunities for service. During the week we don't always have time to get involved in mercy ministry. But Sunday is a day to care for the sick, feed the hungry, and visit prisoners and shut-ins. Since we do all these things in the name of Christ, Sunday is a day of witness to our faith in him. People ought to know that we are Christians by the way we use God's holy day.

A well-known example of using the Lord's Day for witness comes from the life of Eric Liddell, the famous Scottish Olympian who later became a missionary to China. Liddell's story is told in the film *Chariots of Fire*. His best race was the 200 meters, and he was expected to win the gold. However, one of the qualifying heats was scheduled for Sunday. As a devout Presbyterian, Liddell was adamant in his refusal to run, much to the consternation of Britain's racing officials. In the end, Liddell ended up competing in an entirely different event, the 400 meter race. "When I was about to run in the finals," he later wrote, "the trainer handed me a little note. I opened it and read the words, 'Them that honour me will I honour.'"[17] By keeping the Lord's Day holy, Liddell honored God and gave a living testimony of his faith in Jesus Christ. As it turned out, God honored Liddell by giving him the strength to win the Gold Medal at 400 meters. But Liddell's obedience to the fourth commandment made him a champion for Christ even before he approached the starting blocks.

## The Sabbath and the Rest of Life

These are some of the many blessings that come to those who keep God's holy day. Exodus 31 ends by reminding us where this commandment came from: "And he gave to Moses, when he had finished speaking with him on Mount Sinai, the two tablets of the testimony, tablets of stone, written with the finger of God" (v. 18).

Moses had been up on God's mountain for forty days and forty nights (see Deuteronomy 9:11). There God had provided him with the blueprints for the tabernacle (25—31). He had also given him the Book of the Covenant that contained case laws to guide Israel's conduct in daily life (20:22–24). But the most important thing God gave to Moses was the Decalogue—the commandments of his covenant. And this is what the Bible means by "the two tablets of the testimony" (31:18).

These two tablets were supposed to be placed in the ark of the covenant for safekeeping (which is why it was sometimes called "the ark of the Testimony"). In all likelihood, they were two identical copies of the Ten Commandments. This was the ancient custom. Whenever two nations made a covenant, copies were deposited in the throne room of both kings. In this case, Israel's throne and God's throne were one and the same, so both copies were put inside the ark that represented God's rule over Israel.

Both tablets were written in stone, inscribed with the very finger of God. This does not mean that God has hands. Rather, it is a manner of speaking that makes a graphic statement of the divine authorship of the Decalogue. Moses did not make up the Ten Commandments; they came from God. God is the one who wrote the words in stone. Therefore, the commandments come with all the weight of his divine authority. And although it is often ignored today, keeping the Sabbath was one of those commandments. God considered it necessary to a life that is pleasing to him.

A good example of the way that Sabbath-keeping is integral to a life that glorifies God comes from a poem by Seitze Buning. In the poem, Buning reflects on what he learned from watching his Dutch Calvinist parents keep the fourth commandment:

> Were my parents right or wrong
> not to mow the ripe oats that Sunday morning
> with the rainstorm threatening?
>
> I reminded them that the Sabbath was made for man
> and of the ox fallen into the pit.

Without an oats crop, I argued,
the cattle would need to survive on town-bought oats
and then it wouldn't pay to keep them.
Isn't selling cattle at a loss like an ox in a pit?

My parents did not argue.
We went to church.
We sang the usual psalms louder than usual—
we, and the others whose harvests were at stake . . .

for more floods came and more winds blew and beat
upon that House than we had figured on, even,
more lighting and thunder
and hail the size of pullet eggs.
Falling branches snapped the electric wires.
We sang the closing psalm without the organ and in the dark.

Afterward we rode by our oats field,
flattened.

"We still will mow it," Dad said.
"Ten bushels to the acre, maybe, what would have been fifty
if I had mowed right after milking
and if the whole family had shocked.
We could have had it weatherproof before the storm."

Later at dinner Dad said,
"God was testing us. I'm glad we went."
"Those psalms never gave me such a lift as this morning,"
Mother said, "I wouldn't have missed it."
And even I thought but did not say,
How guilty we would feel now if we had saved the harvest.

Then the poem ends on a surprising note, as the writer comments:

The one time Dad asked me why I live in a Black neighborhood,
I reminded him of that Sunday morning.
Immediately he understood.[18]

Most people would fail to see much connection between keeping God's day holy and pursuing racial justice. But we could raise the same question about any of the commandments. What is the relationship between charity and chastity, or between not swearing and not stealing? The answer is that we have one life to give in obedience to God, and God wants all of it. Keeping each commandment is part of keeping all the commandments. Therefore, honoring God on his holy day is integral to the Christian life. It is part of a whole life that is pleasing to God and has his blessing.

# 85

# Unholy Cow

## EXODUS 32:1–6

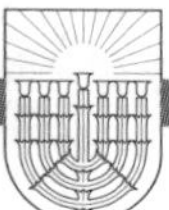

MEANWHILE . . . BACK AT THE CAMP . . . things were getting totally out of hand. Moses was still up on the mountain, meeting with God to receive instructions for building God's holy dwelling, the tabernacle. Moses was also learning the sacred rituals for ordaining his brother Aaron as high priest. It was the ultimate "mountaintop experience": God was revealing his will for Israel's worship.

Then the scene changes. Like a prize-winning novel, the plot of the Bible story unfolds with simultaneous action. Moses had been gone for *ages* (well, at least a month), and while he was gone the pilgrims started getting restless. Where had Moses gone? What was he doing? When was he going to come back and lead them out of the wilderness?

The longer the prophet was away, the more impatient the Israelites became. They started having doubts—not just about Moses, but also about God. Their doubts became murmurs, and their murmurs became complaints, until finally they decided to take matters into their own hands. They went to Aaron, who was second-in-command (the associate pastor, if you will) and said they wanted to make a few changes in their worship service. They told him to get busy making them a new deity. So Aaron very obediently made the only kind of "god" he knew how to make: a golden idol fashioned in the shape of a young bull.

Presumably this golden calf, as it is usually called, was made in the Egyptian style. The Egyptians worshiped any number of bovine deities. They worshiped Hathor, who was represented by the head of a cow, and Isis, the queen of the gods, who had horns on her head.[1] Then there was Menwer, the sacred bull of Ra, whose skin was covered with gold.[2] But according to John Mackay,

> The ultimate in bull worship was probably the Apis bull, considered to [be] the manifestation of Ptah, the creator god worshipped at Memphis in lower Egypt. The bull lived in palatial quarters in the precincts of the temple;

when they worshiped the golden calf. The answer seems to be, both! The second commandment was against worshiping the right God in the wrong way. It prohibited the Israelites from worshiping the true God falsely—namely, by means of an image. This is precisely what Aaron was doing. He did not call the golden calf "Apis" or "Isis." He referred to it as "the Lord" (32:5), using the covenant name of the one true God. By doing this, he could at least say that the Israelites were still worshiping the right God. Yet his sin was just as great. By presenting the graven image as a representation of the one true God, he was violating the second commandment.

The Israelites also broke the first commandment. When they first approached Aaron, they spoke in the plural: "Up, make us gods" (32:1). This was a rejection of monotheism—a belief in one and only one God. The difficulty is that Aaron made only one idol, which has led some scholars to doubt whether the Israelites ever intended to worship more than one god. But their demand speaks for itself: "make us *gods*!" And once they made a golden calf, there would be no stopping them: other gods would surely follow.

The people's desire to worship more than one god is confirmed by their confession of faith: "These are your gods, O Israel, who brought you up out of the land of Egypt!" (v. 4). They were twisting the covenant, which began with God saying, "I am the Lord your God, who brought you out of the land of Egypt, out of the house of slavery" (20:2). There God referred to himself in the singular because he is the only God. But by making the golden calf, the Israelites were adding another deity to their pantheon.

Making the golden calf, then, was doubly disobedient. It was a violation of both of God's first two commandments. G. W. Coats summarizes by saying, "Not only do the people request construction of an object that would serve as leader of the exodus and wilderness journey, an object defined as god and thus an idol that violates the second commandment, but they also identify the object as 'gods' and thus violate the first commandment."[4] This is how we fall into sin: by doing what God tells us not to do. At its most basic level, sin is disobedience to the revealed will of God.

Idolatry wasn't simply what God told the Israelites not to do; it was also what they told God they wouldn't do. And this too is sin: not doing what we promise God that we will do. After Moses had read God's law, the people said, "All the words that the Lord has spoken we will do" (24:3b); "All that the Lord has spoken we will do, and we will be obedient" (24:7b). And when the Israelites said "all," that included the first two commandments. They promised not to worship false gods or to make images of the true god. They made a covenant commitment to serve God alone. Yet the blood of the covenant barely had time to dry before they were dancing around the golden calf, breaking the very laws they had sworn to keep.

How easy it is to tell God that we'll never do something ever again, and then go right ahead and do it! This is especially true with sins of addiction. Gluttons tell God they're going to stop overeating, but then they go on another binge. Sex addicts say they will never use pornography again, but the next thing they know, they're standing in the aisle at the adult bookstore. Drunks swear they've had their last drink. Really. This time they mean it. But sadly they fall off the wagon again.

Why do people do this? And in one way or another we all do it. We all struggle to overcome patterns of habitual sin. We keep getting tempted to commit the same sin again and again. The reason we struggle is because the sin is in our hearts, not in the refrigerator or on the magazine rack. The story of the golden calf helps us see this. Why did the Israelites worship a cow? Because they had never entirely forsaken the gods of Egypt. They had promised to serve the Lord their God, but in their hearts they still cherished their old idolatries. The Bible says, "In their hearts they turned to Egypt" (Acts 7:39). One of the early church fathers, Ephrem the Syrian, wisely commented that the absence of Moses simply gave the Israelites the opportunity to "worship openly what they had been worshiping in their hearts."[5] They didn't even need someone to tempt them with an idol; they simply produced one out of the wickedness of their own hearts.

We do the same thing. Too often in our struggle against sin we focus almost exclusively on our actions. We think we can overcome sin just by stopping doing something. But what our outward sins reveal is the true inward condition of our hearts. Sin is not so much what we do as what we are. Unless we get to the very root of the problem and put sin to death in the heart, we fall right back into the same old sins, doing the very things we swore to God that we would never do again.

To break this pattern, we need to identify and eliminate the idols in our hearts: money, sex, and power; greed, lust, and especially pride. We need to heed the exhortation of the apostle John, who ended his first epistle by saying, "Little children, keep yourselves from idols" (5:21). Or to put it another way—a way that may help us remember the lessons of Exodus 32—*don't have a cow!* Then we need to replace our idolatrous attachments with genuine affection for the Triune God. As A. W. Pink has written: "Man must have an object, and when he turns from the true God, he at once craves a false one."[6] But this statement can also be reversed. The way to reduce our craving for false gods is for our minds and hearts to be intoxicated with the Spirit of the one true God.

## Sin Is Distrust

When do we fall into sin? *When we do not trust God to know what he's doing.* Sin is distrust as well as disobedience. Not trusting God is a sin in itself, but it also leads to other sins as we come up with our own strategies for making life work the way we want it to work.

The proof that the Israelites did not trust God comes in the very first verse:

"When the people saw that Moses delayed to come down from the mountain, the people gathered themselves together to Aaron and said to him, 'Up, make us gods who shall go before us. As for this Moses, the man who brought us up out of the land of Egypt, we do not know what has become of him'" (32:1). The Israelites were not willing to wait for God's instructions on worship. They were too impatient. They knew what they wanted, and they wanted it *NOW*!

God had not told the Israelites when he was going to lead them out of the wilderness. Nor had he told them how long Moses would stay up on the mountain. All they knew was that they were right where God wanted them to be, at least for the moment. And they needed to trust that when it was time for them to move on, God would show them the way.

The Israelites had every reason to believe that God knew what he was doing. He had brought them out of Egypt. He had saved them in the desert. He had given them his law. Every day he provided bread from Heaven. And if they needed any further reassurance that he was there for them, all they had to do was look up and see his glory on the mountain. God was not absent; he was right there with them in their situation.

Yet they doubted. As the weeks passed, and Moses failed to come back down, they started getting anxious. And as they had so often done in the past, they began to grumble against God, until finally they decided that they just couldn't take it any longer. If God was going to abandon them, they complained, then they might as well find some other god to lead them out of the wilderness (as if any other god could!). The proximate cause of the sin of the golden calf was Israel's impatience with God, their unwillingness to trust in his timing.

Israel's distrust also extended to Moses, the man whom God had appointed to serve as their prophet. "As for this Moses," they said, "the man who brought us up out of the land of Egypt, we do not know what has become of him" (32:1b). This was false. The Israelites knew exactly where Moses was: He was up on the mountain with God. By talking this way, they were giving the prophet too much responsibility and too little respect. On the one hand, they described him as the man who had brought them out of Egypt, when in fact their exodus was the work of God. This shows that the Israelites had the wrong expectations. They were counting on a man to save them. This too is sin: trusting anyone or anything else to do what God alone can do. On the other hand, the people failed to honor Moses as their spiritual leader. "This Moses," they called him. Their language was dismissive and disrespectful. They would never say something like this to his face, of course, but now that he was gone, now that his ministry had failed to meet their expectations, they felt justified in setting him aside.

The irony, of course, was that at that very moment everything was going according to God's plan. Moses was getting the instructions Israel needed to build the tabernacle. He would be gone for forty days—the Biblical time of testing. But soon Moses would return, and when he did, the Israelites would build the tabernacle, and God would descend in glory to dwell with his people. Then, when the time was right, he would lead them out of the wilderness and into the Promised Land. God had not abandoned them at all; he was busy preparing for their salvation. But rather than waiting on God or trusting their God-given leader, the Israelites decided to take matters into their own hands.

And this is how sin happens. We fall into sin when we fail to trust that God knows what he's doing and try to work things out on our own. Instead of waiting for him to do something according to his own time frame, we try to speed things up. By setting the agenda, what we are really trying to do is wrest control from God, when what we ought to do instead is wait for him to work.

The trouble is that, like the Israelites, we are often tempted to be impatient. We get impatient for God to heal us or provide for our needs. We get impatient for him to bring spiritual change, either in our own lives or in the lives of others. We get impatient for him to lead us out of the wilderness. But sometimes, for our own benefit, God doesn't want to bring us out of the wilderness. Not yet anyway. And if the wilderness is where God wants us right now, that's where we need to stay, trusting in his goodness and waiting for his timing.

### Sin Is Distortion

Sometimes it isn't only God's timing that we mistrust but the way he does things altogether. This is another way we fall into sin: *by doing things our way rather than his way*. Sin is more than disobedience and distrust—it is distortion. We twist whatever God intends to use for his glory and bend it to our own will.

There were many things the Israelites wanted to do their way instead of God's way. One of them was to worship. The purpose of the exodus was for God's people to worship God the proper way. But rather than waiting for God's word and worshiping the way God told them to worship, they decided to come up with an alternative religion—the Cult of the Golden Calf. God told them not to make any idols, but they decided that rather than worshiping by faith, they wanted a god they could see and touch. So they made a visible representation of the deity.

Meanwhile, God was up on the mountain with Moses, explaining how he really did want to be worshiped. He was drawing up plans for a new worship facility that would satisfy Israel's need to experience his grace in a tangible way, but without turning him into an idol. We become like what we worship; we also become like *how* we worship. Only God's way to worship would preserve his divine majesty. Only God's way to worship would show how sin could be forgiven. And only God's way to worship would point people to Christ by putting the gospel on display.

But the Israelites decided to do things their own way. They wanted to worship in their own style, with their own priest, their own altar, their own sacrifices, their own god, and their own do-it-yourself salvation. What they did was abominable (pun intended)! Rather than worshiping God the way *he* pleased, they did it the way *they* pleased. The worship of the golden calf was idolatrous, immoral, and insulting to God. R. C. Sproul comments: "The cow gave no law and demanded no obedience. It had no wrath or justice or holiness to be feared. It was deaf, dumb, and impotent. But at least it could not intrude on their fun and call them to judgment. This was a religion designed by men, practiced by men, and ultimately useless for men."[7] The contrast between the golden calf and the true worship of God was absolute:

> At every key point the people's building project contrasts with the tabernacle that God has just announced. This gives to the account a heavy ironic cast. (1) The people seek to create what God has already provided; (2) they, rather than God, take the initiative; (3) offerings are demanded rather than willingly presented; (4) the elaborate preparations are missing altogether; (5) the painstaking length of time needed for building becomes an overnight rush job; (6) the careful provision for guarding the presence of the Holy One turns into an open-air object of immediate accessibility; (7) the invisible, intangible God becomes a visible, tangible image; and (8) the personal, active God becomes an impersonal object that cannot see or speak or act. The ironic effect is that the people forfeit the very divine presence they had hoped to bind more closely to themselves.[8]

What made Israel's worship especially dangerous was that some of the things they did were similar to what God had commanded, such as making offerings or sitting down to a covenant meal (see 20:24). However, it was all done in service to their sacred cow. This made it the most dangerous kind of worship—the kind that mixes what is true with what is false. This is what makes theologically liberal churches so deadly today. They still follow the old liturgy, but their teaching about God and Christ is false. People who go to such churches think they have the real thing, but they don't, and they won't ever know it unless they start going to a church that worships the God of the Bible.

Since God is God, he alone has the right to determine how he wants to be worshiped. We should only worship him in the way that he has revealed. Theologians sometimes call this "the regulative principle" for worship. We do not have the right to come up with our own religious rituals. According to the *Philadelphia Confession* (1742), "the acceptable way of worshipping the true God, is instituted by himself, and so limited by his own revealed will, that he may not be worshiped according to the imagination and devices of men, nor the suggestions of Satan, under any visible representations, or any other way not prescribed in the Holy Scriptures."

True worship is according to Scripture, and Scripture tells us to worship God through prayer and praise, through reading and preaching God's Word, through confessing our faith and giving our offerings, and through celebrating the sacraments of baptism and the Lord's Supper. To worship God in any other way may gratify us, but it does not glorify God. We should be careful not to worship God by using images. We should also be careful not to fashion God into our own image, even if we only do this in our minds. We are not free to say, "I like to think of God as . . ." and then invent a deity of our own design.

Another way the Israelites did their own thing involved the use of their gifts. Rather than using them for God and his glory, they used them for their own purposes. We see this from the way the golden calf was made. When the people demanded a god, "Aaron said to them, 'Take off the rings of gold that are in the ears of your wives, your sons, and your daughters, and bring them to me.' So all the people took off the rings of gold that were in their ears and brought them to Aaron" (32:2, 3). Presumably Aaron asked for their earrings because they were so readily accessible. All the people had to do was take them off and hand them over.

Where did these earrings come from in the first place? Back in Egypt the Israelites didn't have any gold; they were slaves. But when they finally left, their former masters gave them treasures of silver and gold (12:35, 36). This plunder was a gift from God, who wanted to make sure they had the resources they needed to build the tabernacle. But the Israelites took the gold and used it to make an idol. This was a flagrant abuse of a divine gift. We commit the same sin when we use all our riches on ourselves rather than investing them to advance the gospel. How much should we give? At least enough so that we have to sacrifice some of the things we want so that God can use our wealth to do what he wants.

Gold was not the only gift the Israelites abused. They also abused the arts. The Bible says that Aaron "received the gold from their hand and fashioned it with a graving tool and made a golden calf" (32:4a). This golden calf was state of the art. Aaron used the latest techniques to make it. Umberto Cassuto describes the ancient process: "First they would make a wooden model, and then overlay it with plating of precious metal. . . . In order to sculpture the finest details on the gold plating, such as the eyes, the hair and the like, artistic work required a sharp and delicate instrument, namely, a graving tool."[9]

The problem was not the artistry that went into the golden calf, but the way Aaron perverted that precious gift. Rather than devoting his skill to the glory of God, he used it to make an idol. This shows how easy it is for God's best gifts to be distorted by sin. Some of the very techniques God wanted Israel's artists to use for the tabernacle could also be used to make idols. This is a reminder to artists to dedicate all their skill to God, lest their work become an end in itself and thus rob God of his glory. But the lesson is for everyone. We all need to make sure that we are using our talents for God and not just for ourselves. The gifts that we prize the most are the most likely to become our gods. Whether our gifts are intellectual, physical, artistic, relational, or occupational, we need to dedicate them to God. If we don't, we are likely to worship the gift rather than its Giver.

The Israelites said they were doing something for God, but it was really for them. This became obvious when, in a desperate attempt to make the best of a bad situation, Aaron tried to use the golden calf as a way to worship the one true God: "When Aaron saw this, he built an altar before it. And Aaron made a proclamation and said, 'Tomorrow shall be a feast to the LORD'" (32:5). By using God's sacred name, Aaron was trying to say that the golden calf was for the glory of God.

People often do this. They use God's name to endorse their agenda. Sometimes they even do it in the church. For example, some people say that Jesus Christ can be glorified through other religions. This is a way of trying to put the name of the true God on a false religion. Or people say that a so-called marriage between homosexuals is beautiful to God. Again, this is contrary to the will of God, and attaching God's name to it does not change that fact. We can't just put God's name on our letterhead and then assume that whatever we do has his blessing.

What the Israelites were doing did *not* have God's blessing. It was not for him, but for them: "And they rose up early the next day and offered burnt offerings and brought peace offerings. And the people sat down to eat and drink and rose up to play" (32:6). It must have been quite a party. The Hebrew word for "play" (*tzachaq*) sometimes has sexual overtones (cf. Genesis 26:8; 39:14). What the Israelites were doing was indecent. Their idolatry led to immorality. Their worship was vulgar and debauched. It degenerated into a wanton orgy of lewd dancing. They weren't worshiping; they were partying. And it wasn't for God's glory at all; it was just for their own sinful pleasure.

This is what happens when we do things our way rather than God's way. Such action contaminates our worship, corrupts our gifts, and compromises our morals. Are we living the way God wants us to live or the way *we* want to live? Are we pleasing God in our worship? Are we serving him with our gifts? Are we honoring him with our bodies? Or are we becoming more and more profane in the way we live?

## Sin Is a Lot of Other Things Too

There are many ways to fall into sin. We fall into sin when we do what God tells us not to do, when we don't trust God to know what he's doing, and when we do things our way rather than his way. And these are not the only ways we fall into sin. Far from it. The story of Israel's unholy cow shows many other ways we go astray.

*We fall into sin when we do what is popular instead of what is right.* This was partly Israel's mistake. By making a golden calf, they were imitating the Egyptians, who worshiped the entire bovine family. But it was also Aaron's mistake. As long as Moses was gone, he was the leader, the one charged with making sure that the people did what was right. But Aaron couldn't stand the pressure. Verse 1 describes how the people "gathered themselves together to Aaron." A better way to say it is that they "crowded" around him. It was a mob scene, with "all the people" (v. 3) trying to intimidate Aaron. They were not there to hear what he had to say but to tell him what they wanted him to do. When they spoke, it was in the imperative, as if they were giving orders. "Up, make us gods," they said (v. 1). "We've waited for Moses long enough; get up and get busy!"

Sometimes people use the same tactics in the church. If they are not in a position of authority, they try to get someone who is in authority to do things the way they think they ought to be done. They pressure their pastors or elders, lobbying for their agenda. They say, "You know, I'm not the only one; many others feel the same way I do." This is why spiritual leaders need to have unfailing courage and uncompromising conviction. When it comes to theology, worship, ministry, and discipline, it is always much harder to do what is right than to do what is popular.

When Aaron faced this challenge, he failed to do what was right. A. W. Pink comments: "It was the first time he had been left in charge of the Congregation, and wretchedly did he acquit himself. Instead of putting his trust in the Lord, the fear of man brought him a snare."[10] To put it another way, when Aaron saw that he couldn't "beat 'em," he decided to "join 'em." He knew better, of course, but instead of defending the one true God, he gave in to the people who were pushing for a new style of worship. He failed to provide godly leadership. Aaron didn't pray about the situation. He didn't consult Israel's elders. He didn't lead the people in true worship or teach them sound theology. He just did as he was told. He tried to say he was doing it for God, of course. This is what spiritual leaders always say. But the truth is that Aaron was too weak to stand up for what was right. In the end, what mattered to him most was not what God said, but what the people would say.

We do the same thing whenever we let people pressure us into doing something we know is wrong. We do it on the playground when kids are talking about something bad. We do it at the office when the numbers don't add up and our boss tells us not to ask any questions. We do it on the weekend when people want us to party. We do it in front of the television when we absorb the attitudes and aspirations of a godless society. We do it on the phone when a friend starts to gossip. And we do it in the church when we compromise our message so people won't get offended. Whenever we do what is popular instead of what is right, we fall into sin. This is desperately important to remember at a time when Christian leaders are claiming "the audience, not the message is sovereign."[11]

Another way we fall into sin is *by forgetting what God has done for us and going back to our old wicked ways*. Exodus 32 becomes all the more shocking when we remember what the people who worshiped the golden calf had seen God do. They had witnessed the plagues that God sent against the Egyptians for worshiping false gods. They had walked through the Red Sea on dry ground. They had conquered their enemies through the power of prayer. They had eaten manna in the wilderness and had drunk water from the rock. They had seen God's glory on the mountain in fire and smoke. The Israelites had seen it all. They had seen the signs; they had witnessed the wonders.

Yet in a matter of weeks they forgot everything that God had ever done for them and started worshiping a cow that couldn't even moo! Then, in an appalling act of revisionist history, they gave the cow credit for what God had done. They said, "These are your gods, O Israel, who brought you up out of the land of Egypt!" (32:4). Their spiritual amnesia astonished the psalmist, who wrote:

> They made a calf in Horeb
> and worshiped a metal image.
> They exchanged the glory of God
> for the image of an ox that eats grass.
> They forgot God, their Savior,
> who had done great things in Egypt,
> wondrous works in the land of Ham,
> and awesome deeds by the Red Sea. (Psalm 106:19–22)

The Israelites forgot what God had done and returned to their old wicked ways.

How quickly we forget. We forget that God gave us life in this world. We forget that he is the source of all our gifts and the origin of all our blessings. We forget that he sent his own Son to die for our sins. We forget that he has put his Spirit into our hearts as a guarantee of eternal life. And when we forget, we turn back to the same old idolatries: money, sex, and power. But these deities will not do anything more for us than the golden calf did for Israel. They are gods that cannot save.

So how *can* we be saved? It is not enough to know what God says. The Israelites knew that, and it still didn't save them. They had the Law. They knew they weren't supposed to make idols or worship other gods. The problem was that they couldn't keep the Law. What they needed, therefore, was the gospel. They needed a Savior to do all the things for them that they couldn't do for themselves. They needed a Savior who would do what God said, who would trust God and his timing, and who would do things God's way rather than his own way, even when it wasn't popular.

They needed Jesus, which is also what we need, of course. Jesus is an obedient Savior; he was obedient unto death (Philippians 2:8). He is a trusting Savior; he trusted that at the right time God would raise him from the dead. He is a submissive Savior; when he knew that he would have to go to the cross, he followed his Father's will rather than his own. And he is a courageous Savior; he defied every temptation and endured the fatal suffering of the cross. Therefore, Jesus is able to save us, even from our own golden idolatries.

Anyone who trusts in Jesus will be saved. And by his grace we are able to avoid falling into sin—not perfectly, of course, but still able. As we grow in godliness, we become more and more able to resist temptation. By grace we are able to do what God says. By grace we are able to trust that God knows what he is doing. By grace we are able to do things his way rather than our way. By grace we have the courage to do what is right, even when everyone else is telling us to do something wrong. And by grace we never forget what Jesus has done to save us, dying for our sins and rising again so we can worship the one true God.

# 86

# Go Down, Moses

EXODUS 32:7–14

MOSES HAD BEEN UP ON THE MOUNTAIN for forty days and forty nights, meeting with Almighty God. He had heard God's law. He had written down God's word. He had seen the plans for God's holy tabernacle. Now it was time for the prophet to go back down. And after all that Moses had seen and heard, we can only imagine his unspeakable joy as he anticipated making his way down the mountain, hand-delivering the Ten Commandments and revealing God's will for Israel.

## Israel Commits Idolatry

Then God told Moses what was happening back at the camp. "Moses," he said, "we need to talk. I hate to tell you this, but while you've been gone, there have been some problems down there. You need to know what's going on." Then God broke the news that while the two of them had been drawing up the plans for a new sanctuary, the Israelites had decided to make some plans of their own. At that very moment, under the direction of their associate shepherd, they were offering ungodly worship to an unholy cow.

God saw how the people were sinning, as he always does. And as far as he was concerned, it was up to Moses to do something about it:

> And the LORD said to Moses, "Go down, for your people, whom you brought up out of the land of Egypt, have corrupted themselves. They have turned aside quickly out of the way that I commanded them. They have made for themselves a golden calf and have worshiped it and sacrificed to it and said, 'These are your gods, O Israel, who brought you up out of the land of Egypt!'" (32:7, 8)

This was a real crisis. Something had gone wrong, badly wrong. Moses had only been gone for a few weeks, and already the people had turned away from

God. The Lord had brought them out of Egypt to worship him, but they had decided to go back to the Pharaohs and their user-friendly gods.

As God explained to Moses what had happened, he laid the blame squarely at Israel's feet. They were the ones who had "corrupted themselves" (v. 7), a word indicating "depraved moral conduct" that makes people "offensive in the sight of God."[1] Their corruption came in several different forms. As a nation, they had "turned aside" from God's law. They had done what God told them not to do and failed to do what he had told them to do, choosing instead to go their own way. They had broken both of God's first two commandments: They worshiped other gods, and they tried to worship the true God with a false image. Their worship was not God ordained but man originated.

None of this should surprise anyone who knows anything about the Israelites. It certainly didn't surprise God, and apparently it didn't surprise Moses either. What *is* surprising is how rapidly Israel fell into sin. God said, "They have turned aside quickly" (v. 8). This shows how different God's sense of timing is from our own. The Israelites couldn't believe how long it was taking Moses to come back down the mountain. But God couldn't believe how quickly the Israelites had fallen into sin. As far as he was concerned, they had sinned early and often.

If any of this sounds familiar, it is because we are tempted to commit the same kinds of sins. We are not fully satisfied with God. We don't trust him to work things out his own way in his own time. So we turn away from his law, coming up with our own strategies for making life work on our terms. We bow to the false gods of success and control, beauty and pleasure. We pay more attention to our occupations and entertainments than we do to serving the only true God.

We also worship the true God falsely. We may not be tempted to make a golden calf, but we *are* tempted to turn the God who is there into the kind of God we would like him to be. We want God to teach our minds but not to transform our hearts. We want him to give us a lift when we worship him on Sunday, but we don't want him to govern all our words and actions the rest of the week. We want him to change others, but we don't want him to change us. We want his love without his holiness and his mercy without his justice.

## God Threatens Judgment

These sins all deserve to be punished, which is exactly what God threatened to do to Israel. He said he was going to punish them for their sins: "'I have seen this people, and behold, it is a stiff-necked people. Now therefore let me alone, that my wrath may burn hot against them and I may consume them, in order that I may make a great nation of you'" (32:9, 10).

"This people," God calls the Israelites, and we are reminded of something they said back in verse 1: "This Moses." Now God dismisses the Israelites with equal disdain, and with good reason. The phrase "stiff-necked" describes a beast of burden that is too stubborn to wear its master's yoke or do what its master says. This is the first time the phrase is used in Exodus, but it becomes one of the Bible's standard ways of referring to the Israelites. What kind of people were they? A stiff-necked people who refused to lower their heads and wear the yoke of obedience to God.

This is a dangerous position for anyone to be in. Stiff-necked people always think they're right and never admit they're wrong. They refuse to listen to good spiritual counsel. They say, "I'm sorry; that's just the way I am," and then they expect everyone else to deal with it. They ask for advice, but they don't follow it. They go ahead and do what they were planning to do anyway. And when they get into trouble, they are unwilling to be corrected. "Yes," they say, "but my situation is different," and then they offer some kind of excuse. When they go through suffering, they complain about it, but they never seem to learn anything from it. They never change. They never grow. And the saddest thing of all is that they don't even know it. Since they never bow in true submission to God, they don't realize how stiff-necked they are.

So don't be stiff-necked! Assume that you might be wrong; and when you are wrong, admit it. If you ask for counsel from someone in spiritual authority, try to follow it. Listen when people correct you, especially if what they're saying makes you angry. This is almost always a sign that there's some truth to what they're saying. Learn from God through suffering. Pursue spiritual transformation by spending time in prayer and the Word. Wear the yoke of Christ with glad submission.

Otherwise God will treat you the way he treated the Israelites. Sometimes God shows stiff-necked people mercy. He uses trials to break us the way a farmer breaks an ox. But this is much more than we deserve. What we deserve is to be punished for our sins, which is what God threatened to do to Israel. He threatened to destroy them. He had given them every chance to obey, but now that they had decided to worship other gods, he had the right to wipe them off the face of the earth.

At this point the whole glorious plan of the exodus seems to be in jeopardy. The Israelites were alienated from God by their sin. Since the beginning of the book, God has referred to them as his people: "I have surely seen the affliction of my people" (3:7); "bring my people, the children of Israel, out of Egypt" (3:10); "let my people go" (5:1). But here he turns the nation over to Moses by switching to the second person possessive. "They are not my people," God says to Moses in essence, "they're *your* people—the people *you* brought up out of Egypt. I don't want them; *you* take them!"

The Israelites were no longer worthy to be called the people of God, but only to be disowned and destroyed. The word used here for destruction (*kalah*) is absolute. God threatened to execute the ultimate sentence, making an end to

Israel once and for all. This would have been perfectly just because sin demands judgment. From the time of Adam, the Bible everywhere insists that "the wages of sin is death" (Romans 6:23). This threat hangs over every stiff-necked person who insists on worshiping other gods. The Bible says, "But because of your hard and impenitent heart you are storing up wrath for yourself on the day of wrath when God's righteous judgment will be revealed" (Romans 2:5).

## God Hints at Grace

Yet even in the threat of judgment, there were signs that God would show grace. It's important to see this because this is one of the passages people use to argue that sometimes God changes his mind. This is one of the arguments of open theism—the dangerous new doctrine that God does not know the future but is working things out as he goes along. On the surface this may seem like a valid way of looking at Exodus 32: First God decided to destroy the Israelites; then he decided not to. Yet we know that the Bible says, "The Glory of Israel will not lie or have regret, for he is not a man, that he should have regret" (1 Samuel 15:29). And when we study Exodus 32 more carefully, we discover that God's will is as settled here as it is anywhere else in Scripture.[2]

It was never God's purpose to destroy the Israelites, but only to save them. Even as he threatened wrath, there were hints that he would show mercy. First there was the simple fact that God commanded Moses to go down. If he really intended to destroy the Israelites, then why send Moses down at all? The answer is that he was planning to save them through the intercession of their mediator. The Israelites had not sinned themselves outside the grace of God. He was sending Moses to pray for their forgiveness.

Then there is the fact that God refers to the Israelites as the people of Moses: "Go down, for your people, whom you brought up out of the land of Egypt . . ." (32:7). By talking this way, God was showing that the people were alienated from him by their sin. If they were going to make a cow and say, "These are your gods, O Israel" (32:4b), then God was going to say to Moses, "These are your people." But he was not trying to shift the blame. Rather, he was helping Moses identify with the Israelites. There is a sense in which they *were* his people. Moses was their spiritual representative before God. So if anyone was going to do anything to help them, it would have to be him. Catch the irony here: Although the people had tried to disown Moses, he was the only one who could save them!

But the biggest hint of God's ultimately gracious purpose for Israel comes in verse 10, where he attaches a condition to his threat of judgment: "Now therefore let me alone, that my wrath may burn hot against them and I may consume them." This does not mean that God can't control his temper. God's wrath is always a pure and just act of his holy will. But here he is speaking about his anger in human terms—not to lower himself to our level, but to help us understand how his justice and mercy interact in our salvation.

The important phrase is "let me alone," which makes it sound as if God is a sulky child. But this is misleading. God is really asking for permission. As the mediator, Moses stands between God and his people, and God will not proceed to punish Israel unless his prophet "allows" him to do it. Under what circumstances would God destroy Israel and start over with Moses? Only if the mediator were to stop praying for his people.

But why would God even say this unless he wanted Moses to keep praying? God did not want to be left alone at all. He was pushing Moses to get involved, to intercede for his people. As Brevard Childs explains it, "God vows the severest punishment imaginable, but then suddenly he conditions it, as it were, on Moses' agreement. 'Let me alone that I may consume them.' The effect is that God himself leaves the door open for intercession. He allows himself to be persuaded. That is what a mediator is for!"[3] This interpretation goes back at least as far as Jerome, who wrote, "Consider the compassionate kindness of God. When he says, 'Let me alone,' he shows that if Moses will continue to importune him, he will not strike. . . . In other words, what does he say? Do not cease your persistent entreaty, and I shall not strike."[4]

By way of comparison, consider the way a frustrated parent might try to get a child to stop leaving belongings all over the house. "Go ahead and leave your toys on the floor," the parent might say. "It's okay—I'll clean them up for you . . . as soon as I get the trash can." Is the parent serious? Will the toys be thrown away? Well, no child is going to wait to find out, which is exactly the point! The parent is trying to get the child to take responsibility for the toys—as it were, to save them. God did the same thing with his prophet. He used the threat of judgment to rouse Moses to make intercession.

## Moses Prays

What God said to Moses was an invitation to intercede, but it was more than an invitation—it was also an examination. God was testing Moses, because in addition to saying that he would destroy everyone back at the camp, God promised to make Moses into a great nation. The prophet would become the new patriarch, a second Abraham, the father of many nations. From then on, the people of God would be known as "the Mosesites" or "the children of Moses."

It was a tempting offer, and thus a real test of the prophet's character. After all, the Israelites deserved to be punished anyway. And who better to become the father of a new nation than Moses, the man who met with God on the mountain? So this was the test: To save Israel, Moses had to turn down the opportunity to make a name for himself. Would he pray for his people, or would he pursue his own ambitions?

Moses passed the test. The Bible doesn't say how tempted he was, or even if he was tempted at all. In fact, it seems like he ignored God's offer altogether. Without a moment's hesitation, Moses began pleading for God to save his people. When "faced with a dictator's dream," writes Everett Fox, "the cloning of an entire nation from himself—he opts for staunchly defending the very people who have already caused him grief through their rebelling, and who will continually do so in the ensuing wanderings."[5] Given the choice between serving himself and saving others, he put others first. This is the mark of a true man of God: He chooses God's greater glory over his own personal good.

The Scripture says that Moses "implored the LORD his God" (32:11a). Instead of leaving God alone, he begged for mercy. This is how Moses prayed:

> O LORD, why does your wrath burn hot against your people, whom you have brought out of the land of Egypt with great power and with a mighty hand? Why should the Egyptians say, "With evil intent did he bring them out, to kill them in the mountains and to consume them from the face of the earth"? Turn from your burning anger and relent from this disaster against your people. Remember Abraham, Isaac, and Israel, your servants, to whom you swore by your own self, and said to them, "I will multiply your offspring as the stars of heaven, and all this land that I have promised I will give to your offspring, and they shall inherit it forever." (vv. 11b–13)

Even after all their ungodliness and all the grief they had caused him, Moses still loved the people of God. He was their mediator, the one who stood in the gap for them before God. And they were his people, the nation he was called to serve. So as long as there was still a chance for God to show mercy, Moses had to take it.

And God *did* show mercy. According to the book of Deuteronomy, Moses prayed for forty days and forty nights (9:25). When he was finished, "the LORD relented from the disaster that he had spoken of bringing on his people" (32:14). Does this mean that God changed his mind? Some people think so. In the words of one scholar, "It certainly seems that Moses, through argument and pleading, has been able to get God to alter his plans. To put it in plain English, Moses gets God to change his mind. There is really no other way to read this, and we should not try to avoid it."[6]

However, there *is* another way to read this, as we have seen. When the Bible says, "the LORD relented," this does not imply that God changed his mind (any more than it implies that God sinned when it speaks of him "repenting"). Furthermore, God gives clear indications that he was planning to show mercy all along. This is why he got Moses involved in the first place. It was so his people could be forgiven. In the words of the psalmist: "Therefore he said he would destroy them—had not Moses, *his chosen one*, stood in the breach before him, to turn away his wrath from destroying them" (Psalm 106:23). So Moses was not changing God's plans; he was carrying them out![7]

Furthermore, "The Hebrew verb used in our verse (*nacham*, usually translated as 'relent' or 'repent') does not always mean to change one's mind, but can also mean 'to be moved to pity/to have compassion for others.'"[8] This is precisely what God had for Israel: compassion for them in their sinful rebellion. "It is not," writes John Mackay, "that God is being forced to adopt a new course of conduct because of some flawed decision of the past or because of some unforeseen circumstance having arisen. It was the Lord himself who opened up the way for the threat against his people to be removed by the appropriate action of the covenant mediator."[9]

## Moses Makes His Case

So how did Moses do it? How did he persuade God to restrain his wrath? Well, notice what Moses did *not* do. He did not try to minimize Israel's sin. He did not offer any excuses. He did not try to defend his people on the basis of their own merits. He did not argue that God's anger wasn't fair. On the contrary, he assumed that the Israelites were guilty, even before he went down to see for himself. And based on that assumption, he knew that God had every right to wipe them out.

This makes Moses' prayer very different from the one that Abraham offered for Sodom and Gomorrah.[10] Abraham's prayer was based on the premise that at least some of the people were righteous. His opening bid was to ask God if he would spare the city for the sake of fifty righteous people. God said he would, and then the negotiations began in earnest, with Abraham getting God to keep lowering the price. By the time he was done, Abraham had worked God all the way down to ten. But he didn't go low enough! God still destroyed the city because there weren't even ten righteous people living there.

Moses didn't try to negotiate with God at all. He started with the assumption that no one was righteous, not even one. He was not on the mountain to intercede for the innocent but for the guilty. Moses was a new kind of mediator, a man who asked God to save the ungodly. Obviously, if he was going to persuade God that this was the right thing to do, he needed to come up with some very persuasive arguments. The people were guilty; why should God save them? Moses made his case by presenting no less than five compelling reasons for God to show mercy—reasons based on God's very character.

First, he appealed to God's *fatherly affection*. God had tried to tell Moses that the Israelites were his (Moses') people, but Moses would have none of it. "O Lord," he said, "why does your wrath burn hot against your people?" (32:11). God said, "I don't want them; you take them." But Moses said, "Oh, no, you don't! They're not my people; they're *your* people. They've always been yours." This was true. God had been saying it since the beginning of Exodus. The reason he had the right to bring them out of Egypt was because they were his people. As he said to Pharaoh, "Israel is my firstborn son" (4:22). This Father-son relationship went back before Moses, even before Israel (Jacob) himself. In his electing grace, God chose his people before the world began. They were his from all eternity.

By reminding God that the Israelites belonged to him by election and redemption, Moses was appealing to God's fatherly affection. They were his children, and nothing they could do would ever change that. It is impossible for any true child of God to sin his or her way out of the Father's love. This promise is for us as much as it was for the Israelites. Everyone who comes to God through faith in his Son will be his child forever. We were chosen in Christ before the creation of the world (see Ephesians 1:4). Even if we sin as badly as the Israelites (or worse!), we are still God's people through faith in Jesus Christ. Jesus said, "No one is able to snatch them out of the Father's hand" (John 10:29b).

Second, Moses appealed to God's *past investment*. He said, "O Lord, why does your wrath burn hot against your people, whom you have brought out of the land of Egypt with great power and with a mighty hand?" (32:11). Moses was reminding God what he had already done for Israel. He had performed miracles, signs, and wonders. He had worked mighty deeds of salvation. He had rescued his people from bondage. So why stop now? It would be such a waste! God was much too deeply involved in the exodus to quit now. How could he destroy the very people he had taken so much trouble to save?[11]

When Moses said this, he was taking the words right out of God's mouth. God often reminded the Israelites what he had done to save them. "I am the Lord your God," he said, "who brought you out of the land of Egypt" (20:2). Now Moses was reminding God of the very thing that God was always reminding the Israelites: He had saved them out of Egypt. Now God needed to make sure that he protected his investment. He couldn't just write the Israelites off; he had to save them to the very end.

As Christians, we are in the same situation. God has gone to a great deal of trouble to bring us to the place we are right now in our pilgrimage. He sent someone to give us the gospel. He helped us see how sinful we really are. He enabled us to believe in Jesus Christ as Savior and Lord. Then he sent his Holy Spirit to change our lives from the inside out. Everything that God has done for us in the past gives us hope that he will bring us all the way to glory, because God always finishes what he starts. As Paul wrote to the Philippians, "He who began a good work in you will bring it to completion at the day of Jesus Christ" (Philippians 1:6). Therefore, if God has done any saving work in our lives—enabling us to repent of our sins, believe in Christ, and live for him—then we may be sure that he will see us through.

In the third place, Moses appealed to God on the basis of his *public reputation*. He asked God to save his people not simply for their sake, but for the sake of his own good name. Remember, this was the reason God saved them in the first place. It was so the Egyptians would see his glory (7:5). So now how would it look if God decided to destroy his people? Moses said, "Why should the Egyptians say, 'With evil intent did he bring them out, to kill them in the mountains and to consume them from the face of the earth'?" (2:12a). God's credibility was on the line. If he destroyed the Israelites now, it would cast doubt on his motives. The Egyptians would misinterpret the whole situation. They would say that God hated his people, that he had brought them out of Egypt only to kill them. If God abandoned them now, his reputation would suffer irreparable damage.

Thus it was out of zeal for God's glory that Moses begged God not to destroy his people. He cared about God's reputation. He wanted to see God exalted among the nations. This gave the strongest possible support to his prayer. Moses was appealing to God's own highest goal, which is to glorify himself. We have the same motivation when we pray for the salvation of family and friends and when we pray for the global work of the gospel through missions. We are asking God to enhance his international reputation, to bring glory to himself by saving sinners.

Fourth, Moses appealed to God on the basis of his *merciful compassion*. This was how his prayer began, with seeking God's favor (32:11), asking God to show unmerited grace to sinners. The appeal for mercy became even more explicit at the end of verse 12, where Moses asked God to turn away from his wrath. There was nothing wrong with God's wrath. It was holy, just, and pure, as it always is. And it was an appropriate response to this situation. The Israelites deserved to be punished for their sins, and there was nothing Moses could say to the contrary.

There was one thing Moses could do, however, and that was to ask God to turn aside his wrath—in a word, to show mercy. Mercy is the most that sinners can hope for. Since it is unmerited favor, it is never something we have a right to demand. God is never obligated to show mercy. However, mercy is one of his essential attributes. He is a God of "mercy" and "steadfast love" (Psalm 25:6), "a gracious and merciful God" (Nehemiah 9:31). Therefore, when we cry out to him for mercy, our prayer strikes a responsive chord in his compassionate heart. When we discover that we are lost in our sins, the thing to do is cry out for mercy the way Moses cried out for Israel.

Moses saved his best argument for last. His final appeal was based on God's *everlasting covenant*: "Remember Abraham, Isaac, and Israel, your servants, to whom you swore by your own self, and said to them, 'I will multiply your offspring as the stars of heaven, and all this land that I have promised I will give to your offspring, and they shall inherit it forever'" (32:13). This time Moses actually quoted God, appealing to him on the basis of his own unbreakable promise. Now *that's* a good argument!

Not that there was anything special about Abraham, Isaac, and Israel. They were ordinary men—sinners like everyone else. But they did have all the promises of God. God had promised to make Abraham a great nation. He had promised him land and seed: a people and a place. He had repeated these promises to Isaac and Jacob. Furthermore, he had sworn to keep them by his very own self, as Moses pointed out. God was bound by the promise of his covenant, and it was utterly impossible for him to go back on his word. He would have to un-God himself to do it. So God *had* to save his people. He promised!

When we approach God on the basis of his covenant, we have the ultimate security. God has promised to save everyone who comes to him through faith in Jesus Christ. We have been saved by the blood of the everlasting covenant (Hebrews 13:20)—the blood that Jesus shed on the cross. And God cannot break his covenant. What a wonderful encouragement this is to anyone who has trouble believing that he or she can still be forgiven. God has promised to save us not just now, but forever. Our salvation is not made secure by our own obedience, which is bound to fail, but by the unbreakable promise of God. As the Scripture says, "If we are faithless, he remains faithful—for he cannot deny himself" (2 Timothy 2:13).

## Go Down, Jesus

When Moses finished interceding for Israel, "the LORD relented from the disaster that he had spoken of bringing on his people" (32:14). What else could he do? Moses was appealing to him on the basis of his love, his plan, his glory, his mercy, and his faithfulness. And since this appeal was based on God's own character, Moses was *not* trying to talk God into doing something he didn't want to do. On the contrary, he was telling God exactly what he wanted to hear. And in the end, God did what he had intended to do from the beginning. He answered the prayer of the mediator whom he had appointed by saving the people he had chosen from all eternity.

This is really the story of our own salvation. God is up on his holy mountain; we are down on earth. And like the Israelites, we are floundering in the folly of our rebellion against God. Our idolatry leads to immorality. What we need is someone like Moses. We need someone to come down and intercede for us—someone who can turn away God's wrath.

The message of the gospel is that God has given us a mediator. When he saw our sin, he wanted to save us, so he sent his Son to intercede for our salvation. As the Scripture says, "For God so loved the world, that he gave his only Son, that whoever believes in him should not perish but have eternal life" (John 3:16). It is as if God said, "Go down, Jesus, go down. Go down because your people—the ones I gave you from all eternity—have become corrupt. They are living in sin. They have turned away from my law to worship other gods. And unless you intercede for them, they will surely be destroyed by my wrath."

And Jesus did come down. He said, "Save them, Father. Save my people [cf. John 17:2], because they are not just my people—they are also your people [cf. John 17:9], the ones you love with a Father's heart. Save them because I died on the cross for their sins, and we should not waste my precious divine blood. Save them because it will bring glory to your name [cf. John 17:1]. Save them because you delight to show mercy. Save them because you promised to save them in the covenant we made before the world began." This is the way that Jesus prays for us. The Bible says, "Christ Jesus is the one who died—more than that, who was raised—who is at the right hand of God, who indeed is interceding for us" (Romans 8:34). Jesus does not plead for us on the basis of our righteousness, but on the merits of his own saving work. For the Bible also says that if we sin, "we have an advocate with the Father, Jesus Christ the righteous. He is the propitiation for our sins" (1 John 2:1b, 2a).

As followers of Jesus Christ, now we are called to intercede for others, to get down on our knees and pray for sinners. We intercede for people who don't know Jesus and for people who do know Jesus but have fallen into sin. And when we pray, we pray like Moses. We appeal to God's fatherly affection, to his love for those who have not yet come into the embrace of his family. We appeal to God on the basis of his redemptive investment. When we see someone caught in sin, we ask God not to waste the work he has already done in their lives but to rescue them. We appeal to God's public reputation. We ask God to save people and keep on saving them so that others will see his glory as their lives are transformed. We appeal to his merciful compassion, to the undeserved favor he shows to sinners. And we appeal to God on the basis of his covenant—his eternal promise to save sinners in Christ. This is our calling as Christians: to pray for sinners the way that Moses prayed for Israel, and the way that Jesus prays for us.

# 87

# Oh, Brother!

## EXODUS 32:15–24

WHEN I WAS A CHILD, someone gave me a record album of Bible sounds. The album contained a series of audio riddles. As we listened, we would hear a sequence of sound effects, and then we would try to figure out which Bible story they told. For example, we would hear the sound of a crackling fire, followed by a rooster crowing three times, and then the sound of a man sobbing. That was an easy one: It was Peter's denial of Christ. Most of the riddles were more difficult, but they opened up a whole new way of listening to the Bible.

Consider some of the great sounds in Scripture. Think of the noise that Gideon and his soldiers made when they attacked the Midianites: blaring trumpets, smashing pots, and battle cries (Judges 7:17–20). Or think of the sound that David's soldiers heard when they attacked the Philistines, the sound of God's army marching in the treetops (2 Samuel 5:24). Then there were the sounds that Elijah heard on God's mountain: wind, earthquake, fire, and the still small voice (1 Kings 19:11, 12). There were all kinds of sounds in the Gospels too: animals lowing in the stable, water splashing into wine jars, wind storming on the lake, silver clinking in a bag, and bloody cries of anguish from the cross. But at the end of days we will hear the happiest sounds ever: the trumpet of God, the last shout of victory, and the chorus of Heaven.

### Moses Goes Down

In Exodus 32 we hear one of the strangest sounds in the Bible. Moses and Joshua heard it as they went back down the mountain. It was such a strange sound that at first Joshua wasn't even sure what it was.

Moses had been meeting with God up on Mount Sinai. The last thing God told him was to go down because the Israelites were worshiping a golden calf. The prophet did as he was told: "Moses turned and went down from the mountain with the two tablets of the testimony in his hand, tablets that were written on both sides; on the front and on the back they were written. The tablets were the work of God, and the writing was the writing of God, engraved on the tablets" (32:15, 16).

These tablets must not have been very large, because they were small enough for Moses to carry. He was bringing them down to deposit in the ark of the covenant. Both tablets were double sided. They were inscribed, front and back, with the words of the Ten Commandments.

The Bible emphasizes that these commandments came from Almighty God. Both the tablets themselves and the writing on them were his handiwork. So what Moses brought down from the mountain was not his own law, but God's law. Moses was not the lawgiver—God was. This is crucial to our whole understanding of the Bible. The Law was never man's word about God, but God's Word to man. This is why it is still binding today. When the church teaches that it is wrong to lie, steal, murder, or have sex outside of marriage, it is not because Christians have a bunch of hang-ups. Rather, these are divine commands that come with the full weight of God's authority.

Knowing that the Law comes from God also helps us understand Exodus 32. The tablets Moses held in his hands included the first two commandments: "You shall have no other gods before me," and "You shall not make for yourself a carved image." In other words, they were inscribed with the very laws that the Israelites were busy breaking. So when Moses came down to confront them, it wasn't just Moses they had to deal with. They had to deal with the God who laid down the law.

On his way down, Moses rejoined Joshua, who had gone halfway up the mountain and was waiting for the prophet's return (cf. 24:13). When the two men got to within earshot of base camp, they heard a sound that Joshua couldn't quite make out. The Israelites were making some kind of noise. "When Joshua heard the noise of the people as they shouted, he said to Moses, 'There is a noise of war in the camp'" (32:17). Spoken like a true general. Joshua was a military man, so naturally he thought that what he heard might have something to do with warfare.

Moses knew that Joshua didn't have it quite right. As they stood there—stopping to listen—what the prophet heard called to mind a verse of poetry, either one he made up on the spot or one that came from some ancient poem: "It is not the sound of shouting for victory, or the sound of the cry of defeat, but the sound of singing that I hear" (v. 18). Moses and Joshua were not hearing shouts of victory after all, or even cries of defeat and dismay. In the words of John Durham, it was neither "the exultant victory-cry of triumph or the keening lamentation of defeat."[1] The sound they heard had nothing to do with warfare at all. It was something else, something different. It was the sound of . . . singing!

This was not a good sign. Even before the two men saw what was happening in the camp, their ears told them that something was amiss. Their very confusion indicated that something was wrong. Not that there was anything wrong with singing. Back at the Red Sea, Moses himself had led the chorus. But that was different, because back then Moses and the Israelites were praising the right God. They sang:

> I will sing to the LORD, for he has triumphed gloriously;
> the horse and his rider he has thrown into the sea. (15:1)

This time the Israelites were singing to an image of a grass-eating, milk-producing, moo-sounding cow. Someone would almost have to be drunk to worship such a deity, and the Israelites probably were. The Scripture says, "The people sat down to eat and drink and rose up to play" (32:6). It was a raucous and indecent celebration, bordering on the obscene. The Israelite camp had become a place of drunken carousing, pagan reveling, and bawdy singing. What Moses and Joshua heard was the sound of people partying.

What a picture this is of the human condition. God has written out his law so we can know how he wants us to live. He has sent a Savior to come down and reveal his will. And what have we been busy doing? We have been breaking his law left and right, making idols, worshiping our own gods, throwing wild parties, and basically living any way we please. Have you been walking with God, or have you been doing your own thing and hoping that God wouldn't notice?

## The End of Idolatry

Sooner or later God will confront our sin, just as Moses confronted the Israelites. Out of his great mercy, and on the basis of his covenant, God had already decided not to destroy the Israelites. However, their sin still needed to be dealt with in a godly way, and this meant that they were going to have to face its consequences. This is always necessary. Forgiveness removes the guilt of sin but not its consequences. Nor should it. God uses the consequences of our sin in a sanctifying way, teaching us never to do the same thing again.

Some Christians believe in immediate sanctification. They assume that all they need to do is confess their sins and then everything can return to normal. They can pick up their marriage right where it left off or go back to their ministry. It is true, of course, that as soon as we confess our sins we are fully and freely forgiven. But this does not mean that we are immune from the consequences of our sin. Sin does real damage, and often we bear its scars long after the guilt of our sin has been taken away. Sin also requires discipline, and the more serious the sin, the more likely it is that God will need to correct us. The ongoing process of sanctification needs to take place. Even after sin is forgiven, it has to be dealt with in a godly way that leads to real progress in godliness.

Dealing with sin effectively takes the kind of godly leadership that Moses gave to Israel. As soon as he saw what the people were doing, he took action: "And as soon as he came near the camp and saw the calf and the dancing, Moses' anger burned hot, and he threw the tablets out of his hands and broke them at the foot of the mountain. He took the calf that they had made and burned it with fire and ground it to powder and scattered it on the water and made the people of Israel drink it" (32:19, 20).

It was one thing to be told what the Israelites were doing and to hear their laughter echo up the mountain, but it was another thing for Moses to see it with his own eyes. It was much worse than he had imagined. Nothing he had heard could possibly have prepared him for what he saw. There was the calf—a golden abomination. There were the people dancing around it, giddy with laughter. The word "dancing" occurs in the plural, which suggests that it was wild and out of control. Not that there is anything wrong with dancing. Miriam and her girls danced by the sea (15:20). It all depends who the dancing is for. In this case, the Israelites were not dancing for the glory of God but for their own carnal pleasure.

When Moses saw everything that was going on at the camp, he was so angry that he smashed the Ten Commandments into a thousand pieces, ground the golden calf into dust, mixed it with water, and made the people drink it. Was this the right thing to do, or was Moses out of control too? Were his actions justified, or did he just lose his temper?

There are at least two indications that Moses' anger was righteous.[2] One is the simple fact that God did not rebuke him for his rage. On another occasion God *did* rebuke Moses. It was in Kadesh, where the Israelites ran out of water (see Numbers 20:1–13). As usual, when the people didn't have what they needed, they blamed Moses. On that occasion the prophet was so fed up with their grumbling and complaining that he lashed out. He spoke angry words and struck a rock in fury. But Moses was angry for himself, not for God, so God punished him for his sin. He did not allow Moses to enter the promised land. But God did not punish him for the way he dealt with the golden calf. This suggests that what he did was right.

This is confirmed in verse 19, where the Bible says that "Moses' anger burned hot." This is the same language that God used back in verse 10 when he threatened to destroy the Israelites. The Hebrew draws a linguistic connection between God and Moses. They both responded to Israel's sin with the same kind of anger. So this was one of those rare situations when someone's anger was actually righteous.

Most of our anger is unrighteous. Like Moses at Kadesh, we get more and more frustrated with something or someone, until finally the anger raging inside us strikes out. Such anger does not come from a zeal for God and his glory; it's all about us and what we're not getting. This is why it is never wise to make a decision, take action, or exercise discipline when we first get angry. Even if some of our indignation is righteous, it is usually mixed up with emotions that are selfish and sinful. If so, then our decisions will be rash, our actions will be impulsive, and our discipline will only vent our anger without leading to holiness. We should wait until we are thinking more clearly and have repented of whatever was sinful about our anger. Then we can do what is right. As the Scripture says, "Be angry and do not sin" (Ephesians 4:26a). One mark of truly righteous indignation is that it does not overrun our reason but stays within the boundaries of obedience to God.

In his anger Moses did not sin, but he did take decisive action. The first thing he did was to dash the tablets to the ground. If he had done this in a fit of rage, it would have been a sin. But Moses broke the tablets as a prophetic act. The Old Testament prophets often did things in public that symbolized Israel's relationship to God. When Moses later recounted this incident he said: "I took hold of the two tablets and threw them out of my two hands and broke them before your eyes" (Deuteronomy 9:17). There at the foot of the mountain—at the very place where the Israelites had sworn to do everything God said (24:3–7)—the prophet demonstrated that they had broken the Law almost as soon as it was given. It was a way of saying that if the Israelites were not prepared to obey the law, they didn't even deserve to have it![3]

By breaking the tablets, Moses showed that the Israelites had broken the whole Law. The Bible says that "whoever keeps the whole law but fails in one point has become accountable for all of it" (James 2:10). Actually, the Israelites stumbled at *more* than one point. But the principle still applies: by worshiping the golden calf, they had broken the whole Law of God.

The next thing Moses did was to destroy the golden calf. He burned it, pulverized it, liquefied it, and then made the people drink it. It is not altogether clear why he made them do this.[4] It may have been another symbolic act. Augustine thought it showed how the people had to swallow their ungodliness.[5] Whatever it meant, Moses gave the Israelites gold water, making them taste the bitterness of their idolatry.

The important thing was to get rid of the idol once and for all. To that end, Moses utterly and completely destroyed the golden calf. Idols are not to be tolerated—they are to be annihilated. We need to do this with our own idolatries. And we are all idolaters. In his commentary on these verses, A. W. Pink defines an idol as

> anything which displaces God in my heart. It may be something which is quite harmless in itself, yet if it absorbs me, if it be given the first place in my affections and thoughts, it becomes an "idol." It may be my business, a loved one, or my service for Christ. Any one or any thing which comes into competition with the Lord's ruling me in a practical way, is an "idol."[6]

Is there anything that displaces God in our hearts? Is there anything that competes with him for our attention? What do we desire? What do we praise? What do we think about? What do we pursue? These are the things that replace God in our hearts, and the only safe way to deal with them is to get rid of them altogether.

All too often Christians try to deal with their idolatries by putting them in the closet rather than taking them out with the trash. We pretend that we have cleaned house, spiritually speaking. But in fact sin is still lurking in the cupboard, ready to come out the next time we are tempted to open the door. The lustful man goes back to look at his pornography; the gossip starts telling rumors again; the greedy man cheats a little on another deal; the unhappy woman goes on another binge of food or alcohol or shopping. Moses never gave the Israelites a chance to go back to the golden calf. In the same way, we need to keep grinding our idols down until they turn to dust. Don't keep dabbling with idols; destroy them!

### Excuses, Excuses

Sooner or later we all have to take responsibility for what we have done. When it came to Israel and the golden calf, there was one man who had to take more responsibility than anyone else. It was Aaron, the brother of Moses, whom God had left in charge while Moses was absent (see 24:14). At some point while he was dealing with Israel's sin, Moses asked his brother to account for his actions. "And Moses said to Aaron, 'What did this people do to you that you have brought such a great sin upon them?'" (32:21).

Here Moses seems almost sympathetic. He knew what the Israelites were like, so he had some idea what Aaron was up against. But how did they get him to do something so wicked? Moses assumed that they must have done something awful to threaten him. However, Moses also held Aaron fully responsible for what he had done. He said, "What did this people do to you that *you* have brought such a great sin upon them?" Calling the golden calf "a great sin," Moses put the blame right where it belonged. No matter what the people had done, Aaron had no excuse. He had to take total responsibility for what happened. As Israel's spiritual leader, he was the one who had led the people into sin.

This shows what responsibility spiritual leaders have before God to keep their people away from sin. It also shows what good pastoral care requires. Moses was sensitive to the temptation Aaron faced; he acknowledged the pressure the man was under. However, he also wanted his brother to take full responsibility for what he had done. This is the right balance. When dealing with sin, spiritual leaders should have compassion for those who have fallen, while at the same time not leaving any room for making excuses.

At this point Aaron should have made a full confession. When his brother came to confront him, he should have said, "It doesn't matter what they did to me, Moses. I was the one who led them into sin. I was their spiritual leader, so it was up to me to help them worship the one true God. God, forgive me—the golden calf was all my fault."

Unfortunately, this is not what Aaron said. Far from it. Instead he said the kinds of things that people usually say when they are confronted with their sin:

> And Aaron said, "Let not the anger of my lord burn hot. You know the people, that they are set on evil. For they said to me, 'Make us gods who shall go before us. As for this Moses, the man who brought us up out of the land of Egypt, we do not know what has become of him.' So I said to them, 'Let any who have gold take it off.' So they gave it to me, and I threw it into the fire, and out came this calf." (32:22–24)

Aaron's halfhearted repentance teaches us how *not* to confess our sins. There were at least three problems with his confession. The first was telling his accuser to back off. Moses was there for Aaron's benefit. He was confronting him with his sin so he could receive forgiveness. But Aaron turned against Moses. He said, "Relax, little brother. Don't get so upset. It's not that big a deal." By telling his brother not to get angry, Aaron made it sound like Moses was the one who had the problem. He was trying to appease Moses without addressing the real issue, which was the wrath of God against his sin.

Sadly, this is often what happens when people are confronted with their sin: They turn against whoever confronts them. "What's your problem?" they say. "Why are you making such a big deal about this?" They turn confronting their sin into a personal issue. Sometimes they accuse their accusers, complaining about the way they were confronted. Sometimes they try to placate their accusers without making a full confession of their sin. Their goal is to get people to leave them alone rather than to deal honestly with their sin before God. This is what Aaron did. Instead of saying, "Brother, I have sinned against God," he said, "Now don't get angry."

The second problem was that Aaron tried to blame others for what he had done. "Well, Moses," he said, "you know how the people are. I realize you've been gone a long time, so in case you forgot, they sin a lot! And by the way, may I point out that you being gone for so long didn't help matters very much either." Then Aaron proceeded to explain how, when Moses failed to return, the Israelites demanded a new deity. Aaron tried to exonerate himself by saying, "The people made me do it!"

Again, this is what people usually do when they are confronted with their sin. First they tell people to back off. Then they shift the blame. And of course there is always somebody to blame: "My parents didn't love me." "My husband didn't care for me." "My wife wasn't meeting my sexual needs." "My elders didn't handle the situation right." "My boss didn't treat me fairly." "He was yelling at me!" "She pushed me!" "They went behind my back." "Everyone was doing it!" Excuses, excuses.

Usually there is some truth to all our excuses. Of course there is! People sin all the time, often in ways that tempt us to sin. This is exactly what happened to Aaron; so what he said was true, as far as it went. And Moses knew it was true. No one knew the people better than he did. However, what the people did was irrelevant to the issue at hand, which was Aaron's own personal sin. No matter how much pressure he was under, he could have resisted. God would have helped him do what was right. So Aaron had to take the blame, and so must we all. No matter what other people have done to us, we may never use that as an excuse for what we have done to them. When it comes to our sin—even if we are provoked—there is no one else to blame.

This is something to remember whenever someone confronts us with our sin. It is so easy to make excuses. There is always someone else to blame. But when it comes to making our confession, this is completely beside the point. What we ought to do is fully confess our sin and leave it at that. What we usually do instead is make a partial confession that is clouded with excuses, more excuses, and all kinds of extenuating circumstances.

The third problem with Aaron's confession is closely related to the second: He refused to admit what he had done. Not only did he blame others, but he also lied about the full extent of his own involvement.

The way to see this is by comparing 32:1–6 with 32:23, 24. In verse 1 the Bible tells us what the Israelites did, while verses 2–6 tell us what Aaron did. Aaron gives Moses his version in verses 23, 24. Verse 23 is an accurate report of what the Israelites did and said—almost word for word. So far, so good. However, after this, Aaron's story gets a little sketchy. God's version (vv. 2–6) carefully explains how Aaron took gold, made an idol, used a tool to make it look like a calf, built an altar, and then organized a worship service. Aaron's story was shorter, because by the time he left out all the incriminating details, there wasn't a whole lot left to say: "So they gave it to me, and I threw it into the fire, and out came this calf" (v. 24b). At first Aaron said, "The people made me do it!" Now it was, "The fire did it!"

Although some of the facts were the same, God's story and Aaron's story were totally different. According to Brevard Childs,

> When Aaron relates the role of the people, he repeats verbatim the entire dialogue as recorded in v. 1 along with its demand for other gods and the abusive reference to Moses. When he comes then to his own role in gathering the gold, the account is considerably abbreviated and minimizes Aaron's own role. The people bring the gold of their own accord, as if it had not been requested by him. When he reaches the crucial point on the actual construction of the calf, Aaron's story diverges completely from the original account. He pictures himself uninvolved. The calf came out all by itself.[7]

When God tells about the golden calf, Aaron plays the starring role. But to hear Aaron tell it, he was a minor character—one of the extras. Furthermore, he treated the golden calf like some kind of spontaneous miracle: "Cow? What cow? Oh, that cow. Well, Moses, I've been wondering about that myself. I don't know how it got here. It was unbelievable! I mean, people took off their jewelry, and the next thing you know, here's this cow, and people are worshiping it!" Idols are always man made, but Aaron tried to make it sound like this one was self-produced.

Today people call this *spin*. The Bible calls it lying. It's a strategy sinners often use to avoid confessing their sin. We downplay our depravity, minimizing the wickedness of what we have done. When we explain what happened, we conveniently leave out the details that might put us in a bad light. And to the extent that we admit that we did anything wrong at all, we want to tell our side of the story, so people will know that what we did wasn't as bad as it looked. We want to make sure they have the right interpretation of what happened—*our* interpretation. Usually, of course, we are only fooling ourselves. Most of our excuses and evasions are about as obvious as Aaron's was, and other people can see what we are trying to hide.

Even if there are times when we can fool people with all our excuses, God never lets us get away with it. He certainly didn't let Aaron get away with it. Aaron said, "Out came this calf." But according to the Word of God, Aaron "received the gold from their hand and fashioned it with a graving tool and made a golden calf" (32:4a). Later God refers to Israel's idol as "the calf, the one that Aaron made" (32:35). After all Aaron's desperate attempts to get Moses to back off, to shift the blame onto the Israelites, and to deny that he had done anything wrong at all, God stated very matter-of-factly that the sin belonged to Aaron after all.

## Who's to Blame?

Whether we admit our sin or not, God always holds us accountable for it. He knows that sin is not something that just happens or that other people make us do. It is what we choose to do out of the idolatry of our own sinful hearts.

If this is true, then we need to own up to our sin. We need to say, "I am the sinner. I am the one who complains about what God hasn't done for me. I am the one who takes what I want, even though it doesn't belong to me. I am the one who curses people under my breath. I am the one who looks down on other people's weakness. I am the one who exaggerates my accomplishments. I am the one who is bitter. I am the one who cannot control his rage. I am the one who uses words to tear people down. I am the one who commits the secret sin that no one else can see. I—I am the sinner."

We need to take the blame the way David did when he prayed, "I know my transgressions, and my sin is ever before me. Against you, you only, have I sinned and done what is evil in your sight" (Psalm 51:3, 4a). We need to pray like the prodigal son, who went back home and said, "Father, I have sinned against heaven and before you" (Luke 15:21a). We need to pray like the tax collector at the temple: "God, be merciful to me, a sinner!" (Luke 18:13).

The reason we need to take the blame is because until we take full responsibility for our iniquity, we can never be saved. Salvation is for sinners. It is for people who know how badly they have broken God's holy law. The Bible says, "The saying is trustworthy and deserving of full acceptance, that Christ Jesus came into the world to save sinners, of whom I am the foremost" (1 Timothy 1:15). The free gift of eternal life is for sinners who confess their sins, admitting they are unrighteous before God.

When we confess our sins, something amazing happens. As soon as we take the blame that we deserve, we can give it all over to Jesus. This is what Jesus was doing when he died on the cross: He was taking the blame for our sin before God. The Bible says, "He himself bore our sins in his body on the tree, that we might die to sin and live to righteousness" (1 Peter 2:24). Jesus is willing to take the blame for us, but first we have to admit that we are the ones who deserve it. Then we can transfer all our guilt over to him.

True spiritual life begins when we fully acknowledge our sin and ask Jesus to save us from it. According to Phillips Brooks, the Christian's

> new life dates from and begins with his sin. . . . Out of his sin, out of the bad, base, cowardly acts which are truly his, out of the weak and wretched passages of his life which it makes him ashamed to remember, but which he forces himself to recollect and own, out of these he gathers the consciousness of a self all astray with self-will which he then brings to Christ and offers in submission and obedience to His perfect will. . . . It is not that the poor creature loves those sins or is glad that he did them, or dreams for an instant of ever doing them again. It is only that through those sins, which are all the real experience he has had, he has found himself, and finding himself, has found his Saviour and the new life. So the only hope for any of us is in a perfectly honest manliness to claim our sins. "I did it, I did it," let me say of all my wickedness. Let me refuse to listen for one moment to any voice which would make my sins less mine. It is the only honest and the only hopeful way, the only way to know and be ourselves. When we have done that, then we are ready for the Gospel, ready for all that Christ wants to show us that we may become, and for all the powerful grace by which He wants to make us be it perfectly.[8]

Isn't it time to stop making excuses? Isn't it time to admit that you are not the person you pretend to be, that in fact you are a natural-born sinner? Unless you confess your sins, you cannot be saved. And until you admit the full extent of your sin, you cannot make the kind of spiritual progress that only comes when you see yourself as you really are, so that God can turn you into the person he wants you to become.

# 88

# Who Is on the Lord's Side?

EXODUS 32:25–35

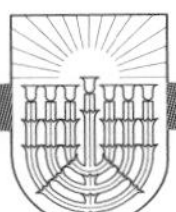

MOSES HAD STARTED TO DEAL with Israel's sin. First he begged God not to destroy his people. Then he smashed the Ten Commandments to show how the Israelites had broken God's law. Next he reduced the golden calf to a pile of dust, which he mixed with water and made the people drink. Moses also confronted Aaron for his role in the rebellion. But the prophet wasn't finished, because the Israelites still hadn't suffered the full consequences for what they had done. Nor had anyone made atonement for their sin. Thus Exodus 32 ends with God demanding the ultimate punishment and Moses desperately grasping for some way to avoid it.

## Taking Sides

As we have seen, Israel's idolatry was indecent: "And when Moses saw that the people had broken loose (for Aaron had let them break loose, to the derision of their enemies) . . ." (32:25). This was the tragic legacy of Aaron and his user-friendly deity. Even after the calf was gone, Israel was still in a state of anarchy. The Hebrew word for "broken loose" (*parua'*) has "the sense of loosening or uncovering."[1] The term is often used for nakedness. Here, at the very least, it means that the Israelites were loose in their morals, and perhaps also that they were committing sexual sin. Their idolatry had led to immorality, as idolatry always does.

Who was responsible for this scandalous situation? The people of Israel were the ones running wild, but Aaron was also to blame, because he "had let them break loose" (v. 25). As Israel's spiritual leader, it was his responsibility to maintain good discipline. But he had failed to deal with the people's sin in a godly, courageous way. The problem was not just that they were sinning, but that no one was holding them accountable. And as long as there was no discipline, the situation would only get worse.

The same principle holds true for the church. When people are running wild, committing scandalous sin, they need to be confronted. This is why many theologians regard discipline as an essential mark of the Christian church. Unless there is good discipline, the church ends up looking exactly like the world, with the result that people both inside and outside the church get confused about what it means to be a Christian.[2]

This is what was so tragic about the Israelites. They were failing to fulfill their God-given calling, which was to glorify God among the nations. Instead they had become an object of scorn and derision—"a laughingstock to their enemies" (v. 25 NIV). This is what happens whenever God's people fail to be godly. Unbelievers are always watching, and whenever they see Christians behaving badly, they make fun of the church. Few things are more destructive to our work and witness than Christians who go out and get drunk, commit sexual sin, tell obscene jokes, and generally bring the name of Christ into disrepute.

When Moses saw that the Israelites were sinning, he realized that he had to do something. "Moses stood in the gate of the camp and said, 'Who is on the LORD's side? Come to me'" (v. 26a). At this point, it wasn't clear if *anyone* was for the Lord. Some have suggested that not all of the Israelites sinned with the golden calf. In fact, most of the ancient rabbis tried to pin the blame on the Egyptians and the other Gentiles in the mixed multitude that came out of Egypt with the Israelites (see 12:38). However, the Bible implicates the entire nation. It says, "All the people took off the rings of gold that were in their ears and brought them to Aaron" (32:3). This was a nationwide rebellion.

From what Moses could see, it didn't look like anyone was on the Lord's side. However, God was willing to show mercy. There was still a way for the people to come and join him. All they had to do was leave their sin behind. So Moses gave them an opportunity. He stood at the entrance to the camp and called for volunteers. "Who is on the LORD's side?" he demanded (v. 26). The only men who answered were the Levites—the members of the prophet's own tribe. They were the ones who rallied to Moses' side, taking their stand with God. To do this, the Levites had to leave the camp of sin. If they had stayed where they were, they would have remained under God's judgment. Simply living with the people of God was not enough to save them. They had to make a personal commitment to serve the living God.

This is a decision that everyone has to make. Are you with God or not? Are you for him or against him? There comes a time when every person has to make a decision. Jesus said, "Whoever is not with me is against me" (Matthew 12:30). If we do not decide for Christ, then we are siding against him.

So the question each person has to ask is, am I with Jesus? Do I believe that he is the divine Son of God—true man as well as very God? Am I trusting in his death on the cross as the full atonement for my sin? Do I believe that he rose from the dead to give me eternal life? Do I serve him as my Lord and praise him as my God? Whoever is not with Jesus is against him. We cannot simply stay where we are, because like the Israelites, we were born in sin. If we want to be with God, we have to leave our sin behind and rally to Jesus.

This is the decision we make when we first come to Christ. It is also a decision we make every day as we live the Christian life. Who is on the Lord's side? Are you with God or not? Are you for him or against him? With every thought we think, every word we speak, and every action we take, we are making our stand. If we do not speak the truth, we are false. If we do not preserve our purity, we are unholy. If we do not promote justice, we are unrighteous. If we do not make sacrifices for others, we are selfish. If we do not walk in humility, we are proud. There is no spiritual neutrality. We must take sides. Every day we are taking a stand, either with God or against him.

Two examples of what it means to be on the Lord's side come from the world of sports and business. In an article called "The Rise and Fall of Kirby Puckett," journalist Frank Deford tried to explain what had led a Hall of Fame baseball player into violent and self-destructive sin. In commenting on the prevalence of sexual sin among professional athletes, Deford quoted a former batboy who said, "With the exception of guys who were devout Christians, virtually everybody had someone on the side."[3] Note the exception: It was the Christians who were different. They were on God's side when it came to chastity and matrimony.

Or consider the courageous example of Sherron Watkins, the energy executive who first called attention to the multi-billion-dollar fraud at Enron. When everyone else was turning a blind eye to corporate theft, she alone was brave enough to say that it was wrong. Is it any surprise to discover that Watkins was raised as a devout Lutheran or that she drew courage from this Scripture: "Consider him who endured from sinners such hostility against himself, so that you may not grow weary or fainthearted" (Hebrews 12:3)?[4] It is not surprising at all, because she was on the Lord's side.

## Putting Idolatry to Death

Once we side with God, we have to be willing to do what he says. This is what it means to be on his side. It means obeying him no matter what. Ordinarily God does not tell us in advance what this will include. All we know is that from now on, everything we are and have is at his disposal, to be used in whatever way he thinks best. But usually we don't know the details.

This was true for the Levites, who could hardly have imagined what God would tell them to do. First Moses told them to come to his side. "And he said to them, 'Thus says the LORD God of Israel, "Put your sword on your side each of you, and go to and fro from gate to gate throughout the camp, and each of you kill his brother and his companion and his neighbor''''' (32:27).

This was a shocking assignment. Notice that it was not Moses' idea; the command came from God. And this was the first thing that God told the Levites to do when they came to his side—to carry out his judgment against Israel's sin. There is no question here as to whether or not this was just. The Israelites had made a blood covenant with God, in which they had promised not to make any idols or have any other gods. Once they broke these commandments, their lives were forfeit. God had every right to put them all to death. If we have trouble understanding this, it is because we do not understand what a wicked thing it is to worship other gods. Moreover, the whole plan of salvation was in jeopardy. Israel was called to be a holy nation through which all the nations of the world would be blessed. But the Israelites had turned away from God, and unless God did something to bring them back, he would no longer have a people to call his own.

Desperate times call for drastic measures. Yet even in his wrath, God remembered to show mercy. Not everyone was killed. The Bible says, "And the sons of Levi did according to the word of Moses. And that day about three thousand men of the people fell" (v. 28). This was a horrific loss of life, but rather than simply thinking about how many perished, we should also consider how many were saved. Three thousand was only one half of 1 percent of Israel's adult male population. God restrained his hand of judgment. Presumably, when the Israelites saw what was happening, most of them stopped sinning against God, and so their lives were spared. In the words of Caesarius of Arles, "Behold true and perfect charity: he ordered the death of a few people in order to save six hundred thousand, with the women and children excepted. If he had not been aroused with zeal for God to punish a few men, God's justice would have destroyed them all."[5] Or as Umberto Cassuto put it, "Better that a few Israelites lose their lives rather than that the entire people should perish."[6]

The Bible doesn't say who was executed, but in all likelihood the Levites only killed the instigators, the men who were most responsible for Israel's sin. When God told them to kill their brothers and neighbors, the point was *not* that each man had to kill his closest friends, but that whoever was guilty had to be punished. The Levites were not to let the ties of blood or friendship hinder them from their service to God. Not even family and friends were to be spared, if they refused to follow God.

The question is why God gave this horrible duty to the Levites. If he had wanted to, God could have punished the people all by himself. Instead he gave the Levites the power to carry out summary executions, which they loyally exercised. The Levites obeyed God by putting unrepentant sinners to death. And they were commended for this. After they had finished their grim work, "Moses said, 'Today you have been ordained for the service of the LORD, each one at the cost of his son and of his brother, so that he might bestow a blessing upon you this day'" (v. 29). Because of their unflinching obedience and unrelenting opposition to sin, God consecrated the Levites for his sacred ministry.

This is a hard passage. It shows that God's claim on us is stronger even than the claims of family and friendship. Jesus said, "Whoever loves father or mother more than me is not worthy of me, and whoever loves son or daughter more than me is not worthy of me. And whoever does not take his cross and follow me is not worthy of me" (Matthew 10:37, 38). This does not mean that we should hate the people in our families. But it does mean that whether they are believers or not, our love for them must submit to our higher love for God.

This passage also teaches us to be ruthless in our pursuit of holiness. God was showing the Levites that if they wanted to serve God in his holy tabernacle, they had to pursue absolute purity among the people of God. The same is true for believers in Jesus Christ. We must put idolatry and immorality to death, not only as individual Christians, but also as a church. Of course, God has not given us the power of the sword. The Bible is perfectly clear about this. "For the weapons of our warfare," wrote the Apostle Paul, "are not of the flesh" (2 Corinthians 10:4a). Our only sword is "the sword of the Spirit, which is the word of God" (Ephesians 6:17). For the Israelites, what drew the distinction between holiness and sin was the sharp edge of a Levite's blade. What draws the distinction for us is the Word of God, which clearly distinguishes right from wrong. And to the extent that we have any power to carry out judgment today, it is only through the exercise of church discipline, in which sin is condemned so that people can grow in godliness. This is one of the differences between the old covenant and the new covenant. Whereas under the old covenant, God's people had the power of the sword, under the new covenant we have the spiritual power of church discipline.

When it comes to idolatry and immorality, there can be no compromise. These sins must be dealt with in a godly way. Whenever Christians are involved in false worship or try to turn God into something he's not or say they can find salvation in someone else or commit scandalous sin—in other words, whenever they do the kinds of things that the Israelites did—they need to be confronted. In the church this sometimes leads to formal discipline. If people refuse to turn away from their sin, they must be cut off from the Body of Christ. So although sinners should never be treated harshly, their sin should always be dealt with firmly, according to the clear teaching of the Bible. And from the Levites we learn that the only people who are qualified to do this are people who are willing to take a stand for God.

## Moses Makes an Offer

One would think that by the time the Levites had finished their work, with all its carnage, God was finished dealing with Israel's sin. The golden calf had been destroyed. Aaron had been confronted. The people had tasted the bitterness of their idolatry. The ringleaders of the rebellion had all been put to death. But there was still a problem, as James Boice explained in his exposition of this passage:

> From a human point of view Moses had dealt with the sin. The leaders were punished. Aaron was rebuked. The allegiance of the people was at least temporarily reclaimed. All seemed to be well. But . . . God still waited in wrath upon the mountain. What was Moses to do? . . . By that time not all of the law had been given, but Moses had received enough of it to know something of the horror of sin and of the uncompromising nature of God's righteousness. Had not God said, "You shall have no other gods before me"? Had not he promised to visit the iniquity of the fathers upon the children to the third and fourth generations? Who was Moses to think that the limited judgment he had begun would satisfy the holiness of such a God?[7]

The people had suffered for their sin, but they had not yet satisfied the wrath of God. How could they? They had broken a blood covenant, which meant that they all deserved to die. Fortunately, God had promised not to destroy them, but what could atone for the guilt of their sin? Was there anything their mediator could do? And if so, what was it? The mediator himself wasn't even sure: "The next day Moses said to the people, 'You have sinned a great sin. And now I will go up to the LORD; perhaps I can make atonement for your sin'" (v. 30). Perhaps Moses could make atonement, but how?

Boice imagines the prophet struggling to figure out what he was going to say to God and then finally getting the first inkling of their salvation:

> The night passed, and the morning came when Moses was to reascend the mountain. He had been thinking. Sometime during the night a way that might possibly divert the wrath of God against the people had come to him. He remembered the sacrifices of the Hebrew patriarchs and the newly instituted sacrifice of the Passover. Certainly God had shown by such sacrifices that he was prepared to accept an innocent substitute in place of the just death of the sinner. His wrath could sometimes fall on the substitute. Perhaps God would accept . . . When morning came, Moses ascended the mountain with great determination. Reaching the top, he began to speak to God.[8]

And this is what Moses said: "Alas, this people has sinned a great sin. They have made for themselves gods of gold. But now, if you will forgive their sin—but if not, please blot me out of your book that you have written" (vv. 31, 32).

This was not the first time Moses had interceded for Israel. He prayed for the people when they were trapped between Pharaoh and the deep blue sea (14:15). He prayed for them at Marah, where the water was bitter (15:25), and again at Rephidim, where there was no water at all (17:4). He prayed for them when the Amalekites attacked and he had to lift his arms all day to win the victory (17:11, 12). Moses prayed, and when he prayed, God answered. He made his people walk on dry land; he gave them sweet water; he delivered them from their enemies. Moses had prayed again just a few days earlier, when he first heard about the golden calf. Arguing on the basis of God's own character and promises, he had persuaded God not to destroy Israel.

Now Moses was praying again. He began by freely confessing Israel's sin, which he had just seen in all its depravity. In fact, the vocabulary of sin appears eight times in just a few short verses. The people had sinned a great sin, but Moses was asking God to forgive them. The trouble was that this time he couldn't come up with any good arguments. On what basis should God forgive people who broke his law? Moses really couldn't think of any suitable reason, so he quickly said, "but if not, please blot me out of your book that you have written" (32:32b).

What did the prophet mean when he asked God to take his name out of his book? What book did he have in mind? John J. Davis mentions two major options: "Many argue that this is a reference to the book of life in which the names of believers are recorded. Others take this book to be 'a register of living men—with reference to the earthly life of this world only and not of the next' (Henry Cowles). This view maintains that the book is a list of those living on earth and 'to be blotted out' of this book means to meet an untimely or premature death."[9]

Both ideas are present in Scripture. For example, when David says, "In your book were written, every one of them, the days that were formed for me, when as yet there was none of them" (Psalm 139:16), he clearly is referring to his natural life span. But the Bible also uses "the Book of Life" to refer to eternal salvation, and that seems to be the way Moses used the phrase here. In the ancient world it was common for kings to keep a register of their citizens. When a census was taken, people's names were written down. When they died, their names were blotted out. Ezekiel referred to this practice when he prophesied, concerning false prophets, "They shall not be in the council of my people, nor be enrolled in the register of the house of Israel" (Ezekiel 13:9; cf. Isaiah 4:3). But the Bible also uses this idea to refer to eternal salvation.

The Book of Life is where God registers the citizens of his heavenly kingdom. When David said of his enemies, "Let them be blotted out of the book of the living; let them not be enrolled among the righteous" (Psalm 69:28), he was asking for justice both in this life and in the life to come. And by the time we get to the New Testament, the Book of Life plainly refers to the eternal life God has promised to his elect. The only people who are allowed to enter God's heavenly kingdom are "those who are written in the Lamb's book of life" (Revelation 21:27; cf. Luke 10:20; Philippians 4:3; Revelation 3:5; 20:12).

Either way, the point is really the same. Whether he was thinking in terms of earthly life or eternal life, Moses was willing to die for his people. This seems all the more remarkable when we remember that God had offered to destroy everyone else and start over with Moses (32:10). But Moses said, "Look, if you have to destroy somebody, destroy me, Lord, but save my people!"[10] Or to put it more provocatively, Moses was willing to be damned if only Israel could be saved.

This shows that Moses was starting to catch on! He was beginning to understand the structure of salvation. When people sinned, they needed a substitute. And the person who had the responsibility to make atonement was the person whom God had chosen to serve as the mediator. Moses was starting to grasp the doctrine of the atonement. In the covenant, sin could be forgiven through the sacrifice of a representative. As long as it was the right person, one man could die for the people's sin. With this thought in mind, he began to pray in a way that no one had ever prayed before. Here was a whole new kind of intercession. Moses was presenting himself as a sacrifice of atonement, offering himself to God as the substitute for Israel's sin.

The offer that Moses made should remind us of the words of Jesus Christ, who said, "The good shepherd lays down his life for the sheep" (John 10:11). Jesus also said, "Greater love has no one than this, that someone lay down his life for his friends" (John 15:13). Moses was a good shepherd: he was willing to lay down his life for his sheep. And he had the greatest of all loves: he would die for his friends.

## God Turns It Down

But God still turned Moses down: "But the Lord said to Moses, 'Whoever has sinned against me, I will blot out of my book. But now go, lead the people to the place about which I have spoken to you; behold, my angel shall go before you. Nevertheless, in the day when I visit, I will visit their sin upon them'" (32:33, 34). And God followed through on his threat, because the Bible says, "Then the Lord sent a plague on the people, because they made the calf, the one that Aaron made" (v. 35).

Up to this point, the whole passage seemed like it was building to a triumphant climax. By the time Moses made his offer, it seemed like the whole plan of salvation was coming together. The chosen mediator was willing to make the ultimate sacrifice. One man would die for the people, and then God would forgive their sin!

Only it didn't work out that way after all. What had all seemed so promising vanished in an instant. The people had sinned, and so had Aaron. To be specific, they had sinned against God. To be sure, God had already promised not to destroy them. By the angel of his presence, he would lead their descendants to the Promised Land. But they would still have to suffer the punishment due to their sins. As John Currid writes, "First, there will be individual responsibility—that is, the person who has sinned against Yahweh will be blotted out of God's book. And, secondly, there is also a collective liability—the sin of the covenant people will rebound on the entire nation."[11]

It is not entirely clear how God punished the Israelites. With what "plague" were they afflicted? Perhaps this simply refers to the fact that this whole generation of Israelites never reached the Promised Land. They died in the wilderness (see Deuteronomy 1:35). Or perhaps this refers to the outbreak of some more immediate, more specific, and more temporary plague—one not mentioned anywhere else in Scripture. Either way, the point is really the same: The people had to bear the punishment for their sin. They could not escape judgment by transferring their guilt over to Moses.

The question is, why not? What went wrong? Why didn't God accept the sacrifice of Israel's mediator? The answer is not stated in Exodus 32, but we know it from the rest of Scripture. Moses could not die for his people's sin because he himself was a sinner. To name just one of his many moral failings, he was a bad-tempered man—so bad tempered that on one occasion he had killed a man. But in order to make atonement for Israel's sin, he had to be perfect. God is willing to let someone die for someone else's sin, but the only sacrifice he can accept is a perfect sacrifice, unstained by sin. So Moses couldn't do it. He came close—perhaps closer than any man had ever come—but he still could not make atonement for sin.

As we read through the Bible we keep looking for a Savior, someone to atone for sin. Eventually we reach the same conclusion as Homer Simpson, who on one episode of *The Simpsons* complained, "This Bible cost 15 bucks! And talk about a preachy book! Everybody's a sinner! . . . Except this guy." Homer was right. Everybody *is* a sinner, except "this guy," Jesus. And he is the only man who could make atonement because he alone is without sin. Jesus Christ lived a perfect life so that he would be qualified to offer himself as the atonement for our sin. Then he died the God-forsaken, God-accursed death of the cross. He was not blotted out of the Book of Life, as Moses had prayed, but for three days he was under the wrath and curse of God. Then on the third day God raised him from the dead, giving eternal life not only to Jesus, but to all who take their stand with him.

The more we study Moses, the more we learn about Jesus. This is the way the Bible works. The story of salvation keeps getting clearer and clearer. The more we read, the more we see the full extent of our sin, and the wrath of God against it. But this does not lead to despair, because we also start to see the forgiveness that God offers through the sacrifice of a Savior.

An illustration may help explain the connection between Moses and salvation in Christ. Think of Moses as the extra who stands in for the star during the filming of a movie. While the stagehands are setting the scene and adjusting the lights, the extra stands right where the star will stand when the filming starts, so that when the star finally takes the stage, everything will be just right. While all this is going on, onlookers can get some idea what the scene will look like, but they don't know the full story. The star is still waiting somewhere backstage.

He won't step in until the last moment, and only then will the scene be played properly.

Something similar happens in the history of salvation. God is the director, and in the Old Testament he is busy setting the stage. Moses is the extra standing in for Jesus, and as we watch him, we see the setup for salvation. Then, when the time is right and everything is ready, Jesus steps onto the stage of the universe. God says, "Action!" and then Jesus starts performing the work of our salvation. He lived a life of perfect obedience. He died a death that atoned for sin. He was raised to live forever. Jesus is the true star of our salvation. Everyone who comes over to his side will be saved. But we do have to come, asking God to forgive our sins and telling him that we want Jesus to be our Savior, because until we do this, we are not on his side at all.

# 89

# With or Without You?

## EXODUS 33:1–11

IN HIS NOVEL *The Hobbit*, J. R. R. Tolkien tells how Bilbo Baggins and a dozen dwarves traveled to the Lonely Mountain, defeated a terrible dragon, and returned home with golden treasures. Their companion for the first part of their journey was Gandalf the Grey, a man of unusual wisdom and extraordinary power. Gandalf served as their guardian and guide, and sometimes their savior.

But Gandalf could not always be with them. Midway through their journey, as the traveling party prepared to enter the forest of Mirkwood, they unexpectedly learned that Gandalf would not be going with them. This unhappy news was greeted with instant dismay: "The dwarves groaned and looked most distressed, and Bilbo wept. They had begun to think Gandalf was going to come all the way and would always be there to help them out of difficulties. . . . They begged him not to leave them. They offered him dragon-gold and silver and jewels, but he would not change his mind."[1] When traveling through dangerous and unfamiliar territory, it is good to have a guide, and devastating to lose one.

### God Cancels His Trip

The loss of a guide explains Israel's distress in Exodus 33. The Israelites had already suffered many painful consequences for their great sin with the golden calf, but now it was time to move on.

> The LORD said to Moses, "Depart; go up from here, you and the people whom you have brought up out of the land of Egypt, to the land of which I swore to Abraham, Isaac, and Jacob, saying, 'To your offspring I will give it.' I will send an angel before you, and I will drive out the Canaanites, the Amorites, the Hittites, the Perizzites, the Hivites, and the Jebusites. Go up to a land flowing with milk and honey." (33:1–3a)

So far, so good. Even after everything the Israelites had done to displease him, God would still make good on his promises. He would give his people blessing after blessing. With Moses as their leader, they would finally leave the wilderness and enter the land that God had promised in the covenant. All their enemies would be defeated. By the power of his avenging angel, God would sweep the land clear of danger. Then the Israelites would take possession of the land in all its abundance. Everything was going to work out after all.

There was only one problem. Although the Israelites were still going to the Promised Land, God had decided not to make the trip. "But I will not go up among you," he said, "lest I consume you on the way, for you are a stiff-necked people" (v. 3b). This verse does not mean that God has trouble controlling his temper. As we have seen throughout Exodus, the Bible sometimes describes God in human terms. This is one of the ways he accommodates himself to our limited understanding. But it does not mean God has the same sinful emotions that we have. When God decides to destroy someone, it is not because he has lost his cool, but because he responds to sin with perfect righteousness. He is a God of holy justice, and this made it too dangerous for him to stay with Israel. It would be safer for them if he didn't go at all.

The problem, of course, was Israel's sin. The Israelites were covenant lawbreakers, or as God so aptly put it, "a stiff-necked people." Like a farm animal that stubbornly refuses to shoulder the plow, the Israelites would not wear the yoke of obedience to God. And under these circumstances, God would not go with them. This was for their own protection. At any moment he might have to judge them for their sin, and then they would perish. The people wanted and needed God to live close to them, and yet he was unable to do this because of their sin.

Perhaps the Israelites should have seen this coming. Since the time he first told Moses to bring Israel out of Egypt, God had been drawing his people closer and closer. He answered their prayers. He provided for their needs. He taught them his law. He even made plans to build his home in the middle of their camp. God was totally committed to this relationship. He was their God, and they were his people.

But at the beginning of chapter 33 there are troubling signs that God and his people had grown apart. In verse 1 God referred to the Israelites as "*the* people" rather than "*my* people." Why the sudden sense of distance? Then in verse 2 he promised to send Israel "an angel." Formerly, God had called his messenger "*my* angel" (23:23; 32:34), implying that the angel represented his very presence. In fact, many people think that the angel may have been the Son of God himself, the Second Person of the Trinity. But now God would send an ordinary angel to do the job, one of the heavenly rank and file.

Then at the end of verse 3 God dropped the bomb: He was not going with them. Among other things, this meant that his plans for the tabernacle were put on hold. The purpose of the tabernacle was to create a sacred space where God could dwell with his people. But God had decided not to go with them—literally, not to go "in their midst." This is the same language that he used back in chapter 25 when he told Moses to build the tabernacle: "Let them make me a sanctuary, that *I may dwell in their midst*" (v. 8). So when God said, "I will not go up among you," he specifically meant there would be no tabernacle at the center of their camp.

The Israelites were desperate to have God go with them. The irony, of course, is that this is why they made the golden calf. They wanted God to be right there with them. But now, because of their sinful idolatry, he would not be with them at all. John Currid notes the irony: "God had given the Hebrews instructions to build a sanctuary so that he would reside among the people. They instead made a calf as a physical representation of gods being with them. Now Yahweh threatens to remove from them the true symbol of his presence."[2]

This is what happens when we worship other gods, especially gods that we can see and touch. Rather than bringing us closer to God, our idols take us farther away. Martin Luther said, "Whatever man *loves*, that is his god. For he carries it in his *heart*; he goes about with it night and day; he sleeps and wakes with it, be it what it may, wealth or self, pleasure or renown."[3] What preoccupies our thoughts? What do we treasure in our hearts? God wants to fill our lives with his presence. But when we carry other things around with us, pursuing them by day and thinking about them at night, there is no room left for God.

The Israelites were facing life without God. There would be no divine presence in their camp—no tabernacle. And without the tabernacle, there would be no altar for sacrifice, no laver for cleansing, no lampstand for light, no table for bread, no incense for prayer, no ark for atonement, and no glory in Israel. The Israelites would have to go it alone. They were still booked for the Promised Land, but God had canceled his reservations. According to Peter Enns,

> The significance of this turn of events cannot be stressed too highly. The whole purpose of the Exodus was for God and his people to be together. God's presence with them will be firmly established in the proposed tabernacle. By saying "go ahead, but you're going without me," the events of the previous thirty-one chapters are being undone. This is not merely a setback; it means the end of the road.[4]

## The People's Response

How would you have responded to the news that God wasn't going? Most people probably think they would be very upset, but I'm not so sure. Consider what God was offering the Israelites: He was offering to bless them without having a relationship with them. But this is exactly what most people want!

It is shocking but true: Most people want God to help them overcome whatever obstacles they are facing in life, and they want to reach a promised land, but they are not all that interested in having a personal relationship with the living God. They would be happy to have God defeat all their enemies and let them into his kingdom, even if he did not give them himself. In fact, this is what some people who claim to be Christians have tried to do. They have made a decision for Christ so they can get into Heaven, but they are not living with him as their Savior and their God.

Even the Israelites knew better. They refused to settle for any blessing apart from God's very presence:

> When the people heard this disastrous word, they mourned, and no one put on his ornaments. For the LORD had said to Moses, "Say to the people of Israel, 'You are a stiff-necked people; if for a single moment I should go up among you, I would consume you. So now take off your ornaments, that I may know what to do with you.'" Therefore the people of Israel stripped themselves of their ornaments, from Mount Horeb onward. (33:4–6)

Word quickly spread throughout the camp: "God's not going with us!" Instantly the people were dismayed. Their distress is indicated both by their attitude and by their actions. They began to cry, partly because they were sad to see God go, but also because they were sorry for their sins. Then they took off their ornaments—meaning their jewelry and other finery—as a symbolic act of repentance. A. W. Pink comments:

> The removal of their ornaments was for the purpose of evidencing the genuineness of their contrition. Outward adornment was out of keeping with the taking of a low place before God. Contrariwise, external attractions and displays show up the absence of that lowliness of spirit and brokenness of heart which are of great price in the sight of God. The more true spirituality declines, the more an elaborate ritual comes to the fore.[5]

Many scholars think that taking off jewelry related in some specific way to idolatry. There seems to be a parallel in Genesis. When Jacob renewed the covenant at Bethel, he told everyone in his family to take off their jewelry, and then he buried it all in the ground, along with all their idols (35:2–4). By taking off their jewelry, they were rejecting their pagan idols and recommitting themselves to serve the one true God.

The Israelites did the same thing at Mount Horeb. And they did it eagerly. God told them to "take off" their ornaments, but the Bible says that they "stripped" (*natzal*) them off, indicating how ready they were to get right with God. This was a sign of genuine repentance. Whenever we realize that something is causing us to sin, we need to get rid of it right away. We also need to make sure that we never go back to it. The Israelites were very careful about this. Once they stripped off their jewelry, they kept it off. According to verse 6, they went without ornaments from Mount Horeb onward. This was a permanent change, which is another sign of genuine repentance: getting rid of sin once and for all. When the Holy Spirit convicts us of any sin, we need to take off whatever is leading us into sin and never put it on again.

Another thing we learn from Israel's ornamentation is the spiritual power of money. We can trace the people's spiritual progress simply by looking at what they did with their gold. Earlier they took off their earrings to make the golden calf, using their wealth to turn away from God. This time they were taking off the rest of their jewelry as a sign that they wanted to worship God alone. They were putting off idolatry. Later they would use the same gold to build the tabernacle (see 35:22). Clearly, the Israelites were making some spiritual progress. Rather than using their wealth to make idols, they were learning to give it up for God and use it for his glory.

What we do with our money and our other possessions is one of the best indicators of our true spiritual condition. Are we spending most of it on ourselves, or are we growing in the grace of generosity? Are we subtly becoming more and more selfish with what we have, or are we making deeper and deeper sacrifices for the kingdom of God? Are we only giving what's left, or are we giving more than we think we can spare, so that God can do his saving work? Jesus said, "Where your treasure is, there your heart will be also" (Matthew 6:21). By examining our patterns of giving and spending, we can see whether our hearts are in the right place or not. A personal bank account or a family budget is a spiritual echocardiogram: it measures the soundness of a person's heart before God.

Israel's heart was in the right place. When the people heard that God was not going with them, they were distressed in the right way and for the right reason. They were not just feeling sorry for themselves. Instead they were repenting of their sin. And they were doing this because they wanted to restore their relationship with God. This was everything to them. As far as they were concerned, if God was not in their midst, then even if they still made it to the Promised Land, they had lost the only thing that really mattered, which was their relationship with God. They didn't want to be led by an angel; they wanted to walk with God.

Their example reminds us to love God more than we love his blessings. Many blessings come from knowing God. There is the blessing of repentance, of being able to see our sin and turn away from it. There is the blessing of forgiveness, of receiving a pardon for all our sin. There is the blessing of justification, of being declared righteous in God's sight. There is the blessing of sanctification, of growing in godliness. There is the blessing of adoption, of having all the rights and privileges of a child of God. There is the blessing of perseverance, of staying with God to the very end. There is the blessing of glorification, of having the free gift of eternal life.

The blessings go on and on forever, but the biggest blessing is God himself. Knowing him is better than anything else we can imagine. We should not focus so much on what he does for us that we neglect who he is to us. How blessed it is to have a personal relationship with the living God. How blessed it is to meditate on his many perfections—his infinite wisdom, power, holiness, goodness, and love. How blessed it is to know him as one God in three Persons. How blessed it is to know the Father as Creator, the Son as Redeemer, and the Spirit as Sustainer of life. How blessed it is to communicate with God every day, to listen to what he is saying to us in his Word, and to tell him all our troubles through prayer.

If we know God—really know him—then all the rest of his blessings will follow. But the first thing, the main thing, the fundamental thing, is to know God in a personal way through Jesus Christ. In his wonderful book *Knowing God*, J. I. Packer writes, "What were we made for? To know God. What aim should we set ourselves in life? To know God. What is the 'eternal life' that Jesus gives? Knowledge of God. . . . What is the best thing in life, bringing more joy, delight, and contentment, than anything else? Knowledge of God."[6] If this is true, then we should keep God at the center of our experience the way the Israelites wanted to keep him at the center of their camp.

## The Tent of Meeting

At this point the Israelites weren't quite sure what would happen next. God had told them that he wasn't going with them. It was too dangerous—not for him, obviously, but for them. Yet they had repented of their sin. They had taken off the ornaments of their idolatry, as God had commanded. Now they were waiting to see what he would do.

The Bible does not resolve their tension right away. Will God go with the Israelites, or will they have to go without him? We don't find out until later in the chapter. While we're waiting, the Bible tells us about Moses and the tent of meeting. Many Bible scholars complain about what they see here as a change of subject. Some say that the next section of Exodus is "completely out of place."[7] The truth, of course, is that what comes next belongs right where the Holy Spirit put it. The Bible brings us to a crucial point in the story of salvation, but instead of resolving things right away, it leaves us hanging in suspense. This is an excellent way to tell a story.

Furthermore, what comes next begins to resolve the problem, because these verses show that there was at least one man who *could* come into God's presence:

> Now Moses used to take the tent and pitch it outside the camp, far off from the camp, and he called it the tent of meeting. And everyone who sought the LORD would go out to the tent of meeting, which was outside the camp. Whenever Moses went out to the tent, all the people would rise up, and each would stand at his tent door, and watch Moses until he had gone into

> the tent. When Moses entered the tent, the pillar of cloud would descend and stand at the entrance of the tent, and the Lord would speak with Moses. And when all the people saw the pillar of cloud standing at the entrance of the tent, all the people would rise up and worship, each at his tent door. Thus the Lord used to speak to Moses face to face, as a man speaks to his friend. When Moses turned again into the camp, his assistant Joshua the son of Nun, a young man, would not depart from the tent. (vv. 7–11)

This "tent of meeting" was not the tabernacle. What makes this somewhat confusing is that elsewhere in Exodus the inner structure of the tabernacle is also called "the tent of meeting" (e.g., 27:21; 40:2). Both tents were places to meet with God. However, at this point, when the tabernacle had not yet been built, Moses had his own private tent of meeting.

One significant difference between the two tents was that whereas the tabernacle stood at the center, Moses pitched this tent outside the camp—*way* outside. The Bible stresses that it was located "far off" from the Israelites. It had to be far away because the Israelites were still under divine judgment. Their camp was still a place of sin, and God had said that he would not dwell in it. So at least for the time being, if the Israelites wanted to meet with God, they had to go outside the camp. They were separated from God by their sin.

Yet God had not entirely abandoned them. The tent of meeting was a temporary tabernacle—an alternative place to meet with God. And what happened at this sanctuary was amazing. Moses would leave the camp and walk out to the tent of meeting. As he was going, the people would stand and worship from a distance. They were looking to their mediator as he went to meet with God. When Moses entered the tent, a pillar of cloud would come down from Heaven and cover the entrance. This was a theophany, a visible manifestation of the glorious presence of God. The glory-cloud showed the people that Moses was meeting with God.

What happened inside the tent of meeting was just as amazing: Moses talked with God. He had talked with God back at the burning bush, and again on top of the holy mountain. But now God was coming down to meet with him in his tent. In grace he was condescending to communicate with his prophet. There at the tent of meeting God spoke with Moses "face to face, as a man speaks to his friend" (33:11). The phrase "face to face" does not mean that Moses could see God, for just a few verses later God would say, "Man shall not see me and live" (33:20). Rather, it is a figure of speech intended to show that God and his prophet enjoyed direct communication. Moses had immediate access to God. This was a level of intimacy and fellowship that no human being had experienced since the day that God banished Adam and Eve from the garden. Moses and God were friends. God told him everything he needed to know about his plans for Israel. He spoke with Moses like a friend with a friend.

This meant that there was still hope. God had told the Israelites that he would not go up in the middle of their camp. But at least he was still talking to their mediator. There was a place, outside the camp, where God would meet with Moses. And anyone who wanted to know God's will could approach the tent of meeting, talk things over with Moses, and then wait for Moses to inquire of God. Although God would not stay in their midst, they could go out and meet with God through their mediator. Even this limited form of contact was an extraordinary privilege. The people were distanced from God by their sin; yet there was still a point of contact, a way for them to connect with God.

## Friends with God

As we consider what Israel had to do to meet with God, we are reminded of the amazing privilege that we have today. Where can we go to meet with God? We don't have to stay at a distance. We don't have to go outside the camp. We don't have to approach the tent of meeting. We don't have to consult with a prophet or a priest. As believers in the Lord Jesus Christ, we have immediate access to God through the presence of his Holy Spirit.

Today the tent of meeting is inside us, because God has come to make his home in us. This is the work of God the Holy Spirit. Jesus has sent the Spirit to live in us. Thus the Apostle Paul prays "that according to the riches of his glory he [God] may grant you to be strengthened with power through his Spirit in your inner being, so that Christ may dwell in your hearts through faith" (Ephesians 3:16, 17a). This means that *we* are the place of God's dwelling. From the very moment that we receive Jesus into our hearts by faith, we are in direct communication with Almighty God.

This is what one of America's founding fathers, John Winthrop, experienced when he first became a Christian. Winthrop wrote: "I was now grown familiar with the Lord Jesus Christ. . . . If I went abroad, he went with me, when I returned, he came home with me. I talked with him upon the way, he lay down with me, and usually I did awake with him: and so sweet was his love to me, as I desired nothing but him in heaven or earth."[8]

This is what happens when someone becomes a Christian. God comes into our lives in a whole new way. He is with us all the time. We have constant communion with him. Now when we read the Bible, God talks to us like a friend with a friend. His Holy Spirit applies his holy Word directly to our minds and hearts. All the promises in the Bible are promises that God makes to us in Christ. All the warnings are warnings to us; all the commandments are commandments to us. God speaks to us in his Word. The communication is two-way, because when we pray, we are speaking back to God. We tell God how much we love him. We confess our sins. We share our worries. We talk over our problems. We ask for help. We speak with God like a friend with a friend. This is what it means to have a personal relationship with Jesus Christ. It means to be in direct and constant communication with Almighty God.

The great Princeton theologian Archibald Alexander wrote, "If Christ be in us there will be communion. . . . He will sometimes speak to us—He will speak comfortably to us—He will give tokens of his love. He will invite our confidence and will shed abroad his love in our hearts. And if Christ be formed within us we cannot remain altogether ignorant of his presence. Our hearts, while he communes with us, will sometimes burn within us."[9]

Now that God is with us and within us, we know that he will never leave us or forsake us, but will stay with us wherever we go. This is the promise that Jesus made to his disciples: "I am with you always, to the end of the age" (Matthew 28:20b). Jesus will never get up and leave our camp. Yet this is exactly what some Christians fear. When we fall into serious sin, we sometimes doubt whether God is still with us. Our sense of guilt is so great that we begin to question our relationship with God: "Does God still love me? Can God still use me? Will God still bless me? Or am I so stiff-necked that he will abandon me?"

The answer is that God never abandons his friends. Every friend of his is a friend forever. God has invested far too much in this friendship to abandon us. Jesus said, "Greater love has no one than this, that someone lay down his life for his friends" (John 15:13). And then he went on to say, "You are my friends . . . I have called you friends, for all that I have heard from my Father I have made known to you" (vv. 14a, 15b). We have the same high privilege that Moses had—to be called a friend of God. But if anything, our privilege is even greater, because we know what sacrifice Jesus made to secure our friendship. He laid down his life for us, dying for our sins on the cross.

As we study the history of salvation, we see God always moving in the direction of closer intimacy with his people. He is always seeking to restore the intimate fellowship we lost through sin. All through Exodus he is trying to find a way to dwell with his people. He can't do it in Exodus 33, but he hasn't given up yet either. He is still meeting with Moses. Soon he will go ahead with his plans for the tabernacle. And by the end of Exodus he will come down to dwell with his people in glory.

The tabernacle was only the beginning. Eventually God came down in the person of his Son and "tabernacled" among us. But he wanted to have an even more intimate relationship with us, so he sent his Spirit to dwell in our hearts by faith. One day he will take us into his very presence. Then, as the Scripture says, we will see him "face to face" (1 Corinthians 13:12a). This has always been God's plan. He wants to draw us into a closer and closer relationship with himself.

God wants to do the same thing in our lives as individual Christians. He wants to develop a deeper, more intimate relationship with us. He wants us to hear his voice speaking in Scripture. He wants us to trust in his promises, depend on his grace, and live by his Spirit. And he wants us to talk to him, growing more intimate with him through prayer.

Do you have this kind of friendship with God? He is inviting you to get to know him by trusting in Jesus. When you receive Jesus Christ into your life by faith, then God is with you. He will never leave you. He will be your friend forever.

# 90

# Under the Shadow of His Hand

EXODUS 33:12–23

IT WAS A GOOD NEWS/BAD NEWS SITUATION. The good news was that the Israelites were still going to the Promised Land, even after the great sin of the golden calf. The bad news was that God wasn't going with them. "Go up to a land flowing with milk and honey," he said, "but I will not go up among you, lest I consume you on the way, for you are a stiff-necked people" (33:3). It was just too dangerous. In his holiness, God might have to destroy the Israelites for their sin.

When the people heard this, they cried tears of repentance and tore off the emblems of their idolatry. Then they waited to see what God would do. Would he stay with them, or would he send them off on their own?

While the Israelites were waiting to find out, Moses went to meet with God. Outside the camp the prophet had pitched a tent of meeting where he could talk things over with God. As Moses went out, the Israelites stood by their own tents and watched to see what would happen. They saw the glory of God come down in a pillar of cloud, and they knew that their mediator was meeting with God.

How they must have wondered what was happening inside that tent! High-level negotiations were taking place, and everyone wanted to know how the talks were going. Would Moses be able to work something out, or would God refuse to make the trip? Israel's destiny depended on what happened in those meetings.

## Stay with Me

At the end of Exodus 33, we are taken inside the tent of meeting to overhear what God and Moses were saying. Their dialogue can be divided into three sections, each of which begins with Moses asking for something from God. In verses 12–14 he asked for something for himself as the mediator, in verses

15–17 he asked for something for Israel as the people of God, and then in verses 18–23 he asked for something for himself as a man who wanted to know God.

First Moses asked for help leading the people of Israel. He said to the Lord, "See, you say to me, 'Bring up this people,' but you have not let me know whom you will send with me. Yet you have said, 'I know you by name, and you have also found favor in my sight.' Now therefore, if I have found favor in your sight, please show me now your ways, that I may know you in order to find favor in your sight" (vv. 12, 13a).

The Bible says that at the tent of meeting God spoke with Moses "as a man speaks to his friend" (v. 11). Here we see Moses speaking to God with the same kind of familiarity. His speech begins with the word "see." So the prophet started something like this: "Now see here, God . . ."

Moses then proceeded to point out what seemed to be an obvious discrepancy between the job he was called to do and the resources he had to carry it out. He still had the same calling to lead Israel to the land of promise. But he couldn't do it on his own. He needed God to go with him. Only now there was some doubt as to whether God would make the trip. So Moses wanted to know who was going with him. Back in verse 2 God promised to send an angel to drive out Israel's enemies, but he hadn't been very specific about the angel's identity. Moses wanted to know *which* angel.

Before God could answer, the prophet went on to make it clear that he would not settle for anything less than the very presence of God. He didn't want any old angel to help him; he wanted the direct guidance of Almighty God. So he begged God to stay with him. "Show me now your ways," he said, "that I may know you" (v. 13a). To lead the people effectively, Moses needed to know the very mind of God. He didn't want God simply to send down orders; he wanted to know the thinking behind God's plans—his ways with his people. To that end, Moses wanted to remain in constant communication with God. This was essential to his spiritual leadership.

As we shall see, the main thing we need to learn from Moses is the way he points us to salvation in Christ. But the prophet also sets an example for our journey in the faith. As we seek to do what God has called us to do, we should pray the way Moses prayed. We should ask God to go with us and to give us intimate knowledge of him. Back in Egypt, Moses had learned (the hard way) how futile it was to do things in his own strength. What we do will only be successful if God is in it. So whenever we do something God has called us to do—whether it is obeying our parents, serving him in our singleness, learning how to be married, working a job, or getting involved in ministry—we need to pray that God will go with us to bless us. Otherwise, all our efforts will be in vain. As Jesus said, "Apart from me you can do nothing" (John 15:5).

When Moses asked God to go with him, he was careful to base his request on one of God's own promises. This was one of the ways he was growing in his prayer life. He was learning the logic of intercession, that the most persuasive prayers argue from premises that God has revealed in his Word. In this case God had said, "I know you by name, and you have also found favor in my sight" (33:12). We do not know when God said this because it is not recorded anywhere else in Scripture. But we can take the prophet's word for it: one of the things God had told Moses when they were talking friend-to-friend was that he knew him and loved him.

This means much more than simply that God knew who Moses was. That would be true of anyone, because in that sense God knows everyone by name. But here the Bible is speaking of a special knowledge that is full of love and favor. According to John Mackay, for God to "know someone by name" is to embrace that person in "a relationship of acceptance and friendship."[1] Moses was an object of covenant grace. God knew him in a loving, saving, and electing way. God knows all his children like this. He knew us in our mother's womb (Psalm 139:13–16). He knew us even before the foundation of the world. He says, "I have loved you with an everlasting love" (Jeremiah 31:3a). Anyone who is friends with God through faith in Jesus Christ is known and loved by the God who rules the universe.

Moses used his favorable standing with God to press for some sort of guarantee that God would stay with him. Earlier he had requested God's presence on the basis of his calling. Now he was asking for it on the basis of his acceptance by God: "If I have found favor in your sight, please show me now your ways, that I may know you in order to find favor in your sight" (33:13). Moses wanted to know the God who knew him.

It is not entirely clear what he meant when he said, "Show me now your ways." Moses may have been asking God to show him the way forward for Israel. If he was going to lead the people, he needed to know where they were going, and only God could show him the way. However, his request might have been more general. To know God's ways is to understand his manner of dealing with people, according to his divine character.

Here again Moses sets the agenda for our own prayers. To serve God effectively, we need to know his ways. Often we want his guidance for specific decisions we have to make. But more than this, we need to know his divine character so that every day we can live in a way that is pleasing to him. Anyone who prays the way Moses prayed will do great things for God. Ask God to be with you. Pray that he will teach you his ways. Seek to know him more intimately. These are prayers that God loves to answer.

God certainly answered these prayers for Moses. God showed him the way. In the words of King David, "He made known his ways to Moses" (Psalm 103:7a). And he promised to stay with Moses: "He said, 'My presence will go with you, and I will give you rest'" (33:14). Literally God said, "My face will go with you." When God said, "my face," he was not identifying a body part but was describing the closeness of his relationship with Moses. This was a promise of God's personal presence. The prophet Isaiah used the same terminology when he said, "The angel of his presence [literally, "the angel of his face"] saved them; in his love and in his pity he redeemed them; he lifted them up and carried them all the days of old" (Isaiah 63:9). God was promising to stay with Moses throughout his journey.

## Go with Us

At the end of his first request, Moses reminded God of his covenant promise to Israel. He was asking God to stay with him as the leader of his people, but he also said, "Consider too that this nation is your people" (33:13b). Moses was hinting that he wanted God to go not only with him, but with the whole nation of Israel.

If this was his request, God seemed to ignore it, because when he told Moses, "My presence will go with you, and I will give you rest" (v. 14), he spoke in the singular. The word "you" does not refer to Israel, therefore, but only to Moses. God was willing to grant Moses some relief by helping him bear the heavy burdens of spiritual leadership, but he had not yet agreed to go up among the Israelites.

This explains why Moses responded to God the way he did: "If your presence will not go with me, do not bring us up from here" (v. 15). At first it may seem like Moses hadn't been paying very good attention. In verse 14 God promised his presence. Moses replied by complaining that if God was not present, Israel would not be able to carry out its mission to the world. But if God had promised to be present, why did Moses raise this issue at all? It sounds as if he was repeating himself.

The answer is that although God had promised to go with him, he had not yet promised to go in the midst of Israel. So Moses was paying attention after all! He was listening so carefully that he picked up on the fact that God had spoken in the singular rather than the plural. And as far as Moses was concerned, that wasn't good enough. The rest of the people needed God every bit as much as he did. So he made a second request that clarified the full intention of his first request. He pleaded for God to go with Israel as a nation.

To persuade God to do this, Moses made his request as forcefully as possible. For starters, he said that unless God agreed to go with them, the Israelites were not even interested in the Promised Land. If God wasn't going, they weren't going either. John Mackay writes,

> If the LORD is not prepared to show his presence with his people—as distinct from merely with Moses himself—then they have lost their special calling and status as the LORD's covenant people, and there is no point in them moving forward to the land. It would be better to remain in the wil-

> derness at Sinai than to enter Canaan without the LORD's full blessing and endorsement.[2]

We can follow their example by making a commitment not to go anywhere without God. We should not set even one foot in a new direction unless we are certain that God will go with us.

When Moses said, "If you don't go, we won't go," he was not resorting to some form of blackmail. He had a serious reason for saying this. Moses understood what the exodus was all about. He knew that it was part of God's plan for saving the world. And he knew that the only way Israel would be able to fulfill its part in that plan was by having God at the center of what they were doing. So he said, "For how shall it be known that I have found favor in your sight, I and your people? Is it not in your going with us, so that we are distinct, I and your people, from every other people on the face of the earth?" (33:16).

Good question. What was it that distinguished the Israelites from other nations as the people of God? It was not their land, because they didn't have any land yet. It was not their wealth, because other nations had more treasure. It was not their culture, because they had been living in slavery. It was not their righteousness, because they could not keep even the most basic commandments. The only thing the Israelites had going for them was their relationship to God. And other people would only know that he was their God if he stayed in their midst.

This is the great divide that runs down the center of the human race. On one side are the people who make their own way through the world, relying on their own talents and pursuing their own goals. But God is not with them. On the other side are those who depend on God's grace and live for God's glory. God is with them; indeed, he is everything to them. And what makes the distinction between those who have God and those who don't is faith in Jesus Christ. This is the great dividing line. Some people have forgiveness for their sins, and some don't. Some people have eternal life, and some don't. Some people have ultimate peace when they face suffering and death, and some don't. The difference is that some people belong to God by faith in Jesus Christ, and others don't. But anyone who wants the comfort of God's presence can have it. There is no need to stay outside. All that God requires is faith in Jesus Christ.

As Moses tried to persuade God to stay with Israel, he did something rather curious. He kept bringing himself into the discussion. He said to God, "For how shall it be known that *I* have found favor in your sight, I and your people? . . . that we are distinct, *I* and your people . . . ?" (v. 16). At first this may sound self-centered. However, Moses understood what it meant to be the mediator of the covenant. He knew that the fate of Israel was tied to his ministry. Somehow his own relationship to God was inextricably linked to their salvation.

This connection between Moses and Israel brings us close to the heart of the gospel. Why did God decide to stay with the Israelites? It was partly because of the promises he had made in the covenant. It also may have had something to do with their repentance, with the way they took off their ornaments as a sign of contrition. But God said he saved the Israelites because he was pleased with their mediator: "This very thing that you have spoken I will do, for you have found favor in my sight, and I know you by name" (v. 17).

Moses was proving to be an effective mediator, and here was another answer to his prayers. He had already persuaded God not to destroy the Israelites but to lead them to the Promised Land. He had also convinced God to stay with him as their guardian and guide. Now God was promising to do what Moses asked him to do in his second request, which was to go in the midst of his people. To be more specific, God was agreeing to go ahead with his plans for the tabernacle and, when it was finished, to come down in glory and live with his people.

God said he would do all this because he was pleased with Moses. When he said, "You have found favor in my sight, and I know you by name" (v. 17), he was speaking again in the singular, referring specifically to Moses. God agreed to go with Israel because he was pleased with his prophet. The Israelites were saved by the merits of their mediator. The grace and love that God elected to show to Moses also extended to them.

God did this so that we would understand the true basis for our salvation. We cannot be saved by what we have done. No one can. We are too sinful to merit salvation. So how can we be saved? Our salvation depends on the pleasure God takes in our mediator. That is to say, our salvation rests on the delight that God takes in the person of his Son and our Savior, Jesus Christ.

This is why the Father's words about the Son were so meaningful. When Jesus came up from his baptism, a voice from Heaven said, "This is my beloved Son, with whom I am well pleased" (Matthew 3:17; cf. 17:5). This is very nearly what God said to Moses: "You have found favor in my sight, and I know you." When he said this, the Father was doing more than simply identifying Jesus as his Son. He was expressing his pleasure in the Son as the acceptable mediator of our salvation. These were more than just words. The Father confirmed his pleasure in the Son by raising him from the dead. The resurrection proved that God was pleased with the perfect life and the atoning death that Jesus offered for sinners.

Frankly, there are times when we wonder how God could ever be pleased with us. We get weighed down by our sin. We feel like failures. We know that we don't even measure up to our own standards, let alone the perfect standard of God. Then we each ask, how could God ever be pleased with someone like me, especially since I know that he is not pleased with my sin? The answer is that God is pleased with Jesus, and therefore he is pleased with anyone who trusts in Jesus. The pleasure God takes in each of us is based on the pleasure that he takes in his own beloved Son. This is the only basis on which God is pleased with anyone. If you want God to be pleased with you, from now until forever, ask Jesus to be your Savior.

Jesus is the Mediator. He does for us what Moses did for Israel, only more perfectly: He prays for our salvation on the basis of his own standing before God. He asks God to accept us not because we're acceptable (we're not), but because *he* is. Jesus says to his Father, "If you are pleased with me, then save my people." And the Father *is* pleased with Jesus. He has said it in his Word, and he has proved it by the resurrection. So he says to Jesus, "I will do the very thing that you have asked. Because I am pleased with you, I will save everyone who trusts in you. O my beloved Son, I will be as pleased with them as I am with you."

## Be Thou My Vision

At this point most people would have been satisfied. God told Moses that his prayer request would be granted. He said, "This very thing that you have spoken I will do" (33:17). God promised to give the prophet exactly what he asked for. But Moses wanted more. Made increasingly confident by the way God answered his first two requests, he said, "Please show me your glory" (v. 18).

This request was not as abrupt as most translations make it sound. In Hebrew it comes across more like an entreaty. But it was still an audacious request. The prophet was asking to see the splendor and radiance of God. Glory is the weightiness of the divine being, and Moses wanted to see it for himself. So with holy boldness he said, "Please show me your glory."

Moses had already seen something of God's glory. He caught his first glimpse at the burning bush, which blazed with fire but was not consumed. He got another glimpse with the seventy elders who saw God (24:9, 10). Then he was covered with glory when he went to the mountaintop and entered the cloud of God's presence (24:15–18). He saw God's glory yet again at the tent of meeting, where the pillar of cloud descended from Heaven (33:9).

But somehow Moses knew there was still more to see. Remember that when he and the elders "saw" God, the only thing they actually saw was the pavement under his feet (24:9, 10). So although he had seen something of God's luminous majesty, he had not yet gazed upon his deity in all its brilliance. Moses wanted a full revelation of God's glory, a visible display of "the essential quality of his being."[3]

Why did Moses make this request? Maybe it was because he understood the meaning of the exodus, that God was saving his people for his glory. If that was the plan, then this seemed like the obvious next step: a full revelation of God's glory. Or maybe it was because Moses wanted to know God more intimately. Only moments before he had said, "Show me now your ways, that I may know you" (33:13). What better way to know God than to see a total revelation of his glory?

Whatever his reasons for asking, Moses wanted to have a personal encounter with the glory of God. And here was God's answer: "I will make all my goodness pass before you and will proclaim before you my name 'The Lord.' And I will be gracious to whom I will be gracious, and will show mercy on whom I will show mercy. But . . . you cannot see my face, for man shall not see me and live" (vv. 19, 20).

It was a yes and no answer. God was willing to reveal his transcendent goodness to Moses. He was willing to announce his sacred divine name (*Yahweh*), just as he had done back at the burning bush. And he was willing to reveal the sovereign grace of his mercy and compassion. This was amazing enough. Moses would have the high privilege of seeing the goodness of God, which is one of the beauties of his divine being. As Stephen Charnock wrote in his famous *Discourses Upon the Existence and Attributes of God*, "Goodness is the brightness and loveliness of our majestical Creator."[4] And God was willing to show his goodness to Moses.

What God was not willing to do was to allow Moses to gaze upon his glory. In other words, he would not give the prophet a direct perception of his divine being. His goodness would pass by (and even this was only for a moment; God would not stand for close scrutiny), but the fullness of his glory would not be seen at all. The reason for this restriction was very simple: If Moses were to see a complete revelation of God in his eternal being, it would be so overwhelming that it would destroy him. God is absolute in his perfection. Moses was a finite, fallen creature, and as such he could not see God and live. No one can. As Augustine said, "No one living in this life can see him as fully as he is."[5] God was willing to show as much of himself as Moses could bear, but there were limits. Some things are beyond our capacity to know. Moses could not see the absolute character of God as he is in himself.

In order to protect Moses from any deadly exposure to his radiant glory, God made some special arrangements. He said, "Behold, there is a place by me where you shall stand on the rock, and while my glory passes by I will put you in a cleft of the rock, and I will cover you with my hand until I have passed by. Then I will take away my hand, and you shall see my back, but my face shall not be seen" (vv. 21–23). Thus Moses was not allowed to look God in the face but only to see, as it were, a fleeting glimpse of the hindquarters of his glory. Here we are dealing with great mysteries. When God talked about his face, his back, and his hand, he was speaking figuratively, of course. He was expressing the invisible majesty of his eternal being in terms of human body parts—physical things that symbolize spiritual realities. God's face refers in some way to the direct revelation of the essence of his divine majesty. To see God's back is to have some lesser experience of his glory, what John Mackay calls "the after-effects of the Lord's presence."[6] We might think of what Moses saw as the contrails of God's glory, the luminous clouds that trailed from his divine being.

God said that as his glory passed by, he would cover Moses with his hand. There was a place in the rock where Moses could hide. There he would be under the shadow of God's care. God would shield him from the radiance of his glory. To put it in a more provocative way, Moses was protected *by* God *from* God. It is important to see this because people often think of being "under the shadow of God's hand" as an image of comfort for the trials of life. Certainly the Bible uses the image this way (e.g., Isaiah 51:16). However, here in Exodus 33 the protection God affords is protection from the greatness of his own glory. In the Bible we see God working out a way of salvation that allows us to know him without being destroyed. We need this protection not because of any deficiency in God, but because of his absolute perfection. The glory of God is more than any mortal can bear.

## Then Face to Face

One wonders whether Moses was tempted to peek. Here was an opportunity no one else had ever been given—a chance to gaze upon the mystery of all mysteries and see the glory of God. One glance would have been fatal, but it still must have been tempting, because this is what human beings have always wanted: a direct experience of Almighty God. This is why people still go on spiritual journeys and why they keep asking ultimate religious questions. It is because we want to know God. We want to understand him. We want to perceive him. In a word, we want to see him.

This is often the way people describe it: They want to *see* God. This was the longing that Job expressed when he said, "In my flesh I shall see God, whom I shall see for myself, and my eyes shall behold, and not another. My heart faints within me!" (Job 19:26b, 27). King David wanted to see the same thing. He said, "As for me, I shall behold your face in righteousness; when I awake, I shall be satisfied with your likeness" (Psalm 17:15). This is what human beings have always longed for. We want to see God so we can know him as he actually is.

This is why it is so wonderful that God sent Jesus to be our Savior. Jesus came so we could see God. There's a story about this in the Gospels. One of the disciples said to Jesus, "Lord, show us the Father, and it is enough for us" (John 14:8). In other words, "Let us see God!" But Jesus said, "Have I been with you so long, and you still do not know me, Philip? Whoever has seen me has seen the Father" (v. 9). The Father and the Son are one. Jesus is God every bit as much as the Father is. So to know him is to know God, to love him is to love God, and to see him is to see God.

As the disciples reflected on their relationship with Jesus, they were amazed to discover that in him they had been seeing God all along. The apostle John wrote, in words that echoed Moses and the exodus, "the Word became flesh and dwelt [literally, "tabernacled"] among us, and we have seen his glory, glory as of the only Son from the Father, full of grace and truth. . . . No one has ever seen

God; the only God, who is at the Father's side, he has made him known" (John 1:14, 18; cf. 2 Corinthians 4:6). John was talking about Jesus, and he was saying that the glory of God has been revealed in him. No one—not even Moses—has seen the face of God, the essence of his eternal being (see John 6:46; 1 John 4:12). But Jesus Christ is God manifested in the flesh. So to know Jesus is to know the God of all glory.

The more we see of Jesus, the more we see of God. This is true figuratively. To "see God" is to perceive his divine attributes and understand his way of salvation. And the way we come to know these things is by studying what the Bible teaches about Jesus Christ. But one day we will literally be able to see Jesus. Jesus Christ has risen from the dead in a glorious body, and when we too have risen, we will be able to see him with our very own eyes: "For now we see in a mirror dimly, but then face to face" (1 Corinthians 13:12a; cf. Matthew 5:8). Only when we ourselves have been raised to glory will we be able to bear the sight of Christ in his glory without being destroyed. In the heart of every believer there is a yearning—yet unsatisfied—to see this promise fulfilled. Even though it is far beyond our comprehension, we know there is still more for us to see, and we long to gaze upon the beautiful face of Jesus Christ. In the meantime we should ask God to show us as much of his glory as presently we can bear.

# 91

# When God Passes By

EXODUS 34:1–7

HAVE YOU EVER WANTED TO SEE SOMEONE really, really badly? In April 2003 my son and I went to see Michael Jordan play professional basketball for the very last time. All we wanted to see was Michael. And we were not the only ones. From the moment Jordan entered Philadelphia's First Union Center, every eye strained to see him. Whether he was shooting or stretching or even just sitting on the bench, everyone was looking at Michael.

According to Exodus, there was someone Moses desperately wanted to see. That "someone" was the God of Israel, in all his glory. Moses had been talking with God in the tent of meeting, but he wanted a fuller revelation of his majesty. He wanted to see God as he is in himself. So he said, "Please show me your glory" (33:18).

In response, God told Moses there were limits to what he could see. Moses was only a man—a sinful man, so he could not endure the direct sight of God's glory. But he could survive a passing glance at God's goodness. So God told him to hide in a cleft in the rock, where God would cover him with his hand. Then God would pass by in all his goodness, and at the last possible moment he would let Moses catch a fleeting glimpse of the backside of his glory. Moses would see what he so desperately wanted to see, something no man had ever seen before: God passing by in glory.

## A New Set of Instructions

Before Moses could see the glory of God, he had to get ready:

> The LORD said to Moses, "Cut for yourself two tablets of stone like the first, and I will write on the tablets the words that were on the first tablets, which you broke. Be ready by the morning, and come up in the morning to Mount Sinai, and present yourself there to me on the top of the mountain. No one

> shall come up with you, and let no one be seen throughout all the mountain. Let no flocks or herds graze opposite that mountain." (34:1–3)

These instructions were meant for Israel's protection. It was not safe for people to touch God's holy mountain. It wasn't even safe for their animals to touch it! This was because of God's supreme holiness. The mountain was made sacred by his presence. He is too dangerous for sinners to approach uninvited and unannounced. So once again, as he did the first time he gave the Ten Commandments, God restricted Israel's access. Only Moses was allowed to go up. He was the mediator, the man chosen to stand before God for the people. But for everyone else there was a sign on the mountain that said, "Don't touch!"

The good news was that God still wanted his people to have his law. The first edition of the Ten Commandments had been destroyed. When Moses came down the mountain and saw the golden calf, he dashed the first set of tablets to the ground, breaking them into a thousand pieces (32:19). Israel had broken the covenant. But God was willing to pick up the pieces of that broken relationship and renew his covenant with his people. So he told Moses to make a fresh set of tablets.

The first time God gave Moses the Law, he also provided the tablets on which it was written. God said, "I [will] give you the tablets of stone, with the law and the commandment, which I have written" (24:12). And this is precisely what God did: "He gave to Moses . . . the two tablets of the testimony, tablets of stone, written with the finger of God" (31:18). The divine origin of these tablets is emphasized again in chapter 32: "The tablets were the work of God, and the writing was the writing of God, engraved on the tablets" (v. 16). God wrote the original Ten Commandments on stones that he provided.

The second time Moses had to bring his own tablets. The Bible doesn't explain why. Perhaps the man-made tablets served as a reminder of Israel's sin. According to Umberto Cassuto, the new tablets showed that Israel had broken the former covenant.[1] He compares this to the second wedding of a couple that has been divorced. When they get remarried, the husband and wife take the same vows they made to one another the first time, but somehow it's not quite the same.

Maybe Cassuto is right. However, a second wedding has a joy all its own. It shows that even a broken covenant can be renewed. And this was the important thing about the new set of tablets: not the tablets themselves, but what was written on them—the Law of God. This was the same law that God gave Moses the first time, a new copy of the Ten Commandments. God said, "I will write on the tablets the words that were on the first tablets" (34:1; cf. Deuteronomy 10:1–4). God was reiterating his covenant with Israel, word for word. He still wanted to have a relationship with his people. And he still wanted them to live by his law, worshiping him alone, honoring his holy day, respecting authority, practicing sexual purity, telling the truth, and keeping all his holy commands.

The way these commands were written is significant. God said that he would do the writing. The Ten Commandments came directly from him, with the full weight of his divine authority. Yet later in the chapter we are told that Moses was the one who wrote down God's law. God said, "Write these words" (34:27), and Moses obeyed: "He wrote on the tablets the words of the covenant, the Ten Commandments" (v. 28b).

This teaches us something very important about how the Bible was written. There is no contradiction between recognizing its human authorship and receiving it as the Word of God. Who wrote the Ten Commandments? Did Moses write them, or did they come from God? Both answers are equally correct. Moses was the author of the book of Exodus, but he was writing under the direct inspiration of the Holy Spirit. Thus the words that he wrote are the very words of God. Liberal theologians try to separate the human from the divine authorship of Scripture, as if God could not use his servants to speak his Word. But the Bible claims to be the Word of God written, even when it was human beings who took pen to paper or stylus to stone. Thus we should receive the Scriptures of the Old and New Testaments as the very Word of God.

## God Came Down

Moses did everything God told him. The Bible tells how he "cut two tablets of stone like the first. And he rose early in the morning and went up on Mount Sinai, as the Lord had commanded him, and took in his hand two tablets of stone" (34:4). Going up early shows the prophet's eagerness to obey. Moses was ready to do God's will. Whenever we know what God wants us to do, we should do it as soon as we can, as Moses did.

The Bible says that Moses went up God's mountain, but even when he reached the very top, God still had to come down to meet him (see v. 5). He is a great God, and no matter how high we reach, he still has to stoop. For us to have an encounter with God at all requires his infinite condescension. He is the Creator; we are only creatures. He is enthroned in Heaven; we dwell on earth below. He's God; we're not. So if he relates to us at all, he must come down.

On this particular occasion God came down in a glorious cloud. This was another theophany—a visible manifestation of the invisible God. Just as God appeared to Moses at the burning bush and the tent of meeting, so he appeared again on the mountain. What is strange is that the Bible says almost nothing about God's appearance. Moses wanted to see God, but rather than telling us what he saw, the Bible tells us what he heard: "The Lord descended in the cloud and stood with him there, and proclaimed the name of the Lord. The Lord passed before him and proclaimed, 'The Lord, the Lord, a God merciful and gracious, slow to anger, and abounding in steadfast love and faithfulness, keeping steadfast love for thousands, forgiving iniquity and transgression and sin'" (vv. 5–7a).

Even Moses had to live by faith and not by sight. He had asked to see the glory, and God showed it to him, or at least a glimpse of it. But what God mainly did was preach a sermon on his divine attributes. Brevard Childs comments, "The revelation of God is in terms of his attributes rather than his appearance."[2] God proclaimed his name to Moses. Then he explained the meaning of his name by listing some of his perfections. He told Moses about his compassion and grace, his patience and love, his faithfulness and forgiveness. This is what God wanted Moses to see: the goodness of his divine nature. And in a way, this was also his glory. For what is the glory of God? It is the weightiness of his being, the totality of his perfections.

Moses wanted to see God. So God said, "All right. Come up here and I'll show you who I am. But if you really want to know me, it's not about seeing what I look like—it's about knowing my infinite perfections, especially as I display them in the salvation of sinners." So God preached his Word to Moses, proclaiming his sacred name and announcing his sovereign attributes. This is what we need as well: not so much to see what God looks like (although one day we will gaze upon his glory in the face of Jesus Christ), but to hear the true words that God has spoken about himself.

## God: A Definition

God started his sermon by repeating his name: "The Lord, the Lord" (34:6). The phrasing almost sounds poetic. God was repeating himself for emphasis. In case there was any doubt, it really was the Lord standing there and talking to Moses.

In most English translations the name of the Lord here is printed in capital and small capital letters to show that this is his special divine name—what Peter Enns calls the "salvation name."[3] God's name is "Yahweh," or "the Lord." This was the sacred name he revealed to Moses at the burning bush, when he said "I am who I am," and "I am has sent me to you" (3:14). God's name testifies to his eternal self-existence and self-sufficiency. Who is God? He is who he is—the covenant Lord. He always has been, and he always will be.

When the Bible speaks of God's name, it is always something more than simply a title. God's name stands for his entire being. It is his nature. It is who he is. So when God passed by Moses and said, "The Lord, the Lord," he was revealing himself as the God of creation and redemption—the God who made and saves his people. And in order to give Moses a fuller revelation of his goodness, he went on to explain the meaning of his sacred name: "The Lord, the Lord, a God merciful and gracious, slow to anger, and abounding in steadfast love and faithfulness, keeping steadfast love for thousands, forgiving iniquity and transgression and sin" (34:6, 7a).

This is one of the most important verses in the entire Bible. We know it's important because it is quoted or referred to dozens of times, especially in the Old Testament.[4] King David prayed, "But you, O Lord, are a God merciful and gracious, slow to anger and abounding in steadfast love and faithfulness" (Psalm 86:15; cf. 103:8; 145:8). The prophet Joel said, "Return to the LORD your God, for he is gracious and merciful, slow to anger, and abounding in steadfast love" (Joel 2:13). Jonah said the same thing when he complained about God's mercy to Nineveh: "I knew that you are a gracious God and merciful, slow to anger and abounding in steadfast love" (Jonah 4:2). The words that God first spoke to Moses became Israel's confession of faith, the people's working definition of God. Whenever anyone wanted to know who God was, they went back to Moses and said, "The Lord is compassionate and gracious, slow to anger, abounding in love and faithfulness."

This divine definition lists seven attributes of God. Each term is rich in its meaning and application. God is "*merciful*." This is a word of sympathy. God cares about our situation. He is sympathetic with our weakness. His heart is drawn to help us whenever we are in need. The Bible says, "As a father shows compassion to his children, so the LORD shows compassion to those who fear him" (Psalm 103:13).

Once when my wife Lisa and I were teaching a premarriage class in our home, our two-year-old son came walking down the stairs. It was long after his bedtime, so I said (rather disapprovingly, even though I was quoting from Dr. Seuss), "You should not be here; you should not be about." A look of distress and dismay crossed his face, and his eyes began to fill with tears. "I'm wet," he whimpered. Immediately I went to pick up my son. I held him in my arms and told him everything would be okay. However imperfectly, this was something like the sympathy of God, who sees what his children need and is drawn to help them. God has a heart full of compassion.

God is also "*gracious*." This is a word of mercy or undeserved favor. People often say they want God to give them what they deserve. If he were to do that, we would all perish in our sins. But God does something better. Rather than giving us what we deserve, he gives us something that we *don't* deserve: the free gift of his grace. Salvation is not based on any merit of our own but only on God's desire to show mercy.

Maxie Dunnam tells the story of a woman who "took a friend with her when she went to a photographer to have her picture taken. The beauty parlor had done its best for her. She took her seat in the studio and fixed her pose. While the photographer was adjusting his lights in preparation for taking the shot, she said to him, 'Now be sure to do me justice.' The friend who had accompanied her said, with a twinkle in her eye, 'My dear, what you need is not justice but mercy.'"[5] This is what we all need, not just in front of the camera lens, but before the all-seeing eye of Almighty God. If we are to be saved at all, it will only be by the undeserved favor of a gracious God.

Next God says he is "*slow to anger*," which is a vivid way of describing his patience. Some of the older translations call it "longsuffering." To say that God is "slow to anger" implies there are times when he does get angry, when he responds to sin with holy wrath. But God is "*slow* to anger." He is not capricious or volatile. And when he acts against evil, he does it righteously and deliberately, not because he loses his temper. John Mackay explains it well:

> *Slow to anger* does not present the LORD as a frustrated deity who eventually loses patience and strikes out against those who have thwarted him. It rather acknowledges that the LORD is reluctant to act against his creation, even when it is in rebellion against him. He waits long to give the sinner opportunity to return in repentance. But he is not forgetful and will not condone sin. At a time of his choosing he will act decisively against it.[6]

The apostle Peter said something similar about God's character in relation to the final judgment: "The Lord is not slow to fulfill his promise as some count slowness, but is patient toward you, not wishing that any should perish, but that all should reach repentance" (2 Peter 3:9).

The merciful, gracious, and long-suffering God abounds in "*love* and *faithfulness*." The Hebrew word for love (*chesed*) is sometimes translated "lovingkindness." It refers specifically to the commitment God has made to his people in the covenant. Here God's covenant love is connected with the Hebrew word for faithfulness (*emet*), which also means "truth" or "truthfulness." The point is that God always follows through on his love. His love is loyal and steadfast. Since he never goes back on a promise, once God promises to love, he keeps on loving. And his love is boundless. It is love without measure and love beyond degree.

Verse 7 repeats the Hebrew word for covenant love (*chesed*) and speaks of God's maintaining this love to thousands. Although the wording is not identical, this seems to echo the second commandment, in which God promised to love "thousands" of those who keep his commandments (20:6). The love of God spreads far and wide; it lasts from generation to generation. God maintains his love. He protects and preserves it. His love endures forever.

Finally, God is "*forgiving*." The Hebrew verb used here (*nasa*) means "to lift or to carry." This gives us a picture of what God does with our sin. He takes it away, lifting the heavy burden of guilt right off our shoulders.

To show how forgiving he is, God lists three things he is willing to forgive: "iniquity and transgression and sin" (34:7). These are three categories of unrighteousness. "Iniquity" (*'awon*) means to "turn aside" from what is right and good. "Transgression" (*pesha'*) is more defiant. John Mackay defines it as a "willful violation of the terms of the covenant, involving not merely disobeying a rule or regulation, but betraying the relationship one has with the covenant King."[7]

Anyone who commits this kind of sin is a traitor to God. The last term ("sin"; *chatta'h*) is the most general. It refers to any kind of moral failure.

The point is that God is willing to forgive any and all kinds of sin. Sometimes we feel so weighed down with guilt that we wonder whether there is any way for God to forgive us. We are tempted to feel that what we have done is so evil that we have fallen beyond the reach of his grace. But however we define what we have done, God is willing to forgive our kind of sinner. He forgives wickedness, rebellion, and sin.

## The God of the Exodus

So this is the God who stood near Moses on the mountain: the compassionate, gracious, patient, loving, faithful, forgiving Lord. This is the God who passed by in glory. And this is the God whom the Israelites worshiped. It's a good thing too, because no other god could have saved them. Only the compassionate and gracious Lord could rescue people like them.

The Israelites needed a compassionate God. They needed someone to hear their cry of distress when they were groaning under their bondage to Pharaoh or when they were hungry and thirsty in the wilderness. And God did hear them. He had compassion on them. He "saw the people of Israel—and God knew" (2:25).

The Israelites needed a gracious God who would treat them better than they deserved. And this is how God treated them all through their journey: with unmerited favor. He rescued them from slavery. He loaded them with treasure. He blessed them with his law. What had the Israelites done to deserve any of this? Absolutely nothing. They were saved by grace.

The Israelites also needed a patient God. They were a bunch of malcontents, always grumbling and complaining. So they needed a God who was slow to anger, who would not give up on them, even when they were hard to love. And speaking of love, they needed a loving God, a God who was faithful to his covenant. And God was faithful. The reason he rescued them from slavery was because he remembered his covenant with Abraham, Isaac, and Jacob (2:24). Moses said it best. After the people walked through the Red Sea on dry ground, he praised God, saying, "You have led in your steadfast love the people whom you have redeemed" (15:13a).

And the Israelites needed a forgiving God. Remember the context: Only days before, the Israelites had worshiped the golden calf. They were guilty of wickedness, rebellion, and sin. Yet Moses had prayed for them. He had begged God, ". . . if you will forgive their sin . . ." (32:32). And God answered the prophet's prayer because he is a forgiving God.

So when God met Moses on the mountain, he revealed himself as the God of the exodus, the God who saved Israel for his glory. He proclaimed in word what he had already demonstrated in deed, that he is "the Lord, the Lord, a

God merciful and gracious, slow to anger, and abounding in steadfast love and faithfulness, keeping steadfast love for thousands, forgiving iniquity and transgression and sin" (34:5–7a). This is the God who saved Israel. He is the only God who could have done it. No other god could have saved people like them.

## God in Christ

Nor can any other god save people like us. The God who passed by Moses in glory is the God whom we need. We need a compassionate God who cares about our situation, a gracious God who gives us what we don't deserve, a patient God who won't give up on us, a loving God who is faithful to his promise, and a forgiving God who takes away our sin.

The wonderful truth of the gospel is that the God of the exodus has given himself to us in Jesus Christ. What God gave to Moses was a definition of his own deity, but it also serves as a fair summary of the character of Jesus Christ. This was the great confession of the early church: "Jesus is Lord" (Romans 10:9).

But what about the rest of the divine attributes that God revealed to Moses? Is Jesus compassionate? Yes, he is. "Compassion" is a word the Gospels often use to describe the way Jesus treated people: "When he saw the crowds, he had compassion for them" (Matthew 9:36a). His compassion was real sympathy, because by becoming a man, Jesus entered into all the misery and suffering of this fallen world. As the Bible says, he is able "to sympathize with our weaknesses" (Hebrews 4:15).

Is Jesus gracious? Yes; the Bible says he is "full of grace and truth" (John 1:14). It says that God has given us an "abundance of grace" through Jesus Christ (Romans 5:17). And when we speak of his grace, we are mainly speaking of the cross where he died for our sins. God treats us better than we deserve. Rather than making us suffer and die for our sins, he accepts the sacrifice that Jesus made on our behalf. This is grace.

Is Jesus patient? Yes; he is slow to anger. To be sure, he does get angry. Just think of what he did to the moneychangers at the temple (John 2:13–16) or the way he responded to the Pharisees who refused to show mercy on the Sabbath (Mark 3:5). Jesus was angry! But he is slow to anger, especially when it comes to his own disciples. Think how patient Jesus was with their repeated failure to understand who he was and what he had come to do.

Is Jesus loving and faithful? Yes again. Everything Jesus did to save us was an act of love. He became a man; he kept God's law; he endured the cross. And he did it all out of love, specifically the love that God has for us in the covenant. Jesus was faithful to do everything that was necessary for our salvation. The Bible says, "In this is love, not that we have loved God but that he loved us and sent his Son to be the propitiation for our sins" (1 John 4:10). Also, Paul prayed that we might know "what is the breadth and length and height and depth" of the love of Christ (Ephesians 3:18). Jesus abounds in love and faithfulness.

Is he forgiving? Yes; with him is full forgiveness. He forgave sinners and tax collectors. He forgave his fallen disciples. He forgave women caught in adultery. He forgave his enemies. He even forgave the men who nailed him to the cross.

Jesus Christ is the very definition of God. If we take the most important statement of God's identity from the Old Testament and compare it to the life of Christ, we see that Jesus is very God of very God. Therefore, when God passed by Moses on the mountain, proclaiming his attributes, he was also telling Moses about God the Son. God was preaching the gospel of Jesus Christ, who is the Lord God of compassion and grace. This was confirmed for Moses on the Mount of Transfiguration, when he saw the glorified Christ (Matthew 17:1–13). There he met the same glorious God whom he had met on Mount Sinai, only this time he met him in the person of his Son.

Do you know this God? Do you know his Son, Jesus Christ? As we study Exodus, we long to see what Moses saw and hear what Moses heard. But the important thing is to know God through Jesus Christ. Are you struggling with suffering? Jesus is full of compassion; he cares about your situation. Are you weighed down with guilt? Jesus is gracious and forgiving. He will treat you better than you deserve, taking away all your sin. Are you filled with doubt and anxiety? Jesus is loving and faithful. He will keep his promises to the very end.

## One Final Attribute

This is probably where we would like to stop, with all the divine attributes that we love to praise: gracious compassion, faithful love, patient forgiveness. However, this is not where God stopped, and we must not stop before he does. God concluded his sermon on the divine attributes by making a strong affirmation of his *justice*: "[He] will by no means clear the guilty, visiting the iniquity of the fathers on the children and the children's children, to the third and the fourth generation" (34:7b).

This is another echo from the second commandment, in which God said, "I the LORD your God am a jealous God, visiting the iniquity of the fathers on the children to the third and the fourth generation of those who hate me" (20:5). The sins of those who rebel against God leave a bitter legacy for the generations that follow. God holds us responsible for our actions not just as individuals but also as families. In Biblical times people generally lived in extended families, with three or even four generations sharing the same home. This helps explain why God held families accountable as families: Generations were living together in community. A good example is the way he punished the families of Korah, Dathan, and Abiram when they rebelled against Moses (Numbers 16:25–34). But even today we are implicated in the sins of others within any covenant community, especially the family.

Talking about God's justice has a way of making people uncomfortable. We would prefer to talk about his love and grace and leave it at that. But this is not all that God is. He is also holy and just. We have to take him whole, not just in parts. And to do this, we have to hold more than one idea in our minds at once. The Bible often forces us to do this. It teaches both the unity and the trinity of the Godhead, the humanity and the deity of Jesus Christ, the divine and the human authorship of Scripture, God's sovereignty and our responsibility, and so forth. One of the marks of sound theology is confessing everything the Bible teaches, not just part of it. This is what distinguishes orthodoxy from heresy. Heretics leave out part of the truth. They believe in the humanity of Jesus Christ but not his deity, they think that human responsibility somehow limits divine sovereignty, and so on.

When it comes to the doctrine of God, we have to believe what God says about himself in his Word: He is a God of justice as well as grace. As Maxie Dunnam puts it, "God is holy love."[8] Many people prefer to think of God as a kindly old grandfather who smiles indulgently on the sins of his grandchildren. This is the deity promoted by liberal theology—a god of unjust love. But this is not the God of the Bible. Our definition of God is not complete unless it includes his divine justice. Indeed, it is only in the context of God's justice that some of his other attributes come to their fullest expression. C. S. Lewis wrote: "Mercy, detached from Justice, grows unmerciful. That is the important paradox. As there are plants which will flourish only in mountain soil, so it appears that Mercy will flower only when it grows in the crannies of the rock of Justice."[9] God does not let sin go unpunished, and this is one of his perfections. In a word, God is righteous. He is a God who punishes—yes, punishes!—sin.

This almost seems like a contradiction. How can the same God forgive and also punish? There seems to be a tension in the very definition of God. How can we resolve it? This is a real problem, because we are among the guilty. To prove this, all we need to do is run down the list of divine attributes and ask if we measure up to God's perfect character. Clearly we don't. We are not merciful and gracious. We are not slow to anger. We are not abounding in love and faithfulness. We are not willing to forgive all kinds of sin. We are not at all the kind of people that God wants us to be. But if that's the case, how can he accept us? After all, he does not leave the guilty unpunished. God is not to be trifled with. Some of his attributes can be deadly.

Some people try to resolve the apparent difficulty by drawing a contrast between the Father and the Son. The God of the Old Testament is a God of justice, they say, but in the New Testament, Christ is a God of love. This is wrong for two reasons. First, it is wrong about what God is like in the Old Testament. As we have seen, the God who led Israel out of Egypt was compassionate and gracious. And, second, when people pit the Father against the Son, they're also wrong about Jesus. Somehow they have the idea that Jesus never condemned anyone for anything, when in fact he often rebuked people for their sins and warned them explicitly about the judgment to come. No one in the Bible talks about Hell more than Jesus. Thus the second half of Exodus 34:7 applies to Jesus every bit as much as the first half.

So how can we reconcile God's justice with his grace? It all seems very confusing until we understand that God worked it all out on the cross. On the cross Jesus died to make atonement for our sin. The Bible says he did this so that God could be "just and the justifier of the one who has faith in Jesus" (Romans 3:26). The crucifixion satisfied God's justice. Jesus paid the debt that we owed because of our sin. But this was also an act of mercy and grace because anyone who trusts in Jesus is fully forgiven. We do not have to die for our own sins; Jesus has already suffered the punishment that we deserve. And because Jesus has done this, God has only grace and mercy for us. And he can give it to us without denying any of his perfections or doing violence to his character. Jesus has satisfied the claims of God's justice. Now everyone who believes in him knows the Lord as the compassionate and gracious God, slow to anger, abounding in love and faithfulness, and forgiving all kinds of sin.

# 92

# God, and God Alone

EXODUS 34:8–17

BE CAREFUL WHAT YOU PRAY FOR because there's always a chance that God might grant your request. This was the experience Moses had at the top of Mount Sinai. The prophet had asked to see God's glory. And God had answered the prophet's prayers, passing by in glory. As he passed by, God also spoke to Moses, proclaiming his name and expounding his attributes. He revealed his compassion, grace, patience, love, faithfulness, forgiveness, and justice.

It was an awesome display of God's majesty, but Moses saw hardly any of it. God showed him what he was there to see, but when the moment actually came, it was too much to bear. Moses could not keep his gaze on the glory of God. Instead, he "bowed his head toward the earth and worshiped" (34:8). The prophet assumed a posture of reverence and submission. He fell down prostrate and put his face in the dust.

This is always the right way to respond to God's glorious goodness. When in doubt, worship! Worship God for his compassionate grace, his covenant love, his patient forgiveness, and even his holy justice. Whenever we catch a glimpse of God's true majesty, we should bow in humble adoration and praise.

## Moses Prays Again

As Moses worshiped, he prayed. This was at least the fifth time the prophet had prayed since the incident with the golden calf. Moses was the mediator, the man appointed to intercede for Israel's sin. Moses was rapidly becoming a full-time defense attorney. In 32:11–13 Moses prayed that God would not destroy the Israelites, but that for the sake of his covenant glory, he would preserve them. In 32:31, 32 he prayed that God would forgive Israel's sin or else blot his name from the Book of Life. In 33:12, 13 he prayed that God would go with him to guide him. Then in 33:15, 16 he prayed that God would be with the Israelites to be their God. Whatever else Moses may have learned in ministry, serving as mediator certainly strengthened his prayer life!

In Exodus 34 we find him at prayer once again. "And he said, 'If now I have found favor in your sight, O Lord, please let the Lord go in the midst of us, for it is a stiff-necked people, and pardon our iniquity and our sin, and take us for your inheritance'" (v. 9). By now this prayer is starting to sound familiar. Moses has made nearly every one of these petitions before. In his former prayers he addressed God as his Lord (32:11), he sought God's favor on the basis of his mediatorial ministry (33:12, 13), he prayed for God's presence (33:15, 16), he confessed Israel's sin (32:31), he begged God's forgiveness (32:32), and he asked God to remember that the Israelites were his people (32:13). Moses was recycling his prayers.

Some Bible scholars object to this. They complain that Exodus is repetitious, that the prayers of Moses are redundant. They point out that God had already promised to do all the things Moses was asking him to do: to forgive his people and go with them on their way. If God had already made these promises, they say, then what was the point in praying about them again?

However, repetition is an essential element of prayer. We often ask God for the same things over and over, including things he has promised to give. Just think of the way Jesus taught us to pray: "thy kingdom come, thy will be done," "give us this day our daily bread," "forgive us our debts," and so forth. These are all things that God has promised his people. We know that his kingdom will come, that he will meet our daily needs, and that he will forgive our sins. Nevertheless, we pray in this way—not in spite of God's promises, but because of them.

Moses had learned to pray within the promises of God. God had promised to be present (33:14), so Moses prayed that he would go with them. God had promised to forgive wickedness and rebellion (34:7), so Moses asked him to pardon Israel's sin. God had promised to take Israel as his treasured possession (19:5; cf. Psalm 33:12), so Moses asked him to make the people his inheritance. The prophet took God's promises—as well as what God had revealed about his character—and made these the basis for his prayers.

God invites us to pray the way Moses prayed. We ought to make our intercession on the basis of his gracious promises and glorious perfections. God has promised never to leave us or forsake us. So we say, "Lord Jesus, I know you said that you would stay with me; so as I enter this new situation, I pray that you will go with me by the power of your Spirit." God has told us that he is a forgiving God in Jesus Christ, so no matter what we have done, we ask him to pardon all our sin. God has also promised to take us as his inheritance. In other words, he has declared that we belong to him in the covenant. We are his possession, and we cannot be taken from him. So we ask God to make us fully his own, begging him to be our God both now and forever. This is the way we should pray and keep on praying. As the Puritan William Gurnall once said: "O Christian, stand to your prayer in a holy expectation of what you have begged upon the credit of the promise."[1]

Moses had several good reasons to pray the way he did. For one thing, he had just been reminded of God's holiness. At the end of his sermon on the divine attributes, God declared that he does not "clear the guilty" (34:7b). This was a sobering declaration of God's holy justice. In the words of one writer, God "is saying that because He is holiness itself, He can never put up with anything that is unholy—that He not only cannot put up with it, He will not put up with it."[2] Naturally, this gave Moses cause for concern. The Israelites were unholy. They had proved this with the golden calf, and thus they deserved whatever punishment God decided to send. Given these circumstances, it only seemed right for Moses to admit—once again—that the people were sinners and to ask—once again—for God's forgiveness.

Only this time Moses went a step further and included himself in the prayer. "Pardon *our* iniquity," he said, "and *our* sin" (34:9). This was real spiritual leadership. As the mediator, Moses was identifying himself with the people in their sin. In the words of Umberto Cassuto, "Moses, out of love for his people, associates himself with the collective deeds of the children of Israel, and includes himself among the transgressors."[3]

This is one of the many ways that Moses shows us the structure of salvation and thus points to the saving work of Jesus Christ. Jesus Christ is our mediator. Although he was not a sinner, he took our sin upon himself so that we could receive forgiveness from God. Therefore, the way for us to escape God's holy wrath and have our sins forgiven is to trust in Jesus Christ: "Everyone who believes in him receives forgiveness of sins through his name" (Acts 10:43).

## The Covenant God Glorified among the Nations

Given the way that Moses prayed within God's promises, it is not surprising that God granted him everything he asked for. God would go with his people. He would forgive their sin. He would claim them as his possession. God would do these things because he had promised to do them, and also because they were in keeping with his character as Israel's gracious and faithful God. This was all included in God's simple response: "Behold, I am making a covenant" (34:10).

When God said this, he did not explicitly say that he would go with his people or forgive their sins or make them his inheritance. He didn't have to. All these things were included in the covenant, which was God's binding promise—his unbreakable commitment—to be everything that Israel ever needed in a God. This included the promise of his presence. It included the forgiveness of their sins. And it included becoming God's eternal inheritance. This was all included in the covenant. Then, as now, to be in the covenant meant having a right to all the blessings of God.

The covenant that God made with Moses and Israel was nothing new. He had made a covenant with them when they first arrived at Mount Sinai. But Moses had broken the first tablets of the Law. So for the covenant to remain in effect, it needed to be reiterated, and Exodus 34 is the repetition of the covenant. First, Moses made a new set of tablets (34:1). Then, under the inspiration of God, he rewrote the Ten Commandments, putting the same words on new tablets (34:28).

This was all very reassuring because it meant that God remained committed to his people. He still wanted to have a relationship with them, even after they had sinned. And the way to reassure them of all this was to remind them of the covenant. Whenever we have any doubts about the love of God, all we need to do is go back to the promises he has made to us in the covenant. This is even more reassuring for us than it was for Israel, because now the covenant has been ratified with the blood of a better mediator. All the promises of God are "Yes" to us in Jesus Christ (2 Corinthians 1:20).

As he reestablished the covenant, God wanted Moses to understand its ultimate purpose. It was the same purpose God has for everything he does: He did it all for his glory. "And he said, 'Behold, I am making a covenant. Before all your people I will do marvels, such as have not been created in all the earth or in any nation. And all the people among whom you are shall see the work of the LORD, for it is an awesome thing that I will do with you'" (v. 10).

By now this plan ought to be very familiar. If we learn nothing else from the book of Exodus, we learn that God saved his people for his glory. He brought Israel out of Egypt in order to display his power and his grace. He never did anything like this for anyone else, before or since. But this was not for Israel's benefit alone. God did it so that other nations would see his majesty.

When God spoke of doing wonders, what kind of wonders did he have in mind? God had already performed many mighty miracles for Israel. He struck their enemies with dreadful plagues. He turned the sea into dry ground. He sent bread from Heaven. And God would continue working wonders. He would lead Israel through the wilderness and then establish his kingdom in the Promised Land. He would dispossess Israel's enemies in the conquest of Canaan. All of this would display his saving power. God's plan was to reveal his glory by showing special favor to the people he had chosen to save. He kept his covenant with them so he would be glorified among the nations.

God has the same purpose today. He wants to "declare his glory among the nations, his marvelous works among all the peoples!" (Psalm 96:3). To accomplish this purpose, he has sent the world a Savior: his own Son, Jesus Christ. Jesus died on the cross for sinners, and then he was buried, but on the third day he rose from the dead. The good news is that now everyone who believes in Jesus receives eternal life. And this good news is for the whole world. According to the Bible, God sent Jesus to be "known to all nations . . . to bring about the obedience of faith" (Romans 16:26b). This was always God's plan in the covenant: to spread his glory throughout the world. As people see the wonder of what God has done to save sinners through Jesus Christ, they join together in giving him the praise. This is what motivates our commitment to world missions: the desire to see God glorified among the nations for his grace in the covenant.

## Against Idolatry

God described his relationship with his people as a covenant. This covenant was all about what God would do to bring glory to himself. However, the covenant also demanded a response. At the same time that God was taking the Israelites to be his people, the Israelites needed to take God to be their God. It was a mutual relationship, and by its very nature, this relationship was exclusive. To have God be their God, the Israelites needed to turn away from every other deity.

God knew how hard this would be for them to do. So he said to them:

> Observe what I command you this day. Behold, I will drive out before you the Amorites, the Canaanites, the Hittites, the Perizzites, the Hivites, and the Jebusites. Take care, lest you make a covenant with the inhabitants of the land to which you go, lest it become a snare in your midst. You shall tear down their altars and break their pillars and cut down their Asherim (for you shall worship no other god, for the LORD, whose name is Jealous, is a jealous God). (34:11–14)

When God told the Israelites not to "make a covenant," he was saying that if they were in a covenant relationship with him, they couldn't make a covenant with anyone else. In the ancient world, "alliances with other peoples were not only alliances with humans but with their gods as well."[4] Therefore, making a covenant with another tribe meant acknowledging the legitimacy of the deities they worshiped.

For most people groups, this wouldn't have posed any difficulty. Most ancient cultures were polytheistic; the people worshiped many gods. But things were supposed to be different in Israel, where God called his people to be radical monotheists. The Israelites were in a covenant relationship with the one and only true and living God. How could they possibly acknowledge—even for a moment—the reality of any other god? Obviously they couldn't; so God commanded them not to make a covenant with the Amorites, Canaanites, Hittites, or anyone else.

Then God went one step further. Not only were the Israelites forbidden to make a covenant with any of these people, but they were also forbidden to use their places of worship. God was planning to drive the Canaanites out of the land. When they left, they would leave their altars behind, as well as their sacred stones and the poles they used for goddess-worship. This would pose a serious temptation for the Israelites. As God said, it would be a "snare" for them (v. 12), like the trap used to catch a bird. If they left the sacred places standing, they would be tempted to worship false gods.

The reason God was so adamantly opposed to any form of idolatry was very simple: He wanted his relationship with his people to be exclusive. He wanted this because of the kind of God that he is. He's jealous! Not only is he jealous, but he is so jealous that "Jealous" is his very name. As God said to Moses, "you shall worship no other god, for the LORD, whose name is Jealous, is a jealous God" (v. 14).

At first "Jealous" may not seem like a very appropriate name for God. This is one of the reasons we need the Bible. If we were to put God's attributes up for a vote, jealousy wouldn't even make the top ten. But rather than coming up with our own ideas about God, we want to know God's ideas about God, as revealed in the Bible. We can trust God to tell us the truth about himself. And one of the things he has said about himself—not just once but dozens of times, and in every part of the Bible—is that he is jealous. It's in the second commandment: "You shall not make for yourself a carved image . . . for I the LORD your God am a jealous God" (20:4, 5). God repeated this claim when he reiterated the covenant in chapter 34: "The LORD . . . is a jealous God" (v. 14).

What does this mean? We usually think of jealousy as spiteful envy, but how could such an attitude be worthy of God? The answer is that there is more than one kind of jealousy. Of course, jealousy can be sinful, and with us, it usually is. The *Oxford English Dictionary* defines the word "jealous" as "afraid, suspicious, or resentful of rivalry in love." This is the way we tend to be: resentful of rivalry. But the primary definition of the word is "fiercely protective."[5] And although God is neither suspicious nor resentful, he certainly is protective, especially when it comes to his relationship with his people. There is nothing God guards more jealously than his love for us and our love for him in the covenant. According to J. I. Packer, "God's jealousy is not a compound of frustration, envy, and spite, as human jealousy so often is, but appears instead as a praiseworthy zeal to preserve something supremely precious." When God told Moses that his name is Jealous, "He meant that He demands from those whom He has loved and redeemed utter and absolute loyalty, and will vindicate His claim by stern action against them if they betray His love by unfaithfulness."[6]

Perhaps the best way to understand the proper jealousy of God is to think in terms of marriage. Even in marriage, jealousy can be sinful. Sometimes husbands and wives have unjust suspicions, petty resentments, and unholy obsessions. And sometimes this leads to such anger and violence that the marriage covenant is destroyed. But there is also a righteous jealousy that nourishes the passion of marriage. By its very nature marriage is an exclusive love relationship, and thus it requires the right kind of jealousy. Indeed, it is impossible to have a godly marriage without it. Jealousy is what makes a wife fiercely protective of her husband's reputation. It is what draws a husband to set aside time for his wife. And it is what banishes the very thought of ever ending up in the arms of another woman, or another man.

This is the kind of jealousy God has for his people: a passionate and protective love. John Calvin wrote:

> God very commonly takes on the character of a husband to us. Indeed, the union by which he binds us to himself when he receives us into the bosom of the church is like sacred wedlock, which must rest upon mutual faithfulness. As he performs all the duties of a true and faithful husband, of us in return he demands love and conjugal chastity. That is, we are not to yield our souls to Satan, to lust, and to the filthy desires of the flesh, to be defiled by them. . . . [T]he Lord, who has wedded us to himself in truth, manifests the most burning jealousy wherever we, neglecting the purity of his holy marriage, become polluted with wicked lusts. But he especially feels this when we transfer to another . . . the worship of his divine majesty, which deserves to be utterly uncorrupted. In this way we not only violate the pledge given in marriage, but also defile the very marriage bed by bringing adulterers to it.[7]

To put it more simply, God cares for us like a faithful husband. Therefore, he is jealous for our love. And when we share our love with anyone else, we are guilty of religious promiscuity. In his excellent book on the theme of spiritual adultery, Ray Ortlund writes: "When the love of Jealous is offended, he burns. His love is not morally indifferent, pouring out its benefits heedless of human response. He expects and requires an ardent and faithful love in return."[8]

All this talk of marriage fits the context of Exodus 34, where God not only describes his relationship with Israel as a covenant, but also warns his people about the danger of spiritual adultery:

> [Take care] lest you make a covenant with the inhabitants of the land, and when they whore after their gods and sacrifice to their gods and you are invited, you eat of his sacrifice, and you take of their daughters for your sons, and their daughters whore after their gods and make your sons whore after their gods. You shall not make for yourself any gods of cast metal. (vv. 15–17)

These verses describe a downward descent into idolatry. If the Israelites made any kind of alliance with pagan nations, they would get invited to participate in idol worship. Then they would face a further temptation: to intermarry with people who worshiped other gods. When their daughters did this, they would go and live with other tribes. But when their sons intermarried, their wives would come and live among the Israelites, bringing their idols with them. This would lead to even more sinful forms of idol worship, possibly including ritual sex with temple prostitutes. As Ray Ortlund explains, the danger unfolds by stages:

> First as a treaty of mutual advantage, then as an invitation to share in worship, then eating of a sacrifice made to a pagan god or goddess, and finally intermarriage with the Canaanites, with the result that all distinctions may in time be expected to dissolve. What begins as an agreement between friends eventuates in the extinction of Israel as a people uniquely covenanted to God.[9]

In the end, the Israelites would be tempted to cast their own idols, just as they did when they flirted with the golden calf.

These warnings turned out to be prophetic. The Israelites never completely drove their enemies out of Canaan. They made treaties with foreign nations (see, e.g., Joshua 9:14, 15). They allowed pagan altars to stand. And as a result, they were seduced into worshiping idols. In doing this, they failed to set a good example for the next generation. Children generally worship what their parents worship. So Israel's sons married women who served other gods, which led the Israelites to commit even more wicked acts of spiritual adultery (e.g., Numbers 25:1, 2). This was Samson's mistake (Judges 14), as well as the downfall of King Solomon (1 Kings 11:1–13). Nothing caused more trouble in Israel than the worship of false gods. Eventually things got so bad that God had to remove his people from the Promised Land.

How did it all start? It all started when the Israelites first entered the land and decided not to destroy the idols that would tempt them to sin. This is what was so tragic: It all could have been avoided. If only the Israelites had obeyed God's command. If only they had refused to make a covenant with anyone else. If only they had been careful not to marry outside their faith. If only they had been as jealous for God as he was for them!

## Loving God Alone

The application is very simple: When it comes to worshiping other gods, there can be no compromise. God wants all our worship and all our praise. He wants us to give the glory to him, and to him alone. Therefore all our idols must be broken, all our sacred stones must be smashed, and all our goddess poles must be cut down.

This does *not* mean that God wants us to vandalize the mosques and temples of strange gods. We do not have the right to destroy other people's property. In a pluralistic society, if someone wants to worship idols, they have the legal right to do so. As Christians we believe in religious tolerance, especially since we know that the kingdom of God never advances by force but only by love. So what *does* God want us to do? He wants us to refuse to make any truce with idolatry in our churches, our families, and our own Christian lives.

We can apply this principle to contemporary theology. Today many people—including some who call themselves evangelicals—think there are many ways to God. They like to think that underneath, all religions are really the same. But God is a jealous God, and when he says that we can only be saved through faith in Jesus Christ, he means it. God sent Jesus to become a man and to be our Savior so that we could know him more intimately. How can we have a relationship with God in any way other than by trusting in Jesus?

We can apply the same principle to our relationships with people from other faiths. We are called to love them, serve them, and befriend them. But the one thing we cannot do is worship with them. To do so would be to deny our covenant relationship to God. This is what is wrong with Christians participating in interfaith worship services. In various ways we can work with people who don't know Christ. But we cannot worship with them. Nor can we serve together in any kind of spiritual alliance. We do not serve the same God, and our God is a jealous God. As the Scripture says, "Do not be unequally yoked with unbelievers" (2 Corinthians 6:14a).

The same principle applies to marriage. The Bible is very explicit about this. God has never allowed his people to marry outside their relationship with him. The reason for this is obvious: Marriage is a covenant, and how can there be a true covenant unless both the husband and the wife are in covenant together with the same God? By implication, this principle also applies to courtship. If dating is preparation for marriage, then Christians should only have serious dating relationships with people it is possible to marry. Non-Christians fail to qualify.

We are called to separate ourselves from idolatry in many ways, but the main place we need to apply this principle is in our own hearts. God wants our relationship with him to be exclusive. To have such a relationship with God, we need to guard our hearts. The greatest threat to our love for God is our attraction to other things. Too often we fail to sense the danger that our affections pose, the way they threaten our very souls. First we make a truce with them, tolerating their presence somewhere in our lives. Soon we are drawn to worship them, and eventually to commit out-and-out spiritual adultery. We do this with money, sex, power, and all the other idols of this age.

What God wants us to do instead is to fall so in love with him that we are unwilling to have any other lovers. But how hard this is for us to do! Not long after arriving in Asia, one missionary wrote:

> I am sitting this morning in the kitchen and I am caught up in two extremes. As I look out onto the makeshift type of kitchen on the porch-like area, I think with such fondness of our comfortable home in the States. I think of how big it was, how there was so much room for the kids to play, of how well our kitchen worked, of how large our refrigerator was, how many products there were to eat, etc., etc. I also think of the incredible convenience of the minivan and the protection of seatbelts. I wonder, "What have I been falling in love with over the last eleven years? Have I been falling

> in love with comfort or have I been falling in love with Jesus?" I fear that all my comforts have started to act like dark sunglasses and I have not seen the glory of my Lord.[10]

What have you been falling in love with? What are you teaching your children to love? Is it comfort? Success? Money? Is it a game or hobby? Is it your work? God is a jealous lover—in every best sense of the word—and he wants you to love him alone.

# 93

# Staying in Covenant Love

EXODUS 34:18–28; 35:1–3

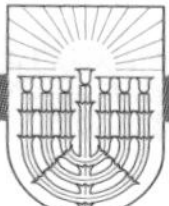

EXODUS 34 IS RATHER PUZZLING. For one thing, it repeats many verses from earlier in Exodus. Verse 18 combines several verses from chapter 12; verses 19, 20 come from chapter 13; verses 22–24 quote chapter 23; and so on. Why did God say these things again, and why did he say them in this order? The list seems almost random. It includes everything from how to redeem a donkey to how to cook a young goat (or how not to).

Another puzzle is the way that the chapter combines two kinds of laws. Some of the commands in Exodus 34 are moral laws straight from the Ten Commandments. God tells his people not to have any other gods (v. 14), not to make graven images (v. 17), and not to work on the Sabbath (v. 21). In other words, he repeats the first, second, and fourth commandments. But other laws in this chapter are ceremonial, not moral. They do not come from the Ten Commandments at all, but from other events in Exodus, as well as from the Book of the Covenant that God gave to Moses after he issued the Ten Commandments (24:7).

At first verses 27, 28 seem like they might help us understand how the chapter fits together, but as it turns out, they only seem to add to the confusion: "And the Lord said to Moses, 'Write these words, for in accordance with these words I have made a covenant with you and with Israel.' So he was there with the Lord forty days and forty nights. He neither ate bread nor drank water. And he wrote on the tablets the words of the covenant, the Ten Commandments."

When God told Moses to "write these words," he seemed to be referring to what he had just said—the various laws he had been repeating. However, the next verse (v. 28) refers explicitly to the Ten Commandments. Are these the same commandments as the ones given in chapter 20, or a new set of laws given in chapter 34? And are they the same words that Moses wrote down in verse 27, or do they form a completely different document? The words in verse

28 were written in stone, but verse 27 does not specify this. Perhaps there were two documents, but if so, which one was the covenant? Then there is a further question: Who wrote these words? In verse 27 Moses does the writing, but verse 28 simply says, "*He* wrote on the tablets." This would seem to refer to Moses. However, back in verse 1 God said that he would write the words on the tablets. So who did the writing?

Different scholars answer these questions in different ways. Some say that Exodus 34 is a different version of the Ten Commandments. They regard Exodus as a loose collection of historical documents, somewhat haphazardly put together. On this interpretation, chapter 34 is an alternative account of God's law for Israel. Others call it a "ritual decalogue"—ten commandments for Israel's worship.[1] They point out that most of the commands in this chapter deal in some way with Israel's annual festivals.

The problem with this way of looking at Exodus 34—apart from seeming to contradict Exodus 20—is that there are more than ten laws here. So the words on the tablets mentioned in verse 28 were not words from this chapter, but the same words that God gave to Moses back in chapter 20: the original Ten Commandments. God was not making a new covenant with Israel; he was reestablishing the covenant he had already made.

But this still leaves us with a question: When God reissued his covenant, why did he repeat only certain commands and not others? Exodus 34 contains excerpts from the rest of God's law that seem somewhat random. God reiterated some of the Ten Commandments but not all of them. Then he added regulations drawn from various parts of the ceremonial law. But how do they all fit together? What is the logic of this passage?

Rather than giving up and deciding that the passage doesn't have much logic (as some scholars do), we want to try and understand the mind of God, who revealed these words by his Holy Spirit. The way to understand them is to remember the context. The Israelites had just committed the great sin of the golden calf. They were guilty of worshiping other gods. Yet in his wonderful mercy and grace, God had forgiven their sin, and now he was giving them a fresh opportunity to live for his glory.

It was in this context that God repeated some of the demands of the covenant. The whole covenant was still in effect. This is why God issued a fresh copy of the Ten Commandments. But he also wanted to help his people keep the covenant in precisely the ways that they had broken it. To that end he gave them a series of regulations—some new and some old—that would keep them from worshiping like Canaanites. These regulations were designed to help the Israelites especially after they entered the Promised Land. According to John Mackay, they were "a sample of the demands of the covenant, dealing with particular areas of living which are seen to be especially hazardous in the light of the defection involving the Golden Calf."[2] The Israelites had fallen into idolatry.

So God repeated some of the moral and ceremonial laws that would help them worship him alone. God was jealous (see 34:14). He loved his people with a fiercely protective love. To help safeguard their love for him in return, he gave them these guidelines for staying in covenant love.

## A Pattern for Worship

God started by telling the Israelites what *not* to do (34:11–17). He told them not to make a covenant with people who worshiped other gods or to make idols or to worship at pagan altars. By obeying these commands, the Israelites would remain spiritually separated from false worship, and this would help them protect their love for God with a holy jealousy.

In addition to telling the Israelites what to avoid, God also had some things he wanted them to practice—things that would help them stay in love with God. We can summarize these regulations in three principles: maintain a regular pattern of worship, enter God's holy rest, and offer God your very best.

The first thing, and perhaps the main thing in this passage, was to maintain a regular pattern of corporate worship. The Israelites nurtured their love for God by gathering to worship him at three pilgrim feasts every year. Exodus 34 mentions all three of these annual festivals.

First came the Feast of Unleavened Bread. God said, "You shall keep the Feast of Unleavened Bread. Seven days you shall eat unleavened bread, as I commanded you, at the time appointed in the month Abib, for in the month Abib you came out from Egypt" (v. 18; cf. 12:17–20; 23:15). This feast began with the Passover meal and lasted one full week afterward. For seven days the Israelites were forbidden to eat anything made with yeast. This symbolized their separation from the spread of sin. Together with Passover, the Feast of Unleavened Bread reminded the Israelites what happened the night that God delivered them from Egypt: they had to leave in such haste that their bread did not have time to rise.

Next came the Feast of Weeks and the Feast of Ingathering. God said:

> You shall observe the Feast of Weeks, the firstfruits of wheat harvest, and the Feast of Ingathering at the year's end. Three times in the year shall all your males appear before the Lord God, the God of Israel. For I will cast out nations before you and enlarge your borders; no one shall covet your land, when you go up to appear before the Lord your God three times in the year. (34:22–24; cf. 23:14–17)

At the Feast of Weeks—also known as the Feast of Harvest or Firstfruits—the first produce from the harvest was presented as an offering to God. Then the Israelites counted off seven weeks from Passover—hence the name: Feast of Weeks. At that time they praised God for the land and its abundant harvest. Then came the Feast of Ingathering, or Feast of Tabernacles. This joyous festival came at the end of the harvest, when all the work was done and the crops were safely gathered in. The Israelites brought large offerings to God, and for one week they lived in makeshift homes (Leviticus 23:41–43). This reminded them of the years they spent in the wilderness, when God provided for their needs day by day.

This was part of Israel's pattern for worship—three pilgrim feasts every year. As it says in Deuteronomy, "Three times a year all your males shall appear before the Lord your God at the place that he will choose: at the Feast of Unleavened Bread, at the Feast of Weeks, and at the Feast of Booths" (16:16). The place that God eventually appointed was Jerusalem. So three times a year the Israelites would go up to that great city for a festival. Naturally they would be tempted to worry about what would happen to their property while they were gone. Maybe their enemies would attack, or perhaps one of their own countrymen would move the boundary stones that marked out their property. But God told his people not to worry. He would take care of them, as he always does when his people do his will.

The pilgrim feasts reminded God's people of the great facts of their salvation. The Feast of Unleavened Bread reminded them how God had rescued them from Egypt, bringing them out of the house of bondage. The other two festivals celebrated God's providential care from the past right up to the present. And keeping these feasts nourished the people in their love for God. They gathered for worship, and as they worshiped, they were reminded in tangible ways of God's saving grace and providential care. Of course, there was always a danger of this becoming an empty ritual. But God appointed these covenant feasts to help his people stay in love by warming their hearts with gratitude and rekindling their religious affections.

The way to apply this to the Christian life is to recognize that all the old feasts have been fulfilled in Christ. At Passover, the people praised God for providing a lamb, and then, as a symbol of their separation from sin, they swept the yeast from their homes. God has provided a lamb for us in Jesus Christ, and his sacrificial death on the cross also demands a life of separation from sin. The Bible says: "Cleanse out the old leaven that you may be a new lump, as you really are unleavened. For Christ, our Passover lamb, has been sacrificed. Let us therefore celebrate the festival, not with the old leaven, the leaven of malice and evil, but with the unleavened bread of sincerity and truth" (1 Corinthians 5:7, 8). We have been saved from sin by trusting in the blood of Jesus Christ, the Lamb who was sacrificed for our sins. Now we need to make a clean sweep, getting rid of sin from our lives. We are called to put away our anger and bitterness and to start living in the love of God.

Jesus also fulfilled the harvest festivals: the Feast of Weeks and the Feast of Ingathering. It was at the Feast of Weeks (known in those days as Pentecost) that Jesus sent his Holy Spirit upon the church and people from many nations were saved. The great harvest of souls had begun. The New Testament also uses the idea of firstfruits to talk about the resurrection. Jesus is "the firstfruits of those who have fallen asleep" (1 Corinthians 15:20). At the end of the world, God will gather everyone who has ever lived for the final harvest of souls. The wicked will be condemned to eternal fire, while the righteous will receive eternal life. And what gives life is the resurrection of Jesus Christ. He was the first to rise from the dead—but only the first. He is the firstfruits of the final harvest, and everyone who trusts in him will live with God forever: "For as in Adam all die, so also in Christ shall all be made alive. But each in his own order: Christ the firstfruits, then at his coming those who belong to Christ" (1 Corinthians 15:22, 23).

The Old Testament festivals were all fulfilled in Jesus. So the way we keep them today is by trusting in him for our salvation. But is there any way for us to maintain a regular pattern for worship like the Israelites? Some Christians do this by keeping the church calendar. They celebrate the "evangelical feasts": the incarnation at Christmas, the atonement at Good Friday, and the resurrection at Easter (as well as the harvest at Thanksgiving). These are all good reasons to worship God, and there is something sensible about reviewing and remembering the great saving acts of God in history. However, we need to recognize that the traditional church calendar is not required in Scripture. God deserves our praise for his great salvation every day. It is as appropriate for us to celebrate the birth of Christ on August 25 as it is on December 25. Jesus Christ is as risen today as he is on Easter Sunday. If Christians want to celebrate on those days, this is certainly appropriate, but it is not set down in Scripture as the annual pattern for our worship.

If God has given us a feast to keep, it is the sacrament of the Lord's Supper. Like Passover, the Lord's Supper reminds us that God has provided a sacrifice for our sins. Like the Feast of Unleavened Bread, it reminds us to sweep the sin from our lives. Like the Feast of Weeks, it reminds us that God has provided bread for us—living bread. And like the Feast of Ingathering, it looks forward to the final harvest, when we will feast with Christ in the kingdom of God.

The Lord's Supper is part of the pattern of worship God has given to help us stay in love. The regular celebration of the sacrament—whether weekly or monthly—reassures us in the covenant. It does not give any special grace that is not directly available to us through faith in God's Word. But it is a more tangible sign and seal of the grace that God has for us in Christ. It is a feast of love in which God displays the extravagance of his affection for us and rekindles our passion for him. Following this pattern of corporate worship helps keep us in the love of God.

## God's Holy Rest

In addition to an annual pattern for worship, the Old Testament people of God also had a weekly pattern. God commanded them to set aside one whole day in seven to worship him. The seventh day of the week—called the Sabbath—was their day to enter God's holy rest.

The Sabbath is a significant theme in the book of Exodus. It is one of the Ten Commandments that God gave to Moses on the mountain (20:8–11). But even before this, the Sabbath principle was taught in the wilderness, where God provided manna six days out of seven (16). The Law was repeated in the Book of the Covenant (23:10–12). Then it showed up again in the context of building the tabernacle (31:12–17). God repeated the command once more in chapter 34: "Six days you shall work, but on the seventh day you shall rest. In plowing time and in harvest you shall rest" (v. 21). Then it shows up yet again at the beginning of chapter 35: "Moses assembled all the congregation of the people of Israel and said to them, 'These are the things that the LORD has commanded you to do. Six days work shall be done, but on the seventh day you shall have a Sabbath of solemn rest, holy to the LORD. Whoever does any work on it shall be put to death. You shall kindle no fire in all your dwelling places on the Sabbath day'" (vv. 1–3).

Today keeping the Sabbath is generally regarded as one of the least important commandments, if it is considered a commandment at all. However, this is not a viewpoint that finds very much support in the book of Exodus, where the Sabbath seems to be one of the *most* important commandments. Indeed, one of the benefits of studying Exodus from beginning to end is to be reminded again and again to receive God's rest.

Each time the Sabbath command is repeated, we learn something new about keeping it. From 4:21 we learn that the Sabbath was to continue without interruption. There were no exceptions—not even during seedtime and harvest. If ever there was a time when it seemed appropriate to break the Sabbath, it was when the weather was perfect for planting or the crops needed to come in from the fields. But even at crucial times in the agricultural calendar, God wanted his people to rest. Rather than depending on their own exertion, they needed to trust him to provide.

Christians honor the Sabbath by keeping the Lord's Day holy. It is always easy to come up with reasons why we deserve an exception: The house needs repair, we are behind in school, a project is due at work. But the only way to enjoy the blessing of the Sabbath is by keeping God's holy rest. And the busier we are, the *more* important this is, not less. Anyone who is too busy to keep the Lord's Day holy should take a Sabbath to rethink his or her priorities. Like everything else in the Christian life, this takes obedience and faith. We need to do what God says and then trust that six days are enough to do whatever work we are truly called to do.

We also learn something new about the Sabbath from the regulations in chapter 35. Earlier in Exodus we learned that God commands us to work six days out of seven, that the Sabbath is a day for resting in him, and that under the old civil law (which is no longer in effect) the sanction for Sabbath-breaking was the death penalty. What is new here is the command not to light a fire on the Sabbath (v. 3). Some orthodox Jewish communities have taken this law and amplified it. They say that it forbids the use of electricity or any other form of power on the Sabbath. But the real point of this regulation is that we need to take a break from the regular daily routine. Apart from works of genuine necessity (and here God gives us freedom of conscience), we should set aside our regular daily work on the Lord's Day, including most of our household chores.

The question is, why does God mention the Sabbath again in this context? What is the fourth commandment doing in a list of ceremonial laws? The answer is that keeping a weekly day of rest nourishes our love for the one true God, and thus it helps us turn away from idols. One of the best ways for the Israelites to stay in love with God and to avoid being seduced by pagan worship was to keep the Sabbath. The same is true for us. The Lord's Day is a weekly festival for worship. It is a day to stop thinking about earthly gain and meditate on the glories of God. It is a day to rest in God's grace.

Honoring God's holy day keeps us in his love. Spending time together is important for any love relationship. This is why husbands and wives should continue to go out on dates. For their love to grow, they need to spend time together. Here God is saying, "Let's get together on our special day—just me and you. I want to hear how you're doing. I want to tell you again how much I love you." Of course, this is something we can do every day of the week. If we want to be reminded of God's love or tell him how we're doing, all we need to do is open our Bibles and pray. Husbands and wives are together every day too, but every wise husband knows how important it is to set aside special time to be with his wife. In the same way, God has set apart one full day in seven for us to rest in his love. The more completely we dedicate this day to him, the more effectively we live for him the rest of the week.

## Giving God Our Very Best

There is more to loving God than sitting down to the Lord's Supper or setting aside a day for worship. To love is to give oneself to the beloved. We see this most supremely in the plan of salvation. The way God showed his love for sinners was by giving his Son to be our Savior. "In this is love," the Scripture says, ". . . God . . . sent his Son to be the propitiation for our sins" (1 John 4:10). If we want to know what love is, all we need to do is look at the cross where Jesus died to save us from our sins.

To love is to give. Thus it is not surprising that when he was teaching the Israelites how to love, God told them to give him the very best they had to offer, starting with their livestock. God said, "All that open the womb are mine, all your male livestock, the firstborn of cow and sheep. The firstborn of a donkey you shall redeem with a lamb, or if you will not redeem it you shall break its neck" (34:19, 20a).

God is the giver of life. Therefore, every creature that comes from the womb belongs to him. The Israelites acknowledged this by offering every firstborn animal as a sacrifice to God. The only exception was the firstborn donkey, which also belonged to God but was not holy enough to be a sacrifice because it was ceremonially unclean. Thus the firstborn donkey was simply put to death, or else redeemed by the blood of a lamb.

Strange to say, God told the Israelites to do the same thing with their sons. He said: "All the firstborn of your sons you shall redeem" (v. 20b). Putting people in the same category as donkeys may not sound very flattering, but it is an accurate picture of our sinful condition.[3] Like donkeys, we are unclean before God and deserve to die in our sins. We are also stubborn, unwilling, and unable to come to God for grace. If we are to be saved, therefore, we must be redeemed. We need a perfect substitute to die in our place.

This was the second time that God told the Israelites to redeem their sons (see 13:13). The ritual was his way of showing that their children really belonged to him (see 4:22; 22:29). They were his, not theirs. However, they were not to be offered as sacrifices. This needs to be emphasized because the Canaanites practiced child sacrifice. Also remember the purpose of this section from Exodus. The Israelites were tempted to serve other gods. To teach them to worship the right God in the right way, God carefully distinguished proper worship from paganism. He had a legitimate claim on every firstborn son. But rather than being sacrificed, they were to be redeemed; a lamb was to be offered as a substitute for every firstborn son.

This ritual was a reminder of what happened at the first Passover, when every firstborn son in Israel was spared from the angel of death. By keeping the rite of redemption, the Israelites declared that they belonged to God by his saving grace. This was also a beautiful picture of the grace that God has for us in Jesus Christ. Jesus is the Lamb who was slain for our redemption. The Bible says, "You were ransomed . . . with the precious blood of Christ, like that of a lamb without blemish or spot" (1 Peter 1:18, 19). Instead of telling us to offer our sons to him, God gave his Son to us! By his death on the cross, Jesus redeemed us so that we could live for God.

The firstborn were not the only ones who belonged to God. Everyone and everything in Israel belonged to him. So God also gave his people this command: "None shall appear before me empty-handed" (34:20b). This general principle applied to all three of the pilgrim feasts. Whenever the people went up to worship, they had to bring something for God. As it says in Deuteronomy, "Every man shall give as he is able, according to the blessing of the LORD your God that he has given you" (16:17).

At the Feast of Unleavened Bread, not showing up empty-handed meant presenting the right kind of offering: "You shall not offer the blood of my sacrifice with anything leavened, or let the sacrifice of the Feast of the Passover remain until the morning" (34:25; cf. 23:18). At the Feast of Weeks and the Feast of Ingathering, it meant offering a tithe from the harvest: "The best of the firstfruits of your ground you shall bring to the house of the Lord your God. You shall not boil a young goat in its mother's milk" (34:26). The last half of this rather puzzling verse probably forbids another Canaanite practice that God wanted his people to avoid—a pagan fertility ritual.[4] What is certain is that in the first half of the verse, God told his people to bring him their very best.

God wants the same from us. He wants the best of our worship. The sacrifice we offer to him is not a lamb or a basket of grain from the harvest, but what the Bible calls "a sacrifice of praise to God, that is, the fruit of lips that acknowledge his name" (Hebrews 13:15). God also wants the best of our possessions. All our stuff belongs to him anyway, and we acknowledge this by giving the first and the best of our income to the church and to the poor. As the Bible says, "On the first day of every week, each of you is to put something aside and store it up, as he may prosper" (1 Corinthians 16:2). For people as wealthy as we are, this means giving generously to support the work of the gospel in our own community and around the world.

But God wants something more than our worship and money. He wants our very lives. This is the way that we show our love for God: by putting our time and our gifts at his disposal—giving him the best of our very selves. A beautiful example comes from the life of Corrie ten Boom, the Dutch Christian whose family saved many Jewish lives during World War II and who endured the horrors of life in a German concentration camp. Corrie had been a Christian for most of her life, but a significant turning point came when she unreservedly offered herself in loving service to God. She prayed, "Lord Jesus, I offer myself for Your people. In any way. Any place. Any time."[5]

This is what it means to belong to God in the covenant—that mutual relationship in which God gives himself to us and we give ourselves to him in return. What God has given to us is far more extravagant than what he gave to Israel. He has given his Son to be our Savior. Now our work, our relationships, our families, our homes, our ministries, our bank accounts, even our vacations—all these things belong to him. It is when we finally learn this that we begin to serve God the way he really wants to be served and love him the way that he has taught us to love.

# 94

# Till We Have Faces

EXODUS 34:29–35

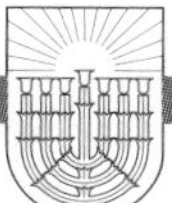

IT WAS TIME FOR MOSES to go back down the mountain. Although it is hard to keep track, the prophet seems to have made this trek at least four other times.[1] He had been going up the mountain to speak with God and then back down again to speak to the people. This time Moses had been at the summit forty days and forty nights—his second journey of this length (see Deuteronomy 10:10). And during this whole time he had been fasting. "So he was there with the LORD forty days and forty nights. He neither ate bread nor drank water" (34:28a). Sustained in some supernatural way, the prophet had been writing down the words of God's covenant with Israel.

As Moses made his descent, he brought down the Law. The Bible says that he "came down from Mount Sinai, with the two tablets of the testimony in his hand" (34:29a). Presumably this refers to the tablets on which God inscribed the Ten Commandments. This was a new set of tablets to replace the ones Moses had destroyed when he saw the golden calf. Notice that there were two of them. Traditionally, Christians have used this fact to make a distinction between the laws that teach us to love God (commandments 1–4) and the laws that teach us to love our neighbor (commandments 5–10)—the "first table" and "second table" of the law. What is more likely is that Moses brought down two complete copies of the Ten Commandments. This is generally the way covenants were established in those days. There was one copy for each party. In this case God was coming down to live with his people, so both copies would be kept in the ark of the covenant.

The first time Moses brought down the Ten Commandments, he was confronted with chaos. But this time the people were ready to receive God's law: "Moses called to them, and Aaron and all the leaders of the congregation returned to him, and Moses talked with them. Afterward all the people of Israel came near, and he commanded them all that the LORD had spoken with him in Mount Sinai" (vv. 31, 32).

First the prophet reviewed the covenant with Israel's elders; then he taught God's law to the entire nation. Perhaps he started with the Ten Commandments and then repeated the regulations from chapter 34—the special commands to help the Israelites stay in covenant love. Then he proceeded to give God's instructions for the tabernacle, running from chapter 35 through the middle of chapter 39. Moses had received these instructions earlier (see 25—30), but the Israelites had not yet heard them because of their great sin with the golden calf.

## The Shining

This all seems very straightforward. Moses came down from Mount Sinai to give Israel God's law, as he had done before. Yet this time a remarkable transformation had taken place. Although the prophet was unaware of it, he had turned glorious: "When Moses came down from Mount Sinai, with the two tablets of the testimony in his hand as he came down from the mountain, Moses did not know that the skin of his face shone because he had been talking with God. Aaron and all the people of Israel saw Moses, and behold, the skin of his face shone, and they were afraid to come near him" (vv. 29, 30).

The prophet was incandescent. He had been in the glorious presence of God, and as a result of his exposure to divine radiation, his face was glowing. Moses was luminous. His countenance was radiant. His skin was shining with a supernatural light. It was the afterglow of God's glory—what John Currid calls "the effulgent splendour of Almighty God."[2]

The way the Bible describes this remarkable light has been the subject of a good deal of discussion. The Hebrew literally says, "The skin of his face sent out horns." Early translations, such as the Vulgate, typically translated this literally and described Moses as "having horns." This explains why medieval and Renaissance artists—such as Michelangelo—typically depicted the prophet with horns on his head![3] But the expression actually refers to rays of light. As a result of his face-to-face encounter with God, Moses had a halo of glory. Dazzling beams of light were shining out from his face.

## The Glory of God

In the face of Moses we see many glorious truths about God, his mediator, ourselves, and the gospel. The first and most obvious thing we see is the glory of God. This is a matter of elementary logic. Why was Moses shining? Because he had been with God. What does this tell us about God? He's glorious!

Although Moses had been with God before, this was the first time he had come away glowing. But then this was the first time that he had been so bold as to ask God to show him his glory. While he was hiding in the cleft of a rock, God had passed by in goodness and grace, proclaiming the greatness of his name. So

Moses' eyes had seen God's glory, and this miraculous display had a lingering effect. The prophet was radiant with reflected glory. The light of God's gracious compassion and faithful love was shining from his face.

Even this was too much for the people to bear: "Aaron and all the people of Israel saw Moses, and behold, the skin of his face shone, and they were afraid to come near him" (34:30). The people were not even looking at the glory of God. All they could see was the afterglow of the reflection of God's glory in the face of a mortal man. And in Aaron's case, the man was his own little brother! Yet the transformation was so dramatic—the light was so dazzling—that they ran away in fear, like rabbits scampering away from the headlights of an oncoming car. The people were in shock and awe. Moses looked like someone from another world, and it was only when he spoke reassuring words that they dared to come near.

Moses could see that they were scared. Whether by the way they were keeping their distance or simply by the whites of their eyes, he could tell how terrified they were. So "when Moses had finished speaking with them, he put a veil over his face" (v. 33). The Bible does not say why the prophet did this. Some have seen it as a sign of modesty: Moses didn't want to dazzle anyone, so he put a cloth over his face. The Apostle Paul regarded this action rather differently. He saw it as a sign of timidity, as we shall see. But in the context of Exodus 34, Moses seems to have put on the veil so as not to frighten anyone.

What does this tell us about the glory of God? It tells us that he is awesomely and supremely glorious. God is infinitely holy, righteous, and just. He is the all-knowing, all-seeing, and all-powerful God. Therefore, even the reflection of his glory strikes fear into the hearts of sinners. What the people saw in the face of Moses was not even the millionth part of God's true glory. But when they saw it, they had to turn away in terror. One commentator explains why the people were so afraid of Moses:

> Because the very glory that shone upon his face searched their hearts and consciences—being what they were, sinners, and unable of themselves to meet even the smallest requirements of the covenant which had now been inaugurated. . . . The glory which they thus beheld upon the face of Moses was the expression to them of the holiness of God. . . . They were therefore afraid, because they knew in their inmost souls that they could not stand before Him from whose presence Moses had come.[4]

What the people saw in Moses' face was the glory of God, and it terrified them.

## The Glory of God's Mediator

The second glorious thing that we see in the face of Moses is the glory of God's mediator. Exodus reveals the glory of God in the salvation of sinners. At each stage of Israel's redemption, God's divine majesty was displayed with more dazzling brightness. He revealed his glory in the burning bush. He revealed it in all the signs and wonders he performed in Egypt. He revealed it in the fire and smoke on the mountain. And he revealed it again in the self-disclosure of his name at the beginning of Exodus 34.

But at the end of this chapter God revealed his glory in a new way. He revealed it in the person of the mediator, as new rays of divine glory shone from Moses' face. The prophet was visibly glorious, and this was not simply a one-time occurrence: "Whenever Moses went in before the LORD to speak with him, he would remove the veil, until he came out. And when he came out and told the people of Israel what he was commanded, the people of Israel would see the face of Moses, that the skin of Moses' face was shining. And Moses would put the veil over his face again, until he went in to speak with him" (vv. 34, 35).

These verses do not simply describe what happened to Moses on the mountain but also what happened afterward. Whenever the prophet entered God's presence—whenever he went into the tent of meeting—he would speak with God face-to-face (see 33:7–11). As long as he was in the tent, Moses left his face uncovered. He had unveiled access to Almighty God. And when he came back out, he radiated God's glory—the same glory that God had given him on the mountain. After a while the glory would fade (see 2 Corinthians 3:13), but every time the prophet went in and out of the tent of meeting, he would shine again with the glory of God.

Once he was back in the camp, Moses would put his veil back on—but not right away. If he had a message from God, he would leave the veil off until he delivered it (vv. 33–35). So whenever the prophet spoke for God, the people could see his glorious face. As Moses did his mediatorial work, he was glorified.

This was necessary because the people had begun to question his authority.[5] At the beginning of chapter 32 they had rejected Moses as their mediator—not for the first time, and not for the last. As a result God needed to reestablish the prophet's authority in some way. He was sending Moses to give the Law. But how would the people know that the Law came from God? How would they know that Moses spoke on his behalf? All it took was one look at the prophet's face. There could be no doubt that he had been with God: He was shining with the reflected radiance of divine glory. As he did his mediatorial work—with the veil still off—the people could see the glory of God shining from his face. This was God's way of authenticating the word that he revealed through his prophet. God gave Moses glory so that the people would listen to him as their mediator in the covenant.

Where do we see the glory of God's mediator today? We see it in the face of Jesus Christ. He is our mediator—the man appointed to stand between us and God for our salvation. And how did God authenticate the ministry of Jesus Christ? He did it in a way similar to what he did for Moses: by revealing Jesus' glory as the mediator.

God did glorious things through the life and ministry of Jesus Christ. Like Moses, Jesus performed many signs and wonders. He also spoke the true words of God. Yet there was a significant difference. Whereas the glory of Moses was only a reflection, the glory of Jesus was inherent. It came from his own glorious person. Jesus is God the Son, and the Scripture says, "He is the radiance of the glory of God" (Hebrews 1:3a). So his glory is not reflected; it radiates from his own divine being. Jesus shines with all the glory of God. In him there is a fullness of glory, compared to which the glory of Moses was only a flicker of light.

We catch a glimpse of the true glory of Jesus Christ in his transfiguration. Jesus went up on the mountain with some of his disciples. And there, the Bible says, "He was transfigured before them, and his face shone like the sun, and his clothes became white as light" (Matthew 17:2). What the disciples saw on that occasion was the true glory of Jesus Christ. The light streaming from his face was the light of his own glory shining through. By the outshining of his glory, Jesus was revealed as God the glorious Son. And why did God do this? He did it so that the disciples would know Jesus as their Savior in the covenant. God said to them, "This is my beloved Son, with whom I am well pleased; listen to him" (Matthew 17:5). The disciples knew that Jesus was their mediator because they could see it in his glorious face.

Jesus' glory was even more fully revealed in his resurrection. Near the end of his life Jesus had prayed for God to restore the glory that was rightfully his. "Father," he prayed, "glorify me in your own presence with the glory that I had with you before the world existed" (John 17:5). The Father answered this prayer by raising Jesus from the dead in a glorious resurrection body. And this is what authenticated his ministry as the Mediator, proving that he is both Savior and Lord. Jesus "was declared to be the Son of God in power . . . by his resurrection from the dead" (Romans 1:4). Therefore, we can identify our mediator by the glory of his resurrection. When we believe that God raised Jesus from the dead, we see the glory of the mediator, Jesus Christ. God has "shone in our hearts to give the light of the knowledge of the glory of God in the face of Jesus Christ" (2 Corinthians 4:6).

## The Glory of God's People

Because he was the mediator, Moses shows us the salvation that we have in Jesus Christ. However, he also shows us something about ourselves. Although he was the mediator, Moses was a man like us. So when we see his glorious face, we see a significant truth about our own salvation. We see that God is able to glorify sinners. And if he is able to glorify sinners, then he is able to glorify us. This is the third glorious thing we see in Moses: the glory of any person who meets with God by faith.

Meeting with God had a remarkable effect on Moses. Every time he had an audience with the King of kings, he came away glorious. This shows that it is possible for sinners to shine with the rays of God's reflected majesty. Being with God has a transforming effect on people. No one who meets God by faith is ever the same again, because when we see God as he is, we become like what he is. In the same way that the moon shines with the light of the sun, the glory of God shines from us. Indeed, this is why we were made: to give glory to God by reflecting his beautiful light. God made us to be glorious.

To glorify God in this way, we need to seek his face. As King David said, "Those who look to him are radiant, and their faces shall never be ashamed" (Psalm 34:5). The glory comes from looking at God. And this is what Moses did: He saw God in his glory. Afterward he wasn't even aware of his own radiance. This was because he hadn't been looking at himself at all; he had been looking at God. He was so absorbed by God's beauty that nothing could distract his gaze. Moses became glorious by taking his eyes off himself and looking to the Triune God. When he did this, he became an entirely different person, almost without realizing it. But other people could see the difference in his very face.

There is a profound spiritual lesson in this. We do not glorify God by looking at ourselves but by looking to him. It is so easy to get lured into a performance-based approach to the Christian life, in which we are always looking at ourselves to see how we are doing spiritually. It is also easy to waste time worrying what we look like to others. Instead we should be looking to Jesus. Only then can we reflect his glory to others. As we look to God, we are transformed by his splendor. And then when people look at us, they see his glory shining through.

In order to shine like this, we need to spend time alone with God. This was true for Moses. He was only radiant when he had been with God, and eventually the glory began to fade, like a flashlight getting low on batteries. In order to shine, Moses needed repeated exposure to the divine radiance of God. The same is true for us. If we are not meeting with God, his glory in us begins to grow dim. If the light came from us, we would not need to meet with God. But the light comes from him, so we need to go to him to get spiritually recharged. This means participating in public worship, including the sacraments. It means reading the Bible and meeting with God through prayer. Anyone who does these things by faith will shine with the light of God. When we see people who radiate the love of God, we can tell that they have been with God in the place of meeting.

Are you shining bright for Jesus? Do you radiate his love, compassion, and grace? If not, then very likely you have been neglecting your time with him in prayer, worship, and the Word. It is by being with Jesus that we become like him, and the more we are with him, the more like him we become.

## The Glory of God's Gospel

The last thing we see in Moses' face is the glory of the gospel. To see this, we need to turn to the New Testament, where the Apostle Paul offers a surprising interpretation of Exodus. To the Corinthians, he writes:

> Now if the ministry of death, carved in letters on stone, came with such glory that the Israelites could not gaze at Moses' face because of its glory, which was being brought to an end, will not the ministry of the Spirit have even more glory? For if there was glory in the ministry of condemnation, the ministry of righteousness must far exceed it in glory. Indeed, in this case, what once had glory has come to have no glory at all, because of the glory that surpasses it. For if what was being brought to an end came with glory, much more will what is permanent have glory. (2 Corinthians 3:7–11)

Here the apostle draws a comparison between the law of Moses and the gospel of Jesus Christ. There was something glorious about the Law. The Israelites could see this in Moses' face, which was shining so brightly that they could hardly bear to look at it. However, the Law could not bring full and final salvation, and thus whatever radiance it had was fading away. Its glory was true but temporary.

How much more glorious, then, is the gospel of Jesus Christ. The gospel is the good news of eternal salvation through the crucifixion and resurrection of Jesus Christ—his death on the cross and his triumph over the tomb. This good news is a ministry of God's Spirit (2 Corinthians 3:8), who alone can give us faith in Christ. This makes the gospel more glorious, because through the gospel the Holy Spirit does a glorious, transforming work in our lives, changing our minds and hearts from the inside out.

The gospel also brings righteousness (2 Corinthians 3:9). Everyone who believes in the obedient life, the atoning death, and the victorious resurrection of Jesus Christ is righteous in God's sight. In the gospel God gives us a perfect righteousness—the righteousness of his own Son. We no longer stand before him condemned by our sin, but perfectly and pristinely righteous. This righteousness is not only perfect, but it is also permanent. The righteousness we have in Christ will last forever. Its glory will never fade away. And in comparison to the Law, this makes the gospel surpassingly glorious. The great theologian Augustine commented that whereas the Law is only "a step to glory," the gospel is "the summit of glory."[6] It is like the difference between the sun and the stars. The stars have a degree of brightness, but when the sun comes out, its radiance fills the sky. So it is with the gospel of Jesus Christ. His glory, and the glory that we have in him, is everlasting.

Another glorious thing about the gospel is that it gives us direct access to God. The Israelites had a relationship with God, but only at a distance. They had to stay off God's holy mountain, they had to stay out of God's holy tabernacle, and they had to look away from God's radiant prophet. Because of their sin, there was always a barrier separating them from the holiness of God. But through the saving work of Jesus Christ, the gospel brings us into God's presence. The Israelites had to go through Moses to get to God. He was their mediator. But we come to God through and in Jesus Christ. And since Jesus *is* God, when we look to Jesus, we are looking directly at God. The apostle writes, "Since we have such a hope, we are very bold, not like Moses, who would put a veil over his face so that the Israelites might not gaze at the outcome of what was being brought to an end" (2 Corinthians 3:12, 13). We see Jesus, and in seeing Jesus, we see the glory of God more directly, more immediately.

This access is only available to sinners who come to God through faith in Jesus Christ. The only way to get to God is through Jesus, so anyone who doesn't know Jesus, doesn't know God—not in a saving way. Without Christ, there is still a veil that keeps people from seeing the glory of God. As Paul went on to say, "To this day, when they read the old covenant, that same veil remains unlifted, because only through Christ is it taken away. Yes, to this day whenever Moses is read a veil lies over their hearts" (vv. 14, 15).

Here Paul is referring specifically to the Jews of his day who rejected Jesus Christ. They still had the law of Moses, which they read every week in the synagogue. But they didn't understand how the Law testified to salvation in Christ. It was as if they had a veil over their hearts that kept them from seeing God's true glory. This was a problem then, and it is still a problem today—not just for Jews who are still outside of Christ, but for everyone who doesn't know Jesus as Savior and Lord. People read the Bible, but they don't understand it. They hear the gospel, but they don't respond to it. And the reason is that the veil of sin keeps them from seeing the truth about God. How can the veil be torn away?

The Bible says, "Only through Christ is it taken away" (v. 14b), and "when one turns to the Lord, the veil is removed" (v. 16). Notice that the Bible uses the passive voice to describe this action. It does not tell us to "remove the veil," but that "the veil *is removed*." We do not do the taking. It is God himself who takes away the veil, by the work of his Holy Spirit. He alone can enable us to understand the Bible, to see Jesus in the Scriptures, and to believe in him for our salvation. If we want to see this for ourselves, all we need to do is ask, saying, "O God, help me understand the Bible. Lead me to the way of salvation. Give me faith in Jesus, so that I can be saved forever."

Once the veil is taken away and we see Jesus, the transformation begins. As it was for Moses, so it is for us: When we see God as he is, we become like what he is. So Paul finishes by saying, "Now the Lord is the Spirit, and where the Spirit of the Lord is, there is freedom. And we all, with unveiled face, beholding the glory of the Lord, are being transformed into the same image from one degree of glory to another. For this comes from the Lord who is the Spirit" (vv. 17, 18).

This is what we were made to do—to reflect the glory of God. The more we see Jesus, the more we reflect his glory. In a world that is dark and often dismal, God is making us shine. And the Bible says that this glory is increasing. Our glory does not fade but is growing brighter by degrees. Everything else in this world seems to grow dim, but the believer in Christ shines ever brighter. God is constantly turning up the wattage, so that we can display his glory with greater and greater radiance.

In this life, shining for Jesus is mainly a metaphor. I say *mainly*, because being with Christ generally does make a difference in our countenance. The more we gaze upon his grace, the more his joy comes shining through, regardless of our circumstances. So some Christians truly are radiant, especially by the end of their lives. However, God's transforming work in us will not be complete until our final resurrection from the dead. Only then will we be fully glorified—body and soul—because only then will we see Jesus face-to-face: "Beloved, we are God's children now, and what we will be has not yet appeared; but we know that when he appears we shall be like him, because we shall see him as he is" (1 John 3:2).

Have you ever hoped that God had something better in store for you? In all the darkness and ugliness of a world scarred by sin, have you ever longed to be more beautiful? We have this longing because God made us to be beautiful—and gloriously so. We are waiting for the dawn of the coming age, when something even more glorious than what happened to Moses will happen to everyone who trusts in Jesus. The shadows will flee, we will shine with the undimmed majesty of God, and our faces will radiate his glory with growing brightness for all eternity. Then the promise of the ancient blessing will be fulfilled: "The Lord bless you and keep you; the Lord make his face to shine upon you and be gracious to you; the Lord lift up his countenance upon you and give you peace" (Numbers 6:24–26).

# 95

# A Heart for Giving

EXODUS 35:4–29

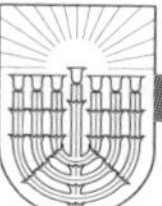

GREAT BUILDINGS ARE NOT BUILT OVERNIGHT. First someone has to decide that there needs to be a building at all. Then someone prepares a rendering—a sketch of what the building will look like when it's finished. This is followed by more detailed blueprints, full of technical specifications. Meanwhile, the builders are gathering the money and materials they need for construction. When all the plans are drawn up and the funding is in place, they can finally break ground. This is followed by the actual construction, which can take months or even years. The last step is to furnish the building. Only then is it ready for occupancy.

As building projects go, the tabernacle in the wilderness was fairly typical. The project started when God told Moses that he wanted to live with his people Israel. God described his dwelling in detail, first showing Moses a prototype and then carefully explaining how to build it. The building would be God's holy tabernacle—a portable tent to serve as the place of his presence on earth. It would be furnished in such a way as to teach the message of salvation. The tabernacle would overwhelm the Israelites with God's awesome holiness, and thus it would show them their need of cleansing. It would also provide atonement for their sin through the sacrifice of blood.

The tabernacle obviously took some time to build, and at the beginning of Exodus 35 most of the work still had to be done. God had drawn up the plans, but Moses had not yet carried them out. There had been an unexpected delay, as there often is with building projects. The people had sinned by setting up an alternative worship service around the golden calf. But God had forgiven their sin through the intercession of Moses, the mediator, and now they were finally ready to start construction.

## The Second Time Around

Exodus 35—39 may seem redundant. In chapters 25—31 God told the Israelites how to build the tabernacle; in chapters 35—39 they actually built it. And since they built it exactly the way God told them to build it, large sections of material are repeated almost verbatim. This does not make for the most interesting reading. In fact, this is one part of the Bible that people are tempted to skim.

Many commentators are negative in their assessment of these chapters. Some see the repetition as a sign that originally there were two versions of Exodus. What we read today is the work of an editor, they say—and not a very skillful one at that. After all, he kept repeating himself! Some scholars regard chapters 35—39 as part of the real book of Exodus. Yet at this point most commentaries get a little sketchy. The commentators don't have much to say about chapters 35—39, except to refer people back to what they said about chapters 25—31! To study this material again, they say, would be tedious and pointless.

However, it is a mistake to skip over anything in the Bible. When God repeats himself, he does it for a reason, and in this case there are good reasons for his repetition. To begin with, repetition was common in ancient literature. This was the accepted way to tell a good story. Repetition builds suspense. In Exodus our sense of anticipation mounts as we wait to see whether God will come down and dwell with his people. Repetition also reinforces the memory. What better way to learn the layout of the tabernacle—and thus the structure of our salvation—than to read about it more than once. Rather than skimming through these chapters, therefore, or skipping them altogether, we should take the time to read them carefully. When God repeats something, he wants us to pay more attention, not less!

Another reason Exodus repeats itself is to showcase Israel's obedience. Like us, the Israelites had a hard time doing what God said. The first time God gave them his plans for the tabernacle, they were too busy doing their own thing to pay attention. But this time they actually obeyed his instructions. This was so surprising that it was worth writing down. God told his people to bring their offerings, build the tabernacle, make the furnishings, and dress the priests. And this is what they did: They brought their offerings, built the tabernacle, made the furniture, and dressed the priests. They followed Moses' instructions precisely, and in doing so, they brought glory to God. God is exalted whenever we do what he tells us to do.

The repetition in Exodus 35—39 also shows how faithful God is. Remember that the people had fallen into serious sin. Would God still love them? The answer is yes! God would keep his promise to live with them and be their God. Thus these chapters stress "two important truths that are hard to believe for those who have fallen in sin. (1) God has not in any way revoked the promise to be fully present among the people. The tabernacle was precisely the sign of this divine presence. (2) God has not in any way revoked the calling and mission given to the people before the fall. Now they understand that God has indeed reinstated them in every respect and mended all that was broken."[1]

We can apply these truths to our own spiritual experience. Since we are so forgetful, we need God to tell us the same thing more than once. We need to read the Bible every day to be reminded of God's goodness and grace, as well as our joyous duty to live for him by serving others. And since sometimes we fall into serious sin, we need to know that God hasn't given up on us. The end of Exodus, with all its repetition, teaches us that there is hope for sinners. Even after all our rebellion, God wants to live in us and use us for his glory.

## Giving What You Have

To make a holy dwelling for God, the Israelites had to have the right materials. Exodus 35 tells how they gathered what they needed for this huge building project. They all had a contribution to make, and from their example we learn what it means to have a heart for giving—offering what we have and what we do for the glorious work of God.

The chapter begins with Moses telling the Israelites—yet again—to honor God's holy day (35:1–3). Before they started their building campaign, the prophet reminded them that God would give them rest. Then he told them to get to work:

> Moses said to all the congregation of the people of Israel, "This is the thing that the LORD has commanded. Take from among you a contribution to the LORD. Whoever is of a generous heart, let him bring the LORD's contribution: gold, silver, and bronze; blue and purple and scarlet yarns and fine twined linen; goats' hair, tanned rams' skins, and goatskins; acacia wood, oil for the light, spices for the anointing oil and for the fragrant incense, and onyx stones and stones for setting, for the ephod and for the breastpiece." (vv. 4–9)

This may sound like a strange way to make a building, but each of these donations was needed somewhere in the tabernacle. The gold, silver, and bronze were used to make the altar, ark, pillars, furniture, and utensils. The linen and yarn were used for the coverings, curtains, and veils. The animal skins covered the tabernacle itself, while the acacia wood was used to construct its framework. The oil, incense, and spices were used by the priests who served inside, with the precious stones adorning the sacred garments of the high priest.

All of these materials came from the Israelites. The people gave from what they had, and in this way they participated in God's work. If God had wanted to, he could have dropped a tabernacle from the sky, but this is not the way he works. He invites us to get involved with what he is doing in the world. In this case God made the plans, but the people did the work. He initiated the tabernacle, but they participated in its construction.

The people started by gathering the right materials, giving God what they had. Of course, everything they had came from him in the first place. In Egypt they had been lowly slaves, but by the grace of God they left with fancy threads and precious stones. On the night of their exodus, the Israelites asked the Egyptians for silver and gold. And their masters gave it to them: "The LORD had given the people favor in the sight of the Egyptians, so that they let them have what they asked. Thus they plundered the Egyptians" (12:36).

In this way God made sure that when it was time to build the tabernacle, the people had something to contribute. They gave generously, bringing their brightest treasures to God. This was important because the materials that went into the tabernacle testified to the majesty of God. According to Patrick Fairbairn, what the people brought

> consisted of the most precious metals, of the finest stuffs in linen manufacture, with embroidered workmanship, the richest and most gorgeous colors, and the most beautiful and costly gems. It was absolutely necessary, by means of some external apparatus, to bring out the idea of the surpassing glory and magnificence of Jehovah as the King of Israel, and of the singular honor which was enjoyed by those who were admitted to minister and serve before Him. But this could only be done by the rich and costly nature of the materials which were employed in the construction of the tabernacle, and of the official garments of those who were appointed to serve in its courts. . . . Such materials, therefore, were used in the construction of the tabernacle, as were best fitted for conveying suitable impressions of the greatness and glory of the Being for whose peculiar habitation it was erected.[2]

The people also gave willingly. God only wanted their offerings if they were willing to give. As the Scripture says, "God loves a cheerful giver" (2 Corinthians 9:7). Thus the collection for the tabernacle was not a tax; it was a freewill offering.

In the church we have a similar opportunity to give something to God. Everything we have comes from him in the first place, and now it is our privilege to use it for his service. When we bring our tithes and offerings, we are supporting God's work through the gospel. Some of our money goes to the building where we meet for worship. Some of it goes to the pastor, so he can devote his life to prayer and the ministry of God's Word. Some of it goes to the other ministry and support staff who help us grow in grace and serve Christ. Some of it goes to outreach among the poor and the lost in the community. And some of it goes to support the work of missions around the world.

It is really God who does all the work, but in his grace he gives us an opportunity to get involved in what he is doing. Giving is one way to get involved.

When it is used properly, money is a great help in ministry, so we should give as much as we can. Since everything we have comes from God anyway, we are only giving back what is rightfully his. But in the act of giving we bring more glory to God. Our gratitude shows that our lives have been touched by his grace. He has given us all the riches of salvation in Jesus Christ. Now we give him what we have, sharing the wealth of his grace with those who are living in spiritual poverty.

## Giving What You Do

We also offer God what we do. Building the tabernacle took more than solid wood and fine linen. It also required the energetic use of people's gifts and talents, especially in the arts and crafts. Moses said:

> Let every skillful craftsman among you come and make all that the LORD has commanded: the tabernacle, its tent and its covering, its hooks and its frames, its bars, its pillars, and its bases; the ark with its poles, the mercy seat, and the veil of the screen; the table with its poles and all its utensils, and the bread of the Presence; the lampstand also for the light, with its utensils and its lamps, and the oil for the light; and the altar of incense, with its poles, and the anointing oil and the fragrant incense, and the screen for the door, at the door of the tabernacle; the altar of burnt offering, with its grating of bronze, its poles, and all its utensils, the basin and its stand; the hangings of the court, its pillars and its bases, and the screen for the gate of the court; the pegs of the tabernacle and the pegs of the court, and their cords; the finely worked garments for ministering in the Holy Place, the holy garments for Aaron the priest, and the garments of his sons, for their service as priests. (35:10–19)

This inventory reminds us how the tabernacle was made. At the center was a large tent covered with curtains and divided into two sections. This is where the sacred furniture went: the altar of incense, the golden lampstand, the table for showbread, and the ark of the covenant, which stood in the Most Holy Place. The tabernacle was surrounded by a white fence that formed a courtyard, and in the courtyard went the large altar where the priests offered sacrifices and the bronze basin for cleansing.

Making all these things required a large number of people with a wide range of skills. To build the tabernacle itself, the Israelites needed to know how to do construction. Making the furniture required the talents of cabinetmakers and metalworkers. Then there were all the fabrics, which required the various skills that go into making cloth. The tabernacle was a special project that demanded special gifts. It was an opportunity for the artists and artisans to shine. But it was not a job for everyone. Only the people who were skilled in these areas were called to help.

This is an important principle that also applies in the church. The Bible teaches that every Christian has spiritual gifts God uses to build his kingdom. We should use the particular gifts that God has given to us: Teachers should teach, leaders should lead, helpers should help, and so on. The Bible says, "Having gifts that differ according to the grace given to us, let us use them: if prophecy, in proportion to our faith; if service, in our serving; the one who teaches, in his teaching; the one who exhorts, in his exhortation; the one who contributes, in generosity; the one who leads, with zeal; the one who does acts of mercy, with cheerfulness" (Romans 12:6–8).

This means that we should do what God has called us to do. It also means that we shouldn't try to do what God has *not* called us to do. Obviously God didn't want people who didn't know how to sew making curtains for his tabernacle. The way they contributed to this project was not by doing but by giving. Each of us needs to be content to do what God has called us to do and to let others do what God has called them to do. The service we offer depends on the gifts we have been given, as confirmed by the church.

As a minister, my calling is to preach—not to conduct the music or organize the children's ministry. And it's a good thing too, because those are not my gifts. What gifts have you been given? How are you using them? Are you doing the job that God has called you to do? Serve the Lord by giving what he has given you to give and doing what he has gifted you to do. As the Scripture says, "As each has received a gift, use it to serve one another, as good stewards of God's varied grace" (1 Peter 4:10).

## Straight from the Heart

The Israelites did this. They gave what they had to give and did what they were skilled to do. And they did it right away: "Then all the congregation of the people of Israel departed from the presence of Moses. And they came, everyone whose heart stirred him, and everyone whose spirit moved him, and brought the LORD's contribution to be used for the tent of meeting, and for all its service, and for the holy garments" (35:20, 21). As soon as they heard what was needed for the tabernacle, they went back to their tents to get it.

This is a moment to savor. It's one of the rare times in Exodus—indeed, in the whole Old Testament—when the people of God actually did what they were told to do. Rather than doing their own thing or worshiping false gods, they obeyed what God commanded. This was marvelous! More than that, it was glorious, because God is highly exalted whenever we do his will.

Not only did the people do the right thing, but they also did it for the right reason. Their obedience came from the heart. The Bible emphasizes this. When Moses told the people to bring what they had, he said, "Whoever is of a generous heart, let him bring the LORD's contribution" (v. 5). And this is how the people gave: willingly, from the heart. This is the kind of giving that God always wants. The heart is the center of a person, the true inner self. More than anything else, what God wants from us is our hearts. No matter what we give or what we do, it is not really for him unless it is an expression of who we are. God wants something more basic than what we have or what we do; he wants us to give him our very hearts.

Giving to God from the heart is one of the true marks of a Christian. Indeed, unless we give from the heart, it is doubtful whether we are Christians at all. When the great Scottish minister Robert Murray M'Cheyne was grieved by what he perceived as a lack of generosity in his congregation, he said to them,

> I am concerned for the poor but more for you. I know not what Christ will say to you in the great day. . . . I fear there are many hearing me who may know well that they are not Christians, because they do not love to give. To give largely and liberally, not grudging at all, requires a new heart; an old heart would rather part with its life-blood than its money. Oh my friends! Enjoy your money; make the most of it; give none away; enjoy it quickly for I can tell you, you will be beggars throughout eternity.[3]

M'Cheyne was right. Generous giving can only come from a new heart—a heart transformed by the grace of God. Generosity is a form of gratitude, and gratitude is the heart's response to grace. We see this in the Israelites. They were so grateful for what God had done for them—delivering them from Egypt, sparing them from the angel of death, and giving them his holy law—that they wanted to do something for him in return. What opened their hearts to give was God's saving grace.

What has God done for you, and what are you giving him in return? Through his death and resurrection, Jesus Christ has rescued you from the Egypt of your sin. He has saved you from eternal death, and he has come into your life to make you holy by grace. How should you respond?

The Israelites responded by giving from their hearts to God. The Bible gives a complete inventory of what they brought:

> So they came, both men and women. All who were of a willing heart brought brooches and earrings and signet rings and armlets, all sorts of gold objects, every man dedicating an offering of gold to the Lord. And every one who possessed blue or purple or scarlet yarns or fine linen or goats' hair or tanned rams' skins or goatskins brought them. Everyone who could make a contribution of silver or bronze brought it as the Lord's contribution. And every one who possessed acacia wood of any use in the work brought it. (vv. 22–24)

The Israelites brought everything that was needed—silver and gold, wood, cloth, and animal skins—and presented it as an offering to the Lord. Giving is an act of worship: We pay for the things we prize. So by giving for the tabernacle, the people were declaring their love for God, offering their hearts to him.

This was a community effort. Without full participation, the tabernacle never would have been built. God only wanted those who were willing to help, and most of the people *were* willing. Nearly everyone participated. The Bible says, "All the men and women, the people of Israel, whose heart moved them to bring anything for the work that the LORD had commanded by Moses to be done brought it as a freewill offering to the LORD" (v. 29).

The Bible singles out two groups of people for special mention. One was a group of women: "Every skillful woman spun with her hands, and they all brought what they had spun in blue and purple and scarlet yarns and fine twined linen. All the women whose hearts stirred them to use their skill spun the goats' hair" (vv. 25, 26). This does not mean that if a woman wants to make a spiritual contribution she has to learn how to sew! What is true today was also true in the time of Moses: Some women knew how to make cloth, and some didn't. The ones who didn't have this gift served the Lord in other ways (including giving him their jewelry, v. 22). The point is that some women had a unique contribution to make in fabricating the tabernacle, and those who had the gift offered it to the Lord.

The reason the Bible singles these women out is to show that their gifts were essential to God's work. Building the tabernacle was a job for both men and women, according to their gifts. The women of Israel were not called to serve as elders or prophets. But rather than getting hung up on what they weren't called to do, these women were eager to do what God *had* called them to do. They are a beautiful example of willing service and joyful submission to God.

The church needs the same kind of women today—women who are willing to serve God from the heart. Unfortunately, some Christians get so caught up in what women *aren't* called to do that they fail to think clearly and creatively about what they *are* called to do. It is true that women are not called to preach or to rule in the church (see 1 Timothy 2:11, 12). But God has poured out his Spirit on every woman who has faith in Christ (Acts 2:17, 18), and with the outpouring of the Spirit come gifts for healing, helping, counseling, encouraging, singing, teaching, and serving God in countless ways. Imagine what the church would be like without the gifts of women. It would not be the church at all—not as God intended it. The work of women is essential to the spiritual vitality of God's people. Therefore women should use whatever gifts they have been given for the glory of God. And they should use them the way their sisters did in the days of Moses—with willing and joyful hearts.

The other people the Bible singles out were Israel's rulers: "And the leaders brought onyx stones and stones to be set, for the ephod and for the breastpiece, and spices and oil for the light, and for the anointing oil, and for the fragrant incense" (35:27, 28). The word "leaders" may refer to Israel's elders. However, the term seems to refer more generally to leaders in the community who presumably had the resources to make the most costly contributions to the tabernacle.

The Bible gives many warnings about the dangers of wealth. Large sums of money tempt us to be selfish and proud. But when financial prosperity is combined with personal godliness, wealth becomes a powerful force for spiritual good. It took a lot of money to build the tabernacle, and in the providence of God some men had a lot of money. But in order to give it up for God, they had to have a heart for giving. They excelled in the grace of giving, willingly bringing their precious gems and priceless spices to the house of God.

This is a wonderful example for wealthy Christians. Money is a powerful tool for advancing the gospel. It can be used to support missionaries, plant churches, start schools, publish literature, broadcast the gospel, show mercy, and provide for the needs of the church. Christians with substantial financial resources have a unique calling to help accomplish great things for the kingdom of God. Of course, there is a sense in which God doesn't need any money at all, any more than he needs any of us. He can get his work done without any help. Yet he gives us an opportunity to participate in his saving work by using our time and our talents—including our money—to serve him. Those of us who have the most should give the most. This is why God has made us rich: so he has more money to use for ministry! As our income rises, so should our commitment to making more and more costly sacrifices for the kingdom of God.

## The Greatest Gift

In the days of Moses, God's people did their giving at the tabernacle. This was the place where they offered God what they had and what they did with willing hearts. Today God's great building project is the church. Once the tabernacle was the place where God lived with his people, but today his dwelling place is the church that he fills with his glorious Spirit. The Bible thus describes the church as "a holy temple in the Lord . . . a dwelling place for God by the Spirit" (Ephesians 2:21, 22). God has called us—both men and women—to help build the church by giving him what we have and what we do from the heart.

As we offer our gifts, we need to remember why we give. We do not give ourselves to God to gain anything in return, but because God has given himself to us in Jesus Christ. A powerful illustration of this amazing truth comes from the life of the Dutch Christian Corrie ten Boom. In her book *The Hiding Place*, Corrie remembers the day her aunt received the news that she had a terminal illness. The woman, whom Corrie called Tante Jans, was well known for her Christian work. She supported charitable causes all over Holland—writing tracts, giving talks, raising funds. Yet she seemed proud of her spiritual achievements, and although people said she was a good woman, somehow she didn't always remind them of Jesus.

Then came the day when medical tests indicated that Tante Jans had only a few weeks to live. The family wondered how she would take the news. "We will tell her together," said Corrie's father, "and perhaps she will take heart from all she has accomplished. She puts great store on accomplishment." So they all filed into her study. When Tante Jans looked up, she gave a little gasp of recognition. Instantly she knew why they were there. The family sought to console her. They told her that she would have a great reward for her labors. They reminded her of all the organizations she had founded, articles she had written, money she had raised, and talks she had given.

But Tante Jans refused to be comforted. Her proud face crumpled; she put her hands over her face and began to cry. "Empty! Empty!" she choked through her tears. "How can we bring anything to God? What does He care for our little tricks and trinkets?" Then something amazing happened. Tante Jans lowered her hands, and with the tears still streaming down her face, she whispered, "Dear Jesus, I thank You that we must come with empty hands. I thank You that You have done all—all—on the Cross, and that all we need in life or death is to be sure of this."[4]

This is how we gain a heart for giving. Not by thinking about how much we have to offer God, but by knowing the Savior who gave himself for us. Do you know Jesus? If not, he offers you the free gift of eternal life. All you have to do is trust in him. And if you do know Jesus, he wants you to give yourself to him. For the sake of his glory, offer him everything you have and everything you are, from the heart.

# 96

# Enough Is Enough!

EXODUS 35:30—36:7

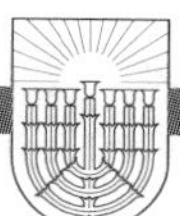

THE ISRAELITES HAD CONSTRUCTED MANY BUILDINGS, but they had never built anything quite like this. Their other buildings were all over Egypt, but this one was out in the wilderness. The others were built on the backs of slaves; this one was made by free hands. The others were made of rock and stone; this one was made with their own treasures. The others were for the glory of Pharaoh; this one was for the glory of God. What was this remarkable building? It was the tabernacle—the house that Israel built as the dwelling place for God.

The tabernacle was no ordinary building. Indeed, there was nothing like it in the world. It was designed by God himself and built to tell the story of his salvation. Its layout and furnishings showed how sinful people could approach a holy God by offering an atoning sacrifice. This was all in preparation for the coming of Jesus Christ. In becoming a man, Jesus became the true tabernacle—the dwelling place of God. And through his death on the cross, Jesus made the atoning sacrifice for our sins, bringing us into a relationship with God that will last forever.

## Artists at Work

Since the tabernacle was an important step in God's eternal plan of salvation, the Bible tells us how it was built. First God gave Moses the plans. Then he invited his people to participate in the building project. The Israelites—both men and women—offered what they had and what they did to God.

At the end of Exodus 35, construction is underway. With heartfelt gratitude for everything God had done to save them out of Egypt, the Israelites began to bring whatever materials were needed for the tabernacle: "All the men and women, the people of Israel, whose heart moved them to bring anything for the work that the Lord had commanded by Moses to be done brought it as a freewill offering to the Lord" (35:29).

Making a building suitable for God's dwelling place required special talents. It took the right people to do the job. So as the Israelites began bringing their gifts and offerings for the tabernacle, Moses made a special announcement:

> See, the Lord has called by name Bezalel the son of Uri, son of Hur, of the tribe of Judah; and he has filled him with the Spirit of God, with skill, with intelligence, with knowledge, and with all craftsmanship, to devise artistic designs, to work in gold and silver and bronze, in cutting stones for setting, and in carving wood, for work in every skilled craft. And he has inspired him to teach, both him and Oholiab the son of Ahisamach of the tribe of Dan. He has filled them with skill to do every sort of work done by an engraver or by a designer or by an embroiderer in blue and purple and scarlet yarns and fine twined linen, or by a weaver—by any sort of workman or skilled designer. Bezalel and Oholiab and every craftsman in whom the Lord has put skill and intelligence to know how to do any work in the construction of the sanctuary shall work in accordance with all that the Lord has commanded. (35:30–36:1)

This is the first time in the Bible that someone is said to be filled with God's Spirit. This shows how important the tabernacle was. God wanted his house built in a special way. To that end, the same Holy Spirit who with the Father and the Son created the world in six days (see Genesis 1:2) was poured out on the men who made the tabernacle.

The outpouring of the Spirit teaches us something about the importance of spiritual gifts in the church. It takes the Holy Spirit to build God's house. In the time of Moses, the Spirit came with special gifts for building the tabernacle. Now as the Holy Spirit dwells in our hearts through faith, he brings gifts such as teaching, evangelism, discernment, leadership, hospitality, and service. These spiritual gifts are for building God's dwelling place on earth (see Ephesians 4:7–13), which today is the church of Jesus Christ. Whatever spiritual gifts we have come from God the Holy Spirit, who calls us to use them in God's house. The Scripture urges us "to excel in building up the church" (1 Corinthians 14:12).

The gifts the Spirit gave for building the tabernacle were mostly artistic. Bezalel, Oholiab, and the other members of Israel's artistic community had a divine calling to make the tabernacle, and with that calling came special gifts from God. This should be a great encouragement to anyone involved in the arts because it shows that some people are called to be artists. Admittedly, the experience of Bezalel and Oholiab was unique. God has never called anyone else to design and build a tabernacle! However, by commissioning these men, God was pronouncing his blessing on the arts. He is a God who takes pleasure in aesthetic beauty. Thus the Christian artist has a legitimate vocation. In the same way that

God called Bezalel and Oholiab by name (35:30, 34), he calls artists today to use their gifts for his glory.

Artists need to respond to God's call with faith and obedience. This is what Bezalel and Oholiab did, with the rest of Israel's artists. Working on the tabernacle was strictly voluntary. God was not a taskmaster like Pharaoh. He only wanted help from people who were willing to serve. Thus the artists who designed and built the tabernacle were ones "in whose mind[s] the LORD had put skill, everyone whose heart stirred him up to come to do the work" (36:2). The artists had to be willing to offer their gifts for God's service. Otherwise they would fail to fulfill their calling. The lesson for us is to do whatever God calls us to do. Anyone who has the high calling of artist should be an artist! This is one form of holy service to God.

These verses also teach that some people are gifted to be artists. Bezalel and Oholiab were given skill to do all kinds of arts and crafts. These men had an eye for design. They knew the techniques of metalwork, woodwork, weaving, and engraving. They were master craftsmen, with all the gifts for making great art: ability, intelligence, insight, and expertise. Presumably Bezalel and Oholiab had this kaleidoscope of talent even before they started working on the tabernacle. God did not choose men who had never created anything before. But this project was so important that he sent his Spirit to enhance their artistry, enabling them to produce an architectural masterpiece.

Notice how the Bible assumes that there are objective standards for artistic excellence. By giving Bezalel and Oholiab special skill for making artistic designs, God was acknowledging that some artists do better work than others. The only people who were qualified to design and build his house were supremely talented artists. God would not settle for bad art! But how can we tell the difference? When the Dutch art critic Hans Rookmaaker sought to resolve this issue, he began by asking if the answer is in the Bible. He wrote:

> If we are seeking as Christians to understand the structures and norms for art, should we not go to the Bible for them? Certainly, but we will not expect to see them explained in detail. . . . God did not give specific laws concerning the arts, nor for any other cultural element. These things belong to human "possibilities": God created them, and made and structured man in such a way that he could discover these possibilities, and gave man the freedom and the task to realize and fulfil them. God left man to use all his possibilities in freedom.[1]

The difference between good art and bad art is not something we learn from the Bible, primarily, but from the world that God has made. What the Bible *does* tell us is that God knows the difference and that he has a taste for excellence.

Bezalel and Oholiab also had a gift for teaching. Bezalel was the artistic director and chief engineer. But he couldn't do all the work himself. He needed other men and women to help. So God gave him the spiritual gifts he needed to establish Israel's first art school. Bezalel was a teacher as well as an artist. Today many people think of the artist as an isolated genius, but that is not how art works, and it is not the Biblical pattern. Like all of God's gifts, art is meant to be shared. One of the ways Bezalel shared his gift was by training apprentices to make fine art. This was not for their benefit alone, but for the whole worshiping community.

Again, this helps us know how to use our spiritual gifts in the church. God has not given us gifts to advance our agenda or enhance our reputation. He has given them to us for the sake of others. If I have a gift for teaching, it is because God wants others to learn; if I have a gift for showing mercy, it is because God wants others to receive his loving care; and so on. We can apply the same principle to the artist. The goal of art is not self-expression or self-indulgence. Rather, like everything else we do, art is for the glory of God and the good of others.

This means that the Christian artist has to practice self-denial as much as any other Christian. It also means that it is possible for someone to be both a good Christian and a good artist. Some Christians think that artists can't be Christians. It is certainly true that many artists—perhaps most—are *not* Christians. This is because art is something that God has given to everyone, not just Christians. It is one of the gifts of his common grace. On the other hand, some artists think that Christians can't be artists—or at least not good artists. They think that Christianity brings out the worst in art, and sometimes it does, but it doesn't have to. Bezalel and Oholiab proved that good art can bring glory to God.

There is something God like in all true art. The Puritan Samuel Mather said, "All the arts are nothing else but the beams and rays of the Wisdom of the first Being in the creatures, shining and reflecting thence upon the glass of man's understanding; and as from Him they come, so to Him they tend."[2] If this is true, then the artist who knows God through faith in Jesus Christ can reflect his glory most clearly and most brightly. Hans Rookmaaker was right when he said:

> Christianity is about the renewal of life. Therefore it is also about the renewal of art. This is how art can be shown its validity through Christianity. It is an expression of Christian understanding, itself a fruit of the Spirit of God, including the emotion, the feeling, the sense of beauty that is bound up with it. It is for Christians to show what is meant by life and humanity; and to express what it means for them to have been "made new" in Christ, in every aspect of their being.[3]

Art can only fulfill this high calling when it is done for God's glory. Sadly, art is often done for its own glory. But for the Christian, art always points to something higher. As a gracious gift of the Holy Spirit, it points to the God of the arts and to his only Son, Jesus Christ.

## Something Beautiful for God

What does the gift of art tell us about God? This is important to ask in connection with the tabernacle. The tabernacle tells us that the call of the artist comes from God and that every artistic gift is to be used for his glory. But it also tells us something about God: he is a God of beauty.

Why else would God have employed so many artists? The tabernacle was a place to go and meet with God; and to fulfill this purpose, it had to communicate his character. As people approached God for worship, they had to have some sense of what he was like. The way the tabernacle described him was through its structure and furniture. But apparently it could only do this accurately if it was beautiful. It had to be made with the finest materials—rich fabrics and precious metals. And these materials needed to be decorated with artistic designs. God called and gifted artists to make everything beautiful. Why? Because he himself is beautiful, and the tabernacle was a place to behold his beauty. As David said, "One thing have I asked of the LORD, that will I seek after: that I may dwell in the house of the LORD all the days of my life, to gaze upon the beauty of the LORD and to inquire in his temple" (Psalm 27:4; cf. 96:6). Our longing for aesthetic beauty is intended to attract us to God.

Although often neglected, beauty is one of God's essential attributes. As Jonathan Edwards said, God's being and beauty are "the sum and comprehension of all existence and excellence."[4] There is beauty in his triune being as Father, Son, and Holy Spirit. What is more beautiful than the intercourse of divine love within the Trinity, the way that each person brings glory to the others? There is beauty in the symmetry of God's divine perfections: His justice is tempered with mercy; his majesty is counterpoised with humility. Then there is the beauty of the world that God has made. There is beauty on the earth and beauty in the skies. Every atom in the universe radiates the power and glory of God. As he considered the world around him, the Dutch theologian Abraham Kuyper asked, "How could all this beauty exist, except created by One Who preconceived the beautiful in His own Being, and produced it from His own Divine perfection?"[5] The poet Gerard Manley Hopkins wrote, "The world is charged with the grandeur of God."[6] And of all the things that God created, nothing is more beautiful than the people he made in his image. Not even the ugliness of our sin can disguise the beauty of his creation.

The most beautiful man of all is Jesus Christ, who is God incarnate, the very Son of God. Jesus is not beautiful because of his physical appearance (see Isaiah 53:2), but because of his perfect obedience to God, his sacrifice on the cross as a servant, and his glorious resurrection from the grave. Jesus is our beautiful Savior—"the radiance of the glory of God" (Hebrews 1:3). And in Jesus, we ourselves are destined to become beautiful. This is the beauty of our salvation. God takes people who have been marred and scarred by sin—both our own sin and the sins of others—and starts to turn our lives into something beautiful, almost like a work of art. The transformation finally will be complete on the day we are presented in heaven like a bride "without spot or wrinkle or any such thing . . . [but] holy and without blemish" (Ephesians 5:27). Then we will be more beautiful than anything we have ever seen or could even imagine. And we will get to see the most beautiful thing of all, which is the glory of God in the face of Jesus Christ.

We serve a beautiful God, who made a beautiful world, which he saved through his beautiful Son, so that we could become his beautiful people and live forever in his beautiful presence. God is so beautiful that everything in his tabernacle had to be beautiful, which is why he poured out his Spirit on Bezalel and Oholiab.

We have not been called to make a beautiful tabernacle, but we can do something beautiful for God, and one of the things we can do is produce beautiful art. We can write beautiful music, design beautiful buildings, and paint beautiful pictures. This is especially important at a time when there is so much ugliness in art. There are still some artists who prize beauty and seek to express it in their work, but beauty is no longer a primary criterion for fine art. There is a good reason for this: It is hard to produce beautiful art in a world that is so often ugly. In the words of one critic, "Much of the energy and effort of our artists and cultural architects has gone into debunking, dismantling, or deconstructing all that is good, beautiful, and respected, to be replaced with the shallow, the ugly, the ephemeral."[7] But in the midst of all the ugliness, Christians have a unique calling to love beauty. We know the beauty of our God. So when we look at the world, we see something more than the ugliness of sin; we also see the beauty of redemption, the once and future glory of the world that God has chosen to save.

In his wonderful little book *Art and the Bible*, Francis Schaeffer explains how the Christian way of looking at the world is to be divided into a major theme and a minor theme. The minor theme resonates with all the ugliness, what Schaeffer calls "the abnormality of the revolting world." Some people have rebelled against God and will never return. Others have turned to God through faith in Christ but are still struggling to overcome their sin. True art will always be honest about the difficulty and discouragement we endure as we live in a fallen world. This is the minor theme. But there is also a major theme, which Schaeffer describes as the "meaningfulness and purposefulness of life" in a world created by God and destined for redemption. We are made in the image of God, and although we are fallen, we can be saved through Christ. This is the major theme, the dominant theme, the beautiful theme.

Both the major theme and the minor theme have their place in art. The problem today is that the minor theme has become dominant, so that ugliness and despair threaten to overwhelm beauty and hope. But the Christian strives to keep both themes in true Biblical perspective. According to Schaeffer,

> The Christian and his art have a place for the minor theme because man is lost and abnormal and the Christian has his own defeatedness. There is not only victory and song in my life. But the Christian and his art don't end there. He goes on to the major theme because there is an optimistic answer. This is important for the kind of art Christians are to produce. First of all, Christian art needs to recognize the minor theme, the defeated aspect to even the Christian life. If our Christian art only emphasizes the major theme, then it is not fully Christian but simply romantic art. . . . On the other hand, it is possible for a Christian to so major on the minor theme, emphasizing the lostness of man and the abnormality of the universe, that he is equally unbiblical. There may be exceptions where a Christian artist feels it is his calling only to picture the negative, but in general for the Christian, the major theme is to be dominant—though it must exist in relationship to the minor.[8]

Keeping both themes in perspective is important for everyone, and especially for artists. We need to see the world as it is, ravaged by sin. But as Christians we are not limited by this. We also have the vision to see what we can become by the grace of God. We see this because we know Jesus Christ, who died the ugliest death when he was crucified for our sins, but who was raised to bring us into a beauty that will never end. And because we know Jesus, we desire to reflect his beauty in the things that we create.

## More Gifts for God

One does not have to be an artist in order to do something beautiful for God. Bezalel, Oholiab, and the other members of Israel's artistic community were not the only ones who used their gifts to glorify God. The whole nation was invited to contribute to the tabernacle, and almost everyone had something valuable to give.

Remember that these donations were entirely voluntary. There was no tax for the tabernacle. Moses didn't even give people the hard sell. He simply said, "Look, God wants us to make him a large tent. Here's what we need to complete the project, and if you have a heart for this, then bring whatever you'd like to give."

This is not an approach that many fund raisers would recommend. The professionals would tell Moses to come up with a better plan: "You can't just tell people to give what they want to give. If you do that, you'll never get enough. You have to make some kind of offer. Tell the people that anyone who brings a gift can be a 'Courtyard Contributor,' but reserve a 'Circle of Honor' in the Holy of Holies for the people who give the most." Or the fund-raisers would advise Moses to tell everyone how much to give: "Don't just take up a collection, Moses; at least give them a suggested donation."

This was the approach that Aaron took when he made the golden calf. He told the people what to give and then he made them give it, saying, "Take off the rings of gold that are in the ears of your wives, your sons, and your daughters, and bring them to me" (32:2). God had a different plan. He wanted Israel's giving to be voluntary, not compulsory. Thus the money for the tabernacle came from a freewill offering.

How well did this plan work? Did the people contribute enough to build the tabernacle? Actually, what they gave was *more* than enough:

> And Moses called Bezalel and Oholiab and every craftsman in whose mind the Lord had put skill, everyone whose heart stirred him up to come to do the work. And they received from Moses all the contribution that the people of Israel had brought for doing the work on the sanctuary. They still kept bringing him freewill offerings every morning, so that all the craftsmen who were doing every sort of task on the sanctuary came, each from the task that he was doing, and said to Moses, "The people bring much more than enough for doing the work that the Lord has commanded us to do." (36:2–5)

The people gave so much that it started to become a problem. As we will learn when we get to chapter 38, they brought more than a ton of gold, three tons of silver, and two tons of bronze (38:21–31). Rather than having too little, the workmen had too much. It was a good problem to have, but it was still a problem. At first it was exciting to see what the people brought: pure gold, fancy cloth, sparkling gems. But they kept bringing more and more every day, until finally there was too much stuff: too much wood, fabric, silver, and gold. So the craftsmen left their work and went to tell Moses what was happening. "Enough already!" they said. "You have to put a stop to this, Moses. It's too much. We don't know what to do with all these contributions."

So the prophet *did* put a stop to it: "So Moses gave command, and word was proclaimed throughout the camp, 'Let no man or woman do anything more for the contribution for the sanctuary.' So the people were restrained from bringing, for the material they had was sufficient to do all the work, and more" (36:6, 7). The Israelites wanted to give so much that Moses had to hold them back.

This sterling example of generosity shows what happens when people who are saved by grace start giving from the heart. We are so grateful for what God has done that we want to keep giving and giving and giving. The story of the tabernacle shows that grace is the best motivation for giving. Rather than giving out of a sense of duty—or even worse, from a sense of guilt—God invites us to give with joyful, grateful hearts. Out of gratitude for what he has done to save us from our sins, he invites us to make freewill offerings to advance the gospel. Many Christians use 10 percent as a useful guideline for their giving. This is the Biblical tithe. But God does not measure our spirituality on a percentage basis. He lavishes his grace on us. He forgives our sins through the death and resurrection of Jesus Christ. He promises an eternal inheritance from the everlasting treasure of his grace. Then he says, "Look, I have a plan for saving the world through the work of my Son. You can help by giving to gospel work. Just offer me whatever your heart tells you to give."

This only works if people's hearts are in the right place. I once spoke with a man who served on the council at his local synagogue. The practice there was to tell people how much they ought to give. Coming from this context, he was amazed to learn that in the church we leave the amount of giving up to the private conscience of our members. He wondered how we could possibly meet our budget. The answer is that we have received the extravagant riches of God's grace in Jesus Christ, and our giving flows out of our gratitude for him. Consider the epitaph of a famous military officer buried at St. Paul's Cathedral in London, which reads: "Sacred to the memory of Charles George Gordon, who at all times and everywhere gave his strength to the weak, his substance to the poor, his sympathy to the suffering, his heart to God."[9] The reason Gordon gave his substance to the poor was because he had first given his heart to God.

The trouble is that so often our hearts are in the wrong place. Our love for money is greater than our love for God, and this keeps us from living with the kind of extravagant generosity that God deserves for his grace. Rather than worshiping God by giving our money away, we hoard it for ourselves. In his book *Money and Power*, Jacques Ellul argues that we idolize money "just as much by being overly anxious and tightfisted about spending it as by wanting lots of it or by worrying about getting enough of it." Ellul also says that the best way to destroy this idol is "to profane money, to take away its sacred character by spending it wisely, but also by giving it freely and graciously."[10]

Free and gracious giving—what John Piper calls "hazardous liberality"[11]—is one sure sign of godliness. There are many examples from the Old Testament. Under King Joash the people kept filling and refilling the royal chest with gold for rebuilding the temple (2 Chronicles 24:8–12). Something similar happened under King Hezekiah. The people brought so many offerings for the temple priests that a huge amount was left over (2 Chronicles 31:10). There are good examples in the New Testament as well, like the woman who poured expensive perfume on Jesus (Matthew 26:7) or the members of the early church who sold their fields and laid the proceeds at the apostles' feet (Acts 4:34, 35). Then there were the Macedonians who (despite their own extreme poverty) gave more than they could spare to help the suffering poor (2 Corinthians 8:1–5). This is what people do when their hearts have been touched by the grace of God: they give and give.

What has God given to us? Everything! Right down to the last precious drop of the Savior's blood. What are we giving him in return? What the Israelites gave was more than enough. But that will never be true for us. How could we ever outgive a God who laid down his life for us by dying on the cross? The most that we can offer is to give our lives back to him, using our spiritual and financial gifts to build his church.

One man who excelled in giving was Adoniram Judson, the pioneer missionary to Burma. On the day Judson was commissioned to go overseas, he also met and fell in love with the beautiful Ann Hasseltine and soon wanted to make a proposal of marriage. But he also knew how costly it would be for her to join him in missionary service. In all likelihood, she would never see her family again. So Judson wrote to Ann's father:

> I have now to ask, whether you can consent to part with your daughter early next spring, to see her no more in this world; whether you can consent to her departure, and her subjection to the hardships and sufferings of missionary life; whether you can consent to her exposure to the dangers of the ocean, to the fatal influence of the southern climate of India; to every kind of want and distress; to degradation, insult, persecution, and perhaps a violent death. Can you consent to all this, for the sake of him who left his heavenly home, and died for her and for you; for the sake of perishing, immortal souls; for the sake of Zion, and the glory of God? Can you consent to all this, in hope of soon meeting your daughter in the world of glory, with the crown of righteousness, brightened with the acclamations of praise which shall redound to her Savior from heathens saved, through her means, from eternal woe and despair?[12]

What a question! And what should a father say to a young man who makes this kind of proposal? In this case, Mr. Hasseltine was wise enough to know that Adoniram Judson really was asking the wrong question. Whether or not he could part with his daughter was beside the point. The real question was whether or not she was willing to give her life to God—all of it, holding nothing back. So he wisely let his daughter make her own decision.

She said yes. But what will you say? You have one life to give to God—only one. It's not enough, but it's all you have, and God is asking you to give it to him as a beautiful gift. And when you do, you will find that it is not so hard for you to give him your money as well.

# 97

# Building in Progress

EXODUS 36:8–38

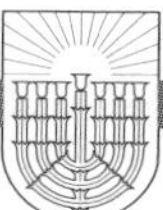

PEOPLE ARE FASCINATED BY the construction of great buildings—especially ones that were built long ago. Visitors to temples, palaces, castles, and cathedrals want to know the facts. Who built this structure, and when? How long did it take? What materials were used in construction? How were they joined together?

One of Philadelphia's architectural landmarks is City Hall, the massive building at the intersection of Broad and Market. It was built by John MacArthur, who served for many years as a deacon of Tenth Presbyterian Church. City Hall is still the tallest masonry structure in the world, built with eighty-eight million bricks covered with marble, granite, and cast iron. Construction started in 1871, but it wasn't until 1894 that the massive bronze statue of William Penn finally stood astride the clock tower. This is just the basic information, but anyone who wants to know more can take the tour and get all the facts. People remember how great buildings were built.

The grand building that the Israelites erected was the tabernacle in the wilderness (and after it, the temple in Jerusalem, which was built on the same basic plan). The Bible gives many fascinating details about this building. Some fifty chapters are dedicated to explaining how the tabernacle was made, what went into it, and what happened inside. This is because it was the most important building ever made—the only one designed by God himself. For five hundred years the tabernacle served as God's portable dwelling place on earth. Thus the Israelites reveled in the facts of its construction. "Tell us again about the tabernacle," they would say. "Read to us from the scroll of Moses. We want to remember every last detail."

We want to know the facts, too, because they are part of our story. In fact, the tabernacle was only the first phase of a construction project that is still underway. It was a place for God to be present with his people, but it was only temporary. When the time was right, God sent his Son, Jesus Christ, to live with us as God's true tabernacle. That was phase two. Phase three is the church that God is now building by his Spirit. We ourselves have become the tabernacle of God—his dwelling place on earth.

### Breaking Ground

It all started with the tabernacle in the wilderness. So if we want to understand what it means for God the Son to tabernacle with us, or for us to be the temple of the Holy Spirit, we need to go back to phase one and see how the tabernacle was built.

The actual construction begins in Exodus 36. God had set apart Bezalel, Oholiab, and other gifted men and women to make this magnificent building. Then to fund the project, Moses issued a call for freewill donations. The Israelites brought extravagant gifts and offered them with heartfelt gratitude to God—more silver and gold, wood and stone, oil and spices, gems and fabric than the workers could even use. Finally it was time for the craftsmen to build the tabernacle, starting with the tent itself:

> And all the craftsmen among the workmen made the tabernacle with ten curtains. They were made of fine twined linen and blue and purple and scarlet yarns, with cherubim skillfully worked. The length of each curtain was twenty-eight cubits, and the breadth of each curtain four cubits. All the curtains were the same size. He coupled five curtains to one another, and the other five curtains he coupled to one another. He made loops of blue on the edge of the outermost curtain of the first set. Likewise he made them on the edge of the outermost curtain of the second set. He made fifty loops on the one curtain, and he made fifty loops on the edge of the curtain that was in the second set. The loops were opposite one another. And he made fifty clasps of gold, and coupled the curtains one to the other with clasps. So the tabernacle was a single whole. (36:8–13; cf. 26:1–6)

These curtains—all made of fine, richly colored linen and joined with golden clasps—formed three walls of the tent that stood at the heart of the tabernacle complex. Inside these curtains went the golden pieces of sacred furniture: the ark of the covenant, the altar of incense, the lampstand of life, and the table of showbread. Because they surrounded the innermost parts of the tabernacle, these curtains were the closest to God's presence, and thus they were the most ornate. They were adorned with cherubim, the holy angels who guard God's heavenly throne. This made the tabernacle a little bit of Heaven on earth. By the flickering light of the lampstand, the priests who served inside the tabernacle could look at the sky-blue curtains and see the wings of hovering angels. Then they would know that this was the place where God was—the throne room of God.

The tabernacle also had a ceiling. And layers of fabric were draped over the walls to protect the sacred furniture. This, too, was the work of skilled craftsmen.

> He also made curtains of goats' hair for a tent over the tabernacle. He made eleven curtains. The length of each curtain was thirty cubits, and the breadth of each curtain four cubits. The eleven curtains were the same size. He coupled five curtains by themselves, and six curtains by themselves. And he made fifty loops on the edge of the outermost curtain of the one set, and fifty loops on the edge of the other connecting curtain. And he made fifty clasps of bronze to couple the tent together that it might be a single whole. And he made for the tent a covering of tanned rams' skins and goatskins. (36:14–19; cf. 26:7–14)

There were four layers in all. First came the beautiful curtains decorated in blue and scarlet. Next came the grayish, brownish curtains of goat hair, followed by the red skins of rams. Over the top went a rugged, weather-resistant tarp made from goatskins. The Bible does not explain the symbolism of these fabrics (if they had any special symbolism at all)—it simply tells how they were made.

In order to support the massive weight of all the curtains, the tabernacle needed a sturdy framework. So while some workers were busy fabricating the tent, others built the wooden structure that supported it.

> Then he made the upright frames for the tabernacle of acacia wood. Ten cubits was the length of a frame, and a cubit and a half the breadth of each frame. Each frame had two tenons for fitting together. He did this for all the frames of the tabernacle. The frames for the tabernacle he made thus: twenty frames for the south side. And he made forty bases of silver under the twenty frames, two bases under one frame for its two tenons, and two bases under the next frame for its two tenons. For the second side of the tabernacle, on the north side, he made twenty frames and their forty bases of silver, two bases under one frame and two bases under the next frame. For the rear of the tabernacle westward he made six frames. He made two frames for corners of the tabernacle in the rear. And they were separate beneath but joined at the top, at the first ring. He made two of them this way for the two corners. There were eight frames with their bases of silver: sixteen bases, under every frame two bases.
>
> He made bars of acacia wood, five for the frames of the one side of the tabernacle, and five bars for the frames of the other side of the tabernacle, and five bars for the frames of the tabernacle at the rear westward. And he made the middle bar to run from end to end halfway up the frames. And he overlaid the frames with gold, and made their rings of gold for holders for the bars, and overlaid the bars with gold. (36:20–34; cf. 26:15–29)

If this seems like too much detail, remember how necessary this information was for the craftsmen who built the tabernacle! The framework they put together consisted of forty-eight upright wooden boards or pillars. These pillars, which were roughly fifteen feet high, were joined by a network of crossbars that made the tabernacle structurally stable. Then the entire framework was covered with gold, suitable for the royal presence of God.

Next Israel's craftsmen made the holy curtain that divided the tabernacle in two, separating the Holy Place from the Most Holy Place: "He made the veil of blue and purple and scarlet yarns and fine twined linen; with cherubim skillfully worked into it he made it. And for it he made four pillars of acacia and overlaid them with gold. Their hooks were of gold, and he cast for them four bases of silver" (36:35, 36; cf. 26:31, 32). This was the innermost veil, which only the high priest was allowed to pass, and only once a year, on the Day of Atonement. It was decorated with cherubim to show that when the high priest passed through the veil, he was entering the throne room of Almighty God.

Finally, Israel's craftsmen fabricated the curtains that went across the entrance to the tabernacle and thus marked the way of approach to God: "He also made a screen for the entrance of the tent, of blue and purple and scarlet yarns and fine twined linen, embroidered with needlework, and its five pillars with their hooks. He overlaid their capitals, and their fillets were of gold, but their five bases were of bronze" (36:37, 38; cf. 26:36, 37).

This is how the tabernacle was built. Amazingly, the Israelites built it exactly the way God told them to build it. Exodus 36 repeats Exodus 26 almost verbatim. In chapter 26 God told Moses how he wanted the tabernacle built. In chapter 36, when the people finally get around to building it, they followed God's instructions down to the last cubit and crossbar. This is a remarkable example of full obedience to the will of God, especially when we remember what happened in between. In chapter 32 the Israelites tried to set up their own way of worship—the golden calf—with disastrous consequences. But this time they did everything just as God said; and as a result, they received a glorious blessing (as we shall see when we get to chapter 40).

When we follow God's instructions, doing what he says to the very best of our ability, we enjoy God's blessing. And in our worship, and in everything else we do, what pleases God is full obedience to his revealed will. Someone once said to the Puritan preacher Richard Rogers, "I like you and your company very well, but you are so precise." Rogers replied, "O Sir, I serve a precise God."[1] Rogers was right: He *is* a precise God. So whatever he tells us to do should be done precisely, down to the last loop on the last curtain.

## The True Tabernacle

It is always important to do what God says. However, it was especially important in this case because of what the building represented. The tabernacle was God's dwelling place on earth—a replica of his sanctuary in Heaven (see Hebrews 8:5; 9:24)—and thus it was the place where people could go and meet with God. As

Tremper Longman writes in his book on Old Testament worship, "The symbolism of the entire structure revolved around one central idea: the Holy God was present in the midst of the camp."[2]

The tabernacle's meaning was communicated, in part, by the materials used for its construction. Bible scholars have different, sometimes conflicting, opinions about the symbolism of this building. But one thing is clear: The closer one came to the center of the tabernacle, the more precious the materials became. This was to show that God was at the center. As Longman explains:

> [T]here was a transition from less precious to more precious materials as one moved from the outside parameter to the Holy of Holies. Bronze was used for the posts of the outermost curtain, but bronze gave way to silver, then to gold, and ultimately to fine gold, used predominately for the furniture in the Holy of Holies. White linen was used on the outer curtain, but eventually this gives way to the fine cloth that was the innermost curtain of the tabernacle. While this served a practical purpose—the less expensive and more utilitarian material on the outside protecting the precious material on the inside—it still reinforced the central symbolic truth of the tabernacle [namely, that this was the place where God was].[3]

God's presence was also revealed by the various terms used to describe the tabernacle—five in all.[4] The Bible calls it "a sanctuary" (25:8)—that is, a holy place set apart for a holy God. It was also termed a "tabernacle" (25:9), which means a dwelling place—in this case, a dwelling place for God. It was referred to as a "tent" (26:36), which indicated that it was portable. When the people were on the move, God went with them. The structure was also called "the tent of meeting" (29:44), which showed that it was a place where people could enter God's presence. Finally, it was called "the tabernacle of the testimony" (38:21). By "testimony," the Bible means the Law of God, which was written in stone and deposited in the ark of the covenant. The tabernacle was a place where God was revealed in his Word.

What all of this means is that the tabernacle was the place where people could go and meet with God. This extraordinary building answered the deepest longing of the human soul. People have always wanted to know where they could have an encounter with the living God. If there is a God, how can I know him? Where can I meet him? Is there any way for me to gain access to the mysteries of his eternal being? At the time of Moses, the answer was to go to the tabernacle. That was the only place where God came down to live with his people.

However, the tabernacle was only the first phase of God's building project. God was not content to have a tabernacle in the wilderness, or even a temple in the city. Because of his ardent love and passionate desire for relationship, he wanted to make even more intimate contact with his people. For although the tabernacle was a marvelous building, it had some definite liabilities. It could only stand in one place at one time, which meant that if people wanted to meet with God, they had to travel to that place. Nor was everyone allowed to enter. Because of God's supreme holiness, only the priests could enter the tabernacle, and only the high priest was permitted to pierce the veil and enter the Most Holy Place where God was.

Then came phase two, as we read in the opening verses of John's Gospel: "In the beginning was the Word, and the Word was with God, and the Word was God. . . . And the Word became flesh and dwelt among us" (John 1:1, 14a). With these staggering words, the Bible breaks ground on the new dwelling place of God. By "the Word," the Scripture means God the Son, the Second Person of the Trinity. He was with God from the beginning, and he *was* God, sharing all the infinite attributes of his divine being. Then the Word became flesh. That is to say, God the Son became a man in the person of Jesus Christ. Theologians call this the incarnation. It means that Jesus is one person with two natures: a divine nature and a human nature. By taking on the flesh of our humanity, he is both God and man.

In order to speak of this awesome mystery, the apostle John chose a phrase ringing with echoes from the exodus. He said, "The Word . . . dwelt among us" (John 1:14). Then, to show what kind of dwelling he had in mind, John used the Greek word for tabernacle, as if to say "The Word *tabernacled* among us." Jesus Christ is the true tabernacle of God. Wherever Jesus is, God is, in person; his divine presence is manifested in the flesh.

This new tabernacle was not made of goat hair and acacia wood. It did not require the twisting of linen and the sewing of curtains. It was not constructed by stretching tents over pillars. This new tabernacle was made of flesh and blood, knit together in the virgin's womb by the miraculous power of God the Holy Spirit. F. B. Meyer wrote: "The tabernacle with its contents was the subject of much divine thought and care. It was not a poor hut run up in an hour. It was not the creation of human fancy. Man was not the creator, but the executor of the divine program and plan. . . . To Him [God] alone must be attributed, also, the pattern of the human life of our Lord, in which the tabernacle was duplicated in flesh and blood."[5] No team of craftsmen, however gifted, could even have attempted this phase of the grand design. Only God could fashion the body of his incarnate Son—bone of our bones and flesh of our flesh, yet very God of very God.

Jesus Christ is the dwelling place of God. This explains the mysterious way that he sometimes spoke about his body. On one occasion the Jewish leaders challenged Jesus to give some miraculous sign that would prove his divine authority. Jesus said, "Destroy this temple, and in three days I will raise it up" (John 2:19). The people thought he was talking about the temple in Jerusalem, so they scoffed at him: "It has taken forty-six years to build this temple, and will you raise it up in three days?" (v. 20). If he had wanted to, Jesus *could* have raised the temple in three days, but that was beside the point: "But he was speaking about the temple of his body" (v. 21).

Sometime after the resurrection, the disciples had one of those Aha! moments. They remembered what Jesus had said about destroying the temple and raising it again, and they finally realized what he was talking about. His body—the physical body that died on the cross for our sins and was raised from the tomb in triumph—was the tabernacle of God. This is how God has made his dwelling among us: by sending his Son into the world to be our Savior.

What this means is that if we want to meet God—if we want to know him and experience him—all we have to do is come to Jesus. He is the true tabernacle. To know him is to know God, and to be with him is to be with God. If we want to meet with God, we do not need to go to any particular place, least of all some special building; all we need do is to believe in Jesus Christ. Presumably this is why God allowed the temple in Jerusalem to be destroyed, as it was by the Romans in AD 70. By the time Jesus had finished suffering and dying for sin, that old temple was obsolete. Jesus Christ is the only temple we need.

Imagine living at the time of Moses—not out in the wilderness between Egypt and Israel, but in some other part of the world. Then imagine someone coming and telling you about the tabernacle. Imagine discovering that there actually was a place where you could go and meet with God, where your sins could be forgiven, and where you could see the glory of Heaven on earth. What would you have done to go and see the tabernacle? What price would you have paid? What distance would you have traveled? What sacrifices would you have made?

What, then, will you do to enter the tabernacle today? Jesus Christ is the true tabernacle, and God is inviting you to enter by trusting in him. Do you believe that Jesus died on the cross for your sins? Will you receive eternal life by trusting in his resurrection from the dead? Ask him to be your Savior and your God. He is inviting you to come in.

## God's Holy Temple

When we come to God through faith in Jesus Christ, something amazing happens: God also comes to us. He sends his Holy Spirit—who is truly God, the Third Person of the Trinity—to live in us. The Bible says that God can "grant you to be strengthened with power through his Spirit in your inner being, so that Christ may dwell in your hearts through faith" (Ephesians 3:16, 17a). By trusting in Christ, we become a dwelling place for God.

This is the third phase of God's building project—the architecture of our salvation. God did not stop with the tabernacle in the wilderness, with the temple in Jerusalem, or even with Jesus Christ, who is the tabernacle incarnate. He wanted to have an even closer relationship with us; so by the abiding presence of his Holy Spirit, he has made his home in the church. Rather than telling us to go somewhere to meet with him, he has come to meet with us! We are a living tabernacle, God's dwelling place on earth. As Adolph Saphir has written, "The tabernacle has no fewer than three meanings. In the first place, the tabernacle is a type, a visible illustration, of that heavenly place in which God has His dwelling. In the second place, the tabernacle is a type of Jesus Christ, who is the meeting-place between God and man. And, in the third place, the tabernacle is a type of Christ in the Church—of the communion of Jesus with all believers."[6]

The New Testament shows this third level of meaning by taking the language of the temple (and remember, the temple was simply a more permanent tabernacle, built on the plan that God gave to Moses, with the same layout and furnishings) and applies it to the church of Jesus Christ. The Apostle Paul describes the church as full of people who are "fellow citizens with the saints and members of the household of God, built on the foundation of the apostles and prophets, Christ Jesus himself being the cornerstone" (Ephesians 2:19, 20). The church is a living building, founded on Christ. What kind of building is it? Paul continues: "In [him] the whole structure, being joined together, grows into a holy *temple* in the Lord. In him you also are being built together into a dwelling place for God by the Spirit" (vv. 21, 22). This was God's plan: to make his dwelling place in the church. Just as God once filled the tabernacle, the temple, and the physical body of Jesus Christ with the radiance of his glory, so now he fills the church with the glorious presence of his Spirit. God is living in us, both individually and corporately. Where is God's dwelling place today? In the church. We have become the tabernacle of God.

When we talk about the church, we are not talking about some sort of building. The church is the people of God. It is a living tabernacle—not made of wood and fabric, but of precious lives transformed by God's grace and filled with God's Spirit. This is one major difference between the tabernacle in the wilderness and God's holy temple, the church. The tabernacle was designed by God, but it was built by human hands. Not so the church, which is built by God's Holy Spirit. Through the preaching of God's Word, the Holy Spirit convinces us that we are sinners and persuades us to trust in Christ for our salvation. Then the Spirit does a transforming work of grace in our lives, giving us spiritual gifts for ministry and changing us from the inside out. This is how God builds his church, working to complete the construction project he began many ages ago.

Our identity as God's tabernacle has many practical implications. It teaches us to have greater respect for the church. We are tempted to think of the church as less important than our own personal relationship with God, when in fact the church is God's dwelling place—an essential part of his plan for saving the world. It is easy for us to see the failings of the church, to complain about them, and even to resent them. The Bible is honest about these things too, but it never loses sight of the fact that God lives in the church by his Spirit. Therefore, the church—for all its weakness—displays his glory.

Knowing that the church is God's tabernacle also teaches us to have more patience with one another. We are still a work in progress, but God is doing his work, and this helps us to be patient with what sometimes seems like a lack of progress. When we look at our brothers and sisters, rather than seeing only their faults, we also see the work of God's Spirit, who is building us together into a beautiful home for God.

These are all valuable lessons. But when the Bible describes the church as a tabernacle or temple, what it usually emphasizes is holiness. A tabernacle is a holy place, set apart for the holy service of God. By making us his tabernacle, God is saying that he wants us to be a holy dwelling place for his Spirit. Just as he once adorned the tabernacle with beauty, so he is now at work to make our lives beautiful in holiness.

The Apostle Paul wrote about this to the Corinthians, when he challenged them to maintain sexual purity: "Flee from sexual immorality. Every other sin a person commits is outside the body, but the sexually immoral person sins against his own body. Or do you not know that your body is a temple of the Holy Spirit within you, whom you have from God?" (1 Corinthians 6:18, 19). Corinth was a den of iniquity in those days, but the Christians there were called to lead holy lives. Through faith in Jesus Christ, they had become a holy temple for God, and this was something to remember whenever they were faced with sexual temptation. It's something for us to remember too. Our bodies are dwelling places for God, who lives in us by his Spirit. Therefore, to look at something we shouldn't look at or touch something we shouldn't touch is to defile God's holy tabernacle. We need to run away from sexual temptation, saying, "That is not for me, because my body is God's temple."

We need to say the same thing whenever we are tempted to compromise our Christianity. Paul also warned the Corinthians not to form spiritual partnerships with people who weren't Christians: "Do not be unequally yoked with unbelievers" (2 Corinthians 6:14). This is a general principle that applies to ministry, courtship, marriage, and any other relationship that requires spiritual cooperation. As followers of the Lord Jesus Christ, we cannot be spiritually united with unbelievers. Why not? The Bible says, "For we are the temple of the living God; as God said, 'I will make my dwelling among them and walk among them, and I will be their God, and they shall be my people'" (v. 16b). If we are part of God's holy temple, then we cannot do spiritual work—for example, start a marriage partnership or carry out any kind of ministry—with people who do not have God's Spirit living in them.

These are only examples. The point is that as followers of Jesus Christ, our lives are like holy tabernacles. They are places where God lives by his Spirit, and which he wants to fill with the beauty of his grace. If that is true, then what kind of lives should we lead? What kinds of things should we think about? What kinds of words should we say? What kinds of things should we do with our bodies? How can we display the glory of the holy God who has come to live in us?

# 98

# In God's House

EXODUS 37:1–29

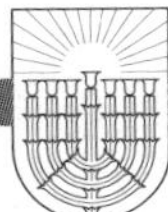

SOME PEOPLE DO NOT FEEL quite at home with God. Sometimes this is because they don't want anyone telling them what to do. Rather than living with God, they want to live on their own. Sometimes they feel like God has let them down. They expect something better out of life, and when they don't get it, they decide that God is to blame. Sometimes they say that they really do want to come home to God—they just don't have time for that right now, so they keep putting God off until later. But many times the reason people aren't at home with God is that they don't really know who he is. They ought to know God, because he has revealed himself in his Word and in his world, but they don't. They need someone to tell them who God is and what it means to have a relationship with him.

One good way to meet God is to visit his house. Sometimes we refer to the church as God's house, but long before God established the church, his home was known as the tabernacle. The tabernacle was a large portable tent, supported by a wooden framework and draped with colorful curtains and animal skins. It was God's house, and as the Israelites made their long trek through the wilderness, they took it with them.

The amazing thing about the tabernacle was that every part of the building revealed something about God. God designed it to show what he is like and what kind of relationship he wants to have with his people. So as we study the tabernacle—and consider how it relates to the person and work of Jesus Christ—we learn what it means to come inside and make our home with God.

## The Ark of the Covenant

In the previous chapter we learned how the tent was made. Here we see what went inside. There were four pieces of sacred furniture in God's house: the ark of the covenant, the table of showbread, the lampstand of life, and the altar of incense. God gave Moses the design for these furnishings back in chapter 25, when the prophet was up on Mount Sinai. Here the Bible matter-of-factly tells how each piece of furniture was actually put together. But we also need to ask what each piece symbolized. What does the furniture in God's house tell us about God and about what it means to live with him?

The first item mentioned in Exodus 37 is the ark of the covenant. Presumably Israel's craftsmen worked on several pieces of furniture at the same time, but the Bible starts with the ark. This was the logical place to begin because it was the most important piece of furniture, the only one that stood in the Holy of Holies.

One sign of the ark's importance is that it was made by Bezalel himself—"the Leonardo da Vinci of the Hebrews."[1] As Israel's artistic director, Bezalel supervised the construction of the entire tabernacle. But when it came time to make the ark of the covenant, he did the work himself:

> Bezalel made the ark of acacia wood. Two cubits and a half was its length, a cubit and a half its breadth, and a cubit and a half its height. And he overlaid it with pure gold inside and outside, and made a molding of gold around it. And he cast for it four rings of gold for its four feet, two rings on its one side and two rings on its other side. And he made poles of acacia wood and overlaid them with gold and put the poles into the rings on the sides of the ark to carry the ark. (37:1–5; cf. 25:10–16)

The ark was a portable wooden box covered with gold and measuring roughly four feet long by two feet wide and two feet high. Three sacred things went with it. Although these items are not mentioned in Exodus 37, they are described elsewhere in the Old Testament. One was manna, the miracle bread that God provided for the Israelites during their forty years of wandering in the wilderness. God had said, "Let an omer of it [manna] be kept throughout your generations, so that they may see the bread with which I fed you in the wilderness, when I brought you out of the land of Egypt" (16:32). So Aaron, the brother of Moses and the high priest of Israel, put a golden jar of manna in the ark as a permanent sign of God's providential care. This bread, supernaturally preserved, reminded the Israelites that God would satisfy all their needs. Who is God? According to the manna in the ark, he is a faithful provider.

The second item in the ark was Aaron's staff. At a time of rebellion, when the Israelites challenged his spiritual authority, God told Moses to gather twelve staffs. These staffs came from the leaders of the twelve tribes of Israel and thus symbolized tribal authority. God miraculously caused Aaron's staff to sprout with buds and blossoms (Numbers 17:8). This confirmed his spiritual leadership, proving that he was Israel's rightful priest. Afterward Aaron's staff was kept with the ark as a permanent reminder of God's authority in Israel (Numbers 17:10). Who is God? According to the staff by the ark, he is the ruler of his people.

The third item was the one that gave the ark its name. It was God's covenant with Israel, written in stone. God told Moses to put a copy of the covenant inside the ark (25:16, 21; cf. Deuteronomy 31:24–26). This covenant—or "testimony," as the Bible sometimes calls it—set the terms for God's relationship with Israel. In the covenant God promised to give his people every blessing of salvation. But he also demanded their obedience to his commandments. He would be their God, and they would be his people. Thus the covenant was a permanent reminder of God's promises to his people and of his law for their lives. Who is God? According to the covenant inside the ark, he is both Savior and Lord.

The ark of the covenant testified that God is our provider and our ruler, our Savior and our Lord. He is the one who gives us our daily bread, who governs us by the authorities he has appointed over us, who grants us all the blessings of salvation, and who tells us how we should live. But the most important thing about the ark was what went on top. Once Bezalel had finished making the box itself,

> he made a mercy seat of pure gold. Two cubits and a half was its length, and a cubit and a half its breadth. And he made two cherubim of gold. He made them of hammered work on the two ends of the mercy seat, one cherub on the one end, and one cherub on the other end. Of one piece with the mercy seat he made the cherubim on its two ends. The cherubim spread out their wings above, overshadowing the mercy seat with their wings, with their faces one to another; toward the mercy seat were the faces of the cherubim. (37:6–9; cf. 25:17–20)

Cherubim are the mighty angels who surround God's glorious throne. They are his guardian angels, the ones who guard the way to his presence. The psalmist addressed God as the one who sits "enthroned upon the cherubim" (Psalm 80:1; cf. 99:1). And according to Samuel, the ark of the covenant was "called by the name of the LORD of hosts who sits enthroned on the cherubim" (2 Samuel 6:2). The cherubim thus showed that the ark was a representation of God's throne. When God descended on the tabernacle, he appeared in a cloud of glory over the cover of the ark, which was the place of his presence and power. Who is God? According to the angels on the ark, he is the ruler of Heaven and earth, who sits enthroned between the cherubim.

This helps explain why the ark was used to lead the Israelites into battle. When Joshua began his conquest of Canaan, the ark led the way. It entered the Jordan River first and parted the waters (Joshua 3). It was also in the middle of the parade that marched around Jericho when the walls fell down (Joshua 6). The ark showed that the God of mighty angels was present in power, leading his people into battle. The King of kings was with his royal armies. This also explains why it was fatal for people to touch the ark (see 2 Samuel 6:1–7) or to use it in any inappropriate way (see 1 Samuel 4, 5). God was present in all the purity and power of his holiness.

The people were *not* holy. They were sinners who had broken God's law for their lives. So there was one more thing that went on the ark: the blood from a sacrifice for sin. Once a year—on the Day of Atonement—the high priest offered a sacrifice for the sins of God's people (see Leviticus 16). First he would slaughter a goat as a sin offering. The goat was a substitute. The people were the ones who deserved to die for their sins, but the animal died in their place. Then the high priest would take the sacrificial blood, enter the Holy of Holies, and sprinkle it on the lid of the ark. In this way he would make atonement for Israel's sin. It was called "the mercy seat" because it was the place where God showed mercy to sinners. The blood was an *expiation*: It removed the guilt of Israel's sin. It was also a *propitiation*: It turned aside God's wrath. When God saw the blood-stained ark, he knew that the demands of his justice had been met. A sacrifice had been made for his people's sin. Who is God? According to the mercy seat, he is the God of mercy and justice, who forgives sinners on the basis of a blood sacrifice.

This was all part of the rich symbolism of the ark. God provides what we need, giving us our daily bread. He governs our lives, directing us by his spiritual authority. He reigns supreme, ruling from his royal throne. And he offers forgiveness, accepting the blood of a substitute as the atonement for our sins.

## The Table, the Lampstand, and the Altar of Incense

The rest of the furniture in God's house was equally symbolic. The ark was the most important piece because it was the place of God's presence, but the other furnishings were also important. Each one teaches us something about God's glory and grace.

The next piece of furniture the Bible mentions is a table for bread:

> He also made the table of acacia wood. Two cubits was its length, a cubit its breadth, and a cubit and a half its height. And he overlaid it with pure gold, and made a molding of gold around it. And he made a rim around it a handbreadth wide, and made a molding of gold around the rim. He cast for it four rings of gold and fastened the rings to the four corners at its four legs. Close to the frame were the rings, as holders for the poles to carry the table. He made the poles of acacia wood to carry the table, and overlaid them with gold. And he made the vessels of pure gold that were to be on the table, its plates and dishes for incense, and its bowls and flagons with which to pour drink offerings. (37:10–16; cf. 25:23–29)

Like everything else inside the tabernacle, this little table and the dishes that went on top were made of gold. Each week the priests would bake twelve loaves of bread, presumably representing the twelve tribes of Israel. On the Sabbath they would set fresh bread on the table, in the presence of God, and then toward the end of the week they would eat it (see Leviticus 24:5–9).

What did this bread teach the Israelites? It taught them that God was their provider. He was the one who gave them grain and provided bread for his priests. On one memorable occasion God even used the bread of the Presence to feed King David and his army (1 Samuel 21:1–6; cf. Matthew 12:3, 4). Since it was an offering to God (Leviticus 24:7), the bread on the table also taught the Israelites to offer themselves for God's service. Just as the twelve loaves were presented to God, so the twelve tribes of Israel were to present themselves before God as his servants.

But the bread also reminded the Israelites that they were bound to God by covenant. Leviticus refers to the bread as "a covenant forever" (Leviticus 24:8), meaning a binding agreement that secures a relationship. In those days, when people made a covenant they usually shared a meal that sealed their fellowship; "sharing a special meal together was an act of friendship and personal communion."[2] We saw this back in Exodus 24, when God confirmed his covenant with Israel. The elders went up on the mountain, where "they beheld God, and ate and drank" (v. 11). They were sharing a meal in God's presence, and this sealed their friendship with him. Similarly, the bread in the tabernacle showed that God communed with his people, relating to them in an intimate way. Who is God? He is our provider and our friend—someone who sits down with us at the table.

The table of showbread was illuminated by the lampstand of life:

> He also made the lampstand of pure gold. He made the lampstand of hammered work. Its base, its stem, its cups, its calyxes, and its flowers were of one piece with it. And there were six branches going out of its sides, three branches of the lampstand out of one side of it and three branches of the lampstand out of the other side of it; three cups made like almond blossoms, each with calyx and flower, on one branch, and three cups made like almond blossoms, each with calyx and flower, on the other branch—so for the six branches going out of the lampstand. And on the lampstand itself were four cups made like almond blossoms, with their calyxes and flowers, and a calyx of one piece with it under each pair of the six branches going out of it. Their calyxes and their branches were of one piece with it. The whole of it was a single piece of hammered work of pure gold. (37:17–22; cf. 25:31–40)

The purpose of the lampstand was to light the tabernacle. Because it was shrouded with so many curtains, the tabernacle was pitch-black. But the lampstand was shining in the darkness. It did this night after night, as the priests continually replenished its oil (Leviticus 24:1–4). The lampstand was a perpetual flame.

Some people think that the lights on the lampstand represented heavenly bodies like the sun, moon, and visible planets. Whether this interpretation is correct or not, it is certainly true that all light comes from God, in whom there is no darkness (1 John 1:5). The lampstand was a symbol of his pure and perfect light. God makes things clear, teaching us to live in the light of his Word. He brings things to light, exposing what is done in secret. He is the revealer and the illuminator.

Notice that the lampstand was covered with buds and blossoms. It looked like a tree of life, and this too was part of its meaning. God is the life giver as well as the light giver. He is the God of both light and life. Just as he once planted the Tree of Life in the garden of Eden, so also he planted the lampstand in the tabernacle as a symbol of his life-giving power. Who is God? According to the golden lampstand, he is the Lord and giver of life. All life and light come from him.

The last piece of furniture in the tabernacle was the altar of incense:

> He made the altar of incense of acacia wood. Its length was a cubit, and its breadth was a cubit. It was square, and two cubits was its height. Its horns were of one piece with it. He overlaid it with pure gold, its top and around its sides and its horns. And he made a molding of gold around it, and made two rings of gold on it under its molding, on two opposite sides of it, as holders for the poles with which to carry it. And he made the poles of acacia wood and overlaid them with gold. He made the holy anointing oil also, and the pure fragrant incense, blended as by the perfumer. (37:25–29; cf. 30:1–5)

This altar was for the burning of sacred incense, which was made according to a special formula and then offered to God both morning and evening (30:7, 8). The altar stood directly in front of the ark of the covenant, separated only by the veil that curtained off the Holy of Holies. Since the ark was just on the other side of the curtain, the altar of incense was called "the altar that is before the Lord" (Leviticus 16:18). When a priest stood at the altar, he was standing in front of the ark, and thus in the presence of God.

The priest offered incense on the altar, and this filled the tabernacle with a pleasing fragrance. The smoking incense represented the prayers of God's people, rising to Heaven. King David said: "O Lord, I call upon you; hasten to me! Give ear to my voice when I call to you! Let my prayer be counted as incense before you, and the lifting up of my hands as the evening sacrifice!" (Psalm 141:1, 2). This interpretation is confirmed by the New Testament, which says that incense represents "the prayers of all the saints" (Revelation 8:3). So the altar of incense was Israel's sweet altar of prayer. There the priest praised God for his holiness, thanked God for his mercy, and presented Israel's petitions before the throne of Heaven. Who is God? According to the altar of incense, he is a God who hears and answers prayer.

This, then, is the God the Israelites encountered when they entered God's house. The tabernacle was furnished so as to show them that God was everything they needed. He was the God of Heaven, who lived with his people on earth. He was the God of truth, who gave them his law. He was the God of guidance, who ruled from his royal throne. He was the God of mercy, who offered forgiveness on the basis of blood. He was the God of providence, who sent bread from Heaven. He was the God of the covenant, who sat down at the table for fellowship. He was the God of life and light, who brightened their way. And he was the God of intercession, who listened to them when they prayed. This was the God who made his home with Israel at the tabernacle.

## At Home with Jesus

The question is, where is God's house today? How can we be at home with him? How can we have a relationship with him? God is everything we need. But where can we find his presence, guidance, forgiveness, provision, revelation, and everything else that comes from living with him?

The answer—as we have seen throughout our studies in the last chapters of Exodus—is that Jesus Christ is the tabernacle of God. God has come to live with us in the person of his Son. In the days of Moses, God made his dwelling in the tabernacle, but this was in preparation for the coming of Christ. The tabernacle held the promise of our salvation. God used it to show the Israelites—and us—what kind of Savior would come.

This was true of the tabernacle as a whole. The whole building was connected to Christ. It demonstrated that God desired to dwell with his people. But the specific details of the tabernacle were also connected to Christ. Each item of furniture testified to the salvation that one day God would provide. Even though Christ had not yet come, there was a sense in which he was already there, woven into the very fabric of the tabernacle. Understand that God has never saved anyone in any way except by the grace of Jesus Christ. The Israelites were saved by trusting in the Savior to come, as he was represented in the tabernacle and in the rituals of the Old Testament. We are saved by trusting simply and directly in Jesus. As Dr. Trimp has written, "In the Old Testament dispensation two things were valid with regard to Christ: *He was there already* and *He still had to come*."[3]

Jesus is our ark of the covenant. First he offered himself as our sacrifice, dying on the cross to make atonement for our sins. Then he sprinkled his very own blood on the mercy seat of Heaven. Now what comes between the righteousness of God and the guilt of our sin is the blood of Jesus Christ. He is "the propitiation for our sins" (1 John 2:2)—the once-and-for-all sacrifice that covers us from the wrath of God. Everyone who trusts in Jesus Christ has God's forgiveness.

After Jesus had finished suffering and dying for sin, God raised him from the dead and exalted him to the highest place in the universe. This means that

Jesus is not just the blood on the mercy seat—he is also the God enthroned between the cherubim. The Savior who died for us now sits on Heaven's throne, reigning as Lord and thus demanding our worship and obedience.

Jesus is our table of showbread. Indeed, he is the bread itself, for Jesus said, "I am the bread of life; whoever comes to me shall not hunger, and whoever believes in me shall never thirst" (John 6:35). Jesus is the one who sustains us, not only by giving us our daily bread, but also by supplying his Spirit as the source of our spiritual life now and forever. Jesus is also the one who sits down with us at the table, welcoming us into his fellowship. Jesus said, "If anyone hears my voice and opens the door, I will come in to him and eat with him, and he with me" (Revelation 3:20). Jesus wants to commune with us in the friendship of his covenant love.

Jesus is our lampstand of life. The Bible says, "In him was life, and the life was the light of men. . . . The true light, which gives light to everyone, was coming into the world" (John 1:4, 9). Jesus is the light of creation, the one who first brought life and light into the world. He is also the light of salvation, showing us the way to eternal life. Jesus said, "I am the light of the world. Whoever follows me will not walk in darkness, but will have the light of life" (John 8:12; cf. 9:5). If we want to have spiritual life—indeed, if we want to live forever—all we have to do is walk in his light.

Jesus is our altar of incense. He prays for us, as he prayed for his disciples in the Gospels (see, e.g., John 17), and his prayers rise like incense before God's throne. The Bible says that Jesus "is able to save to the uttermost those who draw near to God through him, since he always lives to make intercession for them" (Hebrews 7:25). On the basis of his atoning death on the cross, Jesus prays incessantly for our salvation and sanctification. If we want God to hear us, all we have to do is call out to him in the name of Jesus, praying on the basis of his sacrifice for our sins.

Jesus Christ is everything we could ever need. He is the blood sacrifice for all our sins. He is the living bread for all our hunger. He is the friend at the table for all our loneliness. He is the lampstand of life in all our darkness. He is the prayer of intercession in all our desperate troubles. In fact, Jesus is praying for us right now—praying that we will come home to God. We should not stay away but instead trust him for everything, forever.

# 99

# The Courtyard to God

## EXODUS 38:1–31

IN HER BOOK *Maya Mysteries*, Wendy Murray Zoba seeks to understand the bloodiness of the ancient Mayan system of sacrifice. History and archaeology show that the Maya practiced elaborate rituals of atonement, centered around child sacrifice. As Zoba explains it:

> The Maya understood the need for blood, especially the blood. They have shown us there isn't enough human blood in all the world to satisfy the gods. They are telling us the power of the sacrifice cannot be found in the blood of humans sacrificed by human hands. When the warfare increased toward the end of the dynasty, and the Maya all over the lowlands fought their civil wars and took captives, did they send them to the fields to work? No. They cut off their heads and carried them on sticks. For what? What did all that blood avail the ancient Maya?[1]

The answer is, nothing. The Maya thought that offering human sacrifices would bring them closer to God. But the gods were not appeased, even when the bloodletting intensified. Zoba concludes, "The gods were not satisfied," and thus the Maya did not receive forgiveness for their sins.

To us the ancient Mayan rituals seem primitive and barbaric. Yet many people feel the same way about the sacrifices of the Old Testament, and even about the crucifixion of Jesus Christ. Why does the Bible have so much to say about blood—specifically blood sacrifice? At times it almost seems obsessed with the subject. But what do bloody sacrifices have to do with daily life in a postmodern world?

The answer is, "Without the shedding of blood there is no forgiveness of sins" (Hebrews 9:22). This is a universal principle of divine justice for all peoples in all places at all times. The human race has fallen into sin. We have turned against God in rebellion, refusing to obey him and choosing instead to go our own way. As a result we deserve to die. This is what God's justice demands. We have sinned against his infinite majesty, and nothing less than life itself can pay the debt that we owe. Blood is the price for sin. It is the only thing that can make us right with God. Although the Maya were wrong about many things, they were right about this—much "righter" than most people today. Deep down they knew that they could only come to God on the basis of blood. Blood is the way to God.

## God's Front Yard

The question is, by whose blood can we be saved? The tabernacle in the wilderness helps us see the answer. By way of reminder, the tabernacle was the large portable tent that the Israelites built in the wilderness somewhere between Egypt and the Promised Land. It was God's house, symbolizing his dwelling place on earth.

The tabernacle was surrounded by a large rectangular enclosure, measuring roughly 75 feet by 150 feet. The perimeter of this enclosure was marked with a tall fence made of linen fabric stretched across wooden fenceposts. This made a courtyard around the tabernacle. Exodus 38 tells how it was constructed:

> And he made the court. For the south side the hangings of the court were of fine twined linen, a hundred cubits; their twenty pillars and their twenty bases were of bronze, but the hooks of the pillars and their fillets were of silver. And for the north side there were hangings of a hundred cubits, their twenty pillars, their twenty bases were of bronze, but the hooks of the pillars and their fillets were of silver. And for the west side were hangings of fifty cubits, their ten pillars, and their ten bases; the hooks of the pillars and their fillets were of silver. And for the front to the east, fifty cubits. The hangings for one side of the gate were fifteen cubits, with their three pillars and three bases. And so for the other side. On both sides of the gate of the court were hangings of fifteen cubits, with their three pillars and their three bases. All the hangings around the court were of fine twined linen. And the bases for the pillars were of bronze, but the hooks of the pillars and their fillets were of silver. The overlaying of their capitals was also of silver, and all the pillars of the court were filleted with silver. (vv. 9–17)

Like the rest of the tabernacle, the fence around the courtyard was made with costly materials, including fine linen and precious metals. The Bible tells us what went into the tabernacle so we can appreciate its beauty and also learn from the generosity of those who built it. The whole complex was made from materials that the Israelites brought as freewill offerings. With gratitude to God for their deliverance from Egypt, they used their wealth to build God's home.

Exodus 38 ends with an inventory of the treasures they brought, starting with the gold that went inside the tabernacle:

> These are the records of the tabernacle, the tabernacle of the testimony, as they were recorded at the commandment of Moses, the responsibility of the Levites under the direction of Ithamar the son of Aaron the priest. Bezalel the son of Uri, son of Hur, of the tribe of Judah, made all that the LORD commanded Moses; and with him was Oholiab the son of Ahisamach, of the tribe of Dan, an engraver and designer and embroiderer in blue and purple and scarlet yarns and fine twined linen. All the gold that was used for the work, in all the construction of the sanctuary, the gold from the offering, was twenty-nine talents and 730 shekels, by the shekel of the sanctuary. (vv. 21–24)

The Israelites also brought silver, which was used to make the bases for the sanctuary and also to make the hooks and clasps that secured the courtyard fence. This silver came from the price that the men of Israel paid for their redemption (see 30:1–11):

> The silver from those of the congregation who were recorded was a hundred talents and 1,775 shekels, by the shekel of the sanctuary: a beka a head (that is, half a shekel, by the shekel of the sanctuary), for everyone who was listed in the records, from twenty years old and upward, for 603,550 men. The hundred talents of silver were for casting the bases of the sanctuary and the bases of the veil; a hundred bases for the hundred talents, a talent a base. And of the 1,775 shekels he made hooks for the pillars and overlaid their capitals and made fillets for them. (38:25–28)

Finally, the Israelites brought bronze, which was used for the outer fence and for all the sacred objects that stood in the courtyard: "The bronze that was offered was seventy talents and 2,400 shekels; with it he made the bases for the entrance of the tent of meeting, the bronze altar and the bronze grating for it and all the utensils of the altar, the bases around the court, and the bases of the gate of the court, all the pegs of the tabernacle, and all the pegs around the court" (vv. 29–31).

This was a vast quantity of precious metal, amounting to more than a ton of gold, three tons of silver, and two tons of bronze. The Bible gives these facts and figures to show how lavish the tabernacle was and to show how generous the people were in giving their treasure to God. When it comes to showing God how thankful we are that he saved us, no expense should be spared.

This inventory also shows how careful the Israelites were to keep track of God's money. It was their financial statement—an accounting of how much was given and what it was used to make. Obviously, the leaders of Israel wanted to exercise good stewardship of God's resources. As John Currid wisely comments:

> [O]fferings given to God's work must be accounted for. Records must be kept, and what happens to every penny needs to be seen. How often we see churches, or para-church ministries, faltering in this area! We need to be

> careful, for money is a great temptation, and can be an idol that masters its servants. The people in charge of God's work here on earth must be above reproach in the area of finance—this is a great witness to the world and keeps them from condemning us for hypocrisy.[2]

The house God is building today is the church, which is the dwelling place of his Spirit. One way we help build the church is by giving generously to support its work. The offerings we bring pay for workers who lead ministries, pastors who preach the gospel, evangelists who plant new churches, missionaries who cross the world for Christ, and even the building where people come to worship. God uses our material contributions to do the spiritual work of saving sinners. We should give as generously as we are able, and whatever we give should be used wisely. Churches and other Christian ministries should strive to maintain the highest standards of stewardship and accounting.

One part of the courtyard fence deserves special mention—namely, the entrance. The fence separated the camp where the Israelites lived from the tabernacle where God lived. It formed a boundary between the Creator and his creatures. But there was one way to enter. At the front of the tabernacle was an opening thirty feet wide that was covered with a special curtain. The rest of the fence was white. However,

> the screen for the gate of the court was embroidered with needlework in blue and purple and scarlet yarns and fine twined linen. It was twenty cubits long and five cubits high in its breadth, corresponding to the hangings of the court. And their pillars were four in number. Their four bases were of bronze, their hooks of silver, and the overlaying of their capitals and their fillets of silver. And all the pegs for the tabernacle and for the court all around were of bronze. (38:18–20)

The curtain or screen was decorated like this to show that it was the entrance to God's house. Its fabric was identical to the fabric used for the tabernacle itself. This made an obvious connection between the entrance to the courtyard and the doorway to the tabernacle—the place where God was. When the people saw the purple curtain at the front of the courtyard, they knew that it was the entrance to God's house. This was the way to God.

There was only one way to enter. There was no back door to the tabernacle. Nor were people allowed to enter the courtyard by climbing over the fence. There was only one way in. If people wanted to meet with God, they had to enter the way he invited them to enter.

God operates the same way today. There is only one way to salvation, which is by faith in Jesus Christ. People are always coming up with their own ways to God, whether it involves doing good works, keeping a law of obedience, practicing a special form of meditation, or embarking on some sacred pilgrimage. But there is only one way to God. Jesus said, "Enter by the narrow gate. For the gate is wide and the way is easy that leads to destruction, and those who enter by it are many. For the gate is narrow and the way is hard that leads to life, and those who find it are few" (Matthew 7:13a, 14). When Jesus spoke of the narrow gate, he was referring to himself, for he also said, "I am the door. If anyone enters by me, he will be saved" (John 10:9). Jesus Christ is the only way to God.

## The Bloody Altar

When people entered the courtyard to God, they saw two sacred objects. The first was a large bronze altar for sacrifices:

> He made the altar of burnt offering of acacia wood. Five cubits was its length, and five cubits its breadth. It was square, and three cubits was its height. He made horns for it on its four corners. Its horns were of one piece with it, and he overlaid it with bronze. And he made all the utensils of the altar, the pots, the shovels, the basins, the forks, and the fire pans. He made all its utensils of bronze. And he made for the altar a grating, a network of bronze, under its ledge, extending halfway down. He cast four rings on the four corners of the bronze grating as holders for the poles. He made the poles of acacia wood and overlaid them with bronze. And he put the poles through the rings on the sides of the altar to carry it with them. He made it hollow, with boards. (38:1–7)

Like the rest of the tabernacle furnishings, the altar of burnt offering was portable, so that the Israelites could take it with them. The altar was nearly eight feet wide and five feet tall. It was set up like a giant square grill, complete with all the utensils that were needed to tend the fire, remove the ashes, and cook the meat. This is where the Israelites offered their sacrifices to God.

The great bronze altar was in almost constant use. In fact, the priests were required to make sure that its fire was always burning. According to Leviticus, "The fire on the altar shall be kept burning on it; it shall not go out. The priest shall burn wood on it every morning, and he shall arrange the burnt offering on it and shall burn on it the fat of the peace offerings. Fire shall be kept burning on the altar continually; it shall not go out" (Leviticus 6:12, 13).

The reason the priests had to keep the fire burning was because the Israelites had so many sacrifices to offer! Here they presented their whole burnt offerings (see Leviticus 1), both morning and evening (see 29:38–41). This was a sacrifice of atonement, in which the worshiper offered an animal as the substitute for his sins. Here they presented their fellowship offerings (see Leviticus 3). This was a celebration of covenant friendship, in which the fat parts were offered to God, and the rest of the animal was eaten in his presence. Here they presented their sin offerings (see Leviticus 4:1—5:13), which made purification for ritual uncleanness and atoned for specific sins. Here they presented their guilt offerings (see

Leviticus 5:14—6:7) for inadvertent offenses against God's law for holiness. And here, most importantly of all, the high priest offered sacrifices on the Day of Atonement—first for his own sins, then for the sins of all God's people (see Leviticus 16).

The altar of burnt offering was a place of bloody, bloody sacrifice. All these sacrifices were necessary to atone for Israel's sin. In most cases they began with the worshiper placing his hand on the animal's head (e.g., Leviticus 1:4; 3:2; cf. 16:21). This made a symbolic identification between man and beast. It was not the animal that deserved to die, but the worshiper, for he had sinned against God. Yet by placing his hands on the animal, the sinner imputed his guilt to the sacrifice, which then died as his substitute. The worshiper was saying in effect, "This is my sacrifice. Let it be offered in my place, Lord, and may you accept its death as the wages of my sin."

To summarize, the altar of burnt offering is where God provided substitutionary atonement through a sacrifice in blood. As Patrick Fairbairn explained it,

> The ground upon which this merciful arrangement plainly proceeds, is the doomed condition of men as sinners, and the purpose of God to save them from its infliction. Their soul or life has, through sin, been forfeited to God, and, as a debt due to His justice, it should in right be rendered back again to Him who gave it. The enforcement of this claim, of course, inevitably involves the death of transgressors, according to the sentence [that] from the very first hung over the commission of sin, denouncing its penalty to be death. But as God appears in the institution of sacrifice providing a way of escape from this deserved doom, He mercifully appoints a substitute—the soul or life of a beast, for the soul or life of the transgressor; and as the seat of life is in the blood, so the blood of the beast, its life-blood, was given to be shed in death, and served up on the altar of God, in the room of that other and higher but guilty life, which had become due to divine justice. When this was done, when the blood of the slain victim was poured out or sprinkled upon the altar, and thereby given up to God, the sinner's guilt was atoned (covered); a screen, as it were, was thrown between the eye of God and his guilt, or between his own soul and the penalty due to his transgression. In other words a life that had not been forfeited was accepted in the room of the sinner's that was forfeited; and this was yielded back to him as now again a life in peace and fellowship with God—a life out of death.[3]

What the Israelites learned from all this was that in order to come to God, they first needed to present a sacrifice for their sins. No sooner had they entered the courtyard to God than they needed to make atonement. The great bronze altar was the first thing they encountered. It dominated the entrance, reminding them of the wages of their sin and offering them a way to get right with God. Only a blood sacrifice could save them. As they came to offer their sacrifices, again and again they learned that blood was the way to God.

Did all these sacrifices really atone for sin? Yes and no. Yes, because this is the way God told the Israelites to make atonement. But no, because all they offered was the blood of animals, which could not actually atone for the sins of human beings made in his image. The Bible says, "It is impossible for the blood of bulls and goats to take away sins" (Hebrews 10:4). So the altar of burnt offering was only a temporary arrangement. God was teaching the Israelites that the price had to be paid in blood, and at the same time was teaching them to wait for the full and final atonement that only he could provide. The Israelites were saved by believing in the Savior to come, as he was given to them in the sacrifices they offered at the tabernacle.

When the full and final atonement came, it came in the person of God's Son, Jesus Christ, who died on the cross for sinners. This is the amazing fact of our salvation. The debt for our sin needs to be paid in blood, but God does not make us pay the price; he was willing to pay it himself! David Levy writes,

> The Tabernacle with its ordinances was only "a figure for the time then present" (Heb. 9:9) but looked toward Christ's sacrificial death, which was to mediate a new covenant by means of His shed blood for the redemption of mankind (Heb. 9:11–22). . . . The brazen altar stood in the outer court just inside the gate facing the Tabernacle (Exod. 40:6). The sacrificial animals were offered on this altar, and their blood was shed for the sins of the people. The brazen altar typifies Christ's redemptive work on the cross on our behalf, whereby all who put their faith in His shed blood are justified and receive remission of sins (Rom. 3:24–25). Just as it was impossible for the Israelites to come into God's presence without sacrificing at the brazen altar, so it is impossible today for people to come into the presence of God except by the ministry of the cross.[4]

We can only approach God the way the Israelites approached him: by blood. This may sound strange. We are tempted to think we are good enough for God. Why would anyone need to die for us? But the Bible says that we are sinners and that the debt of our sin must be paid in blood. Yet it also says that Jesus "has appeared once for all at the end of the ages to put away sin by the sacrifice of himself" (Hebrews 9:26b). His blood opens up the way to God. Earlier I quoted from Wendy Murray Zoba's book about the mysteries of the Maya, with all their bloody sacrifices. As a Christian, Zoba clearly identifies their tragic mistake: they did not know "the power of the blood of God spilled by God himself."[5]

This is what Jesus offered on the cross: the powerful blood of God. Jesus is God the Son. Therefore, when Jesus bled and died on the cross, he offered the blood of God, which alone is sufficient to atone for all our sins and bring us home to God. If we want the sacrifice of Jesus to count for us, all we need to do is lay our hands on him by faith, saying, "This is my sacrifice. O God, let him be offered in my place. Accept his death as the wages of my sin. And may his blood open up the way for me to come to you."

## The Cleansing Basin

There were two sacred objects in the courtyard. The first was the altar of burnt offering, where sacrifices were offered for Israel's transgressions. This provided atonement as the blood took away the guilt of the people's sin. But there was still a need for cleansing. As the priests went about their daily service to God—bloody as it was—they needed to be washed with water. They did their washing at the bronze basin that stood between the altar of burnt offering and the door of the tabernacle.

Some see a connection here with the events of the exodus. In their deliverance from Egypt, the Israelites received atonement for their sins through the sacrifice of the Passover lamb. Then they passed through the waters of the Red Sea. First atonement, then cleansing—just like the altar and the basin. Vern Poythress comments:

> The altar stands closest to the entrance to the courtyard. After that comes the washing basin, then comes the tabernacle itself with its two rooms. The Israelites' own experience in the immediate past portrays the same sequence. First they are in bondage, in Egypt, then they are delivered through the sacrifice of the Passover lamb, symbolized by the altar. Then they pass through the Red Sea and still live, whereas their enemies are destroyed. The waters of the Red Sea stand for a kind of ceremonial cleansing from their enemies.[6]

The bronze basin symbolized the cleansing power of God's grace in washing away sin. The priests needed constant cleansing because they were engaged in holy service to God. For them it was a matter of life and death. God said, "When they go into the tent of meeting, or when they come near the altar to minister, to burn a food offering to the LORD, they shall wash with water, so that they may not die. They shall wash their hands and their feet, so that they may not die" (30:20, 21a). It was either wash or be killed. Every time the priests offered a sacrifice on the altar, and every time they entered the Holy Place, they needed cleansing.

Like almost everything else at the tabernacle, the bronze basin was a preview of the gospel. According to David Levy, "The laver speaks of Christ as our sanctification. As believer-priests, we are reminded that Christ has sanctified us for His service and is sanctifying us by cleansing us from the daily defilement of sin 'with the washing of water by the word' (Eph. 5:26)."[7] The Bible often describes our salvation in Christ in terms of cleansing from sin. There is a sense in which we receive this cleansing when we first trust in Christ for our salvation. The Bible calls this "the washing of regeneration and renewal of the Holy Spirit"

(Titus 3:5). When God gives us new life in Christ, he washes us clean. This is absolutely necessary. We need to be purified from the pollution of sin. As Jesus said to Peter, "If I do not wash you, you have no share with me" (John 13:8). This is part of the symbolism of Christian baptism, in which water signifies the blood of Jesus that washes away our sin.

Yet we are still sinners, and even after coming to Christ, we have an ongoing need for God's cleansing work in our lives. Like the Old Testament priests, we are called to serve a holy God. In order to serve him in real holiness, we need to be cleansed from the corruption of the sin that we continue to commit. Anyone "who becomes Christ's, and through Christ would dedicate himself to the work and service of God, must be purified from the guilt and pollution of sin—must be regenerated unto holiness of life."[8] In a word, we need to be sanctified. We have been justified by the sacrifice Jesus made for us on the cross. Now we need to be sanctified. We need to be purified. We need God the Holy Spirit to make us holy.

Together, the two sacred objects in the tabernacle courtyard made a powerful statement about salvation. Both of them marked the way to God. First came the altar of atonement, followed by the basin for cleansing. First, justification, then sanctification. First came the atoning blood sacrifice that made sinners right with God by paying the debt of their sin; then came the pure cleansing water that made sinners holy before God by washing away the remaining corruption of their sin.

So it is for the Christian. God has promised that "if we confess our sins, he is faithful and just to forgive us our sins and to cleanse us from all unrighteousness" (1 John 1:9). First we go to the cross, where Jesus offered the atoning blood sacrifice for our sins. Afterward we experience an ongoing work of sanctification as God's Spirit uses God's Word to make us holy. We need to trust God to do this. As we struggle with sin—sometimes almost to the point of despair—the gospel calls us to believe in the power of God's sanctifying grace to cleanse us from sin.

## Mirror, Mirror

One of the remarkable things about the bronze basin was the way it was made. The Bible says, rather matter-of-factly, "He made the basin of bronze and its stand of bronze, from the mirrors of the ministering women who ministered in the entrance of the tent of meeting" (38:8).

There is a story behind this verse—a story we can only guess at because the Bible leaves most of it untold. But apparently there were women who had a special place of service at the tabernacle. We don't know what they did. Maybe they served as greeters or doorkeepers. Perhaps they were singers or musicians of some kind. Maybe they had a ministry of prayer and fasting. Or perhaps they helped in some practical way as people prepared to offer their sacrifices. All we know is that some women were organized to serve God at the tabernacle. There was a place for women to use their gifts for God's glory, as there is in the church today—in countless ways.

We also know that these women owned mirrors, which almost certainly came from Egypt. John Currid comments: "Egypt was well-known in antiquity for making cosmetic objects, in particular, mirrors. Egyptian mirrors consisted of either cast or hammered metal discs, almost always in an elliptical shape. Made mostly of either copper or bronze, they were polished to a radiant sheen. Then they were inserted into a handle made of faience, wood, stone, ivory, or metal. The handles were carved with different types of representations, such as gods."[9]

To understand what happened next, imagine living your whole life in the degradation of slavery. Imagine never having anything to call your own, never possessing anything of beauty, never owning anything nice. Then imagine how much the Israelite women must have envied their Egyptian mistresses, with all their finery and cosmetics. Imagine what it was like to help make another woman beautiful day after day, without having so much as a mirror to see your own face.

Now imagine how the women of Israel felt the night they left Egypt, when the Egyptians put all kinds of treasure into their hands, including those beautiful mirrors. Imagine the buzz of excitement as the women showed one another what their mistresses had given them. Finally they could see how they looked! And finally, perhaps, they could become as beautiful as they had always longed to be.

Then came the day when Moses invited the Israelites to bring their gifts for the tabernacle: gold, silver, and bronze. The people went home to see what they had to offer. And somewhere in Israel there was a woman who looked around her tent and realized that her mirror was made of bronze. In an instant her mind was made up: She would offer it to the Lord! Afterward she may have had some second thoughts, but in her heart she knew that was what God wanted her to give. She talked it over with one or two of her closest friends. Soon there was a community of women who together decided to give up their mirrors for God. For some it must have been a painful sacrifice. No doubt many women were tempted to keep their mirrors, and some of them probably did. After all, there was nothing wrong with wanting to look beautiful.

But to the praise of God, some women were willing to make the sacrifice. Presumably these women cared how they looked. Why else would they have mirrors? But they were not mastered by the vanity of outward appearance. They had caught a glimpse of a beauty that was infinitely more desirable than their own. Rather than idolizing their own appearance, they wanted to see God glorified. They wanted him to be seen to be beautiful, and not themselves. According to an old Jewish commentator—one of the rabbis—"It is the custom of all women to behold their face every morning in a mirror, that they may be able to dress their hair; but lo! there were women in Israel that served the Lord, who abandoned this worldly delight, and gave away their glasses as a free-will offering, for they had no more use of them; but they came every day to the door of the tabernacle of the congregation to pray, and hear the words of the commandments."[10]

As Israel's craftsmen began to work on the tabernacle, they realized that the mirrors were perfect for making the bronze basin. Word of this spread throughout the camp. Everyone who heard what the women had given and how their offering was being used praised God, as Moses did when he wrote down the story. What these women did brought glory to God.

To this day, their example is a challenge to every Christian. It is a challenge to Christian men to see the true beauty of a Christian woman, which is not her outward appearance, but the beauty of a life sanctified by grace. What do you look for in a woman? Do you see what God sees? To look only at the outside is a damaging distortion that does real harm to women and girls by pressuring them to conform to the wrong standards of beauty.

This is also a challenge to Christian women. When you look in the mirror—as every woman does—what do you see? Do you see features you wish you could replace, flaws you wish you could alter, wrinkles and gray hair you wish you could remove? Or do you see a woman loved by God, who has been justified by the blood that Jesus offered on the cross and is being cleansed by the sanctifying work of the Spirit? And what beauty do you desire? Do you wish that God would make you look like someone else? Or do you say, "Lord Jesus, when people look at me, I don't care how beautiful they think I am; I want them to see how beautiful you are"? God has provided atonement and cleansing through Jesus Christ so that his beauty will be revealed in us.

# 100

# Aaron's Wardrobe

EXODUS 39:1–31

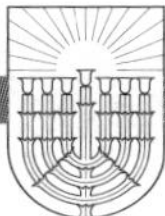

HAVE YOU EVER DONE something so sinful that you wondered if God would ever let you serve him again? Perhaps it was an act of immorality, or perhaps a failure of leadership. Maybe it was something you did against your better judgment, or maybe it was sheer rebellion. But whatever it was—whether it was something recent or something long, long ago—it seemed like such a terrible sin that it ought to permanently disqualify you from serving God.

Aaron did something like that. Although he was chosen to be high priest over the house of God, Aaron committed a terrible sin. The story of his tragic failure was told back in Exodus 32. While his brother Moses was up on the mountain getting the Law from God, Aaron led the Israelites into sin. He set up an alternative worship service—one not ordained by God. With his own hands, he made a golden calf and set it up for the people to worship, in direct violation of the second commandment. And when Moses came down to confront Aaron, he rightly accused him of leading the people into "great sin" (32:21). How could such a man ever serve God again? How could he be worthy to wear the righteous robes of priestly ministry?

Yet Aaron did serve God. He was anointed high priest over the tabernacle—the father of all the priests in Israel. He returned to the very calling he had once desecrated by his sin. And as the mediator, he entered the Most Holy Place, where God was. He not only entered there but also lived to tell about it, for God ordained his ministry as high priest.

Why was a sinner like Aaron allowed to serve the holy God? He was able to serve because although he was fallen, he was also forgiven. In preparation for the priesthood, Aaron's body was washed with holy water (40:12), symbolizing his consecration to God. Then he confessed his sins, placing his hands on the head of a bull and two rams, which were sacrificed to make atonement.

Through the cleansing water and the sacrificial blood, Aaron was set apart to serve.

## Aaron's New Clothes

To carry out his calling as the high priest of Israel, Aaron needed a new wardrobe. Exodus 39 tells how Israel's craftsmen made holy garments for him to wear in the tabernacle. Even after his sin, there was a place for him to serve, and in order to serve there, he had to be suitably dressed: "From the blue and purple and scarlet yarns they made finely woven garments, for ministering in the Holy Place. They made the holy garments for Aaron, as the LORD had commanded Moses" (v. 1).

These priestly robes were made of the same stuff as the tabernacle itself: fine linen, embroidered with blue, purple, and scarlet yarn. These bright colors made a visual connection between the high priest and the place where he served. Vern Poythress describes him as a kind of "vertical replica of the tabernacle."[1] Tremper Longman calls him a "mini-tabernacle"—almost "part of the tabernacle structure itself."[2] The high priest's sacred garments showed that he belonged in God's sanctuary.

There were four main items in Aaron's wardrobe: the ephod, the breastpiece, the robe, and the turban. These clothes and their accessories were introduced back in Exodus 28. In chapter 39 they are described again as Israel's craftsmen make them according to the divine design. Knowing how they were made and what they symbolized shows what a superior priest God has provided for us in Jesus Christ, as well as what kind of holy service he demands from us. Aaron's wardrobe gives us a picture of both Christ and the church that is in Christ.

The first thing the craftsman made was the ephod:

> He made the ephod of gold, blue and purple and scarlet yarns, and fine twined linen. And they hammered out gold leaf, and he cut it into threads to work into the blue and purple and the scarlet yarns, and into the fine twined linen, in skilled design. They made for the ephod attaching shoulder pieces, joined to it at its two edges. And the skillfully woven band on it was of one piece with it and made like it, of gold, blue and purple and scarlet yarns, and fine twined linen, as the LORD had commanded Moses. (39:2–5)

The ephod was such an unusual garment that it became symbolic of the entire priesthood. It was a sort of sleeveless vest that was attached by means of two shoulder straps. The straps were the most important part of the ephod because of what they symbolized: "They made the onyx stones, enclosed in settings of gold filigree, and engraved like the engravings of a signet, according to the names of the sons of Israel. And he set them on the shoulder pieces of the ephod to be stones of remembrance for the sons of Israel, as the LORD had commanded Moses" (vv. 6, 7).

Both shoulder stones bore the names of six of the twelve tribes of Israel (see 28:9, 10). This showed that the priest represented the nation. As he went about his priestly duties, he was carrying the people on his shoulders. Whenever he made sacrifices of atonement, washed in the basin, trimmed the lights on the lampstand, ate the bread of fellowship, offered the incense of prayer, or stood before the ark of the covenant, he was serving God on Israel's behalf. It was not only the priest who had forgiveness, cleansing, illumination, communion, and intercession; these blessings were for all the people of God, as represented by their high priest. Aaron wore the ephod to show that he was bringing God's people into God's presence.

The high priest also wore a breastpiece. As we learned in Exodus 28, this was for casting judgment. There was a pouch inside the breastpiece for the Urim and Thummim—the holy dice that the high priest used to consult the will of God for Israel (28:30). Hence this part of Aaron's wardrobe was called "a breastpiece of judgment" (28:15). Here the Bible explains how it was made:

> He made the breastpiece, in skilled work, in the style of the ephod, of gold, blue and purple and scarlet yarns, and fine twined linen. It was square. They made the breastpiece doubled, a span its length and a span its breadth when doubled. And they set in it four rows of stones. A row of sardius, topaz, and carbuncle was the first row; and the second row, an emerald, a sapphire, and a diamond; and the third row, a jacinth, an agate, and an amethyst; and the fourth row, a beryl, an onyx, and a jasper. They were enclosed in settings of gold filigree. There were twelve stones with their names according to the names of the sons of Israel. They were like signets, each engraved with its name, for the twelve tribes. (39:8–14)

Like the ephod, the breastpiece was a visual representation of Israel. It was decorated with twelve precious and semiprecious stones, each engraved with the name of one of Israel's tribes. Then the breastpiece was attached to the ephod:

> And they made on the breastpiece twisted chains like cords, of pure gold. And they made two settings of gold filigree and two gold rings, and put the two rings on the two edges of the breastpiece. And they put the two cords of gold in the two rings at the edges of the breastpiece. They attached the two ends of the two cords to the two settings of filigree. Thus they attached it in front to the shoulder pieces of the ephod. Then they made two rings of gold, and put them at the two ends of the breastpiece, on its inside edge next to the ephod. And they made two rings of gold, and attached them in front to the lower part of the two shoulder pieces of the ephod, at its seam above the skillfully woven band of the ephod. And they bound the breastpiece by its rings to the rings of the ephod with a lace of blue, so that it should lie on

> the skillfully woven band of the ephod, and that the breastpiece should not come loose from the ephod, as the Lord had commanded Moses. (vv. 15–21)

The golden chains kept the breastpiece where it belonged. Whereas the ephod showed that the high priest carried the people's burdens on his shoulders, the breastpiece showed that he wore their concerns close to his heart. He had a ministry of both support and sympathy.

Next came the high priest's robe—a long, seamless garment of royal blue:

> He also made the robe of the ephod woven all of blue, and the opening of the robe in it was like the opening in a garment, with a binding around the opening, so that it might not tear. On the hem of the robe they made pomegranates of blue and purple and scarlet yarns and fine twined linen. They also made bells of pure gold, and put the bells between the pomegranates all around the hem of the robe, between the pomegranates—a bell and a pomegranate, a bell and a pomegranate around the hem of the robe for ministering, as the LORD had commanded Moses. (vv. 22–26)

The robe was rich in its symbolic significance. It was woven from a single piece of cloth to show what kind of wholeness and integrity God demanded in his priests. The pomegranates were a sign of fruitfulness, because more than almost any other fruit, they are full of seeds. The little golden bells were for safety. The high priest had to wear them when he entered the Holy Place or else he would die (28:35).

To make his wardrobe complete, Aaron was given several accessories, topped off with a turban:

> They also made the coats, woven of fine linen, for Aaron and his sons, and the turban of fine linen, and the caps of fine linen, and the linen undergarments of fine twined linen, and the sash of fine twined linen and of blue and purple and scarlet yarns, embroidered with needlework, as the LORD had commanded Moses. They made the plate of the holy crown of pure gold, and wrote on it an inscription, like the engraving of a signet, "Holy to the LORD." And they tied to it a cord of blue to fasten it on the turban above, as the LORD had commanded Moses. (39:27–31)

It was an extraordinary outfit. No one else has ever worn anything like it. People were stunned when they saw the high priest in his ornate regalia. Everything he wore had symbolic significance. But what was even more striking was the total impression that his strange clothing conveyed. Here was a man who was set apart. His unusual clothing showed that he had a unique calling. The high priest was consecrated for the holy service of God.

Back in Exodus 28, when God told Moses why the high priest needed special clothes, he said, "And you shall make holy garments for Aaron your brother, for glory and for beauty. You shall speak to all the skillful, whom I have filled with a spirit of skill, that they make Aaron's garments to consecrate him for my priesthood" (28:2, 3). These verses mention three things that Aaron's wardrobe was supposed to convey: holiness, glory, and beauty. As David Levy explains, his garments "were to be holy because they were set apart to be worn only during the service in the Tabernacle. They were to be glorious because they exalted the priestly office in the eyes of the people. They were to be beautiful because their colors harmonized with the Tabernacle furnishings. The look of the priest was to match the function of his ministry as he worshiped God in the beauty of holiness."[3]

The high priest's crowning glory was his turban, which had a golden plate summarizing his whole priestly calling. It read, "Holy to the LORD." This was the quintessential attribute of the high priest. He was holy for the people before God. The people were not holy; they kept sinning against God. So how could they enter his holy presence? They couldn't, but they had a priest who could enter on their behalf. As it said right on the man's forehead, he was "Holy to the LORD."

## A Superior Priest

From head to toe, the high priest looked perfect, and he almost was. I say "almost" because he did have some imperfections. As Levy explains,

> The high priest, clothed in the beautiful garments of his office, moved gracefully about the Tabernacle ministering on behalf of Israel. No one was held in higher esteem among the people than he. No one enjoyed greater privilege to experience the sweet fellowship of God's presence than he. No one held a more prominent position on earth than he. Yet, with all of his privilege, position, and prominence, he was not a perfect high priest; he was subject to infirmities and death like all men.[4]

The high priest was also subject to sin. The sign on his forehead said, "Holy to the LORD," but what was in his heart? Did his inward sanctification match his outward ornamentation? According to the psalmist, the high priest was supposed to be "clothed with righteousness" (Psalm 132:9). But holy clothes do not make a man holy, and it was here that the high priest fell short of perfection. He needed to make atonement for his own sins as much as for the sins of anyone else.

This helps us to see what perfect salvation God has provided for us in Jesus Christ. Hebrews calls Jesus our "great high priest" (Hebrews 4:14), "a great priest over the house of God" (Hebrews 10:21). Everyone needs a priest. We need someone to make atonement for our sins; otherwise we would perish. We need someone to usher us into the holy presence of God. And we need someone to pray for us in our trials and temptations. We all need a priest.

When we look at the high priest in Exodus, we see a picture of the priestly ministry of Jesus Christ. Jesus does for us what the high priest did for Israel: He offers the sacrifice for our sins, brings us into God's presence, and prays for what we need. Even Aaron's wardrobe depicted Christ's priestly ministry. Jesus carries us on his shoulders, like the shoulder stones on the ephod. He takes our needs to heart, like the gemstones on the breastpiece. He is robed in royal righteousness, and his perfect life bears this inscription: "Holy to the LORD."

For all the similarities between the high priest in Exodus and the great High Priest of our salvation, what is most important to see is that Jesus is superior in every way. The high priest, with all his fancy clothes, performed a holy ministry for Israel. But what Jesus does for us is vastly superior.

Jesus ministers in a *superior place*. The high priest served in the tabernacle, but Jesus serves in Heaven itself. The Bible says, "We have such a high priest, one who is seated at the right hand of the throne of the Majesty in heaven, a minister in the holy places, in the true tent that the Lord set up, not man" (Hebrews 8:1, 2). Again, it says, "Christ has entered, not into holy places made with hands, which are copies of the true things, but into heaven itself, now to appear in the presence of God on our behalf" (Hebrews 9:24). Therefore, whatever Jesus does on our behalf he does in the most holy place of all, right at the throne of God.

Jesus ministers to us with *superior righteousness*. His righteousness is not external, like a holy set of clothes, but intrinsic to his own holy person. Jesus is clothed with the righteousness of his own perfection: a perfect divine nature and a perfect human nature, unstained by sin. The Bible says, "For it was indeed fitting that we should have such a high priest, holy, innocent, unstained, separated from sinners, and exalted above the heavens. He has no need, like those high priests, to offer sacrifices daily, first for his own sins and then for those of the people" (Hebrews 7:26, 27a). He does not need to offer any sacrifices for his own sins because he is the priest "who has been made perfect forever" (Hebrews 7:28b).

Jesus ministers to us with *superior sympathy*. The high priest carried the people close to his heart. Yet for all his sympathy, he could not understand exactly what they were going through. Only someone who had endured the same temptations and suffered the most severe hardships could really understand. But Jesus has suffered death and endured temptation to the point of victory over Satan; therefore he is able to show us sympathy. Whatever we are going through, Jesus understands: "For we do not have a high priest who is unable to sympathize with our weaknesses, but one who in every respect has been tempted as we are, yet without sin. Let us then with confidence draw near to the throne of grace, that we may receive mercy and find grace to help in time of need" (Hebrews 4:15, 16). Knowing that Jesus cares about our concerns gives us the confidence to take all our troubles to him.

Jesus ministers to us with *superior longevity*. The high priests of Israel are all dead. They are no longer able to help anyone. But by his resurrection, Jesus lives forever, and thus his priestly ministry continues forever. He is our eternal priest. Referring to Israel's priests, the Bible says, "The former priests were many in number, because they were prevented by death from continuing in office, but he holds his priesthood permanently, because he continues forever. Consequently, he is able to save to the uttermost those who draw near to God through him, since he always lives to make intercession for them" (Hebrews 7:23–25).

Best of all, Jesus ministers to us with a *superior sacrifice*. Here is a surprising twist. Whereas the high priests of Israel offered the blood of animals to atone for sin, Jesus shed his own blood when he died on the cross (see Hebrews 9:12). By his free choice he became the sacrificed victim as well as the sacrificing priest. He offered his body unto death to make atonement for our sins. And because Jesus is the sinless Son of God, his sacrifice was perfect. It was sufficient to pay for all our sins. For Israel's priests, making sacrifices became sheer drudgery. They spent their whole lives walking the treadmill of sacrifice, making the same offerings again and again. But once Jesus had offered himself, the whole system of sacrifice was finished forever. He did not enter heaven "to offer himself repeatedly, as the high priest enters the holy places every year with blood not his own . . . he has appeared once for all at the end of the ages to put away sin by the sacrifice of himself" (Hebrews 9:25, 26b).

Jesus is superior in every way. He is not simply our great High Priest—he is our *perfect* High Priest, and everyone who trusts in him will be perfectly saved.

## Our Calling as God's Priests

Why does Jesus do this for us? What is the goal of his priestly ministry? Why does he look down on us with sympathy from the throne of Heaven? What motivates him to pray for us? What was his objective in offering himself as the sacrifice for our sin? The Bible says, "The blood of Christ, who through the eternal Spirit offered himself without blemish to God, [will] purify our conscience from dead works to serve the living God" (Hebrews 9:14). The goal of Christ's priestly ministry is to enable us—as unrighteous as we are—to serve the holy God.

To put this another way, Jesus has become our priest so that we can become God's priests. The New Testament describes the church as a holy and royal priesthood (1 Peter 2:4, 9). It says that the Savior "who loves us and has freed us from our sins by his blood" has "made us a kingdom, priests to his God and Father" (Revelation 1:5b, 6a). Every believer in Jesus Christ is a priest of the Most High God. Therefore, when we see the high priest in all his splendor, we do not simply see Jesus—we also see ourselves.

Serving God as priest is an amazing privilege. Remember that a priest is qualified to enter the holy presence of God. At the tabernacle, most of the people had to stay outside God's sanctuary; only the priests were allowed to enter. But now that God has made us priests, we too are invited to come in. On the basis of the blood that Jesus shed for our sins, we can approach his throne of grace through prayer.

Prayer is a significant part of our priestly ministry. A priest is someone who intercedes for others, and this is our calling as Christians. We pray for people. We pray for our neighbors, interceding for their practical needs and especially for their salvation. We intercede for the local church, praying that the gospel would be preached, sinners would be saved, and saints would grow in the love of Christ. And we pray for the church around the world, interceding for missionaries going overseas, for Christians suffering persecution, and for the unhindered advance of the gospel. This is part of what it means for us to serve God as priests.

But what about offering sacrifices? This was a major part of a priest's job. If we are God's priests, then what sacrifice do we bring? One way to answer this question is to insist that we don't need to bring any sacrifices at all. Jesus made the supreme sacrifice when he died on the cross and atoned for our sins once and for all. No other sacrifice needs to be made. But the Bible says that there are some sacrifices we *can* bring. One is the living sacrifice of ourselves for God's service (Romans 12:1). Another is "a sacrifice of praise" (Hebrews 13:15). We serve God by worshiping him, both publicly and privately. Every time we meet with God in secret or participate in corporate worship, we are fulfilling our priestly duty "to offer spiritual sacrifices acceptable to God through Jesus Christ" (1 Peter 2:5). This is our calling as priests.

In order for us to fulfill our priestly duties—and this is the main lesson to draw from Exodus 39—we need to be holy. Like the high priest of Israel, we have been set apart for the holy service of God. So God says to us what he said to the Israelites: "You shall be holy, for I the LORD your God am holy" (Leviticus 19:2).

Our calling as priests demands complete holiness. We are called to be holy in our daily business, not idling away our time or grasping for unjust gain. We are called to be holy at home, living at peace with our family members and serving them in love. We are called to be holy in our thoughts, not consumed with lust or bitterness or self-pity. We are called to be holy in our speech, not using words that are proud or harsh or manipulative. We are called to be holy in our actions, reaching out in deeds of mercy and preserving our sexual purity. As the Scripture says, "As he who called you is holy, you also be holy in all your conduct" (1 Peter 1:15).

Be holy in *all* you do. Is this a standard that we can keep? Honestly, no. We are unholy. Every day we sin against God in thought and word and deed. We are stained with sin. How then can God accept our service? How can we enter the holy place where God is?

A simple story may help illustrate the difficulty. One memorable Thanksgiving Day I went out to play football in the rain. When I returned home, I started to go into the kitchen, which was the primary functional entrance to our family home. As I opened the door, I was confronted by my mother, who was accompanied by a guard of female relatives brandishing rolling pins, potato mashers, and carving knives. "Don't you dare set one foot in my kitchen!" Mother said. I looked down and realized she was right. I could not enter the house: I was covered with filth!

The same thing is true whenever we seek to enter God's house for worship. We are filthy, having committed the kinds of sins that ought to forbid our entrance. How can a holy God accept our priestly service? Not because we're holy, because we're not. But God *can* do this: He can accept us because Jesus is holy. When we trust in Jesus Christ for our salvation, we are clothed in his righteousness. Now when God sees the service we offer, he does not look at the stains of our sin but at the perfection of his Son.

Ministers have a special need for this kind of holiness because we preach God's holy Word and lead people in holy worship. The English country pastor George Herbert (1593–1633), who was painfully aware of his own need for holiness, wrote a wonderful poem ("Aaron") that relates Exodus 39 to the gospel ministry. Herbert begins by describing Aaron's wardrobe (stanza 1), but soon despairs because he knows that he is not wearing the kind of righteousness that God requires (stanza 2). Then he remembers that he can be clothed in the righteousness of Jesus Christ (stanzas 3 and 4), and as a result by the final stanza he is ready to lead God's people in worship:

Holiness on the head,
Light and perfections on the breast,
Harmonious bells below, raising the dead
To lead them unto life and rest:
Thus are true Aarons dressed.

Profaneness in my head,
Defects and darkness in my breast,
A noise of passions ringing me for dead
Unto a place where is no rest:
Poor priest, thus am I dressed.

Only another head
I have, another heart and breast,
Another music, making live, not dead,
Without whom I could have no rest:
In Him I am well dressed.

Christ is my only head,
My alone-only heart and breast,
My only music, striking me even dead;
That to the old man I may rest,
And be in him new-dressed.

So, holy in my head,
Perfect and light in my dear breast,
My doctrine tuned by Christ (who is not dead,
But lives in me while I do rest),
Come people; Aaron's dressed.[5]

The righteousness of Christ is a preacher's only hope that God will accept his ministry. But this righteousness is not just for ministers, and it is not just for Sundays. It is every Christian's everyday wardrobe. God accepts our service when we are clothed with Jesus Christ, who is the wardrobe of our holiness.

# 101

# Just like God Said

EXODUS 39:32–43

WHEN A BUILDING IS UNDER CONSTRUCTION, there are times when it seems like it will never be finished. But finally, after all the delays (both avoidable and unavoidable), the thing gets built, and it is time for inspection. These days the process is fairly thorough. The mechanical systems are tested. The wiring is checked to see if it is up to code. The structure is analyzed for access and safety. Then there is a final walk-through, with a checklist for work that still needs to be completed. The building can only be used when it passes inspection.

## The Typology of the Tabernacle

Something similar happened at the tabernacle in the wilderness. Once Bezalel, Oholiab, and the rest of Israel's artisans were finished making the various parts of the tabernacle, their work had to be inspected. This was a matter of public safety. The tabernacle was a dwelling place for the living God, who is awesome in holiness and glory. His house had to be made his way, or else the people would be exposed to mortal danger. After all, the last time the Israelites made something for worship, things had ended rather badly. Remember the golden calf?

This time the Israelites wanted to make sure they did everything right. So they brought their work for inspection, piece by piece:

> Then they brought the tabernacle to Moses, the tent and all its utensils, its hooks, its frames, its bars, its pillars, and its bases; the covering of tanned rams' skins and goatskins, and the veil of the screen; the ark of the testimony with its poles and the mercy seat; the table with all its utensils, and the bread of the Presence; the lampstand of pure gold and its lamps with the lamps set and all its utensils, and the oil for the light; the golden altar, the anointing oil and the fragrant incense, and the screen for the entrance of the tent;

> the bronze altar, and its grating of bronze, its poles, and all its utensils; the basin and its stand; the hangings of the court, its pillars, and its bases, and the screen for the gate of the court, its cords, and its pegs; and all the utensils for the service of the tabernacle, for the tent of meeting; the finely worked garments for ministering in the Holy Place, the holy garments for Aaron the priest, and the garments of his sons for their service as priests. (39:33–41; cf. 35:10–19)

The people brought everything needed for the tabernacle and presented it to Moses. They brought the curtains for covering the Tent of Meeting and for separating the Holy Place from the Most Holy Place. These curtains were a sign of the mystery and holiness of God. They brought the ark of the covenant—God's royal throne on earth—and the mercy seat, where blood was sprinkled as an atonement for sin. They brought the table for the bread of the Presence, where the priests communed with God. They brought the golden lampstand, symbolizing God's life and light. They brought the golden altar of incense, where prayer ascended to Heaven like sweet-smelling perfume. They brought the great bronze altar, where animals were sacrificed as a substitute for Israel's sin, as well as the bronze basin for cleansing. And they brought Aaron's wardrobe—the holy garments for the priests to wear as they performed their sacred ministry.

Before seeing whether all these things passed inspection, we should pause to remember what they symbolized about God and about the way of salvation through Christ. The tabernacle was rich in its spiritual significance. Vern Poythress describes it as a "tantalizing visual poem suggesting a multitude of relationships, all tied together in a single structure."[1] This structure was so complex that even after we have studied it carefully, we still have more to learn.

By way of reminder, the tabernacle was God's dwelling place on earth. God called it "my dwelling among you" (Leviticus 26:11). As a replica of Heaven, it taught the Israelites that their God was not some tribal deity, but the Lord God of the universe, who "stretch[es] out the heavens like a tent" (Psalm 104:2). It also taught them about God's character. It taught them that he is a mighty God, attended by angels. He is a holy God, shrouded in mystery. He is a loving God who wants to have a relationship with his people. The tabernacle showed the people that God was the one who would give them life and light, who would provide their daily bread, who would answer their prayers, and who would reveal his law for their lives. Most of all, it taught them to look to God for the forgiveness of their sins.

The tabernacle taught the Israelites all this and more. By doing so, it also taught them about Jesus Christ, who is the true tabernacle—God's dwelling place with humanity. When the Israelites brought the tabernacle to Moses, even if they didn't fully understand it, they were laying out the gospel. Long before Christ came into the world, God was using symbols to teach people about his saving work.

Recognize the wisdom of this. If he had wanted to, God could have sent Jesus to save Adam and Eve right after they sinned. But he had a better plan that would bring him more glory. God allowed human history to unfold in all the misery of its depravity. Meanwhile, through the rituals of the Old Testament, he began to show what it would take to deal with the problem of sin. He did this so we would have a fuller understanding of the total salvation that he has provided for us in Jesus Christ. Consider everything the tabernacle has taught us about holiness, about atonement, about sanctification, and about having a relationship with God. Without the tabernacle, our understanding of these great doctrines of salvation would be impoverished.

We might compare the Old Testament to a picture book in black and white. As we turn the pages, we see images of salvation. But then, when the time was right, God brought Jesus into the story in living color. And having read the opening pages, we see how he fits into the story, filling it with the colors of salvation. This is the way the Bible works. The people, the events, and the institutions of the Old Testament started to reveal the salvation that God eventually provided in Jesus Christ. In his excellent little book *Preaching and the History of Salvation*, Dr. Trimp puts it like this: "In the old you can see the structure of the new."[2]

It is amazing how much the Old Testament teaches us about Jesus Christ. The reason this works is because both testaments were written by the same God, who has been working out his plan of redemption since the beginning of time. As Dr. Trimp goes on to say, "The very same God who revealed Himself in Christ has left traces behind in the history of His Old Testament people. . . . [W]e may see in the facts of the Old Testament an historical dynamic taking shape that moves toward Christ. There is a structural analogy between God's earlier and later work, based upon the one plan of the one God."[3] The Old Testament gives us divinely ordained symbols that reveal the basic truths of salvation in Christ.

In his book on Old Testament typology, Patrick Fairbairn observes that we find in Christ "the centre of Heaven's plan, and the one foundation of human confidence and hope. So that *before* His coming into the world, all things of necessity pointed toward Him; types and prophecies bore testimony to the things that concerned His work and kingdom; the children of blessing were blessed in anticipation of His promised redemption; and *with* His coming, the grand reality itself came, and the higher purposes of Heaven entered on their fulfilment."[4]

How do we connect the Old Testament symbols forward to Christ? We always begin with the history and context of the Old Testament itself. We study its symbolism on its own terms, seeking to understand what God was trying to teach his people in those days. Only then can we make connections with the full story of salvation in Christ. The New Testament helps by explaining many of the connections. The tabernacle is a good example because so many of its details are discussed in Hebrews. The New Testament helps us avoid coming up with arbitrary interpretations that are not really in the Bible.

We also need to remember that not every detail in the Old Testament is symbolic, and therefore not every detail has a specific connection to Christ. For example, we do not need to come up with a connection between the cinnamon in the anointing oil (30:23) and some detail from the life of Christ, or between the wooden framework of the tabernacle and some aspect of the crucifixion. We will only find a valid connection if what we read in the Old Testament is symbolic in its own context. The theologian who understood this principle best was Geerhardus Vos, who wrote:

> A symbol is in its religious significance something that profoundly portrays a certain fact or principle or relationship of a spiritual nature in a visible form. The things it pictures are of present existence and present application. They are in force at the time in which the symbol operates.
>
> With the same thing, regarded as a type, it is different. A typical thing is prospective; it relates to what will become real or applicable in the future. . . .
>
> [T]he things symbolized and the things typified are not different sets of things. They are in reality the same things, only different in this respect that they come first on a lower stage of development in redemption, and then again, in a later period, on a higher stage. Thus what is symbolical with regard to the already existing edition of the fact or truth becomes typical, prophetic, of the later, final edition of the same fact or truth. From this it will be perceived that a type can never be a type independently of its being first a symbol. The gateway to the house of typology is at the farther end of the house of symbolism.
>
> This is the fundamental rule to be observed in ascertaining what elements in the Old Testament are typical, and wherein the things corresponding to them as antitypes consist. Only after having discovered what a thing symbolizes, can we legitimately proceed to put the question what it typifies, for the latter can never be aught else than the former lifted to a higher plane. The bond that holds type and antitype together must be a bond of vital continuity in the progress of redemption. Where this is ignored, and in the place of this bond are put accidental resemblances, void of inherent spiritual significance, all sorts of absurdities will result.[5]

In the case of the tabernacle, nearly everything *was* symbolic. The building clearly represented the house of God, and nearly all its parts symbolized something about his relationship with his people. This is why the tabernacle remains such a rich revelation of the person and work of Jesus Christ.

In his excellent book on the law of Moses and its connection to Christ, Vern Poythress provides no less than eight important lessons that we can draw from the symbolism of the tabernacle:

First, because of its symbolic connection with heaven, the tabernacle reminded the Israelites that God was the true God, the exalted Lord of the whole universe, not simply a god confined to a local spot. . . . Likewise, we should recognize now that God our Father and Christ our Redeemer is the heavenly Lord, the Lord of all. . . .

Second, because the whole universe was God's house, the tabernacle depicted for the Israelites the way in which God's care was demonstrated in their day-to-day circumstances. Food, life, and light all derived from God who had made the whole universe as His dwelling place and their home. Likewise, we today are to see our circumstances and our daily blessings . . . as the provision of our God and our Savior Jesus Christ. . . .

Third, the tabernacle as a unique structure reminded Israel that they had unique privileges. Out of all the nations of the world God chose them to be His people, and condescended to live among them in a special way. Likewise, in New Testament times God dwells in a unique way in the church and in individual Christians. . . .

Fourth, the tabernacle symbolized Eden, and thereby reminded the Israelites of their sinful, lost, separated condition as descendants of Adam. Entrance into Eden was barred to them. And yet they could enter in a sense, when the priest entered as their representative. Hence, the tabernacle spoke both of being lost and also of the promise of overcoming sin through a representative man, ultimately through Jesus Christ our final high priest. . . .

Fifth, the tabernacle symbolized the people of God corporately. Israel as a collective body was called upon to imitate the beauty, order, holiness, and purity of the tabernacle itself. It was to embody beauty, order, holiness, and purity in its own communal living. . . . Likewise, the church in our day is to be holy. The church is not a voluntary association to be governed as its members see fit, but a dwelling place of God. . . . Our families and our homes are to reflect the spiritual purity, beauty, and orderliness that was temporarily pictured through the tabernacle and is now supremely set forth in Jesus Christ Himself. . . .

Sixth, the tabernacle symbolized the people of God individually. The Israelites were commanded to keep their bodies pure, pure first of all from sin but also from ceremonial defilements that symbolized sin. In the New Testament the bodies of Christians are temples of the Holy Spirit. We are "to purify ourselves from everything that contaminates body and spirit, perfecting holiness out of reverence for God" (2 Cor. 7:1). . . .

Seventh, the tabernacle pointed forward to the new Jerusalem, the final dwelling of God with human beings. . . .

Eighth, the tabernacle symbolized God Himself. . . . [T]he Israelites were being instructed by the veils and the not-fully-analyzable symbols to realize that God's character and His purposes were unfathomably deep, and that their salvation rested in God's own character and wisdom. We now know, in the light of fuller revelation, that the God of Israel is our trinitarian God, the one God revealed through the work of Christ as He obeyed the Father through the power of the Holy Spirit. The tabernacle points forward to

> Christ the final dwelling of God with human beings, but also to the Father and the Spirit who in Christ reveal the fullness of the Deity to us.[6]

## With Flying Colors

In order to fulfill its divinely ordained purpose of revealing the character of God and the way of salvation in Christ, the tabernacle had to be made *exactly* the way God said. The man charged with the responsibility of determining whether it met this standard was the prophet Moses. So Moses began to scrutinize the work that the artists had done, examining every curtain and every crossbar to see whether Israel's craftsmanship matched God's design.

Even before hearing his verdict, we know that the tabernacle will pass inspection with flying colors. We know this because the Bible repeatedly tells us that the Israelites made everything the way God told them to make it. Exodus 36, which tells how the tabernacle was made, repeats Exodus 26 almost verbatim. God's instructions were followed down to the last loop on the last curtain and the last hook on the last post. The same is true of Exodus 37, which tells how Bezalel and his colleagues made the furniture, and Exodus 38, which tells how they made the courtyard. All we have to do is compare the account of how the tabernacle was made with God's original instructions and we can see how careful the Israelites were to do what God said.

This becomes even clearer in chapter 39, where we encounter an important phrase. Over and over again the Bible says that Israel's artists made something "as the LORD had commanded Moses." This refrain occurs in verses 1, 5, 7, 21, 26, 29, and 31. The point is that the Israelites made the tabernacle just as God told them to. After describing all the things they made, the Bible summarizes by saying, "Thus all the work of the tabernacle of the tent of meeting was finished, and the people of Israel did according to all that the LORD had commanded Moses" (39:32). The same phrase occurs again at the end of the chapter: "According to all that the LORD had commanded Moses, so the people of Israel had done all the work" (v. 42). Bible scholars call this an *inclusio*. The list of what the people brought for inspection both begins and ends with an affirmation that they did *exactly* what God commanded them to do.

Nevertheless, as a matter of quality control, Moses still needed to examine their work. He was the right man for this job because he had seen the prototype for the tabernacle on God's mountain (26:30). John Durham comments: "Only Moses received Yahweh's instructions on Sinai at first hand, and only Moses was shown by Yahweh the vision of how things were to be, so only Moses can determine whether what Bezalel and his helpers have made is in keeping with Yahweh's intention."[7] To put this in contemporary terms, Moses was the project manager. Since he had met with the architect (namely, God), he was able to tell the contractors (Bezalel and his associates) what their client wanted.

It didn't take Moses long to reach his verdict. Exodus 39 brings construction to a close by saying, "Moses saw all the work, and behold, they had done it; as the LORD had commanded, so had they done it. Then Moses blessed them" (v. 43).

This is a powerful example of full obedience to God, and of the blessing that comes to anyone who does his will. When some scholars read this verse, they hear echoes from the story of creation. At the close of the sixth day, when God had finished making the universe and everything in it, he "saw everything that he had made, and behold, it was very good" (Genesis 1:31; cf. Exodus 39:42). Then God proceeded to bless the work by resting on the seventh day (Genesis 2:2, 3; cf. Exodus 39:43). Something similar happened when Israel finished making the tabernacle. God saw that what the people made was very good, so he gave them his blessing.

When God's work is done in God's way, it always has God's blessing. We can say *God's* blessing because it really was his blessing that the people received. Moses was the one who pronounced the benediction, but he did it on God's behalf. As the mediator, he spoke to the people for God. And when he saw that they had done everything right, he placed God's seal of approval on their work. His blessing was more than a word of encouragement; it meant that the powerful grace of Almighty God would be with them for good.

When God's work is not done in God's way, it does *not* have God's blessing. The Israelites learned this when they worshiped the golden calf. They thought they were doing God's work. They claimed to be worshiping the one true God. But really they were doing their own work their own way, and thus they could not have God's blessing. Rather than waiting for God to reveal his will for their worship, they decided to worship him by images, which were forbidden in the second commandment. As a result, they received God's curse instead of his blessing.

But this time the Israelites got it right. Rather than doing things their own way, they did them God's way. And they did it for the right reason: They wanted to glorify God. After reading this passage, a man who works in architecture and design noted how unusual it is for a project the size of the tabernacle to pass inspection perfectly on the first attempt. He said this would only happen if the workers were highly motivated to please their client. In this case, the client was the God who made Heaven and earth and who had delivered his people from slavery. For him no expense was spared, no corner was cut, no detail was overlooked. The Israelites wanted to please the God of their salvation, and as a result, their work enjoyed the smile of his blessing.

## Jesus Passes Inspection

When God's work is done in God's way, it has God's blessing. How does this principle relate to the saving work of Jesus Christ, and how does it apply to daily Christian living?

Remember that Jesus did the work of our salvation in a physical body, which is the tabernacle of God (see John 1:14). A tabernacle is a place where God dwells. And this is precisely what happened when God the Son became a man in the person of Jesus Christ. He is Immanuel, "God with us" (Matthew 1:23). Thus the body of Jesus is the truest of all tabernacles—the very dwelling place of God. As the Scripture says, "In him the whole fullness of deity dwells bodily" (Colossians 2:9).

Did that tabernacle—the physical body of Jesus Christ—pass inspection? Yes, it did! First it had to pass his inspection. When Jesus came into the world, he examined the flesh and bones of his humanity and said to the Father, "A body have you prepared for me" (Hebrews 10:5). He recognized that in his physical body he would be able to do the whole work of our salvation. He could live a perfect, sinless life and offer a perfect atoning sacrifice in his body.

In order for this sacrifice to be accepted, Christ had to pass the inspection of his Father. The work that he did in the body had to meet God's standard. And so it did. At his baptism, the bodily tabernacle of Jesus Christ was anointed by the Holy Spirit (Matthew 3:16), just as the tabernacle in the wilderness was anointed with oil (30:22–29). Then the Father said, "This is my beloved Son, with whom I am well pleased" (Matthew 3:17). With these words, the Father pronounced his blessing on the Son, just as Moses pronounced God's blessing on the first tabernacle. However, that was only the beginning of Christ's ministry. He still had to withstand the devil, perform miracles, preach the kingdom, and endure all the sufferings of the cross. And Jesus had to do all this without sin. He had to do God's work in God's way. Only then could the Father pronounce his final blessing on the work of the Son.

God gave his benediction by raising Jesus from the dead. After Jesus died on the cross for our sins, God raised him to everlasting life. By the power of the Holy Spirit, the Father brought back to life the bodily tabernacle that he had once prepared for the Son. The resurrection was the Father's declaration that the Son had finished the work of our salvation perfectly: "[Jesus] was declared to be the Son of God in power according to the Spirit of holiness by his resurrection from the dead" (Romans 1:4). The blessing of the resurrection confirmed that Jesus had done God's work in God's way.

Unlike the tabernacle, the salvation we have in Jesus is God's work from beginning to end. The tabernacle in the wilderness was built by human hands. Not so the living tabernacle of Christ's body. God is the one who prepared a body for Jesus Christ. God is the one who offered perfect obedience, in the person of his Son. And God is the one who raised Jesus from the dead by the power of his Holy Spirit. When it came to the bodily tabernacle of Jesus Christ, God did the work, God performed the inspection, and God pronounced the blessing. God did it all so that we would be saved, and he would still get all the glory. We are called simply to trust in Jesus Christ as the tabernacle of our salvation. He is the only

Savior who comes with God's seal of approval. What further recommendation do we need?

## Doing Things God's Way

Jesus did God's work in God's way, and thus he received God's blessing of a triumphant resurrection and ascension to glory. Now through faith in Jesus Christ, we too can share in God's blessing. The two blessings—Christ's blessing and our blessing—are connected. We have already seen how Jesus Christ is the fulfillment of the old tabernacle. But we can take this idea even further, because the Bible also describes the church as a tabernacle (or temple)—God's spiritual dwelling place on earth.

Like the tabernacle, and like Jesus himself, we have been anointed by the Holy Spirit and thus set apart for sacred service. God has taken up residence in us, both as a church and as individual Christians. We are "the household of God" (1 Timothy 3:15; cf. 1 Corinthians 3:9), "a spiritual house" (1 Peter 2:5), "a holy temple in the Lord" (Ephesians 2:21). Jesus said, "If anyone loves me, he will keep my word, and my Father will love him, and we will come to him and make our home with him" (John 14:23). This is true for us not simply as individual Christians but also as the church. Patrick Fairbairn explains that "as the fulness of the Godhead dwells in Christ, He again dwells in the Church of true believers as His fulness; and the idea symbolized in the tabernacle is properly realized, not in Christ personally and apart, but in Him as the Head of a redeemed offspring, vitally connected with Him, and through Him having access even into the holiest."[8] Just as Christ's physical body is the true tabernacle of God, so also his spiritual body—the church—is God's holy dwelling place. The body of Christ is "a dwelling place for God by the Spirit" (Ephesians 2:22).

As God's holy tabernacle, we are called to do God's work in God's way. The church is not a place to do your own thing. It is a spiritual community that glorifies God by doing things just as he said. We are called to follow the Biblical pattern for the church. This means pleasing God in our worship, building our ministry on the solid rock of his Word, bearing one another's burdens, reaching out with deeds of mercy and words of truth, and supporting the global mission of the gospel. And if we do this work in God's way, we will also labor in prayer, depending on God alone to do the spiritual work of ministry.

We can apply this principle in every area of life. Whatever we do should be done God's way, not our own way. This is true at work. God has called us to labor strenuously, serving him and not simply our employer. He has called us to be honest in all our dealings, not seeking our own gain but the good of others. This is God's way to work, and when we work this way, we are under his benediction.

The same is true at school, where we are called to glorify God with our minds. To do this God's way means studying diligently, finishing our homework, resisting the temptation to cheat, respecting our teachers, and showing kindness to our classmates. It means improving our minds for God's sake, and not swelling our own intellectual pride. When we do our schoolwork this way, we have God's blessing.

We also have work to do at home, and this too needs to be done God's way. There is a godly way to be unmarried, living with single-hearted devotion to God and learning to serve others. There is a godly way to be married—the way of submission for wives and sacrifice for husbands. There is a godly way to raise children: not in fear, but in faith; not harshly, but lovingly, training their souls. There is also a godly way for children to respect their parents. It is not by arguing with them or complaining about them, but by willingly and cheerfully obeying them.

God has a way for us to deal with any and every situation in life. There is a godly way to handle success, with humility and gratitude to God. There is also a godly way to handle adversity, not getting bitter about God's providence but trusting in his sovereign care. There is a godly way to celebrate, a godly way to grieve, a godly way to work, and a godly way to rest.

What is God calling you to do? Whatever it is, there are two ways to do it: his way and the wrong way. So often we try to do things our own way, thinking we know best. The results are always disastrous. Instead we should do things God's way, and when we do, we will have his blessing. God will approve of what we have done and will cause it to prosper. He will bless our work itself, and he will bless us in doing it.

## Final Inspection

We work for God knowing that one day there will be a final inspection, what theologians call "the Last Judgment." On that great and terrible day, "we must all appear before the judgment seat of Christ, so that each one may receive what is due for what he has done in the body, whether good or evil" (2 Corinthians 5:10). Jesus said, "Behold, I am coming soon, bringing my recompense with me, to repay each one for what he has done" (Revelation 22:12). Just as the Israelites laid out the tabernacle for Moses, so our lives will be laid out before God, who alone knows all our secrets.

What blessing will we receive then? Have we offered such perfect obedience that we can pass inspection?

God will examine everything that we have done, according to the perfect standard of his justice. For those who have done his work in his way, there will be blessing upon blessing. God has promised that we will receive a fair return for all our labor: "Whatever good anyone does, this he will receive back from the Lord" (Ephesians 6:8; cf. Matthew 16:27). But our good works will not be the basis for our salvation. Although we will be rewarded for them, we will not be saved by them. We cannot be saved by them because even the best of all our efforts cannot meet the standard of God's perfection.

But thankfully, before inspecting us there is something else that God will inspect first. He will inspect the finished work of Jesus Christ, the tabernacle of our salvation. And when he looks at Jesus, he will see the perfect righteousness of the only man who ever did everything just as God commanded. Then God will pronounce his blessing—not simply on Jesus, but also on everyone who trusts in Jesus. The only way to endure the final judgment is to trust in Jesus Christ. When we put our faith in him, he becomes our righteousness (1 Corinthians 1:30), and we are able to pass God's inspection.

# 102

# When Glory Came Down

EXODUS 40:1–38

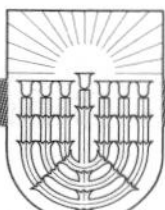

EXODUS BEGAN WITH A PEOPLE ENSLAVED. Under the violent, tyrannical rule of the Pharaohs, the Israelites were bound in chains and forced to build great cities along the Nile. They suffered and died in Egypt, a land that was not their home. But God had a plan for their redemption. According to his covenant promise, he would rescue them from Egypt and lead them to the Promised Land.

God did this for Israel's good and for his glory. All through Exodus we see him working to save his people, and whenever he explains why he is saving them, he says it is for his own glory. Why did God meet with Moses at the burning bush? So the Israelites would know that he is the Lord God of Abraham, Isaac, and Jacob (3:14, 15). Why did God tell Pharaoh to let his people go? So his people could go out in the desert and worship him, giving him the glory of their praise (e.g., 7:16). Why did he cast the armies of Egypt into the depths of the sea? Because, he said, "I will get glory over Pharaoh and all his host, his chariots, and his horsemen. And the Egyptians shall know that I am the LORD, when I have gotten glory over Pharaoh, his chariots, and his horsemen" (14:17b, 18).

In response to these mighty deeds of salvation, the Israelites gave God the glory. As soon as they passed through the sea, they began to sing the song of the horse and rider: "The LORD is my strength and my song, and he has become my salvation; this is my God, and I will praise him, my father's God, and I will exalt him" (15:2). They praised him again when they reached Mount Sinai, where they renewed the covenant and worshiped God for the gift of his law. Then they began to work on the tabernacle—the glorious house of God. This was all in keeping with God's plan, by which his people would be saved for his glory. The exodus was all to the glory of God.

## Setting Up God's Tent

The book reaches its glorious climax with chapter 40. The people had already seen something of God's glory. They had seen it in their deliverance from Egypt. They had seen it in the fire and smoke on the mountain. But they had not yet seen a close, visible manifestation of God's almighty glory. Moses had seen it up on the mountain, and so had Israel's elders. But the people were still waiting for a fuller revelation of God's majesty. They were waiting to see the fulfillment of the promise God made in chapter 29: "I will consecrate the tent of meeting and the altar. Aaron also and his sons I will consecrate to serve me as priests. I will dwell among the people of Israel and will be their God. And they shall know that I am the LORD their God, who brought them out of the land of Egypt that I might dwell among them. I am the LORD their God" (vv. 44–46).

The anticipation builds in the following chapters as the Israelites get to work on the tabernacle. By chapter 40 they are eagerly expecting to see the glory come down. But before they could see it, they needed to erect the tabernacle. Some assembly was required. So "the LORD spoke to Moses, saying, 'On the first day of the first month you shall erect the tabernacle of the tent of meeting'" (40:1, 2). The timing of this was significant: the first day of the first month. In other words, God told Moses to set up the tabernacle on the anniversary of Israel's exodus from Egypt—one year to the very day. This made a clear connection between what happened at the Red Sea and what happened at the tabernacle. The erection of the tabernacle was the culmination of everything that God had been working for since he first brought his people out of Egypt.

God told Moses how to put everything together and where to put it. He followed a deliberate order, working from the inside out. First Moses was to erect the tabernacle. Then he was to set up the furniture that went inside. This was followed by the furniture that went outside, and finally by the fence that went around the perimeter. God said:

> And you shall put in it the ark of the testimony, and you shall screen the ark with the veil. And you shall bring in the table and arrange it, and you shall bring in the lampstand and set up its lamps. And you shall put the golden altar for incense before the ark of the testimony, and set up the screen for the door of the tabernacle. You shall set the altar of burnt offering before the door of the tabernacle of the tent of meeting, and place the basin between the tent of meeting and the altar, and put water in it. And you shall set up the court all around, and hang up the screen for the gate of the court. (vv. 3–8)

Once he had set up the tabernacle, Moses was to set it apart, anointing it for the sacred service of God. God said: "Then you shall take the anointing oil and anoint the tabernacle and all that is in it, and consecrate it and all its furniture, so that it may become holy. You shall also anoint the altar of burnt offering and all its utensils, and consecrate the altar, so that the altar may become most holy. You shall also anoint the basin and its stand, and consecrate it" (vv. 9–11; cf. 30:22–29). In this way, the tabernacle and all its furnishings were dedicated to God.

Moses also needed to consecrate the men who served at the tabernacle. So God reminded him how to ordain Aaron and the other priests: "Then you shall bring Aaron and his sons to the entrance of the tent of meeting and shall wash them with water and put on Aaron the holy garments. And you shall anoint him and consecrate him, that he may serve me as priest. You shall bring his sons also and put coats on them, and anoint them, as you anointed their father, that they may serve me as priests. And their anointing shall admit them to a perpetual priesthood throughout their generations" (vv. 12–15; cf. 29:1–43; 30:30–33). Like the tabernacle itself, the men who served there had to be anointed for the holy service of God.

These were God's final instructions for the tabernacle, which the prophet was careful to follow: "This Moses did; according to all that the LORD commanded him, so he did. In the first month in the second year, on the first day of the month, the tabernacle was erected" (vv. 16, 17). Then, to show that Moses did as he was told, the Bible proceeds to tell how he set up the tabernacle piece by piece. As each piece was put in place, the suspense built: Would God really come down in glory?

Moses started with the tabernacle itself—the Tent of Meeting. This was the holy dwelling place of God, representing his presence with his people. The prophet set it up just the way God said: "Moses erected the tabernacle. He laid its bases, and set up its frames, and put in its poles, and raised up its pillars. And he spread the tent over the tabernacle and put the covering of the tent over it, as the LORD had commanded Moses" (vv. 18, 19). So Moses pitched the Tent of Meeting, just as God said, but the glory did not come down.

Then the prophet "took the testimony and put it into the ark, and put the poles on the ark and set the mercy seat above on the ark. And he brought the ark into the tabernacle and set up the veil of the screen, and screened the ark of the testimony, as the LORD had commanded Moses" (vv. 20, 21). This was the Holy of Holies—the most important part of the tabernacle. The ark of the covenant represented God's throne, and thus it was the place where he ruled in majesty. Inside went the covenant, including the Ten Commandments. Thus the ark showed God's legal authority over Israel. It also showed his grace, because it was covered with the mercy seat, where blood was sprinkled to make atonement for Israel's sin. So Moses put the ark of the covenant in the Holy of Holies, but the glory did not come down.

Next he set up the furniture that went out in the Holy Place, starting with the table of showbread: "He put the table in the tent of meeting, on the north side of the tabernacle, outside the veil, and arranged the bread on it before the LORD, as the LORD had commanded Moses" (vv. 22, 23). This was the bread of the Presence, which was set out as an offering for God, and which the priests ate at the end of each week. It was a reminder of God's provision and a sign of the fellowship that he shared with his people. This was a table of communion, where God offered himself to his people, and his people offered themselves to him. So Moses put the bread on the table, but the glory did not come down.

Then the prophet set up the golden lampstand: "He put the lampstand in the tent of meeting, opposite the table on the south side of the tabernacle, and set up the lamps before the LORD, as the LORD had commanded Moses" (vv. 24, 25). The lampstand flickered with light, showing that in both creation and redemption God is the source of all light. With all its buds and blossoms, the lampstand looked like a tree of life, and thus it was a reminder that God is the origin of life as well as the source of light. So Moses put the lights on the lampstand of life, but the glory did not come down.

He proceeded to set up the altar of incense, which stood between the table and the lampstand, next to the Holy of Holies: "He put the golden altar in the tent of meeting before the veil, and burned fragrant incense on it, as the LORD had commanded Moses. He put in place the screen for the door of the tabernacle" (vv. 26–28). This was Israel's sweet altar of prayer, where intercession ascended to God's throne. On it Moses offered the first incense and the first prayers, but the glory did not come down.

Then it was time to step outside the tabernacle, where there was more furniture to put in place. Moses started with the great bronze altar of sacrifice: "And he set the altar of burnt offering at the entrance of the tabernacle of the tent of meeting, and offered on it the burnt offering and the grain offering, as the LORD had commanded Moses" (v. 29). By making these offerings, Moses inaugurated the system of sacrifice that would atone for Israel's sin and give praise to God. The burning altar was in place, but still the blazing glory did not come down.

Next Moses set up the bronze basin where the priests were consecrated for their sacred duties: "He set the basin between the tent of meeting and the altar, and put water in it for washing, with which Moses and Aaron and his sons washed their hands and their feet. When they went into the tent of meeting, and when they approached the altar, they washed, as the LORD commanded Moses" (vv. 30–32). So the basin was ready. The priests had a place to wash, symbolizing the cleansing power of God's grace and the purity that is required for his service. But still the glory did not come down.

Finally, Moses erected the outer fence that formed a courtyard around the innermost tabernacle: "And he erected the court around the tabernacle and the altar, and set up the screen of the gate of the court" (v. 33a). This curtain or screen separated the tabernacle from the rest of the camp, and thus it showed that the God who lived there was holy—set apart from sinners. But because the curtain formed an entrance, it also showed that there was a way for sinners to approach his holiness.

This is how Moses set up the tabernacle. The Bible summarizes by saying,

"So Moses finished the work" (v. 33b). The prophet did everything right. Over and over again the Bible says that he set up the tabernacle just the way God told him to. Everything was in place. The only thing missing was the one thing that everyone was waiting to see: the glorious presence of God. This was not something that Moses could set in place. With the right instructions, he could put the tabernacle together, but only God could fill it with glory.

## Glory in the Tabernacle

As Moses finished his work, the people watched to see what would happen. They did not have long to wait. The last curtain was tied to the last fence post, the prophet stepped away. "Then the cloud covered the tent of meeting, and the glory of the Lord filled the tabernacle" (v. 34; cf. 1 Kings 8:10). This was the divine seal of approval on all the work that Moses and the Israelites had done: God came down in glory.

The people had seen glimpses of his glory before. They had seen it in the pillar of cloud and fire that protected them from Pharaoh's army and guided them through the wilderness (13:21, 22; 14:19, 20; 16:10). They had seen it in the miracle at the Red Sea, when God was glorified in the deliverance of Israel and the destruction of Egypt. They had seen glory in the fire and smoke on the distant heights of Mount Sinai (24:15–17). Moses had seen the glory too (or at least the back of it) when he met with God on the mountain (33:21–23; 34:5). But neither Moses nor the Israelites had seen the glory come down to earth in all its radiant splendor, as it did when it hovered over the tabernacle, filling that sacred space with glory.

The cloud of God's glory was a theophany—a visible manifestation of the invisible God. God's glory is the weightiness of his divine being, the infinite perfection of his triune deity. Glory is the whole God-ness of God. But on occasion God has made his glory visible in a resplendent cloud of radiant light. It was this glorious cloud that descended on the tabernacle, filling it with light. The form of the verb that the Bible uses for filling (*male'*) is significant because it "reflects a dynamic, ongoing situation."[1] The tabernacle was pulsing with radiation. F. B. Meyer says that this "brilliant light, of surpassing glory, here spoken of as 'the glory of the Lord,' which was undoubtedly the Divine Shechinah, shone from within the Tabernacle itself, so much so that the very curtains were transfigured by its glow and the whole place was transfigured and rendered resplendent with glory."[2]

The glory that filled the tabernacle was a spectacular display of the radiance of God's being. The God of the exodus—the God of power, who made the heavens and the earth; the God of justice, who plagued the Egyptians; the God of love, who kept his covenant with Israel; the God of providence, who led his people through the wilderness; the God of truth, who gave them his law; the God of mercy, who atoned for their sins; the God of holiness, who set them apart for service—this great God was present in glory. When the people looked at the tabernacle, they could see that God was in the house.

Then the Bible says something very surprising. To understand it, we need to remember that the tabernacle was a way to approach God. It was the house where God lived, and because God is holy, it had to be separated from the place where the Israelites lived. But there was a way to enter. There was a courtyard where sinners could make the bloody sacrifices that would bring them into a right relationship with God. And the Tent of Meeting had an entrance—a curtain that allowed the priests to go inside the Holy Place. The tabernacle was designed to give people access. It was a place to meet with the living God.

But when the glory came down, access was denied. Even Moses couldn't get inside! The Bible says, "And Moses was not able to enter the tent of meeting because the cloud settled on it, and the glory of the LORD filled the tabernacle" (40:35; cf. 1 Kings 8:11). The end of Exodus has been moving toward this climactic moment, when the tabernacle would be finished and the people would be able to meet with their God. But when the moment finally came, the tabernacle was filled with such great glory that the mediator couldn't get in!

From this we learn how necessary it is for anyone who wants to meet with God to come with a blood sacrifice for sin. Exodus leads right into Leviticus, which begins with God giving Moses a long list of instructions for making sacrifices at the tabernacle. The only way to approach the God of all glory is to come with a sacrifice of blood. By initially denying Moses entrance, God once again taught his people the necessity of atonement.

We also learn that God is infinitely more glorious than we could ever expect or imagine. After a while we start to get used to God. We become familiar with the vocabulary used to describe his divine attributes. We have heard of his holiness, justice, mercy, and love. We are able to list these terms, and perhaps even to define them, but do we have any idea how glorious God is in the majesty of his triune being? Are we aware of the mortally dangerous perfection of his holiness? Do we sense how overwhelming it is to come into the presence of his glory? Moses knew God better than any man alive; yet when the glory came down, he was not able to enter. Neither can we penetrate God's infinite glory; we can only stand back and worship with reverence and awe.

But then comes another surprise: The great and glorious God of the exodus, "who dwells in unapproachable light" (1 Timothy 6:16), was with his people to save them. The same glorious cloud that kept them away would also stay with them to guide them. This is why God came down in glory—so he could be close to them. Thus the book of Exodus ends with these words: "Throughout all their journeys, whenever the cloud was taken up from over the tabernacle, the people of Israel would set out. But if the cloud was not taken up, then they did not set out till the day that it was taken up. For the cloud of the LORD was on the tabernacle by day, and fire was in it by night, in the sight of all the house of

Israel throughout all their journeys" (40:36–38). These words gave the Israelites assurance that the God of all glory would be present to grant them all the blessings of his saving grace.

Here we see both God's immanence and his transcendence, his nearness as well as the greatness of his glory. God did not just rescue the Israelites from Egypt and then dump them in the wilderness to fend for themselves. On the contrary, he was with his people for good. He wanted to do something more than simply save them; he wanted to have a relationship with them. This was the great comfort that gave them confidence for the future. In all their travels and through all their troubles, God would be with them every step of the way. He would guide them by his glorious light and defend them by his glorious power, leading them night and day until they reached the Promised Land. God saved his people for his glory; and by the glory of his presence, he would lead them to the goal of their salvation.

## Lord of Glory

What God did for Israel was glorious. Their exodus from Egypt was so famous that people are still talking about it today. But as glorious as it was, it cannot compare to the glorious things that God has done for us. The glory in the tabernacle was the climax of Exodus, but not the climax of redemption. It was only the first glimmerings of the glory that God has prepared for us in Jesus Christ.

The book of Exodus really is his story. Jesus is the Moses of our salvation, the mediator who goes for us before God. Jesus is the Lamb of our Passover, the sacrifice for our sins. Jesus is our way out of Egypt, the deliverer who baptizes us in the sea of his grace. Jesus is our bread in the wilderness, the provider who gives us what we need for daily life. Jesus is our voice from the mountain, declaring his law for our lives. Jesus is the altar of our burning, through whom we offer praise up to God. Jesus is the light on our lampstand, the source of our life and light. Jesus is the basin of our cleansing, the sanctifier of our souls. Jesus is our great High Priest, who prays for us at the altar of incense. And Jesus is the blood on the mercy seat, the atonement that reconciles us to God. The great God of the exodus has saved us in Jesus Christ.

As we come to the end of Exodus, we see as well that Jesus is the glory in the tabernacle. This was true from the very moment of his conception. The Bible teaches that the physical body of Jesus Christ is the dwelling place of God: "For in him all the fullness of God was pleased to dwell" (Colossians 1:19). Since glory is one of God's essential attributes, when God caused all his fullness to dwell in Jesus Christ, his glory came down. The Bible says, "And the Word became flesh and dwelt among us, and we have seen his glory, glory as of the only Son from the Father, full of grace and truth" (John 1:14). Jesus Christ is our tabernacle, and as our tabernacle, he is full of the glory of God.

When God the Son came to earth in the person of Jesus Christ, the glory of

God came down from Heaven. As the Scripture says, "He is the radiance of the glory of God" (Hebrews 1:3a). People could not always see his glory, because during his time on earth it was veiled by his humanity. But from time to time they would catch glimpses of it. In his miracles and in his teaching they would see and hear the power and truth of his deity. And on rare occasions God allowed the true glory of Christ to shine out so that people could see it. This happened on the Mount of Transfiguration, where some of the disciples saw Jesus in a bright cloud of radiant glory (Matthew 17:1–5), like the glorious cloud that filled the tabernacle.

But these were only glimpses. No one saw the fullness of his glory until after he died for our sins and God raised him from the dead. Then Jesus was fully revealed in all the glory of God. His disciples could see outwardly what had always been true inwardly—namely, that Jesus radiated the resplendent glory of God.

This was the most glorious thing that anyone has ever seen: the glory of God in the tabernacle of Christ's body. When the disciples saw it, they fell down and worshiped. Think of Thomas. At first he doubted, but the moment he saw the risen Christ, he said, "My Lord and my God!" (John 20:28). What Thomas saw was a greater glory than anything anyone ever saw at the tabernacle. The Bible calls it "the glory that surpasses it" (2 Corinthians 3:10). Thomas saw the glory of God in the person of Jesus. And when he saw Jesus Christ, risen and glorified, he was filled with such amazement and awe that he began to worship him as his Lord and his God. This is what we do as well. As soon as we see that Jesus is the Lord of glory, we are compelled to worship him.

## Entrance to Glory

What is so amazing is that this same glorious Lord Jesus Christ is with us in all the power and comfort of his saving presence. Just as his glory is an even greater glory than the glory revealed at the tabernacle, so also the comfort of his presence is an even greater help to us on our journey. The Lord of glory is with us. His plan was not simply to save us by dying on the cross for our sins, but also to have a relationship with us that will last forever.

To all who trust in him, Jesus has given the promise of his everlasting presence. This is one of the last promises that he gave to his disciples: "And behold, I am with you always, to the end of the age" (Matthew 28:20). Just as God was with the Israelites to the end of their journey, so Jesus has promised to be with us forever. He is in our lives by the presence of his indwelling Spirit. He is guardian and our guide, our help and comfort for the road that lies ahead. In all our travels, and through all our troubles, the God of glory will be with us.

John Currid illustrates this great truth by making a comparison with the British seamen who sailed under Lord Nelson during the Napoleonic Wars:

> Admiral Nelson of the British navy was such a fine seaman and leader of men that sailors loved to serve under him. Sir Robert Stopford, who was sailing with Nelson in the West Indies, wrote home to a loved one that "We are half starved and otherwise inconvenienced by so long out of port, but our reward is that we are with Nelson." So it was with the Israelites who were about to embark into the wilderness, where there was little comfort, little food and little water. Yet, God was with them, and how greatly he would supply all their needs!
>
> This is how we ought to look at life as well. We may be persecuted, or half starved, or put upon by various trials, but our reward is God's presence with us, no matter what our external circumstances.[3]

Whatever troubles we face, we know that we are with Jesus. Or perhaps it is better to say that we know Jesus is with us, and that he will stay with us until we reach the promised land:

> [W]e, too, have been delivered and are waiting to arrive at the final destination. We, like the Israelites, are poised to reach our rest. On this journey, we follow our holy Redeemer as he guides us to the Promised Land. Admittedly, there is no cloud overhead, but we have the Spirit of Christ dwelling in us. He brings us to the goal of our salvation just as surely as the cloud guided the Israelites to their ultimate destination. The people of God should take great comfort in this. The God of Exodus is still guiding. God is present with his people wherever they go, for he still leads and guides them, not to Canaan but to a "better country—a heavenly one" (Heb. 11:16).[4]

As we walk this pilgrim way, we are waiting for an even greater glory to be revealed: the glory of Jesus Christ at the end of the ages. The Bible promises that one day Jesus will come again, and that when he does, he will come on "the clouds of heaven with power and great glory" (Matthew 24:30b; cf. Revelation 1:7). There will be no need for any tabernacle then, because Jesus will take us into the very presence of God, in all his glory (Revelation 21:3, 22): "When Christ who is your life appears, then you also will appear with him in glory" (Colossians 3:4).

This is the message of the exodus, as it is fulfilled in Jesus Christ. Once we were in bondage to sin, enslaved by its tyranny. But through the death and resurrection of Jesus Christ—our Passover Lamb—God has delivered us from the Egypt of our sin. Now he is leading us through our earthly wilderness, with all its difficulties and dangers. The great God of the exodus will never leave us or forsake us. In the church he has set up a sanctuary where even now we may enter his presence for worship. And one day soon Jesus will come down in glory to take us up into the glory that will never end. Everyone who trusts in him will be saved for the glory of God.

*Soli Deo Gloria*!

# Notes

## Chapter One: Into Egypt

1. R. Alan Cole, *Exodus: An Introduction and Commentary*, Tyndale Old Testament Commentaries (Leicester, UK: Inter-Varsity, 1973), pp. 12, 13.
2. Jeffery L. Sheler, *Is the Bible True? How Modern Debates and Discoveries Affirm the Essence of the Scriptures* (New York: HarperCollins, 1999), p. 77.
3. Baruch Halpern, "The Exodus from Egypt: Myth or Reality?" in *The Rise of Ancient Israel* (Washington, DC: Biblical Archaeology Society, 1992), p. 91.
4. Jonathan Kirsch, quoted in *National Review* (January 25, 1999): p. 53.
5. E. L. Doctorow, *City of God* (New York: Random House, 2000), quoted in *Time* magazine (February 14, 2000): p. 82.
6. Abraham Joshua Heschel, quoted in *National Review* (January 25, 1999): p. 53.
7. See Gleason L. Archer Jr., *A Survey of Old Testament Introduction*, rev. ed. (Chicago: Moody, 1974), pp. 215–19, 223, 234; also Howard F. Vos, *Nelson's New Illustrated Bible Manners and Customs: How the People of the Bible Really Lived* (Nashville: Thomas Nelson, 1999), pp. 52–54, 121–24.
8. James K. Hoffmeier, *Israel in Egypt* (Oxford, UK: Oxford University Press, 1999), p. 53.
9. Ibid., p. 114.
10. From the Merneptah Stele, in J. B. Pritchard, ed., *Ancient Near Eastern Texts Relating to the Old Testament* (Princeton, NJ: Princeton University Press, 1955), pp. 376–78.
11. The evidence is summarized in Vos, *Nelson's New Illustrated Bible Manners and Customs*, pp. 121–24.
12. *Papyrus Ipuwer*, quoted in *Biblical Archaeology Review* (May/June 1998): p. 13.
13. For a comprehensive defense of the historicity of Exodus, especially its miracles, see Colin J. Humphreys, *The Miracles of Exodus: A Scientist's Discovery of the Extraordinary Natural Causes of the Biblical Stories* (New York: HarperCollins, 2003).
14. Nahum Sarna, quoted in Sheler, *Is the Bible True?* p. 78.
15. Niels Peter Lemche, *Ancient Israel: A New History of Israelite Society* (Sheffield, UK: JSOT, 1988), p. 109.
16. Umberto Cassuto, *A Commentary on the Book of Exodus*, trans. Israel Abrahams (Jerusalem: Magnes, 1967), p. 9.
17. Jonathan Edwards, *The Works of Jonathan Edwards*, vol. 1 (Edinburgh: Banner of Truth, 1974), p. 119.

## Chapter Two: The New Pharaoh

1. J. B. Pritchard, ed., *Ancient Near Eastern Texts Relating to the Old Testament*, 3rd ed. (Princeton, NJ: Princeton University Press, 1969), p. 470.
2. Umberto Cassuto, *A Commentary on the Book of Exodus*, trans. Israel Abrahams (Jerusalem: Magnes, 1967), p. 12.
3. James K. Hoffmeier, *Israel in Egypt* (Oxford, UK: Oxford University Press, 1999), p. 87.
4. Göran Larsson, *Bound for Freedom: The Book of Exodus in Jewish and Christian Traditions* (Peabody, MA: Hendrickson, 1999), p. 9.

5. Donald Grey Barnhouse, *The Invisible War* (Grand Rapids: Zondervan, 1965), p. 197.

6. See Hoffmeier, *Israel in Egypt*, figure 8.

7. M. Lichtheim, *Ancient Egyptian Literature*, vol. 2 (Berkeley, CA: University of California Press, 1971–1980), pp. 170, 171.

8. Charles H. Spurgeon, "Israel's Cry and God's Answer," *The Metropolitan Tabernacle Pulpit* 45, no. 2631 (Pasadena, TX: Pilgrim, 1977): 337.

9. Charles H. Spurgeon, "Prosperity Under Persecution," *The Metropolitan Tabernacle Pulpit* 17, no. 997 (Pasadena, TX: Pilgrim, 1971), pp. 352, 353.

10. Dan G. McCartney, *Why Does It Have to Hurt?* (Phillipsburg, NJ: P & R, 1998), p. 95.

11. Spurgeon, "Prosperity Under Persecution," p. 351.

12. McCartney, *Why Does It Have to Hurt?* p. 95.

13. Spurgeon, "Prosperity Under Persecution," p. 358.

14. Norman Geisler and Thomas Howe, *When Critics Ask: A Popular Handbook on Bible Difficulties* (Grand Rapids: Baker, 1992), p. 63.

15. Cassuto, *A Commentary on the Book of Exodus*, p. 14.

16. Brevard S. Childs, *The Book of Exodus: A Critical, Theological Commentary* (Louisville: Westminster, 1974), p. 23.

17. John Lightfoot, "A Handful of Gleanings out of the Book of Exodus," in *Works*, vol. 2 (London, 1822), p. 357.

18. Philip Hallie, *Lest Innocent Blood Be Shed* (New York: Harper & Row, 1979), p. 161.

19. Larsson, *Bound for Freedom*, p. 12.

20. Mayen Anyang, quoted in "The Price of a Slave," *Christianity Today* (February 8, 1999): p. 68.

## Chapter Three: The Birth of a Savior

1. Alan Paton, *Cry, the Beloved Country* (New York: Macmillan, 1987), p. 59.

2. Donald Redford gives more than thirty examples in "The Literary Motif of the Exposed Child," *Numen* 14 (1967): pp. 209–28.

3. "The Legend of Sargon," in *Ancient Near Eastern Texts Relating to the Old Testament*, ed. James B. Pritchard, 2nd ed. (Princeton, NJ: Princeton University Press, 1955), p. 119.

4. John Van Seters, "Moses," *Encyclopedia of Religion*, ed. M. Eliade, vol. 10 (New York: Macmillan, 1987), p. 116.

5. David Denby, *The New Yorker*, quoted in *National Review* (January 25, 1999): p. 53.

6. Jonathan Kirsch, quoted in ibid.

7. James K. Hoffmeier, *Israel in Egypt* (Oxford, UK: Oxford University Press, 1999), p. 138.

8. Ibid., pp. 138–40 makes a persuasive case that the vocabulary of the opening section of Exodus is distinctively Egyptian.

9. Göran Larsson, *Bound for Freedom: The Book of Exodus in Jewish and Christian Traditions* (Peabody, MA: Hendrickson, 1999), p. 11.

10. Peter Enns, *Exodus*, NIV Application Commentary (Grand Rapids: Zondervan, 2000), p. 62.

11. Larsson, *Bound for Freedom*, p. 9.

12. John I. Durham, *Exodus*, Word Biblical Commentary (Waco, TX: Word, 1987), p. 17.

13. Umberto Cassuto, *A Commentary on the Book of Exodus*, trans. Israel Abrahams (Jerusalem: Magnes, 1967), pp. 18, 19.

14. Hoffmeier, *Israel in Egypt*, pp. 142, 143.

## Chapter Four: Moses Takes Matters into His Own Hands

1. Peter Enns, *Exodus*, NIV Application Commentary (Grand Rapids: Zondervan, 2000), p. 79.

2. John Calvin, quoted in Brevard S. Childs, *The Book of Exodus: A Critical, Theological Commentary* (Louisville: Westminster, 1974), p. 40.

3. See Childs, *The Book of Exodus*, pp. 40, 41.

4. R. Alan Cole, *Exodus: An Introduction and Commentary*, Tyndale Old Testament Commentaries (Leicester, UK: Inter-Varsity, 1973), p. 59.

5. Göran Larsson, *Bound for Freedom: The Book of Exodus in Jewish and Christian Traditions* (Peabody, MA: Hendrickson, 1999), p. 21.

6. See M. Lichtheim, *Ancient Egyptian Literature*, vol. 2 (Berkeley: University of California Press, 1971–1980), pp. 169–80.

7. A. Erman, *Life in Ancient Egypt* (London: Macmillan, 1894), pp. 68, 69.

8. James S. Ackerman, "The Literary Context of the Moses Birth Story (Exodus 1–2)," in *Literary Interpretations of Biblical Narratives*, ed. Kenneth R. R. Gros Louis (Nashville: Abingdon, 1974), p. 98.

9. Childs, *The Book of Exodus*, p. 37.

10. Ackerman, "The Literary Context of the Moses Birth Story (Exodus 1–2)," p. 102.

## Chapter Five: Moses in the Wilderness

1. Quoted anonymously in Arno C. Gaebelein, *Moses—His First and Second Coming* (New York: Hope, n.d.), n.p.

2. Quoted anonymously in James Montgomery Boice, *Ordinary Men Called by God: A Study of Abraham, Moses, and David* (Grand Rapids: Kregel, 1998), p. 59.

3. John I. Durham, *Exodus*, Word Biblical Commentary (Waco, TX: Word, 1987), p. 24.

4. Boice, *Ordinary Men Called by God*, p. 59.

5. *The Methodist Service Book* (London: Methodist, 1975), D10.

6. Maxie D. Dunnam, *Exodus*, The Communicator's Commentary (Waco, TX: Word, 1987), p. 54.

## Chapter Six: The Burning Bush

1. C. S. Lewis, *That Hideous Strength* (New York: Macmillan, 1946), pp. 288, 289.

2. Nahum Sarna, *The JPS Torah Commentary: Exodus* (Philadelphia: Jewish Publication Society, 1991), p. 12.

3. The arguments in favor of an Arabian site are recounted by Allen Kerkeslager in "Mt. Sinai—in Arabia?" *Bible Review* (April 2000), pp. 32–39, 52.

4. See Joseph J. Hobbs, *Mount Sinai* (Austin, TX: University of Texas Press, 1995), pp. 46–57.

5. Gregory of Nyssa, *The Life of Moses* (New York: Paulist, 1987), p. 60.

6. A. W. Tozer, *The Attributes of God: A Journey into the Father's Heart* (Camp Hill, PA: Christian, 1997), p. 172.

7. John Calvin, *Institutes of the Christian Religion*, ed. John T. McNeill, trans. Ford Lewis Battles, Library of Christian Classics, 20–21 (Philadelphia: Westminster, 1960), 2.8.15.

8. Charles H. Spurgeon, "Israel's Cry and God's Answer," *The Metropolitan Tabernacle Pulpit* 45, no. 2631 (Pasadena, TX: Pilgrim, 1977), p. 343.

## Chapter Seven: The Great I Am

1. Cotton Mather, *A Christian at His Calling*, quoted in Leland Ryken, *Worldly Saints: The Puritans as They Really Were* (Grand Rapids: Zondervan, 1986), p. 27.

2. James Plastaras, *The God of Exodus* (Milwaukee: Bruce, 1966), p. 64.

3. John Calvin, *Institutes of the Christian Religion*, ed. John T. McNeill, trans. Ford Lewis Battles, Library of Christian Classics, 20–21 (Philadelphia: Westminster, 1960), 1.1.1, 2.

4. Umberto Cassuto, *A Commentary on the Book of Exodus*, trans. Israel Abrahams (Jerusalem: Magnes, 1967), p. 36.

5. Peter Enns, *Exodus*, NIV Application Commentary (Grand Rapids: Zondervan, 2000), p. 101.

6. Ibid., p. 103.

7. Herman Bavinck, *The Doctrine of God*, trans. William Hendricksen (Edinburgh: Banner of Truth, 1977), p. 85.

8. Matthew Henry, *Commentary on the Whole Bible*, vol. 1 (New York: Revell, n.d.), p. 284.

9. Alexander Maclaren, *Expositions of Holy Scripture*, vol. 1 (Grand Rapids: Eerdmans, 1952–1959), pp. 23, 24.

## Chapter Eight: Wonders and Signs

1. R. Alan Cole, *Exodus: An Introduction and Commentary*, Tyndale Old Testament Commentaries (Leicester, UK: Inter-Varsity, 1973), p. 72.

2. Brevard S. Childs, *The Book of Exodus: A Critical, Theological Commentary* (Louisville: Westminster, 1974), p. 77.

3. See Gregory Boyd, *God of the Possible* (Downers Grove, IL: InterVarsity, 2000).

4. John D. Currid, *Ancient Egypt and the Old Testament* (Grand Rapids: Baker, 1997), p. 83. See also James K. Hoffmeier, "The Arm of God versus the Arm of Pharaoh in the Exodus Narratives," *Biblica* 67 (1986): pp. 378–87.

5. Umberto Cassuto, *A Commentary on the Book of Exodus*, trans. Israel Abrahams (Jerusalem: Magnes, 1967), p. 44.

6. John I. Durham, *Exodus*, Word Biblical Commentary (Waco, TX: Word, 1987), p. 45.

7. Francis A. Schaeffer, *No Little People* (1974), reprinted in *The Complete Works of Francis A. Schaeffer: A Christian Worldview*, 2nd ed., vol. 3 (Wheaton, IL: Crossway, 1982), p. 8.

8. Göran Larsson, *Bound for Freedom: The Book of Exodus in Jewish and Christian Traditions* (Peabody, MA: Hendrickson, 1999), p. 36.

9. Durham, *Exodus*, p. 46.

## Chapter Nine: Here Am I . . . Send Someone Else

1. Louis Bobe, *Hans Egede: Colonizer and Missionary of Greenland* (Copenhagen: Rosenkilde and Bagger, 1952), pp. 16, 23.

2. This story is recounted in Terry L. Johnson, *When Grace Comes Home: The Practical Difference That Calvinism Makes* (Fearn, Ross-shire, UK: Christian Focus, 2000), pp. 53, 54.

3. Umberto Cassuto, *A Commentary on the Book of Exodus*, trans. Israel Abrahams (Jerusalem: Magnes, 1967), p. 51.

4. Bobe, *Hans Egede*, pp. 23, 29.

## Chapter Ten: Back to Egypt

1. Brevard S. Childs, *The Book of Exodus: A Critical, Theological Commentary* (Louisville: Westminster, 1974), p. 101.

2. S. R. Driver, *Exodus* (1911), quoted in R. Alan Cole, *Exodus: An Introduction and Commentary*, Tyndale Old Testament Commentaries (Leicester, UK: Inter-Varsity, 1973), pp. 77, 78.

3. Peter Enns, *Exodus*, NIV Application Commentary (Grand Rapids: Zondervan, 2000), p. 131.

4. Jon D. Levenson, "Liberation Theology and the Exodus," *Midstream* 35, no. 7 (1989): p. 34.

5. Cornelis Houtman, *Exodus*, Historical Commentary on the Old Testament, trans. Johan Rebel and Sierd Woudstra, vol. 1 (Kampen, Germany: Kok, 1993), p. 430.

6. Charles H. Spurgeon, *The Metropolitan Tabernacle Pulpit* 24 (Pasadena, TX: Pilgrim, 1972): 593.

7. Enns, *Exodus*, p. 134.

## Chapter Eleven: Who Is the Lord?

1. Charles H. Spurgeon, *The Metropolitan Tabernacle Pulpit* 24 (Pasadena, TX: Pilgrim, 1972): pp. 592, 593.

2. James K. Hoffmeier, *Israel in Egypt* (Oxford, UK: Oxford University Press, 1999), p. 115.

3. J. Cerny and A. H. Gardiner, *Hieratic Ostraca I* (Oxford, UK: Printed for the Griffith Institute at the University Press by Charles Batey, 1957), pp. 22, 23, plates 83, 84.

4. Henri Frankfort, *Ancient Egyptian Religion* (New York: Harper, 1948), p. 30.

5. Göran Larsson, *Bound for Freedom: The Book of Exodus in Jewish and Christian Traditions* (Peabody, MA: Hendrickson, 1999), p. 46.

6. Arthur W. Pink, *The Attributes of God* (Grand Rapids: Baker, 1961); A. W. Tozer, *The Attributes of God: A Journey into the Father's Heart* (Camp Hill, PA: Christian, 1997). See also Philip Graham Ryken, *Discovering God in Stories from the Bible* (Wheaton, IL: Crossway, 1999).

## Chapter Twelve: Bricks without Straw

1. J. R. R. Tolkien, *The Hobbit; or There and Back Again*, rev. ed. (New York: Ballantine, 1966), pp. 109, 110.

2. See James K. Hoffmeier, *Israel in Egypt* (Oxford, UK: Oxford University Press, 1999), figure 8. Rekhmire was vizier under Thutmose III, the Pharaoh whose reign corresponds with an early date for the exodus. Perhaps the figures in the relief on Rekhmire's tomb were children of Israel.

3. R. A. Caminos, *Late-Egyptian Miscellanies*, Brown Egyptological Studies, 1 (London: Oxford University Press, 1954), p. 188.

4. Frank J. Yurco, "Merneptah's Canaanite Campaign and Israel's Origins," in *Exodus: The Egyptian Evidence*, eds. Ernest S. Fredrichs and Leonard H. Lesko (Winona Lake, IN: Eisenbrauns, 1997), pp. 27–55 (p. 46).

5. See Alan H. Gardiner, *Late Egyptian Miscellanies*, Bibliotheca Aegyptiaca (Brussels: Édition de la Fondation Égyptologique Reine Élizabeth, 1937), pp. 30, 31; quoted in Hoffmeier, *Israel in Egypt*, p. 115.

6. See Kenneth Kitchen, "From the Brickfields of Egypt," *Tyndale Bulletin* 27 (1976): pp. 143, 144.

7. Brevard S. Childs, *The Book of Exodus: A Critical, Theological Commentary* (Louisville: Westminster, 1974), p. 95.

8. Hoffmeier, *Israel in Egypt*, p. 115.

9. Villiers Stuart, quoted in A. A. McRae, "The Relation of Archaeology to the Bible," *Modern Science and Christian Faith* (Wheaton, IL: Van Kampen, 1950), pp. 215, 216.

10. Andrew Jackson, quoted in Marvin Oaky, *The American Leadership Tradition: The Inevitable Impact of a Leader's Faith on a Nation's Destiny* (Wheaton, IL: Crossway, 2000), p. 64.

11. Howard F. Vos, *Nelson's New Illustrated Bible Manners and Customs: How the People of the Bible Really Lived* (Nashville: Thomas Nelson, 1999), p. 61.

12. George MacDonald, *The Princess and Curdie* (London: J. M. Dent, 1949), p. 25.

13. Peter Enns, *Exodus*, NIV Application Commentary (Grand Rapids: Zondervan, 2000), p. 157.

14. John I. Durham, *Exodus*, Word Biblical Commentary (Waco, TX: Word, 1987), p. 68.

15. Cornelis Houtman, *Exodus*, trans. Johan Rebel and Sierd Woudstra, Historical Commentary on the Old Testament, vol. 1 (Kampen, Germany: Kok, 1993), p. 481.

## Chapter Thirteen: When Trouble Comes

1. Rainer Maria Rilke, *Letters to a Young Poet*, rev. ed. (New York: W. W. Norton, 1962), p. 35.

2. Maxie D. Dunnam, *Exodus*, The Communicator's Commentary (Waco, TX: Word, 1987), p. 94.

3. Godfrey Ashby, *Go Out and Meet God: A Commentary on the Book of Exodus*, International Theological Commentary (Grand Rapids: Eerdmans, 1998), p. 31.

4. John I. Durham, *Exodus*, Word Biblical Commentary (Waco, TX: Word, 1987), p. 70.

5. John Calvin, *Commentaries on the Four Last Books of Moses Arranged in the Form of a Harmony*, trans. C. W. Bingham (Grand Rapids: Baker, 1979), pp. 112, 113.

6. Peter Enns, *Exodus*, NIV Application Commentary (Grand Rapids: Zondervan, 2000), p. 174.

## Chapter Fourteen: The Seven "I Wills" of Salvation

1. See Exodus 6:2, 6–8; 7:5, 17; 8:22; 10:2; 12:12; 14:4, 18; 15:26; 16:12; 20:2; 29:46; 31:13.

2. Brevard S. Childs, *The Book of Exodus: A Critical, Theological Commentary* (Louisville: Westminster, 1974), p. 119.

3. Cornelis Houtman, *Exodus*, trans. Johan Rebel and Sierd Woudstra, Historical Commentary on the Old Testament, vol. 1 (Kampen, Germany: Kok, 1993), p. 503.

4. The story of Calvin's return to Geneva is recounted in T. H. L. Parker, *John Calvin: A Biography* (London: Dent, 1975), pp. 79–81.

## Chapter Fifteen: They Were the Levites

1. See John D. Currid, *A Study Commentary on Exodus*, vol. 1 (Auburn, MA: Evangelical USA, 2000), p. 147.

2. In other words, Amram married his aunt, a practice later forbidden in the Mosaic law (see Leviticus 18:12).

3. Charles H. Spurgeon, *The Treasury of David*, vol. 2 (Grand Rapids: Zondervan, 1968), p. 177.

4. Quoted by Edward Callan in his introduction to Alan Paton, *Cry, the Beloved Country* (New York: Macmillan, 1987), p. xxvii.

5. Francis A. Schaeffer, *No Little People*, in *The Complete Works of Francis A. Schaeffer: A Christian Worldview*, 2nd ed., vol. 3 (Wheaton, IL: Crossway, 1982), p. 12.

## Chapter Sixteen: The Prophet's Prophet

1. Peter Enns, *Exodus*, NIV Application Commentary (Grand Rapids: Zondervan, 2000), p. 181.

2. Marcus A. Brownson, "The Ideal for Our Church," in *The Presbyterian* (April 1, 1937), p. 18.

3. Dwight L. Moody, quoted in Maxie D. Dunnam, *Exodus*, The Communicator's Commentary (Waco, TX: Word, 1987), p. 105.

4. Martin Luther, *What Luther Says: A Practical In-Home Anthology for the Active Christian*, ed. Ewald M. Pass (Saint Louis: Concordia, 1959), p. 1117.

5. R. Kent and Barbara Hughes, *Liberating Ministry from the Success Syndrome* (Wheaton, IL: Tyndale, 1987), pp. 14, 21–23.

6. John D. Currid, *A Study Commentary on Exodus*, vol. 1 (Auburn, MA: Evangelical USA, 2000), pp. 113, 114. See also G. K. Beale, "An Exegetical and Theological Consideration of the Hardening of Pharaoh's Heart in Exodus 4–14 and Romans 9," *Trinity Journal* 5 (1984): pp. 129–54.

7. See Exodus 12:12 and Numbers 33:4, where the word for "vindication" is used again in connection with the final plague.

## Chapter Seventeen: The Staff That Swallowed the Snakes

1. James Montgomery Boice, *Ordinary Men Called by God: A Study of Abraham, Moses, and David* (Grand Rapids: Kregel, 1998), p. 62.

2. Umberto Cassuto, *A Commentary on the Book of Exodus*, trans. Israel Abrahams (Jerusalem: Magnes, 1967), p. 94.

3. For a complete description of ancient Egyptian attitudes about snakes, see John D. Currid, *Ancient Egypt and the Old Testament* (Grand Rapids: Baker, 1997), pp. 86ff.

4. James Henry Breasted, ed., *Ancient Records of Egypt*, vol. 4 (Chicago: University of Chicago Press, 1906–1907), p. 357, quoted in Currid, *Ancient Egypt and the Old Testament*, p. 90.

5. Breasted, *Ancient Records of Egypt*, vol. 4, p. 456, quoted in Currid, *Ancient Egypt and the Old Testament*, p. 90.

6. Pyramid Text 396, quoted in K. Seethe. ed., *Die altägyptischen Pyramidentexten* (Leipzig: J. C. Hinrichs, 1908–1922), quoted in Currid, *Ancient Egypt and the Old Testament*, p. 90.

7. Currid, *Ancient Egypt and the Old Testament*, p. 91.

8. H. Frankfort, *Kingship and the Gods* (Chicago: University of Chicago Press, 1948), p. 108.

9. Göran Larsson, *Bound for Freedom: The Book of Exodus in Jewish and Christian Traditions* (Peabody, MA: Hendrickson, 1999), p. 35.

10. Currid, *Ancient Egypt and the Old Testament*, pp. 92, 93.

11. E. W. Hengstenberg, *Egypt and the Books of Moses* (Edinburgh: Thomas Clark, 1845), p. 100.

12. J. Finegan, *Let My People Go* (New York: Harper, 1963), p. 48.

13. Selwyn Crawford, "Atheist Congregation Discovers Unexpected Success in N. Texas," *Dallas Morning News*, reprinted in *The Philadelphia Inquirer* (July 16, 2000), p. 91.

14. Flavius Josephus, *The Antiquities of the Jews*, in *The Works of Josephus*, trans. William Whiston (Peabody, MA: Hendrickson, 1987), 2.13.3 (p. 72).

15. Charles H. Spurgeon, *The Metropolitan Tabernacle* 9, no. 521 (Pasadena, TX: Pilgrim, 1969), pp. 409.

16. Currid, *Ancient Egypt and the Old Testament*, p. 98.

17. "Book of the Dead," Spell 30B, in R. O. Faulkner, *The Egyptian Book of the Dead* (New York: Macmillan, 1972), quoted in Currid, *Ancient Egypt and the Old Testament*, p. 97.

## Chapter Eighteen: River of Blood

1. James Montgomery Boice, *Psalms: An Expositional Commentary; Vol. 2: Psalms 42–106* (Grand Rapids: Baker, 1996), pp. 849, 850.

2. J. B. Pritchard, ed., *Ancient Near Eastern Texts Relating to the Old Testament*, 3rd ed. (Princeton, NJ: Princeton University Press, 1955), p. 272.

3. See Greta Hort, "The Plagues of Egypt," *Zeitschrift für die alttestamentliche Wissenschafft* 69 (1957): pp. 84–103; 70 (1958): pp. 48–59. Hort's arguments are helpfully summarized in James K. Hoffmeier, *Israel in Egypt* (Oxford, UK: Oxford University Press, 1999), pp. 146–49. See also Colin J. Humphreys, *The Miracles of Exodus: A Scientist's Discovery of the Extraordinary Natural Causes of the Biblical Stories* (New York: HarperCollins, 2003), pp. 111–49.

4. See Deuteronomy 4:34; Psalm 78:11, 12, 42–51; 105:26–36; and Jeremiah 32:20.

5. Pritchard, *Ancient Near Eastern Texts Relating to the Old Testament*, p. 441.

6. Herodotus, quoted in John D. Currid, *A Study Commentary on Exodus*, vol. 1 (Auburn, MA: Evangelical USA, 2000), p. 164.

7. Donald Grey Barnhouse, *The Invisible War* (Grand Rapids: Zondervan, 1965), p. 202.

8. Currid, *A Study Commentary on Exodus*, vol. 1, p. 164.

9. J. L. Foster, "Thought Couplets in Khety's 'Hymn to the Inundation,'" *Journal of Near Eastern Studies* 34, no. 1 (1975): pp. 1–29.

10. Umberto Cassuto, *A Commentary on the Book of Exodus*, trans. Israel Abrahams (Jerusalem: Magnes, 1967), p. 99.

11. See Richard Dawkins, *River out of Eden* (New York: Basic, 1995).

## Chapter Nineteen: Why the Frogs Croaked

1. Weldon Kees, "The Coming of the Plague," in Robert Atwan and Laurance Wieder, eds., *Chapters into Verse: Poetry in English Inspired by the Bible* (New York: Oxford University Press, 1993), p. 124.

2. Umberto Cassuto, *A Commentary on the Book of Exodus*, trans. Israel Abrahams (Jerusalem: Magnes, 1967), p. 100.

3. Greta Hort, "The Plagues of Egypt," *Zeitschrift für die alttestamentliche Wissenschafft* 69 (1957): pp. 84–103; 70 (1958): pp. 48–59; see especially vol. 69, pp. 96–98. For a different explanation, see Colin J. Humphreys, *The Miracles of Exodus: A Scientist's Discovery of the Extraordinary Natural Causes of the Biblical Stories* (New York: HarperCollins, 2003), pp. 119–21.

4. W. M. Flinders Petrie, *Egypt and Israel* (London: SPCK, 1911), pp. 35, 36.

5. James Montgomery Boice, *Ordinary Men Called by God: A Study of Abraham, Moses, and David* (Grand Rapids: Kregel, 1998), p. 65. Here is how Harry Rimmer imagined it in *Dead Men Tell Tales* (Berne, IN: Berne Witness, 1939):

> Like a blanket of filth the slimy, wet monstrosities covered the land, until men sickened at the continued squashing crunch of the ghastly pavement they were forced to walk upon. If a man's feet slipped on the greasy mass of their crushed bodies, he fell into an indescribably offensive mass of putrid uncleanness, and when he sought water to cleanse himself, the water was so solid with frogs, he got no cleansing there. (p. 105)

6. Charles H. Spurgeon, "Take Away the Frogs" (No. 3340), *The Metropolitan Tabernacle Pulpit* (Pasadena, TX: Pilgrim, 1972).

7. John D. Currid, *A Study Commentary on Exodus*, vol. 1 (Auburn, MA: Evangelical USA, 2000), p. 173.
8. Ibid.
9. Spurgeon, "Take Away the Frogs."

## Chapter Twenty: The Finger of God

1. Philo of Alexandria, quoted in Godfrey Ashby, *Go Out and Meet God: A Commentary on the Book of Exodus*, International Theological Commentary (Grand Rapids: Eerdmans, 1998), p. 44.
2. Umberto Cassuto, *A Commentary on the Book of Exodus*, trans. Israel Abrahams (Jerusalem: Magnes, 1967), p. 93.
3. R. Alan Cole, *Exodus: An Introduction and Commentary*, Tyndale Old Testament Commentaries (Leicester, UK: Inter-Varsity, 1973), pp. 92, 93.
4. Louis Berkhof, *Systematic Theology*, 4th ed. (Grand Rapids: Eerdmans, 1941), p. 176.
5. Joseph P. Free, *Archaeology and Bible History* (Wheaton, IL: Van Kampen, 1950), p. 84.
6. John D. Currid, *Ancient Egypt and the Old Testament* (Grand Rapids: Baker, 1997), pp. 113–17.
7. J. A. Wilson, *The Burden of Egypt* (Chicago: University of Chicago, 1951), p. 48.
8. "The Prophecy of Neferti," quoted in James K. Hoffmeier, *Israel in Egypt* (Oxford, UK: Oxford University Press, 1999), p. 152.
9. John J. Davis, *Moses and the Gods of Egypt: Studies in the Book of Exodus* (Grand Rapids: Baker, 1971), p. 103.
10. Göran Larsson, *Bound for Freedom: The Book of Exodus in Jewish and Christian Traditions* (Peabody, MA: Hendrickson, 1999), p. 62.

## Chapter Twenty-One: Lord of the Flies

1. Charles H. Spurgeon, "Take Away the Frogs," *The Metropolitan Tabernacle Pulpit*, no. 3340 (Pasadena, TX: Pilgrim, 1972).
2. Göran Larsson, *Bound for Freedom: The Book of Exodus in Jewish and Christian Traditions* (Peabody, MA: Hendrickson, 1999), p. 63.
3. John J. Davis, *Moses and the Gods of Egypt: Studies in the Book of Exodus* (Grand Rapids: Baker, 1971), p. 106.
4. Donald Grey Barnhouse, *The Invisible War* (Grand Rapids: Zondervan, 1965), p. 206.
5. Charles H. Spurgeon, "A Divine Challenge!" *The New Park Street Pulpit* 5 (Pasadena, TX: Pilgrim, 1975), p. 285.
6. R. Alan Cole, *Exodus: An Introduction and Commentary*, Tyndale Old Testament Commentaries (Leicester, UK: Inter-Varsity, 1973), p. 95.
7. Spurgeon, "A Divine Challenge!" p. 287.
8. Charles H. Spurgeon, "All or None; or, Compromises Refused: A Sermon with Five Texts," *The Metropolitan Tabernacle Pulpit* 31, no. 1830 (Pasadena, TX: Pilgrim, 1972), p. 161.
9. Jeanette Howard, *Out of Egypt* (Tunbridge Wells, UK: Monarch, 1991), pp. 217–19.

## Chapter Twenty-Two: A Plague on Your Livestock

1. John J. Davis, *Moses and the Gods of Egypt: Studies in the Book of Exodus* (Grand Rapids: Baker, 1971), p. 113.
2. Greta Hort, "The Plagues of Egypt," *Zeitschrift für die alttestamentliche Wissenschafft* 69 (1957): pp. 84–103 (p. 100). Colin J. Humphreys, *The Miracles of Exodus:*

*A Scientist's Discovery of the Extraordinary Natural Causes of the Biblical Stories* (New York: HarperCollins, 2003), pp. 123–25 argues that the livestock were killed off by a combination of African horse sickness and a related virus known as bluetongue, both of which are transmitted by the *Culicoides* midge.

3. John D. Currid, *A Study Commentary on Exodus*, vol. 1 (Auburn, MA: Evangelical USA, 2000), p. 194.

4. Hort, "The Plagues of Egypt," p. 100.

5. C. F. Keil and F. Delitzsch, *The Pentateuch, Biblical Commentary on the Old Testament*, vol. 1 (Grand Rapids: Eerdmans, 1949), p. 487.

6. Currid, *A Study Commentary on Exodus*, vol. 1, p. 192.

7. The discovery is described in Davis, *Moses and the Gods of Egypt*, pp. 113, 114.

8. Ibid., pp. 114, 115.

9. Jonathan Edwards, *A History of the Work of Redemption*, in *The Works of Jonathan Edwards*, vol. 1 (1834; repr. Edinburgh: Banner of Truth, 1974), pp. 532–619.

10. John I. Durham, *Exodus*, Word Biblical Commentary (Waco, TX: Word, 1987), p. 119.

11. Hudson T. Armerding, "The Understanding Heart," in *A Word to the Wise* (Wheaton, IL: Tyndale, 1980), pp. 83–88.

## Chapter Twenty-Three: Can't Stand That Itch!

1. *Midrash Sekhel Tov*, quoted in Göran Larsson, *Bound for Freedom: The Book of Exodus in Jewish and Christian Traditions* (Peabody, MA: Hendrickson, 1999), p. 58.

2. Greta Hort, "The Plagues of Egypt," *Zeitschrift für die alttestamentliche Wissenschafft* 69 (1957): pp. 84–103 (p. 101). Colin J. Humphreys, *The Miracles of Exodus: A Scientist's Discovery of the Extraordinary Natural Causes of the Biblical Stories* (New York: HarperCollins, 2003) believes that whatever the disease was, it was carried by the stable fly (p. 126).

3. Hort, "The Plagues of Egypt," p. 102.

4. Quoted in J. B. Pritchard, ed., *Ancient Near Eastern Texts Relating to the Old Testament* (Princeton, NJ: Princeton University Press, 1955), p. 369.

5. John D. Currid, *Ancient Egypt and the Old Testament* (Grand Rapids: Baker, 1997), p. 111.

6. John J. Davis, *Moses and the Gods of Egypt: Studies in the Book of Exodus* (Grand Rapids: Baker, 1971), p. 115.

7. John D. Currid, *A Study Commentary on Exodus*, vol. 1 (Auburn, MA: Evangelical USA, 2000), p. 196.

8. R. Alan Cole, *Exodus: An Introduction and Commentary*, Tyndale Old Testament Commentaries (Leicester, UK: Inter-Varsity, 1973), p. 97.

9. The complete text of Pascal's prayer is published by Robert Scott and George W. Gilmore in *World's Devotional Classics*, vol. 6 (New York: Funk and Wagnalls, 1916), pp. 182–97.

## Chapter Twenty-Four: The Worst Hailstorm Ever

1. James K. Hoffmeier, *Israel in Egypt* (Oxford, UK: Oxford University Press, 1999), p. 148.

2. Umberto Cassuto, *A Commentary on the Book of Exodus*, trans. Israel Abrahams (Jerusalem: Magnes, 1967), p. 117.

3. See Hoffmeier, *Israel in Egypt*, pp. 150, 151.

4. John D. Currid, *Ancient Egypt and the Old Testament* (Grand Rapids: Baker, 1997), pp. 207, 208.

5. Charles H. Spurgeon, "Take Away the Frogs," *The Metropolitan Tabernacle Pulpit*, no. 3340 (Pasadena, TX: Pilgrim, 1972).

6. Daniel Defoe, *Robinson Crusoe*, quoted in Philip Zaleski, "The Strange Shipwreck of Robinson Crusoe," *First Things* 53 (May 1995): pp. 38–44.

## Chapter Twenty-Five: Something to Tell Your Grandchildren

1. Laura Ingalls Wilder, *On the Banks of Plum Creek*, rev. ed. (New York: HarperCollins, 1953), pp. 194–204.

2. Charles H. Spurgeon, *The Metropolitan Tabernacle Pulpit* 43 (Pasadena, TX: Pilgrim, 1976): p. 68.

3. Abraham Kuyper, quoted in *Modern Reformation* (January/February 2001): p. 22.

4. John J. Davis, *Moses and the Gods of Egypt: Studies in the Book of Exodus* (Grand Rapids: Baker, 1971), p. 120.

5. See also Deuteronomy 28:38; 1 Kings 8:37; 2 Chronicles 7:13; and Amos 7:1–3.

6. Daniel DaCruz, "Plague Across the Land," *Aramco World* (November/December 1967): p. 21.

7. *Chicago Tribune*, March 25, 1988, quoted in James K. Hoffmeier, *Israel in Egypt* (Oxford, UK: Oxford University Press, 1999), p. 148.

8. London *Times*, June 19, 2001, quoted in Colin J. Humphreys, *The Miracles of Exodus: A Scientist's Discovery of the Extraordinary Natural Causes of the Biblical Stories* (New York: HarperCollins, 2003), pp. 131, 132.

9. J. H. Breasted, ed., *Ancient Records of Egypt*, 5 vols. (1906), quoted in John D. Currid, *A Study Commentary on Exodus*, vol. 1 (Auburn, MA: Evangelical USA, 2000), p. 215.

10. Wilder, *On the Banks of Plum Creek*, pp. 216, 217.

## Chapter Twenty-Six: Heart of Darkness

1. Alfred Lansing, *Endurance: Shackleton's Incredible Voyage* (New York: Carroll & Graf, 1959), p. 38.

2. Stephen Quirke, *The Cult of Ra: Sun-Worship in Ancient Egypt* (New York: Thames & Hudson, 2001), p. 7.

3. Quoted in ibid., p. 25.

4. Quoted in ibid., p. 161.

5. Ibid., pp. 7, 19, 117.

6. Quoted in Rick Gore, "Pharaohs of the Sun," *National Geographic* (April 2001), p. 38.

7. Kurt Sethe, *Urkunden der 18. Dynastie*, 19.6–8, quoted in Hoffmeier, *Israel in Egypt*, p. 153.

8. *Papyrus Sallier I*, quoted in Hoffmeier, *Israel in Egypt*, p. 153.

9. Quoted in Quirke, *The Cult of Ra*, p. 20.

10. *Stela for Amen-em-het III*, quoted in J. B. Pritchard, ed., *Ancient Near Eastern Texts Relating to the Old Testament* (Princeton, NJ: Princeton University Press, 1955), p. 431.

11. *Papyrus Anastasi II*, 5.7ff., quoted in Göran Larsson, *Bound for Freedom: The Book of Exodus in Jewish and Christian Traditions* (Peabody, MA: Hendrickson, 1999), p. 71.

12. Colin J. Humphreys, *The Miracles of Exodus: A Scientist's Discovery of the Extraordinary Natural Causes of the Biblical Stories* (New York: HarperCollins, 2003), pp. 134–36.

13. Peter Enns, *Exodus*, NIV Application Commentary (Grand Rapids: Zondervan, 2000), p. 231.

14. Charles H. Spurgeon makes a similar application in "All or None; or, Compromises Refused: A Sermon with Five Texts," *The Metropolitan Tabernacle Pulpit* 31, no. 1830 (Pasadena, TX: Pilgrim, 1976), p. 164.

15. Jeanette Howard, *Out of Egypt* (Tunbridge Wells, UK: Monarch, 1991), pp. 218, 219.

16. Charles H. Spurgeon, "The Question Between the Plagues," *The Metropolitan Tabernacle Pulpit* 43, no. 2503 (Pasadena, TX: Pilgrim, 1976), p. 66.

## Chapter Twenty-Seven: The Deadliest Plague

1. Fleming James, *Personalities of the Old Testament* (New York: Scribners, 1939), p. 14.

2. Nahum Sarna, quoted in Colin J. Humphreys, *The Miracles of Exodus: A Scientist's Discovery of the Extraordinary Natural Causes of the Biblical Stories* (New York: HarperCollins, 2003), p. 137.

3. Maya Müller, "Afterlife," trans. Robert E. Shillenn and Jane McGary, *The Oxford Encyclopedia of Ancient Egypt*, ed. Donald B. Redford, vol. 1 (Oxford, UK: Oxford University Press, 2001), p. 32.

4. Umberto Cassuto, *A Commentary on the Book of Exodus*, trans. Israel Abrahams (Jerusalem: Magnes, 1967), p. 133.

5. Jonathan Edwards, *The End for Which God Created the World*, quoted in John Piper, *God's Passion for His Glory: Living the Vision of Jonathan Edwards* (Wheaton, IL: Crossway, 1998), p. 124.

## Chapter Twenty-Eight: The First Passover

1. From the Hermetic Writings, attributed to Hermes Trismegistus and cited in Barbara Mertz, *Red Land, Black Land* (New York: Dell, 1966), p. 251.

2. J. A. Motyer, "Old Testament Covenant Theology" (lecture, Theological Students Fellowship, London, 1973), p. 13.

3. David Smale, "Along for the Ride," *Sharing the Victory* 19, no. 2 (October 2000): pp. 19–21.

4. Jonathan Edwards, *A History of the Work of Redemption*, ed. John F. Wilson, in *The Works of Jonathan Edwards*, vol. 9 (New Haven, CT: Yale University Press, 1989), n.p.

5. Geerhardus Vos, *Biblical Theology* (Grand Rapids: Eerdmans, 1948), p. 120.

6. Flavius Josephus, *The Wars of the Jews*, 6.9.3, in *The Works of Josephus*, trans. William Whiston (Peabody, MA: Hendrickson, 1987), p. 749.

7. Charles H. Spurgeon, "The Sacred Love Token," *The Metropolitan Tabernacle Pulpit* 21, no. 1251 (Pasadena, TX: Pilgrim, 1971), pp. 483, 484.

## Chapter Twenty-Nine: A Feast to Remember

1. Dr. Davis made this comment on the floor of the Presbyterian Church in America's General Assembly in Dallas, TX (June 2001).

2. John I. Durham, *Exodus*, Word Biblical Commentary (Waco, TX: Word, 1987), p. 159.

3. Arthur W. Pink makes this case in *Gleanings in Exodus* (Chicago: Moody, 1981), p. 93.

4. John L. Mackay, *Exodus* (Fearn, Ross-shire, UK: Christian Focus, 2001), pp. 213, 214.

## Chapter Thirty: Out of Egypt

1. Dr. Seuss, *Marvin K. Mooney, Will You Please Go Now!* (New York: Random, 1972).

2. John D. Currid, *A Study Commentary on Exodus*, vol. 1 (Auburn, MA: Evangelical USA, 2000), p. 257.

3. Arthur F. Holmes, *Building the Christian Academy* (Grand Rapids: Eerdmans, 2001), pp. 18, 19.

4. Augustine's ideas are summarized in David J. Hesselgrave, "Third Millennium Missiology and the Use of Egyptian Gold," *Journal of the Evangelical Theological Society* 42, no. 4 (December 1999): p. 581.

5. Nigel Goodwin, quoted in Makato Fujimura, "Form and Content," in *It Was Good: Making Art to the Glory of God*, ed. Ned Bustard (Baltimore: Square Halo, 2000), p. 58.

6. For a full discussion of these places, see John D. Currid, *Ancient Egypt and the Old Testament* (Grand Rapids: Baker, 1997), pp. 125–29.

7. Charles Krahmalkov, "Exodus Itinerary Confirmed by Egyptian Evidence," *Biblical Archaeology Review* 20, no. 5 (1994): p. 56.

8. Samuel R. Driver, *The Book of Exodus*, Cambridge Bible (Cambridge, UK: Cambridge University Press, 1911), p. xlv.

9. N. H. Snaith, "Numbers," in M. Black and H. H. Rowley, eds., *Peake's Commentary on the Bible* (London: Nelson, 1962), p. 254.

10. James Hoffmeier, quoted in Kevin D. Miller, "Did the Exodus Never Happen?" *Christianity Today* (September 7, 1998): p. 48.

11. Michael Feiler, *Walking the Bible: A Journey by Land Through the Five Books of Moses* (New York: HarperCollins, 2001): p. 202.

## Chapter Thirty-One: This Do in Remembrance of Me

1. Charles H. Spurgeon, "The Exodus," *The New Park Street Pulpit* 2, no. 55 (Pasadena, TX: Pilgrim, 1975): p. 9.

2. Göran Larsson, *Bound for Freedom: The Book of Exodus in Jewish and Christian Traditions* (Peabody, MA: Hendrickson, 1999), pp. 90, 91.

3. Charles H. Spurgeon "The Blood of Sprinkling and the Children," *The Metropolitan Tabernacle Pulpit* 33, no. 1988 (London: Banner of Truth, 1969): pp. 587, 588.

## Chapter Thirty-Two: The Redemption of Sons

1. Benjamin Breckinridge Warfield, "'Redeemer' and 'Redemption,'" in *The Person and Work of Christ*, ed. Samuel G. Craig (Philadelphia: P & R, 1950), pp. 325–48 (p. 325).

2. James B. Jordan, *The Law of the Covenant: An Exposition of Exodus 21–23* (Tyler, TX: Institute for Christian Economics, 1984), p. 251.

3. This insight comes from Peter Enns, *Exodus*, NIV Application Commentary (Grand Rapids: Zondervan, 2000), p. 255.

4. William J. Dumbrell, *Covenant and Creation: A Theology of Old Testament Covenants* (Nashville: Thomas Nelson, 1984), p. 100.

5. *The Heidelberg Catechism with Commentary* (Philadelphia: United, 1963), n.p.

## Chapter Thirty-Three: Between the Desert and the Sea

1. See James K. Hoffmeier, *Israel in Egypt* (Oxford, UK: Oxford University Press, 1999), pp. 164–72.

2. Claude Jarvis, quoted in Joseph J. Hobbs, *Mount Sinai* (Austin, TX: University of Texas Press, 1995), p. 55.

3. Hoffmeier, *Israel in Egypt*, p. 170.

4. Colin J. Humphreys, *The Miracles of Exodus: A Scientist's Discovery of the Extraordinary Natural Causes of the Biblical Stories* (New York: HarperCollins, 2003), pp. 224–43 seeks to pinpoint the precise location of this attack.

5. John D. Currid, *A Study Commentary on Exodus*, vol. 1 (Auburn, MA: Evangelical USA, 2000), p. 296.

6. Peter Enns, *Exodus*, NIV Application Commentary (Grand Rapids: Zondervan, 2000), p. 273.

7. Charles H. Spurgeon, "Direction in Dilemma," *Metropolitan Tabernacle Pulpit* 9, no. 541 (Pasadena, TX: Pilgrim, 1973), p. 654.

## Chapter Thirty-Four: The Great Escape

1. Charles H. Spurgeon, "Forward! Forward! Forward!" *Metropolitan Tabernacle Pulpit* 10, no. 548 (Pasadena, TX: Pilgrim, 1973): pp. 13.

2. See Bernard Batto, "The Reed Sea: *Requiescat in Pace*," *Journal of Biblical Literature* 102, no. 1 (1983): pp. 27–35.

3. James K. Hoffmeier, *Israel in Egypt* (Oxford, UK: Oxford University Press, 1999), pp. 207–15. For yet another explanation, see Colin J. Humphreys, *The Miracles of Exodus: A Scientist's Discovery of the Extraordinary Natural Causes of the Biblical Stories* (New York: HarperCollins, 2003), pp. 172–205, who argues that the Israelites crossed the Gulf of Aqaba, which in those days was called *yam suph*, meaning "Sea of Reeds," and later was called the Red Sea.

4. Brevard S. Childs, *The Book of Exodus: A Critical, Theological Commentary* (Louisville: Westminster, 1974), p. 236.

5. Umberto Cassuto, *A Commentary on the Book of Exodus*, trans. Israel Abrahams (Jerusalem: Magnes, 1967), pp. 167, 168.

6. Joseph J. Hobbs, *Mount Sinai* (Austin, TX: University of Texas Press, 1995), p. 55. Similarly, Colin J. Humphreys, *The Miracles of Exodus*, attributes Israel's salvation to meteorological conditions known as "wind setup" and "wind setdown." Humphreys locates the event at the Gulf of Aqaba rather than the Gulf of Suez.

7. This is a major theme in Peter Enns, *Exodus*, NIV Application Commentary (Grand Rapids: Zondervan, 2000).

8. Cassuto, *A Commentary on the Book of Exodus*, p. 168.

9. Donald Bridge, *Signs and Wonders Today* (Leicester, UK: Inter-Varsity, 1985), p. 17, quoted in John D. Currid, *A Study Commentary on Exodus*, vol. 1 (Auburn, MA: Evangelical USA, 2000), p. 307.

10. For a description of how the wave may have developed, see Humphreys, *The Miracles of Exodus*, pp. 255–57.

11. J. B. Pritchard, ed., *Ancient Near Eastern Texts Relating to the Old Testament*, 3rd ed. (Princeton, NJ: Princeton University Press, 1969), p. 431.

12. Pharaoh himself may have been among the victims. His demise is not mentioned here in Exodus, but it seems to be confirmed by the psalmist, who describes how God "overthrew Pharaoh and his host in the Red Sea" (Psalm 136:15).

13. Enns, *Exodus*, p. 287.

14. Alistair McGrath, *The Mystery of the Cross* (Grand Rapids: Zondervan, 1988), p. 24.

## Chapter Thirty-Five: The Song of Salvation

1. The story is briefly recounted in Andrew F. Walls, *The Missionary Movement in Christian History: Studies in the Transmission of Faith* (Maryknoll, NY: Orbis, 1996), p. 86.

2. John Currid argues this case persuasively in *A Study Commentary on Exodus*, vol. 1 (Auburn, MA: Evangelical USA, 2000), pp. 309–23.

3. Brevard S. Childs, *The Book of Exodus: A Critical, Theological Commentary* (Louisville: Westminster, 1974), p. 246.

4. Thomas Moore, "Sound the Loud Timbrel," in Robert Atwan and Laurance Wieder, eds., *Chapters into Verse: Poetry in English Inspired by The Bible*, vol. 1 (New York: Oxford University Press, 1993), p. 129.

5. Quoted in David Van Biema, "In Search of Moses," *Time* magazine (December 14, 1998): p. 87.

6. *Babylonian Talmud, Megilla* 10b, quoted in Göran Larsson, *Bound for Freedom: The Book of Exodus in Jewish and Christian Traditions* (Peabody, MA: Hendrickson, 1999), p. 109.

7. Mariano DiGangi, "Faithful in Commitment to the Lost," in *Faithful Witness: The Urbana 84 Compendium*, ed. James McLeish (Downers Grove, IL: InterVarsity, 1985), pp. 123–31 (p. 125).

8. Timothy Keller, "Why We Need Artists," in *It Was Good: Making Art to the Glory of God*, ed. Ned Bustard (Baltimore: Square Halo, 2000), pp. 79–87 (p. 85).

9. William Hammond, "Awake, O Soul, and Sing," 1745.

## Chapter Thirty-Six: A Bitter Complaint

1. Dietrich Bonhoeffer, *Life Together*, trans. John W. Doberstein (San Francisco: Harper & Row, 1954), p. 53.

2. John L. Mackay, *Exodus* (Fearn, Ross-Shire, UK: Mentor, 2001), p. 278.

3. Colin J. Humphreys, *The Miracles of Exodus: A Scientist's Discovery of the Extraordinary Natural Causes of the Biblical Stories* (New York: HarperCollins, 2003), pp. 267–71.

4. John Calvin, *Commentaries on the Four Last Books of Moses*, Calvin's Commentaries, vol. 2 (Edinburgh; repr. Grand Rapids: Baker, 1999), p. 265.

5. See Humphreys, *The Miracles of Exodus*, pp. 271–73.

6. Calvin, *Commentaries on the Four Last Books of Moses*, vol. 2, p. 265.

7. Charles H. Spurgeon, "Marah Better Than Elim," *Metropolitan Tabernacle Pulpit* 39, no. 2301 (Pasadena, TX: Pilgrim, 1973), p. 151.

8. Nathan Stone, *Names of God* (Chicago: Moody, 1944), p. 72.

9. John Buchan, *Witch Wood* (Edinburgh: Canongate, 1995), p. 9.

## Chapter Thirty-Seven: Bread from Heaven

1. George W. Coats, *Rebellion in the Wilderness* (Nashville: Abingdon, 1968), p. 249.

2. Herodotus, quoted in R. Alan Cole, *Exodus: An Introduction and Commentary*, Tyndale Old Testament Commentaries (Leicester, UK: Inter-Varsity, 1973), p. 131.

3. F. S. Bodenheimer, "The Manna of Sinai," *Biblical Archaeologist* 10 (1947): pp. 1–6.

4. John J. Davis, *Moses and the Gods of Egypt: Studies in the Book of Exodus* (Grand Rapids: Baker, 1971), p. 181.

5. Göran Larsson, *Bound for Freedom: The Book of Exodus in Jewish and Christian Traditions* (Peabody, MA: Hendrickson, 1999), p. 115.

6. Maxie D. Dunnam, *Exodus*, The Communicator's Commentary (Waco, TX: Word, 1987), p. 195.

7. Virginia Pritchard, "Five Loaves and Five Turkeys!" *Focus on the Family* (November 1999), pp. 14, 15.

## Chapter Thirty-Eight: A Sabbath for Man

1. Clement of Rome, "The Recognitions of Clement," in *The Twelve Patriarchs et al.*, eds. Alexander Roberts and James Donaldson, Ante-Nicene Fathers, vol. 8 (1886; repr. Peabody, MA: Hendrickson, 1994), p. 87.

2. Joseph A. Pipa, *The Lord's Day* (Fearn, Ross-shire, UK: Christian Focus, 1997), pp. 97–105 makes a persuasive case that the term "Sabbath" in Colossians 2:17 refers to the Jewish Sabbath and does not apply to the Christian celebration of the Lord's Day.

3. Peter Enns, *Exodus*, NIV Application Commentary (Grand Rapids: Zondervan, 2000), p. 325.

4. John D. Currid, *A Study Commentary on Exodus*, vol. 1 (Auburn, MA: Evangelical USA, 2000), p. 336.

5. Richard B. Gaffin Jr., "A Sign of Hope," *New Horizons* (March 2003).

6. Walter Brueggeman, *Christian Century* (May 24–31, 1999), quoted in *Christianity Today* (September 6, 1999).

7. Nan Chase, "Ancient Wisdom," *Hemispheres* (July 1997): p. 118.

## Chapter Thirty-Nine: That Rock Was Christ

1. Gerhard Von Rad, *Old Testament Theology*, trans. D. M. G. Stalker, vol. 1 (New York: Harper & Row, 1962), p. 12.

2. C. S. Lewis, *God in the Dock: Essays on Theology and Ethics*, ed. Walter Hooper (Grand Rapids: Eerdmans, 1970), p. 244.

3. John Calvin, *Commentaries on the Four Last Books of Moses*, Calvin's Commentaries, vol. 2 (Edinburgh; repr. Grand Rapids: Baker, 1999), p. 288.

4. Umberto Cassuto, *A Commentary on the Book of Exodus*, trans. Israel Abrahams (Jerusalem: Magnes, 1967), p. 202.

5. Ibid., p. 203.

6. Edmund P. Clowney Jr., "God on Trial," *Christianity Today* (February 24, 1978): pp. 16, 17.

## Chapter Forty: Lift Up Your Hands

1. Charles H. Spurgeon, "War with Amalek," *The Metropolitan Tabernacle Pulpit* vol. 12, no. 712 (Pasadena, TX: Pilgrim, 1970), p. 534.

2. Nahum Sarna, *The JPS Torah Commentary: Exodus* (Philadelphia: Jewish Publication Society, 1991), p. 95.

3. G. W. Coats, *Exodus 1–18* (Grand Rapids: Eerdmans, 1998), p. 141.

4. John D. Currid, *A Study Commentary on Exodus*, vol. 1 (Auburn, MA: Evangelical USA, 2000), p. 366.

5. See Brevard S. Childs, *The Book of Exodus: A Critical, Theological Commentary* (Louisville: Westminster, 1974), pp. 310–12.

6. John Calvin, *Commentaries on the Four Last Books of Moses*, Calvin's Commentaries, vol. 2 (Edinburgh; repr. Grand Rapids: Baker, 1999), p. 293.

7. Dante Alighieri, *Inferno*, Canto 3, lines 52–54.

8. Sabine Baring-Gould, "Onward, Christian Soldiers," 1865.

## Chapter Forty-One: Family Reunion

1. John Calvin, *Commentaries on the Four Last Books of Moses*, Calvin's Commentaries, vol. 2 (Edinburgh; repr. Grand Rapids: Baker, 1999), p. 297.

2. Norman P. Grubb, *C. T. Studd: Athlete and Pioneer* (Grand Rapids: Zondervan, 1933), p. 16.

## Chapter Forty-Two: Israel Gets Organized

1. Maxie D. Dunnam, *Exodus*, The Communicator's Commentary (Waco, TX: Word, 1987), p. 229.

2. Peter Enns, *Exodus*, NIV Application Commentary (Grand Rapids: Zondervan, 2000), p. 372.

3. *The Book of Church Order of the Presbyterian Church in America*, 5th ed. (Atlanta: Committee for Christian Education and Publications, 1990).

4. Roger Beardmore, ed., *Shepherding God's Flock* (Harrisonburg, VA: Sprinkle, n.d.), pp. 105, 106.

## Chapter Forty-Three: Kingdom of Priests

1. Larry Williams, *The Mountain of Moses* (Solana Beach, CA: CTI). For a sensational account of a recent attempt to prove that Mount Sinai is Jabal al Lawz in modern-day Saudi Arabia, see Howard Blum, *The Gold of Exodus* (New York: Simon & Schuster, 1998). Colin J. Humphreys has made a much more persuasive case that Mount Sinai is the Arabian Mount Bedr in *The Miracles of Exodus: A Scientist's Discovery of the Extraordinary Natural Causes of the Biblical Stories* (New York: HarperCollins, 2003).

2. John Lloyd Stephens, quoted in Bruce Feiler, *Walking the Bible: A Journey by Land through the Five Books of Moses* (New York: HarperCollins, 2001), p. 251.

3. This is highlighted in John Durham's outline of Exodus: "Israel in Egypt" (1:1—13:16), "Israel in the Wilderness" (13:17—18:27), "Israel at Sinai" (19:1—40:38). See John I. Durham, *Exodus*, Word Biblical Commentary (Waco, TX: Word, 1987), p. xxx.

4. J. R. R. Tolkien, *The Hobbit, or There and Back Again*, rev. ed. (New York: Ballantine, 1966), p. 270.

5. John L. Mackay, *Exodus* (Fearn, Ross-Shire, UK: Mentor, 2001), p. 326.

6. Ibid., p. 322.

## Chapter Forty-Four: Don't Touch!

1. Michael Horton, *In the Face of God* (Dallas: Word, 1996), p. 53.

2. Ibid., p. 53.

3. Annie Dillard, *Teaching a Stone to Talk* (New York: Harper & Row, 1982), pp. 40, 41.

4. John L. Mackay, *Exodus* (Fearn, Ross-Shire, UK: Mentor, 2001), p. 330.

5. John Calvin, *Commentaries on the Four Last Books of Moses*, Calvin's Commentaries (Edinburgh; repr. Grand Rapids: Baker, 1999), p. 324.

6. See Meredith G. Kline's groundbreaking *Treaty of the Great King* (Grand Rapids: Eerdmans, 1963), and also William J. Dumbrell's summary of recent research in *Covenant and Creation: A Theology of Old Testament Covenants* (Nashville: Thomas Nelson, 1984), pp. 94–96.

7. John Calvin, *Commentaries on the Four Last Books of Moses*, Calvin's Commentaries (Edinburgh; repr. Grand Rapids: Baker, 1999), p. 324.

8. Bruce Feiler, *Walking the Bible: A Journey by Land Through the Five Books of Moses* (New York: HarperCollins, 2001), p. 248.

9. These words come from the second stanza of Charles Wesley's famous hymn, "Hark! the Herald Angels Sing."

## Chapter Forty-Five: Smoke on the Mountain

1. John Calvin, *Commentaries on the Four Last Books of Moses*, Calvin's Commentaries (Edinburgh; repr. Grand Rapids: Baker, 1999), pp. 326, 327.

2. Maxie D. Dunnam, *Exodus*, The Communicator's Commentary (Waco, TX: Word, 1987), p. 245.

3. John Milton, "On the Morning of Christ's Nativity" (1629), stanza 17, in *The Oxford Book of Christian Verse*, ed. Lord David Cecil (Oxford, UK: Oxford University Press, 1940), p. 171.

4. Francis A. Schaeffer, *The God Who Is There* (1968), in *The Complete Works of Francis A. Schaeffer: A Christian Worldview, Vol. 1, A Christian View of Philosophy and Culture* (Wheaton, IL: Crossway, 1982).

5. These examples are cited by S. R. Driver in *The Book of Exodus* (Cambridge, UK: Cambridge University Press, 1911), pp. 176, 177.

6. The most Biblically and scientifically persuasive attempt has been made by Colin J. Humphreys in *The Miracles of Exodus: A Scientist's Discovery of the Extraordinary Natural Causes of the Biblical Stories* (New York: HarperCollins, 2003), pp. 82–93.

7. Colin Humphreys argues that "volcanic gases being forced under pressure through cracks in rocks" sometimes make a trumpeting sound (p. 90). He wisely does not attempt to explain what Moses called "the voice of God" (19:19 NIV).

8. Francis A. Schaeffer, *He Is There and He Is Not Silent* (1972), in *The Complete Works of Francis A. Schaeffer: A Christian Worldview, Vol. 1, A Christian View of Philosophy and Culture* (Wheaton, IL: Crossway, 1982).

9. John L. Mackay, *Exodus* (Fearn, Ross-Shire, UK: Mentor, 2001), p. 336.

10. This connection is made by Peter Enns in *Exodus*, NIV Application Commentary (Grand Rapids: Zondervan, 2000), p. 391.

11. I owe this insight to my colleague Richard Phillips.

12. Philip Edgcumbe Hughes, *A Commentary on the Epistle to the Hebrews* (Grand Rapids: Eerdmans, 1977), p. 543.

13. Enns, *Exodus*, 403.

14. John Newton, "Let Us Love, and Sing, and Wonder" (1774).

## Chapter Forty-Six: Written in Stone

1. James Patterson and Peter Kim, *The Day America Told the Truth* (New York: Plume, 1992), p. 201.

2. "Religion Is Gaining Ground, but Morality Is Losing Ground," *Emerging Trends* 23, no. 7 (September 2001), pp. 1, 2.

3. It is also possible to interpret the second person singular as a collective addressing the nation of Israel as a corporate person. But even if the entire nation is in view, the effect of the singular is to personalize the Law.

4. The dilemma is posed in *Euthyphro*, where Plato has Socrates ask, "Do the gods love an act because it is pious, or is it pious because the gods love it?" See Samuel Enoch Stumpf, *Socrates to Sartre: A History of Philosophy*, 3rd ed. (New York: McGraw-Hill, 1982), p. 38.

5. Arthur W. Pink, *The Ten Commandments* (Swengel, PA: Reiner, 1961), p. 5.

6. Peter Enns, *Exodus*, NIV Application Commentary (Grand Rapids: Zondervan, 2000), p. 371.

7. Ted Koppel, quoted in Cal Thomas, *Los Angeles Times* (1994).

8. Ernest C. Reisinger, *The Law and the Gospel* (Phillipsburg, NJ: P&R, 1997), p. 54.

9. Over against covenant theology, classic dispensational theology believes in the future restoration of Israel as a nation under God, complete with the rebuilding of the temple and the reestablishment of the Old Testament sacrificial system.

10. John Calvin, *Institutes of the Christian Religion,* trans. Ford Lewis Battles, 2 vols., Library of Christian Classics, 20–21 (Philadelphia: Westminster, 1960), 4.20.14.

11. John Calvin, *John Calvin's Sermons on the Ten Commandments*, ed. and trans. Benjamin W. Farley (Grand Rapids: Baker, 1980), p. 24.

12. Reisinger, *The Law and the Gospel*, p. 69.

## Chapter Forty-Seven: A Multiuse Item

1. Jochem Douma, *The Ten Commandments: Manual for the Christian Life*, trans. Nelson D. Kloosterman (Phillipsburg, NJ: P&R, 1996), p. 4.

2. Martin Luther, as recounted in Michael S. Horton, *The Law of Perfect Freedom* (Chicago: Moody, 1993), p. 263.

3. Thomas Watson, *The Ten Commandments* (1890; repr. Edinburgh: Banner of Truth, 1965), p. 14.

4. J. C. Ryle, *Holiness* (1879; repr. Durham, UK: Evangelical, 1979), p. 26.

5. John Calvin, *Institutes of the Christian* Religion, quoted in R. C. Sproul, *The Soul's Quest for God* (Wheaton, IL: Tyndale, 1992), pp. 111, 112.

6. *Stone v. Graham*, quoted by Ronald B. Flowers, *Liberty* (July/August 2000): p. 4.

7. John Calvin, *Institutes of the Christian* Religion, trans. Ford Lewis Battles, 2 vols., Library of Christian Classics, 20–21 (Philadelphia: Westminster, 1960), 2.7.6.

8. Augustine, quoted in Calvin, *Institutes*, 2.7.9.

9. Martin Luther, *Lectures on Galatians, 1535*, trans. and ed. Jaroslav Pelikan, Luther's Works, vol. 26 (St. Louis: Concordia, 1963), p. 327.

10. John Calvin, quoted in Ernest C. Reisinger, *The Law and the Gospel* (Phillipsburg, NJ: P&R, 1997), p. 28.

11. Charles Spurgeon, *Parables and Miracles*, vol. 3 (Grand Rapids: Baker, 1993), p. 413.

12. Baloo, *National Review* (October 11, 1999): p. 51.

13. Luther, *Lectures on Galatians*, vol. 26, p. 309.

14. Donald Grey Barnhouse, *Exposition of Bible Doctrines, Taking the Epistle to the Romans as a Point of Departure; Vol. II: God's Wrath, Romans 2:1–3:20* (Grand Rapids: Eerdmans, 1953), pp. 275, 276.

15. Archibald Alexander, quoted in David B. Calhoun, *Princeton Seminary, Vol. 1: Faith and Learning, 1812–1868* (Edinburgh: Banner of Truth, 1994), p. 276.

## Chapter Forty-Eight: Interpreting God's Law

1. Baloo, *National Review* (August 28, 2000): p. 58.

2. John Calvin, *Institutes of the Christian Religion*, trans. Ford Lewis Battles, 2 vols., Library of Christian Classics, 20–21 (Philadelphia: Westminster, 1960), 2.8.7.

3. Francis Turretin, *Institutes of Elenctic Theology*, trans. George Musgrave Giger, ed. James T. Dennison, Jr., 3 vols. (Phillipsburg, NJ: P&R, 1992–1997), 11.3.9.

4. Thomas Watson, *The Ten Commandments* (1890; repr. Edinburgh: Banner of Truth, 1965), p. 45.

5. Umberto Cassuto, *A Commentary on the Book of Exodus*, trans. Israel Abrahams (Jerusalem: Magnes, 1967), p. 240.

6. Quoted in Jochem Douma, *The Ten Commandments: Manual for the Christian Life*, trans. Nelson D. Kloosterman (Phillipsburg, NJ: P&R, 1996), p. 352.

7. Turretin, *Institutes of Elenctic Theology*, 11.6.3.

8. Ernest C. Reisinger, *The Law and the Gospel* (Phillipsburg, NJ: P&R, 1997), pp. 74, 75.

9. Watson, *The Ten Commandments*, pp. 46, 47.

10. See Reisinger, *The Law and the Gospel*, pp. 73, 74.

11. J. Gresham Machen, *What Is Faith?* (New York: Macmillan, 1925), p. 152.

## Chapter Forty-Nine: The First Commandment

1. Jochem Douma, *The Ten Commandments: Manual for the Christian Life*, trans. Nelson D. Kloosterman (Phillipsburg, NJ: P&R, 1996), p. 16.

2. Godfrey Ashby, *Go Out and Meet God: A Commentary on the Book of Exodus*, International Theological Commentary (Grand Rapids: Eerdmans, 1998), p. 88.

3. John Calvin, *Institutes of the Christian Religion,* trans. Ford Lewis Battles, 2 vols., Library of Christian Classics, 20–21 (Philadelphia: Westminster, 1960), 2.8.16.

4. Martin Luther, quoted in Maxie D. Dunnam, *Exodus*, The Communicator's Commentary (Waco, TX: Word, 1987), p. 253.

5. Thomas Watson, *The Ten Commandments* (1890; repr. Edinburgh: Banner of Truth, 1965), p. 55.

6. Matthew Henry, *Commentary on the Whole Bible*, vol. 1 (New York: Revell, n.d.), n.p.

7. Robert Bellah et al., *Habits of the Heart* (New York: Harper & Row, 1985), p. 221.

8. Oscar Wilde, quoted in Michael S. Horton, *The Law of Perfect Freedom* (Chicago: Moody, 1993), p. 56.

## Chapter Fifty: The Second Commandment

1. Rob Schenck, *The Ten Words That Will Change a Nation: The Ten Commandments* (Tulsa, OK: Albury, 1999), p. 32.

2. Christopher J. H. Wright, *Deuteronomy*, New International Biblical Commentary (Peabody, MA: Hendrickson, 1996), pp. 71, 72.

3. Quoted in John R. W. Stott, *The Message of Acts*, The Bible Speaks Today (Leicester, UK: Inter-Varsity, 1990), p. 277.

4. E. M. Blaiklock, *The Acts of the Apostles: An Historical Commentary*, Tyndale New Testament Commentary (Grand Rapids: Eerdmans, 1959), p. 137.

5. John Calvin, *Institutes of the Christian Religion*, trans. Ford Lewis Battles, 2 vols., Library of Christian Classics, 20–21 (Philadelphia: Westminster, 1960), 1.11.8.

6. Nahum M. Sarna, *The JPS Commentary on Exodus* (Philadelphia: Jewish Publication Society, 1991), p. 110.

7. Neil Postman, *Amusing Ourselves to Death: Public Discourse in the Age of Show Business* (New York: Penguin, 1985), p. 9.

8. Walter Brueggemann, *Theology of the Old Testament: Testimony, Dispute, Advocacy* (Philadelphia: Fortress, 1997), pp. 184, 185.

9. Michael S. Horton, *The Law of Perfect Freedom* (Chicago: Moody, 1993), p. 54.

10. John Calvin, *The Acts of the Apostles*, trans. W. F. G. McDonald and John W. Fraser, Calvin's New Testament Commentaries, eds. David W. Torrance and Thomas F. Torrance, vol. 2 (Grand Rapids: Eerdmans, 1973), pp. 121, 122.

11. Wright, *Deuteronomy*, p. 71.

## Chapter Fifty-One: The Third Commandment

1. Göran Larsson, *Bound for Freedom: The Book of Exodus in Jewish and Christian Traditions* (Peabody, MA: Hendrickson, 1999), p. 145.

2. Brevard S. Childs, *The Book of Exodus: A Critical, Theological Commentary* (Louisville: Westminster, 1974), p. 410.

3. Jochem Douma, *The Ten Commandments: Manual for the Christian Life*, trans. Nelson D. Kloosterman (Phillipsburg, NJ: P&R, 1996), pp. 74, 75.

4. Thomas Watson, *The Ten Commandments* (1890; repr. Edinburgh: Banner of Truth, 1965), p. 91.

5. Gary North, *Chronicles: A Magazine of American Culture* (December 1992): p. 15.

6. John Calvin, *Institutes of the Christian Religion*, trans. Ford Lewis Battles, 2 vols., Library of Christian Classics, 20–21 (Philadelphia: Westminster, 1960), 2.8.22.

7. Martin Luther, *The Small Catechism* (1529), in *The Book of Concord: The Confessions of the Evangelical Lutheran Church*, eds. Robert Kolb and Timothy J. Wengert, trans. Charles Arand, et al. (Minneapolis: Fortress, 2000), pp. 345–75 (p. 352).

8. Rob Schenck, *The Ten Words That Will Change a Nation: The Ten Commandments* (Tulsa, OK: Albury, 1999), pp. 53, 54.

9. Stephen L. Carter, *God's Name in Vain: The Wrongs and Rights of Religion and Politics* (New York: Basic, 2000), pp. 12, 13.

10. David F. Wells, *God in the Wasteland: The Reality of Truth in a World of Fading Dreams* (Grand Rapids: Eerdmans, 1994), p. 88.

11. Donald W. McCullough, *The Trivialization of God: The Dangerous Illusion of a Manageable Deity* (Colorado Springs: NavPress, 1995).

12. William Shakespeare, *Hamlet, Prince of Denmark*, Act 3, Scene 4, Lines 100–1.

## Chapter Fifty-Two: The Fourth Commandment

1. Bill Gates, quoted by Walter Isaacson, "In Search of the Real Bill Gates," *Time* (January 13, 1997): p. 7.

2. Lance Morrow, quoted in Mark E. Dever, "The Call to Work and Worship," *Regeneration Quarterly* (Spring 1996): p. 5.

3. Thomas Watson, *The Ten Commandments* (1890; repr. Edinburgh: Banner of Truth, 1965), p. 93.

4. Umberto Cassuto, *A Commentary on the Book of Exodus*, trans. Israel Abrahams (Jerusalem: Magnes, 1967), p. 244.

5. See James T. Dennison Jr., *The Market Day of the Soul: The Puritan Doctrine of the Sabbath in England, 1532–1700* (New York: University Press of America, 1983).

6. Watson, *The Ten Commandments*, p. 97.

7. Ibid., p. 95.

8. Ibid., p. 99.

9. Leland Ryken, *Redeeming the Time: A Christian Approach to Work and Leisure* (Grand Rapids: Baker, 1995), p. 178.

10. Martin Luther, "Treatise on Good Works," trans. W. A. Lambert, in *Luther's Works*, ed. Helmut T. Lehmann, vol. 44 (Philadelphia: Fortress, 1966), p. 72.

11. Ignatius, *Letter to the Magnesians*, quoted in Jochem Douma, *The Ten Commandments: Manual for the Christian Life*, trans. Nelson D. Kloosterman (Phillipsburg, NJ: P&R, 1996), p. 139.

12. Benjamin Breckinridge Warfield, *Selected Shorter Writings* (Phillipsburg, NJ: P&R, 1970), p. 319.

13. Eugene Peterson, "The Pastor's Sabbath," *Leadership* (Spring 1985): pp. 55, 56.

14. Watson, *The Ten Commandments*, p. 101.

15. David C. Searle, *And Then There Were Nine* (Fearn, Ross-Shire, UK: Christian Focus, 2000), p. 67.

16. The best book on this subject is Leland Ryken's *Redeeming the Time*, previously cited.

17. See Dennison, *The Market Day of the Soul*, p. 94.

18. Robert G. Rayburn, "Should Christians Observe the Sabbath?" quoted in a sermon by George W. Robertson at Covenant Presbyterian Church in St. Louis, Missouri.

## Chapter Fifty-Three: The Fifth Commandment

1. Annie Gottlieb, *Do You Believe in Magic?* (New York: Time, 1987), pp. 234, 235.

2. John Calvin, *Institutes of the Christian Religion,* trans. Ford Lewis Battles, 2 vols., Library of Christian Classics, 20–21 (Philadelphia: Westminster, 1960), 2.8.11.

3. John I. Durham, *Exodus*, Word Biblical Commentary (Waco, TX: Word, 1987), p. 290.

4. Augustine, quoted in *Exodus, Leviticus, Numbers, Deuteronomy*, ed. Joseph T. Lienhard, Ancient Christian Commentary on Scripture, vol. 3 (Downers Grove, IL: InterVarsity, 2001), p. 106.

5. Rob Schenck, *The Ten Words That Will Change a Nation: The Ten Commandments* (Tulsa, OK: Albury, 1999), p. 88.

6. Calvin, *Institutes*, 2.8.35.

7. Thomas Watson, *The Ten Commandments* (1890; repr. Edinburgh: Banner of Truth, 1965), p. 130.

8. Ecclesiasticus 3:12, 13.

9. Michael S. Horton, *The Law of Perfect Freedom* (Chicago: Moody, 1993), p. 134.

10. Socrates, quoted in Fran Sciacca, *Generation at Risk*, rev. ed. (Chicago: Moody, 1991), p. 25.

## Chapter Fifty-Four: The Sixth Commandment

1. Dick Wright, *Christianity Today* (March 11, 2002): p. 15.

2. Jochem Douma, *The Ten Commandments: Manual for the Christian Life*, trans. Nelson D. Kloosterman (Phillipsburg, NJ: P&R, 1996), p. 216.

3. Stephen L. Carter, *God's Name in Vain: The Wrongs and Rights of Religion and Politics* (New York: Basic, 2000), p. 126.

4. *Christianity Today* (February 4, 2002), p. 80.

5. Thomas Watson, *The Ten Commandments* (1890; repr. Edinburgh: Banner of Truth, 1965), p. 141.

6. John Calvin, quoted in Michael S. Horton, *The Law of Perfect Freedom* (Chicago: Moody, 1993), p. 175.

7. J. L. Koole, *De Tien Geboden*, quoted in Douma, *The Ten Commandments: Manual for the Christian Life*, p. 213.

8. Vincent Canby, *New York Times*, quoted in Michael Medved, *Hollywood vs. America* (New York: HarperCollins, 1992): p. 187.

9. Medved, *Hollywood vs. America*, pp. 188–90.

10. See Parents Television Council, *Special Report: What a Difference a Decade Makes* (March 30, 2000).

11. Dave Grossman, "Trained to Kill," *Christianity Today* (August 19, 1998): pp. 2, 3.

12. Wesley J. Smith, *Culture of Death: The Assault on Medical Ethics in America*, reviewed by Richard M. Doerflinger in *First Things*, no. 115 (August/September 2001): pp. 68–72 (p. 68).

13. Malcolm Potts, quoted in W. Wilson Benton's sermon "Life Is for Living" (April 18, 1993).

14. John Calvin, *Commentaries on the Four Last Books of Moses*, Calvin's Commentaries (Edinburgh; repr. Grand Rapids: Baker, 1999), pp. 41, 42.

15. John Calvin, *Institutes of the Christian Religion,* trans. Ford Lewis Battles, 2 vols., Library of Christian Classics, 20–21 (Philadelphia: Westminster, 1960), 2.8.39.

16. Martin Luther, *Large Catechism*, quoted in Horton, *The Law of Perfect Freedom*, pp. 157, 158.

17. John MacArthur Jr., *The MacArthur New Testament Commentary, Matthew 1–7* (Chicago: Moody, 1985), p. 293.

18. Calvin, *Institutes*, 2.8.39.

## Chapter Fifty-Five: The Seventh Commandment

1. See Leland Ryken, *Worldly Saints: The Puritans as They Really Were* (Grand Rapids: Zondervan, 1986), pp. 40, 41.

2. Ibid., p. 53.

3. Douglas Wilson, *Fidelity: What It Means to Be a One-Woman Man* (Moscow, ID: Canon, 1999), p. 53.

4. C. S. Lewis, *Mere Christianity* (New York: Macmillan, 1952), pp. 95, 96.

5. David Murray, testimony before the Senate Subcommittee on Oversight of Government Management, Restructuring, and the District of Columbia (May 8, 1997), p. 2.

6. Terry Fisher, quoted in Michael Medved, *Hollywood vs. America* (New York: HarperCollins, 1992), pp. 111, 112.

7. Martin Luther, *The Large Catechism*, trans. Robert H. Fischer (Philadelphia: Fortress, 1959), p. 36.

8. Wendell Berry, interviewed in *Modern Reformation* (November/December 2001): p. 40.

9. R. Kent Hughes, "Set Apart to Save: Sexual Conduct," (sermon, College Church, Wheaton, IL, December 2, 2001), p. 5.

10. Greg Gutfield, "The Sex Drive," *Men's Health* (October 1999), quoted in *Leadership* (Summer 2000): p. 69.

11. Anonymous, quoted in Hughes, "Set Apart to Save: Sexual Conduct," p. 5.

12. Thomas Watson, *The Ten Commandments* (1890; repr. Edinburgh: Banner of Truth, 1965), p. 160.

13. Martyn Lloyd-Jones, *Studies in the Sermon on the Mount* (Grand Rapids: Eerdmans, 1984), p. 261.

## Chapter Fifty-Six: The Eighth Commandment

1. T. Cecil Myers, *Thunder on the Mountain* (Nashville: Abingdon, 1965), pp. 119, 120, quoted in Maxie D. Dunnam, *Exodus*, The Communicator's Commentary (Waco, TX: Word, 1987), p. 251.

2. Rob Schenck, *The Ten Words That Will Change a Nation: The Ten Commandments* (Tulsa, OK: Albury, 1999), p. 155.

3. George W. Robertson, "The Eighth Commandment," *Leader to Leader* (July/August 1997): p. 3.

4. Martin Luther, quoted in Michael S. Horton, *The Law of Perfect Freedom* (Chicago: Moody, 1993), p. 206.

5. John Calvin, quoted in Peter Lewis, *The Message of the Living God*, The Bible Speaks Today (Downers Grove, IL: InterVarsity, 2000): p. 158.

6. John Calvin, *Institutes of the Christian* Religion, trans. Ford Lewis Battles, 2 vols., Library of Christian Classics, 20–21 (Philadelphia: Westminster, 1960), 2.8.45.

7. Martin Luther, *The Large Catechism* (Philadelphia: Fortress, 1959), p. 39.

8. See Scott Adams, *Dilbert and the Way of the Weasel* (New York: HarperBusiness, 2002).

9. George Barna, *The Barna Report, 1992–93* (Ventura, CA: Regal, 1992), p. 117.

10. Martin Luther, quoted in Horton, *The Law of Perfect Freedom*, 206.

11. Martin Luther, quoted in Dunnam, *Exodus*, p. 265.

12. John Calvin, *Commentary on Genesis*, quoted in Horton, *The Law of Perfect Freedom*, p. 204.

13. *Issues and Answers: Gambling*, The Christian Life Commission of the Southern Baptist Convention (November 1993).

14. Jerry Bridges, *The Discipline of Grace: God's Role and Our Role in the Pursuit of Holiness* (Colorado Springs: NavPress, 1994), p. 88.

15. R. Kent Hughes, "Set Apart to Save: Materialism," (sermon, College Church, Wheaton, IL, November 4, 2001).

16. A. W. Tozer, *Born after Midnight* (Harrisburg, PA: Christian, 1959), p. 107.

17. John Chrysostom, *On Wealth and Poverty*, trans. Catherine Roth (New York: St. Vladimir's Seminary, 1984), pp. 49–55.

18. Martin Luther, *Luther's Works: Lectures on Galatians, 1535, Chapters 1–4*, ed. Jaroslav Pelikan, vol. 26 (Saint Louis: Concordia, 1963), p. 277.

19. Ibid., vol. 26, pp. 277, 278.

### Chapter Fifty-Seven: The Ninth Commandment

1. O'Leary's tragic downfall is documented in Gary Smith, "Lying in Wait," *Sports Illustrated* (April 8, 2002): pp. 70–87.

2. The survey, conducted by Colorado's Avert Inc., is mentioned by Jeffrey Kluger in "Pumping Up Your Past," *Time* magazine (June 10, 2002).

3. Paul Gray, quoted in Michael S. Horton, *The Law of Perfect Freedom* (Chicago: Moody, 1993), pp. 225, 226.

4. Jochem Douma, *The Ten Commandments: Manual for the Christian Life*, trans. Nelson D. Kloosterman (Phillipsburg, NJ: P&R, 1996), pp. 315, 316.

5. Ibid., pp. 316, 317.

6. This form of the well-known saying comes from Göran Larsson, *Bound for Freedom: The Book of Exodus in Jewish and Christian Traditions* (Peabody, MA: Hendrickson, 1999), p. 153.

7. Thomas Watson, *The Ten Commandments* (1890; repr. Edinburgh: Banner of Truth, 1965), pp. 169, 170.

8. George Orwell, as seen on a Philadelphia bumper sticker.

9. Paul Gray, quoted in Horton, *The Law of Perfect Freedom*, p. 225.

10. "Churched Youth Survey," Barna Research Group (1994).

11. Charles Colson, "Post-Truth Society," *Christianity Today* (March 11, 2002): p. 112.

12. John Calvin, *Institutes of the Christian* Religion, trans. Ford Lewis Battles, 2 vols., Library of Christian Classics, 20–21 (Philadelphia: Westminster, 1960), 2.8.47.

13. William Barclay, in Maxie D. Dunnam, *Exodus*, The Communicator's Commentary (Waco, TX: Word, 1987), p. 266.

### Chapter Fifty-Eight: The Tenth Commandment

1. Mark Buchanan, "Trapped in the Cult of the Next Thing," *Christianity Today* (September 6, 1999): p. 64.

2. John L. Mackay, *Exodus* (Fern, Ross-shire, UK: Christian Focus, 2001, p. 354.

3. Thomas Watson, *The Ten Commandments* (1890; repr. Edinburgh: Banner of Truth, 1965), p. 174.

4. John D. Currid, *A Study Commentary on Exodus*, vol. 2 (Auburn, MA: Evangelical USA, 2000), p. 49.

5. Anonymous, quoted in Maxie D. Dunnam, *Exodus*, The Communicator's Commentary (Waco, TX: Word, 1987), p. 267.

6. Watson, *The Ten Commandments*, p. 178.

7. Recounted in Michael S. Horton, *The Law of Perfect Freedom* (Chicago: Moody, 1993), p. 167.

8. Martin Luther, *Large Catechism*, quoted in ibid., p. 241.

9. Francis A. Schaeffer, *True Spirituality* (Wheaton, IL: Tyndale, 1971), p. 8.

10. F. B. Meyer, *Elijah* (Fort Washington, PA: Christian Literature Crusade, 1992), p. 135.

11. Jeremiah Burroughs, *The Rare Jewel of Christian Contentment* (1648; repr. Edinburgh: Banner of Truth, 1964), p. 18.

12. Horton, *The Law of Perfect Freedom*, p. 247.

### Chapter Fifty-Nine: The End of the Law

1. John Bunyan, *The Pilgrim's Progress* (New York: New American Library, 1964), pp. 26, 27.

2. Umberto Cassuto, *A Commentary on the Book of Exodus*, trans. Israel Abrahams (Jerusalem: Magnes, 1967), p. 252.

3. Charles H. Spurgeon, "The Mediator—the Interpreter, " *The Metropolitan Tabernacle Pulpit* 35, no. 2097 (1890; repr. London: Banner of Truth, 1970), p. 409.

4. Ibid., p. 409.

5. David Brainerd, quoted in Ernest C. Reisinger, *The Law and the Gospel* (Phillipsburg, NJ: P&R, 1997), p. 78.

6. John Murray, *Principles of Conduct: Aspects of Biblical Ethics* (Grand Rapids: Eerdmans, 1957), pp. 185, 186.

7. Martin Luther, *Luther's Works: Lectures on Galatians, 1535, Chapters 1–4*, ed. Jaroslav Pelikan, vol. 26 (Saint Louis: Concordia, 1963), p. 130.

8. Thomas Watson, *The Ten Commandments* (1890; repr. Edinburgh: Banner of Truth, 1965), p. 44.

9. Samuel Bolton, *The True Bounds of Christian Freedom* (1645; repr. London: Banner of Truth, 1964), pp. 71, 72.

10. Reisinger, *The Law and the Gospel*, p. 36.

11. Thomas Ascol, in the "Foreword" to ibid., p. xi.

## Chapter Sixty: The Altar of God

1. Rabbi David Wolpe, quoted in Kristin E. Holmes, "The Exodus and Historical Doubts," *The Philadelphia Inquirer* (March 24, 2002).

2. *National Review* (July 17, 2000): p. 58.

3. John Seabrook, *Nobrow: The Culture of Marketing—The Marketing of Culture* (New York: Alfred A. Knopf, 2000), p. 5.

4. John L. Mackay, *Exodus* (Fearn, Ross-Shire, UK: Mentor, 2001), p. 362.

5. Tremper Longman III, *Immanuel in Our Place: Seeing Christ in Israel's Worship*, The Gospel According to the Old Testament (Phillipsburg, NJ: P&R, 2001), pp. 80, 81.

6. Ibid., p. 90.

7. Martin Luther, *Luther's Works: Lectures on Galatians, 1535, Chapters 1–4*, ed. Jaroslav Pelikan, vol. 26 (Saint Louis: Concordia, 1963), p. 277.

## Chapter Sixty-One: Bound for Freedom

1. Godfrey Ashby, *Go Out and Meet God: A Commentary on the Book of Exodus*, International Theological Commentary (Grand Rapids: Eerdmans, 1998), p. 98.

2. John D. Currid, *A Study Commentary on Exodus*, vol. 2 (Auburn, MA: Evangelical USA, 2000), p. 57.

3. This principle is explained in James B. Jordan, *The Law of the Covenant: An Exposition of Exodus 21–23* (Tyler, TX: Institute for Christian Economics, 1984), pp. 87–90.

4. Brevard S. Childs, *The Book of Exodus: A Critical, Theological Commentary* (Louisville: Westminster, 1974), p. 468.

5. This is the interpretation offered by Jordan, *The Law of the Covenant*, p. 77.

6. John L. Mackay, *Exodus* (Fearn, Ross-Shire, UK: Mentor, 2001), p. 359.

7. Ambrose, "Letter 1(7).14," in *Exodus, Leviticus, Numbers, Deuteronomy*, ed. Joseph T. Lienhard, Ancient Christian Commentary on Scripture, vol. 3 (Downers Grove, IL: InterVarsity, 2001), p. 110.

8. The story is told by Leith Anderson in *A Church for the 21st Century* (Minneapolis: Bethany House, 1992), p. 216.

## Chapter Sixty-Two: An Eye for an Eye

1. Göran Larsson, *Bound for Freedom: The Book of Exodus in Jewish and Christian Traditions* (Peabody, MA: Hendrickson, 1999), p. 167.

2. Ibid., p. 165.

## Chapter Sixty-Three: Property Law

1. Alan Greenspan, quoted in *The Gazette* (July 17, 2002): p. A8.

2. Hammurabi's Code, quoted in John D. Currid, *A Study Commentary on Exodus*, vol. 2 (Auburn, MA: Evangelical USA, 2000), p. 91.

3. Nehama Leibowitz, *Studies in Shemot* (Jerusalem: The World Zionist Organization, 1976), pp. 361, 362.

4. R. Kent Hughes, *Luke*, vol. 2, Preaching the Word (Wheaton, IL: Crossway, 1998), p. 222.

5. *Westminster Confession of Faith*, 15.2.

## Chapter Sixty-Four: Good Laws from a Great God

1. Umberto Cassuto, *A Commentary on the Book of Exodus*, trans. Israel Abrahams (Jerusalem: Magnes, 1967), p. 288.

2. Göran Larsson, *Bound for Freedom: The Book of Exodus in Jewish and Christian Traditions* (Peabody, MA: Hendrickson, 1999), p. 171.

3. Roland de Vaux, *Ancient Israel*, vol. 1 (New York: McGraw Hill, 1965), p. 27.

4. This view is defended by James Jordan in *The Law of the Covenant: An Exposition of Exodus 21–23* (Tyler, TX: Institute for Christian Economics, 1984), pp. 146–49.

5. John J. Davis, *Moses and the Gods of Egypt* (Grand Rapids: Baker, 1971), p. 231.

6. John L. Mackay, *Exodus* (Fearn, Ross-Shire, UK: Mentor, 2001), p. 391.

7. Peter Enns, *Exodus*, NIV Application Commentary (Grand Rapids: Zondervan, 2000), p. 451.

8. Anna Nicole Smith, quoted in *Time* magazine (August 19, 2002): n.p.

9. John Ed Bradley, "The Best Years of His Life," *Sports Illustrated* (August 12, 2002): pp. 136–48 (p. 138).

10. R. Alan Cole, *Exodus: An Introduction and Commentary*, Tyndale Old Testament Commentaries (Leicester, UK: Inter-Varsity, 1973), p. 177.

11. These statistics come from Ken Rudy, *Entertaining Angels: A Guide to Loving the Foreigner* (2001), pp. 1, 2.

12. Fred Bailey, *International Student Ministries Guide* (InterVarsity, 1984), quoted in Rudy, *Entertaining Angels: A Guide to Loving the Foreigner*, pp. 2, 3.

13. Mackay, *Exodus*, p. 394.

## Chapter Sixty-Five: The People's Court

1. Gary Smith, "The Ball (An American Story)," *Sports Illustrated* (July 29, 2002): pp. 62–79.

2. John L. Mackay, *Exodus* (Fearn, Ross-Shire, UK: Mentor, 2001), p. 398.

3. Anonymous, quoted in John D. Currid, *A Study Commentary on Exodus*, vol. 2 (Auburn, MA: Evangelical USA, 2000), p. 116.

4. Clement of Alexandria, *Stromateis*, 2.18.90, in *Exodus, Leviticus, Numbers, Deuteronomy*, ed. Joseph T. Lienhard, Ancient Christian Commentary on Scripture, vol. 3 (Downers Grove, IL: InterVarsity, 2001), pp. 117, 118.

5. Wendell Berry, *A Timbered Choir: The Sabbath Poems, 1979–1997* (New York: Counterpoint, 1999).

6. John I. Durham, *Exodus*, Word Biblical Commentary (Waco, TX: Word, 1987), p. 331.

7. Tom Neven, "A Doer of the Word," *Focus on the Family* (September 2000): pp. 1–4.

## Chapter Sixty-Six: Three Pilgrim Feasts

1. Geoffrey Chaucer, *The Canterbury Tales*, trans. Nevill Coghill (London: Cresset, 1992), p. 17.

2. Quoted by Göran Larsson in *Bound for Freedom: The Book of Exodus in Jewish and Christian Traditions* (Peabody, MA: Hendrickson, 1999), p. 188.

3. James B. Jordan, *The Law of the Covenant: An Exposition of Exodus 21–23* (Tyler, TX: Institute for Christian Economics, 1984), p. 186.

4. Tremper Longman III, *Immanuel in Our Place: Seeing Christ in Israel's Worship*, The Gospel According to the Old Testament (Phillipsburg, NJ: P&R, 2001), pp. 197, 198.

5. Godfrey Ashby, *Go Out and Meet God: A Commentary on the Book of Exodus*, International Theological Commentary (Grand Rapids: Eerdmans, 1998), p. 113.

6. Larsson, *Bound for Freedom*, p. 181.

7. John J. Davis, *Moses and the Gods of Egypt* (Grand Rapids: Baker, 1971), p. 236.

8. Betty Stam, as quoted by Elisabeth Elliott in "Glorifying God in Mission," *Evangelicals Now* (November 1998): p. 9.

## Chapter Sixty-Seven: Guardian Angel

1. Umberto Cassuto, *A Commentary on the Book of Exodus*, trans. Israel Abrahams (Jerusalem: Magnes, 1967), p. 306.

2. Tertullian, "Answer to the Jews," 9.23, in *Exodus, Leviticus, Numbers, Deuteronomy*, ed. Joseph T. Lienhard, Ancient Christian Commentary on Scripture, vol. 3 (Downers Grove, IL: InterVarsity, 2001), p. 119.

3. Augustine, "Against Faustus, a Manichaean," 16.19, in *Exodus, Leviticus, Numbers, Deuteronomy*, ed. Joseph T. Lienhard, vol. 3, p. 119.

4. Nahum Sarna, *The JPS Torah Commentary: Exodus* (Philadelphia: Jewish Publication Society, 1991), p. 148.

5. John L. Mackay, *Exodus* (Fearn, Ross-Shire, UK: Mentor, 2001), p. 408.

6. Ibid., pp. 407, 408.

7. John J. Davis, *Moses and the Gods of Egypt* (Grand Rapids: Baker, 1971), p. 238.

8. Ibid., p. 238.

9. Godfrey Ashby, *Go Out and Meet God: A Commentary on the Book of Exodus*, International Theological Commentary (Grand Rapids: Eerdmans, 1998), p. 115.

10. Mackay, *Exodus*, p. 413.

## Chapter Sixty-Eight: The Blood of the Covenant

1. John L. Mackay, *Exodus* (Fearn, Ross-Shire, UK: Mentor, 2001), p. 417.

2. W. R. Smith, *The Religion of the Semites*, rev. ed. (Edinburgh: 1894), pp. 312–18.

3. Mackay, *Exodus*, p. 420.

4. O. Palmer Robertson, *The Christ of the Covenants* (Grand Rapids: Baker, 1980), p. 135.

5. John D. Currid, *A Study Commentary on Exodus*, vol. 2 (Auburn, MA: Evangelical USA, 2000), p. 137.

6. Robertson, *The Christ of the Covenants*, p. 4.

7. Peter Enns, *Exodus*, NIV Application Commentary (Grand Rapids: Zondervan, 2000), p. 490.

8. J. A. Motyer, *Old Testament Covenant Theology* (lectures, Theological Students Fellowship, London, 1973), p. 19.

9. Charles Haddon Spurgeon, "The Blood of the Everlasting Covenant," in *The New Park Street Pulpit*, vol. 5 (1859; repr. Pasadena, TX: Pilgrim, 1975), pp. 419, 420.

## Chapter Sixty-Nine: They Saw God

1. John L. Mackay, *Exodus* (Fearn, Ross-Shire, UK: Mentor, 2001), p. 420.

2. These examples are quoted in ibid., 421.

3. Maimonides, quoted in Brevard S. Childs, *The Book of Exodus: A Critical, Theological Commentary* (Louisville: Westminster, 1974), p. 506.

4. John D. Currid, *A Study Commentary on Exodus*, vol. 2 (Auburn, MA: Evangelical USA, 2000), p. 139.

5. John I. Durham, *Exodus*, Word Biblical Commentary (Waco, TX: Word, 1987), p. 344.

6. C. F. Keil and F. Delitzsch, *The Pentateuch*, Commentary on the Old Testament, vol. 2 (Grand Rapids: Eerdmans), p. 159.

7. John Owen, *Meditations and Discourses Concerning the Glory of Christ* (London, 1691), p. 5.

8. Currid, *A Study Commentary on Exodus*, vol. 2, p. 140

9. Meredith G. Kline, *Treaty of the Great King* (Grand Rapids: Eerdmans, 1963), p. 19.

10. C. S. Lewis, *The Last Battle* (London: Bodley Head, 1956), pp. 173–77.

## Chapter Seventy: Freewill Offering

1. Randy Alcorn, *Money, Possessions and Eternity* (Wheaton, IL: Tyndale, 1989), pp. 399, 400.

2. William Walsham How, "We Give Thee but Thine Own," 1864.

3. John D. Currid, *A Study Commentary on Exodus*, vol. 2 (Auburn, MA: Evangelical USA, 2000), p. 150.

4. R. Alan Cole, *Exodus: An Introduction and Commentary*, Tyndale Old Testament Commentaries (Leicester, UK: Inter-Varsity, 1973), p. 189.

5. Currid, *A Study Commentary on Exodus*, vol. 2, p. 150.

6. Umberto Cassuto, *A Commentary on the Book of Exodus*, trans. Israel Abrahams (Jerusalem: Magnes, 1967), p. 325.

7. Peter Enns, *Exodus*, NIV Application Commentary (Grand Rapids: Zondervan, 2000), p. 509.

8. Petrus Dathenus, *The Pearl of Christian Comfort*, trans. Arie W. Blok, Reformed Experiential Thought, vol. 3 (Grand Rapids: Reformation Heritage, 1997), p. 31.

9. John L. Mackay, *Exodus* (Fearn, Ross-Shire, UK: Mentor, 2001), p. 430.

10. "The Baptist Temple: Some History," as described in the GeoCities website.

## Chapter Seventy-One: The Ark of the Covenant

1. M. R. DeHaan, *The Tabernacle* (Grand Rapids: Zondervan, 1955), p. 13.

2. The comment goes at least as far back as the Dutch commentator Herman Witsius, who is quoted in Brevard S. Childs, *The Book of Exodus: A Critical, Theological Commentary* (Louisville: Westminster, 1974), p. 547.

3. Tremper Longman III, *Immanuel in Our Place: Seeing Christ in Israel's Worship*, The Gospel According to the Old Testament (Phillipsburg, NJ: P&R, 2001), p. 25.

4. John L. Mackay, *Exodus* (Fearn, Ross-Shire, UK: Mentor, 2001), p. 442.

5. Ibid., p. 445.

6. Umberto Cassuto, *A Commentary on the Book of Exodus*, trans. Israel Abrahams (Jerusalem: Magnes, 1967), p. 331.

7. John D. Currid, *A Study Commentary on Exodus*, vol. 2 (Auburn, MA: Evangelical USA, 2000), p. 154.

8. Mackay, *Exodus*, p. 448.

9. Ibid., p. 449.

## Chapter Seventy-Two: The Bread of the Presence

1. Clericus, cited in Brevard S. Childs, *The Book of Exodus: A Critical, Theological Commentary* (Louisville: Westminster, 1974), pp. 538, 539.

2. Philo, quoted in John L. Mackay, *Exodus* (Fearn, Ross-Shire, UK: Mentor, 2001), p. 431.

3. Origen, as summarized in Childs, *The Book of Exodus: A Critical, Theological Commentary*, p. 548.

4. See Arthur W. Pink, *Gleanings in Exodus* (Chicago: Moody, 1981), pp. 216, 233, 234.

5. Gregory the Great, "Pastoral Care," in *Exodus, Leviticus, Numbers, Deuteronomy*, ed. Joseph T. Lienhard, Ancient Christian Commentary on Scripture, vol. 3 (Downers Grove, IL: InterVarsity, 2001), p. 123.

6. Kevin J. Conner, quoted by Makoto Fujimura, "Form and Content," in Ned Bustard, ed., *It Was Good: Making Art to the Glory of God* (Baltimore: Square Halo, 2000), pp. 49–60 (p. 51).

7. J. F. Cramer, quoted in Childs, *The Book of Exodus: A Critical, Theological Commentary*, p. 548.

8. Umberto Cassuto, *A Commentary on the Book of Exodus*, trans. Israel Abrahams (Jerusalem: Magnes, 1967), p. 320.

9. Mackay comments:

> One general principle that has often been put forward is that if some object or arrangement differed between the Tabernacle and the Temple, then no particular significance ought to be attached to details given regarding it. For instance, in the Temple cedar wood was used in place of the acacia of the Tabernacle. There was therefore no particular symbolic significance in the fact that acacia wood had originally been used. Cedar and acacia were simply the best woods available at the time. (*Exodus*, p. 433)

10. Ibid., p. 450.

11. James Strong, *The Tabernacle of Israel* (1888; repr. Grand Rapids: Kregel, 1987), pp. 63, 64.

12. Cassuto, *A Commentary on the Book of Exodus*, p. 336.

13. John J. Davis, *Moses and the Gods of Egypt: Studies in Exodus*, 2nd ed. (Grand Rapids: Baker, 1986), p. 265.

14. Vern Poythress, *The Shadow of Christ in the Law of Moses* (Phillipsburg, NJ: P&R, 1991), pp. 19, 20.

15. M. R. DeHaan, *The Tabernacle* (Grand Rapids: Zondervan, 1955), pp. 92, 93.

16. Kent and Barbara Hughes, *Common Sense Parenting* (Wheaton, IL: Tyndale, 1995), pp. 15, 16; rev. ed. later reprinted as *Disciplines of a Godly Family*, (Wheaton, IL: Crossway, 2004).

### Chapter Seventy-Three: The Golden Lampstand

1. Umberto Cassuto, *A Commentary on the Book of Exodus*, trans. Israel Abrahams (Jerusalem: Magnes, 1967), p. 343.

2. John I. Durham, *Exodus*, Word Biblical Commentary (Waco, TX: Word, 1987), p. 364.

3. This insight comes from S. Ridout, as quoted in Arthur W. Pink, *Gleanings in Exodus* (Chicago: Moody, 1981), p. 213.

4. Carol Myers, quoted in Peter Enns, *Exodus*, NIV Application Commentary (Grand Rapids: Zondervan, 2000), p. 515.

5. John D. Currid, *A Study Commentary on Exodus*, vol. 2 (Auburn, MA: Evangelical USA, 2000), p. 160.

6. J. Gerald Janzen, *Exodus*, Westminster Bible Companion (Louisville: Westminster/John Knox, 1997), p. 198.

7. Vern Poythress discusses this interpretation in *The Shadow of Christ in the Law of Moses* (Phillipsburg, NJ: P&R, 1991), p. 18.

8. See ibid., p. 16.

9. John L. Mackay, *Exodus* (Fearn, Ross-Shire, UK: Mentor, 2001), p. 456.

10. Charles Wesley, "Hark! the Herald Angels Sing" (1739, 1753).

11. M. R. DeHaan, *The Tabernacle* (Grand Rapids: Zondervan, 1955), p. 103.

12. J. B. Phillips, "The Angels' Point of View," in *New Testament Christianity* (New York: Macmillan, 1956), pp. 15–19.

13. Quoted without attribution in David M. Levy, *The Tabernacle: Shadows of the Messiah* (Bellmawr, NJ: Friends of Israel Gospel Ministry, 1993), p. 47.

## Chapter Seventy-Four: The Tabernacle of God

1. "High Flight," John Gillespie Magee Jr. (September 3, 1941).

2. John J. Davis, *Moses and the Gods of Egypt* (Grand Rapids: Baker, 1971), p. 258.

3. Vern Poythress, *The Shadow of Christ in the Law of Moses* (Phillipsburg, NJ: P&R, 1991), p. 38.

4. John L. Mackay, *Exodus* (Fearn, Ross-Shire, UK: Mentor, 2001), p. 466.

5. David M. Levy, *The Tabernacle: Shadows of the Messiah* (Bellmawr, NJ: Friends of Israel Gospel Ministry, 1993), p. 71.

## Chapter Seventy-Five: The Altar in the Courtyard

1. Vern Poythress, *The Shadow of Christ in the Law of Moses* (Phillipsburg, NJ: P&R, 1991), pp. 11, 12.

2. John D. Currid, *A Study Commentary on Exodus*, vol. 2 (Auburn, MA: Evangelical USA, 2000), p. 180.

3. Poythress, *The Shadow of Christ in the Law of Moses*, p. 16.

4. Umberto Cassuto, *A Commentary on the Book of Exodus*, trans. Israel Abrahams (Jerusalem: Magnes, 1967), p. 362.

5. Paul Kiene, *The Tabernacle of God in the Wilderness of Sinai* (Grand Rapids: Zondervan, 1977), p. 35.

6. M. R. DeHaan, *The Tabernacle* (Grand Rapids: Zondervan, 1955), p. 49.

7. James Strong, *The Tabernacle of Israel* (1888; repr. Grand Rapids: Kregel, 1987), p. 126.

8. Patrick Fairbairn, *The Typology of Scripture*, vol. 2 (Grand Rapids: Zondervan, n.d.), pp. 207, 208.

9. Currid, *A Study Commentary on Exodus*, vol. 2, p. 187.

10. Arthur W. Pink, *Gleanings in Exodus* (Chicago: Moody, 1981), p. 213.

11. Poythress, *The Shadow of Christ in the Law of Moses*, p. 44.

12. Pink, *Gleanings in Exodus*, p. 242.

13. John Owen, quoted in Currid, *A Study Commentary on Exodus*, vol 2, p. 183.

## Chapter Seventy-Six: A Priest before God

1. Flavius Josephus, cited in John J. Davis, *Moses and the Gods of Egypt* (Grand Rapids: Baker, 1971), p. 264.

2. Peter Enns, *Exodus*, NIV Application Commentary (Grand Rapids: Zondervan, 2000), p. 555.

3. Carolyn Custis James, *When Life and Beliefs Collide: How Knowing God Makes a Difference* (Grand Rapids: Zondervan, 2001), p. 75.

4. Göran Larsson, *Bound for Freedom: The Book of Exodus in Jewish and Christian Traditions* (Peabody, MA: Hendrickson, 1999), p. 219.

5. However, on the Day of Atonement the high priest wore white linen; see Leviticus 16:4.

## Chapter Seventy-Seven: Knowing God's Will

1. Göran Larsson, *Bound for Freedom: The Book of Exodus in Jewish and Christian Traditions* (Peabody, MA: Hendrickson, 1999), p. 220.

2. Edward Dennett, quoted in Arthur W. Pink, *Gleanings in Exodus* (Chicago: Moody, 1981), p. 265.

3. For a list of possible interpretations, see John J. Davis, *Moses and the Gods of Egypt* (Grand Rapids: Baker, 1971), pp. 275, 276.

4. John L. Mackay, *Exodus* (Fearn, Ross-Shire, UK: Mentor, 2001), p. 481.

5. Umberto Cassuto, *A Commentary on the Book of Exodus*, trans. Israel Abrahams (Jerusalem: Magnes, 1967), p. 379.

6. Sinclair B. Ferguson, *Discovering God's Will* (Edinburgh: Banner of Truth, 1982), p. 35.

7. Ibid., p. 34.

8. John Newton, *Letters of John Newton* (Edinburgh: Banner of Truth, 1960), pp. 81, 82.

## Chapter Seventy-Eight: Fit for a Priest

1. Donald Smarto, *Pursued: A True Story of Crime, Faith, and Family* (Downers Grove, IL: InterVarsity, 1990), p. 105.

2. Ibid., pp. 105, 106.

3. Ibid., pp. 119, 120.

4. Flavius Josephus, "The Antiquities of the Jews," in *The Works of Josephus*, trans. William Whiston (Peabody, MA: Hendrickson, 1987), *Jewish Antiquities*, 3.7.3 (pp. 157, 158).

5. John L. Mackay writes:

> Although ancient tradition dating back at least to the time of the translation of the Septuagint in the third century B.C. has understood this as referring to a "plate," it is [a] word that ordinarily indicates a flower, and so it may well have been flower shaped, or had a floral decoration. (*Exodus* [Fearn, Ross-Shire, UK: Mentor, 2001], p. 483)

6. *The Letter of Aristeas*, quoted in Göran Larsson, *Bound for Freedom: The Book of Exodus in Jewish and Christian Traditions* (Peabody, MA: Hendrickson, 1999), p. 223.

7. John D. Currid, *A Study Commentary on Exodus*, 2 vols. (Auburn, MA: Evangelical USA, 2000), p. 206.

8. Arthur W. Pink, *Gleanings in Exodus* (Chicago: Moody, 1981), p. 259.

9. "Tziim," Francis Brown, ed., with S. R. Driver and Charles A. Briggs, *The New Brown-Driver-Briggs Gesenius Hebrew and English Lexicon* (Peabody, MA: Hendrickson, 1979), p. 844.

10. Mackay, *Exodus*, p. 486.

11. Soltau, in Pink, *Gleanings in Exodus*, pp. 276, 277.

12. Smarto, *Pursued*, p. 122.

## Chapter Seventy-Nine: The Ordination of Priests

1. This insight comes from John Currid, *A Study Commentary on Exodus*, vol. 2 (Auburn, MA: Evangelical USA, 2000), p. 224.

2. Ibid., vol. 2, p. 218.

3. Bede, quoted in *Exodus, Leviticus, Numbers, Deuteronomy*, ed. Joseph T. Lienhard, Ancient Christian Commentary on Scripture, vol. 3 (Downers Grove, IL: InterVarsity, 2001), p. 132.

4. Charles Simeon, quoted in Ian S. Barter, "Charles Simeon of Cambridge," *Banner of Truth*, no. 455–456 (August/September, 2001): pp. 29–44 (p. 31).

5. Martin Luther, *The Babylonian Captivity of the Church*, quoted in Currid, *A Study Commentary on Exodus*, vol. 2, p. 217.

6. John J. Davis, *Moses and the Gods of Egypt* (Grand Rapids: Baker, 1971), p. 279. This interpretation goes back at least two thousand years. According to the ancient Jewish commentator Philo, "The fully consecrated must be pure in words and actions and in his life; for words are judged by the hearing, the hand is a symbol of action, and the foot of the pilgrimage of life" (quoted in Göran Larsson, *Bound for Freedom: The Book of Exodus in Jewish and Christian Traditions* [Peabody, MA: Hendrickson, 1999], p. 229).

## Chapter Eighty: The Big Picture

1. J. A. Motyer, "Old Testament Covenant Theology" (lectures, Theological Students Fellowship, London, 1973), p. 20.

2. John Paton, quoted in John D. Currid, *A Study Commentary on Exodus*, vol. 2 (Auburn, MA: Evangelical USA, 2000), p. 232.

3. John Shelby Spong, *Why Christianity Must Change or Die* (San Francisco: HarperCollins, 1999), p. 95.

4. Currid, *A Study Commentary on Exodus*, vol. 2, p. 239.

5. Ibid.

## Chapter Eighty-One: Sweet Altar of Prayer

1. John D. Currid, *A Study Commentary on Exodus*, vol. 2 (Auburn, MA: Evangelical USA, 2000), pp. 240, 241.

2. Göran Larsson, *Bound for Freedom: The Book of Exodus in Jewish and Christian Traditions* (Peabody, MA: Hendrickson, 1999), p. 234.

3. Tremper Longman III, *Immanuel in Our Place: Seeing Christ in Israel's Worship*, The Gospel According to the Old Testament (Phillipsburg, NJ: P&R, 2001), p. 58.

4. See Peter Enns, *Exodus*, NIV Application Commentary (Grand Rapids: Zondervan, 2000), p. 537.

5. John I. Durham, *Exodus*, Word Biblical Commentary (Waco, TX: Word, 1987), p. 400.

6. C. W. Slemming, *Made According to the Pattern* (Fort Washington, PA: Christian Literature Crusade, 1974), p. 114.

7. David M. Levy, *The Tabernacle: Shadows of the Messiah* (Bellmawr, NJ: Friends of Israel Gospel Ministry, 1993), p. 59.

8. Patrick Fairbairn, *The Typology of Scripture*, vol. 2 (Grand Rapids: Zondervan, n.d.), p. 317.

9. M. R. DeHaan, *The Tabernacle* (Grand Rapids: Zondervan, 1955), p. 105.

10. Amy Carmichael, *Gold by Moonlight* (Fort Washington, PA: Christian Literature Crusade, 1970), pp. 157, 158.

11. Arthur W. Pink, *Gleanings in Exodus* (Chicago: Moody, 1981), p. 284.

12. Fairbairn, *The Typology of Scripture*, p. 317.

## Chapter Eighty-Two: Bought with a Price

1. Lorene Cary, *The Price of a Child* (New York: Vintage, 1995).

2. Note that the atonement money paid during a census was different from the later temple tax mentioned in Nehemiah 10:32 and Matthew 17:24–27.

3. Arthur W. Pink, *Gleanings in Exodus* (Chicago: Moody, 1981), p. 290.

4. See 30:16; also 21:30, where the language of redemption is used in a similar way.

5. John J. Davis, *Moses and the Gods of Egypt* (Grand Rapids: Baker, 1971), pp. 265, 266.

6. David M. Levy, *The Tabernacle: Shadows of the Messiah* (Bellmawr, NJ: Friends of Israel Gospel Ministry, 1993), p. 36.

7. John L. Mackay, *Exodus* (Fearn, Ross-Shire, UK: Mentor, 2001), p. 510.

8. John D. Currid, *A Study Commentary on Exodus*, vol. 2 (Auburn, MA: Evangelical USA, 2000), p. 256.

## Chapter Eighty-Three: Art for God's Sake

1. Emily Cottrill, quoted by Lucas McFadden in "Freedom of Expression? The Plight of Wheaton Artists," *The Record* (September 27, 2002): pp. 6, 7.

2. This insight comes from Frank E. Gaebelein, *The Christian, the Arts, and Truth*, ed. D. Bruce Lockerbie, A Critical Concern Book (Portland: Multnomah, 1985), p. 64.

3. R. Alan Cole, *Exodus: An Introduction and Commentary*, Tyndale Old Testament Commentaries (Leicester, UK: Inter-Varsity, 1973), p. 210.

4. John I. Durham, *Exodus*, Word Biblical Commentary (Waco, TX: Word, 1987), p. 410.

5. Ibid., p. 410.

6. Leland Ryken, *The Liberated Imagination: Thinking Christianly About the Arts*, The Wheaton Literary Series (Wheaton, IL: Harold Shaw, 1989), pp. 54–57.

7. John Calvin, quoted in Abraham Kuyper, *Calvinism: Six Stone Foundation Lectures* (Grand Rapids: Eerdmans, 1943), p. 153.

8. Ralph Waldo Emerson, "The Rhodora," quoted in Ryken, *The Liberated Imagination*, p. 85.

9. Henri Matisse, quoted in George Steiner, *Real Presences* (Chicago: University of Chicago, 1991), p. 209.

10. Jonathan Edwards, *The Nature of True Virtue*, quoted in Ryken, *The Liberated Imagination*, p. 70.

11. Matthew Bridges, "Crown Him with Many Crowns," 1851.

12. Francis A. Schaeffer, *Art and the Bible* (Downers Grove, IL: InterVarsity, 1973), p. 30.

13. Ibid., p. 31.

## Chapter Eighty-Four: God's Holy Day

1. Benton Johnson, "On Dropping the Subject: Presbyterians and Sabbath Observance in the Twentieth Century," in *The Presbyterian Predicament*, eds. Milton J. Coalter, John M. Mulder, and Louis B. Weeks (Louisville: Westminster/John Knox, 1990).

2. John D. Currid, *A Study Commentary on Exodus*, vol. 2 (Auburn, MA: Evangelical USA, 2000), p. 264.

3. Göran Larsson, *Bound for Freedom: The Book of Exodus in Jewish and Christian Traditions* (Peabody, MA: Hendrickson, 1999), p. 238.

4. Peter Enns, *Exodus*, NIV Application Commentary (Grand Rapids: Zondervan, 2000), pp. 509, 544.

5. Michael Horton, *A Better Way: Rediscovering the Drama of God-Centered Worship* (Grand Rapids: Baker, 2002), p. 195.

6. Enns, *Exodus*, p. 545.

7. These early sources are quoted by D. James Kennedy in *God's Absolute Best for You* (Fort Lauderdale, FL: Coral Ridge Ministries, 2001), p. 82.

8. R. Alan Cole, *Exodus: An Introduction and Commentary*, Tyndale Old Testament Commentaries (Leicester, UK: Inter-Varsity, 1973), p. 211.

9. Traditional Jewish prayer, quoted by Marva J. Dawn, *Keeping the Sabbath Wholly: Ceasing, Resting, Embracing, Feasting* (Grand Rapids: Eerdmans, 1989), p. 2.

10. John Calvin, *Sermons on Deuteronomy*, quoted in Joseph A. Pipa, *The Lord's Day* (Fearn, Ross-Shire, UK: Christian Focus, 1997), p. 147.

11. Richard Bauckham and Trevor Hart, *Hope against Hope: Christian Eschatology in Contemporary Context* (London: Darton, Longman & Todd, 1999), p. 178.

12. In *Keeping the Sabbath Wholly*, Marva Dawn gives a wonderful explanation of all that it means to cease and to rest. Both Dawn and Pipa have good practical suggestions for making the Sabbath a delight, as does Karen Mains in *Making Sunday Special* (Waco, TX: Word, 1987).

13. Leonard Doohan, *Leisure: A Spiritual Need* (Notre Dame, IN: Ave Maria, 1990), p. 46.

14. Dawn, *Keeping the Sabbath Wholly*, pp. 3, 4.

15. Stephen Carter raises this question in *God's Name in Vain: The Wrongs and Rights of Religion in Politics* (New York: Basic, 2000), p. 119.

16. J. C. Penney, quoted in Kennedy, *God's Absolute Best for You*, p. 85.

17. Currid, *A Study Commentary on Exodus*, vol. 2, p. 123.

18. Sietze Buning, "Obedience," in *Purpaleanie and Other Permutations* (Orange City, IA: Middleburg, 1995); used by permission.

## Chapter Eighty-Five: Unholy Cow

1. John D. Currid, *A Study Commentary on Exodus*, vol. 2 (Auburn, MA: Evangelical USA, 2000), p. 271.

2. Stephen Quirke, *The Cult of Ra: Sun-Worship in Ancient Egypt* (New York: Thames & Hudson, 2001), p. 36.

3. John L. Mackay, *Exodus* (Fearn, Ross-Shire, UK: Mentor, 2001), p. 529.

4. G. W. Coats, "The Golden Calf in Psalm 22," *Horizons in Biblical Theology* 9 (1987): p. 1.

5. Ephrem the Syrian, "Homily on Our Lord," 17.3–18.1, in *Exodus, Leviticus, Numbers, Deuteronomy*, ed. Joseph T. Lienhard, Ancient Christian Commentary on Scripture, vol. 3 (Downers Grove, IL: InterVarsity, 2001), p. 140.

6. Arthur W. Pink, *Gleanings in Exodus* (Chicago: Moody, 1981), p. 316.

7. R. C. Sproul, *Grace Unknown: The Heart of Reformed Theology* (Grand Rapids: Baker, 1997), pp. 19, 20.

8. Donald Fretheim, *Exodus*, Interpretation (Louisville: John Knox, 1991), pp. 280, 281.

9. Umberto Cassuto, *A Commentary on the Book of Exodus*, trans. Israel Abrahams (Jerusalem: Magnes, 1967), p. 412.

10. Pink, *Gleanings in Exodus*, p. 317.

11. George Barna, *Marketing the Church* (Colorado Springs: NavPress, 1988), p. 145.

## Chapter Eighty-Six: Go Down, Moses

1. John L. Mackay, *Exodus* (Fearn, Ross-Shire, UK: Mentor, 2001), p. 532.

2. See Jonathan Master, "Exodus 32 as an Argument for Traditional Theism," *Journal of the Evangelical Theological Society* 45, no. 4 (December 2002): pp. 585–98.

3. Brevard S. Childs, *The Book of Exodus: A Critical, Theological Commentary* (Louisville: Westminster, 1974), p. 567.

4. Jerome, quoted in *Exodus, Leviticus, Numbers, Deuteronomy*, ed. Joseph T. Lienhard, Ancient Christian Commentary on Scripture, vol. 3 (Downers Grove, IL: InterVarsity, 2001), pp. 141, 142.

5. Everett Fox, *Now These Are the Names: A New English Rendition of the Book of Exodus* (New York: Schocken, 1986), p. 181.

6. Peter Enns, *Exodus*, NIV Application Commentary (Grand Rapids: Zondervan, 2000), p. 572.

7. R. Alan Cole, *Exodus: An Introduction and Commentary*, Tyndale Old Testament Commentaries (Leicester, UK: Inter-Varsity, 1973), p. 217.

8. John D. Currid, *A Study Commentary on Exodus*, vol. 2 (Auburn, MA: Evangelical USA, 2000), p. 277.

9. Mackay, *Exodus*, p. 536.

10. See Genesis 18:16–33. Göran Larsson compares the two prayers in *Bound for Freedom: The Book of Exodus in Jewish and Christian Traditions* (Peabody, MA: Hendrickson, 1999), pp. 248, 249.

11. Godfrey Ashby, *Go Out and Meet God: A Commentary on the Book of Exodus*, International Theological Commentary (Grand Rapids: Eerdmans, 1998), p. 132.

## Chapter Eighty-Seven: Oh, Brother!

1. John I. Durham, *Exodus*, Word Biblical Commentary (Waco, TX: Word, 1987), p. 430.

2. John L. Mackay, *Exodus* (Fearn, Ross-Shire, UK: Mentor, 2001), pp. 538, 539.

3. Peter Enns, *Exodus*, NIV Application Commentary (Grand Rapids: Zondervan, 2000), p. 574.

4. Many contemporary scholars draw a connection between Exodus 32 and Numbers 5, where a woman suspected of adultery drinks bitter water to determine whether she is innocent or guilty. However, this interpretation seems strained; there is no evidence in Exodus 32 that Moses made the Israelites endure a trial by ordeal.

5. Augustine, *Explanation of the Psalms*, 35.26, in *Exodus, Leviticus, Numbers, Deuteronomy*, ed. Joseph T. Lienhard, Ancient Christian Commentary on Scripture, vol. 3 (Downers Grove, IL: InterVarsity, 2001), p. 143.

6. Arthur W. Pink, *Gleanings in Exodus* (Chicago: Moody, 1981), p. 327.

7. Brevard S. Childs, *The Book of Exodus: A Critical, Theological Commentary* (Louisville: Westminster, 1974), p. 570.

8. Phillips Brooks, "The Fire and the Calf," *Twenty Centuries of Great Preaching*, ed. Clyde E. Fant Jr., and William M. Pinson Jr., vol. 6 (Waco: TX: Word, 1971), pp. 170, 171.

## Chapter Eighty-Eight: Who Is on the Lord's Side?

1. John J. Davis, *Moses and the Gods of Egypt* (Grand Rapids: Baker, 1971), p. 290.

2. See Mark Dever, *Nine Marks of a Healthy Church* (Wheaton, IL: Crossway, 2000), pp. 153–79.

3. Frank Deford, "The Rise and Fall of Kirby Puckett," *Sports Illustrated* (March 17, 2003): pp. 61, 62.

4. Chris Seay, *The Tao of Enron* (Colorado Springs: NavPress, 2002), pp. 115–21.

5. Caesarius of Arles, Sermon 40.1, in *Exodus, Leviticus, Numbers, Deuteronomy*, ed. Joseph T. Lienhard, Ancient Christian Commentary on Scripture, vol. 3 (Downers Grove, IL: InterVarsity, 2001), p. 143.

6. Umberto Cassuto, *A Commentary on the Book of Exodus*, trans. Israel Abrahams (Jerusalem: Magnes, 1967), p. 421.

7. James Montgomery Boice, *Foundations of the Christian Faith* (Downers Grove, IL: InterVarsity, 1986), pp. 253, 254.

8. Ibid., p. 254.

9. Davis, *Moses and the Gods of Egypt*, pp. 290, 291.

10. Boice, *Foundations of the Christian Faith*, p. 254. The Apostle Paul offered virtually the same prayer when he said, "I could wish that I myself were accursed and cut off from Christ for the sake of my brothers, my kinsmen according to the flesh. They are Israelites" (Romans 9:3, 4a).

11. John D. Currid, *A Study Commentary on Exodus*, vol. 2 (Auburn, MA: Evangelical USA, 2000), p. 292.

## Chapter Eighty-Nine: With or Without You?

1. J. R. R. Tolkien, *The Hobbit, or There and Back Again*, 4th ed. (Boston: Houghton Mifflin, 1978).

2. John D. Currid, *A Study Commentary on Exodus*, vol. 2 (Auburn, MA: Evangelical USA, 2000), p. 295.

3. Martin Luther, quoted in Chris Seay, *The Tao of Enron* (Colorado Springs: NavPress, 2002), p. 120.

4. Peter Enns, *Exodus*, NIV Application Commentary (Grand Rapids: Zondervan, 2000), p. 578.

5. Arthur W. Pink, *Gleanings in Exodus* (Chicago: Moody, 1981), p. 334.

6. J. I. Packer, *Knowing God* (Downers Grove, IL: InterVarsity, 1973), p. 29.

7. John I. Durham, *Exodus*, Word Biblical Commentary (Waco, TX: Word, 1987), p. 443.

8. John Winthrop, quoted in Leland Ryken, *Worldly Saints: The Puritans as They Really Were* (Grand Rapids: Zondervan, 1986), pp. 206, 207.

9. Archibald Alexander, quoted in Andrew Hoffecker, *Piety and the Princeton Theologians* (Grand Rapids: Baker, 1984), p. 34.

## Chapter Ninety: Under the Shadow of His Hand

1. John L. Mackay, *Exodus* (Fearn, Ross-Shire, UK: Mentor, 2001), p. 555.

2. Ibid., p. 556.

3. John D. Currid, *A Study Commentary on Exodus*, 2 vols. (Auburn, MA: Evangelical USA, 2000), p. 304.

4. Stephen Charnock, *Discources upon the Existance and Attributes of God* (London: Henry G. Bohn, 1845), p. 539, http://babel.hathitrust.org/cgi/pt?id=hvd.ah697k;view=1up;seq=9.

5. Augustine, "Letter 147.20," in *Exodus, Leviticus, Numbers, Deuteronomy*, ed. Joseph T. Lienhard, Ancient Christian Commentary on Scripture, vol. 3 (Downers Grove, IL: InterVarsity, 2001), p. 149.

6. Mackay, *Exodus*, p. 559.

## Chapter Ninety-One: When God Passes By

1. Umberto Cassuto, *A Commentary on the Book of Exodus*, trans. Israel Abrahams (Jerusalem: Magnes, 1967), p. 438.

2. Brevard S. Childs, *The Book of Exodus: A Critical, Theological Commentary* (Louisville: Westminster, 1974), p. 596.

3. Peter Enns, *Exodus*, NIV Application Commentary (Grand Rapids: Zondervan, 2000), p. 584.

4. Göran Larsson, *Bound for Freedom: The Book of Exodus in Jewish and Christian Traditions* (Peabody, MA: Hendrickson, 1999), p. 259.

5. Maxie D. Dunnam, *Exodus*, The Communicator's Commentary (Waco, TX: Word, 1987), p. 372.

6. John L. Mackay, *Exodus* (Fearn, Ross-Shire, UK: Mentor, 2001), p. 563.

7. Ibid., p. 564.

8. Dunnam, *Exodus*, p. 371.

9. C. S. Lewis, *God in the Dock*, quoted by Richard A. Kauffman in *Christianity Today* (May 2003): p. 60.

## Chapter Ninety-Two: God, and God Alone

1. William Gurnall, quoted by Michael F. Ross in *God Our Redeemer*, a devotional guide produced by Mission to North America and published by the Christian Education and Publications Committee of the Presbyterian Church in America (2003), p. 13.

2. John A. Redhead, *Getting to Know God* (Nashville: Abingdon, 1954), pp. 25, 26.

3. Umberto Cassuto, *A Commentary on the Book of Exodus*, trans. Israel Abrahams (Jerusalem: Magnes, 1967), p. 441.

4. Godfrey Ashby, *Go Out and Meet God: A Commentary on the Book of Exodus*, International Theological Commentary (Grand Rapids: Eerdmans, 1998), p. 137.

5. Joyce M. Hawkins and Robert Allen, eds., *The Oxford Encyclopedic English Dictionary* (Oxford, UK: Clarendon, 1991), p. 762.

6. J. I. Packer, *Knowing God* (Downers Grove, IL: InterVarsity, 1973), pp. 153, 155.

7. John Calvin, *Institutes of the Christian Religion*, ed. John T. McNeill, trans. Ford Lewis Battles, 2 vols., Library of Christian Classics, 20–21 (Philadelphia: Westminster, 1960), 22.8.18.

8. Raymond Ortlund Jr., *God's Unfaithful Wife: A Biblical Theology of Spiritual Adultery*, New Studies in Biblical Theology, vol. 2 (Downers Grove, IL: InterVarsity, 2002), pp. 30–31.

9. Ibid., pp. 31, 32.

10. Correspondence from Heidi Shepard, ministering in Asia with InterServe (April 2003).

## Chapter Ninety-Three: Staying in Covenant Love

1. John I. Durham, *Exodus*, Word Biblical Commentary (Waco, TX: Word, 1987), p. 458.

2. John L. Mackay, *Exodus* (Fearn, Ross-Shire, UK: Mentor, 2001), p. 567.

3. Arthur W. Pink develops this point in *Gleanings in Exodus* (Chicago: Moody, 1981), p. 361.

4. See John D. Currid, *A Study Commentary on Exodus*, vol. 2 (Auburn, MA: Evangelical USA, 2000), pp. 122, 123.

5. Corrie ten Boom, with John and Elizabeth Sherrill, *The Hiding Place* (Washington Depot, CT: Chosen, 1971), p. 73.

## Chapter Ninety-Four: Till We Have Faces

1. See Exodus 19:3, 7, 20, 25; 20:21; 24:9, 13; 32:15; 34:4.

2. John D. Currid, *A Study Commentary on Exodus*, vol. 2 (Auburn, MA: Evangelical USA, 2000), p. 322.

3. See R. Mellinkoff, *The Horned Moses in Medieval Art and Thought* (Berkeley, CA: University of California Press, 1970).

4. Ed. Dennett, quoted in Arthur W. Pink, *Gleanings in Exodus* (Chicago: Moody, 1981), p. 370.

5. This interpretation comes from John I. Durham, *Exodus*, Word Biblical Commentary (Waco, TX: Word, 1987), p. 466.

6. Augustine, quoted in William Barclay, *The Letters to the Corinthians*, Daily Study Bible (Edinburgh: Saint Andrew, 1954), pp. 214, 215.

## Chapter Ninety-Five: A Heart for Giving

1. Göran Larsson, *Bound for Freedom: The Book of Exodus in Jewish and Christian Traditions* (Peabody, MA: Hendrickson, 1999), pp. 265, 266.

2. Patrick Fairbairn, *The Typology of Scripture*, vol. 2 (Grand Rapids: Zondervan, n.d.), p. 207.

3. Robert Murray M'Cheyne, *Sermons of M'Cheyne* (Edinburgh: n.p., 1848), p. 482.

4. Corrie ten Boom, with John and Elizabeth Sherrill, *The Hiding Place* (Washington Depot, CT: Chosen, 1971), p. 42.

### Chapter Ninety-Six: Enough Is Enough!

1. H. R. Rookmaaker, *Modern Art and the Death of a Culture* (Wheaton, IL: Crossway, 1994), p. 235.

2. Samuel Mather, quoted in Leland Ryken, *Worldly Saints: The Puritans As They Really Were* (Grand Rapids: Zondervan, 1986), p. 169.

3. Rookmaaker, *Modern Art and the Death of a Culture*, p. 229.

4. Jonathan Edwards, quoted in Frank E. Gaebelein, *The Christian, the Arts, and Truth: Regaining the Vision of Greatness*, Critical Concerns (Portland: Multnomah, 1985), p. 65.

5. Abraham Kuyper, *Calvinism: Six Stone Foundation Lectures* (Grand Rapids: Eerdmans, 1943), p. 156.

6. Gerard Manley Hopkins, "God's Grandeur," in *The Oxford Book of Christian Verse*, ed. Lord David Cecil (Oxford, UK: Oxford University Press, 1940), p. 495.

7. Stuart McAllister, quoted in Ned Bustard, *It Was Good—Making Art to the Glory of God* (Baltimore: Square Halo, 2000), pp. 13, 14.

8. Francis A. Schaeffer, *Art and the Bible* (Downers Grove, IL: InterVarsity, 1973), pp. 56–58.

9. John D. Currid, *A Study Commentary on Exodus*, vol. 2 (Auburn, MA: Evangelical USA, 2000), p. 336.

10. Jacques Ellul, *Money and Power*, trans. LaVonne Neff (Downers Grove, IL: InterVarsity, 1984), pp. 106–16. The quotations here come from Marva Dawn's summary of Ellul's work in *Keeping the Sabbath Wholly: Ceasing, Resting, Embracing, Feasting* (Grand Rapids: Eerdmans, 1989), p. 185.

11. John Piper, *Don't Waste Your Life* (Wheaton, IL: Crossway, 2003), p. 111.

12. Courtney Anderson, *To the Golden Shore: The Life of Adoniram Judson* (Grand Rapids: Zondervan, 1956), p. 83.

### Chapter Ninety-Seven: Building in Progress

1. Richard Rogers, quoted in Leland Ryken, *Worldly Saints: The Puritans as They Really Were* (Grand Rapids: Zondervan, 1986), p. 5.

2. Tremper Longman III, *Immanuel in Our Place: Seeing Christ in Israel's Worship*, The Gospel According to the Old Testament (Phillipsburg, NJ: P&R, 2001), p. 32.

3. Ibid., pp. 33, 34.

4. See David M. Levy, *The Tabernacle: Shadows of the Messiah* (Bellmawr, NJ: Friends of Israel Gospel Ministry, 1993), p. 18.

5. F. B. Meyer, *Devotional Commentary on Exodus* (Grand Rapids: Kregel, 1978), p. 302.

6. Adolph Saphir, quoted in Arthur W. Pink, *Gleanings in Exodus* (Chicago: Moody, 1981), p. 180.

### Chapter Ninety-Eight: In God's House

1. Godfrey Ashby, *Go Out and Meet God: A Commentary on the Book of Exodus*, International Theological Commentary (Grand Rapids: Eerdmans, 1998), p. 142.

2. Vern Poythress, *The Shadow of Christ in the Law of Moses* (Phillipsburg, NJ: P&R, 1991), p. 20.

3. C. Trimp, *Preaching and the History of Salvation: Continuing an Unfinished Discussion*, trans. Nelson D. Kloosterman (Scarsdale, NY: Westminster Discount Book Service, 1996), p. 44.

### Chapter Ninety-Nine: The Courtyard to God

1. Wendy Murray Zoba, *Maya Mysteries*, as quoted in *Books & Culture* 8, no. 1 (January/February 2002): p. 28.

2. John D. Currid, *A Study Commentary on Exodus*, vol. 2 (Auburn, MA: Evangelical USA, 2000), p. 355.

3. Patrick Fairbairn, *The Typology of Scripture*, vol. 2 (Grand Rapids: Zondervan, n.d.), p. 266.

4. David M. Levy, *The Tabernacle: Shadows of the Messiah* (Bellmawr, NJ: Friends of Israel Gospel Ministry, 1993), p. 20.

5. Zoba, *Maya Mysteries*, p. 28.

6. Vern Poythress, *The Shadow of Christ in the Law of Moses* (Phillipsburg, NJ: P&R, 1991), p. 24.

7. Levy, *The Tabernacle: Shadows of the Messiah*, p. 20.

8. Fairbairn, *The Typology of Scripture*, vol. 2, p. 260.

9. Currid, *A Study Commentary on Exodus*, vol. 2, pp. 349, 350.

10. Aben-ezra, quoted in Fairbairn, *The Typology of Scripture*, vol. 2, p. 258.

## Chapter One Hundred: Aaron's Wardrobe

1. Vern Poythress, *The Shadow of Christ in the Law of Moses* (Phillipsburg, NJ: P&R, 1991), p. 53.

2. Tremper Longman III, *Immanuel in Our Place: Seeing Christ in Israel's Worship*, The Gospel According to the Old Testament (Phillipsburg, NJ: P&R, 2001), p. 125.

3. David M. Levy, *The Tabernacle: Shadows of the Messiah* (Bellmawr, NJ: Friends of Israel Gospel Ministry, 1993), p. 160.

4. Ibid., p. 186.

5. George Herbert, "Aaron," in *Chapters into Verse: Poetry in English Inspired by The Bible; Vol. 1: Genesis to Malachi*, eds. Rovert Atwan and Laurance Wieder (Oxford, UK: Oxford University Press, 1993), pp. 138, 139.

## Chapter One Hundred One: Just like God Said

1. Vern Poythress, *The Shadow of Christ in the Law of Moses* (Phillipsburg, NJ: P&R, 1991), p. 29.

2. C. Trimp, *Preaching and the History of Salvation: Continuing an Unfinished Discussion*, trans. Nelson D. Kloosterman (Scarsdale, NY: Westminster Discount, 1996), p. 67.

3. Ibid., p. 69.

4. Patrick Fairbairn, *The Typology of Scripture*, vol. 1 (Grand Rapids: Zondervan, n.d.), p. 48.

5. Geerhardus Vos, *Biblical Theology: Old and New Testaments* (Grand Rapids: Eerdmans, 1948), pp. 144, 146.

6. Poythress, *The Shadow of Christ in the Law of Moses*, pp. 35–37.

7. John I. Durham, *Exodus*, Word Biblical Commentary (Waco, TX: Word, 1987), p. 496.

8. Fairbairn, *The Typology of Scripture*, vol. 2, p. 217.

## Chapter One Hundred Two: When Glory Came Down

1. John D. Currid, *A Study Commentary on Exodus*, vol. 2 (Auburn, MA: Evangelical USA, 2000), p. 369.

2. F. B. Meyer, *Devotional Commentary on Exodus* (Grand Rapids: Kregel, 1978), p. 473.

3. Currid, *A Study Commentary on Exodus*, vol. 2, p. 371.

4. Peter Enns, *Exodus*, NIV Application Commentary (Grand Rapids: Zondervan, 2000), p. 602.

# Scripture Index

# General Index

# Index of Sermon Illustrations